PAUL ROMNEY, Ph. D.
Historian, Consultant

JOWITT'S
DICTIONARY OF ENGLISH LAW

AUSTRALIA
The Law Book Company Ltd.
Sydney : Melbourne : Brisbane

CANADA AND U.S.A.
The Carswell Company Ltd.
Agincourt, Ontario

INDIA
N. M. Tripathi Private Ltd.
Bombay

ISRAEL
Steimatzky's Agency Ltd.
Jerusalem : Tel Aviv : Haifa

MALAYSIA, SINGAPORE, BRUNEI
Malayan Law Journal (Pte) Ltd.
Singapore

NEW ZEALAND
Sweet & Maxwell (N.Z.) Ltd.
Wellington

PAKISTAN
Pakistan Law House
Karachi

JOWITT'S
DICTIONARY
OF
ENGLISH LAW

By
THE LATE THE RIGHT HONOURABLE THE
EARL JOWITT

and

CLIFFORD WALSH, LL.M.
Solicitor of the Supreme Court

SECOND EDITION

By

JOHN BURKE
Barrister
Sometime Editor of Current Law

VOLUME 2

L — Z
with Bibliography

LONDON
SWEET & MAXWELL LIMITED
1977

First edition	.	.	.	1959
Second impression	.	.	1965
Third impression	.	.	1972
Fourth impression	.	.	1974
Second edition	.	.	.	1977
Second impression	.	.	1978
Third impression	.	.	1980
Fourth impression	.	.	1982

Published in Great Britain by
Sweet & Maxwell Limited of
11 New Fetter Lane London
Law Publishers and printed in
Great Britain
by Page Bros (Norwich) Ltd

ISBN 0 421 23090 8

L

L.C.J., Lord Chief Justice.

L.J., Lord Justice of Appeal.

L.S., *locus sigilli*, the place of the seal.

£.s.d., *librae* (pounds), *solidi* (shillings), *denarii* (pence).

Label [Lat. *labellum*], a narrow slip of paper or parchment affixed to a deed, writing, or writ, hanging at or out of the same; and an appending seal is called a label (Jacob).

As to the labelling of foods and drugs see the Food and Drugs Act, 1955, ss. 6, 7.

Labina, watery land.

Laborariis, De. Under the Statute of Labourers (*q.v.*) there were two forms of this writ, one against a man having no apparent means of livelihood who refused to take employment, and the other against a man who refused to serve for the summer with a master living in the town where he had served during the winter (Reg.Orig. 189). In each case the erring labourer was to be committed to gaol until he had seen the error of his ways.

See SUPER STATUTO VERSUS SERVANTES.

Labour and National Service, Ministry of. The Ministry of Labour was established pursuant to the new Ministries and Secretaries Act, 1916, s. 1. By s. 2 of that Act there were transferred to this new ministry the powers and duties of the Board of Trade under the Conciliation Act, 1896, the Labour Exchanges Act, 1909, the Trade Boards Act, 1909, and the National Insurance (Unemployment) Acts, 1911 to 1916. The Ministry was dissolved and its functions transferred to the Secretary of State for Employment by S.I. 1968 No. 729. See LABOUR EXCHANGE.

Labour exchange. The Labour Exchanges Act, 1909, empowered the Board of Trade to establish and maintain labour exchanges, *i.e.*, offices or places of employment used for the purpose of collecting and furnishing information, either by the keeping of registers or otherwise, respecting employers who desire to engage workpeople and workpeople who seek employment. This function of the Board of Trade was transferred to the Minister of Labour and National Service (*q.v.*) by the New Ministries Act, 1916. The 1909 Act was repealed and replaced by the Employment and Training Act, 1948.

Labour Exchanges are now termed Employment Offices.

Labourer. It has been judicially decided that a parish clerk or a bailiff or a carpenter is not a labourer and that a labourer is a man who digs and does other things of that kind with his hands (*Morgan* v. *L.G.O.C.* (1884) 13 Q.B.D. 832). But a farmer who does manual work on his own farm is not a labourer (*R.* v. *Silvester* (1864) 33 L.J.M.C. 79). A driver of a motor omnibus is engaged in manual labour (*Smith* v. *Associated Omnibus Co.* [1907] 1 K.B. 916). Professional footballers are not employed by way of manual labour (*Re Professional Players of Association Football* [1928] W.N. 96). See LABOURING CLASSES; MASTER AND SERVANT.

Labourers, Statute of. This was the statute 1349, 23 Edw. 3, passed after about half the population had died of the Black Death. It recited that many of the people had died of the pestilence and that many, seeing the necessity of masters and great scarcity of servants, would not serve unless they received excessive wages and that some were rather willing to beg in idleness than by labour to get their living, and enacted that everyone under sixty, except traders, craftsmen, those with private means and landowners, should work for anyone willing to employ them at the wages paid from 1340 to 1346. Justices of Labourers were constituted to administer the statute. It was repealed by the Statute Law Revision Act, 1863 (Putnam, *Enforcement of the Statutes of Labourers*). See LABORARIIS, DE; SUPER STATUTO VERSUS SERVANTES, ETC.

Labouring a jury, tampering with a jury (Co.Litt. 157b).

Lace, a measure of land equal to one pole, used in Cornwall.

Orders are made with reference to the lace industry under the Industrial Organisation and Development Act, 1947, s. 9.

Lace making is regulated by Home Work Orders under the Factories Act, 1961, s. 133. Gold and silver lace is to be sold by troy weight (Weights and Measures Act, 1963, s. 10 (2)). The Gold and Silver Thread Acts, 1741 and 1788, were repealed by the Hallmarking Act, 1973. See PLATE.

Lacerta, a fathom.

Laches [Fr. *lâcher*, to loosen], slackness, negligence or unreasonable delay in pursuing a legal remedy whereby the party forfeits the benefit upon the principle *vigilantibus non dormientibus jura subveniunt*. In the old books the term is chiefly used with reference to rights of entry. Thus, while the doctrine of descent cast (*q.v.*) was in force, if an infant was disseised of land, and the disseisor died in possession, the infant was not deprived of his right of entry, as a person of full age would have been, because no laches could be imputed to an infant in such a case (Litt. 402, 726). See DISABILITY; INTRUSION.

At the present day " laches " is generally used to denote unreasonable delay in enforcing an equitable right. Thus if a person discovers that he has been induced by fraud to enter into a transaction, and then waits an unnecessary time before taking proceedings to set it aside, this laches will disentitle him to relief. He is, however, entitled to a reasonable time for the purpose of making inquiries, and obtaining advice, etc. Where an equitable right of action is analogous to a legal right of action, and there is a provision in the Limitation Act, 1939, fixing a limit of time for bringing actions at law to enforce such claims, the court will by analogy apply the same limit of time to proceedings taken to enforce the equitable right (*Peele* v. *Gurney* (1873) L.R. 6 H.L. 384). See ACQUIESCENCE.

Lacta, a defect in the weight of money.

Lacuna, a ditch or dyke; a furrow for a drain; a blank in writing.

Lada, purgation, exculpation. There were three kinds: (1) That wherein the accused cleared himself by his own oath, supported by the oaths of his consacramentals (compurgators), according to the number of which the *lada* was said to be either simple or threefold; (2) Ordeal; (3) Corsned. See CORSNED BREAD.

Also, a service which consisted in supplying the lord with beasts of burden; or, as defined by Roquefort: *Service qu'un vassal devoit à son seigneur, et qui consistoit à faire quelques voyages par ses bêtes de somme* (Anc.Inst.Eng.).

Also, a lath, or inferior court of justice; also a course of water, or a broadway.

Lade, or **Lode,** the mouth of a river.

Laden in bulk, freighted with a cargo which is neither in casks, boxes, bales, nor cases, but lies loose in the hold, being defended from wet or moisture by a number of mats and a quantity of dunnage. Cargoes of corn, salt, etc., are usually so shipped. As to the carriage of grain, see the Merchant Shipping (Safety Convention) Act, 1949, s. 24.

Lading. See BILL OF LADING.

Lady [Sax. *hlaef*, loaf; *dig,* day; *daegee,* kneader; *weardige,* keeper.] It was the fashion for the lady of the manor, once a week or oftener, to distribute to her poor neighbours, with her own hands, a certain quantity of bread. The title is borne by the wives of knights, and of all barons and knightly degrees above them, either in their own right or by courtesy, except the wives of bishops. See DAME.

" Lady " is the recognised courtesy title of the daughters of dukes, marquises, and earls (as, *e.g.,* [the] Lady Jane Sheepshanks) and of the wife of anyone entitled to the courtesy of lord (as, *e.g.,* [the] Lady George Gaunt). It is the customary title of the wife of a knight or of a baronet (as [the] Lady Warrington); but the formal title of those ladies is, for instance, Dame Theodora Warrington: and, except formally, a marchioness, viscountess, or baroness is always spoken of or to as, for instance, Lady Farintosh instead of as the Marchioness of Farintosh.

Lady Day, March 25, being the Annunciation of the Blessed Virgin, and one of the usual quarterly days for the payment of rent, etc. Lady Day, under the old style, was April 6. See ANNUNCIATION, FEAST OF; OLD LADY DAY.

Lady of Grace; Lady of Justice. See ST. JOHN, ETC.

Lady-court, the court of a lady of the manor.

Lady's friend. See NEXT FRIEND.

Laedorium, reproach (Girald.Camb. c. 14).

Laen-land. In the late Anglo-Saxon period this, as distinguished from boc-land and folkland (*q.v.*)—both of which were held, but on different titles, from the king—meant land held of a superior other than the king. It thus corresponded more or less to land which, after the Norman Conquest, was held of, not by, a tenant, *in capite*.

Laesae majestatis, Crimen, the crime of injured majesty, treason (Glanville, c. 11; 4 Bl.Comm. 75).

There is no modern equivalent in our law, although *lèse-majesté*, the French translation of the Latin expression, is well known in Continental law: but *lèse-majesté* includes many offences against the sovereign, such as mere insult, which are of much less gravity than treason.

Laesio fidei, breach of faith. The ecclesiastical courts down to the middle of the fifteenth century claimed that in matters such as non-payment of debt and breach of contract they had a general jurisdiction, inasmuch as a *laesio fidei* came into question. The growth of the equitable jurisdiction of the Chancellor, and the steady resistance of the judges generally, eventually put an end to this claim and such suits were prohibited by the Constitutions of Clarendon, 1164, c. 15.

Laesio ultra dimidium vel onormis, the injury sustained by one of the parties to an onerous contract when he had been over-reached by the other to the extent of more than one-half of the value of the subject-matter, *e.g.*, when a vendor had not received half the value of property sold, or the purchaser had paid more than double value.

Laet [*litus, lidas, letus*], one of a class between servile and free (Palgrave 354).

Laetare Jerusalem, Lent or Easter offerings, so called from these words in the hymn of the day. They are also denominated *quadragesimalia* (Cowel). See QUADRAGESIMALS.

Laethe, or **Lathe,** a division or district peculiar to the county of Kent (Spelman). See LATHE.

Lafordswic [Sax. *hlaford*, lord, *swic*, betrayal], a betraying of one's lord or master.

Laga, law.

Lagan or **Ligan** [Sax. *liggan*], goods tied to a buoy and sunk in the sea; also a right which the chief lord of the fee had to take goods cast on shore by the violence of the sea (Bract. 1, 3, c. ii; 5 Co. Rep. 106b).

Also the goods themselves; included in " wreck " by the Merchant Shipping Act, 1894, s. 510. See DROITS OF ADMIRALTY; FLOTSAM; JETSAM.

Lage; Laga; Lagh [Sax.], law. The word is found in compound forms such as Danelage.

Lage-day, a day of open court; the day of the county or hundred court (Hilliard's note to Touch. 92; Cowel; Elph. 591).

Lage-man, a juror (Cowel).

Lagen, a measure of six sextarii or seven quarts (2 Fleta, c. viii).

Lagh [Sax. *laga*], law.

Laghslite, breach of law; a punishment for breaking the law.

Lagon. See LAGAN.

Lagos, a West African settlement of the Crown, now part of Nigeria.

Lagotrophy [λαγως, a hare; τρεφω, to nourish], a warren of hares.

Lagu, law; also used to express territory or district in which a particular law was in force, as *Denalagu, Mercna lagu*, etc. (Praefatio ad Wilk. L. Anglo-Sax. 16).

Lahman, or **Lagemannus,** a lawyer (1 *Domesday* 189).

Lah-slit, a mulct for offences committed by the Danes (Anc.Inst.Eng.).

Laia, a roadway in a wood (1 Dugd. Mon. 483).

Laic [λαός, people], one who is not in holy orders, or not engaged in the ministry of religion.

Lairwite, or **Lecherwite,** a fine for adultery or fornication, especially with an unfree woman, anciently paid to the lords of some manors (4 Co.Inst. 206).

Laisser-faire, freedom of action as opposed to State planning and restriction.

Laity [λαός, people], the people, as distinguished from the clergy.

As to the House of Laity, see NATIONAL ASSEMBLY OF THE CHURCH OF ENGLAND.

Lambarde, William. Born 1536, admitted to Lincoln's Inn in 1556, appointed a bencher of the Inn in 1578, became a master in Chancery in 1592, and died in 1601. He published in 1568 his *Archaionomia,* a paraphrase of the Anglo-Saxon laws and of the laws of William the Conqueror; in 1581 he published his *Eirenarcha; or of the Office of the Peace*, which was for long the standard work on the subject; and in 1635 he published his *Archion,* or discourse upon the High Courts of Justice in England.

Lambeth degrees, degrees conferred by the Archbishop of Canterbury, by virtue of the statute 1534, 25 Hen. 8, c. 21, ss. 2, 3. He has authority to confer all the usual degrees in arts, divinity, law and medicine, with or without examination, upon either laymen or clergymen. Recipients of such degrees may wear the academic costume of the university to which the archbishop who grants them may belong. A Lambeth degree in medicine does not entitle the holder to be registered as a medical practitioner (Medical Act, 1956, Sch. 3), and the holder of such a degree who uses it for the purpose of implying that he is duly registered or that he is recognised by law as a physician commits an offence punishable upon summary conviction (s. 31).

Degrees in divinity are those usually conferred by the archbishop: and such a degree is most usually given in the case of a bishop or other high dignitary who happens not to have obtained the corresponding degree at one of the universities.

The stamp duty on faculties for Lambeth degrees was abolished by the Finance Act, 1948, s. 75.

Lame duck, a cant term on the Stock Exchange meaning that a broker or jobber cannot fulfil his contracts; it is libellous (*Morris* v. *Langdale* (1800) 2 Bos. & Pul. 284).

Lammas, the gule or first day of August, and the second of the four cross quarter-days of the year. The term is said to be derived from a custom by which the tenants of the Archbishop of York were obliged, at the time of Mass, on August 1, to bring a live lamb to the altar. In Scotland they are said to wean lambs on this day. It may be corrupted from *latter-math*. Others derive it from a Saxon word, signifying loaf-mass, because on that day our forefathers made an offering of bread composed of new wheat.

Old Lammas Day is August 12, which corresponds to August 1 of the time before the calendar was reformed.

Lammas lands, open arable and meadow lands, which are held by a number of owners in severalty during a portion of the year, and which after the severalty crop has been removed are commonable not only to the owners in severalty but to other classes of commoners, *e.g.*, inhabitants of the parish, tenants and inhabitants of a manor, freeman or householders of a borough, or the owners or occupiers of ancient tenements within the parish, usually termed tofts (*Baylis* v. *Tyssen-Amherst* (1877) 6 Ch.D. 500). They derive their name from the former practice of keeping them open from Lammas Day to Lady Day next ensuing. The date of opening them is now August 12. See COMMON.

Lampern, the river lamprey, an eel-like fish. It is excluded from the prohibition on using eel baskets at close seasons (Salmon and Freshwater Fisheries Act, 1975, s. 21 (1) (*b*)).

Lancaster, a county of England erected into a palatine in the reign of Edward III, and granted by him to his son John for life, that he should have *jura regalia* and a king-like power to pardon treasons, outlawries, etc., and make justices of the peace and justices of assize within the county, and that all processes and indictments should be in his name. It is now vested in the Crown. It had a separate Chancery Court. See CHANCERY COURT OF LANCASTER; COUNTY PALATINE; DUCHY COURT OF LANCASTER; DUCHY OF LANCASTER; HERALD.

Lanceti, vassals who were obliged to work for their lord one day in the week, during autumn, with fork, spade or flail, at the lord's option (Spelman).

Land, in its restrained sense, means soil, but in its legal acceptation it is a generic term, comprehending every species of ground, soil or earth, whatsoever, as meadows, pastures, woods, moors, waters, marshes, furze, and heath; it includes also houses, mills, castles, and other buildings; for with the conveyance of the land, the structures upon it pass also. And besides an indefinite extent upwards, it extends downwards to the globe's centre, hence the maxim, *Cujus est solum ejus est usque ad caelum et ad inferos*; or, more curtly expressed, *Cujus est solum ejus est altum* (Co.Litt. 4a).

In an Act of Parliament passed after 1850 " land " includes messuages, tenements and hereditaments, houses, and buildings of any tenure (Interpretation Act, 1889, s. 3). By the Law of Property Act, 1925, s. 205 (1) (ix), " land " for the purposes of the Act includes land of any tenure, and mines and minerals, whether or not held apart from the surface, buildings or parts of buildings (whether the division is horizontal, vertical or made in any other way), and other corporeal hereditaments; also a manor, an advowson, and a rent and other incorporeal hereditaments, and an easement, right, privilege, or benefit in, over, or derived from land; but not an undivided share in land. A conveyance of land did not pass tithe rentcharge by implication (*Public Trustee* v. *Duke of Lancaster* [1927] 1 K.B. 516).

Water, by a solecism, is held to be a species of land; *e.g.*, in order to recover possession of a pool or rivulet of water, the action must be brought for the land— *e.g.*, ten acres of " land covered with water "—and not for the water only (*Hampton Urban Council* v. *Southwark Water Company* [1900] A.C. 3).

Land is divisible both horizontally (see CLOSE) and vertically. Therefore one man may be entitled to the surface of land, and another to the minerals under it (see EASEMENT), or one man may have a fee simple in one storey of a house, while the rest may belong to another.

Land is a tenement and a hereditament, and, therefore, belongs to the class of real property. See HEREDITAMENT; REAL ESTATE; TENEMENT.

Rights in respect of land are of two kinds—(i) rights of ownership, although theoretically land is not the subject of ownership according to English law (see ESTATE; TENURE); and (ii) rights *in alieno solo*, which include easements and profits (*q.v.*).

In the old books, and in fines and the like, the word " land " strictly signified nothing but arable land, the reason given being that arable land was considered more beneficial to the country than pasture.

See ACCUMULATION; EJECTMENT; LANDLORD AND TENANT; POSSESSION; SEISEN; VENDOR AND PURCHASER.

Land and Natural Resources, Ministry of. The Ministry was dissolved and most of its functions transferred to the Ministry of Housing and Local Government and thence to the Secretary of State for the Environment (S.I. 1967 No. 156; 1970 No. 1681). As to functions previously transferred to the Ministry see S.I. 1965 Nos. 143, 319, 1120.

Land Authority for Wales. See the Community Land Act, 1975, ss. 8–14, Sch. 3.

Land certificate. See CERTIFICATE.

Land charge. The Land Charges Registration and Searches Act, 1888, provided that a land charge should be void against a purchaser for value of the land charged therewith, unless it was registered in the register of charges mentioned in that Act, since transferred to the Land Registry by virtue of the Land Charges Act, 1900, repealed by the Land Charges Act, 1925. The Act of 1925 was amended by a number of Acts including the Matrimonial Homes Act, 1967, s. 2, Sch. and the Land Registration and Land Charges Act, 1971. The statute law has been consolidated by the Land Charges Act, 1972. The system of compulsory registration of charges over land has been greatly extended. Purchasers of land must search for such charges, both in the Land Registry and the local registries. The search is essential for the ascertainment of title.

Five registers are kept at the Land Registry at Kidbrooke, London, S.E.3: (a) land charges, (b) pending actions, (c) writs and orders affecting land (d) deeds of arrangement affecting land, (e) annuities (now closed and transferred to Class E), together with an index (Act of 1972, s. 1).

The register of land charges is made up as follows (see s. 2 of the Act): Class A, statutory land charges; Class B, similar charges not made on the application of any person, if created or conveyed after

1925, and not being local land charges; Class C (not being a local land charge) (i) puisne mortgages, (ii) limited owner's charges, (iii) general equitable charges, (iv) estate contracts, if created after 1925 or if created before 1926, acquired under a conveyance made on or after that date; Class D, (i) Inland Revenue charges for capital transfer tax (Finance Act, 1975, Sch. 12 para. 18); (ii) restrictive covenants created after 1925 except covenants in leases; (iii) equitable easements, rights and privileges created after 1925; Class E, annuities created before 1926 and registered after 1925; Class F, charges affecting any land by virtue of the Matrimonial Homes Act, 1967 (see MATRIMONIAL HOME).

Pending actions, writs and orders affecting land and deeds of arrangement must be registered anew every five years (ss. 5–8). Failure to register charges created after 1888 under Class A avoids the charge against any purchaser of land if not registered before completion of purchase; under Class B or Class C so far as regards mortgages, limited or statutory owner's charges and equitable charges, failure to register avoids the charge against any purchaser of the land charged or any interest therein; failure to register estate contracts or charges in Class D avoids the charge only against the purchaser of a legal estate for money or money's worth. Under Class F failure to register avoids the charge against any purchaser of the land charged or any interest therein. " Purchaser " under the Land Charges Act, 1972, means any purchaser for valuable consideration unless he is referred to otherwise, e.g., as a purchaser for money's worth.

Personal search of the land charges registers may be made on payment of a fee (Act of 1972, s. 9) but it is the practice to obtain a certificate of official search which protects a purchaser against any entry made after the date of the certificate, provided the purchase is completed before the expiration of fifteen days after the date of the certificate (ss. 10, 11).

The procedures and forms for registration and search are prescribed by the Land Charges Rules, 1974 (No. 1286).

Registration of land charges under the Land Charges Act, 1972, must not be confused with registration of charges on registered land or notice of incumbrances or equitable interests on or in registered land which can be registered or noted under the Land Registration Act, 1925. Registration under the Land Charges Act, 1972, or under the Companies Act, 1948, does not, as against registered purchasers or incumbrances, protect charges which should be registered or noted under the Land Registration Act, 1925, s. 14. See CHARGE; DRAINAGE; IMPROVEMENT OF LAND; LOCAL LAND CHARGES; NOTICE.

Land Commission. This was created by the Land Commission Act, 1967, to collect betterment levy and was abolished by the Land Commission (Dissolution) Act, 1971.

Land Commissioners, the commissioners formerly called Copyhold Inclosure and Tithe Commissioners. By the Settled Land Act, 1882, s. 26, a certificate of the commissioners that an improvement within that Act had been effected was authority to trustees to pay for the improvement out of capital money.

The powers and duties of the Land Commissioners were transferred to the Board of Agriculture by the Board of Agriculture Act, 1889. See COPYHOLD COMMISSIONERS.

Land drainage. The statute law relating to land drainage was consolidated by the Land Drainage Act, 1930, amended by the Land Drainage Act, 1961, the Agriculture (Miscellaneous Provisions) Act, 1968, and the Land Drainage (Amendment) Act, 1976. All matters relating to land drainage are under the general supervision of the regional water authority acting through regional and local land drainage committees (Water Act, 1973, s. 19, Sch. 5). A water authority may raise revenue by means of drainage charges (Drainage Rates Acts, 1958 and 1963; Land Drainage Act, 1961; Finance Act, 1963, Sch. 12 para. 23, Sch. 13 Pt. IV; Water Resources Act, 1963, Sch. 13 paras. 12, 13, Sch. 14; Agriculture (Miscellaneous Provisions) Act, 1968, Schs. 6, 8; Water Act, 1973, Schs. 5, 8, 9); S.I. 1974 No. 595, art. 315).

Water authorities exercise a general

supervision over land drainage but discharge their functions through regional land drainage committees (Water Act, 1973, s. 19).

The Coal-Mining (Subsidence) Act, 1957, authorises the carrying out of remedial or preventive measures in connection with land drainage affected or likely to be affected by subsidence.

See COAST PROTECTION; DRAIN; SEWER WATER.

Land gabel, a tax or rent issuing out of land. The land gabel mentioned in Domesday was at the rate of a penny a year for each house (Spelman).

Land improvement. See IMPROVEMENT OF LAND.

Land registries. See REGISTRATION OF TITLE TO LAND.

Land societies. See FREEHOLD LAND SOCIETIES.

Land tax, a tax laid upon land and houses, which by the statute 1688, 1 Will. & Mary, c. 3, superseded all the former methods of taxing either property or persons in respect of their property, whether by tenths or fifteenths, subsidies on land, hydages, scutages or tallages. It was a tax the burden of which fell on the beneficial proprietor. Land tax was abolished by the Finance Act, 1963, s. 68, together with the officers of Land Tax Commissioner, Clerk to the Land Tax Commissioners and collector of land tax. For Acts consequentially repealed see the Act of 1963, Sch. 14 Pts. V, VI.

Land tenants, terre-tenants: see the statute 1340, 14 Edw. 3, st. 1, c. 3. See TERRE-TENANT.

Land Transfer Acts. See REGISTRATION OF TITLE TO LAND.

Land values duties, duties imposed by the Finance (1909–10) Act, 1910, ss. 1–42. They were increment value duty, reversion duty, undeveloped land duty and mineral rights duty (*q.v.*). They have all been abolished (Finance Act, 1920, s. 57; Finance Act, 1967, Sch. 16 Pt. VIII).

Landa, an open field, a field cleared from wood.

Land-agende, Land-hlaford, or **Land-rica,** a proprietor of land; lord of the soil (Anc.Inst.Eng.).

Land-boc [Sax.; Lat. *libellus de terra*], the deed or charter by which lands were held (Spelman).

Land-cheap, a customary fine paid in some manors on the alienation of copyholds.

Landea, a ditch, in marshy lands, to carry water into the sea (Du Cange).

Landefricus, a landlord; a lord of the soil.

Landegandman, a copyholder, an inferior tenant of a manor (Spelman).

Landimers [Lat. *agrimensores*], measurers of land (Tomlin).

Landirecta, rights which charged the land whoever possessed it. See TRINODA NECESSITAS.

Landlocked, an expression sometimes applied to a piece of land belonging to one person and surrounded by land belonging to other persons, so that it cannot be approached except over their land (*London Corp.* v. *Riggs* (1880) 13 Ch.D. 798). See EASEMENT.

Landlord, he of whom land or tenements are held; who has a right to distrain for rent in arrear, etc. (Co.Litt. 57).

Landlord and tenant. A tenancy arises when the owner of an estate in land, called the lessor or landlord, agrees expressly or by implication to allow another person, called the lessee or tenant, to enjoy the exclusive possession and use of the land for a period less than the landlord's estate in it, generally upon payment of rent. The landlord's estate is called the reversion, and at common law a power of distress for rent is incident to the reversion.

Leases or tenancies may be for any agreed period such as for years or less, *e.g.*, for a year, half-year, quarter or week; from year to year; at will; on sufferance; or they may arise upon estoppel; or exist by force of a statute (see RENT RESTRICTION; LEASE). In a narrower sense the words "tenancy" and "landlord and tenant" are generally restricted to a lease of a house or land for occupation purposes. If nothing appears to the contrary, either expressly or by implication, in the lease or agreement, the landlord is not liable for any repairs and the tenant is bound to use the premises in a tenant-like manner and to restore the premises to the landlord at the end of the term in the state in which they were when he entered upon them subject to the deterioration which would ensue naturally during the term, having regard to the purpose for which they were let, and the tenant's implied agreement for tenant-like user of the premises. Beyond these obligations a tenant is not under any implied obligation to repair or reinstate the premises if destroyed or damaged by the act of God, natural decay, or by tempest or fire (*Yellowly* v. *Gower* (1855) 11 Exch. 174; *Standen* v. *Christmas* (1883) 10 Q.B. 135). The landlord is not under any implied obligation to repair or under any warranty that the premises are fit for the purposes for which they are taken except as to fitness upon letting furnished premises (*Collins* v. *Hopkins* [1923] 2 K.B. 617), or as to fitness and repair in the case of small houses. See the Housing Act, 1957, s. 6; London Government Act, 1963, Sch. 8 para. 2; *McCarrick* v. *Liverpool Corporation* [1947] A.C. 219. His only implied obligation is that the tenant shall quietly enjoy and possess the premises during the term free from disturbance by the landlord or by persons claiming against him or by paramount title, though it is said that in any letting short of a demise by deed the implied warranty does not extend to disturbance by title paramount (*Markham* v. *Paget* [1908] 1 Ch. 697; *Jones* v. *Lavington* [1903] 1 K.B. 253).

Another implied obligation on the tenant's part is that he is liable to an action of debt for the rent.

All these implied warranties and obligations arise out of privity of estate, so that if the reversion on the one hand or the lease on the other is assigned, the original lessor or lessee is no longer bound by these obligations, which devolve with the reversion and the land upon the respective assignees, but if the obligation in any form is expressed by way of covenant or agreement, the implied covenant is excluded as a rule and the obligation becomes binding by privity of contract, so that the original contractors are bound during the whole term to each other by contract and to the assignees by privity of estate only;

thus a lessee is liable for the rent and covenants notwithstanding assignment, while assignees being only bound by privity of estate, their obligations cease upon assignment over. Further, assignees are only bound by covenants running with the land, such as to pay rent, repair, not to assign or otherwise touching and concerning the thing demised; they are not bound by privity of estate by their predecessor's personal undertakings which do not affect the premises comprised in the lease, although, of course, if the assignee has covenanted with his assignor to the like effect, he becomes bound by his personal contract with the latter.

Formerly, covenants in respect of things having reference to the subject-matter of the lease not in existence at the date of covenant would not bind assigns unless they were named, but the word " assigns " in such covenants is not now necessary under the Law of Property Act, 1925, s. 79, in leases made after 1925; on the other hand, the benefit of such covenants passed to assigns without their being named by the Conveyancing Act, 1881, s. 58, repealed and reproduced as amended by the Law of Property Act, 1925, s. 78, in leases made after the commencement respectively of the Acts of 1882 and 1925, according to their respective provisions.

Houses are usually let at an " inclusive " or " exclusive " rent. " Inclusive " means that the landlord undertakes to pay the rates. " Exclusive " means that the burden of rates as well as the payment of rent falls upon the tenant. As a rule, the usual and proper covenants and agreements by the tenant in an exclusive lease are to pay the rent, rates and outgoings except landlord's taxes, and to keep and deliver up the premises in repair or good tenantable repair. An unqualified covenant to keep in repair means to reinstate and keep the premises in the state when the covenant begins to operate (*Walker* v. *Hatton* (1842) 10 M. & W. 249), even though destroyed by fire, etc. " Good tenantable repair " was explained in *Proudfoot* v. *Hart* (1890) 25 Q.B.D. 42, as such repair as having regard to the age, character and locality of the house would make it reasonably fit for the occupation of a reasonably minded tenant of the class who would be likely to take it. These covenants are frequently supplemented by undertakings to paint at agreed periods, to insure, not to assign or underlet without the landlord's permission, as modified by the Landlord and Tenant Act, 1927, s. 19 (1) (*a*), and otherwise. The measure of damages for breach of a covenant to repair is the amount by which the reversion has been diminished (Landlord and Tenant Act, 1927, s. 18; *Jaquin* v. *Holland* [1960] 1 W.L.R. 258).

In all leases and tenancy agreements the landlord, as a rule, qualifies his implied covenant for quiet possession so as to exclude his liability for acts of persons under a paramount title.

Apart from agreement or condition terminating the lease or proviso for re-entry, the tenant has an exclusive right to a possession of the premises for the whole term, even against the landlord, and when the landlord is under any obligation in regard to the premises, the tenant generally agrees to allow the landlord at all reasonable times to inspect and enter for the agreed purposes. Further, even if the tenant fails to pay the rent or commits breaches of covenant, the landlord cannot enter unless the lease or agreement contains a proviso for re-entry in those events (Common Law Procedure Act, 1852, s. 210; Judicature Act, 1925, s. 99 (1) (*f*) (*g*), Sch. 1). As to relief against forfeiture for non-payment of rent, see the Judicature Act, 1925, s. 46; as to forfeiture for breach of covenant, see the Law of Property Act, 1925, s. 146, as amended by the Landlord and Tenant Act, 1927, s. 18.

The provisions of the Landlord and Tenant Act, 1927, which gave a right to payment of compensation for loss of goodwill or a new lease in lieu thereof are repealed by the Landlord and Tenant Act, 1954, which gives a right to a continued tenancy irrespective of the existence of goodwill. See also the Law of Property Act, 1969, ss. 1–15, Sch. 1.

A landlord may oppose the grant of a new tenancy on the ground that he intends to occupy the property comprised in the tenancy for the purposes of his own business (Landlord and Tenant Act, 1954, s. 30; Law of Property Act, 1969, s. 6). See Woodfall, *Landlord and Tenant*.

In any proceedings in which a tenant of a dwelling alleges a breach on the part of the landlord of a repairing covenant, the court may order specific performance of the covenant. (Housing Act, 1974, s. 125.) Where a landlord is liable to maintain or repair premises, the landlord owes to all persons who might reasonably be expected to be affected by defects in the state of the premises a duty to take care that they are reasonably safe from personal injury or from damage to their property caused by a defect in the premises (Defective Premises Act, 1972, s. 4).

The identity of the landlord of a dwelling must be disclosed to the tenant on request (Housing Act, 1974, s. 121). If the landlord of a dwelling assigns his interest the assignee is under an obligation to give notice of that fact to the tenant (s. 122).

See AGRICULTURAL HOLDING; DANGEROUS PREMISES; DISTRESS; FIXTURES; HOLDING OVER; INVITEE; LEASE; LICENCE TO ASSIGN; NOTICE TO QUIT; OCCUPIERS' LIABILITY; RENT; TENANCY; TENANT; TERM.

Land-man [Lat. *terricola*], a terre-tenant (Blount).

Landmark, an object fixing the boundary of an estate or property.

Landrail, included in the definition of game in the Game Licences Act, 1860, s. 2.

Land-reeve, a person whose business it is to overlook a farm or estate, to attend to the woods and hedge-timber, and to the state of the fences, gates, buildings, private roads, drift-ways, and watercourses, and to the stocking of commons, and encroachments of every kind, and to prevent or detect waste and report the same to the manager or land-steward. See REEVE.

Lands Clauses Acts, the Lands Clauses Consolidation Act, 1845, the Lands Clauses Consolidation Acts Amendment Act, 1860, the Lands Clauses Consolidation Act, 1869, the Lands Clauses (Umpire) Act, 1883, and the Lands Clauses (Taxation of Costs) Act, 1895.

These Acts formed a code under which

land could be compulsorily acquired for public or quasi-public purposes, but only by way of the incorporation of the Acts with a special Act passed for a particular purpose. Such a special Act may be one for the acquisition of land for purposes of national defence or official purposes, or the acquisition of land for local or municipal purposes by public bodies, or the acquisition of land for commercial purposes of public utility by private persons or private corporations.

The procedure laid down by the Lands Clauses Acts continues to apply to notices to treat but generally the procedure for the acquisition of land is now governed by the Acquisition of Land (Authorisation Procedure) Act, 1946, and in certain cases the special parliamentary procedure laid down by the Statutory Orders (Special Procedure) Act, 1945, applies. See ACCOMMODATION WORKS; COMPENSATION; NOTICE TO TREAT; SUPERFLUOUS LANDS.

Lands Tribunal, a tribunal set up under the Lands Tribunals Act, 1949, with jurisdiction to determine, in place of the official arbitrators, questions relating to compensation for the compulsory acquisition of land and other matters referred to in s. 1 (3) of the Act, including the extinguishment or modification of restrictive covenants under the Law of Property Act, 1925, s. 84, as amended by the Law of Property Act, 1969, s. 28.

The jurisdiction of the Tribunal in respect of compensation for land compulsorily acquired is now exercised under the Land Compensation Act, 1961, ss. 1–4. See COMPENSATION.

The Tribunal has a discretion as to costs which must be exercised judicially; reasons must be given for any departure from the usual rule that a successful party will not be ordered to pay the costs of an unsuccessful party (*Pepys* v. *London Transport Executive* [1975] 1 W.L.R. 234). See also the Tribunals and Inquiries Act, 1971, Sch. 1 and ADMINISTRATIVE TRIBUNALS.

Lands, tenements and hereditaments, the most comprehensive description of real property. See HEREDITAMENT; LAND; TENEMENT.

Landscape areas. The Town and Country Planning (Landscape Areas Special Development) Order, 1950 (No. 729), made under the Town and Country Planning Act, 1947, s. 13, designates certain areas of natural beauty wherein the design and appearance of all buildings, including those for agriculture and forestry, are under control. For power to make development orders, see the Town and Country Planning Act, 1971, s. 24.

Land-steward, a person who overlooks or has the management of a farm or estate.

Land-waiter, an officer of the custom-house, whose duty was, upon landing any merchandise, to examine, taste, weigh, or measure it, and to take an account thereof. In some ports he also executed the office of a coast-waiter. Land-waiters were occasionally styled searchers, and attended and joined with the patent-searcher in the execution of dockets for the shipping of goods to be exported to foreign parts; where drawbacks on bounties were to be paid to the merchant on the exportation of goods, they, as well as the patent-searchers, certified the shipping thereof on the debentures (Encyc.Londin.). See TIDEWAITER.

Langdale's (Lord) Act, the Wills Act, 1837.

Langeman, a lord of a manor (1 Co. Inst. 5).

Langeolum [Lat. *lana*], an undergarment made of wool, formerly worn by the monks, which reached to their knees (1 Dugd.Mon. 419).

Languidus, in ill-health; a return made by a sheriff to a writ, when the removal of a person in his custody would endanger his life. See DUCES TECUM LICET LANGUIDUS.

Lanis descrescentia Walliae traducendis absque custuma, a writ which lay to the customer of a port to permit one to pass wool without paying custom, it having been paid before in Wales (Reg. Brev. 279).

Lano niger, a base coin in the reign of Edward I (Mem. in Scac.).

Lapidation, the act of stoning a person to death.

Lapis marmorious, a marble stone about twelve feet long and three feet broad, placed at the upper end of Westminster Hall, where was also a marble chair erected on the middle thereof, in which the sovereign sat at the coronation dinner, and at other times the Lord Chancellor (Orig.Jurid.).

Lapse [Lat. *lapsus*], error; failing in duty.

As a general rule, when a person to whom property has been devised or bequeathed dies before the testator, the devise or bequest fails or lapses, and the property goes as if the gift had not been made; consequently, if a testator bequeaths £100 to A (or to A " his executors or administrators ") and the residue of his property to B, then, if A dies during the lifetime of the testator, the legacy lapses and falls into the residue, that is, it goes to B on the testator's death. There are, however, some exceptions to this rule. Thus if property is given to several persons as joint tenants, on the death of one of them during the lifetime of the testator the whole goes to the survivors. And if property is given to a person in tail who dies before the testator, leaving issue capable of taking under the entail, the property goes as if the devisee had died immediately after the testator (Wills Act, 1837, s. 32; Law of Property Act, 1925, s. 130). And if a testator gives property to a child or other descendant of himself, and such descendant dies leaving issue who survive the testator, the gift does not lapse but takes effect as if the person to whom the gift was made had died immediately after the testator (Wills Act, 1837, s. 33) (*Re Basioli* [1953] Ch. 367). This rule applies to illegitimate children or other issue (Family Law Reform Act, 1969, s. 16).

In ecclesiastical law, a lapse occurs when a benefice becomes void and the patron neglects to present within six months after the avoidance. In such a case the patronage devolves from the patron to the bishop (see COLLATION) and on the neglect of the bishop to the metropolitan, and on the neglect of the metropolitan to the Crown.

In criminal proceedings, " lapse " is used in the same sense as " abate " in civil procedure, that is to say, it means that the proceedings come to an end

from the death of the accused or some other event. The death of the complainant or prosecutor does not cause a lapse (*R.* v. *Truelove* (1880) 5 Q.B.D. 336). See ABATEMENT OF CRIMINAL PROCEEDINGS.

Lapsus calami, a slip of the pen; see *Re Powell-Cotton's Resettlement* [1957] Ch. 159, at p. 163.

Lapwing. See WILD BIRDS.

Larboard, the port, or left-hand, side of a ship looking forward, as opposed to the starboard, or right-hand side.

Larceny [Fr. *larcin;* Lat. *latrocinium*], contracted from latrociny, the unlawful taking and carrying away of things personal, with intent to deprive the rightful owner of the same. The offence of larceny at common law was abolished by the Theft Act, 1968, s. 32, and by Sch. 3 Pt. I the Larceny Acts, 1861 and 1916 were repealed. See now THEFT. See also ADVERTISEMENT; ANIMALS FERAE NATURAE; BLACKMAIL; BURGLARY; DECEPTION; EMBEZZLEMENT; FALSE PRETENCE; GRAND LARCENY; HANDLING STOLEN GOODS; HOUSEBREAKING; JOY-RIDING; MISAPPROPRIATION; PETIT LARCENY; ROBBERY.

Lardarius regis, the king's larderer, or clerk of the kitchen.

Larding money [Lat. *lardarum*], a small customary annual payment made by the tenants of the manor of Bradford, in Wiltshire, to their lord for liberty to feed their hogs with the masts of the lord's wood, the fat of a hog being called lard; or a commutation for some customary service of carrying salt or meat to the lord's larder (1 Dugd.Mon. 321).

Larks. See WILD BIRDS.

Larrons [Lat. *latro*], thieves.

Lascar, a native Indian sailor; the term is also applied to tent-pitchers, inferior artillery-men, and others.

Agreements by masters or owners of ships with lascars are regulated by the Merchant Shipping Act, 1894, s. 125, reproducing the Merchant Shipping Act, 1854, s. 544, and saving the Lascars Act, 1823, ss. 25-34.

Lashite or **Lashlite,** a kind of forfeiture during the government of the Danes in England.

Lassence v. Tierney, Rule in. This rule, as stated by Lord Davey in *Hancock*

v. *Watson* [1902] A.C. 14, is that if, on an absolute gift to one beneficiary, trusts are engrafted in favour of other beneficiaries which fail, the absolute gift takes effect so far as the trusts have failed to the exclusion of the residuary legatee or next-of-kin as the case may be.

Last [Sax. *haelstan*; Fr. *lest*], a burden; a weight or measure of fish, corn, wool, leather, pitch, etc. See DAKIR.

Last court, an obsolete administrative assembly in the Cinque Ports constituted of the bailiffs (*q.v.*) and jurats (*q.v.*); a court held by the twenty-four jurats in the marshes of Kent, and summoned by the bailiffs, whereby orders were made to lay and levy taxes, impose penalties, etc., for the preservation of the marshes.

Last day of term. Before the abolition of term (*q.v.*) it was the custom of the common law courts on the last day of each term that the junior bar should move its motions first, and that they should begin with the barrister junior in point of standing and end with the senior. The inner bar then moved, but in order of seniority.

Last heir. He to whom land came for want of heirs, whether the king or the lord, was formerly known as the last heir (7 Bract. c. 17). See ESCHEAT.

Last resort. A court from which there is no appeal is called the court of last resort.

Lastage or **Lestage** [Lat. *lastagium*], a toll payable by traders attending fairs and markets; the ballast or lading of a ship; also, custom paid for wares sold by the last, as herrings, pitch, etc.

In London it was one of the metage (*q.v.*) dues.

Lastatinus, an assassin or murderer (Wals.).

Lata culpa dolo aequiparatur. (Gross negligence is tantamount to fraud.) It has been said that this maxim does not hold in English law; negligence, however great, does not of itself constitute fraud (*Le Lievre* v. *Gould* [1893] 1 Q.B. at p. 498), but a statement made with a reckless disregard of its truth or untruth has the same effect as a statement which is wilfully untrue.

Latching, an underground survey.

Latent [Lat. *latens*], hidden, concealed; secret. See AMBIGUITY.

Latent defect, a defect which could not previously to an accident have been avoided by care or discovered by reasonable examination.

Latera, sidesmen, companions, assistants.

Laterare, to lie sideways, in opposition to lying endways, used in descriptions of lands.

Lath, Lathe, Lada, a part of a county. In some counties there is an intermediate division between the shire and the hundred—as lathes in Kent, and rapes in Sussex—each of them containing three or four hundreds or wapentakes.

Lathreeve, Ledgreeve, or **Tritin-greve,** an officer under the Saxon government who had authority over a lathe.

Latimer [Fr. *latinier*, *latiner*], an interpreter (2 Co.Inst. 515). It is suggested that it should be *latiner*, because he who understood Latin might be a good interpreter. Camden makes it signify a Frenchman or interpreter (Britan. 598).

Latin, the language of the ancient Romans.

There are said to be three sorts of law Latin: good Latin, allowed by the grammarians and lawyers; false or incongruous Latin, which in times past would abate original writs though it would not make void any judicial writ, declaration, or plea, etc.; and words of art, known only to the sages of the law, and not to grammarians, called lawyers' Latin.

By the statute 1362, 36 Edw. 3, st. 1, c. 15, it was enacted that all pleas should be pleaded, adjudged, etc., in the English language, but be entered and enrolled in Latin. The records of the courts continued to be entered in Latin until the statute 1731, 4 Geo. 2, c. 26, which provided that both the pleadings and the records should thenceforth be framed in English (1 P. & M. 58; 2 H.H.E.L. 477).

See FALSE LATIN; FRENCH.

Latin information, an information and action by the Crown, the Duchy of Lancaster or the Duke of Cornwall in the nature of civil proceedings to recover a debt or damages for a tort or otherwise (see *Att.-Gen.* v. *Valle-Jones* [1935] 2 K.B. 209), abolished by the Crown Proceedings Act, 1947, Sch. 1. An English information was an information in equity on the revenue side of the Queen's

Bench Division. See ENGLISH INFORMATION.

Latin side. See CHANCERY.

Latinarius, one able to translate Latin (*Domesday*).

Latitat (he lies hid), a writ whereby all persons were originally summoned to answer in personal actions in the King's Bench; so called because it was supposed by the writ that the defendant lurked and lay hid, and could not be found in the county of Middlesex (in which the court was holden) to be taken by bill, but had gone into some other county, to the sheriff of which this writ was directed to apprehend him there (Fitz.N.B. 78; *Termes de la Ley*). It was abolished by the Uniformity of Process Act, 1832. See BILL OF MIDDLESEX.

Lator [Lat. *latus*], a bearer, a messenger.

Latro; Latrocinium. These words generally meant respectively a robber (*latro*) and *latrocinium* (robbery): but in Leg. W. 1 *latro* is used as meaning one having exclusive local jurisdiction in cases of robbery and in a charter of Henry I *latrocinium* is used in the same sense.

Latrocination [at. *latro*, a robber], the act of robbing; a depredation.

Latrociny, larceny.

Latter-math, a second mowing; the after-math.

Laudare, to advise or persuade; to arbitrate.

Laudatio, testimony delivered in court concerning an accused person's good behaviour and integrity of life. It resembled the practice which prevails in our trials of calling persons to speak to a prisoner's character. The least number of the *laudatores* among the Romans was ten.

Laudator, an arbitrator.

Laudibus Legum Angliae, De. Sir John Fortescue, who had been some time chief justice of the King's Bench in the reign of Henry VI, is said to have written this work, while in exile with the Prince of Wales, and others of the Lancastrian party, in France. He was then made Chancellor; and in that character he supposes himself holding a conversation with the young prince on the nature and excellence of the laws of England compared with the civil law and the laws of other countries. He considers at length the mode of trying matters of fact by jury, and shows how it excels that by witnesses. He informs us that some of our princes wished to introduce the civil law merely for the sake of governing in the arbitrary way allowed by that law, which declares, *quod principi placuit legis habet vigorem*. He then proceeds to examine some other points of difference between the civil and common law, always deciding in favour of our own. He concludes his book with a short account of the societies where the law of England was studied, the degrees and ranks in the profession, with the manner in which they were conferred; to these are subjoined some short remarks on the conduct and delay of suits (4 Reeves 113). See FORTESCUE.

Laudimium, the fiftieth part of the value of an estate paid by a new proprietor to the tenant for investiture or leave to take possession (Civil Law).

Laudum, an arbitrament or award (Wals.).

Laughe, frank-pledge (2 Reeves 17).

Launcegay, a kind of ancient weapon, prohibited by the statute 1383, 7 Rich. 2, c. 13.

Laund or **Lawnd,** an open field without wood (Blount).

Laundry. The Factories Act, 1961, s. 175 (2) (*a*), provides that a "factory" includes a laundry carried on as ancillary to another business or incidentally to the purposes of a public institution.

The Act controls the period of employment of women in laundries (s. 110) and contains other regulations (s. 71) for their proper management.

Sending infected articles which have not been properly disinfected or without proper notice to laundries, private or public, is prohibited by Public Health Act, 1936, s. 152; London Government Act, 1963, s. 40; Local Government Act, 1972, Sch. 14 para. 14.

A local authority may supply laundry facilities in connection with housing (Housing Act, 1957, s. 95).

Laureate or **Laureat** [Lat. *laurea*], an officer of the household of the sovereign, whose business formerly consisted only in composing an ode annually, on the sovereign's birthday, and on the new year; and sometimes also, though rarely, on the occasion of any remarkable victory (Warton's *Hist. of English Poetry*).

The title is derived from the circumstance that in classical times and in the Middle Ages the most distinguished poets were solemnly crowned with laurel. From this the practice found its way into our universities; and it is for that reason that Selden, in his *Titles of Honour*, speaks of the laurel crown as an ensign of the degree of mastership in poetry. A relic of the old university practice of crowning distinguished students of poetry exists in the term "Laureation," which is still used at St. Andrew's University to signify the taking of the degree of Master of Arts.

See POET LAUREATE.

Laurels, pieces of gold, coined in 1619, with the king's head laureated, *i.e.*, with a laurel wreath round it.

Lavatories. As to lavatories in factories and workships, see the Public Health Act, 1936, s. 46 (amended by the Factories Act, 1937, Sch. 6; Offices, Shops and Railway Premises Act, 1963, Sch. 2); as to public lavatories, see the Public Health Act, 1936, ss. 87–89 (amended by the Public Health Act, 1961, s. 80; Local Government Act, 1972, Sch. 14 paras. 9, 10); as to lavatories in shops, offices, etc., see the Offices, Shops and Railway Premises Act, 1963, s. 9.

Turnstiles in public lavatories have been removed under the Public Lavatories (Turnstiles) Act, 1963.

Lavatorium, a laundry or place to wash in; a place in the porch or entrance of cathedral churches, where the priest and other officiating ministers were obliged to wash their hands before they proceeded to divine service.

Lavina. See LABINA.

Law [Lat. *lex, ligare*, to bind; Sax. *lage, lagea, lah*; Fr. *loi*; Ital. *legge*], a rule of action to which men are obliged to make their conduct conformable; a command, enforced by some sanction, to acts or forbearances of a class. A principle of conduct observed habitually by an individual or a class. When sufficiently formulated or defined to be observed uniformly by the whole of a class it may become a custom; or it may be imposed on all individuals who consent or are unable to resist its application and the sanction or penalty which is imposed for non-compliance, and in that case it become a law. If, in addition, the law and its sanction are imposed by, or by authority of a sovereign, the law becomes "positive." Short of positive law the principle may be called a moral or social law. Generally speaking, jurisprudence is concerned only with positive law, and law in its ordinary legal sense means positive law. See LEX.

Law is used in two principal senses, the idea common to both of them being uniformity of action. In one sense "law" is merely the expression for a uniformity of action which has been observed: as when we speak of the laws of gravitation, or say that crystals are formed according to certain laws: here the law follows from the uniformity. In the other sense, the law produces the uniformity, that is, the law is a rule of action. To this latter class belong the law of nature (using that term in the sense of rules imposed, as Blackstone puts it, on man by his Maker) and laws of human origin. Human laws again are either (i) social (such as the so-called laws of honour, morality, etc.), or (ii) political, the latter being divisible into (a) international law, and (b) positive law, that is to say, law capable of judicial enforcement, or law in the technical sense of the word.

In its widest sense, law is an aggregate of rules enforceable by judicial means in a given country; thus, we speak of the law of England as opposed to the law of France or the civil law. This kind of law is called territorial or municipal law to distinguish it from international law.

With reference to its origin, law is derived from judicial precedents (see STARE DECISIS), from legislation or from custom. That part of the law of England which is derived from judicial precedents is called common law, equity, or admiralty, probate or ecclesiastical law, according to the nature of the courts by which it was originally enforced. That part of the law which is derived from legislation is called the statute law:

many statutes are classed under one of the divisions above mentioned, because they have merely modified or extended portions of it, while others have created altogether new rules. That part of the law which is derived from custom is sometimes called the customary law (see CUSTOM).

The ordinary, but not very useful, division of law into written and unwritten, rests on the same principle. The written law is the statute law, the unwritten law is the common law (*q.v.*).

With reference to its subject-matter, law is either public or private. Public law is that part of the law which deals with the State, either by itself or in its relations with individuals, and is called constitutional, when it regulates the relations between the various divisions of the sovereign power; and administrative, when it regulates the business which the State has to do; the most important branches of the latter class are the criminal law and the law for the prevention of crimes; the law relating to education, public health, the poor, etc.; ecclesiastical law; and the law of judicial procedure (courts of law, evidence, etc.).

Private or civil law deals with those relations between individuals with which the State is not directly concerned: as in the relations between husband and wife, parent and child, and the various kinds of property, contracts, torts, trusts, legacies, the right recognised by the rules of admiralty law, etc. (See ADMIRAL; ADMIRALTY ACTION; COMMON LAW; EQUITY.) Even here, however, the courts take cognisance, to a certain extent, of the indirect effects of private conduc on the community in general; they accordingly refuse to sanction contracts which are immoral, or in restraint of trade or marriage, or are otherwise against public policy. See PUBLIC POLICY.

Law is also divided by the Benthamite school into substantive and adjective. Substantive law is that part of the law which creates rights and obligations, while adjective law provides a method of enforcing and protecting them. In other words, adjective law is the law of procedure.

In a narrower sense, " law " signifies a rule of law, especially one of statutory origin; and hence, in its narrowest sense, " law " is equivalent to " statute "; as when we speak of the Poor Law, the Corn Laws, etc.

Law is also sometimes used as opposed to equity, and then means the principles followed in common law courts in contradistinction to those which were administered only in courts of equity before the Judicature Acts (*q.v.*).

The law of foreign countries is a question of fact in English courts. See FOREIGN LAW.

See FACT; MAKE HIS LAW; RESPONDEAT OUSTER.

Law Christian, the ecclesiastical law as distinguished from the common law.

Law Commission, a body consisting of a chairman and four other commissioners appointed by the Lord Chancellor, to promote the systematic development, simplification and modernisation of the law (Law Commissions Act, 1965).

Law Courts, the Royal Courts of Justice (*q.v.*).

Law day, " a leet or sheriffes tourn " (*Termes de la Ley.* See LAGE-DAY.

Law List, a list of barristers, solicitors, and other legal practitioners. It has been published annually since 1801. The Solicitors Act, 1974, s. 18, made the list prima facie evidence that any solicitor whose name appears therein holds the prescribed certificate for the current year and that any solicitor whose name does not appear therein does not hold such certificate. Publication of the *Law List* in one volume ceased with the 1976 edition. Thereafter information should be sought from the Law Society and the Senate of the Inns of Court and the Bar.

Law Lords, the Lord Chancellor, the Lords of Appeal in Ordinary (*q.v.*), ex-Lord Chancellors, and other peers who have held high judicial office.

Law, Martial. See MARTIAL LAW.

Law merchant [*lex mercatoria*], that part of the law of England which governs mercantile transactions. It is founded upon the general custom of merchants of all nations, which, though different from the general rules of the common law, has been gradually engrafted into it and made to form part of it. See CUSTOM.

Law of marque. See LETTERS OF MARQUE.

Law of nations, the old-fashioned equivalent for international law (*q.v.*) or, more strictly, public international law. It is a literal translation of the Latin phrase *jus gentium*, which, however, did not mean the law governing the conduct of States in their relations with one another, but those rules of law which are common to all civilised nations: *vocaturque jus gentium, quasi quo jure omnes gentes utuntur.*

Law of nature. See JUS; LAW.

Law of Property Act, 1925. This Act, with the amending Acts of 1926, 1929, 1932, 1964 and 1969, consolidated and effected changes in the land laws with the object of simplifying the transfer and conveyance of land. It abolished all legal estates or tenures in land except an estate in fee simple in possession and a term of years absolute in land or in certain incorporeal hereditaments arising out of or annexed to or charged upon the legal estate in land. Any number of these legal estates can exist in respect of the same piece of land or incorporeal hereditament; for instance, land may be held in fee simple, leased and mortgaged at the same time. All other estates and interests in land are reduced to equitable interests. All mortgages of the same legal estate under the statutory conditions are legal estates, none being for the whole fee simple or the term, but each for a term taken out of the fee or original term which remains in the mortgagor and so that each subsequent mortgage overlaps the previous one and takes up some of the residue of the legal estate still remaining in the mortgagor. See MORTGAGE.

The chief legal estates converted into equitable interests from January 1, 1926, are tenancies in common or in undivided shares in land (see UNDIVIDED SHARES IN LAND); limited estates, less than the fee or entire term, *e.g.*, entailed estates, estates for life or in remainder whether vested or contingent; and legal estates of infants in fee simple, a legal estate not being capable of being held by an infant (see INFANT). The object of these changes was that the entirety of the legal estate should be in the hands of an owner or joint owners of full age able to deal with the whole estate without the concurrence of holders of equitable interests in favour of a purchaser for value by means of an expedient which is generally termed " the curtain " (*q.v.*). In the case of trustees for sale as to undivided shares; the tenant for life or other statutory owner of the fee in trust for limited or settled estates and infants' estates; personal representatives as to the estate of the deceased, whether testate or intestate; mortgagees; or an order of the court, the whole of the legal estate in the fee simple or term may (subject to the Law of Property Act, 1925, s. 2 (3)) be conveyed free from, *i.e.*, so as to overreach, equitable interests to a purchaser for value without disclosing, or putting him upon inquiry concerning the equitable interests or title to the same so withheld from his notice (Law of Property Act, 1925, ss. 1, 2). A person not included in the classes referred to, *e.g.*, a sole beneficial owner in possession of his property, selling it in exercise of his powers as such owner, cannot take advantage of the curtain except in so far as it may have been properly used in connection with any link in his own title. See LAND CHARGE; MORTGAGE; REGISTRATION OF TITLE TO LAND.

The registration of equitable interests and some legal charges under the Land Charges Act, 1972, has to some extent preserved the legal rights against the land of the owners of these equities (see LAND CHARGE). Subject to the Acts all equitable interests are preserved (Law of Property Act, 1925, s. 3).

Notwithstanding these changes, the old law of real property as it existed on December 31, 1925, is still in force subject to express statutory modification in regard to the equitable interests to which the old legal estates in land have been reduced, and the old law is applicable for the purpose of ascertaining the title of the persons claiming land or any interest therein before 1926.

See ABSTRACT OF TITLE; COMMON; CONDITIONS OF SALE; ESTATE; LEASE; MORTGAGE; NOTICE; PERPETUITY.

Law of the staple, the law merchant (*q.v.*).

Law Officers of the Crown. These,

more generally described as the Law Officers, are the Attorney-General (*q.v.*) and the Solicitor-General (*q.v.*). Down to 1872 the Advocate-General (*q.v.*) was also included in the expression. The Scottish Law Officers are the Lord Advocate and the Solicitor-General.

Law reports, reports of judgments of courts on points of law, published for the purpose of being used as precedents (see REPORTS). Prior to 1865, these reports were all executed and published as mere private speculations, one reporter or pair of reporters being usually, though not always, accredited by the chief judge of each court. In 1865 the Incorporated Council of Law Reporting for England and Wales began to publish monthly the reports called *The Law Reports*. These have no monopoly and any report made by a member of the Bar and published on his responsibility may be cited in argument.

The Scottish reports of civil cases from 1907 onwards are known as " Session Cases " and are published annually. They are cited thus, *e.g.*: 1934 S.C. 121; House of Lords cases are cited thus, *e.g.*: 1934 S.C.(H.L.) 33. The reports prior to 1907 are in five series, referred to by the names of the editors—Shaw, Dunlop, Macpherson, Rettie and Fraser. They are cited by the number of the volume in the series, and the initial of the editor, thus, *e.g.*: 12 R. 121. Scottish cases are also reported in the *Scots Law Times* (S.L.T.).

Transcripts of all judgments in the Court of Appeal are filed in the Bar Library. Copies may be obtained from the Official Association of Shorthand Writers on payment of the usual charges. See 117 S.J. 206. Summaries of unreported decisions are published from time to time in the monthly parts of *Current Law* and are printed in the *Current Law Year Book* from 1973 onwards.

The Incorporated Council of Law Reporting is a charity (*Incorporated Council of Law Reporting for England and Wales* v. *Att.-Gen.* [1972] Ch. 73).

Law Society. On the decay of the Inns of Chancery, which in their later aspect were the Inns specially appropriated to attorneys, a society was formed called the Society of Gentlemen Practisers in the several Courts of Law and Equity. It was established in 1739, and was active and prosperous, at least until 1810. In 1819 another society, called the Metropolitan Law Society, came into existence, the object of both societies being the prevention of abuses amongst solicitors, attorneys and proctors. In 1825, a society, known as the Law Society, was formed by Mr. Bryan Holme, a member of the Society of Gentlemen Practisers. This society received a charter of incorporation in 1831; it was thenceforth known as the Incorporated Law Society; and the societies which had preceded it became defunct. The Incorporated Law Society received in 1845 a further charter, in which it is referred to as " The Society of Attorneys, Solicitors and Proctors, and others, not being barristers, practising in the Courts of Law and Equity of the United Kingdom." Under the Solicitors Act, 1843, s. 2, the society was made registrar of attorneys and solicitors: the custody of the roll of solicitors, which previously had been with the Clerk of the Petty Bag (*q.v.*), was transferred to it by the Solicitors Act, 1888, s. 5. For the functions of the Law Society under the Solicitors Act, 1974, see SOLICITORS.

The charters already referred to were supplemented by others granted in 1872, 1903, 1909 and 1954. In the charter of 1903 the society is described as the Law Society: that is now its official description and is used in the Solicitors Act, 1974.

The society first instituted lectures for students in 1833.

Every person who is or has been a practising solicitor in England or Ireland, or a writer to the signet, or writer in Scotland, is qualified to become a member of the society. Non-practising solicitors are eligible for membership (Solicitors Act, 1974, s. 76). If a solicitor's name is struck off the roll, that solicitor ceases to be a member of the society. A member who is suspended from practice is not entitled to the rights and privileges of the society. The Council of the society have further rights of suspension (s. 78). Annual subscriptions are payable for membership (s. 77).

The Council of the society may

appoint committees for general or special purposes (s. 79). The Council has general power to act on behalf of the society (s. 80).

The Law Society has a right to be heard on matters of principle affecting the duties of solicitors generally (*Pearson* v. *Pearson* (*Queen's Proctor Showing Cause*) [1969] 1 W.L.R. 722).

The Council of the society examines Bills brought into Parliament, and makes such remarks and suggestions as appear to it necessary and organises opposition to such as appear to affect injuriously the rights and privileges of members. The society has long been active in supporting legal reforms, and is now usually referred to for suggestions and remarks on Bills affecting the principles of practice of the law, and upon new rules and orders. Many reforms in law and practice have been initiated, and numerous Acts of Parliament have originated with or have been supported by the Society. Questions of professional practice and etiquette are referred to the Council, and they also assist members of the society by giving information on new points of law or practice, and by obtaining judicial decisions on doubtful questions of general interest. The Council also advise members through the Scale Committee on questions relating to costs.

A provincial meeting is usually held in the autumn of each year on the invitation of one of the country law societies. At these meetings an address by the president and other papers are read and discussed; and social gatherings, entertainments and excursions are arranged.

Provincial law societies on somewhat similar lines have been established in various parts of the country.

See COLONIAL ATTORNEYS RELIEF ACTS.

Law spiritual [*lex spiritualis*], the ecclesiastical law (Co.Litt. 344).

Law suit, an action or litigation.

Law terms. See TERM.

Lawday, a court-leet, or view of frank-pledge; a day on which courts, more especially the old courts of the shire and the hundred, were held; hence used for the sitting of such a court or for the court itself.

Lawful. The natural meaning in a statute of the words " it shall be lawful " is permissive only, but if the words are used to effectuate a legal right, they are compulsory (*Julius* v. *Bishop of Oxford* (1880) 5 App.Cas. 182).

Lawful day, a day on which legal business may be done. See DIES NON.

Lawful heirs; Lawful issue; Heirs lawfully begotten. In these expressions the words " lawful " or " lawfully begotten " are mere redundances and do not affect the meaning of the words " heir " or " issue " (*q.v.*).

Lawing of dogs, the cutting of several claws of the forefeet of dogs in the forest, to prevent their running at deer. See EXPEDITATE.

Lawless court, a manor court which belonged to the honour of Raleigh, held on King's Hill, at Rochford, in Essex, on Wednesday morning next after Michaelmas Day, yearly, at cock-crowing, at which court they whispered and had no candle, nor any pen nor ink, but a coal; and he who owed suit or service there, and did not appear, forfeited double his rent (Cam.Brit.).

Lawless man [*ex lex*], an outlaw.

Lawyer, a person learned in the law, as a barrister or solicitor.

Lay [λαός], not clerical; not professional; regarding or belonging to the people, as distinct from the clergy or a particular profession.

Lay or ley also means a rate. In Tudor times on receipt of a precept from the high constable the reeve laid a lay or rate on the landowners of the district sufficient to collect the sum mentioned in the precept.

Lay corporations, bodies politic; they are either: civil, created for temporal purposes; or eleemosynary, created for charitable purposes.

Lay days, Laying days, running or consecutive days; a term used as to the time of loading and unloading ships. They are the days which are allowed by a charterparty for loading and unloading the ship. If the vessel is detained beyond the period allowed, demurrage (*q.v.*) becomes payable. See CHARTERPARTY.

Lay impropriators, lay persons to whose use ecclesiastical benefices have been annexed. At the dissolution of the monasteries by the statutes 1535, 27 Hen.

8, c. 28, and 1539, 31 Hen. 8, c. 13, the appropriations of the several parsonages which belonged to them were given to the Crown. The same had been done in former reigns when the alien priories were dissolved and given to the Crown. From these two roots have sprung all the lay impropriations or secular parsonages, they having been afterwards granted out from time to time by the Crown to laymen. See APPROPRIATION; IMPROPRIATION; LAY RECTOR.

Lay investiture, the putting of a bishop into possession of the temporalities of his see. This takes place when he performs homage (q.v.).

Lay people, jurymen.

Lay rector, a person holding by title under lay impropriation. As to the lay rector's liability to repair, see *Morley* v. *Leacroft* [1896] P. 92, and *Stuart* v. *Haughley Parish Church Council* (1935) 104 L.J.Ch. 314. As to the right to occupy a seat in the chancel of a church, see *Stileman-Gibbard* v. *Wilkinson* [1897] 1 Q.B. 749.

Laye [Old Fr. *ley*], law.

Lay-fee, lands held in fee of a lay lord, and subject to the ordinary services, as distinguished from lands held in frankalmoign discharged from such services.

Laystall [Sax.], a place for dung or soil.

Lazar [Old Fr. *lazare* from *Lazarus* of the New Testament (Luke xvi, 20)], a leper, any person infected with a nauseous and pestilential disease.

Lazaret, or **Lazaretto,** places where quarantine is to be performed by persons coming from infected countries; to escape from them was punishable by a fine of £200, and for a quarantine officer to permit any person to leave them without an order of the Privy Council was a felony under the Quarantine Act, 1825, repealed by the Public Health Act, 1896, itself repealed and replaced by the Public Health Act, 1936.

Le Roy (or **la Reine**) **le veult.** (The King (or the Queen) wills it.) The form of the royal assent (q.v.) to public Bills in Parliament.

Le Roy (or **la Reine**) **n'est lié par aucun statut s'il ne fut expressement nommé.** (The King (or the Queen) is not bound by any statute unless expressly named therein.)

Le Roy (or **la Reine**) **remercie ses bons sujets, accepte leur bénévolence et ainsi le veut.** (The King (or the Queen) thanks his (or her) loyal subjects, accepts their benevolence, and wills it thus.) The form of the royal assent (q.v.) to a Bill of supply.

Le Roy (or **la Reine**) **s'avisera.** (The King (or the Queen) will consider of it.) The form of words used to express a denial of the royal assent (q.v.).

Le salut du peuple est la suprême loi. Montesquieu's translation of *Salus populi est suprema lex* (q.v.).

Le serement du visconte (the oath of the sheriff), an enactment printed in the *Statutes of the Realm* as of uncertain date, and in the *Statutes at Large* as 1306, 34 Edw. 1.

Lea or **Ley,** a pasture (Co.Litt. 4b).

Lead. When fines (q.v.) and recoveries (q.v.) were used as modes of conveying land any complicated limitations, such as those in settlements, which might be required were effected by deeds specifying the uses to which the lands were to be held. If the deed was executed before the fine or recovery it was called a deed to lead to the uses; if afterwards it was called a deed to declare the uses (2 Bl. Comm. 363).

To lead evidence is to adduce or call evidence.

Lead mines. See MINERALS.

Lead works. The Factories Act, 1961, ss. 74, 75, restricts the employment of women and young persons in certain processes involving lead manufacture or the use of lead compounds.

Leader, the leading counsel in a case, as opposed to a junior.

Leader of the opposition, in relation to either House of Parliament, that member of that House who is for the time being leader in that House of the party in opposition to Her Majesty's Government, having the greater numerical strength in the House of Commons (Ministerial and Other Salaries Act, 1975, s. 2). As to salaries see Sch. 2.

Leading case, a judicial decision or precedent settling the principles of a branch of law. Thus *Coggs* v. *Bernard* (1703) 2 Ld.Raym. 909, is a leading case on the law of bailments (*q.v.*). John William Smith published a selection of leading cases in 1837, principally illustrating rules of the common law. White and Tudor published a collection of leading cases in equity in 1949. See RULING CASES.

Leading question, a question which suggests to a witness the answer which the party examining desires him to give. Such questions are only allowed to be put (except in cross-examination) as to matters not in dispute and such preliminary inquiries as the name and address of the witness.

If a witness shows himself decidedly adverse to the party calling him it is in the discretion of the court to allow him to be examined as if on cross-examination. See HOSTILE WITNESS.

Lead-mining. See BARMOTE COURT; KING'S FIELD.

League [Fr. *ligue*; Lat. *ligo*], a treaty of alliance between different States or parties. It may be offensive, or defensive, or both. It is offensive when the contracting parties agree to unite in attacking a common enemy; defensive when the parties agree to act in concert in defending each other against an enemy.

Also a measure equal to three English miles, or 3,000 geometrical paces.

League of Nations (Société des Nations), a conventional assembly which was set up in 1920, with a membership of 58 States. The Covenant, consisting of 26 articles at the beginning of each of the peace treaties, was its charter, pledging these States to promote international co-operation, and achieve peace and security by accepting obligations not to go to war, and to respect treaties. It was superseded after the war of 1939–45 by the United Nations Organisation.

Leakage, an allowance made to merchants for the leaking of casks or the waste of liquors.

Leal, loyal, belonging to law.

Leap-year, otherwise called bissextile (*bis* and *sextilis* (*dies*)) from its introduction to make up the loss of the six hours by which the course of the sun annually exceeds the 365 days allowed for.

Leap-year, which happens every fourth year, thus consists of 366 days instead of 365 by the addition of a day to the 28 days in other years of February. The day thus added was by Julius Caesar appointed to be the day before February 24, which among the Romans was the sixth of the calends, and which on this occasion was reckoned twice, hence the term bissextile. See CALENDAR.

Lease [Lat. *locatio*, the letting of property; Fr. *laisser*, to let; Sax. *leapum, leasum*, to enter lawfully], sometimes also called demise (*demissio*), a grant of property for life, or years, or from year to year or at will, by one who has greater interest in the property.

A lease is in effect a conveyance or grant of the possession of property (generally but not necessarily land or buildings) to last for a term of years or other fixed period, or at will, and usually with the reservation of a rent. The person who grants the lease is called the lessor, the person to whom it is granted being the lessee. It is essential to a lease that it should be for a less estate or term than the lessor has in the property, for if it comprises his whole interest it is a conveyance or assignment and not a lease. Again, if the intention of the parties is that the grantee is not to be entitled to exclusive possession of the property, the grant is a licence and not a lease.

The ancient operative words were " demise, lease, and to farm let," or " demise and lease."

The Law of Property Act, 1925, makes a distinction between leases for years which are legal estates if they consist of terms of years absolute and leases for life which were converted into merely equitable interests if created under a settlement, but by s. 149 of the Act leases for life at a rent or in consideration of a fine were converted into terms of 90 years, terminable by notice as therein provided.

Until 1926, under a lease for years, except a lease operating under the Statute of Uses, 1535, the lessee must have entered into the leased premises, for before entry he had only an *interesse termini* by virtue of his common law assurance, a right which could be assigned, but not surrendered, and which did not prevent the merger of two estates by its interposition, nor itself occasion a merger. The interest in a term *in futuro* was also called the *interesse termini*. By the Law of Property Act, 1925, s. 149, the doctrine of *interesse termini* was abolished and all terms of years absolute take effect from the date fixed for commencement of the term without actual entry. A term at a rent or in consideration of a fine limited to take effect more than 21 years from the date of its creation is void. A contract for such a term is also void but leases of an equitable interest under a settlement or a power to mortgage in a settlement, or by way of indemnity and for like purposes under a settlement, are excepted from the prohibition, and a further exception is made by s. 149 (5), which saves legal terms taking effect in reversion expectant on a larger term.

The Law of Property Act, 1925, ss. 51–55, reproducing and amending the Statute of Frauds, 1677, ss. 1–3, and the Real Property Act, 1845, s. 3, requires that for the purposes of creating a legal estate all leases are to be by deed except leases taking effect in possession for a term not exceeding three years and at the best rent which can be reasonably obtained without taking a fine; such excepted leases may be made otherwise than by deed, *i.e.*, by parol. The doctrine of part performance is not affected (s. 55 (*d*)). Under that doctrine leases which would be void because they are not made by deed may be enforceable as an agreement upon the same terms as if the lease had been granted (*Walsh* v. *Lonsdale* (1882) 21 Ch.D. 9). Further, all agreements for a lease except a lease which may be made by parol must be evidenced by writing (Law of Property Act, 1925, s. 40, reproducing part of the Statute of Frauds, 1677, s. 4), unless the agreement has been partly performed and is specifically enforceable (*Maddison* v. *Alderson* (1883) 8 App.Cas. 467). Agreements which are not in writing and not specifically enforceable are interests at will only (Law of Property Act, 1925, s. 54). Possession by the tenant and receipt of rent by the landlord are good evidence of a tenancy.

By the Judicature Act, 1925, s. 56, causes for the specific performance of contracts for leases are assigned to the Chancery Division.

A lease for years or at will is a chattel interest. See CHATTEL; ESTATE; LEASEHOLDS.

Where a person who is himself a lessee grants a lease of the same property to another person for a shorter term, it is called an underlease or sublease or a derivative lease.

A concurrent lease, or lease of a reversion, is one granted for a term which is to commence before the determination of a previous lease of the same land to another person. If under seal, it operates as an assignment of the reversion during the continuance of the previous lease, so that the new lessee is entitled to the rent and covenants under the previous lease; and after the expiration of that lease, it (the concurrent lease) operates as a lease in possession.

A lease in reversion is a lease which is not to take effect in possession immediately, and the term " reversionary lease " is sometimes used in the same sense: but strictly speaking a reversionary lease is one to take effect from the expiration or determination of a previous lease.

With reference to the right or authority under which they are granted, leases are made (1) under a right or power incident to the lessor's estate; thus a tenant in fee has power to grant leases for any term; or (2) under a power of appointment or, formerly, a limitation to uses, as where land was limited to A and his heirs, to such uses as B should by demise appoint (see POWER); or (3) under a statutory power, *e.g.*, under the Settled Land Act, 1925.

As to leases by estoppel, see ESTOPPEL.

A lease by deed in the ordinary form consists of the following parts: the premises, the habendum, the reddendum, the lessee's covenants, the lessor's covenants and the proviso for re-entry. The covenants vary according to the nature of the lease, but ordinarily they include covenants by the lessee for payment of the rent, and if the lease is one of a building, to repair and insure it, or if it is one of a farm or mine, to manage it in a proper manner; there is also generally a covenant by the lessee not to underlet or assign the lease without the lessor's consent, and not to carry on certain trades or occupations, and a covenant by the lessor for quiet enjoyment which merely guarantees the lessee against entry by the lessor and those claiming under him. The covenant implied by statute (see COVENANT) guarantees the lessee against entry by all persons whatsoever: it will be excluded if there is an express covenant.

The rent and covenants are always binding on the original lessee and his representatives, notwithstanding any assignment which he may make. On an assignment of leaseholds, therefore, the assignee is bound to enter into a covenant with the assignor to indemnify him against this liability. The assignee is himself also liable for rent unpaid or covenants broken during his tenancy provided the covenants run with the land (see COVENANT); but when he assigns to another, his liability ceases so far as regards future rent or breaches of covenant.

See also DISCLAIMER.

Leases are generally prepared in two parts, known as the lease and the counterpart: the lease is executed by the lessor alone, and is kept by the lessee; the counterpart is executed by the lessee alone, and is kept by the lessor. It is customary for the lessee to pay the whole costs of preparing the lease, but see now the Costs of Leases Act, 1958.

Leases are in some cases subject to statutory provisions; such are leases at a rack-rent by tenants for life (see EMBLEMENTS), leases under the Ecclesiastical Leases Act, 1842, and leases subject to the Agricultural Holdings Act, 1948, or the Rent Restriction Acts.

As to stamp duties, see the Finance Act, 1972, s. 125; Finance Act, 1974, s. 49, Sch. 11 para. 10.

See ATTORNMENT; BUILDING LEASE; DEMISE; DISTRESS; GAME; INTERESSE TERMINI; LANDLORD AND TENANT; LEASEHOLDS; RENT; TERM; USE AND OCCUPATION.

Lease and release, a mode of conveying freehold land which derived its effect from the Statute of Uses, 1535, compounded of a lease for a year at common law, or a bargain and sale for a year under the Statute of Uses, 1535, and a common

law release. This mode of conveying freehold land was used to evade the Statute of Enrolments, 1535, which was passed to prevent land from being conveyed secretly by bargain and sale (*q.v.*). The statute required only bargains and sales of estates of inheritance or freehold to be enrolled, and therefore it soon became the practice on a sale of land for the vendor to execute a lease to the purchaser for a year by way of bargain and sale, which under the Statute of Uses, 1535, gave him seisin of the land without entry or enrolment, and then the vendor released his reversion to the purchaser by a deed known as a release, thus vesting in him the fee simple in possession without entry or livery of seisin. The lease and the release were executed on the same day, the release being dated for the following day and being executed after the lease. The consideration for the lease was a nominal sum of five or ten shillings, which was never paid, the real consideration being stated in the release.

Before 1535 conveyance of lands of all tenures by lease and release had been practised: but the method differed from that used afterwards, there being first the lease, then an actual entry on the land by the bargainee or lessee, and then the release. It was the Statute of Uses, 1535, that rendered actual entry unnecessary and so made the later form of lease and release practicable. The repeal of the Statute of Uses, 1535, by the Law of Property Act, 1925, Sch. 7, renders it now impracticable.

Before the Statute of Frauds, 1677, it was not necessary that the lease and release should be in or evidenced by writing.

The lease and release was preferable to a bargain and sale, and to a covenant to stand seised to uses, because it effected a transfer of the legal estate under the rules of the common law, and therefore the declarations of uses upon it did not have to be confined to persons from whom a consideration moved. It was also preferable to a bargain and sale, and still more to a feoffment, because no additional ceremony was necessary to its operation and the transfer of property in land could be effected by it anywhere and instantaneously. Where the subject of conveyance was land in reversion or remainder, it was also preferable to a mere deed of grant, as it made it unnecessary for the grantee, if his title were called in question, to prove that there was a particular estate in existence at the time of the grant.

By the statute 1841, 4 & 5 Vict. c. 21, conveyance by release without a lease was made effectual; and by the Real Property Act, 1845, s. 2 (replaced by the Law of Property Act, 1925, s. 51), the immediate freehold of corporeal tenements is deemed to lie in grant as well as in livery, and the conveyance by lease and release thus became obsolete.

Lease back. Where land is sold and leased back there is a limitation on the tax reliefs which may be claimed (Income and Corporation Taxes Act, 1970, s. 491; Finance Act, 1972, s. 80). For further provisions as to leasing assets see the 1970 Act, ss. 492–495; Finance Act, 1971, s. 49, Sch. 8 para. 16.

Leaseholds, lands held under a lease for years. They are personal estate, being chattels real. But for the purposes of the Administration of Estates Act, 1925, real estate includes leaseholds. By the Wills Act, 1837, s. 26, a general devise of land, or lands and tenements, or the like, will include the testator's leasehold estates, unless a contrary intention appears.

Tenants of houses (other than flats or maisonettes held on long leases at low rents) who fulfil the necessary residential qualifications can acquire the freehold compulsorily or obtain an extension of fifty years on the term of their leaseholds (Leasehold Reform Act, 1967, ss. 1–37; Rent Act, 1968, Schs. 15, 17; Housing Act, 1969, s. 82; Housing Act, 1974, s. 118).

Leasing, or **Lesing,** gleaning.

Leasum, lawful.

Leave and licence, a defence to an action in trespass setting up the consent of the plaintiff to the act complained of.

Leave to defend. The repealed Bills of Exchange Act, 1855, commonly called Keating's Act, allowed actions on bills or notes commenced within six months after they were due, to be by writ of summons in a form provided by the Act, and, unless the defendant within twelve days obtained leave to appear and defend the action, allowed the plaintiff to sign judgment on proof of service. This procedure was abolished in 1880.

Under R.S.C., Ord. 14, r. 1, where a statement of claim has been served on a defendant and that defendant has entered an appearance the plaintiff may, on filing an affidavit stating that in his belief there is no defence to the action, apply for leave to enter judgment. Unless the defendant shows that he has a good defence an order may be made empowering the plaintiff to enter judgment. See JUDGMENT.

Leave to move to set aside or vary a judgment might formerly be given by the judge at the trial of an action, when some point of law was raised, the decision of which affected the fate of the action; the motion was heard by a Divisional Court. This practice was abolished by the Appellate Jurisdiction Act, 1876, s. 17. See MOTION FOR JUDGMENT; TRIAL.

Leccator, a debauched person (Cowel).

Lecherwite [Sax. *legum*, to lie with; *wite*, penalty], a fine for adultery or fornication, paid to the lords of certain manors (4 Co.Inst. 206). See LAIRWITE.

Lectrinum, a pulpit (3 Dugd.Mon. 243).

Lecture, in the Copyright Act, 1956, Sched. VIII para. 9, includes address, speech and sermon; " delivery " in the case of a lecture, includes delivery by means of any mechanical instrument.

Lecturer [Lat.*praelector*], an instructor, a reader of lectures; also a clergyman who assists rectors, etc., in preaching, etc. See the Lecturers and Parish Clerks Act, 1844.

Ledger-book, a book in the prerogative courts, considered as their rolls.

Ledgreve or **Ledgrave.** See LATHREEVE.

Ledo, the rising water or increase of the sea.

Leeman's Acts, the Banking Companies (Shares) Act, 1867, and the Borough Funds Act, 1872, so called after the introducer, Mr. George Leeman, M.P. for York.

Leet, court, an inferior court in manors. See COURT LEET.

Lega or **Lacta,** the alloy of money.

Legable [Lat. *legabilis*], capable of being bequeathed.

Legacy [Lat. *legatum*], a gift of personal property by will. The person to whom the property is given is called the legatee, and the gift or property is called a bequest (*q.v.*). The legatee's title to the legacy is not complete until the executor has assented to it. See Assent.

Legacies are of three kinds, specific, demonstrative and general.

A specific legacy is a bequest of a specific part of the testator's personal estate. Thus, a bequest of "the service of plate which was presented to me on such an occasion," is specific, and so also is a bequest of "£100 Consols standing in my name at the Bank of England." A specific legacy must be paid or retained by the executor in preference to the general legacies, and must not be sold for the payment of debts until the general assets of the testator are exhausted (see Assets). On the other hand, a specific legacy is liable to ademption (*q.v.*), unless it is given in such a way as to refer to the state of the property at the testator's death; thus, a bequest of "the black horses which I shall be possessed of at my death" is specific, but it takes effect if the testator leaves property answering the description, although he may have sold the black horses which he had at the date of his will (*Bothamley* v. *Sherson* (1875) L.R. 20 Eq. 309).

A demonstrative legacy is a gift of a certain sum directed to be paid out of a specific fund; thus, " I bequeath to A the sum of £50 to be paid out of the £100 Consols in my name " is a demonstrative legacy. Such a legacy is not adeemed by the testator selling or disposing of the fund in his lifetime, while it also has the advantage of being paid in priority to the general legacies if the fund is sufficient.

A general legacy is one payable only out of the general assets of the testator: as where he bequeaths to A £100 sterling, or £100 Consols, without referring to any particular stock, although he may have £100 Consols standing in his name. So a legacy of a mourning ring of the value of £10 merely amounts to a general legacy of £10, with a direction to the executor to purchase a ring. A general legacy is liable to abatement or total failure if the residuary estate is not sufficient to pay the testator's debts and other legacies (see Abatement of Lega-

cies) unless it is given for valuable consideration, *e.g.*, to a wife in consideration of her releasing her dower.

Where personal property is bequeathed to trustees to be held upon trust, *e.g.*, to pay the income to A for life, this is called a trust legacy.

Where a legacy is given to an infant or person beyond the seas, the executor may pay the amount into court under R.S.C., Ord. 92, r. 2, and Supreme Court Funds Rules, r. 40, and when the legatee comes of age, or returns, he may have it paid out to him on making an application by petition or summons.

When a testator by the same testamentary instrument, or by different testamentary instruments, has bequeathed more than one legacy to the same person, the question arises whether he intended the second legacy to be cumulative, *i.e.*, in addition to the first, or substitutional for it. If by different instruments he has given legacies of equal, greater, or lesser sums to the same person, the court, considering that he who has given more than once must, prima facie, be intended to mean more than one gift, awards to the legatee all the legacies. If, however, they are not given *simpliciter*, but the motive of the gift is expressed, and in such instruments the same motive is expressed, and also the same sum is given, the court considers these two coincidences as raising a presumption that the testator did not by a subsequent instrument mean another gift, but a repetition only of the former gift. See Cumulative Legacies.

Pecuniary legacies bear interest from the expiration of twelve months from the testator's death; the executor may pay them before, but he is not compelled to do so. See R.S.C., Ord. 44, r. 19.

Subject to the particular construction of the will, if a legacy is bequeathed to a person to be paid or payable at the age of twenty-one, or any other age or certain determinate term, and the legatee dies before that age, this is such an interest vested in the legatee immediately on the testator's death that it goes to his executor or administrator, it being *debitum in praesenti*, though *solvendum in futuro*, the time being annexed to the payment and not to the gift itself; but if a legacy is bequeathed to a person at twenty-one, or if, or when, or in case, or provided he shall attain twenty-one, or at any future definite period, and he dies before that age or period, the legacy lapses, these expressions being construed as annexing the time to the substance of the legacy, so that the right of the legatee is made to depend upon his being alive at the time fixed for its payment. The giving of interest on a legacy to a legatee, or a provision for his maintenance until the time for payment of the legacy, provided it is equal in amount to the interest, as a rule, vests the legacy; but not, it seems, where the legacy is payable out of land. See MAINTENANCE.

In the civil law a legacy was an injunction given to the heir to pay or give over a part of the inheritance to a third person.

See CUMULATIVE LEGACIES; EXECUTOR; IN TERROREM; LAPSE; MARSHALLING; MORTMAIN; SATISFACTION; WILL.

Legacy duty. A duty of trifling amount was first imposed on legacies of the value of £20 and upwards by the statute 1779, 20 Geo. 3, c. 28, s. 1; and by the Legacy Duty Act, 1796, s. 1, a duty was imposed on legacies of the like value and also upon every part of any residuary personal estate of the value of £100, the rate of the duty running from 2 per cent. in the case of any brother, sister, nephew, or niece, to 6 per cent. in the case of a stranger. The incidence and the rate of duty were subsequently varied by a multiplicity of Acts and it was abolished by the Finance Act, 1949, s. 27.

Legal, lawful; according to law; according to the common law as opposed to equitable.

Legal aid. The law relating to legal aid and advice was consolidated by the Legal Aid Act, 1974, which repealed the Legal Aid and Advice Acts, 1949 to 1972. The persons eligible for legal advice and assistance are persons whose disposable income does not exceed £28·00 a week or who are in receipt of supplementary benefit or family income supplement and whose disposable capital does not exceed £250. These figures are subject to alteration by regulations (s. 1: S.I. 1974 No. 1302). Legal aid may be obtained by persons whose disposable income does not exceed £1,175 a year but a person may be refused legal aid if his disposable

capital exceeds £1,200, and it appears that he could afford to proceed without legal aid. Regulations may substitute other figures for those specified above (s. 6). Contributions are payable by persons receiving advice or assistance (s. 4; S.I. 1974 No. 1184) or legal aid (s. 9; S.I. 1974 No. 1303). Solicitors and counsel are remunerated out of the legal aid fund (s. 10, Sch. 2). Panels of solicitors and barristers willing to give advice or assistance or to act for persons receiving legal aid are formed under s. 12. The scope and general conditions of legal advice and assistance are given in s. 2 and of legal aid in s. 7, Sch. 1. The costs of successful unassisted parties in legally aided proceedings may be ordered by the court out of the legal aid fund (ss. 13, 14). The legal aid scheme is run by the Law Society in consultation with the General Council of the Bar (ss. 15, 16). The functions of the Law Society include the establishment and administration of the legal aid fund (s. 17). Proceedings may be taken under s. 23 for misrepresentation by a person seeking advice or assistance or legal aid. Rights of a legally aided person to indemnity may inure to the legal aid fund (s. 24).

The circumstances in which a court may make an order for legal aid in criminal proceedings and in proceedings relating to children and young persons are dealt with in ss. 28–31. An order for legal aid may be made when the court considers it desirable to do so in the interests of justice and a person is entitled to an order when committed on a charge of murder or where the prosecutor appeals or applies for leave to appeal from the criminal division of the Court of Appeal or the Courts-Martial Appeal Court to the House of Lords. But a court is not to make an order for legal aid unless a person requires assistance in meeting the costs of proceedings. A doubt whether a legal aid order should be made should be resolved in favour of the person asking for legal aid (s. 29). Contributions may be required from persons receiving legal aid (ss. 32–36; S.I. 1968 No. 1265; 1975 No. 64). The costs of legal aid are payable out of the legal aid fund in the case of proceedings in magistrates' courts and by the Secretary of State in other cases (s. 37). As to assigning solicitors and counsel to act for a legally aided person see s. 38. See Practice Note dated June 4, 1974; [1974] 1 W.L.R. 774.

An unassisted husband who successfully defends a divorce petition brought by his legally aided wife who relied upon serious allegations as to his conduct may properly be awarded costs against the legal aid fund (*Stewart* v. *Stewart* [1974] 1 W.L.R. 877).

Legal assets. See ASSETS.

Legal charge. See MORTGAGE.

Legal custody. Any person required or authorised by or under the Criminal Justice Act, 1948, to be taken to any place or to be kept in custody, while being so taken or kept, is deemed to be in legal custody; a constable while taking or keeping any such person as aforesaid has all the powers, authorities, protection and privileges of a constable as well beyond his constablewick as within it (s. 66).

Legal estate. See ESTATE.

Legal executive. The Institute of Legal Executives provides a recognised qualification and status for persons employed by solicitors in private practice or by a solicitor employed as such in any office, department, corporation or undertaking whether governmental, public, municipal, colonial, foreign, commercial or otherwise. Fellows of the Institute are described as " legal executives " and are entitled to the use of the letters " F.Inst. L.Ex."

A legal executive is ineligible for jury service. See JURY.

Legal fiction. See FICTION.

Legal medicine. See FORENSIC MEDICINE.

Legal memory. See MEMORY.

Legal quay, a place appointed for the loading and unloading of goods liable to duties. In 1558 an Act was passed enacting that to prevent smuggling, goods except fish were to be handled only during daylight, and only on appointed, or " legal," quays, in London and certain other ports. The London legal quays were all on the north side of the Thames, between London Bridge and the Tower. There were " sufferance " wharves south of the Thames, but their privileges were merely permissive and of uncertain duration.

Legal tender. See TENDER.

Legalis homo, a lawful man, a person who stands *rectus in curia*, not outlawed, excommunicated, or infamous.

Legalis moneta Angliae, lawful money of England (Co.Litt. 207).

Legalise; Legalisation. When an act which is prima facie illegal becomes legal, it is said to be legalised: thus many acts done upon a man's own property, which are injurious to the adjoining land and consequently actionable as nuisances, may be legalised by prescription. See EASEMENT.

When the execution of a document is attested by a notary, consul, magistrate, or the like, it is sometimes said to be legalised. This expression is borrowed from the French.

Legamannus. See LAGE-MAN.

Legantine, or **Legatine Constitutions,** ecclesiastical laws enacted in national synods, held under the Cardinals Otho and Othobon, legates from Pope Gregory IX, and Pope Clement IV, about 1220 and 1268.

Legatarius partiarius, a legatee to whom the testator had instructed his heir to give a share of the *hereditas*, called a *legatum partitionis* because the legatee divided the inheritance with the heir (Civil Law).

Legatary [Lat. *legatum*], a legatee.

Legate, a deputy, an ambassador, the Pope's nuncio.

There are three kinds: legates *a latere*, being such as the Pope commissions to take his place in councils, and so called because he never gives this office to any but his favourites and confidants, who are always *a latere* (at his side); legates *de latere* or *legati dati*, those entrusted with apostolical legation, and acting under a special commission; and *legati nati*, legates by virtue of their offices, as the Archbishop of Canterbury in former times (Encyc.Londin.).

Legatee, one who has a legacy left to him.

Legation, an embassy or mission.

Legator, one who makes a will, and leaves legacies.

Legatory, the part of a freeman's

personal estate of which he could dispose by will. See CUSTOM OF LONDON.

Legatum, a legacy given to the church or an accustomed mortuary.

Legatum generis, a legacy of a thing in general terms as belonging to a class, *e.g.*, a slave (Civil Law).

Legatum nominis, a legacy of a debt (Civil Law).

Legatum optionis, a legacy of choice, as where the testator directed the legatee to choose from among his slaves or other property (Civil Law).

Legatum partitiones, a legacy where the legatee divided the inheritance with the heir (Civil Law).

Legatum poenae nomine, a legacy by way of penalty, to constrain the heir to do or not to do something (Civil Law).

Legatus regis vice fungitur a quo destinatur et honorandus est sicut ille cujus vicem gerit (12 Co.Rep. 17). (An Ambassador fills the place of the king by whom he is sent, and is to be honoured as is he whose place he fills.)

Legem facere, to make law or institute legal proceedings on oath. See Selden's *Notes on Hengham's Summae*, 133.

Legem ferre or **rogare,** to propose a law (Civil Law).

Legem habere, to be capable of giving evidence or instituting legal proceedings upon oath. See OATH.

Legem sciscere, to give consent and authority to a proposed law, applied to the consent of the people (Civil Law).

Leger, Leiger, or **Ledger** [Dut. *legger*, to lie], anything that lies in a place; as, a ledger-book, a book that lies in a counting-house; leger-ambassador, a resident ambassador.

Legergeld; Legerwite. See LAIRWITE.

Leges Edwardi Confessoris. See EDWARD THE CONFESSOR, LAWS OF.

Leges et constitutiones futuris certum est dare formam negotiis non ad facta praeterita revocare: nisi nominatim et de praeterito tempore et adhuc pendentibus negotiis cautum sit (Cod. 1, 14, 7). (It is clear that laws and ordinances settle the course of future transactions and do not refer to bygone matters, unless their provisions relate expressly both to a past time and to matters hitherto pending.) This maxim of the civil law applies also in our law with the insertion of the words

" or impliedly " after " expressly." See LEX PROSPICIT, ETC.

Leges Henrici Primi. See HENRY I, LAWS OF.

Leges posteriores priores contrarias abrogant (1 Co.Inst. 25b). (Later laws abrogate prior contrary laws.) See GENERALIA SPECIALIBUS NON, ETC.; LEGES ET CONSTITUTIONES, ETC.

Legiosus, litigious, subjected to a course of law.

Legis constructio non facit injuriam (Co.Litt. 183a). (The law is construed so as not to work a wrong.) See CONSTRUCTIO LEGIS.

Legislation, the making of law; any set of statutes.

Legislative Committee. See NATIONAL ASSEMBLY, ETC.

Legislature, the power which makes laws. See PARLIAMENT.

Legitimacy; Legitimate. " Legitimate " signifies " lawful." The word is applied especially to children to signify that they have been born in lawful wedlock (Co. Litt. 244a).

By the Matrimonial Causes Act, 1973, s. 45, any person who is a British subject, or whose right to be deemed a British subject depends wholly or in part on his legitimacy or on the validity of any marriage, may, if he is domiciled in England or Northern Ireland or claims any real or personal estate in England, petition the High Court for a decree declaring that he is the legitimate child of his parents, and that the marriage of his father and mother or of his grandfather and grandmother was a valid marriage or that his own marriage was a valid marriage.

Children of a voidable marriage which has been annulled (see NULLITY) are deemed legitimate (Matrimonial Causes Act, 1973, s. 16, Sch. 1 para. 12). Children of a void marriage may be legitimate by reason of the Legitimacy Act, 1976, s. 1, Sch. 1.

A declaration of legitimacy obtained under the Legitimacy Declaration Act, 1858, extends to a peerage claim (*The Ampthill Peerage* [1976] 2 W.L.R. 777).

See BASTARD; CHILD; LEGITIMATION; LYNDHURST'S ACT; MULIER; PALLIO COOPERIRE.

Legitimatio. Children of concubinage

could be legitimated *per subsequens matrimonium* (Civil Law).

Legitimation, the making legitimate of a person born illegitimate. By reason of the Statute of Merton, 1235 (*q.v.*), legitimation was unknown to English law until 1926. An illegitimate child was legitimated, on the subsequent marriage of his parents, by the Legitimacy Act, 1926, s. 1, as amended by the Legitimacy Act, 1959, s. 1, provided that his father was at the date of the marriage domiciled in England and Wales. These sections have been repealed and replaced by the Legitimacy Act, 1976, s. 2, Schs. 1, 2. A child of a void marriage may be legitimated by s. 1, Sch. 1. As to legitimation by extraneous law, see s. 3; as to property see ss. 5, 6. As to adopted children, see s. 4; Adoption Act, 1976, ss. 39, 47; ADOPTION.

Any person claiming that he or his parent or any remoter ancestor became or has become a legitimated person may apply by petition to the High Court or the county court for a decree to that effect (Matrimonial Causes Act, 1973, s. 45 (2) (3)). The proceedings may be heard in camera (s. 45 (9)).

As to re-registration of births see the Births and Deaths Registration Act, 1953, s. 14, the Legitimation (Re-Registration of Birth) Act, 1957, and the Legitimacy Act, 1976, s. 9, Schs. 1, 2. See Jackson, *Formation and Annulment of Marriage,* 35 *et seq.*

Baptismal registers are to be annotated to show subsequent legitimation (Baptismal Registers Measure, 1961).

Legitime, that portion of a parent's estate of which he cannot disinherit his children without a legal cause (Civil Law). See LEGITIM.

Legitime imperanti parere necesse est (Jenk.Cent. 120). (It is necessary to obey him who gives an order as of right.) See JUS NON HABENTI, ETC.

Legitimi haeredes, the agnates because the inheritance was given to them by a law of the Twelve Tables (Civil Law).

Legrewita. See LAIRWITE (*q.v.*).

Legruita, a fine for criminal conversation with a woman.

Leibnitz. Gottfried Wilhelm Leibnitz was born on July 3, 1646, at Leipzig, and died at Hanover on November 14, 1716. He wrote *Methodus nova jurisprudentiae, Codex juris gentium diplomaticus, Observationes de principiis juris,* and numerous miscellaneous works.

Leidgrave, an officer under the Saxon government who had jurisdiction over a lath. See LATH.

Leigh, a meadow.

Leipa, one who escapes or departs from service (Spelman).

Lent [Sax. *lenten,* spring], the time from Ash Wednesday to Easter Day. The forty days of Lent are days of fasting or abstinence. See FAST DAY.

Leod, the people, nation, country, etc.

Leodium, liege.

Leoht-gescot [*symbolum luminis*], a tax for supplying the church with lights (Anc.Inst.Eng.).

Leonina societas, a partnership in which one of the partners has " the lion's share," *i.e.*, all the profits while another bears all the losses.

Lep and lace, a custom in the manor of Writtle, in Essex, that every cart which went over a place called Greenbury within that manor (unless it was the cart of a nobleman), should pay 4d. to the lord (Blount).

Leporarius, a greyhound (Cowel).

Leporium, a place where hares are kept (2 Dugd.Mon. 1035).

Leproso amovendo, a writ which lay to remove a leper or lazar who thrust himself into the company of his neighbours in any parish, either in the church, or at other public meetings, to their annoyance (Reg. Brev. 237).

Leprosy. This is a notifiable disease (Public Health (Leprosy) Regulations 1966 (No. 12)).

Les Estatus de Excestre, the Statutes of Exeter. Two enactments are printed under these collective titles in the *Statutes of the Realm* as of uncertain date, and in the *Statutes at Large* as 1286, 14 Edw. 1.

Les Estatuz de la Jeuerie, the Statutes of Jewry. An enactment is printed under these titles in the *Statutes of the Realm* as of uncertain date and in the *Statutes at Large* as the Statutum de Judeismo. See JEWS.

Les Estatuz del Eschekere the Statutes of the Exchequer. An enactment is printed in the *Statutes of the Realm* as of uncertain date, and in the *Statutes at Large*, as 1266, 51 Hen. 3, st. 4, 5.

Les lois ne se chargent de punir que les actions extérieures. (Laws charge themselves with punishing overt acts only.) So long as an act rests in bare intention it is not punishable.

Les Prélats, Seigneurs, et Communes en ce présent Parlement assemblées, au nom de touts vos autres sujets, remercient très humblement votre Majesté, et prient à Dieu vous donner en santé bonne vie et longue. (The prelates, lords and commons, in this present Parliament assembled, in the name of all your other subjects most humbly thank your Majesty, and pray to God to grant you in health a good and long life.) This is the form of words used by the clerk in an act of grace or indemnity, which originates with the Crown, or, so to speak, has the royal assent before it is agreed to by the two Houses.

Lesbianism, unnatural sexual practices between women, so called from the poetess, Sappho of Lesbos. An imputation of lesbianism is an imputation of unchastity within the meaning of the Slander of Women Act, 1891 (*Kerr* v. *Kennedy* [1942] 1 K.B. 409). It may amount to cruelty to a husband if his health suffers thereby (*Gardner* v. *Gardner* [1947] 1 All E.R. 630; *Spicer* v. *Spicer* [1954] 1 W.L.R. 1051).

Leschewes, trees fallen by chance, or windfalls (Brooke Abr. 341).

Lèse-majesté. See LAESAE MAJESTATIS.

Leshchewes, windfalls (Brooke Abr. 341).

Lesotho. The colony of Basutoland became an independent kingdom under the name of Lesotho (Lesotho Independence Act, 1966).

Lespegend. Used in the forged *Constitutiones de Foresta* (see CANUTE, LAW OF) as the title of a minor officer of the forest who took care of the vert and venison therein.

Lessa, a legacy (1 Dugd.Mon. 562).

Lessee, the person to whom a lease is made or given.

Lessons, Table of. By the Prayer Book (Table of Lessons) Act, 1871, the use of a revised table of lessons to be read in church was authorised and directed to be inserted in the Prayer Book in lieu of the existing table. The Revised Tables of Lessons Measure, 1922, provides an alternative table.

Lessor, one who lets anything to another by lease.

Lessor of the plaintiff. See EJECTMENT.

Lestage, lastage (*q.v.*).

Lestagefry, lestage-free, or exempt from the duty of paying ballast-money.

Lestagium, lastage or lestage; a duty laid on the cargo of a ship.

Leswes or **Lesues,** pastures (*Domesday*; Co.Litt. 4b).

Let. "Without let or hindrance" means without obstruction.

Leta, a court-leet.

Letare Jerusalem. See QUADRAGESIMALS.

Lethal weapon, deadly weapon.

Letherwite. See LAIRWITE.

Letter. With regard to contracts entered into by letter, the rule is, that an acceptance by letter takes effect from the date of posting the acceptance.

The recipient or lawful possessor of letters has all the rights in them incident to property except that he is not entitled to publish them or a paraphrase of them (*Philip* v. *Pennell* [1907] 2 Ch. 577; *Oliver* v. *Oliver* (1861) 31 L.J.C.P. 4).

Letter missive. In ecclesiastical law, this is a document sent with the *congé d'élire* to the dean and chapter, containing the name of the person whom they are to elect. See CONGÉ D'ÉLIRE.

When a peer was made a defendant in the Court of Chancery, the Lord Chancellor sent a letter missive to him, to request his appearance, together with a copy of the bill, petition, and order; if he neglected to appear to this, he was then served with a copy of the bill and a citation to appear and answer; if he continued still in contempt, a sequestration nisi, which was made absolute in the usual way, issued immediately against his lands and goods, without any of the arresting processes of attachment, etc., which could not affect a lord of Parliament.

See BILL OF COMPLAINT.

Letter of absolution, the mode formerly resorted to by an abbot for the release of his brethren, in order to qualify them for entering into some other order of religion.

Letter of allotment. See ALLOT.

Letter of attorney. See POWER OF ATTORNEY.

Letter of credit, an authority by one person (A) to another (B) to draw cheques or bills of exchange (with or without a limit as to amount) upon him (A) with an undertaking by A to honour the drafts on presentation. An ordinary letter of credit also contains the name of the person (A's correspondent) by whom the drafts are to be negotiated or cashed: when it does not do so, it is called an open letter of credit.

A letter of credit is in fact a proposal or request to the person named therein, or (in the case of an open letter) to persons generally, to advance money on the faith of it, and the advance constitutes an accceptance of the proposal, thus making a contract between the giver of the letter of credit and the person cashing or negotiating the draft, by which the former is bound to honour the draft. See AGREEMENT.

Letters of credit are sometimes used in conjunction with circular notes, in which case the letter of credit is called a letter of indication. Circular notes are forms of drafts, generally for some specific amount, given with the letter and requiring to be signed by the bearer. Circular notes are chiefly used by persons travelling abroad, and may be obtained from almost any banker.

See CONFIRMED CREDIT.

Letter of exchange, bill of exchange (*q.v.*).

Letter of licence, an agreement between a debtor and his creditors that the latter should for a specified time suspend their claims, and allow the debtor to carry on his business at his own discretion. Down to the virtual abolition by the Debtors Act, 1865, of arrest for debt, it also contained an agreement by the creditors not to arrest the debtor. It was usually contained in a provision that the business should be carried on under the inspection and control of persons nominated by the creditors, who were called inspectors, and the agreement then became, and was termed, a deed of inspectorship.

The object of these instruments was to avoid bankruptcy proceedings. Neither of them is known in the present law of bankruptcy.

See BANKRUPTCY; COMPOSITION.

Letter-claus (*literae clausae*), close letter, so called in contradistinction to letters patent, because the former is commonly sealed up with the royal signet, or privy seal, whereas letters patent are left open and sealed with the broad seal.

Letters close. See CLOSE ROLLS; LETTER-CLAUS.

Letters of administration. Where a person possessed of property, whether real or personal, dies intestate, or without an executor, the Family Division will grant to a proper person an authority under the seal of the court, called letters of administration, by which the grantee, the administrator, becomes clothed with powers and duties similar to those of an executor (*q.v.*). In addition to the oaths taken by the administrator, which are similar to those taken by an executor (see PROBATE), he may be required to produce sureties. See ADMINISTRATION BOND.

If the deceased died wholly intestate, simple letters of administration are granted to one of the next-of-kin (*e.g.*, the widow or children of the deceased), or, if they renounce, to a creditor or other person. If a will of the deceased exists, but no executor has been appointed, or the executor appointed predeceases the testator, or refuses or becomes incapable to act, the court will grant (as a general rule, to the person having the greatest interest under the will, *e.g.*, the residuary legatee) letters of administration with the will annexed (*cum testamento annexo*), a grant which is similar to probate of the will.

As to limited grants of letters of administration, see GRANT OF PROBATE.

Letters of business, instruments under the Sign Manual addressed by the Crown to the Convocation of the Province of York or Canterbury and conveying to Convocation the desire of the Crown that some special business therein mentioned should be considered by Convocation. Such letters have from an early date been issued upon various occasions.

Letters of marque or **mark,** extraordinary commissions issued, either in time of open war or in time of peace, after all attempts to procure legal redress had failed, by the Lords of the Admiralty, or the vice-admirals of a distant province, to the commanders of merchant ships, authorising reprisals for reparation of the damages sustained by them through enemies at sea. They were either " special," to make reparation to individuals, or " general," when issued by the government of one State against all the subjects of another; the former have long been obsolete; the latter kind seems to be an authorisation of privateering (q.v.) and therefore to be no longer allowed (See COUNTERMARQUE; REPRISALS). The stamp duty on letters of marque and reprisal was abolished by the Finance Act, 1949, Sch. 8.

Letters of request. In ecclesiastical practice, where a diocesan court (q.v.) has jurisdiction in a case, but the plaintiff wishes the cause to be instituted in the provincial court (q.v.), he may apply to the judge of the former court for letters of request; and when the judge has signed them, and they have been accepted by the judge of the provincial court, a decree issues under his seal, calling upon the defendant to answer to the plaintiff in the suit. See REQUEST, LETTERS OF.

The term " letters of request " is now more generally applied to the " request to examine witnesses in lieu of a commission," which may be made under R.S.C., Ord. 70, to the courts of foreign countries or British colonies, in which are persons whose evidence is required in a proceeding in this country. See ROGATORY LETTERS.

Letters of safe-conduct. No subject of a nation at war with this country can, by the law of nations, come into the realm, or travel upon the high seas, or send his goods and merchandise from one place to another, without danger of being seized, unless he has letters of safe-conduct, which must be granted under the Great Seal, and enrolled in Chancery. But passports or licences from ambassadors abroad are now more usually obtained, and are of equal validity. See ALIEN ENNEMI.

Letters patent, or **Letters overt** [Lat. *literae patentes*], writings of the sovereign, sealed with the Great Seal, whereby a person or company is enabled to do acts or enjoy privileges which he or it could not do or enjoy without such authority. They are so called because they are open with the seal affixed and ready to be shown for confirmation of the authority thereby given. Peers are sometimes created by letters patent, and letters patent of precedence were granted to barristers. See CLOSE ROLLS; GRANT; GREAT SEAL; WARRANT.

A patent right is a privilege granted by the Crown to the first inventor of any new contrivance in manufactures, that he alone shall be entitled, during a limited period, to make articles according to his own invention (Statute of Monopolies, 1623).

To be the subject of a patent right an article must be material and capable of manufacture: an idea or scientific law or hypothesis cannot be patented. It must be new within the United Kingdom and not known to the public at the date of grant and show some utility. The person applying for the patent must be the true and first inventor of it; yet where the secret is acquired abroad by one who afterwards introduces it into the realm, he is considered by the law as the true inventor.

The various statutes regulating the procedure for obtaining a patent were consolidated, with amendments, by the Patents Act, 1949.

Applications may be made at once for a complete specification or for a provisional specification. The provisional specification protects the inventor pending the examination of the complete specification when lodged and during formalities required for the grant of the letters patent on the complete specification, which must be lodged within 12 months of first application. Opposition to the grant is heard by the Comptroller subject to appeal. The grant entitles the patentee to all rights and profits in the invention. Upon infringement of the patent the patentee can protect his right by injunction and a claim for damages. The patent is valid for 16 years with a further period of 7 to 14 years if the High Court decides that the invention has not been sufficiently remunerated. The patent is subject to certain rights of the Crown which may be reserved on the grant, and if the invention is likely to be useful in war the authorities may acquire it upon compensation agreed by the Treasury. The patent may be registered in such foreign countries as are parties to a convention with this country, within 12 months, and it is assignable under seal either absolutely or with time or regional limits. Upon death, the patent rights vest in the personal representatives. See PATENTS.

Letters rogatory. See ROGATORY LETTERS.

Letting scheme. This is similar to a building scheme (*q.v.*). It must be proved that restrictions imposed by a common lessor were intended to be for the benefit of all the properties intended to be let (*Kelly* v. *Battershill* [1949] 2 All E.R. 830).

Lettres de cachet. See CACHET.

Lettres d'État, letters formerly issued in France in favour of government officials suspending legal proceedings against them.

Leuca, a measure of land, the extent of which is not precisely known: some say 1,500 paces. Ingulphus, p. 910, says 2,000 paces. In 1 Dugd.Mon. 313, it is 480 perches. Spelman says a mile.

Leucata, a space of ground as much as a mile contains (1 Dugd.Mon. 768). And so it seems to be used in a charter of William the Conqueror to Battle Abbey.

Leukaemia. This disease was held not to be attributable to war service in *Kincaid* v. *Ministry of Pensions* [1948] L.J.R. 1581.

Levant Company. After certain persons had opened up trade with the Sultan (or the Grand Signior, as he was then called), Elizabeth I granted them a monopoly of that trade in 1581. James I incorporated them in 1605, by a charter which confirmed their monopoly, gave them the right of choosing the consuls and vice-consuls in all places in the Levant Seas, and gave them power to fine and imprison members of the company. In 1643 the Long Parliament gave them the further right of nominating the ambassador at Constantinople. These privileges of the company were confirmed by the statute 1753, 26 Geo. 2, c. 13. The company actually nominated and paid the ambassador until 1803, and the consuls in Turkey until 1825, when the charter was surrendered.

Levant et couchant [Lat. *levantes et cubantes*], where cattle have been so long on the land of another that they have lain down and risen to feed; supposed to be a day and a night (*Termes de la Ley*).

When land to which a right of common of pasture is annexed can maintain during the winter by its produce, or requires to plough and manure it, a certain number of cattle, those cattle are said to be levant and couchant on the land. The origin of this double definition of levancy and couchancy probably was that the number requisite to plough and manure was the limit to common appendant, and the capacity of wintering was the limit to common appurtenant (*Bennett* v. *Reeve* (1740) Willes 231). It appears that the courts have adopted the latter admeasurement as the more liberal in both cases, but they have never denied the right of common appendant to be admeasured by its original standard (*Carr* v. *Lambert* (1866) L.R. 1 Ex. 165). It is therefore commonly said that cattle levant and couchant are such as the produce of the land will maintain during the winter, without reference to their being required for its tillage. Levancy and couchancy is one of the standards for ascertaining the number of cattle which each commoner may put on the common. See COMMON.

If cattle escape from A's land into B's land by default of B (as for want of his keeping a sufficient fence), they cannot be distrained for rent by B's landlord until they have been levant and couchant on the land, that is, until they have been at least one night there. If they escape by default of A, they may be distrained immediately (*Jones* v. *Powell* (1826) 5 B. & C. 647).

Levari facias, a writ of execution which commanded the sheriff to levy a judgment debt on the lands and goods of the debtor by seizing and selling the goods, and receiving the rents and profits of the lands until the debt was satisfied. This writ had been practically superseded before 1883 by the writ of *elegit* (*q.v.*); and the Bankruptcy Act, 1883, s. 146 (2), enacted that it should no longer be issued in any civil proceeding. The writ of *sequestrari facias* (*q.v.*) is in the nature of a *levari facias*, and was hence sometimes called a *levari facias de bonis ecclesiasticis.*

Levée en masse, an organised or spontaneous rising of the civil population against the enemy.

Level crossing. The driver and fireman of a train may assume that people approaching a level crossing will look out for the trains (*Lloyds Bank* v. *British Transport Commission* [1956] 1 W.L.R. 1279). Running trains through a level crossing imposes on those doing so a general duty of care towards persons lawfully on the level crossing which extends not only to positive operations but also to keeping the crossing in reasonably adequate condition (*Commissioner for Railways* v. *McDermott* [1967] 1 A.C. 169).

For statutory provisions, see the Railways Clauses Consolidation Act, 1845, ss. 46, 47, 59–62, 75; *Copps* v. *Payne* [1950] 1 K.B. 611 and the Transport Act, 1968, ss. 123, 124.

Levitical degrees. These degrees of affinity are referred to in the statute 1540, 32 Hen. 8, c. 38, s. 2, and are set forth in Leviticus, c. 18. Marriage within them is prohibited except, since 1907, in the case of a deceased wife's sister, since 1921, with a deceased husband's brother, and, since 1931, between persons and their nephews and nieces by marriage. See AFFINITY; DECEASED WIFE'S SISTER, ETC.

Levy [Lat. *levo*], the act of raising money or men. To levy execution is to raise a sum of money by a writ of execution against the property of a judgment debtor. See EXECUTION; FIERI FACIAS.

Levy Board. See HORSERACE BETTING LEVY BOARD.

Lex, law. In the civil law it was a resolution adopted by the Roman *populus* (patricians and plebeians) in the *comitia*, on the motion of a magistrate of senatorial rank, as a consul, a praetor, or a dictator.

Lex Angliae est lex misericordiae (2 Co.Inst. 315). (The law of England is a law of mercy.) This is said by Coke in connection with the Statute of Gloucester, 1278, c. 9, which was passed in relief of those committing homicide by misadventure or in self-defence.

Lex Angliae nunquam matris sed semper patris conditionem imitari partum judicat (Co.Litt. 123). (The rule of the law of England is that the offspring shall always follow the condition of the father; never that of the mother.) And so if a villein took a free woman to wife the children of the marriage were villeins. See PARTUS SEQUITUR, ETC.

Lex Angliae sine Parliamento mutari non potest (2 Co.Inst. 619). (The law of England cannot be changed except by Parliament.) See PROCLAMATIONS, ROYAL.

Lex beneficialis rei consimili remedium praestat (2 Co.Inst. 689). (A beneficial law affords a remedy for cases both of which are on the same footing.) See IN CONSIMILI CASU.

Lex Brehonia, the Brehon or Irish law, abolished by King John.

Lex citius tolerare vult privatum damnum quam publicum malum (Co. Litt. 125, 132). (The law is more willing to tolerate a private loss than a public evil.) Thus, no action lies for anything said by a Member of Parliament in Parliament, or by an advocate in the course of judicial proceedings or by a witness in the witness-box, or by one official of another in a report: for if such actions lay, Parliament, the courts and the public services could not be carried on.

Lex deraisnia, the proof of a thing which one denies to be done by him where another affirms it, defeating the assertion of his adversary, and showing it to be against reason or probability; this was used among the Romans as well as the Normans (Cowel).

Lex dilationes semper exhorret (2 Co. Inst. 240). (The law always abhors delays.) This is a comment by Coke on the Statute of Westminster I, 1275, c. 40, passed for the relief of persons who had been delayed of their rights by false vouching to warranty. See LEX REPROBAT, ETC.

Lex domicilii, the law of the country where a person has his domicile (*q.v.*).

Lex est dictamen rationis (Jenk.Cent. 117). (Law is the word of reason.)

Lex est exercitus judicum tutissimus ductor (2 Co.Inst. 526). (The law is the safest guide of all the judges.)

Lex est ratio summa, quae jubet quae sunt utilia et necessaria, et contraria prohibet (Co.Litt. 319). (Law is the supreme science which commands those things which are useful and necessary, and forbids what is contrary thereto.)

Lex est sanctio justa, jubens honesta, et prohibens contraria (2 Co.Inst. 588). (Law is a sacred sanction, commanding what is proper and forbidding what is not.) This is a quotation from Bracton.

Lex est tutissima cassis, sub clypeo legis nemo decipitur (2 Co.Inst. 56). (The law is the safest helmet; under the shield of the law no man is deceived.)

Lex ferenda, the law which it is desired to establish.

Lex fingit ubi subsistit aequitas (11 Co. Rep. 90). (The law has recourse to fictions when the resources of equity come to an end.) See FICTION.

Lex fori, the law of the place of action. The forms of remedies, modes of proceeding, rules of evidence and execution of judgments are regulated by the law of the place where the action is instituted, the *lex fori*. See LEX LOCI.

Lex Hortensia, a law passed in 287 B.C. which provided that *plebescita* should bind the whole Roman people equally with *leges.*

Lex hostilia de furtis, a Roman law which provided that a prosecution for theft might be carried on without the owner's intervention.

Lex injusta non est lex. (Any interpretation of the law which makes the law work injustice is bad law.) See AEQUUM ET BONUM, ETC.

Lex intendit vicinum vicini facta scire (Co.Litt. 78b). (The law holds that one neighbour knows what another does.)

Lex judicialis, an ordeal (Leg. Hen. 1).

Lex Julia majestatis, a Roman law promulgated by Augustus, comprehending all the ancient laws that had before been enacted to punish transgressors against the State.

Lex lata, the law that is in force.

Lex loci, the law of the place. The expression is chiefly used in the following phrases: *lex loci* [*celebrati*] *contractus* is the law of the place where a contract was made: *lex loci solutionis* is the law of the place of payment, that is, of the place where, by the terms of the contract, payment is to be made: *lex loci actus* is the law of the place where a transfer of property or some similar formal act has been performed: *lex loci rei sitae* is the same as *lex situs* (*q.v.*): *lex loci delicti* is the law of the place where a tort or wrong has been committed: *lex fori* is the law of the place where judicial proceedings have been taken to enforce an obligation, etc. Unless otherwise provided by statute questions of evidence are determined by the *lex fori* and not by the *lex loci contractus.* Thus, copies of foreign documents, though admissible in a foreign court, will be rejected unless complying with English law. See INTERNATIONAL LAW; JURISDICTION; LOCUS REGIT ACTUM.

Lex loci actus, the law of the place where a legal act takes place, *e.g.*, where a will is made.

Lex loci celebrationis, the law of the place where a marriage is celebrated.

Lex loci contractus, the law of the place of the contract. Generally speaking, the validity of a contract is decided by the law of the place where it was made. If valid there, it is, by the general law of nations (*jure gentium*), held valid everywhere, by the tacit or implied consent of the parties. The rule is founded not merely in the convenience, but in the necessities of nations; for otherwise it would be impracticable for them to carry on an extensive intercourse and commerce with each other.

The same rule applies to the invalidity of contracts; if void or illegal by the law of the place of the contract, they are generally held void and illegal everywhere. This would seem to be a principle derived from the very elements of natural justice. The code expounds it: *Nullum enim pactum, nullam conventionem, nullum contractum, inter eos videri volumus subsecutum, qui contra-*

hunt lege contrahere prohibente (Just. Inst. i, 14, 5). But no nation is bound to recognise or enforce any contracts injurious to its own interests, or its subjects (*Ogden* v. *Ogden* [1908] P. 46). In the absence of specific provision in a contract, the test to determine the proper law of the contract would be the system of law with which the transaction had the closest and most real connection (*Whitworth Street Estates (Manchester)* v. *James Millar and Partners* [1969] 1 W.L.R. 377; *Compagnie Tunisienne de Navigation S.A.* v. *Compagnie D'Armement Maritime S.A.* [1969] 1 W.L.R. 1338). See also the Supply of Goods (Implied Terms) Act, 1973, ss. 5, 6, 13. See CONFLICT OF LAWS.

Lex loci delicti, the law of the place of the tort or wrong.

Lex loci rei sitae, the law of the place where the thing is situate, sometimes also called *lex situs.* As to real or immovable property, the general rule of the common law is that the laws of the place where such property is situate exclusively govern in respect to the power to contract, the rights of the parties, the modes of transfer, and the solemnities which should accompany them (*Freke* v. *Lord Carbery* (1873) L.R. 16 Eq. 461; *Bank of Africa* v. *Cohen* [1909] 2 Ch. 129). The title, therefore, to real property can be acquired, passed, and lost only according to the *lex loci rei sitae.*

Lex loci solutionis, the law of the place of payment.

Lex mercatoria, the law merchant, the mercantile law or general body of European usages in commercial matters. See CUSTOM.

Lex merciorum. See MERCEN-LAGE.

Lex necessitatis est lex temporis, scilicet, instantis (Hob. 159). (The law of necessity is the [only] law for the time, that is to say, for the instant.) See NECESSITAS EST LEX, ETC.

Lex neminem cogit ad vana seu inutilia peragenda. See LEX NON PRAECIPIT, ETC.

Lex neminem cogit ostendere quod nescire praesumitur (Lofft 569). (The law compels no one to disclose that which he is presumed not to know.) This maxim would seem to apply to privileged communications.

Lex nil frustra facit (Jenk.Cent. 17). (The law does nothing in vain.) See INUTILIS LABOR, ETC.

Lex non a rege est violanda (Jenk. Cent. 7). (The law is not to be violated by the king.) This is said as a gloss on an ancient decision that the king's justices ought not to comply with any royal command which was repugnant to the law.

Lex non cogit ad impossibilia (Co.Litt. 231b). (The law does not compel the impossible.) See IMPOTENTIA EXCUSAT, ETC.; LEX NON INTENDIT, ETC.

Lex non curat de minimis (Hob. 88). (The law takes no heed of trifles.) See DE MINIMIS, ETC.

Lex non debet deficere conquerentibus in justitia exhibenda (Co.Litt. 197). (The law ought not to make default in dispensing justice to those who seek it.)

Lex non deficit in justitia exhibenda (Jenk.Cent. 31). (The law does not fail to dispense justice.)

Lex non favet delicatorum votis (9 Co. Rep. 57b). (The law does not favour the wishes of the fastidious.) Thus, although an action may lie for "erecting a hogstye so near the house of a neighbour that the air thereof is corrupted," or for depriving his house of light or air, no action will lie because of the erection of any building which interferes with the view from a house.

Lex non intendit aliquid impossibile (12 Co.Rep. 89). (The law does not mean anything that is impossible.) See LEX NON COGIT, ETC.

Lex non praecipit inutilia (Co.Litt. 127b). (The law does not enjoin useless things.)

Lex non requirit verificari quod apparet curiae (9 Co.Rep. 54). (The law does not require that which is apparent to the court to be verified.) In Co.Litt., at 303b, Coke says "That which is apparent to the court by necessary collection out of the record need not be averred": and this maxim would seem to mean that, rather than "facts need not be proved of which the court takes judicial notice."

Lex non scripta, the unwritten law; that is to say, the common law. See LAW.

Lex plus laudatur quando ratione probatur (Litt.Epil.). (The law is most worthy of approval when it is in accordance with reason.)

Lex posterior derogat priori (Mackeldey, Civ. L. 5). (A later Act overrules an earlier one.) See CONSTITUTIONES TEMPORE, ETC.; LEGES POSTERIORES, ETC.; PRIORES LEGES, ETC.

Lex prospicit non respicit (Jenk.Cent. 284). (The law looks forward, not backward.) No statute is retrospective in its action except by express provision or necessary implication. See LEGES ET CONSTITUTIONES, ETC.; NOVA CONSTITUTIO, ETC.

Lex punit mendacium (Jenk.Cent. 15). (The law punishes falsehood.)

Lex regia, the statute by which the Roman people vested the supreme power in the emperor.

Lex rejicit superflua, pugnantia, incongrua (Jenk.Cent. 133). (The law rejects such things as are superfluous, contradictory, and incongruous.)

Lex reprobat moram (Jenk.Cent. 35). (The law disapproves of delay.) See LEX DILATIONES, ETC.

Lex respicit aequitatum (Co.Litt. 24b). (The law regards equity.)

Lex sacramentalis, compurgation (*q.v.*): see Leg. Hen. 1, c. 9.

Lex scripta, the written law; that is to say, statute law. See LAW.

Lex scripta si cesset, id custodiri oportet quod moribus et consuetudine inductum est; et si qua in re hoc defecerit, tunc id quod proximum et consequens ei est; et si id non appareat, tunc, jus quo urbs Romana utitur servari oportet (7 Co.Inst. 19). (If the written law is silent, that which is drawn from manners and customs ought to be observed; and if that is in any matter defective, then that which is next and analogous to it; and if that does not appear, then the law which Rome uses should be followed.) The last maxim of Coke is so far followed at the present day that, in cases where there is no precedent of the English courts, the civil law is always heard with respect, and often, though not necessarily, followed.

Lex semper dabit remedium (Jacob 69). (The law will always give a remedy.) See DAMNUM SINE, ETC.; IN NOVO, ETC.; UBI JUS, ETC.

Lex semper intendit quod convenit rationi (Co.Litt. 78b). (The law always intends what is in accordance with reason.) See LEX EST RATIO, ETC.; LEX NON COGIT, ETC.

Lex situs, the law of the place where property is situated. The general rule is, that lands and other immovables are governed by the *lex situs*, that is, by the law of the country in which they are situated. See LEX LOCI; LEX LOCI REI SITAE.

Lex specialis derogat generali. (A special statute overrules a general one.)

Lex spectat naturae ordinem (Co.Litt. 197). (The law has regard to the order of nature.) Thus, the law will not compel a man to demand that which he cannot, in the nature of things, recover. See LEX NON COGIT, ETC.

Lex succurrit ignoranti (Jenk.Cent. 15). (The law assists the ignorant.) But not if their ignorance is ignorance of law. See IGNORANTIA FACTI, ETC.

Lex talionis, the law of retaliation; the primitive law embodied in the phrase "an eye for an eye, a tooth for a tooth." It survived in the shape of capital punishment for murder. The statute 1363, 37 Edw. 3, c. 18, made a curious attempt to apply it by enacting that he who preferred an accusation should be put under sureties (which Lambarde calls sureties of taliation) to undergo, in the event of the accusation being found to be false and malicious, the punishment to which the accused person, if found guilty, would have been liable; but the statute 1364, 38 Edw. 3, c. 9, repealed this enactment, and provided instead that the false accuser should be imprisoned until he had paid damages to the accused and a fine to the king. Except in this instance, the *lex talionis* has never, apart from murder, been incorporated in our law.

Lex terrae, the law of the land.

Lex terrena, the common law when regarded as the law of earthly origin, and contrasted with the law Christian or spiritual law.

Lex uno ore omnes alloquitur (2 Co. Inst. 184). (The law speaks to all with one voice.) This is quoted in connection with the Statute of Westminster I, 1275, c. 14, which provided that the one law should prevail throughout the whole land. See NIHIL IN LEGE, ETC.

Lex Wallensica, the ancient laws of Wales.

Ley or **Loi,** law; the oath with compurgators; also a meadow.

Ley gager, a wager of law; one who commences a lawsuit (Cowel).

Leyerwite. See LAIRWITE.

Leze-majesty, an offence against sovereign power; treason; rebellion. See LAESAE MAJESTATIS.

Liabilities adjustment, the procedure alternative to bankruptcy provided by the Liabilities (War-time Adjustment) Acts, 1941 and 1944, applicable to debtors whose financial affairs were adversely affected by war circumstances.

Liability, the condition of being actually or potentially subject to an obligation, either generally, as including every kind of obligation, or, in a more special sense, to denote inchoate, future, unascertained or imperfect obligations, as opposed to debts, the essence of which is that they are ascertained and certain. Thus when a person becomes surety for another, he makes himself liable, though it is unascertained in what obligation or debt the liability may ultimately result. See LIMITATION OF LIABILITY.

Liard, a farthing.

Libel [Lat. *libellus*; Fr. *libelle*], defamation in a permanent form. False defamatory words, if written and published, constitute a libel. Everything printed or written, which reflects on the character of another, and is published without lawful justification or excuse, is a libel, whatever the intention may have been (*O'Brien* v. *Clement* (1846) 15 M. & W. 435). A statement in a talking film is a libel and not merely a slander (*Youssopoff* v. *Metro-Goldwyn-Mayer Picture Corporation* (1934) 50 T.L.R. 581). Wireless broadcasts are to be treated as publications in a permanent form (Defamation Act, 1952, s. 1). As to publication by dictation, etc., to a typist, see *Osborn* v. *Boulter & Son* [1930] 2 K.B. 226. All contumelious matter that tends to degrade a man in the opinion of his neighbours, or to make him ridiculous, will amount to

libel when conveyed in writing, or by picture, effigy, or the like (*Monson* v. *Tussauds* [1894] 1 Q.B. 671). A writing of fictitious character which incidentally contains the name of a real person may be a libel (*Jones* v. *Hulton* [1910] A.C. 20). The term also includes such writings as are of a blasphemous, treasonable, seditious, or immoral kind. As to the averment in an indictment for obscene libel, see *R.* v. *Barraclough* [1906] 1 K.B. 201.

A public libel is one which tends to produce evil consequences to society, because it is blasphemous (see BLASPHEMY), or obscene (*q.v.*), or seditious (*q.v.*). The publication of such a libel is a misdemeanour. To this class also belong libels on the Houses of Parliament, which are contempts or breaches of privilege; libels on courts of justice, or on persons concerned in proceedings before courts, which are contempts of court (*q.v.*); and libels on foreign rulers, ambassadors, etc.

Private libels are of two kinds. A defamatory libel, or a libel on the character of an individual, is a false and defamatory writing, picture, broadcast or the like, published concerning a certain person, and which either brings him within the danger of the law by accusing him of a crime, or has a tendency to injure him in his profession or calling, or by holding him to scorn, ridicule, hatred or execration, impairs him in the enjoyment of general society. A defamatory libel is a civil injury, giving rise to a right of action for damages by the person defamed. It is also a misdemeanour, and makes the offender punishable criminally by fine and imprisonment. The question whether a publication is libellous or not is one of mixed fact and law, and rests with the jury, subject to the judge's direction as to the law (see FACT); and this applies in criminal as well as in civil proceedings. See FOX'S LIBEL ACT.

Both the author and the publisher of a libel are liable to be sued or indicted; but it is a defence in either case that the matter complained of was written or printed on a privileged occasion. Privilege may be absolute, as in the case of statements in judicial proceedings, in

LIBEL

Parliament, or by Ministers of the Crown in advising their sovereign (*Dawkins* v. *Lord Rokeby* (1873) L.R. 8 Q.B. 255), or in connection with investigations by the Commissions for Local Administration (*q.v.*) (Local Government Act, 1974, s. 32). Privilege may be qualified, *i.e.*, upon an occasion which justified the publication of it, *e.g.*, that the defendant was giving a character of a servant. No privilege, however, attaches to information supplied by a trade protection society to its customers for the purposes of profit and not from sense of duty if such information is injurious to the character of another. The mere fact of a contract to supply information does not create such a duty or common interest that communications made in fulfilment of the contractual obligations are privileged. The underlying principle is the common convenience and welfare of society, and not the convenience of individuals (*Macintosh* v. *Dunn* [1908] A.C. 390). The Law of Libel Amendment Act, 1888, as amended by the Defamation Act, 1952, ss. 7, 8, Sch., gives privilege to fair and accurate newspaper reports or broadcasts of proceedings of a court, or public meeting (*Standen* v. *South Essex Recorders* (1934) 50 T.L.R. 365; *Cook* v. *Alexandra* [1974] Q.B. 279). See NEWSPAPERS. As to reports and broadcasts of committal proceedings see the Criminal Justice Act, 1967, s. 5. As to performances of a play see the Theatres Act, 1968, ss. 4, 7.

Proof of malice will rebut a defence of qualified privilege but not a defence of absolute privilege. A statement honestly believed to be true and not made for any improper motive cannot be said to have been made maliciously because of the unreasonableness of the belief (*Horrocks* v. *Lowe* [1975] A.C. 135).

It is a good defence to an action of libel that the statement was true (*M'Pherson* v. *Daniels* (1829) 10 B. & C. at p. 272). A defence that the plaintiff assented to a publication which was made may also be good, on the principle *volenti non fit injuria* (*Chapman* v. *Lord Ellesmere* [1932] 2 K.B. 431). As to the discretion of the judge in awarding or withholding costs upon a verdict for nominal damages, see *Martin* v. *Benson* [1927] 1 K.B. 771. But to be a defence to an indictment, a plea of justification on the ground of the truth of the libel must further allege that its publication was for the public good (Libel Act, 1843, s. 6); but if the libel is blasphemous or seditious, no evidence of its truth will be received (*R.* v. *M'Hugh* [1901] 2 Ir.R. 569). See APOLOGY; BLACKMAIL; DEFAMATION; FAIR COMMENT; INNUENDO; JUSTIFICATION; MALICE; NEWSPAPERS; PRESS; PRIVILEGE; PUBLICATION; SLANDER.

If a person falsely and maliciously publishes statements calculated to injure the property (*e.g.*, the business) of another, this, though not a libel, gives rise to an action for malicious falsehood.

The issue of a writ for libel cannot be used as a gag to prevent discussion and in a proper case the statement of claim will be struck out under R.S.C., Ord. 18, r. 19 (*Wallersteiner* v. *Moir* [1974] 1 W.L.R. 991).

In the ecclesiastical courts, the first plea in a plenary cause (not being a criminal cause) is termed the libel, and runs in the name of the party, or his proctor, who alleges and propounds the facts on which the demand is based. See PLEA.

Libellant; Libellee, the persons by and against whom respectively a libel is filed in an ecclesiastical court. Formerly the terms applied also to the persons by and against whom proceedings were brought in the old Court of Admiralty.

Libelli famosi, scurrilous publications of a libellous nature. See LIBEL.

Libellus conventionis, the statement of a plaintiff's claim in a petition presented to the magistrate, who directed an officer to deliver it to the defendant (Civil Law).

Liber albus, the White Book of London (*q.v.*).

Liber assisarum, a compilation of selected cases from the manuscript year books of the reign of Edward III, first printed about 1517. Coke styles it a book of great authority (1 Co.Inst. 198b.) There is another book called *Abridgment of the Book of Assizes,* printed about 1510, containing cases of the reigns of Edward III, Richard II, Henry IV, Henry V and Henry VI.

Liber Eliensis. The only known ancient copy of the *Inquisitio Eliensis* (*q.v.*) is the document called the *Liber Eliensis* which is in the library of Trinity College, Cambridge.

Liber feudorum, a code of the feudal law, compiled by direction of the Emperor Frederick Barbarossa, and published at Milan, in 1170.

Liber foederum. See TESTA DE NEVILL.

Liber homo, a freeman.

Liber judicialis Alfredi, the Dooms of Alfred. See ALFRED, DOOMS OF.

Liber niger domus regis, the black book of the king's household, the title of a book in which there is an account of the household establishment of Edward IV, and of the musicians retained in his service for his private amusement and for the service in his chapel.

Liber niger scaccarii; Liber niger parvus. See BLACK BOOK OF THE EXCHEQUER.

Liber quadripartitus, a translation of the old dooms into Latin made about the year 1118. The first part contains the old English laws, the second some important State papers. The third and fourth parts, dealing respectively with legal procedure and theft, are not extant (Liebermann, *Quadripartitus*).

Liber ruber scaccarii. See RED BOOK OF THE EXCHEQUER.

Libera, a livery or delivery of so much corn or grass to a customary tenant, who cut down or prepared the said grass or corn, and received some part or small portion of it as a reward or gratuity.

Libera batella, a free boat; the right of fishing with a boat in waters where no general public right of fishing existed.

Libera chasea habenda, a writ granted to a person for a free chase (*q.v.*) belonging to his manor, after proof made by inquiry of a jury that the same belonged to him (Reg.Brev. 36).

Libera piscaria, a free fishery. See FISHERY.

Libera wara, a free measure of ground.

Liberam legem amittere, to lose one's free law (called the villainous judgment (*q.v.*)), to become discredited or disabled as juror and witness, to forfeit goods and chattels and lands for life, to have those lands wasted, houses razed, trees rooted up, and one's body committed to prison. It was formerly pronounced against conspirators.

Liberata pecunia non liberat offerentem (Co.Litt. 207). (Money being set free does not set free the party offering.) This means that a refusal of a tender does not free the debtor from the debt in respect of which the tender is made: but of course he can plead tender (*q.v.*).

Liberate, a writ which lay for the payment of a yearly pension or other sum of money, granted under the Great Seal, and addressed to the treasurer and chamberlain of the Exchequer; also a writ to the sheriff for the delivery of possession of lands and goods extended or taken upon the forfeiture of a recognisance; also a writ which issued out of Chancery, directed to a gaoler, for delivery of a prisoner who had put in bail for his appearance (Fitz.N.B. 432).

When execution had been issued on a statute staple by a writ in the nature of an extent, the lands, tenements and chattels of the conusor or debtor were not delivered to the conusee or creditor, but were seized by the sheriff "into the king's hands," and in order to get possession of them the conusee had to sue out a writ called a liberate, which commanded the sheriff to deliver them into his hands. See EXTENT.

Liberate rolls, rolls in the Record Office containing lists of the writs of allocate (*q.v.*), computate (*q.v.*), and liberate (*q.v.*) which were issued between 1201 and 1436.

Liberatio, money, meat, drink, clothes, etc., yearly given and delivered by the lord to his domestic servants (Blount).

Liberation, payment (Civil Law).

Libertas, freedom; the capacity to possess the rights and fulfil the duties of a free person (Civil Law).

Libertas directa, the setting free of his own slave by a master, as when he appointed his slave as a tutor (Civil Law.)

Libertas ecclesiastica, church liberty, or ecclesiastical immunity.

Libertas est naturalis facultas ejus quod cique facere libet, nisi quod de jure aut vi prohibetur (Co.Litt. 116). (Liberty is the power given by nature of

1093

doing what each man pleases, unless it be a thing the doing of which is prevented by the law or by actual force.) This is cited in a disquisition on villeinage.

Libertas est res inestimabilis (Jenk. Cent. 52). (Liberty is a priceless thing.)

Libertas fideicommissaria, where a testator appointed as a tutor another man's slave, entrusting his heir to purchase and enfranchise the slave (Civil Law).

Libertate probandi, De, a writ which lay for one who, being claimed as a villein, offered to prove that he was free: it required the sheriff to take security from him to appear and prove his freedom before the justices and directed that upon such security being given the alleged villein should go unmolested pending the decision of the matter (Fitz. N.B. 77). See NATIVO HABENDO, DE.

Libertates regales ad coronam spectantes ex concessione regum a corona exierunt (2 Co.Inst. 496). (Royal franchises pertaining to the Crown are alienated from the Crown by grant from the kings.) This is said by Coke in connection with the *Statutum de quo warranta,* 1289, which applied to all *jura regalia* vested in subjects.

Libertatibus allocandis, De, a writ which lay for a citizen or burgess impleaded contrary to his right to be impleaded only within his city or borough (Reg.Orig. 262).

Libertatibus exigendis in itinerere, De, a writ which lay to the justices in eyre directing them to allow a man to appear by an attorney (Reg.Orig. 19).

Liberticide, a destroyer of liberty.

Libertinum ingratum leges civiles in pristinam servitutem redigunt; sed leges Angliae semel manumissum semper liberum judicant (Co.Litt. 137b). (The civil laws reduce an ungrateful freedman to his original slavery, but the laws of England regard as free for ever a man who has ever been made a free man.)

Libertinus, a freedman; a man who had been set free from slavery by manumission. *Libertini* fell originally into three classes: full Roman citizens, *Latini funiari,* and *dediticii* (Civil Law).

Liberty, an authority to do something which would otherwise be wrongful or illegal. Thus, if a man grants to another trees growing on land, that implies a liberty to cut them and carry them away. (See FREE ENTRY, EGRESS AND REGRESS.) Such a liberty may be either personal to the grantee, or it may be inherent or annexed to property so as to pass with it on an assignment. See LICENCE.

" Liberty " is also used as equivalent to "franchise" (*q.v.*), both as denoting a right and as denoting the place where the right is exercisable. Thus, the Liberty of the Savoy is a place subject to a franchise. Each of the Inns of Court was originally a liberty. As to writs of execution within a liberty, see MANDAVI BALLIVO; NON OMITTAS.

The privileged districts, called liberties from being exempt from the sheriff's jurisdiction, having separate commissions of the peace, and not being incorporated boroughs, might, by Order in Council, be united with the counties in which they were situate upon petition of the justices of the liberty or of the courts, under the Liberties Act, 1850.

The Municipal Corporations Act, 1888, s. 48 (1), provided that every liberty and franchise of a county should form for the purpose of that Act part of the county of which it formed part for the purposes of parliamentary elections.

Liberty of the press. This simply means that such a thing as an *imprimatur* (*q.v.*) is now unknown to our law, and that every man may print and publish what he pleases, although, of course, he will be liable to a prosecution if he prints anything which is a criminal libel, or which is obscene, blasphemous or seditious, and to civil proceedings if he prints defamatory matter. See PRESS.

Liberty of the rules. In certain circumstances prisoners in the King's Bench, Fleet, and Marshalsea prisons obtained permission to live outside the actual prisons but within certain adjacent areas known as the Rules. This, which was called the Liberty of the Rules, was abolished, together with the prisons, by the Queen's Prisons Act, 1842. See QUEEN'S PRISON.

Liberty of the subject. See ACT OF SETTLEMENT; BILL OF RIGHTS; HABEAS CORPUS; MAGNA CARTA; PETITION OF RIGHT, 1628.

Liberum tenementum, a freehold or frank tenement (*q.v.*). The defendant in an action of trespass to land could plead that the *locus in quo* was the close, soil and freehold of the defendant. This was called the plea of avowry of *liberum tenementum.* It was construed as admitting the actual possession of the plaintiff, but as containing by implication an assertion of a right of possession in the defendant as owner of the freehold (*Delaney* v. *Smith* [1946] K.B. 393).

The plea of *liberum tenementum* was the only case of usual occurrence in more modern practice in which the allegation of a general freehold title in lieu of a precise allegation of title was sufficient. It was sustained by proof of any estate of freehold, whether in fee, in tail, or for life only, and whether in possession or expectant on determination of a term of years, but it did not apply to the case of a freehold estate in remainder or reversion expectant on a particular estate of freehold, nor to copyhold tenure.

Liblac [Lat. *venecifium*], witchcraft, particularly that kind which consisted in the compounding and administering of drugs and philtres (Leg.Athel. 6).

Liblacum, bewitching any person; also a barbarous sacrifice (Leg.Athel. 6).

Libra pensa, a pound of money by weight.

It was usual in former days, not only to sell the money, but to weigh it; because many cities, lords, and bishops, having their mints, coined money, and often very bad money, too, for which reason, though the pound consisted of twenty shillings, they weighed it (Encyc. Londin.).

In early times, and more especially during periods of debasement of the currency, there was sometimes used as a measure of money a pound which, instead of being the twenty shillings or two hundred and forty silver pennies making up the customary pound, was an actual pound weight of pure silver. See SILVER COINS.

Libraries. Free public libraries, at the expense of the ratepayers, were established by the Public Libraries Acts, 1855 and 1890. These Acts were consolidated by the Public Libraries Act, 1892. The law is now contained in the Public Libraries and Museums Act, 1964, and the Local Government Act, 1972, ss. 206–208, Sch. 30.

For exemption from capital transfer tax, see the Finance Act, 1975, Sch. 6 para. 12.

Librata terrae, a measure of land containing four oxgates (*q.v.*), each of which seems to have contained thirteen or fourteen acres.

In the time of Henry III, the owner of fifteen *libratae terrae* was liable to receive knighthood, which was then regarded as undesirable owing to the attendant expenses.

Libripens, a scalesman (Civil Law).

Licence [Lat. *licentia*], a permission given by one man to another to do some act which without such permission it would be unlawful for him to do. It is a personal right, and is not transferable, but dies with the man to whom it is given. It can as a rule be revoked at will by the licensor unless the licensee has given consideration for it. As to the nature and effect of the licence granted to the purchaser of a ticket for a theatre or other similar entertainment, see *Hurst* v. *Picture Theatres* [1915] 1 K.B. 1; *Allen & Sons* v. *King* [1916] 2 A.C. 54. It may be either written or oral; when written, the paper containing the authority is often called a licence. A licence amounting to or coupled with an interest in an incorporeal hereditament should be under seal (*Wood* v. *Leadbitter* (1845) 13 M. & W. 838), or it may be revocable (*Lowe* v. *Adams* [1901] 1 Ch. 598); whether it is revocable or not is a question of construction (*Winter Garden Theatre* (*London*) v. *Millennium Productions* [1948] A.C. 173). See AUTHORITY; LIBERTY.

A licence passes no interest, and therefore if A grants to B the right to fasten barges to moorings in a river, this does not amount to a demise, nor give the licensee an exclusive right to the use of the moorings, nor render him liable to be rated as the occupier of part of the bed of the river (*Watkins* v. *Milton Overseers* (1868) L.R. 3 Q.B. 350). If a person by deed grants an exclusive licence for the use of land, this may amount to a lease, or to the grant of an incorporeal hereditament (*Hooper* v. *Clark* (1867) L.R. 2 Q.B. 200; *Addiscombe Garden Estates* v. *Crabbe* [1958] 1 Q.B. 513). A mere licence is always revocable, but when a licence comprises, or is connected with, a grant of an interest, it is generally irrevocable: thus, a licence by A to hunt in his park is revocable; but a licence to hunt and take away the deer when killed is in truth a grant of the deer with a licence annexed to come on the land, and if the grant is good the licence is irrevocable. So a licence may be irrevocable if granted for valuable consideration.

A licence is necessary before doing many acts, as to marry without publication of banns, or to drive a motor vehicle on the road. See DRIVING LICENCES.

A marriage licence is an authority enabling two persons to be married. Such licences are of three kinds. A special licence is granted by the Archbishop of Canterbury, and enables the parties to be married in any church or chapel or other meet and convenient place (Marriage Act, 1949, s. 5). An ordinary licence is granted by any archbishop or bishop for the marriage of persons within his diocese in a church or chapel in which banns may lawfully be published. The effect of the ordinary licence is merely to legalise marriage without banns: the grant of such a licence would appear to be entirely in the discretion of the bishop and the only remedy in case of refusal is to have recourse to either banns or a special licence. A superintendent registrar's licence is one granted by the superintendent registrar of the district in which the parties, or one of them, reside, authorising the solemnisation of a marriage between them according to the rites of the Church of England, or the usages of the Quakers or Jews, etc., or such form as they think fit to adopt. See BANNS OF MARRIAGE; MARRIAGE.

There are numerous other varieties of licence: see GAME LICENCE; INTOXICATING LIQUORS; LOCAL TAXATION LICENCES; MOTOR CAR; MUSIC AND DANCING LICENCES; PATENTS.

Licence to arise (Licentia surgendi), the liberty or space of time allowed by the court to a tenant who has been essoined

de malo lecti (see ESSOIN) in a real action to arise from his bed and appear. It was also the title of a writ used in the matter (5 Bract.; 6 Fleta, c. 10).

Licence to assign. A landlord cannot exact a fine or sum of money in the nature of a fine from his tenant as a condition of granting him a licence to assign or underlet (Law of Property Act, 1925, s. 144), and by the Landlord and Tenant Act, 1927, s. 19, covenants not to assign or underlet without licence or consent are subject to the provisos that the licence or consent is not to be unreasonably withheld, and that if a lease is for more than forty years and is made for building, improvement, or alteration of buildings, with the exception of some public or similar buildings, no licence or consent is required for an assignment or underletting effected more than seven years before the end of the term, provided that notice in writing of the transaction is given to the lessor within six months after the transaction is effected. A licence to assign is unreasonably withheld if withheld on the ground of colour, race or ethnic or national origins (Race Relations Act, 1965, s. 5).

Licence to Convocation. The statute 1533, 25 Hen. 8, c. 19, provides that Convocation cannot enact any canons or constitutions without the sovereign's assent and licence. Such assent and licence are given by the document known as a licence to Convocation.

Licensed victualler. The publican is the licensed victualler *par excellence*. The term may be applied to any person selling any kind of intoxicating liquor under a licence from the justices of the peace. See INTOXICATING LIQUORS; VICTUALLER.

Licensee, a person to whom a licence has been granted; one to whom permission to enter premises has been given, but who has no common interest with the occupier of the premises (*Mersey Docks* v. *Procter* [1923] A.C. 253). The common law rule is that the occupier of the premises must warn the licensee of concealed dangers known to the occupier, but this must now be read subject to the Occupiers' Liability Act, 1957, which provides that the occupier must take such care as is reasonable to see that the licensee will be reasonably safe in using the premises for the purposes for which he is permitted to be there. See NEGLIGENCE.

Licensing Acts, the Acts restraining printing except by licence (see PRESS); also the Acts regulating the sale of intoxicating liquors (*q.v.*).

Licensing authority, the body which grants, or declines to grant, justices' licences for the sale of intoxicating liquor (*q.v.*) by retail.

Licentia concordandi, the king's licence or permission for which the king's silver (*q.v.*) was paid on the passing of a fine (2 Bl.Comm. 350).

Licentia loquendi (Li. lo.), leave to imparl (*q.v.*).

Licentia surgendi, licence to arise (*q.v.*).

Licentia transfretandi, a writ which was directed to the warden of a channel port commanding him to permit the passage overseas of such persons as had obtained the royal licence (Reg.Brev. 193).

Licentiate, one who has licence to practise any art or faculty.

Licet [Lat.], it is lawful; although.

Licet dispositio de interesse futuro sit inutilis, tamen fieri potest declaratio praecedens quae sortiatur effectum, interveniente novo actu (Bac.Max.Reg. 14). (Although the grant of a future interest is inoperative, yet it may become a declaration precedent, which will take effect on the intervention of some new act.) The settlement of after-acquired property illustrates this maxim.

Licet saepius requisitus, although often requested.

Licita bene miscentur, formula nisi juris obstet (Bac.Max.Reg. 24). (Things permitted are properly united unless a rule of law intervenes.) A common case was a grant of a rent by a tenant for life and the remainderman.

Licitation [Lat. *licere*, to set a price for sale], the act of exposing for sale to the highest bidder.

Licking of thumbs, a form by which bargains were completed.

Lidford law, a sort of Jedburgh justice, whereby a person was first punished and then tried. Lidford (now Lydford), in Devonshire, had rather a bad name:

but there is no evidence that, in the ordinary course, an alleged felon was first executed and then tried there.

Lie. An action " lies " if, on the facts of the case, it is competent in law, and can properly be instituted or maintained. Waifs, estrays, etc., which the persons entitled thereto may seize are said to lie in franchise. Property is said to lie in grant when it is capable of being disposed of by deed; it is said to lie in livery when it is capable of being disposed of by delivery.

Liege [Fr. *lige*; Ital. *ligio*], bound by some feudal tenure; a subject. See HOMAGE.

Liege homage, an acknowledgement which included fealty and the services consequent upon it.

Liege-lord, a sovereign; superior lord.

Liegeman, he who owes allegiance.

Lieges or **Leger,** a resident ambassador.

Lieges or **Liege people.** See LIEGE.

Lien [Fr. *lien;* Lat. *ligamen; ligare,* to bind], a right by which a person is entitled to obtain satisfaction of a debt by means of property belonging to the person indebted to him. It answers to the *tacita hypotheca* of the civil law. It is neither a *jus in re*, nor a *jur ad rem, i.e.,* it is not a right of property in the thing itself, nor a right of action to the thing itself. A lien is a species of security (see RIGHT; SECURITY), but differs from a mortgage, charge or the like in this respect, that in the case of a mortgage or charge the origin of the debt is immaterial (*e.g.,* it may be a loan, a debt for goods sold, etc.), while a lien can only be a security on property which is or has been the subject of a transaction between the parties; thus, if A sells lands to B, A has a lien on them for the unpaid purchase-money, unless he expressly or impliedly waives his right; and a seller of goods who is an " unpaid seller " within the meaning of the Sale of Goods Act, 1893, s. 38, has such lien on the goods as is provided by ss. 39, 41–48 of that Act.

Liens arise either by operation of law or by agreement between the parties. Liens arising by operation of law (liens by implication, implied liens) are those which arise from the relation of the parties, without express or tacit stipulation, and by the rules of the common law (as in the case of the vendor's lien for unpaid purchase-money mentioned above), or by the rules of equity (equitable liens), or under the provisions of a statute (statutory liens). Liens by agreement between the parties (conventional liens) are those created intentionally in cases where the relation between the parties is not such as to give rise to a lien by operation of law, as where a carrier stipulates for a general lien on goods sent him for transmission (*Wiltshire Iron* v. *G.W. Ry.* (1871) L.R. 6 Q.B. 776). The intention to create the lien may be express, or it may be implied, *e.g.*, from a previous course of dealings between the parties. See IMPLICATION.

Liens are either particular, as a right to retain a thing for some charge or claim growing out of, or connected with, the identical thing; or general, as a right to retain a thing not only for such charges or claims but also for a general balance of accounts between the parties in respect to other dealings of the like nature.

General liens are not favoured by the law, but particular liens, on the other hand, are favoured by the law.

A retaining (or possessory) lien is the right of the creditor to retain possession of his debtor's property until his debt has been satisfied; thus, if a person takes a watch to a watchmaker to be repaired, the watchmaker has a lien on the watch for his remuneration, *i.e.*, has the right of retaining it until his charges are paid. In this instance the lien is a particular lien, because it exists only as a security for the particular debt incurred in respect of the watch itself, while a general lien is available as a security for all debts arising out of similar transactions between the parties; thus, if a solicitor has possession of title deeds belonging to his client, he has a general lien on them, that is, he is entitled to retain them until he is paid the whole amount owing to him from the client for professional services up to that time; so has an accountant (*Woodworth* v. *Conroy* [1976] 2 W.L.R. 338). (See CHARGE.) General liens exist only in pursuance of a usage to that effect in the particular trade or business, the principal instances being in the case of solicitors, bankers, innkeepers, wharfingers and factors.

A charging lien is a right to charge property in another's possession with the payment of a debt or the performance of a duty: an instance of this is the equitable lien of a vendor of land for the unpaid purchase-money. A charging lien can be enforced by bringing an action (formerly by filing a bill in equity) for a sale of the property (*Walter* v. *Ware Ry.* (1866) L.R. 1 Eq. 195). The important distinction between a possessory and a charging lien is that in the case of the former, if the creditor gives up possession of the property, he loses his lien, while it follows from the nature of a charging lien that the property need not be in the creditor's possession.

There are also various forms of maritime lien, or lien on a ship, freight, etc., some of which are possessory, and some charging; thus, a shipowner has, independently of contract, a possessory lien on goods carried in his ship for the freight due in respect of them. If a ship is injured in a collision by the negligence of the other ship, the owners of the former have a maritime (charging) lien on the latter for the damage (*The Charles Amelia* (1867) L.R. 2 A. & E. 330); so the master of a ship has a maritime (charging) lien on the ship and freight for his wages and disbursements (Merchant Shipping Act, 1894, s. 167); this is an instance of a statutory lien, or lien created by statute. A maritime charging lien can be enforced by proceedings in the Admiralty Court (*q.v.*), in which distress and sale of the ship may be ordered.

"Lien" formerly denoted *obligatio*, generally, a warranty (*Termes de la Ley*).

To create a valid lien it is essential that the person through whom it is acquired should himself either have the absolute ownership of the property, or at least a right to vest it; for *nemo plus juris ad alium transferre potest, quam ipse habet*. There must also be an actual or constructive possession by the party asserting it, with the express or implied assent of the party against whom it is asserted. It must not be inconsistent with the express terms or the clear intent of the contract.

A lien attaches only to certain and

liquidated demands, and not to those which sound only in damages, unless, indeed, a special contract exists. The debt or demand for which the lien is asserted must be due to the person claiming it in his own right, and not merely as agent. It must also, in the absence of a special agreement, be a debt or demand due from the person for whose benefit the party is acting, and not from a third person, although the goods may be claimed through him.

A lien may be waived by act of or agreement between the parties, by which it is surrendered or becomes inapplicable. It is lost by relinquishing possession (*Hartley* v. *Hitchcock* (1816) Stark. 408; *Great Eastern Ry.* v. *Lord's Trustee* [1909] A.C. 109).

A lien on goods is not lost when the demand in respect of which it was acquired can no longer be enforced by action on account of the Limitation Act, 1939, for the Act does not put an end to the debt but only to the remedy by action.

A lien is a mere right of retainer, which may be used as a defence to an action for the recovery of the property, or as a matter of title or special property, to reclaim the property by action in case of unlawful dispossession. A lien does not import a right of sale. Sometimes a court of equity decreed a sale as a part of its own system of remedial justice; and courts of Admiralty constantly decree a sale to satisfy maritime liens, such as liens for seamen's wages, repairs of foreign ships, salvage, and other claims of a kindred nature (see MARITIME LIEN), and exceptions occur under statute, *e.g.*, the Innkeepers Act, 1878, and the Hotel Proprietors Act, 1956, s. 2 (2). The owner has a right to dispose of the property, subject to the lien, and the person to whom he conveys it will have a title to it upon discharging the lien.

The Disposal of Uncollected Goods Act, 1952, confers a right of sale of unclaimed goods left for repair.

By the Sale of Goods Act, 1893, s. 41, the unpaid seller of goods in possession of them may retain possession of them until payment or tender of the price where the goods have been sold without any stipulation as to credit, or where the goods have been sold on credit, but the term of credit has expired, or where the buyer has become insolvent, *i.e.*, has ceased to pay his debts or cannot pay them, whether he has committed an act of bankruptcy or not.

Equitable liens are not necessarily possessory. They are charges arising by implication of equity on the property in the hands of anyone who holds it with notice subject to any formalities which may be required by law such as registration (see LAND CHARGE; NOTICE). Such charges may be enforced by sale under order of the court, and in cases where the lien is not possessory, may be defeated like other charges under the Limitation Act, 1939.

By the Judicature Act, 1925, s. 56 (1) (*b*), causes for the sale and distribution of the proceeds of any property subject to lien are assigned to the Chancery Division.

Lien of a covenant, the commencement of a covenant stating the names of the covenantors and covenantees, and the character of the covenant, whether joint or several.

Lieu [Fr.], place, room; in lieu of means instead of.

Lieu conus, a castle, manor, or other notorious place, well known, and generally taken notice of by those who dwell about it (2 Lil. Abr. 641).

Lieutenancy, Commission of. In the reign of Edward VI commissions of lieutenancy, which were practically the same as the earlier commissions of array (*q.v.*), began to be issued and were addressed to the then newly created lieutenants (or lords lieutenant (*q.v.*)) of the counties. They continued to be issued from time to time up to the period of the Civil War. After the Restoration they fell into disuse as the result of the creation of the militia (*q.v.*) system.

Lieutenant [Fr. *lieu*, a place; *tenant*, holding], a deputy; *locum tenens*; one who acts by vicarious authority; a naval and military rank. See LORD LIEUTENANT.

Life. The law presumes the continuance of a given state of facts unless it is shown either that it has terminated or that in the inevitable course of events it must have terminated. Once the fact of life on a given date has been established, the law will presume its continuance unless there is evidence, or a presumption of fact recognised by the law, to the contrary effect. There is no presumption that any human life must terminate within any specified period. See ABSENCE FOR SEVEN YEARS; COMMORIENTES; DEATH; PRODUCTION; TENANT FOR LIFE.

Life annuity, an annual payment during the continuance of any given life or lives. See ANNUITY; LAND CHARGE; RENT; SETTLED LAND.

Life assurance, a transaction whereby a sum of money is secured to be paid upon the death of the person whose life is assured, or upon the failure of one out of two or more joint lives. See ASSURANCE; INSURANCE; INTEREST; POLICY OF ASSURANCE.

Life, Expectation of. Damages recoverable for personal injuries include damages for loss of normal expectation of life. See EXPECTATION OF LIFE.

Life interest, an interest for one's own life, or the life of another (*pur autre vie*). See SETTLED LAND.

Life peer. Until 1958, no such thing as a life peerage with a right to a seat in the House of Lords was known to the law except in the case of the Lords of Appeal in Ordinary (*q.v.*).

Life peers may now be created under the Life Peerages Act, 1958.

Life tenant, a person who holds property beneficially during his lifetime. See SETTLED LAND.

Lifeboats. Lifeboats and their crews are maintained by the Royal National Life Boat Institution whose regulations are set out in *The Cayo Bonito* [1904] P. 310. Where the services of lifeboat crews are required only for salvage of property they may rank as salvors.

Life-saving appliances (including lifeboats) must be carried by ships in accordance with the Merchant Shipping (Safety Convention) Act, 1949, s. 2.

Harbour authorities are under an obligation to maintain lifeboats and rocket apparatus (Harbours, Docks and Piers Clauses Act, 1847, ss. 16, 17; Harbours Transfer Act, 1862, s. 5).

Ligan [Fr. *lier*, to tie], a wreck consisting of goods sunk in the sea, but tied to a cork or buoy, in order that they may be found again (5 Co.Rep. 106). See DROITS OF ADMIRALTY; JETSAM.

Ligeance, the true and faithful obedience of a subject to his sovereign; also the dominion and territory of a liege-lord. See ALLEGIANCE.

Ligeantia est vinculum fidei: ligeantia est legis essentia (Co.Litt. 129). (Ligeance is the bond of fidelity, and the essence of the law.) Coke cites this maxim in connection with the rule that in an action by an alien against a subject the defendant could plead as a defence that the plaintiff was born " out of the ligeance."

Ligeas, a liege.

Light. No right to have the access of light to one's windows free from any obstruction exists at common law, but by virtue of the Prescription Act, 1832, uninterrupted enjoyment of light for twenty years, commonly called " ancient lights " constitutes an absolute and indefeasible right to it, unless the enjoyment took place under some deed or written consent or agreement (*Hyman* v. *Van den Bergh* [1908] 1 Ch. 167). See ANCIENT LIGHTS; PRESCRIPTION.

The Prescription Act, 1832, did not alter the previous law as to ancient lights (*Colls* v. *Home and Colonial Stores* [1904] A.C. 179). The right is to uninterrupted access of such light only as is ordinarily required for ordinary purposes and not to light peculiarly appropriate to the particular purpose for which the light has been used (*Price* v. *Hildich* [1930] 1 Ch. 500) but account may be taken of the nature of the locality and of modern lighting standards (*Ough* v. *King* [1967] 1 W.L.R. 1547).

Compensation for depreciation of the value of land due to artificial lighting of public works may be claimed under the Land Compensation Act, 1973. See NUISANCE.

If two tenements belong to a common landlord, the right to light can be acquired by one tenement, not only against the other tenement, but also against the landlord (*Morgan* v. *Fear* [1907] A.C. 425; *Foster* v. *Lyons & Co.* [1927] 1 Ch. 219).

Light dues, amounts payable by the owner of a ship for the purpose of maintaining lighthouses and similar navigation marks.

Light railway, a railway on which not more than eight tons weight may be brought upon the rails by any one pair of wheels, and on which the speed of trains may not exceed twenty-five miles an hour.

Light railways were formerly authorised by the Board of Trade under the Regulation of Railways Act, 1868, s. 27. The Light Railways Act, 1896, established a Light Railway Commission for the purpose of authorising light railways, with special aid from the Treasury. By the Light Railways Act, 1912, the powers of the Light Railway Commissioners were continued. Most light railways were acquired by the Transport Commission under the Transport Act, 1947, Sch. 3.

Lighter. The Merchant Shipping Act, 1921, s. 1, applied the provisions of the Merchant Shipping Act, 1894, relating to the registry of ships and limitation of liability of the owners or ships to lighters and barges. As to unsafe lighters, see s. 2; Merchant Shipping (Liability of Shipowners and Others) Act, 1958, Sch.

Lightermen. See WATERMEN.

Lighthouse, a building from which lights are shown to guide ships at sea. The power of erecting and maintaining them is a branch of the royal prerogative. At common law no one but the Crown could erect beacons, lighthouses and seamarks. Many of the rights of the Crown with regard to such matters were at one time delegated by letters patent to the Lord High Admiral. The advent of the Trinity House (*q.v.*) resulted in all the powers of the Crown being vested in them. They began with beacons (*q.v.*), and ultimately developed the lighthouse system. By the Harbours, Docks and Piers Clauses, etc. Act, 1847, s. 78, lighthouses are not to be erected without the sanction of Trinity House. The management of lighthouses is regulated by the Merchant Shipping Act, 1894, ss. 634–675, as amended by the Merchant Shipping (Mercantile Marine Fund) Act, 1898, which created a General Lighthouse Fund in substitution for the Mercantile Marine Fund (*q.v.*) and, subject to the rights of persons having authority over local lighthouses, is vested in the following bodies: as to lighthouses in England, Wales, the Channel Islands, and the adjacent seas and islands, and in Gibraltar, in the Trinity House; in Scotland and the adjacent seas and islands, and in the Isle of Man, in the Commissioners of Northern Lighthouses; and in Ireland and the adjacent seas and islands, in the Dublin Corporation. See also the Harbours Act, 1964, ss. 29, 30, Sch. 6.

The Act of 1898 provides that light dues are to be levied with respect to the voyages made by ships, or by way of periodical payment, and no longer with respect to the lights which a ship passes, or from which it derives benefit, prescribes a scale of light dues and rules for levying them, and enacts that the expenses of colonial lights are to be paid out of the General Lighthouse Fund. See FALSE LIGHTS.

Lighting and Watching Act. The Lighting and Watching Act, 1833, was an Act which could be adopted in any parish.

The Act was repealed as to the metropolis by the Sanitary Act, 1866, s. 35, and was superseded by the Public Health Act, 1875, s. 163, in districts where that Act was in force.

The Act was repealed by the Parish Councils Act, 1957.

Lights on vehicles. The requirements of lights on vehicles are now the subject of construction and use regulations made under the Road Traffic Act, 1972, s. 40, as amended by the Road Traffic Act, 1974, s. 9.

Ligius, a person bound to another by a solemn tie or engagement; the relation of a subject to his sovereign.

Lignagium, a right of cutting fuel in woods; also a tribute or payment due for the same (Jacob).

Lignamina, timber fit for building (Du Cange).

Ligula, a copy or transcript of a court-roll or deed.

Liguritor, a flatterer; perhaps a glutton.

Lime. Contributions towards the cost of spreading lime on agricultural land may be paid under the Agriculture Act, 1937, s. 1 (as subsequently amended); Agricultural Lime Scheme, 1966 (No. 794); Local Authorities, etc. (Miscellaneous Provisions) (No. 2) Order, 1974 (No. 595).

As to the standards of measurement,

etc. on the sale of agricultural liming materials, agricultural salt and inorganic fertilisers, see the Weights and Measures Act, 1963, s. 21, Sch. 7 Pt. III.

Limitation. To limit an estate or interest is to mark out the extreme period during which it is to continue, and the clause by which this is done in a conveyance, will, etc., is called a limitation. Thus, if there is a gift to A for life, and after his death to B, this is a limitation of a life interest to A, and of the remainder to B. (See WORDS OF LIMITATION.) Hence a limitation is opposed to a condition or defeasance, which may put an end to an interest before the time fixed for its extreme duration, though the difference is sometimes one of form only; thus, if A devises land to his widow for life, on condition that she does not marry again, the same result is produced as if he devised it to her during widowhood, which is a collateral limitation.

A conditional limitation is where one interest is limited to end and another to commence on the doing of some act or the happening of some event. Thus, if there if a gift to A until B returns from Rome, and on that event to C, or if there is a gift to A provided that when B returns from Rome it shall immediately vest in C, in either case the limitation to C is a conditional limitation. But in the specific and more accurate use of the term, a conditional limitation is where an interest is limited to commence in defeasance of a preceding interest as opposed to a contingent remainder, which awaits the regular determination of the preceding interest. See REMAINDER.

A collateral limitation is one which marks the extreme duration of an interest, and at the same time indicates an uncertain event the happening of which will put an end to it before the expiration of that period. Thus, a limitation to a woman during widowhood is a collateral limitation, because it gives her an interest for life, but makes it determinable on her marrying again. No interest could be limited in expectancy on the determination of a fee simple, however limited or conditional it might be (see REVERTER; RIGHT OF ENTRY),

except in a will or under the Statutes of Uses, 1535. A conditional or collateral limitation by way of use was sometimes called a shifting or springing use (see USE); when created by will it is called an executory devise. See EXECUTORY INTERESTS.

Limitation of actions. By various statutes, of which the first was the Limitation Act, 1623, and the principal succeeding ones, the Real Property Limitation Act, 1833, the Civil Procedure Act, 1833, the Real Property Limitation Act, 1874, now replaced by the Limitation Act, 1939, as amended by the Law Reform (Limitation of Actions, etc.) Act, 1954, the Limitation Act, 1963, and the Limitation Act, 1975, certain periods are fixed within which, upon the principle *interest reipublicae ut sit finis litium*, actions must be brought or proceedings taken.

Limitation, as a measure of time prescribed by statute within which proceedings to enforce a right must be taken, is of two kinds, namely (1) where on the expiration of the time the right itself is barred, as in the case of a person who has been out of possession of land for twelve years (Limitation Act, 1939, s. 16), although he may be ignorant of the fact that another is in possession (*Rains* v. *Buxton* (1880) 14 Ch.D. 537); and (2) where on the expiration of the time the remedy is barred, but not the right; thus, in the case of a simple contract debt which has remained unpaid and unacknowledged for six years, the creditor's right to bring an action to recover it is gone (Limitation Act, 1939, s. 2 (1)), but the debt exists for other purposes: hence he can exercise a right of lien to recover it, but not a set-off or counterclaim, because that is in the nature of a cross-action.

The period allowed in each case runs from the time when the right of action accrued. In certain cases, however, persons under disability have an extended time allowed them, calculated from the time the disability ceased, provided the whole time allowed does not exceed a certain maximum period. The disabilities recognised for this purpose are infancy and unsoundness of mind (s. 22; Limitation Act, 1975, s. 2).

If the person liable to be sued gives the creditor a written and signed acknowledgment of the debt, this has the effect of extending the period of limitation, so that it runs only from the acknowledgment, or the last acknowledgment, if there were several (s. 23 (4)). See ACKNOWLEDGMENT.

The Judicature Act, 1873, s. 25, provided that no claim by a *cestui que trust* against his trustee for any property held on an express trust or in respect of any breach of such trust should be held to be barred by any Statute of Limitations, but the Limitation Act, 1939, s. 19, provides that actions by beneficiaries against trustees for breach of trust are barred after six years from the date when the cause of action accrued, except in cases of fraud or retention or conversion of property.

The Act binds the Crown (Limitation Act, 1939, ss. 30 (1), 32; Crown Proceedings Act, 1947, Sch. 2).

The period of limitation in actions for personal injuries is, in general, three years from the date on which the cause of action accrued or the date, if later, of the plaintiff's knowledge. If, however, the person injured dies before the three years have expired, the period, as respects the cause of action surviving for the benefit of the estate of the deceased (by virtue of s. 1 of the Law Reform (Miscellaneous Provisions) Act, 1934) is three years from the date of the death or the date of the personal representative's knowledge, whichever is the later (Limitation Act, 1939, s. 2A, added by the Limitation Act, 1975, s. 1). The court has power to override these time limits (Act of 1939, s. 2D, added by the Act of 1975, s. 1).

The other principal periods of limitation are as follows: torts, other than torts involving personal injuries, six years; simple contracts, six years; specialty debts and judgments, twelve years (Act of 1939, s. 2); recovery of land by the Crown or a spiritual or eleemosynary corporation sole, thirty years; recovery of land by other persons, twelve years (Act of 1939) s. 4.

As to the recovery of damages for the death of a person, see CAMPBELL'S (LORD) ACT.

For the purposes of the Limitation Acts, any damage for which a person is liable under ss. 2 to 4 of the Animals Act, 1971, is to be treated as due to his fault (Act of 1971, s. 10).

A possessory title may be forced on a purchaser (*Re Sands and Thompson* (1833) 22 Ch.D. 614).

A title under the Limitation Act, 1939, can be acquired to land although it has been registered under the Land Registration Act, 1925, s. 75, if the claimant satisfies the registrar and obtains registration in his own name. The Law of Property Act, 1925, s. 12, expressly saves the operation of the statutes and general law affecting the limitation of actions.

No advantage can be taken of a statute of limitation in an action unless an issue thereon is raised by the pleadings: R.S.C., Ord. 18, r. 8.

At common law there is no period of limitation for prosecution of criminal offences except where they are punishable on summary conviction, in which cases the period is six months, by the Magistrates' Courts Act, 1952, s. 104, and there are many other statutory limitations on prosecutions of indictable offences. There is no period of limitation for proceedings to claim a peerage before the Committee of Privileges of the House of Lords.

Treason must, in general, be prosecuted within three years.

Limitation of liability. As to companies with limited liability, see COMPANIES; CONTRIBUTORY.

A shipowner is not liable at all for loss of or damage to goods on the ship in certain cases, *e.g.*, when caused by fire (Merchant Shipping Act, 1894, s. 502), and is not liable for loss of life or injury to persons or things caused by or on board the ship in other cases beyond a certain amount for each ton of the ship's tonnage, (s. 503 as amended by the Merchant Shipping (Liability of Shipowners and Others) Act, 1958), except in certain cases mentioned (see YACHTS). If the damages actually sustained exceed the amount thus arrived at, they are paid into court, and distributed among the claimants in proportion to their claims. The claimants are said to prove against the fund in court just as creditors prove against an insolvent estate. These limitations of liability only apply to cases where the loss or injury has not been caused by the shipowner's actual fault or privity (ss. 502, 503).

Where two vessels are injured by collision, and both are to blame, so that the enactment as to apportioning the liability for the damage applies (see COLLISION OF SHIPS), and one of them obtains a limitation of his liability under the Merchant Shipping Act, 1894, a set-off is allowed between the amounts of the respective damages. Thus, suppose the ships A and B come in collision, and both are equally to blame, and the half-damage payable by A is £14,000 and that payable by B is £2,000, then if there were no limitation of liability, A would be liable to B for the difference, namely, £12,000; and if ship A obtains a judgment limiting its liability to £5,000, then ship B is entitled to set off the £2,000 against the £14,000, and to prove against the £5,000 for the balance of £12,000 (*Chapman* v. *Royal Netherlands* (1879) 4 P.D. 157).

See CARRIERS ACT; INNKEEPER.

Limited administration, a special and temporary administration of certain specific effects of a testator or intestate granted under varying circumstances.

Limited companies. Under the Companies Act, 1948, limited liability means that the members are not liable beyond the unpaid-up part (if any) of the nominal amount of the shares in respect of which they are registered in the books of the company. When a share has been fully paid up, no further liability exists. As to shares which have not been fully paid up, see CONTRIBUTORY.

Limited executor, an executor whose appointment is qualified by limitations as to the time or place wherein, or the subject-matter whereon, the office is to be exercised, as distinguished from one whose appointment is absolute, *i.e.,* certain and immediate, without any restriction in regard to the testator's effects or limitation in point of time.

Limited owner, a tenant for life, in tail or by the curtesy, or other person not having a fee simple in his absolute dis-

position. The legal estates of limited owners were reduced to equitable interests by the Law of Property Act, 1925, ss. 1, 4. See SETTLED LAND.

The Limited Owners' Residences Act, 1870, as amended by the Limited Owners' Residences Act, 1870, Amendment Act, 1871, enabled the tenant for life of a settled estate to charge the estate with the expense of building a mansion house to the extent of two years' rental of the estate (*Re Dunn* [1877] W.N. 39).

A limited owner's charge is a charge arising under the Finance Act, 1894, in favour of a tenant for life who has paid estate duty in respect of the estate; it is registrable under the Land Charges Act, 1972, s. 2 (1), Class C (ii).

Limited partnership. See PARTNERSHIP.

Limogia, enamel (Du Cange).

Linarium, a flax plat, where flax is grown (Du Cange).

Lincoln, Statute of, the statute 1316, 9 Edw. 2, st. 2, relating to sheriffs.

Lincoln's Inn, one of the four Inns of Court. See INNS OF COURT.

Lincoln's Inn Fields, a square containing a public park, now under the control of the London Boroughs of Camden and Westminster. The statute 1735, 8 Geo. 2, c. 26, authorised the enclosure of the land and the levying of a rate for its maintenance upon the houses forming the square in which the fields lay. This enactment was passed because the fields had become a receptacle for refuse and a resort of dangerous persons. It appears from the preamble to the Act that the Society of Lincoln's Inn had no proprietary interest in the land (Williams, *Early Holborn*).

Lindesfern, or **Lindesfarne,** Holy Island in Northumberland, which was formerly a bishop's see (4 Co.Inst. 288).

Lindsey. See RIDING.

Line, succession of relations; boundary; the twelfth part of an inch.

Line throwing apparatus. See the Merchant Shipping Act, 1894, s. 427, as substituted by the Merchant Shipping (Safety Convention) Act, 1949, s. 2.

Linea recta semper praefertur transversali (Co.Litt. 10b). (The direct line is always preferred to the collateral.) Thus the eldest son of a deceased eldest son is the heir of a grandfather rather than a surviving younger brother of the deceased eldest son.

Lineage [Fr. *lignage*], race, progeny, family, ascending or descending.

Lineal consanguinity, that relationship which subsists between persons descended in a right line, as grandfather, father, son, grandson. See CONSANGUINITY.

Lineal descent, the descent of an estate from ancestor to heir in a right line. See DESCENT.

Lineal warranty, where the heir derived, or might by possibility have derived, his title to the land warranted, either from or through the ancestor who made the warranty; as where a father or an elder son in the life of the father released to the disseisor of themselves, or of the grandfather, with warranty, this was lineal to the younger son (Litt. 703). It was abolished by the Fines and Recoveries Act, 1833, s. 14. See WARRANTY.

Linen. As to trade marks on linen, see the Trade Marks Act, 1938, s. 93.

Liqueur. See SPIRITS.

Liquid assets, cash or property of a readily realisable nature, *e.g.*, government securities. See ASSETS.

Liquidated. A sum is said to be liquidated when it is fixed or ascertained. The term is usually employed with reference to damages (*q.v.*). See WRIT OF SUMMONS.

Liquidated damages, the amount agreed upon by a party to a contract to be paid as compensation for the breach of it, and intended to be recovered, whether the actual damages sustained by the breach are more or less, in contradistinction to a penalty (*Kemble* v. *Farren* (1829) 6 Bing. 141). See DAMAGES; PENALTY.

Liquidated demand. Where an action is brought for a debt or liquidated demand only, the writ must be endorsed with a statement of the amount claimed and for costs and also with a statement that further proceedings will be stayed if, within the time limited for appearing, the defendant pays the amount claimed to the plaintiff, his solicitor or agent or into court (R.S.C., Ord. 6, r. 2 (1) (*b*)). See LEAVE TO DEFEND.

Liquidation. Under the Bankruptcy Act, 1869, a debtor unable to pay his debts might present a petition stating that he was insolvent, and thereupon summon a general meeting of his creditors. If the meeting passed a special resolution declaring that the affairs of the debtor were to be liquidated by arrangement, and not in bankruptcy, the creditors appointed a trustee, with or without a committee of inspection, and the property of the debtor vested in the trustee and became divisible among his creditors, in the same way as if he had been made bankrupt. The subsequent proceedings generally followed the same course as those in an ordinary bankruptcy, except that the close of the liquidation and the discharge of the trustee were fixed by the creditors. The theory of the proceeding was that the affairs of the estate were brought under the immediate control of the creditors, without the delays and expenses caused by the supervision of the court as in bankruptcy.

Liquidation is not now known to the bankruptcy law, the only alternative to bankruptcy being an arrangement (*q.v.*) effected either privately or through the court.

The liquidation of a company is now known as winding up (*q.v.*): but the person who carries out the winding up is known as a liquidator (*q.v.*).

Liquidator, a person appointed to carry out the winding up of a company (see WINDING UP). In the case of a member's voluntary winding up, with or without supervision, one or more liquidators are appointed by the company (Companies Act, 1948, s. 235). In the case of a creditor's voluntary winding up, the creditors and the members each nominate a liquidator, the liquidator of the creditors having preference (s. 294). Where a company is being wound up subject to supervision, the court may appoint additional liquidators (s. 314). In the case of a compulsory winding up by the court a provisional liquidator may be appointed by the court as soon as a petition for winding up has been presented (s. 238). After the winding-up order is made, the official receiver is *ex officio* the provisional liquidator until he or some other person is appointed as liquidator (s. 239).

The duties of a liquidator are to get in and realise the property of the company, to pay its debts, and to distribute the surplus (if any) among the members. The chief difference between a liquidator in a winding up by the court and a liquidator appointed in a voluntary winding up is that the former cannot as a rule take any important step in the winding up without the sanction of the court, while the latter is not so restricted, and also does as of course various things which, in a winding up by the court, are done either by the court or by the liquidator under a general authority of the court, *e.g.*, settling the list of contributories and making calls.

Liquor licences. See INTOXICATING LIQUORS.

Lis [Lat.], a suit, action, controversy, or dispute.

Lis alibi pendens, a suit pending elsewhere. The fact that proceedings are pending between a plaintiff and defendant in one court in respect of a given matter is frequently a ground for preventing the plaintiff from taking proceedings in another court against the same defendant for the same object and arising out of the same cause of action. As a general rule, the plaintiff is put to his election which suit he will pursue, and the other is either dismissed, or the proceedings in it are suspended until the other is decided. This applies more especially where both proceedings are in British courts. Where one proceeding is in a British and the other in a foreign court, the court will consider whether in one of them relief is obtainable which could not be obtained at all, or so easily, in the other.

Lis mota, existing or anticipated litigation. The phrase is used chiefly with reference to declarations or statements made under such circumstances that they are admissible in evidence notwithstanding the rule against hearsay evidence; thus a pedigree drawn up by a member of a family is admissible after his death as evidence of the facts stated in it, unless it can be shown that it was drawn up after litigation was in contemplation (*post litem motam*). The phrase is also used in questions of privileged communications. See CONFIDENTIAL COMMUNICATIONS; PRIVILEGE.

Lis pendens, a pending suit, action, petition or the like. The old doctrine of *lis pendens* was that if property was in question in a suit or action, it could not be alienated during the pendency of the suit or action, even to a purchaser or mortgagee without notice. A *lis pendens* may be registered under the Land Charges Act, 1972, s. 5. The registration of a *lis pendens* does not create an incumbrance on the property, but merely gives intending purchasers or mortgagees notice of the litigation. The registration ceases to have effect after five years unless renewed (s. 8). The court may, on the determination of the proceedings or if satisfied that the proceedings are not prosecuted in good faith, make an order directing the vacation of the registration (s. 10).

Listed stock, securities approved for admission to trading on the Stock Exchange.

Lit de justice. See BED OF JUSTICE.

Literae clausae; Literae patentes. See CLOSE ROLLS.

Literae de coketto. See COCKET.

Literae humaniores, Greek, Latin, general philology, logic, moral philosophy, metaphysics; the name of one of the principal courses of study in the university of Oxford.

Literal contract, a written agreement subscribed by the contracting parties (Civil Law).

Literal proof, written evidence.

Literarum obligatio or **expensilatio,** an obligation created by an entry in the account book (*codex*) of the creditor with the consent of the debtor, charging the debtor as owing a certain sum (Civil Law).

Literary and scientific institutions. The Literary and Scientific Institutions Act, 1854, as amended, affords facilities for procuring and settling sites and buildings in trust for institutions established for the promotion of literature, science, or the fine arts, or for the diffusion of useful knowledge, and makes provisions for improving the legal conditions of such institutions. As to the proper purposes of these institutions, see *Re Bad-*

ger [1905] 1 Ch. 568. As to relief from rates see the General Rate Act, 1967, s. 40.

Literary work. See COPYRIGHT.

Literate, one not being a university man, or a pupil of a theological college, who is up to the educational standard required for admission to orders of the Church of England.

Literatura. *Ad literaturam ponere* means to put children to school. This liberty was anciently denied to those parents who were servile tenants, without the lord's consent; the prohibition against the education of sons arose from the fear that a son, being bred to letters, might enter into holy orders, and so stop or divert the services which he might otherwise do as heir to his father (Paroch.Antiq. 401).

Lithographs. These are included under engravings for purposes of copyright (Copyright Act, 1956, s. 48). See COPYRIGHT.

Litigant, one engaged in a law-suit.

Litigation, judicial contest; law-suit.

Litigious. In ecclesiastical law, a church or benefice is said to be litigious when two patrons present to it by several titles, because then the bishop does not know under which presentation to admit, even if they both present the same clerk. See JUS PATRONATUS; QUARE IMPEDIT.

Litis aestimatio, the measure of damages.

Litis contestatio, in the ecclesiastical courts, the issue of an action; in the civil law, a submission to the decision of a *judex.* See CONTESTATION OF SUIT.

Litis nomen omnem actionem significat, sive in rem, sive in personam sit (Co. Litt. 292). (The word *lis* signifies every action whether it be *in rem* or *in personam.*) See IN REM.

Litispendence [Lat. *lis,* strife; *pendere,* to hang], the time during which a law-suit is going on.

Litre has the meaning from time to time assigned by order of the Board of Trade (Weights and Measures Act, 1963, Sch. 1 Pt. IV). For definition see S.I. 1963 No. 1354. A hectolitre is one hundred litres. A decilitre is one-tenth of a litre. A centilitre is one-hundredth of a litre. A millilitre is one-thousandth of a litre (*ibid.*).

Litter. It is an offence to drop or leave litter in any place in the open air to which the public have access without payment (Litter Act, 1958; Dangerous Litter Act, 1971). The offence of depositing and leaving litter is not a continuing offence. Accordingly it must be proved that the litter was deposited within six months before information laid (*Vaughan v. Briggs* [1960] 1 W.L.R. 622).

Local authorities have power to provide litter bins (Public Health Act, 1961, s. 51; Local Government Act, 1972, Sch. 14 para. 41, Sch. 30); so have highway authorities (Highways Act, 1959, s. 156).

A co-ordinated effort to deal with the problem of litter is envisaged by the Control of Pollution Act, 1974, s. 24.

Little Easter Sunday, Low Sunday (*q.v.*).

Little goe, a species of lottery (*q.v.*). mentioned in the Gaming Act, 1802, s. 2.

Littleton. Thomas Littleton seems to have been born about the beginning of the fifteenth century. He was called to the bar at the Inner Temple. He was made serjeant-at-law in 1453 and judge of the Common Pleas in 1466, was knighted in 1475 and died on August 23, 1481. The celebrated *Treatise on Tenures* which he wrote for the use of his son is still quoted as an authority on the law of real property, and is made valuable by the equally celebrated *Commentary* of Sir Edward Coke, known as *Coke upon Littleton.* There is also a commentary on it by an unknown writer, which is pronounced by Hargrave to be a very methodical and instructive work.

Liturgy [λειτουργια, a public service], the Book of Common Prayer used in the established church, as confirmed by the Act of Uniformity, 1662.

The Prayer Book (Table of Lessons) Act, 1871, passed to amend the law relating to the Table of Lessons and Psalter contained in the Prayer Book, provides a new Table of Lessons, and the Act of Uniformity Amendment Act, 1872, provides a shortened form of Morning and Evening Prayer. An alternative Table of Lessons is provided by the Revised Tables of Lessons Measure, 1922. See ACT OF UNIFORMITY; PRAYER BOOK.

Livelode, maintenance, support.

Liverpool Court of Passage. See COURT OF PASSAGE.

Livery [Fr. *livrer*], the act of giving seisin or possession, superseded by the Real Property Act, 1845, s. 2. It also means simply delivery, as a horse is said to stand at livery where the livery stable keeper delivers him to the owner for use as required. In London it means the collective body of liverymen, and also the privilege of a particular company or society.

It also means release from wardship, and the writ by which possession was obtained. Formerly, when an infant heir of land had been in ward to the king by reason of a tenure *in capite ut de corona*, he was obliged on attaining twenty-one to sue livery, that is, to obtain delivery of the possession of the land, for which (in the case of a general livery) he paid half-a-year's profit of the land. Livery was either general, that is, in the ordinary form, which had several disadvantages, or special, that is, granted by the king as a matter of grace, by which those disadvantages were avoided and for which the heir had to pay more (Co.Litt. 77a).

As to the mode by which a tenant *in capite ut de honore* obtained his lands, see OUSTERLEMAIN.

See CAPITE, TENURE IN; COMPANIES, CITY; GUARDIAN; KNIGHT'S SERVICE.

Livery of seisin, a public solemnity or overt ceremony which was formerly necessary to convey an immediate estate of freehold in lands or tenements: that is, an estate of freehold in possession, or an estate of freehold only kept out of possession by a chattel interest (*i.e.*, a term of years) preceding it (Co.Litt. 48a; Shepp. Touch. 209).

If before the Statute of Uses, 1535, a tenant in fee wished to convey his estate to another, he could only do so by a feoffment (*q.v.*) which operated by livery of seisin. At the present day simpler means of conveyance are available, and livery of seisin is abolished (Law of Property Act, 1925, s. 51).

Livery of seisin was a transfer of the feudal possession of land, and it was therefore essential that it should be made either in the presence or with the assent of all persons having a right to the possession as against the feoffor, such as lessees for years.

There were two kinds of livery of seisin, *viz.*, a livery in deed and a livery in law. A livery in deed was where the feoffor was on the land to be conveyed, and orally requested or invited the feoffee to enter, or formally handed to him any object, such as the ring or hasp of the door of the house, or a branch or twig of a tree, or a turf of the land, and declared that he delivered it to him by way of seisin of all the lands and tenements contained in the deed of feoffment. A livery in law or livery within the view was when the feoffor said to the feoffee, being in view of the house or land, " I give you yonder land to you and your heirs, and go enter into the same, and take possession thereof accordingly," and the feoffee entered accordingly in the lifetime of the feoffor. See HEREDITAMENT.

Livery stable. See RIDING ESTABLISHMENTS.

Liverymen, members of such of the City companies as are livery companies. See COMPANIES, CITY.

Livery-office, an office appointed for the delivery of lands.

Lives, Lease for. A lease to A during the life of another or the lives of others was a tenure of very long standing in England, chiefly in the west and the north, or where the lease was granted by a corporation, and in Ireland. Now such a lease is either a lease for 90 years determinable by notice after any event determining the term under the original demise as provided by the Law of Property Act, 1925, s. 149, if the lease is at a rent or in consideration of a fine, or is a converted copyhold lease for life without right of perpetual renewal under the Law of Property Act, 1922. In all other cases it is an equitable interest and governed by the Settled Land Act, 1925. The tenant under the lease was called a tenant *pur autre* (or *auter*) *vie*, and the person during whose life the lease was to last, the *cestui que vie*. By the Cestui que Vie Act, 1666, there is a prima facie presumption of death after seven years' absence; and by the Cestui que Vie Act, 1707, an order may be made by the Chancery Division for the production of the *cestui que vie* on an application by the person interested (*Re Isaacs* (1838) 1 My. & C. 1; *Re St. John's Hospital* (1868) 18 L.T. 12). The lease for lives was abolished on the Duchy of Cornwall estates by the Duchy of Cornwall Management Act, 1863. It was at one time very common in Inns of Court leases. See AUTRE VIE, ESTATE PUR.

Livestock. The Agriculture Act, 1967, makes provision for the livestock and livestock products industries and for the payment of calf and beef cow subsidies (ss. 1–25). " Livestock " is defined as cattle, sheep and pigs (s. 25 (1)). Buildings used for livestock are exempted from rates (General Rate Act, 1967, ss. 1–4). " Livestock " for this purpose includes any mammal or bird kept for the production of food or wool or for the purpose of its use in the farming of land (s. 1 (3)). As to the welfare of livestock see the Agriculture (Miscellaneous Provisions) Act, 1968, ss. 1–8. As to injuries to and damage by livestock, see ANIMALS, LIABILITY FOR.

See AGRICULTURAL MARKETING BOARDS; ANIMALS, DISEASES OF; BULL; CATTLE; HILL FARMING; POULTRY.

Living. See BENEFICE.

Living memory. See MEMORY.

Lloyd's. A number of merchants, shipowners, underwriters, and insurance brokers were accustomed to meet, about the time of James II, in a coffee-house in Tower Street, in the City of London, kept by one Lloyd. This informal assemblage gradually formed itself into the association through which the insurance of the British mercantile marine is effected, and which furnishes the commercial world with a complete record, in the publication entitled *Lloyd's List*, of daily events in the shipping world, such as casualties and sailings. Lloyd's Signal Station Act, 1888, empowered Lloyd's to establish shipping signal stations with telegraphic communication. But Lloyd's was made by itself, not by Parliament, although Parliament did in fact incorporate and regulate it by Lloyd's Act, 1871. Many of the usages recognised by Lloyd's as obtaining between shipowners and underwriters have been recognised by the courts also. The Insurance Companies Act, 1974, s.

12 (4) excludes members of Lloyd's from the operation of Part II of that Act provided they comply with the requirements of s. 73 of the Act.

Insurance at Lloyd's can be effected to cover loss arising not merely from maritime disasters but from almost every conceivable event, such, for instance, as the birth of twins. See Wright, *History of Lloyd's*.

Special provisions with regard to taxation are contained in the Income and Corporation Taxes Act, 1970, s. 330, Sch. 10; Finance Act, 1973, ss. 39, 40, Sch. 16.

Lloyd's bonds, instruments invented about the middle of the last century by Mr. J. H. Lloyd, a member of the bar, intended to assist railway companies in carrying out their schemes, by indirectly enlarging their borrowing powers, which were limited by the Acts creating them, the Railway Regulation Act, 1844, s. 19, and the Companies Clauses Consolidation Act, 1845. A Lloyd's bond was merely an admission under seal of a debt due from some railway company to the party in whose favour it was executed, with a covenant to pay the debt with interest. It was an account stated under seal with a covenant to pay. The obligee was able to go into the market and obtain cash upon the faith of these instruments. They were generally used (and could only legally be used) for paying contractors and others who had done work or supplied materials, etc., for the company, and could not be given for a mere loan of money to the company. See Tarrant, *Lloyd's Bonds*.

Lloyd's Register. *Lloyd's Register of British and Foreign Shipping* is published annually by the Society of Lloyd's Register, an unincorporated society which has existed in its present form since 1834. The society, which is quite distinct from " Lloyd's," is voluntarily maintained by those interested in shipping, and is managed by a committee consisting of shipowners, merchants, and underwriters. The register is an alphabetical list of ships, classified according to materials, mode of construction, state of repair, etc. The classification is indicated by letters and numerals—such as " 100 A1," which are those used for the highest class. The society publishes rules in accordance with which vessels must be constructed in order to be classed in the register.

The society is officially recognised: see, for instance, the Merchant Shipping Act, 1894, ss. 429, 443.

Lloyd's Register is quite distinct from *Lloyd's List,* as to which see LLOYD'S.

Load line, an imaginary line along the side of a ship below which the vessel must not sink when loaded. Effect was given to the International Convention respecting load lines, 1930, by the Merchant Shipping (Safety and Load Line Conventions) Act, 1932, and to the International Convention on Load Lines, 1966, by the Merchant Shipping (Load Lines) Act, 1967. Ships of war, fishing boats and pleasure yachts are exempt. See PLIMSOLL MARK.

Loadmanage, the pay to a pilot for conducting a ship from one place to another. See LODEMANAGE.

Loadsman, one who, after a ship had been brought to a port by a pilot, took the ship to her berth in the port (Jacob). See LODEMANAGE.

Loan [Sax. *hloen*], anything lent or given to another on condition of return or repayment. See MONEYLENDER.

A gratuitous loan is a class of bailment called *commodatum* in the civil law, and denominated by Sir William Jones as a loan for use (*prêt à usage*), to distinguish it from *mutuum*, a loan for consumption.

The borrower has the right to use the thing during the time and for the purpose agreed upon by the parties. The loan is to be considered as strictly personal, unless from other circumstances a different intention may fairly be presumed. The borrower must take proper care of the thing borrowed, use it according to the lender's intention, and restore it at the proper time, and in a proper condition.

The lender must suffer the borrower to use and enjoy the thing lent during the time of the loan, according to the original intention, without any molestation or impediment, under the peril of damages. He must reimburse the borrower any extraordinary expenses to which he has been put for the preservation of the thing lent. He is bound to give notice to the borrower of defects of the thing lent; and if he does not, but conceals them, and an injury occurs to the borrower thereby, the lender is responsible. Where the thing has been lost by the borrower, and, after he has paid the value thereof, is restored to the lender, the latter must return either the price paid or the thing; for, by such payment of the loss, the property is effectively transferred to the borrower.

For exemption from stamp duty on transfer of loan capital, see Finance Act, 1976, s. 126.

See BORROWING CONTROL; BORROWING POWERS; CONSUMER CREDIT; LOCAL LOANS; MONEYLENDER; MORTGAGE.

Loan capital duty, abolished and replaced by capital duty (Finance Act, 1973, ss. 48, 49).

Loan commissioners. In the Public Works Loans Act, 1875, s. 4, this expression means the Public Works Loan Commissioners (*q.v.*).

Loan societies, institutions established for the purpose of advancing money on loan to the industrial classes, and receiving back payment for the same by instalments, with interest. They are exempt from the provisions of the Consumer Credit Act, 1974, see s. 16.

By the Loan Societies Act, 1840, forms of proceeding of a similar nature to those prescribed in the Acts regulating savings banks and friendly societies are requisite to enable loan societies to avail themselves of this Act. Their rules require certification by the Registrar of Friendly Societies.

These societies are entitled to issue debentures for money deposited with them, and these are exempted from stamp duty. They are also placed on the same footing with savings banks, in the event of the death of a claimant intestate, as regards dispensing with the production of letters of administration.

With respect to the recovery of loans, the Act provides a form of note to be signed by the borrower and two sureties; and upon failure in payment, the person liable may be summoned before any justice of the peace, who may levy by distress and sale of the goods. The society (by its treasurer) may proceed against the person liable, in any county court having jurisdiction, and where the sum due happens to exceed the amount for which the court has jurisdiction, may recover such part of the debt as that court can give judgment for, in lieu of the whole.

An abstract of the accounts is to be made out yearly and sent to the proper authority, to be laid before Parliament.

For amendments see the Administration of Estates (Small Payments) Act, 1965; Finance Act, 1970, Sch. 8 Pt. V; Finance Act, 1971, Sch. 14 Pt. VI; Courts Acts, 1971, Sch. 11 Pt. IV.

Lobsters. The minimum sizes of crabs and lobsters that may be landed, sold or possessed for sale may be prescribed under the Sea Fish (Conservation) Act, 1967, as amended by the Sea Fisheries Act, 1968. See FISHERIES.

Local Act. See ACT OF PARLIAMENT.

Local actions, those referring to some particular locality, as actions for trespass to land, in which the venue had to be laid in the county where the cause of action arose.

Real actions and the mixed action of ejectment were local: but personal actions were for the most part transitory, *i.e.,* their cause of action might be supposed to arise anywhere, but when they were brought for anything in relation to realty, they were then local.

See COUNTY COURTS; VENUE.

Local allegiance, allegiance due from an alien or stranger as long as he continues within the sovereign's dominions and protection; it ceases the instant such alien transfers himself from this kingdom to another, unless he happens to have obtained a British passport (*Joyce* v. *D.P.P.* [1946] A.C. 347). But if an alien, seeking the protection of the Crown, and having a family and effects here, should, during a war with his native country, go thither, and there adhere to the enemy for purposes of hostility, he may be dealt with as a traitor (Fost. 115). See ALIEN.

Local and personal Acts. See ACT OF PARLIAMENT.

Provisions in local and personal Acts giving double and treble costs, and allowing the general issue to be pleaded, and special matter to be given in evidence, are repealed by the Limitation of Actions and Costs Act, 1842, ss. 1, 3. The same Act provides for uniformity of notice of action in such actions (one month in all cases) and equalises the periods of limitation under such Acts. By the Interpretation Act, 1889, s. 9, every statute made after 1850 is to be taken to be a public one, and judicially noticed as such, unless the contrary is expressly declared.

Local authority. This expression is of modern origin. In the definition clauses of numerous Acts passed during the last hundred years, it is declared to mean, for the purposes of each of those Acts, the persons or bodies who respectively give effect to the Acts in various areas. In the Local Government Act, 1972, the general definition of a local authority is a county council (*q.v.*), the Greater London Council (*q.v.*), a district council (*q.v.*), a London borough council (see LONDON), a parish council (*q.v.*) or (in Wales) a community council (see COMMUNITIES) (s. 270 (1)), but this Act like other Acts contains special definitions of the expression local authority for the purposes of different provisions of the Act.

As to the qualifications for nomination and election to and membership of a local authority, see the Local Government Act, 1972, ss. 2–8, 15, 16.

Miscellaneous powers are conferred on local authorities by the Local Authorities (Land) Act, 1963, as amended.

The Public Bodies (Admission to Meetings) Act, 1960, provides for the admission of the press and certain other members of the public to the meetings of local authorities and other bodies exercising functions (s. 1 (1)). The Local Government Act, 1972, s. 100, extended the Act of 1960 to the meetings of committees, joint committees and advisory committees of local authorities. A body may, by resolution, exclude the public whenever publicity would be prejudicial to the public interest (Act of 1960, s. 1 (2) (3)). The bodies to which the Act applies are specified in Sch. 1 to the Act of 1960, amended by the London Government Act, 1963, Sch. 18 Pt. II; Local Government Act, 1972, Sch. 30; National Health Service Reorganisation Act, 1973, Schs. 4, 5; Water Act, 1973, Sch. 3. Where a local authority arranges a meeting to which s. 1 of the Act of 1960, applies, it is their duty to provide reasonable accommodation for the public, but if an unexpectedly large number of persons arrive so that the room chosen in good faith is insufficient, then certiorari will not go to quash any decision reached (*R.* v. *Liverpool City Council, ex p. Liverpool Taxi Fleet Operators' Association* [1975] 1 W.L.R. 701).

For exemption from tax, see the Income and Corporation Taxes Act, 1970, s. 353. For definition of local authority for tax purposes see the Finance Act, 1974, s. 52. For exemption of local authorities from the Consumer Credit Act, 1974, see ss. 16, 189 (1). See CONSUMER CREDIT.

Local boards of health. These were authorities formed under various Local Government Acts for carrying out in their respective districts the provisions of those Acts; also authorities formed by order of the Local Government Board under the Public Health Act, 1875, s. 272, Sch. 2, to be sanitary authorities for the execution of the provisions of that Act. Under the Local Government Act, 1894, s. 21, the local boards became urban district councils.

Local Commissioner. See the Local Government Act, 1974, s. 23. See COMMISSIONS FOR LOCAL ADMINISTRATION.

Local education authority. For the purposes of the Education Act, 1902, the council of every county and of every county borough was the local education authority, except that for the purposes of elementary education the council of a borough with a population of 10,000, or of an urban district with a population of 20,000, was the local education authority of that borough or district (Education Act, 1902, s. 1). This enactment was replaced by the Education Act, 1921, s. 3 (1) (2), which was practically identical. Now, however, by the Education Act, 1944, s. 6 (1), the local education authorities are the county councils, except where a joint board is established under s. 117 (5).

Local government, the system of government under which the administration of local affairs is in the hands of the local authority (*q.v.*).

For the administration of local govern-ment, England (exclusive of Greater London, the Isles of Scilly, the county of Monmouth and the county borough of Newport) is divided into local government areas known as counties (see COUNTY) and in those counties there are local government areas known as districts (see DISTRICT). Counties are divided into metropolitan counties and non-metropolitan counties. Districts are divided into parishes (see PARISH). The former administrative counties, boroughs, urban districts, rural districts and parishes cease to exist as such together with their councils. So do the corporations of boroughs (Local Government Act, 1972, s. 1, Sch. 1).

Wales (including the former administrative county of Monmouth and the county borough of Newport) is divided into counties, districts and communities (*q.v.*) (s. 20, Sch. 4).

The Local Government Act, 1972, came into force on April 1, 1974. It created new local government structures. Earlier Acts were the Local Government Act, 1858, which dealt mainly with public health, the Local Government Act, 1888, which established county councils, the Local Government (Transfer of Powers) Act, 1903, the Local Government Act, 1894, which established parish meetings, parish councils and district councils, the Local Government Act, 1929, which transferred the functions of guardians of the poor to county and county borough councils, the Local Government Act, 1933, which consolidated the law with amendments and listed the administrative counties, county boroughs and non-county boroughs, the Parish Councils Act, 1957, the Local Government Act, 1958, which provided machinery for the review of the organisation of local government, the Local Government (Records) Act, 1963, the Local Government (Financial Provisions) Act, 1963, the Local Government (Pecuniary Interests) Act, 1964, the Local Government Act, 1966, the Parish Councils and Burial Authorities (Miscellaneous Provisions) Act, 1970, the Local Authorities (Goods and Services) Act, 1970, the Local Authority Social Services Act, 1970, the Local Authorities (Qualification of Members) Act, 1971. See BOROUGH; COUNTY

BOROUGH; COUNTY COUNCIL; DISTRICT; PARISH.

As to changes in local government areas, see the Local Government Act, 1972, ss. 46–78. As to changes of name, see ss. 74–77. As to local government franchise, see the Representation of the People Act, 1949, ss. 2–5, 22–54; Representation of the People Act, 1969, ss. 1, 24, Sch. 1 para. 6, Sch. 2 para. 1.

The Local Government Act, 1974, makes provision for the revision of the system of local government finance.

Local Government Board, a board established by the Local Government Board Act, 1871, for the purpose of concentrating in one department of the Government the supervision of the laws relating to the public health, the relief of the poor, and local government. The powers and duties of the Local Government Board were transferred to the Ministry of Health by the Ministry of Health Act, 1919, s. 11, and are now exercised by the Secretary of State for the Environment (*q.v.*). See ENVIRONMENT, SECRETARY OF STATE FOR THE.

Local knowledge. Justices may and ought to take into consideration matters which they know of their own knowledge and particularly matters in regard to locality whether it be on land or in water (*Ingram* v. *Percival* [1969] 1 Q.B. 548), provided it is of a general nature (*Reynolds* v. *Llanelly Associated Tinplate Co.* [1948] 1 All E.R. 306 (county court judge).

Local land charges. A local land charge is (1) a charge acquired by a local authority, water authority or new town development corporation under the public health, highways or similar Acts being a charge binding on successive owners of the land; (2) a prohibition of or restriction on the use of land imposed by a local authority on or after January 1, 1926, or enforceable by a local authority under any covenant or agreement made with them on or after that date being a prohibition or restriction binding on successive owners of the land; (3) a prohibition of or restriction on the use of land imposed by a Minister of the Crown or government department on or after the Local Land Charges Act, 1975, came into force or enforceable under any

covenant made with him or them, being a prohibition or restriction binding on successive owners of the land affected; (4) a positive obligation affecting land enforceable by a Minister of the Crown, government department, or local authority under any similar covenant or agreement; (5) a charge or other matter expressly made a local land charge by any other statute (Local Land Charges Act, 1975, s. 1). This Act replaced the Land Charges Act, 1925, s. 15 as amended. The Act of 1975 was expressed to commence on a date fixed by the Lord Chancellor (s. 20 (3)). The following are not local land charges: (a) a prohibition or restriction enforceable under a covenant or agreement made between a lessor and a lessee; (b) a positive obligation enforceable under a covenant or agreement made between a lessor and a lessee; (c) a prohibition or restriction under a covenant or restriction made for the benefit of a Minister of the Crown, government department or local authority; (d) a prohibition or restriction embodied in any bye-laws; (e) a condition or restriction subject to which planning permission was granted or deemed to have been granted before the commencement of the Act; (f) a condition or restriction embodied in a scheme under the Town and Country Planning Act, 1932, or any enactment repealed by that Act; (g) a prohibition or restriction in a forestry dedication covenant; (h) a general prohibition or restriction (Act of 1975, s. 2). Local land charges registers are kept by district councils, London borough councils and the Common Council of the City of London (including the Inner Temple and Middle Temple) (ss. 3–7). Searches in the register may be personal (s. 8) or official (s. 9). Compensation may be claimed for non-registration or a defective official search (ss. 10, 11). Office copies of entries in the register are evidence (s. 12). A solicitor, trustee, personal representative, agent or other person in a fiduciary position is not answerable for loss occasioned by reliance on an erroneous official search or an erroneous office copy of an entry in the register (s. 13).

A local authority is vicariously liable to anyone who suffers damage due to its clerk's negligence in issuing a local land charges search certificate (*Ministry of Housing and Local Government* v. *Sharp* [1970] 2 Q.B. 223).

Local loans. Borrowing by local authorities by way of public loan is regulated by the Local Loans Act, 1875, the Local Loans Sinking Funds Act, 1885, and the Local Government Act, 1972, ss. 111, 172, Sch. 13.

By the Local Authorities Loans Act, 1945 (as amended), local authorities may borrow from the Public Works Loan Commissioners under the Public Works Loans Act, 1875, as amended. Provision is made from time to time for the grant of money for the purpose of local loans out of the Local Loans Fund: see *e.g.* the Public Works Loans Act, 1967.

As to the rate of interest see the National Loans Act, 1968, s. 6, and the Housing Finance Act, 1972, Sch. 11 Pt. IV.

Loans under s. 3 of the National Loans Act, 1968, may be made by the Public Works Loan Commissioners (Finance Act, 1975, s. 55).

Local planning authority. See TOWN AND COUNTRY PLANNING.

Local taxation licences. Licences the proceeds of which are collected by county councils under the Local Government Act, 1888, s. 20, Sch. 1 and the Finance Act, 1908, s. 6, as amended by subsequent legislation.

Local valuation courts, courts which hear appeals against objections to rating proposals. Appeal lies to the Lands Tribunal (*q.v.*) (General Rate Act, 1967, ss. 76, 77, 82–92; General Rate Act, 1970, s. 1; Local Government Act, 1972, Sch. 13 paras. 29, 30).

Local venue. See VENUE.

Locatarius, a depositee.

Locatio, hire, a letting-out.

Locatio conductio, hiring, a bailment for reward or compensation. See HIRE.

Locatio custodiae, the receiving of goods on deposit for reward.

Locatio mercium vehendarum, a contract for the carriage of goods for hire.

Locatio operis, or **operis faciendi,** the hiring of labour and services.

Locatio rei, the hiring of a thing.

Location, a contract for the temporary use of a chattel, or the service of a person, for an ascertained hire.

Location of Offices Bureau. This was set up under the Location of Offices Bureau Order, 1963 (No. 792). The Bureau has a duty to encourage decentralisation and diversion of office employment from congested areas in Central London to suitable centres elsewhere.

Locator, a letter of a thing or services for hire.

Lock hospital, a hospital for the treatment of venereal disease.

Locke's Act, the Solicitors Act, 1860, amending the law as to the admission, etc., of solicitors.

Locke King's Act, the Real Estate Charges Act, 1854, so called from the Member of Parliament by whom the Bill was introduced. The Act was amended by the Real Estate Charges Acts, 1867 and 1877.

The Acts provided that when any person died entitled to any estate or interest in land (including leaseholds) which was charged at the time of his death with the payment of money by way of mortgage, or with equitable charges or liens for unpaid purchase-money, and he did not signify a contrary intention, his heir or devisee should not be entitled to have the mortgage debt discharged out of his personal estate (as was the old rule), but should take the land subject to the debt. The Acts were replaced and extended to all forms of real and personal property by the Administration of Estates Act, 1925, ss. 35, 55 (1) (xvii). See EXONERATION; MARSHALLING.

Lockman, an officer in the Isle of Man who executes the orders of the governor, much like our under-sheriff. Also an old Scots term for the hangman; so called because one of his dues consisted in taking a small ladleful or lock of meal out of every caskful exposed in the market.

Lock-out, a refusal by an employer to continue to employ workpeople with a view to compelling them to accept terms affecting their employment.

The expression "lock-out" was elaborately defined in the repealed s. 167 (1) of the Industrial Relations Act, 1971.

Lock-up. This expression occurred in the Police Constables Act, 1842, s. 22, which speaks of lock-up houses for the temporary confinement of persons. See also the Lock-up Houses Act, 1848, and the Petty Sessions and Lock-up Houses Act, 1868, ss. 6–10.

Loco citato, Loc. cit., at the passage quoted.

Lococession, the act of giving place.

Locomotives. The Locomotives Act, 1865, s. 3, provided that every locomotive on a highway must be preceded by a man on foot with a red flag, and contained provisions as to the number of men to be employed. This enactment was repealed in these respects by the Locomotives Act, 1878, s. 29.

The Road Traffic Act, 1972, s. 190, defines a light locomotive as a mechanically propelled vehicle (*q.v.*) which is not constructed itself to carry a load, other than the following articles, that is to say, water, fuel, accumulators and other equipment used for the purpose of propulsion, loose tools and loose equipment and the weight of which unladen does not exceed $11\frac{1}{2}$ tons but does exceed $7\frac{1}{4}$ tons.

The same section defines a heavy locomotive as a mechanically propelled vehicle (*q.v.*) which is not constructed itself to carry a load other than any of the articles aforesaid and the weight of which unladen exceeds $11\frac{1}{2}$ tons. See MOTOR CAR.

As regards locomotives on railways, see ENGINES; STEAM ENGINES.

Loculus, a coffin, a purse.

Locum tenens, one who, under lawful authority, acts in the execution of an office held by another; a deputy.

Locus in quo, the place where, the place in which; the place where a thing is alleged to have been done or to have happened.

Locus partitus, a division made between two towns or counties, to make trial where the land or place in question lies (4 Fleta, c. 15).

Locus poenitentiae, a place or chance of repentance, a power of drawing back from a bargain before any act has been done to confirm it in law.

Locus regit actum, the place governs the act; that is, the act is governed by the law of the place where it is done.

In private international law the rule is that when a legal transaction complies with the formalities required by the law of the country where it is done, it is also valid in the country where it is to be given effect to, although by the law of that country other formalities are required. There are many exceptions to the rule, the principal being with reference to land and other immovables. See DOMICILE; LEX LOCI.

Locus sigilli, abbrev. L.S., the place of the seal, as designated by an O at the foot of a document requiring a seal.

Locus standi, a place to stand on. To say that a person has no *locus standi* means that he has no right to appear or be heard in such-and-such a proceeding.

The phrase is used in parliamentary practice with reference to the question whether a person who objects to a private Bill has the right to appear by counsel and summon witnesses to support his objection before the select committee. It is also used in opposition proceedings in the Patent Office. See REFEREE.

Locust. The control of locusts is the subject of international conventions: see Cmd. 7650, 8820, 9002; Cmnd. 128, 600, 1353, 3402.

Lodemanage; Loadmanage, a charge for piloting a ship.

The Cinque Ports pilots were formerly known as lodesmen (see LOADSMAN), loatsmen or leadmen (the latter name being connected with the use of the lead used to take soundings, and the others being apparently of similar derivation through the Flemish word *loot* meaning lead). They formed a society, with a warden and masters, which was under the jurisdiction of the Court of Lodemanage, which was a branch of the Court of Admiralty of the Cinque Ports (*q.v.*). The property of the Court of Lodemanage and of the Society of Cinque Ports Pilots was transferred to the Trinity House by the Pilotage Law Amendment Act, 1853, s. 10; and s. 4 of the same Act made the Cinque Ports pilots subject to the same rules, etc., as Trinity House pilots.

Lodge. To lodge documents is to file or leave them with the appropriate official.

Lodger, a person who occupies rooms in a house of which the general possession remains in the landlord. If, therefore, a house is divided into sets of rooms, each of which has an outer door opening on to a common staircase, while the entrance to that staircase either has no street-door, or has a door under the control of a porter acting as the servant of the collective tenants, then each set of rooms is not a lodging, but a separate hereditament, and each tenant has a rateable occupation. See RATE.

Goods belonging to a lodger are exempt from distress for rent owing by the lodger's landlord to the superior landlord. To entitle himself to this exemption, the lodger must serve on the superior landlord a declaration, with an inventory of the goods distrained on, stating that the goods are his, and undertaking to pay to the landlord any rent due or to accrue from the lodger to his immediate landlord (Law of Distress Amendment Act, 1908, s. 1).

A person who occupied unfurnished lodgings of the yearly value of £10 was entitled to be registered as a voter at parliamentary elections; but this lodger-franchise was abolished in 1918. See ELECTORAL FRANCHISE.

For powers of the local authority in respect of houses in multiple occupation see the Housing Act, 1957, s. 90; Housing Act, 1961, ss. 12–23; Housing Act, 1964, ss. 64–91; Housing Act, 1969, ss. 58–64.

Lodging houses, Common. The term is defined in the Public Health Act, 1936, s. 235, as meaning a house (other than a public assistance institution) provided for the purpose of accommodating by night poor persons, not being members of the same family, who resort thereto and are allowed to occupy one common room for the purpose of sleeping or eating. As to the test of sleeping and having meals in a common room, see *Langdon* v. *Broadbent* (1877) 37 L.T. 434. As to its use by persons of the poorer classes, see *L.C.C.* v. *Hankins* [1914] 1 K.B. 490. The Act provides for their registration and inspection.

Log, a record, called the official log book in a form approved by the Department of Trade, is to be kept in every ship registered in the United Kingdom.

The making of the log book is prescribed by the Department of Trade (Merchant Shipping Act, 1970, s. 68).

Logating. "Logating in the field" is mentioned in the preamble to the statute 1541, 33 Hen. 8, c. 9, as one of sundry new and crafty games with which men occupied themselves instead of practising archery. Loggat was a game in which a stake was fixed to the ground and the players threw from a distance "loggats" (spherical masses of wood with long handles), which they tried to leave as near the stake as possible.

Logia, a small house, lodge or cottage (1 Dugd.Mon. 400).

Logium, a lodge, hovel or outhouse.

Logomachy, a contest of words.

Loitering. Persons found loitering and suspected of intending to commit an arrestable offence may be arrested without warrant (Vagrancy Act, 1824, s. 4; Criminal Law Act, 1967, Sch. 2). See *Ledwith* v. *Roberts* [1937] 1 K.B. 232; *Christie* v. *Leachinsky* [1947] A.C. 573; *Cosh* v. *Isherwood* [1968] 1 W.L.R. 48.

Loitering or soliciting by a common prostitute is punishable under the Street Offences Act, 1959, s. 1.

Loitering by a postman is an offence under the Post Office Act, 1953, s. 59.

Lollardy [Old Ger. *lullen, lollen,* or *lallen,* to sing with a low voice], a term brought from Belgium and given to the early Protestants (the followers of Wycliffe) in the reign of Edward III. The Lollards closely resembled the Puritans of the reign of Elizabeth I (Stow, *Annals,* 425).

London, the metropolis of England.

The administrative county of London was created by the Local Government Act, 1888, ss. 40 (1), 100. The City of London was included only for certain administrative purposes.

The London Government Act, 1963, effected a reorganisation. It created thirty-two new London boroughs (s. 1; Local Government Act, 1972, Sch. 30). The area comprising the areas of the London boroughs, the City and the Inner Temple and Middle Temple constitutes the administrative area of Greater London (1963 Act, s. 2 (1)). The constitution and membership of the Greater London Council and of the London borough councils are prescribed by the 1972 Act, s. 8, Sch. 2. The county of Middlesex ceased to exist (1963 Act, s. 3). The Greater London Council is the highway authority for metropolitan roads and the council of a London borough or the Common Council are the highway authorities for other roads (1963 Act, s. 16).

Public health in London is regulated by the Public Health Acts applied to London by the London Government Act, 1963, s. 40, Sch. 11 Pt. II.

As to transport in London, see the Transport (London) Act, 1969, and the Transport (London) Amendment Act, 1969.

The City of London contains a little more than a square mile, the precise area being 671 acres. The government of the City remains much as it was in the Middle Ages. It is vested in the Lord Mayor, the aldermen, the common councillors or councilmen and the City companies.

The title of Lord Mayor has existed from 1354. Before that date, as from, at any rate, 1189, the office had existed under the title of Mayor. The Lord Mayor is selected by the Court of Aldermen out of the two aldermen nominated for the office by the Court of Common Hall. The presentation and swearing of the Lord Mayor takes place in the Queen's Bench Division before the judges of that division on the second Saturday in November in every year (City of London (Various Powers) Act, 1959, s. 5).

The office of alderman has existed from the thirteenth century. There are twenty-six aldermen, one of them being the Lord Mayor, each of whom represents one of the wards. The office is for life, except in case of insolvency, conviction of crime or other good cause. Each of them is elected by the constituents of his ward, except the alderman of the Ward of Bridge Without, or Southwark, who is always the senior alderman, there being no electors, and consequently no election in that ward. Each candidate for aldermanship must be a freeman of the city.

The Court of Aldermen consists of all the aldermen, presided over by the Lord Mayor or his *locum tenens*, thirteen being a quorum.

The Court of Common Council or the Court of the Lord Mayor, Aldermen and Commoners of the City of London in Common Council assembled dates from, at any rate, 1275. It consists of, besides the Lord Mayor and the aldermen, two hundred and six common councillors, the latter being elected annually by the ward-motes of the twenty-five wards which have constituencies. The administration of the City is in the hands of the Court of Aldermen and the Court of Common Council. There is also a third municipal body, the Meeting or Assembly of the Mayor, Aldermen and Liverymen of the several Companies of the City of London in Common Hall assembled, generally called the Court of Common Hall. This court consists of the Lord Mayor, or, in his absence, one of the sheriffs, four aldermen at the least, the sheriffs and all the freemen of the City who are livery-men of the City companies: it nominates two aldermen for the office of Lord Mayor, and elects the sheriffs and certain other City officers, but takes no further part in the administration of the City.

See CENTRAL CRIMINAL COURT; CHAMBERLAIN OF THE CITY, ETC.; COMPANIES, CITY; CUSTOM OF LONDON; FOREIGN ATTACHMENT; GREATER LONDON COUNCIL; GUILDHALL SITTINGS; MAYOR'S, ETC., COURT; RATIONABILI PARTE BONORUM, DE.

London commissioners to administer oaths in Chancery. Under the statute 1853, 16 & 17 Vict. c. 78, s. 2, the Lord Chancellor was empowered to appoint solicitors whose offices were within ten miles of Lincoln's Inn Hall—the habitation of the old Court of Chancery—to administer oaths, etc., in Chancery. This enactment was repealed by the Commissioners for Oaths Act, 1889. See COMMISSIONERS FOR OATHS.

London Court of Bankruptcy. This court was established by the Bankruptcy Act, 1869. It had jurisdiction throughout the City of London and the metropolitan county court districts. The Judicature Act, 1873, s. 16, transferred its jurisdiction to the Supreme Court. See BANKRUPTCY COURTS.

London Gazette. See GAZETTE.

London, Port of. The port of London includes all the water lying between

Teddington, in Middlesex, and an imaginary straight line drawn from the pilot mark at the entrance of Havengore Creek, in the county of Essex, to the land's end at Warden Point, in the Isle of Sheppey, in the county of Kent, but does not include any part of the river Medway, which is within the jurisdiction of the Medway Conservators, or any part of the river Swale, or any part of the river Lea, which is within the jurisdiction of the Lea Conservancy Board, or any part of the Grand Junction Canal (Port of London Act, 1908, ss. 490–495). The Port of London Act, 1908, put the port under the authority of a port authority thereby created, and transferred to the port authority the undertakings of the London and India Docks Company, the Surrey Commercial Dock Company and the Millwall Dock Company. The port is now administered under the Port of London Act, 1968. See also the Port of London Authority Revision Order, 1967 (No. 1197), made under the Harbours Act, 1964.

London Sessions. The sittings of the Central Criminal Court (*q.v.*) are sometimes called the London Sessions. See HICKS HALL.

London Sittings, the Guildhall Sittings (*q.v.*).

London Transport Board. See BRITISH TRANSPORT COMMISSION.

Long-distance blockade. The distance from the coast of a blockading force is irrelevant as long as the blockade (*q.v.*) is effective. See PAPER BLOCKADE.

Long Parliament. The Long Parliament met on November 30, 1640. It impeached the Earl of Strafford, thirteen bishops and six of the judges. It passed the Triennial Act, 1642, abolished ship-money, the Star Chamber and the High Commission Courts, and declared impressment illegal. It issued the appeal to the country known as the Grand Remonstrance. It was dissolved in 1658.

Long Quinto. There are two Year Books 5 Edw. 4. The longer of the two is known as the Long Report or Long Quinto. It is sometimes cited as " L.5."

Long terms. See ENLARGEMENT.

Long vacation. See VACATION.

Longa possessio parit jus possidendi et tollit actionem vero domino (Co.Litt. 110b). (Prolonged possession produces the right of possession, and takes away the right of action from the true owner.)

Longum tempus et longus usus, qui excedit memoriam hominum, sufficit, pro jure (Co.Litt. 115). (Long time and long use, which exceeds the memory of man, suffices in law.) See MEMORY.

Lopwood, a right in the inhabitants of a parish within a manor to lop for fuel at certain periods of the year the branches of trees growing upon the waste lands of the manor. The right can only be created by Crown grant or Act of Parliament. See PRESCRIPTION; PROFIT A PRENDRE.

Loquela, an imparlance; a declaration. See IMPARLANCE.

Loquela sine die, a respite to an indefinite time; an indefinite adjournment (*q.v.*).

Lord [Sax. *hlaford, laford,* lord; *hlaf,* a loaf of bread; *ford,* to give, because such great men kept extraordinary houses, and fed all the poor; for which reason they were called givers of bread], monarch, governor, master.

In the law of real property, a lord is a person of whom land is held by another as his tenant. The relation between the lord and the tenant is called tenure (*q.v.*), and the right or interest which the lord has in the services of his tenant is called a lordship or seignory (*q.v.*).

Under the feudal system, the grantor of land, who retained the dominion or ultimate property, was called the lord, and the grantee, who had only the use and possession, was called the vassal or feudatory.

If before the statute *Quia Emptores,* 1289, A conveyed land to B to hold of himself (A), and B conveyed it to C to hold of himself (B), A would be called lord paramount, B mesne lord and C tenant paravail (see MESNE). The statute *Quia Emptores,* 1289, having abolished subinfeudation, no person can now create a lordship (see SUBINFEUDATION). The only lords of any importance at the present day are lords of manors (see MANOR). But the Crown is sovereign lord, or lord paramount, of all the land in England, and in that character sometimes becomes entitled to land by escheat (*q.v.*).

High court judges are addressed as " My Lord " in court, and out of court are addressed by barristers as " Judge " and by others as " Sir."

See DUKE; EARL; HOUSE OF LORDS; LORD IN GROSS; MARQUIS; VERY LORD.

Lord Advocate. See ADVOCATE, LORD.

Lord Chamberlain. See CHAMBERLAIN, LORD.

Lord Chancellor. See CHANCELLOR, LORD.

Lord Chief Baron. See BARON.

Lord Chief Justice. See JUSTICE.

Lord Great Chamberlain. See CHAMBERLAIN, LORD GREAT.

Lord High Admiral. See ADMIRAL.

Lord High Commissioner, the representative of the sovereign at the General Assembly of the Church of Scotland.

Lord High Steward. When a person was impeached, or when a peer was indicted for treason or felony, one of the lords was appointed Lord High Steward, and acted as speaker *pro tempore* (see CERTIORARI; IMPEACHMENT). If a peer was indicted for treason or felony while the House of Lords was not sitting, the indictment was removed into the Court of the Lord High Steward, which was instituted by commission from the Crown, summoning all the peers of Parliament; in it the Lord High Steward was sole judge on points of law, and the peers summmoned were triers and judges of fact only. This court, which has not sat since 1688, was quite distinct from the Court of the Lord Steward of the Queen's Household (*q.v.*). The privilege of peers to be tried by the House of Lords for treason or felony was abolished by the Criminal Justice Act, 1948, s. 30.

The commission recited the indictment and gave power to receive and try it *secundum legem et consuetudinem Angliae*. When the indictment was regularly removed by certiorari, the Lord High Steward addressed a precept to a serjeant-at-arms, to summon the lords to attend and try the indicted peer. All the peers who had a right to sit and vote were summoned 21 days before the trial, and every lord appearing and taking the oath might vote upon the trial. The decision was by a majority, but a majority could not convict, unless it consisted of twelve or more.

The office of Lord High Steward was not at first hereditary, but at an early period it became so in the family of the Earls of Leicester. When Simon de Montfort, who held that title, was killed in 1265, it, and his other honours, were forfeited to the Crown. After various regrants, it finally merged in the Crown in 1407; and since then there has been no Lord High Steward, except when an appointment has been made *pro hac vice*, that is to say, for a special occasion. The appointment was made, upon an address from the House of Lords requesting that a High Steward be appointed, by commission under the Great Seal. When the peers assembled for a trial the commission was read by the Clerk of the Crown in Chancery, and the High Steward was then presented with his staff of office by the heralds. At the conclusion of the proceedings, the High Steward broke his staff and declared the commission dissolved, whereupon his office determined.

Lord High Treasurer. See LORD TREASURER; TREASURY.

Lord in gross, he who is lord, not by reason of any manor, but as the king in respect of his crown, etc. Very lord (*q.v.*) is he who is immediate lord to his tenant; and very tenant he who holds immediately of that lord. So that, where there is lord paramount, lord mesne, and tenant, the lord paramount is not very lord to the tenant.

Lord Justice-Clerk, the second judicial officer in Scotland.

Lord Justice-General, the highest judicial officer in Scotland, head of the High Court of Justiciary. The office is united with that of the Lord President of the Court of Session.

Lord Keeper, or Keeper of the Great Seal, was originally another name for the Lord Chancellor. (See CHANCELLOR, LORD.) After Henry II's reign the offices were sometimes divided; now, there cannot be a Lord Chancellor and Lord Keeper at the same time, for by the statute 1562, 5 Eliz. 1, c. 18, they are declared to be the same office. Down to 1760 the Great Seal was sometimes held by a Lord Keeper instead of by a Lord Chancellor, but since that date there has been no Lord Keeper.

Lord-lieutenant. The office of "lieutenants of counties" was created about the reign of Henry VIII or Edward VI for the purpose of having a representative of the Crown in each county, to keep it in military order. For this purpose they had the power of raising militia.

The Crown appoints a lord-lieutenant for each county in England and Wales and for Greater London (Local Government Act, 1972, s. 218 (1)). Formerly the Letters Patent relative to these appointments used the words "Her Majesty's Lieutenant of and in the county of —" but these dignitaries were normally referred to as lord-lieutenants. The Act of 1972 adopts the customary title. The lord-lieutenant formerly appointed twenty deputy-lieutenants (Militia Act, 1882, s. 30 (2); Deputy Lieutenants Act, 1918, s. 1; Administration of Justice Act, 1964, s. 18 (3)). These appointments are now made by the Crown (Act of 1972, s. 218 (1)). During the absence or disability of the lord-lieutenant the Crown may authorise any three deputy-lieutenants to act for him. The lord-lieutenant may appoint any deputy-lieutenant to act for him during absence or disability and he is known as a vice lord-lieutenant (Act of 1882, ss. 31, 32; Act of 1972, s. 218 (2) (3)).

A recruit for the Territorial Army or Royal Auxiliary Air Force may be attested by a lord-lieutenant or deputy-lieutenant (Auxiliary Forces Act, 1953, s. 12 (3)).

In the City of London the Lord Mayor, although not entitled lord-lieutenant, is *ex officio* head of the city lieutenancy, and recommends to the Crown the names of persons to fill vacancies therein. The provisions of the Local Government Act, 1972, relating to the appointment of a lord-lieutenant of Greater London do not apply to the City of London (s. 218 (8)).

Lords-lieutenant are appointed for life or *quamdiu se bene gesserint.*

Lord-Lieutenant was the title of the governor or viceroy of Ireland.

See CUSTOS ROTULORUM; LIEUTENANCY, COMMISSION OF.

Lord Lyon King of Arms, the principal Officer of Arms in Scotland. His duties are both ministerial and judicial, and include control of all arms, badges, and signs armorial, the execution of royal proclamations, the appointment and control of messengers-at-arms, the granting of certificates in connection with changes of name, etc. Under him are three heralds, and three pursuivants.

Lord Mayor's Court in London. An inferior court, formly held before the lord mayor and aldermen. Its practice and procedure were amended by the Mayor's Court of London Procedure Act, 1857. In this court the recorder presided, or, in his absence, the common serjeant, or the assistant judge appointed under the Borough Courts of Record Act, 1872, The Mayor's and City of London Court Act, 1920, amalgamated the City of London Court (the jurisdiction of which was that of a county court) with the Mayor's Court. See MAYOR'S AND CITY OF LONDON COURT.

Lord Ordinary, a judge of the Court of Session (*q.v.*).

Lord paramount. See PARAMOUNT.

Lord President of the Council, the president of the Privy Council. The office is held by such person, being a member of one House of Parliament or the other, as the king or queen in council, from time to time, orally declares to be the Lord President of the Council. His salary is from £7,500 to £9,500 unless he is in the Cabinet when it is £13,000 a year (Ministerial and other Salaries Act, 1975, s. 1, Sch. 1). In point of precedence he ranks next after the Prime Minister.

Lord Privy Seal. Before the Reformation this office was usually held by a churchman. Since then it has usually been held by a lay peer. Until recent times the Privy Seal had to be affixed to documents, especially letters patent, which were to pass the Great Seal (*q.v.*). But the Patents, Designs and Trade Marks Act, 1883, made the use of the seal of the Patent Office sufficient for the purposes of that Act. The Crown Office Act, 1877, authorised the use of a wafer Privy Seal instead of the actual Privy Seal: the Great Seal Act, 1884, s. 3, altogether abolished the use of the Privy Seal. The Lord Privy Seal has, as such, no official duties whatever to discharge unless he is a peer, in which case he is *ex officio* a member of the House of Lords Offices Committee, a body which looks after the domestic arrangements of that House. His salary is between £7,500 and £9,500 a year unless he is in the Cabinet when it is £13,000 a year (Ministerial and other Salaries Act, 1975, s. 1, Sch. 1). The office had been without salary down to 1900, when Lord Salisbury assumed it (with a salary of £2,000) on his becoming Prime Minister (*q.v.*), which was not then a recognised office, and which carried no salary. The office is generally conferred upon some politician whom it is desired to include in the Cabinet without his holding an office involving official functions. See CLERKS OF THE PRIVY SEAL.

Lord Steward of the Queen's Household. This is an office quite distinct from that of the Lord High Steward (*q.v.*). He is mentioned in the statute 1532, 24 Hen. 8, c. 13; his title was changed to that of Great Master of the Household in 1540, but the title of Lord Steward of the Queen's Household was revived by the statute 1554, 1 Mar. c. 4, and has ever since been in use. He originally presided over the now-abolished Court of the Lord Steward of the Queen's Household (*q.v.*), and was, in theory, one of the two judges of the Palace Court (*q.v.*); he still appoints the Coroner of the Queen's Household (see CORONER); but his main function from the beginning was, and still is, to supervise the servants and the arrangements of the royal household, as regards all matters not entrusted to the Master of the Household (*q.v.*), or the Lord Chamberlain (*q.v.*), or not relating to the Chapels Royal. The office is not hereditary: it was formerly always held by a peer, who was always a member of the political party which was in office for the time being, but in 1924 it was decided that the office should not be political, and should be in the gift of the monarch personally.

Lord Treasurer. The full title of this officer was the Lord High Treasurer and Treasurer of the Exchequer. As Lord High Treasurer, he was appointed by receiving a white staff from the king; as Treasurer of the Exchequer, he was appointed by letters patent. The office, which dates from the earliest Norman period, was never hereditary. It was in early times always held by some one

person; in 1612 it was put in commission; from then until 1714 it was sometimes held personally and was sometimes in commission; and since 1714 has always been in commission. The Commissioners constitute the Treasury Board, which never meets now, but which used to meet, in gradually diminishing numbers, until the middle of the last century. It now consists of the First Lord of the Treasury, that is, the Prime Minister, who exercises as regards finance only a general supervision; the Chancellor of the Exchequer, who is for all practical purposes the Lord Treasurer and five junior Lords. The Board is assisted by a Chief Secretary, a Parliamentary Secretary who is the Chief Whip, a Financial Secretary and a Minister of State, all of whom are Members of Parliament. See TREASURY.

Lord Warden. See CINQUE PORTS.

Lords' Act, the Debtors Imprisonment Act, 1758, so called from having originated in the House of Lords.

Lord's Day Act, the Sunday Observance Act, 1677. See SUNDAY.

Lords, House of. See HOUSE OF LORDS.

Lords Justices. As regards Ireland, the Lords Justices were commissioners for executing the office of Lord Lieutenant who were sworn in during a vacancy in that office and during any absence from Ireland of the Lord Lieutenant. They could not be Roman Catholics (Roman Catholic Relief Act, 1829, s. 12).

As regards England, from 1253 Lords Justices were from time to time appointed; these were frequently individual barons or individual members of the royal family, the Earl of Pembroke, for instance, being appointed in 1285 and John, Duke of Bedford, being appointed in 1421. After 1688 commissioners were appointed from time to time under the Great Seal to exercise, during the absence of the sovereign from the realm, such of the royal functions as were delegated to them. They were always chosen from amongst such peers, spiritual or temporal, as were members of the Privy Council. See REGENCY.

Lords Justices of Appeal, the ordinary judges of the Court of Appeal. Prior to the Judicature Act, 1873–75, there were two Lords Justices of Appeal in Chancery, to whom an appeal lay from a vice-chancellor by the Court of Chancery Act, 1851. See SUPREME COURT OF JUDICATURE.

Lords Marchers, those noblemen who lived on the marches of Wales or Scotland, who had their laws and power of life and death, like petty kings. They were abolished by the statute 1535, 27 Hen. 8, c. 26. See MARCHES.

Lords of Appeal in Ordinary, persons appointed by the Crown for the purpose of aiding the House of Lords in the hearing and determination of appeals; they must have held high judicial office for two years, or have been practising barristers or advocates for at least fifteen years; they are barons for life, and are entitled to sit and vote in the House of Lords (Appellate Jurisdiction Acts, 1876 to 1947). High judicial office means the office of Lord Chancellor, paid judge of the Judicial Committee, or judge of the superior courts of Great Britain or Northern Ireland. They are *ex-officio* members of the Court of Appeal, but need not sit therein unless at the request of the Lord Chancellor they consent so to do (Judicature Act, 1925, s. 6 (2)). The maximum number of Lords of Appeal in Ordinary is eleven. The number may be increased by Order in Council (Administration of Justice Act, 1968).

Lords of Erection. On the Reformation in Scotland, the king, as proprietor of benefices formerly held by abbots and priors, gave them out in temporal lordships to favourites, who were termed Lords of Erection.

Lords of Parliament, those who have seats in the House of Lords.

Lords of Regality, persons to whom rights of civil and criminal jurisdiction in Scotland were given by the Crown.

Lords of Session, the judges of the Court of Session in Scotland, otherwise known as Senators of the College of Justice.

Lords spiritual, the archbishops and bishops who have seats in the House of Lords.

Lords temporal, lay peers who have seats in the House of Lords. See HOUSE OF LORDS.

Loriners [Lat. *lorum*, a rein], one of the London livery companies; the guild of bridle, bit and spur makers.

Lorry area. Parking areas for heavy goods vehicles off highways may be provided by highway authorities under the Highways Act, 1971, s. 30. Such areas are called " lorry areas."

Loss. In the law of marine insurance, the losses which arise from the various perils insured against may be either total or partial; they are total when the subject-matter of the insurance is wholly destroyed or injured to such an extent as to justify the owner in abandoning it to the insurer, and partial when the thing insured is only partially damaged or where, in the case of an insurance on goods, the owner of them is called upon to contribute to a general average. Total losses may again be divided into actual and constructive total losses. Actual total losses arise where the ship or cargo is totally destroyed or annihilated, or where they are placed by any of the perils insured against in such a position that it is wholly out of the power of the assured to procure their arrival. Thus, where by means of a peril insured against, a ship founders or is actually destroyed, or even where she is so much injured that she becomes a wreck, the loss is total and actual, although the form of the ship may still remain (*Cambridge* v. *Anderton* (1823) 2 B. & C. 691); and in these cases the assured may recover for a total loss without abandonment. Losses are constructively total when the subject-matter of the insurance, although still in existence, is either actually lost to the owners or beneficially lost to them, and notice of abandonment has been given to the underwriters. Thus, where the ship, although existing as a ship, is captured (*Mullet* v. *Sheddon* (1810) 13 East 304) or laid under an embargo, and has not been recaptured or restored before action brought, so that she is lost to the owners, or where she is so damaged by a peril insured against as to be unnavigable, and is so situated that either she cannot be repaired without incurring an expense greater than her value when repaired, the assured may abandon and treat the loss as total. See ABANDON-

MENT OF SHIP; INSURANCE; POLICY OF INSURANCE.

Loss leaders, goods sold at a price far below the manufacturers' recommended price in order to attract custom to the place of sale. In an action for allegedly unlawful withholding of supplies contrary to s. 2 (1) of the Resale Prices Act, 1964 (see RESALE), an interlocutory injunction will not be granted against the defendant suppliers if they make out a prima facie case that they had reasonable cause to believe their goods to have been used as loss leaders (*J.J.B. (Sports)* v. *Milbro Sports* [1975] I.C.R. 73).

Loss of consortium. See CONSORTIUM.

Loss of earnings. See DAMAGES.

Loss of Employment. See DAMAGES.

Loss of expectation of life. See EXPECTATION OF LIFE.

Loss of law. A man " lost his law " and became incompetent to testify if he was defeated in trial by battle, or reduced to villeinage (9 H.H.E.L. 191).

Loss of profits. See DAMAGES.

Loss of publicity. Damages for wrongful dismissal may include damages for loss of publicity (*Marbé* v. *Edwardes* [1928] 1 K.B. 269; *Clayton* v. *Oliver* [1930] A.C. 209).

Loss of services. See PER QUOD SERVITUM AMISIT.

Lost bill of exchange, cheque, or promissory note. The Bills of Exchange Act, 1882, s. 69, replacing the statute 1698, 9 & 10 Wm. 3, c. 17, s. 3, enacts that if a bill of exchange, or cheque, or note, is lost before it is overdue, the person who was the holder of it may apply to the drawer to give him another bill, or cheque, or note of the same tenor, giving security to the drawer, if required, to indemnify him if the bill, or cheque, or note alleged to have been lost is found again. By s. 70 of the same Act, in any action or proceeding on a bill, or cheque, or note, the court may order that the loss of the instrument shall not be set up, provided an indemnity is given to the satisfaction of the court against the claims of any other person upon the instrument.

Lost document. The ordinary rule is that a document is proved by the production of the original, but on proof that a document has been destroyed, or cannot be found after a proper search made, it may be proved by secondary evidence of a copy or oral evidence of its contents.

Lost grant. Before the Prescription Act, 1832, a claim to an easement could in theory only be supported either where it had been enjoyed from time immemorial, or where the claimant could prove that it had been created by a deed of grant. But after the Limitation Act, 1623, had limited the time for bringing actions for possession of land to twenty years, the courts adopted the same period as sufficient to give rise to an easement, on the presumption that it had been created by a deed of grant which had been lost, and juries were directed so to find in cases in which no one had the faintest belief that any grant had ever existed, and where the presumption was known to be a mere fiction (*Angus* v. *Dalton* (1878) 3 Q.B.D. at p. 105). This presumption of a lost grant lost some of its importance after the passing of the Prescription Act, 1832, but it remains one of the methods by which an easement may be acquired. Twenty years' uninterrupted enjoyment of an easement raises a presumption of a lost grant rebuttable only by evidence that the making of such a grant was impossible (*Tehidy Minerals* v. *Norman* [1971] 2 Q.B. 528). See Gale, *Easements.*

Lost or not lost, words inserted in a maritime policy of insurance to prevent the operation of the rule that if a ship is lost at the time of insurance, the policy is void, although the assured did not know of the loss. The words operate to make the underwriter liable, even where the subject-matter of insurance had not vested in the assured at the time of the occurrence of the loss (Marine Insurance Act, 1906, s. 6 (1)), but not where, at the time that the assurance was effected, the assured knew of the loss and the insurer did not; for instance, if a merchant, having bought goods at sea, were to insure them " lost or not lost," the policy would entitle him to recover from the underwriter in respect of a loss sustained during the voyage, but before the purchase and without the knowledge of the merchant when he insured. See INSURANCE; LOSS; POLICY OF INSURANCE.

Where the subject-matter of the insurance has arrived in safety before the insurance was effected, the " lost or not lost " clause makes the premium non-returnable unless the insurer, when effecting the policy, knew of such safe arrival (Marine Insurance Act, 1906, s. 84 (3) (*b*)).

Lost property. See the London Hackney Carriage Act, 1853, s. 11 (amended by the London Passenger Transport Act, 1933, s. 106, Sch. 16; Customs and Excise Act, 1952, ss. 44, 318, Sch. 10 Pt. II; Criminal Justice Act, 1967, Sch. 3 Pt. I; the Civil Aviation Act, 1949, s. 56 (extended by the Airports Authority Act, 1965, s. 16); the Road Traffic Act, 1960, s. 160 (1) (i).

Lot, a contribution or duty; a dole (*q.v.*). See SCOT AND LOT.

Lot and cope [A.S. *hlot*, tribute; *ceap*, market, sale], duties payable to the Crown in respect of lead mines in the High Peak, Derbyshire. Lot was every thirteenth dish of lead; cope was a payment of sixpence a load (Pettus, *Fodinae Regales*).

Lot meads, common meadows divided yearly and distributed by lot among the owners, the share of each being called a dole. The owner of a dole may have a freehold in the soil, or he may only have *vestura terrae*.

A lot mead or lot meadow is an open field divided into lots or doles. See DOLE; OPEN FIELDS.

These lot meads seem to have originated in certain manors where a piece of meadow land was periodically allotted to the freehold tenants of the arable land in the manor (1 *Conveyancer* (N.S.) 53).

See INHERITANCE; SEVERALTY.

Loth, the thirteenth dish of lead in the mines of Derbyshire, which belonged to the Crown. See LOT AND COPE.

Lotherwite or **Leyerwit,** a privilege to make amends for lying with a bond-woman without licence. See LAIRWITE.

Lots, parcels of land under one ownership put up separately at one sale. By the Law of Property Act, 1925, s. 45 (5), it is an implied condition of the sale that a purchaser of two or more lots held wholly or partly under the same title shall not have a right to more than one abstract of the common title, except at his own expense. As a rule the purchaser of the largest lot in value is entitled to the documents of title on completion where all the lots have been sold.

As to the position of a bidder purchasing a wrong lot by mistake, see *Van Praagh* v. *Everidge* [1903] 1 Ch. 434.

Lottery, a game of chance; a distribution of prizes by lot or chance (*Taylor* v. *Smetten* (1883) 11 Q.B.D. 207). Lotteries were first made unlawful by the statute 1698, 10 Wm. 3, c. 23.

The Lotteries and Amusements Act, 1976 (repealing ss. 41–50 of the Betting, Gaming and Lotteries Act, 1963, as amended) declares that, subject to the provisions of the Act, all lotteries which do not constitute gaming are unlawful (s. 1) and promotion of a lottery is an offence (s. 2). Exempt are small lotteries incidental to certain entertainments (s. 3), private lotteries (s. 4), lotteries of art unions (s. 25 (6)), lotteries promoted by registered societies or by local authorities (ss. 5–13). As to pool competitions see POOL COMPETITIONS. Prize competitions conducted in or through newspapers or in connection with any trade or business or the sale of any article to the public are exempt when success depends to a substantial degree upon the exercise of skill (s. 14). Amusements with prizes may also be exempt (ss. 15–17). For powers of Secretary of State see ss. 18, 24; for search warrants, s. 19; for penalties and forfeitures, ss. 20, 21.

A physical lot is not essential to a lottery (*Barclay* v. *Pearson* [1893] 2 Ch. 154).

Loud-speakers. See NOISE.

Loughborough's (Lord) Act, the Accumulations Act, 1800. See ACCUMULATION.

Lourcurdus, a ram, or bell-wether.

Love day, the day on which any dispute was amicably settled between neighbours; or a day on which one neighbour helped another without hire.

Lovite, a formally affectionate term for a subject of the king when addressed or referred to in certain formal documents.

Low Sunday, the Sunday next after Easter.

Lowbote, a recompense for the death of a man killed in a tumult.

Low-water mark, that part of the seashore to which the waters recede when the tide is lowest.

Lubbock's Act, the Bank Holiday Act, 1871. See BANK HOLIDAYS.

Lucid interval, an interval of sanity separating two attacks of insanity. Perfect sanity is not required to constitute a lucid interval: it is sufficient that the person knows what he is doing, and that his act is not affected by a delusion (*q.v.*), and that he has capacity sufficient for the doing of the particular act. An act done during a lucid interval is as valid, and involves the same liabilities and responsibilities, as the act of a sane man. See COURT OF PROTECTION; HOMO POTEST, ETC.; MENTAL HEALTH.

Lucrative succession. Before an heir incurred liability through *praeceptio hereditatis* (*q.v.*), it had to be shown that he had received the grant by a lucrative succession, *i.e.*, that it was pure gain to him and that he had given no consideration (Civil Law).

Lucri causa [Lat.], for the purpose of gain.

Lucrum, a small slip or parcel of land.

Lucrum cessans, loss of prospective profits.

Luggage. See PASSENGERS' LUGGAGE.

Luminare, a lamp or candle set burning on the altar of any church or chapel, for the maintenance whereof land and rent-charges were frequently given to parish churches, etc. (Ken.Glos.).

Luminising, an industrial process in respect of which health and safety regulations are made under the Factories Act, 1961, s. 76.

Lump, The. Self-employed sub-contractors in the building industry usually supplying labour only who were excused deduction of tax at source. Abuse of this system is countered by the Finance Act, 1971, ss. 28–31, and the Finance (No. 2) Act, 1975, ss. 68–71. See also S.I. 1975 No. 1960; 1976 No. 1126; *Ferguson* v. *John Dawson and Partners* [1976] 1 Lloyd's Rep. 143.

Lunacy; Lunatic. These terms are no longer used in law. See MENTAL HEALTH.

Luncheon vouchers. See MEAL VOUCHERS.

Lundress [Fr. *Londres*, London], a sterling silver penny, which was only coined in London (Lowndes, *Essay on Coins* 17).

Lupanatrix, a bawd or strumpet (3 Co. Inst. 206).

Lupinum caput gerere, to be outlawed, and have one's head exposed like a wolf's, with a reward to him who should take it. See CAPUT LUPINUM.

Lupulicetum, a hop garden (1 Co.Inst. 4).

Lurgulary, casting any corrupt or poisonous thing into the water.

Lushburgers or **Luxemburgers,** base coin made abroad and passed off in this country as English money in the reign of Edward III. The Treason Act, 1351, made it treason to bring such coin into the realm (3 Co.Inst. 1).

Luxury. See SUMPTUARY LAWS.

Lych gate, the gate into a churchyard, with a roof or awning hung on posts over it to cover the body brought for burial, when it rests underneath.

Lyef-yeld, or **Lef-silver,** a small fine paid by a customary tenant to his lord, for leave to plough or sow.

Lying by. A person who, by his conduct, may fairly be supposed to acquiesce in a transaction, may be prevented from having it set aside by reason that he has been " lying by " (*Nana* v. *Nana* [1958] A.C. 95). See LACHES.

Lying in franchise, waifs, wrecks, estrays, and the like, which may be seized without suit or action.

Lying in grant, or **in livery.** See GRANT.

Lynches, or **Linces,** the banks between the terraces formed where a common field is on a hillside by ploughing, so as to turn the sod downhill; also the terraces themselves.

Lynch-law, the procedure whereby an offender is tried and executed by a self-appointed body of citizens acting generally in defiance of the law, alleging as an excuse either the slowness of the regular legal procedure, or the neglect of the duly constituted authorities to put it in force, or that no duly constituted authorities exist. Lynch-law was often practised in the United States of America.

Lyndhurst's (Lord) Act, the Marriage Act, 1835, which provided that marriages between persons within the prohibited degrees, which had previously been only voidable, should be void; also the Nonconformist Chapels Act, 1844, and the Execution Act, 1844.

Lyndwood's Provinciale. See CANON LAW.

Lyon King-of-Arms. See LORD LYON KING-OF-ARMS.

Lyon's Inn. See INNS OF CHANCERY.

Lytton's (Lord) Act, the Dramatic Copyright Act, 1833.

M

M, the brand or stigma of a person convicted of manslaughter and admitted to the benefit of clergy (*q.v.*). It was burned on the brawn of the left thumb.

M.B.E. See BRITISH EMPIRE, ETC.

M.R., Master of the Rolls (*q.v.*).

M.V.O. See ROYAL VICTORIAN, ETC.

Mace, an ornamental staff borne as a symbol of authority, upon occasions of State, before certain persons, such as the Lord Chancellor, the Speaker of the House of Commons, the Lord Mayor, the Chancellors of Universities, etc. The Speaker's mace is on the table of the House while the Speaker is in the chair; when his place is occupied by the Chairman of Committees while the House is in committee, the mace lies under the table.

In the City of London the Serjeant-at-Mace executed the process of the Mayor's Court.

Mace-greff [*machecarius*], one who buys stolen goods, particularly food, knowing them to have been stolen (Brit. c. xxix).

Mace-proof, secure against arrest.

Machecollare, or **Machecoulare,** to machicolate a castle, *i.e.,* to make an aperture over a gate or other passage through which scalding liquid or ponderous or offensive things may be cast upon the assailants (Co.Litt. 5a).

Machinery. The Factories Act, 1961, contains provisions as to the fencing and cleaning of machinery. See FACTORIES.

McNaghten's (or **M'Naghten's** or **Macnaughton's**) **Case, Rules in.** In *R.* v. *McNaghten* or *M'Naghten* or *Macnaughton* (1843) 4 St.Tr.(N.S.) 847, a discussion took place in the House of Lords upon the direction to the jury by Tindal C.J. in the trial of McNaghten, and as a result a series of questions was put to the judges. The answers of the majority constitute the " McNaghten Rules," and have been accepted as laying down the law as to insanity with reference to criminal responsibility. The rules have been the subject of much discussion and criticism by political, medical, and legal writers. The main rule laid down is that in order to establish a defence on the ground of insanity, it must be proved that, at the time of committing the act, the person accused was labouring under such a defect of reason, from disease of the mind, as not to know the nature and quality of the act he was doing, or, if he did know it, that he did not know that he was doing what was wrong. The onus of proving insanity lies on the defence. Irresistible or uncontrollable impulse is not a symptom from which insanity may be inferred (*Att.-Gen. for South Australia* v. *Brown* [1960] A.C. 432).

As to the relation of insanity to diminished responsibility see DIMINISHED RESPONSIBILITY; SPECIAL VERDICT.

Mactator, a murderer.

Mad Parliament. See PARLIAMENTUM INSANUM.

Madness. See DIMINISHED RESPONSIBILITY; INSANITY; McNAGHTEN'S CASE; MENTAL HEALTH; SPECIAL VERDICT.

Maec-burgh, kindred, family.

Maegth. In Anglo-Saxon times a man's kindred were known as the *maegth.* See MAG-BOT.

Maere [Sax. *mer*], famous, great, noted; as *Aelmere,* all famous (Gibs. Camd.).

Mag-bot; Maeg-bote, compensation for homicide paid to the kindred of the deceased (Leg. Canuti, c. 2).

Magic, witchcraft, sorcery. See WITCHCRAFT.

Magis de bono quam de malo lex intendit (Co.Litt. 78b). (The law favours a good rather than a bad construction.) Where the words used in an agreement are susceptible of two meanings, the one agreeable to, the other against, the law, the former is adopted. Thus a bond conditioned " to assign all offices " will be construed to apply to such offices only as are assignable.

Magister, a master or ruler; a person who has attained to some eminent degree in science.

Magister ad facultates, an ecclesiastical officer who grants dispensations.

Magister navis, the master of a ship.

Magister rerum usus (Co.Litt. 229). (Use is the master of things.) See MINIME MUTANDA, ETC.

Magister societatis, the manager of a partnership.

Magistracy, the body of officers who administer the laws; the office of a magistrate.

Magistrate, a person charged with duties of government, and being either supreme, namely, the sovereign, or subordinate, namely, one of the officers who are appointed by or are subject to the sovereign; a judicial officer having a summary jurisdiction in matters of a criminal or quasi-criminal nature. Magistrates are of two kinds, honorary and stipendiary. The former class consists of justices of the peace; the latter class includes the magistrates appointed to act in certain populous places in lieu of the ordinary justices. These stipendiary magistrates have wider powers than ordinary justices. See METROPOLITAN STIPENDIARY MAGISTRATE; STIPENDIARY MAGISTRATES.

As to the jurisdiction of magistrates, see JUSTICES OF THE PEACE. As to their liability for acts committed by them, see CORAM NON JUDICE; JUDGE.

Magna assisa eligenda, De. The first species of extraordinary trial by jury is that of the grand assize, which was instituted by Henry II, by way of alternative offered to the choice of the tenant or defendant in a writ of right, instead of the custom of duelling. The writ issued to the sheriff to return four knights, who were to elect and choose twelve others to be joined with them, and these, all together, formed the grand assize or great jury, which was to try the matter of right (3 Bl.Comm. 351). It was abolished by the Real Property Limitation Act, 1833. See ASSISE, GRAND.

Magna Carta, the charter granted by King John in 1215. It was reissued in 1216, 1217, and 1225. It was afterwards re-enacted and confirmed by Parliament over thirty times down to the reign of Henry VI.

This Great Charter is based substantially upon the Saxon common law, which flourished in this kingdom until the Norman invasion consolidated the system of feudality. The barons assembled at St. Edmund's Bury, in Suffolk, in the latter part of the year 1214, and there swore to withdraw their allegiance from the Crown, and openly rebel, unless King John confirmed by a formal charter the ancient liberties of England; and they then engaged to demand this of the king in the early part of the ensuing year, arming themselves in the meantime, so as to compel the king, if necessary, to confirm those liberties which had been confirmed by the charters of his predecessors, and his own disregarded oath. As the first step the barons disclaimed all allegiance to him, were formally absolved from their oaths of fidelity, and chose for their general Robert Fitzwalter, with the title of Marshal of the Army of God and of the Holy Church. After the fortress of Bedford had surrendered to them, and they were in possession of the metropolis, by private agreement with the citizens, the king sent a message to them to desire that a place and time of meeting might be fixed for the purpose of his complying with their demands. The meadow called Runnymede, or Runemede (from the Saxon word *rune,* signifying council), situated on the southwest bank of the Thames, between Staines and Windsor, was selected for the interview. The conferences between the king and the armed barons opened on Monday, June 15, 1215, and closed on the following Friday. Articles of agreement were drawn up and sealed, and were reduced to the form of a charter, to which the Great Seal was affixed, and the instrument was given by the king's hand as a confirmation of his own act, but it was not signed by him. This event took place on a small island, still called Magna Carta Island, situated in the Thames, not far from Aukerwyke, in Buckinghamshire. Many originals of the Great Charter were made, for the purpose of depositing one in every diocese. Two of these are in the British Museum, and it is said there are two others in existence, one in the cathedral at Salisbury, and the other in that at Lincoln.

Magna Carta was not firmly established as the common law of the realm for nearly a century after the conferences at Runnymede, during which period the country was kept in a constant state of alarm and excitement by the struggles of the barons' war, but at length this constitutional barrier against legal encroachments was finally secured to the people by its solemn confirmation by Edward I. No fewer than thirty-two Acts of Parliament were obtained from 1267 to 1416, for the purpose of fixing the Great Charter as the guarantee of freedom of political opinion.

The Great Charter, as set forth in the statutes at large, is expressed to be made in 1225 and confirmed in 1297. The original Latin is printed in the statute book in one column, and an English translation of it in another.

The Great Charter is in fact a collection of statutes in thirty-seven chapters, which are for the most part declaratory of ancient customs. The 1st chapter is a confirmation of liberties in these words: "First, we have granted to God, and by this our present charter have confirmed for us and our heirs for ever, that the Church of England shall be free and shall have her whole rights and liberties inviolable. We have granted also and given to all the freemen of our realm, for us and our heirs for ever, these liberties, underwritten, to have and to hold to them and their heirs, of us and our heirs for ever."

The 2nd chapter relates to the relief of the Crown's tenants of full age: " If any of our earls or barons, or any other, which holdeth of us in chief by knight's service, die, and at the time of his death his heir be of full age, and oweth to us relief, he shall have his inheritance by the old relief; that is to say, the heir or heirs of an earl, for a whole earldom, by one hundred pounds; the heir or heirs of a baron, for a whole barony, by one hundred marks; the heir or heirs of a knight, for one whole knight's fee, one hundred shillings at the most, and he that hath less shall give less, according to the old custom of the fees."

The Great Charter only aimed at modifying the grievances of feudalism, which created the military tenure of knight's service. Cromwell abolished this military tenure by intermitting the Court of Wards in 1645, and this was confirmed by the statute 1660, 12 Car. 2, c. 24.

The statute did away with the effect of the next four chapters of the Great Charter. The 3rd chapter relates to the wardship of an infant heir of an earl, baron, or knight; the 4th chapter prohibits the guardian from wasting the lands of his ward, and from destroying his tenants; the 5th chapter compels such guardians to keep in repair such lands; and the 6th chapter provides that such heirs shall be married without disparagement.

The 7th chapter concerned widows and dower. See DOWER. It was repealed by the Administration of Estates Act, 1925, Sch. 2 Pt. I and the Statute Law (Repeals) Act, 1969.

The 8th chapter related to Crown debts. It was repealed by the Statute Law (Repeals) Act, 1969.

The 9th chapter enacts that: " The City of London shall have all the old liberties and customs which it hath been used to have. Moreover, we will and grant that all other cities, boroughs, towns, and the barons of the five ports, and all other ports, shall have all their liberties and free customs."

The 10th chapter prohibited excess distress for more service for a knight's fee than was due. It was repealed by the Statute Law Revision Act, 1948.

The 11th chapter enacted that " Common Pleas shall not follow our court, but shall be holden in some place certain." See COMMON PLEAS. It was repealed by the Civil Procedure Acts Repeal Act, 1879.

The 12th chapter related to assizes, and provided that: " Assizes of novel disseisin and of mortdauncestor shall not be taken but in the shires, and after this manner; if we be out of this realm, our chief justicers shall send our justices through every county once in the year, which, with the knights of the shires, shall take the said assizes in those counties; and those things that at the coming of our foresaid justicers, being sent to take those assizes in the counties, cannot be determined, shall be ended by them in some other place in their circuit; and those things which for difficulty of some articles cannot be determined by them, shall be referred to our justicers of the bench, and there shall be ended."

A novel disseisin was so called to distinguish it from an ancient disseisin, and it arose in this way: The judges in the olden time, when travelling was perilous and slow, went their circuits but once in seven years; all disseisins then or dispossessings of the lawful owners of land which took place before the last circuits were ancient, but all disseisins since were novel. Mortdauncestor was an action brought against a person who had taken possession of property after the death of an ancestor, and before his heir-at-law had entered into their occupancy.

This 12th chapter was repealed by the Civil Procedure Acts Repeal Act, 1879.

The 13th chapter related to assizes of darrein presentment, a method of trying the right to present a priest to an ecclesiastical benefice. It was repealed by the Statute Law Revision Act, 1863.

The 14th chapter was directed against excessive fines, and provided that: " A freeman shall not be amerced for a small fault, but after the manner of the fault, and for a great fault after the greatness thereof, saving to him his contenement; and a merchant likewise, saving to him his merchandise; and any other's villein than ours shall be likewise amerced, saving his wainage, if he fall into our mercy. And none of the said amerciaments shall be assessed but by the oath of honest and lawful men of the vicinage. Earls

and barons shall not be amerced but by their peers, and after the manner of their offence. No man of the church shall be amerced after the quantity of his spiritual benefice, but after his laytenement, and after the quantity of his offence."

A man's contenement is that which is absolutely necessary for his support and maintenance, as his tools and instruments of trade; and wainage is that which is necessary for the labourer and the farmer, for the cultivation of his land, as carts, and implements of husbandry.

This 14th chapter was repealed by the Criminal Law Act, 1967, Sch. 3 Pt. I.

The 15th and 16th chapters related to the making of bridges and defending of riverbanks. They were repealed by the Statute Law Repeals Act, 1969.

The 17th chapter enacted that: " No sheriff, constable, escheator, coroner, nor any other our bailiffs, shall hold pleas of our Crown." It was repealed by the Statute Law Revision Act, 1892.

The 18th chapter enacted that: " If any that holdeth of us lay-fee do die, and our sheriff or bailiff do show our letters-patents of our summons for debt, which the dead man did owe to us, it shall be lawful to our sheriff or bailiff to attach and inroll all the goods and chattels of the dead, being found in the said lay-fee, to the value of the same debt, by the sight of lawful men, so that nothing thereof shall be taken away, until we be clearly paid off the debt, and the residue shall remain to the executor to perform the testament of the dead, and if nothing be owing unto us, all the chattels shall go to the use of the dead, saving to his wife and children their reasonable parts." It was repealed by the Crown Proceedings Act, 1947, Sch. 2 and S.I. 1949 No. 1836.

The 19th, 20th, and 21st chapters related to purveyance for a castle, doing of castle ward, and taking of horses, carts, and woods for the service of the royal castles. They were repealed by the Statute Law Revision Act, 1863.

The 22nd chapter declared thus: " We will not hold the lands of them that be convict of felony but one year and one day, and then those lands shall be delivered to the lords of the fee."

The addition of the day to the year appears to have been intended to prevent any dispute about whether the year is to be calculated as inclusive or exclusive of its last day. By the Forfeiture Act, 1870, escheat and forfeiture for treason or felony were abolished. The 22nd chapter was repealed by the Statute Law Revision Act, 1948.

The 23rd chapter enacted that: "All wears from henceforth shall be utterly put down by Thames and Medway, and through all England, but only by the sea-coasts." It is obvious that wears in navigable rivers would be obstructive of free communication. See WEAR. It was repealed by the Statute Law (Repeals) Act, 1969.

The 24th chapter related to the writ *praecipe in capite*. It was repealed by the Statute Law Revision Act, 1863.

The 25th chapter directed that: "One measure of wine shall be through our realm, and one measure of ale, and one measure of corn, that is to say, the quarter of London; and one breadth of dyed cloth, russets, and haberjects, that is to say, two yards within the lists, and it shall be of weights as it is of measures." It was repealed by the Statute Law Revision Act, 1948.

The 26th, 27th, and 28th chapters, related to the writ of inquisition of life and member, and the old feudal tenures and wager of law. The 26th chapter was repealed by the Offences against the Person Act, 1828, s. 1. The 27th and 28th chapters were repealed by the Statute Law Revision Act, 1863.

The 29th chapter is as follows: "*Nullus liber homo capiatur vel imprisonetur aut disseisiatur de libero tenemento suo vel libertatibus vel liberis consuetudinibus suis, aut utlagetur aut exuletur aut aliquo modo destruatur, nec super eum ibimus nec super eum mittemus nisi per legale judicium parium suorum, vel per legem terrae. Nulli vendemus, nulli negabimus aut differemus rectum vel justiciam.* (No freeman shall be taken or imprisoned, or be disseised of his freehold, or liberties or free customs, or be outlawed or exiled, or any otherwise destroyed; nor will we pass upon him, nor

condemn him, but by lawful judgment of his peers, or by the law of the land. To no man will we sell, to no man deny, to no man delay, justice or right.)

The 30th chapter enacted that: "All merchants if they were not openly prohibited before shall have their safe and sure conduct to depart out of England, to come into England, to tarry in and go through England, as well by land as by water, to buy and sell, without any manner of evil tolts [*i.e.,* extortions], by the old and rightful customs, except in time of war. And if they be of a land making war against us, and be found in our realm at the beginning of the wars, they shall be attached without harm of body or goods, until it be known unto us, or our chief justice, how our merchants be intreated there in the land making war against us; and if our merchants be well intreated there, theirs shall be likewise with us." It was repealed by the Statute Law (Repeals) Act, 1969.

The 31st, 32nd, and 33rd chapters relate to the royal escheat, the lord's services, and the patronage of abbeys. They were repealed by the Statute Law Revision Acts, 1863 and 1887.

The 34th chapter provided that no man should be taken or imprisoned upon the appeal of a woman for the death of any other than her husband. It was repealed by the Statute Law Revision Act, 1863.

The 35th chapter related to county courts, sheriffs' turns, and leets. It was repealed by the Sheriffs Act, 1887.

The 36th chapter enacted that: "It shall not be lawful from henceforth to any to give his land to any religious house, and to take the same land again to hold of the same house. Nor shall it be lawful to any house of religion to take the lands of any, and to lease the same to him of whom it received them. If any from henceforth give his lands to any religious house, and thereupon be convict, the gift shall be utterly void, and the land shall acrue, to the lord of the fee." It was repealed by the Statute Law Revision Act, 1863. See CHARITABLE USES; MORTMAIN.

The concluding chapter sets forth that its establishment was bought from the Crown, like most of our great liberties, with a fifteenth of our movable property, in consideration of which the king grants "for us and our heirs, that neither we nor our heirs shall attempt to do anything whereby the liberties contained in this charter may be infringed or broken. And if anything should be done to the contrary, it shall be held of no force or effect."

See 2 Hallam, *Middle Ages* 326; McKechnie, *Magna Carta.*

Magna Charta et Charta de Foresta sont appellés les deux grandes chartres (2 Co.Inst. 570). (Magna Carta and the Charter of the Forest are called the two great charters.)

Magna precaria, a great or general reap day, or day of harvesting (Tomlin).

Magnum centum, the great hundred, a measure of number containing one hundred and twenty.

Magnum concilium. See GREAT COUNCIL.

Magnus Portus. In the Middle Ages this meant the town and harbour of Portsmouth.

Maiden, an instrument formerly used in Scotland for beheading criminals. It consisted of a broad piece of iron about a foot square, very sharp in the lower part, and loaded above with lead. At the time of execution it was pulled up to the top of a frame about eight feet high, with a groove on each side for it to slide in. The prisoner's neck being fastened to a bar underneath, and the sign being given, the maiden was let loose, and the head severed from the body. It was the prototype of the guillotine. See HALIFAX GIBBET LAW.

Maiden assize, circuit, sessions, formerly one at which no prisoner was sentenced to death, but later one at which there was no defendant for trial. See GLOVES.

Maiden rent, a fine of a noble (see GOLD COINS) anciently paid on marriage by every tenant of the manor of Builth in Radnorshire; formerly erroneously supposed to have been in commutation of the mythical *jus primae noctis* (*q.v.*).

Maignagium [Fr. *maignem*], a brasier's shop, or perhaps a house.

Maihematus, maimed or wounded.

Mail [Fr. *malle*, a trunk], a bag of letters carried by the post, or the vehicle which carries the letters; also armour.

As to theft from mails, see the Post Office Act, 1953, ss. 53, 55–59, 70, 72, 87 (1); Theft Act, 1968, s. 14, Sch. 2 Pt. I, Sch. 3 Pt. I.

Mailcert, a certificate by a representative of a belligerent or a neutral State exempting matters sent by post from contraband control. See NAVICERT.

Maile, a kind of ancient money, or silver halfpence; a small rent (Jacob).

Maiming, depriving of any necessary part. See MAYHEM.

Main road. See HIGHWAY; ROAD.

Mainad, a false oath, perjury.

Maine-port, a small tribute, commonly of loaves of bread, which in some places the parishioners paid to the rector in lieu of small tithes (Cowel).

Mainour, Manour, or **Meinour,** a thing taken away which was found in the hand (*in manu*) of the thief who took it. The phrase "found (or taken) with the mainour" meant to be caught in possession of stolen goods. Later the phrase "taken with (or in) the mainour (or manner)" meant to be found in the commission of any unlawful act, and meant the same as to be taken *in flagrante delicto*. See HAND-HABHENDE; INFANGTHET.

Mainovre, or **Mainoeuvre,** a trespass committed by hand: see the statute 1383, 7 Ric. 2, c. 4.

Mainpast. See MANUPASTUS.

Mainpernable, that which may be held to bail: see the Statute of Westminster I, 1275, c. 15.

Mainpernor. See MAINPRISE.

Mainprise [Fr. *main*, hand; *pris*, taken]. The writ of mainprise, *manucaptio*, was a writ directed to the sheriff, commanding him to take sureties for a prisoner's appearance, usually called mainpernors, and to set him at large (3 Bl.Comm. 128; Fitz.N.B. 250).

Mainprise literally means a taking into the hand, and is used in the old books to signify the process of delivering a person to sureties or pledges (mainpernors) who undertook to produce him again at a future time. Bail applied only to cases where a man was arrested or imprisoned, while a man could be mainperned not only in such cases but also where he had not been arrested or imprisoned, *e.g.*, in an appeal of felony and other obsolete proceedings (4 Co.Inst. 179; *Termes de la Ley*).

Mainpernors were not bound by recognisances to the Crown, as bailsmen were and are, and they could not, like bailsmen, relieve themselves of responsibility by seizing and remitting to custody the man for whom they had gone security.

See BAIL; MANUCAPTIO.

Main-rent, vassalage.

Mainsworn, forsworn.

Maintainors, persons who second or support a cause in which they are not interested, by assisting either party with money, or in any other manner. See MAINTENANCE AND CHAMPERTY.

Maintenance, the supply of necessaries, such as food, lodging, clothing, etc.

Where property is being administered in an action or other proceeding in the Chancery Division, and the persons absolutely or presumptively entitled to it are incompetent to support themselves (as where they are infants or of unsound mind), the court will direct a proper portion of the income to be expended for their maintenance.

A maintenance clause in a marriage settlement or will, by which property is given to infants on their attaining majority, or the like, is one which authorises the trustees to expend part or the whole of the income of the property in maintaining and educating the infants during their minority. By the Conveyancing and Law of Property Act, 1860, s. 26, this power was given to the trustees of all settled property. That enactment was repealed by the Conveyancing Act, 1881, s. 71, and was replaced by s. 43 of the latter Act, which in turn was replaced and extended by the Trustee Act, 1925, s. 31, and the Administration of Estates Act, 1925, s. 47 (1) (ii). The Legitimacy Act, 1976, s. 8, places a legitimated child in the same position as a legitimate child in respect of maintenance given by any Act. See ACCUMULATION.

On a petition for divorce, nullity of marriage or judicial separation either party to the marriage may be ordered to make periodical payments for the maintenance of the other from the presentation of the petition to the determination of the suit (Matrimonial Causes Act, 1973, s. 22). After the decree, permanent financial provision may be ordered either in the form of periodical or lump sum payments (s. 23). Financial provision may also be ordered for a child of the family (ss. 23, 52). Orders may be made for the transfer and settlement of property and for the variation of settlements (s. 24).

In making an order the court is to have regard to all the circumstances of the case including (a) the income, earning capacity, property and other financial resources which each of the parties to the marriage has or is likely to have in the foreseeable future, (b) the financial needs, obligations and responsibilities which each of the parties to the marriage has or is likely to have in the foreseeable future, (c) the standard of living enjoyed by the family before the breakdown of the marriage, (d) the age of each party to the marriage and the duration of the marriage, (e) any physical or mental disability of either party, (f) the contributions made by each party to the welfare of the family, including any contribution made by looking after the home or caring for the family, (g) in the case of divorce or nullity of marriage, the value to either of the parties to the marriage of any benefit (*e.g.*, a pension) which, by reason of the dissolution of the marriage, that party will lose the chance of acquiring. The general aim is to place the parties, so far as is practicable and, having regard to their conduct, just to do so, in the financial position in which they would have been if the marriage had not broken down and each had properly discharged his or her financial obligations and responsibilities towards the other (s. 25). See *Harris* v. *Harris* (1973) 4 Fam. Law 10, for a case awarding maintenance at less than the amount arrived at under the " one-third " rule.

Quite apart from any other matrimonial proceedings either party to a marriage may apply to the court for financial relief in the event of wilful neglect by the other party to maintain her or him or a child of the family (s. 27). But a wife's uncondoned adultery bars her right to maintenance under this section (*Gray* v. *Gray* [1976] 3 W.L.R. 181). The maximum terms for which orders for financial provision may be made are set out in s. 28. All orders come to an end on re-marriage of the party in whose favour the order is made (s. 28, Sch. 1 para. 15). The upper age limit in respect of financial provision for children is eighteen, with an extension in favour of children whose education or training is continuing (s. 29). Orders may be varied or discharged (s. 31). See also the Inheritance (Provision for Family and Dependants) Act, 1975, ss. 14–18. Arrears of more than twelve months cannot be enforced without leave of the court (Act of 1973, s. 32). In exceptional circumstances an order for repayment may be made (ss. 33, 38, Sch. 1 para. 16). Orders are registrable for enforcement in other parts of the United Kingdom and for enforcement in magistrates' courts and by an attachment (*q.v.*) of earnings order (Sch. 2 paras. 3, 10 (2)). Any provision in a maintenance agreement restricting the right to apply to the court for an order for financial provision is void (s. 34). Maintenance agreements may be altered by the court (ss. 35, 36). Transactions designed to defeat the objects of the Act are rendered void (s. 37). The court has power to make orders dealing with the welfare, custody and education of the children of the family (ss. 41, 42).

For the jurisdiction of a magistrates' court to order maintenance, see MATRIMONIAL PROCEEDINGS IN MAGISTRATES' COURTS. As to the maintenance of a minor, see GUARDIAN.

Maintenance orders are registrable and enforceable under the Maintenance Orders Act, 1958, as amended by the Administration of Justice Act, 1970, s. 48, Sch. 11. As to reciprocal enforcement, see the Maintenance Orders (Reciprocal Enforcement) Act, 1972; Affiliation Proceedings (Amendment) Act, 1972.

Earnings may be attached in order to satisfy maintenance orders. See the Attachment of Earnings Act, 1971, as amended by the Maintenance Orders (Reciprocal Enforcement) Act, 1972, Sch.

Proceedings to enforce certain maintenance orders are assigned to the Family Division (*q.v.*) of the High Court (Administration of Justice Act, 1970, s. 1, Sch. 1). As to the taxation of maintenance payments, see the Finance Act, 1974, s. 15.

Maintenance and champerty. At common law maintenance is an officious intermeddling in a suit which in nowise concerns one, by assisting either party with money or otherwise to prosecute or defend it; maintenance is both actionable and indictable (*Bradlaugh* v. *Newdegate* (1883) 11 Q.B.D. 1), and invalidates contracts involving it. Maintenance includes champerty (*q.v.*), which occurs where the assistance is given in consideration of a promise of part of the thing in suit. By the civil law it was a species of *crimen falsi* to enter into any confederacy, or do any act to support another's law-suits, by money, witnesses, or patronage (4 Bl.Comm. 134).

Maintenance is either *ruralis* (in the country) as where one assists another in his pretensions to lands, by taking or holding the possession of them for him, or where one stirs up quarrels or suits in the country; or it is *curialis* (in a court of justice) where one officiously intermeddles in a suit depending in any court, which does not belong to him, and with which he has nothing to do (2 Rol.Abr. 115).

Maintaining suits in the spiritual courts is not within the statutes relating to maintenance (Cro.Eliz. 549).

A man may lawfully maintain a suit in which he has any interest, actual or contingent; and also a suit of his near kinsman, servant, or poor neighbour, out of charity and compassion, with impunity (Bac.Abr.).

Further, any legitimate common interest will justify a person or persons jointly subscribing to pay the expenses of a suit, even when it is carried on by a third party (*Martell* v. *Consett Iron Co.* [1955] Ch. 363). A person will not be guilty of maintenance in indemnifying his customers from actions brought against them by a trade rival (*British*

Cash, etc., Conveyors v. *Lamson Store Service Co.* [1908] 1 K.B. 1006). An action for maintenance does not lie without proof of special damage. The success of the maintained action is not a bar to the right of action for maintenance (*Neville* v. *London Express Newspaper* [1919] A.C. 368).

This offence was punishable at common law, and also by the statute 1377, 1 Ric. 2, c. 4, by fine and imprisonment; and by the statute 1540, 32 Hen. 8, c. 9, by a forfeiture of £10. The offence of maintenance was abolished by the Criminal Law Act, 1967, s. 13, and s. 14 of that Act provides that no person shall be liable in tort for maintenance or champerty, but the abolition of criminal and civil liability does not affect any rule of law as to the cases in which a contract is to be treated as contrary to public policy or illegal.

Maisnada, a family (2 Dugd.Mon. 219).

Maison de Dieu. See MEASON-DUE.

Maisura, a house or farm.

Majestas. This is defined by Ulpian (Dig. 48, tit. 4, s. 1) as *crimen illud quod adversus populum Romanum vel adversus securitatem ejus committitur.* He then gives various instances of the crime of *majestas,* some of which nearly correspond to treason in English law; but all the offences included under *majestas* comprehend more than our term treason. One of the offences included in *majestas* was the effecting, aiding in or planning the death of a *magistratus populi Romani,* or of one who had *imperium* or *potestas.* Though the phrase *crimen majestatis* was used, the complete expression was *crimen laesae majestatis.*

Majesty, a title of sovereigns. It was first used among ourselves in the reign of Henry VIII. See HIGHNESS.

Major haereditas venit unicuique nostrum a jure et legibus quam a parentibus (2 Co.Inst. 56). (A greater inheritance comes to every one of us from legal right and the laws than from our parents.) " The law," Coke goes on, " is the best birthright the subject hath."

Major regalia, the greater rights of the Crown, such as regard the royal character and authority.

Majority, the full age of eighteen years. See FULL AGE.

It also means the greater number. In a deliberative body, questions are ordinarily decided by a majority of those present at a meeting (*q.v.*) and voting, provided that the whole number present is not less than a certain quorum (*q.v.*) of the whole body.

The principle that the majority of members is entitled to control a company is embodied in the rule in *Foss* v. *Harbottle* (1843) 2 Hare 461.

Majus continet minus (Jenk.Cent. 208). (The greater contains the less.) See IN TOTO, ETC.; OMNE MAJUS, ETC.

Majus dignum trahit ad se minus dignum (Co.Litt. 355). (The more worthy draws with it the less worthy.) Merger is an obvious illustration of this maxim. See CUI LICET, ETC.; OMNE MAJUS, ETC.

Majus est delictum seipsum occidere quam alium (3 Co.Inst. 54). (It is a greater crime to kill one's self than to kill another.) This was the view prevailing anciently. See SUICIDE.

Majus jus. In the reign of Edward III this was a proceeding in some customary manor courts for the trial of a right to land (Cowel).

Make his law. A man was said to make his law when he performed that law which he had formerly bound himself to; that is, cleared himself of an action commenced against him, by his oath and the oaths of his neighbours. See COMPURGATION; WAGER OF LAW.

Maker, the person who signs a promissory note; by making it he engages that he will pay it according to its tenor, and is precluded from denying to a holder in due course the existence of the payee and his then capacity to endorse (Bills of Exchange Act, 1882, s. 88).

Mal, a prefix, meaning bad, wrong, fraudulent; as maladministration, malfeasance, malpractice, malversation, etc.

Mal grato, in spite; unwillingly.

Mala, a mail, or port-mail; a bag to carry letters, etc.

Mala fide, in bad faith.

Mala fides, bad faith; the opposite to bona fides, good faith.

Mala grammatica non vitiat chartam. Sed in expositione instrumentorum mala grammatica quoad fieri possit evitanda est (6 Co.Rep. 39). (Bad grammar does not vitiate a deed. But in the interpretation of instruments, bad grammar is to be avoided so far as may be.) That is to say, an interpretation is not necessarily erroneous because it involves an ungrammatical use of words; but such a construction is not to be adopted without actual necessity. See CLERICAL ERROR; MENS TESTATORIS, ETC.

Mala in se, acts which are wrong in themselves, such as murder, as opposed to *mala prohibita* (*mala quia prohibita*), that is to say, those acts (such as smuggling) which are only wrong because they are prohibited by law. The distinction was formerly of importance with reference to the exemption of ambassadors, which, according to the earlier writers, only extended to *mala prohibita*; but this is no longer the case. See AMBASSADOR.

Mala praxis, where a medical practitioner injures his patient by neglect, want of skill, or for experiment. Ordinary cases of *mala praxis* give rise to a right of action for damages (*Seare* v. *Prentice* (1807) 8 East 348). (See TORT.) In cases of gross misconduct the practitioner may be indicted.

Mala prohibita, wrongs which are prohibited by human laws, but are not necessarily *mala in se* (*q.v.*) or wrongs in themselves.

Malandrinus, a thief or pirate (Walsing. 338).

Malawi. See the Malawi Independence Act, 1964; Malawi Republic Act, 1966.

Malaysia. See the Malaysia Act, 1963.

Malberge [*mons placiti*], a hill where the people assembled at a court, like our assizes, which by the Scots and Irish were called parley hills (Du Cange).

Male servants. An excise licence had formerly to be taken out each year for every male servant who during the year, or any part of it, was employed as *maître d'hôtel*, house steward, master of the horse, groom of the chambers, *valet de chambre*, butler, under-butler, clerk of the kitchen, confectioner, cook, house porter, footman, page, waiter, coachman, groom, motor-car driver, postilion, stable-boy, gardener, under-gardener, park-keeper, gamekeeper, under-gamekeeper, huntsman, or whipper-in (Revenue Act, 1869, ss. 18, 19 (3); Motor Car Act, 1903, s. 13; Road Traffic Act, 1930, s. 118), whether he was employed for the purpose of a trade or business or not: but no licence was required for soldiers or sailors employed as servants by officers, or for a servant, other than one driving a carriage let for more than twenty-eight days, employed at a livery stable of which entry had been made, or for a driver employed to drive a public stage or hackney carriage for the licensee thereof (Revenue Act, 1869, s. 19 (5)), or for servants employed at any house of public entertainment or at a boarding-house (Customs and Inland Revenue Act, 1873, s. 4 (4), or where a male servant who did not live in his employer's house was employed in one of the taxable capacities for only an inconsiderable part of each day, or where a male servant living with his employer in a non-taxable employment was employed only occasionally in a taxable capacity (Customs and Inland Revenue Act, 1876, s. 5); but, except in cases coming within these exemptions the licence was required in respect of every servant employed in a taxable capacity for any time, however short. The duty on the licence was 15s. per annum.

The licences for male servants (as well as those for armorial bearings and for carriages) were known as establishment licences, and were also included in the larger category of local taxation licences.

The taxes on male servants and on armorial bearings and carriage duties were abolished by the Finance Act, 1937, s. 5, and the Finance Act, 1944, ss. 6, 49, Sch. 5 Pts. I, II.

Malecreditus, one of bad credit, who is not to be trusted (1 Fleta, c. xxxviii).

Maledicta expositio quae corrumpit textum (4 Co.Rep. 35). (It is a bad exposition which corrupts the text). That is to say, which substitutes other words for those actually used in the statute.

Malediction, a curse such as was anciently annexed to donations of lands made to churches or religious houses,

MALEDICTION

against those who should violate their rights.

Malefaction, a crime, an offence.

Malefactor, a contemptible or formidable wretch; one who commits a *malum in se*.

Maleficia non debent remanere impunita; et impunitas continuum affectum tribuit delinquendi (4 Co.Rep. 45). (Evil deeds ought not to remain unpunished; and impunity is a continual inducement to the commission of crime.) See INTEREST REIPUBLICAE NE MALEFICIA, ETC.

Maleficia propositis distinguuntur (Jenk.Cent. 290). (Evil deeds are distinguished from evil purposes.) See IN CRIMINALIBUS VOLUNTAS, ETC.

Maleficium, waste; damage; injury (Civil Law).

Maleson, or **Malison** [Lat. *malum*, evil; *sonus,* a sound], a curse (Bailey).

Malesworn, or Malsworn, forsworn (Cowel).

Maletent, Maletoute [Low Lat. *mala tolta,* bad tax], a toll for every sack of wool; see the statute 1297, 25 Edw. 1, c.7.

Malfeasance, the doing of an unlawful act, *e.g.,* a trespass. See MISFEASANCE; NONFEASANCE; TORT.

Malice [Lat. *malitia*], a formed design of doing mischief to another, technically called *malitia praecogitata,* or malice prepense or aforethought. It is either express, as when one with a sedate and deliberate mind and formed design kills another, which formed design is evidenced by certain circumstances discovering such intentions, as lying in wait, antecedent menaces, former grudges, and concerted schemes to do him some bodily harm; or implied, as where one wilfully poisons another, when the law presumes malice, though no particular enmity can be proved. The nature of implied malice is also illustrated by the maxim, *Culpa lata dolo aequiparatur*—when negligence reaches a certain point it is the same as intentional wrong. Everyone must be taken to intend that which is the natural consequence of his actions; if any one acts in exactly the same way as he would do if he bore express malice to another, he cannot be allowed to say he does not.

Malice in common acceptance means ill-will against a person, but in its legal sense it means a wrongful act done intentionally without just cause or excuse (*Bromage* v. *Prosser* (1825) 4 B. & C. at p. 255; *McPherson* v. *Daniels* (1829) 10 B. & C. 272). So long as a person believes in the truth of what he says and is not reckless, malice cannot be inferred from the fact that his belief is unreasonable, prejudiced or unfair (*Horrocks* v. *Lowe* [1972] 1 W.L.R. 1625).

Ill-will or improper motive is often called actual or express malice, or malice in fact, to distinguish it from malice in law, which merely denotes absence of legal excuse. To amount to murder, a killing must be committed with malice aforethought. " Aforethought " does not necessarily imply premeditation, but it implies intention, which must necessarily precede the act intended. See HOMICIDE; MANSLAUGHTER; MURDER; PREPENSE.

Malice constituted by a proved intention to inflict grievous bodily harm (*q.v.*) has not been abolished by s. 1 (1) of the Homicide Act, 1957 (*D.P.P.* v. *Smith* [1961] A.C. 290).

In the law of defamation the defence that the occasion was one of qualified privilege may be rebutted by establishing actual malice in the defendant, for he is not entitled to protection if he uses such an occasion for some indirect and wrong motive (*Clark* v. *Molyneux* (1877) 3 Q.B.D. 246). But the malice of one co-defendant is not to be imputed to another (*Egger* v. *Viscount Chelmsford* [1965] 1 Q.B. 248). Similarly, proof of actual malice will defeat the defence of fair comment (*q.v.*).

An act lawful in itself is not converted by malice into an actionable wrong (*Allen* v. *Flood* [1898] A.C. 1).

Malicious arrest, where a person maliciously and without reasonable cause procures another to be arrested. He thereby makes himself liable to an action for damages. The term is practically confined to cases of arrest in civil cases (*i.e.,* for debt, etc.) which have now become rare. See ARREST; DEBTORS ACT; FALSE IMPRISONMENT; MALICE; TORT.

Malicious damage. See DAMAGE, CRIMINAL.

Malicious falsehood. See LIBEL.

Malicious injuries to property. The Malicious Damage Act, 1861, which dealt with these offences has been repealed and replaced by the Criminal Damage Act, 1971. See DAMAGE, CRIMINAL.

Malicious injuries to the person. Everyone who unlawfully and maliciously wounds or causes any grievous bodily harm to any person, or shoots or attempts to shoot him with intent in any such case to maim, disfigure, disable or do some grievous bodily harm to him, is liable to imprisonment for life (Offences against the Person Act, 1861, s. 18).

Malicious prosecution, a prosecution, preferred maliciously, without reasonable or probable cause; the remedy is an action on the case, in which damages may be recovered. Damage must be pleaded and proved (*Berry* v. *British Transport Commission* [1962] 1 Q.B. 306). The allegation of want of reasonable and probable cause must be expressly proved and cannot be implied; it is for the judge, not the jury, to determine upon it (*Abrath* v. *North Eastern Ry.* (1886) 11 App.Cas. 247; *Cox* v. *English, Scottish and Australian Bank* [1905] A.C. 168). *Animus injuriae* cannot be inferred from the mere fact that the prosecution has failed (*Corea* v. *Peiris* [1909] A.C. 549).

Malignare, to malign or slander; also to maim.

Malins' (Sir Richard) Act, the Married Women's Reversionary Interest Act, 1857, enabling married women to dispose of reversionary interests in personalty (see now the Law of Property Act, 1925, ss. 167, 169); also the Infant Settlements Act, 1855.

Malitia praecogitata, malice aforethought. See MALICE.

Malitia supplet aetatem (Dyer, 104b). (Malice supplies the want of age.) A child between 10 (Children and Young Persons Act, 1933, s. 50; Children and Young Persons Act, 1963, s. 16 (1)) and 14 years of age can be convicted of a crime if, and only if, it is affirmatively shown that he had sufficient capacity to know that the act which he did was wrong (*R.* v. *Owen* (1830) 4 C. & P. 236). See AGE; CHILDREN.

Mallum, Mallus. See METHEL.

Malt mulna, a quern or malt mill (Mat.Par.).

Malt-shot, Malt-scot, a payment for making malt (Somner).

Malt-tax, a tax abolished by the Inland Revenue Act, 1880, which substituted a duty on beer.

Malta. See the Malta Independence Act, 1964; Malta Republic Act, 1975.

Malum in se. See MALA IN SE.

Malum non praesumitur (4 Co.Inst. 72). (Evil is not presumed.)

Malum prohibitum. See MALA PROHIBITA.

Malum quo communius eo pejus. (The more common an evil is, the worse.)

Malus usus est abolendus, quia in consuetudinibus non diuturnitas temporis, sed soliditas rationis est consideranda (Co.Litt. 141). (A usage which is bad in law ought to be abolished, because, in dealing with customs, it is not the length of time for which they have prevailed but the validity of the argument which can be advanced that has to be considered.)

Malveilles [Fr. *malveillance*], ill-will; crimes and misdemeanours; malicious practices.

Malveis procurers, jury-packers: those who procured the appointment of jurors who were not impartial (*Articuli super Chartham,* c. 10).

Malveisa, a warlike engine to batter and beat down walls (Mat.Par.).

Malveisin [Fr. *mauvais voisin*], an ill neighbour, a warlike engine so called (Mat.Par.).

Malversation, misbehaviour in an office, employment or commission, as breach of trust, extortion, etc.

Man, Isle of (Mona), in the Irish Sea, off the coast of Cumberland, Westmorland, and Lancashire, granted by Henry IV and James I to members of the Stanley family, whose successor in the female line, the Duke of Athol, sold it to the Crown for £70,000, being about ten years' purchase of the annual revenue, by the Isle of Man Purchase Act, 1765. Since 1290, the island has been under the protection of the English Crown, which for long delegated its rights to a succession of nobles. They, from 1406 to 1649, were known as Kings of Man: in 1649 the title was changed to Lord of Man. The island was never incorporated with Great Britain. It is a dominion, though not a foreign dominion, of the Crown. The bishop—known as the Bishop of Sodor and Man—has a seat, although not a vote, in the House of Lords: but otherwise the island is entirely without any parliamentary representative. Parliament, however, can and occasionally does legislate for it: but in the absence of express provision it is not affected by any statute, and it makes its own laws subject to its own constitution, being legislated for by its own parliament, called the House of Keys.

It is included in the expression British Islands unless the contrary intention appears (Interpretation Act, 1889, s. 18 (1)).

The Isle of Man Act, 1958, enables the island to regulate its own customs, duties, finances, harbours, mines and quarries.

See KEYS; TYNWALD, COURT OF.

Man of straw, one who is incapable of justifying any financial credit that may be reposed in him; one who is not worth suing.

Man trap. Engines to catch trespassers are unlawful, unless set in a dwelling-house for defence between sunset and sunrise (Offences against the Person Act, 1861, s. 31). " Engine " means a mechanical contrivance. It does not include an electrical device (*R.* v. *Munks* [1964] 1 Q.B. 304).

Mana, an old woman (Jacob).

Manacle [Lat. *manus*], chain for the hands; shackle.

Management and Administration Department, the name given to the office of the Master in Lunacy by the Management of Patients' Estates Rules, 1934 (No. 269). It was renamed the Court of Protection (*q.v.*) by the Patients' Estates (Naming of Master's Office) Order, 1947 (No. 1235).

Manager, superintendent, conductor, director.

In Chancery practice, when a receiver (*q.v.*) is required for the purpose not only of receiving rents and profits or getting in outstanding property but of carrying on or superintending a trade or business, he is usually denominated a " manager," or a " receiver and manager." The most usual cases in which managers are appointed are those which relate to partnerships or to mines or collieries. In a case where the trade or property is abroad, or in one of the colonies, and the manager must necessarily be resident there, it is usual to add to the order

directing the appointment of a manager an order for the appointment of one or more consignee or consignees resident in this country, to whom the produce of the property in question may be remitted, and by whom it may be disposed of.

In bankruptcy, a special manager of the business of the debtor until a trustee is appointed may be appointed, on the application of any creditor, by the official receiver under the Bankruptcy Act, 1914, s. 10; and the official receiver, when acting as interim receiver under s. 8 of the Act, can, of his own motion, appoint a special manager.

Under the Companies Act, 1948, s. 127, the official receiver, when he becomes the liquidator of a company, may, if satisfied that a special manager is required, apply to the court for a special manager to be appointed, and the court may thereupon appoint a special manager.

In parliamentary practice, where the two Houses of Parliament have a conference (*e.g.,* to settle amendments to a bill as to which there is a difference between the two Houses), each House appoints managers to represent it, and the conference is held between the managers. As to managers of an impeachment, see IMPEACHMENT.

Managing clerk. A managing clerk to a solicitor may be admitted as a solicitor or unadmitted. He conducts matters under his principal's supervision. An unadmitted clerk is usually considered to be entitled to be called a managing clerk after he has had ten years' experience in a solicitor's office. See LEGAL EXECUTIVE.

Managing director, a director appointed to be in charge of the management of a company. There is no principle of law which prevents the managing director of an employer company from being a member of a trade union of employees (*Boulting* v. *Association of Cinematograph, Television and Allied Technicians* [1963] 2 Q.B. 606).

Managing owner of ship, one of several co-owners, to whom the others, or those of them who join in the adventure, have delegated the management of the ship. He has authority to do all things usual and necessary in the management of the ship and the delivery of the cargo, to enable her to prosecute her voyage and earn freight, with the right to appoint an agent for the purpose. He is not entitled to make an extra profit for himself by accepting secret commission (*Williamson v. Hine* [1891] 1 Ch. 390).

Under the Merchant Shipping Act, 1894, s. 59, the name and address of the managing owner for the time being of every registered British ship must be registered, or, if there is no managing owner, the ship's husband (*q.v.*) or other person to whom the management of the ship is entrusted, must be registered.

Managium, a mansion-house or dwelling-place.

Manbote, compensation or recompense paid for homicide, more especially to the overlord when the deceased was unfree. The manbote in that case was, however, less than that payable to the relations of a freeman.

Manca; Mancus; Mancusa, a square gold coin, current about the time of the Conquest and value for thirty silver pennies (Spelman). It must have been a continental coin, there being no English gold coinage before the reign of Henry III. See GOLD COINS.

Manceps [Lat.], a farmer of the public revenues; one who sold an estate with a promise of keeping the purchaser harmless; one who bought an estate by outcry; one who undertook a piece of work and gave security for the performance.

Manche-present, a bribe; a present from the donor's own hand.

Manchester became a municipal borough in 1838 and a county borough by the Local Government Act, 1888. Its bishopric was established by the Ecclesiastical Commissioners Act, 1847.

Under the Local Government Act, 1972, Greater Manchester is a metropolitan county (s. 1, Sch. 1 Pt. I).

Manchester Registry. See TRADE MARKS.

Mancipate, to enslave; to bind; to tie.

Mancipatio. Every father, in the Roman law, had such an authority over his son, that before the son could be released from his subjection and made free he must be twice sold and bought, his natural father being in the first instance the vendor. The vendee was called *pater fiduciarius*. After this

fictitious bargain, the *pater fiduciarius* sold him again to his natural father, who could then, but not till then, manumit or make him free. The imaginary sale was called *mancipatio*; and the act of giving him liberty, or setting him free, was called *emancipatio*.

Mancipatio also meant selling or alienating lands by the balance, or money paid by weight, and in the presence of five witnesses. This mode of alienation took place only among Roman citizens, and only in respect of certain estates situated in Italy, which were called *mancipia*. It was abolished by Justinian, when he obliterated the distinction between things *mancipi* and things *nec mancipi*.

Manciple [Lat. *manceps*], a clerk of the kitchen, or caterer, especially in colleges.

Mandamus [Lat. we command], a prerogative order issued in certain cases to compel the performance of a duty.

The order of mandamus was substituted for the writ of mandamus by the Administration of Justice (Miscellaneous Provisions) Act, 1938, s. 7; see R.S.C., Ord. 53.

The order of mandamus issues from the Queen's Bench Division where the injured party has a right to have anything done, and has no other specific means of compelling its performance, especially where the obligation arises out of the official status of the respondent. Thus, it is used to compel public officers to perform duties imposed upon them by common law or by statute (*e.g.,* to make a rate) or to compel inferior courts to proceed in matters within their jurisdiction (see PROCEDENDO; PROHIBITION); it is also applicable in certain cases where a duty is imposed by Act of Parliament for the benefit of an individual.

The remedy of mandamus to a tribunal is not to be excluded (Tribunals and Inquiries Act, 1971, s. 14).

By the Judicature Act, 1925, s. 45 (1), replacing the Judicature Act, 1873, s. 25 (8) an interlocutory mandamus may be granted in any case in which it appears to the court to be just or convenient. See INJUNCTION.

The High Court has jurisdiction to make an order of mandamus to the Crown Court (*q.v.*) except in relation to that court's jurisdiction in matters relating to trial on indictment (Courts Act, 1971, s. 10 (5)).

Originally mandamus was the generic name for a class of writs varying in their form and object, but totally different from the later prerogative writ which, for the sake of distinction, was called a special mandamus. In the fourteenth and the beginning of the fifteenth century the writ was in form a mere letter-missive from the sovereign; during the latter half of the fifteenth century the writ was directed to issue on a petition to Parliament for redress; it thus became in form a parliamentary writ, and, being then chiefly used to enforce restitution to public offices, was commonly known as the writ of restitution; finally it became an original writ, issuable by the King's Bench in all cases where there was a legal right, but no other specific remedy (Tapping, *Mandamus*).

There was also a writ of mandamus ordering the sheriffs to take into the hands of the king the lands of a king's widow (*q.v.*) who had married without the royal licence; and there was another writ of mandamus which in certain cases was used instead of a *diem clausit extremum* (*q.v.*) (Fitz.N.B. 253).

Mandant, the principal in the contract of mandate.

Mandata licita strictam recipiunt interpretationem, sed illicita latam et extensam (Bac.Max.Reg. 16). (Lawful orders receive a strict interpretation, unlawful orders a wide and extended one.) Thus if A gives a lawful authority to B, then only such acts as are clearly within that authority are held to be the acts of A: but if C employs D to poison E, and D, contrary to the letter of his instructions, but within the spirit of them, takes it upon himself to strangle E, then C will still be guilty of murder of E (*Parkes* v. *Prescott* (1869) L.R. 4 Ex. 182).

Mandatarius terminos sibi positos transgredi non potest (Jenk.Cent. 53). (A mandatory cannot exceed the limits imposed upon him.) See MANDATA LICITA, ETC.

Mandatary [Lat. *mandatarius*], he to who a mandate, charge, or command-

ment is given; also he who obtains a benefice by mandamus.

Mandate, a direction or request. Thus, a cheque is a mandate by the drawer to his banker to pay the amount to the holder of the cheque.

The word mandate is also used as an equivalent for *mandatum,* a bailment of goods, without reward, to be carried from place to place, or to have some act performed about them. The person employing is called in the civil law *mandans* or mandator, and the person employed *mandatarius* or mandatory. The distinction between a mandate and a deposit is that in the latter the principal object of the parties is the custody of the thing; and the service and labour are merely accessory. In the former, the labour and service are the principal objects of the parties, and the thing is merely accessory. Three things are necessary to create a mandate: that there should exist something which should be the subject of the contract, or some act or business to be done; that it should be done gratuitously; and that the parties should voluntarily intend to enter into the contract. A mandatary incurs three obligations: to do the act which is the object of the mandate, and with which he is charged; to bring to it all the care and diligence that it requires; and to render an account of his doings to the mandator. A mandator contracts to reimburse a mandatory for all expenses and charges reasonably incurred in the execution of the mandate, and also to indemnify him for his liability on all contracts which arise incidentally in the proper discharge of his duty. The contract of mandate may be dissolved either by the renunciation of the mandatory at any time before he has entered upon its execution, or by his death; for, being founded in personal confidence, it is not presumed to pass to his representatives, unless there is some special stipulation to that effect. But if the mandate is partly executed, there may in some cases arise a personal obligation on the part of the representatives to complete it.

In early times, before the independence of the superior courts had been established, the Crown controlled their actions by mandates or orders to pursue such and such a course.

The granting of royal mandates to judges for interfering in private causes constituted a branch of the royal prerogative which was given up by Edward I. The Bill of Rights, 1688, declared the pretended power of suspending or dispensing with laws as formerly exercised, by regal authority without consent of parliament, to be illegal.

Mandated territories, countries and islands the regulation of which was entrusted by mandate of the League of Nations to governments willing and able to take over their government and development. Countries governed under mandate included Palestine, parts of Togoland, the Cameroons, and East Africa, by Great Britain; South West Africa, by South Africa; part of New Guinea, by Australia; Nauru Island and the Samoa Islands, by New Zealand; part of East Africa, by Belgium; the Caroline Islands, by Japan; and parts of Togoland, the Cameroons, Syria and Lebanon, by France. See TRUST TERRITORIES.

Mandati dies, Maundy Thursday.

Mandati, Panes de, loaves of bread given to the poor upon Maundy Thursday.

Mandator, director. See MANDATE.

Mandatory, perceptive; directory.

Mandatory injunction, an injunction requiring the performance of some act, *e.g.,* the removal of a building or obstruction.

For the principles governing the grant of a mandatory injunction see *per* Lord Upjohn in *Redland Bricks* v. *Morris* [1970] A.C. 652. As to application for an injunction, see R.S.C., Ord. 29, s. 1.

Mandatum, a fee or retainer given by the Romans to the *procuratores* and *advocati. Mandatum* is also used in the sense of a command from a superior to an inferior. See BAILMENT; MANDATE.

Mandavi ballivo (I have commanded the bailiff). Where a sheriff receives a writ which has to be executed within a place which is a liberty he commands the bailiff of the liberty to execute the writ and afterwards makes the return *mandavi ballivo,* setting out also what return has been made by the bailiff. If the bailiff has not made a return, the sheriff should return that fact accordingly (*mandavi ballivo, qui nullum dedit responsum*).

Manentes [Lat. *manere,* to continue], tenants, those who had to stay on the land, that is to say, villeins.

Manerium, a manor (*q.v.*).

Manerium dicitur a manendo, secundum excellentiam, sedes magna, fixa, et stabilis (Co.Litt. 58). (A manor is so called from *manendo,* according to its excellence, a seat, great, fixed, and firm.)

Mangonare, to buy in a market (Leg. Etheld. c. 24).

Mangonellus, a warlike instrument for casting stones against the walls of a castle.

Mania, mental alienation.

Mania a potu, otherwise denominated *delirium tremens,* a disease induced from the intemperate use of spirituous liquors or certain other diffusible stimulants.

Manifest. In the case of a merchant vessel this is a list of the goods making up her cargo, with the names of the shippers; see the Revenue Act, 1884, s.3.

Manifesta probatione non indigent (7 Co. Rep. 40). (Things manifest do not require proof.)

Manifesto. In international law this is a declaration by which a State gives notice to its own citizens and to neutrals of the existence of a state of war between it and another State. The term is also applied to any public declaration by a sovereign, government, or party as to their conduct or course of action.

Manner, or **Mainour** [Fr. *manier*]. To be taken with the mainour is where a thief is taken with the stolen goods about him—as it were in his hands; that is, *in flagrante delicto*. In such a case he might be brought into court, arraigned and tried, without indictment (4 Bl. Comm. 308). See MAINOUR.

Manning, a man's work for one day; used in old leases reserving to the lessor so many mannings in each year from the lessee.

Mannire, to cite any person to appear in court and stand in judgment there: it was different from *bannier;* for though both of them were citations, this was by the adverse party and that was by the judge. See BANNIER AD PLACITA.

Mannus, a horse.

Manoeuvres, Military. See MILITARY MANOEUVRES.

Manopus, goods taken in the hands of an apprehended thief. See MANU OPERA.

Manor [Lat. *manerium*. Fr. *manoir*, habitation; Lat. *manendo*, abiding there, because the lord usually resided there], an estate in fee simple in a tract of land granted by the sovereign to a subject in consideration of certain services to be performed. The *tenementales* were granted out; the *dominicales* (whence the term demesne) were reserved to the lord; the barren lands which remained formed the wastes; the whole fee was termed a lordship or barony and the court appendant to the manor the court baron. Every manor (with some doubtful and unimportant exceptions) is of a date prior to the statute *Quia Emptores,* 1289.

A manor was made by the owner of an estate in fee carving out other estates in fee to be held by other freeholders as his tenants. A manor consisted of demesnes and services: of demesnes, that is, of lands of which the freeholder, the lord of a manor, was seised in his demesne as of fee; of services, namely, of such yearly rent, called rent service, and other services as he reserved in the grant to his tenants of portions of land, which once were his, to be held by them and their heirs of him and his heirs. Of the demesne, the lord was seised; of the lands held by free tenants by rent or other services, the tenants themselves were seised, each man in his own demesne as of his own fee. Two free tenants, at least, were necessary to constitute a manor; but there might be as many more as the lord could procure to become his men.

Copyholds formed no part whatever of the essence of a manor. The lord of a manor might have copyholders or not.

If a copyhold tenement had by immemorial custom been treated by the tenant as if it were itself a manor, *e.g.*, by holding courts, granting part of it to be held of himself as copyhold, etc., this formed a customary or copyhold manor, and the tenant was called a customary lord, although, as far as regards the principal manor, he was himself merely a copyholder of that manor, and paid fines,

etc., like the other tenants (Co.Litt. 58b; 11 Co.Rep. 17).

A court baron was an essential part of a manor, and this court could not be held without at least two freeholders as suitors. If there were not two suitors, the manor became a reputed manor and continued to have certain manorial rights and franchises. "Manor" includes a lordship and a reputed manor or lordship (Law of Property Act, 1925, s, 205 (1) (ix)).

The land legislation of 1925 did not disturb the property in fee simple or many of the valuable rights incident to a manor, such as mines, minerals, lime, clay, stone, gravel pits or quarries, franchises, royalties and privileges in respect of fairs, chase or warren, fisheries and hunting and shooting, but manorial courts were abolished, the lord's right to escheat transferred to the Crown or the Duchy of Lancaster or of Cornwall and rent and other services except grand and petty serjeanty commuted and extinguished. See COPYHOLD; MANORIAL DOCUMENTS.

It is now generally supposed that manors were not a creation of the Norman Conquest, but an adaptation to the Norman rules of tenure of the institutions known as village communities which existed among the Saxons (Hone, *Manor*; Webb, *Manor and Borough*; Ault, *Private Jurisdiction in England*).

Manorial documents, court rolls, surveys, maps, terriers, documents and books relating to the boundaries, franchises, wastes, customs or courts of a manor but not deeds or evidence of title to the manor, are placed under the superintendence of the Master of the Rolls. They may remain in the possession or under the control of the lord of the manor but he is not entitled to destroy or damage them. The Master of the Rolls has power to direct the documents to be sent to the Public Record Office or local institutions undertaking to be responsible for the preservation and indexing of the documents and the Master of the Rolls may make rules for these purposes. (Law of Property Act, 1922, s. 144A; inserted by the Law of Property (Amendment) Act, 1924, Sch. 2).

Manorial incidents. See MANOR.

Manorial waste. See COMMON.

Manpower Services Commission. See the Employment and Training Act, 1973.

Man-queller [Sax. *man, cwellan*], a murderer.

Manrent, a kind of bond between lord and vassal, by which protection was stipulated on the one hand, and fidelity with personal service on the other.

Mansa, or **Mansum,** a mansion or house (Spelman).

Manse, a house or habitation, either with or without land; the dwelling-house of a clergyman (Paroch.Antiq. 431).

Manser, a bastard.

Mansion [Lat. *mansio, a manendo*], the lord's house in a manor. Alongside this meaning of the word there had grown up the meaning of any dwelling-house: thus the statute 1498, 11 Hen. 7, c. 9, s. 2, speaks of " every . . . mansion or dwelling place." But this " mansion " included all buildings within the curtilage of a dwelling-house, and the whole " mansion " in this sense was the subject of burglary (*q.v.*) until the Criminal Law Act, 1826, s. 13, excluded from the definition of the " dwelling-house " which can be the subject of burglary any structure between which and the inhabited house there is no covered communication, and thereby made a clear distinction between a dwelling-house and a mansion. See MESSUAGE; PRINCIPAL MANSION HOUSE.

Mansion-house, a dwelling-house (3 Co.Inst. 64).

The Settled Land Act, 1882, gave a tenant for life a power to sell settled land, but by the Settled Land Act, 1890, s. 10, the principal mansion-house (unless it was usually occupied as a farmhouse, or its site with its park, etc., did not exceed twenty-five acres in extent) was not to be sold, exchanged, or leased by such tenant for life without the consent of the trustees of the settlement, or an order of the Chancery Division. Now, by the Settled Land Act, 1925, s. 65, the mansion and park may be sold without the consent of the trustees or leave of the court unless the settlement otherwise provides. For the meaning of the term principal mansion-house, see *Gilbey* v. *Rush* [1906] 1 Ch. 11. See LIMITED OWNER.

Manslaughter, the crime of unlawful homicide, without malice (*q.v.*) afore-thought, either express or implied (1 Hale P.C. 466).

Manslaughter is of two kinds: (1) involuntary, where a man by accident kills another in the course of doing an unlawful and dangerous act, with intent to commit an assault (*R.* v. *Lamb* [1967] 2 Q.B. 981), or where a man, by culpable neglect of a duty imposed·upon him is the cause of the death of another; and (2) voluntary, where, upon a sudden quarrel, two persons fight, and one kills the other, or where a man greatly provokes another by personal violence, and the other immediately kills him.

Manslaughter is punishable, at the discretion of the court, by imprisonment for life (Offences against the Person Act, 1861, s. 5). As to children and young persons see the Children and Young Persons Act, 1933, s. 53. As to causing death by dangerous driving see the Road Traffic Act, 1972, s. 1, Sch. 4. See DANGEROUS DRIVING.

Upon an indictment for murder, the jury, if they find that malice aforethought has not been proved, can bring in a verdict of manslaughter.

A high degree of negligence is required before a charge of manslaughter can be established; the breach of a statutory duty causing death is not necessarily man-slaughter (*Andrews* v. *Director of Public Prosecutions* [1937] A.C. 576).

A person suffering from abnormality of mind who would but for the Homicide Act, 1957, s. 2, be liable to be convicted of murder is to be convicted instead of manslaughter (s. 2 (3)). See DIMINISHED RESPONSIBILITY.

A person who aided, abetted, counselled or procured a person to commit suicide may be charged with and found guilty of manslaughter (Suicide Act, 1961, s. 2 (2)).

As to a defence of drunkenness see *R.* v. *Howell* [1974] 2 All E.R. 806. See DRUNKENNESS.

Mansuetae naturae [Lat., of a tame nature], domesticated. It was usually necessary to prove scienter in order to recover damages in respect of harm done by an animal *mansuetae naturae*. See ANIMALS, LIABILITY FOR.

Mansum capitale, the manor-house or lord's court (Paroch.Antiq. 150).

Mansum presbyterium, the dwelling-house of a clergyman, sometimes called *presbyterium.*

Mansura, the habitation of people in the country (*Domesday*).

Mansus, a farm (Selden, *Tithes,* 62).

Mantea, a long robe or mantle.

Mantheoff [Lat. *mannus,* a horse; Sax. *theft,* a thief], a horse-stealer (Leg. Alb.).

Manticulate, to pick pockets.

Manu forti, with strong hand.

Manu opera, stolen goods taken from a thief caught in the act; cattle or any implements used in husbandry (1 Dugd. Mon. 977).

Manualia beneficia, daily distributions of meat and drink to the canons and other members of cathedral churches for their subsistence.

Manualis obedientia, sworn obedience or submission upon oath.

Manucaptio, a writ which lay for a man taken on suspicion of felony, etc., who could not be admitted to bail by the sheriff or others having power to let to mainprise (Fitz.N.B. 249). See MAINPRISE.

Manucaptor, one who stands bail for another.

Manufacture, anything made by art.

Manumission, the act of giving freedom to slaves. Among the Romans it was performed in three several ways: when with his master's consent a slave had his name entered in the census or public register of the citizens; when the slave was led before the praetor, and the magistrate laid his wand (*vindicta*) on his head; and when the master, by his will, gave his slave freedom. Among us, in the time of the Conqueror, villeins were manumitted by their master delivering them by the right hand to the viscount or sheriff in full court, showing them the door, giving them a lance and a sword, and proclaiming them free. Others were manumitted by charter. There was also an implied manumission, as when the lord made an obligation for payment of money to the bondman at a certain day, or sued him where he might enter without suit, and the like (Jacob).

Manung, or **Monung,** the district within the jurisdiction of a reeve, apparently so called from his power to exercise therein one of his chief functions, *viz.,* to exact (*amanian*) all fines (Anc.Inst.Eng.).

Manupastus, a domestic; perhaps the same as *hlafaeta* (Anc.Inst.Eng.).

Manupes, a foot of full and legal measure.

Manurable, admitting of tillage.

Manure. See the Control of Pollution Act, 1974, Sch. 3 para. 7. See POLLUTION.

As to artificial manures, see FERTILISERS AND FEEDING STUFFS.

Manus, an oath, from the ceremony of laying the hand on the book; also, the person taking an oath, or compurgator.

Manus mediae et infimae homines, men of a mean condition, or of the lowest degree.

Manutenentia, the writ which was issued against anyone guilty of the crime of maintenance (Reg.Brev. 182).

Manwryth, the value or price at which a man was estimated, according to his degree; apparently synonymous with *wergeld.* It occurs only in the laws of Hlothaere and Eadric (Anc.Inst.Eng.).

Map, a graphic delineation of territory. See ORDNANCE SURVEY; PLAN.

Mara, a mere, lake, or great pond, which cannot be drawn dry (Par.Antiq. 418; Dugd.Mon. 666).

Marcatus, the rent of a mark by the year anciently reserved in leases, etc.

Marchandises avariées [Fr.], damaged goods.

Marchers, Lords. From a time soon after the Conquest, the English kings permitted their nobles to conquer and to hold such parts of Wales as they could. Each noble—there were 137 of them in 1536—was given *jura regalia,* or sovereign rights, within the area held by him; this went on until the conquest of Wales in 1282. Each of such nobles was known as a lord marcher and his territory was called a lordship marcher. The territory held by them included approximately the former Welsh counties of Brecknock, Denbigh, Glamorgan, Montgomery, Pembroke, and Radnor, the English county of Monmouth, and parts of Shropshire, Herefordshire, and Gloucestershire. The statute 1354, 28 Edw. 3,

c. 11, declared their territories perpetually annexed to the English Crown; and their quasi-sovereign position was abolished by the statute 1535, 27 Hen. 8, c. 26. See COURT OF THE COUNCIL, ETC.; WALES.

Marches, the boundary between England and Wales and that between England and Scotland. Powerful nobles were appointed by the Crown to act as wardens of the marches to prevent invasion (Pease, *Lord Wardens of the Marches*; Nicolson, *Leges Marchiarum*). See COURT OF THE COUNCIL OF THE MARCHES; DEFENSIVA; DIES MARCHIAE; MARCHERS, LORDS.

Marches, Court of, a tribunal in Wales, where pleas of debt or damages, not above the value of £50, were tried and determined (Cro.Car. 384).

Marchet, Marchetta, Merchetum, Merchetae [Norm.Fr. *marché, marchette*; Lat. *mercatus,* buying and selling], a pecuniary fine paid by the tenant to his lord for the marriage of one of the tenant's daughters. This custom obtained, with some difference, throughout all England and Wales, as also in Scotland. It is also denominated *gwahrmerched, i.e.,* maid's-fee (Co.Litt. 117b, 140a).

According to the old writers, no free man could be liable to pay such a fine, but only villeins, and therefore it could not be claimed by custom against all the tenants of a manor. But in later times a free man could take lands to hold by the service of marchet, if he liked to do so (Bract. 208b; Litt. 194, 209).

The fine was in respect of any loss of service which the lord might sustain. The idea that it was in any way connected with the mythical *jus primae noctis (q.v.)* —as that expression is commonly understood—is said to be quite without foundation; but see *Boerii Decisiones Burgidalenses,* fo. 532, cited at p. 423 of C. P. Cooper's *Catalogue of Books on Foreign Law,* 1849, from which it appears that in France some seigneurs had this right which was there termed *Markette, Marketa, Marquette, Merchet* or *Mercheta.*

Marchioness [Lat., *marchio*], a dignity in a woman answerable to that of marquess in a man, conferred either by creation, or by marriage with a marquess.

Mare Clausum, the title of a celebrated work by Selden, written in answer to the treatise called *Mare Liberum.*

Mare Liberum, a famous treatise by Grotius, to show that all nations have an equal right to use the sea.

Mareschall, or **Mareshal,** a marshal.

Marettum [Fr. *maret, marais,* a fen or marsh], marshy ground overflowed by the sea of great rivers (Co.Litt. 5).

Margarine. As to standards of measurement. etc., on the sale of margarine see the Weights and Measures Act, 1963, s. 21, Sch. IX.

For food standards and labelling see the orders made under the Food and Drugs Act, 1955, ss. 4, 7, 123.

Marginal notes, the notes in the margins of Acts of Parliament which shortly indicate the subject-matter or the substance of each section. They are not considered by Parliament and are not part of the Act, and anyone printing the Act is at liberty to alter them as he may think fit (*Sutton* v. *Sutton* (1883) 22 Ch. D. 513; *Att.-Gen.* v. *Great Eastern Ry.* (1879) 11 Ch.D. 465). A marginal note is not the subject of debate or amendment in Parliament, and it follows that during the passage of a Bill amendments may be made to a clause which extends its effect beyond the scope of the marginal note, which, nevertheless remains unamended. The note, therefore, would then become actually misleading if used as a guide to construction (*R.* v. *Bates* [1952] 2 All E.R. 842; *Chandler* v. *D.P.P.* [1964] A.C. 763).

It is permissible to approach a consideration of the general purpose of an Act and the mischief at which it is aimed with the marginal note in mind (*Stephens* v. *Cuckfield R.D.C.* [1960] 2 Q.B. 373).

In some private Acts the marginal notes may form part of the Act (*Re Woking, etc., Act, 1911* [1914] 1 Ch. 300).

Marinariorum capitaneus, an admiral or warden of the ports (Par.Antiq.).

Marinarius, a mariner or seaman (Par. Antiq.).

Marine, a general name for the navy of a kingdom or state; as also the whole economy of naval affairs, or whatever respects the building, rigging, arming, equipping, navigating, and fighting of ships. It comprehends also the government of naval armaments, and the state of all the persons employed therein, whether civil or military. Also one of the marines. See MARINES, ROYAL.

Marine boards. See the Merchant Shipping Act, 1894, ss. 244–245; S.I. 1972 No. 1977.

Marine insurance. See INSURANCE.

Marine Society. This society, which now carries on the *Warspite* training establishment, was formed in 1756 for the purpose of training boys to the sea-service. It was incorporated by the statute 1772, 12 Geo. 3, c. 67.

Marine store dealer. The business of a marine store dealer was regulated by the Merchant Shipping Act, 1894, ss. 538–542, but these sections have been repealed and replaced by the Scrap Metal Dealers Act, 1964. See SCRAP METALS.

Marine survey, an inspection of a ship carried out by a marine surveyor, *e.g.,* for purposes of insurance.

Mariner. Any mariner or seaman, being at sea, may make a nuncupative will (Statute of Frauds, 1677, s. 22; Wills Act, 1837, s. 11; Wills (Soldiers and Sailors) Act, 1918). See ACTUAL MILITARY SERVICE.

Marines, Royal, a military force drilled as infantry, whose special province is to serve on board ships of war when in commission. The force was first established about the middle of the 18th century. When serving on board ship, their discipline is regulated by the Naval Discipline Act, 1957, and when on shore, by the Army Act, 1955.

Marischal, an officer in Scotland, who, with the Lord High Constable, possessed a supreme itinerant jurisdiction in all crimes committed within a certain space of the court, wherever it might happen to be.

Mariscus, a marshy or fenny ground (*Domesday*; Co.Litt. 5a).

Maritagio amisso per defaltam, De, a writ which anciently lay under the Statute of Westminster II, 1285, c. 4, for a tenant in frank-marriage who had lost through his default the land so held by him.

Maritagium, the power which the lord had of disposing of his infant ward in marriage; also land given as a marriage portion; also a dowry of any kind. See FRANKMARRIAGE; MARRIAGE.

Maritagium est aut liberum aut servitio obligatum; liberum maritagium dicitur ubi donator vult quod terra sic data quieta sit et libera ab omni seculari servitio (Co.Litt. 21). (A marriage portion is either free or bound to service; it is called frank-marriage when the giver wills that land thus given be exempt from all secular service.)

Maritagium habere, Maritare, to have the free disposal of an heiress in marriage.

Marital [Lat. *maritus*], pertaining to a husband; incident to a husband.

Marital rights, rights of a husband. The expression was chiefly used to denote the right of a husband to property which his wife was entitled to during the treaty of marriage. If, after the engagement to marry, she made a voluntary conveyance of any part of that property without notice to the intended husband, it was considered a fraud on his marital rights, and therefore liable to be set aside, although he might not have known that she was entitled to the property; but since the Married Women's Property Act, 1882, this doctrine of fraud on marital rights has become obsolete. (See JUS MARITI.) The expression marital rights is now used as synonymous with conjugal rights (*q.v.*).

Maritima Angliae. In ancient patents running from Edward II to Henry VIII, this is used as meaning the sea coast. It it also said to mean the profits and emoluments of the sea which were anciently collected by the sheriff but were afterwards granted to the Lord High Admiral. See COSTERA.

Maritima incrementa, alluvion (*q.v.*), when caused by the action of the sea.

Maritime courts. These were formerly the High Court of Admiralty and its court of appeal, the Judicial Committee of the Privy Council. But by the Judicature Act, 1873, ss. 16, 34, the jurisdiction of the High Court of Admiralty was transferred to and vested in the High

Court of Justice. See ADMIRALTY COURT. Courts of Vice-Admiralty are established in British possessions beyond the seas, with jurisdiction over maritime causes, including those relating to prize (Colonial Courts of Admiralty Act, 1890; Statute of Westminster, 1931, ss. 5, 6).

Maritime frontiers, the outer limit of territorial waters.

Maritime law, the law relating to harbours, ships, and seamen. No system or code of maritime law has ever been issued by authority in Great Britain. The laws and practices that obtain are founded on the practice of merchants, the principles of the civil law, the laws of Oleron and Wisby, the works of jurisconsults, the judicial decisions of our own and foreign countries, etc.

The decisions of Lord Mansfield did much to fix the principles of the maritime law of England as also did those of Lord Stowell. The decisions of the latter chiefly have reference to questions of neutrality, and of the conflicting pretensions of belligerents and neutrals. It has been alleged that he favoured the claims of belligerents.

See ADMIRAL; ADMIRALTY; AFFREIGHTMENT; BILL OF LADING; CHARTERPARTY; CONSOLATO DEL MARE; DOMESDAY OF IPSWICH; HANSEATIC, ETC.; INSURANCE; LIEN; MERCHANT SHIPPING; OLERON, ETC.; RHODES, ETC.; UNDERWRITER; WHITE BOOK OF LONDON; WISBY, ETC.

Maritime lien, a claim which attaches to the *res, i.e.,* the ship, freight, or cargo. A maritime lien consists in the substantive right of putting into operation the Admiralty Court's executive function of arresting and selling the ship, so as to give a clear title to the purchaser and thereby enforcing distribution of the proceeds among the lien creditors in accordance with their several priorities and subject thereto rateably (*The Tolten* [1946] P. 135). It may arise *ex delicto, e.g.,* compensation for damage by collision, or *ex contractu,* for services rendered to the *res*; but it is strictly confined to services such as salvage, supply of necessaries to the ship, and seamen's wages (*The Ripon City* [1897] P. 226). Thus for ordinary work done upon a ship, such as repairs, there will be no maritime lien, but there may be a possessory lien so long as possession is retained (*Ex p. Willoughby* (1881) 16 Ch.D. 604). The privilege when once it attaches will not be affected by any change in the possession of the *res* (*The Henrich Björn* (1886) 11 App.Cas. 270; *Foong Tai & Co.* v. *Buchheister & Co.* [1908] A.C. 458).

Maritime territory, territorial waters (*q.v.*).

Mark [Welsh, *marc*; Sax., *mearc*; Dut., *merche*; Fr., *marque*], a token; an impression; a proof; evidence; licence of reprisals; a coin of the value of 13s. 4d.; a Scottish coin of the value of 1s. 2d.

As a measure of weight the mark was always two-thirds of the pound weight, just as, in the monetary system, it was two-thirds of the pound sterling.

In commerce it means a certain character struck or impressed on various kinds of commodities, to show the place where they were made, and the person who made them, or to witness that they have been viewed and examined by the officers charged with the inspection of manufactures; or to show that the duties imposed thereon have been paid. It is also used to indicate the price of a commodity. If anyone uses the mark of another to do him damage, an action will lie, and an injunction may be obtained. See TRADE MARKS.

Those who are unable to write, sign a cross, for their mark, when they execute any document. See MARKSMAN.

Market, Mercat [Lat. *mercatus*], a public time and place of buying and selling; also purchase and sale. It differs from the *forum*, or market of antiquity, which was a public market-place on one side only, the other sides being occupied by temples, theatres, etc.

A market can only be set up by virtue of a royal grant, or by long and immemorial usage, which presupposes a grant.

See the Markets and Fairs Clauses Act, 1847, and the Markets and Fairs (Weighing of Cattle) Acts, 1887 to 1926.

As to disturbance of a market, see *Goldsmid* v. *Great Eastern Ry.* (1884) 9 App.Cas. 927; *Att.-Gen.* v. *Horner* (*No. 2*) [1913] 2 Ch. 140. In *City of London Fruit Corporation* v. *Lyons, Sons & Co.*

[1936] Ch. 78, it was held that any member of the public has a right of access to a franchise market on payment of tolls and observance of bylaws for the purpose of conducting sales, and that a sale by auction in the vicinity was not a disturbance. See MARKETS AND FAIRS.

Market, Court of the clerk of the, the court of the clerk of the market was incident to every fair and market in the kingdom, to punish misdemeanours therein, as a court of *piepoudre* was to determine all disputes relating to private or civil property. The object of this jurisdiction was principally the recognisance of weights and measures, to try whether they were according to the true standard thereof, which standard was anciently committed to the custody of the bishop, who appointed some clerk under him to inspect abuses; and hence this officer, though usually a layman, was called the clerk of the market (4 Bl.Comm. 275).

His functions are now discharged by inspectors of weights and measures. See WEIGHTS AND MEASURES.

Market garden, a holding cultivated, wholly or mainly, for the purpose of the trade or business of market gardening (Agricultural Holdings Act, 1948, ss. 67–69; Agriculture Act, 1958, Sch. 1 para. 17, Sch. 2 Pt. II).

With regard to what were at common law fixtures and the absolute property of the landlord, a market gardener may before the determination of his tenancy remove fruit trees and fruit bushes planted, but not permanently set out; and if he fails to do so, they become the property of the landlord without any compensation being payable (Agricultural Holdings Act, 1948, s. 67 (1) (c)). Any tenant is entitled to remove and retain any engine, machinery, fencing or other fixture affixed by him to the holding, and any building erected by him thereon for which he is not entitled to compensation, and which he was under no obligation to erect, provided that he has given a month's previous notice in writing to the landlord, and that the landlord has not within such month elected to purchase at the fair value to an incoming tenant (s. 13).

Market geld, the toll of a market.

Market, Open. The normal rule upon the compulsory acquisition of land is that its value is to be the value if sold by a willing seller in the open market (Land Compensation Act, 1961, s. 5 (2); *Horn* v. *Sunderland Corporation* [1941] 2 K.B. 26). The same formula is used in the Coal Industry Nationalisation Act, 1946, s. 14 (4) (*Priestman Collieries* v. *Northern District Valuation Board* [1950] 2 K.B. 398).

Market overt, open market. Market overt in ordinary market towns is only held on the special days provided for the particular town, by charter or prescription; but in the City of London every day, except Sunday, is market day. The market place, or spot of ground set apart by custom for the sale of particular goods, is also in ordinary towns the only market overt, but in the City of London every shop in which goods are exposed publicly for sale is market overt, though only for such things as the owner professes to trade in (2 Bl.Comm. 449).

That part of London not within the City does not appear to have the privilege of market overt.

The doctrine of market overt is that all sales of goods made therein are binding not only on the parties but also on all other persons: so that if stolen goods are sold in market overt, the purchaser, if acting in good faith, acquires a valid title to them against the true owner (Sale of Goods Act, 1893, s. 22 (1)). If, however, the thief is convicted, a restitution order may be made. See RESTITUTION OF STOLEN GOODS.

A sale in market overt does not destroy the true owner's title unless made openly between sunrise and sunset (*Reid* v. *Commissioner of Police of the Metropolis* [1973] 1 Q.B. 551).

The doctrine of market overt does not apply to goods belonging to the Crown, and in the case of horses it is subject to statutory restrictions. See HORSE.

Market price. See VALUE.

Marketable security. For the purposes of the Stamp Act, 1891, the expression " marketable security " is defined by s. 82 of that Act as a security of such description as to be capable of being sold in any stock market in the United Kingdom (*Brown* v. *I.R.C.* [1895] 2 Q.B.

598). Stamp duty under this heading is abolished (Finance Act, 1973, s. 49, Sch. 22 Pt. V.

Markets and fairs. At common law a market or a fair is a franchise or privilege to establish meetings of persons to buy and sell. The privilege is in each case derived either from royal grant or from prescription implying such grant. It may be possessed by a lord of a manor or by a municipal corporation or other body corporate. The franchise carries with it the right to restrain, by *scire facias* (*q.v.*) or by injunction, any person from setting up another market or fair so near as to interfere with the exercise of the franchise. A disturbance of a market occurs where a person (a) sets up a rival market or (b) does some act whereby the market owner is deprived of the benefit of his franchise (*Scottish Co-operative Wholesale Society* v. *Ulster Farmers' Mart Co.* [1960] A.C. 63). The franchise also implied the right to hold a court of pie powder (*q.v.*); but the right to levy tolls (*q.v.*) is not implied and exists only where given by the grant, though it may be established by prescription (*Att.-Gen.* v. *Colchester Corporation* [1952] Ch. 586).

The difference between a fair and a market is that the fair is the larger gathering, and is held, say, only once or twice a year, while a market is held once or twice a week (2 Co.Inst. 406).

In course of time many fairs had ceased to fulfil any useful purpose, and had become mere gatherings of undesirable persons. The Fairs Act, 1871, empowered the Home Secretary to abolish any fair upon the representation of the justices of the petty sessional district in which it was held, and with the consent of the owner of the franchise. Under the Fairs Act, 1873, the Home Secretary may alter or lessen the days on which a fair is held upon the like representation of the justices, or upon the representation of the franchise owner.

The holding of unlawful fairs within the metropolitan police district can be summarily prevented under the Metropolitan Fairs Act, 1868.

In the great modern centres of population, markets are held either under special local Acts, generally embodying the Markets and Fairs Clauses Act, 1847. Powers are given for the provision and regulation of markets by the Food and Drugs Act, 1955, Part III.

As to the exercise of franchises and prescriptive rights formerly exercised in cities, boroughs or urban or rural districts, see S.I. 1974 No. 482, art. 17.

The owner of the market is under no obligation to provide stalls or pens. His duty is limited to providing a space in which buyers and sellers can meet and conduct their trading (*Brackenborough* v. *Spalding U.D.C.* [1942] A.C. 310).

The "hiring fairs" or "mops," still occasionally held for the purpose of the making of agreements between employer and domestic servants or farm labourers, are not fairs or markets in the legal sense. See STATUTE FAIR.

Marketzeld. See MARKET GELD.

Markpenny, a penny anciently paid at the town of Maldon by those who had gutters laid or made out of their houses into the streets (Jacob).

Marksman, a person who cannot write, and therefore makes his mark X in executing instruments, which mark is sufficient signature of a will (*In b. Clarke* (1858) 1 Sw. & Tr. 22) or of a writing which the Statute of Frauds, 1677, requires to be signed (*Baker* v. *Dening* (1838) 8 A. & E. 94).

Where a person who cannot write is desirous of subscribing his name to a document, another person writes it for him, and he identifies it as his signature by inscribing over it, or near it, a mark, usually a cross. He is hence called a marksman. It seems that if there is any peculiarity about the mark, the evidence of a person who is acquainted with the mark usually made by the alleged maker of the particular mark in question is admissible to prove it as the handwriting of the marksman, but not otherwise. See HANDWRITING.

Marlborough. See BLENHEIM.

Marlebridge, Statute of, the statute 1267, 52 Hen. 3, whereof cc. 1, 2, 4 and 15 (all dealing with distress) are still in force. The statute was passed at Marlborough, then known as Marlebridge or Marlberge.

Marque [Sax. *mearc*; Lat. *signum*], a mark; a sign; reprisals. See COUNTER-MARK; LETTERS OF MARK.

Marquis, or **Marquess** [Fr. *marquis*; Lat. *marchio*; Ger. *margrave*], one of the second order of nobility, next in order to a duke. The first marquis was Robert de Vere, Earl of Oxford, whom Richard II in 1386 made Marquis of Dublin.

A marquis is styled by the sovereign in royal commissions, etc., "our right trusty and entirely beloved cousin." His title is "most honourable."

The wife of a marquis is formally styled marchioness, but is informally known as Lady Carabas, or as the case may be; and his sons (other than the eldest son, who takes by courtesy the next lower title—usually an earldom—of the family) are by courtesy entitled to the prefix of "lord," while his daughters are entitled in like manner to the prefix of "lady." During his life the eldest son of his eldest son bears by courtesy the title of the family next in rank after that used by the eldest son. See LADY; LORD; PEERAGE.

Marquisate, the seignory of a marquis.

Marriage, the voluntary union for life of one man and one woman to the exclusion of all others (*Hyde* v. *Hyde* (1866) L.R. 1 P. & D. 130, 133), for the purpose of living together and procreating children (Ayliffe's *Parergon*, 2nd ed. 360; but see *Baxter* v. *Baxter* [1948] A.C. 274, 286), entered into in accordance with the rules as to the consanguinity (*q.v.*) or affinity (*q.v.*) of the parties, and their capacity to enter into and perform the duties of matrimony, and in accordance with the rites or formalities required either by the law of England or the place where the marriage takes place.

A marriage must be a Christian marriage, which, generally speaking, is to be taken as meaning monogamous but a polygamous marriage, valid according to the *lex loci,* may be the subject of matrimonial relief (Matrimonial Causes Act, 1973, ss. 11, 47).

As to capacity to marry, see CONSENSUS, ETC.

Marriage, to some extent, is a contract: the agreement of the parties is essential to a valid marriage (see AGREEMENT); but when it has been solemnised, marriage creates a personal relation and a status (*Niboyet* v. *Niboyet* (1878) 4 P.D. 1).

Under the canon law, as it existed before the rupture with Rome in the reign of Henry VIII, a marriage could be validly celebrated by a public celebration of the marriage service in a church, known as a celebration *in facie ecclesiae,* or by a clandestine celebration anywhere conducted by one in priest's orders. The common law adopted the canon law as stated above, but there was no need for the intervention of church or priest, openly or secretly, or at all. In early canonical theory, a marriage did not exist until the man and woman concerned had become one flesh, and this was the basis of Peter Lombard's theory, developed in the twelfth century, and adopted fully into English law, concerning *sponsalia,* or espousals. *Sponsalia per verba ae praesenti,* a promise of present marriage was a recognised marriage; *sponsalia per verba de futuro* became an effective marriage when sexual intercourse took place between the parties. The Council of Trent, in 1563, modified the canon law in a manner immaterial from the point of view of the English law, which of course took no cognisance of the proceedings of the Council. But after the Reformation the common law put those in priest's or deacon's orders of the Church of England on the same footing as those in priest's orders of the Roman and Eastern Churches. The Convocation of the Province of Canterbury in 1603 passed certain canons, known as the Canons of 1603, which laid down, among other things, that before the celebration of a marriage there must either be a licence or a publication of banns. But these canons, although binding to the extent that persons who violated them were liable to ecclesiastical censure, were never part of the law of the land, which therefore down to 1754 remained what it had been before the Reformation. A number of clergymen officiating in churches and chapels which were free from the visitation of the ordinary found it to their profit to celebrate marriages without banns or licence: but after the Commissioners for Ecclesiastical Causes had, about 1684, taken action against such clergymen, marriages of this kind ceased to be celebrated on a large scale by anyone who had anything to lose and the business passed mainly into the hands of the Fleet (*q.v.*) parsons, the process being accelerated by the statutes 1694, 6 & 7 Will. 3, c. 6; 1695, 7 & 8 Will. 3, c. 35; and 1711, 10 Anne, c. 19, s. 176, which imposed pecuniary penalties for marrying, or getting married, without either licence or banns. The profits, however, were large, and many clandestine marriages continued to take place even outside the Fleet and its purlieus until Lord Hardwicke's Act, 1753, made it impossible to contract any valid clandestine marriage. That Act provided that a marriage celebrated without publication of banns or licence should be void; that a marriage celebrated elsewhere than in a parish church or public chapel in which banns were usually published should be void in the absence of a special licence from the Archbishop of Canterbury for its celebration elsewhere; and that anyone solemnising a marriage without banns or licence should be guilty of felony, punishable with fourteen years' transportation. The Act had, however, unfortunate effects. It made invalid marriages of dissenters and Roman Catholics celebrated according to the rites of their respective communions, which antecedently had been valid. Such marriages had been valid in the case of Roman Catholics, because a Roman Catholic priest was recognised by the common law as being in priest's orders; and they were valid, in the case of dissenters, by force of the Toleration Act, 1688. But Lord Hardwicke's Act, 1753, gave the Church of England the sole right of celebrating valid marriages; and this state of things continued until it was terminated by the enactment of the Marriage Act, 1837.

As to the interest acquired by each of the spouses in the personalty of the other, see ADMINISTRATION; DISTRIBUTION; JUS MARITI; NEXT-OF-KIN.

A husband was formerly liable for all the debts and liabilities of his wife contracted before the marriage, but this rule was broken down by the Married Women's Property Act, 1870, s. 12, which provided that a husband should not be liable for his wife's ante-nuptial debts. See MARRIED WOMEN'S PROPERTY.

The Marriage Acts, 1823 and 1826, were consolidated by the Marriage Act, 1949, and the statute law is contained in the Marriage Acts, 1949 to 1970. These are the Marriage Act, 1949, the Marriage Act, 1949 (Amendment) Act, 1954, the Marriage Acts (Amendment) Act, 1958, the Marriage (Secretaries of Synagogues) Act, 1959, the Marriage (Enabling) Act, 1960, the Marriage (Wales and Monmouthshire) Act, 1962, and the Marriage (Registrar General's Licence) Act, 1970. See also the Family Law Reform Act, 1969, s. 2.

S. 5 of the Act of 1949 sets out the four methods by which marriages according to the rites of the Church of England may be solemnised: by publication of banns (*q.v.*); by special licence granted by the Archbishop of Canterbury or any person authorised by virtue of the Ecclesiastical Licences Act, 1533; by common licence granted by the appropriate ecclesiastical authorities; and by certificate of a superintendent registrar, this method not being exclusive to Church of England marriages, but applying also to other forms of marriage. Marriages of Quakers, Jews, Roman Catholics and Protestant dissenters are specially provided for. The Marriage Act, 1949 (Amendment) Act, 1954, deals with marriage in registration districts in which neither party to the marriage resides. See also the Marriage Acts (Amendment) Act, 1958 (registration of places of worship). Ss. 6 (4), 9, 11 (2), 15 (1) (*b*), 16 (1) (*b*), 35 (3), 72 of the Marriage Act, 1949, have been extended to Wales and Monmouthshire (Marriage (Wales and Monmouthshire) Act, 1962).

A clergyman of the Church of England or the Church in Wales is not bound to solemnise the marriage of a divorced person whose former spouse is still living or to permit such a marriage in his church (Matrimonial Causes Act, 1965, s. 8 (2)).

Where a man and woman have lived together as man and wife there is a rebuttable presumption that they lived together in consequence of a valid marriage and not in a state of concubinage (*Re Taylor* [1961] 1 W.L.R. 9).

MARRIAGE

A person born biologically male cannot contract a valid marriage as a woman despite a sex-change operation (*Corbett* v. *Corbett* (*orse. Ashley*) [1971] P. 110).

Proceedings for a declaration as to the validity of a marriage or as to a person's matrimonial status are assigned to the Family Division (*q.v.*) of the High Court (Administration of Justice Act, 1970, s. 1, Sch. 1).

As to marriages governed by foreign law or celebrated abroad under English law see the Matrimonial Causes Act, 1973, s. 14.

The Foreign Marriage Acts, 1892 to 1947, provide for the marriage of British subjects abroad; these Acts provide for what are known as diplomatic and consular marriages. A marriage between parties one of whom at least is British may be validly solemnised before an ambassador, governor, high commissioner, resident, consul or other marriage officer at that person's residence in a foreign country. S. 22 of the Act of 1892, as replaced and amended by s. 2 of the Act of 1947, provides for naval, air force and military marriages abroad where one of the parties is a member of the forces serving in the territory where the marriage takes place, or is employed in certain capacities in that territory. See also the Family Law Reform Act, 1969, s. 2 (1) (*a*) (persons under 21). The Colonial Marriages Act, 1865, makes colonial marriages valid everywhere, subject to certain restrictions. The Marriage of British Subjects (Facilities) Act, 1915 (amended by the Marriage of British Subjects (Facilities) Amendment Act, 1916; Marriage Act, 1939, s. 2), facilitates marriage between British subjects resident in the United Kingdom and British subjects resident in other parts of H.M. dominions or in British protectorates.

Marriage of British subjects with foreigners at home and abroad is facilitated by the Marriage with Foreigners Act, 1906. As to persons under twenty-one, see the Family Law Reform Act, 1969, s. 2 (1) (*b*).

Under the Royal Marriages Act, 1772, no descendant of George II, other than the issue of princesses married into foreign families, may contract matrimony without the previous consent of the sovereign, provided, however, that any such descendant, being over the age of twenty-five, may, upon giving twelve months' notice to the Privy Council, contract a marriage of which the sovereign disapproves unless in the meantime both Houses of Parliament expressly declare their disapproval.

Marriage formerly signified not only the union of man and wife, but also the right of a guardian by tenure to bestow his ward in marriage, which the law gave to the lord, not for his benefit only, but so that he should match the ward in a good family without disparagement (see MARITAGIUM). If an infant tenant by knight's service refused such a marriage, the lord was entitled to the value of the marriage, that is, to the amount which he would have received for giving his ward in marriage; but a guardian in socage could make no profit by the marriage of his ward (Litt. 110, 123).

See AFFINITY; AGE; BIGAMY; BREACH OF PROMISE; CONSANGUINITY; CONSORTIUM; DECEASED WIFE'S SISTER OR DECEASED BROTHER'S WIDOW; DISPARAGEMENT; DIVORCE; FLEET MARRIAGES; FORFEITURE OF MARRIAGE; GRETNA GREEN MARRIAGE; HUSBAND AND WIFE; INFANT; MARITAL RIGHTS; MARRIED WOMEN'S PROPERTY; MORGANATIC MARRIAGE; NECESSARIES; RESTRAINT OF MARRIAGE; SETTLEMENT; SURVIVORSHIP.

Marriage articles, the heads of an agreement for a marriage settlement. Expressions and limitations in these articles are allowed a more liberal meaning consistently with intention than formal conveyances and settlements.

Marriage brokage, a consideration paid for contriving a marriage, and illegal as contrary to public policy, so that money paid under it may be recovered back (*Herman* v. *Charlesworth* [1905] 2 K.B. 123).

Marriage officer, an official who can celebrate marriages in British possessions abroad as well as in foreign countries. The term includes an ambassador, minister or *chargé d'affaires*; or, under appointment in writing by the ambassador, etc., the *locum tenens* of the ambassador, etc., or any secretary of the embassy; and, if holding a warrant from the Secretary of State, any British consul,

consul-general, vice-consul, pro-consul, consular agent, governor, high commissioner or resident (Foreign Marriage Act, 1892, ss. 11, 24).

Marriage, Promise of. See BREACH OF PROMISE.

Marriage settlement, an arrangement made before marriage, and in consideration of it, whereby real or personal property is settled for the benefit of the husband and wife and the issue of the marriage. There is an express saving for such a settlement in the Married Women's Property Act, 1882, s. 19. The Married Women's Property Act, 1907, invalidates a settlement made by a female infant unless confirmed after attaining 21, but without prejudice to settlements under the Infants Settlement Act, 1855.

Marriage settlements of land not by way of trust for sale are settlements within the meaning of the Settled Land Act, 1925, s. 1, and must be effected by two instruments, the vesting deed and the trust instrument. Settlements of land on trust for sale should also be effected by two deeds, the conveyance on trust for sale and the trust instrument. See SETTLED LAND; TRUST INSTRUMENT; VESTING INSTRUMENT.

Marriage settlements vary according as the property settled consists of real or personal estate. If it consists of real estate the property may be settled on the husband or the wife, according to the source of the property, for life, with remainder to the first and other sons in tail with remainder to the daughters in tail, and the wife or husband and younger children being respectively provided for by a jointure or determinable life interest and portions charged on the estates; or it may be conveyed to trustees upon trust for sale and to hold the proceeds upon the trusts declared by a deed of even date, which declares the trusts of the proceeds in practically the same form as a settlement of personal estate. If the property to be settled consists of personal estate, as stocks or shares, it is assigned to trustees upon trust for sale and to invest and pay the income to the husband and wife, according to the source of the fortune, successively for life, and on the death of the survivor to hold the capital in trust for the issue of the marriage as the

parents or the survivor may appoint, and in default of appointment for the children equally.

On granting a decree of divorce or nullity or judicial separation or at any time thereafter the Family Division may make an order varying for the benefit of the parties to the marriage and of the children of the family any ante-nuptial or post-nuptial settlement made on the parties to the marriage and may make an order extinguishing or reducing the interest of either of the parties to the marriage under such settlement (Matrimonial Causes Act, 1973, s. 24). Settlements may also be varied under the Inheritance (Provision for Family and Dependants) Act, 1975, s. 2 (1) (*f*).

Marriage value, the value of a leasehold interest in land when merged with the freehold reversion (*Trocette Property Co.* v. *Greater London Council* (1974) 28 P. & C.R. 408, C.A.).

Marriage, Value of, a fine which a tenant holding by knight's service had on his marriage to pay to his lord. As to the writs available to the lord, see FORFEITURE OF MARRIAGE; VALUE OF MARRIAGE.

Marriages, Registration of. See REGISTRATION OF MARRIAGES.

Married women's property. At common law a husband became on his marriage absolutely entitled to all choses in possession belonging to his wife in her own right (including those acquired after marriage), and to the whole of the rents and profits of her lands during the continuance of the marriage, except in so far as such property was the separate estate (*q.v.*) of the wife. This rule was broken down in part by the Matrimonial Causes Act, 1857, ss. 21, 25, the Married Women's Property Act, 1870, ss. 1, 7, 8, the Married Women's Property Act (1870) Amendment Act, 1874, the Married Women's Property Act, 1882, the Married Women's Property Act, 1893, and the Bankruptcy Act, 1914, ss. 125, 168, Sch. 6.

Proceedings under the Married Women's Property Act, 1882, s. 17, as to the title to property are assigned to the Family Division (*q.v.*) of the High Court (Administration of Justice Act,

1970, s. 1, Sch. 1). See HUSBAND AND WIFE.

The Law of Property Act, 1925, s. 170, provides that a married woman is able to acquire as well from her husband as from any other person, and hold, any interest in property real or personal either solely or jointly with any other person (whether or not including her husband) as a trustee or personal representative, in like manner as if she were a *feme sole* and that no interest in such property shall vest or be deemed to have vested in the husband by reason only of the acquisition by his wife. A married woman is able, without her husband, to dispose of, or to join in disposing of, any interest in real or personal property held by her solely or jointly with any other person (whether or not including her personal representatives) as trustee or personal representative, in like manner as if she were a *feme sole*. This does not prejudicially affect any beneficial interest of the husband.

The Law Reform (Married Women and Tortfeasors) Act, 1935, s. 1 (amended by the Law Reform (Husband and Wife) Act, 1962, Sch.), provides that a married woman shall be capable of acquiring, holding, and disposing of, any property, and be capable of rendering herself, and being rendered, liable in respect of any tort, contract, debt or obligation and be capable of suing and being sued in tort or in contract or otherwise and be subject to the law relating to bankruptcy and to the enforcement of judgments and orders, in all respects as if she were a *feme sole*. S. 3 of the Act abolished a husband's liability for a wife's torts committed by her before or after the marriage, and for any contract entered into, or debt or obligation incurred, by her before the marriage.

If any question arises as to the right of a husband or wife to money derived from any allowance made by the husband for the expenses of the matrimonial home or for similar purposes, or to any property acquired out of such money, the money or property shall, in the absence of any agreement between them to the contrary, be treated as belonging to the husband and wife in equal shares (Married Women's Property Act, 1964).

A husband and wife living together may jointly elect that the wife's earned income shall be taxed as if she were a single person (Finance Act, 1971, s. 23, Sch. 4; Finance Act, 1976, s. 36 (10)).

The Married Women (Restraint upon Anticipation) Act, 1949, abolished restraints upon anticipation or alienation attached to the enjoyment of property by a woman.

See ADMINISTRATION; HUSBAND AND WIFE; NECESSARIES; PARAPHERNALIA; SEPARATE ESTATE.

Marrow, author of a book written in the reign of Henry VII, and said to be still in manuscript, on the office of justice of the peace, quoted by later writers, such as Fitzherbert and Lambard.

Marshal, or **Mareschal,** an officer who has the care or command of horses.

An officer called a marshal attends each High Court judge on circuit. He is the personal officer of the judge and performs the duties of secretary. He is appointed for each circuit by the judge; the judge pays his travelling expenses, and he receives a small fee out of public funds for each day during the circuit. He formerly had to swear the grand jury (*q.v.*). He is usually a recently-called barrister and only acts as marshal at the beginning of his career. A scheme to enable pupils to sit as marshals in county courts has been introduced.

The Marshal of the Admiralty Court (*q.v.*) is entrusted with the following duties: execution of all warrants issued by the court; appraisement and sale of condemned ships and cargoes; removal of ships, *sub judice*, from port to port on removal being ordered; receipt and subsequent payment into court of all money arising out of execution of process; ascertaining the sufficiency or otherwise of bail; and the custody of embargoed ships.

The Marshal of the Marshalsea was the keeper of the Marshalsea Prison (*q.v.*).

Marshal, Earl. See EARL MARSHAL.

Marshal of the King's Household. This officer is mentioned in the statute 1353,

27 Edw. 3, st. 2, c. 6. He was quite distinct from the Earl Marshal. Apart from his duties in the administration of the royal household he, along with the Steward of the King's Household, adjudicated in the Court of the Marshalsea (*q.v.*), and both of them were nominally judges of the Palace Court (*q.v.*). The office of Marshal of the King's Household no longer exists.

Marshal of the Queen's Bench, an officer who had the custody of the Queen's Bench Prison. The statute 1841, 5 & 6 Vict. c. 22, abolished this office, and substituted an officer called Keeper of the Queen's Prison.

Marshalling. In the administration of the estates of deceased persons, marshalling consists of arranging the assets so as to give effect to the priority of debts. In the distribution of assets, marshalling takes place where there are two claimants, A and B, and two funds, X and Y, both of which are available to satisfy A's claim, but only Y is available for that of B, and A is compelled to have recourse to the X fund in order that the Y fund may be left for B. Or, what is the same thing, if A has been paid out of the Y fund, B is allowed to have recourse to the X fund, against which he had originally no claim. Thus, if a legacy is given to A charged on real estate, and another not so charged is given to B, the personal estate not being sufficient to pay both, A will be compelled to satisfy his legacy wholly or partially out of the real estate, so that B's legacy may be paid in full out of the personalty.

These doctrines have not been affected by the vesting of real property in personal representatives (Administration of Estates Act, 1925, s. 2) except that (by s. 34 of the Act) some alteration is made in the order of administration of solvent estates. See ADMINISTRATION.

A testator was formerly said to " marshal his own assets " in favour of a charity when he directed a legacy to a charity to be paid out of his pure personal estate, for the law did not marshal assets in favour of charities, and, therefore, without such a direction, the legacy would have abated in the proportion of the impure to the pure personalty. See ABATEMENT OF LEGACIES; MORTMAIN.

The doctrine of marshalling also applies to mortgages. Thus, if the owner of two estates mortgages them both to one person, A, and then one of them to another, B, without B having notice of A's mortgage, B may insist that A's debt shall be satisfied out of the other estate (the one not mortgaged to B) so far as it will extend.

Marshalsea, Court of the, a court originally held before the Steward and Marshal of the Royal Household, to administer justice between the sovereign's domestic servants, that they might not be drawn into other courts, and their service become lost. It held pleas of all trespasses committed within the verge of the court (twelve miles round the sovereign's residence) where only one of the parties was in the royal service (in which case the inquest was taken by a jury of the country); and of all debts, contracts, and covenants where both of the contracting parties belonged to the royal household, and then the inquest was composed of men of the household only. But this court being ambulatory, Charles I erected a new court of record, called the *curia palatii*, or Palace Court, to be held before the steward of the household and knight marshal, and the steward of the court or his deputy, with jurisdiction to hold plea of all manner of personal actions whatsoever which should arise between any parties within twelve miles of the royal palace at Whitehall, not including the city of London.

The court was held once a week for causes under £20, together with the ancient Court of Marshalsea, in the borough of Southwark, and a writ of error lay thence to the Court of Queen's Bench. It was abolished by the County Courts Act, 1849.

Marshalsea Prison, a debtors' prison, used down to 1842, when it, the Queen's Bench Prison (*q.v.*), and the Fleet Prison (*q.v.*) were abolished and replaced by the Queen's Prison (*q.v.*). It had originally been the prison of the Court of the Marshalsea, and had been in existence from, at any rate, the year 1300. See DEBT, IMPRISONMENT FOR.

Mart, a market, a place of public traffic or sale.

Marten's Act, the Public Health (Interments) Act, 1879.

Martial law, the law as administered down to 1521 in the Court of Chivalry (*q.v.*); military law (*q.v.*); acts done for the purpose of defeating invaders or rebels; the supersession of ordinary law and the temporary government of a country or parts of it by military tribunals when this is done in pursuance of a proclamation by the Crown or of notice by the military authorities, but if it is done under the authority of statute, there is no martial law.

Martial law is now usually and properly used in the fourth of the senses mentioned above. The expression in this sense is, however, something of a misnomer. Martial law in this sense is, in fact, no law at all. It is not merely extra-legal; it is also illegal (1 Bl.Comm. 413).

There is no provision for any such law in our legal system; and acts done in pursuance of it require to be covered by an Act of Indemnity in order to protect from legal proceedings those by or by whose orders such acts were done: see *e.g.*, the Indemnity Act, 1920, relating to acts done in the war of 1914–18.

Martial law was prohibited by the Petition of Right, 1628, but was authorised in Ireland by the statutes 1803, 43 Geo. 3, c. 117, and 1833, 3 & 4 Wm. 4, c. 4, and the Restoration of Order in Ireland Act, 1920. It was proclaimed in Jamaica without authority by Governor Eyre in 1865, but was followed by a Jamaica Act of Indemnity, which was held good in *Phillips* v. *Eyre* (1870) L.R. 6 Q.B. 1.

Martinmas, the feast of St. Martin of Tours, on November 11, sometimes corrupted into *martilmas* or *martlemas*. It is the third of the four cross quarter-days of the year. It was formerly sometimes called Martinmas in Winter, in order to distinguish it from the feast of the Translation of St. Martin, July 4. In many parts of England it was the general time of hiring farm servants. Church-scot (*q.v.*) used to be paid on this day. See OLD MARTINMAS.

Martyria, a figure of rhetoric, by which the speaker brings his own experience in proof of what he advances.

Masagium, a messuage.

Masculine. Statutes passed prior to 1850 frequently declare that words in them which import the masculine gender shall be deemed to include females, unless there is something in the Act inconsistent therewith. By the statute 1850, 13 & 14 Vict. c. 21, s. 4, this provision was made general. See now the Interpretation Act, 1889.

Mass. A gift for masses for the souls of the dead is not void for superstition (*Bourne* v. *Keane* [1919] A.C. 815). See SUPERSTITIOUS USES, ETC.

The infliction of a " mass punishment " is unlawful unless authorised in some way by statute (*Patterson* v. *District Commissioner for Accra* [1948] A.C. 341, 350).

Massachusetts Company. See COMPANIES, CHARTERED.

Massamore, Massy more, Massamora, an ancient name for a dungeon, derived from the Moorish language, perhaps as far back as the time of the Crusades.

Master [Dut. *meester*; Fr. *maistre*; [Lat. *magister*], a director; a governor; a teacher; one who has servants; the head of a college; the captain of a ship; an officer of the Supreme Court.

Master and servant. In modern statutes it is usual to speak of employer and employee instead of master and servant. The relation of master and servant exists where one person, for pay or other valuable consideration, enters into the service of another and devotes to him his personal labour for an agreed period. The test of such a service seems to be, first, that the servant is bound to obey the reasonable commands of his master to do all acts falling within the scope of his employment, and secondly, that the master has the power of dismissing the servant on his neglecting his duty, or for incompetence or gross misconduct, or on giving notice of dismissal in accordance with the express or implied terms of the contract.

It would also seem that the service must be exclusive, *i.e.*, that the servant cannot work for anyone else, without his master's permission, unless his service is limited to certain times or otherwise (*Lumley* v. *Gye* (1853) 2 E. & B. 216).

Servants are sometimes divided into menial (*q.v.*) or domestic (*q.v.*) servants, labourers and workmen, and apprentices. The rules of law as to the respective rights and duties of the master and servant in the absence of express agreement vary to some extent according to the nature of the employment.

The master may bring an action against any person who injures his servant, if he thus loses the services of his servant, and thereby suffers actual damage (see SERVICE, CONTRACT OF; TORT), and the master has an action against any person who knowingly entices away a servant or harbours and detains him after having been apprised of the contract.

On the other hand, the servant is frequently the agent of his master for certain purposes, and accordingly has power to bind him by his acts (see AGENT); and if the servant in the course of his employment tortiously causes injury to any person, the master is liable. Therefore, if a servant in driving his master's vehicle on his master's business injures a person by negligent driving, the master is liable in damages to that person, even although the servant may have gone out of his proper course for his own business or amusement; but if the servant takes the vehicle out without his master's orders and for his own business or amusement, then the master is not liable for his negligence.

A master owes a duty to his servant to exercise due care and skill in respect of the adequacy of plant, the competence of fellow employees, and the propriety of the system of work (*Wilsons & Clyde Coal Co.* v. *English* [1938] A.C. 57). The common law liability of the master has been extended by the Employer's Liability (Defective Equipment) Act, 1969. Where an employee suffers personal injury in the course of his employment in consequence of a defect in equipment provided by his employer and the defect is attributable wholly or partly to the fault of a third party (whether identified or not), the injury is deemed to be also attributable to negligence on the part of the employer. The employer is at liberty to plead contributory negligence on the part of the employee (s. 1).

It is the duty of every employer to ensure so far as is reasonably practicable, the health, safety and welfare at work of all his employees (Health and Safety at Work etc. Act, 1974, s. 2). It is the duty of an employer to ensure, so far as practicable, that persons not in his employment are not exposed to risks. Self-employed persons are under a similar obligation (s. 3). General duties of care are imposed on persons concerned with premises with regard to persons other than their employees (s. 4). There is obligation on designers, manufacturers, importers or suppliers of articles with regard to their safety in use (s. 6). It is the duty of an employee at work to take reasonable care for his own safety and that of others (s. 7). Interference with safety appliances is prohibited (s. 8). No charge may be levied in respect of safety precautions (s. 9). Regulations and approved codes of practice may be made under ss. 15, 16. Failure to observe a code of practice does not render a person liable to any civil or criminal proceedings but is admissible in evidence (ss. 17, 47). As to enforcement, see ss. 18–28. As to offences, see ss. 33–42. As to appeals in connection with licensing provisions, see s. 44. As to default powers, see s. 45. See further the Employment Protection Act, 1975, s. 116, Sch. 15.

The Contracts of Employment Act, 1972 (as amended by the Employment Protection Act, 1975, Sch. 16 Pt. II), lays down the minimum periods of notice to terminate employment and requires employers to give to their employees written statements concerning the main terms of their contracts of employment. Employees affected by the Act must, for their part, give not less than one week's notice to terminate contracts of employment. An employee who participates in a strike or is locked out by his employer loses that week for purposes of remuneration but not for purposes of reckoning continuity of employment. An employee is an individual who has entered into or works under a contract with an employer, whether the contract be for manual labour, clerical work or otherwise, be expressed or implied, oral or in writing, and whether it be a contract of service or of apprenticeship.

A Crown servant is not within the Act (*Wood* v. *Leeds Area Health Authority* (*Training*) [1974] I.C.R. 535).

See also the Local Government Act, 1972, s. 256 (2); the Social Security Act, 1973, s. 91, and the Trade Union and Labour Relations Act, 1974, Sch. 5 and the Amendment Act of 1976; the Employment Protection Act, 1975, ss. 85, 89, 120, 122, Schs. 5, 11.

Sex discrimination is rendered unlawful. See SEX DISCRIMINATION.

A master must insure against liability for bodily injury or disease sustained by his servant arising out of and in the course of his employment (Employers' Liability (Compulsory Insurance) Act, 1969).

Contracts of service are exempt from stamp duty (Finance Act, 1964, s. 23).

The Employment and Training Act, 1973, established the Manpower Services Commission and the Employment Services Agency and reformed the arrangements for providing employment and training services. See further the Employment Protection Act, 1975, s. 115, Sch. 14.

A servant may be a joint tortfeasor within the meaning of the Law Reform (Married Women and Tortfeasors) Act, 1935, s. 6; though a servant does not undertake to indemnify a master against liability for his (the servant's) negligence, but merely to use the best of his ability, the servant may be liable to contribute a proportion of the damages resulting from his own negligence (*Jones* v. *Manchester Corporation* [1952] 2 Q.B. 852; *Lister* v. *Romford Ice and Cold Storage Co.* [1957] A.C. 555).

Under the Employers and Workmen Act, 1875, justices of the peace had jurisdiction in many cases where questions arose as to the rights or liabilities of either party to a contract of service, and county courts also had jurisdiction in some of those matters. The Act was repealed by the Statute Law (Repeals) Act, 1973. The Employment Protection Act, 1975, contains provisions entitling an employee to a " guaranteed payment " where he is not provided with work (ss. 22–33), provisions in favour of women employees who become pregnant (ss. 34–52). An employee is entitled to a written statement of reasons for his dismissal (s. 70) and an itemised pay statement (s. 81).

See COMMON EMPLOYMENT; COUNCIL OF CONCILIATION; EMBEZZLEMENT; FACTORIES; FALSE CHARACTER; JUS TERTII; MALE SERVANTS; TRUCK ACTS; WORKMEN'S COMPENSATION ACT. Generally as to dismissal see MISCONDUCT; REDUNDANCY; TRADE UNIONS; GOLDEN HANDSHAKE.

Master in Lunacy. See COURT OF PROTECTION.

Master of the Bench, the full title of a bencher (*q.v.*) of any one of the four Inns of Court.

Master of the Buckhounds, one of the officers of the royal household down to 1901, when the royal buckhounds were abolished and the office of Master of the Buckhounds ceased to exist. The Master had been one of the officers who went in and out with the Ministry. His function was to act as master of the packs of staghounds which, at the cost of the Civil List, hunted the country to the west of Windsor. The Master was always a peer. He was in theory a subordinate of the Master of the Horse.

Master of the Court of Wards and Liveries, the chief official of the Court of Wards and Liveries (*q.v.*). His office was abolished, along with the court, in 1660.

Master of the Crown Office, the Crown coroner and attorney in the criminal department of the Court of Queen's Bench, who prosecuted at the relation of some private person or common informer, the Crown being the nominal prosecutor: see the statute 1843, 6 & 7 Vict. c. 20. He is now an officer of the Supreme Court. See CROWN OFFICE.

Master of the Faculties, an officer under the archbishop, who grants licences and dispensations, etc. The judge of the provincial Court of Canterbury and York became *ex officio* Master of the Faculties on the first vacancy occurring after the passing of the Public Worship Regulation Act, 1874. See ARCHES, DEAN OF THE.

Master of the Horse. This official was originally in actual charge of the royal stables. That, however, is now entrusted to a permanent official known as the

Crown Equerry. The Master of the Horse, who is always a peer of high rank, is one of the three principal officers of the household, the first being the Lord Steward (*q.v.*) if and when that functionary exists, and the second being the Lord Chamberlain (*q.v.*). The Master of the Horse, like the Lord Chamberlain and other chief officers of the household, goes in and out with the Ministry. His chief present function is to attend the sovereign on State occasions.

Various holders of the office during the last three hundred years have claimed to act as Serjeant of the Silver Scullery when a coronation took place.

Master of the Household. The officer of the royal household who is now styled the Lord Steward (*q.v.*), was anciently sometimes styled the Grand Master of the King's Household, but the latter title has been disused for centuries, and the title of Master of the Household is now applied to the head of the Department of that name. The management of the household is in the hands of this officer. See BOARD OF GREEN CLOTH; SENESCHAL.

Master of the King's Musters. See MUSTER-MASTER GENERAL.

Master of the Mint. Before 1870 there was an official known as the Master of the Mint who had charge of the Mint (*q.v.*): there was a Deputy Mint Master: and each of them was paid a salary. Now under the Coinage Act, 1971 (as amended by the Government Trading Funds Act, 1973, s. 7), the Chancellor of the Exchequer is styled the Master Worker and Warden of the Mint and there is a Deputy Master of the Mint appointed by the Treasury.

Master of the Ordnance, an officer dating from the reign of Henry VIII, to whom was entrusted the care of the king's artillery and ordnance or munitions of war. His modern representative in normal times is the Master-General of the Ordnance, a military officer who is a member of the Ministry of Defence. See ORDNANCE, BOARD OF.

Master of the Posts. Henry VIII created this officer for the purpose of making arrangements to have post-horses provided in such places and in such numbers as to ensure the speedy transit of the king's letters. In the reign of Elizabeth I the transmission of foreign correspondence, which had previously been arranged by merchants, was entrusted to the Master of the Posts, whose title was changed to Chief Postmaster. Between 1635 and 1660 the Crown and the Cromwellian authorities asserted the sole right to carry letters, and the Chief Postmaster became the Postmaster General for Foreign Parts. See POST OFFICE.

Master of Reports and Entries, an officer of the Court of Chancery. The office was abolished by the Court of Chancery Act, 1855, s. 5.

Master of the Rolls [*magister rotulorum*], originally the chief of a body of officers called the Masters in Chancery, of whom there were eleven others, including the Accountant-General. The Master of the Rolls was originally keeper of the records and acted as assistant to the Lord Chancellor, like the other Masters in Chancery. Subsequently, in the reign of Edward I, he acquired judicial authority in matters within the jurisdiction of the Court of Chancery, and in the reign of Henry VI bills for relief were addressed to him as well as to the Lord Chancellor. In more modern times, any suit, petition, etc., could be heard in the first instance by the Master of the Rolls, as well as by the Vice-Chancellors. But down to 1827 the Master of the Rolls sat in the evening from six to ten o'clock, the theory being that he, as being only the deputy of the Lord Chancellor, ought not to sit at the same time as the Lord Chancellor, who up to then had dealt with such matters as now come before a judge of the Chancery Division. Until 1873 he was qualified to sit in the House of Commons (see OFFICE OF PROFIT). By the Judicature Act, 1873, s. 5, the Master of the Rolls was made a member of the High Court of Justice, and by s. 6 an *ex officio* member of the Court of Appeal, while under the Judicature Act, 1881, s. 2 (now the Judicature Act, 1925, s. 6 (2), he became a judge of the Court of Appeal only, but he still retains his non-judicial duties as custodian of the records. He admits solicitors of the Supreme Court. See SOLICITORS. His powers as to matters formerly appertaining to the Petty Bag Office were preserved by the Solicitors

MASTER

Act, 1888, s. 5. He is Chairman of the Advisory Council on Public Records and is responsible for the records of the Chancery of England. (Public Records Act, 1958, ss. 1, 7).

Master of the Seal Office, an officer of the Court of King's Bench who kept the great seal for sealing of writs in this court and the Common Pleas.

Master of the Temple, the clergyman of the Temple Church. His salary is paid partly by the Crown and partly by the two Temples; and the Temples provide him with a residence near the Temple Church. The nomination is in the hands of the Crown. These arrangements are provided for by the lease from James I under which the Temples are held. See READER.

Master of the Wardrobe, an officer of the royal household who had charge of the robes of deceased kings and queens in the Tower of London and of all curtains, bedding, cloth for liveries, etc., in the palaces of the reigning sovereign. He is mentioned in the statute 1597, 39 Eliz. 1, c. 7. He has disappeared, although the Mistress of the Robes (*q.v.*) remains.

Master of the Wards, the judge of the Court of Wards and Liveries (*q.v.*): see the statute 1540, 32 Hen. 8, c. 46, s. 2.

Masters Extraordinary. The full title of these officers was Masters Extraordinary in Chancery; and under that designation they were abolished by the statute 1853, 16 & 17 Vict. c. 78, which created the London Commissioners (*q.v.*) and the commissioners for oaths (*q.v.*) to perform the duties vested in the Masters Extraordinary. Masters Extraordinary were first heard of in the reign of James I (*Hargrave's Law Tracts* 294).

Masters in Chancery. The full title of these officers, whose office was of great antiquity (see CLERKS OF THE ROBE), was Masters in Ordinary of the High Court of Chancery. They were eleven in number, or twelve including the Master of the Rolls (*q.v.*). They were assistants of the Lord Chancellor, and also of the Master of the Rolls after the latter had acquired judicial authority. Down to the end of the eighteenth century they occasionally sat in court with the Lord Chancellor and the Master of the Rolls; but subsequently they sat only in

chambers for the discharge of functions which were partly ministerial and partly judicial. They, except one who received a salary of about £300 in addition to fees, were, in 1798, paid only by fees—many of immemorial origin—the amounts whereof averaged, in the case of different Masters, from about £1,300 to about £1,100 a year (*Commons Committee's Reports* (1803), vol. 13, p. 224). The Court of Chancery Act, 1852, after reciting that proceedings before the Masters were attended with great delay and expense, abolished them by s. 1, and s. 16 provided for the appointment of eight Chief Clerks (*q.v.*), two being appointed by the Master of the Rolls and two by each of the three Vice-Chancellors.

The Masters in Ordinary were so called in order to distinguish them from the Masters Extraordinary (*q.v.*). See HATS IN COURT.

Masters of Requests. See COURTS OF REQUESTS.

Masters of the Queen's Bench, Common Pleas and Exchequer. The Superior Courts (Officers) Act, 1837, provided that there should be in each of these courts five officers, to be called the Masters of each court, to conduct the civil business thereof. In exercise of powers given by the Judges Chambers (Despatch of Business) Act, 1867, s. 1, rules were made empowering any of these Masters to transact all business, with certain specified exceptions, which a judge of the court might transact in chambers. The Judicature Act, 1873, s. 77, attached them to the Supreme Court. Upon the establishment of the Central Office (*q.v.*) by the Judicature Officers Act, 1879, they became, under that Act, Masters of the Supreme Court (*q.v.*). See PROTHONOTARY.

Masters of the Supreme Court. These at present consist of the Masters in the Chancery Division, who are the Chief Clerks (*q.v.*) and the Clerks of Record and Writs (*q.v.*) under another name; the Masters of the Queen's Bench Division, who occupy the same positions and do practically the same work as did the Masters of the Queen's Bench, Common Pleas and Exchequer (*q.v.*) (the present number is ten of whom the senior master is also Queen's Remembrancer (*q.v.*). One of the other masters is also Queen's Coroner (*q.v.*) and Master of the Crown Office); and the seven Masters of the Supreme Court who carry out in the Central Office (*q.v.*) the taxation of the costs (*q.v.*) of all cases in the Chancery and Queen's Bench Divisions. In the Queen's Bench Division a master, and in the Family Division a registrar, may transact all such business and exercise all such authority and jurisdiction as may be transacted by a judge in chambers except as regards (a) matters relating to criminal proceedings, other than applications to which R.S.C., Ord. 79, r. 10 (2) relates; (b) matters relating to the liberty of the subject; (c) proceedings to which Ord. 57 applies and with respect to which a judge in chambers has jurisdiction; (d) subject to Ord. 50, r. 9, para. (2), Ord. 51, r. 2, and Ord. 89, r. 1 (3), proceedings for the grant of an injunction or other order under the Judicature Act, 1925, s. 45; (e) appeals from district registrars; (f) applications for review of a taxing master's decision; (g) applications under the Judicature Act, 1925, s. 51, for leave to institute or continue legal proceedings; (h) any other matter or proceeding which by any of the rules of the Supreme Court is required to be heard only by a judge. A master or registrar may grant an injunction in agreed terms (R.S.C., Ord. 32, r. 11). A master also has all the jurisdiction and powers conferred upon a judge of the High Court by the Bills of Sale Act, 1878, s. 14, the Married Women's Property Act, 1882, s. 17, the Arbitration Act, 1950, the Partnership Act, 1890, s. 23, the Administration of Justice (Miscellaneous Provisions) Act, 1933, s. 6 (1), or the County Courts Act, 1959. Most of the interlocutory proceedings in a cause are decided by masters or registrars from whom there is generally a right of appeal to a judge and in some cases, direct to the Divisional Court.

The Masters of the Chancery Division, have, subject to the right of any party to have an adjournment to the judge in person, all the powers of a judge in chambers except such as are reserved to a judge (R.S.C., Ord. 32, r. 14; Practice Direction (Chancery: Powers of Mas-

ters) [1970] 1 W.L.R. 762). Since January, 1972, the Masters of the Supreme Court and assistant masters are appointed by the Lord Chancellor, with the concurrence of the Minister for the Civil Service as to numbers and salaries (Courts Act, 1971, s. 26).

Mast-feeding, pannage (*q.v.*).

Masura, a decayed house; a wall; the ruins of a building; a certain quantity of land, about four oxgangs.

Mate, the deputy of the master in a merchant ship. There are sometimes several mates of various grades. See BILL OF LADING.

Matelotage [Fr. *matelot*], the hire of a ship or boat.

Materfamilias, the mother or mistress of a family (Civil Law).

Material; Materiality. The question of whether an untrue representation or a concealment makes voidable a contract to the subject-matter of which it relates, or whether an erasure or alteration avoids a written instrument, depends in general upon whether the misrepresentation, concealment, erasure or alteration is material and the question whether it is material depends partly on the facts of the case and partly on the nature of the transaction. Thus, altering the date of a cheque is a material alteration. So, if during the negotiation of a marine insurance, a statement is made which has no real bearing on the risk, but, which, nevertheless, influences the mind of the underwriter, as, for instance, an assertion that previous insurances have been obtained on the same ship at a low premium, the misrepresentation will entitle the insurer to avoid the policy. See UBERRIMAE FIDEI.

The making of a material change in the use of any buildings or other land is development within the meaning of the Town and Country Planning Act, 1971, s. 22 (1). The expression is not defined in the Act.

Maternal. See DESCENT.

Maternity benefit. See the Social Security Act, 1975, ss. 12, 21–23.

Masterta, a maternal aunt; the sister of one's mother.

Matertera magna, a great maternal aunt.

Math, a mowing.

MATRICIDE

Matricide, slaughter of a mother; one who has slain his mother. See PARRICIDE.

Matriculate, to enter a university.

Matrimonial causes, suits for the redress of injuries respecting the rights of marriage. They were formerly a branch of the ecclesiastical jurisdiction, but were transferred to the jurisdiction of the Court for Divorce and Matrimonial Causes by the Matrimonial Causes Act, 1857.

" Matrimonial cause " means any action for divorce, nullity of marriage, judicial separation, jactitation of marriage or restitution of conjugal rights (Judicature Act, 1925, s. 225).

Matrimonial causes are assigned to the Family Division (*q.v.*) of the High Court (Administration of Justice Act, 1970, s. 1, Sch. 1). Any county court may be designated a divorce county court with jurisdiction to hear undefended matrimonial causes (Matrimonial Causes Act, 1967, s. 1; Courts Act, 1971, s. 45 (3)).

See ADULTERY; ALIMONY; ASSISE; CONJUGAL RIGHTS; DIVORCE; FAMILY DIVISION; HUSBAND AND WIFE; JUDICIAL SEPARATION; MAINTENANCE; MARRIAGE; NULLITY OF MARRIAGE.

Matrimonial home. A spouse not entitled by virtue of any estate, interest, contract or enactment to occupy the matrimonial home is given protection from eviction or exclusion by the Matrimonial Homes Act, 1967, s. 1. A spouse who has an equitable interest in the matrimonial home is also within the protection (s. 1 (9), added by the Matrimonial Proceedings and Property Act, 1970, s. 38). This protection amounts to a charge on the matrimonial home (Act of 1967, ss. 2–6, Sch., as amended by the Law of Property Act, 1969, Sch. 2 Pt. II, and the Land Charges Act, 1972, Schs. 3, 5). See LAND CHARGE. A wife who owns the matrimonial home jointly with her husband is not within the Act of 1967. She must rely on her common law rights (*Gurasz* v. *Gurasz* [1970] P. 11). As to the effect of the husband's bankruptcy, see *Re Turner, A Bankrupt* [1974] 1 W.L.R. 1556. See also *Baynham* v. *Baynham* [1968] 1 W.L.R. 1890 (right of spouse who leaves to return); *Miles* v. *Bull* [1969] 1 Q.B. 258 (sale over wife's head).

The matrimonial home may be the subject of a property adjustment order under the Matrimonial Causes Act, 1973, s. 24. See the Family Division Practice Direction dated January 27, 1971 [1971] C.L.Y. 5453; Practice Note dated December 14, 1972 [1972] C.L.Y. 1682. Where the matrimonial home is the sole or principal asset and the wife and children are living in it, the wife may be given the sole right to occupy it to the exclusion of her husband for the purpose of providing a home for the children and while that subsists (*Allen* v. *Allen* [1974] 1 W.L.R. 1171). After that, if the house is sold, husband and wife should ordinarily receive their shares absolutely. Unless the wife has remarried or is definitely going to remarry, prospective remarriage should be ignored (*S.* v. *S.* [1976] Fam. 18). An assignable contractual weekly tenancy is property for this purpose (*Hale* v. *Hale* [1975] 1 W.L.R. 931).

A deserted wife is not in rateable occupation of the matrimonial home (*Malden and Coombe Corporation* v. *Bennett* [1963] 1 W.L.R. 652); her husband is (*Des Salles d'Epinoix* v. *Kensington and Chelsea Royal London Borough Council* [1970] 1 W.L.R. 179). But a divorced wife who remains in sole and exclusive possession of the matrimonial home is the rateable occupier (*Mourton* v. *Hounslow Borough Council* [1970] 2 Q.B. 362).

Matrimonial proceedings in magistrates' courts. The law was consolidated by the Matrimonial Proceedings (Magistrates' Courts) Act, 1960.

A married woman or a married man may apply by way of complaint (*q.v.*) to a magistrates' court for an order against the other party to the marriage on any of the following causes of complaint arising during the subsistence of the marriage, that is to say, that the defendant (a) has deserted (see DESERTION) the complainant, (b) has been guilty of persistent cruelty (*q.v.*) to (i) the complainant or (ii) an infant child of the complainant or (iii) an infant child of the defendant who at the time of the cruelty was a child of the family, or (c) has been found guilty (i) on indictment of any offence which involved an assault (*q.v.*) upon the complainant, or

(ii) by a magistrates' court of an offence against the complainant under the Offences against the Person Act, 1861, ss. 20, 42, 43 or 47 (bodily injury, common assault, aggravated assaults on females and boys), being in the case of the said s. 42 (common assault) an offence for which the defendant has been sentenced to imprisonment or any other form of detention (see BORSTAL TRAINING; DETENTION) for a term of not less than one month, or (iii) of, or of an attempt to commit, an offence under the Sexual Offences Act, 1956, ss. 1–29 (see SEXUAL OFFENCES), or under the Indecency with Children Act, 1960 (see INDECENCY), against an infant child (see s. 16 (1)) of the complainant, or against an infant child of the defendant who at the time of the commission or attempt to commit the offence was a child of the family, (d) has committed adultery (q.v.), or (e) while knowingly suffering from a venereal disease has insisted (see Rigby v. Rigby [1944] P. 33) on or has without the complainant being aware of the presence of that disease permitted sexual intercourse between the complainant and the defendant, or (f) is for the time being an habitual drunkard (q.v. and s. 16 (1)) or drug addict (see s. 16 (1)), or (g) being the husband, has compelled his wife to submit herself to prostitution or has been guilty of such conduct as was likely to result and has resulted in the wife's submitting herself to prostitution, or (h) being the husband, has wilfully (q.v.) neglected to provide reasonable maintenance for the wife or for any child (s. 16 (1)) of the family who is or would but for that neglect have been a defendant (s. 16 (1)), or (i) being the wife, has wilfully (q.v.) neglected to provide, or to make a proper contribution towards, reasonable maintenance for the husband or for any child (s. 16 (1)) of the family who is or would but for that neglect have been a dependant (s. 16 (1)), in a case where, by reason of the impairment of the husband's earning capacity through age, illness or disability of mind or body, and having regard to any resources of the husband and wife respectively which are, or should properly be made available for the purpose, it is reasonable in all the circumstances to expect the wife to contribute (Matrimonial Proceedings (Magistrates' Courts) Act, 1960, s. 1 (1)). As to jurisdiction, see s. 1 (2) (3); Administration of Justice Act, 1964, Sch. 3.

On the hearing of a complaint the court may make a matrimonial order containing any one of the following provisions: (a) a provision that the complainant be no longer bound to cohabit with the defendant (which provision while in force has effect in all respects as a decree of judicial separation (q.v.)), (b) a provision that the husband shall pay to the wife such weekly sum as the court considers reasonable in all the circumstances of the case (see Roberts v. Roberts [1970] P. 1; Brasman v. Brasman (1975) 5 Fam. Law 85), (c) where by reason of the impairment of the husband's earning capacity (see McEwan v. McEwan [1972] 1 W.L.R. 1217) through age, illness or disability of mind or body, it appears to the court reasonable in all the circumstances so to order, a provision that the wife shall pay to the husband such weekly sum as the court considers reasonable in all the circumstances of the case, (d), (e), (f) provisions as to the custody of any child of the family who is under the age of sixteen years, (g) a provision for access, (h) provision for the maintenance of any child of the family (Matrimonial Proceedings (Magistrates' Courts) Act, 1960, s. 2 (1); Maintenance Orders Act, 1968, Sch.; Local Government Act, 1972, Sch. 23 para. 10; Matrimonial Causes Act, 1973, s. 18 (3)). Special provisions apply when the defendant is an habitual drunkard or drug addict (Act of 1960, s. 2 (2)). If adultery is complained of the court must be satisfied that it has not been condoned or connived at or conduced to by wilful neglect or misconduct (s. 2 (3)). The magistrates may refuse to make an order in a case more suitable for the High Court (Act of 1960, s. 5). Interim orders may be made under s. 6. Matrimonial orders are suspended until the parties cease to cohabit and cease to have effect if they resume cohabitation (Act of 1960, s. 7; Matrimonial Proceedings and Property Act, 1970, ss. 30, 33). Matrimonial orders may be revoked, revived or varied (Act of 1960, ss. 8–10).

An appeal lies to the High Court from decisions of the magistrates (s. 11). The time limit for a complaint of adultery is normally six months from the date when the act of adultery first became known to the complainant (s. 12). Payment of any sum directed to be paid by a matrimonial order is enforced in the same way as under an affiliation (*q.v.*) order (Act of 1960, s. 13; Criminal Justice Act, 1967, Sch. 3; Matrimonial Proceedings and Property Act, 1970, s. 32). As to repayment of sums paid after cessation of a matrimonial order by reason of remarriage, see ss. 7 (4), 13A; Matrimonial Proceedings and Property Act, 1970, ss. 30, 31.

Matrimonium, property descending *ex parte materna* (*q.v.*) (Blount).

Matrimonium subsequens legitimos facit quoad sacerdotium non quoad successionem propter consuetudinem regni quae se habet in contrarium (Co.Litt. 345). (A subsequent marriage makes children legitimate as regards holy orders, but not (because of the custom of this kingdom, which is to the contrary effect as regards succession to lands.) The canon law forbade the ordination of bastards, but it held that persons born out of wedlock were legitimated by a subsequent marriage of their parents; the common law recognised no such legitimation (see ANTENATI), but the law was changed by the Legitimacy Act, 1926. See LEGITIMATION. See Jackson, *Formation and Annulment of Marriage,* 35, 68.

Matrimony, marriage; the nuptial state; the contract of man and wife. See HUSBAND AND WIFE; MARRIAGE.

Matrina, a godmother.

Matrix ecclesias, the mother church, *i.e.,* the cathedral, so called in relation to the parochial churches within the same diocese, or a parochial church in relation to chapels depending on it (Leg. Hen. 1, c. 19).

Matron, a married woman; a mother of a family; a female superintendent, as the matron of a school, hospital or a prison.

Matrons, Jury of. See JURY OF MATRONS.

Matter. See ACTIONS AND MATTERS, ETC.

Maturiora sunt vota mulierum quam virorum (6 Co.Rep. 71). (The promises of women are made earlier than those of men.) This merely means that the minimum age for a valid marriage was less for a women than for a man. See CONSENSUS, ETC.

Maturity, the time when a bill of exchange or promissory note becomes due.

Maundy Thursday [Sax. *maund,* an alms-basket; Lat. *dies mandati,* the day of the command], the day preceding Good Friday, on which princes give alms. See ALMONER.

The fineness of maundy coins is laid down by the Coinage Act, 1971, s. 1, Sch. 1.

Mauritius. See the Mauritius Independence Act, 1968, as amended by the Finance Act, 1969, Sch. 21 Pt. IX; Civil Aviation Act, 1971, Sch. 11.

Maxim [Lat. *maximum*], an axiom; a general principle; a leading truth so called, *quia maxima est ejus dignitas et certissima auctoritas atque quod maxime omnibus probetur* (because its dignity is the greatest and its authority the most certain, and because it is universally approved by all) (Co.Litt. 11).

Modern opinion, however, does not rate maxims so highly, and Lord Esher M.R., in *Yarmouth* v. *France* (1887) 19 Q.B.D. at p. 653, in connection with *volenti non fit injuria,* went so far as to say that they are almost invariably misleading, and for the most part so large and general in their language that they always include something which really is not intended to be included in them. Similarly, Mr. Justice Stephen (Hist.Crim.Law, 94) wrote " They are rather minims than maxims, for they give not a particularly great, but a particularly small, amount of information. As often as not the exceptions and qualifications are more important than the so-called rules." While they mostly serve as good indexes to the law, they are mostly bad abstracts of it. See *Broom's Legal Maxims*; *Mews' Digest*; *Encyclopaedia of the Laws of England*; and *Bouvier's Law Dictionary* (where about 1,500 are collected, including duplicates). Bacon collected 800, but published 25 only. His introduction to them begins with the celebrated " I hold every man to be a debtor to his own profession."

Maxime, a maxim (Co.Litt. 11).

Mayhem, the deprivation of a member proper for defence in fight, as an arm, leg, finger, eye, or fore-tooth; yet not a jaw-tooth, or an ear, or a nose, because they have been supposed to be of no use in fighting. One circumstance peculiar to an action for mayhem was that the court might, on view of the wound, increase the damages awarded by the jury (3 Salk. 115; 3 Bl.Comm. 121).

It was originally both a civil injury and a criminal offence, but by modern statutes the law relating to felonious maiming and wounding has been amended, so that there is no legal difference between depriving a person of a member proper for his defence in fight and causing him any other grievous bodily harm (see MALICIOUS INJURIES TO THE PERSON), except that everyone has a right to consent to the infliction upon himself of any bodily harm not amounting to a mayhem.

Mayhem, as a civil injury, seems still to exist, but the use of the word is obsolete.

See APPEAL OF FELONY.

Mayhemavit, he has maimed.

Mayor [Brit. *meyr*; *miret*, to keep; Old Eng. *maier*, power; Lat. *major*; Fr. *maire*], the annual chief magistrate of a borough. If a district (*q.v.*) has conferred on it the status of a borough (*q.v.*) the chairman and vice-chairman of the council are entitled to the style of mayor and deputy mayor of the borough (Local Government Act, 1972, ss. 3–5, 245). The chief officer of a London borough is the mayor (Sch. 2 Pt. I para. 1 (2)). He may appoint a deputy mayor (Sch. 2 Pt. I para. 5). A parish or community which resolves to become a town has a town mayor and deputy town mayor (s. 245 (6)). As to the Lord Mayor of London, see LONDON.

Mayor, Aldermen and Burgesses, prior to the Local Government Act, 1972, the name of a municipal corporation of a borough to which the Municipal Corporations Act, 1882, applied; see s. 8 of that Act (replaced, except as to London) by the Local Government Act, 1933, s. 17 (by which " citizens " was sub-stituted\for " burgesses " in the case of a city), replacing the Municipal Corporations Act, 1835, s. 6.

Mayoralty, the office of a mayor. See LONDON; MAYOR; STAPLE.

Mayor's and City of London Court, a court formed in 1921 by the amalgamation of the Mayor's Court of London (*q.v.*) and the City of London Court (*q.v.*) (Mayor's and City of London Court Act, 1920). The court as constituted immediately before January 1, 1972, was abolished. The City of London becomes a county court district and its court has the normal county court jurisdiction, but the county court so established is to be known as the Mayor's and City of London Court and its judge (*i.e.*, the circuit judge (*q.v.*) assigned to the district) is to be known as the judge of the Mayor's and City of London Court (Courts Act, 1971, s. 42, Sch. 5). The courthouse also retains its name (Courts Act, 1971, s. 29).

Mayor's Court of Bristol. By charter dated August 8, 1373, Edward III regularised this court, which had assumed a jurisdiction analogous to that of the Mayor's Court of London. Within three hundred years from the date of the charter, the Bristol court had fallen into disuse. See CONCESSIT SOLVERE. It was abolished by the Local Government Act, 1972, Sch. 28.

Mayor's Court of London, an inferior court which had jurisdiction in civil matters where the whole cause of action arose within the City of London, which did not for this purpose include Southwark or the river Thames; if, however, the debt or damage claimed in an action did not exceed £50, the court had jurisdiction, provided that the defendant dwelt or carried on business within the City at the time the action was brought, or within six months previously, or that part of the cause of action arose within the city (Mayor's Court of London Procedure Act, 1857, s. 12). Actions of ejectment, and actions under the Bills of Exchange Act, 1882, might be brought in the court, and also certain proceedings peculiar to the city. It was the Court of Appeal from the Chamberlain Court (see CHAMBERLAIN OF THE CITY OF LONDON).

The court had two "sides" or divisions, a legal and an equitable, but of late years the equitable jurisdiction had almost fallen into disuse. It had no jurisdiction in replevin (*q.v.*).

The judge of the court was the Recorder, or, in his absence, the Common Serjeant (Mayor's Court of London Procedure Act, 1857, s. 43), or the assistant judge appointed under the Borough, etc., Courts of Record Act, 1872. The lord mayor and the aldermen were in theory the judges; but they never sat.

See MAYOR'S AND CITY OF LONDON COURT; COMMON PLEADER, ETC.

Mead, metheglin (*q.v.*); a meadow.

Mead-silver, an annual payment of one penny an acre formerly paid by the parishioners of Cobham as a composition for tithe-hay, that is to say, tithes of hay.

Meal-rent, a rent formerly paid in meal (Jacob).

Meals for children. A local education authority may provide at the public expense milk, meals and other refreshment for pupils attending schools and county colleges maintained by them when the schools or colleges are open for instruction (Education Act, 1944, s. 49; Education (Milk) Act, 1971, s. 1). The authority may also provide for boarding accommodation, taking into account the religious denomination of the person with whom the child will reside (Education Act, 1944, s. 50; Education Act, 1946, s. 14, Sch. 2 Pt. I; Education (Miscellaneous Provisions) Act, 1948, Sch. 1 Pt. I). The authority may also provide for the clothing of pupils so as to ensure that they are sufficiently clad while pupils at the school. The authority may recover the cost of boarding accommodation and clothing, taking into account the means of the parents, and may recover any sum so payable summarily as a civil debt (Education Act, 1944, ss. 51, 52; Education (Miscellaneous Provisions) Act, 1948, Sch. 2). The authority may provide, or assist in providing, facilities for recreation and social and physical training for pupils of schools and colleges in their area, including camps, holiday classes, playing fields, play centres and other places (including playgrounds, gymnasiums and swimming baths not appropriated to any school or college); Education Act, 1944, s. 53.

Meal vouchers. By an Extra Statutory Concession these are treated as exempted from taxation under the following conditions (a) that vouchers are non-transferable and used for meals only; (b) that where any restriction is placed on their issue to employees, they are available to lower paid staff; and (c) that the value of any vouchers or part of a voucher does not exceed 15 new pence for each working day: Statement by the Chancellor of the Exchequer H.C. Vol. 598 col. 13.

The foregoing concession is not affected by the taxation of vouchers under the Finance (No. 2) Act, 1975, ss. 36, 37.

Mean, or **Mesne** [Lat. *medius*], a middle between two extremes, whether applied to persons, things, or time. See MESNE.

Mease; Mese [Lat. *messuagium*], a messuage or dwelling-house (Fitz.N.B. 2).

Mease also means a customary measure of herrings, containing in various places 500, 525, 612 or 615 fish.

Meason-due [Fr. *maison de Dieu*], a house of God; a monastery, religious house, almshouse or hospital: see the statute 1597, 39 Eliz. 1, c. 5.

Measure [Lat. *mensura*], that by which anything is measured; the rule by which anything is adjusted or proportioned. Magna Carta, 1215, c. 25, prescribed one measure of wine, ale, and corn through the realm.

See WEIGHTS AND MEASURES.

Enactments of the National Assembly of the Church of England (*q.v.*), now the General Synod are called Measures.

Measure of damages, the test which determines the amount of damages to be given. The general rule is that in contract the plaintiff recovers such damages as arise naturally from the breach in the usual course of things, and such as may be supposed to have been in contemplation of the parties as the probable result of a breach (*Hadley* v. *Baxendale* (1854) 9 Exch. 341; *Victoria Laundry* v. *Newman Industries* [1949] 2 K.B. 528). The measure of damages in negligence is the damage which could have been foreseen by a reasonable man. It is not enough that the damage was a direct consequence of the negligent act (*Overseas Tankship (U.K.)* v. *Mort's Dock and Engineering Co., The Wagon Mound* [1961] A.C. 388, not following *Re Polemis and Furness, Withy & Co.* [1921] 3 K.B. 560). See also *Smith* v. *Leech Brain & Co.* [1962] 2 Q.B. 405. The same rule applies in nuisance (*Overseas Tankship (U.K.)* v. *Miller Steamship Co. Pty.* [1967] 1 A.C. 617). In some cases vindictive or exemplary damages can be given, *e.g.*, libel or slander. The actual loss cannot always be recovered, as the whole or a portion of the loss may be too remote a consequence of that which constitutes the cause of action. Though unable to prove actual loss, a plaintiff may sometimes be entitled to nominal damages, *e.g.*, for breach of an agreement to lend money. In actions of contract, the difference between the market price and the contract price of the subject-matter at the date the contract is broken will as a rule give the measure of damages. Profits upon an expected resale cannot be recovered unless such resale was in the contemplation of the parties at the time of making the contract. In assessing general damages for future economic loss the likelihood of future depreciation in the purchasing power of money cannot be taken into account (*Gollan* v. *Duncan* [1961] N.Z.L.R. 60).

Damages for breach of contract for the sale of land are regulated as a rule on the following principles. In an open contract or in the absence of the usual conditions, upon breach by the purchaser the vendor cannot recover the price by way of damages but he may recover his loss, if any, upon a resale and his expenses, giving credit for the deposit, if any. Upon breach by the vendor, if the breach complained of is that he has failed to show title on an open contract, the purchaser cannot recover his loss upon the contract, but only his expenses. If however, the breach has been caused by failure to make good a title which he has expressly undertaken to sell or if he has not perfected his title where he could have done so reasonably, or has committed a breach of trust by selling or where he has been prevented from completing by his own default, the purchaser may recover the amount of his loss and any other damages which he may have suffered by the breach.

Damages for personal injuries should include a sum for the loss of the amenities of life (*Olivier* v. *Ashman* [1960] 1 W.L.R. 924) and the sum awarded may be substantial (*H. West & Son* v. *Shephard* [1964] A.C. 326). Social security benefits are to be taken into account (Law Reform (Personal Injuries) Act, 1948, s. 2, as amended).

In assessing damages in cases of severe personal injury the fact that the plaintiff may be unable to enjoy personally any award of damages is not relevant, except that ignorance will be an element in the assessment of damages for pain and suffering (*Wise* v. *Kaye* [1962] 1 Q.B. 638). But the fact that the plaintiff will be supported by the National Health Service will be ignored (*Daish* v. *Wauton* [1972] 2 W.L.R. 29).

The sum awarded for personal injuries should not be out of all proportion to the sum awarded in another case in respect of similar injuries (*Bastow* v. *Bagley & Co.* [1961] 1 W.L.R. 1494).

Income tax is taken into account in assessing damages for lost income but not if the sum awarded is itself chargeable to tax (*British Transport Commission* v. *Gourley* [1956] A.C. 185; *Diamond* v. *Campbell-Jones* [1961] Ch. 22; *Parsons* v. *B.N.M. Laboratories* [1964] 1 Q.B. 95; *Bold* v. *Brough* [1964] 1 W.L.R. 201).

Damages for innocent misrepresentation may be recovered as an alternative to rescission (Misrepresentation Act, 1967, s. 2), including loss of bargain (*Watts* v. *Spence* [1975] 2 W.L.R. 1039).

Unemployment benefit received by the plaintiff in an action for wrongful dismissal must be brought into account (*Parsons* v. *B.N.M. Laboratories* [1964] 1 Q.B. 65).

See DAMAGES; EXPECTATION OF LIFE.

Measurer, or Meter, an officer in the City of London who measured woollen cloths, coals, etc. In respect of their metage (*q.v.*) rights the corporation of the City of London was the measurer for the Port of London. See AULNAGER.

Measuring money, a duty exacted, in addition to alnage, on cloth. It was abolished in the reign of Henry IV (Rot. Parl. 11 Hen. 4). See ALNAGE.

Meat. The Shops Act, 1950, ss. 61, 62, provide for the compulsory closing of retail meat traders' shops on Sunday, with exemption in respect of Jewish retail dealers in meat, who may keep open on Sunday under licence, on giving notice to the local authority and displaying notices as provided by the Act, but they must not keep open on Saturday. See UNSOUND FOOD.

As to standards of measurement etc. on the sale of meat and food containing meat, see the Weights and Measures Act, 1963, s. 21, Sch. 4 Pts. I, II.

Meat and Livestock Commission. See the Agriculture Act, 1967, ss. 1–9 as amended.

Mechanically propelled vehicle. See MOTOR CAR; MOTOR CYCLE; MOTOR TRACTOR; MOTOR VEHICLE.

Mederia, a house or place where metheglin or mead was made.

Mediae et infimae manus homines, men of a middle and base condition (Blount).

Medianus homo, a man of middle fortune.

Mediate testimony, secondary evidence (*q.v.*).

Mediation, reconciliation of claims of States by a third power.

Mediators of questions, six persons appointed under the statute 1353, 27 Edw. 3, st. 2, c. 24, who decided questions arising between merchants as to whether wool was marketable or properly packed, etc.

Medical benefit. See the Social Security Act, 1975, s. 14.

Medical Council. See GENERAL MEDICAL COUNCIL.

Medical inspection. It is the duty of the Secretary of State to make provision for the medical and dental inspection and treatment of pupils in attendance at schools maintained by local education authorities (National Health Service Reorganisation Act, 1973, s. 3).

The court will exercise its inherent jurisdiction to grant a stay of proceedings if, in litigation over damages for per-sonal injuries, the plaintiff unreasonably refuses to submit to a medical examination (*Edmeades* v. *Thames Board Mills* [1969] 2 Q.B. 67).

For the rules to be observed in medical inspections in nullity proceedings, see Practice Direction (P.D.A.) Medical Inspection in Nullity Proceedings, dated February 19, 1963 [1963] 1 W.L.R. 310).

Medical jurisprudence. See FORENSIC MEDICINE.

Medical officer of health. Under the Local Government Act, 1933, ss. 103, 106–112, medical officers of health could be appointed by urban and rural authorities and county councils. Under the Local Government Act, 1972, s. 112, a local authority may appoint such officers as are thought necessary. See also Public Health Act, 1936, s. 3, Sch. 1; Food and Drugs Act, 1955, s. 86; London Government Act, 1963, ss. 40, 42, 74 (1), Sch. 4 para. 17.

Medical practitioner. The Medical Act, 1956, and the Medical Act, 1956 (Amendment) Act, 1958, apply to both physicians and surgeons. They are amended by the Medical Act, 1969.

The phrase "medical practitioner" covers all aspects of medical practice, including consultancy (*Lyn-Perkis* v. *Jones* [1969] 1 W.L.R. 1293).

The correct test of negligence of an ordinary medical practitioner is the standard of the ordinary competent practitioner exercising ordinary professional skill (*Chin Keow* v. *Government of Malaysia* [1967] 1 W.L.R. 813).

It is an offence for any person to pretend falsely that he holds any medical or surgical qualification (*Younghusband* v. *Luftig* [1952] 2 All E.R. 72). Unless there is such false pretence, no unqualified person commits any offence by merely practising medicine or surgery: but he does so at the risk of civil or criminal proceedings in respect of such consequences as may result if he treats a patient without proper skill; and he, like a qualified but unregistered medical practitioner, cannot recover in any court for medical attendance or for medicine which he has both prescribed and supplied (Medical Act, 1956, s. 27).

Under by-law clxxii of the Royal College of Physicians (*q.v.*) no registered medical practitioner who is a fellow of that college may sue for his fees; and it is provided by the Medical Act, 1956, s. 27, that this by-law is a bar to any proceedings by such fellow for recovery of his expenses, charges or fees.

Registered medical practitioners are exempt from serving in any corporate or parochial office (Medical Act, 1956, s. 30).

Medical practitioners are excusable as of right from jury service. See JURY.

See INFAMOUS CONDUCT; NATIONAL HEALTH SERVICE; ROYAL COLLEGE OF PHYSICIANS; ROYAL COLLEGE OF SURGEONS, ETC.

Medical Research Council. See the Science and Technology Act, 1965, s. 1; the Biological Standards Act, 1975.

Medicine, Professions supplementary to. The Professions Supplementary to Medicine Act, 1960, provides for the regulation of chiropodists, dietitians, medical laboratory technicians, occupational therapists, physiotherapists, radiographers and remedial gymnasts. Orthoptists were added by S.I. 1966 No. 990.

Medicines. See the Medicines Acts, 1968 and 1971.

Medico-legal, relating to the law concerning medical questions.

Medietate linguae, De. See JURY.

Medio acquietando, a judicial writ to distrain a lord for the acquitting of a mesne lord from a rent which he had acknowledged in court not to belong to him (Reg.Jur. 129).

Mediums. The Fraudulent Mediums Act, 1951, provides for the punishment of persons who fraudulently purport to act as spiritualistic mediums or to exercise powers of telepathy, clairvoyance or other similar powers for reward.

Medletum, Medlea, Medlefe, Medleta [Fr. *mêler*, to meddle], a sudden scolding at and beating one another (Bract. 1, 3, c. xxxv).

Med-sceat, a bribe; hush-money (Anc. Inst.Eng.).

Medsypp, a harvest supper or entertainment given to labourers at harvest-home.

Meeting, an assembly of persons whose consent is required for anything to decide, by a proper majority of votes, whether or not that thing shall be done.

At common law in the absence of other provisions a corporation is bound by the majority present at a regular corporate meeting and not only by an absolute majority of the corporation; this does not apply to companies (*Perrott and Perrott* v. *Stephenson* [1934] 1 Ch. 171).

Meetings of seditious societies are restrained by the Seditious Meetings Act, 1817. In *Thomas* v. *Sawkins* [1935] 2 K.B. 249, the right of the police was upheld to enter private premises to attend a meeting to which the public were invited, in reasonable anticipation of misdemeanours or breach of the peace. See PUBLIC MEETING.

In the law of bankruptcy the most important kind of meeting is the first meeting of creditors, which is held as soon as possible after a receiving order has been made, for the purpose of deciding whether a composition or scheme of arrangement shall be accepted or whether the debtor shall be adjudged bankrupt (Bankruptcy Act, 1914, s. 13). A trustee in bankruptcy is bound to have regard to the directions of the creditors in administering the estate (s. 79 (1)); he may from time to time summon general meetings of the creditors for the purpose of ascertaining their wishes (s. 79 (2)); and he is required to do so if one-sixth in value of the creditors so demand. A general meeting may also be held for the purpose of removing the trustee or appointing a new trustee (s. 95).

In the law of companies, meetings are of three kinds, statutory, ordinary and extraordinary, or, as the two latter are also called, general and special. Ordinary or general meetings are usually held at stated times and for the transaction of business generally. Extraordinary or special meetings are held as occasion may require for the transaction of some particular business, which ought to be specified in the notice convening the meeting. The one meeting may be both ordinary and extraordinary. Every company having a share capital is bound to hold a general meeting, known as a statutory meeting, not less than one month or more than three months after it is entitled to commence business and to hold an annual general meeting once at least in each year and not more than fifteen months after the last such meeting. If a company holds its first annual general meeting within eighteen months of its incorporation, it need not hold it in the year of its incorporation or in the following year (Companies Act, 1948, ss. 130, 131).

A single person cannot constitute a meeting (*Sharp* v. *Dawes* (1877) 2 Q.B.D. 26).

See LOCAL AUTHORITY; PUBLIC MEETING; RESOLUTION; SEDITION; WHARNCLIFFE MEETING.

Megawatt. See WATT.

Megbote [Sax.], a recompense for the murder of a relation.

Meigne, or **Maisnader,** a family.

Meiny, Meine, or **Meinie,** the royal household; a retinue; see the statute 1377, 1 Ric. 2, c. 4.

Meldfeoh, the recompense due and given to him who made discovery of any breach of penal laws committed by another person, called the promoter's (*i.e.,* informer's) fee (Leg.Inae, c. 20).

Melieur serra prize pour le roy (Jenk. Cent. 192). (The best shall be taken for the king.)

Melior est conditio defendentis. (The position of the defendant is the stronger.)

Melior est conditio possidentis et rei quam actoris (4 Co.Inst. 180). (The position of the possessor is the better; and that of the defendant is better than that of the plaintiff.) See IN AEQUALI JURE, ETC.; IN PARI CAUSA.

Melior est conditio possidentis, ubi neuter jus habet (Jenk.Cent. 118). (The condition of the possessor is better [than that of one seeking to oust him] where neither of them has a clear title [to the matter in dispute].)

Melior est justitia vere praeveniens, quam severe puniens (3 Co.Inst. Epil.). (The justice which is really preventive is better than the justice which punishes severely.) See JUSTITIA EST DUPLEX, ETC.

Meliorating waste. See WASTE.

Meliorem conditionem suam facere

potest minor, deteriorem nequaquam (Co. Litt. 337). (A minor is able [in law] to make his condition better, but not by any means to alter it for the worse.) This means that within certain limits the law protects a minor against his own improvidence. See INFANT; MINOR ANTE, ETC.; SUCCURRITUR, ETC.

Melius est omnia mala pati quam malo consentire (3 Co.Inst. 23). (It is better to suffer every ill than to consent to ill.)

Melius [or **satius**] **est petere fontes quam sectari rivulos.** (It is better to go to the fountain head than to follow streamlets.) See COMPENDIA, ETC.

Melius inquirendum, Ad, a writ for a second inquiry, where partial dealing was suspected; and particularly of what lands or tenements a man died seised, on finding an office for the king (Fitz.N.B. 255). See AD MELIUS INQUIRENDUM.

Member of Parliament. See HOUSE OF COMMONS.

Members, places where anciently a custom house was kept, with officers or deputies in attendance. They were lawful places of exportation or importation (Beawes. Lex Mer., 6th ed., vol. i, p. 246).

Membrum, a slip or small piece of land.

Memoranda rolls. These rolls, now in the Record Office, date from 1199 to 1848. They were compiled by the King's Remembrancer and the Treasurer's Remembrancers for the use of the barons of the Exchequer.

Memorandum. In a policy of marine insurance the memorandum is a clause inserted to prevent the underwriters from being liable for injury to goods of a peculiarly perishable nature and for minor damages. It began as follows: " N.B.—Corn, fish, salt, fruit, flour and seed are warranted free from average, unless general or the ship be stranded "; meaning that the underwriters are not to be liable for damage to these articles caused by seawater or the like. See AVERAGE; POLICY OF INSURANCE.

To the particulars and conditions of sale of land which is to be sold by auction there is always appended a memorandum setting out that such and such a person has been declared the purchaser of the property, at such and such a price, and this is signed by the purchaser and by the auctioneer as agent for the vendor. See CONDITIONS OF SALE; PARTICULARS OF SALE.

Memorandum in error, a document alleging error in fact, accompanied by an affidavit of such matter of fact (Common Law Procedure Act, 1852, s. 158). See ERROR.

Memorandum in writing. See STATUTE OF FRAUDS.

Memorandum of alteration. Formerly where a patent was granted for two inventions, one of which was not new or not useful, the whole patent was bad, and the same rule applied when a material part of a patent for a single invention had either of those defects. To remedy this, the statute 1835, 5 & 6 Will. 4, c. 83, empowered a patentee (with the fiat of the Attorney-General) to enter a disclaimer, or a memorandum of an alteration in the title or specification of the patent, not being of such a nature as to extend the exclusive right granted by the patent; and the Patent Law Amendment Act, 1852, s. 39, provided that thereupon the memorandum was deemed to be part of the letters patent or the specification. Subsequently, the Patents, Designs and Trade Marks Act, 1883, s. 18, provided that either an applicant for a patent or a patentee might apply in writing at the Patent Office for leave to amend his specification by way of correction, disclaimer, or alteration (but not by way of enlargement or of substituting a practically different specification), and that the amendment, if leave therefor was obtained pursuant to the section, should form part of the specification; see now the Patents Act, 1949, ss. 29, 30. See DISCLAIMER.

Memorandum of association. See ASSOCIATION, MEMORANDUM OF.

Memorial, that which contains the particulars of a deed, etc., and is the instrument registered, in the case of a deed which must be registered. The registration of a deed or other document is effected by leaving it at the registry together with a memorial under the hand and seal of one of the parties to the deed. The memorial is an abstract of the material parts of the deed, with the parcels (*q.v.*) at full length, and concludes with a statement that the party desires the deed to be registered. The execution of the deed and memorial is proved by the oath of an attesting witness.

" Memorial " also signifies a petition or statement submitted to a person or body.

Memory. In the old books, when a person alleges in legal proceedings that a custom or prescription has existed from time whereof the memory of man runneth not to the contrary, that is as much as to say that no man then alive has heard any proof of the contrary. This is also called time of living memory, as opposed to time of legal memory, which runs from the commencement of the reign of Richard I (July 6, 1189, or September 3, 1189), because the Statute of Westminster I, 1275, c. 8, fixed that period as the time of limitation for bringing certain real actions (Litt. 170; 2 Co.Inst. 238, 239; 2 Bl.Comm. 31). See ANCIENT MESSUAGES; CUSTOM; LIMITATION OF ACTIONS; LOST GRANT; PRESCRIPTION.

Menaces. As to making an unwarrantable demand with menaces see BLACKMAIL, the common law offence of obtaining property by threats was abolished by the Theft Act, 1968, s. 32.

Menagium, a family (Wals. 66).

Mendlefe. See MEDLETUM.

Menial servants [Lat. *moenia*, walls; Mid. Eng. *meine*, a household], servants employed in or about a house. The housekeeper of a large hotel, a steward and a resident governess are not menial servants, for they are not in strictness servants at all: but a huntsman, a head gardener, a pot-boy, and a man employed to do work about a garden and stables, all come within the definition. The fact that a servant lives elsewhere than in his employer's house does not prevent his being a menial servant; but it prevents his coming within the meaning of the expression " domestic servant " (*q.v.*).

In the absence of an express agreement the engagement of a menial or of a domestic servant is by the year; but the engagement is terminable during the course of the year by a month's notice on either side or by the payment of a month's wages in lieu of notice (*Turner* v. *Mason* (1845) 14 M. & W. 112).

Mens rea, a guilty mind. Although as a general rule there must be a mind at fault before there can be a crime, it is not an inflexible rule, and a statute may relate to such a subject-matter and may be so framed as to make an act criminal whether there has been an intention to break the law or otherwise do wrong or not. See Actus non Facit Reum Nisi Mens Sit Rea; Assault; Intention.

Mens testatoris in testamentis spectanda est (Jenk.Cent. 277). (In construing wills regard is to be had to the intention of the testator.) See Verba Intentioni, etc.

Mensa [Lat.], table; viands for household consumption; patrimony, or goods and necessaries (Jacob).

Mensa et thoro. See Divorce.

Mensalia, parsonages or spiritual livings united to the tables of religious houses, and called mensal benefices amongst the canonists (Blount).

Mensura regalis, the standard measure of capacity used when the clerk of the markets (*q.v.*) still had functions to perform: see the statute 1640, 16 Car. 1, c. 19.

Mental deficiency. The Mental Health Act, 1959 (as amended), now provides a single code to cover both mental illness and mental deficiency. See Mental Health. By the Mental Deficiency Act, 1927, s. 1, the following were deemed to be mental defectives: idiots, that is to say, persons in whose case there exists mental defectiveness of such a degree that they are unable to guard themselves against common physical dangers; imbeciles, that is to say, persons in whose case there exists mental defectiveness which, though not amounting to idiocy, is yet so pronounced that they are incapable of managing themselves or their affairs or, in the case of children, of being taught to do so; feeble-minded persons, that is to say, persons in whose case there exists mental defectiveness which, though not amounting to imbecility, is yet so pronounced that they require care, supervision and control for their own protection or for the protection of others or, in the case of children, that they appear to be per-

manently incapable by reason of such defectiveness of receiving proper benefit from instruction in ordinary schools; and moral defectives, that is to say, persons in whose case there exists mental defectiveness coupled with strongly vicious or criminal propensities and who require care, supervision and control for the protection of others.

Mental defectiveness was defined as meaning a condition of arrested or incomplete development of mind existing before the age of eighteen years, whether arising from inherent causes or induced by disease or injury.

Mental health. The Mental Health Act, 1959, repealed the Lunacy and Mental Treatment Acts, 1890–1930, and the Mental Deficiency Acts, 1913–1938, and provided a single code to cover both mental illness and mental deficiency. There is now a whole new language dealing with mental disorder. " Lunatic," " criminal lunatic," " person of unsound mind," " idiot," " imbecile," " feeble-minded person," " moral defective," " lunatic asylum," " judge in lunacy " and " master in lunacy " are terms which have been discarded (some of them by reason of the Mental Deficiency Act, 1927).

" Mental disorder " means mental illness, arrested or incomplete development of mind, psychopathic disorder and any other disorder or disability of the mind, and " mentally disordered " has an equivalent meaning. " Psychopathic disorder " means a persistent disorder of mind (whether or not including subnormality of intelligence) which results in abnormally aggressive or seriously irresponsible conduct on the part of a person and requires or is susceptible to medical treatment. But promiscuity or immoral conduct is not by itself to be classed as mental disorder (Mental Health Act, 1959, ss. 1, 4).

The Act of 1959 provides for the registration and conduct of mental nursing homes and residential homes for mentally disordered persons (ss. 14–24). These sections impose fines for breach of the obligations imposed thereby and these were increased by the Criminal Justice Act, 1967, s. 92, Sch. 3 Pt. I.

The compulsory admission of patients

to hospitals (including certain nursing homes) for observation and for treatment is regulated by the Mental Health Act, 1959, ss. 25–29 (amended by the Family Law Reform Act, 1969, s. 1 (3), Sch. 1 Pt. I and the Children and Young Persons Act, 1969, s. 72 (3), Sch. 5 para. 39). Applications for the admission of a patient may be made by the nearest relative of the patient or by a mental welfare officer. A mental welfare officer cannot make an application in the face of an objection by the nearest relative until the functions of that relative have been transferred to some other person by order of a county court (Act of 1959, ss. 27, 52–54). An application must be supported by the medical recommendations of two medical practitioners (Act of 1959, s. 28). Emergency admissions may be made under s. 29. Psychopathic and sub-normal patients who are liable to be dangerous may be detained under the Mental Health (Amendment) Act, 1975.

The procedure for reception of a patient into guardianship is regulated by ss. 33–35 of the Act of 1959. A guardianship application may be made in respect of a patient on the grounds that he is suffering from mental disorder, i.e., mental illness or severe subnormality or, in the case of a patient under the age of twenty-one, psychopathic disorder or subnormality, and that his disorder warrants his reception into guardianship. It must also be shown that it is necessary in the interests of the patient or for the protection of other persons that the patient should be received into guardianship. Local health authorities may act as guardian. The approval of the local health authority is necessary for any other person to be appointed guardian (Act of 1959, s. 33). No guardianship application may be made in respect of an infant who is a ward of court (s. 58 (3)). See WARD. Applications for the reception of a patient into guardianship may be made by the nearest relative of the patient or a mental welfare officer and must be forwarded on the written recommendations of two medical practitioners (ss. 26–28, 33 (5)). A guardian has all such powers as would be exercisable if he were the father of a patient fourteen years old (s. 34). A patient

received into guardianship may apply to a Mental Health Review Tribunal (see below) within six months or when he attains the age of sixteen (s. 34 (5)).

Mental Health Review Tribunals are established under s. 3 and applications may be made to the appropriate Tribunal for the discharge of a patient from hospital or guardianship (ss. 37, 122–124). Patients may be granted leave of absence from hospital (s. 39). Patients who absent themselves from hospital without leave may be taken into custody and returned to hospital (ss. 40, 139, 140). The discharge of patients from hospital or guardianship is regulated by s. 47. Special provision is made by s. 58 as regards wards of court.

A patient who requires treatment for mental disorder may be admitted to any hospital or mental nursing home by agreement and without any formality. He may remain in hospital or a mental nursing home by agreement after he has ceased to be liable to be detained therein. This applies to an infant over sixteen who is capable of expressing his own wishes (Mental Health Act, 1959, s. 5).

As to local authority services for the prevention, care and after care of mental disorder, see the Mental Health Act, 1959, ss. 8–10, Health Services and Public Health Act, 1968, ss. 12, 78, Sch. 3 Pt. I, Children and Young Persons Act, 1969, s. 72, Sch. 5 para. 37, Local Authority Social Services Act, 1970, Education (Handicapped Children) Act, 1970.

The Crown Court and magistrates' courts may make orders authorising the detention in hospital or reception into guardianship of persons convicted before them of offences punishable with imprisonment for which a penalty is not fixed by law and are found to be suffering from mental disorder. A magistrates' court may also make such orders in certain categories of mental disorder without convicting (Mental Health Act, 1959, ss. 60, 62–64; Children and Young Persons Act, 1963, s. 64 (3), Sch. 5; Criminal Procedure (Insanity) Act, 1964, s. 5 (3), Sch. 1 para. 2 (1), (3); Criminal Appeal Act, 1968, ss. 6 (2), 52, Sch. 1 para. 2, Sch. 5 Pt. I; Children and Young Persons Act, 1969, ss. 1 (5), 2, 72 (3), (4), Sch. 5 paras.

40, 41, Sch. 6; Courts Act, 1971, Sch. 8 para. 38).

Where a patient is admitted to hospital under an order made by the High Court or the Crown Court or transferred to a hospital by direction of the Secretary of State, the court or the Secretary of State may impose special restrictions for the protection of the public. The patient cannot be discharged without the consent of the Secretary of State and he may not appeal to the Mental Health Review Tribunal (Mental Health Act, 1959, ss. 65, 66; Criminal Procedure (Insanity) Act, 1964, s. 5 (3), Sch. 1, para. 2 (1); Criminal Appeal Act, 1968, ss. 6 (2), 52, Sch. 1 para. 2, Sch. 5). Magistrates' courts may commit an offender in custody to quarter sessions to enable a restriction order to be made (Mental Health Act, 1959, ss. 67, 68; Criminal Justice Administration Act, 1962, s. 15 (1), (3); Children and Young Persons Act, 1963, s. 19; Criminal Justice Act, 1967, s. 103 (2), Sch. 7 Pt. I).

Institutions for treatment under conditions of special security, known as "special hospitals" are provided under ss. 97–99 of the Mental Health Act, 1959. See SPECIAL HOSPITAL.

Where an accused is not responsible for his actions a jury may return a special verdict of not guilty by reason of insanity. See SPECIAL VERDICT.

If the question arises whether the accused is fit to plead, that is whether he is under a disability which constitutes a bar to his being tried, that question is, in general, to be determined at once by a jury. (See R. v. Podola [1960] 1 Q.B. 325.) The court may, however, postpone consideration of the question until any time up to the opening of the case for the defence. There is a right of appeal against a finding that the accused is unfit for trial (Criminal Procedure (Insanity) Act, 1964, s. 4; Criminal Appeal Act, 1968, ss. 15, 16, 54, Sch. 7). If the accused is found to be under a disability the court must make an order that he be admitted to such hospital as may be specified by the Secretary of State (Criminal Justice (Insanity) Act, 1964, s. 5, Sch. 1; Criminal Appeal Act, 1968, ss. 6, 52, 54, Schs. 1, 5, 7). The burden of proving disability to stand trial lies with

the side which puts it forward (R. v. Podola [1960] 1 Q.B. 325; R. v. Robertson [1968] 1 W.L.R. 1767). As a rule it is in the interest of the defendant to postpone the question of fitness to plead until after arraignment (R. v. Webb [1969] 2 Q.B. 79).

The property of persons under a disability is protected by a department of the Supreme Court called the Court of Protection (formerly the Management and Administration Department). See COURT OF PROTECTION.

Visitors appointed by the Lord Chancellor (known as the Lord Chancellor's Visitors) visit patients for the purpose of investigating matters relating to the capacity of any patient to manage and administer his property and affairs. A Visitor may interview a patient in private and he may make a private medical examination of the patient and is entitled to see any medical reports relating to the patient. The Master and Deputy Master of the Court have the like powers (Mental Health Act, 1959, ss. 108, 109).

The Board of Control has been dissolved and its functions are now vested in the Secretary of State for Social Services.

The Mental Health Act, 1959, contains provisions as to forgery of documents, false statements, etc. (s. 125); the ill-treatment of patients (s. 126); sexual offences (ss. 127, 128; Sexual Offences Act, 1967, s. 1 (4); Family Reform Act, 1969, s. 1 (3), Sch. 1 Pt. I); assisting patients to absent themselves without leave etc. (Mental Health Act, 1959, s. 129); prosecutions (s. 131); emergency reception of patients (s. 132); pocket money for patients in hospital (s. 133); patients' correspondence (ss. 36, 134); search warrants (s. 135); mentally disordered persons found in public places (s. 136); mentally disordered members of parliament (s. 137); pay, pensions, etc., of mentally disordered persons (s. 138; Parliamentary and Other Pensions Act, 1972, s. 20 (2)); provisions as to custody, conveyance and detention of patients (Mental Health Act, 1959, ss. 139, 140; Criminal Justice Act, 1967, s. 72 (3)); protection of persons acting under the Act (Mental Health Act, 1959, s. 141).

A probation order may be made where

the condition of an offender does not warrant his detention in pursuance of a hospital order under Part V of the Mental Health Act, 1959 (Powers of Criminal Courts Act, 1973, s. 3).

Mental hospitals. See MENTAL HEALTH.

Mentiri est contra mentem ire (3 Buls. 260). (To lie is to go against the mind.) That is to say, a lie is a statement which he who makes it knows to be untrue. See Os, ETC.; SERMO EST, ETC.

Mepris, neglect; contempt.

Mer, or **Mere,** a fenny places, or piece of water.

Mera noctis, midnight.

Merannum, timbers; wood for building.

Mercable [Lat. *mercor*], to be sold or bought.

Mercantile agent. The Factors Act, 1889, s. 1, defines a mercantile agent as a mercantile agent having in the customary course of his business as such agent authority either to sell goods or to consign goods for the purpose of sale, or to buy goods or to raise money on the security of goods. A mercantile agent has implied authority to pledge the goods entrusted to him (*Weiner* v. *Gill* [1906] 2 K.B. 574; *Weiner* v. *Harris* [1910] 1 K.B. 285; *Kempler* v. *Bravingtons* (1925) 133 L.T. 680). See AGENCY.

Mercantile law, the law relating to bills of exchange, contracts of affreightment, marine insurance, etc. See CUSTOM.

Mercantile Marine Fund. The Merchant Shipping Act, 1894, s. 676, provided that a number of fees and other receipts, including light dues, mentioned in that section should be paid into the Mercantile Marine Fund; and s. 677 provided that the fund should be charged with the expenses of a large number of services relating to ships, including the lighthouse service. The Merchant Shipping (Mercantile Marine Fund) Act, 1898, abolished the Mercantile Marine Fund. It enacted that the receipts specified in s. 676 of the Act of 1894, other than light dues, should be paid into the Exchequer; that the light dues should be paid into a fund called the General Lighthouse Fund; and that the expenses incurred by a general lighthouse authority under s. 531 of the Act of 1894, and various other expenses in connection with

lighthouses, etc., should be charged to the General Lighthouse Fund.

Mercat [Lat. *mercatus*], market; trade.

Mercative, belonging to trade.

Mercatores de Venicia, an unincorporated society of Merchants of Venice trading in England in the time of Henry VIII (Madox, *Firma Burgi*).

Mercature, the practice of buying and selling.

Mercedary [Lat. *mercedula*, a small fee], one who hires.

Mercenarius, a hireling or servant.

Mercen-lage [*lex Merciorum*], the law of the kingdom of Mercia, which covered the counties of Gloucester, Worcester, Hereford, Warwick, Oxford, Chester, Salop and Stafford (1 Bl.Comm. 65; Tomlin).

Merchandise marks. See TRADE DESCRIPTION.

Merchant [Fr. *marchand*], one who traffics to remote countries, one who deals in the purchase and sale of goods. (*Josselyn* v. *Parson* (1872) L.R. 7 Exch. 127).

Merchant Adventurers. This association grew out of the rivalry between a number of English merchants and the Hanse. In 1505 Henry VII conferred on them the title of the Fellowship of Merchant Adventurers. At that time their chief centre was Calais. Subsequently they moved to Antwerp. In 1564 Elizabeth I granted them a charter incorporating them as the Governor, Assistants and Fellowship of the Merchant Adventurers of England with liberty to trade in the north of Germany. They then operated chiefly from Hamburg, and came to be known as the Hamburg Company. By the end of the seventeenth century they had ceased to be an active body (Clawson & Keene, *Early Chartered Companies*; Lingelbach, *Merchant Adventurers of England*). See HANSE; STEELYARD.

Merchant's risk. See RISK.

Merchant shipping. The statute law was consolidated by the Merchant Shipping Act, 1894 (replacing the Merchant Shipping Act, 1854). The law is contained in the Merchant Shipping Acts, 1894 to 1970: see s. 101 of the Merchant Shipping Act, 1970.

For restrictions on the transfer of

ships, see the Emergency Laws (Re-enactments and Repeals) Act, 1964, s. 16; S.I. 1969 No. 1836.

Merchantable, marketable. Where goods are sold in the course of business, there is an implied condition that the goods are of merchantable quality except (a) as regards defects specifically drawn to the buyer's attention before the contract is made or if the buyer examines the goods before the contract is made, as regards defects which that examination ought to reveal (Sale of Goods Act, 1893, s. 14 (2); Supply of Goods (Implied Terms) Act, 1973, s. 3).

Merchants, Statute of, the statute 1285, 13 Edw. 1, st. 3. See ACTON BURNEL, STATUTE OF.

Merchenlage. See MERCEN-LAGE.

Merchet, a fine or composition paid by inferior tenants to the lord for liberty to dispose of their daughters in marriage. See MARCHET.

Merciament, an amerciament, penalty or fine.

Mercimoniatus Angliae, customs duties in the early Norman period (1 Knighton, c. 5).

Mercy, In. See AMERCIAMENT.

Mercy, Prerogative of. See PARDON; PREROGATIVE.

Mercy, Recommendation to. Before the abolition of the death penalty, it was common for a jury, in finding the accused guilty of murder, to accompany their verdict by a recommendation of the prisoner to the mercy of the Crown on certain named grounds. Such a recommendation has no legal effect whatever, but is usually attended to, although persons have been hanged in spite of it.

Merger [Lat. *mergere*, to sink], an annihilation, by act of law, of a particular in an expectant estate consequent upon their union in the same person without an intervening estate in another person, thus accelerating into possession the expectant which swallows up the particular estate. It is the drowning of one estate in another, and differs from suspension, which is but a partial extinguishment for a time; while extinguishment, properly so termed, is the destruction of a collateral thing in the subject itself out of which it is derived. In order that there may be a merger, the two estates which

are supposed to coalesce must be vested in the same person at the same time and in the same right (*Re Radcliffe* [1892] 1 Ch. 231). An entailed interest, however, is an exception to the rule; for a man may have in his own right both an entailed interest and a reversion in fee; and the entailed interest will not merge in the fee (2 Bl.Comm. 177).

The doctrine of merger probably results from the maxim *nemo potest esse dominus et tenens*; or perhaps from the inconsistency, but for it, of one person owning two interests in fact, whilst one of them, in law, includes the time or duration of both.

When the same person has a legal estate in the fee, and is also entitled to the trust or beneficial ownership of that estate, the trust will merge in the legal ownership, but, on the other hand, the legal estate can never be extinguished in the equitable ownership.

Merger is either absolute or qualified, for an interest as against one person may be extinguished, whilst as against another it may still have existence.

Before the passing of the Real Property Act, 1845 (repealed and reproduced by the Law of Property Act, 1925, s. 139), the doctrine worked great hardship in cases where the immediate reversion on a lease was a leasehold term; leaseholds, however long their term, being considered an inferior or less estate than a freehold, if the leasehold reversion became merged in an estate for life or other freehold estate, any sublease was terminated and the rent of the sublease and all remedies for it were lost. The Act of 1845, s. 9, declared that when the reversion on a lease became merged, the next estate was to be deemed the reversion. See APPORTIONMENT.

In order to effect a merger there must be two interests at least in the same property, or in the same part of the same property, which must vest in the same person; the several interests must be immediately expectant upon each other; the more remote interest must be without any intervening vested interest or contingent remainder created in the same instant of time and by the same means which originated the other interest, and the determination or acquisition of an intermediate interest may be the cause of merger, as between interests kept distinct by means of such intermediate interest; the interest in reversion or remainder must be larger than the preceding interest; there cannot be a merger as between equal estates of freehold.

Under the Law of Property Act, 1925, s. 88, foreclosure by a mortgagee will merge the mortgage term into and vest the fee simple in the mortgagee subject to any prior mortgage term, and a similar consequence, *mutatis mutandis*, follows upon foreclosure of a leasehold term (s. 89).

By the Law of Property Act, 1925, s. 185, reproducing the Judicature Act, 1873, s. 25 (4), it is provided that there shall not be any merger by operation of law only of any estate the beneficial interest in which would not be deemed to be merged or extinguished in equity. In equity merger is, and always has been, a question of the intention of the parties (*Capital, etc., Bank* v. *Rhodes* [1903] 1 Ch. 652).

As to the merger of charges on property, the general rule is that if the benefit of the charge and the property subject to it vest in the same person, equity will treat the charge as kept alive or merged according to whether it is of advantage or of no advantage to the person in whom the two interests have vested that the charge should be kept alive (*Whiteley* v. *Delaney* [1914] A.C. 132). The Law of Property Act, 1925, s. 116, enacts that, subject to this rule in equity, a mortgage term when discharged by payment shall become a satisfied term and shall cease.

When an engagement has been made by simple contract, and then the same engagement is made by deed, the simple contract is merged and extinguished in the deed. If an action is brought and judgment recovered, the right of action is said to be merged in the judgment (*Aman* v. *Southern Ry.* [1926] 1 K.B. 59).

When a right belonging to the Crown by virtue of its prerogative (such as the right to wreck) is granted to a subject as an appendancy to land, then if the land comes into the hands of the Crown, the right merges in the *jus coronae*, and does not pass by a grant of the land, but must be created again. Rights vested in the Crown otherwise than *jure coronae* (such as warrens, fairs, etc.) do not merge (9 Co.Rep. 24).

The Fair Trading Act, 1973, regulates and restricts business mergers (ss. 57–77). See MONOPOLIES AND MERGERS COMMISSION.

Merit, Order of, an order instituted in 1902. Members bear no titles, but rank next after G.C.B.'s (see BATH) and are entitled to append the initials O.M. to their names and to wear a badge. The badge distinguishes military from civil members by a difference in design.

Merito beneficium legis amittit, qui legem ipsam subvertere intendit (2 Co. Inst. 53). (He justly loses the benefit of law who purposes to overturn the law itself.) Against those who attempted to subvert the laws there lay a writ in the nature of a commission *ad capiendum impugnatores juris regis et ad ducendum eos ad Gaolam de Newgate* and this was *lex terrae* to take a man without answer or summons.

Meritorious consideration, one founded upon some moral obligation. See CAUSE OF ACTION; CONSIDERATION.

Merits. A person is said to have a good cause of action or defence on the merits when his claim or defence is based on the real matters in question, and not on any technical ground. Thus, before the Judicature Acts, 1873–75, a defence based on the misjoinder or non-joinder of parties by the plaintiff would not have been a defence on the merits. The term " merits " is to be understood in a technical sense, and is not confined to strictly moral and conscientious defences; thus defences of the Statute of Frauds, 1677, s. 4, or the Limitation Act, 1939, and of bankruptcy and infancy, are defences on the merits.

If a defendant inadvertently allows judgment to go by default, the court will not, as a rule, set the judgment aside under R.S.C., Ord. 13, r. 9, and allow him to defend unless he makes an affidavit of merits, that is, an affidavit showing that he has a substantial ground of defence to the action. A like affidavit has to be made by a defendant seeking to resist an application for judgment under Ord. 14.

Merk. See MARK.

Mero motu. See EX MERO MOTU.

Merry-go-rounds. See WHIRLIGIG.

Merseum, a lake; also a marsh or fenland.

Merse-ware, the ancient name for the inhabitants of Romney Marsh, Kent.

Mersey. As to collisions in the sea channels leading to the Mersey, see the Mersey Channels Act, 1897. The Mersey Docks and Harbour Board is the harbour authority for Liverpool and Birkenhead (Mersey Docks Consolidation Act, 1858; Mersey Docks Act, 1881). The Minister for Transport became Commissioner of the Conservancy (Minister of Transport Act, 1919, s. 2; S.I. 1970 No. 1681).

Mertlage, a church calendar or rubric.

Merton, Statute of, the statute 1235, 20 Hen. 3, the earliest statute in the Statute-book, so called because it was enacted at the priory of Merton, in Surrey. Its principal unrepealed provisions allow the inclosure or approvement of commons by lords of manors, and declare the illegitimacy of children born before marriage. It was in connection with the latter provision that the barons declared against any alteration, notwithstanding the request of the bishops that the law should be altered. *Omnes comites et barones,* runs the statute, *una voce responderunt quod nolunt leges Angliae mutare quae usitatae sunt et approbatae.* The Legitimacy Act, 1976, does not affect succession to dignities or titles of honour (Sch. 1 para. 4). See BASTARD; INCLOSURE; LEGITIMATION.

Mescroyants, unbelievers.

Mese, a house and its appurtenances.

Mesnality, a manor held under a superior lord.

Mesnalty, the right of the mesne; the tenure or seignory of a mesne lord. If there was a lord paramount, a mesne lord, and a tenant paravail, and the lord paramount purchased the tenancy of the tenant paravail in fee, then the seignory of the mesnalty was extinct (Litt. 231).

Mesne [Lat. *medius*] (pronounced "mean"), middle, intervening, intermediate. Thus in framing an assignment of a lease which has already passed through several hands since it was ori-ginally granted, it is usual to refer to all the assignments before the last as "mesne assignments." So if property is mortgaged first to A and then to B, and is subsequently mortgaged to A a second time, B is said to be a mesne incumbrancer, or to have a mesne incumbrance, because his mortgage stands between the two mortgages to A. See PRIORITY; TACKING. In the old books "mesne" often denotes "mesne lord" (Co.Litt. 152b).

Mesne lord, a lord who holds of a superior lord, and of whom an inferior (tenant paravail) holds.

Mesne process, writs intervening in the progress of a suit or action between its beginning and end, as contradistinguished from primary and final process. Thus, the *capias* or mesne process was issued after a writ of summons, which was the primary process, and before a *capias ad satisfaciendum,* which was the final process, or process of execution. See IMPRISONMENT.

By the Judgments Act, 1838, s. 1, the power of arrest upon mesne process was relaxed, and confined to the case of a debtor about to quit England, and where the amount of the debt was £20 or upwards; and the Debtors Act, 1869, s. 6, enacts that a person shall not be arrested upon mesne process in any action. Nevertheless, where a plaintiff has good cause of action against the defendant to the amount of £50 or upwards, and the defendant is about to quit England, and the absence of the defendant from England will materially prejudice the plaintiff in the prosecution of his action, a judge may order the defendant to be arrested unless or until security be found.

Mesne profits, profits derived from land whilst the possession of it has been improperly withheld: that is, the yearly value of the premises. Mesne profits are the rents and profits which a trespasser has, or might have, received or made during his occupation of the premises, and which therefore he must pay over to the true owner as compensation for the tort which he has committed. A claim for rent is therefore liquidated, while a claim for mesne profits is unliquidated.

The jury are not bound by the amount of the rent, but may give extra damages.

But ground-rent paid by the defendant should be deducted from the damages. A plaintiff may recover in this action the costs of the action of ejectment.

As to the date from which mesne profits are assessable, see *Elliott* v. *Boynton* [1924] 1 Ch. 236.

A claim for arrears of rent and mesne profits may be joined with a claim for possession (R.S.C., Ord. 13, rr. 4, 5).

Mesne, Writ of, a writ which lay when the lord paramount distrained on the tenant paravail; the latter had a writ of mesne against the mesne lord (Litt. 142).

Messarius [Lat. *messis*], a chief servant in husbandry; a bailiff (2 Dugd. Mon. 832).

Messe thane, one who said Mass; a priest.

Messenger, one who carries an errand; a forerunner.

Messengers are certain officers employed under the direction of the Secretaries of State, and always ready to be sent with dispatches, foreign and domestic (now called Queen's Messengers). They were employed with the secretaries' warrants to arrest persons for treason, or other offences against the State, which did not so properly fall under the cognisance of the common law, and, perhaps, were not properly to be divulged in the ordinary course of justice (2 Hawk.P.C. c. xvi, s. 9).

In bankruptcy there was a sort of sheriff's officer, known as the messenger, whose duty it was to execute the decrees and processes of the court. He and his staff were transferred by the Bankruptcy Act, 1883, to the Board of Trade.

There was a messenger or pursuivant of the Great Seal, who, amongst other things, had to do with writs for the election of members of Parliament. His office was abolished as a separate office by the Great Seal (Offices) Act, 1874, s. 4, which provided that his duties as to writs for the election of members of Parliament should be transferred to such officer as the Lord Chancellor should select, and that the officer so selected might bear the title of Messenger of the Great Seal. The officer is now the Clerk of the Chamber and Officer in Charge, Crown Office.

The Messengers of the Exchequer were four officers attached to that court who acted as pursuivants to the Lord Treasurer.

In the seventeenth and eighteenth centuries the Stationers' Company had an officer, known as the Messenger of the Press, whose duty it was to search, at first for unlicensed, and subsequently for seditious, printings.

Messina, harvest.

Messis sementem sequitur. (Harvest follows the sower.) See EMBLEMENTS.

Messuage [Low Lat. *messuagium*; Fr. *maison*], a dwelling-house with its outbuildings and curtilage and adjacent land assigned to the use thereof (Co.Litt. 5b, 56b).

In *Monks* v. *Dykes* (1839) 4 M. & W. 567, it was said that a messuage and a dwelling-house are substantially the same thing, and therefore if rooms are so occupied as to be in fact a dwelling-house, they may be described as a messuage.

As a word of conveyance, " messuage " includes not only the buildings but also the curtilage, orchard and garden belonging thereto. A " capital messuage " is the chief mansion house of an estate. See MANSION.

Metachronism [μετά; χρονος], an error in computation of time.

Metage, the act of measuring. The Corporation of the City of London had under charter and by prescription been in receipt of a large income arising from their right of compulsory metage, at first of all merchandise, and finally only of grain, brought into the Port of London. The dues which they levied for measuring the grain were known as fillage and lastage. The Metage on Grain (Port of London) Act, 1872, abolished compulsory metage and fillage and lastage, and provided that for thirty years a duty at the rate of three-sixteenths of a penny on each hundredweight of grain should be paid to the corporation. The Act, which provided that the proceeds of the duty should be applied to the preservation of open spaces for public use, was amended by the City of London (Various Powers) Act, 1877.

Metalliferous mines. See MINERALS.

Metals, Dealers in old. See SCRAP METALS.

Metayer system. Under this system land is divided in small farms, among single families, the landlord generally supplying the stock and receiving, in lieu of rent, a fixed proportion of the produce. This proportion, which is generally paid in kind, is usually (as is implied in the words *métayer, mezzajuólo* and *medietarius*) one-half (1 Mill, Pol.Econ. 296, 363; Smith, Wealth of Nat., 3, c. ii).

Mete, meat, in the sense of food generally. It occurs in several compounds, such as metecorn (an allowance for food to servants or to customary tenants in return for their labour), metegavel (a rent paid in food, etc.). The word also meant to measure, and occurs in this sense in compound forms, such as mete-wand (a measuring-rod), etc.

Metecorn, a measure or portion of corn given by a lord to customary tenants as a reward and encouragement for labour.

Metegavel, a meat-tax, a tribute or rent paid in victuals.

Meter [Sax. *mete*], an instrument of measurement, as a gas meter or an electricity meter.

Metes and bounds. Where a widow was entitled to dower (*q.v.*) of land, her share was ascertained and set apart to be held by her in severalty, and she was then said to hold it by metes and bounds, that is, by measurement and boundaries (Litt. 36). See ADMEASUREMENT.

Metewand or **Mete yard**, a staff of a certain length wherewith measures are taken.

Metheglin, an alcoholic fluid made by fermenting honey, water and spices, mentioned in the statute 1663, 15 Car. 2, c. 9.

Methel [Sax. *mathlian,* to speak, to harangue], speech, discourse (Anc.Inst. Eng.).

Methyl alcohol. See the Customs and Excise Act, 1952, ss. 115, 121.

Methylated spirits. See the Customs and Excise Act, 1952, ss. 116–121, 172, and the Hydrocarbon Oil (Customs and Excise) Act, 1971.

Metre. The yard (*q.v.*) or the metre is the unit of measurement of length in the United Kingdom (Weights and Measures Act, 1963, s. 1). Metre has the meaning assigned to it from time to time by the Department of Trade. The Weights and Measures (International Definitions) Order 1963 (S.I. 1963 No. 1354) defined the meanings of metre, litre, kilogramme, ampere, watt, volt and ohm in terms which reproduce in English the international definitions of these units. Subdivisions of a metre are decimetre (one tenth of a metre), centimetre, (one hundreth of a metre), and millimetre (one thousandth of a metre) (Weights and Measures Act, 1963, s. 10, Sch. 1 Pt. I). A square metre is a superficial area equal to that of a square each side of which measures one metre (s. 10, Sch. I Pt. II). A square decimetre is one hundredth of a square metre. A square centimetre is one hundredth of a square decimetre. A square millimetre is one hundredth of a square centimetre (*ibid.*). An are is one hundred square metres. A decare is ten ares. A hectare is 100 ares (*ibid.*). A cubic metre is a volume equal to that of a cube each edge of which measures one metre. A cubic decimetre is one thousandth of a cubic metre. A cubic centimetre is one thousandth of a cubic decimetre (s. 10, Sch. 1, Part III).

Metric system, a system of weights and measures in which the unit is multiplied or divided by ten. The Weights and Measures Act, 1963, prescribes metric units of measurement in addition to imperial units. The length of a yard (*q.v.*) is stated as a proportion of a metre (*q.v.*) and the pound as a proportion of a kilogramme (*q.v.*) (ss. 1, 2, 3-5, 10, Schs. 1–3). Further weights were added by S.I. 1968 No. 320; 1970 No. 1709. The metric ton is to be known as the tonne or metric tonne (S.I. 1970 No. 1709). See also S.I. 1971 No. 827. See CARAT.

Metric ton. See KILOGRAMME.

Metropolis, the principal city, being the seat of government, in any kingdom.

Metropolitan, an archbishop. The primate and metropolitan of all England is the Archbishop of Canterbury.

Metropolitan Board of Works, a board appointed for the better local management of the metropolis, and constituted and authorised under the Metropolis Management Act, 1855, and many subsequent Acts. The board had the care and management of all grounds and gardens dedicated to the use of the inhabitants in the metropolis, the superintendence of the drainage, the regulation of the street traffic, and generally of the buildings of the metropolis. The board was superseded by the London County Council (Local Government Act, 1888, s. 40 (8)). See LONDON.

Metropolitan borough councils. See LONDON.

Metropolitan counties. See LOCAL GOVERNMENT.

Metropolitan courts, the county courts of the districts which, together with the City of London, form the London Bankruptcy District. See BANKRUPTCY COURTS.

Metropolitan police district, the area under the charge of the Metropolitan Police. See the London Government Act, 1963, s. 76; S.I. 1974 No. 482, art. 11.

Metropolitan stipendiary magistrate. Under the Administration of Justice Act, 1964, s. 10 (replacing the relevant provisions of the Metropolitan Police Acts, 1829 to 1959) the Crown may appoint salaried magistrates to execute the duties of justices of the peace within any London commission area and for the counties of Essex, Hertfordshire, Kent and Surrey, from amongst barristers and solicitors of not less than seven years' standing.

The number of metropolitan magistrates may not exceed sixty or such larger number as may be specified by Order in Council (Administration of Justice Act, 1973, s. 2 (6)), Sch. 5 Pt. II. A metropolitan magistrate may be removed from office by the Lord Chancellor for inability or misbehaviour (Act of 1964, s. 10 (4) (c)).

The Lord Chancellor may assign a metropolitan stipendiary magistrate to a petty sessional division in the inner London area but that does not preclude him from exercising jurisdiction for any other division of the inner London area (Act of 1964, s. 10 (4)). One of the metropolitan stipendiary magistrates is designated by the Lord Chancellor to be Chief Metropolitan Stipendiary Magistrate (Act of 1964, s. 10 (3)).

A metropolitan stipendiary magistrate can do all things for which two ordinary magistrates are required (Act of 1964, s. 9 (4)).

A barrister may be appointed chief clerk to any metropolitan stipendiary court (Criminal Justice Administration Act, 1962, s. 11 (1)). And see CLERK TO THE JUSTICES.

The metropolitan magistrates' courts are: Bow Street, Clerkenwell, Great Marlborough Street, Greenwich, Woolwich, Marylebone, North London, Old Street, Camberwell Green, Tower Bridge, Lambeth, Thames, Wells Street, West London, South Western.

Metteshep or **Mettenschep,** an acknowledgment paid in a certain measure of corn; a fine or penalty imposed on tenants for not doing their customary service of cutting the lord's corn.

Meubles meublant [Fr.] household furniture.

Meya, a mow or heap of corn (Blount, Ten. 130).

Mice. See RATS AND MICE.

Micel-gemote. See MICHEL-GEMOTE.

Michael Angelo Taylor's Act, the Metropolitan Paving Act, 1817, introduced into the House of Commons by Mr. Michael Angelo Taylor, who, among other things, was admitted to Lincoln's Inn in 1770 at the age of twelve years, and was called to the Bar four years afterwards.

Michaelmas, September 29, the feast of the Archangel Michael and All Angels. It is one of the customary quarter-days, and gives its name to the autumn sittings of the High Court, though they commence on October 1, and to the Michaelmas term of the Inns, though it commences on November 5. See OLD MICHAELMAS DAY.

Michaelmas term. This began on November 2 and ended on November 25. The division of the legal year into terms was abolished so far as regards the administration of justice by the Judicature Act, 1873, s. 26.

Michel-gemote, the great meeting or ancient parliament of the kingdom (1 Bl. Comm. 147).

Michel-synoth, the great council of the Saxons (1 Bl. Comm. 147).

Michery, theft, cheating.

Middle Temple. See INNS OF COURT.

Middle-man, an intermediary between wholesale merchants and retail dealers; a distributor from producer to consumer.

Middlesex. Much of the ancient county of Middlesex was absorbed into the county of London by the Local Government Act, 1888, and the county of Middlesex ceased to exist under the London Government Act, 1963, s. 3. See LONDON.

The Act of 1888 provided for a sheriff of Middlesex (ss. 46 (6), 113). For the preceding seven hundred years the duties of sheriff had been performed in Middlesex by the sheriffs of the City of London.

The Middlesex Deeds Registry was a registry of assurances relating to land situate in the county of Middlesex. It was regulated by the Middlesex Registry Act, 1708, but that statute did not apply to copyholds, leases at a rack-rent, or leases not exceeding twenty-one years, or to any instrument made after the passing of the Land Charges Act, 1900, which was capable of registration under that Act or under the Land Charges Registration and Searches Act, 1888 (Land Charges Act, 1900, s. 4). The Middlesex Deeds Register was closed by the Land Registration Act, 1936, and the Middlesex Deeds Act, 1940. See also the Land Registration and Land Charges Act, 1971, s. 14.

Middlesex, Bill of, a writ resorted to by the Court of King's Bench in order to enlarge its jurisdiction in civil causes, which was formerly confined to actions of trespass, or other injury alleged to have been committed *vi et armis*. But it might always hold pleas of any civil action other than an action real, provided the defendant was an officer of the court, or in the custody of the marshal, or prison-keeper of the court. In proceedings against prisoners or officers of the court, the actions were said to be commenced by bill, in all other cases by original writ (3 Bl.Comm. 285). See BILL OF MIDDLESEX.

Midsummer Day, the summer solstice, which is on June 24, and the feast of St. John the Baptist, a festival first mentioned by Maximus Tauricensis, A.D. 400. It is one of the four usual quarter-days for the paying of rent. See OLD MIDSUMMER DAY.

Midwife, a person following the profession of delivering women of children. The Medical Act, 1956, ss. 10, 11, requires as a qualification for registration as a medical practitioner, and for the recovery of professional charges, the passing of a qualifying examination in medicine, surgery, and midwifery.

The Midwives Act, 1951 (which consolidated the Midwives Acts, 1902 to 1950), provides for the constitution and functions of the Central Midwives Board and for the regulation of midwives. See also the National Health Service Reorganisation Act, 1973, Schs. 4, 5. The central authority is the Department of Health and Social Security. See HEALTH, MINISTRY OF.

Midwives are excusable as of right from jury service. See JURY. As to sex discrimination, see the Sex Discrimination Act, 1975, s. 20.

Mile, a measure of length containing 1,760 yards (Weights and Measures Act, 1963, s. 10, Sch. 1 Pt. I). The statute 1592, 13 Eliz. 1 c. 6, s. 8 provided that the mile should contain eight furlongs (*q.v.*) and every furlong 40 luggs or poles, and every lugg or pole (*q.v.*) $16\frac{1}{2}$ feet. The mile everywhere has always contained 320 rods (see ROD), poles, perches or luggs but varied in different parts of the country as the length of the perch (*q.v.*) varied locally. A square mile is 640 acres (*q.v.*) (Weights and Measures Act, 1963, s. 10, Sch. 1 Pt. II).

Mileage, travelling expenses which are allowed to witnesses, sheriffs, and bailiffs and others.

Mileometer. See ODOMETER.

Miles [Lat.], a soldier; particularly, a knight.

Milestones. Railway companies were required by the Railways Clauses Consolidation Act, 1845, to set up the posts marking the miles, quarter-miles, and half-miles which are to be seen along railways. No corresponding obligation was imposed on highway authorities, who however were empowered by the Highway Rate Assessment and Expenditure Act, 1882, s. 6, to expend money on maintaining, replacing or setting up milestones along any highway. The trustees of turnpike roads had been required under various repealed statutes to erect milestones at distances of one mile.

Militare, to be knighted.

Military Asylum of Chelsea, an institution for the reception of children of soldiers, now called the Duke of York's Royal Military School.

Military courts, the Court of Chivalry and courts-martial. See COURT, CHIVALRY OF; COURT-MARTIAL.

Military feuds, the genuine or original feuds which were in the hands of military men, who performed military duty for their tenures. See TENURE.

Military forces. See ARMY; MILITIA; RESERVE FORCES.

Military law. As distinguished from civil law, military law is the law relating to and administered by military courts, and is concerned with the trial and punishment of offences committed by officers, soldiers and other persons (*e.g.*, sutlers and camp followers) who are from circumstances subjected for the time being to the same law as soldiers. But the term is frequently used in a wider sense and as including not only the disciplinary but also the administrative law of the army, as, for instance, the law of enlistment and billeting.

Military manoeuvres. These may be authorised by Order in Council under the Manoeuvres Act, 1958, which consolidated the Ministry Manoeuvres Acts, 1897 and 1911, and the relevant portions of the Land Powers (Defence) Act, 1958.

Military necessity, the doctrine according to which military needs justify departures from usages, as distinct from laws, of warfare.

Military objective, an object of which the destruction or injury would constitute a distinct military advantage to the belligerent (Hague Rules, 1923).

Military offences, those offences which are cognisable by the courts military, as insubordination, sleeping on guard, desertion, etc., as well as any civil crime, with special provisions in the case of manslaughter, treason or rape.

Military service. See NATIONAL SERVICE.

Military tenures. The various tenures by knight's service, grand serjeanty, cornage, etc., are frequently called military tenures, from the nature of the services which they involved. See SERVICE; TENURE.

Military testament, an informal will made by a soldier on active service. By the Wills Act, 1837, s. 11, a soldier or sailor on active service may dispose of his personal estate as he might have done before that Act. The Wills (Soldiers and Sailors) Act, 1918, extends this right to make wills without formalities to realty. As to seamen and marines, see also the Navy and Marines (Wills) Act 1953. See NUNCUPATIVE WILL; WILL.

Militia, the national soldiery, as distinguished from the regular forces or standing army, being the inhabitants, or, as they have been sometimes called, the trained bands of a town or county, who were armed on short notice for their own defence. The force which was raised after the Restoration of 1660 was a substitute for those which had been raised under the commissions of array (*q.v.*) and lieutenancy (*q.v.*). The name had been in use during the Civil War, but the force was for the first time regularly raised under the authority of the statute 1662, 14 Car. 2, c. 3, which empowered the lords lieutenant (*q.v.*) of counties to raise and train troops within their counties for service as the king might direct. The statute 1757, 30 Geo. 2, c. 25, provided that the men required for the militia should be selected by a system of balloting. This system of balloting fell in abeyance after 1815, except as regards two years in the reign of William IV: but for this, until the enactment of the statute 1829, 10 Geo. 4, c. 10, there would appear to have been no statutory sanction. As a substitute for the balloting system, voluntary enlistment was introduced: but this again was not put upon a regular footing until the enactment of the statute 1852, 15 & 16 Vict. c. 50. The succession of Acts for the suspension of the ballot ended with the enactment of the Militia (Ballot Suspension) Act, 1865, which, though only a temporary Act, was kept in force by the annual Expiring Laws Continuance Acts. This Act of 1865 provided, however, by s. 2, that the militia ballot might be revived by Order in Council. The Militia Act, 1882, s. 12 (as amended by the Reserve Forces and Militia Act, 1898, s. 2), made the militia available only for service in the United Kingdom, except as regards those members of the force who might voluntarily offer to serve elsewhere. The militia in the old sense has now disappeared. The Territorial Army and Militia Act, 1921, s. 2, enacted that the portion of the army reserve previously called the special reserve should be called the militia. Men subjected to compulsory military training under the Military Training Act, 1939, were also known as militiamen. The Army Reserve Act, 1950, s. 2, provided that where a man who has never served in the regular forces is enlisted into the first class of the army reserve, he shall serve therein as a militia-man. See RESERVE FORCES.

The word militia was also used to mean knighthood.

Milk. See DAIRIES.

Milk for meat, an arrangement that the agister of cows should take their milk in exchange for their pasturage. In *London and Yorkshire Bank* v. *Belton* (1885) 15 Q.B.D. 457, it was held that under such an agreement the farmer was taking a " fair price " for the grass within the Agricultural Holdings Act, 1883, s. 45, now the Agricultural Holdings Act, 1948, s. 19, by which live-stock taken in to be fed at a fair price are exempted from distress for rent.

Milk Marketing Board, a board set up to regulate the marketing of milk under the powers given by the Agricultural Marketing Act, 1931, s. 1 and the Agricultural Marketing Act, 1958, s. 1.

Mill dam. Every proprietor may divert the waters of a stream for the purpose, for example, of turning a mill: but then he must carry the water back into the stream so that the other proprietors may in their turn have the benefit of it. The use of the stream must not interfere with the equal common right of his neighbours (*Wright* v. *Howard* (1823) 1 Sim. & St. 203). On navigable rivers mill dams erected since Magna Carta, 1215, are illegal (*Rolle* v. *Whyte* (1868) L.R. 3 Q.B. 286).

Millbank Penitentiary, a prison erected near Westminster as provided by the statutes 1812, 52 Geo. 3, c. 44, and 1813, 53 Geo. 3, c. 162, for the purpose of confining convicted offenders. Further provisions for its regulation were made by the statutes 1816, 56 Geo. 3, c. 63, and 1819, 59 Geo. 3, c. 136. Its demolition was authorised by the Housing of the Working Classes Act, 1885.

Milleate or **Mill-leat,** a trench to convey water to or from a mill: see the statute 1609, 7 Jac. 1, c. 19.

Milled money, money with regular marking on the edge of coins; coined money.

Mill-holms, low meadows and other fields in the vicinity of mills, or watery places about mill dams.

Milligramme. See KILOGRAMME.

Millilitre. See LITRE.

Millimetre. See METRE.

Minage, a toll or duty paid for selling corn by a measure called a mina (Jacob).

Minare, to dig mines.

Minator, a miner.

Minator carucae, a ploughman.

Minatur innocentibus, qui parcit nocentibus (4 Co.Rep. 45). (He threatens the innocent who spares the guilty.) The leaving of law-breakers unpunished is a menace to law-abiding persons. See IMPUNITAS, ETC.

Mine [Wel. *mwyn, mwy*; *maen,* a stone], an excavation or cavern in the earth; an excavation made for the purpose of getting coal or other minerals (*q.v.*).

The inspection and regulation of mines is provided for by the Mines and Quarries Acts, 1954 to 1971. See also S.I. 1974 Nos. 2012, 2013; the Local Government Act, 1974, Sch. 8; the Sex Discrimination Act, 1975, s. 21, and COAL MINES.

As to the rating of mines, see the General Rate Act, 1967, ss. 35, 36; Local Government Act, 1974, s. 19, Sch. 3 para. 7.

Mineral rights duty, a duty imposed by the Finance (1909–10) Act, 1910, ss. 20, 21, on the rental value of minerals. The duties were abolished by the Finance Act, 1967, Sch. 16 Pt. VIII.

Mineral waters. See TABLE WATERS.

Minerals, those parts of the earth which are capable of being got from underneath the surface for the purpose of profit. The term therefore includes coal, metal ores of all kinds, stone, slate, and coprolites, but not the common clay, sand, or gravel found in the upper soil. It includes all substances of commercial value which can be got from beneath the earth, either by mining or quarrying, except common clay (*Glasgow* v. *Farie* (1888) 13 App.Cas. 657), or sandstone (*N.B. Ry.* v. *Budhill Coal and Sandstone Co.* [1910] A.C. 116); but china clay is a mineral (*G.W. Ry.* v. *Carpalla China Clay Co.* [1910] A.C. 83): see also *Waring* v. *Foden* [1932] 1 Ch. 276.

In the Mines and Quarries Act, 1954, the term " minerals " includes " stone, slate, clay, gravel, sand and other natural deposits except peat " (s. 182 (1)).

By the Law of Property Act, 1925, s. 205 (1) (ix), mines and minerals include any strata or seam of minerals or substances in or under any land and the powers of working and getting the same, but not an undivided share thereof.

A mine is a work for the excavation of minerals by means of pits, shafts, levels, tunnels, etc., as opposed to a quarry, where the whole excavation is open. See also the definitions in the Mines and Quarries Act, 1954, s. 180.

While unsevered, minerals form part of the land, and as such are real estate. When severed, they become personal chattels.

Royal mines are mines of gold or silver, and belong to the Crown, in whosesoever land they may be found (1 Bl.Comm. 295).

In other cases, mines and minerals other than coal (see COAL MINES) belong prima facie to the owner of the surface of the land, though they may be, and frequently are, held by different persons. Minerals under copyhold land belonged to the lord, though he could not work them without the tenant's consent, except by a local custom. (See COPYHOLD.) Facilities for the working of minerals may be obtained under the Mines (Working Facilities and Support) Acts, 1923 to 1974. See, as to the principles on which compensation is awarded, *Re National Coal Board's Application* [1960] Ch. 192. Further rights to withdraw support in order to enable coal to be worked are contained in the Coal Act, 1938, Sch. 2; Coal Act, 1943, s. 11, Sch. 2, and the Coal Industry Act, 1975, s. 2. In many places, customs or prescriptions exist by virtue of which persons are entitled to work mines in land the freehold of which is vested in another person (Houghton, *Compleat Miner*; Gough, *Mendip Mining Laws*). See BARMOTE COURT; GALE; GOLD-MINES; STANNARIES; TIN-BOUNDING.

As to the rights of adjoining owners in respect of minerals, see BARRIER; BOUNDARY; BOUNDS; EASEMENT; SUPPORT.

Obligations are imposed on mine owners for the protection of the public and of persons employed in mines by the Mines and Quarries Act, 1954. See COAL MINES; FENCE.

For safety provisions, see the Health and Safety at Work etc. Act, 1974, and orders made thereunder.

Provision is made with regard to the opencast working of ironstone by the Mineral Workings Acts, 1951 and 1971, and the Local Government Act, 1974, s. 35, Sch. 6 para. 19, Sch. 8.

In relation to the winning and working of minerals the provisions of the Town and Country Planning Act, 1971, are modified. See s. 264 and the Town and Country Planning Development Order, 1963, Pt. III.

A Secretary of State may make contributions up to £50 million towards expenditure incurred on searching for, or on discovering and testing, mineral deposits in Great Britain or in the sea bed and subsoil of the territorial waters of the United Kingdom adjacent to Great Britain or in that of any area for the time being designated under s. 1 (7) of the Continental Shelf Act, 1964. The term " mineral deposits " includes any natural deposits capable of being lifted or extracted from the earth (Mineral Exploration and Investment Grants Act, 1972).

For provisions for the protection of persons working on oil-rigs, etc., see the Mineral Workings (Offshore Installations) Act, 1971; Offshore Installations (Diving Operations) Regulations, 1974 (No. 1229).

Minim. One-sixtieth of a fluid drachm (Weights and Measures Act, 1963, s. 10, Sch. 1 Pt. IV) but a minim is no longer a unit of measurement (s. 10 (9)).

Minime mutanda sunt quae certam habent interpretationem (Co.Litt. 229, 365). (Things which have a settled interpretation are to be altered as little as possible.) See A COMMUNI, ETC.; MAGISTER RERUM, ETC.; PERICULOSUM EST, ETC.

Miniment or **Muniment,** the evidences of title. See MUNIMENT.

Minimum lending rate. See BANK RATE.

Minimum subscription, the minimum cash to be raised by the issue of shares offered to the public for subscription. This must be stated in the prospectus and application therefor received before allotment of shares. The amount includes the minimum required, in the opinion of the directors, for property to be bought by the proceeds of the issue, preliminary expenses, repayment of loans for those purposes, and working capital (Companies Act, 1948, s. 47).

Minimum wage. In early times wages were regulated by statutes (Kelsall, *Wage Regulations under the Statute of Artificers*). See LABOURERS, STATUTE OF.

The system of establishing by statute a wage which is to be the lowest paid was introduced in modern times by the Trade Boards Act, 1909, which applied only to certain trades (mentioned in the Schedule to the Act), the men and women employed in which were understood to be unable to secure adequate wages by negotiation with their employers, and to such other trades as might be brought within the Act by Order in Council. In 1912 a minimum wage was established for coal-miners (see COAL MINES). During the war of 1914–18 the payment of prescribed wages was made obligatory in a number of industries connected with the supply of munitions of war by Acts of temporary operation. The Corn Production Act, 1917, Pt. II, established for agricultural workers a minimum wage, which was to be fixed by the Agricultural Wages Board constituted under s. 5 of the Act. The Corn Production (Repeal) Act, 1921, s. 5, provided machinery by which standard rates of wages could be fixed, and enacted that these rates should be paid to agricultural workers unless the contract for service specified a lower rate, and unless such lower rate was approved by the body which fixed the standard rate or by a court in which proceedings for the recovery of wages at the standard rate were being taken. Today most industries have minimum-wage provisions.

See AGRICULTURAL WAGES BOARD; TRADE BOARDS.

Mining lease, a lease for mining purposes, that is, the searching for, winning, working, getting, making merchantable, carrying away, or disposing of mines and minerals, or purposes connected therewith; the term includes a grant or licence for mining purposes (Law of Property Act, 1925, s. 205 (1) (xiv)).

Minister, an agent; one who acts not by an inherent authority but under another.

In politics the term means one to whom a sovereign entrusts the administration of government. See MINISTRY.

The functions and styles and titles of Ministers may be altered under the Ministers of the Crown Act, 1975.

The number of Ministers entitled to sit and vote in the House of Commons is ninety-five (House of Commons (Disqualification) Act, 1975, s. 2, Sch. 2).

A Minister of State is a member of Her Majesty's Government in the United Kingdom, appointed at a salary, who neither has charge of any public department nor holds any other specified office (House of Commons Disqualification Act, 1975, s. 9). The salary of a Minister of State is between £7,500 and £9,500 a year unless he is a member of the Cabinet, when it is £13,000 (Ministerial and other Salaries Act, 1975, s. 1, Sch. 1).

Quoad the Church of England a minister includes anyone in priest's orders having a cure of souls. It is now principally applied to the clergy of the various nonconformist bodies. As to sex discrimination, see the Sex Discrimination Act, 1975, s. 19.

Ministers plenipotentiary and envoys extraordinary form the second class of foreign envoys. They are distinguished from ambassadors by not being regarded as the personal representatives of their heads of State. Ministers resident form the third class, and are distinguished from ministers plenipotentiary by not being entitled to be addressed as "Excellency."

Ministerial is opposed to judicial or discretionary. Thus, a ministerial office or duty is one which merely involves the following of instructions; in other words, one which can be performed without the exercise of more than ordinary skill, prudence, or discretion, *e.g.*, the payment or receipt of money, the execution of a deed, or the like; while a judicial or discretionary office or duty involves the exercise of judgment or discretion (*q.v.*).

Ministrant, the party cross-examining a witness under the old system of the ecclesiastical courts.

Ministry. This means not merely the members of the Cabinet but also all holders of offices who go in and out with the Government. Thus the Solicitor-General is always a member of the Ministry, but is never in the Cabinet. See MINISTER.

The term is also used with reference to a department of the Government to denote the Minister and his associated subordinates.

The salaries payable to holders of ministerial offices are regulated by the Ministerial and other Salaries Act, 1975.

Minor. A person who is not of full age (*q.v.*) may be described as a minor instead of as an infant (Family Law Reform Act, 1969, s. 12).

As to consent by a minor over sixteen to surgical, medical or dental treatment, see the Family Reform Act, 1969, s. 8.

Minor ante tempus agere non potest in casu proprietatis, nec etiam convenire; differetur usque aetatem; sed non cadit breve (2 Co.Inst. 291). (A minor before majority cannot act in a case of property, not even to agree; it should be deferred until majority; but a writ does not fail.) This is a passage from Bracton which is quoted by Coke with special reference to the Statute of Gloucester, 1278, c. 2.

Minor canon, any vicar, vicar choral, priest vicar, or senior vicar being a member of the choir in any cathedral or collegiate church (Ecclesiastical Commissioners Act, 1840, s. 93). The term minor canon is used only at St. Paul's and Hereford Cathedrals.

Minor interests, interests not capable of being disposed of or created by registered dispositions and capable of being overridden unless protected as provided by the Land Registration Act, 1925, and all rights which are not registered or protected on the register and are not overriding interests (s. 3 (xv)).

Minor jurae not potest (5 Bract. 340; Co.Litt. 172). (A minor cannot swear.) It was never literally true. Thus in Bracton's time the oath of allegiance could be required of a person over twelve; but even after the time of Coke an infant could not upon his oath make his law in an action of debt. See WAGER OF LAW.

The Children and Young Persons Act, 1933, s. 38, provides for reception of the unsworn evidence of a child of tender years.

Minor minorem custodire non debet; alios enim praesumitur male regere qui seipsum regere nescit (1 Fleta 10; Co.Litt. 88). (A minor cannot be guardian to a minor, for he is presumed to direct others badly who knows not how to direct himself.) This refers to guardianship under the feudal system.

Minor, qui infra aetatem xii annorum fuerit, utlagari non potest, nec extra legem poni, quia ante talem aetatem non est sub lege aliqua (3 Bract. 125; Co.Litt. 128). (A minor who is under twelve years of age cannot be outlawed, nor placed without the law, because, before such age, he is not under any law.)

Minora regalia, the revenue of the Crown, as opposed to its dignity and power.

Minories. See PRIVILEGED PLACES.

Minority [*Lat. minor*], the state of being under age, *i.e.*, eighteen years; also, the smaller number.

Minority and lesion. See LESION.

Mint [Lat. *moneta*; Sax. *mynet*, money; *mynetian*, to coin], the place where money is coined.

The Mint, or place in which money is manufactured, existed in the Tower of London so far back as Anglo-Saxon times. From early times there were also provincial mints at various towns, and down to the fall of Cardinal Wolsey grants of coining rights were frequently made to ecclesiastical persons. The coining at the principal Mint in the Tower was done by contractors from the thirteenth century down to 1851. In 1325 the officers of the Mint were incorporated by royal charter, which placed the management in the hands of a master (the contractor for the time being) and various other officers. The Mint remained in the Tower until 1810, when it was removed to its present site on Tower Hill. In 1851 contractors ceased to be employed, and the Mint became in all respects a Government Department, managed by public officials. It is now regulated by the Coinage Act, 1971. See MASTER OF THE MINT; PYX; SEGNIORAGE.

As to the finance of the Royal Mint see the Government Trading Funds Act, 1973, s. 7, and the Royal Mint Trading Fund Order, 1975 (No. 501).

The Mint was also a place of privilege in Southwark, near the King's Prison, where persons formerly sheltered themselves from justice under the pretext that it was an ancient palace of the Crown. It was also known as Suffolk Place. It was suppressed by the Statute 1723, 9 Geo. 1, c. 28.

Mintage, that which is coined or stamped.

Mint-mark. The masters and workers of the Mint, in the indentures made with them, agree to make a privy mark in the money they make, of gold and silver, so that they may know which moneys were of their own making; after every trial of the pyx, having proved their moneys to be lawful, they are entitled to their *quietus* under the Great Seal, and to be discharged from all suits or actions; they then change the privy mark, so that the moneys from which they are not yet discharged may be distinguished from those for which they are; they use the new mark until another trial of the pyx. See PYX.

Mint-master, one who manages the coinage. See MASTER OF THE MINT.

Minute, sixty seconds, or the sixtieth part of a degree or hour; also notes or records of a transaction. Thus, the record of the proceedings at a meeting of directors or shareholders of a company is called the minutes. Minutes must be made, in the proper book, of all general meetings and of all meetings of directors and managers of a company (Companies Act, 1948, s. 438).

When the parties to an action, petition, or other proceeding in the Chancery Division are agreed as to the order or judgment which should be made on an application to the court, they usually (especially if the matter is complicated) draw up beforehand minutes of the order or judgment (formerly called " minutes of order "), containing in outline all the provisions which are thought necessary. The minutes are afterwards put into the form of an order by the registrar.

Formerly, in Chancery suits, when an order or decree had been made, the registrar did not draw it up in full in the first instance, but framed an outline giving the substance of the order, copies of which were delivered to the parties, to be settled by them in his presence, if necessary. For many years the practice has been to draw up the order or decree complete in the first instance, and copies of the draft are delivered to the parties. In practice these copies are still called " minutes "; and when any dispute arises on the form of the order which has to be referred to the Court, the cause is put into the paper " to be spoken to on the minutes." See ENTER; PASS; SETTLE.

Mirror des Justices. This singular work has raised much doubt and difference of opinion concerning its antiquity. Some have pronounced it older than the Conquest, other have ascribed it to the time of Edward II. It was first published in 1642.

This book, which bears the name of Andrew Horne, and is written with very little precision, treats of all branches of the law, whether civil or criminal. Besides this, it gives a cursory retrospect of some changes ordained by former kings, and enumerates a list of abuses, as the author terms them, of the common law, proposing, at the same time, what he considers corrections. He does the same with Magna Carta, 1215, the Statute of Merton, 1235, the Statute of Marlbridge, 1267, and some principal statutes in the reign of Edward I (2 Reeves, c. xii, 358).

The best edition is that of Whitaker, published, with an introduction by Maitland, by the Selden Society in 1893.

Misa, a compact, a firm peace.

Misadventure, Excusable homicide by, also termed homicide *per infortunium*; it arises where a man, doing a lawful act, without any intention of hurt, unfortunately kills another, as where a person is at work with a hatchet, and the head of it flies off and kills a bystander, or is shooting at a mark and undesignedly kills a man, for the act is lawful, and the effect is merely accidental. So where a parent is moderately correcting a child, a master his apprentice or scholar, or an officer punishing a criminal, and happens to occasion his death, it is only misadventure, for the act of correction was lawful; but if he exceeds the bounds of moderation, in the manner, the instrument, or the quantity of punishment, and death ensues, it is manslaughter at least, and in some cases, according to the circumstances, murder, immoderate correction being unlawful (Fost. 275). See INFORTUNIUM, HOMICIDE PER.

Misallege, to cite falsely as a proof or argument.

Misappropriation, the misdemeanour which is committed by a banker, factor, agent, trustee, etc., who fraudulently deals with money, goods, securities, etc., entrusted to him, or by a director or public officer of a corporation or company who fraudulently misapplies any of its property. See FRAUD; PUBLIC OFFICER.

Miscarriage, a failure of justice; abortion (*q.v.*).

Mischief. The word is often used as referring to the object or purpose of a statute, as where it is said that the office of the judge is to make such construction as will suppress the mischief and advance the remedy (*Heydon's Case* (1584) 3 Co. Rep. 7b), and to suppress all evasions for the continuation of the mischief (*Magdalen College Case* (1616) 11 Co. Rep. 71b).

Mischievous animals. See ANIMALS, LIABILITY FOR.

Miscognisant, ignorant of, unacquainted with.

Misconduct. There is no fixed rule of law defining the degree of misconduct which will justify summary dismissal of a servant. The servant must have disregarded an essential condition of the contract of service. A single act of disobedience to an order is not necessarily a sufficient justification for summary dismissal (*Laws* v. *London Chronicle (Indicator Newspapers*) [1959] 1 W.L.R. 698).

Miscontinuance, cessation, intermission. Down to 1833, when the entry of continuances (*q.v.*) was abolished, there was said to be a discontinuance (*q.v.*) when no continuance was entered; when the continuance was entered up, but irregularly, there was said to be a miscontinuance. There was, therefore, a distinction between the two terms, although they are sometimes erroneously said to be of identical meaning (2 Hawk.Pl.Cr. 299).

Misdemeanour. An indictable offence. All distinctions between misdemeanour and felony have been abolished and all indictable offences (including piracy) are now governed by the rules relating to misdemeanours (Criminal Law Act, 1967, s. 1).

Like statutory misdemeanours to which no express punishment is attached, common law misdemeanours are punishable by fine or imprisonment or both.

Misdescription. In certain cases, when a contract contains a material misdescription, that is, when the description of the subject-matter of the contract is incorrect or misleading in a material and substantial point, the contract is voidable at the option of the party misled, independently of fraud, concealment, or misrepresentation (*q.v.*). Thus, in a contract of fire insurance, if the building is so described by the assured as to make the risk appear less than it really is, the insurer is entitled to avoid the contract. So, in a sale of land, a misdescription materially affecting the value, title, or character of the property sold will make the contract voidable at the purchaser's option. The test of materiality seems to be whether, if the subject-matter had been correctly described, the party misled would have entered into the contract.

A wrong description does not affect the validity of the transaction if there is no mistake as to the identity of the person or thing intended to be described, as where a person is called by a wrong name, the maxim being *falsa demonstratio non nocet* (*q.v.*).

Misdescription of Fabrics. The Fabrics (Misdescription) Act, 1913, prohibits the sale of any textile fabric with a misleading description as to its inflammability.

Misdirection, an error in law made by a judge in charging a jury or, when sitting alone, putting the wrong questions to himself to answer: See R.S.C., Ord. 59, r. 11. See NEW TRIAL.

Mise [Fr., *mise, mise en gage,* stake-money], disbursement, costs; a tax or tallage, etc.; also, the issue in a writ of right. It is sometimes corruptly used for *mease* or *mees, i.e.,* a messuage.

Mise in the writ of right was the same thing as the issue in an ordinary action, and was so called because the tenant "put" himself upon the grand assise (*q.v.*), that is, chose it as the mode of trial (Co.Litt. 294b).

The word was also applied to certain taxes payable in Wales and in the adjoining areas: see *e.g.,* the statutes 1535, 27 Hen. 8, c. 26, s. 23, and 1548, 2 & 3 Edw. 6, c. 36, s. 52.

It was also used in the old personal action where the judgment was *pro misis et custagiis* (for charges and costs) such and such a sum.

Mise-book, a book formerly kept in the County Palatine of Chester for entries as regards the payment of mise (*q.v.*) (Tomline).

Mise-money, money paid by way of contract or composition to purchase any liberty, etc. (Blount).

Miselli, leprous persons.

Misera est servitus, ubi jus est vagum aut incertum (4 Co.Inst. 246). (Obedience to the law is a hardship, where the law is vague and uncertain.) This maxim is quoted by Coke as a comment on the jurisdiction exercised by the Council of the North—until the common law courts intervened—under instructions which were kept secret so that the king's subjects were unaware of their position with regard to the Council.

Miserabile depositum, an involuntary deposit under pressing necessity (Civil Law).

Miserere, have mercy; the name and first word of one of the penitential psalms, being that which was commonly used to be given by the ordinary to such condemned malefactors as were allowed the benefit of clergy, whence it is also called the Psalm of Mercy (Jacob). See NECK VERSE.

Misericordia, an arbitrary amerciament (*q.v.*) or punishment imposed on any person for an offence. It is thus called, according to Fitzherbert, because it ought to be but small and less than that required by Magna Carta (Anc.Inst. Eng.).

It also meant a discharge of all manner of amerciaments which a person might incur in the forest. See CAPIAS PRO FINE.

Misericordia communis, a fine set on a whole county or hundred.

Misericordia domini regis est, qua quis per juramentum legalium hominum de vicineto eatenus amerciandus est, ne aliquid de suo honorabili contenemento amittat. (The mercy of our lord the king is that by which every one is to be amerced by a jury of good men from his immediate neighbourhood, lest he should lose any part of his own honourable tenement.)

Misevenire, to fail or succeed ill; to fail in one's defence or in purgation (Leg.Canut.).

Misfeasance [Norm.Fr., *mis,* wrongly; *fere,* to do], the improper performance of a lawful act, as where a person is guilty of negligence in performing a contract. A misfeasor is a person who does a misfeasance. In the old books misfeasance was used especially to signify trespasses and other offences in parks, forests, etc. (2 Co.Inst. 198). As to the distinction between misfeasance and nonfeasance, see *McClelland* v. *Manchester Corporation* [1912] 1 K.B. 118; *Guilfoyle* v. *Port of London Authority* [1932] 1 K.B. 336; *Coleshill* v. *Manchester Corporation* [1928] 1 K.B. 776. As to misfeasance proceedings in the course of a winding up against directors, promoters, managers or others, see the Companies Act, 1948, s. 333; *Re Morecambe Bowling* [1969] 1 W.L.R. 133. See MALFEASANCE; NONFEASANCE; TORT.

Mishering. See ABISHERING.

Misjoinder, where persons are wrongly joined as plaintiffs or defendants in an action: in other words, where persons are made parties who ought not to be. The rule before the Judicature Acts, 1873–75, was that in an action of contract a misjoinder of plaintiffs led only to increased costs, while a misjoinder of defendants was fatal; and that in an action of tort a misjoinder of plaintiffs or defendants led only to increased costs. No action can now be defeated by reason of the misjoinder or non-joinder of parties (R.S.C., Ord. 15, r. 6). See JOINDER; PARTIES.

Misnomer, a misnaming. Down to 1834, a plea in abatement (q.v.) lay for a misnomer in civil proceedings, and down to the enactment of the Criminal Law Act, 1826, a misnomer in an indictment was fatal. Now in either case an amendment (q.v.) can be made. *Nil facit error nominis cum de corpore vel persona constat* (a mistake in the name does not matter when there is no mistake in the body or person) (11 Co.Rep. 21.).

As to misnomer of a juror, see *R.* v. *Mellor* (1858) Dears. & B. 468.

See IDEM SONANS.

Mispleading, omitting anything essential to the action or defence. See JEOFAIL.

Misprision [Fr. *mépris*], neglect, negligence, oversight. In its larger sense, it is used to signify every considerable misdemeanour which has not a certain name given to it by the law; and it is said that a misprision is contained in every treason or felony whatsoever, and that one who is guilty of felony or treason may be proceeded against for a misprision only (Staundford, *Plees del Coron.*).

Upon the same principle, while the Court of Star Chamber existed, it was held that the sovereign might remit a prosecution for treason, and cause the delinquent to be censured in that court, merely for a high misdemeanour, as in the case of the Earl of Rutland, 1601, concerned in Essex's rebellion. Every great misdemeanour, according to Coke, which has no certain term appointed by the law, is sometimes called a misprision. The term is, however, rarely if ever used in this sense, it being now practically confined to the two phrases " misprision of treason " and " misprision of felony."

Misprision of treason is where a person who knows that some other person has committed high treason does not within a reasonable time give information thereof to the High Court or a justice of the peace. At common law the punishment is imprisonment for life and forfeiture of the offender's goods, etc.; but prosecutions for the offence are now unknown.

Misprision of felony was where a person who knows that some other person has committed felony conceals or procures the concealment thereof. The distinction between felony and misdemeanour has now been abolished and all indictable offences are now governed by the rules relating to misdemeanours (Criminal Law Act, 1967, s. 1). It follows that the offence of misprision of felony has lapsed. See COMPOUNDING.

Misprisions are divided in the textbooks into two kinds: —

(1) Negative, the concealment of what ought to be revealed; such is misprision of treason, the bare knowledge and concealment of treason without any degree of assent, for any assent makes the party a principal; as the concealment, construed to be aiding and abetting, did at common law; but it was enacted by the statute 1554, 1 & 2 Ph. & M. c. 10, that a bare concealment of treason should be only held a misprision. The Treason Act, 1695, s. 3, provides that there must be two witnesses to support the case (1 Hale, P.C. 374).

Theftbote, and concealing treasure-trove, were each of them species of negative misprision. It was not an element of the offence that the concealment should be for the benefit of the accused nor that it should consist of a positive act (*Sykes* v. *D.P.P.* [1962] A.C. 528).

(2) Positive, otherwise denominated contempt of high misdemeanours, such as the maladministration of such high officers as are in public trust and employment, usually punishable by parliamentary impeachment; also, embezzlement of the public money, punishable by fine and imprisonment; also, such contempts of the executive magistrate as demonstrate themselves by some arrogant and undutiful behaviour towards the sovereign and government. To endeavour to dissuade a witness from giving evidence, to disclose an examination before the Privy Council, or to advise a prisoner to stand mute (all of which are impediments to justice), are high misprisions and contempts, punishable by fine and imprisonment (4 Bl.Comm. 119).

Misprisions of clerks are mistakes made by clerks, etc., in writing or keeping records.

Misrecital, a wrong recital. If it be in the beginning of a deed, which goes not to the end of a deed, it shall not hurt, but if it go to the end of a sentence, so that the deed is limited by it, it is vicious (Cart. 149).

Misrepresentation may be *suggestio falsi*, in a matter of substance essentially material to the subject, whether by acts or by words or by manoeuvres or by positive assertions, or material concealment (*suppressio veri*) whereby a person is misled and damnified.

Fraudulent misrepresentation is a representation contrary to the fact, made by a person with knowledge of its falsehood, or without belief in its truth, or recklessly, not caring whether it is true or false, and being the cause of the other party's entering into the contract (*Derry* v. *Peek* (1889) 14 App.Cas. 337). A misrepresentation by an agent from whom the facts have been withheld by his principal does not amount to fraudulent misrepresentation by the principal (*Armstrong* v. *Strain* [1952] 1 K.B. 232). See DECEIT; DOLUS DANS LOCUM CONTRACTUI; FRAUD.

Innocent misrepresentation is where the person making the representation believed it to be true.

When a person has been induced to enter into a contract by misrepresentation, he may in general either affirm the contract and insist on the misrepresentation being made good, if that is possible, so as to be put in the same position as if it had been originally true, or rescind the contract, or rely upon the misrepresentation as a defence to an action on the contract. Misrepresentation makes a contract only voidable and not void unless it produces mistake excluding true consent (*error in substantia*) (see MISTAKE). If the representation was a term of the contract damages are recoverable for breach of contract. By the Statute of Frauds Amendment Act, 1828, no action lies in respect of any representation of the credit, trade, dealings, etc., of another to obtain credit for that other, unless it is in writing, signed by the party to be charged (*Hirst* v. *West Riding Banking Co.* [1901] 2 K.B. 560).

As to rescission and damages for innocent misrepresentation see the Misrepresentation Act, 1967. See RESCIND; RESCISSION.

Missa, the mass.

Missae presbyter, a priest in orders.

Missal, the mass-book.

Misstaicus, a messenger.

Missura, the ceremonies used in the Roman Catholic Church to recommend and dismiss a dying person.

Mistake, misapprehension as to the existence of a thing, arising either from ignorance or from a false belief on the point.

Mistake of law (*error* or *ignorantia juris*) is a mistake as to a general rule of law: as where a testator thinks that to disinherit his heir it is necessary to give him a nominal bequest, or where a person does not know that a contract for the sale of land must be evidenced by writing. The general rule is that such a mistake is no excuse and does not affect the transaction. Thus, in the first case the executor could not refuse to pay the bequest, and, in the second, the contract would be unenforceable by action for want of written evidence.

Mistake of fact (*error* or *ignorantia facti*) is either as to the existence of a fact or as to the existence of a right depending on questions of mixed law and fact. If there is a mistake of fact, the contract is void.

Questions of foreign law being questions of fact, a mistake as to foreign law is a mistake of fact. See FACT.

If a person signs a document by mistake, thinking it to be a document of another nature, his signature is ineffectual, because he did not intend to sign it (*Foster* v. *MacKinnon* (1867) L.R. 4 C.P. 704): he can plead *non est factum* (*q.v.*) (it is not his deed). If A and B enter into a contract of sale for an estate called Dale, there being in fact two estates called Dale, A meaning one and B the other, the consent or common intention necessary to constitute a contract is absent, and there is no contract (*Raffles* v. *Wichelhaus* (1864) 2 H. & C. 906). As a general rule, unilateral mistake has no legal effect (*Tamplin* v. *James* (1880) 15 Ch.D. 215). Money paid under a mistake of fact may be recovered back (*Kelly* v. *Solari* (1841) 9 M. & W. 54). If a mistake occurs in expressing the terms of an agreement, it will, as a general rule, be corrected, either when proceedings are taken to enforce it or by substantive proceedings taken for the purpose. As to whether a mistake as to the identity of one contracting party by the other can render the contract null and void, see *Gallie* v. *Lee* [1969] 2 Ch. 17. See RECTIFICATION.

In criminal cases a mistake of fact may be an excuse, as when a man, intending to do a lawful act, does that which is unlawful, acting upon an honest and reasonable belief in the existence of facts, which, if true, would make his act lawful.

Mistery, Mystery [Fr. *métier*], a trade or calling.

Mistress, the proper style of the wife of an esquire or a gentleman.

Mistress of the Robes, a lady of high rank who is, theoretically, the chief personal attendant of the queen, whether the queen be a queen consort or a queen regnant, but whose duties are purely formal. Her attendance is required only on rare occasions of State. During the first years of the reign of Queen Victoria it became the rule that the Mistress of the Robes went in and out with the Ministry of the day. (See BEDCHAMBER.) The corresponding official as regards the king is the Groom of the Stole. His office would appear to be at present in abeyance. There is no rule that the holder goes in and out with the Ministry.

Mistrial, an erroneous trial.

Misuser, abuse of any liberty or benefit which works a forfeiture of it.

Mitigation. Where a defendant or prisoner proves facts tending to reduce the damages or punishment to be awarded against him, he is said to show facts in mitigation of damages or of sentence, as the case may be.

Mitre Court. See PRIVILEGED PLACES.

Mittendo manuscriptum pedis finis, a writ which was addressed to the treasurer and chamberlain of the Exchequer to search for and transmit the foot of a fine acknowledged before justices in eyre, into the Common Pleas (Reg.Brev. 14).

Mitter le droit, to pass a right. See RELEASE.

Mitter l'estate, to pass an estate. See RELEASE.

Mittimus (we send), a writ used in sending a record or its tenor from one court to another. Thus where *nul tiel record* was pleaded in one court to the record of another court of equal or superior jurisdiction, the tenor of the record was brought into Chancery by certiorari (*q.v.*), and thence sent by *mittimus* into the court where the action was. The necessity for the writ ceased in certain cases by force of the Crown Debts Act, 1801, ss. 5, 6, and in the remaining cases by force of the Judicature Act, 1873, s. 76. The effect of these enactments was to make an exemplification (*q.v.*) available in every case in which a *mittimus* had previously been required. See TESTE.

Mittimus was also a precept or command in writing directed to the gaoler or keeper of some prison for the receiving and safe keeping of an offender charged with any crime, until he should be delivered by due course of law.

Mittre à large, to set or put at liberty.

Mixed actions, actions partaking of the nature of real and personal actions, by which some property is demanded and also damages for a wrong sustained.

Mixed Arbitral Tribunal, a temporary tribunal, consisting of three members, established under the Treaty of Peace Order, 1919, pursuant to the Treaty of Peace Act, 1919, relating to the Treaty of Versailles.

Mixed contract, one in which one of the parties confers a benefit on the other, and requires of the latter something of less value than what he has given; as a legacy charged with something of less value than the legacy itself (Civil Law).

Mixed government, a form of government combining monarchy, aristocracy, and democracy.

Mixed laws, those which concern both persons and property.

Mixed personalty, impure personalty. See PERSONALTY.

Mixed property, a compound of realty and personalty.

Mixed questions [Fr. *questions mixtes*], those which arise from the conflict of foreign and domestic laws.

Mixed questions of law and fact, cases in which the jury (if there is one) are to find the particular facts, and the court is to decide upon the legal quality of those facts by the aid of established rules of law, independently of any general inference or conclusion to be drawn by the jury.

Mixed subjects of property, such as fall within the definition of things real, but which are attended nevertheless with some of the legal qualities of things personal, as emblements, fixtures, and shares in public undertakings connected with land. Besides these, there are others which, though things personal in point of definition, are, in respect of some of their legal qualities, of the nature of things real; such are animals *ferae naturae*, charters and deeds, court rolls and other evidences of the title to land, together with the chests in which they are contained, ancient family pictures, ornaments, tombstones, coats of armour, with pennons and other ensigns, and especially heirlooms.

Mixed tithes, tithes of wool, milk, pigs, etc., consisting of natural products, but nurtured and preserved in part by the care of man.

Mobile homes. See CAMPING.

Mobilia sequuntur personam. (Movables follow the person.) Thus, the law of a man's domicile usually governs the descent of his personal property and his testamentary dispositions thereof.

Mobilisation. See RESERVE FORCES.

Mobles [Fr. *meubles*; Lat. *mobilia*], movable goods; furniture.

Mock auction. A mock auction is defined in the Mock Auctions Act, 1961, as a sale of goods by competitive bidding at which a lot is sold to a person for less than the amount of his highest bid or part of the price is repaid or credited to him or at which the right to bid is restricted or stated to be restricted to persons who have bought or agreed to buy one or more articles or at which any article is given away or offered as a gift (s. 1 (3)). The Act applies to any plate, plated articles, linen, china, glass, books, pictures, prints, furniture, jewellery, articles of household or personal use or ornament or any musical or scientific instrument or apparatus (s. 3 (2)). Nothing in the Act derogates from any right of action or other remedy (whether civil or criminal) in proceedings instituted otherwise than under the Act (s. 3 (6)). For penalties, see s. 1 (1).

At common law there is a mock auction where an auction is held with confederates who pose as bona fide bidders but who really make only sham bids in order to induce other persons to bid. It is a conspiracy (*q.v.*) to defraud and an indictable offence.

Mockadoes, a kind of cloth made in England, mentioned in the statute 1580, 23 Eliz. 1, c. 9.

Model, a representation or copy of a thing. In the Copyright Act, 1956, works of sculpture include casts and models (s. 48). See COPYRIGHT.

Small or model buildings were held to be buildings within the meaning of the Town and Country Planning Act, 1947 (*Buckinghamshire County Council* v. *Callingham* [1952] 2 Q.B. 515).

As to noise from model aircraft, see NOISE.

Moderata misericordia, a writ founded on Magna Carta, 1215, which lay for him who was amerced in a court, not of record, for any transgression beyond the quality or quantity of the offence; it was addressed to the lord of the court, or his bailiff, commanding him to take a moderate amerciament (*q.v.*) of the parties (New Nat.B. 167; Fitz.N.B. 76).

Moderator, a president or chairman.

Modiatio, a certain duty paid for every tierce of wine (2 Dugd.Mon. 194).

Modius, a measure, usually a bushel.

Modius terrae vel agri, a quantity of ground containing in length and breadth 100 feet (3 Dugd.Mon. 200).

Modo et forma, in manner and form, a phrase formerly used in pleading. It was the nature of a traverse to deny the matter of fact in the adverse pleading in the manner and form in which it was alleged, and, therefore, to put the opposite party to prove it to be true in manner and form as well as in general effect. The plea of *non est factum* and the replication *de injuria* were the only negative traverses not pleaded *modo et forma.* These words were in no case strictly essential, so as to render their omission a cause of demurrer.

Modus, a particular method of tithing. See MODUS DECIMANDI.

Modus calumpniandi essoniarum (the manner of challenging essoins). An enactment is printed under this title in the *Statutes of the Realm* amongst the *Statutes of Uncertain Date*, and in the *Statutes at Large* as 1319, 12 Edw. 2, st. 2.

Modus de non decimando non valet. (An agreement not to take tithes avails not.)

Modus decimandi, where there existed by custom a particular manner of tithing, that is, of paying tithes, different from the general rule. This was sometimes a pecuniary compensation, such as twopence an acre for the tithe of land; sometimes it was a compensation in work and labour, as that the parson should have only the twelfth cock of hay, and not the tenth, in consideration of the owner's making it for him, or the like (2 Bl. Comm. 29).

A too large modus was called a " rank " modus, and the Tithe Act, 1832, required evidence of usage for thirty years.

Moduses have been commuted in all cases. See COMPOSITION; NON DECIMANDO DE; RANK; TITHES.

Modus et conventio vincunt legem (2 Co.Rep. 73; Co.Litt. 19). (Custom and agreement overrule law.) An agreement may be made, if the parties to a contract so desire, which will overrule the law, but this does not apply to cases in which " contracting out " is prohibited by statute, or to cases in which their agreement would derogate from the rights of the public or be against public policy. See PACTA, ETC.; PERPETUA, ETC.; PRIVATORUM, ETC.

Modus faciendi homagium et fidelitatem (the manner of doing homage and fealty). An enactment is printed under this title in the *Statutes of the Realm* amongst the *Statutes of Uncertain Date*, and in the *Statutes at Large* as 1324, 17 Edw. 2, st. 2.

Modus legem dat donationi (Co.Litt. 19; Plow.Com. 251). (Agreement gives law to the gift.) That is to say, the agreement for the transfer of land settles the conditions upon which the land is to be held. But this rule, which dates from the time of Fleta, has limitations. See MODUS ET CONVENTIO, ETC.

Modus levandi fines (the manner of levying of fines). An enactment is printed under this title in the *Statutes of the*

Realm amongst the *Statutes of Uncertain Date*, and in the *Statutes at Large* as 1325, 18 Edw. 1, st. 4. See CONGÉ D'ACCORDER; FINE.

Moerda [Teut.], the secret killing of another; murder (4 Bl.Comm. 194).

Moidore, a gold coin of Portugal.

Moiety [Lat. *medietas*; Fr. *moitié*], half. The word is, however, occasionally used to signify any fractional part, such as a third, fourth, etc.

Mole drainage, a method of draining land by forming an artificial mole-run some inches below the surface by drawing a mole plough (a round plug attached to a coulter) through the ground. It is an improvement for which a tenant of an agricultural holding may claim compensation from his landlord (Agricultural Holdings Act, 1948, s. 52, Sch. 4 para. 1).

Molendinum, a mill.

Molendum, grist; a certain quantity of corn sent to a mill to be ground.

Molestation. Molesting a person by following him in a persistent or disorderly manner, or by hiding his property, or by besetting his place of work or residence, with the view of compelling him to do, or abstain from doing, an act, is forbidden by the Conspiracy and Protection of Property Act, 1875, s. 7, repealing the statute 1871, 34 & 35 Vict. c. 32. The term " molest " was used in the Act of 1871, but is omitted from the Act of 1875. See COMBINATION; INTIMIDATION; TRADE UNIONS.

In separation deeds between husband and wife there are generally mutual covenants against molestation. In such a case molestation implies not merely annoyance but an intention to annoy (*Hunt* v. *Hunt* (1898) 67 L.J.Q.B. 18); proceedings taken bona fide for the purpose of obtaining a divorce are not molestation.

Molitura, Molta, the toll or multure paid for grinding corn at a mill.

Molitura libera, a free grinding or liberty of a mill without paying toll, a privilege which the lord generally reserved to his own family (Paroch.Antiq. 236). See FARINAGIUM.

Moll Flanders' Act, the Disorderly Houses Act, 1751.

Molliter manus imposuit, a defence set up to an action for battery where the defendant alleged that the battery complained of was lawful and that " he laid hands on the plaintiff gently," that is, used no more force than was necessary: as where a churchwarden turned a man out of church to prevent him from disturbing the congregation.

Molman, a man subject to do service. See GAVELMAN.

Molmutian (or **Molmutin**) **laws,** the laws of Dunvallo Molmutius, sixteenth king of the Britons, who is said to have reigned about 400 B.C. These were the first published laws in Britain, and, together with those of Queen Mercia, were translated into Latin by Gildas, a British historian of the sixth century (Usher, Primord. 126).

Molneda, Mulneda, a mill-pond or pond (Paroch.Antiq. 135).

Molta, Moltura. See MOLITURA.

Mona, the Isle of Anglesey; also the Isle of Man.

Monachus, a monk. As to liability of Roman Catholic monks to banishment, see JESUITS; ROMAN CATHOLICS.

Monarchy [μόναρχος], a government in which the supreme power is vested in a single person. Where a monarch is invested with absolute power, the monarchy is termed despotic; where the supreme power is virtually in the laws, though the majesty of government and the administration are vested in a single person, it is a limited monarchy. It is hereditary where the regal power descends immediately from the possessor to the next heir by blood, as in our country; or elective, as was formerly the case in Poland.

Monasteries Dissolution Acts, the statutes 1535, 27 Hen. 8, c. 28; 1539, 31 Hen. 8, c. 13; 1540, 32 Hen. 8, cc. 7, 24. As to the liability to banishment of members of Roman Catholic religious orders (not being nunneries), see JESUITS; ROMAN CATHOLICS.

Monasticon Anglicanum, a monumental work by Sir William Dugdale, Garter Principal King-at-Arms, originally published in Latin. It contains a history of the abbeys and other monasteries, hospitals, friaries, and cathedral and collegiate churches with their depen-dencies in England and Wales, and also of all such Scottish, Irish and French monasteries as were connected with religious houses in England. The best modern edition is that published in 1817–30, under the editorship of Caley, Ellis and Bandinel.

Monetagium, Monya, or **Moneyage,** called also *focagium,* a certain tribute paid by tenants to their lord every third year, that he should not change the money which he had coined, when it was lawful for certain great men to coin money, but not of silver and gold, in their territories (Hale, Hist. 217).

It also meant a mintage, and the right of coining or minting money.

Monetandi jus comprehenditur in regalibus quae nunquam a regio sceptro abdicantur (Dav. 18). (The right of coining money is included in those rights of royalty which are never separated from the kingly sceptre.)

Money, that which passes freely from hand to hand throughout the community in final discharge of debts and full payment for commodities, being accepted equally without reference to the character or credit of the person who offers it and without the intention of the person who receives it to consume it or apply it to any other use than in turn to tender it to others in discharge of debts or payment for commodities (*Moss* v. *Hancock* [1899] 2 Q.B. 111).

In *Re Emerson* [1929] 1 Ch. 128, a gift of " the residue of money at the time of my death " was held to include the residuary personal estate. In *Re Mellor* [1929] 1 Ch. 446, a gift of " the remainder of any moneys " following an express direction to pay debts was held to carry both real and personal property. In *Re Collings* [1933] Ch. 920, it was held that " money " in its strict legal sense included money on deposit account at a bank. In *Perrin* v. *Morgan* [1943] A.C. 399, it was held that " all moneys of which I die possessed " included investments. " Ready money " does not normally include money for which a substantial period of notice is required. " Cash " may mean ready money or just money (*Re Stonham* [1963] 1 W.L.R. 238).

See EARMARK; GOODS.

Money Bill, a bill which in the opinion of the Speaker of the House of Commons contains only provisions dealing with all or any of the following subjects, namely, the imposition, repeal, remission, alteration or regulation of taxation; the imposition, for the payment of debt or other financial purposes, of charges on the Consolidated Fund or the National Loans Fund, or on money provided by Parliament, or the variation or repeal of any such charges; supply; the appropriation, receipt, custody, issue or audit of accounts of public money; the raising or guarantee of any loan or the repayment thereof; or subordinate matters incidental to those subjects or any of them (Parliament Act, 1911, s. 1 (2); National Loans Act, 1968, s. 1 (5)). Taxation, public moneys, and loans by local authorities for local purposes are not within the definition. This is the first and only statutory definition of the expression " money Bill," although the expression had been well understood for centuries much in the sense of the definition. For hundreds of years it had been settled that money Bills could originate only in the House of Commons: in the seventeenth century the Commons claimed that the Lords could reject but not alter a money Bill, and this claim came in course of time to be admitted by the Lords: then the Commons claimed that the Lords could not reject such a bill: finally, when the Finance Bill of 1909 was rejected by the Lords, the Parliament Act, 1911, was passed by the Commons and was forced through the Lords by the threat to create enough new peers to swamp the opposition. The effect of that Act is that any bill certified by the Speaker to be a money Bill within the meaning of the definition must be presented for the royal assent at the end of the session in which it passes the Commons, whether it is or is not passed by the Lords (s. 1 (1)).

Money broker, a money changer; a scrivener or jobber; one who lends or raises money to or for others.

Money counts. Simple contracts, express or implied, resulting in mere debts, are of so frequent occurrence as causes of action, that certain concise forms of counts were devised for suing upon them. These were, before the Judicature Acts, 1873–75, called the *indebitatus*, or common money counts, or money counts. See ASSUMPSIT; COUNT.

Money had and received. When a person receives money which in justice and equity belongs to another, as a rule a debt is created and the money can be recovered by an action for money had and received to the use of the plaintiff (*Moses* v. *Macferlan* (1760) 2 Burr. 1005; *Marriott* v. *Hampton* (1797) 7 T.R. 269; *Barclays Bank* v. *Cole* [1967] 2 Q.B. 738). But the action cannot be extended beyond the principles illustrated in the decided cases (*Sinclair* v. *Brougham* [1914] A.C. 398 at p. 453). The cause of action arises when the money is received and not earlier (see *Bowling* v. *Cox* [1926] A.C. 751). See QUASI-CONTRACT.

Money into land. In equity, land articled or devised to be sold, and turned into money, is considered as money, and money articled or bequeathed to be invested in land, has, in equity, many of the qualities of real estate, upon the ground that equity regards substance and not form, and will further the intention of parties.

By the Settled Land Act, 1925, s. 75 (5), replacing the Settled Land Act, 1882, s. 26 (5), capital money arising under the Act while remaining uninvested or unapplied and investments thereof are for all purposes of disposition, transmission and devolution to be treated as land and are to be held for and go to the same persons successively in the same manner and for and on the same estates, interests and trusts as the land wherefrom the money arises would, if not disposed of, have been held and have gone under the settlement; s. 78 contains provisions as to personal estate settled by reference to capital money or on trusts corresponding with the settlement of the land. These provisions do not relate to or affect money arising on a trust for sale.

Before 1926, money agreed or directed to be laid out in land so fully became land as not to be personal assets, to be subject to the curtesy of the husband and the dower of the wife, to pass as land by will, if subject to the real use at the time the will was made and not to pass as money by a general bequest to a legatee, though it would by a particular description, as so much money to be laid out in land, or by a bequest of all the testator's estate in law and equity. But equity would not consider money as land, unless the covenant or direction to lay it out in land was imperative. The Administration of Estates Act, 1925, puts real and personal estate on the same footing as regards the order of administration.

The Fines and Recoveries Act, 1833, s. 71, enacts that lands to be sold of any tenure where the money arising from the sale is subject to be invested in the purchase of lands to be settled, so that any person, if the lands were purchased, would have an entailed interest therein, and also money subject to be invested in the purchase of lands to be settled, so that any person, if the lands were purchased, would have an entailed interest therein shall, for the purposes of the Act, be treated as the lands to be purchased, and be considered subject to the same interests as the lands to be purchased would have been actually subject to; by the Law of Property Act, 1925, s. 130, an entailed interest may be created in personalty as well as in real property.

Money of account, the currency in which a debt is expressed or a liability to pay damages is calculated. It is also called " money of contract " or " money of measurement." It is contrasted with " money of payment " which is the currency in which the debt or liability is to be discharged. See Dicey, *Conflict of Laws.* See GOLD CLAUSE.

Money orders, orders for the payment of money which may be purchased from the Post Office for the remission of small sums of money through the post. Postal orders are money orders in a special form (Post Office Act, 1969, ss. 70, 71.

Money paid. See ASSUMPSIT; QUASI-CONTRACT.

Moneylender. The Money-lenders Act, 1900, and the Moneylenders Act, 1927, were repealed by the Consumer Credit Act, 1974. A loan by a moneylender is a " personal credit agreement " within the meaning of s. 8 (1) and if the loan does not exceed £5,000 is a " consumer credit agreement " within s. 8 (2) and a " regulated agreement " within s. 8 (3). It may amount to a " restricted-use credit " or an " unrestricted use credit " (s. 11), and it may constitute a " debtor-creditor-supplier agreement " or a " debtor-creditor agreement." See Sch. 2 Examples 8, 9, 11, 12, 19.

A moneylender must obtain from the Director of Fair Trading a licence under ss. 21 *et seq.*

If the county court finds a credit bargain extortionate it may reopen the credit agreement so as to do justice between the parties (ss. 137–140, 189 (1)).

As to advertising by a moneylender see ss. 43–47.

See CONSUMER CREDIT.

Monger [Sax. *mangian,* to trade], a dealer or seller. It is seldom or never used alone, or otherwise than after the name of some commodity, to express a seller of such commodity. Also, a little fishing vessel: see the statute 1571, 13 Eliz. 1, c. 11.

Moniers, or **Moneyers,** ministers of the Mint; bankers.

Moniment, a memorial, superscription or record.

Monism, the doctrine according to which international law is either inferior or superior to municipal law, but according to which both international law and municipal law form part of one legal order.

Monition, a summons or citation. In admiralty practice, a monition was a formal order of the court commanding something to be done by the person to whom it was directed, and who was called the person monished. Thus, when money was decreed to be paid, a monition might be obtained commanding its payment. A monition was granted either on motion or on application in chambers, and, if not obeyed, might be enforced by attachment (*q.v.*). A monition also meant the process, analogous to a writ of summons, by which a cause for the condemnation of a ship as prize was formerly commenced. Monitions in either of these senses are now unknown: in admiralty, the judge has the same powers of injunction, etc., as in other divisions: and every cause in prize is commenced by writ of summons.

In ecclesiastical appeals to the Privy Council (and formerly also in admiralty appeals), as soon as the petition of appeal is lodged, a monition for process issues, calling upon the judge and officers of the court below to transmit the proceedings in the cause to the registry of the appellate court. See PROCESS.

Monitions in divorce practice are now disused, orders having taken their place.

In ecclesiastical procedure, a monition is an order monishing or warning the party complained against to do or not to do a certain act under pain of the law and contempt thereof (*Dale's Case* (1882) 7 App.Cas. 240). Thus, there may be a monition for personal answers (see ANSWER), for payment of costs, requiring a clergyman to reside, etc. A monition may also be appended to a sentence inflicting a punishment for a past offence: in that case the monition forbids the repetition of the offence (*Martin* v. *Maconochie* (1879) 4 Q.B.D. 697). See ADMONITION; DUPLEX QUERELA.

Monitory letters, letters from an ecclesiastical authority with regard to scandals and abuses within the cognisance of the ecclesiastical courts. They are not, however, a recognised part of the procedure of such courts.

Monmouthshire. This was made one of the counties of England by the statute 1535, 27 Hen. 8, c. 26. A number of Acts provide that it shall be treated as part of Wales for certain purposes, *e.g.*, the Ministry of Health Act, 1919, s. 11 (3), the Census (Great Britain) Act, 1910, s. 4 (1) (*e*), the Welsh Church Act, 1914, s. 1, the Welsh Intermediate Education Act, 1889, the Ministry of Agriculture and Fisheries Act, 1919, s. 6, etc. The administrative county of Monmouthshire and the county borough of Newport were excluded from England and included in Wales by the Local Government Act, 1972, ss. 1, 20. These areas form part of the new counties of Gwent and Mid Glamorgan (Sch. 4).

Monocracy, government by one person.

Monogamy [μόνος, single; γάμος, marriage], marriage of one husband to one wife.

Monomachy [μόνος, single; μαχη, a fight], a duel; a single combat.

It was anciently allowed by law, for the trial or proof of crimes. It was even permitted in pecuniary causes, but it is now forbidden both by the civil and canon laws.

Monomania, insanity upon a particular subject.

Monopolies and Mergers Commission. This body is created by the Fair Trading Act, 1973 (replacing the Monopolies Commission). Its functions are to investigate and report on the existence or possible existence of a "monopoly situation" in respect of the supply of goods and services or in relation to exports, with respect to the transfer of a newspaper or newspaper assets and with respect to a "merger situation" qualifying for investigation

Monopoly [μόνος, single; πυλέω, to sell], the exclusive privilege of selling any commodity; a licence or privilege allowed by the Crown, for the sole buying, selling, making, working, and using of anything.

Such grants were common before the Stuarts, and were very oppressive and injurious during the reign of Elizabeth I. The power of granting monopolies was a part of the prerogative. They were abolished by the Statute of Monopolies, 1623, which declared all monopolies void, with an exception for patents (*q.v.*) for fourteen years for the sole working or making of any new manufacturers within the realm, to the first inventors.

Ancient franchises (*q.v.*) existing either by grant or prescription, such as the tolls of a bridge, ferry, or market, are not within the statute.

See RESTRICTIVE TRADE PRACTICES.

Monopoly value. Conditions were formerly attached to the grant of a new justices' on-licence (see ON-LICENCE) for the purpose of securing monopoly value to the public. This requirement was abolished by the Finance Act, 1959, s. 5.

Monster, an animal which has not the shape of mankind, but, in any part, evidently bears the resemblance of the brute creation, has no inheritable blood, and cannot be heir to any land, although it be brought forth in marriage; but, though it have deformity in any part of its body, yet, if it have human shape, it may be an heir (Co.Litt. 7b; 2 Bl.Comm. 246).

Monstrans de droit (manifestation or plea of right), one of the common law methods of obtaining possession or restitution from the Crown or either real or personal property preferred either on the common law side of the Court of Chancery, or in the Exchequer (3 Bl. Comm. 256).

Where the Crown was in possession under a title the facts of which were already set forth upon record, a party aggrieved might proceed in *monstrans de droit, i.e.*, might make, in opposition to such recorded title, a claim of right, grounded upon certain facts relied upon by him, without denying those relied upon by the Crown, and praying judgment of the Crown whether, upon those facts, the Crown or the subject had the right. If the right was determined against the Crown, the judgment was that of *ouster le main* or *amoveas manus*, by which judgment the Crown was instantly out of possession, and it therefore needed no actual execution.

The remedy was practically superseded by the petition of right (*q.v.*), and now an ordinary action lies under the Crown Proceedings Act, 1947. See OUSTERLE-MAIN; TRAVERSE.

Monstrans de faits ou records (showing of deeds or records). After the plaintiff in an action on, for instance, a bond, had delivered his declaration (*q.v.*) he was bound under the old common law practice to exhibit his bond. *Monstrans de faits* differed from *oyer de faits* in that he who pleaded the deed or record, or declared upon it, had to show it, and the defendant might demand *oyer* of the same. See PROFERT.

Monstraverunt, a writ which lay for tenants in ancient demesne when required to perform services to which they were not liable.

Monstrum, a box in which relics are kept; also, a muster of soldiers.

Montague Close. See PRIVILEGED PLACES.

Montesquieu. Charles de Sécondat, Baron de la Brède et de Montesquieu, was born on January 1, 1689, and died on February 10, 1755. He wrote *L'Ésprit des Lois*, and various historical and other works.

Montgomery's Act, the Entail Improvement Act, 1770.

Month [Sax. *monath*, moon, which was formerly written mone, as month was written moneth], the period in which that planet moneth, *i.e.*, completeth its orbit.

It is lunar, the time between the change and change, or the time in which the moon returns to the same point, being twenty-eight days; or solar, that period in which the sun passes through one of the twelve signs of the zodiac; or calendar, by which we reckon time, consisting unequally of thirty or thirty-one days, except February, which consists of twenty-eight, and in leap year of twenty-nine days. The calendar month is also called usual, natural, civil, political.

In an Act of Parliament passed after 1850, the word "month," which was formerly taken to mean lunar month unless calendar month was specified, means calendar month unless there is something to show that lunar month is intended (Interpretation Act, 1889, s. 3). The same rule applies to any judgment, order, direction or document formerly part of the proceedings of the Supreme Court (R.S.C., Ord. 3, r. 1). At common law and in equity it meant twenty-eight days (2 Bl.Comm. 141; *Kodak (Australia) Pty.* v. *Hally* [1960] Q.S.R. 452.

In ecclesiastical matters it means a calendar month. By R.S.C., Ord. 64, r. 1, where the time for doing any act or taking any proceeding is limited by months, not expressed to be lunar months, such time is to be computed by calendar months.

By the rule of the commercial world a month is deemed to be a calendar month; and this rule is applied to bills of exchange and promissory notes by the Bills of Exchange Act, 1882, s. 14 (4); but in legal documents which came into operation before 1926, the primary meaning of month was lunar month, and there was no general exception making it mean calendar month in commercial documents; it could only bear that meaning where, according to the ordinary rules of construction of documents, a secondary meaning could be admitted (*Bruner* v. *Moore* [1904] 1 Ch. 305; *Phipps & Co.* v. *Rogers* [1925] 1 K.B. 14).

The Law of Property Act, 1925, s. 61, enacts that in all deeds, contracts, wills, orders and other instruments executed, made or coming into operation after 1925, "month" means calendar month unless the context otherwise requires.

As to how a calendar month is to be computed, see *Radcliffe* v. *Bartholomew* [1892] 1 Q.B. 161.

Monumenta quae nos recorda vocamus sunt veritatis et vetustatis vestigia (Co.Litt. 118). (The written documents which we call records are the footprints of truth and antiquity.) Coke is here speaking of the dignity of courts of record.

Monuments. See ANCIENT MONUMENTS.

Monya. See MONETAGIUM.

Moor, an officer in the Isle of Man, who summons the courts for the several sheadings. The officer is similar to our bailiff of a hundred.

Mooring. A long-standing claim to the ownership of a tidal creek may, even without actual proof of title, be very strong evidence in favour of finding possession in the claimant sufficient to found an action of trespass against third parties merely establishing moorings there (*Fowley Marine (Emsworth)* v. *Gafford* [1968] 2 Q.B. 618).

Anchoring is a contravention of a by-law prohibiting mooring (*Evans* v. *Godber* [1974] 1 W.L.R. 1317).

Moot [Sax. *gmot, emot*], meeting. See GEMOTE.

Moots are exercises in pleading, and in arguing doubtful cases and questions, by the students of an Inn of Court (*q.v.*) before the benchers of the Inn. They were, like bolts (*q.v.*), also held in the Inns of Chancery up to the time when these institutions ceased to perform educational functions. At one time the performance of a specified number of moots before and after call was essential for qualification as and retaining qualification as a barrister (Dugd.Orig. 311–324). See BARRISTERS.

Moot case, or **Moot point,** a case or point unsettled and disputable, such as properly affords a topic of disputation.

Moot-hall, or **Moot-house,** council-chamber, hall of judgment, town-hall.

Moot-hills, hills of meeting, on which our British ancestors held their great courts.

Moot-man, one of those who used to argue the reader's cases in the Inns of Court. See MOOT CASE.

Mop. See MARKETS AND FAIRS; STATUTE FAIR.

Mora, delay. Mere delay has no legal result where express or implied promptness could not have been exacted, but the onus of proof increases on those responsible as the delay itself increases.

Mora also means a moor, marsh land, a heath, fen land, barren and unprofitable ground (Co.Litt. 5a).

Mora debitoris non debet esse creditori damnosa (Pothier). (Delay on the part of one under a duty ought not to be injurious to him to whom the duty is owing.) This is a qualification of the principle embodied in the maxim *Damnum sentit dominus* (*q.v.*). Thus, where there is delay in giving or taking delivery of goods sold, then the goods, as from the date of the commencement of the delay, are at the risk of the party in default as regards any loss which might not have been incurred but for the default. (Sale of Goods Act, 1893, s. 20).

Mora mussa, a watery or boggy moor; a morass (1 Dugd.Mon. 306).

Mora reprobatur in lege (Jenk.Cent. 51). (Delay is disapproved in law.)

Moral actions, those in which men have knowledge to guide them and a will to choose for themselves (1 Rutherford Inst.Nat.Law, c. i).

Moral consideration. A mere moral consideration will not support a promise by parol. See CONSIDERATION.

Moratorium, an authorised postponement of payment of debts.

Moratur in lege (he tarries in the law), he demurs; for in a demurrer the party demurring did not go on with his case but elected to stand or fall by the judgment of the court upon the point raised on demurrer (*q.v.*).

Moravians, otherwise called Herrnhuters or United Brethren, a sect of Christians exempted from military service in America by the statute 1748, 22 Geo. 2, c. 30, and allowed by that statute and by the Quakers and Moravians Acts, 1833 and 1838 (since super-seded by the Oaths Act, 1888), to give evidence on affirmation instead of oath.

More or less (*sive plus sive minus*). These words, in the expression " be the same more or less," are used in con-tracts for the sale of land and convey-ances to cover any slight inaccuracy in the area as stated. The description would run, " containing ten acres be the same more or less." They would, however, cover only a very slight deficiency in the area: what precisely they cover has never been accurately laid down; and for any considerable deficiency the pur-chaser would be entitled to an abatement of the agreed price (*Cross* v. *Eglin* (1831) 2 B. & Ad. 106). The more general form now is " ten acres or thereabouts."

Morganatic marriage, a marriage between two persons of unequal rank which is valid and indissoluble, but in which the spouse of lower rank does not assume the rank of the other and of which the children do not inherit the dignity nor, as of right, the possessions of the spouse of higher rank. Such a mar-riage is unknown to English law, but is recognised by the laws of various foreign states. Such marriages have not infre-quently been contracted by royal per-sonages, most of whom have been men: they have sometimes occurred in the case of women of royal rank who have married subjects.

Morgangani, or **Morgangiva** [Sax. *morgen*, morning; *gifan*, gift], a gift on the morning after the wedding; dowry; the husband's gifts to his wife on the day after the wedding (Leg.Canut., c. 99; Leg.Hen. 1, c. 70).

Morina, murrain; also the wool of sick sheep, and those dead with the mur-rain (2 Fleta, c. 79, par. 6).

Morling, or **Mortling**, wool from the skin of dead sheep.

Mormonism, a social system prevail-ing in Utah, in the United States, whereby plurality of wives was recog-nised. These marriages were not recog-nised by English law (*Hyde* v. *Hyde* (1866) L.R. 1 P. & D. 130), nor were they legal according to the law of the United States. See WORSHIP, PLACE OF.

Morosus, marshy. See MORA.

Morphine. See DRUGS, DANGEROUS.

Mors dicitur ultimum supplicium (3 Co.Inst. 212). (Death is denominated the extreme penalty.) Because, Coke explains the law is satisfied by the execu-tion of judgment of death and has the body buried instead of leaving it on the gallows. Coke had not anticipated hanging in chains.

Mors omnia solvit (Jenk.Cent. 160). (Death clears all scores.) But not always. See ACTIO PERSONALIS, ETC.

Morsellum, or **Morsellus terrae**, a small parcel or bit of land (Dugd.Mon. 282).

Mort d'ancestor. See ASSISE OF MORT D'ANCESTOR.

Mortality. See BILLS OF MORTALITY.

Mortgage [Old Germ. *wetti*, *ved*, a bond; Lat. *vadium*, pledge; Fr. *mort*, dead; *gage*, pledge], a dead pledge; a thing put into the hands of a creditor.

A mortgage is the creation of an interest in property, defeasible (*i.e.*, annullable) upon performing the condi-tion of paying a given sum of money, with interest thereon, at a certain time. This conditional assurance is resorted to when a debt has been incurred, or a loan of money or credit effected, in order to secure either the repayment of the one or the liquidation of the other. The debtor, or borrower, is then the mort-gagor, who has charged or transferred his property in favour of or to the credi-tor or lender, who thus becomes the mort-gagee. If the mortgagor pays the debt or loan and interest within the time men-tioned in a clause technically called the proviso for redemption, he will be entitled to have his property again free from the mortgagee's claim; but if he did not comply with such proviso, at common law he lost the property to the mortgagee. In equity, however, until the mortgage has been foreclosed, or unless the property has been sold under powers to satisfy the debt, it has always been redeemable upon payment of the debt or loan, with interest and expenses, at any period within twelve (formerly twenty) years after the last recognition of the mortgage security by the mortgagee; and this because equity deems the non-compliance with the proviso for redemption a penalty, against which it always relieves when practicable.

Seeing that in by far the greater number of loan transactions the mortgagor never performs the condition in the proviso for redemption, they have been denominated mortgages, as the pledge is then dead or lost (*mortuum vadium*) to the mortgagor at law. A mortgage differs from a vifgage (*vivium vadium*), so called because neither loan nor property is lost, for the creditor enters into possession of the property and receives its proceeds in satisfaction of his debt, with interest, upon which the debtor becomes entitled to his own again. A Welsh mortgage is one in which the creditor receives the proceeds of his security in satisfaction of the interest of his debt, the principal remaining due and the estate never becoming forfeited, but redeemable at any time; and the creditor not being entitled to sue at law in the absence of a covenant or bond, or to foreclose in equity. If property were conveyed to a mortgagee and his heirs until out of its rents the loan and interest had been received, this would have been in the nature of a Welsh mortgage, and might be compared to a tenancy by *elegit*.

Equity will not suffer any compact to infringe the right of redeeming a mortgage. The right or equity of redemption is the chief and inseparable incident of a mortgage—an incident unextinguishable, save by a foreclosure decree, a sale by the mortgagee under a power, express or implied, in that behalf, a legislative provision, or unreasonable delay. (See CLOG ON EQUITY OF REDEMPTION.) A provision rendering a mortgage irredeemable for a short term, such as five or seven years, is, however, allowed (*Biggs* v. *Hoddinott* [1898] 2 Ch. p. 311). In *Davis* v. *Symons* [1934] Ch. 442, a covenant not to redeem for twenty years was not allowed, and redemption was allowed in six months. A provision in a mortgage by a company postponing the date for redemption for forty years was held valid in *Knightbridge Estates Trust* v. *Byrne* [1940] A.C. 613.

Every kind of property may be mortgaged except the salaries and emoluments of public functionaries; full pay and half-pay of naval and military men; retiring allowances of persons liable to serve again; commissions in the army; and church livings with cure of souls, and other statutory exceptions.

While an increase in the rate of interest upon default of regular payment is a penalty, and is not admissible, the reservation of a higher rate, with an abatement for punctual payment, may be made.

The Real Estate Charges Acts, 1854 and 1877, provided that the heir or devisee of real estate should not claim payment of mortgages out of personal assets; and the Real Estate Charges Act, 1867, provided that in construing wills a general direction to pay debts out of personalty should not include mortgage debts, unless an intention to that effect was expressed or implied. These Acts, commonly called Locke King's Acts, were repealed and reproduced in an amended form, to give effect to the assimilation of real and personal property by the Administration of Estates Act, 1925, s. 35. This provision now relates to any property, whether real or personal, including entailed interests.

The Law of Property Act, 1925, ss. 93, 95, 96, gives a mortgagor power to require the mortgagee to transfer the mortgage debt instead of reconveying, power to inspect title deeds, and power to pay off one mortgage, where there are mortgages to the same person of different properties, without paying off the others, unless the power is excluded by the terms of the mortgage. See CONSOLIDATION.

The Law of Property Act, 1925, s. 99, confers on mortgagors and mortgagees in possession extensive powers of leasing, but powers of leasing were commonly provided for before the Act by express terms in the mortgage deed.

The Law of Property Act, 1925, ss. 101, 103–109, confers on mortgagees powers of sale, insurance, and to appoint a receiver.

The Law of Property Act, 1925, s. 102, enables a mortgagee of an undivided share in land to exercise such powers of sale, etc., as a mortgagee of a share in the land possessed before 1925; for the effect of the powers of a mortgagee upon sale or foreclosure, over the fee simple or term remaining in the mortgagor and against subsequent incumbrancers, see ss. 88, 89.

A mortgagee, however, cannot sell the mortgagor's beneficial interest apart from the legal title (*Hunter* v. *Hunter* [1936] A.C. 202); and he cannot sell to himself (*Williams* v. *Wellingborough Borough Council* [1975] 1 W.L.R. 1327).

The Law of Property Act, 1925, ss. 117–120, Sch. 4, provides forms of charge by way of legal mortgage, and statutory charge by way of legal mortgage and forms of transfer and other forms including forms of receipt on discharge. This receipt by the Law of Property Act, 1925, s. 115, operates as a surrender, reconveyance or transfer of the mortgaged property subject to prior incumbrances (if any). The vesting effect of a receipt in this form (without other reconveyance) applies to any class of property. The receipt need not be by deed and should be endorsed on or attached to the mortgage.

The Law of Property Act, 1925, s. 97, together with the Land Charges Act, 1925, s. 10, introduced alterations in the substantive law of mortgage. By the Law of Property Act, 1925, ss. 85, 86, all mortgages of a fee simple existing on January 1, 1925, were converted into terms of 3,000 years from that day, the reversion in fee remaining in the mortgagor. Mortgages of a legal term were converted into mortgages less a few days, leaving the leasehold reversion in the mortgagor, the term of each subsequent then-existing mortgage in either case being for a day longer than the term of the prior incumbrance. In the same manner mortgages after 1925 can only be effected by the creation of a term of years, leaving the freehold or leasehold reversion, as the case may be, in the mortgagor. Such mortgages carry the right to possess the documents of title subject to claims of prior mortgagees, and may be effected by a charge by way of legal mortgage (Law of Property Act, 1925, s. 87, Sch. 5). Mortgages made after 1925, though creating a legal estate, must be registered under the Land Charges Act, 1972, s. 2, in the Land Registry, unless the mortgage is accompanied by a deposit of the documents of title. The absence of documents affects any purchaser (including a registered mortgagee) with notice of a prior title. Mortgages without the deeds obtain priority not necessarily by order of the date of creation but according to date of registration (Law of Property Act, 1925, s. 97). First and any subsequent mortgages which are not accompanied by the title deeds and not registered are void as against a purchaser for value if registration is not effected before completion of the purchase. Legal mortgages made before 1926 do not lose priority and bind the purchaser if he is affected with notice. Such mortgages may and should be registered unless the mortgagee holds the deeds. Mortgages and charges registered under the Companies Act, 1948, are not affected by these provisions. In regard to registered land, see REGISTRATION.

All causes for redemption or foreclosure of mortgages are assigned to the Chancery Division.

As to the power of trustees to invest in mortgages of land, see the Trustee Investments Act, 1961, s. 1, Sch. 1. Upon appointment of new trustees, the land mortgaged must be expressly conveyed or transferred to them (Trustee Act, 1925, s. 40 (4)). See EQUITABLE MORTGAGE; LAND CHARGE; NOTICE.

A sub-mortgage is a mortgage by a mortgagee of his mortgage debt with a transfer of the mortgage security; the original mortgagee is called sub-mortgagor in respect of the sub-mortgage. A further charge is an agreement that a subsisting mortgage shall be a security for a further advance by the mortgagee. A further security is a mortgage of some additional property, or a grant of additional remedies to secure a subsisting mortgage debt.

An equitable mortgage is one which passes only an equitable interest, either because the form of transfer or conveyance used is an equitable one, or because the mortgagor's interest is equitable.

A legal mortgage of an estate in fee simple is effected by a demise for a term of years absolute, subject to a proviso for cesser on redemption, or a legal charge by deed (Law of Property Act, 1925, s. 85 (1)). A legal mortgage of a leasehold interest is effected by a sublease or a legal charge by deed (Law of Property Act, 1925, s. 86 (1)).

Equitable mortgages exist where there is an agreement to create a legal mortgage or a deposit of title deeds or an equitable charge.

A mortgagor in possession is in the same position as an ordinary landowner, except that he must not prejudice the security by committing waste. He is entitled to collect rents under leases granted before the mortgage, until the mortgagee gives the tenants notice of the mortgage; and, under the Law of Property Act, 1925, s. 98, he may bring actions in his own name in respect of the possession or rents of the land, or for damages in respect of any trespass or other wrong done to the land. The mortgagor's power of leasing is commonly restricted by the mortgage.

A mortgagor in possession or receipt of the rents and profits of any land, as to which the mortgagee has given no notice of intention to enter into possession or receipt of the rents and profits, may sue for such possession, or such rents and profits, or to prevent or recover damage for any wrong thereto, in his own name (Judicature Act, 1873, s. 25 (5) replaced by the Law of Property Act, 1925, s. 98); but see *Turner* v. *Walsh* [1909] 2 K.B. 484.

A mortgagee in possession is bound to account to the mortgagor for the rents and profits which he has received, or ought with proper management to have received, and is liable for waste. The principle is that he must get no advantage out of the mortgage other than the payment of principal, interest and costs, and he is made to account not only for what he has actually received, but also for what he might have received but for his own wilful default or neglect.

A mortgagee in possession has statutory power to grant leases and to accept leases within the limits applicable to a mortgagor in possession (Law of Property Act, 1925, ss. 99, 100): he also has power, in the case of a mortgage by deed, to cut and sell timber ripe for cutting and not planted for shelter or ornament. He has power to insure the property, where the mortgage is by deed, against loss or damage by fire. He retains his right to sue on the personal covenant to repay, and may pursue all his remedies at one and the same time. Provided that the mortgage is by deed he has certain restricted powers of sale exercisable where notice requiring payment of the mortgage debt has been given and there is three months' default thereafter or where interest is two months in arrear after being due or where there is a breach of some provision (other than the covenant to pay the loan and interest) which is contained in the mortgage deed or in the Law of Property Act, 1925, and which imposes an obligation upon the mortgagor (s. 103). The mortgagee may also appoint a receiver, (s. 109), or foreclose the mortgage (s. 88). He has a right to possession of title deeds (s. 85), a right to tack further advances, and a right to consolidate where there are two or more mortgages by the same mortgagor held by the same mortgagee.

Mortgage interest is subject to control under the Rent Act, 1968, Pt. VIII (ss. 93–99), as amended by the Courts Act, 1971, Sch. 11 Pt. II. The control does not apply to mortgages created on or after December 8, 1965, or in certain cases of mortgages of long tenancies, on or after November 28, 1967.

Where a dwelling-house is the subject of a mortgage, the court may postpone the operation of an order for possession to give the mortgagor additional time to fulfil his obligations (Administration of Justice Act, 1970, s. 36) and the jurisdiction of the county court is extended (ss. 37–39). See also the Administration of Justice Act, 1973, s. 8, and the Consumer Credit Act, 1974, Sch. 4 para. 30.

Mortgages of land are in most cases excluded from the operation of the Consumer Credit Act, 1974: see s. 16. Where not so excluded a mortgage of land (including any security charged on land) securing a consumer credit agreement (see s. 8) or a consumer hire agreement (see s. 15) is enforceable only under an order of the court (s. 126). The transferee of a mortgage of registered land which falls within the Act is protected by s. 177. *Cf.* the Land Registration Act, 1925, s. 33 (3).

As to the abolition of stamp duty on mortgages, see the Finance Act, 1971, s. 64, Sch. 14 Pt. VI.

Mortgagee, he who takes a mortgage as security for a loan.

Mortgagor, he who gives a mortgage as security for a loan.

Morth [Sax.], murder, answering exactly to the French *assassinat* or *meurtre de guetapens.*

Morthlaga, a murderer.

Morthlage, murder.

Mortis causa donatio. See DONATIO MORTIS CAUSA.

Mortmain [Fr. *mort*, dead; *main*, hand], such a state of possession of land as makes inalienable; whence it is said to be in a dead hand—in a hand that cannot shift away the property. It takes place upon alienation to any corporation, sole or aggregate, ecclesiastical or temporal (Co.Litt. 2b; 2 Bl.Comm. 268).

The statutes prohibiting alienation in mortmain, in the strict sense of the word, that is, alienation of land to corporations, are Magna Carta, 1215, the statute *De Viris Religiosis*, 1279, the Statute of Westminster II, 1285, and the statute 1391, 15 Ric. 2, c. 5. These statutes were supplemented by the Charitable Uses Act, 1735 (the Mortmain Act), replaced by the Mortmain and Charitable Uses Act, 1888, supplemented by the Mortmain and Charitable Uses Act, 1891. The whole law relating to mortmain was abolished by the Charities Act, 1960, ss. 38, 39, Schs. 5, 7.

Mortuaries, places for the reception of dead bodies before interment. The Public Health Act, 1875, ss. 141, 142, empowered every local sanitary authority to provide a mortuary, and to cause dead bodies to be removed to it in cases where their retention in dwelling-houses might be prejudicial to the health of the inmates: see now Public Health Act, 1936, s. 198; London Government Act, 1933, s. 40.

In ecclesiastical law, mortuaries were a kind of ecclesiastical heriot, being a customary gift claimed by and due to the minister in very many parishes on the death of his parishioners. Like lay heriots,

they were originally only voluntary bequests to the church, being intended as a kind of expiation and amends to the clergy for personal tithes and other duties not paid by the deceased in his lifetime. It was usual in ancient times to bring the mortuary to church along with the corpse when it was brought to be buried, and thence it was sometimes called a corse-present. In the laws of Canute it was called soul-scot or *symbolum animae* (2 Bl.Comm. 425). Mortuaries were abolished by the Ecclesiastical Jurisdiction Measure 1963, s. 82 (3).

Mortuum vadium, a dead pledge or mortgage. See MORTGAGE.

Moss-troopers. See BLACKMAIL.

Most-favoured nation clause, a stipulation in a treaty according to which one party grants to the other party the same treatment as it has granted, or may grant, to a third State.

Mote, a meeting, an assembly; used in composition as *burgmote, folkmote,* etc. See GEMOTE.

Mote-bell, the bell which was used by the Saxons to summon people to the court.

Moteer, a customary service or payment at the mote or court of the lord, from which some were exempted by charter or privilege.

Motel. The Alberta District Court of Canada held that a motel which did not serve food was not an inn at common law (*King* v. *Barclay* (1960) 24 D.L.R. (2d) 418). See INNKEEPER.

Mother-church [*primaria ecclesia*]. See MATRIX ECCLESIAS.

Mothering, a custom of visiting parents on mid-Lent Sunday (Jacob).

Motibilis, one who may be removed or displaced; also, a vagrant (5 Fleta, c. vi).

Motion, an application to a court or a judge. Some motions are employed to obtain a judgment on the main question in an action (see MOTION FOR JUDGMENT); but these are not motions in the sense in which the word is commonly used, namely, to denote an interlocutory application in an action. As a general rule, a motion is an oral application made by counsel in open court, as opposed to a petition, which is a written application, and to a summons, which is made in chambers, unless it is an originating summons. See SUMMONS.

Except where an application by motion may properly be made *ex parte* (*q.v.*), no motion may be made without previous notice to the parties affected thereby. If, however, the court is satisfied that the delay caused by proceeding in the ordinary way would or might entail irreparable or serious mischief, the court may make an order *ex parte* on such terms as to costs or otherwise, and subject to such undertaking, if any, as it thinks just. Any party affected by such an order may apply to the court to set it aside. Unless the court gives leave to the contrary, there must be at least two clear days (*q.v.*) between the service of a motion and the day named in the notice for hearing the motion (R.S.C., Ord. 8, r. 2). As to motions to a divisional court see Ord. 57, r. 2.

Applications for an injunction may be made *ex parte* on affidavit where the case is one of urgency. Otherwise the application must be made by motion or summons (R.S.C., Ord. 29, r. 1). An application for the appointment of a receiver may be made by summons or motion. An application for an injunction may be made *ex parte* on affidavit (Ord. 30, r. 1).

A motion of course is a motion which is granted by the court as a matter of course.

In Chancery practice, if counsel is unable to make a motion on the day for which notice has been given, he is entitled, as a matter of right, " to save the motion," that is, to adjourn it to the next motion day by mentioning it to the court, without the consent of the other side; but in cases where the motion was listed by special leave he can do this only with the consent of the other side or with the leave of the court.

If counsel does not either bring on or save his motion on the day for which notice has been given (provided of course he has had an opportunity of being heard), the motion is said to be abandoned, and the other party is entitled to his costs of it. See LAST DAY OF TERM.

As to motions by way of appeal, see APPEAL.

Motion for decree. Under the practice of the old Court of Chancery the most usual mode of bringing on a suit for hearing when the defendant had answered was by motion for decree. To do this the plaintiff served on the defendant a month's notice of his intention to move for a decree. (See DECREE; FURTHER CONSIDERATION.) Now the plaintiff merely replies and the action is set down for trial under R.S.C., Ord. 34.

Motion for judgment. Motion for judgment is necessary in the Chancery Division where an action is ordered to be set down without pleadings as a short cause on motion for judgment. See R.S.C., Ord. 8, rr. 1–5, notes. There is an option to apply by motion or summons on judgment in default of defence (Ord. 19, r. 7); on judgment on admissions (Ord. 27, r. 3); on leave under Ord. 77, r. 9 in proceedings against the Crown. As to admiralty orders see Ord. 75.

Motion for a new trial. See TRIAL.

Motion in arrest of judgment. See ARREST OF JUDGMENT.

Motive, a state of mind; an incentive; an object. It is relevant evidence of intention.

Motor car. The Road Traffic Act, 1972, s. 190, defines a motor car as a mechanically propelled vehicle (*q.v.*) not being a motor cycle (*q.v.*) or an invalid carriage (*q.v.*) which is constructed itself to carry a load or passengers and the weight of which unladen (a) if it is constructed solely for the carriage of passengers and their effects, is adapted to carry not more than 7 passengers exclusive of the driver and is fitted with tyres of the prescribed type, and does not exceed 3 tons; (b) if it is constructed or adapted for use for the conveyance of goods or burden of any description, does not exceed 3 tons or $3\frac{1}{2}$ tons in the case of a vehicle carrying gas containers or plant for the purpose of its propulsion; (c) does not exceed $2\frac{1}{2}$ tons in a case falling within neither of those categories.

A heavy motor car is a mechanically propelled vehicle (not being a motor car), which is constructed to carry a load or passengers, and the weight of which unladen exceeds $2\frac{1}{2}$ tons.

A person under sixteen may not drive a motor cycle (*q.v.*) or invalid carriage (*q.v.*). A person under seventeen may not drive a motor car or tractor used primarily for farming. A person under twenty-one may not drive a heavy locomotive, light locomotive (see LOCOMOTIVE), motor tractor (*q.v.*) or heavy motor car. Regulations may modify these restrictions (Road Traffic Act, 1972, ss. 4, 96); European Communities Act, 1972, Sch. 4; Road Traffic Act, 1974, Sch. 5 Pt. II). See DRIVING LICENCES.

Users of motor vehicles must be insured against third party risks (Road Traffic Act, 1972, s. 143). A person may be convicted of using a car on a road without an insurance policy where it has broken down, the battery removed, and jacked up so that the wheels are off the ground (*Elliott* v. *Grey* [1960] 1 Q.B. 367). A motor car ceases to be a mechanically propelled vehicle only when there is no reasonable prospect of ever making it mobile again (*Law* v. *Thomas* (1964) 62 L.G.R. 195).

Once a car becomes the subject-matter of a retail sale and purchase, is registered with the local authority, has the number plates affixed and is driven out of the distributor's or the dealer's premises, the car ceases to be a new car (*Morris Motors* v. *Lilley* [1959] 1 W.L.R. 1184).

For penalties for tampering with motor vehicles, see the Road Traffic Act, 1972, s. 29, Sch. 4.

Motor car and motor cycle trials and "scrambles" on footpaths or bridleways have to be authorised by the local authority (Road Traffic Act, 1972, s. 35).

It is an offence to drive a motor vehicle on a footpath or bridleway without lawful authority (s. 36).

The Vehicles (Excise) Act, 1971, consolidated the law relating to excise duties on mechanically propelled vehicles and to the licensing and registration of such vehicles. It was amended by the Finance Acts, 1971, ss. 6, 7 and 1972, s. 128, the Road Traffic Act, 1972, Sch. 7 and S.I. 1974 Nos. 168, 482, art. 19. See *Pilgram* v. *Dean* [1974] 1 W.L.R. 601; *Binks* v. *Department of the Environment* [1975] R.T.R. 318. See EXCISE.

Motor cycle. The Road Traffic Act, 1972, s. 190, defines a motor cycle as a mechanically propelled vehicle (*q.v.*) not being an invalid carriage (*q.v.*) with less than four wheels the weight of which unladen does not exceed 8 cwt.

As to licences to ride a motor cycle, see DRIVING LICENCES.

Pillion riding is regulated under the Road Traffic Act, 1972, s. 16. The pillion rider must sit astride on a proper seat. Not more than one pillion rider is permitted; for penalties see Sch. 4 and the Road Traffic Act, 1974; Sch. 5 Pt. III. Motor cyclists and their pillion riders must wear crash helmets (Road Traffic Act, 1972, ss. 32, 33; S.I. 1974 No. 844).

As to "scrambles," see MOTOR CAR.

Motor Insurers' Bureau, an incorporated body which is under agreement with the Minister for Transport to satisfy any unsatisfied judgment arising from any liability required to be covered by insurance (see MOTOR CAR). It is a condition of recovery from the Bureau that notice of proceedings should be given to the Bureau either before action or within 21 days of the commencement of proceedings. The address of the Bureau is 60 Watling Street, London, E.C.4.

Authorised insurers are required to be members of the Motor Insurers' Bureau (Road Traffic Act, 1974, s. 20).

As to making the Bureau a party see *Fire, Auto and Marine Insurance Co.* v. *Greene* [1964] 2 Q.B. 687; *White* v. *London Transport* [1971] 2 Q.B. 721.

The Bureau is liable to pay a third party who has been deliberately injured by a driver (*Hardy* v. *Motor Insurers' Bureau* [1964] 2 Q.B. 745). Where a claimant has been refused payment and does not appeal he cannot bring an action for the amount claimed (*Persson* v. *London County Buses* [1974] 1 W.L.R. 569).

Motor racing. A person who promotes or takes part in a race or trial of speed between motor vehicles (*q.v.*) on a public highway is guilty of an offence (Road Traffic Act, 1972, s. 14). For prosecution and punishment, see Sch. 4 and the Road Traffic Act, 1974, Sch. 5 Pt. III. As to information as to identity of drivers, see the Road Traffic Act, 1972, s. 168. Motor rallies are regulated under s. 15.

Motor tractor. The Road Traffic Act, 1972, s. 190, defines a motor tractor as a mechanically propelled vehicle (*q.v.*) which is not constructed itself to carry a load other than the following articles, that is to say, water, fuel, accumulators and other equipment used for the purpose of propulsion, loose tools and loose equipment and the weight of which unladen does not exceed 7¼ tons.

Motor vehicle. The Road Traffic Act, 1972, s. 190, defines a motor vehicle as a mechanically propelled vehicle intended or adapted for use on roads. A vehicle on tow does not cease to be a mechanically propelled vehicle (*Cobb* v. *Whorton* [1971] R.T.R. 392; *Norton* v. *Leach* [1972] R.T.R. 416).

As to the regulation of the construction and use of motor vehicles and their equipment, see the Road Traffic Act, 1972, ss. 40–83, Sch. 4; Road Traffic Act, 1974, Sch. 2 Pt. II, Sch. 5 Pt. III, Sch. 6 paras. 14, 15, Sch. 7. As to lights see Lights on Vehicles. As to the power of the police to stop a motor vehicle, see the Act of 1972, s. 59; to demand names and addresses, ss. 162, 164, 168, Sch. 4; Act of 1974, Sch. 5 Pt. III. As to excise licences, see Excise. As to the regulation of foreign vehicles, see the Road Traffic (Foreign Vehicles Act, 1972; the European Communities Act 1972, Sch. 4; the Road Traffic Act, 1974, Sch. 7.

A badge is required to be issued by local authorities for display on motor vehicles used by disabled persons (Chronically Sick and Disabled Persons Act, 1970, s. 21).

The unauthorised dumping of abandoned motor vehicles is an offence. They may be removed and disposed of by local authorities who may recover the expense of so doing (Civic Amenities Act, 1967, ss. 19–22; Local Government Act, 1972, Sch. 14 para. 45, Sch. 19 paras. 33–35, Sch. 30; Airports Authority Act, 1975, s. 14).

Where a motor vehicle which has been let under a hire-purchase (*q.v.*) agreement or has been agreed to be sold under a conditional sale agreement is disposed of by the hirer or buyer before the property in the vehicle has become vested in him, a private purchaser of the vehicle who acts in good faith and without notice of the agreement is protected (Hire-Purchase Act, 1964, ss. 27–29, as substituted by the Consumer Credit Act, 1974, Sch. 4 para. 22).

Motor vehicles more than three years old require the production of a Ministry of Transport Services test certificate before an excise licence is issued (Road Traffic Act, 1972, s. 52; S.I. 1966 No. 973; 1969 Nos. 418, 419). An authorised vehicle examiner owes a duty of care, enforceable by action, to carry out the M.O.T. test carefully and to deliver an accurate certificate (*Artingstoll* v. *Hewen's Garages* [1973] R.T.R. 197).

As to roadside tests, see the Road Traffic Act, 1972, ss. 53–55.

A person who takes a motor vehicle onto a public road remains in charge of it until he has taken it off the road again or has put it in the charge of someone else (*Woodage* v. *Jones* (*No. 2*) [1975] R.T.R. 119).

Motor-ways are " special roads " (*q.v.*) within the meaning of the Highways Act, 1959, s. 11. See the Motorways Traffic Regulations, 1959 (S.I. 1959 No. 1147).

Motu proprio, the commencing words of a certain kind of papal rescript.

Moult, a mow of corn or hay (Paroch. Antiq. 401).

Movable dwelling. See Camping.

Movables, goods, furniture, personalty.

Mulct, a fine of money or a penalty.

Mulier [Norm.Fr. *mulieré*; Lat. *mulier*, a woman], a woman; a virgin; a wife; a legitimate child (1 Co.Inst. 243; 2 Bl. Comm. 248).

Mulier is applied in the old books to a son, daughter, brother, sister, etc., to signify one born in lawful wedlock, or legitimate, as opposed to a bastard. The expression was formerly of importance in what was called the case of bastard *eigné* and *mulier puisné* (elder son a bastard and younger son legitimate), which occurred where a man had a bastard son, and afterwards married and had a legitimate son. If the father died and the bastard entered on his land and died seised of it, so that it descended to his issue, the *mulier puisné* was barred of his right to the land (Litt. 399 *et seq.*).

Littleton, favouring the argument for *legitimatio per subsequens matrimonium*, states that in the opinion of some it was necessary for the bastard *eigné* to be born of a woman with whom his father later contracted a valid marriage (Jackson, *Formation and Annulment of Marriage* 38).

The doctrine seems to have been abolished by the Real Property Limitation Act, 1833, s. 39. See BASTARD.

Mulieratus, a legitimate son (Glanvil).

Mulieres ad probationem status hominis admitti non debent (Co.Litt. 6). (Women ought not to be admitted to prove the status of a man.) This refers to the question whether the man was a villein.

Mulierty, lawful issue, because begotten *e muliere* (of a wife), and not *e concubina* (Co.Litt. 352).

Mullones foeni, cocks or ricks of hay.

Mulmutin laws. See MOLMUTIAN LAWS.

Mulneda, a place to build a water-mill (2 Dugd.Mon. 284).

Multa, or **Multura, episcopi,** a fine which was paid to the king by the bishops, that they might have power to make their wills; and that they might have the probate of other men's wills, and the granting of administrations (2 Co.Inst. 291).

Multa conceduntur per obliquum, quae non conceduntur de directo (6 Co.Rep. 47). (Many things are allowed by a side-wind which was not allowed directly.)

Multa in jure communi, contra rationem disputandi, pro communi utilitate introducta sunt (Co.Litt. 70). (For the sake of the public good many things which are logically indefensible have been made part of the common law.)

Multa multo exercitamentis facilius quam regulis percipies (4 Co.Inst. 50). (There are many things which you will learn much more easily from practice than from rules.) Coke is here speaking of parliamentary procedure.

Multifariousness. Under the practice of the old Court of Chancery, a bill of complaint was open to a demurrer for multifariousness when it attempted to embrace too many objects or causes of suit. See JOINDER.

Multipartite [Lat. *multus*, many; *pars*, a part], divided into several parts.

Multiple occupation. As to the management of houses in multiple occupation, see the Housing Act, 1961, ss. 12–23; Housing Act, 1969, ss. 58–64, Sch. 10.

Multiplicata transgressione, crescat poenae inflictio (2 Co.Inst. 479). (Where wrongdoing is multiplied the infliction of punishment increases also.) This seems to mean that habitual offenders should get heavy sentences.

Multiplication. The "multiplication" of gold and silver was made felony by the statute 1403, 5 Hen. 4, c. 4. This multiplication was the imaginary or pretended manufacture of gold or silver out of other metals. See PHILOSOPHERS' STONE.

Multiplicity. A bill in equity might have been objectionable for an undue dividing or splitting up of a single cause of suit, and thus multiplying subjects of litigation. Equity discourages unreasonable litigation. It would not, therefore, permit a bill to be brought for a part of a matter only where the whole was the proper subject of one suit (Judicature Act, 1873, s. 24 (7), now Judicature Act, 1925, s. 43); as to inferior courts, see Judicature Act, 1873, ss. 89–91, now Judicature Act, 1925, ss. 201–203.

Multiply. When a thing is divided into several parts, and something which was dependent on or annexed to it thenceforward becomes dependent on or annexed to each part of it, the accessory is said to be multiplied. Thus, if a copyhold tenement for which a heriot was due to the lord on the death of each successive tenant was divided into parcels and conveyed to different persons, the heriot was multiplied, *i.e.,* a heriot was due for each parcel.

Multitudinem decem faciunt (Co.Litt. 257). (Ten make a multitude.) So at least some have said, remarks Coke, who is considering what precisely is meant by the word "multitude" where it was said that someone occupied premises with a multitude of people. Coke himself says that the question is one for the discretion of the judges.

Multitudo errantium non parit errori patrocinium (11 Co.Rep. 75). (The fact that many persons have made any given mistake does not tend to show that it is right.)

Multitudo imperatorum perdit curiam (2 Co.Inst. 219). (A multitude of masters destroys a court.) Quoted by Coke as a comment on the provisions against extortion by officers of the court which are contained in the Statute of Westminster I, 1275, c. 30. It is not an authority for the proposition that cases are better heard by a single stipendiary magistrate than by a multiplicity of justices.

Multo, a wether sheep. *Multones auri* (golden sheep), mentioned in a patent of Edward I, were French gold coins which sometimes circulated in England.

Multo fortiori. See A FORTIORI.

Multure [Fr. *moulture;* Lat. *molere,* to grind], a grist or grinding; the corn ground; also the toll or fee due for grinding. See MOLITURA.

Mum, a species of fat ale brewed from wheat and bitter herbs, mentioned in revenue Acts.

Mumming, antic diversions of the Christmas holidays, suppressed in Queen Anne's time; see the statute 1511, 3 Hen. 8, c. 9.

Mund [A.S.], protection, peace, whence *mundbryc,* breach of the peace (Leg. Hen. 1, c. 37).

Mundbriech, a privilege to raise banks on any person's land to secure the common interest from inundations.

Mundbryce [A.S.], trespass against one's lord; compensation for breach of the peace (2 Holds., H.E.L. 88).

Mundbyrd, Mundeburde, a receiving into favour and protection.

Munera, portions of lands distributed to tenants and revocable at the lord's will, under our early feudal system.

Municipal [Lat. *municipalis, munus;* office; *capere,* to take or hold], belonging to a corporation.

Municipal corporation, a body of persons in a town having the powers of acting as one person, of holding and transmitting property, and of regulating the government of the town. Such corporations existed in the chief towns of England (as of other countries from very early times), deriving their authority from incorporating charters granted by the Crown. They were regulated by the Municipal Corporations Acts, 1835 and 1882 and the Local Government Act, 1933.

Municipal corporations of every borough outside Greater London ceased to exist on April 1, 1974 (Local Government Act, 1972, s. 1 (1)). See DISTRICT.

Municipal law, that which pertains solely to the citizens and inhabitants of a State, and is thus distinguished from political law and the law of nations.

Muniment [Lat. *munire,* to fortify], support, defence, record; a deed or writing upon which claims and rights are founded and depend; evidences, charters.

Muniment-house, or **Muniment-rooms,** a house or room of strength in cathedrals, collegiate churches, castles, colleges, public buildings, etc., purposely made for keeping deeds, charters, writings, etc. (3 Co.Inst. 170).

Munitions of war. As to keeping secret patents for their invention, see the Patents Act, 1949, s. 18. As to supplying them to foreign States at peace with this country, for the purpose of hostilities between themselves, see the Foreign Enlistment Act, 1870. As to the establishment of a Ministry of Munitions during the war of 1914–18, see the Ministry of Munitions Act, 1915. It was abolished by the Ministries of Munitions and Shipping (Cessation) Act, 1921. In the war 1939–45, the production of munitions was under the control of the Ministry of Supply. See CONTRABAND.

Munus publicum, a public office.

Murage [Lat. *murus,* a wall], money paid to keep walls in repair.

It is mentioned in the statute 1275, 3 Edw. 1, c. 30, as having been granted by the Crown to certain citizens and burgesses *por lor vile enclose* (for the enclosing of their town). It was a toll, or the right to levy a toll, for the erection or maintenance of town walls, upon persons passing through the town (Moore, *Foreshore*).

Muratio, a town or borough surrounded with walls (Jacob).

Murder [Sax. *morthor, morthen;* Low Lat. *murdrum*], when a person of sound memory and discretion unlawfully kills any reasonable creature in being, with malice aforethought, either express or implied (3 Co.Inst. 47; 4 Bl.Comm. 195).

The person committing the offence must be conscious of doing wrong, and able to discern between good and evil. See DRUNKENNESS; MCNAGHTEN'S CASE.

Death must result within a year and a

day after the cause of death administered (*R. v. Dyson* [1908] 2 K.B. 454).

The killing must be with malice aforethought express or implied and malice is implied by a proved intention to inflict grievous bodily harm (*D.P.P.* v. *Smith* [1961] A.C. 290; *Hyam* v. *D.P.P.* [1975] A.C. 55). Where a person kills another in the course or furtherance of some other offence, the killing amounts to murder only if done with the same malice aforethought as is required for a killing to amount to murder when not done in the course or furtherance of another offence. A killing done in the course of or for the purpose of resisting an officer of justice, or of resisting or avoiding or preventing a lawful arrest (*q.v.*), or of effecting an escape or rescue from legal custody, is treated as a killing in the course or furtherance of an offence (Homicide Act, 1957, s. 1).

A man can be guilty of murder although he did not intend to harm his victim, if he intended to do an act which a reasonable man would say was likely to cause death (*D.P.P.* v. *Smith* [1961] A.C. 290) but this principle does not apply to attempted murder (*R.* v. *Grimwood* [1962] 2 Q.B. 621).

The Offences against the Person Act, 1861, s. 1, provided that every person convicted of murder should suffer death as a felon. The Homicide Act, 1957, s. 5, enacted that the death penalty should be confined to capital murders as defined in that section and to cases of repeated murder within s. 6. These sections and s. 1 of the Act of 1861 were repealed by the Murder (Abolition of Death Penalty) Act, 1965. See CAPITAL OFFENCES; CAPITAL PUNISHMENT.

On an indictment for murder, a person found not guilty of murder may be found guilty of manslaughter or of causing grievous bodily harm or of any offence of which he may be found guilty under an enactment specifically so providing or of assisting in the murder or of an attempt to murder or of an attempt to commit any other offence of which he might be found guilty but may not be found guilty of any offence not included above (Criminal Law Act, 1967, s. 6 (2)). Enactments specifically providing for alternative verdicts are the Infant Life Preservation Act, 1929, s. 2 (2) (which allows a verdict of child destruction), the Infanticide Act, 1938, s. 1 (2) (which allows a verdict of infanticide), the Suicide Act, 1961, s. 2 (2) (see below).

As to diminished responsibility, see DIMINISHED RESPONSIBILITY.

A person who aided, abetted, counselled or procured a person to commit suicide may be charged with and found guilty of murder (Suicide Act, 1961, s. 2 (2)). See SUICIDE.

As to the punishment for attempted murder, see *R.* v. *White* [1910] 2 K.B. 124.

A murderer is disqualified from deriving any benefit under the will of his victim (*In the Estate of Hall* [1914] P. 1; *Re Callaway* [1956] Ch. 559). The rule applies to manslaughter (*Re Peacock* [1957] Ch. 310) but does not apply where the person who killed another was insane (*Re Batten's Will Trusts* (1961) 105 S.J. 529). It does apply where he is suffering from diminished responsibility (*Re Giles, Giles* v. *Giles* [1972] Ch. 544).

Murdrum, the secret killing of another; also the amercement to which the vill wherein it was committed, or, if that were too poor, the whole hundred, was liable (4 Bl.Comm. 195).

As to the rates of compensation for murder amongst the Anglo-Saxons, see 2 Hall, *Mid. Ages,* 133.

See ENGLECERY.

Muriatic acid gas. See ALKALI WORKS.

Murorum operatio, the service of work and labour done by inhabitants and adjoining tenants in building or repairing the walls of a city or castle; their personal service was commuted into murage (*q.v.*).

Muscovy Company, a company, also known as the Russia Company, which originated in the reign of Edward VI, and which in 1555 received a charter authorising discovery and colonisation as well as granting the monopoly of the Russia trade. It had a quasi-official position in Russia, and until, upon the execution of Charles I, it lost the favour of the Tsar, it was predominant amongst the foreign traders there. It levied, with the consent of the Russian Government, certain duties upon exports from Russia to

England, and out of the proceeds paid the English consuls in Russia and defrayed the expenses of the Anglican chapels at St. Petersburg and Moscow.

Museum. Museums and art galleries may be maintained by local authorities who may make a charge for admission (Public Libraries and Museums Act, 1964, ss. 12–15; Local Government Act, 1972, s. 208, Sch. 30).

The Museums and Galleries Admission Charges Act, 1972, enables charges for admission to the British Museum, the National History Museum, the National Museum of Antiquities of Scotland and the National Galleries of Scotland.

For exemption from capital transfer tax see the Finance Act, 1975, Sch. 6 para. 12.

Mushrooms. A person who picks mushrooms growing wild on any land does not steal what he picks unless he does it for reward or for sale or other commercial purpose. " Mushroom " includes any fungus (Theft Act, 1968, s. 4 (3)). Nor is he guilty of an offence under the Criminal Damage Act, 1971. See s. 10 (1).

Music. The Copyright Act, 1956, s. 2, provides for copyright in musical works. See COPYRIGHT.

Music and dancing licences. The grant of these in London and Westminster and within twenty miles thereof is regulated by the Home Counties (Music and Dancing) Licensing Act, 1926, as amended by the London Government Act, 1933, Sch. 18, the Local Government Act, 1972, s. 204 (7), Sch. 29 para. 27, Sch. 30 and the Local Government Act, 1974, s. 35, Sch. 6 para. 3. A right of appeal with respect to a licence is given by the Act of 1972, s. 207 (8), Sch. 25 Pt. II. In Greater London the licence is to be granted by the Greater London Council (London Government Act, 1963, Sch. 12). There is a saving for licensed premises (Licensing Act, 1964, s. 182 (1)) and cinemas (Cinematograph Act, 1952, s. 7). As to Sunday entertainments see SUNDAY.

Under the adoptive Public Health Acts Amendment Act, 1890, s. 51, a house or garden, whether licensed for the sale of liquor or not, may not be kept for public dancing, singing, music, or other public entertainment of the like kind, without a licence from the justices having power to grant licences for the sale of intoxicating liquor.

An adoptive Act, the Private Places of Entertainment (Licensing) Act, 1967 (amended by the Theatres Act, 1968, Sch. 2, the Courts Act, 1971, Sch. 9 Pt. I, and the Local Government Act, 1972, Sch. 29 para. 27, Sch. 30) enables a local authority to control private music and dancing conducted for gain.

Musicians in London streets. The Metropolitan Police Act, 1864, s. 1, replacing the Metropolitan Police Act, 1839, s. 57, enacts that any householder within the Metropolitan Police District, personally, or by his servant, or by any police constable, may require any street musician or street singer to depart from the neighbourhood of the house of such householder, on account of the illness or on account of the interruption of the ordinary occupations or pursuits of any inmate of such house, or for other reasonable or sufficient cause, and that every person who shall sound or play upon any musical instrument or shall sing in any thoroughfare or public place near any such house after being so required to depart, shall be liable to a penalty of not more than forty shillings, or, in the discretion of the magistrate before whom he shall be convicted, may be imprisoned for any time not more than three days and in default of payment for not more than one month (*R.* v. *Hopkins* [1893] 1 Q.B. 621), and that it shall be lawful for any constable belonging to the Metropolitan Police Force to take into custody without warrant any person who shall offend as aforesaid, provided that he shall be given into custody by the person making the charge and provided also that the person making a charge for an offence against the Act shall accompany the constable who shall take into custody any person offending as aforesaid to the nearest police station-house, and there sign the charge sheet kept for such purpose.

Musk rats. Power to prohibit or control the importation or keeping of musk rats is contained in the Destructive Imported Animals Act, 1932.

Mussa, a moss or marsh ground; a

1213

place where sedges grow; a place over-run with moss.

Mussels. See ANIMALS, FERAE NATURAE; FISHERY.

Muster-book, a book in which the forces are registered (*Termes de la Ley*).

Muster-Master General, an officer who kept lists of the forces of the Crown to prevent frauds. He is mentioned in the statute 1592, 35 Eliz. 1, c. 4, and in 1802 there was still a Commissary and Muster-Master General.

Muta canum [Fr. *meute*], a mew or kennel of hounds, one of the mortuaries (*q.v.*) to which the Crown was entitled at a bishop's decease (2 Bl.Comm. 426).

Mutation, a French death duty. *Droits de mutation par décès,* is a duty payable on transmission of property on death (*Re Scott* [1914] 1 Ch. 848).

Mutatis mutandis, with the necessary changes in points of detail.

Mute. A prisoner is said to stand mute when, being arraigned for treason or mis-demeanour, he either makes no answer at all, or answers foreign to the purpose, or with such matter as is not allowable, and will not answer otherwise. In the first case, a jury must be sworn to try whether the prisoner stands mute of malice (*i.e.*, obstinately) or by visitation of God (*e.g.*, being deaf or dumb). (*R.* v. *Sharp* [1957] Crim.L.R. 821.) If he is found mute by visitation of God, the trial proceeds as if he had pleaded not guilty; if he is found mute of malice, or if he will not answer directly to the indict-ment, the court orders a plea of not guilty to be entered, and the trial proceeds accordingly (Criminal Law Act, 1967, s. 6 (1) (*c*)). See PEINE FORTE ET DURE.

Muthlach, murder.

Mutilation, deprivation of a limb or any essential part. See MAYHEM.

Mutiny Act, a statute annually passed from 1689 to 1879, to punish mutiny and desertion, and for the better payment of the army and their quarters.

The Bill of Rights, 1688, declares that raising or keeping a standing army within the kingdom in time of peace, unless with the consent of Parliament, is against the law. Therefore, to enable the army to be kept up, an Act of Parliament was annually passed authorising this to be done. This annual Act contained elaborate provisions for the enlistment, payment and billeting of soldiers, for the punishment of mutiny and desertion, and generally for the government of the Army, and was hence called the Mutiny Act; but these provisions were con-solidated in the Army Discipline and Regulation Act, 1879; and, therefore, in the annual Act it was sufficient to provide that the Army Discipline and Regulation Act, 1879, should remain in force for one year. The Act of 1879 was supplemented and amended by various Acts, especially the Regulation of the Forces Act, 1881, and was itself replaced by the Army Act, 1881. The last-men-tioned Act was annually re-enacted, fre-quently with amendments, by an Army and Air Force (Annual) Act, which also fixed the number of men to be main-tained in the army during the current year. The Army and Air Force (Annual) Act for the time being in force was the authority for the existence of the army. This is now provided for by the Army Act, 1955, and the Air Force Act, 1955, which are continued on an annual basis by orders made under powers contained in the Armed Forces Act, 1971, s. 1.

Mutual credits; Mutual dealings; Mutual debts. The phrase "mutual credits" used in the Bankruptcy Act, 1914, denotes such dealings between two persons as must in their nature terminate, or have a tendency to terminate, in debts. The Act provides by s. 31 that where there have been mutual credits, mutual debts, or other mutual dealings between the bankrupt and one of his creditors, an account shall be taken of what is due from the one party to the other in respect of such mutual deal-ings and the sum due from the one party shall be set off against the sum due from the other party, and the balance of such account, and no more, shall be claimed or paid on either side respectively (*Eberle's Hotel Co.* v. *Jonas* (1887) 18 Q.B.D. 459). The effect produced by the mutual credit clause is, therefore, a species of set-off (*q.v.*), but it differs from the ordinary set-off between solvent persons in having for its object, not to prevent cross actions, but to avoid the injustice, which would otherwise arise, of compelling a creditor to pay the trustee in bankruptcy the full amount of the debt due from him to the bankrupt, while the creditor would perhaps only receive a small dividend under the bankruptcy on the debt due from the bankrupt to him. The set-off provided by s. 31 of the Bankruptcy Act, 1914, cannot be excluded by agreement (*Rolls Razor* v. *Cox* [1967] 1 Q.B. 552; *National Westminster Bank* v. *Halesowen Presswork and Assemblies* [1972] A.C. 785).

Mutual promises, concurrent considerations, which will support each other, unless one or the other be void; in which case, there being no consideraion on the one side, no contract can arise. See CONSIDERATION; PROMISE.

Mutual wills, wills made by two persons who leave their effects reciprocally to the survivor. Either will may be revoked during the joint lives, but revocation is ineffective if the benefit of the other will has been taken (*Stone* v. *Hoskins* [1905] P. 194; *In the Estate of Heys* [1914] P. 192; *Re Green* [1951] Ch. 148).

Mutuality. In every agreement the parties must, as regards the principal or essential part of the transaction, intend the same thing; that is, each must know what the other is to do: this is called mutuality of assent.

In a simple contract arising from agreement, it is sometimes of the essence of the transaction that each party should be bound to do something under it: this requirement is called mutuality; thus, an agreement by A to refer a question between himself and B to arbitration is not enforceable unless B also agrees to be bound by the award; and an agreement by C with D to learn a trade is not binding unless there is also an undertaking by D to teach him. This may be called mutuality of obligation.

Mutuality of remedy is where each party can enforce the contract against the other; thus, a vendor of land can enforce specific performance of the contract by the purchaser, because the purchaser could have done the same to him.

Mutuari, to borrow.

Mutuation, the act of borrowing.

Mutuatus. If a man owed another person money and had a note for it without seal, an action of debt lay upon a *mutuatus*; but in this there might be wager of law, which there could not be in an action on the case, on an implied promise of payment (*Jacob*). See COMPURGATION.

Mutus, silent, not having anything to say.

Standing mute is when a person, being arraigned, either cannot speak, or refuses to answer or plead. See MUTE; PEINE FORTE ET DURE.

To advise a prisoner to stand mute is a contempt of court. See MISPRISION.

Mutus et surdus, dumb and deaf.

Mutuum, a loan whereby the absolute property in the thing lent passes to the borrower, it being for consumption, and he being bound to restore, not the same thing, but other things of the same kind. Thus, if corn, wine, money, or any other thing which is not intended to be returned, but only an equivalent in kind, is lost or destroyed by accident, it is the loss of the borrower; for it is his property, and he must restore the equivalent in kind, the maxim *ejus est periculum cujus est dominium* applying to such cases.

In a *mutuum* the property passes immediately from the mutuant or lender to the mutuary or borrower, and the identical thing lent cannot be recovered or redemanded.

Mynster-ham [*ecclesiae mansio*], monastic habitation; perhaps the part of a monastery set apart for purposes of hospitality or as a sanctuary for criminals (Anc.Inst.Eng.).

Mystery [Fr. *mestier*], an art, trade, or occupation.

Myxomatosis, a disease deadly to rabbits. Knowingly using or permitting the use of an infected rabbit to spread the disease is punishable on summary conviction with a fine of £20, or on a subsequent conviction, £50 (Pests Act, 1954, s. 12).

N

N. L. See NON LIQUET.

Nadgairs, sometime, lately; a word used in the title page of Anderson's *Reports.*

Nail, an old measure, sometimes of weight, in which case it was usually eight pounds and was used with regard to cheese, beef, etc., and sometimes of length, in which latter case it was two-and-a-half inches and was used for cloth.

Naked contract. See NUDUM PACTUM, ETC.

Nam; Naam; Namium [Sax. *nam*, to take], the taking or distraining of another man's goods. The term, in its Latinised form, is found in the laws of Canute, c. 18; and in the Anglo-French form of *naam* it is found in Britton (1290) and in the *Termes de la Ley* (1641). *Naam vif* meant a distress of cattle; *naam mort* was a distress of other chattels (Horne, *Mirror*, lib. 2; 2 Co.Inst. 140; Spelman).

Namium vetitum was the proceeding which lay where distress had been unlawfully concealed or carried out of the country; and *namium repetitum* was a second distress (2 Co.Inst. 140; 3 Bl. Comm. 149).

Namation, a later form of *nam* (*q.v.*).

Name [Lat. *nomen*; Fr. *nom*; Goth. *namo*; Sax. *nama*; Dut. *naem*], the discriminative appellation of an individual.

Proper names are either Christian names, as being given at baptism, or surnames, from the father (4 Co.Rep. 170).

A Christian name may be altered at confirmation with the consent of the bishop, and the bishop is directed by a constitution of 1281 to change " wanton names " at confirmation. In Blunt's *Church Law,* 2nd ed., p. 60, two post-Reformation instances are given of a bishop changing a Christian name at confirmation, and it is said that cases still occur where this is done.

Marriage confers a name upon a woman, which is not lost by her divorce, and she can acquire another only by obtaining it by repute obliterating her name by marriage (*Fendall* v. *Goldsmid* (1877) 2 P.D. 263). As to retainer of a title, see *Cowley* v. *Cowley* [1901] A.C. 450.

Anyone may take on himself whatever surname or as many surnames as he pleases, without an Act of Parliament or royal licence. But a man cannot have two names of baptism as he may have divers surnames (Co.Litt. 3a).

The assumption by a stranger of a name the patronymic of a family is no ground of action (*Du Boulay* v. *Du Boulay* (1869) L.R. 2 C.P. 430). Names may be changed by Act of Parliament, by royal licence, or by deed poll. As to practice see the Enrolment of Deeds (Change of Name) Regulations, 1949 (S.I. 1949 No. 316); Enrolment of Deeds (Change of Name) (Amendment) Regulations, 1969 (S.I. 1969 No. 1432); Enrolment of Deeds (Change of Name) (Amendment) Regulations, 1974 (No. 1937). See SURNAME.

The surname of a minor can be changed only by agreement between the parents or, in the absence of agreement, by a decision of the court (*Y.* v. *Y.* (*Child: Surname*) [1973] Fam. 147).

The addition of " & Co." was held to be a change of name in *Evans* v. *Piauneau* [1927] 2 K.B. 374. As to business names see the Registration of Business Names Act, 1916. See BUSINESS NAMES, REGISTRATION OF; CHRISTIAN NAME; COMPANIES; DIRECTOR; GOODWILL; TRADE NAME.

Name and arms clause, a clause sometimes inserted in a will or settlement by which property is given to a person, for the purpose of imposing on him the condition that he shall assume the surname and arms of the testator or settlor, with a direction that if he neglects to assume or discontinues the use of them, the estate shall devolve on the next person in remainder. Owing to the difficulty of ascertaining with sufficient precision the nature of the assumption and use postulated by the clause, the condition may be void for uncertainty (*Re Murray* [1955] Ch. 69), but not always. See *Re Howard's Will Trusts* [1961] Ch. 507; *Re Neeld* [1962] Ch. 643; *Re Neeld* [1969] 1 W.L.R. 998.

Namium, a distress. See NAM.

Namium vetitum, an unjust taking of

the cattle of another and driving them to an unlawful place, pretending damage done by them (3 Bl.Comm. 149). See NAM; REPLEVIN.

Nantes, Edict of, an edict for the security of Protestants, made by Henry IV of France, and revoked by Louis XIV, October 2, 1685.

Narr [Lat. *narratio*], a declaration in an action (Jacob).

Narratio, the oral claim of a plaintiff in the courts. It was also called the *conte* or tale.

Narrator, a pleader or reporter. A *serviens narrator* was a serjeant-at-law (2 Fleta, c. 37).

Narrow seas, those running between two coasts not far apart. The term is sometimes applied to the English Channel.

The Firth of Forth is also " narrow waters " as far as collision regulations are concerned (*Screw Collier Co.* v. *Kerr* [1910] A.C. 165).

Narrow-land, selion of land (*q.v.*).

Natal. As to the union of the colonies of Natal, the Cape of Good Hope, the Transvaal, and the Orange River Colony, see the South Africa Act, 1909. The Union was established on May 30, 1910. See DOMINION.

Natale, the state and condition of a man.

Nathwyte. See LAIRWITE.

Nation, a people distinguished from another people, generally by their language, or government; an assembly of men of free condition, as distinguished from a family of slaves.

National Assembly of the Church of England, the Assembly constituted in accordance with the constitution set forth in the appendix to the addresses presented by the Convocations of Canterbury and York on May 10, 1919, and laid before Parliament (Church of England Assembly (Powers) Act, 1919, s. 1 (1)). This assembly was known as the Church Assembly. It has been renamed the General Synod of the Church of England and reconstituted (Synodical Government Measure, 1969, s. 2, Sch. 2). The General Synod consists of the Convocations (*q.v.*) of Canterbury and York joined together in a House of Bishops (the Upper House) and a House of Clergy (the Lower House) and having added to them a House of Laity. The General Synod meets at least twice a year. The General Synod appoints a Legislative Committee to which all measures which it is desired to become law are referred (Sch. 2).

The Act of 1919 (as amended by the Synodical Government Measure, 1969, s. 2 (2)) provides that there is to be constituted at the commencement of each Parliament a committee of both Houses of Parliament styled the Ecclesiastical Committee, consisting of fifteen peers nominated by the Lord Chancellor and fifteen members of the House of Commons nominated by the Speaker (s. 2); that every Measure passed by the General Synod shall be submitted by the Legislative Committee to the Ecclesiastical Committee, who are to report thereon to Parliament (s. 3); and that upon each House of Parliament resolving that such Measure be presented for the royal assent it shall have the force of an Act of Parliament upon the royal assent being signified as in the case of Acts of Parliament (s. 4).

See Cripps' *Law relating to the Church and Clergy.*

See MEASURE.

National assistance. See the National Assistance Act, 1948; the National Assistance (Amendment) Acts, 1951 and 1959; the National Assistance Act, 1948 (Amendment) Act, 1962; the Ministry of Social Security Act, 1966; the Tribunals and Inquiries Act, 1971; and the Social Security Act, 1975.

National Biological Standards Board. See the Biological Standards Act, 1975.

National Coal Board. See COAL MINES.

National College of Physical Training for England. See the Physical Training and Recreation Act, 1937, s. 7.

National debt, the money owing by Government to certain members of the public, the interest of which is paid out of the taxes raised by the whole of the public. It is regulated by the National Debt Act, 1870. Certain enactments relating to the National Debt were consolidated by the National Debt Act, 1958, replaced by the National Debt Act, 1972. See FUNDS, PUBLIC.

National defence contribution, a tax on the profits of trades or business imposed by the Finance Act, 1937, ss. 19–25. It was renamed the profits tax by the Finance Act, 1946, s. 44. See PROFITS TAX.

National Enterprise Board. This was established by the Industry Act, 1975, with enormous powers of acquisition and interference with British industry.

National Film Finance Corporation, a body having power to make loans for financing films (Cinematograph Film Production (Special Loans) Acts, 1949 to 1957).

National Freight Corporation. See the Transport Act, 1968, ss. 1–5.

National Gallery. This was established in pursuance of a Treasury Minute dated March 24, 1824. It is, apart from gifts, dependent on the Treasury. The Tate Gallery was made a separate institution by the National Gallery and Tate Gallery Act, 1954.

For exemption from capital transfer tax, see the Finance Act, 1975, Sch. 6 para. 12.

National health service. See the National Health Service Acts, 1946, 1951, 1952, 1961, and 1966; the National Health Service (Amendment) Act, 1949; the Health Visiting and Social Work (Training) Act, 1962; the National Health Service Contributions Acts, 1965 and 1970; and the National Health Service (Reorganisation) Act, 1973.

As to control, etc. of executive councils, joint committees, tribunals and service committees, see the Tribunals and Inquiries Act, 1971, Sch. 1. As to the control of prices of medical supplies see the Emergency Laws (Re-enactments and Repeals) Act, 1964, s. 5; S.I. 1968 No. 1699.

National Industrial Relations Court. This court was set up by the Industrial Relations Act, 1971. It attracted the particular hatred of the Trade Union Congress and was abolished by the Trade Union and Labour Relations Act, 1974, ss. 1, 21–24.

National insurance. Social security under the National Insurance Acts and the National Insurance (Industrial Injuries) Acts is replaced by the scheme under the Social Security Act, 1975. As to the control, etc. of tribunals and commissioners, see the Tribunals and Inquiries Act, 1958, Sch. 1 and ADMINISTRATIVE TRIBUNALS.

National judges. Judges of the International Court of Justice retain the right to sit in a case involving their own countries. If necessary *ad hoc* judges nominated by the parties are appointed. See Lauterpacht, *Development of International Law by the International Court.*

National Land Fund. See the Finance Act, 1946, ss. 48–51, and the Historic Buildings and Ancient Monuments Act, 1953, s. 7.

National library. See BRITISH LIBRARY.

National Loans Fund. See the National Loans Act, 1968, as amended.

National Maritime Museum. See the National Maritime Museum Act, 1934.

National parks, tracts of country in England and Wales designated by order of the National Parks Commission as national parks under the National Parks and Access to the Countryside Act, 1949, ss. 1–14. The Act of 1949 was supplemented and amended by the Countryside Act, 1968, under which the National Parks Commission became the Countryside Commission. Powers are conferred on local authorities to provide country parks with facilities for sailing, boating, bathing and fishing, facilities on common land and camping and picnic sites (ss. 6–10; Local Government Act, 1972, Schs. 21, 30).

See also the Local Government Act, 1974, ss. 7, 9, 35, 42, Schs. 6–8.

Ten national parks have been established: the Peak District, the Lake District, Snowdonia, Dartmoor, Pembrokeshire Coast, North York Moors, Yorkshire Dales, Exmoor, Northumberland and Brecon Beacons.

The Commission has, under the Act, power to submit for the approval of the Secretary of State for the Environment proposals for long-distance routes for use on foot or on horseback (ss. 51–58). Those being established are: the Pennine Way, South-west Peninsular Coastal Path, Pembrokeshire Coastal Path, and a path following the line of Offa's Dyke. A South Downs route is being planned.

The Commission may, subject to confirmation by the Minister, designate areas of outstanding natural beauty to which some of the provisions of the Act relating to national parks apply (ss. 87, 88). The following areas have been established: Anglesey, Arnside and Silverdale, Cannock Chase, Chichester Harbour, Chilterns, Cornwall, Cotswolds, Dedham Vale, East Devon, North Devon, South Devon, Dorset, Forest of Bowland, Gower, East Hampshire, South Hampshire Coast, Kent Downs, Lincolnshire Wolds, Lleyn, Malvern Hills, Mendip Hills, Norfolk Coast, Northumberland Coast, Quantock Hills, Shropshire Hills, Solway Coast, Suffolk Coast and Heaths, Surrey Hills, Sussex Downs, North Wessex Downs, Isle of Wight, Wye Valley. See the Annual Reports of the National Parks Commission.

National Research Development Corporation. See the Development of Inventions Act, 1967, ss. 1–4 and the Industry Act, 1975, s. 26.

National savings. See the War Loan (Supplemental Provisions) Act, 1915, the War Loan Act, 1919, the Finance Act, 1923, s. 33, and the Finance Act, 1932, s. 23 and the National Debt Act, 1972.

National Savings Bank. This is the successor of the Post Office Savings Bank. It is under the control of the Director of Savings (see SAVINGS, DIRECTOR OF) and is regulated by the National Savings Bank Act, 1971, as amended by the Superannuation Act, 1972, Sch. 6.

National savings certificates. See the National Debt Act, 1972, s. 8.

National Savings Stock Register. See the National Debt Act, 1972, ss. 2–7.

National service. Compulsory military service was imposed during the war of 1939–45 by the National Service (Armed Forces) Act, 1939. See now the National Service Acts, 1948 to 1955, which are in abeyance. See s. 61 of the Act of 1948 and S.I. 1953 No. 1771.

The Ministry of National Service was dissolved in 1959 and its functions transferred to the Ministry of Labour (S.I. 1959 Nos. 1769, 1970) and thence to the Secretary of State for Employment (S.I. 1968 No. 729).

National Steel Corporation. See the Iron and Steel Act, 1967, ss. 1–8; S.I. 1967 No. 1107.

National Theatre. See the National Theatre Acts, 1949 and 1974, and the National Theatre and Museum of London Act, 1973.

National treatment, treatment of foreigners on the same footing as nationals of one's own country.

National Trust. This is the name given to the National Trust for Places of Historic Interest or Natural Beauty incorporated by the National Trust Act, 1907, for the purposes of promoting the permanent preservation of lands and tenements (including buildings) of beauty or historic interest, and as regards lands, for the preservation of their natural aspects, features and animal and plant life. The National Trust is a charity: see the National Trust Charity Scheme Confirmation Act, 1919. Its purposes were extended by the National Trust Act, 1937, to include the preservation of buildings of national interest or architectural, historic or artistic interest or places of natural interest or beauty and the protection and augmentation of the amenities of such buildings and places and their surroundings, the preservation of furniture and pictures and chattels having national or historic or artistic interest, and the access to and enjoyment of the same by the public. The powers of the Trust were enlarged accordingly.

Further provision with respect to the transfer of settled lands to the National Trust was made by the National Trust Act, 1939. For exemption from capital transfer tax see the Finance Act, 1975, Sch. 6 para. 12, and acquisition under the Community Land Act, 1975, see s. 41.

National water council. See WATER.

National waters, inland waters, historical waters (*q.v.*), and the sea landwards of the base line (*q.v.*).

Nationalisation. See BANK OF ENGLAND; COAL MINES; ELECTRICITY; GAS; IRON AND STEEL; RAILWAY.

Nationality, that quality or character which arises from the fact of a person's belonging to a nation or State. Nationality determines the political status of the individual, especially with reference to allegiance (*q.v.*), while domicile determines his civil status. Nationality arises either by birth or by naturalisation (*q.v.*). See BRITISH SUBJECT.

Nations, Law of. The principal offences against the law of nations are: violations of safe conducts; infringements of the rights of ambassadors; and piracy. See INTERNATIONAL LAW.

Nativi de stipite; Nativi de conventione. A *nativus*, or native, meant a bondman or villein. In Cornwall at the time of Henry I *nativi de stipite* (natives of stock) were bondmen by birth, while *nativi de conventione* were bondmen by contract (Leg.Hen. 1, c. 76).

Of a native of stock in the time of Edward III it was said that when he died his lord had his chattels, and his last born son had the land by fine, and he could not send his son to school, nor marry his daughter, without licence of the lord. This system held good legally as late as the reign of Elizabeth I. See CONFESSION; NEIFE.

Nativitas, the servitude, bondage or villeinage of woman (Leg.Wm. 1).

Nativo habendo, De, a writ in the nature of a writ of right, which lay for a lord whose villein had run away. It required the sheriff to apprehend the villein and restore him to the lord, and upon it the question was tried as to whether the alleged villein was a free man or the villein of the lord (Reg.Orig. 7, 8; Fitz.N.B. 77; New Nat. Brev. 171, 172). See LIBERTATE PROBANDI, DE.

Nativus, a servant-born (Spelman). See NEIFE.

Natura Brevium. This was the *Natura Brevium* of the reign of Edward III, a compilation giving the original writs then in use. After Fitzherbert (*q.v.*) had brought out his *New Natura Brevium* about 1531, the earlier list was known as the *Old Natura Brevium*.

Natura non facit saltum; ita nec lex (Co.Litt. 238). (Nature takes no leap; neither does law.) Coke is pointing out that various preliminary steps to a writ of entry *sur disseisin* must be taken.

Natura non facit vacuum, nec lex supervacuum (Co.Litt. 79). (Nature does nothing useless and the law does nothing superfluous.)

Naturae vis maxima (Noy, Max. 26).

(The force of nature is very great.) Quoted as a comment upon the *Articuli super Cartas,* 1300, c. 11, which sanctioned as between relations what as between others would have been champerty (*q.v.*).

Natural affection, that love which a person has for his kindred. It is held to be good, though not valuable, consideration for certain purposes. See CONSIDERATION.

Natural allegiance, that perpetual attachment which is due from all natural-born subjects to their sovereign; local allegiance is temporary only, being due from an alien or stranger born for so long a time as he continues within the sovereign's dominions and protection (Fost. 184).

Allegiance may be owed after an alien has left this country if he has become possessed of a British passport (*Joyce* v. *D.P.P.* [1946] A.C. 347).

Natural child, the child in fact, the child of one's body. Some children are both the natural and legitimate offspring of a marriage, *i.e.,* those duly born in wedlock. Some are the legitimate but not the natural offspring of a marriage, *i.e.,* those who are born in wedlock, and never bastardised, although begotten in adultery and in fact the natural children of a stranger. See Shakespeare's *King John,* Act i, sc. 1.

Some are natural children only; *i.e.,* bastards, born out of wedlock, and those born in wedlock, who are bastardised, and hence the word is popularly more often used as though it were simply equivalent to bastard. See BASTARD; LEGITIMATION.

Natural Environment Research Council. This was created by the Science and Technology Act, 1965, to take over the work of the Nature Conservancy and the National Oceanographic Council. It continues the work of the latter council but in other respects has been replaced by the Nature Conservancy Council (*q.v.*) (Act of 1965, ss. 1, 3; Nature Conservancy Council Act, 1973, s. 1, Schs. 2, 4).

Natural equity. See EQUITY.

Natural gas. This may be supplied in accordance with a licence granted by the Secretary of State for Energy (Petroleum (Production) Act, 1934, s. 4; Gas Act,

1972, Sch. 6 para. 2). See also the Continental Shelf Act, 1964. See CONTINENTAL SHELF.

Natural History Museum. This was created by the British Museum Act, 1963, s. 8, as a museum separate from the British Museum (*q.v.*).

Natural infancy, a period of non-responsible life, which ends with the tenth year of a person's age (Children and Young Persons Act, 1933, s. 50; Children and Young Persons Act, 1963, s. 16 (1)).

Natural justice, the rules to be followed by any person or body charged with the duty of adjudicating upon disputes between, or upon the rights of, others. The chief rules are to act fairly, in good faith, without bias, and in a judicial temper, and to give each party an opportunity of adequately stating his case. The rules of natural justice do not apply to administrative acts (*Schmidt* v. *Secretary of State for Home Affairs* [1969] 2 Ch. 149).

The requirements of natural justice can be complied with without an oral hearing (*Brighton Corporation* v. *Parry* (1972) 70 L.G.R. 576).

See BIAS; INTEREST, DISQUALIFICATION FOR.

Natural law, rules derived from God, reason or nature, as distinct from man-made law.

Natural obligations, duties which have a definite object, but are not necessarily subject to any legal obligation.

Natural persons, human beings, as distinguished from artificial persons or corporations recognised by the law.

Natural rights, those rights which supplement the direct rights, *e.g.*, of ownership (*q.v.*), by imposing duties on other persons. Thus every owner of land has prima facie the right to prevent his neighbours from polluting the air passing over his land, and from disturbing, diminishing or polluting the water flowing through his land; he is also entitled to so much support from his neighbour's land as is necessary to keep his own land at its natural level. These are called natural rights, as opposed to acquired rights, such as easements, profits *à prendre*, franchises, etc. See ACCESS; AIR; NAVIGATION; SUPPORT ; WATER.

Natural use. The rule of absolute liability for the escape of things liable to do damage if they escape does not apply to things brought on to land in the course of a natural use of the land.

Natural-born subjects, those who are born within the dominions of the Crown and within the allegiance of the sovereign. See ALIEN; ALLEGIANCE; BRITISH SUBJECT; NATIONALITY; NATURALISATION.

Naturale est quidlibet dissolvi eo modo quo ligatur (Jenk., Cent. 70; Broom, 592). (It is natural for a thing to be unbound in the same way as it was bound.) Thus an obligation is made void by a release, a record by a record, a deed by a deed, a parol promise by a parol promise and an Act of Parliament by an Act of Parliament. See EODEM LIGAMINE, ETC.; LEX ANGLIAE SINE, ETC.; NIHIL TAM CONVENIENS, ETC.

Naturales liberi, natural children, children not born in lawful wedlock as opposed to *legitime*; children born as opposed to adopted (Civil Law).

Naturalisation. This takes place when a person becomes the subject of a State to which he was before an alien. The effect of naturalisation is that the naturalised subject thereby acquires all political and other rights, powers and privileges, and becomes subject to all obligations to which natural-born members of the State are entitled and subject, except that he cannot divest himself of his obligations towards the State of which he was formerly a subject, without the consent of that State. See EXPATRIATION.

Down to the enactment of the Naturalisation Act, 1844, an alien could become a British subject only by force of a special Act of Parliament. Under that Act and subsequently under the Naturalisation Act, 1870, which replaced it, an alien could become a British subject upon receiving from the Home Secretary a certificate of naturalisation; and since 1844, naturalisation by special Act has occurred in only a few cases.

The Act of 1870 was repealed by the Status of Aliens Act, 1914, which, as amended, governed naturalisation until the British Nationality Act, 1948. S. 10 (1) of that Act provides that the Home Secretary may, if application therefor is made to him in the prescribed manner by any alien or British protected person of full age and capacity who satisfies him that he is qualified under the provisions of Sch. 2 to the Act for naturalisation, grant to him a certificate of naturalisation; and that the person to whom the certificate is granted shall, on taking an oath of allegiance, be a citizen of the United Kingdom and colonies by naturalisation as from the date on which that certificate is granted.

Sch. 2 to the Act provides that the qualifications for naturalisation of an alien are: that he has either resided in the United Kingdom or been in Crown service in the United Kingdom, or partly the one and partly the other, throughout the period of twelve months immediately preceding the date of the application; that during the seven years immediately preceding such period of twelve months he has resided in the United Kingdom or any colony, protectorate, United Kingdom mandated territory or United Kingdom trust territory or been in Crown service as aforesaid, or partly the one and partly the other, for periods amounting in the aggregate to not less than four years; that he is of good character; that he has sufficient knowledge of the English language; and that he intends in the event of a certificate being granted to him to reside in the United Kingdom or in any colony, protectorate or United Kingdom trust territory, or to enter into or continue in Crown service under the United Kingdom, or service under an international organisation of which the United Kingdom is a member, or service in the employment of a society, company or body of persons established in the United Kingdom or established in any colony, protectorate or United Kingdom trust territory. The Home Secretary has power to take into account certain other qualifications in certain cases, and there are special provisions as to protected persons and others. See further the Commonwealth Immigrants Act, 1962, ss. 12 (2), 20; the Guyana Independence Act, 1966, s. 4 (2); the West Indies Act, 1967, s. 12, Sch. 3 para. 4 (3) (a).

See ALIEN; ALLEGIANCE; BRITISH SUBJECT; DENIZEN; NATIONALITY.

Nature conservation. The Nature Conservancy was created by royal charter on March 23, 1949. It was replaced first by the Natural Environment Research Council established under the Science and Technology Act, 1965, and then by the Nature Conservancy Council under the Nature Conservancy Council Act, 1973. The functions of the Council are the establishment of nature reserves, providing advice on the development and implementation of policy on nature conservation and the dissemination of knowledge, the support of research and the statutory functions of the Nature Conservancy. Nature conservation means the conservation of flora, fauna, or geological or physiological features. The property of the Natural Environment Research Council was transferred to the Nature Conservancy Council by S.I. 1974 No. 1241. The establishment of nature reserves is facilitated by the National Parks and Access to the Countryside Act, 1949, ss. 15–26. For particulars of the nature reserves so established, see Whitaker's *Almanack*. See also the Countryside Act, 1968, ss. 15 (1), 37, 46 (2); Conservation of Seals Act, 1970; the Water Act, 1973, s. 22; and the Badgers Act, 1973, as amended by the Nature Conservancy Council Act, 1973, Sch. 1.

Nature, Law of, certain rules of conduct supposed to be so just that they are binding upon all mankind. See NATURAL JUSTICE; NATURAL LAW.

Naufrage [Lat. *naufragium*], shipwreck.

Naulage [Lat. *naulum*], the freight of passengers in a ship (Johns.; Webster).

Nautae [Lat.], sailors; carriers by water.

Nautical Almanack. See the Nautical Almanack Act, 1828.

Navagium, a duty of certain tenants to carry their lord's goods in a ship (1 Dugd.Mon. 922).

Naval courts, courts held abroad in certain cases to inquire into complaints by the master or officers or seamen of a British ship, or as to the wreck or abandonment of a British ship, or when it is required in the interests of the owners of the ship or cargo (Merchant Shipping Act, 1894, s. 480). A naval court consists of three, four or five members, being naval officers, consular officers, masters of British merchant ships or British merchants (s. 481). It has power to supersede the master of the ship with reference to which the inquiry is held, to discharge any of the seamen, to decide questions as to wages and send home offenders for trial or try certain offences in a summary manner (s. 483). A naval court is quite distinct from a naval court-martial.

Naval discipline. See NAVY.

Naval reserves, originally volunteer forces, the naval coast volunteers (Naval Volunteers Act, 1853), the royal naval reserve (Royal Naval Reserve (Volunteer) Act, 1859, and succeeding Acts) and the royal naval volunteer reserve, formed under the Naval Forces Act, 1903. The royal naval volunteer reserve was abolished by the Reserve Forces Act, 1966. The royal naval reserve and the royal naval special reserve remain in being.

Navicert, a certificate by a representative of a belligerent in a neutral State exempting a ship or her cargo from contraband control.

Navicularis [Lat.], a sea captain.

Navigable; Navigation. The right of navigation is the right of the public to use an arm of the sea, a river, or other piece of water, as a highway for shipping, boating, etc., including the right to anchor in it (*Gann* v. *Free Fishers* (1866) 11 H.L.C. 192). It is a right of way and not a right of property, and therefore the owner of the bed of a river over which the public have by user acquired a right of navigation may erect any structure on it which does not interfere with the navigation warranted by that user (see HIGHWAY). In the case, however, of estuaries and navigable tidal rivers, the beds of which are prima facie vested in the Crown, the ownership of the soil is wholly subject to the public right of navigation, and no part of it can be used so as to derogate from or interfere with that right. A river which is subject to a right of navigation is said to be " navigable."

The question whether a river is navigable or not seems to depend partly on its size and the formation of its bed, and partly on the use to which it has been put; if a river will admit ships and it has been used for shipping purposes by the public, it is a navigable river, whether it is tidal or non-tidal, and whether it flows through or over private land or land belonging to the Crown. As a rule, however, an arm of the sea or a tidal river with a broad and deep channel is deemed navigable.

Power to divert navigable watercourses and to construct bridges over and tunnels under navigable waters is contained in the Highways Act, 1971, ss. 10–13.

As to navigation on the sea, see HIGH SEAS.

Where the public have acquired the right of navigation on a private or non-tidal river, the original exclusive right of the riparian owners to fish in it is not thereby affected (*Smith* v. *Andrews* [1899] 2 Ch. 678). See FISHERY.

Obstructing the navigation of a navigable water is a public nuisance. See NUISANCE.

See MOORINGS; Coulson & Forbes on *Waters*.

Navigation Acts, Acts restricting the import or export of goods except in British bottoms, *i.e.,* in ships the owners of which and the large proportion of the crews of which were British, passed for the protection of British shipping and commerce as against foreign countries. The first Navigation Act was passed during the Commonwealth, in 1651, to restrain the competition of the Dutch marine, and its restrictions were repeated in the statute 1660, 12 Car. 2, c. 18, sometimes styled the *Charta Maritima*, but earlier statutes of the same nature, *e.g.,* 1381, 5 Ric. 2 stat. 1, c. 3, had been passed in the reigns of Richard II, Henry VII, and Elizabeth I. All the Navigation Acts were repealed in 1849.

Navy [Lat. *navis*, a ship], an assemblage of ships, commonly ships of war; a fleet.

The discipline of the navy was formerly regulated by rules, articles, and orders, first enacted by the authority of Parliament soon after the Restoration, but it is now regulated by the Naval Discipline Act, 1957 (as amended).

Full time serving members of the Royal Navy are excusable as of right from jury service. So too are members of the Women's Royal Naval Service, Queen Alexandra's Royal Naval Nursing Service or any Voluntary Aid Detachment serving with the Royal Navy. See JURY.

Navy agency. See SHIP'S AGENT.

Navy bills, bills of exchange which certain officers of the navy were authorised to draw for their pay, etc., or which various naval authorities were authorised to draw in payment for stores, etc. No such bills are now in use. The Acts authorising them were repealed by the Admiralty, etc., Acts Repeal Act, 1865.

Ne admittas (that you admit not). While the old writ of *quare impedit* (*q.v.*) or assize of *darrein presentment* (*q.v.*) was available, a plaintiff who had sued out that writ could then sue out another writ, known as the writ of *ne admittas*, prohibiting the bishop from admitting, pending the decision of the case, the clerk whom the defendant had presented (Reg.Orig. 31; Fitz.N.B. 37; 3 Bl.Comm. 428).

Ne baila pas (he did not bail). In detinue, this meant a plea by the defendant that the chattels in question had not been delivered to him by the plaintiff.

Ne disturba pas. In the action of *quare impedit,* if the bishop and the clerk who had been presented pleaded *ne disturba pas,* the proceedings determined as against them. Now the bishop and the clerk usually disclaim title and leave the alleged owner of the advowson to fight the action.

The plea *ne disturba pas* in the action of *quare impedit* was the general issue appropriate to that action. See ISSUE.

Ne dona pas, or **Non dedit,** the general issue in a formedon (*q.v.*). It denied the gift in tail to have been made in manner and form as alleged, and was therefore the proper plea if the tenant meant to dispute the fact of the gift, but did not apply to any other case.

Ne exeat regno, a writ which issues from the Chancery Division to restrain a person from going out of the kingdom without licence of the Crown, or leave of the court. It is a high prerogative writ, which was originally applicable to purposes of State only, but was afterwards extended and confined to private transactions. It is or may be employed when a person, against whom another has an equitable claim for a sum of money actually due, is about to leave the country for the purpose of evading payment, and the absence of the defendant would materially prejudice the plaintiff in the prosecution of his action; but it would appear to be confined now to persons coming within the Debtors Act, 1869, s. 6 (*Drover* v. *Beyer* (1879) 13 Ch.D. 242).

Ne injuste vexes, a writ founded on Magna Carta, 1215, c. 10, which lay for a tenant distrained by his lord for more services than he ought to perform; it was a prohibition to the lord unjustly to distrain or vex his tenant; in a special use it was where the tenant had prejudiced himself by doing greater services, or paying more rent without constraint, than he needed; by reason of the lord's seisin, the tenant could not avoid it by avowry, but was driven to his writ for remedy (Reg.Orig. 4; Fitz.N.B. 10; New Nat.Br. 22).

It was abolished by the Real Property Limitation Act, 1833, s. 35.

Ne judex ultra petita partium. (A judge should not award to a party more than the party seeks to obtain.)

Ne luminibus officiatur, a servitude restraining the owner of a house from obstructing the light of his neighbour.

Ne recipiatur, a caveat against receiving and setting down an action for trial which the defendant might formerly enter when the action had not been entered in due time.

Ne rector prosternat arbores in ceriterio (that the rector do not cut down trees in the churchyard), an enactment printed under this title in the *Statutes of the Realm* among the *Statutes of Uncertain Date,* and in the *Statutes at Large* as 1361, 35 Edw. 1, st. 2.

Ne relessa pas (he did not release), a replication (*q.v.*) filed in reply to an answer (*q.v.*) in which the defendant alleged that the plaintiff had released.

Ne unques [Law Lat.], never.

Ne unques accouplé; Ne unques accoupié, a plea in which the fact of marriage was denied.

Ne unques executor (never an executor), a pleading which declared that the defendant (or plaintiff) was not and never was executor (or administrator) as alleged.

Ne unques indebitatus (never indebted) (*q.v.*), another form of *nunquam indebitatus* (*q.v.*). See NIL DEBET.

Ne unques seisie que dower, a plea by which a defendant denied that the husband of a widow was at or after her marriage seised of such an estate in lands as to entitle her to dower.

Ne unques son receiver (never his receiver). In an action for an account this was the plea by which a defendant denied that he had ever received anything for the plaintiff.

Ne varietur (let it not be changed). These words are sometimes written by foreign notaries and translators on copies or translations of documents furnished by them.

Neat, or **Net,** the weight of a pure commodity alone, without the container cask, bag, dross, packing, etc., opposed to gross weight, tare as opposed to *brut*; also undiluted; in accounts, a sum of money after deduction of all stated outgoings or expenses or other deductions.

Neat cattle, oxen or heifers.

Neat-land, land let out to the yeomanry.

Nec per vim, nec clam, nec precario, not by violence, stealth or permission. User as of right, in order to found a title by prescription must be *longus usus nec per vim, nec clam, nec precario.*

Nec tempus nec locus occurrit regi (Jenk.Cent. 190). (Neither time nor place affects the king.) In a decision that no grant of rights of criminal jurisdiction by the king could preclude him from prosecuting any pleas of the Crown in any place within the realm, this maxim is quoted only *quoad* the words *nec locus.* See NULLUM TEMPUS, ETC.

Nec veniam, effuso sanguine, casus habet (3 Co.Inst. 57). (Where blood is spilled the case is unpardonable.) This is quoted only as fortifying the proposition that the unlawful throwing of a missile into a crowded street so that someone is killed constitutes murder though there was no intention to kill.

Nec vi, nec clam, nec precario, not by violence, stealth or permission. See NEC PER VIM, ETC.

Necation [Lat. *neco*], the act of killing.

Necessaries. Notwithstanding the general rule that an infant is incapable of binding himself by a contract (Infants Relief Act, 1874), he must pay a reasonable price for necessaries sold and delivered to him (Sale of Goods Act, 1893, s. 2); they must be suitable to his condition in life and to his actual requirements at the time of sale and delivery. The same rule applies to a person of unsound mind. See INFANT.

There is a presumption of fact that a wife living with her husband has his authority to pledge his credit for articles of household use suitable to the degree and estate of her husband, so as to make him liable to the tradesmen, unless he has sufficiently supplied her with articles of the kind in question, or unless she has a separate income. She may be held out by the husband as having his authority to buy other things, *e.g.,* if he has allowed her to purchase such things on credit and paid for them, when he will be liable to the tradesmen unless they have notice that she is not authorised to pledge his credit for such things. But see AGENT OF NECESSITY.

In the case of ships, the term " necessaries " means such things as are fit and proper for the service in which the ship is engaged, and such as the owner, being a prudent man, would have ordered if present; e.g., anchors, rigging, repairs, victuals. The master may hypothecate the ship for necessaries supplied abroad so as to bind the owner.

In the criminal law, wilful neglect to provide necessaries for children or apprentices is a common law misdemeanour, and it is also an offence, as regards apprentices, under the Conspiracy and Protection of Property Act, 1875, s. 6, and, as regards children not over the age of sixteen, under the Children and Young Persons Act, 1933, s. 1, want of means not being a defence.

Necessary representation. States and other corporate entities must be represented by individuals as media through whom alone they can act.

Necessitas est lex temporis et loci (Hale P.C. 54). (Necessity is the law when and where it exists.) But Hale quotes this maxim only to dissent and says that if a person being under necessity for want of victuals or clothes steals another person's goods, it is felony. So where starving sailors in an open boat kill and eat one of their number, they are guilty of mur-

der (*R.* v. *Dudley* (1885) 14 Q.B.D. 273).
Where a man is a free agent, necessity is
never a justification for the doing of a
criminal act, although it may justify the
doing of an act which is merely a civil
wrong.

**Necessitas inducit privilegium quoad
jura privata** (Bac.Max. 5). (Necessity
gives a privilege as to private rights.)

Necessitas non habet legem (Plowd. 18).
(Necessity has no law.) This is true only
as regards the doing of acts which are not
criminal. See NECESSITAS EST, ETC.

**Necessitas publica major est quam
privata** (Bac.Max. 5; Noy, Max. 34).
(Public necessity is greater than private.)

Necessitas quod cogit defendit. (Necessity defends what it compels.) See NECES-
SITAS EST, ETC.

Necessity, agent of. See AGENT OF
NECESSITY.

Necessity, Homicide by, a species of
justifiable homicide, because it arises
from some unavoidable necessity, without
any will, intention, or desire, and without
any inadvertence or negligence in the
party killing, and therefore without any
shadow of blame; as, for instance, by
virtue of such an office as obliges one, in
the execution of public justice, to put a
malefactor to death who has forfeited his
life to the laws of his country; but to kill
a man in order to eat him, and so escape
death by hunger, is murder (*R.* v. *Dudley*
(1885) 14 Q.B.D. 273). See JUSTIFIABLE
HOMICIDE.

Neck verse, the words *Miserere mei
Deus,* with which the fifty-first Psalm
begins. When a prisoner claimed benefit
of clergy (*q.v.*) a paper on which these
words were printed in black letters was
handed to him. If he could either read
them, or recite them as if he were able
to read them, he was held to be able
to read and to be entitled to benefit of
clergy (Kiralfy, *Source Book of English
Law,* 12, 13).

Negatio conclusionis est error in lege
(Wing. 268). (The negation of a conclusion is error in law.) It is the premises
upon which the conclusion is based that
ought to be traversed.

**Negatio destruit negationem, et ambo
faciunt affirmativum** (Co.Litt. 146). (A
negative destroys a negative, and both
make an affirmative.) Yet where the law
considers that a negative was in fact
intended, it will hold that there is really
a negative, for *mala grammatica non
vitiat cartam (q.v.)*.

Negative. In general a negative cannot
be proved or testified by witnesses (2 Co.
Litt. 662).

Where one party charges another with
a culpable omission or breach of duty,
the person who makes the charge is
bound to prove it, though it may involve
a negative, for it is not to be presumed
that a person has acted illegally till the
contrary is proved. Where the presumption is in favour of a defendant, the plaintiff must disprove the defence, though he
may have to prove a negative.

In summary proceedings any exception, etc., may be proved by the defendant, but need not be negatived in the
information (Magistrates' Courts Act,
1952, s. 81).

Negative conflict of jurisdiction, a
declaration of incompetence on the part
of two or more institutions.

Negative pregnant, in pleading, is
where a person gives an evasive answer to
an allegation of his opponent by answering it literally, without answering the
substance of it. Thus, if it is alleged that
A received a certain sum of money, and
he denies that particular amount, this is
a negative pregnant, because the substance of the allegation is the receipt of
some money, and not the particular
amount received. A should, therefore,
answer either that he did not receive any
money at all, or state how much he
received. Similarly, when something is
alleged to have happened under certain
circumstances, it is not sufficient to deny
that it happened under those particular
circumstances; but the party must state
whether it happened at all. It is laid down
by R.S.C., Ord. 18, r. 13, that each party
must deal specifically with each allegation
of fact of which he does not admit the
truth, except damages.

Where a traverse is of a negative averment so that it is clear that it is intended
to set up an affirmative case, particulars
of the affirmative case must be given
(*I.R.C.* v. *Jackson* [1960] 1 W.L.R. 873).

Negilldare or **Neggildare,** to claim
kindred (Leg.Hen. 1, c. 70; Leg.Inae, ss.
7, 8).

Negligence. Negligence has two meanings in the law of tort; it may mean either a mental element which is to be inferred from one of the modes in which some torts may be committed, or it may mean an independent tort which consists of breach of a legal duty to take care which results in damage, undesired by the defendant, to the plaintiff.

A person must take reasonable care to avoid acts or omissions which he can reasonably foresee would be likely to injure persons who are so closely and directly affected by his act that he ought reasonably to have them in contemplation (*Donoghue* v. *Stevenson* [1932] A.C. 562). This, however, is only a very general statement. Whether a person has been guilty of actionable negligence is a question of fact or law or of mixed fact and law, depending entirely upon the nature of the duty which the person charged with negligence has failed to comply with or perform in the particular circumstances of each case.

The question of negligence may be one entirely of law, where the case falls within a general settled rule or principle of law; more often it is one of law and fact, though it is sometimes of fact only where it is left to the jury to decide whether the defendant has shown a want of care which would have been expected in the ordinary course of events in the circumstances.

The onus of proving negligence rests on the plaintiff; in some cases *res ipsa loquitur, i.e.,* the thing resulting from it speaks for itself, as in the case of a railway collision (*Carpue* v. *London, Brighton, and South Coast Ry.* (1844) 5 Q.B. 747).

If the plaintiff has been guilty of contributory negligence, in other words, if with ordinary care he might have avoided the consequence of the defendant's negligence, he could not formerly recover any damages (*Butterfield* v. *Forester* (1809) 11 East 60; *British Columbia Electric Railway* v. *Loach* [1916] 1 A.C. 719); now however the damages are reduced according to the degree of blame (Law Reform (Contributory Negligence) Act, 1945; Carriage by Air Act, 1961, s. 6).

In the civil law there are three degrees of negligence: *lata culpa,* gross neglect; *levis culpa,* ordinary neglect; and *levissima culpa,* slight neglect. These distinctions, however, have no place in English law, except to some extent in the law of bailments (*Coggs* v. *Bernard* (1703) 2 Ld. Raym. 909).

Damages for negligence not exceeding £20 may be recovered by local authorities summarily as a civil debt (Public Health Act, 1961, s. 81; London Government Act, 1963, s. 40, Sch. 11 Pt. I para 40; Local Government Act, 1966, s. 28 (4)).

See ACT OF GOD; ANIMALS, LIABILITY FOR; CONTRIBUTORY NEGLIGENCE; DANGEROUS CHATTELS; DANGEROUS PREMISES; DANGEROUS THING, ESCAPE OF; ESTOPPEL; MASTER AND SERVANT; VOLENTI NON FIT INJURIA.

Negligentia semper habet infortuniam comitem (Co.Litt. 246). (Negligence always has misfortune for a companion.)

Negoce [Lat. *negotium*], business, trade, management of affairs.

Negotiable instruments. An instrument is said to be negotiable when any person who has acquired it in good faith and for value can enforce the contract contained in it or the right of property of which it is evidence against the person originally liable on it, although the person from whom he acquired it may have had a defective title or none at all. In the first of these respects, negotiable instruments were always an exception to the rule that choses in actions were not assignable; and, in the latter respect, they are an exception to the rule which denies to the transferee of property a title superior to that of the person from whom he receives it. Moreover, the benefit of the contract or other right is attached to the possession of the document, which, according to ordinary rules, would be only evidence of the right. Negotiable instruments are, therefore, altogether anomalous institutions. They exist primarily for the convenience of commerce.

Negotiability is either absolute or qualified. When an instrument is transferable so as to give the transferee all the rights originally created by it without affecting him with any equities between prior holders, its negotiability is said to be absolute; an ordinary bill of exchange, promissory note or cheque is an instance. Thus, if A, being indebted to B, gives B a promissory note on the condition that it is to be regarded as a security only, and is not to be negotiated before a certain time, B may nevertheless transfer it to C for value; and if C has no notice of the arrangement between A and B, he may enforce payment of it against A (*Ex p. Swan* (1868) L.R. 6 Eq. 344). So if B steals a bill and transfers it to C for value, and C has no notice of the theft, C may enforce it against the parties liable on it, although B had in fact no title to transfer. When an instrument is transferable only to certain persons, or in a certain manner, or so as to make the transferee take it subject to equities affecting it in the hands of prior holders, while preserving the other incidents of negotiability, its negotiability is said to be qualified or restrained. Thus, in the first instance given above, if the promissory note were transferred after its due date, the transferee would take subject to the arrangement between A and B. See CHEQUE; EQUITY.

" Negotiable " is also used in a wide sense to denote an instrument transferable from one person to another by indorsement or delivery, but wanting in the essential of giving the transferee a good title notwithstanding any defect of title in his transferor. This quality is also called *quasi*-negotiability, to distinguish it from negotiability in the true sense. See BILL OF LADING; DEBENTURE; EXCHEQUER BILLS; SCRIP.

Promissory notes were made negotiable by the statute 1704, 3 & 4 Anne, c. 8, and placed in all respects upon the same footing with inland bills of exchange.

The Bills of Exchange Act, 1882, contains the law as to negotiation of bills of exchange, promissory notes, and cheques. S. 31 declares that these instruments are negotiated when they are transferred from one person to another in such a manner as to constitute the transferee the holder of them, and s. 32 enumerates the conditions under which an indorsement may operate as a negotiation, as that the indorsement must be written on the bill itself, and be signed by the indorser, and must be an indorsement of the entire bill. A cheque or bill marked " pay cash or order " is not within the Act and is not a negotiable instrument

(*North and South Insurance Co.* v. *National Provincial Bank* (1936) 105 L.J.K.B. 163). See BILL OF EXCHANGE; NOT NEGOTIABLE.

Negotiate. To negotiate a bill of exchange, promissory note, cheque or other negotiable instrument for the payment of money is to transfer it for value by delivery or indorsement.

Negotiation, treaty of business, whether public or private.

Negotiorum gestio. This, in the civil law, meant the interference of one in the affairs of another merely from benevolence and without authority. In English law a man so interfering has usually no claim on the other in respect of what he may do. Liabilities are not to be forced upon people behind their backs (*Falcke* v. *Scottish Insurance* (1887) 34 Ch.D. 249).

The civil law raised a *quasi*-mandate, by implication, for the benefit of the owner in many of such cases. Nor is an implication of this sort wholly unknown to the common law, as where there has been a subsequent ratification of the acts by the owner; and sometimes where unauthorised acts are done, positive presumptions are made by law for the benefit of particular parties. Thus, if a stranger enters upon an infant's lands and takes the profits, the law will oblige him to account for them, for it will be presumed that he entered to take them in trust for the infant (*Wall* v. *Stanwick* (1887) 34 Ch.D. 763).

As the *negotiorum gestor* interferes without any actual mandate, there is good reason for requiring him to exert the requisite skill and knowledge to accomplish the object or business which he undertakes, to do everything which is incident to or dependent upon that object or business, and to finish whatever he has begun.

Neife, a woman born in villeinage (Litt. 186; 2 Bl.Comm. 94).

Originally the word signified a villein of either sex, and *nayfté* meant the status of a villein. It is derived from the Latin *nativus*, there having been apparently at one time a distinction between villeins by birth and freemen who had become villeins, *e.g.*, by confession

in a court of record (Brit. 77b). See CON-
FESSION; NATIVI DE STIPITE.

Neifty, Writ of, a writ which lay for a
lord who claimed a woman for his *neife*
(*q.v.*) (Tomlin). See NATIVITAS.

Nem. con.; Nem. dis. Anything unanimously agreed to in the House of Commons is recorded as having been agreed
to *nem. con.*, that is to say *nemine
contradicente* (no one saying otherwise).
In a like case in the House of Lords the
term used in *nem. dis.*, that is to say,
nemine dissentiente (without anyone dissenting).

Nembda [Teut.], a jury (3 Bl.Comm.
350).

**Neminem oportet esse sapientiorem
legibus** (Co.Litt. 97). (No man ought to
be wiser than the laws.) No man ought
to set himself up as being wiser than
the law which is the perfection of reason,
because by many successions of ages it
has been fined and refined by an infinite
number of grave and learned men.

**Nemo admittendus est inhabilitare
seipsum** (Jenk., Cent. 40). (No one is to
be permitted to incapacitate himself.)
Quoted in connection with a decision that
a man could not plead that his own deed
had been executed while he was *non
compos mentis.*

Nemo agit in seipsum (Jenk., Cent. 40).
(No one takes proceedings against himself.) A man cannot be at once *actor*
(plaintiff) and *reus* (defendant) in a legal
proceeding. See IDEM AGENS, ETC.

**Nemo aliquam partem recte intelligere
potest antequam totum iterum atque
iterum perlegit** (3 Co.Rep. 59b). (No one
can properly understand a part until he
has read the whole again and again.)
See NOSCITUR A SOCIIS.

**Nemo allegans turpitudinem suam est
audiendus.** (No one who alleges his own
guilt can be heard.)

**Nemo cogitur rem suam vendere,
etiam juste pretio** (4 Co.Inst. 275). (No
one is compelled to sell his property,
even for the full value.) Coke was writing
before the days of compulsory purchase.
Nowadays, not only may a man be compelled to sell his property against his
will, but he may not even receive its full
value. See ID QUOD NOSTRUM, ETC.

**Nemo contra factum suum proprium
venire potest** (2 Co.Inst. 66). (No one
can come against his own deed.) A
grantor cannot derogate from his own
grant.

**Nemo dat qui non habet; Nemo dat
quod non habet** (Jenk., Cent. 250). (No
one gives who possesses not.) The general
rule is that no man can give another any
better title than he himself has. This
is the rule both as to realty, except where
the Settled Land Act, 1925, or other
enactments apply, and as to chattels,
except where the true owner is estopped
by his conduct from denying the purported title of the vendor (Sale of Goods
Act, 1893, s. 21 (1)), where under the
Factors Act, 1889, there is statutory
authority for an apparent owner to sell,
where the sale is made under a statutory
power or where the sale is in market
overt.

Nemo de domo sua extrahi debet (D.
50, 17, 103). (No one can be dragged
out of his own house.) This is a maxim of
the civil law; it has never applied to this
country. See DOMAS SUA, ETC.

Nemo debet bis puniri pro uno delicto
(4 Co.Rep. 43a). (No one should be
punished twice for one fault.) A decision
of a competent court upon any given set
of facts—so that the plea of *autrefois
convict* (*q.v.*), or the plea of *autrefois
acquit* (*q.v.*) is available—is a bar to any
subsequent prosecution. But where a
man is convicted of common assault and
the injured person subsequently dies, a
prosecution for manslaughter is not
barred, because here there is an additional
fact.

**Nemo debet bis vexari, si constat
curiae quod sit pro una et eadem causa**
(5 Co.Rep. 61). (No man ought to be
twice vexed, if it is proved to the court
that it is for one and the same cause.)
No man should be twice sued or twice
prosecuted upon one and the same set of
facts, if there has been a final decision
of a competent court.

But an abortive trial without a verdict,
as if a jury is discharged for inability to
agree, may be followed by a new trial, as
was held in *Winsor* v. *R.* (1866) L.R. 1
Q.B. 390, where the prisoner was hanged
after a second trial for murder.

NEMO

See Interest Reipublicae ut Sit, etc.; Nemo Debet bis Puniri, etc.; Res Judicata, etc.

Nemo debet esse judex in propria causa (12 Co. Rep. 114). (No one should be judge in his own cause.) In *Dimes* v. *Grand Junction Canal Co.* (1852) 3 H.L.C. 759, the judgment of Lord Chancellor Cottenham was set aside on the ground of his having been a shareholder in the defendant company. See Aliquis, etc.; Nemo Potest Esse, etc.

Nemo debet locupletari aliena jactura. (No one ought to be enriched by another's disaster.) See *Fletcher* v. *Alexander* (1868) L.R. 3 C.P. 381.

Nemo est haeres viventis (Co.Litt. 22b). (No one is the heir of anyone who is alive.) See Heir.

Nemo ex alterius incommodo debet locupletari (Jenk., Cent. 4, 8). (No man ought to be made rich out of another's injury.)

Nemo ex dolo suo proprio relevetur, aut auxilium capiat. (No one is relieved or aided by his own fault.) See Nullus Commodum, etc.

Nemo ex proprio dolo consequitur actionem. (No one obtains a cause of action by his own fraud.) See Fraus et Dolus, etc.

Nemo ex suo delicto meliorem suam conditionem facere potest (D. 50, 17, 134). (No one can improve his position by his own wrongdoing.) English law also acts on this principle; and so where the existence of a cause of action is, by the fraud of the person who creates it, concealed from the person who could take advantage of it, then the Limitation Act, 1939, will begin to run only as from the date when the fraud is or could reasonably have been discovered. See Fraus et Dolus, etc.

Nemo militans Deo implicetur secularibus negotiis (Co.Litt. 70). (No man warring for God should be associated with secular business.) Quoted in connection with the rule that one holding of the king in escuage should not himself render military service, but should send a substitute.

Nemo nascitur artifex (Co.Litt. 97). (No one is born a skilled workman.) Quoted in connection with the observation that knowledge of the common law was to be acquired only by long study, observation and experience.

Nemo patriam in qua natus est exuere nec ligeantiae debitum ejurare possit (Co.Litt 129). (A man cannot abjure his native country, nor the allegiance he owes his sovereign.) This is no longer the case. See Alienage; Naturalisation.

Nemo potest contra recordum verificare per patriam (2 Co.Inst. 380). (No man can take the verdict of a jury as to the correctness of any decision.) See Judicium Semper Pro, etc.

Nemo potest esse simul actor et judex. (No one can be at once suitor and judge.) A man cannot sue either before himself or his deputy. See Nemo Debet Esse, etc.; Nemo Sibi Esse, etc.

Nemo potest esse tenens et dominus (Gilb.Ten. 142). (No man can be tenant and lord.) Cited in connection with the rule that if an eldest brother had enfeoffed the second brother and received homage, and if the second brother had died without issue, then the land descended to the next youngest brother and not to the eldest.

Nemo potest facere per alium, quod per se non potest (Jenk. 237). (No one can do through another what he cannot do himself.)

Nemo potest mutare consilium suum in alterius injuriam (D. 50, 17, 75). (No one can change his counsel to the injury of another.) This was applied by the Roman lawyers as meaning that legislation should not be retrospective.

Nemo potest plus juris ad alium transferre quam ipse habet (Co.Litt. 309). (No one can transfer a greater right to another than he himself has.) See Nemo Dat, etc.

Nemo praesumitur alienam posteritatem suae praetulisse (Wing. 285). No one is presumed to have preferred another's posterity to his own.) Quoted in connection with a doctrine of the old law as to warranty of land. It has no application now.

Nemo praesumiture esse immemor suae aeternae salutis, et maxime in articulo mortis (6 Co.Rep. 76). (No one is presumed to be forgetful of his own eternal welfare, and more particularly in the moment of death.) Quoted, not in connection with the admissibility of dying declarations, to which it would naturally seem to apply, but as showing that fraud is not to be imputed to a testator in connection with his will.

Nemo praesumitur malus. (No one is presumed to be bad.)

Nemo prohibetur pluribus defensionibus uti (Co.Litt. 304). (No one is forbidden to use several defences.) A defendant may raise as many distinct and separate defences as he thinks proper; but see R.S.C., Ord. 19, r. 27.

Nemo punitur pro alieno delicto (Wing. 336). (No one is punished for the fault of another.) Quoted in connection only with the doing of civil wrongs.

Nemo punitur sine injuria, facto, seu defalta (2 Co.Inst. 287). (No one is punished unless for some injury, deed, or default.) See ACTUS LEGIS NEMINI FACIT INJURIAM.

Nemo sibi esse judex vel suis jus dicere debet (C. 3, 5, 1). (No one ought to be his own judge, or to decide matters in which he is interested.) See NEMO DEBET ESSE JUDEX, ETC.

Nemo tenetur ad impossibilia (Jenk., Cent. 7). (No one is required to do what is impossible.) See IMPOTENTIA, ETC.; LEX NON COGIT, ETC.

Nemo tenetur armare adversarium contra se (Wing. 665). (No one is bound to arm his adversary against himself.) Wingate applies the maxim to obsolete law as to replevin and the challenging of jurors.

Nemo tenetur divinare (4 Co.Rep. 28). (No one is bound to be a prophet.)

Nemo tenetur prodere seipsum. (No one is bound to betray himself.)

The Evidence Act, 1851, s. 5, made parties admissible witnesses in actions, but expressly saved criminal proceedings from its operation; but a series of enactments, e.g., the Licensing Act, 1872, s. 51. the Criminal Law Amendment Act, 1885, s. 20, and the Law of Libel Amendment Act, 1888, s. 9, and finally the Criminal Evidence Act, 1898, made defendants competent, but not compellable, to give evidence.

Nemo tenetur seipsum accusare (Wing. 486). (No one is bound to incriminate himself.) No one is bound to give any evidence which in the opinion of the court will expose him to any penalty or forfeiture reasonably likely to þe sued for, or to any punishment.

Nephew [Lat. *nepos*], the son of a brother or sister, or half-brother or half-sister; in special cases, a great-nephew (*Weeds* v. *Bristow* (1886) L.R. 2 Eq. 333), or nephew by marriage (*Sherratt* v. *Mountford* (1873) L.R. 8 Ch. 928), and even an illegitimate nephew (*In the Goods of Ashton* [1892] P. 83).

Neptis, a grand-daughter (*Whitlock* v. *Whitlock* (1924) 40 T.L.R. 566).

Nervous shock. Injury to health due to nervous shock is a form of bodily injury for which damages may be claimed (*Hambrook* v. *Stokes* [1925] 1 K.B. 153), provided the consequence is not too remote (*Bourhill* v. *Young* [1943] A.C. 92; *King* v. *Phillips* [1953] 1 Q.B. 429).

Net. See NEAT.

Net annual value. See ANNUAL VALUE.

Net Book Agreement. This is not contrary to the public interest (*Re Net Book Agreement, 1957* [1962] 1 W.L.R. 1347).

Net profits, clear profits after all deductions (*Watson* v. *Haggitt* [1928] A.C. 127).

Nether House. Used during the sixteenth and seventeenth centuries as meaning the House of Commons.

Nets. A custom for fishermen to spread their nets to dry on the lands of a private owner at all times seasonable for fishing is good, as was held of two fishermen of Walmer in Kent in *Mercer* v. *Denne* [1904] 2 Ch. 534.

Neutralisation, exclusion by treaty of a territory from a region of war, as, e.g., of the Ionian Islands in the Crimean War; involving the status of neutrality, as, e.g., in the case of Switzerland; assimilation of an artificial waterway linking oceans to natural straits, as, e.g., in the case of the Kiel Canal under the Treaty of Versailles.

Neutrality, the status of a power not at war in relation to the belligerents, involving the duty of impartiality on the part of the neutral State. See FOREIGN ENLISTMENT ACT.

Never indebted, Plea of, a species of traverse which occurred in actions of debt on simple contract, and was resorted to when the defendant meant to deny in point of fact the existence of any express contract to the effect alleged in the declaration, or to deny the matters of fact from which such contract would by law be implied. By R.S.C., Ord. 18, r. 13, a defendant may not deny generally the facts alleged by the plaintiff, but must deal specifically with each allegation which he does not admit. See PLEADING.

Nevis. See the West Indies Act, 1967.

New assignment, a form of pleading which sometimes arose from the generality of the declaration, when, the complaint not having been set out with sufficient precision, it became necessary, from the evasiveness of the plea, to reassign the cause of action with fresh particulars. It most frequently occurred in actions of trespass, as where two assaults had been committed, one of which was justifiable and the other indefensible; or in trespass *quare clausum fregit,* when the defendant claimed a right of way.

Under the common law practice before the Judicature Acts, 1873–75, where the declaration in an action was ambiguous and the defendant pleaded facts which were literally an answer to it, but not to the real claim set up by the plaintiff, the plaintiff's course was to reply by way of new assignment, that is, to allege that he brought his action not for the cause supposed by the defendant, but for some other cause to which the plea had no application. Under the present practice, a plaintiff in such a case would amend his statement of claim. See AMENDMENT.

New building. Under the Roads Improvement Act, 1925, s. 11, new building includes any additions to an existing building.

The question whether any building is a new building is in general one of fact (*Ballard* v. *Horton's Estates* (1926) 24 L.G.R. 449); so also in the case of tem-

porary buildings (*Rodwell* v. *Wade* (1924) 23 L.G.R. 174; *Keeling* v. *Wirral R.D.C.* (1925) 23 L.G.R. 201).

The Public Health Acts Amendment Act, 1907, s. 23, contained a definition of a new building, but this section was repealed by the Public Health Act, 1936; provisions relating to buildings and building by-laws are contained in Part II of the Act. " New building " is not defined, but s. 62 provides for the application of by-laws for the construction, materials, space for, lighting, ventilation, and dimensions of rooms for human habitation, also height of existing buildings, when altered, extended or changed.

New development. See DEVELOPMENT.

New England Company, a colonising company founded in 1620 (Scott, *Joint Stock Companies*).

New Forest, a royal forest in Hampshire which has existed as such since the time of the Conqueror. It contains about 92,000 acres, of which about 63,000 acres are, strictly speaking, forest. Some 27,000 acres belong to private persons, parts of which are subject to certain forest rights of the Crown (Lewis, *Historical Inquiries concerning Forests*).

Forest law has been abrogated, except so far as it relates to the appointment and functions of verderers (*q.v.*) by the Wild Creatures and Forest Laws Act, 1971.

Provision is made for the government of the New Forest by the New Forest Act, 1877 (40 & 41 Vict. c. cxxi), the New Forest Act, 1879 (42 & 43 Vict. c. cxciv), and the New Forest Acts, 1949, 1964 and 1970. See also the Local Government Act, 1974, Sch. 8.

New Inn. See INNS OF CHANCERY.

New Parishes. The New Parishes Acts, 1843 to 1844, were passed to make better provision for the spiritual care of populous parishes. They are replaced by the New Parishes Measure, 1943 (as amended). See BLANDFORD'S ACT; ECCLESIASTICAL COMMISSIONERS; PEEL'S ACTS.

New streets. See the Highways Act, 1959, ss. 157–172; Local Government Act, 1972, s. 188 (4).

New Style. The modern system of

computing time was introduced into Great Britain in 1752 by the Calendar (New Style) Act, 1750, September 3 of that year being reckoned as September 14. See CALENDAR; NEW YEAR'S DAY.

New towns. The creation of new towns was provided for by the New Towns Act, 1946. This Act and subsequent legislation were consolidated in the New Towns Act, 1965 (amended by the Statutory Corporations (Financial Provisions) Act. 1974, and the New Towns Act, 1975). For particulars of new towns, see Whitaker's *Almanac.*

New trial. If any defect of judgment happens from causes wholly extrinsic, *i.e.,* arising from matters foreign to or *dehors* the record, the only remedy (except formerly error *coram nobis* or *vobis* in a few cases) is to apply to the court for a new trial, which is in substitution for a bill of exceptions. But the court must be satisfied that there are strong probable grounds to suppose that the merits have not been fairly and fully discussed, and that the decision is not agreeable to the justice and truth of the case before it will grant a new trial.

The following is a summary of the cases in which a new trial may be granted. They are all subject to the rule that in an action of contract, unless some right independent of the damages is in question, the amount in dispute must be £20 at least for the court to interfere.

(1) Mistakes, etc., of a judge as where he misdirects the jury or himself or improperly nonsuits the plaintiff, or admits or rejects evidence by which means the result of the trial or inquiry has been different from what it otherwise would have been. But a new trial may not be granted on the ground of misdirection or of the improper admission or rejection of evidence, or because the verdict of the jury was not taken upon a question which the judge at the trial was not asked to leave to them, unless in the opinion of the court to which the application is made some substantial wrong or miscarriage has been thereby occasioned by the trial of the action (R.S.C., Ord. 59, r. 11).

(2) Default or misconduct of an officer of the court, as where a cause is, by mistake, entered in a wrong list, and the cause is tried as undefended in the defendant's absence.

(3) Default or misconduct of the jury, as where a juror has been sworn by a wrong surname, and it has been productive of some injustice, or if the jury find a verdict against the weight of evidence, but in this case, more than in any other, the court will be very reluctant to grant a new trial. A new trial may also be granted for excessive damages or for the smallness of the damages, if out of all proportion to the injury, or for the misconduct of the jury, as if they had eaten or drunk at the expense of the party for whom they had afterwards found a verdict, or if they determine their verdict by lot, or if any of them had declared that the plaintiff should never have a verdict.

(4) Absence, etc., of counsel or solicitor. The instances are very rare in which the court has granted a new trial on this ground.

(5) Default or misconduct of the opposite party. If a party, for whom a verdict is afterwards given, delivers to the jury, after they have left the box, evidence which had not been adduced in court, a new trial will be granted, or if he has laboured the jury, or used improper influence with them, or misled or taken by surprise the opposite party, and also where no notice of trial has been given, but if the defendant appears to defend, this irregularity is waived.

(6) Default or misconduct of witnesses. The general rule is that a new trial will not be granted on the ground that evidence has not been given which might have been given at the trial, for the plaintiff ought, if unprepared with his evidence, either to make application to postpone the trial before the jury are sworn, or should withdraw his record and not take the chance of a verdict. The court has granted a new trial where it appeared clearly that the plaintiff's case was a mere fiction supported by perjury, which the defendant could not at the time of the trial be prepared to answer.

(7) Discovery of new evidence after the trial. A new trial will seldom be granted where a verdict has been given against a

party, or a plaintiff has been nonsuited for want of evidence which might have been produced at the trial, because it would tend to introduce perjury. But if new evidence has been discovered after the trial, the court will grant a new trial (usually upon payment of costs) if necessary in order to do justice between the parties; but the discovery of witnesses who can contradict those produced on the former trial seems to be no ground for a new trial, nor will the court grant a new trial to let a party into a defence of which he was apprised at the first trial.

(8) Where one of several issues, etc., has been wrongfully decided. A new trial may be ordered on any question in an action, whatever the grounds for the new trial, without interfering with the finding or decision upon any other question (R.S.C., Ord. 59, r. 11 (3)).

(9) Where there has been a previous new trial. If the jury on the second trial finds for the party against whom the former verdict was given, the court, if the case is doubtful, or the second verdict does not accord with the justice of the case, may be induced to grant a third trial, but this is entirely in the discretion of the court, even after two concurring verdicts.

(10) Where a party has been taken by surprise.

The time for applying for a new trial runs from the verdict of the jury, and not from the giving of judgment (*Greene* v. *Croome* [1908] 1 K.B. 277).

The motion must be made to the Court of Appeal (Judicature Act, 1925, s. 30 (1), replacing the Judicature Act, 1890, s. 1).

The Court of Appeal may order a new trial where an appeal against conviction has been allowed on the ground of new evidence (Criminal Appeal Act, 1968, ss. 7, 8, 23, Sch. 2).

New Year's Day. From the seventh to the twelfth century, the year began on Christmas Day; from the twelfth century as regards the Church, and from the fourteenth century as regards the law, it began on March 25; and since the Calendar Act, 1751 (see CALENDAR), it has begun on January 1.

In Scotland the year was, by a proclamation of November 27, 1599, ordered thenceforth to commence in that kingdom on January 1 instead of March 25.

New Zealand, Bishopric of. This was constituted by the statute 1852, 15 & 16 Vict. c. 88.

New Zealand Company. See COMPANIES, CHARTERED.

Newgate. The New Gate of the City of London, which was built in the reign of Henry I, was used as a prison from at any rate 1188. It was rebuilt as a prison about 1420. In 1780 it was destroyed by the Gordon rioters. In 1783 it was rebuilt; and it was used both for criminals and debtors until 1815, after which year only criminals were confined in it. In 1881 it ceased to be used as a prison except during the actual sittings of the Central Criminal Court. In 1902 it was pulled down (Griffith, *Chronicles of Newgate*).

News. Spreading false news to make discord between the sovereign and nobility, or concerning any great man of the realm, was punishable by the statutes 1275, 3 Edw. 1, c. 34; 1378, 2 Ric. 2, st. 1, c. 5; and 1388, 12 Ric. 2, c. 11; these statutes were repealed by the Statute Law Revision Act, 1887. See SEDITION.

Newspapers, periodical publications containing intelligence of passing events. They have from time to time been the subject of enactments for their general regulation. The principal of these were the statutes 1819, 59 Geo. 3, c. 9, and and 1836, 6 & 7 Wm. 4, c. 76. But these and other statutes were repealed by the Newspapers, Printers and Reading Rooms Repeal Act, 1869.

The Newspaper Libel and Registration Act, 1881, provides for the establishment of a register of proprietors of newspapers (s. 8), and for annual returns being made by the printers and proprietors of every newspaper, giving particulars of its title and its proprietors (s. 9). The returns are entered in the register, which is open to public inspection (s. 13). A newspaper is anything within the popular meaning of that word which is published in England or Ireland at intervals not exceeding twenty-six days (s. 1). For the purpose of the Defamation Act, 1952, s. 7, the period is thirty days, and the meaning is any paper containing public news or observations thereon.

The Judicial Proceedings (Regulation of Reports) Act, 1926, makes it an offence to print or publish in relation to judicial proceedings any indecent matter, or indecent medical, surgical, or physiological details calculated to injure public morals (s. 1 (1) (*a*)). The same Act by s. 1 (2) (as amended by the Domestic and Appellate Proceedings (Restriction of Publicity) Act, 1968, s. 2 and the Matrimonial Causes Act, 1973, Sch. 2 para. 7, Sch. 3) restricts the publication of particulars in respect of matrimonial causes and proceedings for declarations of legitimacy and the like. No prosecution under this Act may be commenced without the sanction of the Attorney-General (s. 1 (3)).

The Children and Young Persons Act 1933, s. 39, prohibits, on direction of the court, publication of any particulars leading to the identification of any child or young person concerned in proceedings arising out of any offence against decency or morality. S. 49, as amended by the Children and Young Persons Act, 1969, s. 10, prohibits the publication of particulars leading to the identification of any child or young person involved in juvenile court proceedings, except with the authority of the court or Secretary of State. The Criminal Justice Act, 1967, s. 3, as amended by the Children and Young Persons Act, 1969, Sch. 5 para. 56, restricts the matter which may be included in a report or broadcast of committal proceedings in a magistrates' court.

Under the Libel Act, 1845, s. 2, the defendant in any action for a libel contained in a public newspaper may plead an apology and payment into court.

The Law of Libel Amendment Act, 1888, s. 3, enacts that newspaper reports of proceedings in any court are privileged unless they contain blasphemous or indecent matter. This section applies only to courts exercising judicial authority within the United Kingdom (Defamation Act, 1952, s. 8). The section applies to broadcasting (Act of 1952, s. 9 (2)). No criminal prosecution for a libel contained in a newspaper can be commenced without the leave of a judge in chambers (Act of 1888, s. 8). Charges of libel contained in newspapers may be tried summarily (Act of 1881, ss. 4, 5).

By the Defamation Act, 1952, s. 7 (1), Sch. Pt. I, the following reports are privileged without explanation or contradiction unless malice is proved: a fair and accurate report of any public proceedings of the legislature of any part of H.M. dominions outside Great Britain; a like report of public proceedings of an international organisation of which the United Kingdom is a member, or is represented thereat; a like report of public proceedings in an international court; a like report of court proceedings in H.M. dominions outside the United Kingdom or of court-martial proceedings outside the United Kingdom held under the Naval Discipline Act, 1957, the Army Act, 1955, or the Air Force Act, 1955; a like report of public proceedings in a public inquiry by the government or legislature of any part of H.M. dominions outside the United Kingdom; a fair and accurate copy of or extract from registers kept in pursuance of an Act of Parliament and open to inspection by the public, or of other documents open by the law of the United Kingdom to public inspection; and court notices or advertisements in the United Kingdom. S. 7 (2), Sch. Pt. II, deal with statements which are privileged subject to explanation or contradiction; they cover fair and accurate reports of various kinds of associations, public meetings, inquiries and general meetings of public companies, within the United Kingdom.

The Fair Trading Act, 1973 (replacing the Monopolies and Mergers Act, 1965, s. 8) contains special provisions regulating and restricting newspaper mergers (Act of 1973, ss. 57–62).

The National Enterprise Board (*q.v.*) are prohibited from publishing newspapers (Industry Act, 1975, s. 9).

See APOLOGY; CONTEMPT OF COURT; IN CAMERA; LIBEL; PRESS; PRINTERS.

Nexi, persons free-born, who, for debt, were delivered bound to their creditors, and obliged to serve them until they could pay their debts (Civil Law).

Next friend. An infant (*q.v.*) who desires to bring an action must, as a rule, do so through the intervention of a person called a next friend, who is generally a relation (R.S.C., Ord. 80, r. 2). Proceedings on behalf of a patient, *i.e.*, a person who by reason of mental disorder is incapable of managing and administering his property and affairs, must also be brought by his next friend (rr. 1, 2). Every next friend is responsible for the propriety of the proceedings taken in his name. See GUARDIAN.

For the practice in the Family Division, see the Matrimonial Causes Rules, 1971, r. 105.

A married woman may be either a next friend or a guardian *ad litem* (R.S.C., Ord. 80, r. 3).

The phrase " next friend " or *prochein amy*, as applied to an infant heir in socage, meant next of blood (Litt. 123; Co.Litt. 88a).

Next-of-kin, those who are next in degree of kindred to a deceased person, *i.e.*, are most closely related to him in the same degree. The degrees of kindred are reckoned according to the civil law, both upwards to the ancestor and downwards to the issue, each generation counting for a degree. Thus, from father to son is one degree, from grandfather to grandson or vice versa is two degrees, and from brother to brother is two degrees, namely one upwards to the father and one downwards to the other son: so from uncle to nephew, or vice versa, is three degrees. See DESCENT.

Prior to the Administration of Estates Act, 1925, the next-of-kin of a person who died intestate signified those persons who were entitled to his personal property, after payment of his debts, under the Statutes of Distribution, 1670, and 1685. If the intestate left a widow and any child or children or descendant of any child, the widow took the first £500 and, as regards anything over that amount, she took a third and the issue took two-thirds *per stirpes* (*q.v.*), subject to the rules as to advancement (*q.v.*). If he left no widow his issue took the whole in the same manner. If he left a widow but no issue, the widow took the first £500, and as regards anything over that amount, she took a half, and the other half, or if there was no widow, the whole, went as follows: first to the father, if living; then to the mother, brothers and sisters, or such of

them as were living, in equal shares, the children of any deceased brother or sister standing in their parent's place, provided the mother or any brother or sister of the deceased was living; and if there was no mother, brother or sister living, then to those who were next of kindred to the deceased in the same degree. The husband of a woman dying intestate took the whole of her personal property. For the modern rules, see DISTRIBUTION.

When a testator gave his property to the " next-of-kin " of himself or another, the expression was construed to mean next-of-kin in the strict sense of next in degree of kindred, and therefore did not include persons claiming by representation, *e.g.*, children of a deceased brother (*Akers* v. *Sears* [1896] 2 Ch. 802), unless there was an express or implied reference to the Statutes of Distribution. Even then " next-of-kin " did not include the husband or wife of the deceased (*Re Jeffery's Trusts* (1872) L.R. 14 Eq. 136).

Next presentation, the right to present to the first vacancy of a benefice. When an advowson was sold during an existing incumbency, the right of next presentation passed to the grantee, unless the owner had already sold it to someone else, which he might do before the Benefices Act, 1898. But when a vacancy had actually occurred, the right of presenting to it was always considered to be of such a personal nature that it could not be sold, and if, therefore, the owner sold the advowson at such a time, the next presentation did not pass to the grantee. If the owner of the advowson died intestate during a vacancy, the next presentation formerly went to his executor, while the advowson went to his heir. Now, both pass to the executor. A next presentation, when held separately from the advowson, is personal estate. A clerk could not purchase a next presentation even if the benefice were filled, with a view of presenting himself. The sale of next presentations is abolished and the transfer of rights of patronage of a benefice regulated by the Benefices Act, 1898, and the Benefices Act, 1898 (Amendment) Measure, 1923. See also the Pastoral Measure, 1968, ss. 32, 67–73. See AVOIDANCE; SIMONY.

Nexum, a formal transfer of ownership of a thing; an obligation (Civil Law).

Nicking of horses. See DOCKING AND NICKING OF HORSES.

Nicole, an ancient name for Lincoln.

Niece [Lat. *neptis*], the daughter of a brother or sister; it may mean great-niece, or niece by marriage. See NEPHEW.

Nief. See NEIFE.

Nient comprise (not contained), an exception taken to a petition, because the thing desired was not contained in the deed or proceeding upon which the petition was founded. Thus, in a petition to be put into possession of lands whereof a recovery had been had, it was open to the defendant to take the exception that they were not included (*nient comprise*) in the lands to which the judgment related (Tomlin; *New Book Entries*; Jacob).

Nient culpable (not guilty), a plea in criminal prosecutions (4 Bl.Comm. 339).

It was in use so late as the eighteenth century. The customary abbreviation in the court records was *nient cul.* See NON CULPABILIS.

Nient dedire [Norm. Fr., not deny], to disown nothing, to suffer judgment by not denying or opposing it, *i.e.,* by default. In the old common law practice, when a suggestion (*q.v.*) was entered on the record in an action, and the opposite party did not wish to deny it, he made an entry on the record to that effect, which operated as a confession of the truth of the suggestion, and was called a *nient dedire*.

Nient le fait (not his deed), a plea which denied that an alleged deed had been duly signed, sealed and delivered. It was also used to deny that a bond was the valid bond of the defendant. See NON EST FACTUM.

Niger liber, the black book or register in the Exchequer; chartularies of abbeys, cathedrals, etc.

Nigeria. See the Nigeria Independence Act, 1960; Nigeria Republic Act, 1963.

Night, the time of darkness between sunset and sunrise. See DAY.

The Night Poaching Act, 1828, s. 12, provides that for the purposes of that Act night commences one hour after sunset and ends one hour before sunrise. This means local sunset and sunrise.

Under the Customs and Excise Act, 1952, s. 307 (1), night is between 11 p.m. and 5 a.m. In the National Insurance (Old Persons' and Widows' Pensions and Attendance Allowance) Act, 1970, s. 4 (2) (*a*), " night " is not defined by a " sunset to sunrise " rule but depends upon the coming of night according to the domestic routine of the household under consideration, that is, the principal period of inactivity during the hours of darkness (*R.* v. *National Insurance Commissioner, ex p. Secretary of State for Social Services* [1974] 1 W.L.R. 1290).

In the time of the Saxons, time was computed not by days but by nights; and so it continued till the reign of Henry I, as appears by his laws (Leg.Hen. 1, cc. 66, 76), and hence a sennight, *septem noctes*, is a week, and a fortnight, *quatuordecem noctes*, is two weeks (Tomlin).

Night-house, the name sometimes given to a refreshment-house before the Licensing Act, 1872.

Nightline, a line fastened at one end to a peg on the banks of a river or lake, with a weight at the other end, the intermediate line carrying baited hooks. The weighted end is thrown overnight into the water and is drawn in next day with such fish, if any, as may have been hooked.

Nightwalkers, such persons as sleep by day and walk by night, being oftentimes pilferers, or disturbers of the peace: see the statute 1331, 5 Edw. 3, c. 14. They may be arrested by the police, and committed to custody till the morning (2 Hale, P.C. 90).

The offence of being a common nightwalker was abolished by the Criminal Law Act, 1967, s. 13.

Nihil; Nil, an endorsement by a sheriff upon a writ; it signifies that the defendant has no goods upon which the sheriff can levy, or none of any value. See CLERK OF THE NIHILS; NIHILS; TOT.

Nihil aliud potest rex in terris, cum sit Dei minister et vicarius, quam quod de jure potest (11 Co.Rep. 74). (The king, since he is the minister and vicar of God, is incapable of doing anything in the world except what he is of right empowered to do.) This is a quotation from Bracton which Coke, apparently with an eye on James I, introduces into the judgment in the *Magdalen College Case*. See REX NON POTEST PECCARE.

Nihil capiat per billam (that he take nothing by his bill). See NIHIL CAPIAT PER BREVE.

Nihil capiat per breve (that he take nothing by his writ). Where an issue, arising upon a declaration or temporary plea, was decided for the defendant, the judgment was, generally, that the plaintiff take nothing, etc., and that the defendant go thereof without day, etc., which was a judgment of *nihil capiat*, etc. (Co.Litt. 363a).

Nihil consensui tam contrarium est quam vis et metus (Dig. 50, 17, 116). (Nothing is so opposed to consent as force and fear.) There is no consent when an act is done under duress (*q.v.*).

Nihil dat qui non habet. (He gives nothing who has nothing.) A gift of anything by one other than the owner is a nullity. See NEMO DAT, ETC.

Nihil dicit (he says nothing), the judgment which a plaintiff had against a defendant who failed to put in an answer to the plaintiff's plea by the day assigned. See DEFAULT.

Nihil facit error nominis cum de corpore constat (11 Co.Rep. 21). (A mistake as to the name has no effect when there is no mistake as to who is the person meant.) The maxim is cited by Coke as explaining the decision that a grant made to the king by the title of Sovereign Lord James, omitting the word "king," was good. See FALSA DEMONSTRATIO, ETC.

Nihil habet forum ex scena (Bacon). (The court has nothing to do with what is not before it.)

Nihil habuit in tenementis (he had no interest in the tenements), a plea denying the lessor's title pleaded in an action of debt only, brought by a lessor against a lessee for years, or at will, without deed or occupation by the lessee, for if the lessee had become tenant he would have been estopped from denying his landlord's title.

Nihil in lege intolerabilius est, eandem rem diverso jure censeri (4 Co.Rep. 93a). (Nothing in law is more intolerable than that like cases should be decided upon different constructions of the law.) See LEX UNO, ETC.

Nihil infra regnum subditos magis conservat in tranquillitate et concordia quam debita legum administratio (2 Co.Inst. 158). (Nothing more preserves in tranquillity and concord those subject to the royal authority than a due administration of the laws.)

Nihil praescribitur nisi quod possidetur (Hale, *De Jure Maris*, 32). (No right can be acquired by prescription except in respect of what is owned.) This applies to anyone other than the sovereign or a grantee of the sovereign. The public have no common law right of bathing in the sea and, as incident thereto, of crossing the seashore for that purpose. See FORESHORE.

Nihil quod est contra rationem est licitum (Co.Litt. 97). (Nothing is lawful which is contrary to reason.)

Nihil quod inconveniens et licitum est (Co.Litt. 97). (Nothing which is inconvenient is lawful.) But Coke really quotes this maxim only as meaning that an argument drawn from inconvenience is forcible in law. For although he says that the law cannot suffer anything which is inconvenient, yet he continues, it is better to suffer an inconvenience which is peculiar to one than an inconvenience which may prejudice many. See NECESSITAS PUBLICA, ETC.

Nihil simul inventum est et perfectum (Co.Litt. 230). (Nothing is invented and perfected at the same moment.) Coke quotes this as illustrating the gradual development of the forms used in conveyancing.

Nihil tam conveniens est naturali aequitati quam unumquodque dissolvi eo ligamine quo ligatum est (2 Co.Inst. 359). (Nothing is so much in agreement with natural justice as that everything should be loosed by the same means as bound it.) See NATURALE EST, ETC.

Nihil tam conveniens est naturali aequitati quam voluntatem domini volentis rem suam in alium transferre ratam habere (1 Co.Rep. 100). (Nothing is so consonant to natural justice as to give effect to the intentions of an owner who desires to transfer his property to another.) This is a quotation from Bracton which is cited in the argument for the defendant in *Shelley's Case* (1581) 1 Co.Rep. 936.

Nihil tam proprium est imperii quam legibus vivere (2 Co.Inst. 63). (Nothing is so characteristic of the royal power as the fact that it is exercised in accordance with the laws.)

Nihil temere novandum (Jenk., Cent. 167). (Rash innovations should be avoided.) See NOVITAS, ETC.

Nihils, or **Nichils,** debts to the Crown which a sheriff, when making up his accounts for the Exchequer, said were nothing worth and illeviable, for the insufficiency of the parties from whom due. Sheriffs' accounts are now audited by such persons, etc., as the Treasury directs (Sheriffs Act, 1887, s. 22).

Nil debet (he owes nothing), the plea of the general issue (*q.v.*) in actions of debt not founded on specialty. By rules made in 1834 the plea of *nil debet* was abolished, and it was provided that the defendant in actions of debt on simple contract, other than actions on promissory notes or bills of exchange, should plead that he never was indebted in manner and form as in the declaration alleged. This plea was known as *nunquam indebitatus*. But the rules of 1834 were made under the authority of the statute 1831, 2 & 3 Will. 4, c. 39, s. 1 of which provided that no rule made thereunder should deprive anyone of the power of pleading the general issue where the power had been given by statute. In 1853, however, by rules made under the authority of the Common Law Procedure Act, 1852, it was provided that the plea of *nil debet* should not be allowed in any action, and the plea (also known as *nunquam indebtitatus*) that the defendant never was indebted as alleged was substituted not only for that prescribed by the rules of 1834 but also for the plea of *non assumpsit* in certain cases; and it was provided also that the new plea, when used instead of the *non assumpsit* plea, should operate as a denial of the matters of fact from which the liability of the defendant was alleged to arise. R.S.C., Ord. 18, r. 13, provides that no defendant can deny generally, and that he must deal specifically with every allegation of fact (except as regards damages) which he does not admit. *Nunquam indebitatus* is consequently abolished.

Nil dicit, Judgment by. See DEFAULT.

Nil habuit in tenementis (he had no interest in the tenements), a plea to be pleaded only in an action of debt, which was brought by a lessor against a lessee for years or at will without deed; it put the plaintiff to strict proof of his title (12 Viner 184).

Nimia subtilitas in jure reprobatur (4 Co.Rep. 5; Wing 26). (Over-great subtlety in the law is condemned.) See SIMPLICITAS, ETC.

Nimium altercando veritas amittitur (Hob. 344). (If you argue overmuch the true view is lost.)

Nimmer, a thief; a pilferer.

Nisan, the Babylonish name for Abib, the first sacred and seventh civil month of the Jewish year.

Nisi. A decree, order, rule, declaration, or other adjudication of a court is said to be made nisi when it is not to take effect unless the person affected by it fails to show cause against it within a certain time, that is, unless he appears before the court, and gives some reason why it should not take effect. See ABSOLUTE; DECREE; RULE.

Orders (or rules) nisi were much used in the common law courts before the Judicature Acts, 1873–75. See ORDER.

Nisi prius, unless before. In the practice of the High Court, a trial at *nisi prius* was where an action was tried by a jury before a single judge, either at the sittings held for that purpose in London and Middlesex, or at the assizes (*q.v.*). Formerly all common law actions were tried at bar, that is, before the full court, consisting of several judges; and, therefore, the writ for summoning the jury commanded the sheriff to bring the jurors from the county where the cause of action arose to the court at Westminster. But it was provided by Magna Carta, 1215, that assizes of novel disseisin and mortdauncestor (which were the most common remedies of that day) should thenceforward instead of being tried at Westminster, in the superior courts, be taken in their proper counties, and for this purpose justices were to be sent into every county once a year to take these assizes there. These local trials, being convenient, were applied to other actions:

for by the statute 1285, 13 Edw. 1, c. 30, as the general course of proceedings, writs of *venire* for summoning juries to the superior courts were in the following terms: *Praecipimus tibi quod venire facias coram justiciariis nostris apud Westm. in Octavis Sancti Michaelis nisi talis et talis, tali die et loco, ad partes illas venerint duodecim, etc.* Thus the trial was to be had at Westminster only "unless before" that day it took place in the county before the justices appointed to take the assizes. This clause of *nisi* or *nisi prius* was not retained in the *venire*, but it occurred in the record and the judgment roll. It was enforced by the statute 1340, 14 Edw. 3, c. 16, which authorised a trial before the justices of assize, in lieu of the superior court, and gave it the name of a trial at *nisi prius* (2 Co.Inst. 424).

See Banc; Bar, Trial at; Civil Side; Record; Trial.

Nisi prius record, an instrument in the nature of a commission to the judges at *nisi prius* for the trial of a cause, written on parchment and delivered to the officer of the court in which the cause was to be tried. Any variance between the record and the issue had to be objected to at the time of trial, but the judges had power to amend variances. See Record; Trial.

Nitro-glycerine. See Explosives.

No case to answer. A submission that there is no case to answer may properly be made and upheld (a) when there is no evidence to prove an essential element in the alleged offence; (b) when the evidence adduced by the prosecution has been so discredited as a result of cross-examination or is so manifestly unreliable that no reasonable tribunal could safely convict upon it. Apart from these two situations a tribunal should not in general be called upon to reach a decision as to conviction or acquittal until the whole of the evidence which either side wishes to tender has been placed before it. If, however, a submission is made that there is no case to answer, the decision should depend not so much on whether the adjudicating tribunal (if compelled to do so) would at that stage convict or acquit, but on whether the evidence is such that a reasonable tribunal might convict. If a

reasonable tribunal might convict on the evidence so far laid before it, there is a case to answer (Practice Direction (Submission of No Case) [1962] 1 W.L.R. 227).

A submission of no case to answer on the basis of insufficient evidence, or that it would be unsafe to leave the matter to the jury, should be made in the absence of the jury (*R. v. Falconer-Atlee* (1973) 58 Cr.App.R. 348).

No par value. Shares have been issued by some American companies which are of no nominal value but represent that proportion of the company's net assets which remains after deducting the nominal value of other classes of shares.

Nobiliores et benigniores presumptiones in dubiis sunt praeferendae (Reg. Jur.Civ.). (In cases of doubt, the more generous and more favourable presumptions are to be preferred.)

Nobility, a division of the people, comprehending dukes, marquesses, earls, viscounts, and barons. These had anciently duties annexed to their respective honours; they are created either by writ, *i.e.*, by royal summons to attend the house of peers, or by letters patent, *i.e.*, by royal grant of any dignity and degree of peerage.

Noble. See George-Noble; Gold Coins.

Nocent, guilty; criminal.

Noctanter (by night), a writ which issued out of Chancery, and returned to the King's Bench, for the prostration of inclosures, etc. Under the Statute of Westminster I, 1285, c. 46, which provided that where a hedge or ditch was overthrown the neighbouring vills (*q.v.*) should be liable for damages if they did not indict the offenders, a writ known as *noctanter* lay to the sheriff, and was the first step in the proceedings for the recovery of damages. The above-mentioned provision was repealed by the statute 1826, 7 & 8 Geo. 4, c. 27; and this put an end to the issue of the writ.

Formerly an indictment for burglary was defective unless it set out that the act charged had been done *noctanter*.

Noctes, Noctem de firma, entertainment of meat and drink for so many nights (*Domesday*). See Firma.

Nocumento amovendo, a writ of abatement issued where a defendant was indicted and convicted for obstructing a highway, or for other nuisances (Mather, *Sheriff Law*).

Nodfyrs, or **Nedfri** [Sax. *neb*, necessary], necessary fire (Spelman).

Noise. An action may lie for a nuisance by noise, as by ringing bells (*Soltau* v. *De Held* (1851) 2 Sim.(N.S.) 133); user of a stable (*Ball* v. *Ray* (1873) L.R. 8 Ch. 467); or printing works (*Polsue* v. *Rushmer* [1907] A.C. 121); or hotel kitchen (*Vanderpant* v. *Mayfair Hotel Co.* [1930] 1 Ch. 138). As to nuisance caused by rifle practice, see *Hawley* v. *Steele* (1877) 6 Ch.D. 521. See MUSICIANS IN LONDON STREETS.

Where noise (including vibration) amounting to a nuisance (*q.v.*) exists or is likely to occur or recur the district council (*q.v.*), or the council of a London borough or the Common Council of the City of London, as local authority may serve a notice requiring the abatement of the nuisance or prohibiting or restricting its occurrence or recurrence and requiring the execution of such works or the taking of such other steps as are necessary. The notice is served on the person responsible for the nuisance, alternatively on the owner or occupier of the premises involved. The person served with a notice may appeal to the magistrates within twenty-one days. Contravention of a notice is an offence. It is a defence to show that the best practicable means (see s. 72) have been used to prevent noise. Alternatively the local authority may sue for an injunction in the High Court notwithstanding that the local authority have suffered no damage from the nuisance (Control of Pollution Act, 1974, ss. 58, 70, 73). These provisions take the place of the Noise Abatement Act, 1960, s. 1.

An occupier of premises may complain to a magistrates' court on the ground that he is aggrieved by noise amounting to a nuisance (Control of Pollution Act, 1974, ss. 59, 70). Special provisions apply to the control of noise on construction sites (ss. 60, 61). With exceptions for police, fire brigades and ambulances, etc., the use of loud-speakers in streets is prohibited between 9 p.m. and 8 a.m. on the following morning and at any time for the purpose of advertising any entertainment, trade or business. Further exceptions relate to radios in cars, horns in cars, fairgrounds and cases of emergency. Ice cream, etc. vans are exempt if they do not create an annoyance (s. 62). Noise abatement zones may be established under s. 63, Sch. 1. Local authorities are required to inspect their areas (s. 57) and keep a register of noise levels (s. 64) which may not be exceeded (s. 65) and may be required to be reduced (s. 66). As to new buildings, see s. 67. As to plant and machinery, see s. 68. As to the execution of works, see s. 69. As to the publication of codes of practice, see s. 71. Noise from model aircraft is within the Act (s. 73 (4)). For penalties see ss. 74, 87 (2).

Compensation for noise arising from the use of public works may be claimed under the Land Compensation Act, 1973, ss. 1–19. Power to insulate buildings against noise caused or expected to be caused by the construction or use of public works is given by ss. 20, 21.

Noise Advisory Council, a non-statutory body whose reports are published by H.M.S.O.

Noka, a half ingate, generally 7½ acres.

Nolens volens, whether willing or unwilling

Nolle prosequi (to be unwilling to prosecute), a proceeding in the nature of an undertaking by the plaintiff when he had misconceived the nature of the action, or the party to be sued, to forbear to proceed in a suit altogether, or as to some part of it, or as to some of the defendants. It differed from a *non pros.*, which put a plaintiff out of court with respect to all the defendants. (See DISCONTINUANCE.) In criminal prosecutions by indictment or information, a *nolle prosequi* to stay proceedings may be entered by leave of the Attorney-General at any time before judgment: it is not equivalent to an acquittal and is no bar to a new indictment for the same offence.

A *nolle prosequi* is usually entered in cases where the accused person cannot be produced in court to plead or stand his trial owing to physical or mental incapacity which is expected to be permanent. Either the prosecution or the accused person can apply to the Attorney-General for his direction that a *nolle prosequi* should be entered and such application is made quite informally, *e.g.*, by letter. This power of the Attorney-General is not subject to any control by the court (*R.* v. *Comptroller of Patents* [1899] 1 Q.B. 909, 914). If the office of Attorney-General is vacant, the Solicitor-General may act (Law Officers Act, 1944, s. 1).

Nolumus leges Angliae mutari. (We decline to have the laws of English changed.) See MERTON, STATUTE OF.

Nom de plume. An employee who acquires a reputation under a *nom de plume* is, in the absence of some clear term to the contrary, entitled to use it after the employment has discontinued (*Forbes* v. *Kemsley Newspapers* [1951] 2 T.L.R. 656). There is no copyright in a *nom de plume* but it may be protected by a passing-off action (Copinger, *Copyright*).

Nomen collectivum, a collective name, that is to say, a designation covering persons of a particular class (such as the word " children ") or indicating one of a particular class (such as the words " eldest male issue "). See PERSONA DESIGNATA.

Nomen generalissimum, a most universal term, as land.

Nomina ministorum, a roll formerly sent by the clerk of the peace to the sheriff containing a list of all the county justices. This was sent by the under-sheriff with the return of the precept giving notice of the assize to all justices of the peace, to the clerk of assize, who at the sitting handed it to the sheriff, who handed it to the judge, who handed it back unopened to the clerk, who returned it to the under-sheriff who restored it to the clerk of the peace (106 J.P. 183). See JUSTICES OF THE PEACE.

Nomina sunt mutabilia, res autem immobiles (6 Co.Rep. 66). (Names can be changed but things remain the same.)

Nomina villarum (the names of the vills), the title of the various lists of vills, *i.e.*, townships, towns or villages, which from time to time were compiled for public purposes. The title is more particularly applied to the lists which all the sheriffs furnished in 1316 of the vills in their respective counties and of the owners of the vills. The original lists for nine of the southern counties are still preserved. A transcript of all the lists was made by order of Henry VII and copies of this still exist. The lists had been made for the purpose of enabling Edward II to raise one man from each vill in accordance with the authorisation of the Parliament of Lincoln.

The name is also applied to the lists contained in the Testa de Nevill (*q.v.*), and to reports made in the reign of Charles II by the bailiffs of the liberties of various towns as to the claims of the lords thereof to estreats, etc.

Nominal damages. See DAMAGES.

Nominal partner, one who has not any actual interest in the trade or business, or its profits; but by allowing his name to be used holds himself out to the world as apparently having an interest. See HOLDING OUT; PARTNERSHIP.

Nominate contracts, those distinguished by particular names (Civil Law).

Nominatim, by name; expressed one by one.

Nomination, the act of mentioning by name.

A member, not being under the age of sixteen, of a friendly society may by writing under his hand delivered at or sent to the registered office of the society, nominate any person to whom any sum of money payable on his death is to belong. The nomination may be revoked or varied and is revoked by the marriage of the nominator (Friendly Societies Act, 1974, ss. 66–70). Similar powers of nomination are given by the Industrial and Provident Societies Act, 1965, ss. 23–27 amended by the Administration of Estates (Small Payments) Act, 1965; Family Law Reform Act, 1969, ss. 19 (2), 24 (4) (*g*).

In ecclesiastical law, the owner of an advowson may grant the right of nomination to another, and then the grantor is bound to present for institution any clerk whom the grantee shall name. (See PRESENTATION.) No Roman Catholic can nominate (Presentation of Benefices Act, 1713, s. 1). A nominator must appoint his clerk within six months after avoidance; if he does not, and the patron presents his clerk before the bishop has taken any benefit of the lapse, he is obliged to admit such clerk (Plowd. 529).

As regards parliamentary, municipal and local government elections, nomination is the written proposal of a person as a candidate for a vacancy. Such nominations are the subject of various statutory provisions. See, *e.g.*, the Representation of the People Act, 1969, s. 12, Sch. 1 paras. 5, 6; Local Government Act, 1972, s. 79.

Nominativus pendens, a nominative case grammatically unconnected with the rest of the sentence in which it stands. The opening words in the form of a deed *inter partes* (" This deed," etc., down to " whereas "), though an intelligible and convenient part of the deed, having regard to the predicate " witnesseth " or " now this deed witnesseth," are sometimes of this kind.

Nomine poenae (under the description of a penalty). Additional rent, known as a penal rent, payable to the landlord under a covenant in a lease which is to become operative in the event of non-performance of conditions in the lease, was formerly said to be payable *nomine poenae*. Formerly it might be made payable in all leases in, for instance, the event of non-payment of rent on the appointed days. The Agricultural Holdings Act, 1948, s. 15, precludes the landlord of an agricultural holding from recovering as penal rent any greater sum than is sufficient to cover the actual loss sustained by reason of breach of the condition.

Nominis umbra, the shadow of a name, *e.g.*, a one-man company.

Nomocanon [νόμος, law; χανών, a rule], a collection of canons and imperial laws relative or conformable thereto. The first nomocanon was made by Johannes Scholasticus in 554. Photius, patriarch of Constantinople, in 883, compiled another nomocanon, or collation of the civil laws with the canons; this is the most celebrated.

It also means a collection of the ancient canons of the apostles, councils, and fathers, without any regard to imperial constitutions. Such is the nomocanon by Cotelier (Encyc.Londin.).

Nomographer [νόμος, law; γράφω, to write], one who writes on the subject of laws.

Nomotheta [Gk.], a law-giver, or law commissioner.

Nomethetical, legislative.

Non acceptavit, he did not accept. Before the Judicature Acts, 1873–75, this was the name of the plea, in an action of *assumpsit* against an alleged acceptor of a bill of exchange, by which the acceptance of the bill was denied.

Non accipi debent verba in demonstrationem falsam quae competunt in limitationem veram (Bac.Max. 13). (Words capable of being read as amounting to a limitation which was obviously intended are not to be read in a sense which makes them a false description.) Thus, where the parish of Hurst lies both in Wiltshire and Berkshire, and in the Berkshire part A owns the lands of Callis, they will pass under a devise of the lands of " Callis situate in the parish of Hurst in the county of Wiltshire," because the words " in the county of Wiltshire " can and should be taken as referring to " the parish of Hurst " and not to Callis.

Non accrevit infra sex annos, the plea of the Statute of Limitation, 1623, when the action did not accrue on the promise but subsequently to it. See NON ASSUMPSIT INFRA SEX ANNOS.

Non alio modo puniatur aliquis, quam secundum quod se habet condemnatio (3 Co.Inst. 217). (A person may not be punished otherwise than in accordance with the sentence.) So, as Coke continues, *non licet felonem pro felonia decollari* (it is unlawful that a felon should be decapitated for felony.)

Non aliter a significatione verborum recedi oportet quam cum manifestum est aliud sensisse testatorem (Dig. 32, 69). (There should be no departure from the ordinary meaning of words except in so far as it appears that the testator meant something different.)

Non assumpsit (he did not promise), a plea by way of traverse, which occurred in the action of *assumpsit*. This plea operated as a denial of the existence of any express promise to the effect alleged in the declaration, or of the matters of fact from which the promise alleged would be implied by law, and thus raised the general issue. See ISSUE; NIL DEBET.

Non assumpsit infra sex annos (he did not promise within six years), the plea by which the Statute of Limitations, 1623, was pleaded.

Non bis in idem (not twice tried for the same offence). See AUTREFOIS ACQUIT; AUTREFOIS CONVICT.

Non cepit modo et forma (he did not take in the manner and form alleged), the plea which was used by the defendant in the action of replevin to plead the general issue. It was a plea by way of traverse and it applied to the case where the defendant had not taken the cattle or goods, or where he did not take them or have them in the place mentioned in the declaration, the place being a material point in this action.

Non compos mentis (not sound of mind). There were said to be four species: *ideota* (an idiot), who from his birth, by a perpetual infirmity, is *non compos mentis*; he who by sickness, grief, or other accident, wholly loses his memory and understanding; a lunatic who has sometimes his understanding and sometimes not, *aliquando gaudet lucidis intervallis*, and therefore he is called *non compos mentis* so long as he has not understanding; and he who by his own vicious act for a time deprives himself of his memory and understanding, as he who is drunken, but that kind of *non compos mentis* gives no privilege or benefit to him or to his heirs (Co.Litt. 247a). See DRUNKENNESS; IDIOCY; INSANITY; MENTAL HEALTH.

There are, however, certain offences which cannot be committed without *mens rea* or intent to commit the crime; and so therefore a man who kills another while in *delirium tremens* cannot be convicted of murder or manslaughter. See NON SANAE MEMORAE.

Non concessit (he did not grant), the plea by which a stranger to a deed put in issue the title of the grantor in the deed and also the operation of the deed; also the plea by which the defendant denied that the Crown had granted to the plaintiff by letters patent the rights claimed by the plaintiff. It did not deny the grant of a patent, but of the patent as described in the plaintiff's declaration (3 Burr. 1544; 6 Co.Rep. 15b).

Non constat, it is not clear; it does not follow; there are no grounds for assuming.

Non culpabilis, a form of plea of not guilty, formerly used in criminal cases. The usual abbreviation on the minutes of the court was *non cul.* (16 Viner 1). See NIENT CULPABLE.

Issue was joined on the plea by the abbreviation *prit.*, *i.e.*, *paratus*, ready to prove the accused guilty, and, eventually, the officer of the court began to apply these abbreviations to the accused, " *Culprit*, how wilt thou be tried? " See CULPRIT.

Non damnificatus (not injured), a plea in an action of debt on an indemnity bond, or bond conditioned to keep the plaintiff harmless and indemnified, etc. It was in the nature of a plea of performance, being used where the defendant meant to allege that the plaintiff had been kept harmless and indemnified, according to the tenor of the condition (2 Lil.Abr. 224).

Non dat qui no habet. (He cannot give who has not.)

Non debeo melioris conditionis esse quam auctor meus a quo jus in me transit (Dig. 50, 17, 175). (I ought not to be in a better position than my assignor, from whom the right passes to me.) See NEMO DAT, ETC.

Non debet alteri per alterum iniqua conditio inferri (Dig. 50, 17, 74). (An unjust condition ought not to be imposed upon one man by another.)

Non debet cui plus licet quod minus est non licere (Dig. 50, 17, 21). (It is lawful for a man to do a less thing if he is entitled to do a greater thing [which includes the less].) This is the equivalent in the civil law of our maxim *Cui licet*, etc. See MAJUS CONTINET, ETC.; OMNE MAJUS, ETC.

Non decimando, De. A prescription *de non decimando* was a claim to be exempt from tithes and to pay no compensation in lieu of them. Such a prescription could be set up only by spiritual persons or by corporations or persons claiming under them, and until 1832 it was necessary to prove that the land in question had been immemorially exempt from tithes. But by the Tithe Act, 1832, non-payment of tithes during a certain period (thirty years in some cases and sixty in others) was sufficient to establish a prescriptive exemption. See TITHES.

Non decipitur qui scit se decipi (5 Co. Rep. 60). (He is not deceived who knows himself to be deceived.) See VOLENTI, ETC.

Non definitur in jure quid sit conatus (6 Co.Rep. 42). (No definition of an attempt is given by the law.)

Non demisit (he did not demise), a plea available before the Judicature Acts, 1873–75, to a defendant in an action of debt for rent when the plaintiff in his declaration did not aver that the demise was by indenture: it could not be used when the plaintiff declared an indenture. In replevin (q.v.) it was a plea in bar to an avowry for arrears of rent.

Non detinet (he does not detain). In the old action of detinue the defendant could use the plea of *non detinet* in order to plead that he did not detain the goods specified in the plaintiff's declaration; but if he did use the plea he was estopped from pleading that they were not the goods of the plaintiff.

Non differunt quae concordant re tametsi non in verbis iisdem (Jenk., Cent. 70). (Those things that agree in substance, though not in the same words, are not different from one another.)

Non distringendo, De, a writ to prevent distraint; it was formerly available in many cases (Reg. of Writs).

Non est arctius vinculum inter homines quam jusjurandum (Jenk., Cent. 126). (As between men there is nothing more binding than an oath.) See JURATO, ETC.

Non est disputandum contra principia negantem (Co.Litt. 343). (One cannot dispute against a man who denies first principles.)

Non est factum (it is not his deed), the law Latin form of *nient le fait* (q.v.). This was a plea by way of traverse, which occurred in debt on bond or other specialty, and also in covenant. It denied that the deed mentioned in the declaration was the defendant's deed; under this. the defendant might contend at the trial that the deed was never executed in point of fact, but he could not deny its validity in point of law

(*Howatson* v. *Webb* [1908] 1 Ch. 1). See ASSUMPSIT; MODO ET FORMA; PLEADING.

Non est factum is a defence in an action founded on a document (whether under seal or not) when there has been a mistake as to the very nature of the transaction. The defence is not available when the mistake is as to the contents of the document but not as to its nature (*Muskham Finance* v. *Howard* [1963] 1 Q.B. 904; *Mercantile Credit Co.* v. *Hamblin* [1965] 2 Q.B. 242; *Saunders* (*Executrix in the Estate of Rose Maud Gallie*) v. *Anglia Building Society* [1971] A.C. 1004; *United Dominions Trust* v. *Western* [1976] Q.B. 513).

Non est inventus (he is not found), the return (sometimes abbreviated to N.E.I.), which was made by the sheriff upon a writ commanding him to arrest a person who was not within his bailiwick. See ATTACHMENT; CAPIAS; RETURN.

Non est recedendum a communi observantia (2 Co.Rep. 74). (There should be no departure from common usage.) See A COMMUNI, ETC.

Non est regula quin fallit (Plow.Com. 162). (There is no rule without exceptions.) See EXCEPTIO PROBAT, ETC.

Non facias malum ut inde fiat bonum (11 Co.Rep. 74). (You are not to do evil in order that good may come thereof.)

Non impedit clausula derogatoria quo minus ab eadem potestate res dissolvantur a qua constituuntur (Bac.Max. 19; Broom. 347). (A derogatory clause does not prevent things from being destroyed by the same power as created them.)

If an Act of Parliament contained a clause that it should not be lawful for Parliament, during a space of seven years, to repeal the Act, such a clause, which is technically termed *clausula derogatoria*, would be void; for one Parliament cannot bind another, and Parliament may alter, amend or repeal during any session even an Act which it has passed earlier in that session (Interpretation Act, 1889, s. 10). See PERPETUA, ETC.

Non implacitando aliquem de libero tenemento sine breve, a writ which prohibited bailiffs, etc., from distraining or impleading any man touching his freehold, without the king's writ (Reg.Orig. 171; Tomlin).

Non in legendo sed in intelligendo leges consistunt (8 Co.Rep. 167). (The laws consist not in reading but in understanding.) Understanding and not mere knowledge of the letter of the law is required of a lawyer.

Non infregit conventionem (he committed no breach of covenant), a plea which raised a substantial issue in an action for non-repair according to covenant, whether there was a want of repair or not. See PLEADING.

Non intromittendo, quando breve praecipe in capite sub dole impetratur, a writ, which ceased to be available when the Court of Wards and Liveries (*q.v.*) was abolished, which issued to the justices of the King's Bench or in eyre commanding them not to give any benefit under the writ *praecipe in capite* to one who had obtained that writ under pretence of entitling the king to lands, and directing them to put such person to his writ of right (Reg.Orig. 4).

Non jus, sed seisina, facit stipitem (6 Fleta, c. 14). (Not right, but seisin, makes the stock of descent.) See SEISIN; SEISNA, ETC.

Non liquet, it is not clear. In the civil law the *judices* or judges, instead of deciding a case, could, if the facts did not point to a definite conclusion, write N.L. (*non liquet*) on their tablets and leave the case for decision at some future time. No similar finding has ever been open to an English jury: the nearest thing to it is the Scottish verdict " not proven," which, however, is a bar to any further trial.

Non merchandizanda victualia, a writ addressed to justices of assize, to inquire whether the magistrates of a town sold victuals in gross or by retail during the time of their being in office, which was contrary to an obsolete statute, and to punish them if they did (Reg.Brev. 184).

Non molestando, De, a writ which lay for one molested notwithstanding that the writ of protection (*q.v.*) had issued to him (Reg.Brev. 184).

Non observata forma infertur adnullatio actus (Coke, De jure Reg.Eccl. 4a; 5 Co.Rep. 20). (Non-observance of the prescribed formalities involves the invalidity of the proceeding.) Quoted by Coke in connection with the deprivation of a clerk pursuant to the Act of Uniformity, 1558.

Non obstante, notwithstanding. About the year 1250, the Crown began to issue licences to do such and such a thing *non obstante* any law to the contrary. At a later period, such licences were frequently given in order to enable corporations to hold lands in contravention of the mortmain statutes (Vaugh. 347; Plowd. 501).

This contined to be done, in spite of protests, until at last James II resolved to dispense with the provisions of the Test Act, 1672. This and other things led to the Revolution of 1688, after which the Bill of Rights, 1688, enacted that any dispensation *non obstante* should be wholly void and without effect. See MORTMAIN.

Non obstante veredicto, notwithstanding the verdict. Upon an application for a new trial, the Court of Appeal, if satisfied that the findings of the jury cannot stand and that it has all the necessary evidence before it, may set aside the judgment of the court below and enter judgment, notwithstanding the verdict (Judicature Act, 1925, s. 30; R.S.C., Ord. 59, rr. 2, 11).

Non officit affectus nisi sequatur effectus (1 Rol.Rep. 226). (The intention is not hurtful unless an effect follows.) See AFFECTUS PUNITUR, ETC.; VOLUNTAS IN, ETC.

Non omittas (that you omit not), a clause usually inserted in writs of execution, directing the sheriff not to omit to execute the writ by reason of any liberty, because there were many liberties or districts in which the sheriff had no power to execute process unless he had special authority. Such authority was given by this clause, the full form of which was *non omittas propter libertatem* (do not omit because of any liberty) (Fitz.N.B. 68, 74; Tomlin).

If a writ does not contain a *non omittas* clause, the sheriff directs his mandate either to the lord or the bailiff of the liberty, by whom the writ is executed and returned.

Non omne quod licet honestum est. (Not all things which are lawful are honourable.)

Non omnium quae a majoribus nostris constituta sunt ratio reddi potest (Dig. 1, 3, 20). (A reason cannot be given for all the laws that have been established by our ancestors.) See CONTRA NEGANTEM, ETC; QUI RATIONEM, ETC.

Non placet, it is not approved.

Non plevin, default in replevying (*q.v.*) land within due time: see the statute 1335, 9 Edw. 3, c. 2.

Non ponendis in assisis et juratis, a writ which issued to free a person from serving on assizes or as a juror (Fitz. N.B. 165).

Non possessori incumbit necessitas probandi possessiones ad se pertinere (C. 4, 19, 2; Broom). (A person in possession is not bound to prove that what he possesses belongs to him.) This applies only as against a person other than the true owner. See IN PARI, ETC.; MELIOR EST CONDITIO, ETC.

Non potest adduci exceptio ejusdem rei cujus petitur dissolutio (Bac.Max. 2). (When the validity of any matter is in question, then he who seeks to uphold it cannot plead it in bar of proceedings taken to upset it.)

Non potest probari quod probatum non relevat (Broom). (That cannot be proved, which, if proved, is immaterial.)

Non potest rex gratiam facere cum injuria et damno aliorum (3 Co.Inst. 236). (The king cannot confer a favour on one man to the injury and damage of others.) Thus no pardon can be granted in respect of a common nuisance which remains unabated (2 Hawk.P.C.).

Non procedendo ad assisam rege inconsulto, a writ to stop the trial of a cause appertaining to one who was in the royal service, etc., until the pleasure of the king was known (Reg.Brev. 220).

Non procedendo ad captionem assisae rege inconsulto, a writ which issued to stop proceedings at an assize until the pleasure of the king was known.

Non pros., an abbreviation for *non prosequitur,* he does not follow up. Judgment *non pros.* was available for the defendant in an action when the plaintiff failed to take the proper steps within the prescribed time. The modern equivalents are an order (under R.S.C., Ord. 19, r. 1) of dismissal for want of prosecution, where the plaintiff fails to deliver his statement of claim, or an order of dismissal (under R.S.C., Ord. 25, r. 1 (4) or Ord. 78, r. 5) if the plaintiff does not take out a summons for directions, or (under R.S.C., Ord. 34, r. 2 (2)) where the plaintiff does not set down the action for trial.

Non quod dictum est, sed quod factum est, in jure inspicitur (Co.Litt. 36). (Not what is said, but what is done, is regarded in law.) This is quoted in connection with the proposition that there can be valid delivery of a deed without any words spoken.

Non quod voluit testator, sed quod dixit in testamento inspicitur. (Not what the testator wished, but what he said, is considered in construing a will.) Difficulties arise from confounding the testator's intention with his meaning. Intention may mean what the testator intended to have done, whereas the only question in the construction of wills is the meaning of the words.

Non refert an quis assensum suum praefert verbis, an rebus ipsis et factis (10 Co.Rep. 52). (It matters not whether a man gives his assent by his words, or by his acts and deeds.) See INDEX, ETC.

Non refert quid notum sit judici, si notum non sit in forma judicii (3 Buls. 115). (It matters not what is known to the judge, if it is not known judicially.)

Non residentia pro clericis regis, a writ enjoining a bishop not to molest, by reason of non-residence, a clerk who was absent in the service of the king (Reg. Orig. 58).

Non sane memory (Non sanae memoriae). In the old system of pleading this was an exception (*q.v.*) whereby it was pleaded that the person who had done an act was not of sound memory when he did it. See NON COMPOS MENTIS.

Non sequitur, it does not follow.

Non solent quae abundant vitiare scripturas (Dig. 50, 17, 94). (Surplusage does not vitiate writings.) See SURPLASAGIUM, ETC.; UTILE, ETC.

Non solvendo pecuniam ad quam clericus mulctatur pro non residentia, a writ prohibiting the bishop from enforcing a fine imposed for non-residence upon a clerk who was absent on the king's service (Reg.Orig. 59).

Non sum informatus, I am not informed; that is to say, I have no instructions to defend. Upon this being filed by the attorney appearing for a litigant, it formerly enabled the plaintiff to have judgment. See COGNOVIT; WARRANT OF ATTORNEY.

Non tenuit. In the old action of replevin (*q.v.*) this was a plea in bar to an avowry for arrears of rent; it set out that the plaintiff did not hold in the manner and form alleged in the avowry (Rose, Real Act. 628).

Non term; non terminus. In the sixteenth century, and earlier, these expressions meant the period between one term (*q.v.*) and another. Any such period was also known as the time or days of the king's peace (Lamb.Archa. 126).

Non valet confirmatio, nisi ille, qui confirmat, sit in possessione rei vel juris unde fieri debet confirmatio; et eodem modo, nisi ille cui confirmatio fit, sit in possessione (Co.Litt. 295). (Confirmation is without effect unless he who confirms is either in possession of the thing itself or of the right of which confirmation is to be made, and, in like manner, unless he to whom confirmation is made is in possession.) See CONFIRMATION.

Non videntur qui errant consentire (Dig. 50, 17, 116; Broom). (Those who are mistaken are not deemed to consent.) Where an agreement has been made or an act done under a mistake of a material fact, then relief can be obtained in equity. See MISTAKE.

Non videtur consensum retinuisse si quis ex praescripto minantis aliquid immutavit (Bac.Max. 22). (He is not deemed to have consented who has altered anything at the command of anyone using threats.) See NIHIL CONSENSUI, ETC.

Non videtur quisquam id capere, quod ei necesse est alii restituere (Dig. 50, 17, 51). (No one is deemed to take that which he must give up to another.) In these circumstances, he is in fact a mere conduit pipe.

Non-ability, inability; an exception against a person (Fitz.N.B. 35, 65). See DISABILITY.

Non-acceptance, the refusal of acceptance. See ACCEPTANCE OF GOODS.

Non-access. Access is presumed during wedlock; but this presumption may be encountered by proof of circumstances showing that sexual intercourse did not take place within such a time that the husband could be the father. If non-access for above nine months is proved, by showing that the husband and wife were separated from one another, any child of the wife conceived during and born after that period is a bastard unless the court can be induced to adopt a large view of the period of gestation (*Preston-Jones* v. *Preston-Jones* [1951] A.C. 391). As to the admissibility of evidence by husband or wife of non-access, see the Matrimonial Causes Act, 1973, s. 48. See ACCESS.

Non-act, a forbearance from action; the contrary to act.

Nonae et decimae, payments formerly made to the church by the tenants of church farms, *nonae* being rent, and *decimae* tithes (Blount).

Non-age, minority. See INFANT.

Nonagium; Nonage, the ninth part of the movables of a deceased which was paid for pious uses to the clergy of his parish (Blount).

Non-appearance, the omission of timely and proper appearance; a failure of appearance. See APPEARANCE; DEFAULT.

Non-belligerency, discrimination by a neutral between belligerents. It is illegal under international customary law (Schwarzenberger, Int.Law).

Non-business days. See BUSINESS DAY.

Non-claim. At common law, the levying of a fine (*q.v.*) barred the right of all persons, whether parties, privies or strangers, unless they put in their claim within, at first, a year and a day. This was called being barred by non-claim. Alterations were afterwards made in the time allowed for claiming, but now no continual or other claim preserves any right of making an entry or distress or of bringing an action (Real Property Limitation Act, 1833, s. 11).

There was also a non-claim in a writ of right.

Non-combatants, civilian population.

Nonconformist, anyone who is not in communion with the Church of England; but it is more generally used as meaning Protestant dissenters, as distinguished from persons such as Roman Catholics on the one hand and professed atheists on the other. See DISSENTERS; RECUSANTS.

Non-contentious. See CONTENTIOUS BUSINESS.

Non-delivery. See DELIVERY.

Non-direction, omission on the part of a judge to enforce a necessary point of law upon a jury. The Judicature Act, 1875, s. 22, preserved the right of any party to have the issues for trial by jury left to the jury, with a proper and complete direction to the jury upon the law, and as to the evidence applicable to such issues (*Young* v. *Hoffman Manufacturing Co.* (1907) 76 L.J.K.B. 993). See NEW TRIAL.

Non-disclosure. See CONCEALMENT.

Non-existing grant. See LOST GRANT.

Nonfeasance, the neglect or failure of a person to do some act which he ought to do. The term is generally used to denote, not a breach of contract, but rather a failure to perform a duty towards the public whereby some individual sustains special damage peculiar to himself, as where a highway authority permits a road to become worn into a dangerous hole. If they had purported to repair the hole and then opened it to the public in a dangerous state, there would be a misfeasance (*q.v.*). The exemption from civil liability enjoyed by the highway authority was abrogated by the Highways (Miscellaneous Provisions) Act, 1961, s. 1 (1) but absence of negligence is a defence (s. 1 (2) (3)). See MALFEASANCE; TORT.

Non-intromittant clause, a clause in the charter of a borough which exempted the borough from the jurisdiction of the justices of the peace appointed for the county in which the borough was situated (*R.* v. *Sainsbury* (1791) 4 T.R. 451).

Non-issuable pleas, pleas upon which a decision would not determine the action upon the merits, such as a plea in abatement (*q.v.*). See PLEA; PLEADING.

Non-joinder, where a person who ought to be made party to an action is omitted. The general rule is that, in an action on a contract, all the parties to it who are entitled or liable jointly should be joined as plaintiffs and defendants, and that, in an action of tort, persons who have a joint interest ought to sue

jointly for an injury to it: persons who have a separate interest, but sustain a joint injury, may sue either jointly or separately. Joint wrongdoers may be sued either jointly or separately. See JOINT; MISJOINDER.

Non-joinder is cured by making an application to the court to add the necessary parties (R.S.C., Ord. 15, r. 6).

Non-juror, one who (conceiving the Stuart family unjustly deposed) refused to swear allegiance to those who suceeded them.

By the statute 1714, 1 Geo. 1, st. 2, c. 13, any two justices of the peace might summon and tender oaths to any person whom they suspected to be disaffected; and every person refusing the same, properly called a non-juror, was adjudged a popish recusant convict and subject to severe penalties which in the end might amount to the alternative of abjuring the realm or suffering death as a felon (4 Bl.Comm. 124). See RECUSANTS.

Non-justiciable disputes, disputes which are not considered by the parties to be capable of settlement by a judicial international institution.

Non-provided school, a voluntary school (*q.v.*).

Non-residence. In ecclesiastical law, this is where a spiritual person holding a benefice does not keep residence in it. It is in ordinary cases an offence, and is punishable by monition and sequestration of the benefice, by forfeiture of part of the income of the benefice, and by the compulsory appointment of a curate. Licences for non-residence may be granted by the bishop in certain cases (Pluralities Act, 1838, ss. 42–51).

As applied to a trading corporation, non-residence signifies that it has no place of business in England. The question is of importance with reference to the liability of such a corporation to be sued in this country, and to the manner in which it should be served with process. (See DOMICILE; JURISDICTION.) It should be served not with the writ but with notice thereof (R.S.C., Ord. 11, r. 5). See RESIDENCE.

As to the liability of non-residents to income tax, capital gains tax and corporation tax, see the Taxes Management

Act, 1970, ss. 78–85; Income and Corporation Taxes Act, 1970, ss. 49–51.

Nonsuit [*non est prosecutus*]. The judge orders a nonsuit when the plaintiff fails to make out a legal cause of action or fails to support his pleadings by any evidence; whether the evidence which he gives can be considered any evidence at all of a cause of action is a question of law for the judge. Before 1875 the advantage of this practice (which was peculiar to the common law courts) was that the plaintiff could, on paying all costs, bring another action against the defendant for the same cause of action; but under Ord. 41, r. 6, of the R.S.C., 1875, any judgment of non-suit, unless the court otherwise directed, had the same effect as a judgment on the merits, that is, it barred the plaintiff from bringing another action for the same cause; but in case of mistake, surprise or accident, a judgment of nonsuit might be set aside by the court. Order 41, r. 6, was cancelled in 1883 and there is now in strictness no such thing as a nonsuit in the High Court. A plaintiff cannot now elect to be nonsuited, and if he offers no evidence it is the duty of the court to direct the jury to find a verdict for the defendant, and the usual consequences of such verdict will follow (*Fox* v. *Star Newspaper Co.* [1900] A.C. 19); but a judge cannot order a non-suit on plaintiff's opening without the consent of his counsel (*Fletcher* v. *L. & N.W. Ry.* [1892] 1 Q.B. 122). The term is still loosely used instead of the term " judgment for the defendant," where the judge withdraws the case from the jury and directs a verdict for the defendant. Nonsuit still applies in the county court (C.C.R., 1936, Ord. 23, r. 3).

See DISCONTINUANCE.

Non-summons, failure to serve a summons. The statute 1588, 31 Eliz. 1, c. 3, s. 2, provided that the process in a real action known as summons upon the lands should be proclaimed upon the local church door fourteen days at the least before the day the summons was returnable. If the provisions were not complied with the defendant could wage his law of non-summons (Saund. 45c).

Non-tenure, a plea in bar to a real action, denying that the defendant held the land mentioned in the plaintiff's count or declaration, or denying that he held some particular part of it. It was either general, where he denied ever having been tenant of the land in question, or special, where it was alleged that he was not a tenant on the day whereon the writ was sued out.

Non-user, where a person ceases to exercise a right. The term is principally used with reference to easements, profits *à prendre*, and similar rights, which may be extinguished by non-user for a certain number of years, which apparently must be not less than twenty; but the non-user must be of such a nature as to show an intention to abandon the right, as where it amounts to acquiescence in an unlawful interruption. See INTERRUPTION.

A public officer is liable to forfeiture for non-user or neglect to perform the duties of his office if special damage is proved (Co.Litt. 233a; 2 Bl.Comm. 153).

None effect. See VOID.

Nones, days in the Roman calendar, so called because they reckoned nine days from them to the Ides; the seventh day of March, May, July, and October, and the fifth day of all other months (Kenn.Paroch.Antiq. 92).

Nook [*nocata terrae*], a measure of land which appears to have sometimes meant twelve and a half acres, but which, according to Noy's *Complete Lawyer* (1651), contained two fardels (*q.v.*) or one-fourth of a yardland (*q.v.*).

Norfolk groat, a farthing.

Normal [Lat. *norma*, a rule or precept], opposed to exceptional. That state wherein any body most exactly comports in all its parts with the abstract idea thereof, and is most exactly fitted to perform its proper functions, is entitled normal.

Normandy. See GRAND COUSTUMIER, ETC.

Norman-French, the tongue in which several formal proceedings of State are still carried on. The language, having remained the same since the date of the Conquest, at which it was introduced into England, is very different from the French of this day, retaining peculiarities which at that time distinguished every province from the rest. A peculiar mode of pronunciation (considered authentic) is believed to have been handed down and preserved by the officials, who have, on particular occasions, to speak the tongue. Norman-French was the language of our legal procedure till the statute 1362, 36 Edw. 3, c. 15. See FRENCH.

Norroy [Fr. *nord*; *roy*], the title of the third of the three kings-at-arms, or provincial heralds. See HERALD.

North Britain, Scotland.

North Sea Fisheries Convention, an agreement arrived at on May 6, 1882, between Great Britain, Belgium, Germany, France, Denmark and Holland for the purpose of regulating the fisheries of the North Sea outside territorial waters.

North's Act, the statute 1773, 13 Geo. 3, c. 63, relating to the East India Company.

Northampton, Assize of. In 1176, at the Council of Northampton, Henry II divided the kingdom into six circuits, to each of which three itinerant justices were assigned.

Northampton, Statute of, the statute 1328, 2 Edw. 3, enacted at Northampton.

Northern Ireland, that part of Ireland other than the part known successively as the Irish Free State, Eire and the Republic of Ireland. By the Government of Ireland Act, 1920, s. 1, Northern Ireland consists of six counties: Antrim, Armagh, Down, Fermanagh, Londonderry, and Tyrone, including the boroughs of Belfast and Londonderry, with representation in the Parliament of the United Kingdom and Northern Ireland, and a Parliament of Northern Ireland, consisting of the sovereign, a Senate and a House of Commons. The supreme authority of the Imperial Parliament is preserved.

Representative government in Northern Ireland was suspended by the Northern Ireland (Temporary Provisions) Act, 1972. See the Northern Ireland Constitution Act, 1973 (as amended).

Acts of Parliament apply to Northern Ireland unless expressly excluded. See IRELAND.

Northstead, Manor of. See CHILTERN HUNDREDS, ETC.

Norwich Guildhall Court. This court was abolished on January 1, 1972, by the Courts Act, 1971. s. 43. See also Sch. 5 para. 12.

Noscitur a sociis. (A man is known from his associates.) So also the meaning of a word can be gathered from the context: where there is a string of words and the meaning of one of them is doubtful, that meaning is given to it which it shares with the other words. So, if the words "horse, cow, or other animal" occur, "animal" is held to apply to brutes only. See EJUSDEM GENERIS.

Noscitur ex socio, qui non cognoscitur ex se (Moore 817). (He who cannot be known from himself may be known from his associate.)

Nosocomi, managers of pauper hospitals (Civil Law).

Nostrum est judicare secundum allegata et probata (1 Dyer 12). (It is our duty to decide according to what is pleaded and proved.) See JUDICIS EST JUDICARE, ETC.; NON REFERT QUID, ETC.

Not guilty, the appropriate plea to an indictment where the prisoner wishes to raise the general issue (see ISSUE; PLEA), that is to say, when he wishes to deny everything and to let the prosecution prove what they can. It was also a plea used in common law actions of tort under the old practice, when the defendant simply denied that he had committed the wrong complained of (see ISSUE). Under the present system of pleading, a defendant must deal specifically with all allegations made by the plaintiff which he does not admit, and therefore a plea of not guilty is no longer permissible in civil proceedings.

There were formerly certain public and private Acts of Parliament which provided (principally for the protection of constables, inspectors, and other public officers) that in actions for anything done in pursuance of such Acts or in execution of the powers and authorities thereof, the defendant might plead not guilty, which entitled him to give the special matter in evidence at the trial; that is, he might prove the facts of the case and show that he acted in pursuance of the statute, so that such a plea had the same effect as if he had pleaded the facts and his defence specifically. This was called pleading "not guilty by statute," but the defendant could not plead any other defence without leave; and he had to insert in the margin of the plea the words "by statute," together with the year, chapter, and section of the Act or Acts on which he relied and to specify whether they were public or private. The right to plead not guilty by statute in such cases was taken away by the Public Authorities Protection Act, 1893, s. 2. The right to plead not guilty under any local or personal Act passed had previously been taken away by the Limitation of Actions and Costs Act, 1842, s. 3, known as Pollock's Act. See Non Culpabilis.

Not negotiable. These words are sometimes added as part of the crossing of a cheque, with the result that, by the Bills of Exchange Act, 1882, s. 81, no one who takes the cheque can have or can give a better title than the person had from whom he took it (*G.W. Ry.* v. *London and County Bank* [1901] A.C. 422).

A warrant for interest on war stock signed by the chief accountant of the Bank of England and crossed "& Co., not negotiable," directing the bank's cashiers to pay a certain sum to the order of a certain person is a cheque within the meaning of the Bills of Exchange Act, 1882, and a warrant for payment of a dividend within s. 95 of the Act. A banker in good faith and without negligence receiving payment for a customer who has no title is entitled to the protection of s. 82 of the Act (*Slingsby* v. *Westminster Bank* [1931] 1 K.B. 173; *Importers Company* v. *Westminster Bank* [1927] 2 K.B. 297; *Jones* v. *Waring and Gillow* [1926] A.C. 670).

Notarial act, a written certification or authentication under the signature or official seal of a notary of any document or entry; any instrument, attestation or certificate by a notary in the execution of his office.

Notary or **Notary public.** [Fr. *notaire*; Lat. *notarius*], an officer who takes notes of anything which may concern the public; he makes a record of proceedings in an ecclesiastical cause; he attests deeds or writings to make them authentic in another country; he is principally employed in mercantile affairs, as to make protests of bills of exchange, etc.

(see Legalisation). He cannot permit another to act in his name, and in London he must be free of the Scriveners' Company. The Court of Faculties makes the appointment in accordance with the Public Notaries Acts, 1801 to 1843, and the Master of that court has inherent jurisdiction to strike a notary public off the roll (*Re Champion* [1906] P. 86); as to its jurisdiction in the case of the colonies, see *Bailleau* v. *Victorian Society of Notaries* [1904] P. 180 and the Administration of Justice Act, 1969, s. 29. See Faculty.

As to notarial acts abroad see the Consular Relations Act, 1968, s. 10, Sch. 1 art. 5 (*f*).

A qualified solicitor (see Solicitors) may practice as a solicitor in all matters relating to applications to obtain notarial faculties (Solicitors Act, 1974, s. 19 (1) (*d*)). References in any enactment to a duly certificated notary public are to be construed as a reference to a notary public who either (a) has in force a practising certificate as a solicitor duly entered in the Court of Faculties (see Faculties, Court of) in accordance with rules made by the Master of Faculties or (b) has in force a practising certificate as a notary public issued by the Court of Faculties (ss. 87 (1), 89 (7)).

Notation, the act of making a memorandum of some special circumstance on a probate or letters of administration; thus where probate is granted of the will of a testator who died domiciled in England and it appears that part of the estate is in Scotland, then a notation of the fact that the testator died domiciled in England is made on the probate in order that recognition may be given to the grant in Scotland under the Confirmation and Probate Amendment Act, 1858.

Note a bill, To. When a foreign bill has been dishonoured, it is usual for a notary public to present it again on the same day, and if it is not then paid, to make a minute, consisting of his initials, the day, month, and year, and reason, if assigned, of non-payment. The making of this minute is called noting the bill. See Noting.

Note of a fine, a brief of a fine made by the chirographer before it was engrossed. It was abolished by the Fines and Recoveries Act, 1833.

Note of allowance. Under the Common Law Procedure Act, 1852, s. 149, either party to an action might deliver to one of the masters a memorandum alleging error in law, whereupon the master delivered to the party a note of the receipt thereof. A copy of this note, known as a note of allowance, together with a statement of the error relied on, might then be served on the other side to ground proceedings in error (*q.v.*).

Proceedings in error in law were deemed a *supersedeas* of execution from the service of the copy of such note, together with the statement of the grounds of error intended to be argued (Common Law Procedure Act, 1852, s. 150).

Note of hand, a promissory note. See PROMISSORY NOTE.

Notes, Judge's. See JUDGE'S NOTES; SHORTHAND WRITERS.

Notice, knowledge or cognisance. To speak of a court taking judicial notice (*q.v.*) of a fact means that the court recognises the fact without evidence to prove it. Thus the courts notice the political constitution of the government, the existence and title of every State and sovereign recognised by this country, the dates of the calendar, etc.

To give notice of a fact to a person is to bring it to his knowledge: when the circumstances are such that he is either actually aware of the fact, or might or ought to be aware of it, he is said to have notice of it.

Notice is actual (express), constructive, or imputed. Actual or express notice is that given in plain words from one person to another, either orally or in writing. Certain legal rights are registrable under the Land Charges Act, 1972, and if not registered are void against a purchaser even if the purchaser knows of them; certain equitable rights are also registrable, with the same effect. If legal rights are not registrable they are good against the whole world irrespective of notice or absence of notice: if equitable rights are not registrable, they are good against the whole world except a bona fide purchaser of the legal estate without notice of such equitable rights. Where registration is required, registration constitutes actual notice of the right in question to the whole world.

Constructive notice is where knowledge of the fact is presumed from the circumstances of the case: a person is held to have constructive notice of facts to a knowledge of which he would have been led by inquiry such as men of business under similar circumstances would reasonably have made.

Imputed notice, sometimes classified as constructive notice, is notice to an agent, solicitor, etc., on the presumption that the agent did his duty by communicating the notice to his principal; therefore that presumption may be rebutted if it appears that the agent was a party to fraud, or otherwise acted in such a way as to raise a presumption that he would not communicate the notice to his principal.

The equitable doctrine of notice was that a person who purchased an estate, although for valuable consideration, after notice of a prior equitable right, made himself a mala fide purchaser, and was not enabled, by getting in the legal estate, to defeat that right, but was held to be a trustee for the benefit of the person whose right he sought to defeat. Thus if a vendor contracted with two different persons, for the sale to each of them of the same estate, and the person with whom the second contract was made acquired notice of the first contract, and then procured a conveyance of the legal estate in pursuance of his own contract, the court would order him to convey the property to the first purchaser. Today such a contract is registrable as an estate contract; if registered it is notice to the person taking the conveyance; if not registered it would not affect the person taking the conveyance even though he knows of it.

A purchaser with notice may protect himself by purchasing the title of another bona fide purchaser for valuable consideration without notice; for, otherwise, such bona fide purchaser would not enjoy the full benefit of his own unexceptionable title. If a person who has notice (except in the case of a charity) sells to another who has no notice, and is a bona fide purchaser for valuable consideration, the

NOTICE

latter may protect his title, although it was affected with the equity arising from notice in the hands of the person from whom he derived it; for, otherwise, no man would be safe in any purchase, but would be liable to have his own title defeated by secret equities, of which he could have no possible means of making a discovery (*Le Neve* v. *Le Neve* (1747) Amb. 436). This decision went far to nullify the Middlesex Registry Act, 1708, and the principle of it is not to be applied in the construction of a modern statute: see *Re Monolithic Building Co.* [1915] 1 Ch. 643, where it was held that the Companies (Consolidation) Act, 1908, s. 93, now the Companies Act, 1948, s. 95, avoided an unregistered mortgage as against a subsequent registered incumbrancer, even with express notice. The principle on which this case was decided has become statutory under the Law of Property Act, 1925, s. 199, and the Land Charges Act, 1972. See CONSTRUCTIVE NOTICE; LAW OF PROPERTY ACT, 1925.

The doctrine of constructive trust was narrowed down by the Conveyancing Act, 1911, s. 13, reproduced by the Law of Property Act, 1925, s. 112, which provides that a 10s. (50p) stamp on a transfer of mortgage does not by itself give notice of a trust. The Law of Property Act, 1925, s. 113, absolves persons dealing in good faith with a mortgagee or with the mortgagor after discharge of the mortgage from any duty to inquire into the trusts of the mortgage money even if he has notice of the trust, and under the Trustee Act, 1925, s. 28, a trustee or personal representative acting for one trust or estate is not in the absence of fraud affected by notice obtained through acting for another.

Subject to the foregoing limitations on the doctrine and effect of notice, a purchaser of a legal estate or equitable interest in land will be affected by every and any right, equity, or incumbrance of which he has actual or constructive notice. As to the length of title in which notice will be imputed, see *Re Cousins* (1886) 31 Ch.D. 671, and the Law of Property Act, 1925, s. 44; Law of Property Act, 1969, s. 23.

By the Law of Property Act, 1925, s. 198, registration under the Land Charges Act, 1972, according to the statutory requirements constitutes notice of the instrument or matter registered, but this relates only to instruments and matters which must be registered. Notwithstanding the Law of Property Act, 1925, s. 198 (under which registration of a land charge is deemed to constitute actual notice), a purchaser is not deemed to have notice of the charge unless he, or his counsel, solicitor or other agent had actual knowledge of it. A purchaser is not precluded from rescinding a contract for the purchase of land on discovering an undisclosed registered land charge (Law of Property Act, 1969, s. 24, reversing the rule in *Re Forsey and Hollebone's Contract* [1927] 2 Ch. 379). As to compensation for loss due to undisclosed land charges see the Act of 1969, s. 25.

Whether or not an instrument or matter has been registered, the absence of the documents of title to the property by itself constitutes notice in all cases in which the same are material, and so does the occupation of land or any title or claim of an occupier, though the notice does not necessarily mean notice of an adverse claim.

Purchasers for value are affected by notice, actual or constructive (Law of Property Act, 1925, s. 205 (1) (xvii), of mortgages effected before 1926 (Law of Property Act, 1925, Sch. 1 Pts. VII, VIII), trusts, settlements and equities of every kind created or arising before 1926, restrictive covenants and equitable easements created before 1926, and estate contracts made before 1926, unless the benefit has been acquired after 1925 and not registered. On the other hand, purchasers for value will not be affected by notice of the following conveyances and transactions of which the legal title or effect has not been perfected by registration under the Land Charges Act, 1972, before completion of the purchase: land charges in Class A of s. 2 of that Act created after 1888 or acquired after 1888, and not registered within the first year after conveyance; land charges in Class B of s. 2; charges in Class C of s. 2, where the charge is created or transferred after 1925, including mortgages, not excepting first mortgages not completed by possession of the title deeds and required to be registered; any equitable charge acquired after 1925 which is registrable under Class C (ii) and (iii) of s. 2, and under Class D of s. 2, charges for death duties on deaths after 1925, restrictive covenants made after 1925, and equitable easements arising after 1925. Further, purchasers for money or money's worth of a legal estate will not, but all other purchasers will, be affected by notice of an unregistered estate contract within s. 2, including contracts to make a settlement of land made or acquired after 1925. The Land Charges Act, 1972, does not apply to registered land, with a few exceptions. See ANNUITY; LAND CHARGE; REGISTERED LAND.

A purchaser for valuable consideration, without notice of a prior equitable right, who obtains the legal estate at the time of his purchase, is entitled to priority in equity, as well as at law, according to the maxim: " Where conflicting equities are equal, the law shall prevail." Nor will equity prevent a bona fide purchaser without notice from protecting himself against a person claiming under a prior equitable title, by getting in the outstanding legal estate, because, as the equities of both are equal, the purchaser should not be deprived of the advantage of his superior activity or diligence. And where he has merely the best right to call for the legal estate, he is entitled to the protection of equity (*Bassett* v. *Nosworthy* (1673) Rep. *temp.* Finch 102). The application of this doctrine has been modified by the Land Charges Act, 1972, the Land Registration Act, 1925, and the Law of Property Act, 1925, and by the fact that not only the first but all subsequent legal mortgages of a legal estate are now legal estates, and tacking or getting in the legal estate by a subsequent mortgagee and squeezing out an intervening mortgagee has been abolished by the Law of Property Act, 1925, s. 94, except in regard to further advances under the statutory conditions. See FURTHER ADVANCE; MORTGAGE.

Notice of a memorandum relating to restrictive covenants or easements endorsed on one of the title deeds which are not handed to a purchaser under a title common to other parties will affect purchasers of other parts of the land under the same title (Law of Property Act, 1925, s. 200), but without pre-judice to any obligation to register as land charges, restrictive covenants of freehold land, estate contracts and equitable easements, liberties or privileges created or registrable after 1925 (Land Charges Act, 1972, s. 2). Notice of a previous assent or conveyance on the probate or grant of administration will constitute notice to subsequent purchasers under the same title (Administration of Estate Act, 1925, s. 36). By the Law of Property Act, 1925, ss. 137, 138, trustees who have received notices of equitable interests are obliged to produce them to any person interested in the equitable interest, at the cost of the latter.

In regard to priority of charges, the Law of Property Act, 1925, s. 97 (as amended by the Law of Property Act, 1969, ss. 16, 17, Sch. 2 Pt. II; Land Charges Act, 1972, Sch. 3 para. 1), provides that every mortgage affecting a legal estate in land after 1925, whether legal or equitable (not being a mortgage protected by deposit of documents relating to the legal estate affected), is to rank according to its date of registration as a land charge. Mortgages and charges of registered land do not come within this rule. See DEARLE v. HALL, RULE IN; LAND CHARGE; MORTGAGE; PRIORITY; REGISTRATION OF TITLE TO LAND.

An entry on the register affects the registered proprietor of registered land and persons deriving title under him with notice of the estate, claim or other matter comprised in the notice (Land Registration Act, 1925, s. 48). Leases exceeding 21 years, annuities or rentcharge, severance of mines or minerals, land charges and deposits of land certificates are among the matters of which notice may be entered on the register.

As to notice of the assignment of a chose in action, see CHOSE.

See LIS PENDENS; PRIORITY; REGISTRATION OF TITLE ETC.; TACKING.

Notice in lieu of service. See SUMMONS.

Notice of accident. See ACCIDENT; ACCIDENTS, NOTICE OF.

Notice of action. By numerous statutes, *e.g.,* by the Poor Law Amendment Act, 1834, it was enacted that no action should be brought against persons acting in pursuance of these statutes, until the expiration of a certain time after notice in writing had been given to the defendant that such action would be brought. This requirement was abrogated by the Public Authorities Protection Act, 1893. But where notice of action is required under a local or personal Act, such notice must still be given.

Notice of admission. Notice of admission of fact is given under R.S.C., Ord. 27, r. 2. See ADMISSION.

Notice of breaches. See PARTICULARS OF BREACHES AND OBJECTIONS.

Notice of claim. See CITATION.

Notice of dishonour. The Bills of Exchange Act, 1882, s. 49, contains rules as to notice of dishonour.

The notice must be given by or on behalf of the holder or of an indorser himself liable.

The notice may be given in writing or by personal communication. If written it need not be signed, and an insufficient written notice may be supplemented by an oral communication.

The notice may be given as soon as the bill is dishonoured, and must be given within a reasonable time thereafter. In the absence of special circumstances notice is not deemed to have been given within a reasonable time unless, when the person giving and the person to receive notice reside in the same place, the notice is given or sent off in time to reach the latter on the day after the dishonour of the bill, and where the person giving and the person to receive notice reside in different places, the notice is sent off on the day after the dishonour of the bill if there is a post at a convenient hour on that day, and if there is no such post on that day, then by the next post thereafter. See BILL OF EXCHANGE.

Notice of intended prosecution. See the Road Traffic Act, 1972, s. 179; *Groome* v. *Driscoll* [1969] 3 All E.R. 1638n; *Nicholson* v. *Tapp* [1972] 1 W.L.R. 1044.

Notice of motion. Unless the court gives leave for shorter notice, there must be at least two clear days between the service of a notice of motion and the day named in the notice for hearing of the motion (R.S.C., Ord. 8, r. 2). As to the exclusion of Saturday, Sunday, a bank holiday, Christmas Day or Good Friday see Ord. 3, r. 2. See MOTION.

Notice of objections. See PARTICULARS OF BREACHES AND OBJECTIONS.

Notice of trial. Notice of trial is no longer necessary in any action; but in Queen's Bench actions for trial out of London, the plaintiff must give the defendant seven days' notice of his intention to lodge with the District Registrar for the place of trial his certificate of readiness (Practice Direction (Trial out of London), para. (2) [1964] 1 W.L.R. 1272).

If a plaintiff does not, within the period fixed, set down the action for trial, the defendant may set down the action for trial or may apply to the court to dismiss the action for want of prosecution (R.S.C., Ord. 34, r. 2).

Notice of writ of summons, etc. In an action in the High Court, when the plaintiff has obtained leave, under R.S.C., Ord. 11, r. 1, to serve a writ or a notice of a writ on a defendant out of the jurisdiction then, unless service is to be effected in Scotland, Northern Ireland, the Isle of Man or the Channel Islands, the leave granted is leave to serve out of the jurisdiction a notice of the writ and not the writ (Ord. 11, r. 3). This is done because it is considered inappropriate to serve a foreigner in a foreign State with a mandate in the Queen's name. Service out of the jurisdiction of an originating summons, petition, notice of motion is permissible with the leave of the court under Ord. 11, r. 9.

If the defendant has gone out of the jurisdiction to evade service, substituted service may be ordered under Ord. 65, r. 4 (*Re Urquhart* (1890) 24 Q.B.D. 723). See SERVICE OF PROCESS.

Notice to admit. The parties to a suit may agree to admit at the trial documents and facts.

Notices to admit or produce documents may be served under R.S.C., Ord. 27, r. 5. Notice to admit facts may be given under r. 2. See ADMISSIONS (IN CIVIL PROCEEDINGS).

Notice to proceed. In a cause or matter in which there has been no proceeding for a year, the party who desires to proceed must give the other party a month's notice of his intention to do so (R.S.C., Ord. 3, r. 6).

Notice to produce. At any time before the trial of an action, any party to an action or other proceeding may give any other party notice to produce for his inspection any document referred to in the pleadings or affidavits of the party to whom the notice is given: and if he refuses to produce it without good cause, an order for inspection may be obtained from the court (Ord. 24, rr. 10, 11).

See DISCOVERY; INSPECTION; PRODUCTION.

Notice to quit. Where there is a tenancy of land or tenements from year to year, or other like indefinite period, a notice to quit is required, to enable either the landlord or the tenant to determine the tenancy without the consent of the other. As a general rule, no particular form is required.

In some cases the length of notice required is fixed by special agreement between the lessor and lessee, in other cases it is fixed by a local custom, and in other cases by the general law of the land. Where a tenancy from year to year exists, without a special agreement or local custom as to its determination, half a year's notice, expiring at the end of the first or some other year of the tenancy, must be given; thus, if the tenancy commenced on March 25, notice to quit must be given on or before September 29, expiring on March 25 following (*Quartermaine* v. *Selby* (1888) 5 T.L.R. 223). In the case of an agricultural holding a notice to quit is void if it purports to terminate the tenancy earlier than twelve months from the end of the year of the tenancy during which the notice is served (Agricultural Holdings Act, 1948, s. 23) and the tenant may serve a counternotice, in which case the notice to quit does not operate unless the Agricultural Land Tribunal (*q.v.*) consents to its operation (s. 24, as amended by the Agriculture Act, 1958, s. 3, and the Agriculture (Miscellaneous Provisions) Act, 1963, s. 19 (6)). By the Rent Act, 1957, s. 16, no notice by a landlord or a tenant to quit any premises let as a dwelling is valid unless given not less than four weeks before the date on which it is to take

effect. See also the Rent Act, 1968, s. 12 (4). The notice must be in writing, and contain such information as may be prescribed (Housing Act, 1974, s. 123).

If a tenant continues in possession by consent after his lease has expired, or rent has been received, a notice must be given before he can be ejected, for the law implies a tacit renovation of the contract, and in such cases the tenant usually holds from year to year upon the former terms. No fresh notice, however, is necessary where a tenant, after having given or been given a notice, contumaciously or wilfully holds over, and becomes liable for double rent according to the Distress for Rent Act, 1737, s. 18. Where a lessee holds under a void demise, no notice is necessary; but where a lease, granted by a tenant for life under a limited power of leasing which exceeded his power, was void, and not capable of being confirmed by the remainder-man, but the remainder-man received money as rent after the death of the tenant for life, it was held to be an admission of a tenancy from year to year, and that a notice to quit had to be given before any ejectment could be brought.

If the tenant dies his personal representatives have the same interest in the land as their testator or intestate had, and are, therefore, entitled to the same notice to quit.

No notice to quit is necessary where the tenant does an act which amounts to a disavowal of the title of the lessor; as where the tenant has attorned to some other person, or answered an application for rent by saying that his connection as tenant with the party applying has ceased.

An oral notice to quit by a tenant under a parol lease is sufficient, but where a power is given to determine a lease on giving a notice in writing, it cannot be determined on giving an oral notice.

A notice to quit given by a mortgagor before default was held a good notice to determine the tenancy; and a notice given to a steward of a corporation is sufficient, without additional evidence that he had an authority under seal from the corporation for such purpose. A receiver appointed by the court, with a general authority to let the lands to tenants from year to year, has authority to determine such tenancies by a regular notice to quit. A mere agent to receive rents has no implied authority to give a notice to quit, but an agent to receive rents and let has authority to determine a tenancy. An agent ought to have authority to give such notice at the time when it begins to operate; for a recognition subsequent to that date of the authority will not make the notice good (*Doe* d. *Mann* v. *Walters* (1830) 10 B. & C. 625). A notice to quit by an agent of an agent is not sufficient without a recognition by the principal. A notice on an under-tenant, given by the original lessor, is not good.

The common form of notice by a landlord, in the case of a tenancy from year to year, which was held to be good in *Hirst* v. *Horn* (1840) 6 M. & W. 393, is as follows: " I hereby give you notice to quit and deliver up possession of the premises   which you hold of me as tenant thereof on the   day of   next or at the expiration of the year of your tenancy which shall expire next after the end of one-half year from the service of this notice. Dated this   day of 19 . A. B."

The notice should be clear and certain, neither ambiguous nor optional (*Phipps* v. *Rogers* (1924) 40 T.L.R. 845).

Leaving a notice to quit at the tenant's house with a servant, without further proof of its having been explained to the servant or that it came to the tenant's hands, is not sufficient.

If a landlord receives or distrains for rent due after the expiration of a notice to quit it is a waiver of that notice, and giving a second notice to quit may amount to waiver of a notice previously given. If a landlord has given a notice to quit, and the tenant holds over, the landlord cannot waive his notice and distrain for rent subsequently accruing. If, at the end of the year (where there has been a tenancy from year to year), the landlord accepts another person as his tenant in substitution for the former tenant, without any surrender in writing, such acceptance and substitution is a surrender and dispenses with a notice to quit.

In order to determine a periodic tenancy (*e.g.*, a tenancy from week to week or from quarter to quarter), a notice to quit must be one which expires at the end of a period of the tenancy (*Queen's Club Gardens* v. *Bignell* [1924] 1 K.B. 117; *Bathavon R.D.C.* v. *Carlile* [1958] 1 Q.B. 461).

Under the Rent Restriction Acts the service of a notice to quit on a controlled tenant terminates the contractual tenancy, but the tenant is entitled to remain in possession as a statutory tenant and no order for possession can be made against him unless the conditions in the Acts are satisfied. See RENT RESTRICTION.

Notice to third party, *i.e.*, to a person not being a party to the writ of summons in an action. See CITATION; THIRD PARTY.

Notice to treat, the notice which a public body having compulsory powers for the purchase of land is bound to give to the persons interested in any land which it is empowered and desires to purchase. The notice demands particulars of the estate and interest of the persons to whom it is given, and states that the public body is willing to treat for the purchase of the land (Lands Clauses Consolidation Act, 1845, s. 18). If the parties do not agree as to the compensation to be paid the amount is settled by the Lands Tribunal (*q.v.*). A notice to treat may be withdrawn under the Land Compensation Act, 1961, s. 31, on payment of compensation.

Noting, the making of a memorandum or note on a bill of exchange by a notary which states that he has presented the bill for payment or acceptance, and that it has been dishonoured. It consists of his initials and charges, and the date, and, in the case of foreign bills, is considered as preparatory to a formal protest (*q.v.*). The duty of a notary in protesting a bill consists in three parts: demanding, noting and protesting. To preserve the recourse against the drawer or indorser of an inland bill it is not necessary to note or protest it. Noting is for business purposes generally taken as showing due presentment. The expenses of noting can be recovered as liquidated damages (Bills of Exchange Act, 1882, s. 57).

Although, in the case of inland bills of exchange, neither noting nor protesting is necessary, the rule is different in the case of a dishonoured foreign bill, which should be taken to a notary on the day it is refused acceptance or payment, and it is his business to note, demand, and protest it; and notice of this must be sent the same day to the drawer and indorsers, with a copy of the bill, if the drawer and indorsers are abroad, but mere notice is sufficient if they are in England. A bill must be noted not later than the next succeeding day of business after the day of dishonour (Bills of Exchange Act, 1882, s. 51; Bills of Exchange (Time of Noting) Act, 1917). See PROTEST.

Notorious. In the law of evidence, matters deemed notorious do not require to be proved. There does not seem to be any recognised rule as to what matters are to be deemed notorious; cases have occurred in which the state of society or public feeling has been treated as notorious, *e.g.*, during times of sedition.

Nova causa interveniens, a new cause intervening. In general, consequences cease to be direct if they are interrupted by a new intervening cause. See NOVUS ACTUS INTERVENIENS.

Nova constitutio futuris formam imponere debet non praeteritis (2 Co. Inst. 292). (A new law ought to regulate what is to follow, not the past.) It is a general principle that no statute shall be construed so as to have a retrospective operation, unless its language is such as plainly to require that construction; and this involves the subordinate rule that a statute is not to be construed so as to have a greater retrospective operation than its language renders necessary. Except in special cases, an Act ought to be construed so as to interfere as little as possible with vested rights; and where the words admit of another construction, they should not be so construed as to impose disabilities not existing at the passing of the Act. See LEX PROSPICIT, ETC.

Nova custuma, an imposition or duty. See ANTIQUA CUSTUMA.

Nova oblata. See OBLATA.

Nova statuta, the statutes from the year 1327 to 1483. They were first printed in 1485 by Maclinia; and they were reprinted by Pynson about twenty years later. See ANTIQUA STATUTA; VETERA STATUTA.

Novae Narrationes (new counts). The collection called *Novae Narrationes* contains pleadings in actions during the reign of Edward III. It was first printed about the year 1515. It consists principally of declarations, but there are sometimes pleas and subsequent pleadings. The *Articuli ad Novas Narrationes* is usually subjoined to this book, and is a treatise on the method of pleading. It first treats of actions and courts, and then goes through each particular writ, and the declaration upon it, accompanied with directions and illustrated by precedents (3 Bl.Comm. 297; 3 Reeves, c. xvi, 152).

See ARTICULI AD NOVAS NARRATIONES; NARRATIO.

Novale, land newly converted from pasture to tillage; also fallow land, that is to say, land which lies untilled after either two years or one year of tillage (Tomlin).

Novatio, the renewal or remaking of an existing obligation; the transmutation of an obligation so that it ceases to exist and is renewed as a new obligation. The preceding obligation might have been contracted in any form; the new obligation had to be *verbis* or *literis* and bound either civilly or naturally (Civil Law).

Novatio non praesumitur. (A novation is not presumed.)

Novation, where the promisee in a contract agrees to accept another person as the person to be bound in lieu of the original promisor. Where a company or partnership transfers its liabilities to another company or partnership the question frequently arises whether there has been a novation, that is, whether the creditors or promisees have agreed to accept the liability of the new company or partnership in discharge of the old company or partnership. Slight evidence is sufficient to show that a creditor who continues his dealings with incoming partners accepts the new firm as his debtors instead of the old firm (*Smith* v. *Patrick* [1901] A.C. 282). A novation of a contract includes a release of an existing debt (*Re United Railways of Havana and Regla Warehouses* [1961] A.C. 1007).

Novel disseisin, recent disseisin. See ASSISE OF NOVEL DISSEISIN.

NOVELLAE

Novellae, those constitutions of the civil law which were made after the publication of the Theodosian Code; sometimes the Julian edition only is meant.

The *Novellae, or Novellae Constitutiones,* form a part of the *Corpus Juris.* Most of them were published in Greek, and their Greek title is Αὐτοχράτορος Ἰουστινιάνον Αὐγούστον Νεαραί Διατάξεις. Some of them were published in Latin, and some in both languages.

The first of these *Novellae* of Justinian belongs to the year 535, and the latest to the year 565, but most of them were published between the years 535 and 539. These *Constitutiones* were published after the completion of the second edition of the Code, for the purpose of supplying what was deficient in that work. Indeed, it appears that on the completion of his second edition of the new Code, Justinian designed to form many new constitutions which he might publish into a body by themselves, so as to render a third revision of the Code unnecessary, and that he contemplated giving to this body of law the name of *Novellae Constitutiones* (Just. in Cod., cordi nobis, s. 4).

It does not, however, appear that any official compilation of these new constitutions appeared in the lifetime of Justinian. The Greek text of the *Novellae,* as we now have them, consists of 168 *Novellae,* of which 159 belong to Justinian, and the rest to Justin II and Tiberius; they are generally divided into chapters. There is a Latin epitome of these *Novellae* by Julian, a teacher of law at Constantinople, which contains 125 *Novellae.* The epitome was probably made in the time of Justinian, and the author was probably Antecessor, at Constantinople. There is also another collection of 134 *Novellae* in a Latin version made from the Greek text. This collection is generally called *Liber Authenticorum;* the compiler and the time of the compilation are unknown. This collection was made independently of the Greek compilation. It is divided into nine *collationes,* and the *collationes* are divided into *tituli.* The most complete work on the history of the *Novellae* is by Biener, *Geschichte der Novellen.* See CORPUS JURIS CIVILIS.

Novelty. An objection to a patent on the ground that the invention is not new or original is called an objection for want of novelty. Only the first inventor is entitled to apply for a patent (Patents Act, 1949, s. 1 (1)). A design also is to be registered only if it is either new or original (Registered Designs Act, 1949, s. 1 (2)); but the degree of novelty required in the case of a design is less than that required in the case of a patent. See DISCLAIMER; PATENTS; PUBLICATION.

Novitas non tam utilitate prodest quam novitate perturbat (Jenk., Cent. 167). (A new thing does not produce by its utility a benefit commensurate with the disturbance caused by its novelty.) See NIHIL TEMERE, ETC.; OMNIS INNOVATIO, ETC.

Noviter ad notitiam perventa, matters newly come to the knowledge of a party.

Noviter perventa, or *noviter ad notitiam perventa,* in ecclesiastical procedure, are facts newly come to the knowledge of a party to a cause. Leave to plead facts *noviter perventa* is generally given, in a proper case, even after the pleadings are closed, or on appeal.

Novum judicium non dat jus novum, sed declarat antiquum; quia judicium est juris dictum et per judicium jus est noviter revelatum quod diu fuit velatum (10 Co.Rep. 42). (A new judgment does not make new law, but declares the old law; because a judgment is the enunciation of law, and by judgment the law is newly revealed which was previously hidden.) This maxim is based on the theory that within the common law—which had "neither fault nor flaw"—there was an amorphous body of law, covering every conceivable case, which had only to be put into shape by the judges in their judgments. The law was in fact the Sleeping Beauty and the judge was the Fairy Prince. See DORMIT, ETC.

Novus actus interveniens, a new act intervening. A person is not liable for damage done if the chain of causation between his act and the damage is broken by the intervening act of a third person unless it is a foreseeable consequence of his own act (*Liesbosch Dredger* v. *Edison* [1933] A.C. 449; *Haynes* v. *Harwood* [1935] 1 K.B. 153; *Perry* v. *Kendricks Transport* [1956] 1 W.L.R. 85; *Baker* v.

T. E. Hopkins & Son [1959] 1 W.L.R. 966).

Novus homo, a pardoned criminal or discharged insolvent; a *parvenu.*

Noxa sequitur caput. (Guilt follows the person.) In the civil law the purchaser of a slave or an animal which had done damage took over the liability to make good the damage.

Noxal action, an action for damage done by a slave or an animal (Civil Law).

Noxious plants. See WEEDS, INJURIOUS.

Nuces colligere, to gather hazel nuts. This was formerly one of the services imposed by lords upon their inferior tenants (Paroch.Antiq. 495).

Nuclear power. See ATOMIC ENERGY.

Nuda pacta obligationem non parit (Dig. 2, 14, 7, s. 4). (A naked promise does not beget an obligation.)

Nudi consensus obligatio contrario consensu dissolvitur (Dig. 50, 17, 35). (The binding force of a contract made without consideration is terminated by an agreement to the contrary effect.)

Nudum pactum, a bare agreement, that is to say, an agreement made without consideration and upon which, unless it is under seal, no action will lie, the maxim being *ex nudo pacto non oritur actio* (Noy, Max. 24). See CONSIDERATION.

Nudum pactum est ubi nulla subest causa praeter conventionem; sed ubi subest causa, fit obligatio, et parit actionem (Plow. 309). (A contract is a naked contract (*nudum pactum*) where there is no consideration except the agreement: but where there is consideration the contract becomes binding and constitutes a cause of action.)

Nuisance [Fr. *nuire*, to hurt], something noxious or offensive; any unauthorised act which, without direct physical interference, materially impairs the use and enjoyment by another of his property, or prejudicially affects his health, comfort, or convenience.

Nuisance may be distinguished from negligence in that nuisance is an act or omission causing injury, the injury itself giving rise to an action for damages, while a person suffering from damage due to negligence must prove that the damage was caused by some want of care, according to its degree which was required in the particular circumstances of the case.

Actions against persons or public undertakings for damage under statutory powers are generally founded on negligence. Where the actual method of exercising the power creating a nuisance is indicated by the statute, negligence in the authorised method may be actionable. The onus appears to be on a defendant pleading that the nuisance was inevitable and compulsory by statute to show that care was used to prevent a nuisance when conforming with the statute (*Manchester Corporation* v. *Farnsworth* [1930] A.C. 171). If the power is permissive only, due care must be exercised not to infringe the rights of other people; while statutory powers which are without prejudice to such rights may give rise to an action for damages without any proof of negligence.

Nuisance is of two kinds, public and private.

A public or common nuisance is an act which interferes with the enjoyment of a right which all members of the community are entitled to, such as the right to fresh air, to travel on the highways, not to be exposed to danger to health from infectious diseases, unwholesome food, etc. Hence, if a person carries on a manufacture from which noxious fumes are emitted, or exposes for sale unwholesome food, or stops up or obstructs a highway, or allows buildings belonging to him near a highway to become ruinous, he commits a public nuisance. " A public nuisance is a nuisance which is so widespread in its range or so indiscriminate in its effect that it would not be reasonable to expect one person to take proceedings on his own responsibility to put a stop to it, but that it should be taken on the responsibility of the community at large ": *per* Denning L.J. in *Att.-Gen.* v. *P.Y.A. Quarries* [1957] 2 Q.B. 169.

For a public nuisance to be established, the prosecution must prove that the act complained of affected a considerable number of persons or a section of the public. Actual rather than potential danger or risk must be proved (*R.* v. *Madden* [1975] 1 W.L.R. 1379 (bomb hoax)).

A public nuisance may give rise to proceedings of different kinds: it may give ground for an indictment; it may give ground for a civil action for an injunction, formerly called an information, by the Attorney-General, either of his own motion or at the instance of some person aggrieved, called the relator; or it may give rise to an action at the suit of some private individual who is specially injured by it beyond the rest of the public, for a public nuisance may be a tort as well as a crime.

A private nuisance is an unlawful interference with a person's use or enjoyment of land, or of some right over, or in connection with it. Thus, if a man builds a house so close to mine that his roof overhangs mine, and the water flows off his roof upon mine, this is a nuisance, for which an action will lie; similarly, if my neighbour carries on a noisy or offensive trade, or if anyone injuriously interferes with my watercourse, market, ferry, or the like. The use of premises for purposes of prostitution may amount to a nuisance (*Thompson-Schwab* v. *Costaki* [1956] 1 W.L.R. 335).

The remedy for a nuisance is by abatement (*q.v.*), or by an action for damages, injunction, or mandamus. See ASSISE OF NUISANCE; DISTURBANCE; NOCUMENTO AMOVENDO; PRESCRIPTION; TORT.

Where there is statutory immunity from actions of nuisance arising out of the use of public works, compensation for depreciation of the value of land due to noise, vibration, smell, fumes, smoke, artificial lighting or the discharge of liquid or solid substances may be claimed under the Land Compensation Act, 1973, ss. 1–19. A claim may be made in respect of the use of a highway whether or not an action for nuisance arises (ss. 1 (6), 17)).

Compensation is not payable on any claim unless the amount of the compensation exceeds £50 (s. 7). Disputes as to compensation are referred to the Lands Tribunal (s. 16). Power to mitigate the injurious effect of public works is contained in ss. 20–28.

Any premises in such a state as to be a nuisance or injurious to health, any animal so kept, any chimney (not being the chimney of a private dwelling-house) sending forth black smoke in such quantity as to be a nuisance, and other nuisances described in the Public Health Act, 1875, s. 91, reproduced and extended by the Public Health Act, 1936, ss. 91–100, and by s. 107 (offensive trades), s. 108 (fried fish), may be dealt with summarily by complaint before the justices by a local authority, who are bound to inspect their district to detect nuisances, to serve notices requiring abatement, and to make complaint to the justices on the notices not being complied with. As to the metropolis, see the London Government Act, 1963, s. 40, Sch. 11 Pt. I para. 36. See also the Clean Air Act, 1956, the Public Health Act, 1961, s. 26 (defective premises), s. 27 (ruinous and dilapidated buildings and neglected sites), s. 28 (new buildings overreaching adjacent chimneys), s. 29 (demolitions), s. 30 (cellars and rooms below subsoil water level), ss. 31, 32 (food storage accommodation), s. 33 (bathrooms), s. 34 (accumulation of rubbish), ss. 35–37 (filthy or verminous premises or articles). See also the G.L.C. (General Powers) Act, 1967, s. 25; Civic Amenities Act, 1967, s. 26; Local Government Act, 1972, Sch. 14 para. 37; Control of Pollution Act, 1974, Sch. 2 paras. 11, 12.

Dust, effluvia or steam caused by any trade, business, manufacture or process which is prejudicial to the health of, or a nuisance to, the inhabitants of the neighbourhood is a statutory nuisance (Public Health Act, 1936, s. 92 (1) (*d*); Public Health Act, 1961, s. 72). See AMENITIES.

Something which began by not being a nuisance cannot grow into one by mere lapse of time (*Radstock Co-operative & Industrial Society* v. *Norton-Radstock U.D.C.* [1968] Ch. 605).

Recurring public nuisances may be restrained by a prohibition order issued by the local authority followed, if necessary, by a nuisance order made by the justices (Public Health (Recurring Nuisances) Act, 1969). Once a statutory nuisance has been proved, justices are bound to make a nuisance order under the Public Health Act, 1936, s. 94 (2) but have a wide discretion as to the extent and timing of remedial work ordered and may have regard to the imminence of demolition of the premises in question (*Nottingham City District Council* v. *Newton* [1974] 1 W.L.R. 923). See INJUNCTION; NOISE; SMOKE.

Nul prendra advantage de son tort demesne (2 Co.Inst. 713). (No man shall profit by wrong that he does.) See Ex Turpi Causa Non Oritur Actio; Nullus Commodum Capere Potest de Injuria Sua Propria.

Nul tiel agard (no such award), a plea traversing an award. Under this plea a defendant could not object to the award in point of law (1 Salk. 72).

Nul tiel record, Issue of, a traverse that there was no such record. This was the proper form of issue whenever a question arose as to what had judicially taken place in a superior court of record.

It was the plea of a plaintiff on the defendant's alleging matters of record in bar of the plaintiff's action. It was sometimes the plea of a defendant, as in an action on a judgment (Tomlin).

See Failure of Record; Judgment; Mittimus; Record, Trial by.

Nul tort, Plea of, a traverse in a real action that no wrong was done; it was a species of the general issue.

Null and void, void (*q.v.*).

Nulla bona (no goods), the name given to the return made by a sheriff, sequestrator, or other officer, to a writ or warrant authorising him to seize the chattels of a person, when he has been unable to find any to seize. It is a not infrequent return to a writ of *fieri facias* (*q.v.*).

Nulla curia quae recordum non habet potest imponere finem, neque aliquem mandare carceri; quia ista spectant tantummodo ad curias de recordo (8 Co.Rep. 60). (No court which has not a record can impose a fine, or commit any person to prison; because those powers belong only to courts of record.) This does not apply to statutory courts such as magistrates' courts.

Nulla impossibilia aut inhonesta sunt praesumenda; vera autem et honesta et possibilia (Co.Litt. 78). (Things which are impossible or shameful are not to be presumed, but rather things which are true and seemly and possible.) Coke is speaking of the question whether a will was obtained by collusion.

Nulla pactione effici potest ut dolus praestetur (Dig. 2, 14, 27). (By no contract can it be arranged that a man shall be indemnified against responsibility for his own fraud.)

Nulla poena sine lege. (There should be no punishment without previous legal authority.)

Nullity of marriage. A defective marriage may be either void *ipso jure*, or merely voidable. A void marriage is one which will be regarded by every court in any case in which the existence of the marriage is in issue as never having taken place, and can be so treated by the parties to it without the necessity of any decree annulling it; whereas a voidable marriage is one that will be regarded by every court as a valid subsisting marriage until it is annulled by decree of a court of competent jurisdiction (*De Reneville* v. *De Reneville* [1948] P. 100). A void marriage may be put in issue at any time, even after the parties to it are dead, but a voidable marriage can probably only be put in issue by one of the parties to it.

A marriage which took place before August 1, 1971, is void *ipso jure* in the following cases: where at the time of the ceremony of marriage one spouse was already married and the other party to the previous marriage was still alive and the marriage was still subsisting; possibly where the marriage was entered by threats or duress; where there was a mistake as to identity or the nature, but not the effect, of the ceremony; where one spouse was insane at the time of the ceremony; where the parties were within the prohibited degrees of consanguinity and affinity; where there was non-observance of the due forms and ceremonies; in case of non-age; possibly where one spouse was intoxicated at the time of the ceremony; and where the marriage was a sham.

A marriage which took place before August 1, 1971, is voidable on any of the following grounds: (1) impotence, *i.e.,* inability of one of the parties to consummate it; (2) probably where the marriage was induced by threats or duress, or where one of the parties was in a state of intoxication at the time of the ceremony; (3) wilful refusal of the other party to consummate it; (4) where either party was at the time of the marriage of unsound mind or a mental defective within the meaning of the Mental Deficiency Acts, 1913 to 1938, or subject to recurrent fits of insanity or epilepsy; (5) where either party was at the time of the marriage suffering from venereal disease in a communicable form; and (6) where the wife was at the time of the marriage pregnant by some person other than the petitioner (Matrimonial Causes Act, 1965, s. 9 (1)).

The court must not grant a decree in cases (4), (5) or (6) unless it is satisfied that the petitioner was at the time of the marriage ignorant of the facts alleged, that proceedings were instituted within a year from the date of the marriage, and that marital intercourse with the consent of the petitioner has not taken place since the discovery by the petitioner of the existence of the grounds for a decree (Matrimonial Causes Act, 1965, s. 9 (2); Nullity of Marriage Act, 1971, ss. 3 (4), 7 (3)).

Where a decree of nullity is granted in respect of a voidable marriage any child who would have been the legitimate child of the parties to the marriage if it had been dissolved instead of being annulled at the date of the decree is deemed to be their legitimate child notwithstanding the annulment (Matrimonial Causes Act, 1965, s. 11). See Jackson, *Formation and Annulment of Marriage.*

A marriage which takes place after July 31, 1971, is void on the following grounds only, that is to say (a) that it is not a valid marriage because (i) the parties are within the prohibited degrees of relationship (see AFFINITY), or (ii) either party is under the age of sixteen, or (iii) the parties have knowingly and wilfully intermarried in disregard of the rules laid down by s. 49 of the Marriage Act, 1949, and s. 13 of the Marriage (Registrar General's Licence) Act, 1970; (b) that at the time of the marriage either party was already lawfully married; (c) that the parties are not respectively male and female; if in the case of a polygamous marriage entered into outside England and Wales, that either party was domiciled in England and Wales (Matrimonial Causes Act, 1973, s. 11).

A marriage which takes place after July 31, 1971, is voidable on the following grounds only, that is to say (a) that the marriage has not been consummated owing to the incapacity of either party to consummate it; (b) that the marriage has not been consummated owing to the wilful refusal of the respondent to consummate it; (c) that either party did not validly consent to it, whether in consequence of duress, mistake, unsoundness of mind or otherwise; (d) that at the time of the marriage either party, though capable of giving a valid consent, was suffering (whether continuously or intermittently) from mental disorder (see MENTAL HEALTH) of such a kind or to such an extent as to be unfitted for marriage; (e) that at the time of the marriage the respondent was suffering from venereal disease in a communicable form; (f) that at the time of the marriage the respondent was pregnant by some person other than the petitioner (Matrimonial Causes Act, 1973, s. 12). As to marriages before August 1, 1971, see Sch. 1 Pt. II.

Whatever the date of the marriage, the court may not grant a decree on the ground that the marriage is voidable if the petitioner, knowing that it was open to him to have the marriage avoided, led the respondent reasonably to believe that he would not seek to do so; if it would be unjust to the respondent to grant a decree. Without prejudice to the above, the court may not grant a decree on the grounds mentioned in paragraph (c), (d), (e) or (f) of s. 12 above unless proceedings are instituted within three years of the date of the marriage. Without prejudice to the above, the court may not grant a decree on the grounds mentioned in paragraph (e) or (f) of s. 12 above unless satisfied that the petitioner was at the time of the marriage ignorant of the facts alleged (s. 13). A decree of nullity granted after July 31, 1971, in respect of a voidable marriage operates to annul the marriage only as respects any time after the decree has been made absolute and the marriage, notwithstanding the decree, is treated as if it had existed up to that time (Matrimonial Causes Act, 1973, s. 16).

It was held in *Re D'Albroy's Trusts* [1968] 1 W.L.R. 120, that a decree absolute of nullity operated retrospectively so as to nullify the marriage for all purposes, but the Matrimonial Causes

Act, 1973, Sch. 1 para. 12 provides that where a decree of nullity was granted on or before July 31, 1971, in respect of a voidable marriage, any child who would have been a legitimate child of the marriage if at the date of the decree it had been dissolved instead of being annulled is deemed to be legitimate. As to the legitimacy of a child born of a void marriage see the Legitimacy Act, 1976, s. 1. See BASTARD.

Every decree of nullity is, in the first instance, a decree nisi. The decree is normally made absolute after the expiration of three months from the grant of the decree nisi but it may be expedited (Matrimonial Causes Act, 1973, ss. 1 (5), 15; Matrimonial Causes (Decree Absolute) General Order, 1957, Sch. 1 para. 1). The court is not to make a decree absolute unless satisfactory arrangements have been made for the welfare of the children of the family (Matrimonial Causes Act, 1973, s. 41). The court has power to make orders for the custody and education of the children of the family under the age of eighteen (Matrimonial Causes Act, 1973, s. 42). If necessary a child can be committed to the care of a local authority (s. 43) or be made the subject of a supervision order (s. 44).

The court has jurisdiction to entertain proceedings for nullity of marriage if (and only if) either of the parties to the marriage (a) is domiciled in England and Wales on the date when the proceedings are begun, or (b) was habitually resident in England and Wales throughout the period of one year ending with that date, or (c) died before that date and either (i) was at death domiciled in England and Wales or (ii) had been habitually resident in England and Wales throughout the period of one year ending with the date of the death (Domicile and Matrimonial Proceedings Act, 1973, s. 5). And see DOMICILE.

The evidence of a husband or wife is admissible to prove that marital intercourse did or did not take place between them during any period (Matrimonial Causes Act, 1973, s. 48 (1)) but a husband or wife is not compellable in any criminal proceedings to give such evidence (Matrimonial Causes Act, 1965, s. 43 (1); Civil Evidence Act, 1968, s. 16 (4)).

Evidence on the question of sexual capacity is heard in camera unless the court otherwise directs (Matrimonial Causes Act, 1973, s. 48 (2)).

As to medical inspections in nullity proceedings see Practice Direction (P.D.A.) [1963] 1 W.L.R. 310.

Proceedings for nullity are assigned to the Family Division (*q.v.*) of the High Court (Administration of Justice Act, 1970, s. 1, Sch. 1).

See DECREE; DIVORCE.

Nullius filius, the son of no one; a bastard (*q.v.*).

Nullius hominis auctoritas apud nos valere debet, ut meliora non sequeremur si quis attulerit (Co.Litt. 383). (The authority of no man ought so to prevail with us that we should not adopt better things, if another bring them.) Quoted in connection with a point on which Littleton differed from Newton, C.J., the latter being in the wrong.

Nullum arbitrium (there was no such award), the usual plea, also called *nul tiel agard* (*q.v.*), of a defendant sued on an award, that no award was made.

Nullum crimen sine lege. (There should be no crime without previous law making the deed a crime.)

Nullum crimen sine poena. (There should be no crime without punishment.)

Nullum exemplum est idem omnibus (Co.Litt. 212). (No example is the same to all.) No precedent is the same for all cases: that is to say, alterations in the forms of conveyances are necessary to fit them for particular cases.

Nullum fecerunt arbitrium (they never submitted to arbitration), the plea of a defendant sued upon an award, which denied that there had been an arbitration (Bac.Abr.Arbitr.).

Nullum iniquum est in jure praesumendum (Hard. 61). (The doing of anything contrary to justice is not to be presumed in law.) See IN ODIUM SPOLIATORIS, ETC.

Nullum simile est idem (4 Co.Rep. 18; Co.Litt. 3a). (A thing which is similar to another thing is not the same as that other thing.) One should not be misled by analogies. Another form of the maxim is *nullum simile est idem nisi quatuor pedibus currit*, that is to say, things similar to one another are not the same unless they are on four feet with one another; and yet another form is, *nullum simile quatuor pedibus currit*, that is to say, no simile is exactly on all fours with any other. See ARGUMENTUM A SIMILE, ETC.; TALIS NON, ETC.

Nullum tempus aut locus occurrit regi (2 Co.Inst. 273). (Time never runs against the Crown.) No laches can be imputed to the sovereign, whose time and attention are supposed to be occupied by the cares of government; and therefore the ordinary statutes of limitations did not bind the Crown. But by the Crown Suits Act, 1769, commonly called the Nullum Tempus Act, and the Crown Suits Act, 1861, the common law rule was altered and the Crown was barred by lapse of time in cases within those Acts.

The Limitation Act, 1939, applies to the Crown, but the Act does not apply to Crown proceedings for recovery of tax or duty or interest, or to forfeiture proceedings under the Customs and Excise Act, 1952, or to any proceedings in respect of the forfeiture of a ship: the Act applies to the Crown in right of the Duchy of Lancaster, and to proceedings by or against the Duke of Cornwall (s. 30). The Act does not apply to an action or arbitration for which a period of limitation is prescribed by any other enactment (s. 32).

See NEC TEMPUS, ETC.

Nullus commodum capere potest de injuria sua propria (Co.Litt. 148). (No one can gain an advantage by his own wrong.) The maxim goes much further than to say merely that no man shall profit by his own fraud: he is not allowed to profit by his own mistake, and so where he grants a lease believing that he has a sufficient estate to grant it and purporting to grant thereout, he will not be heard to say that he did not grant it under a power which in fact made the lease valid. See EX TURPI CAUSA NON ORITUR ACTIO; NEMO EX, ETC.; NUL PRENDRA, ETC.

Nullus videtur dolo facere qui suo jure utitur (Dig. 50, 17, 55). (No one is to be deemed a wrongdoer who merely avails himself of his legal rights.)

Numbering. Power is given to local authorities to number houses in streets (Towns Improvement Clauses Act, 1847, ss. 64, 65; Public Health Act, 1875, s.

160; Rural District Councils (Urban Powers) Order, 1949 (No. 2088)).

Nummata, the price of anything in money, as *librata* is the price of a thing by computation of pounds.

Nummata terrae, an acre of land (Spelman).

Nun (*monialis*), a female bound by vows of celibacy, living in company with other nuns in a nunnery or convent. Nuns are excepted from jury service. See JURY.

Nunc pro tunc (now for then). The court sometimes directs a proceeding to be dated as of an earlier date than that on which it was actually taken, or directs that the same effect shall be produced as if it had been taken at an earlier date. Thus, it will direct a judgment to be ante-dated if the entry of it has been delayed by the act of the court, or if the plaintiff has died between the hearing and the date when the judgment was delivered. This is called entering a judgment *nuc pro tunc*. See R.S.C., Ord. 42, r. 3, notes.

Nuncio, a messenger, servant, etc.; a spiritual envoy from the Pope.

Nuncupare heredem, to name an heir publicly before witnesses (Civil Law).

Nuncupate, to declare publicly and solemnly.

Nuncupative will, a verbal testament depending merely upon oral evidence, being declared by the testator *in extremis* before a sufficient number of witnesses and afterwards reduced to writing (2 Bl.Comm. 500).

The Statute of Frauds, 1677, restricted nuncupative wills, except when made by mariners at sea, and soldiers in actual service. Nuncupative wills are abolished by the Wills Act, 1837, s. 9, but with a proviso by s. 11 that any soldier being in actual military service (*q.v.*), or any marine or seaman being at sea, may dispose of his personal estate, as he might have done before the Act. A will made by a soldier under s. 11 accordingly requires no attestation, and s. 15, avoiding gifts to attesting witnesses,..has no application to such a will (*Re Limond* [1915] 2 Ch. 240). The Wills (Soldiers and Sailors) Act, 1918, enlarges the class of persons to whom s. 11 of the Act applies, and extends the right to make wills, without the formalities required by the Act of 1837, to real property in the case of persons within this class. See the Navy and Marines (Wills) Act, 1953, as to the disposal of money and effects under the control of the Admiralty which belonged to certain classes of deceased members of the navy and marines.

Nundination, traffic at fairs and markets; any buying and selling.

Nunquam crescit ex post facto praeteriti delicti aestimatio (Bac.Max.Reg. 8). (Once an offence has been committed its gravity is not increased by any subsequent event.) This is a maxim of Paulus (Dig. 50, 17, 138) which Bacon uses to illustrate the proposition that if A slandered B, a commoner, and B afterwards became a peer, proceedings for *scandalum magnatum* would not be available to B, whose only remedy would be an action on the case. He does not quote it as an authority for the doctrine that penal statutes should not be retrospective.

Nunquam indebitatus. See NEVER INDEBTED, PLEA OF; NIL DEBET.

Nunquam res humanae prospere succedunt ubi negliguntur divinae (Co.Litt. 95). (Human things never prosper where divine things are neglected.) Quoted in an encomium of tenure in frankalmoign.

Nuper obiit, a writ which lay for a sister and co-heir, deforced by her coparcener of lands or tenements whereof their father, brother, or any other common ancestor died seized of an estate in fee simple (Reg.Orig. 226; Fitz.N.B. 197).

It was one of the many writs abolished by the Real Property Limitation Act, 1833, s. 36.

Nuper vicecomes, an ex-sheriff. See DISTRINGAS.

Nuptiae, marriage. *Nuptiae justiae*, legal marriage, was that form of marriage which gave the father *potestas* over the children. The conditions were consent of the parties duly expressed, puberty, and *connubium*, the legal power of contracting marriage (Civil Law).

Nuptial, pertaining to marriage; constituting marriage; used or done in marriage.

Nuptias non concubitus sed consensus facit (Dig. 50, 17, 30). (It is consent, not cohabitation, which makes a marriage.) See CONSENSUS NON, ETC.

Nurseries. Day nurseries for children may be provided in open spaces under the London County Council (General Powers) Act, 1939, s. 71.

Persons maintaining foster children are required to give notice to the local authority (Children Act, 1958, s. 3; Children and Young Persons Act, 1969, s. 53, Sch. 6).

Education authorities may provide nursery schools under the Education Act, 1944, ss. 8, 9; Education (Miscellaneous Provisions) Act, 1948, ss. 3, 4.

Nursery garden. Nursery grounds are within the definition of agricultural land in the General Rate Act, 1967, s. 26 (3).

Nurses. The enactments relating to nurses were consolidated by the Nurses Act, 1957, which provides for a General Nursing Council for England and Wales, for a register of nurses, a roll of assistant nurses and a list of persons neither registered nor enrolled and for the training of nurses. It has been amended by the Nurses (Amendment) Act, 1961, the Teachers of Nursing Act, 1964, the Nurses Act, 1967, and the Nurses Act, 1969. As to nurses' training institutions, see the Tribunals and Inquiries Act, 1958, Sch. 1.

Nurses are excusable as of right from jury service. See JURY.

The enactments relating to agencies for the supply of nurses were consolidated by the Nurses Agencies Act, 1957. It regulates the conduct of agencies for the supply of nurses and the licensing of agencies. It was amended by the Nurses (Amendment) Act, 1961, Sch. 1 para. 12, Sch. 2; the London Government Act, 1963, Sch. 17 para. 17, and the Local Government Act, 1972, Sch. 29 para. 30, Sch. 30.

Nursing homes must be registered and inspected under the Nursing Homes Act, 1975.

Nurture. See GUARDIAN.

Nurus [Lat.], a daughter-in-law.

O

O.B.E. See BRITISH EMPIRE, ETC.

O.E.E.C. See ORGANISATION FOR EUROPEAN ECONOMIC CO-OPERATION.

O.M. See MERIT, ETC.

O. Ni. the course of the Exchequer was that as soon as a sheriff or escheator entered into his account for issues, amerciaments, etc., to mark upon his head O NI, which is as much as to say, *oneratur nisi habet sufficientem exonerationem*, and presently he became the king's debtor and a *debet* was set upon his head, and thereupon the parties *paravaile* became debtors to the sheriff or escheator and discharged against the king (4 Co.Inst. 116).

The effect of this seems to have been that the sheriff, unless he could show cause to the contrary, became himself liable to pay the moneys which he was empowered to get in, but had his remedy over against those who should have paid such moneys.

O.T.C. See OVERSEAS TRADE CORPORATION.

Oath [Sax. *ath*], an appeal to God to witness the truth of a statement. It is called a corporal oath where a witness, when he swears, places his right hand on the Holy Evangelists. It is called a promissory oath when it relates not to past events but to an intention to do something in the future, as in the case of an oath of allegiance.

The Christian religion, though it prohibits swearing, accepts oaths required by legal authority. All who believe in a God, the avenger of falsehood, have always been admitted to give evidence, but the old rule was that all witnesses must take an oath of some kind. Gradually, however, the legislature relaxed this rule, and the privilege of affirming instead of taking an oath was universally granted by the Oaths Act, 1888, by which any person who objects to being sworn and states, as the ground of such objection, either that he has no religious belief, or that the taking of an oath is contrary to his religious belief, is permitted to make his solemn affirmation instead of taking an oath. By s. 3, if an oath has been duly taken, the fact that the person taking it had no religious belief does not affect its validity. S. 5 provides that if a person desires to swear with uplifted hand, in the form and manner in which an oath is usually administered in Scotland, he shall be permitted so to do without further question.

The Oaths Act, 1909, s. 2, enacts that the person taking the oath shall hold the New Testament, or, in the case of a Jew, the Old Testament, in his uplifted hand, and shall say or repeat after the officer administering the oath the words " I swear by Almighty God that . . .," followed by the words of the oath. In the case of children under fourteen the words are " I promise before Almighty God that . . ." (Children and Young Persons Act, 1963, s. 28).

The Statutory Declarations Act, 1835, abolishes unnecessary and extra-judicial oaths, and empowers any justice of the peace, notary public, or other officer authorised to administer an oath to take voluntary declarations in the form specified in the Act (s. 18, Sch.).

Promissory oaths are those required to be taken by persons on their appointment to certain offices, as the oath of allegiance, of which the form is, " I, ——, do swear that I will be faithful and bear true allegiance to Her Majesty Queen Elizabeth II, her heirs and successors, according to law."

By the Promissory Oaths Act, 1868, a number of unnecessary oaths were abolished, and declarations substituted. That Act also provides forms of the oath of allegiance, judicial oath, and official oath to be taken by particular officers. The Promissory Oaths Act, 1871, repeals a number of Acts already impliedly repealed.

The Parliamentary Oaths Act, 1866, requires the oath of allegiance to be taken by members of Parliament before sitting or voting, and the Promissory Oaths Act, 1868, substitutes a new form of oath, but does not otherwise alter the Act of 1866. By the Act of 1866 a Quaker or other person permitted by law to affirm may make affirmation instead of oath, but an atheist, although permitted by law to affirm in a court of justice, could not affirm under this Act. In *Clarke* v. *Bradlaugh* (1881) 7 Q.B.D. 38, the House of Commons, when Bradlaugh was first elected, refused to allow him to make oath, so that he could not take his seat; but on being re-elected to a subsequent Parliament, he made oath without objection.

The Oaths Act, 1888, allows an affirmation in all places and for all purposes. Affirmations may be made when it is not reasonably practicable without inconvenience and delay to administer an oath in the manner appropriate to a person's religious belief (Oaths Act, 1961).

The Interpretation Act, 1889, s. 3, enacts that in every Act passed after 1850 the expressions " oath " and " affidavit " shall, in the case of persons for the time being allowed by law to affirm or declare instead of swearing, include affirmation and declaration, and the expression " swear " shall, in the like case, include affirm and declare.

Every court, judge, justice officer, commissioner, arbitrator or other person having authority to hear evidence may administer an oath to a witness (Evidence Act, 1851, s. 16).

Oaths may be administered by and affidavits sworn before commissioners of oaths (*q.v.*). For other powers of administering oaths see the Commissioners for Oaths Act, 1889, s. 2 (court officers); Bankruptcy Act, 1914, s. 72 (official receiver). By the Perjury Act, 1911, s. 15, " oath " includes " affirmation " and " declaration," and " swear " includes " affirm " and " declare." See PERJURY.

The Oaths and Evidence (Overseas Authorities and Countries) Act, 1963, authorises the administration of oaths and notarial acts by representatives of, and other persons empowered by the authorities of, countries overseas, and by representatives of Her Majesty in posts overseas. British ambassadors, ministers and other diplomatic officers may administer oaths (Commissioners for Oaths Act, 1889, s. 6; Oaths and Evidence (Overseas Authorities and Countries) Act, 1963, s. 3; S.I. 1965 No. 1129). See also the Consular Relations Act, 1968, s. 10.

The administering of unlawful oaths is an offence (Unlawful Oaths Act, 1797; Unlawful Oaths Act, 1812).

See AFFIDAVIT; COMPURGATION; DEPOSITION; EX OFFICIO OATH; FALSE SWEARING; MAKE HIS LAW; RECUSANTS.

Oath ex officio. See EX OFFICIO OATH.

Oath helper. See COMPURGATION.

Oath of allegiance. See OATH.

Oath of office. See PROBATE.

Oats. See GUARANTEED PRICES.

Ob contingentiam. See CONTINGENCY.

Obedience; Obedientia. In the canon law, as it applied before the Reformation, this meant not merely compliance with a command, but a monastic office or the administration of it.

Obedientia est legis essentia (11 Co. Rep. 100). (Obedience is the essence of law.)

Obedientiarius, a monastic officer.

Obit. [Lat. *obiit, obivit,* he died], a funeral solemnity or office for the dead; the anniversary office.

It meant either a requiem mass celebrated while the corpse was in the church before interment or a mass celebrated annually for the repose of the soul of a deceased person. Many churches held lands and received annual payments in consideration of the annual celebration of obits: all such lands and payments were confiscated to the Crown by the statutes 1547, 1 Edw. 6, c. 14, ss. 4, 5, and 1663, 15 Car. 2, c. 9.

As to post-obit bonds, see BOND.

Obiter dictum an opinion not necessary to a judgment and therefore not binding as a precedent. See DICTUM.

Objection. If a document, or question to a witness, tendered by one party is objected to, all the counsel on the side objecting may be heard against the admissibility, and all on the other side may be heard in support; the senior counsel on the first side is heard in reply. The same course is followed on an objection to an indictment.

When a party is dissatisfied with a taxation of his bill of costs, he carries in objections in writing, which are replied to by the taxing officer (R.S.C., Ord. 62, r. 33).

See EXCEPTION.

OBJECTS

Objects of a power, the persons in whose favour a power of appointment may be exercised.

Objurgatrices, scolds, or unquiet women, punished with the cucking-stool. See CASTIGATORY.

Oblata, gifts or offerings made to the king by any of his subjects. In the Exchequer it signified old debts, brought as it were together from precedent years, and put on the present sheriff's charge (Jacob; Pract.Excheq. 78).

Oblata terrae, half an acre, or, as some say, half a perch of land (Spelman).

Oblate rolls. See FINE ROLLS.

Oblations, or **Obventions,** offerings or customary payments made to the minister of a church, including fees on marriages, churchings, burials, mortuaries, etc. (*q.v.*), and Easter offerings (2 Co.Inst. 389).

Easter offerings are assessable to income tax (*Cooper* v. *Blakiston* [1909] A.C. 104).

The Baptismal Fees Abolition Act, 1872, makes it illegal for any clergyman of the Church of England or any parish clerk, etc., to demand any fee for baptism or for the registry thereof; but it does not prohibit the acceptance of any such fees spontaneously offered.

The ceremonies at the coronation of the sovereign include the oblation to the sovereign of a pall or altar-cloth of gold and a wedge of gold weighing one pound and the oblation of the Sword of State. The first of these oblations was omitted at the last five coronations, to the loss of the Lord Chamberlain, who is entitled to the pall and the wedge after the oblation, if he claims them.

Obligatio civilis, a statutory obligation, or one recognised by the *jus civile* (Civil Law).

Obligatio literarum. See LITERARUM OBLIGATIO.

Obligatio praetoria, or **honoraria,** an obligation established by the praetor in the exercise of his jurisdiction (Civil Law).

Obligatio verborum. See VERBORUM OBLIGATIO.

Obligation, the relation between two persons, one of whom can take judicial proceedings or other legal steps to compel the other to do or abstain from doing a certain act. Although it includes both the right of the one and the duty of the other, the term is more frequently used to denote the latter. See RIGHT.

Obligations are either perfect or imperfect. A perfect obligation is one which can be directly enforced by legal proceedings in the ordinary way: thus, if A contracts to pay B £50, B can enforce the obligation by bringing an action against A. An imperfect obligation is one which cannot be directly enforced but still has some legal effects.

An obligation may have been originally perfect, but have become imperfect from the remedy having been taken away: thus, if an action on a simple contract is not brought within the time prescribed by the Limitation Act, 1939, the remedy by action is gone, although the right still exists, and may become available in certain cases; for instance, if a debt is barred by the statute, the creditor may nevertheless, if he has the chance, obtain payment of it by a lien or by appropriation of payment, or the remedy may be revived by an acknowledgment by the debtor. An obligation is imperfect if no proceedings can be taken on it, because it does not satisfy the requirements of the law in regard to form or otherwise: thus, by the Law of Property Act, 1925, s. 40, no action can be brought on a contract for the sale of land so long as the contract is not evidenced by writing signed by the party to be charged; but the contract nevertheless exists and, therefore, money paid under it cannot be recovered back merely on the ground of its not being enforceable by action. Solicitors, medical practitioners, etc., cannot recover remuneration for their services unless they have complied with the Acts requiring them to take out certificates (*q.v.*).

In the technical sense of the term, an obligation is the same thing as a bond. In the case of a conditional bond, the operative part is sometimes called the obligation, to distinguish it from the condition. See BOND.

Obligee, the person in whose favour an obligation or bond is entered into; a creditor.

Obligor, he who enters into an obligation or bond; a debtor.

Obliqua oratio, the manner of reporting a speech in which " he," not " I," stands for the speaker in giving his words; and hence the words " you," " your," never occur, and every sentence begins with the word " that " expressed or understood, but generally expressed in the first sentence only. It is opposed to the *oratio directa,* sometimes called a speech in the first person, in which the very words of the speaker are given.

Obnoxious. An act is said to be obnoxious to a statute when it is caught by the prohibition of the statute.

Obreption. In ecclesiastical law, this is the obtaining of a faculty, dispensation, etc., by means of a false statement. See SUBREPTION.

Obscenity. The law relating to obscene publications was given new statutory form by the Obscene Publications Act, 1959, which repealed the Obscene Publications Act, 1857, and superseded the common law offence of publishing an obscene article. The Act of 1959 was amended by the Obscene Publications Act, 1964, and the Criminal Justice Act, 1967, s. 25.

The statutory test of obscenity (superseding the common law definition in *R.* v. *Hicklin* (1868) L.R. 3 Q.B. 360) is as follows: An article is deemed to be obscene if its effect or where the article comprises two or more distinct items, the effect of any one of its items is, if taken as a whole, such as to tend to deprave and corrupt persons who are likely, having regard to all relevant circumstances, to read, see or hear the matter contained or embodied in it (Act of 1959, s. 1 (1); *R.* v. *Clayton and Halsey* [1963] 1 Q.B. 163; *R.* v. *Calder and Boyars* [1969] 1 Q.B. 151; *R.* v. *Anderson* [1972] 1 Q.B. 304). Obscenity and depravity are not confined to sex (*John Calder (Publications)* v. *Powell* [1965] 1 Q.B. 509). " Article " means any description of article containing matter to be read or looked at or both, any sound record and any film or other record of a picture or pictures (Act of 1959, s. 1 (2)). Included in the definition of obscene article are things used for producing such an article, *e.g.,* photographic negatives, stencils and moulds (Act of 1964,

s. 4, overruling *Straker* v. *D.P.P.* [1963] 1 Q.B. 926).

The Obscene Publications Act, 1959, is concerned not only with the protection of the innocent from corruption, but also with the protection of the less innocent from further corruption (*D.P.P.* v. *Whyte* [1972] A.C. 849).

A person publishes an article who (a) distributes, circulates, sells, lets on hire, gives or lends it, or who offers it for sale or for letting out on hire; or (b) in the case of an article containing or embodying matter to be looked at, or a record, shows, plays or projects it (Act of 1959, s. 2 (3)). This does not apply to a public cinematograph showing or to television or sound broadcasting (s. 2 (3), proviso). See *Att.-Gen.'s Reference* (No. 2 of 1975) [1976] 1 W.L.R. 710.

Any person who, whether for gain or not, publishes an obscene article or who has an obscene article for publication for gain (whether gain to himself or gain to another) is liable (a) on summary conviction to a fine not exceeding £100 or to imprisonment for a term not exceeding six months; (b) on conviction on indictment to a fine or imprisonment for a term not exceeding three years or both (Act of 1959, s. 2 (1); Act of 1964, s. 1 (1)). A person is deemed to have an article for publication for gain if with a view to such publication he has the article in his ownership, possession or control (Act of 1964, s. 1 (2)). Summary proceedings must be brought within 12 months (Act of 1959, s. 2 (2)) and a prosecution on indictment within two years of the commission of the offence (Act of 1959, s. 2 (3)). Wholesalers, distributors, booksellers and other persons innocently disseminating or holding obscene articles are protected by the 1959 Act, s. 2 (5) and the 1964 Act, s. 1 (3) (*a*). As to republication, see the 1959 Act, s. 2 (6), the 1964 Act, s. 1 (3) (*b*), and *R.* v. *Barker* [1962] 1 W.L.R. 349.

A person publishing an article is not to be proceeded against for an offence at common law consisting of the publication of any matter contained in the article where it is of the essence of the offence that the matter is obscene (1959 Act, s. 2 (4)) but that provision does not exclude prosecution for a conspiracy to corrupt public morals which is a crime at common law (*Shaw* v. *D.P.P.* [1962] A.C. 220).

Powers of search, seizure and forfeiture are contained in the Act of 1959, s. 3, the Act of 1964, s. 1 (4) (5) and the Courts Act, 1971, Sch. 8 para. 37. See *Morgan* v. *Bowker* [1964] 1 Q.B. 507. No warrant to search for and seize obscene articles is to be issued except on an information laid by or on behalf of the Director of Public Prosecutions or by a constable (Criminal Justice Act, 1967, s. 25). Appeal lies to quarter sessions against an order for forfeiture but this does not exclude the right to appeal to the Divisional Court by way of case stated (Act of 1959, s. 3 (5); *Burke* v. *Cooper* [1962] 1 W.L.R. 700).

The defendant may set up as a defence that publication is justified as being for the public good on the ground that it is in the interest of science, literature, art or learning or other objects of general concern. Expert evidence may be called to this defence by either side (Act of 1959, s. 4; *D.P.P.* v. *A. and B.C. Chewing Gum* [1967] 2 All E.R. 504; *R.* v. *Calder & Boyars* [1969] 1 Q.B. 151; *R.* v. *Penguin Books* [1961] Crim.L.R. 176; but see *R.* v. *Staniforth and Grantham* [1975] Crim.L.R. 291 to the contrary).

It is an offence under the Post Office Act, 1953, s. 11 (as amended by the Post Office Act, 1961, Sch.; Criminal Justice Act, 1967, Sch. 3 Pts. I, II; Post Office Act, 1969, Sch. 4 para. 2 (3), Sch. 11 Pt. II) to send in a postal packet any indecent or obscene article or to place on the packet any words, marks or designs of a grossly offensive or of an indecent or obscene character. The offence is punishable on summary conviction by fine not exceeding £100 and on conviction on indictment to imprisonment for twelve months. See *R.* v. *Stanley* [1965] 2 Q.B. 32; *R.* v. *Straker* [1965] Crim.L.R. 239.

As to exposing obscene publications or any indecent exhibition to view in public places see the Vagrancy Act, 1824, s. 4 and the Town Police Clauses Act, 1847, s. 28.

See INDECENCY; INDECENT ADVERTISEMENTS; INDECENT EXPOSURE.

Obscuritas pacti nocet ei qui apertius loqui potuit. (Ambiguity in contract works against the party who could have expressed himself more clearly.)

Obsignatory, ratifying and confirming.

Obsolescence. See the Capital Allowances Act, 1968; Finance Act, 1971, ss. 40–54; Finance Act, 1972, ss. 67–69; Finance Act, 1975, s. 13; Finance Act, 1976, ss. 39–43.

Obsolete, invalid by virtue of discontinuance; said of a law or practice which has ceased to be enforced or be in use by reason of change of manners and circumstances, as wager of battel (*q.v.*), the punishment of the stocks (*q.v.*), the provision of the Gaming Act, 1540, by which labourers and others are forbidden to play cards or other specified games except at Christmas, but are allowed to play them at Christmas in their masters' houses and in their masters' presence; and that of the Statute of Westminster II, 1285, c. 34, by which elopement with a nun from her convent, although the nun consents is punishable by three years' imprisonment and fine. (See STATUTE LAW REVISION.) But however absurd and, in common language obsolete, an English statute may be, it does not become legally obsolete by mere non-user, though the fact of non-user may be important when the question is whether there has been a repeal by implication (*The India* (No. 2) (1864) 33 L.J. Adm. 193).

Wager of battel survived till 1819 and required a statute, or was deemed to require one, for its abolition, and so did pressing to death for want of a plea, and the inquiry whether the prisoner fled for his crime in criminal cases (see PEINE FORTE ET DURE; FLY FOR IT), but the view expressed in *R.* v. *Ramsay and Foote* (1883) 48 L.T. 735, to the effect that "law grows," would usually be taken at the present day. A thorough examination of enactments by the Law Commission (*q.v.*) has resulted in the repeal of a large number of obsolete enactments.

Obstetricante manu, by the hand of a midwife, said of evidence of a child helped out by his nurse, etc.

Obstriction, obligation; bond.

Obstructing justice, an offence of a very high and presumptuous nature; but more particularly so, when it is an obstruction of an arrest upon criminal process; and it has been held that the party opposing such arrest becomes thereby *particeps criminis,* that is, an accessory in felony, and a principal in high treason (4 Bl.Comm. 128).

Obstruction, wilful obstruction without lawful authority or excuse, of a highway is an offence under the Highways Act, 1959, s. 121. *Mens rea* is not an element in the offence (*Arrowsmith* v. *Jenkins* [1963] 2 Q.B. 561). See also the Town Police Clauses Act, 1847, s. 28; the Motor Vehicles (Construction and Use) Regulations, 1973 (Nos. 24, 1347, 1706) arts. 114–116; the Road Traffic Regulation Act, 1967, s. 80; Transport Act, 1968, s. 131; Road Traffic Act, 1972, Sch. 7; Fixed Penalty (Procedure) Regulations 1974 No. 1475; *Solomon* v. *Durbridge* (1956) 120 J.P. 231 (parked car). Obstruction of the highway may constitute a public nuisance (see NUISANCE.).

Vehicles causing an obstruction may be dealt with under the Removal and Disposal of Vehicles Regulations, 1968 (No. 43). See also the Functions of Traffic Wardens Order, 1970 (No. 1958).

Whether or not the user amounting to obstruction is or is not an unreasonable use of the highway is a question of fact depending on all the circumstances, including the length of time the obstruction continues, the place where it occurs, the purpose for which it is done and whether it does in fact cause an obstruction as opposed to a potential obstruction (*Nagy* v. *Weston* [1965] 1 W.L.R. 280, *per* Lord Parker C.J.).

Making a " U " turn may amount to obstruction (*Wall* v. *Williams* [1965] Crim.L.R. 50).

Obstruction of a police constable in the execution of his duty is an offence under the Police Act, 1964, s. 51 (3). Any act which makes it more difficult for the police to carry out their duty may amount to obstruction (*Hinchcliffe* v. *Sheldon* [1955] 1 W.L.R. 1207 (shouting warnings that the police were about)). A policeman may arrest the offender with-

out a warrant if he reasonably apprehends a breach of the peace (*Piddington* v. *Bates* [1961] 1 W.L.R. 162 (insisting on joining pickets)), or has statutory authority for making the arrest (*Gelburg* v. *Miller* [1961] 1 W.L.R. 153 (refusal to move motor car or give name and address)). A continuous moving line of pickets crossing the highway can amount to an obstruction (*Tynan* v. *Balmer* [1967] 1 Q.B. 91). See PICKETING.

It is not obstruction (contrary to the Police Act, 1964, s. 51 (3)) for a suspected person to refuse to answer questions put by the police when there is no legal duty to answer. Nor is it obstruction to refuse to accompany the police to the police station without being arrested. It is otherwise if false information is given (*Rice* v. *Connolly* [1966] 2 Q.B. 414).

For cases of obstruction by sitting in the highway by way of protest see *R.* v. *Moule* (1964) 108 S.J. 100; *R.* v. *Adler* [1964] Crim. L.R. 304. Obstruction of a member of Her Majesty's armed forces in the execution of his duty is an offence under the Army Act, 1955, s. 193; Air Force Act, 1955, s. 193.

Obstruction of a local authority enforcing a notice requiring the execution of works is an offence under the Housing Act, 1957, s. 10.

See PICKETING.

Obstructive building, a building which by reason of its contact with or proximity to other buildings is dangerous or injurious to health (Housing Act, 1957, s. 72). For powers of local authorities in regard to obstructive buildings, see *Jackson* v. *Knutsford Urban D.C.* [1914] 2 Ch. 686.

Obtaining credit. As to an undischarged bankrupt obtaining credit, see the Bankruptcy Act, 1914, s. 155. Obtaining credit by fraud is an offence under the Theft Act, 1968, s. 16.

Obtemperandum est consuetudini rationabili tanquam legi (4 Co.Rep. 38). (A reasonable custom is to be obeyed as if it were law.) This is said of a custom of a manor.

Obtest, to call solemnly upon, to adjure; to protest.

Obventions, offerings; tithes and oblations. See OBLATIONS.

Occasio. In the time of Fleta this meant a levy made by a lord on those holding of him for war or other urgent necessity.

Occasional licence. See LICENCE.

Occasionari, to be charged or loaded with payments or occasional penalties.

Occasiones, assarts. See ASSART.

Occultatio thesauri inventi fraudulosa (3 Co.Inst. 133). (The concealment of discovered treasure is fraudulent.) It is in fact a misdemeanour. See THESAURUS, ETC.; TREASURE TROVE.

Occupancy, mere possession or use either by agreement or otherwise without other claim to the ownership or enjoyment of property; also taking possession of land to which no one else lays claim or without leave of the owner.

Property in goods and chattels may be acquired by occupancy. It has been said that anybody authorised by the Crown may seize to his own use such goods as belong to an alien enemy. All persons may, on their own lands, or in the seas, generally exercise the right to pursue and take any fowl or insect of the air, any fish or inhabitant of the waters, and any beast or reptile of the field. The exceptions to this right are royal fish, such as whales, sturgeons, etc., animals of forest, chase, or free warren, and fish belonging to a several or free fishery.

Occupancy, as a mode of acquiring title to personal property, is of comparatively little importance in English law, being principally confined to the case of goods unclaimed or thrown away (see DERELICT; ESTRAYS; WAIF), and game or animals *ferae naturae* (*e.g.,* fish in the sea or a river) when taken by the finder or pursuer (2 Bl.Comm. 402). See GAME.

As regards land the doctrine of occupancy was formerly of some importance. If A granted land to B during the life of C, and B died before C, then there was no one entitled to the land, because A had parted with his right during C's life, and B's estate had determined with his own death; therefore anyone might enter on the land and retain possession during the remainder of C's life. A person so entering was called an occupant, or, more commonly, a general occupant, because anyone might enter in this manner. This doctrine of general or common occupancy was abolished by the Statute of Frauds, 1677, s. 12, replaced by the Wills Act, 1837, ss. 3, 6.

If A granted land to B and his heirs during the life of C, and B died before C, B's heir might enter and hold possession, and in such case he was called a special occupant, having a special right of occupation by the terms of the grant (2 Bl.Comm. 258). Special occupancy was abolished by the Administration of Estates Act, 1925, s. 45. See AUTRE VIE; CONFUSION; POSSESSION.

Occupant, he who is in possession of a thing. See OCCUPANCY.

Occupatile, that which has been left by the right owner, and is now possessed by another.

Occupatio, the taking possession of a thing belonging to no one, *res nullius,* but capable of being owned (Civil Law).

Occupatio bellica, taking possession of enemy territory in war.

Occupatio pacifica, taking possession of the territory of another State in time of peace with its consent.

Occupation [Lat. *occupatio*; *capere,* to seize], possession; the act of taking possession; also, trade or mystery.

In its usual sense, occupation is where a person exercises physical control over land. Thus, the lessee of a house is in occupation of it so long as he has the power of entering it and staying there at pleasure and of excluding all other persons (or all except one or more specified persons) from the use of it. Occupation is therefore the same thing as actual possession (*Hadley* v. *Taylor* (1866) L.R. 1 C.P. 53). See POSSESSION; USE AND OCCUPATION.

Permissive occupation is where the occupier has merely a licence or permission from the person entitled to the occupation (*Parker* v. *Leach* (1866) L.R. 1 P.C. 312).

In the law of rating, occupation signifies actual use and enjoyment, as distinguished from mere possession. Thus a freeholder is in possession of the minerals beneath the surface of his land, and of a house which is to let, whether empty or in the custody of a caretaker, but he is not in occupation of them for the purpose of rating. To constitute a rateable occupation, it must be exclusive as well as beneficial; therefore lodgers (*q.v.*), licensees, and servants are not rateable occupiers.

In the law of parliamentary and municipal elections, occupation of a dwelling-house, lands, or lodgings, was one kind of qualification for being registered as a voter (known as an inhabitant occupier); but this qualification is now gone. See ELECTORAL FRANCHISE.

In a technical sense, occupation was a term of art, and signified a putting out of a man's freehold in time of war: it was the same as disseisin in time of peace.

Such occupation, however, did not produce a descent cast as a disseisin did (Litt. 412; Co.Litt. 249b). See DESCENT CAST.

Being a prisoner detained at one of H.M. Prisons is not an " occupation, service or employment " entitling the prisoner to be registered as an absent voter (*Donnelly* v. *Edinburgh Electoral Registration Officer,* 1964 S.L.T.(Sh.Ct.) 80).

Occupation lease, a lease made for the convenience of personal occupation.

Occupative, possessed, used, employed.

Occupavit, a writ which lay for him who was ejected from his freehold in time of war, as the writ of *novel disseisin* lay for one disseised in time of peace.

Occupier, the person residing in or upon or having a right to reside in or upon any house, land or place, formerly rateable to the poor rate under the Poor Relief Act, 1601, and as inhabitant occupier entitled to the parliamentary franchise; now a person liable to pay rates by reason of occupation of premises under the General Rate Act, 1967.

As to the liability of the occupier of a factory (*q.v.*) see the Factories Act, 1961, ss. 160–163. As to the liability of an occupier to persons entering premises, see OCCUPIERS' LIABILITY. See also INVITEE; LICENSEE.

Occupiers' liability. The Occupiers' Liability Act, 1957, s. 2, provides that an occupier of premises owes the same duty, " the common duty of care ", to all his visitors (*i.e.,* licensees and invitees (s. 1 (2)) but not trespassers) except in

so far as he is free to and does extend, restrict, modify or exclude the duty. The common duty of care is a duty to take such care as in all the circumstances of the case is reasonable to see that the visitor will be reasonably safe in using the premises for the purposes for which he is invited or permitted by the occupier to be there. Under s. 3, where an occupier is bound by contract to permit third parties to enter his premises he cannot restrict or exclude the common duty of care. Thus if a landlord of premises such as a block of offices retains under his control the passages, stairways and lifts he will owe the common duty of care to the persons living with or visiting his tenants. By s. 1, the common duty of care is substituted for the duties owed by an occupier at common law to his visitors. S. 5 introduces the common duty of care into contractual relationships. The Act binds the Crown (s. 6). " Occupation " for the purposes of the Act is synonymous with control, and the occupier is the person with immediate control and supervision of the premises and the power of permitting and prohibiting the entry of others (*Wheat* v. *E. Lacon & Co.* [1966] A.C. 552).

Damages under the Act include damages in respect of consequent financial loss (*A.M.F. International* v. *Magnet Bowling* [1968] 1 W.L.R. 1028).

Under the Defective Premises Act, 1972, s. 7, a duty of care is placed on the landlord for defects in the state of the premises which he has let where he has an obligation or right to remedy such defects. The duty is owed to all persons who might reasonably be expected to be affected by such defects.

Ochlocracy [ὄχλος, a multitude; κράτος, power or command], a form of government wherein the populace has the whole power and administration in its own hand; a democracy; mob-rule.

Octave, the eighth day after a festival, both days being counted; thus the octave of Easter is the following Sunday, Low Sunday (3 Bl.Comm. 277).

Octo tales. See DECEM TALES; TALES.

Odhal, allodial (*q.v.*).

Odio et atia, a writ called *breve de bono et malo,* addressed to the sheriff to inquire whether a man committed to prison upon suspicion of murder was committed on just cause of suspicion, or only upon malice and ill-will; and if, upon the inquisition, it was found that he was not guilty, then there issued another writ to the sheriff to bail him (Reg.Brev. 133; Tomlin). The practice now is to issue a habeas corpus.

Odiosa et inhonesta non sunt in lege praesumenda; et in facto quod in se habet et bonum et malum, magis de bono quam de malo praesumendum est (Co.Litt. 78). (Odious and dishonest things are not to be presumed in law; and in an act which partakes both of good and bad, the presumption should be in favour of what is good rather than what is bad.)

Odometer, a device for measuring the distance travelled by a wheel. In a motor vehicle the odometer is usually embodied in the speedometer. If the odometer on a car being sold does not give the true mileage of the car, a disclaimer by the car seller, must, in order to excuse him from the charge of applying a false trade description (see Trade Descriptions), neutralise the odometer reading by being as bold, precise and compelling as the odometer itself (*Zawadski* v. *Sleigh* [1975] R.T.R. 113; *Simmons* v. *Potter* [1975] R.T.R. 347; *R.* v. *Hammerton's Cars* (1976) *The Times,* July 15).

Oeconomicus, executor (Matt.Par.).

Oecumenical. See ECUMENICAL.

Of course. A step in an action or other proceeding is said to be of course when the court or its officers have no discretion to refuse it, provided the proper formalities have been observed. In this sense the issue of a writ of summons is a matter of course. (See WRIT OF SUMMONS.) An order of course means an order made on an *ex parte* application to which a party is entitled on his own statement and at his own risk. An order of course improperly obtained may be set aside.

Off-licence, a justices' licence authorising the sale of intoxicating liquor for consumption off the premises for which the licence is granted (Licensing Act, 1964, s. 1 (2) (*b*)).

Off-shore installations. See SHIP-BUILDING.

Offa. See ANGLO-SAXON LAWS.

Offence. The word " offence " has no technical meaning in English law, but it is commonly used to signify any public wrong, including, therefore, not only crimes or indictable offences, but also offences punishable on summary conviction. The word is used as part of the titles of various Acts, such as the Offences against the Person Act, 1861; and in various enactments such as the Powers of Criminal Courts Act, 1973, it is used as a comprehensive term to cover anything which a court may deal with.

Offensive trade, the trade or business of blood boiler, blood drier, bone boiler, fat extractor, fat melter, fellmonger, glue maker, gut scraper, rag and bone dealer, size maker, soap boiler, tallow melter or tripe boiler, or any other trade, manufacture or business declared to be an offensive trade by order as provided by the Public Health Act, 1936, s. 107; see also the London Government Act, 1963, s. 40 (3), Sch. 11 Pt. I para. 20. See ALKALI WORKS; NUISANCE.

Offensive weapons. It is an offence to carry an offensive weapon in a public place without lawful authority or reasonable excuse, proof of which lies on the accused (Prevention of Crime Act, 1953, s. 1 (1); *R.* v. *Jura* [1954] 1 Q.B. 503; *Evans* v. *Wright* [1964] Crim.L.R. 466; *Grieve* v. *Macleod* [1967] Crim.L.R. 424; *Ohlson* v. *Hylton* [1975] 1 W.L.R. 724). Powers of arrest without warrant are conferred on a constable by the Act (s. 1 (3)). Offences are punishable on summary conviction with a fine of £200 or three months' imprisonment or both; on indictment with a fine or two years' imprisonment or both (s. 1 (1); Criminal Justice Act, 1967, s. 92, Sch. 3 Pt. I).

" Public place " (*q.v.*) includes any highway and any other premises or place to which at the material time the public have or are permitted to have access, whether on payment or otherwise. " Offensive weapon " means any article made or adapted for use for causing injury to the person, or intended by the person having it with him for such use by him (Prevention of Crime Act, 1953, s. 1 (4)). The court may order the forfeiture or disposal of any weapon in respect of which an offence has been committed (s. 1 (2)).

Although the original purpose of a person carrying an article may be innocent, if the article is subsequently used to intimidate someone it can be said to be an offensive weapon (*Woodward* v. *Koessler* [1958] 1 W.L.R. 1255; *Farrell* v. *Rennicks* (1959) 75 Sh.Ct.Rep. 113; *R.* v. *McMahon* [1961] Crim.L.R. 622). It must be proved that the accused knew that he was in possession of an offensive weapon (*R.* v. *Cugullere* [1961] 1 W.L.R. 858). If the article is not an offensive weapon *per se* the onus is on the prosecution to prove that the person carrying it intended to use it to cause injury (*R.* v. *Petrie* [1961] 1 W.L.R. 358; *R.* v. *Edmonds* [1963] 2 Q.B. 142; *R.* v. *Gibson* [1963] Crim.L.R. 281; *R.* v. *Allamby* [1974] 1 W.L.R. 1494).

It is an offence to make, import, sell, hire, offer to sell or hire, expose or have in possession for sale or hire, lend or give to any other person a "flick knife" or "gravity knife." The penalty for a first offence is a fine not exceeding £50 or imprisonment for not more than three months or both; for a subsequent offence, £200 or six months' imprisonment or both (Restriction of Offensive Weapons Acts, 1959 and 1961, overruling *Fisher* v. *Bell* [1961] 1 Q.B. 394). A flick knife, sometimes known as a flick gun, is a knife which has a blade which opens automatically by hand pressure applied to a button, spring or other device in or attached to the handle. A gravity knife is a knife which has a blade which is released from its handle or sheath by the force of gravity or centrifugal force and which when released is locked in place (Act of 1959, s. 1).

Offer. Every agreement in substance consists of an offer made by one party and its unconditional acceptance by the other. An acceptance with conditions or new terms added is in effect a counter-offer, and does not operate as an acceptance of the original offer. An offer may be withdrawn at any time before it has been unconditionally accepted; and if the person to whom an offer is made refuses it, or neglects to accept it within a reasonable time, it lapses and he cannot afterwards revive it by purporting to accept

it. Where A makes an offer to B in the belief (known to B) that B is X there is no offer capable of acceptance by B (*Cundy* v. *Lindsay* (1878) 3 App.Cas. 459; *Ingram* v. *Little* [1961] 1 Q.B. 31). But see *Lewis* v. *Averay* [1972] 1 Q.B. 198. See ACCEPTANCE; AGREEMENT; LETTER.

An offer of shares or debentures to the public must comply with the provisions of the Companies Act, 1948, s. 45. See PROSPECTUS.

Offerings, personal tithes, payable by custom to the parson or vicar of a parish, either occasionally, as at sacraments, marriages, churching of women, burials, etc.; or at constant times, as at Easter, Christmas, etc.; see the statutes 1548, 2 & 3 Edw. 6, cc. 13, 20, 21, and the First Fruits and Tenths Measure, 1926. Voluntary Easter offerings received by an incumbent are profits accruing to him and are assessable to income tax (*Cooper* v. *Blakiston* [1909] A.C. 104). See OBLATIONS.

Offertory; Offertorium. During the Communion Service, while the portion known as the offertory sentences is being read, the churchwardens or other fit persons go round amongst the congregation and make a collection. Before the Reformation the collection made at the part of the mass known as the offertory was for the use of the priest; the offertory since the Reformation has been applicable to such pious and charitable uses as the minister and churchwardens think fit.

Off-going crop. See AWAY GOING CROP.

Office, the right and duty to exercise an employment: thus, we speak of the office of a trustee, executor, guardian, director, sheriff, etc. Offices are either public or private. A public office is one which entitles a man to act in the affairs of others without their appointment or permission. Public offices are granted either for life or (as in the case of a judge of the High Court) during good behaviour (*dum*—or *quamdiu*—*bene se gesserit*), or (as in the case of nearly all offices held of the Crown) during the pleasure of the appointor (*durante bene placito*), and some few offices, such as that of Earl Marshal (*q.v.*), are capable of being granted to a man and his heirs, in which case they are incorporeal hereditaments, or of being entailed, in which case they are also tenements (4 Co.Litt. 20a; 2 Bl.Comm. 36).

Public offices are either offices of trust, which cannot be performed by deputy, or ministerial offices, which may be performed by deputy.

As to obtaining offices by desert only, the statute 1388, 12 Ric. 2, c. 2, enacted that the Chancellor, the Treasurer, the judges of the King's Bench and the Common Pleas, the Barons of the Exchequer and all others called to ordain, name, or make justices of the peace, sheriffs, or other officers or Ministers of the king should be sworn not to do so for any gift or brocage, favour or affection. The maxim is *officia magistratus non debent esse venalia* (the offices of a magistrate ought not to be saleable) Co.Litt. 234a).

The statute was repealed by the Promissory Oaths Act, 1871, having been superseded by the Promissory Oaths Act, 1868.

The sale of offices is also prohibited by the Sale of Offices Acts, 1551 and 1809. In *Sterry* v. *Clifton* (1850) 19 L.J.C.P. 237, it was held that certain official clerkships of attorneys might be considered partnership property.

" Office " is frequently used in the old books as an abbreviation for inquest of office (*q.v.*); when the jury on inquest of office had found the facts to be inquired into, and the verdict or inquest had been returned, the office was said to be found and returned.

See AMOTION; DEMISE; OATH; PUBLIC OFFICER; PUBLIC OFFICE, SALE OF.

Office copy, a transcript of a proceeding filed in the proper office of a court under the seal of such office. Office copies of writs, records, pleadings and documents filed in the High Court are admissible in evidence (R.S.C., Ord. 38, r. 10). See COPY.

Office development. In addition to the normal control over office development by the need to obtain planning permission (see DEVELOPMENT), the Town and Country Planning Act, 1971, imposes a temporary special control over office development (ss. 73–86, Sch. 13; S.I. 1974 No. 482, art. 12, Sch.). A builder of office premises which exceed in floor space the prescribed limits must first obtain an office development permit (O.D.P.) from the Secretary of State for the Environ-

ment, and he may attach restrictions to the permit. No appeal lies against a refusal to grant an office development permit and no compensation is payable for such refusal. A planning application will not be granted unless accompanied by such permit. The present exemption limits are 10,000 square feet. These restrictions apply to all land within the metropolitan area and to such other areas to which they are applied by order of the Secretary of State. They have been applied to most thickly populated areas. Ss. 73–86 of the Act of 1971 are due to expire on August 4, 1977 but Parliament may determine otherwise (s. 86 (1); Town and Country Planning (Amendment) Act, 1972, ss. 5, 6). See also LOCATION OF OFFICES BUREAU.

Office found, the decision of an inquest of office (*q.v.*), to the effect that the Crown was entitled to the lands or chattels in question (Kitch 177).

Office of profit. The Act of Settlement, 1700, s. 3, provided that no person having an office or place of profit under the Crown could be a member of the House of Commons. The Succession to the Crown Act, 1707, s. 24, enacted that persons holding any office or place of profit under the Crown created after October 25, 1705, and persons holding various offices specified in the section, should be incapable of being elected or sitting as members of the House; s. 25 enacted that any member accepting any office of profit from the Crown which did not come within s. 24 should cease to be a member but could be re-elected; s. 27 enacted that the acceptance of any new or other commission in the army or navy should not disqualify or cause a member to lose his seat.

This enactment, if it stood by itself, would have disqualified for membership nearly all the members holding salaried political offices. A number of Acts passed since 1705, while creating new offices, declared that the holders thereof should not be ineligible for election. The present position is regulated by the House of Commons Disqualification Act, 1975. Not more than 95 holders of ministerial offices may sit (s. 2).

A member vacates his seat by accepting the stewardship of the Chiltern Hundreds or the Manor of Northstead. See CHILTERN HUNDREDS.

Office of the judge. In ecclesiastical law it is said that " the office of the judge is promoted " when criminal proceedings are taken. The meaning of the expression is, that inasmuch as all spiritual criminal jurisdiction is in the hands of the bishop or ordinary (*judex ordinarius*), his office or function is set in motion whenever such proceedings are instituted. The person taking the proceedings is known technically as *promotor officii judicis*; he is *promotor necessarius* when the machinery of the court is set in motion by the ordinary *ex mero motu* (*q.v.*) and he is *promotor ordinarius* in other cases.

Officers of the Supreme Court. By the Judicature Act, 1873, s. 77, the officers of the various courts whose jurisdiction was by that Act transferred to the High Court or the Court of Appeal were attached to the Supreme Court; by the Judicature Act, 1875, these officers were attached to the divisions which represented the courts of which they were formerly officers; and by the Judicature (Officers) Act, 1879, they were transferred to the Central Office of the Supreme Court. See now the Judicature Act, 1925, ss. 105, 221–232.

Offices. The Offices, Shops and Railway Premises Act, 1963, as amended, sets standards of health, welfare and safety for employees in the premises referred to. Premises are to be kept clean, at a reasonable temperature, properly ventilated and lit, with sanitary conveniences, washing facilities, drinking water, accommodation for clothing, sitting facilities, seats for sedentary work, eating facilities (ss. 1–15). The premises and machinery are to be made safe to work in (ss. 16, 17). Young persons are not to be exposed to damage in cleaning machinery (s. 18). Persons working at dangerous machines are to be trained and supervised (s. 19). Noise and vibration are to be kept at reasonable levels (s. 21). Dangerously heavy work is prohibited (s. 23). First aid must be provided (ss. 24–27). Fire precautions must be taken (ss. 28–44). Exemptions may be granted from some requirements of the Act (ss. 45, 46). No levy may be made on employees to pay for compliance with the Act (s. 47).

Accidents must be notified (s. 48). There is an obligation to notify the appropriate authority that persons are to be employed (s. 49). Employees are to be given all necessary information (s. 50). The Act of 1963, was amended by the Health and Safety at Work etc. Act, 1974 and orders made thereunder.

The Community Land Act, 1975, contains power for the Secretary of State to acquire unoccupied office premises (ss. 28–36).

Offices of the Supreme Court. The offices of the Supreme Court are to be open every day except Saturdays and Sundays, Good Friday, the Tuesday after Easter Sunday, Christmas Day, bank holidays (*q.v.*) and such other days as the Lord Chancellor, with the concurrence of the Lord Chief Justice, the Master of the Rolls and the President of the Family Division may direct (R.S.C., Ord. 64, r. 7).

As to the vacations in the offices of the Supreme Court, see VACATION.

Official, formal; authorised.

In the civil law, an official is a minister of, or attendant upon, a magistrate. In the canon law, he is the person to whom a bishop commits the charge of his spiritual jurisdiction; there is one in every diocese, called *officialis principalis, i.e.,* chancellor; the rest, if there are more, are *officiales foranei, i.e.,* commissaries. In English ecclesiastical law he is the person whom the archdeacon appoints as his substitute (Wood, Inst. 30, 505). See DIOCESAN COURTS.

Official assignees, certain persons from the class of merchants or accountants who were appointed by the Lord Chancellor under the Bankruptcy Acts, 1849 and 1861, to act in bankruptcies, one of whom had to be an assignee of the bankrupt's estate and effects, together with the assignee or assignees chosen by the creditors. All the personal estate, the profits of the realty, and the proceeds of all such estates as were sold were received by such official assignees alone, and paid into the Bank of England to the credit of the Accountant in Bankruptcy. These officials ceased to exist under the system of bankruptcy introduced in 1869, but the official receivers established by the Act of 1883 resemble them. See ASSIGNEE.

Official Custodian for Charities. The Official Custodian for Charities was constituted by the Charities Act, 1960. He takes the place of both the Official Trustee of Charity Lands (constituted by the Charitable Trusts Act, 1853, ss. 47–50 and the Charitable Trusts Act, 1855, s. 15) and the Official Trustees of Charitable Funds (constituted by the Charitable Trusts Act, 1853, s. 51, the Charitable Trusts Act, 1855, s. 18 and the Charitable Trusts Act, 1887, s. 4). He is a corporation sole and has an official seal. Such officer of the Charity Commissioners as they may from time to time designate is the Official Custodian for Charities. He is subject to the directions of the Commissioners (Charities Act, 1960, s. 3). As to property vested in the Official Custodian, see ss. 16, 17.

Official liquidators. Under the Companies Act, 1862, s. 92, after a winding-up order had been made, official liquidators were appointed for the purpose of carrying out the winding up under the direction of the court. There is now no such thing as an official liquidator. See LIQUIDATOR.

Official log-book, a log-book in a certain form, and containing certain specified entries required by the Merchant Shipping Act, 1894, ss. 239, 240, re-enacting the Merchant Shipping Act, 1854, ss. 280–282, to be kept by all British merchant ships, except those exclusively engaged in the coasting trade. The entries are admissible as evidence.

Official managers, persons formerly appointed, under statutes now repealed, to superintend the winding up of insolvent companies under the control of the Court of Chancery.

Official oath, the form of oath set out in the Promissory Oaths Act, 1868, s. 3, which, under s. 5 of that Act, must be taken by all Ministers and other high officers of State, including, under various Acts passed since 1868, Ministers whose offices have been created since that date. This oath is quite distinct from the oath of office, as to which see PROBATE.

Official Petitioner. The Director of Public Prosecutions acts as Official Petitioner in relation to cases in which a criminal bankruptcy (q.v.) order is made (Powers of Criminal Courts Act, 1973, s. 41).

Official principal, an ecclesiastical officer whose duty it is to hear causes between party and party, as the delegate of the bishop or archbishop by whom he is appointed. He generally also holds the office of vicar-general (q.v.). The Auditor of the Chancery Court of York (q.v.) is the Official Principal of the Archbishop of York (Ecclesiastical Jurisdiction Measure, 1963, s. 13 (1)). The Chancellor of a diocese is the official principal of the bishop of that diocese. The Official Principal of the province of Canterbury is called the Dean of Arches. See ARCHES, DEAN OF THE.

Official receivers, officers appointed by the Department of Trade under the Bankruptcy Act, 1914, ss. 70–75, replacing the Bankruptcy Act, 1883, s. 66, to act as interim receivers and managers of bankrupts' estates, pending the appointment of trustees in bankruptcy. The report of an official receiver is absolutely privileged (*Bottomley* v. *Brougham* [1908] 1 K.B. 584; *Burr* v. *Smith* [1909] 2 K.B. 306). The official receiver becomes provisional liquidator on the making of a winding-up order (Companies Act, 1948, s. 239). See LIQUIDATOR.

Where the Official Receiver, as liquidator, agrees to execute a conveyance to a third party, the high standard of conduct imposed on him by virtue of his office requires him to comply with his promise although there is no contract and no estoppel (*Re Wyvern Developments* [1974] 1 W.L.R. 1097).

Official referee. Under the Administration of Justice Act, 1956, ss. 9, 10 (replacing the Judicature Act, 1925, s. 125), official referees could be appointed by the Crown on the recommendation of the Lord Chancellor. Their jurisdiction and the class of case referred to them were prescribed by rules of court made under s. 15 of the Act of 1956 (replacing ss. 88 and 89 of the Act of 1925).

The office of official referee was abolished by the Courts Act, 1971, s. 25 and the functions of official referees are discharged by such of the circuit judges (see CROWN COURT) as the Lord Chancellor appoints. The persons holding office as official referees on January 1, 1972, became circuit judges. (Act of 1971, s. 16, Sch. 2).

A circuit judge discharging the functions of an official referee will continue to be addressed as " Your Honour."

Official secrets. Legislation to prevent the disclosure of official secrets began with the Official Secrets Act, 1889. In 1878 a clerk in the Foreign Office was employed to copy a secret agreement between Great Britain and Russia. He took a copy for his own use and gave it to a London newspaper, in which it was published: he was arrested on an obviously untenable charge of larceny: and he was discharged because he had committed no offence known to the law. The facts in the case would have constituted a breach of official trust punishable under s. 12 of the Act of 1889. That Act also covered various cases of improperly obtaining or endeavouring to obtain information as to military or naval matters. It was repealed and re-enacted with amendments by the Official Secrets Act, 1911, which is amended by the Official Secrets Act, 1920. It is made an offence to spy in a prohibited place, or wrongfully to communicate codes, plans, models, documents, or information relating to such a place, or to munitions of war, or which are used in such a place. There are provisions as to arrest, harbouring of spies, and issue of search warrants. The fact that a person charged with an offence has been in communication with any person reasonably suspected of being an agent of a foreign power, or has in his possession the address of any such person, is evidence against him. A Secretary of State may require the production of any document relating to a telegram or cable or wireless message. Every person who carries on the business of receiving letters, postal packets, or telegrams for other persons must be registered with the police and keep a record of the letters, etc., passing through his hands, and must not give up a letter, etc., unless a receipt is signed, or written instructions for delivery are given, by the addressee.

The mischief aimed at by s. 1 of the Official Secrets Act, 1911, is not limited to espionage. It includes sabotage (*Chandler* v. *D.P.P.* [1964] A.C. 763).

Doing an act as a result of which the communication of official secrets is possible, even if not probable, is an offence (*R.* v. *Bingham* [1973] Q.B. 870).

The Official Secrets Act, 1920, s. 6 (as substituted by the Official Secrets Act, 1939), enables a chief officer of police to take action if satisfied that there is reasonable ground for suspecting that an offence under s. 1 of the Act of 1911 has been committed and for believing that any person is able to furnish information as to the offence. See also the European Communities Act, 1972, s. 11 (disclosure of classified Euratom information).

See IN CAMERA.

Official Solicitor. The Official Solicitor of the Court of Chancery was an officer whose functions consisted of protecting the Suitors Fund (*q.v.*) and of administering so much of that fund as came under the spending power of the court. He was transferred to the High Court by the Judicature Act, 1873, s. 77, which made no change in the title of his office: in view, however, of the fact that the Court of Chancery is gone, he is now known as the Official Solicitor of the Supreme Court. When so directed, he acts for persons suffering under a disability; he acts generally as solicitor in cases in which the Chancery Division requires his services as solicitor; he visits persons in custody for contempt.

Official Trustee of Charity Lands. See OFFICIAL CUSTODIAN OF CHARITIES.

Official Trustees of Charitable Funds. See OFFICIAL CUSTODIAN OF CHARITIES.

Official use, an active use, which imposed some duty on the legal owner or feoffee to uses, as a conveyance to A with directions for him to sell the estate and distribute the proceeds amongst B, C, and D. To enable A to perform this duty he kept the legal estate under the Statute of Uses, 1535.

Officiality, the court or jurisdiction of which an official is head.

Officiariis non faciendis vel amovendis, a writ addressed to municipal corporations commanding them not to admit such and such a one to office or to remove him from office (Reg.Orig. 126).

It was superseded by the writ of *quo warranto* (*q.v.*).

Officina justitiae, the workshop of justice. The common law side of the Chancery was so called, inasmuch as all original writs issued from it although returnable to the common law courts (4 Co.Inst. 80). See CHANCERY.

Officio, Ex, by virtue of his office; *e.g.,* the Lord Chief Justice of England is a member of the Court of Appeal, *ex officio.*

Officio, Ex, oath, an oath whereby a person might be obliged to make his answer to any matters alleged against him, and extending originally even to criminal charges. It was derived from the practice of the ecclesiastical courts (3 Bl.Comm. 447).

Officious will, a will by which the testator fulfils the duty (or *officium*) of providing for his family (Civil Law). See INOFFICIOUS, ETC.

Officit conatus si effect ussequatur (Jenk., Cent. 55). (An attempt becomes harmful if the effect follows.) See ATTEMPT.

Officium nemini debet esse damnosum. (An office ought to be injurious to no one.)

Ohm, a measure of electrical resistance. See the Weights and Measures Act, 1963, s. 10, Sch. 1 Pt. VI; S.I. 1963 No. 1354.

Oil. See PETROLEUM. As to the standards of measurement etc. on the sale of liquid fuel and lubricating oil see the Weights and Measures Act, 1963, s. 21, Sch. 7 Pt. I.

As to oil pollution, see the Prevention of Oil Pollution Act, 1971; POLLUTION.

Old age pensions. The Old Age Pensions Act, 1908, introduced a system under which, with few exceptions, everyone on reaching the age of seventy became entitled to a weekly pension of 5s. during his life where his yearly means from other sources did not exceed £21, and to a rate of pension sinking by sums of 1s. a week according as the yearly means exceeded £21 but did not exceed £31 10s. Where the yearly means exceeded £31 10s. there was no pension.

The Act of 1908 was amended by the Old Age Pensions Act, 1911, and other Acts. Such pensions are now known as retirement pensions. See the Social Security Act, 1975, ss. 12, 27–30, 39, 40.

Old Bailey, the Central Criminal Court (*q.v.*).

Old Christmas Day, January 6, which represents December 25 of the period before the reform of the calendar (*q.v.*).

Old Lady Day, April 6, which represents March 25 of the period before the reform of the calendar (*q.v.*).

Old Lammas Day. See LAMMAS.

Old Martinmas, November 24, which represents November 11 of the period before the reform of the calendar (*q.v.*).

Old metals. See SCRAP METALS.

Old Michaelmas Day, October 11, which represents September 29 of the period before the reform of the calendar (*q.v.*).

Old Midsummer Day, July 6, which represents June 24 of the period before the reform of the calendar (*q.v.*).

Old rent, accustomed rent (*q.v.*).

Old style. See CALENDAR; NEW YEAR'S DAY.

Old Tenures, a treatise, attributed to the reign of Edward III, dealing with tenures of land. It is called the *Old Tenures* to distinguish it from Littleton's well-known *Treatise on Tenures.* It is printed in the 11th and 12th editions of *Coke upon Littleton.*

Oleron, Laws of. This compilation, also known as the Rolls (or Lois or Jugements) of Oleron, derives its name from an island off the coast of the *département* of Charente Inférieure in France. It contains a collection of the customs of the sea which formed in the twelfth century something in the nature of a code of international maritime law for the Atlantic, corresponding to the Laws of Wisby (*q.v.*) for the Baltic and the Consolato del Mare (*q.v.*) for the Mediterranean. The compilation is alleged to have been made about 1150 for Eleanor of Aquitaine, then the wife of Louis VII of France, and afterwards, in 1152, the wife of Henry II of England. The earliest known copy, called *La Charte D'Oleroun des Juggements de la Mer,* and dating apparently from the fourteenth century, is contained in the *Liber Memorandorum* which is preserved in the Guildhall of the City of London. *The Rutter of the Sea,* by Thomas Petyt, printed in 1536, contains a translation entitled the *Laws of Ye Yle of Oleron & Ye Judgementes of Ye*

See; this appears to have been made from the *Purple Book of Bruges*, which is a version slightly altered to give it a local Flemish colour. An earlier translation, by Robert Copeland, had appeared in 1528. Translations are also to be found in Malyne's *Lex Mercatoria* and Justice's *Sea Laws*. See Selden, Dom.Mar. c. 14; 37 L.Q.R. 326.

Oligarchy, a form of government wherein the administration of affairs is lodged in the hands of a few persons.

Olympiad, a Grecian epoch: the space of four years.

Ombudsman. See COMMISSIONS FOR LOCAL ADMINISTRATION; PARLIAMENTARY COMMISSIONER.

Omittance, forbearance.

Omne crimen ebrietas et incendit et detegit (Co.Litt. 247). (Drunkenness both kindles and uncovers every crime.)

Omne jus aut consensus fecit aut necessitas constituit aut firmavit consuetudo (D. 1, 3, 40). (Mutual consent has made, or necessity has established, or usage has fixed, every rule of law.) This statement of a Roman jurist does not apply to English law.

Omne majus continet in se minus (5 Co. Rep. 115; Jenk., Cent. 208). (The greater contains the less.) Thus tender of a sum larger than a debt is good tender; but only if change is not required. See IN MAJORE, ETC.; MAJUS CONTINET, ETC.

Omne quod solo inaedificatur solo cedit (Just.Inst. 2, 1, 29). (Everything which is built into the soil is merged therein.) See AEDIFICATIO, ETC.; QUICQUID PLANTATUR, ETC.

Omne sacramentum debet esse de certa scientia (4 Co.Inst. 279). (Every oath ought to be of certain knowledge.) It is perjury (*q.v.*) for a witness to give evidence as to a matter of which he knows nothing (Perjury Act, 1911, s. 1).

Omne testamentum morte consummatum est (Co.Litt. 322; 3 Co.Rep. 29). (Every will is completed by death.) Until the death of the testator it is of no effect.

Omnes licentiam habent his, quae, pro se indulta sunt, renunciare (C. 1, 3, 51). (Everyone has liberty to renounce those things which are granted for his benefit.) Similarly, *quilibet potest renunciare juri*

pro se introducto (every person may decline to take advantage of a law made for his own benefit) (2 Co.Inst. 183). See WAIVER.

Omnes sorores sunt quasi unus haeres de una haereditate (Co.Litt. 67). (All sisters are, as it were, one heir to one inheritance.) They all took as coparceners (*q.v.*).

Omnes subditi sunt regis servi (Jenk., Cent. 126). (All subjects are the king's servants.) Quoted as a comment on a decision of the Exchequer that in an action of trespass or debt or in which outlawry lay, " servant " was not a good description since every man is a servant of the law and of the king.

Omnia delicta in aperto leviora sunt (8 Co.Rep. 127). (All offences are less grave when they are committed openly.)

Omnia praesumuntur contra proferentem. See *St. Edmundsbury and Ipswich Diocesan Board of Finance* v. *Clark* (*No. 2*) [1975] 1 W.L.R. 468.

Omnia praesumuntur contra spoliatorem (Broom, Max. 80). (All things are presumed against a wrongdoer.) This maxim embodies the grounds of the decision in *Armory* v. *Delamirie* (1722) 1 Str. 504, where it was held that where A had unlawfully detained jewels (of which only the size was proved) the property of B, then the jewels must unless produced be presumed to have been of the finest quality. See IN ODIUM, ETC.

Omnia praesumuntur legitime facta donec probetur in contrarium (Co.Litt. 232). (All things are presumed to have been legitimately done, until the contrary is proved.) Where there is question of official acts there is a rebuttable presumption that all necessary conditions, precedents and formalities have been complied with. See EX DIUTURNITATE, ETC.

Omnia praesumuntur rite et solemniter esse acta (Co.Litt. 6). (All things are presumed to be correctly and solemnly done.) That is to say, they are presumed to be done correctly until the contrary is proved. See EX DIUTURNITATE, ETC.

Omnia quae jure contrahuntur, contrario jure pereunt (D. 50, 17, 100). (All things which are made by a law perish as the result of a contrary law.) See LEGES POSTERIORES, ETC.; NATURALE EST, ETC.

Omnia quae sunt uxoris sunt ipsius viri; no habet uxor potestatem sui, sed vir (Co. Litt. 112). (All things which belong to the wife belong to the husband; it is not the wife but the husband who has control of the wife's property.) This is no longer so since the statutory alterations in the position of married women (q.v.). See UXOR NON, ETC.

Omnibus (for all), a public vehicle. For the purposes of the Town Police Clauses Acts, 1847 and 1889, the term " omnibus " when used in these Acts is defined in s. 3 of the Act of 1889. For the purposes of the Metropolitan Public Carriage Act, 1869, there is no definition of the term " omnibus," but the term " stage carriage " as defined in s. 4 of that Act, includes everything known as an omnibus.

Omnibus poenalibus judiciis et aetati est imprudentiae succurritur (D. 50, 17, 108). (In all criminal proceedings assistance is given to age and imprudence.) That is to say, the rigour of the law is mitigated in the case of offenders who are of tender age or who, for any reason, have not such intent as is necessary to constitute a crime. See CATCHING BARGAIN; CHILDREN; FIRST OFFENDER; INFANTICIDE; PROBATION OF OFFENDERS.

Omnis actio est loquela (Co.Litt. 292). (Every action is a complaint.) So a release of all *loquelae* was a release of all *actiones*.

Omnis conclusio boni et veri judicii sequitur ex bonis et veris praemissis et dictis juratorum (Co.Litt. 226). (Every conclusion arrived at in a proper and good judgment is the conclusion to be drawn from the premises which have been properly and reasonably found by the jurymen.) Coke is speaking of a special verdict. See VERDICT.

Omnis consensus tollit errorem (2 Co. Inst. 123). (Every assent removes error.)

Omnis innovatio plus novitate perturbat quam utilitate prodest (2 Buls. 338). (Every innovation causes more confusion by what is new in it than good by what is useful in it.) See JUDICIS EST JUS, ETC.; MISERA, ETC.; VIA, ETC.

Omnis interpretatio si fieri potest ita fienda est in instrumentis, ut omnes con-trarietates amoveantur (Jenk., Cent. 96). (If possible, deeds are to be so interpreted that all inconsistencies are got rid of.)

Omnis nova constitutio futuris temporibus formam imponere debet, non praeteritis (2 Co.Inst. 95). (Every new law should regulate the future and not the past.) See LEGES ET CONSTITUTIONES, ETC.

Omnis privatio praesupponit habitum (Co.Litt. 339). (Every deprivation presupposes former possession.) Quoted in support of the proposition that an estate tail could not be discontinued except by one seised by force of the entail. See DISCONTINUANCE; NEMO DAT, ETC.

Omnis querela et omnis action injuriarum limitata est infra certa tempora (Co.Litt. 114). (Every plaint and every action for injuries is limited within certain times.) Quoted from Bracton by Coke in connection with the common law rule as to time within the memory (q.v.) of living men.

Omnis ratihabitio retrotrahitur et mandato priori aequiparatur (Co.Litt. 207). (Every ratification of an act already done has a retrospective effect, and is equal to a previous request to do it.) Quoted in connection with the proposition that an unauthorised payment of a debt by a stranger is to be deemed payment by the debtor as on the date of actual payment if the debtor subsequently ratifies it. See RATIFICATION.

Omnium, the aggregate of certain portions of different stocks in the public funds.

Omnium contributione sarciatur quod pro omnibus datum est (4 Bing. 121). (That which is given for all is made good by the contribution of all.) This is the principle on which the doctrine of general average is founded. See AVERAGE.

On-licence, a justices' licence for the sale of any intoxicating liquor for consumption on the premises (Licensing Act, 1964, s. 1).

Oncunne, accused (Du Cange).

One-armed bandit. A jocular term for a type of gaming machine. See FRUIT MACHINE.

One hundred thousand pound clause. In a recovery (q.v.), or common recovery, it was at one time the practice for the tenant for life to convey to the tenant to the praecipe (*q.v.*) for the life of the tenant for life, subject to the proviso that, unless £100,000 should be paid on the day after the time within which the recovery was to be suffered, the use should cease. As the sum specified—it might be any sum —was always far in excess of the value of the estate, the effect of this proviso (known as " the one hundred thousand pound clause ") was to work an avoidance of the estate of the tenant to the praecipe; and this avoidance in no way affected the validity of the recovery, it being necessary only that there should be a tenant to the praecipe when the recovery was suffered.

Onerando pro ratione portionis, De, a writ which lay for a joint tenant, or a tenant in common, who had been distrained for more rent than he was liable to pay (Reg.Orig. 182). See now the implied powers conferred by the Law of Property Act, 1925, s. 190.

Onerari non debet (he ought not to be burdened), a form of commencement of a pleading, substituted in some few cases for *actionem non* (1 Saund. 290, n. *b*).

Oneris ferendi, a servitude entitling the dominant tenement to a right of support (Civil Law).

Onerous. A contract, lease, share or other right is said to be onerous when the obligations attaching to it counterbalance or exceed the advantage to be derived from it, either absolutely or with reference to the particular possessor.

As to disclaimer of onerous property by a trustee in bankruptcy, see DIS-CLAIMER.

Onslow's Act, the Habeas Corpus Act, 1816.

Onus episcopale, ancient customary payments from the clergy, to their diocesan bishop, of synodals, pentecostals, etc. See EPISCOPALIA.

Onus importandi, the charge of importing merchandise, mentioned in the statute 1660, 12 Car. 2, c. 28.

Onus probandi, the burden of proof. See BURDEN OF PROOF; PROOF.

Op. cit. [*opere citato*], in the work just referred to.

Open account, one which has not been stated or settled between the parties. See ACCOUNT, SETTLED; ACCOUNT STATED; FALSIFY.

Open cheque, one not crossed, payable either to bearer or to order.

Open contract, a complete contract of which the meaning admits the implications of law without special conditions, or except so far as such conditions may modify those implications, as a contract to sell land without mentioning the day for completion of the purchase, or without stipulations as to title or otherwise (Vendor and Purchaser Act, 1874, ss. 1, 2; Conveyancing Act, 1881, s. 3, reproduced with amendments by the Law of Property Act, 1925, ss. 44, 45). See CONTRACT FOR SALE OF LAND.

Open court. Every court of justice is open to every subject of the Crown (*Scott v. Scott* [1913] A.C. 417 at p. 440). By statute the place where justices try offences summarily is an open court (Magistrates' Courts Act, 1952, s. 98 (4)). So also is the place where they determine to commit a prisoner for trial unless any enactment contains an express provision to the contrary (see *e.g.*, the Official Secrets Act, 1920, s. 8) or where the interests of justice otherwise require (Criminal Justice Act, 1967, s. 6). Whether a coroner's court is an open court is a matter of doubt (*Garnett v. Ferrand* (1827) 6 B. & C. 611). The general rule is that all courts of justice are open to all so long as there is room (*R. v. Lewes Prison Governor* [1917] 2 K.B. 254; *McPherson v. McPherson* [1936] A.C. 177). See IN CAMERA; JUVE-NILE COURT.

Open cover, an informal unstamped agreement by which a marine insurance company undertakes to issue a policy on cargo not yet shipped as soon as the cargo is actually shipped and the premium has been paid. The policy will be issued not only to the person who received the open cover but also to any person who produces it to the company. Effect is given as a matter of course to such agreements; but they cannot be enforced in law.

Open door, the principle of the treatment of parties to a treaty and their nationals in a third country on a footing of equality with other parties to the treaty.

Open fields or **meadows,** fields which are undivided, but belong to separate owners; the part of each owner is marked off by boundaries until the crop has been carried, when the pasture is shared promiscuously by the joint herd of all the owners. This system of agriculture is still in operation at Laxton in Nottinghamshire, where a jury is elected every year to see that the landmarks are still in place (Seebohm, *English Village Community*; Elton, *Commons*, 31). See DOLE; LOT MEADS; SELION OF LAND; SEVERALTY; SHACK.

Open law [*lex manifesta*], the making or waging of law: see Magna Carta, c. 21.

Open policy, one in which the value of the ship or goods insured is to be ascertained in case of loss. See POLICY.

Open space. By the Metropolitan Open Spaces Acts, 1877 and 1881, the Metropolitan Board of Works, succeeded by the London County Council (Local Government Act, 1888, s. 40 (8)), had power to acquire and hold for the use of the public any open spaces within the metropolis. These Acts were extended, with amendments, to urban sanitary districts, and, with the consent of the Local Government Board, to rural sanitary districts, by the Open Spaces Act, 1887; and the Open Spaces Act, 1890, empowered the trustees of land held upon trust for the purposes of public recreation to transfer it to the local authorities of their districts for those purposes. The Open Spaces Act, 1906, consolidates these Acts and by s. 20 enacts that the expression " open space " means any land, whether inclosed or not, on which there are no buildings or of which not more than one-twentieth part is covered with buildings, and the whole or the remainder of which is laid out as a garden or is used for purposes of recreation, or lies waste and unoccupied. See also the London County Council (General Powers) Act, 1926, s. 11. As to the requirements for a faculty from the consistory court under this Act to convert a closed churchyard into an open space, see *Bermondsey Borough Council* v. *Mortimer* [1926] P. 87.

A covered railway platform is not an open space within the meaning of the Public Order Act, 1936, s. 9. *Quaere* whether a stand at a racecourse or football ground is an open space (*Cooper* v. *Shield* [1971] 2 Q.B. 334).

Square gardens in cities and boroughs are protected by the Town Gardens Protection Act, 1863, within which statute it was held in 1868 that Leicester Square in London did not come (*Tulk* v. *Metropolitan Board of Works* (1868) L.R. 3 Q.B. 682); see also the London Squares Preservation Act, 1931. The Local Government Act, 1933, s. 174, provided for the compulsory acquisition of open spaces. See also the Housing Act, 1957, s. 150; New Towns Act, 1965, ss. 7 (2), 8 (3), 21; Town and Country Planning Act, 1968, s. 31; Town and Country Planning Act, 1971, ss. 121, 129.

For powers of local authorities to manage parks and open spaces see the Public Health Act, 1961, ss. 52–54; London Government Act, 1963, s. 58 (1); Local Government Act, 1972, Sch. 14 para. 42, Sch. 30; S.I. 1966 No. 1305, art. 5.

As to open spaces held in undivided shares, see the Law of Property Act, 1925, s. 39, Sch. 1 Pt. V para. 5, and *Re Bradford* [1928] Ch. 138, and *Re Townshend* [1930] 2 Ch. 328.

See LOCAL IMPROVEMENTS; NATIONAL PARKS; NATIONAL TRUST.

Open theft [Sax. *open theof*], a theft that is manifest (Leg.Hen. 1, c. 13).

Opencast mining. See COAL MINES; MINERALS.

Opening biddings. Where estates were sold under a decree of a court of equity, the court considered itself to have a greater power over the contract than if the contract were made between party and party; and as the aim of the court was to obtain as great a price as possible for the estate, it would open the biddings after the estate was sold, and put up the estate for sale again.

The Sale of Land by Auction Act, 1867, s. 7, abolished this practice (under which biddings were opened even more than once) with an exception for cases of fraud or improper management of a sale, in which, upon the application of any person interested in the land, the court may open the biddings, and may hold a bidder bound by his bidding, or discharge him from being the purchaser and order the land to be resold (*Delves* v. *Delves* (1875) L.R. 20 Eq. 77).

Opening the case. On a trial before a jury the party who upholds the affirmative of the issue begins, in conformity with the civil law maxim, *ei incumbit probatio, qui dicit, non qui negat*; *cum, per rerum naturam, factum negantis probatio nulla sit* (Cod. 4). See RIGHT TO BEGIN.

Opening the pleadings, stating briefly at a trial before a jury the substance of the pleadings. This is usually done by the junior counsel for the plaintiff at the commencement of the trial. In the Chancery Division, the trial or hearing commences with the speech of the plaintiff's senior counsel, which is called the opening.

Opentide, the time after corn is carried out of the fields (Brit.).

Operarii, tenants of small portions of a manor who held by the service of doing a stipulated number of days' work in the year for the lord (Tomlin).

Operatio, a day's work due to the lord by an *operarius* (Paroch.Antiq. 320).

Operative part. In a conveyance, lease, mortgage, or other formal instrument, the operative part is that which carries out the main object of the instrument. Thus, in a conveyance or lease, the operative part consists of the operative words of conveyance or demise and the parcels; sometimes everything which follows the recitals (*q.v.*) is called the operative part, for the term has no fixed meaning.

Operative words. In the original sense of the phrase, operative words are words which have an operation or effect in the creation or transfer of an estate. Thus, in a gift of land to A and B and the heirs of the body of A, the word " heirs " is an operative word, because it creates an estate of inheritance in A; and the words " of the body " are operative words, because their effect is to limit an entailed interest (Co.Litt. 26a). (See HEIR.)

More often, however, such words are called words of limitation (*q.v.*), and the term " operative words " is applied to those words which pass an estate. Thus, the words enfeoff, grant, bargain and sell, demise, alien, release and confirm are, or were, used in conveyances of freehold land as operative words, that is, for the purpose of effecting an alienation of the land from the grantor to the grantee.

Opetide, the ancient time of marriage, from Epiphany to Ash Wednesday.

Opinion. The judgments delivered in the House of Lords by the Law Lords are technically known as opinions or speeches. The mere expression of opinions by any judge as to matters not decided in a case are known as *dicta* or *obiter* (see DICTUM). The advice given by counsel upon the facts set out in a case submitted to him is known as an opinion. See ADVICE OF COURT.

Statements of opinion may be admissible in evidence under the Civil Evidence Act, 1972, s. 1. See HEARSAY. A statement of opinion by a witness on any relevant matter including an issue in the proceedings, if made as a way of conveying relevant facts personally perceived by him is admissible as evidence of what he perceived (Civil Evidence Act, 1972, s. 3 (2) (3)). As to the opinions of expert witnesses, see EXPERT EVIDENCE.

Opium. See DRUGS, DANGEROUS.

Oportet quod certa res deducatur in judicium (Jenk., Cent. 84). (A thing which is certain must be brought to judgment.) That is to say, there must be no doubt as to what precisely it is that the court has to decide. Quoted in connection with a decision of the Exchequer on a double plea. See DUPLICITY.

Opposer, an officer of the Green Wax (*q.v.*) in the Exchequer, whose office was abolished before 1798; he does not appear in the list of Green Wax officials at that time.

Opposite, an old word for opponent.

Opposition. See LEADER OF THE OPPOSITION.

Oppression, the common law misdemeanour committed by a public officer who, under colour of his office, wrongfully inflicts upon any person any bodily harm, imprisonment or other injury. In 1762 the offence was held to have been committed where justices refused licences to publicans who had not voted as the justices wished (3 Burr. 1317). Prosecutions for the offence are now unknown.

A minority shareholder of a company may petition the court for relief from oppression under the Companies Act, 1948, s. 210. The conditions for success are stated in *Re H. R. Harmer* [1959] 1 W.L.R. 62.

Opticians. See the Opticians Act, 1958.

As to charges for optical work see the National Health Service Act, 1951, Sch.; National Health Service Act, 1961; National Health Service Reorganisation Act, 1973, Sch. 4 para. 59.

Optima est legis interpres consuetudo (Lofft. 237; D. 1, 3, 37). (Custom is the best interpreter of the law.)

Optima est lex quae minimum relinquit arbitrio judicis; optimus judex qui minimum sibi (Bac.Aphor. 46). (That system of law is best which confides as little as possible to the discretion of a judge; that judge the best who trusts as little as possible to himself.) This does not mean that a judge should be weak; what it does mean is that he should not rely upon his own views where there is law to guide him. See DISCRETIO EST, ETC.

Optima legum interpres est consuetudo (Plow.Com. 336). (Custom is the best interpreter of the laws.) This is a maxim of the civil law which was quoted by Chief Baron Saunders in 1568 in connection with the question whether the Crown was entitled to mines of copper if the copper contained gold or silver.

Optima statuti interpretatrix est (omnibus particulis ejusdem inspectis) ipsum statutum (8 Co.Rep. 117; Wing. 239). (The best interpreter of a statute is (all the separate parts being considered) the statute itself.) See INJUSTUM EST, ETC.

Optimacy, nobility; men of the highest rank.

Optimus interpres rerum usus (2 Co. Inst. 282). (The best interpreter of things is usage.) A wider form of *Optima legum, etc. (q.v.)*. But evidence of usage is inadmissible to vary, though admissible to explain, a written contract; and evidence of the existence of a custom which is bad in law is never admissible. See Ex NON SCRIPTO, ETC.; MALUS USUS, ETC.

Optimus interpretandi modus est sic leges interpretari ut leges legibus concordant (8 Co.Rep. 169). (The best mode of interpretation is so to interpret laws that they may accord with each other.) See ACT OF PARLIAMENT.

Optimus legum interpres consuetudo (4 Co.Inst. 75). (Custom is the best interpreter of the laws.)

Option, the privilege (acquired for a consideration) of calling for delivery or of making delivery of, or both, within a specified time, of some particular stock or article at a specified price to a specified amount. An option is valid if—which is not always the case—it is intended that the stock or article shall actually change hands.

An option, exercisable by notice in writing, is not validly exercised by the posting of a letter which is not received (*Holwell Securities* v. *Hughes* [1974] 1 W.L.R. 155). An agreement giving first refusal to purchase registered land does not constitute an interest in land, nor does it constitute a minor interest capable of binding third parties by virtue of the Land Registration Act, 1925, s. 3 (xv) (*Murray* v. *Two Strokes* [1973] 1 W.L.R. 823).

A clause giving the lessee the option of purchasing the reversion for a fixed sum within a limited number of years, or at any time during the term, is sometimes inserted in leases. Such an option is exempted from the rule against perpetuities regardless of the length of the term (Perpetuities and Accumulations Act, 1964, s. 9 (1)). Other options to buy land are valid for twenty-one years only (s. 9 (2)). If the option is granted without time limit it will be valid if exercised within twenty-one years (s. 3). The liability of the person granting the option ceases at the end of twenty-one years and cannot be enforced in contract (s. 10). But these rules do not apply to instruments taking effect before the commencement of the Act (s. 15 (5)). Accordingly a clause giving an option to purchase at any time during a ninety-nine years' lease granted before the commencement of the Act offends against the law of perpetuities and cannot be specifically enforced (*Woodall* v. *Clifton* [1905] 2 Ch. 257; *Worthing Corporation* v. *Heather* [1906] 2 Ch. 532).

The sum of £1 is a perfectly sufficient valuable consideration for the grant of an option to purchase (*Mountford* v. *Scott* [1975] 2 W.L.R. 114).

Options to purchase a legal estate (including options to renew a lease) must be registered in the Land Registry under the Land Charges Act, 1972, as estate contracts (*q.v.*), or they will be void against a purchaser for value (with or without notice), for money or money's worth; but the grantee of the option will be entitled to damages against the grantor if he has put it out of his power to perform the contract (*Wright* v. *Dean* [1948] Ch. 686). A tenant for life may grant an option to purchase or to take a lease exercisable over any period not exceeding ten years (Settled Land Act, 1925, s. 51). The Law of Property Act, 1925, s. 149 (3), prohibits the granting of a lease at a rent or upon payment of a fine to take effect more than twenty-one years from the date of the instrument purporting to create it except in regard to terms or interests under a settlement or under equitable powers for a mortgage, indemnity, etc. An option to renew a lease exercisable more than twenty-one years after its creation is not rendered void by this provision (*Weg Motors* v. *Hales* [1962] Ch. 49). The Law of Property Act, 1922, Sch. 15 para. 7 (2), avoids any contract to renew a lease for more than sixty years from the expiration of the lease.

In ecclesiastical law, an archbishop had a customary prerogative to name a clerk or chaplain of his own, to be provided for by each bishop of his province who was consecrated by him. In lieu of this right, it was usual for the bishop to make over by deed to the archbishop the next presentation of such dignity or benefice within the bishop's see and disposal, as the archbishop should choose: hence, this was called his option. This privilege was abolished by the Ecclesiastical Commissioners Act, 1840, s. 42, which forbade a spiritual person to assign any patronage or presentation belonging to him by virtue of his office.

Optional writ, any original writ which commanded the defendant to do the thing required or show cause why he had not done it (3 Bl.Comm. 274).

Ora, a Saxon coin or a Danish coin introduced into England by the Danish invaders, said to be worth sixteen or twenty pence, although from the Laws of Edward the Elder and Guthrum (*circa* 920), c. 7, it would appear to have been at one time worth something like thirty pence. In Domesday Book the word is used as meaning an ounce.

Oraculum, a decision by a Roman emperor.

Oral, delivered by the mouth; not written.

Oral pleading, pleadings by word of mouth in the presence of the judges. This was the original mode of pleading; it was, however, except in criminal cases, superseded by written pleadings in the reign of Edward III.

Orando pro rege et regno. Before the Reformation, while there was no standing collect for a Parliament in session, it was customary for a new Parliament to petition the king to require the clergy to offer up prayers for the kingdom and for a good understanding between the king and Parliament; and thereupon the writ *De orando pro rege et regno* (to pray for the king and the kingdom) was issued to the clergy. It does not appear to have been used much later than the reign of Edward III (Nichols. Engl.Hist. 66).

Orangemen, a party in Ireland who adhere to the views of William of Orange.

Oratio, an address by the emperor to the senate stating what he wished them to embody in a *senatus consultum* (Civil Law).

Oratio obliqua. See OBLIQUA, ORATIO.

Orator [Lat. *orare*, to pray], a petitioner; a plaintiff in a bill, or information, in Chancery was so called before the statute 1852, 15 & 16 Vict. c. 86.

Oratrix, or **Oratress,** a female petitioner; a female plaintiff in a bill in Chancery was formerly so called.

Orbation, privation of parents or children; poverty.

Orchards. See GARDENS.

Orchestra. A local authority has power to maintain a band or orchestra (Local Government Act, 1972, s. 145).

Orcinus, pertaining to *Orcus*, the nether world, or death; a freedman who had received freedom directly from the will of his master, having been the slave of the testator at the date of the will as well as at the date of his death (Civil Law).

Ordeal [Sax. *ordal*; *or*, great; *dele*, judgment], an ancient manner of trial in criminal cases practised among the Saxons, who affected to believe that God would actively interpose to establish an earthly right. There were four sorts: campfight, *duellum*, or combat (see BATTLE, TRIAL BY); fire ordeal; hot water ordeal; and cold water ordeal.

Ordeal was distinguished by the appellation of *judicium Dei*, and sometimes by that of *vulgaris purgatio*, to distinguish it from the canonical purgation, which was by the oath of the party. Fire ordeal was confined to persons of rank, while water ordeal was open to the common people. Fire ordeal was performed either by taking up in the hand a piece of red-hot iron of one pound weight in the case of single ordeal, or three pounds' weight in the case of triple ordeal, or else by walking barefoot and blindfold over nine red-hot ploughshares laid lengthwise, at unequal distances; if the party escaped unhurt he was adjudged innocent; if otherwise, he was condemned as guilty. Water ordeal was performed either by plunging the bare arm up to the wrist or elbow in boiling water and taking out a stone, or by casting the suspected person into a river or pond of cold water; and if in the former instance his arm was burnt, or if in the latter instance he floated without any effort to swim, it was deemed evidence of his guilt; if otherwise, of his innocence. The ordeal was abolished in the reign of Henry III, when the more rational process of trying the guilt or innocence of an accused person by means of compurgation (*q.v.*) was substituted for it (Lea, *Superstition and Force*; Goitein, *Primitive Ordeal*; Snell, *Customs of Old England*).

See APPEAL OF FELONY; BATTLE, TRIAL BY; BIER RIGHT; CORSNED BREAD.

Ordel, ordeal.

Ordelfe, Ordeffe, Oredelf, a liberty whereby a man claimed ore found in his own land; also, the ore lying under land.

Ordels, the right of administering oaths and adjudging trials by ordeal within a precinct or liberty.

Order, mandate, precept; command; also a class or rank.

In its simplest sense, an order is a mandate or direction. Thus, bills of exchange, cheques, etc., are said to be drawn to order when the payee is entitled to transfer the right to claim payment to any person whom he may direct. See BEARER; BILL OF EXCHANGE; DELIVERY ORDER; NEGOTIABLE.

More commonly, however, order signifies a direction or command by a court of judicature, and directions or commands termed " rules " are included in " orders." As a general rule, " order " is opposed to " judgment," and therefore denotes orders made in summary proceedings on petition or summons (see SUMMARY), and orders made in actions on interlocutory applications, whether before or after final judgment (see INTERLOCUTORY). Such are the ordinary orders for discovery and production of documents, orders for time, etc., made in the course of almost every action. See RULE.

As to orders of course, see OF COURSE.

Orders are also issued by subordinate legislative authorities. Such are Orders in Council (*q.v.*), or orders issued by the Privy Council in the name of the Queen, either in exercise of the royal prerogative or in pursuance of an Act of Parliament. The Rules of the Supreme Court under the Judicature Act, 1925, are grouped together in the form of orders, each order dealing with a particular subject-matter.

Order and disposition. When goods are in the order and disposition of a bankrupt, they go to his trustee, and have gone so since the time of James I. The Bankruptcy Act, 1914, s. 38, provides that all goods being at the commencement of the bankruptcy in the possession, order or disposition (that is, in the possession or apparent control) of the bankrupt in his trade or business, by the consent and permission of the true owner, of which goods and chattels the bankrupt is reputed owner, shall be divisible amongst his creditors: the section, however, provides that choses in action, other than debts due or growing due to the bankrupt in the course of his trade or business, shall not be deemed goods within the meaning of the section. See POSSESSION; REPUTED OWNERSHIP.

Order in Council, an order made by the Queen by and with the advice of the Privy Council.

Some Orders in Council are made under statutory authority. The issue of Orders in Council is expressly authorised by various modern statutes, the effect of this authorisation being to give the government a power to legislate, subject in many cases to the right of Parliament to nullify the Order in Council by an address disapproving thereof. See Statutory Rules, etc.

Other Orders in Council are made by virtue of the royal prerogative (*q.v.*). Thus the civil service is regulated to some extent by Orders in Council made under the prerogative.

Order of Council. An Order in Council (*q.v.*) is an order made by the sovereign by and with the advice of the Privy Council: an Order of Council is an order made by the Privy Council without the concurrence of the sovereign.

The Municipal Corporations Act, 1883, s. 6, provided for the issue of Orders of Council: but the section was not acted on. The Acts relating to dentists, medical men, chemists and veterinary surgeons, however, contain provisions which authorise the issue of Orders of Council for certain purposes, *e.g.,* Medical Act, 1956, ss. 49–51.

Order of course, an order made on an *ex parte* application, and to which a party is entitled as of right on his own statement and at his own risk.

Order of discharge, an order made under the Bankruptcy Act, 1914, s. 26, by a court of bankruptcy, the effect of which is to discharge a bankrupt from all debts, claims, or demands provable under the bankruptcy, except Crown debts, debts incurred by fraud, and certain judgments (s. 28).

Order, Payable to. A bill of exchange or cheque payable to order is payable to the person named thereon or as he may direct by his indorsement.

Orders, Holy. See Holy Orders.

Orders other than of knighthood. See Companions of Honour; Crown of India; Distinguished Service Order; Imperial Service Order; Merit, Order of; St. John, etc.; Victoria and Albert, Etc.

Ordinacio de Conspiratoribus, the statute 1305, 33 Edw. 1, st. 2.

Ordinance. The difference between an Act of Parliament and an ordinance in Parliament is that the ordinance lacks the threefold consent of lords, commons, and Crown, and is ordained by one or two of them (4 Co.Inst. 25; Co.Litt. 159b).

The enactments which were passed during the period between the outbreak of the Civil War and the Restoration (1642–1660) were all passed without the consent of the Crown, and are known as ordinances.

According to some old writers, an ordinance was in the nature of a declaration by the Crown in answer to a petition by the Commons, on a question as to the law applicable to a given case, while a statute was an enactment of new law.

In modern times the term ordinance is applied to the instrument by which the sovereign creates a new order of knighthood, and to what correspond in Crown colonies to Acts of Parliament here and in the Dominions and self-governing colonies.

Ordinance of the Forest. See Ordinatio Forestae.

Ordinandi lex, the law of procedure as distinguished from the substantive part of the law.

Ordinarius ita dicitur quia habet ordinariam jurisdictionem, in jure proprio, et non propter deputationem (Co.Litt. 96). (The ordinary is so called because he has an ordinary jurisdiction in his own right, and not a deputed one.)

Ordinary, a civil law term for any judge having authority to take cognisance of causes in his own right, and not by deputation; it was used in the Statute of Westminster II, 1285, c. 19, to indicate one who had ordinary or exempt and immediate jurisdiction in ecclesiastical causes (Co.Litt. 344).

The name is applied to the bishop of a diocese when exercising the ecclesiastical jurisdiction annexed to his office, he being *judex ordinarius* within his diocese. The archbishop is the ordinary of the whole province to visit and receive appeals from inferior jurisdictions (2 Co.Inst. 398; 9 Co.Rep. 41; Wood's Inst. 25). See Bishop; Judge Ordinary.

The name is also applied to a commissary or official of a bishop or other ecclesiastical judge having judicial power; an archdeacon; an officer of the royal household.

Ordinary conveyances, those deeds of transfer which are entered into between two or more persons, without an assurance in superior court of justice. See DEED.

Ordinary of assize and sessions, a deputy of the bishop of the diocese, appointed to give malefactors their neck-verses, and judge whether they read or not; also to perform divine service for them, and assist in preparing them for death. See NECK VERSE.

Ordinary of Newgate, the clergyman who attended upon condemned malefactors in that prison to prepare them for death; he recorded the behaviour of such persons, and it was the custom of the ordinary to publish a small pamphlet upon the execution of any remarkable criminal.

Ordinatio Forestae, the statutes 1305, 33 Edw. 1, st. 5, and 1306, 34 Edw. 1, st. 5, regarding causes and matters of the forest (2 Reeves, c. ix, 104, 106).

Ordinatio pro statu Hiberniae, the statute 1324, 17 Edw. 2, st. 1, concerning Ireland (2 Reeves, c. ix, 99).

Ordination, the conferring of holy orders. The first thing necessary on application for holy orders is the possession of a title, that is, an assurance from a rector or vicar to the bishop that, provided the bishop finds the person fit to be ordained, the rector or vicar will take him for his curate, with a stated salary. The candidate is then examined by the bishop or his chaplain respecting both his faith and his erudition; and various certificates are necessary, particularly one signed by the clergyman of the parish in which he has resided during a given time. The candidate has to comply with the requirements of the Clerical Subscription Act, 1865 (see CLERICAL SUBSCRIPTION; and of the Clergy (Ordination and Miscellaneous Provisions) Measure, 1964, s. 1); a clerk must have attained his twenty-third year before he can be ordained a deacon, and his twenty-fourth to receive priest's orders (Ordination of the Ministers Act, 1571, s. 3; Clergy Ordination

Act, 1804, s. 1; Canon 34), unless being over twenty-three years he has a faculty from the Archbishop of Canterbury (Clergy (Ordination and Miscellaneous Provisions) Measure, 1964, s. 2). See also the Overseas and Other Clergy (Ministry and Ordination) Measure, 1967.

In the Presbyterian and Congregational Churches ordination means the act of establishing a licensed preacher over a congregation with pastoral charge and authority, or the act of conferring on a man the powers of a settled minister of the gospel, without the charge of a particular church, but with general powers whenever he may be called upon to officiate.

See ADMISSION; BENEFICE; RECTOR; VICAR.

Ordinatione contra servientes, De, a writ which lay against a servant for leaving his master contrary to the Statute of Labourers, 1349 (Reg.Orig. 189).

Ordines, a general chapter or other solemn convention of the religious of a particular order.

Ordines majores et minores. The holy orders of priest, deacon, and sub-deacon, any of which qualified for presentation and admission to an ecclesiastical dignity or cure, were called *ordines majores*; and the inferior orders of chanter, psalmist, ostiary, reader, exorcist and acolyte were called *ordines minores*; persons ordained to the *ordines minores* had their *prima tonsura* different from the *tonsura clericalis* (Cowel).

Ordinum fugitivi, those of the religious who deserted their houses, and, throwing off the habits, renounced their particular order in contempt of their oath and other obligations (Par.Antiq. 388).

Ordnance, Board of, a body of officials, also called the Ordnance Office, which from the sixteenth century provided the munitions of war required for the army and the navy, and more especially for the navy, the army until after the Restoration having no regular establishment in time of peace. The office was in the Tower of London, and it superintended and disposed of all the arms, instruments, and utensils of war, both by sea and land, in all the magazines, garrisons, and forts of Great Britain. The head of the Board was the Master of the Ordnance (*q.v.*), who afterwards developed in the Master-General of the Ordnance. The Board grew into an important separate department. For many years before 1828 the Master-General of the Ordnance was a member of the Cabinet, and necessarily a member of one House of Parliament or the other. The Board was divided into two distinct branches, the civil and the military, by the Superannuation Act, 1834. Up to 1855 the Board remained independent of the Secretary for War, and was represented in Parliament by two of its members. In 1855 its powers were transferred to the Secretary for War by the Ordnance Board Transfer Act, 1855. The Master-General of Ordnance is a member of the Ministry of Defence.

As to the finance of Royal Ordnance Factories see the Government Trading Funds Act, 1973.

Ordnance debentures, bills payable by the treasurer of the Board of Ordnance which that body formerly issued in payment for stores, etc., purchased by them. See ORDNANCE, BOARD OF.

Ordnance survey, a survey of the United Kingdom, made under the authority of the Ordnance Survey Act, 1841. The work was originally entrusted to the Board of Ordnance (see ORDNANCE, BOARD OF), from whom it passed in 1855 to the Secretary of State for War, in 1870 to the Commissioners of Works (under the Survey Act, 1870), and in 1889 to the Board of Agriculture (under the Board of Agriculture Act, 1889). The work is done by the Ordnance Survey Department under its own Director-General.

For definition of ordnance map, see the Interpretation Act, 1889, s. 25; for use of ordnance maps in the Land Registry, see the Land Registration Act, 1925, s. 76. As to boundaries, see *Davey* v. *Harrow Corporation* [1958] 1 Q.B. 60.

Ordo, that rule which monks were obliged to observe.

Ordo albus, the white friars or Augustines. The Cistercians also wore white.

Ordo niger, the black friars. The Cluniacs also wore black.

Ore tenus, by word of mouth. See DEMURRER.

Orfgild [Sax. *orf*, cattle; *gild*, recompense], a delivery or restitution of cattle; a restitution made by the hundred or county for any wrong done by one who was in pledge, or rather a penalty for taking away cattle (Lamb.Arch. 125; Cowel; Blount).

Organisation for European Economic Co-operation and Development (O.E.C.D.), an organisation set up by the Convention for European Economic Co-operation (Cmd. 7388) signed in Paris on April 16, 1948. See the O.E.C.D. Support Fund Act, 1975.

Orgild, without recompense; as where no satisfaction was to be made for the death of a man killed, so that he was judged lawfully slain (Spelman).

Orige. See ORWIGE.

Origin. A declaration as to the place in which goods were manufactured or grown, made before a prescribed person by a shipper of the goods before they are actually shipped, is known as a certificate of origin. This must be produced in most foreign countries before the goods can be unloaded.

As to domicile of origin, see DOMICILE.

Original. See BILL OF COMPLAINT; CONVEYANCE; EVIDENCE; ORIGINAL WRIT; TITLE; WRIT.

Original and derivative estates. An original is the first of several estates bearing to each other the relation of a particular estate and a reversion. An original estate is contrasted with a derivative estate; and a derivative estate is a particular interest carved out of another estate of larger extent.

Original bills in equity. See BILL IN CHANCERY.

Original writ, or Original [Lat. *breve originale*], the beginning or foundation of a real action at common law.

It was a mandatory letter issuing out of the common law, or ordinary, jurisdiction of the Court of Chancery, under the Great Seal, and in the sovereign's name, addressed to the sheriff of the county where the injury was committed, containing a summary statement of the cause of complaint, and requiring him to command the defendant to satisfy the claim, and, on his failure to comply, then to summon him to appear in one of the superior courts of common law. In some cases it simply required the sheriff to enforce the appearance. Original writs differed from each other in their tenor, according to the nature of the plaintiff's complaint, and were conceived in fixed and certain forms. Many of these are of a remote antiquity; others are of later origin. The ancient writs had provided for the most obvious kinds of wrong; but, in the progress of society, cases of injury arose new in their circumstances, so as not to be reached by any of the writs then known in practice; and it seems that either the clerks of the Chancery (who prepared the original writ) had no authority to devise new forms for such cases, or they were remiss in its exercise. Therefore, by the Statute of Westminster II, 1285, c. 24, it was provided that as often as it should happen in the Chancery that in one case a writ was found, and in a like case, falling under the same right, and requiring like remedy, no writ was to be found, the clerks of the Chancery should agree in making a writ or adjourn the complaint till the next Parliament, and write the case in which they could not agree, and refer it to the next Parliament. See CASE.

The following original writs were issued, not *ex debito justitiae*, but *ex mera gratia*, and were sometimes denominated discretionary writs: *de ventre inspiciendo*; *supplicavit*; certiorari; prohibition; writs of error in criminal cases: *ad quod damnum*; *scire facias*, to repeal letters patent, etc. (Mad.Eq. b. 8.)

Originalia rolls, rolls running from 1236 to 1837, in which were recorded the estreats sent from the Chancery to the Exchequer. They were so called to distinguish them from records which contain the judgments of the barons of the Exchequer.

Originating summons, a summons without writ, returnable in the chambers of a judge of the High Court. Summonses of this description are very frequently issued in the Chancery Division for the determination of questions arising in the administration of an estate or trust, without the administration of the whole estate or trust; for settling quesions between vendors and purchasers (see VENDOR AND PURCHASER SUMMONS); for foreclosure or redemption of mortgages; for determining

questions of construction of a written instrument, and for numerous other purposes. If the question raised is one requiring argument it is generally adjourned into court; if it is a simple matter the judge will determine it in chambers. The summons may be taken out by any person interested, and is served on the persons whose rights are sought to be affected. See SUMMONS.

An originating summons can probably be issued to determine whether a tribunal's finding is right in law even though its decision is by statute "final" (*Punton* v. *Ministry of Pensions* [1963] 1 W.L.R. 186).

Origine propria neminem posse voluntate sua eximi manifestum est (Cod. 10, 38, 4). (It is manifest that no one is able, of his own will, to get rid of his proper origin.) No one could at common law divest himself of his natural allegiance. See NATURALISATION; NEMO PATRIAM, ETC.

Ornamental grounds. The Town Gardens Protection Act, 1863, provides for the protection of gardens and ornamental grounds in cities and boroughs. See GARDENS; OPEN SPACE.

Ornamental timber. Cutting down ornamental timber by the tenant for life is a species of equitable waste (*q.v.*) (*Micklethwaite* v. *Micklethwaite* (1857) 1 De G. & J. 504).

Ornaments rubric, the rubric of the Prayer Book which directs just before the order for Morning Prayer that such ornaments of the Church and of ministers shall be retained and be in use as were authorised by the Act of Uniformity, 1548.

The meaning of this rubric was held to be that vestments of ministers as celebrants cannot be worn, though prescribed by the first Prayer Book of Edward VI, which had the authority of the Act of Uniformity, 1548 (*Clifton* v. *Ridsdale* (1887) 2 P.D. 276).

Stations of the Cross introduced for devotional purposes may be illegal ornaments (*Re St. Mary, the Virgin, West Moors* [1963] P. 390) if they are intended or likely to be used for superstitious purposes (*Re St. Augustine's, Brinksway* [1953] P. 364).

Ornest, trial by battle, which does not seem to have been used in England before the time of the Conqueror, though originating in the kingdoms of the North, where it was practised under the name of *holmgang*, from the custom of fighting duels on a small island or *holm* (Anc.Inst.Eng.).

Orphan, fatherless child or minor, or one deprived of both father and mother.

The Lord Chancellor is the general guardian of all orphans and minors throughout the realm. See GUARDIAN; WARD.

In London the Lord Mayor and Aldermen had in their Court of Orphans the custody of the orphans of deceased freemen, and also the keeping of their land and goods; accordingly the executors and administrators of freemen leaving such orphans had to exhibit inventories of the estate of the deceased, and give security to the Chamberlain for the orphan's part or share.

Guardians' allowances are payable under the Social Security Act, 1975, s. 38.

Orphan dues. The statute 1693, 5 & 6 W. & M., c. 10, imposed a duty of four shillings per tun on all sorts of wines imported into the Port of London, for the relief of orphans and others in London.

Acts of William IV and Victoria provided for similar duties on coals, culm and cinders imported to any place within twenty miles of London. The duties were removed by the statute 1861, 24 & 25 Vict. c. 42, which provided for their termination in 1872.

Orphanotrophi, managers of houses for orphans (Civil Law).

Ortelli, used in the Carta de Foresta, c. 6, as meaning the claws of a dog's foot (Kitch.).

Ortolagium, a garden plot or hortilage.

Orwige [*sine wita*], without war or feud, such security being provided by the laws, for homicides under certain circumstances, against the *foehth*, or deadly feud, on the part of the family of the slain (Anc.Inst.Eng.).

Os demonstrat quod cor ruminat (3 Buls. 260). (The mouth shows what it is that the heart is thinking.) See SERMO EST, ETC.

Osborne Estate. See the Osborne Estate Acts, 1902 and 1914.

Osborne Morgan's Act, the Burial Laws Amendment Act, 1880.

Ostensible, apparent.

Ostensio, a tax which was paid by merchants, etc., for leave to show or expose their goods for sale in markets (Du Cange; Anc.Inst.Eng.).

Osteopathy, a theory which assumes that disease is caused by deformation of the skeleton and consequent interference with the adjacent nerves and blood-vessels. The Medical Act, 1956, s. 27, does not prevent an osteopath who is not a registered medical practitioner from recovering fees for treatment as distinct from diagnosis or advice (*Macnaghten* v. *Douglas* [1927] 2 K.B. 292).

Ostium ecclesiae, Dower ad. See AD OSTIUM ECCLESIAE, ETC.

Oswald's Law, a law made by King Edgar about 964 at the suggestion of St. Oswald, the bishop of Worcester. During the anarchy produced by the Danish invasions, the parochial clergy had become to a large extent non-celibate and the monasteries had in many cases been broken up. Under Oswald's Law, celibacy became again the rule amongst the clergy and the monasteries were restored.

Oswald's Law Hundred, a hundred in Worcestershire containing about 300 hides of land which St. Oswald obtained from King Edgar as an endowment for St. Mary's Church in Worcester. It was exempt from the sheriff's jurisdiction (Camd.Brit.).

Ottawa Agreements. See the Ottawa Agreements Act, 1932, the Finance Act, 1937, s. 3, and the Import Duties Act, 1958.

Otter, a small board weighted on one edge so that it floats upright, which is attached to a line in the same way as an ordinary kite is attached to the string; when pushed out from the bank of a lake or river it works through the water parallel to anyone walking along the bank and holding the line; on the line are flies to catch fish. The use of any " otter lath or jack " for the capture of salmon, trout or freshwater fish is prohibited by the Salmon and Freshwater Fisheries Act, 1975, s. 1.

Oulter le mer, beyond the seas. This was one of the recognised essoins (*q.v.*).

Ounce. One sixteenth part of the imperial pound (Weights and Measures Act, 1963, s. 10, Sch. 1 Pt. V). See POUND. An ounce troy is 480 grains (*ibid.*). See TROY WEIGHT. A fluid ounce is one-twentieth of a pint (s. 1, Sch. 1 Pt. IV). See GALLON; PINT. The apothecaries' ounce was also 480 grains (Sch. 1 Pt. V) but it is no longer a unit of measurement. See APOTHECARIES' WEIGHT.

Ourlop, the lierwite or fine paid to the lord by an inferior tenant when his daughter was debauched.

Oust, to dispossess.

Ouster, dispossession; a wrong or injury which may be sustained in respect of hereditaments, corporeal or incorporeal, carrying with it the deprivation of possession; for thereby the wrongdoer gets into the actual occupation of the land or hereditament, and obliges him who has a right to seek his legal remedy in order to gain possession and damage for the injury sustained. An ouster may be either rightful or wrongful. A wrongful ouster is a disseisin (*q.v.*) (Co.Litt. 153b, 181a).

Ouster of the freehold was effected by abatement, intrusion, disseisin, discontinuance or deforcement.

Ouster of chattels real consisted first of amotion of possession from estates held by statute, recognisance, or *elegit,* which happened by a species of disseisin or turning out of the legal proprietor before his estate was determined, by raising the sum for which it was given to him in pledge; and secondly, of amotion of possession from an estate of years, which took place by a like kind of disseisin, ejection, or turning out of the tenant from the occupation of the land during the continuance of his term (3 Bl.Comm. 167, 198).

See DEFORCEMENT.

Ouster le mer. See OULTER LE MER.

Ousterlemain [Lat. *amovere manum*], a writ directing the seisin or possession of land to be delivered out of the hands of the Crown into those of a person entitled to it. It was the mode by which an heir in ward of land held of the Crown *ut de honore* obtained possession of it on attaining majority (Co.Litt. 77a). See LIVERY; WARDSHIP.

Ousterlemain also meant a judgment on a *monstrans de droit,* deciding that the Crown had no title to a thing which it had seized (Staunf.Prerog. 77b). See AMOVEAS MANUS, ETC.; CAPITE, TENURE IN.

Out of court, deprived of all right to have one's case so much as considered by the court. A plaintiff in an action at common law must have declared within one year after the service of a writ of summons, otherwise he was out of court, unless the court had, by special order, enlarged the time for declaring. See now R.S.C., Ord. 3, r. 6.

Outas. See UTAS.

Outcry, used in the seventeenth and eighteenth centuries as a synonym for auction. See OUTROPER.

Outer bar, junior barristers, who plead outside the bar, as opposed to Queen's Counsel, who plead within it.

Outfangthef. The franchise of outfangthef, according to Britton, was the right of a lord to bring into his own jurisdiction and to hang upon his own gallows one of his own men who had been condemned for theft by someone else. Bracton and Fleta, on the other hand, say that it meant the right of the lord to try thieves who had come into the lord's jurisdiction after stealing elsewhere; and Rastell (1579) says that it meant the right of the lord to bring back into his jurisdiction and to try there any man of his own who had stolen elsewhere: see the statute 1555, 1 & 2 Ph. & M. c. 15. See INFANGTHEFT.

Outgoings, payments which have to be made out of the gross returns of a property or business before its net proceeds can reach the owner, as a drainage rate on land, or the salaries of clerks in the management of a business.

Outgoings is a most comprehensive general expression in a lessee's covenant to pay taxes and other charges (*Stockdale* v. *Ascherberg* [1904] 1 K.B. 447; *Greaves* v. *Whitmarsh* [1906] 2 K.B. 340; *Howe* v. *Botwood* [1913] 2 K.B. 387; *Henman* v. *Berliner* [1918] 2 K.B. 236). As to a head landlord's indemnity, see *Dependable Upholstery* v. *Brasted* [1932] 1 K.B. 291.

Outhest, or **Outhorn,** a calling men out to the army by sound of horn (Jacob).

Outhouses, buildings belonging to and adjoining dwelling-houses.

Outland. In Saxon times this meant the parts of a manor or estate which were let to tenants; inland meant the part—corresponding to the modern demesne and home-farm—which the lord retained for his own use (Spelman).

Outland bill, a bill of exchange used in connection with foreign trade.

Outlaw [Sax. *utlaghe*; Lat. *utlagatus*], a person put out of the law, or deprived of its benefits by judgment of outlawry (*q.v.*). In the reign of Alfred, and until a good while after the Conquest, no man could be outlawed but for felony, the punishment whereof was death. But in the beginning of the reign of Edward III, it was resolved by the judges, for avoiding of inhumanity and of effusion of blood, that it should not be lawful for any man but the sheriff having lawful warrant therefor to put to death any man outlawed, though it were for felony (Co. Litt. 128b).

Up to then an outlaw was *caput lupinum* (*q.v.*). See Snell, *Customs of Old England*. See WAIF; WAIVED.

Outlawry [Lat. *utlagaria*], the being put out of the law for contempt in wilfully avoiding the execution of the process of the king's court.

Outlawry had long been obsolete in civil proceedings, and was formally abolished by the Civil Procedure Acts Repeal Act, 1879, in civil proceedings. In criminal proceedings it was practically disused, but was formally kept alive by the Forfeiture Act, 1870, which Act, while abolishing forfeiture for felony, provided that nothing therein should affect the law of forfeiture consequent on outlawry. It was abolished by the Administration of Justice (Miscellaneous Provisions) Act, 1938.

The maxim applicable to outlaws was let them be answerable to all, and none to them; *utlagatus est quasi extra legem positus; caput gerit lupinum* (an outlaw is, as it were, placed outside the law; he bears the head of a wolf) (7 Co.Rep. 14).

Accordingly, any person outlawed was *civiliter mortuus.* He could hold no property given or devised to him; and all the property which he held before was for-feited. He could neither sue on his contracts, nor had he any legal rights which could be enforced; while, at the same time, he was personally liable upon all causes of action. He could, however, bring actions *in autre droit,* as executor, administrator, etc., because in such actions he only represented persons capable of contracting, and under the protection of the law (*Ex p. Franks* (1831) 7 Bing. at p. 767).

Where an indictment had been found against a person and summary process proved ineffectual to compel him to appear, process of outlawry could be issued. The preliminary process of issuing successively writs of *venire facias ad respondendum, distringas* and *capias ad respondendum* was first gone through; and if the defendant still eluded justice, a writ of *exigent* was awarded, by which the sheriff was required to proclaim the defendant and call him on five county court days (of the old sheriff's county court) one after another upon pain of outlawry: a writ of proclamation was also issued and executed. If the defendant still failed to appear, judgment of outlawry was pronounced by one of the coroners for the county: judgment could also be signed in the Crown Office, and a *capias utlagatum* (*q.v.*) issued. See QUINT-EXACT.

The outlaw became liable to imprisonment, forfeited his property to the Crown (his goods immediately and his chattels real and the profits of his land upon office found) (see OFFICE), was incapacitated from maintaining civil proceedings and became subject to other disabilities (3 Bl.Comm. 284). See ATTAINER.

There were two kinds of outlawry in civil proceedings, one (called outlawry on mesne process) which was used to compel a defendant to appear in an action, the other (called outlawry after judgment) which was a means of execution to enforce a judgment. The former was abolished by the Common Law Procedure Act, 1852, s. 24; the latter by the Civil Procedure Acts Repeal Act, 1879, s. 3.

See GLOVES.

Outparters, stealers of cattle; see the statute 1421, 9 Hen. 5, st. 1, c. 7. See OUTPUTTERS.

Outpenny. See INPENNY, ETC.

Outputters, such as set watches for the robbing of any manor-house; perhaps the same as outparters (Cowel).

Outputers or outputters were persons in the franchise of Redesdale who maintained and equipped robbers operating in the adjacent counties of Northumberland, Cumberland and Westmorland: see the statute 1421, 9 Hen. 5, st. 1, c. 7. See INTAKER.

Outriders, bailiffs errant employed by sheriffs to ride throughout the counties or hundreds to summon persons to the old county or hundred court; mentioned in the statute 1340, 14 Edw. 3, st. 1, c. 9.

Outrooper; Outroper, an auctioneer. This was at one time a title of the officer of the City of London now known as the Common Crier and Serjeant-at-Arms. A charter of 1638 created an office, called outroper or common crier, for the selling of household stuff, apparel, leases and other things by open and public claim, commonly called outcry (*q.v.*) and sale.

Outstanding. Where land is vested in a trustee or mortgagee, the *cestui que trust* or mortgagor can only deal with the beneficial or equitable interest, the legal estate in the land being, as it is said, outstanding in the trustee or mortgagee. If the trust or mortgage is satisfied without the legal estate being revested in the *cestui que trust* or mortgagor, and he contracts to sell the land, the purchaser may require him to get in the legal estate, that is, to obtain a reconveyance of it from the trustee or mortgagee.

Outstanding term, a term in gross at law, which, in equity, might be made attendant upon the inheritance, either by express declaration or by implication. See the Satisfied Terms Act, 1845, extended by the Law of Property Act, 1925, s. 5, Sch. 1 Pt. II para. 1, to outstanding terms out of leaseholds, vesting the outstanding terms in the immediate reversion; for the law before 1926, see *Re Moore and Helm* [1912] 2 Ch. 105, and for conditions of sale, see the Law of Property Act, 1925, s. 42 (3).

Outstroke. The right of conveying minerals to the surface from one mine through another mine is known (as regards the mine through which the minerals are brought) as outstroke and (as regards the mine from which the minerals are brought) as instroke.

Outworker, a person to whom materials are supplied to work on in his own home. For an examination of the position of an outworker, see *Westall Richardson* v. *Roulson* [1954] 1 W.L.R. 905. Lists of outworkers are to be kept in certain trades (Factories Act, 1961, s. 133).

Ovelty, a kind of equality of service in subordinate tenures (Fitz.N.B. 36).

Over. In conveyancing, the word "over" is used to denote a contingent limitation intended to take effect on the failure of a prior estate.

Thus, in what is commonly called the name and arms clause (*q.v.*) in a will or settlement, there is generally a proviso that if the beneficiary fails to comply with the condition the estate is to go to someone else; this is a limitation or gift over.

Overcrowding. By the Housing Act, 1957, s. 77, it is provided that a dwelling-house shall be deemed to be overcrowded at any time when the number of persons sleeping in the house either is such that any two of those persons being ten years old or more of opposite sexes and not living together as husband and wife sleep in the same room, or is, in relation to the number and floor area of the rooms of which the house consists, in excess of the permitted number as defined in Sch. 6 to the Act.

Overcrowding is an offence on the part of the occupier as well as the landlord. Local authorities are under a duty to cause inspections to be made. Licences to exceed the permitted numbers may be granted.

Overcyted, or **Overcyhsed,** proved guilty, or convicted (Blount).

Overdraft, the amount a customer has been permitted by his bank to draw in excess of the money paid in. Security for repayment is usually demanded.

The granting of an overdraft is a transaction falling within the scope of the Consumer Credit Act, 1974. See Sch. 2, Examples 6, 17, 18, 23. See BANKER; CONSUMER CREDIT.

Overdue, past the time of payment.

By the Bills of Exchange Act, 1882, s. 36, where an overdue bill is negotiated, it can only be negotiated subject to any defect of title affecting it at its maturity, and thenceforward no person who takes it can acquire or give a better title than that which the person from whom he took it had. A bill payable on demand is deemed to be overdue when it appears on the face of it to have been in circulation for an unreasonable length of time. What is an unreasonable length of time is a question of fact. Except where an indorsement bears date after the maturity of the bill, every negotiation is prima facie deemed to have been effected before the bill was overdue.

Overdue ship, a ship of which news has not been received for such a time as to give rise to the presumption or probability that she has been lost.

Overhead wires. See the London Overground Wires Act, 1933. See also the Electric (Supply) Act, 1919, s. 21, as amended by the Electricity (Supply) Act, 1926, Sch. 6, the Town and Country Planning Act, 1947, Sch. 8, the Electricity Act, 1947, Sch. 4 and the London Government Order 1970 (No. 211).

Overhernissa, contumacy or contempt of court (Leg.Aethel. c. 25).

Overreaching clause, a clause in a resettlement which saved the powers of sale and leasing annexed to the life interest created by the original settlement, when it was desired to give the tenant for life the same estate and powers under the resettlement. The clause was so called because it provided that the resettlement should be overreached by the exercise of the old powers. If the resettlement were executed without a provision to this effect, the powers annexed to the estate for life created by the original settlement would be gone after the resettlement: but this ceased to be of much importance because the powers given to a tenant for life by the Settled Land Acts, 1882 to 1890, remained notwithstanding the resettlement: see now the Settled Land Act, 1925. See RESETTLEMENT.

Overreaching conveyance. Under the Law of Property Act, 1925, it is possible for estate owners (*q.v.*) to sell the land in question free from prior incumbrances: the third party rights are trans-ferred to the purchase-money obtained on the sale. Trustees acting under an *ad hoc* trust for sale have similar powers. See REGISTRATION OF TITLE, ETC.; TRUST FOR SALE.

Overriding interests. See the Land Registration Act, 1925, s. 70. See REGISTRATION OF TITLE TO LAND.

Overriding trust, a trust which takes precedence of other trusts previously declared.

Overrule, to set aside the authority of a former decision.

Oversamessa, a fine for failure to pursue a robber or a murderer (3 Co.Inst. 116).

Oversea companies, companies incorporated outside Great Britain which establish a place of business within Great Britain (Companies Act, 1948, s. 406).

Overseas aid. See the Overseas Aid Acts, 1966 and 1968.

Overseas Development, Ministry of. This ministry was dissolved by S.I. 1970, No. 1682 but was re-established by the Ministers of the Crown Act, 1974, s. 3 (3). See now the Ministers of the Crown Act, 1975, s. 7, Sch. 2. For further functions see the Minister of Overseas Development Order 1974 (No. 1264).

Overseas Food Corporation. This was set up by the Overseas Resources Development Act, 1948. It was dissolved by the Overseas Resources Development Act, 1954, and its undertaking transferred to the Tanganyika Agricultural Corporation.

Overseas Resources Development. See COLONIAL DEVELOPMENT.

Overseers. The statute 1572, 14 Eliz. I, c. 5, created the office of overseer in order that they might assist the churchwardens in the care of the poor. The Poor Relief Act, 1601, repealed the sections of the Act in 1572 which related to overseers, and provided that in every parish two or more justices living in or near the parish should annually nominate under their hands and seals the churchwardens, and from two to four householders of the parish, to be overseers of the poor. The Poor Law (Overseers) Act, 1814, provided that the nomination should be made on March 25 or within fourteen days thereafter. Churchwardens were, by the Poor Law Amendment Act, 1866, s. 12 (except in rural parishes, in which case their jurisdiction ceased by virtue of the Local Government Act, 1894), overseers of the poor, and they joined with the overseers in making poor rates; but the churchwardens, having distinct business of their own, usually left the care of the poor to the overseers, though anciently they were the sole overseers of the poor. The overseers originally not only levied the poor rate but also expended it. Their duties regarding rating were transferred to the rating authority by the Overseers Order, 1927. Assistant overseers could be appointed with a salary under the Poor Relief Act, 1816. Overseers were abolished by the Rating and Valuation Act, 1925, s. 1, and the poor law was abolished by the National Assistance Act, 1948.

Formerly it seems to have been common for a testator after appointing an executor to appoint an overseer, who had no power to intermeddle with the administration, but only to counsel, persuade and advise the executor.

Oversewenesse. See OVERHERNISSA.

Overt, open. See MARKET OVERT.

Overt act, an open act, or one consisting of something stronger than mere words, and evidencing a deliberate intention in the mind of the person doing it. The phrase is chiefly used in the law of treason, it being a rule that a treasonable intention is not punishable unless it is evidenced by some overt act. Thus, to provide weapons or ammunition for the purpose of killing the sovereign, or to assemble and consult on the means of doing so, is an overt act of treason: but the mere speaking of words is not an overt act (4 Bl.Comm. 79).

The term is also used in the law of criminal conspiracy to signify any act done by conspirators in pursuance of their intention; the unlawful agreement of which the conspiracy consists constitutes an overt act.

Overt word, a word the meaning of which is clear and beyond doubt.

Overture, an opening; a proposal.

Ovrages, or **Ouvrages,** day's work.

Ovres, acts, deeds, or works (8 Co. Rep. 131).

Owe; Owing. To owe a sum of money is to be under an obligation to pay it either at once or at some future time, and such a debt is said to be " owing " as opposed to " payable." See DUE.

Owel, equal.

Owelty, equality. Where an exchange of two pieces of land of unequal value is made, and a sum of money or some other compensation is given by the owner of the less valuable land to the owner of the other land, this compensation is said to be given for owelty, or equality, of exchange, that is, to equalise the value.

Owlers; Owling. Owlers were people who carried wool, etc., to the sea at night—when owls are abroad—for the purpose of exporting it in contravention of the statute 1662, 14 Car. 2, c. 18, s. 8, and owling was the offence which they committed by so doing.

Owner. For the purposes of the Public Health Act, 1936, s. 343, and the Factories Act, 1961, s. 176, an owner is the person for the time being receiving the rack-rent of the premises in connection with which the word is used, whether on his own account or as agent or trustee, or who would receive it if the premises were let at a rack-rent (*Kensington Corporation* v. *Allen* [1926] 1 K.B. 576). For the purposes of serving a purchase notice under the Town and Country Planning Act, 1971, s. 180, an owner does not include a freeholder who has let the land at less than a rack-rent (*London Corporation* v. *Cusack-Smith* [1955] A.C. 337).

An estate owner is defined by the Law of Property Act, 1925, s. 205 (1) (ix), as the owner of a legal estate, but an infant is not capable of being an estate owner. An estate owner is the person having the power to give a legal title to the whole of the estate (see ESTATE) for the purposes of sale, mortgage, lease or otherwise. This includes an absolute beneficial owner, a tenant for life, statutory owners (*q.v.*), trustees for sale, and personal representatives and mortgagees in exercise of their paramount powers. The legal title so disposed of is subject to all such equities, liabilities, charges and obligations (if any) attaching to the estate as may be binding on the transferee and the estate after it has been disposed of.

The word "owner" in the Police (Property) Act, 1897, s. 1 (1), as amended by the Criminal Justice Act, 1972, s. 58, should be given its ordinary, popular meaning, that is a person entitled to the goods in question or whose goods they are: possession is not enough (*Raymond Lyons & Co.* v. *Metropolitan Police Commissioner* [1975] Q.B. 321).

Owner's risk. See RISK.

Ownership, the most extensive right allowed by law to a person, of dealing with a thing to the exclusion of all other persons, or of all except one or more specified persons. It is therefore a right *in rem.* (See RIGHT.) Ownership is essentially indefinite in its nature, but in its most absolute form it involves the right to possess and use or enjoy the thing, the right to its produce and accessions, and the right to destroy, encumber, or alienate it: or, as the civilians express it, ownership gives the *jus utendi, fruendi, et abutendi*; but the exercise of these rights may be restricted in various manners, and the owner may part with them or limit them in favour of other persons; so long, however, as the grantees have only definite rights of user over the thing, and the original owner retains an indefinite right, he is still owner; but if he parts with the indefinite right and retains only a definite one (*e.g.,* a right of way, in the case of land), he ceases to be owner. Ownership may exist either in corporeal or incorporeal things. Thus, a man may be owner of an annuity, patent, or copyright, as well as of land or furniture.

With reference to the right of user and alienation, ownership is either absolute (*dominium plenum*), or not (*minus plenum*).

Ownership is said to be absolute when it is subject only to those restrictions which are imposed by law on all owners, and are therefore implied in the idea of ownership. These restrictions may arise from the duties of the owner of the thing towards his neighbours and the world at large which forbid him to make it hurtful or dangerous to those who happen lawfully to come into contact with it.

(See NATURAL RIGHTS; NUISANCE.) Restrictions on alienation exist in the case of persons under disability, and are also imposed by the rule against perpetuities. In English law absolute ownership can only exist in chattels, as all land is subject theoretically to the obligations of tenure; but practically the fee simple in land gives absolute ownership. See ESTATE; FEE; TENURE.

Restricted ownership occurs where either concurrent or successive rights of user are vested in persons other than the owner; thus land may be subject to easements or rights of common (*q.v.*), or the right of user possessed by the owner for the time being may be restricted by the fact that he has only a limited interest in it, as in the case of a joint tenant, tenant for life, or lessee. See WASTE.

Ownership may be divided among several persons in various manners, so that each is owner to a limited extent, either successively, *i.e.* one after another, or concurrently, *i.e.* at the same time. As to its duration, ownership may be absolute or unlimited (*dominium perpetuum*), as in the case of an estate in fee simple, or limited (*dominium temporale*), that is, liable to determine at a certain time or on the happening of a given event, as in the case of a lessee or tenant for life. As to the time of enjoyment, ownership may be present, as in the case of an interest in possession, or deferred, as in the case of an interest in reversion or remainder. Ownership is called sole or several, where one person only is entitled to the thing at the same time. Concurrent ownership, where several persons are entitled to the thing at the same time, takes the form either of co-ownership, or of nominal and beneficial ownership. Co-ownership occurs where several persons are entitled to the possession, user and benefit of one thing, *pro indiviso,* no one being entitled to any specific part of it, and the right of user of each being subject to a similar right in the others; as in the case of joint tenancy and tenancy in common (*q.v.*). Nominal and beneficial ownership occurs where two persons are owners in respect of one thing, although one of them either cannot derive any benefit from it at all, or has only exactly defined rights over it, while the other has the real benefit of the thing. Each is considered owner for certain purposes. Thus, A may be the owner of a thing as against all the world except B, while with regard to B he may have no rights of ownership at all, being bound, by virtue of a personal relation between them, to allow B to have the use and profits of the property, or even to deal with the property as B may direct. As the rules of the common law only recognise A's rights to the property and ignore those of B, A is called the legal owner, while B is called the equitable owner, because his rights are only recognised by virtue of the doctrines of equity. The legal owner is the nominal owner, the equitable the beneficial owner. See EQUITY; MORTGAGE; TRUST.

As to general and special, ordinary and privileged, ownership, see PROPERTY.

See INTEREST; TITLE.

Oxfild, a restitution made by a hundred or county for any wrong done by one who was within the same (Lamb. Arch. 125).

Oxford Group, a religious movement (with no connection with Oxford or Oxford University) which failed to establish exemption from income tax as a body of persons formed for charitable purposes only (*Oxford Group* v. *I.R.C.* [1949] 2 All E.R. 537).

Oxford University. See UNIVERSITY COURTS.

Oxgang; Oxgate; Osken, twelve to fifteen acres, as much land as one ox could plough in a year. The plough team contained eight oxen: the land which they could plough in one year was known as the carucate (*q.v.*); and the oxgang was one-eighth part of the carucate, it being taken that the one ox could plough one-eighth part of the land which the whole team could plough. But a single ox never ploughed alone; and the oxgang was really so much land as a single ox ought, in theory, to plough (1 P. & M. H.E.L. 347). See LIBRATA TERRAE.

Oyer, to hear. In the old common law practice, a defendant was said to demand or crave oyer of a deed pleaded by the plaintiff when, previous and preparatory to pleading in bar, he asked that it should be read to him, the generality of defendants in early times being considered incapable of reading themselves; the record then generally went on to set out the deed in full as having been read to the defendant. This copy or setting out of the deed was also called the oyer (Co.Litt. 35b, 121b; 3 Bl.Comm. 299). See PROFERT.

Oyer was abolished by the Common Law Procedure Act, 1852, s. 55.

Oyer was used in the reign of Edward I as meaning an assise.

Oyer and terminer [Old Fr.], to hear and determine (Britt. 10a).

The commission of oyer and terminer was the commission which issued to certain judges of the High Court and other persons as their authority to inquire, hear, and determine all treasons, felonies, and misdemeanours committed within the county into which they were sent. This commission only authorised them to proceed upon an indictment found at the same assizes, for they must first " inquire " (formerly by means of the grand jury), before they could " hear and determine " by the help of the petty jury. (See JURY.) Their power to try other prisoners was conferred by the commission of gaol delivery (*q.v.*). See ASSISE; CENTRAL CRIMINAL COURT; GAOL DELIVERY.

References to a court of oyer and terminer are to be construed as references to the Crown Court (Courts Act, 1971, Sch. 8).

Oyer de record, hear the record. This was a petition that the court, for greater certainty, should refer to any record which was relied on in a proceeding.

Oyez (hear ye), the introduction to any proclamation or advertisement given by the public criers. It is pronounced *oh! yes!* See NORMAN-FRENCH.

Oysters. Oyster beds are protected under the Sea Fisheries (Shellfish) Act, 1967, s. 7. Oysters may not, in general, be sold between May 14 and August 4 (s. 16; Sea Fisheries Shellfish Act, 1973, s. 1). " Sea fish " includes shellfish (Act of 1967, s. 22 (2)).

For offences in relation to the taking or destroying of fish see the Theft Act, 1968, Sch. 1 para. 2.

An action *in rem* will lie for damage caused by the negligent grounding of a ship on an oyster bed (*The Swift* [1901] P. 168), and a claim will lie for damage caused by the discharge of a sewer causing contamination (*Foster* v. *Warblington U.D.C.* [1906] 1 K.B. 648). See CRABS AND LOBSTERS.

P

P.A., particular average. See AVERAGE.

P.A.Y.E. See PAY-AS-YOU-EARN.

P.C., prime cost sum. In specifications for building and engineering works it is usual to provide that such and such an article is to be provided at the " p. c. " of such and such a sum. Here the prime cost means the net price actually paid by the contractor. He is not entitled to buy the article at the price which a private purchaser would pay and to deduct for himself any trade discount or, apart from special custom, any discount for cash, which may be allowed to him.

P.C. is also a contraction of Privy Council (*q.v.*) or Privy Councillor; also of police constable.

P.P.I. See POLICY PROOF OF INTEREST.

Paage [Old Fr. *paage*; Low Lat. *paagium*], a toll for passage through another's land.

Pacare, to pay.

Pacatio, payment.

Pace, a measure of length containing two feet and a half or three feet. The geometrical pace is five feet long; the common pace is the length of a step, the geometrical is the length of two steps, or the whole space passed over by the same foot from one step to another.

The Latin word *pace* means with the leave of.

Paceatur, let him be freed or discharged.

Pacific blockade, blockade by way of reprisals in a state of peace. It must not affect ships other than those of the State against which the blockade is directed.

Pacific islanders. The kidnapping of Pacific islanders for forced labour was dealt with by the Pacific Islanders Protection Acts, 1872 and 1875.

Pack of wool, a horse load, which consists of 17 stone and 2 pounds, or 240 pounds weight (1 Fleta 2, c. xii).

Package. Duties known as package, scavage, balliage, and porterage had been levied in the port of London for hundreds of years on goods exported or imported by aliens or by denizens (*q.v.*) who were the sons of aliens, under the authority of charters granted by Edward IV and Charles I, until they were abolished, at an expense of about £140,000, under the statute 1833, 3 & 4 Will. 4, c. 66. See SCHOLANDA.

Packway, a way along which there was a right of leading pack-horses. See BRIDLEPATH..

Pact, or Pactio [Fr. *pacte*; Lat. *pactum*], a contract, bargain, covenant.

Pacta conventa qua neque contra leges neque dolo malo inita sunt omnimodo observanda sunt (C. 2, 3, 29). (Compacts which are not illegal, and do not originate in fraud, must in all respects be observed.) See MODUS ET, ETC.

Pacta dant legem contractui (Halk. 118). (Agreements constitute the law of the contract.) See MODUS ET, ETC.

Pacta privata juri publico derogare non possunt (7 Co.Rep. 23). (Private compacts cannot derogate from public right.) See CONVENTIO, ETC.

Pacta quae contra leges constitutionesque vel contra bonos mores fiunt nullam vim habere indubitati juris est (C. 2, 3, 6). (It is undoubted law that agreements which are contrary to the laws and constitutions or contrary to good morals have no force.) See MODUS ET, ETC.; PRIVATORUM CONVENTIO, ETC.

Pacta quae turpem causam continent non sunt observanda (Dig. 2, 14, 27). (Agreements containing a disgraceful cause are not to be observed.) Wherever the consideration which is the ground of the promise, or the promise which is the consequence or effect of the consideration, is unlawful, the contract is void. See ALLEGANS SUAM TURPITUDINEM, ETC.; EX DOLO, ETC.

Pacta sunt servanda. (Contracts are to be kept.)

Pacta tertiis nec nocent nec prosunt. (Contracts do not impose any burden nor confer any benefit upon a third party.)

Pactional damage, agreed pre-estimated damages, liquidated damages.

Pactis privatorum juri publico non derogatur. (No derogation from public right is effected by agreements between individuals.) See PACTA PRIVATA, ETC.

Pacto aliquid licitum est, quod sine pacto non admittitur (Co.Litt. 166a). (By special agreement things are allowed which are not otherwise permitted.)

Pactum constitutae pecuniae, an agreement by which a person appointed to his creditor a certain day, or a certain time, at which he promised to pay; or an agreement by which a person promised to pay a creditor (Civil Law).

Pactum de contrahendo, an undertaking to negotiate or conclude a contract.

Pactum de non petendo, an agreement made between a creditor and his debtor that the creditor would not demand from the debtor the debt due. By this agreement the debtor was freed from his obligation (Civil Law).

Pactum de quota litis, an agreement by which a creditor promised to pay a portion of a debt difficult to recover, to a person who undertook to recover it (Civil Law).

Pactum, Nudum. See NUDUM PACTUM.

Padder, a robber, a foot highwayman or foot-pad.

Paddock [Sax. *panne*, a park], a small inclosure for deer or other animals.

Pagus, a county (Jacob).

Pains and Penalties, Bills of, Acts of Parliament to condemn particular persons for treason or felony, or to inflict pains and penalties beyond or contrary to the common law, to serve a special purpose. They are in fact new laws, made *pro re nata.* It is an incident of such bills that persons who are to be affected by them are entitled by custom to be heard at the bar of the House in person or by counsel. But on a bill to disfranchise the borough of St. Albans, this claim was disallowed. See BILL OF PAINS AND PENALTIES.

Paintings. Works of painting are included in artistic work for the purposes of the Copyright Act, 1956, s. 3. See COPYRIGHT.

Pairing, a practice which is said to have originated in the time of Cromwell, whereby two members of the House of Commons, or other deliberative assembly, of opposite opinions, agree to absent themselves from voting on a particular division or during a given period.

Pais, or **Pays,** country, the people out of whom a jury is taken; a corruption of *pagus.* See IN PAIS.

Pais, Conveyances in, conveyances between two or more persons " in the country," *i.e.,* upon the land to be transferred. See FEOFFMENT.

Pais, Estoppel in. See ESTOPPEL.

Pais, Trial by, a trial by the country, *i.e.,* a jury.

Pakistan. The Indian Independence Act, 1947, set up two independent Dominions in India known respectively as India and Pakistan. Both were independent republics which accepted the Crown as the symbol of the free association of the independent nations who are members of the Commonwealth. This did not, however, imply allegiance to the Crown or affect the sovereignty of the republic. Pakistan is no longer a member of the Commonwealth. See Pakistan Act, 1973; Pakistan Act, 1974. See Gledhill, *Pakistan.*

Palace. A palace, which is a royal residence, is privileged from the execution of legal process within its precincts; but the privilege does not, it seems, extend to a royal palace, *e.g.,* Hampton Court, which is not a royal residence (*Att.-Gen.* v. *Dakin* (1869) L.R. 4 H.L. 338; *Combe* v. *De la Bere* (1881) 22 Ch.D. 316).

Palace Court, a court established under letters patent granted by James I, and continued under this patent until 1631, when a new patent was granted. To remove doubts as to the validity of the second patent, fresh letters patent were granted in 1665. It had jurisdiction in personal actions to any amount arising between any parties within twelve miles of Whitehall, except as regards actions arising in the City of London or actions within the jurisdiction of the Court of the Marshalsea (*q.v.*) or of the courts at Westminster, but cases of importance were generally removed into the King's Bench or Common Pleas. The judges were the Lord Steward and the Marshal of the King's Household—neither of whom ever sat—and the steward of the court or his deputy. The deputy was a barrister and the sole real judge. The number of barristers practising was limited to four, each of whom paid £41 6s. 6d. for his seat, and of attorneys to six who paid £141 6s. 6d. each. It was abolished by the County Courts Act, 1849 (Buckley, *Marshalsea and Palace Courts*). See LORD STEWARD OF THE QUEEN'S HOUSEHOLD.

Palace of Westminster, the official designation of the block of buildings containing the Houses of Parliament, the offices connected with them, and the residences of various officers of the two Houses. The buildings are theoretically a royal palace in which the Houses are permitted to meet: see the statute 1538, 28 Hen. 8, c. 12.

Palagium, a duty to lords of manors for exporting and importing vessels of wine at any of their ports (Jacob).

Palatine Courts, the Court of Common Pleas at Lancaster, the Chancery Court of Lancaster, the Chancery Court of Durham, and the Courts of Pleas at Durham, and the Courts of the County Palatine of Chester (which were abolished by the Law Terms Act, 1830). See CHANCERY COURT, ETC.; COUNTY PALATINE; COURT; COURT OF PLEAS.

Palestine. British jurisdiction in Palestine was terminated by the Palestine Act, 1948. The Jewish portion of Palestine became the State of Israel.

Palfridus, a palfrey, a horse to travel on.

Paling-man, a merchant denizen, or one born within the English pale.

Pallio cooperire, to cover with the *pallium*. It is stated, on the authority of Robert Grosseteste, the bishop of Lincoln (1175–1253), that in his time, at the marriage of persons with children born before the marriage, it was the custom for the parents and the children to stand beneath a cloth, or *pallium*, spread over their heads *in signum legitimationis* (to signify the legitimation of the children). The statement is made in an epistle written in 1236 (the year that the barons declined to permit *antenati* (*q.v.*) to be legitimated by a subsequent marriage), in the hope of getting the barons to make the marriage law of England the same as that of the Church (*Chronicles of Great Britain and Ireland,* vol. 25, p. 13). See MERTON, STATUTE OF.

Palm Sunday, the Sunday before Easter.

Palm tree justice. An expression used to describe a form of justice dispensed by a cadi sitting under a palm tree without the advantage of books or precedents. See, for an example of the use of the term, *Gissing* v. *Gissing* [1969] 2 Ch. 85, *per* Edmund Davies L.J.

Palmer's Act, the Central Criminal Court Act, 1856 (repealed), which was passed specially for the purpose of securing a fair trial for William Palmer, of Rugeley, Staffordshire, a poisoner, against whom there was a strong local feeling in the town at which, in the absence of special legislation he would necessarily have been tried.

See HINDE PALMER'S ACT.

Palmistry, the telling of fortunes from the lines on the palm of the hand. It seems to have been introduced into England by the gypsies (see EGYPTIANS), who are described in the statute 1530, 22 Hen. 8, c. 10, as practising it. Under the Vagrancy Act, 1824, s. 4, anyone telling fortunes by palmistry is punishable as a rogue and a vagabond (*q.v.*).

Pamphlet [Fr. *par un filet,* by a thread], a small book, usually printed in the octavo form, and stitched. The statute 1711, 10 Ann., c. 19, s. 113, as to the printers of pamphlets, was repealed by the Inland Revenue Repeal Act, 1870. See PRINTERS.

Pandectae, or **Digesta.** In the last month of the year 530, Justinian, by a constitution addressed to Tribonian, empowered him to name a commission for the purpose of forming a code out of the writing of those jurists who had enjoyed the *jus respondendi,* or, as it is expressed by the emperor, *autiquorum prudentium quibus auctoritatem conscribendarum interpretand-arumque legum sacratissimi principes praebuerunt.* The compilation, however, comprises extracts from some writers of the republican period. Ten years were allowed for the completion of the work. The instructions of the emperor were to select what was useful, to omit what was antiquated or superfluous, to avoid unnecessary repetitions, to get rid of contradictions and to make such other changes as should produce out of the mass of ancient juristical writings a useful and complete body of law (*jus antiquum*); the work was to be named *Digesta,* a Latin term indicating an arrangement of materials; or *Pandectae,* a Greek word expressive of the comprehensiveness of the work. It was also declared that no commentaries should be written on this compilation, but permission was given to make *paratitla,* or references to parallel passages, with a short statement of their contents. It was also declared that abbreviations (*sigla*) should not be used for forming the text of the Digest. The work was completed in January, 533, as appears by a constitution, both in Greek and Latin, which confirmed the work, and gave to it legal authority.

The number of writers from whose works extracts were made is thirty-nine.

Justinian's plan embraced two principal works, one which was to be a selection from the jurists, and the other from the *Constitutiones.* The first, the Pandects, was intended to contain the foundation of the law; it was the first work since the Twelve Tables which in itself, and without supposing the existence of any other, might serve as a central point of the whole body of the law. It may be properly called a code, and the first complete code since the Twelve Tables, though a large part of its contents is not law, but is dogmatic, or is taken up with the investigation of particular cases. Instead of the insufficient rules of Valentinian III, the excerpts in the Pandects are taken immediately from the writings of the jurists and arranged according to their matter. The code also has a more comprehensive plan than the earlier codes, since it comprises both rescripts and edicts. These two works, the Pandects and the Code, may be considered as the completion of Justinian's designs. The *Institutiones* cannot be viewed as a third work; independent of both, it serves as an introduction to them, or as a manual. The *Novellae* are single and subsequent additions or alterations, and it is merely an accidental circumstance that a third edition of the code was not made at the end of Justinian's reign, which would have comprised the *Novellae* which had permanent application.

The Pandects are divided into fifty books, each book containing several titles, divided into laws, and the laws generally into several parts or paragraphs.

In order to prevent the circulation of incorrect editions, three Ultramontane and three Citramontane scholars were chosen every year in the University of Bologna, and termed *pecarii;* they were excused from all other *munera publica,* and held their sessions once a week for the purpose of correcting imperfect copies in possession of circulating libraries; a fine of five *soldi* was imposed on all possessors of defective books, together with the expenses of correction, for which purpose every doctor or scholar was obliged to lend his own perfect copy, under pain of a fine of five *lire;* hence the term *exempla correcta et bene emendata.* Books thus corrected were advertised by the bedel (1 Colqu.R.C.L. 67–73). See CORPUS JURIS CIVILIS; DIGEST.

Pandoxator, a brewer.

Pandoxatrix, a woman who brews and sells ale.

Panel [Lat. *panellum;* Fr. *panneau,* a square or panel], a little part, or rather a schedule or page, containing the names of jurors summoned to serve as upon a trial; empannelling a jury means entering them into the sheriff's roll or book (Co. Litt. 158b; Jacob).

The term was often applied to the list of such medical practitioners as had agreed to administer the medical benefit under the National Health Insurance Acts. Those entitled to be treated by such a medical practitioner are known as panel patients.

The word is used to denote a list of any authoritative persons or consultants where determination or advice is required by statute, as under the Acquisition of Land (Assessment of Compensation) Act, 1919, the Law of Property Act, 1925, s. 84, and the Landlord and Tenant Act, 1927. See JURY.

Panel of arbitrators, the permanent court or tribunal established under the Hague Arbitration Convention. See HAGUE CONFERENCE.

Pannage; Pawnage Low Lat. *pannagium*; Fr. *panage*], food that swine feed on in the woods, as mast of beech, acorns, etc., sometimes called *pawnes.*

A common of pannage is the right of feeding swine on mast, acorns, etc., at certain seasons in a commonable wood or forest. It does not prevent the owner of the wood from lopping and cutting down the trees in the ordinary course of management (*Chilton* v. *London* (1878) 7 Ch.D. 562). Pannage also meant the money paid for agisting (*q.v.*) swine. There was also a common of after-pannage, or the right of feeding swine after the right of pannage had been exercised. The name was also given to the money received by the agisters for the hogs permitted to feed in the royal forests: see the Statute of Westminster II, 1285, c. 25 (Cromp.Jurisdn. 155; Manwood, c. 12).

" Pannage " is also a corrupted form of *pavagium* (*q.v.*). See DANGERIA.

Pannagium est pastus porcorum, in nemoribus et in silvis, de glandibus, etc. (1 Buls. 7). (Pannage is a pasture of hogs, in woods and forests, upon acorns, and so forth.)

Pannel. See PANEL.

Pannellation, the act of empannelling a jury.

Pannier-man; Pannier. In the Inns of Court one of the Inn servants used a horse with panniers to convey the supplies of provisions required for use in hall, and was known as the pannier-man.

The servants of the Inner Temple who wait at dinner were colloquially known as panniers.

Pannus, a garment made with skins (2 Fleta, c. xiv).

Pantomime, a dramatic performance in which gestures take the place of words (*Lee* v. *Simpson* (1847) 3 C.B. 871). But the word is also used to describe Christmas theatrical entertainments.

Papal bull. The bull is a circular leaden seal with, on one side, the images of St. Peter and St. Paul and, on the other side, the name of the reigning Pope, and the date of his accession. It is affixed to certain documents issued by the Pope; and from this fact these documents themselves have acquired the title of bulls.

The introduction into the kingdom of papal bulls was made treason by the statute 1571, 13 Eliz. 1, c. 2. That statute, in so far as it imposed punishment, was repealed by the Religious Disabilities Act, 1846, which, however enacted that it should not be lawful to bring bulls into the country. See PRAEMUNIRE.

Paper. As to the paper on which proceedings in the Supreme Court must be printed, see PARCHMENT; PRINTING, ETC.

Paper blockade, a blockade declared by a belligerent which cannot or does not effectually enforce it.

Paper book, the issues in law, etc., upon special pleadings, formerly made up by the clerk of the papers, who was an officer for that purpose, but afterwards by the plaintiff's attorney or agent (3 Bl.Comm. 317; Jacob).

In proceedings on a writ of error in a criminal case, the paper books were copies of the proceedings, with a note of the points intended to be argued, delivered to the judges by the parties two days before the argument.

Paper credit, credit given on the security of any written obligation purporting to represent property.

Paper days. Before the Judicature Acts, 1873–75, there were in each of the common law courts certain days known as Special Paper Days on which the courts heard the cases entered for argument in a list called the Special List. In the Queen's Bench there were Crown Paper Days, or days for business on the Crown side.

Paper duty. This was repealed by the Customs and Inland Revenue Act, 1861.

Paper money, bank notes, bills of exchange, and promissory notes. On the outbreak of the war with Germany in August, 1914, the Government issued currency notes for £1 and 10s. respectively. The first issued were soon called in, others of better design and less easy to imitate being substituted. Currency notes were commonly called Treasury notes, and were legal tender for the payment of any amount (Currency and Bank Notes Act, 1914). See BANK NOTES; CURRENCY NOTES.

Paper Office; Paper Mill. An Office of H.M. Papers and Records for Business of State and Council, was established in 1578. This office, also known as the Paper Office, existed until 1854 at a number of different addresses in and about Whitehall. Upon the death in 1854 of the then keeper of the State papers, the Paper Office became merged in the Public Record Office (*q.v.*).

In the Court of King's Bench there was an office known as the Paper Office or Paper Mill. In it were kept the records of the court pending their removal to the Treasury of the Exchequer, in which latter office all records of the courts were finally deposited. See CLERK OF THE PAPER OFFICE.

Paper, Revenue, a list kept in the Queen's Remembrancer's Department of the Central Office of the Supreme Court of appeals by way of petition or case stated from decisions of the Commissioners of Income Tax and from other decisions relating to taxation. Cases in the list are heard before a judge of the Chancery Division. See the Redistribution of Business (Revenue Paper) Order, 1962 (No. 2877) and R.S.C., Ord. 34, r. 3, notes.

Paper, Special, a list kept in the Queen's Bench Division on matters set down for argument on points of law. See Directions given by the Lord Chief Justice on December 9, 1958 [1958] 1 W.L.R. 1291; R.S.C., Ord. 34, r. 4, notes.

Papist [Lat. *papa*, a pope], one who, adhering to the communion of the Church of Rome, maintains the supreme ecclesiastical power of the Pope, as contradistinguished from English Protestants who in statutes, canons, and the 36th Article of Religion maintain the supreme ecclesiastical power of the sovereign. From the time of the Reformation Papists, either under that title or under the title of persons professing the Popish religion, or of Popish recusants convict, were subjected, by one statute after another, to various civil and religious disabilities, the removal of which began in 1788, and was to a great extent completed by the Roman Catholic Emancipation Act, 1829, which Act and other Acts, the earliest being an Act of 1791, speak of them as Roman Catholics. See RECUSANTS; ROMAN CATHOLICS.

Par, state of equality; equal value. Par value is the face value of a security or share as contrasted with its market price or selling value. See EXCHANGE.

Par in parem imperium non habet (Jenk.Cent. 174). (An equal has no authority over an equal.) This is cited by Jenkins in connection with a decision—which is now obviously bad law—that one justice cannot commit another for a breach of the peace. But as regards courts, the maxim holds good: thus there is no jurisdiction in one section of the Crown Court (*q.v.*) to examine or review anything done by another section (*R. v. Slatter* [1975] 1 W.L.R. 1084).

Paracium, the tenure which existed between parceners when they held of a lord in unequal shares. It was due from the younger to the elder of them, but without homage or service (Co.Litt. 163a).

Parage; Paragium, equality; the equality referred to is that of blood, name, or dignity. When a fief was divided unequally amongst brothers, the younger held of the elder *ex jure et titula paragii* (by right and title of equality) just as in a corresponding case parceners (see PARACIUM) held the one of the other.

It also meant a marriage portion.

Paragraph, a part of section of a statute, pleading, affidavit, etc., which contains one article, the sense of which is complete.

Paramount, superior; having the highest jurisdiction, as lord paramount, the supreme lord of the fee; the sovereign.

Title paramount means a superior title; for instance, A purports to convey to B land which really belongs to C, and C ejects B from the land, B is said to be evicted by title paramount, meaning a title superior to that granted to him by A (Co.Litt. 173b). See EVICTION BY TITLE PARAMOUNT.

In the law of tenure, if A held land in fee of B, and B held the same land in fee of C, then C was the lord paramount, and he had the seignory paramount, as opposed to A, the tenant paravail, and B the mesne, whose seignory was called the mesnalty (*q.v.*) (Litt. 583).

Paramountcy, the relationship of the sovereign as Emperor of India to the rulers of the native States, terminated by the Indian Independence Act, 1947.

Paraphernalia; Bona paraphernalia [Gk. παρά, beyond; φερνή, dower], jewellery and ornaments given by a husband to his wife before or during marriage. Whether these were meant to be absolute gifts or were merely paraphernalia for her adornment as a spouse was a question of fact (*Tasker* v. *Tasker* [1895] P. 1). Before the Married Women's Property Act, 1882, they differed from property held by the wife for her separate use in that the husband might dispose of them during his life and they were liable for his debts, while they differed from her ordinary chattels in that the husband had no power to dispose of them by will, so that if she survived him she was entitled to them, subject to his debts (11 Vin.Abr. 176).

Paraphernalia were deemed gifts *sub modo* only, *i.e.*, for the purpose of being worn by the wife as ornaments of her person, and it was otherwise in the case of wearing apparel purchased by the wife with money supplied by the husband (*Masson, Templier & Co.* v. *De Fries* [1909] 2 K.B. 831). But if the like articles were bestowed upon her by her father, or by a relative, or even by a stranger, before or after marriage, they were deemed absolute gifts to her separate use; and then, if received with the husband's consent, he could not, nor could his creditors, dispose of them, any more than they could of any other property received and held to her separate use. See HUSBAND AND WIFE; MARRIED WOMEN'S PROPERTY.

The better opinion would seem to be that the doctrine of paraphernalia is now gone, and that, while the wife may own some chattels and the husband may own others, there is no such mixed and partial ownership as was known to the doctrine.

Parasceve, the sixth day of the last week in Lent, called Good Friday. It is a *dies non juridicus.*

Parasitus, a domestic servant (Blount).

Parasynexis, a conventicle, or unlawful meeting (Civil Law).

Paratitla, an abbreviated explanation of some titles or books of the Code or Digest (Civil Law). See PANDECTAE.

Paravail [Fr. *par*; *avayler*, to dismiss; *aval*, below], the lowest tenant of a fee; or he who is immediate tenant to one who holds of another; he who has avail and profit of the land (2 Co.Inst. 296).

Paravail means inferior or subordinate. Thus, where A is indebted to B, and B is indebted to C, B is the primary debtor and A is the sub-debtor or debtor paravail (Keilway, 187).

The term was chiefly used with reference to the tenure of estates in land, a tenant paravail being a tenant who held land in fee of another and had no tenant who held of him, as opposed to a mesne lord (*q.v.*) and a lord paramount (*q.v.*).

Parcel, a part or portion of land.

Every piece of copyhold land formed parcel of the manor to which it belonged; that is to say, so far as the freehold was concerned, the copyholds belonged to the lord, and formed part of his lands, although his beneficial interest in them was comparatively small, being subject to the customary estates of the tenants. See COPYHOLD; DEMESNE; MANOR.

The word was also applied to the accounts of the escheators. See PARCEL MAKERS.

Parcel makers, two officers in the Exchequer who formerly made the parcels of the escheators' accounts, wherein they charged them with everything they had levied for the sovereign's use within the time of their being in office, and delivered the same to the auditors, to make up their accounts therewith (Prac.Exch. 99).

Parcels, the technical term for the description of the property dealt with by a conveyance, mortgage, or other assurance.

In a conveyance, lease or other deed dealing with property, that part which follows the operative words is called the parcels. It contains the description, either expressly or by reference, of the property dealt with, and in the case of land generally begins with some such words as " All that piece or parcel of land," Sometimes the full description is contained in a recital or in a schedule to the deed, and there is often a reference to a plan drawn on the deed. As to a purchaser's right to have the property conveyed to him by reference to a plan, see *Re Sansom* [1910] 1 Ch. 741; *Re Sparrow* [1910] 2 Ch. 60. There is no general rule that if the parcels of a conveyance are ambiguous a plan forming part of the conveyance cannot be used to resolve the ambiguity unless the conveyance refers to the plan (*Leachman* v. *L. & K. Richardson* [1969] 1 W.L.R. 1129). See ABSTRACT OF TITLE; ABUTTALS; DEED; OPERATIVE PART; PARCEL; PREMISES.

Parcels, Bill of, a list of the articles comprised in a consignment of goods, with the prices of the articles. It is sent by a seller to a purchaser.

Parcenary, the tenure of lands by parceners, coparcenary. See COPARCENER.

Parcener, coparcener (*q.v.*).

Parchment [Lat. *pergamena*], skins of sheep dressed for writing, so called because invented at Pergamos, in Asia Minor, by King Eumenes, when paper, which was in use in Egypt only, was prohibited by Ptolemy to be transported into Asia. Until recent years it was used for deeds and was used for writs of summons previously to November 1, 1875. See the Judicature Act, 1875. Indictments may be on durable paper (Indictments Act, 1915, Sch. 1). Prior to the Judicature Act, 1875, all writs of summons had from time immemorial been written on parchment. Writs of summons are now partly printed and partly written or typewritten on paper of a prescribed size (R.S.C., Ord. 66, r. 2). Down to April 1, 1916, all inquisitions (or records of the findings of coroners' inquests) were invalid where murder, manslaughter or *felo de se* was found, unless set out on parchment (Coroners Act, 1887, s. 18 (2)), but now the use of parchment is unnecessary in

any case (Indictments Act, 1915, s. 9, Sch. 2). See PROBATE.

Deeds were written on parchment until the typewriter came into general use after the war of 1914–18, since when they have been typed on durable paper known as parchment substitute.

Parco fracto, De, a writ for damages caused by a pound-breach (*q.v.*) (Reg. Orig. 166).

Pardon is where the Crown releases a person from the punishment which he has incurred for some offence. A pardon may be granted either before or during a prosecution, in which case it may be pleaded in bar, or after conviction, in which case it may be pleaded in arrest of judgment or in bar of execution, so that the offender is discharged from punishment. Some offences, however, cannot be pardoned, *e.g.,* a common nuisance while it remains unredressed (see NON POTEST REX, ETC.). To preserve the liberty of the subject, the committing any man to prison out of the realm is, by the Habeas Corpus Act, 1679, made a *praemunire* (*q.v.*) unpardonable by the Crown. The sovereign cannot pardon where private justice is principally concerned in the prosecution of offenders: *non potest rex gratiam facere cum injuria et damno aliorum.* At common law the Crown could not pardon an offence against a penal statute after information brought; for thereby the informer had acquired a private property in his part of the penalty. But the Remission of Penalties Act, 1859, enabled the Crown to remit penalties for offences, although payable to parties other than the Crown; and a special power of a similar character, limited to offences against the Sunday Observance Act, 1781, was conferred by the Remission of Penalties Act, 1875. Proceedings by common informers were abolished by the Common Informers Act, 1951. By the Act of Settlement, 1701, no pardon under the Great Seal is pleadable to an impeachment by the Commons in Parliament. But after the impeachment has been solemnly heard and determined the prerogative of pardon may be extended to the person impeached.

The effect of a pardon is to make the offender a new man (*novus homo*), to acquit him of all corporal penalties and forfeitures annexed to the offence pardoned, and not so much to restore his former as to give him new credit and capacity. Nevertheless the judgment remains formally unreversed.

A pardon is granted by warrant under the Great Seal (which is now never used for the purpose) or under the Sign Manual (see the Criminal Law Act, 1967, s. 9). Pardons are granted by the Crown only upon the advice of the Home Secretary. The Home Secretary, before deciding any question as to a pardon, may take the opinion of the Court of Appeal on the matter (Criminal Appeal Act, 1968, ss. 17, 49). See PREROGATIVE OF MERCY.

Pardoners, persons who carried about the Pope's indulgences, and sold them to any who would buy them.

Parens est nomen generale ad omne genus cognationis (Co.Litt. 80). (Parent is a name general to every kind of blood-relationship.) This is merely Littleton's explanation of *parentes* in the Statute of Merton, 1235, c. 6, where that word is in fact used in the same sense as the modern French *parents*.

Parens patriae. The sovereign, as *parens patriae*, has a kind of guardianship over various classes of persons, who, from their legal disability, stand in need of protection, such as infants, idiots, and mental patients.

Parent and child. The relation of parent and child is not one which is much interfered with by the law, almost the only duties arising from it which are capable of legal enforcement being those of maintenance and education. Every parent is bound to provide necessaries for his children if he able to do so and they are unable to support themselves; and is bound to send them to school, but they are to be educated, so far as is compatible with efficiency and the avoidance of unreasonable expenditure, in accordance with the wishes of their parents (Education Act, 1944, s. 76). The children of a poor person not able to work were bound to maintain him or her if they were able to do under the Poor Relief Act 1601, s. 7, but the National Assistance Act, 1948, s. 42, while imposing liability on a man and wife to maintain one another and their children, imposes no corresponding liability on children to maintain their parents. These obligation of maintenance are enforceable only as public duties, and not by the person liable to be maintained. See MAINTENANCE; POOR LAW.

As regards third persons, the relation gives the parent the right of protecting the person and property of his child, and vice versa.

See BASTARD; GUARDIAN; INFANT.

Parent company, a holding company (*q.v.*).

Parentela. This, or the fuller form *de parentela se tollere*, signified a reunciation of kindred and of all rights of inheritance from them, effected in court before twelve men, who made oath that they believed it to be done for good cause (Leg.Hen. 1, c. 88).

Parenthesis, a part of a sentence occurring in the middle thereof, and usually inclosed between marks like ( ), the omission of which part would not injure the grammatical construction of the rest of the sentence.

Parenticide [Lat. *parens*, a father; *caedere*, to kill], one who murders a parent.

Parentis, In loco, in place of a parent; the position of a person undertaking the office and duty of a father to make provision for a child of another (*Powys* v. *Mansfield* (1837) 3 My. & Cr. 359).

Parergon, one work executed in the intervals of another; a subordinate task. It is the title of a work on the canons, by Ayliffe.

Pares, a person's peers or equals; as the jury for trial of causes, who were originally the vassals or tenants of the lord, being the equals or peers of the parties litigant. Magna Carta, 1215, s. 39, provides against the condemnation of a freeman *nisi per legale judicium parium suorum, vel per legem terrae.*

The lawyers of the seventeenth century contended that this reference to the judgment of his peers was in effect a declaration of the right to be tried by a jury. But that was going too far. The jury which they knew was unknown in 1215. What the *judicium parium suorem* meant was the judgment of the *pares curtis* or other vassals of the lord of the defendant.

Pares curiae, the vassals of a superior attending his court.

Pari passu [Lat.], with equal step, equally, without preference.

Paribus sententiis reus absolvitur (4 Co.Inst. 64). (When opinions are equal, a defendant is acquitted.) When opinions are equal means when the court is equally divided. The maxim was relied on by the Star Chamber in a case where the court was divided four and four. On the hearing of an appeal the order appealed against stands in the event of an equal division of the court. In cases of summary jurisdiction the proper course is for equally divided justices to adjourn the hearing (*R. v. Herts JJ.* [1926] 1 K.B. 191); but they may dismiss the case and so bar a further prosecution. See SEMPER PRAE-SUMITUR PRO NEGANTE, ETC.

Parish [Low Lat. *parochia*; Fr. *paroisse*; Gk. παροικία, habitation], the particular charge of a secular priest. *Parochia est locus quo degit populus alicujus ecclesiae* (a parish is a place in which the people of a particular church reside). It is that circuit of ground which is committed to the care of one parson or vicar, or other minister having cure of souls therein (1 Bl.Comm. 111).

A definition of "parish" for ecclesiastical purposes in given in the Synodical Government Measure, 1969, Sch. 3 para. 44 (1). See also the Parish Councils Act, 1957, s. 14 (2), Local Government Act, 1958, s. 66 (1), Ecclesiastical Fees Measure, 1962, s. 1.

A parish has been since the middle of the seventeenth century a division for civil as well as for ecclesiastical purposes: thus the collection and application of the poor rate was parochial. Down to the early part of the last century the ecclesiastical and civil parish in nearly every case covered the same area but by 1923 there was about 15,000 civil parishes and about 14,000 ecclesiastical parishes and the areas coincided in only about 4,000 cases. This was the effect of many statutes by which provision is made for the subdivision of parishes into districts or parishes for ecclesiastical, poor law and taxation purposes, and for the amalgamation of detached portions of parishes. See CHAPEL; ECCLESIASTICAL COMMIS-SIONERS; OVERSEERS; PERAMBULATION; POOR LAW.

Parishes were divided into urban parishes and rural parishes (Local Government Act, 1933, s. 1 (2) (*f*)). Under the reorganisation of local government (*q.v.*) in England effected by the Local Government Act, 1972, rural parishes continue to exist as parishes. Boroughs (*q.v.*) and urban districts (see DISTRICT) became parishes (Local Government Act, 1972, s. 1, Sch. 1). Every parish in England has a parish meeting (*q.v.*) and in most cases a parish council (*q.v.*).

A parish may by resolution take on itself the status of a town. The council will thereupon bear the name of the council of the town, the chairman and vice-chairman will become the town mayor and deputy town mayor and the parish meeting will become the town meeting (s. 245). As to former boroughs regaining the status of boroughs see BOROUGH.

A pastoral scheme may provide for the creation of new benefices or parishes, for the dissolution of existing benefices or parishes, for the alteration of the areas of existing benefices or parishes or the definition of their boundaries and for the creation of new extra-parochial places, the incorporation in parishes of existing extra parochial places or the alteration or definition of the boundaries of existing extra-parochial places (Pastoral Measure, 1968, s. 16).

A place not included in a parish is called extra-parochial. Such places are, however, now in substantially the same position for civil purposes as if they were parishes. See TITHES.

See Toulmin Smith, *The Parish*; Steer, *Parish Law*.

See PAROCHIAL CHURCH COUNCIL.

Parish apprentices. Parish apprentices originated with the Poor Relief Act, 1601, s. 4, which provided that the churchwardens and overseers of the poor of any parish might, with the assent of two justices, bind as apprentices the children of parents unable to maintain them. Poor children were afterwards bound as apprentices by boards of guardians acting in accordance with the orders of the Ministry of Health under the Poor Law Amendment Act, 1844, s. 12; by s. 13 of that Act, no person could be compelled to take a parish apprentice; under the statute 1696, 8 & 9 Will. 3, c. 30, parishioners had been precluded from refusing to take apprentices whom the parish required them to receive. The Poor Law Amendment Act, 1844, was repealed by the Poor Law Act, 1927. Further provision was made by the Poor Law Act, 1930, ss. 59–66, 69, and the Merchant Shipping Act, 1894, s. 393. The poor law was abolished by the National Assistance Act, 1948. A local authority may with the consent of the Home Secretary arrange for the emigration of children in its care under the Children Act, 1948, s. 17, and may make contributions towards the cost of training, etc., under s. 20 of that Act as amended by the Children and Young Persons Act, 1969, Sch. 5 para. 15.

Parish boundaries. The ecclesiastical parish in most parts of England was simply the old Anglo-Saxon tun or township, or two adjoining townships in one only of which was there a church. It originated long before the period of statute law, and so was a creation of the common law. It became the custom for the parishioners to " beat the bounds," that is to say, to perambulate or walk round the parish in order to perpetuate the memory of the boundaries. This was done during the three days known as Rogation Days (*q.v.*) which precede Ascension Day (*q.v.*). The 19th Injunction of Elizabeth I, while forbidding religious processions generally, sanctioned perambulation and subsequent prayer in the parish church. The proper expenses of perambulation once in every three years were payable out of the rates (Poor Law Amendment Act, 1844, s. 60), but no charge for refreshments was allowed.

Perambulations still take place in many parishes, but their necessity or utility has to a large extent ceased by reason of the fact that in the great majority of parishes the boundaries were fixed under statutory powers during the last century (*e.g.*, Public Health Act, 1875, s. 278; Divided Parishes and Poor Law Amendment Act, 1876; Local Government Act, 1933, s. 141).

Apart from other evidence, the exact line followed in a perambulation will be held to mark the parish boundary.

Parish clerk. The parish clerk is coeval with the parish. The office is of extreme antiquity—next in dignity to the clergy, says Leland; but it is a temporal office (*Lawrence* v. *Edwards* [1891] 2 Ch. 72). In early times he kept the parish school, accompanied the priest when visiting the sick, and assisted in the services of the church. After the Reformation he sat under or in front of the officiating minister and recited the responses in the church services. Now he assists the minister at baptisms, marriages and funerals, in connection with the two latter of which he receives fees.

Before the Reformation the appointment of the clerk lay with the vicar or rector. Canon 91 of the Canons of 1606 confirmed this arrangement. In some places, under an ancient custom, the parishioners themselves have the right of making the appointment; and Canon 91 does not override such a custom (*Jermyns' Case* (1624) 2 Cro. 670). But the custom was modified by the Lecturers and Parish Clerks Act, 1844, which provided that, where the minister did not himself appoint, the appointment was subject to his consent (s. 3). Where the parishioners appointed, they acted through the vestry or the churchwardens. He is now appointed by the incumbent and the parochial church council jointly; the remuneration and terms depend on the custom of the particular parish and on the agreement made with him (Parochial Church Councils (Powers) Measure, 1956, s. 7 (iii)).

The Company of Parish Clerks is the most ancient in the City of London; yet they stand at the bottom of the list, and have neither livery nor the privilege of making their members free of the City. See COMPANIES; CITY.

The foregoing applies only to the parish clerk of the ecclesiastical parish known to the common law. The clerks of the many churches erected under the Church Building Acts, 1818 and 1819, and under the New Parishes Acts, 1843,

1844 and 1856, and the New Parishes Measure, 1943, are known simply as clerks and have not the same status as the parish clerk proper.

Parish constables. See the Parish Constables Act, 1872, by which provision was made for their abolition. See CONSTABLES.

Parish council. This was established by the Local Government Act, 1894 (later the Local Government Act, 1933, ss. 43–55), for every rural parish.

Under the Local Government Act, 1972, there is a parish council for every parish or group of parishes which had a parish council before April 1, 1974, or was a borough or district council which, under the Act became a parish. Where a parish has no parish council the establishment of a parish council is a function of the district (*q.v.*) council. The district council may dissolve the parish council of a small parish and may make orders grouping parishes, dissolving groups and separating parishes from groups (ss. 9–12).

A parish council consists of a chairman and parish councillors. It is a body corporate. It need not have a common seal. Where it has no seal instruments may be signed and sealed by members of the council (s. 14). The chairman is elected annually by the council from among the councillors. He continues in office, unless he resigns or becomes disqualified, until his successor becomes entitled to act as chairman. He may receive an allowance for his expenses. The council may appoint a vice-chairman (s. 15).

The number of parish councillors is such number, not less than five, as is fixed by the district council. They are elected by the local government electors for the parish. Elections are to be held in 1976 and 1979 and every fourth year thereafter. All the councillors return together. Where a parish is divided into wards there is a separate election for each ward (s. 16). Meetings of a parish council are regulated by Sch. 12 Pt. II.

Parish councils have power to acquire land by agreement (s. 124). Land may be acquired compulsorily on behalf of a parish council by the district council (s. 125). Powers of appropriation and disposal are contained in ss. 126, 127. As to the provision of buildings, see s. 133. As to the use of schoolrooms, see s. 134. As to expenses, see s. 150. As to custody of documents, see ss. 226, 227.

A parish council may become a town council or a borough council. See PARISH.

Under the Parish Councils Act, 1957, a parish council has power to provide seats and shelters in roads, and public clocks (ss. 1 (1) (2), 2, 5), to pay reasonable expenses (s. 6 (1) (2)). A parish council is a local authority in respect of open spaces (*q.v.*) (s. 8).

Parish meeting. This was established for every rural parish by the Local Government Act, 1894 (later the Local Government Act, 1933, ss. 43–55, 77, Sch. 3 Pt. VI).

Under the Local Government Act, 1972, there is a parish meeting in every parish (s. 9). Where the population of a orders grouping parishes, dissolving parish is small, the parish meeting may apply to the district council (*q.v.*) to dissolve the parish council. A parish meeting may apply to the district council for groups or separating parishes from groups (ss. 10–12).

The parish meeting consists of the local government electors for the parish. Any act of a parish meeting may be signified by an instrument signed by the person presiding and two other local government electors present at the meeting. If an instrument under seal is required the instrument may be signed by those persons and sealed with the seal of the parish council or, if there is no parish council, with the seal of the parish trustees (*q.v.*) or, if the trustees have no seal, with the seals of those persons (s. 13). In a parish not having a parish council, the parish meeting is to elect a chairman for the year (s. 15 (10)). A parish meeting for a parish ward is conducted as if it were a meeting of the whole parish (s. 17). In a parish not having a separate parish council the parish meeting may discharge their functions by means of a committee of local government electors (s. 108) and may have the functions of a parish council conferred on the meeting by the district council (*q.v.*) (s. 109). As to expenses see s. 150; as to the custody of documents, see s. 226. As to the conduct of parish meetings see Sch. 12 Pt. III.

No poll can be demanded at a parish meeting except on a question formally put to the meeting by a proposition or amendment to a resolution (*Bennett* v. *Chappell* [1966] Ch. 391).

Parish officers, churchwardens, and formerly overseers and constables.

Parish priest, the parson; a minister who holds a parish as a benefice, called, if the predial tithes were unappropriated, rector, and if appropriated, vicar.

Parish register, the register of marriages, baptisms and burials which Canon 70 of the Canons of 1603 requires to be kept in every church and chapel of the Church of England. The keeping of this register is also directed by the Parochial Registers Act, 1812, s. 1; but the Births and Deaths Registration Act, 1836, s. 1, repealed so much of the Act of 1812 as related to the entry of marriages in this register. See REGISTRATION, ETC.

Parish trustees. In a parish not having a separate parish council, the chairman of the parish meeting and the proper officer of the district council are a body corporate by the name of " The Parish Trustees of ——." They need not have a common seal but if they have no seal any act of theirs which requires to be signified by an instrument under seal may be signified by an instrument signed and sealed by the persons who are the parish trustees (Local Government Act, 1972, s. 13). The parish trustees acting with the consent of the parish meeting may dispose of parish land in any manner they wish (s. 127). As to the use of a schoolroom see s. 134.

Parishioner, a resident in the common-law ecclesiastical parish. Down to the Reformation the word had reference only to religious status: afterwards, when the parish became an area for civil purposes, the word parishioner acquired a civil meaning. In its civil meaning it includes not only the residents in a parish but also non-resident occupiers of land who pay rates. At common law parishioners paying scot and lot (*q.v.*) formed the vestry (*q.v.*).

Paritor [Lat. *apparitor*], a beadle; a summoner to the courts of civil law.

Park [Lat. *parcus*; *parcere*, to spare], a place of privilege for wild beasts of venery, and other wild beasts of the forest and chase, who have protection there, so that no man may hurt or chase them without licence of the owner. A park differs from a forest in that a subject may hold a park by prescription or royal grant. It differs from a chase because a park must be enclosed; if it lies open, it is a good cause of seizing it into the sovereign's hands, as a free chase may be if it lies enclosed. For a park three things are required; a grant thereof; enclosure by pale, wall, or hedge; and beasts of a park, such as buck, does, etc. (*Howard's Case* (1626) Cro.Car. 59).

Franchises of park were abolished by the Wild Creatures and Forest Laws Act, 1971.

As to the application of the Road Traffic enactments to the Royal Parks see S.I. 1974 No. 797.

The word "park," as used in the Settled Land Acts, is not confined to an ancient legal park, but includes an ordinary private park (*Pease* v. *Courtney* [1904] 2 Ch. 509). A park, in the popular sense of the word, namely, one erected without lawful warrant, is sometimes called a nominative park by the old writers but now, even in Acts of Parliament, it is called simply a park. The parks forming part of the demesnes of the Crown are called royal parks. As to the management of the royal parks, see the Parks Regulation Act, 1872; the London Parks and Works Act, 1887; the Parks Regulation (Amendment) Act, 1926; the Agriculture (Miscellaneous Provisions) Act, 1968, s. 48 and the Parks Regulation (Amendment) Act, 1974. See DEMESNE.

As to the exemption of parks from rating, see the General Rate Act, 1967, s. 44. See NATIONAL PARKS; OPEN SPACE.

Park-bote, to be quit of enclosing a park or any part thereof (4 Co.Inst. 308; Cowel).

Possibly, however, it means the repair of the fence or wall of a park. See BOTE.

Parker, a park-keeper.

Parking. Parking offences may be subject to a fixed penalty without prosecution (Road Traffic Regulation Act, 1967, s. 80; Transport Act, 1968, s. 131, Sch. 18;

PARKING

Road Traffic Act, 1972, Sch. 7; Road Traffic Act, 1974, Sch. 6 para. 8). By the Road Traffic Act, 1974, ss. 1, 3–5 liability is fixed on the owner of the vehicle.

As to parking on Sunday on a single yellow line, see *Derrick* v. *Ryder* [1972] R.T.R. 480. As to leaving a car park without paying, see *Davies* v. *Hackett* [1973] R.T.R. 8. Leaving a car, without putting a coin in a parking meter, for any reason whatever is an offence (*Strong* v. *Dawtry* [1961] 1 W.L.R. 841 (absence for two minutes to get change)). As to penalties in respect of parking, see the Road Traffic Act, 1974, Sch. 5 Pt. II, Sch. 7. The vehicle owner may be made liable for excess parking charges (ss. 2–5).

If a vehicle is parked on the highway it becomes an unnecessary obstruction if left there too long (*Solomon* v. *Durbridge* (1956) 120 J.P. 231). Bad parking may give rise to a liability in negligence (*Chop Seng Heng* v. *Thevannasan S/O Sinnapan* [1975] 3 All E.R. 572).

It is an offence to park a heavy commercial vehicle on the verge of a road or on any land between two carriageways or on a footway. It is an offence to park any other vehicle on the verge of an urban road or on any land between two carriageways of an urban road or on a footway (*q.v.*) comprised in an urban road (Road Traffic Act, 1972, ss. 36A, 36B; Heavy Commercial Vehicles (Controls and Regulations) Act, 1973, s. 2; Road Traffic Act, 1974, s. 7).

In order to facilitate the cleaning of streets, a district council or a London borough council or the Common Council of the City of London may prohibit parking of vehicles in the street during specified hours of any day (Control of Pollution Act, 1974, s. 23).

Forgery of a parking meter ticket is punishable under the Road Traffic Regulation Act, 1967, ss. 86, 90; Transport Act, 1968, s. 127; Road Traffic Act, 1974, Sch. 5 Pt. IV para. 3.

Adequate steps must be taken to bring to the notice of a customer a condition in a car park ticket excluding liability for injury to the customer (*Thornton* v. *Shoe Lane Parking* [1971] 2 Q.B. 163).

A movable stall with wheels but no mechanical means of propulsion may be a "vehicle" for the purposes of parking regulations (*Boxer* v. *Snelling* [1972] R.T.R. 472).

Parking places. Power to provide parking places for vehicles off highways, on highways without payment and on highways for payment is contained in the Road Traffic Regulation Act, 1967, ss. 28–45, amended by the Transport Act, 1968, s. 127, Sch. 14 Pt. VI, Sch. 18 Pt. II, the Highways Act, 1971, s. 9, S.I. 1967 No. 414, the Local Government Act, 1972, Schs. 19, 30, the Local Government Act, 1974, s. 35, Sch. 6 para. 20. Parish councils may provide parking places (Road Traffic Regulation Act, 1967, ss. 46–50; Local Government Act, 1972, Sch. 19 para. 22).

Power to make charges for parking in Royal Parks is contained in the Act of 1967, s. 51. Charges may be made for removing and storing vehicles and abandoned vehicles may be disposed of (Act of 1967, ss. 52, 53; Transport Act, 1968, Sch. 14 Pt. VI paras. 25, 26; Local Government Act, 1972, Sch. 19 para. 23).

As to the control of off-street parking in London see the Transport (London) Act, 1969, s. 36, Sch. 5; Land Commission (Dissolution) Act, 1971, Sch. 2 para. 5; Tribunals and Inquiries Act, 1971, Sch. 3; Town and Country Planning Act, 1971, Sch. 23 Pt. II.

As to the parking of heavy goods vehicles see LORRY AREAS; PARKING.

The power of making designation orders was vested in local authorities by S.I. 1967 No. 414.

Stands for hackney carriages and omnibuses may be fixed under the Town Police Clauses Act, 1847, s. 68, the Town Police Clauses Act, 1889, s. 6, and the Public Health Act, 1875, s. 171. Parking places for public service vehicles are regulated under the Road Traffic Regulation Act, 1967, s. 33, as amended by the Transport Act, 1968, Sch. 14 Pt. VI paras. 18–20, Sch. 18 Pt. II.

Conditions may be imposed on the grant of planning permission (*q.v.*) as to the provision of facilities for the parking, loading, unloading or fuelling of vehicles and the imposition of such conditions is not a subject of compensation (Town and

Country Planning Act, 1971, s. 147 (2) (*c*).

Regulations may be made under the Road Traffic Act, 1972, exempting vehicles standing or parked on any road with respect to which a speed limit applies or on any road verge or in any parking place or any stand for hackney carriages (s. 78 (1) (*d*)).

Parliament [Fr. *parler*, to speak], the legislature of the United Kingdom of Great Britain and Northern Ireland (Royal and Parliamentary Titles Act, 1927, s. 2), consisting of the sovereign, and the three estates of the realm, *i.e.*, the lords spiritual and temporal (called the House of Lords or Upper House of Parliament), and the persons elected by the people (called the House of Commons, or Lower or Nether House of Parliament). Twelve members are returned to the House of Commons by Northern Ireland (Representation of the People Act, 1948, Sch. 1 Pt. IV).

As to pensions of members of Parliament, see the Parliamentary and other Pensions Act, 1972.

Until the reign of Henry IV both Houses sat together (4 Co.Inst. 5).

The word parliament was first applied to general assemblies of the State, under Louis VII in France, about the middle of the twelfth century. The earliest mention of it in the statutes is in the preamble to the Statute of Westminster I, 1275. See ACT OF PARLIAMENT; CHILTERN HUNDREDS, ETC.; CONTEMPT OF PARLIAMENT; ELECTORAL FRANCHISE; HOUSE OF COMMONS; HOUSE OF LORDS; IMPEACHMENT; KNIGHT; PREROGATIVE; PROROGATION; TRENNIAL ACTS.

Parliament de la Bonde, the Parliament of the Band. This was the Parliament held in London in 1321. The Earl of Lancaster and other great barons wore coloured bands as distinguishing marks when they attended, in order to procure a sentence of forfeiture and exile against the Despensers.

Parliament House, the buildings comprising the courts, etc., of the Court of Session in Edinburgh.

Parliament rolls. See ROLLS OF PARLIAMENT.

Parliamentary agents, persons (usually solicitors) who transact the technical business involved in passing private Bills through the Houses of Parliament. They are required to sign a prescribed declaration and to give security for compliance with the rules of the House of Commons.

Parliamentary Commissioner, an official appointed under the Parliamentary Commissioner Act, 1967, for the investigation of administrative action taken on behalf of the Crown. The departments and authorities subject to investigation are listed in Sch. 2 to the Act as amended by Order in Council (see s. 4). Complaints must be made in writing to a member of parliament who may if he thinks fit refer them to the commissioner (ss. 5, 6). If the commissioner thinks that there has been injustice which is not being remedied he may lay before Parliament a special report upon the case (s. 10 (3)). Matters not subject to investigation are specified in s. 5 and Sch. 3, as amended by the Fugitive Offenders Act, 1967, s. 21 (4). The Parliamentary Commissioner is a member of the Commissions for Local Administration (*q.v.*) (Local Government Act, 1974, s. 23 (2); see also s. 33).

The following were added to Sch. 2 to the Act: Department of Energy; Department of Industry; Department of Trade; Department of Prices and Consumer Protection (S.I. 1974 No. 692).

Mandamus does not lie to the Parliamentary Commissioner to investigate a complaint (*Re Fletcher's Application* [1970] 2 All E.R. 527n.).

Parliamentary committees. These consist of committees of the whole House, standing or sessional committees, select committees and joint committees.

A committee of the whole House, whether in the Lords or the Commons, is really the House of Lords or the House of Commons, as the case may be, presided over by a chairman instead of by the Lord Chancellor or the Speaker. In the House of Commons, there are the Committee of Supply and the Committee of Ways and Means. These committees do not legislate. They merely pass resolutions on financial matters. But a resolution of the Committee of Ways and Means which varies or renews taxation has, under the Provisional Collection of

Taxes Act, 1968, statutory effect for a limited period.

The standing or sessional committees and the select committees consist in each House of a certain number of members who perform various functions in connection with Bills.

Joint committees consist of equal numbers of members of each House. Since 1864 they have frequently been constituted; but between 1695 and 1864 there had been no such committee.

Not only any Bill but any subject that is brought under the consideration of either House, may, if the House thinks proper, be referred to a committee for the purpose of making inquiries, by the examination of witnesses or otherwise, into matters which could not be conveniently inquired into by the whole House; and when the inquiry is ended, the committee, through their chairman, make a report to the House of the result. All private Bills are referred to committees of each House before they are sanctioned by that House. Their reports are not absolutely binding upon the House, but the House seldom reverses their decision.

As to the power of such committees to administer oaths to witnesses, see the Parliamentary Witnesses Oaths Act, 1871.

Parliamentary deposits. Under the standing orders of both Houses of Parliament, the promoters of private Bills providing for parliamentary powers over the property of others are required to deposit in court sums bearing a certain proportion to the estimated cost of the works proposed, the object being to place a check of speculative promotion and to provide security for persons whose property may be injuriously affected.

Parliamentary privilege. See PRIVILEGE.

Parliamentary secretary includes a person holding ministerial office (however called) as assistant to a member of Her Majesty's Government in the United Kingdom but not having departmental responsibilities (House of Commons Disqualification Act, 1975, s. 9; Ministerial and other Salaries Act, 1972, s. 1 (6) (a)).

Parliamentum diabolicum, the Dia-

bolical Parliament. This was the Parliament held at Coventry in 1459. The Duke of York (afterwards Edward IV) and many of his chief adherents were attainted by it, but its proceedings were annulled by the succeeding Parliament (Holingshed, Chron.).

Parliamentum indoctorum, the Lack-learning Parliament. This was the Parliament held at Coventry in 1404, for membership of which as knights of the shire all lawyers and persons skilled in the law were declared disqualified through the insertion of a prohibition to that effect in the writ of summons framed by Lord Chancellor Beaufort.

Parliamentum insanum, the Mad Parliament. This was the Parliament held at Oxford in 1258, distinguished for the extreme character and the violence of its proceedings. It drew up the set of articles known as the Provisions of Oxford, under which all the powers of government were placed in the hands of a kind of representative oligarchy (Stubbs, Sel.Ch. 369).

Paroche, Parochia, a parish.

Parochial chapels, places of public worship in which the rites of sacrament and sepulture are performed. See CHAPEL.

Parochial charities. See the Charities Act, 1960, s. 37; Local Government Act, 1972, s. 210 (9), Sch. 30.

Parochial church council. The establishment in every parish of a parochial church council was provided for by the Parochial Church Councils (Powers) Measure, 1921. It was amended by the Parochial Church Councils (Amendment) Measure, 1949, and these two Measures were consolidated with further amendments by the Parochial Church Councils (Powers) Measure, 1956 (amended by the Synodical Government Measure, 1969, s. 6). Parochial church councils are bodies corporate and their primary duty is to co-operate with incumbents in the initiation, conduct and development of church work, both within the parish and outside. Certain powers, duties and liabilities of the vestry and of the church-wardens are transferred to the parochial church council. See also the Pastoral Measure, 1968, Sch. 3 para. 12.

Such a council is quite distinct from

the parish council (*q.v.*), and is in no way concerned with secular matters.

As to meetings to elect representatives to the ruridecanal conference, see *Mulholland* v. *St. Peter, Roydon, Parochial Church Council* [1969] 1 W.L.R. 1842.

Parochian, a parishioner.

Parol, or Parole [Fr. *parole*], by word of mouth; but the expression is also made use of to denote writings not under seal.

The pleadings in an action were, when they were given *viva voce* in court, frequently termed the parol.

In its technical sense, as applied to a legal transaction, the word means that the transaction has been effected without the solemnity of a deed. Therefore an assignment of chattels, or a contract, or a lease, which is either oral or reduced into a writing not under seal, is called a parol assignment, contract or lease (see CONTRACT). Similarly in the law of evidence, where the contents of a document are brought before the court either orally or by means of a copy, this is called adducing parol evidence of its contents. Parol evidence also sometimes means extrinsic evidence. See EVIDENCE; PAROL EVIDENCE.

As to demurrer of the parol, see DEMUR.

" Parol " literally means verbal or oral. In early times few persons could write, and therefore when a document was required to record a transaction the parties put their seals to it and made it a deed. Transactions of less importance were testified by word of mouth or by parol, and this use of " parol," to signify the absence of a deed, remained after simple writing without sealing had come into use. See PAROLE.

Parol agreements, such as are either by word of mouth or are committed to writing, but are not under seal. The common law draws only one great distinction, *viz.*, between instruments under seal and instruments not under seal.

Parol arrest. Any justice of the peace may, by word of mouth, authorise any one to arrest another who is guilty of a breach of the peace in his presence.

Parol demurrer. This was abolished by the Debts Recovery Act, 1830, s. 10. See DEMUR.

Parol evidence, testimony by the mouth of a witness; also extrinsic evidence, whether oral or otherwise, relating to a transaction contained in a written instrument.

It is a general rule that oral evidence cannot be substituted for a written instrument, where the latter is required by law, or to give effect to a written instrument defective in any particular essential to its validity; nor to contradict, alter, or vary a written instrument, required by law, or agreed upon by the parties, as the authentic memorial of the facts which it recites. But parol evidence is admissible to defeat a written instrument on the ground of fraud, mistake, etc., or to apply it to its proper subject, or, in some instances, as ancillary to such application to explain the meaning of doubtful terms, or to rebut presumptions arising extrinsically. In these cases the parol evidence does not usurp the place of written evidence, but either shows that the instrument ought not to be allowed to operate at all, or is essential in order to give to the instrument its legal effect.

The general rule with regard to the admission of parol evidence to explain the meaning of, or to add to, vary, or alter the express terms of a deed, is that it is not admissible (*Henderson* v. *Arthur* [1907] 1 K.B. 10), except where, although the deed is clearly expressed, some ambiguity arises from extrinsic circumstances; where the language of a charter or deed has become obscure from antiquity; where the grant is uncertain owing to a want of acquaintance with the grantor's estate; where it is important to show a consideration or a different consideration consistent with, and not repugnant to, that stated in the deed itself; where it becomes necessary to show a different time of delivery from that at which the deed purports to have been made; where it is sought to prove a customary right not expressed in the deed, but not inconsistent with any of its stipulations; or, where fraud or illegality in the formation of the deed is relied on, to avoid it. If a clause in a deed is so ambiguously or defectively expressed that the court cannot collect the meaning of the parties, it is void on account of uncertainty.

Parole, a promise made by a prisoner of war, when he has leave to go anywhere, to return at a time appointed, or not to take up arms till exchanged; the practice of releasing prisoners of war on an undertaking that they will not serve again during the war. The government members of whose forces are so released on parole is not bound to confirm their undertaking, but in that case those released must be sent back again into captivity (Holland, *Lectures*, 338).

Parole Board. See the Criminal Justice Act, 1967, ss. 59–64, Sch. 2; Criminal Justice Act, 1972, s. 35, Sch. 5, Sch. 6 Pt. II.

As to further offences by prisoners on parole see Practice Direction December 19, 1975 [1975] C.L.Y. 525.

Parricide, the killing of a father, also called patricide, and, in some old writers, of a mother or a child. The killing of a mother is of course more properly known as matricide. No such offence as parricide or matricide is known to English law; the offence is murder or manslaughter; it did not come within the old offence of petty treason (*q.v.*). The punishment in the civil law was more severe than for any other kind of homicide; after being scourged, the delinquent was sewn up in a leathern sack with a live dog, a cock, viper and an ape, and so cast into the sea (4 Bl.Comm. 202).

Pars enitia. See ENITIA PARS.

Pars pro toto, the name of a part used to represent the whole; as the roof for the house, ten spears for ten armed men, etc.

Pars rationabilis, a reasonable part. See RATIONABILI PARTE BONORUM, DE; REASONABLE PARTS.

Parson [Lat. *persona*, person; *parochianus*, parish priest], a parish priest. A parson, anciently written persone, is so called because the parson *omnium personam in ecclesia sustinet*. A parson, *persona ecclesiae*, is one who has full possession of all the rights of a parochial church. He is called parson, *persona*, because he personates or represents the Church. He is sometimes called the rector or governor of a church but the appellation parson is the most legal, most beneficial, and most honourable title that a parish priest can enjoy (3 Bl.Comm. 384).

Persona impersonata, parson impersonee, is a rector who is in full possession of the parochial church whether presentative or impropriate (Co.Litt. 300). The rector of a presentative advowson is not a complete parson until he has been inducted (*q.v.*), while in the case of an impropriate advowson the rector is perpetual parson.

A parson is a corporation sole. He has the freehold for life of the parsonage-house, the glebe and formerly tithes and other dues. But these are sometimes appropriated, that is to say, the benefice is perpetually annexed to some spiritual corporation, either sole or aggregate, being the patron of the living, which the law esteems equally capable of providing for the service of the church as any single private clergyman (1 Bl.Comm. 384).

Many appropriations, however, are in the hands of lay persons, who are usually styled, by way of distinction, lay impropriators. In all appropriations there is generally a spiritual person attached to the church, under the name of vicar, to whom the spiritual duty or cure of souls belongs, in the same manner as to the rector in parsonages not appropriate or rectories, and to whom a portion of the income of the benefice is assigned.

The method of becoming a parson or vicar is much the same. There are four requisites: holy orders, presentation, institution, and induction. A parson or vicar may cease to be so by death, by cession in taking another benefice, by consecration to a bishopric, by resignation, or by deprivation (1 Bl.Comm. 388, 392).

See ADVOWSON; RECTOR; VICAR.

Parson imparsonee [Lat. *persona impersonata*], a clerk presented, instituted, and inducted into a rectory, and thus in full and complete possession of the church (1 Bl.Comm. 391; Co.Litt. 300a).

Parson mortal; Parson immortal. Before the Reformation, the rector of a church appointed for his own life was called parson mortal (*persona mortalis*), but any collegiate or conventional body to which the church was for ever appropriated was styled parson immortal (*persona immortalis*) (Cartul.Rading. 182; Jacob).

Parsonage, the benefice of a parish; the parson's house. Strictly, it means the parochial church with the residence of the incumbent, the glebe (*q.v.*) and, formerly, the tithes (*q.v.*); but it is commonly applied to the house only. The repair of parsonage houses is now a function of the Parsonages Board of the diocese (Repair of Benefice Buildings Measure, 1972). See also GLEBE.

The law relating to the sale, purchase and improvement of parsonage houses and of other property belonging to benefices was consolidated by the Parsonages Measure, 1938, amended by the Church Property (Miscellaneous Provisions) Measure, 1960, ss. 1–4).

See DILAPIDATION; GILBERT ACTS.

Part. See RIDING.

Part; Party. A person who takes part in a legal transaction or proceeding is said to be a party to it. Thus, if an agreement, conveyance, lease, or the like, is entered into between A and B, they are said to be parties to it; and the same expression is often, though not very correctly, applied to the persons named as the grantors or releasors in a deed-poll (*q.v.*).

Parties to formal instruments are divided into classes or parts according to their estates or interests in the subject-matter of the transaction; thus, if A mortgages land to B, C and D, and they all agree to sell it to E and F, the conveyance would be made between A of the first part, B, C and D of the second part, and E and F of the third part. As to the distinction between parties and privies, see PRIVY.

See PARTIES.

Part payment, payment of part of a debt. Such a payment (independently of its effect in satisfying the debt *pro tanto*) has the effect of reviving a debt (or rather the balance of a debt) which would otherwise be barred by the Limitation Act, 1939. Part payment by one joint debtor after the expiration of the period of limitation does not revive the debt against the others (Limitation Act, 1939, s. 25).

Part payment was formerly an alterna-tive to written evidence necessary to make enforceable by action a contract for the sale of goods of the value of £10 or over (Sale of Goods Act, 1893, s. 4), but there are now no special requirements in relation to such a contract (Law Reform (Enforcement of Contracts) Act, 1954, s. 2).

Part performance, the equitable doctrine recognised by the Law of Property Act, 1925, s. 40, that where a contract for the sale or other disposition of land or an interest in land is not evidenced by writing, it may nevertheless be enforced by a decree of specific performance if it has been partly carried into effect, as where the plaintiff has entered into possession of the land. See PERFORMANCE.

Partes finis nihil habuerunt, De, an exception (*q.v.*) taken against a fine levied, upon the ground that the parties to the fine had no estate in the lands (3 Co.Rep. 88).

Partial insanity, mental unsoundness always existing, although only occasionally manifest, such as monomania (*Smith* v. *Tebbitt* (1867) L.R. 1 P. & D. 398).

Partial loss. See ABANDONMENT OF CARGO; LOSS.

Partibility. See GAVELKIND.

Particata terrae, a rood (*q.v.*) of land (Spelman).

Particeps criminis, one who has a share in a crime: an accessory (*q.v.*).

Particeps fraudis, a partner in fraud.

Particula, a small piece of land.

Particular average. See AVERAGE.

Particular estate, an estate granted or carved out of a larger estate.

Particular lien. See LIEN.

Particular tenant, the owner of a particular estate. See ESTATE.

When a particular tenant conveyed by a feoffment, fine, or recovery, a greater estate than the law entitled him to convey, a forfeiture ensued to the person in immediate remainder or reversion. If a tenant for his own life alienated by feoffment for the life of another or in tail or in fee, these being estates which either must or might have lasted longer than his own, his creating them was not only beyond his power, and inconsistent with the nature of his interest, but was also a forfeiture of his own particular estate to him in remainder or reversion, who was entitled to enter immediately.

Fines and recoveries having been abolished and a feoffment having no longer a tortious operation (Real Property Act, 1845, s. 4), a tenant, by creating a larger interest than he had in the property, did not after the passing of that Act incur a forfeiture, for such a creation was then void as to the excess, and good for his own interest. The Real Property Act, 1845, was repealed by the Law of Property Act, 1925, and conveyance by feoffment was abolished by s. 51 of that Act. See FEOFFMENT.

Particularity, in a pleading, affidavit, or the like, is the allegation of particulars or details. An excess or deficiency of particularity in a pleading is equally a defect; the latter entitles the opposite party either to an order for particulars (q.v.), or to an order requiring the other party to amend his pleading (see AMENDMENT), while the former may lead to a disallowance of cost for prolixity (R.S.C., Ord. 41, r. 6, note).

Particulars, the details of the claim or of the defence in an action which are necessary in order to enable the other side to know what case he has to meet. They are intended to make quite clear the case of the party who furnishes them. Interrogatories (q.v.) and discovery (q.v.), on the other hand, relate to the evidence upon which the case of the other party depends.

The courts have a general jurisdiction, independently of statute, to order a detailed statement of the demand in any litigation, or of any defence, to be given that surprise may be avoided, and substantial justice promoted. The necessity for application for particulars has become less frequent since the Judicature Acts, 1873–75, as a statement of claim containing the material facts on which the plaintiff relies is substituted for the declaration under the old practice, which only contained a legal statement of the plaintiff's cause of action. See R.S.C., Ord. 18, r. 12.

See BILL OF PARTICULARS.

Particulars of breaches and objections. It was provided by the Patent Law Amendment Act, 1852, s. 41, that in an action for the infringement of letters patent, the plaintiff was bound to deliver with his declaration particulars of the breaches which he complained of, and that the defendant in an action for infringement, and the prosecutor in any proceedings by *scire facias* (q.v.) to repeal letters patent, were bound to deliver with the plea or declaration particulars of any objections to the validity of the patent on which they meant to rely at the trial. This enactment was repealed by the Patents Designs and Trade Marks Act, 1883, now itself repealed, and there is now no such requirement. See PATENTS.

Particulars of sale. When land or houses are sold by auction it is usual to prefix to the conditions of sale (q.v.) a description of the property, giving the area, the tenure, the tenancy or tenancies if the property or any of it is let, easements or incumbrances affecting it, any outgoings, the name of the auctioneer and the place and time of sale, and the name of the vendor. The particulars and conditions of sale and the memorandum (q.v.) form the contract of sale.

It is the duty of a vendor to make himself acquainted with the peculiarities and incidents of the property he is going to sell, and when he describes it for the information of the purchaser to describe everything material to be known in order to judge of its nature and value, and any substantial variation from the description will render the contract voidable (*Flight* v. *Booth* (1834) 1 Bing.N.C. 77). If there is anything connected with the property important to be known which cannot be discerned or may be misapprehended by inspection, it ought to be stated in the particulars. On the sale of property of any considerable size the particulars are usually accompanied by a plan. In sales by auction the conditions of sale are generally printed at the end of the particulars and followed by a short printed form of contract. See CONDITIONS OF SALE.

Parties, persons concerned in any deed or act; litigants. In a legal proceeding, the parties are the persons whose names appear on the record. In Chancery practice, persons who are not parties, but who are affected by certain orders of the court, can be made parties by being

1322

served with notice of such orders. (See NOTICE OF JUDGMENT.) In an action, the parties are divided into plaintiffs and defendants, and, if necessary, they are distinguished according to the manner in which they were introduced into it.

In the case of a petition, the parties consist of the petitioners and the respondents. In the case of a summons, the persons at whose instance it is issued are called the applicants, and the persons to whom it is addressed the respondents.

Parties to a proceeding are also divided into necessary and proper. Necessary parties are those who are interested in the subject-matter of the proceedings, and in whose absence, therefore, it could not be fairly dealt with: proper parties are those who, though not interested in the proceedings, are made parties for some good reason; thus, where an action is brought to rescind a contract, any person is a proper party to it who was active or concurring in the matters which gave the right to rescind.

R.S.C., Ord. 15, makes provision as to the joinder of parties and the consequences of misjoinder and nonjoinder. All persons may be joined as plaintiffs in whom the right to any relief claimed is alleged to exist, whether jointly, severally, or in the alternative. Two or more defendants may be joined, in case the plaintiff is in doubt as to the person from whom he is entitled to redress. Trustees, executors, and administrators may sue and be sued on behalf of or as representing the property or estate of which they are the trustees or representatives, without joining any of the parties beneficially interested in the trust or estate. Where there are numerous parties having the same interest in one action, one or more of such parties may sue or be sued, or may be authorised by the court to defend in such action, on behalf of or for the benefit of all parties so interested. No cause or matter is defeated by reason of the misjoinder or nonjoinder of parties, and the court may in every cause or matter deal with the matter in controversy, so far as regards the rights and interests of the parties actually before it. The court or a judge may, at any stage of the proceedings, either upon or without the application of either party, and on such terms as may appear to the court or a judge to be just, order that the names of any parties improperly joined, whether as plaintiffs or as defendants, be struck out, and that the names of any parties, whether plaintiffs or defendants, who ought to have been joined, or whose presence before the court may be necessary in order to enable the court effectually and completely to adjudicate upon and settle all the questions involved in the action be added. See JOINDER; MISJOINDER; NONJOINDER.

Ord. 15, r. 6, allows the introduction of third parties in cases where the defendant claims any remedy over against any other person. See THIRD PARTY.

By the Judicature Act, 1925, s. 225, replacing the Judicature Act, 1873, s. 100, the word " party " includes every person served with notice of or attending any proceeding, although not named on the record.

As to change of parties by death, etc., see ABATEMENT.

In criminal cases the parties are the prosecutor and the prisoner or defendant.

Parties to a cause, civil or criminal, have a right to be present, in any case, throughout the trial. See WITNESS.

As to the parties to a bill of exchange, and as to the " parts " of foreign bills of exchange, see BILL OF EXCHANGE.

Partition, the act of dividing.

Before 1926 all co-owners of land might make partition, and coparceners were compellable to do so by common law. Co-owners, other than coparceners or copyholders, were compellable to make partition by the statutes 1539, 31 Hen. 8, c. 1, and 1540, 32 Hen. 8, c. 32, the latter statute applying to joint tenants and tenants in common holding for life or years.

Co-owners of copyhold were first enabled to make partition by the Copyhold Act, 1841, s. 85, re-enacted by the Copyhold Act, 1894, s. 87.

With a view to the more convenient and perfect partition or allotment of the premises, equity frequently decreed a pecuniary compensation to one of the parties for owelty, *i.e.,* equality of partition, so as to prevent any injustice or inequality, as where one party had laid out large sums in improvements on the estate.

For an order for partition of a wall separating the gardens of two adjoining houses, see *Mayfair Property Co.* v. *Johnson* [1894] 1 Ch. 508.

Partition took place where land belonging to joint tenants, tenants in common, coparceners or heirs in gavelkind was divided among them in severalty, each taking a distinct part. Partition was either voluntary, that is, by agreement between the parties, or compulsory. Voluntary partition was effected either by a deed, which varied according to the nature of the property and the tenancy, or by obtaining an order of exchange from the Ministry of Agriculture and Fisheries, which took effect without any further conveyance. Compulsory partition was effected by an action for partition in the Chancery Division (Judicature Act, 1873, s. 34), in which case the details were generally settled by a scheme (*q.v.*) in chambers.

By the Partition Act, 1868, s. 3, it was provided that in a suit for partition, where by reason of the nature of the property or the number of the parties interested, or of any other circumstance, a sale of the property and a distribution of the proceeds would be more beneficial for the parties interested than a division of the property, the court might, on the request of any of the parties interested, and notwithstanding the dissent or disability of any other of them, direct a sale of the property. The Partition Act, 1876, further amended the law. Co-owners, coparceners and all others entitled to undivided shares in land having been deprived of their legal title to a legal estate by the Law of Property Act, 1925, ss. 1 (6), 34, and the Settled Land Act, s. 36, the entirety becoming vested in trustees for sale, the Partition Acts, 1868 and 1876, were repealed, and the Law of Property Act, 1925, s. 28 (3), provides that where the net proceeds of sale have become absolutely vested in persons of full age in undivided shares (whether or not such shares may be subject to a derivative trust) the trustees for sale may partition the land remaining unsold or any part thereof or provide for payment of any

equality money subject to the consents in the section provided for. Trustees not having power to invest in land may obtain the requisite power under the Trustee Act, 1925, s. 57.

A party asking for a sale was not compellable to part with his share to his co-owners at a valuation (*Pitt* v. *Jones* (1880) 5 App.Cas. 651).

See COMMISSION OF PARTITION.

Partition, Deed of. When an estate was held in community by joint tenants, tenants in common, coparceners, or joint heirs in gavelkind, and they were desirous of dividing it into distinct portions, to be exclusively enjoyed by each, and were not under legal disability, they could accomplish their object by a deed of partition. By the Real Property Act, 1845, s. 3, the partition of any tenements except copyhold was void unless made by deed. Sometimes, instead of agreeing as to their several allotments, a reference was made to a person to divide the estate into the required portions, and one mode of effecting this division was to convey the whole estate to the proposed referee upon trust to convey the several allotments to the respective parties according to his award.

In Kent, where the land was of gavelkind tenure, these partitions were called shifting, from the Saxon, *shiftan,* to divide.

Deeds of partition are now made under the Law of Property Act, 1925, s. 28 (3). See PARTITION.

Partition of chattels. The court may order partition of chattels owned in undivided shares upon application by the persons interested in a moiety or upwards (Law of Property Act, 1925, s. 188).

Partition, Writ of. This was abolished by the Real Property Limitation Act, 1833, s. 36. See PARTITIONE FACIENDA, DE.

Partitione facienda, De. When an inheritance descended to more than one heir, and they could not agree to a partition, the writ *de partitione facienda* lay for any of them. It was abolished by the Real Property Limitation Act, 1833, s. 36. The writ was a common law writ. Its abolition left the Court of Chancery with exclusive jurisdiction in partition (*q.v.*), and that jurisdiction was confirmed to the Chancery Division by the Judicature Act, 1873, s. 34.

Partnership, the relation which subsists between persons carrying on a business with a view to profit (Partnership Act, 1890, s. 1 (1)). The Partnership Act, 1890, is a codifying Act, which, in effect, transferred the law of the subject from the region of reported cases to that of statute, the Partnership Act, 1865, known as Bovill's Act, and a small part of the Mercantile Law Amendment Act, 1856, being the only previous statutory enactments on the subject.

The Partnership Act, 1890, sets out and declares with little variation the pre-existing law, the chief amendment being that contained in s. 23, which deprived a judgment creditor of an individual partner of the right to issue execution against the property of the partnership, but gave such creditor power to obtain an order charging the judgment debtor's interest in the partnership.

The Partnership Act, 1890, s. 1, which defines partnership as the relation which subsists between persons carrying on business in common with a view to profit, excludes from this definition a company incorporated under the Companies Acts or by statute or by letters patent or by royal charter and a company working within the Stannaries (*q.v.*).

At common law, as well as under the Act of 1890, the following are the characteristic marks of a partnership: every partner is entitled and bound to take part in the conduct of the business, unless it is otherwise agreed between them (s. 24 (6)); every partner is liable for the debts of the partnership to the whole extent of his property (s. 9), and as between the partners, each partner is bound to contribute to the debts in proportion to his share of the profits (s. 24 (1)); as regards third persons, the act of every partner, within the ordinary scope of the business, binds his co-partners, whether they have sanctioned it or not (ss. 5, 6); the relation between the partners being personal, no one of them can put a stranger in his place without the consent of the others (s. 24 (7)).

Where no time for the duration of the partnership is fixed, it is called a partnership at will, and may be dissolved at the pleasure of any partner at a moment's notice (s. 32 (*c*)). As to other modes of dissolving a partnership, see DISSOLUTION.

When a partner dies or retires, and the partnership agreement provides that the partnership shall not thereby be dissolved, the remaining partners are called the continuing partners. A retiring partner (and the estate of a deceased partner) is not liable for the partnership debts contracted after his connection ceased, provided, in the case of a retiring partner, that notice of the fact is given. No notice is required in the case of a dormant partner. As to bankruptcy of partners, see CONVERSION IN BANKRUPTCY; FIRM; JOINT.

Partnerships are of two kinds. A general partnership is where the business includes all transactions of a particular class, as where A and B agree to carry on the business of bankers, grocers, etc. A particular or special partnership is where the parties agree to share the profits of one particular transaction, as where A and B agree to join in selling a particular cargo of goods, or in working a particular patent.

A sub-partnership is where a partner in a firm makes a stranger a partner with him in his share of the profits of that firm. Thus, if A and B carry on business as A, B & Co. and B agrees with C to give him a share of the profits received from the business of A, B & Co., C is a sub-partner with B but not a partner in the firm of A, B & Co. See FIRM.

A quasi-partnership, or partnership as regards third persons, is where one person is liable for the debts of another as if he were his partner, although no true partnership exists. The cases in which this occurs are referable to one of two principles. The first is that where a person carries on business as agent for another, the latter is liable to third persons for the debts of the business. Before 1865, the doctrine was carried much further, so as to make every person who received a share of the profits of a business liable for its debts, but it became the tendency to hold that an agreement entitling one person to share the profits made by another gave rise to nothing more than a presumption that the relation of principal and agent existed between them, and the passing of the Partnership Act, 1865, deprived the question of much of its importance. By the operation of this Act, a person who merely lent money to a firm, in consideration of receiving a share of the profits, was not a partner even as regards third persons, but in popular language he was sometimes called a dormant partner, or *commanditaire* (*q.v.*), and the effect of s. 2 (3) of the Act of 1890 is identical. The second principle under which a person may be subjected to the liabilities of a partner is that where a person holds himself out to third persons as a partner in the firm, he is liable to those persons for debts contracted by the firm (Partnership Act, 1890, s. 14 (1)); such a person is called an ostensible partner. Generally, the " holding out " consists in his allowing his name to appear in the firm as if he were a partner, and he is then sometimes called a nominal partner. The mere continuance of a business after a partner's death in the old firm name does not make the estate or the personal representatives of the deceased partner liable for partnership debts contracted after his death (s. 14 (2)).

A limited partnership is one in which, although there must be one or more partners responsible for all the liabilities of the partnership, there may be one or more partners who are under no liability if they contribute an agreed sum for partnership purposes (Limited Partnership Act, 1907, s. 4 (2)) provided that they take no part in the management (s. 6), and that the partnership is registered as a limited partnership (s. 8). A limited partnership is not dissolved by the death of a limited partner, and in the case of his becoming of unsound mind the court will not consider this a ground for dissolution of the partnership unless his share cannot be otherwise ascertained and realised (s. 6 (2)). The bankruptcy law applies to limited partnerships as if they were ordinary partnerships, and if all the general partners become bankrupt the assets of the partnership vest in the trustee (Bank-

ruptcy Act, 1914, s. 127). See COM-MANDITE.

The expression " salaried partner " is not a term of art and whether such a partner is a partner in the true sense depends on the substance of the relationship and the facts of the particular case (*Stekel* v. *Ellice* [1973] 1 W.L.R. 191).

For limitations on the number of persons in a partnership see the Companies Act, 1948, ss. 429, 434; Companies Act, 1967, ss. 119–121.

As to the taxation of partnership retirement annuities, see the Finance Act, 1974, s. 16.

As to sex discrimination, see the Sex Discrimination Act, 1975, s. 11.

See PART-OWNERS.

Part-owners, persons who are entitled to property jointly, or in common, or in coparcenary.

They have a distinct, or at least an independent, although an undivided, interest in the property. If the property is in land, by the Law of Property Act, 1925, s. 1, a legal estate is not capable of subsisting or of being created in an undivided share in land and the beneficial interest in the property is merely equitable (see UNDIVIDED SHARES). Neither of them can transfer or dispose of the whole property, or act for the others as partners can in relation thereto; each can merely deal with his own share, and to the extent of his own several right and interest. It is an entirely different relation from partnership.

Part-owners differ from partners in several respects, the principal of which are: that a partner is the agent of his co-partners within the ordinary scope of the business, so that he has power to bind them towards third persons even against their will, while a part-owner, in the absence of a special agreement, has no such power, and can only deal with his own interest in the property; and that a part-owner can transfer his interest to a stranger, while a partner cannot without the consent of his co-partners. The term " part-owners " in this relation chiefly occurs in the law of merchant shipping. Part-owners of ships are tenants in common, with distinct and undivided interests, and each is the agent of the others, as to the ordinary repairs, employment, and business of the ship, in the absence of any known dissent. The property in a ship is by the Merchant Shipping Act, 1894, s. 5, divided into 64 shares, the limit having been raised from 32, by which it was fixed by the Act of 1854, to 64 by the Act of 1880. Difficult questions often arise as to whether the co-owners of a vessel are partners in respect of her, either generally or for a particular voyage. See MANAGING OWNER.

Partridge. There may be theft of partridges reared by a hen, though uncooped (*R.* v. *Shickle* (1868) L.R. 1 C.C.R. 158). See GAME.

Partus sequitur ventrem (I. 2, 1, 19). (The offspring follow the dam.) This was a rule of the civil law. It never prevailed in England. See LEX ANGLIAE NUNQUAM, ETC.

Party. See PART; PARTIES.

Party and party costs, costs in an action recoverable from the unsuccessful party. They are limited to costs incurred of necessity. For other scales of costs, see R.S.C., Ord. 62, rr. 28 and 29, and COSTS.

Party jury, used in the statute 1662, 14 Car. 2, c. 11, s. 13, as meaning a jury *de mediate linguae.* See JURY.

Party wall. The common use of a wall separating adjoining lands of different owners is prima facie evidence that the wall and the land on which it stands belongs to the owners of those adjoining lands in equal moieties as tenants in common, or would so belong if tenancy in undivided shares in a legal estate had not been done away with by the Law of Property Act, 1925. Now under the Law of Property Act, 1925, s. 38, Sch. 1 Pt. V, a party wall of this class is considered to be severed vertically into two moieties, each moiety being subject to a cross easement in favour of the owner of the other moiety, corresponding to those which would have subsisted if a valid tenancy in common had been created.

At common law, a party wall was a wall of which the two adjoining owners were tenants in common (*Wiltshire* v. *Sidford* (1836) 1 M. & R. 404), and in the absence of evidence to the contrary such tenancy

would be presumed. But at common law it might also mean a wall divided longitudinally into two strips, one belonging to each of the neighbouring owners (*Matts* v. *Hawkins* (1813) 5 Taun. 20); or a wall which belonged entirely to one of the adjoining owners, but was subject to an easement or right in the other to have it maintained as a dividing wall between the two tenements (*Sheffield etc. Soc.* v. *Jarvis* [1871] W.N. 208); or as is now provided by the Law of Property Act, 1925, s. 38, Sch. 1 Pt. V, a wall divided longitudinally into two moieties, each moiety being subject to a cross easement in favour of the owner of the other moiety (*Watson* v. *Gray* (1880) 14 Ch.D. 192).

Party walls in London are subject to the provisions of the London Building Acts as modified by the London Government Act, 1963, s. 43.

Outside London, building regulations may be made under the Public Health Act, 1961, ss. 4–11.

Parum differunt quae re concordant et cum adsunt testimonia rerum quid opus est verbis? (2 Bulst. 53). (Verbal differences are of little account when there is substantial agreement; and when you have facts to bear witness what use is there of words?)

Parum est latam esse sententiam nisi mandetur executioni (Co.Litt. 289). (It is not enough that judgment be pronounced unless it be carried to execution.) See EXECUTIO EST, ETC.; JURIS EFFECTUS, ETC.

Parum proficit scire quid fieri debet si non cognoscas quomodo sit facturum (2 Co.Inst. 503). (It avails little to know what ought to be done if you do not know how it is to be done.) Cited in connection with the somewhat vague provisions of the statute *Quia Emptores*, 1289, c. 2, as to apportionment.

Parvise, an afternoon's exercise or moot for the instruction of young students—bearing the same name originally with the *Parvisae* (little-go) of Oxford (*Selden's Notes on Fortescue*, c. li; Tomlin).

Pas [Fr.], precedence; the right of going foremost.

Pasch [Heb. *pasahh*], the passover.

Pascha clausum, the octave of Easter, or Low Sunday (*q.v.*) which closes that solemnity.

Pascha floridum, the Sunday before Easter, called Palm Sunday (*q.v.*).

Paschals; Paschal rents; Pascha rents, yearly tributes paid by the clergy to the bishop or archdeacon at their Easter visitations; quadragesimals (*q.v.*).

Pascua, land used mainly for the pasturing of cattle, such as land which is not farmed and is mountain, moor or marsh (3 Lindwood, Prov.Angl. c. 18).

Pascuage; Pascuagium, the grazing or pasturing of cattle, sometimes used as the equivalent of pannage (*q.v.*) (Mon. Ang. 2, 23).

Pascuum, feeding; wheresoever cattle are fed (Co.Litt. 4b). See PASTURA.

Pasnage, or **Pathnage.** See PANNAGE.

Pass. In conveyancing, to pass is to transfer or be transferred. Thus, we may either say that a conveyance by a person entitled to make it passes the estate limited by it (see OPERATIVE WORDS), or that the estate passes by the conveyance.

In the practice of the Chancery Division when the draft (or minutes) of an order or judgment has been settled by the registrar in the presence of the parties, it is left for engrossment, and when it has been engrossed, the parties again attend to examine the engrossment with the draft; if it is correct they sign it, and this is generally called " passing " the order, but strictly speaking the passing is performed by the registrar, who places his initials at the end: after which the order is entered (*q.v.*) (see MINUTE). In simple cases, an order not affecting the rights of the parties *inter se* may be settled and passed by the registrar without notice to the parties (R.S.C., Ord. 42, r. 7). When an account has been brought into chambers and vouched, the master is said to have passed or allowed it, with or without disallowances or surcharges. The term " pass " is also applied to the accounting party who brings in the account.

As to the passing of Acts of Parliament, see ACT OF PARLIAMENT.

Passage, the easement of passing over a piece of private water, analogous to a right of way over land. See EASEMENT; WAY.

Passage, Court of. See COURT OF PASSAGE.

Passagio, De, a writ which was issued to keepers of the ports to authorise passage overseas (Reg.Orig. 193; Tomlin).

Passagium regis, a voyage or expedition to the Holy Land made by the kings of England in person.

Passator, one who controlled or who could levy toll for the use of a ford, ferry or bridge across a river (Cowel).

Passenger ship, a ship propelled by mechanical power carrying passengers to, from or between any places in the United Kingdom except steam ferries working in chains (Merchant Shipping Act, 1894, ss. 267, 743; Merchant Shipping Act, 1906, s. 13).

Passengers, persons conveyed from one place to another.

The Merchant Shipping Act, 1894, s. 267, defines a passenger as any person carried in a ship other than the master, the crew, the owner, and the family and servants of the owner.

In some respects, passengers by ship may be considered as a portion of the crew. They may be called on by the master or commander of the ship, in case of imminent danger, either from tempest or enemies, to lend their assistance for the general safety; and in the event of their declining, may be punished for disobedience. As the authority arises out of the necessity of the case, it must be exercised strictly within the limits of that necessity (*Boyce* v. *Bayliffe* (1807) 1 Camp. 58).

A passenger is not, however, bound to remain on board a ship in the hour of danger, but may quit it if he has an opportunity; and he is not required to take upon himself any responsibility as to the conduct of the ship; if he incurs any responsibility, and performs extraordinary services, in relieving a vessel in distress, he is entitled to a corresponding reward. The goods of passengers contribute to general average.

A passenger in a motor car who contributes to the expenses may thereby make himself liable for the negligence of the driver (*Scarsbrook* v. *Mason* [1961] 3 All E.R. 767).

The London Hackney Carriages Act,

1843, s. 2, contains a definition of " passenger " for the purposes of that Act.

See CARRIERS; NEGLIGENCE; PUBLIC SERVICE VEHICLES; RAILWAY.

Passengers' luggage. A passenger by railway or by public transport is entitled to take with him a reasonable amount of ordinary luggage without extra charge. The luggage must be for the passenger's personal use and of the kind usually taken by a passenger while away from home. The liability of a common carrier in respect of passengers' luggage is that of a carrier of goods. See Kahn-Freund, *Law of Inland Transport.*

Passiagiarius, a ferry-man (Jacob).

Passim, in various places. Used as a very general reference to an author, book, statute, etc.

Passing off, the wrong committed by a person who sells goods or carries on business, etc., under such a name, mark, description or otherwise in such a manner as to mislead the public into believing that the goods or business, etc., are those of another person. The latter person has a right of action in damages or for an account, and for an injunction to restrain the defendant for the future.

A High Court judge at first instance may seek guidance from the European Court upon the interpretation of any article of the EEC Treaty in interlocutory proceedings to restrain a passing off (*Löwenbräu München* v. *Grunhalle Lager International* [1974] C.M.L.R. 1).

Passing-ticket, a kind of permit, being a note or check which the toll-clerks on some canals give to the boatmen, specifying the lading for which they have paid toll.

Passive debt, a debt upon which, by or without agreement between the debtor and creditor, no interest is payable, as distinguished from an active debt, *i.e.,* a debt upon which interest is payable. In this sense the terms " active " and " passive " are sometimes applied to debts due from defaulting foreign governments. This use of the terms is to be distinguished from the French use of *actif* (assets) and *passif* (liabilities).

Passive resisters, persons who, as a protest against the expenditure of a local

authority in connection with an object of which they disapprove, decline to pay that part of a rate attributable to such expenditure, and by such passive resistance force the local authority to recover the sum withheld by distress and sale or other process. Passive resistance was resorted to especially in connection with the operation of the Education Act, 1902. See *R.* v. *Gillespie* [1904] 1 K.B. 174.

Passive trust, a trust as to which the trustee has no active duty to perform. Passive uses were resorted to before the Statute of Uses, 1535, in order to escape from the provisions of the common law, and equitable interests were, after the statute, revived under the form of trusts. In order to guard against the forfeiture of a legal estate for life, passive trusts, by settlements, were resorted to, also trusts to preserve contingent remainders; and passive trusts were created in order to prevent dower.

Where an active trust was created, without defining the quantity of the estate to be taken by the trustee, the courts endeavoured in the case of devises by will and executory contracts to give by construction the quantity originally requisite to satisfy the trust in every event, although the general rule was that the same words of limitation were necessary to convey either a legal or an equitable estate in fee simple in a grant by deed to trustees as were required in any other grant of the legal estate in fee (*Re Moncton's Settlement* [1913] 2 Ch. 636; *Re Bostock's Settlement* [1921] 2 Ch. 693). But if a larger estate was expressly given, the courts could not reject the excess; and although the estate taken, whether expressly or constructively, might not have exceeded the original scope of the trust, yet, if eventually no estate, or a less estate, were actually wanted, the legal ownership remained wholly or partially vested in the trustee as a merely passive trustee. By the Law of Property Act, 1925, Sch. 1 para. 3, the legal estate existing on January 1, 1926, in a bare trustee became vested in the person of full age who at that date was entitled to require the legal estate to be vested in him subject to any mortgage term subsisting or created by the Act upon the conditions and subject to the provisions of the Schedule, and to the provisions of the Law of Property (Amendment) Act, 1926, in favour of a purchaser without notice from the trustee. See BARE TRUSTEE.

Passive use, a permissive use. See PASSIVE TRUST; USE.

Passport, a licence for the safe passage of anyone from one place to another, or from one country to another. Passports are issued by the Foreign Office to (i) citizens of the United Kingdom and colonies, (ii) British subjects without citizenship, (iii) British protected persons. Applications are made on forms obtainable at any of the Passport Offices at Clive House, 70–78 Petty France, London, S.W.1; India Buildings, Water Street, Liverpool; Olympia House, Upper Dock Street, Newport, Gwent; 55 Westfield Road, Peterborough; First Floor, Empire House, 131 West Nile Street, Glasgow, or any Employment Office or main Post Office. An applicant must be recommended and identified by a person holding a certain position, *e.g.,* a justice of the peace, barrister, solicitor or physician.

A combination to procure a passport taken out in one name but to be used in another is an indictable misdemeanour (*R.* v. *Brailsford and McCulloch* [1905] 2 K.B. 730). Forgery of a passport is a misdemeanour under the Official Secrets Act, 1920, s. 1. Forgery of a passport or obtaining a passport under false pretences is an indictable offence under the Criminal Justice Act, 1925, s. 36, as amended by the Criminal Justice Act, 1967, s. 92 (8). The offence is triable summarily (Magistrates' Courts Act, 1952, Sch. 6).

Allegiance is owed by a holder of a British passport (*Joyce* v. *D.P.P.* [1946] A.C. 347).

To justify police action in taking and withholding a passport where no one has been arrested or charged it must be shown that the police reasonably believe that the passport holder has himself committed the crime or is implicated in it (*Ghani* v. *Jones* [1970] 1 Q.B. 693).

Past debt, a debt which is in existence before the doing of some subsequent act in the law relating to it, *e.g.,* a debt which is secured by a promissory note given

after the advance had been made and not when it originally was made.

Pastitium, pasture land (*Domesday*).

Pastor [Lat., a shepherd], applied to a minister of the Christian religion, who has charge of a congregation, hence called his flock.

Pastoral schemes. See the Pastoral Measure, 1968; Sharing of Church Buildings Measure, 1970.

Pastura, pasture. The difference between *pastura* and *pascuum* was that *pastura* meant the ground itself and *pascuum* the feeding, so that the demand in a *praecipe* had to be for *pastura* and not *pascuum* (Co.Litt. 4b). See PASCUUM.

Pasturage; Pasture. " Pasture " means both land employed for the pasturage of cattle, etc., and the right of pasture (Co. Litt. 4b).

A right of pasture is the right of feeding animals on the grass and other wild herbage, and the leaves, mast, acorns, etc., of trees growing on land belonging to another person. Rights of pasture are of three kinds, several, common, and seignorial.

A several pasture is one which entitles the person having the right to exclude the owner of the land from feeding his beasts on it (Co.Litt. 122a).

Such a right may be created by grant or prescription (*Davies* v. *Du Paver* [1952] 2 All E.R. 991). Sheepheaves (*q.v.*) seem to be several rights of pasture.

A common of pasture is where the person having the right can only exercise it in common with the owner of the soil. As to the varieties of common of pasture, see COMMON.

A seignorial right of pasture occurs in the case of a fold-course (*q.v.*).

By the Inclosure Act, 1845, s. 113, any land directed to be inclosed under that Act may be set apart to be stocked and depastured in common by the persons interested therein. The valuer acting in the matter is to ascertain and allot the stints or rights of pasturage of the persons interested, the numbers and kinds of animals to be admitted to the pasture, the times during which the animals may be kept on the pasture, etc. Such a pasture is called a regulated pasture. See FIELD REEVE; SHACK; STINT; VESTURE.

The laying down of pasture is an

improvement for which a tenant is entitled to compensation on quitting. See COMPENSATION FOR IMPROVEMENTS.

Pastus, the maintenance by tenants of the king and other great men at certain times, or as often as they should make a progress to their lands. It was often commuted to money payments (1 Mon.Angl. 123).

Patent agent. No person may describe himself as a patent agent unless he is registered pursuant to the Patents Act, 1949, s. 88.

Patent ambiguity, a doubt apparent upon the face of an instrument. It can only be explained by argument on the construction of the instrument and not by parol evidence. See AMBIGUITY.

Patent Bill Office. The Attorney-General's Patent Bill Office was the office in which were formerly prepared the drafts of all letters patent other than those for inventions. The draft patent was called a bill (*q.v.*), and the officer who prepared it was called the Clerk of the Patents to Her Majesty's Attorney and Solicitor General. By the Great Seal Act, 1851, warrants were substituted for bills, and by the Great Seal Act, 1880, the duty of preparing such warrants was transferred to the Clerk of the Crown in Chancery (*q.v.*). See PRIVY SEAL.

Patent medicines. Under the Medicine Stamp Acts, 1802 and 1804, duties were imposed on each bottle or package of patent or proprietary medicines according to the price. These duties were payable by the manufacturers and collected by means of labels of appropriate amounts, so affixed to the packages as to be destroyed when they were opened. The duties were doubled by the Finance Act, 1915. The Schedule to the Medicine Stamp Act, 1812, exempted from duty medicinal drugs vended entire (*i.e.,* without mixture or composition with any other drug or ingredient) by a medical practitioner, chemist or druggist, or by the holder of a patent medicine licence; and medicinal drugs, though mixtures or compositions, if not within the definition of patent medicine, if sold by a medical practitioner, chemist or druggist. An annual licence had to be taken out by every dealer in or maker of proprietary medicines which were liable to duty (Medicine Stamp Act, 1802, s. 9; Medicine Stamp Act, 1812, s. 1, Sch.; Customs and Inland Revenue Act, 1875). The medicine duties were repealed by the Pharmacy and Medicines Act, 1941, s. 14.

See DRUGS, DANGEROUS; POISON.

Patent of precedence, letters patent formerly granted to certain barristers as a mark of distinction which entitled them to rank among those who had been appointed queen's counsel.

Patent Office. The only Patent Office now existing is that relating to patents, designs and trade marks. See PATENTS.

The Great Seal Patent Office was the office in which the Clerk of the Patents affixed the Great Seal (*q.v.*) to the many documents upon which it formerly was required. Although the office of the Clerk of the Patents (*q.v.*) had been abolished by the Lord Chancellor's Pension Act, 1832, s. 2, provided that this should be without prejudice to the rights of anyone entitled to the office either in possession or reversion; and the office in fact existed until it was finally abolished and the duties were transferred to the Clerk of the Crown in Chancery (*q.v.*) under the Great Seal (Offices) Act, 1874, s. 6.

Patent rolls. See CLOSE ROLLS; ROLL.

Patentee, one who has a patent. The offices of patentee and deputy patentee of the Subpoena Office were abolished by the statute 1853, 15 & 16 Vict. c. 87, s. 27.

Patent-right, the exclusive privilege granted by the Crown to the first inventor of a new manufacture of making articles according to his invention. See PATENTS.

Patents. A patent means letters patent for an invention (Patents Act, 1949, s. 101). A patent is obtained by making to the Patent Office an application accompanied by a specification (*q.v.*). If the specification is provisional, the complete specification must be lodged within twelve months of the date of the application, or such further time not exceeding three months as the Comptroller may direct (s. 3). The provisional specification secures priority as from the date of the application: for, on acceptance, every patent is sealed as from the date of the application (s. 13).

A patent, when granted, is sealed with

the seal of the Patent Office (s. 19). Its normal duration is sixteen years (s. 22) but this may be extended by five, or in exceptional cases ten, years on the ground of inadequate remuneration (s. 23), or war loss (s. 24).

Patents are assignable, and assignments, as well as licences, are to be registered in the register of patents (s. 74). In addition to licences which the patentee may grant, there are, since 1919, licences which any patentee must grant, upon certain terms, if his patent is endorsed by the Comptroller with the words "licence of right" (s. 37). Such endorsement is one of the means of preventing abuse of the monopoly given by the patent. As to the revocation of patents, see s. 42.

The Patents Act, 1957, provides for an extension of the period prescribed in the Patents Act, 1949, s. 12, within which an application for a patent is required to be put in order. The Patents and Designs (Renewals, Extension and Fees) Act, 1961, extended the period for payment of renewal fees.

The remedy for infringement of a patent is an action for damages or an injunction, or both. See INFRINGEMENT.

A patent will be granted only for something which is both novel (see NOVELTY; PUBLICATION) and of utility; but utility means merely utility for the purpose indicated by the patentee, although that purpose may itself be useless.

For taxation in connection with patent rights and know-how see the Income and Corporation Taxes Act, 1970, ss. 378–388; Finance Act, 1970, s. 36, Sch. 8 Pt. VII; Finance Act, 1971, ss. 37, 38, 69, Sch. 14 Pt. II.

Patent agents are privileged from giving discovery or evidence of matters communicated to them in professional confidence (Civil Evidence Act, 1968, s. 15).

See COMMISSIONERS OF PATENTS; DISCLAIMER; PARTICULARS OF BREACHES AND OBJECTIONS; SCIRE FACIAS; TITLE.

Patents Appeal Tribunal. See the Patents Act, 1949, ss. 9, 14, 85, 87. No appeal from a decision of the Tribunal lies to the Court of Appeal; it is an inferior court (*q.v.*) and certiorari (*q.v.*) is the only remedy of a person aggrieved (*Baldwin & Francis* v. *Patents Appeal Tribunal* [1959] A.C. 663).

Pater est quem nuptiae demonstrant (Dig. 2. 4. 5). (He is the father whom marriage indicates.) See FILIATIO, ETC.; SEMPER PRAESUMITUR PRO LEGITIMATIONE, ETC.

Pater et mater non sunt de sanguine puerorum (3 Co.Rep. 40). (The father and the mother are not of the blood of their children.) This meant that land could not descend from a child to a parent. See HAEREDITAS NUNQUAM, ETC.

Paterfamilias, one who was *sui juris* and the head of a family (Civil Law).

Paternity. Any presumption of law as to the legitimacy or illegitimacy of any person may, in civil proceedings, be rebutted on a balance of probabilities rather than by proof beyond a reasonable doubt (Family Law Reform Act, 1969, s. 26). Where in civil proceedings, paternity is in question a blood test may be ordered (ss. 20–25). For a discussion of the law on the subject of paternity and the cases in which it may be shown that the child is not that of the husband, see *Russell* v. *Russell* [1924] A.C. 687. Evidence of a spouse to prove non-access during marriage was formerly inadmissible but such evidence is now admissible (Matrimonial Causes Act, 1973, s. 48). A husband has always been able to give evidence that he had never had intercourse with his wife before the marriage (*Poulett Peerage* [1903] A.C. 395). It becomes a question, when a widow marries immediately after the death of her husband, and she is delivered of a child at the expiration of ten months from the death of the first husband, as to the paternity of the child. Blackstone and Coke say, that if a man dies and his widow soon after marries again, and a child is born within such a time as that by the course of nature it might have been the child of either husband, in this case he is said to be more than ordinarily legitimate, for he may, when he arrives at years of discretion, choose which of the fathers he pleases. But Hargrave suggests that the circumstances of the case, instead of the choice of the issue, should determine who is the father. The Romans forbade a woman to marry until after the expiration of ten months from her husband's decease, which term was prolonged to twelve by Gratian and Valentinian. The French code adopted the same rule, *viz.*, after ten months. It was also established under the Saxon and Danish governments. It was the law in this country until the Conquest. See ACCESS; AFFILIATION; BASTARD; LEGITIMACY.

Path. See FOOTPATH; NATIONAL PARKS.

Patibulary [Lat. *patibulum*], belonging to the gallows.

Patibulated, hanged on a gibbet.

Patient, a person suffering or appearing to suffer from mental disorder (Mental Health Act, 1959, s. 147 (1)); a person incapable, by reason of mental disorder, of managing and administering his property and affairs (ss. 101, 119, 138). He was known, before the Mental Treatment Act, 1930, as a lunatic.

Patria, the country; the men or jury of a neighbourhood (Cowel). See COUNTRY.

Patria laboribus et expensis non debet fatigari (Jenk.Cent. 6). (A jury ought not to be harassed by labours and expenses.) This relates to the jury in an assize of novel disseisin.

Patria potestas, paternal power. It was acquired by birth, legitimation or adoption. It was lost by the death of the father, by the father or son suffering loss of freedom or citizenship, by the son attaining certain dignities, and by emancipation (Civil Law).

Patrial. See IMMIGRATION.

Patriarch, the chief bishop over several countries or provinces, as an archbishop is of several dioceses (God. 20).

Patriciatus, the patriciate, from the time of Constantine the highest rank at court (Civil Law).

Patricide, the murder, or murderer, of a father. See PARRICIDE.

Patricius, a title of the highest honour, conferred on those who enjoyed the chief place in the emperor's esteem (Civil Law).

Patrimonium. Things *in nostro patrimonio* were things belonging to individuals; things *extra nostrum patrimonium* were things belonging not to individuals but to all men (*communes*), to the State (*publicae*), to corporate bodies (*universitatis*), or to no one (*nullius*) (Civil Law).

Patrimony, an hereditary estate or right descended from ancestors.

Patrinus, a godfather.

Patriotic Fund. Commissioners were appointed under the sign manual, dated October 7, 1854, for the purpose of raising and applying a fund known as the Patriotic Fund for the relief of officers and men in the naval and military service of the Crown who might lose their lives in the Crimean War. A number of Acts, entitled the Patriotic Fund Acts, 1867 to 1899, were passed to regulate the application of the fund. The Patriotic Fund Reorganization Act, 1903, established a body corporate, entitled the Royal Patriotic Fund Corporation, and transferred all the property of the original fund to this new body upon trust for the widows, children and dependants of officers and men of the navy and army. The constitution of the Royal Patriotic Fund Corporation was amended by S.I. 1974 No. 595, art. 3. See also the Royal Patriotic Fund Corporation Act, 1950.

Patritius, an honour conferred on men of the first quality in the time of the Saxon kings.

Patron, one who has the disposition of an ecclesiastical benefice (see ADVOWSON); among the Romans an advocate or defender (see CLIENT).

Patronage, the right of presenting to a benefice. A disturbance of patronage is a hindrance or obstruction of a patron to present his clerk to his benefice, the remedy for which was the real action of *quare impedit* (*q.v.*). See BENEFICE. It also means the right of appointing to any office (*q.v.*).

Patronage Secretary, the chief Government Whip. See WHIP.

Patronatus, patronage.

Patronum faciunt dos, aedificatio, fundus (Dod.Adv. 7). (Endowment, building, and dedication to religious purposes are necessary to make one the founder of a church or religious house.) But this is merely what Joan de Garlandia says in *Synonymis* without reference to English law (Du Cange.)

Patruelis, a cousin-german by the

1333

father's side; the son or daughter of a father's brother (Civil Law).

Patruus, an uncle by the father's side, a father's brother; *magnus,* a grandfather's brother, great-uncle; *major,* a great-grandfather's brother; *maximus,* a great-grandfather's father's brother.

Pauper, a person in receipt of relief under the poor laws; a person suing or defending an action *in forma pauperis.* See DISPAUPER; DIVES; GUARDIANS OF THE POOR; IN FORMA PAUPERIS; OVERSEERS; PARISH; POOR LAW; POOR PERSONS; SETTLEMENT OF PAUPERS.

Pauper, Assignment to a, an assignment to a man of straw. See STRAW, MAN OF.

Pauperies, mischief occasioned by an animal; damage done without *injuria* or wrongful intent (Civil Law). See ACTIO NOXALIS.

Pavagium; Pavage, a toll levied to meet the cost of paving streets or other highways (Plac.Parl. 35 Ed. I).

Pawn or **Pledge** [Lat. *pignus*], a bailment of goods by a debtor to his creditor, to be kept till the debt is discharged.

A mortgage of goods is in the common law distinguishable from a mere pledge or pawn. By a mortgage the whole legal title passes conditionally to the mortgagee; and if the goods are not redeemed at the stipulated time, the title becomes absolute at law although equity allows redemption. But in a pledge, a special property only passes to the pledgee, the general property remaining in the pledgor. Also, in the case of a pledge, the right of a pledgee is not consummated except by possession; and, ordinarily, when that possession is relinquished, the right of the pledgee is extinguished or waived. But, in the case of a mortgage of personal property the right of property passes by the conveyance to the mortgagee, and possession is not or may not be essential to create or support the title.

The things which may be the subject of pawn are, ordinarily, goods and chattels; but money, debts, negotiable instruments, choses in action, and indeed any other valuable things of a personal nature, such as patent-rights and manuscripts, may by the common law be delivered in pledge. It is not indispensable that the pledge should belong to the pledgor; it is sufficient if it is pledged with the consent of the owner. By the pledge of a thing, not only the thing itself is pledged, but also, as accessory, the natural increase thereof. If the pledgor has only a limited title to the thing, as for life or for years, he may still pawn it to the extent of his title; but when that expires, the pledgee must surrender it to the person who succeeds to the ownership. See FACTOR.

It is of the essence of the contract that there should be an actual delivery of the thing to the pledgee; for until delivery, the whole contract is executory, and the pledgee acquires no right of property in the thing. But there need not be an actual manual delivery, as it is sufficient if there are any of those acts or circumstances which, in construction of law, are deemed sufficient to pass the possession of property, as the key to a warehouse. As possession is necessary to complete the title, so by the common law the title determines if the pledgee loses the thing pledged, or delivers it back to the pledgor unless for a temporary or special purpose.

It is also of the essence of the contract that the thing should be delivered as a security for some debt or engagement. It may be delivered as security for a future debt or engagement, as well as for a past debt; for one or for many debts and engagements; upon condition or absolutely; for a limited time or for an indefinite period. It may also be implied from circumstances, as well as arise by express agreement, and it matters not what is the nature of the debt or the engagement. The pledge is understood to be a security for the whole and for every part of the debt or engagement. It is indivisible; *individua est pignoris causa.*

The pledgee or pawnee acquires, in virtue of the pawn, a special property in the thing, and is entitled to the exclusive possession of it during the time and for the objects for which it is pledged. The pledgee has a right to sell the pledge when the pledgor fails to perform his engagement. He might have filed a bill in equity against the pledgor for a sale, and he may proceed to sell *ex mero motu,* upon giving due notice of his intention to the pledgor. If several things are pledged, each is deemed liable for the whole debt or engagement; and the pledgee may proceed to sell them from time to time, until the debt or other claim is discharged. The possession of the pawn does not suspend the right to sue for the whole debt or other engagement without selling the pawn, for it is only a collateral security. A pawnee cannot become the purchaser at the sale. A pledgee cannot alienate the property absolutely, nor beyond the title actually possessed by him, unless in special cases. He may deliver the pawn into the hands of a stranger for safe custody, without consideration; or he may sell or assign all his interest in the pawn, or he may convey the same interest conditionally, by way of pawn, to another person, without destroying or invalidating his security.

As to the pawnee's title to use the pawn, if the pawn is of such a nature that the due preservation of it requires some use, then such use is not only justifiable, but is indispensable to the faithful discharge of the duty of the pawnee. If the pawn is of such a nature that it will be worse for the use, such, for instance, as clothes, the use is prohibited to the pawnee. If the pawn is of such a nature that the keeping is a charge to the pawnee, as a cow or horse, then the pawnee may milk the cow and use the milk, and ride the horse by way of recompense for the keeping. If the use will be beneficial to the pawn, or is indifferent, then it seems that the pawnee may use it. If the use will be without any injury, and yet the pawn will thereby be exposed to extraordinary perils, then the use is impliedly interdicted.

The pawnee is liable for ordinary neglect in keeping the pawn. He must return the pledge and its increments, if any, after the debt or other duty has been discharged. He must render a due account of all the income, profits, and advantages derived by him from the pledge, in all cases where such an account is within the scope of the bailment.

If the pledge is conveyed by way of mortgage, so that the legal title passes unless the pledge is redeemed at the stipulated time, the title of the pledgee becomes absolute at law; and the pledgor

has only an equitable right to redeem. If, however, it is a mere pledge, as the pledgor has never parted with the general title, he may, at law, redeem, notwithstanding he has not strictly complied with the condition of his contract. If, when the pledgor applies to redeem, the pledge has been sold by the pledgee without any proper notice to the pledgor, no tender of the debt due need be made before bringing an action therefor: for the party has incapacitated himself to comply with his contract to return the pawn. Subject to the pledgee's right, the owner has a right to sell or assign his property in the pawn. As the general property of goods pawned remains in the pawnor, and the pawnee has a special property only, either may maintain an action against a stranger for any injury done to it, or for any conversion of it. Goods pawned are not liable to be taken in execution in an action against the pawnor, at least not unless the bailment is terminated by payment of the debt, or by some other extinguishment of the pawnee's title, except in case of the Crown, and then subject to the pawnee's right. By the act of pawning, the pawnor enters into an implied engagement of warranty that he is the owner of the property pawned. The pawnor must reimburse to the pawnee all expenses and charges which have been necessarily incurred by the pawnee in the preservation of the pawn, even though by some subsequent accident these expenses and charges may not have secured any permanent benefit to the pawnor.

The contract of pledge is put an end to or extinguished by payment of the debt or discharge of the engagement for which the pledge was given; by satisfaction of the debt in any other mode, either in fact or by operation of law, as, for instance, by receiving other goods in payment or discharge of the debt; by taking a higher or different security for the debt, without any agreement that the pledge shall be retained therefor (this is called *novatio* in the civil law); by extinguishing the debt, which also extinguishes the right to pledge; by the thing perishing; or by any act of the pledgee which amounts to a release or waiver of the pledge. See PAWNBROKER.

PAWNAGE

Pawnage, or **Pannage.** See PANNAGE.

Pawnbroker, one who lends money on goods which he receives upon pledge.

The Pawnbrokers Acts, 1872 to 1960, were repealed by the Consumer Credit Act, 1974, s. 192, Sch. 5. In their place ss. 114–122 of the Act of 1974 relate to pledges taken under regulated agreements, that is (s. 189 (1)), a consumer credit agreement (s. 8) or a consumer hire agreement (s. 15). See CONSUMER CREDIT. These provisions cover a wider range of transactions than are traditionally associated with the concept of " pawnbroking."

" Pawn " means any article subject to a pledge. " Pledge " means the pawnee's rights over an article taken in pawn. " Pawnee " and " pawnor " include any person to whom the rights and duties of the original pawnee or the original pawnor, as the case may be, have passed by assignment or operation of law (s. 189 (1)).

At the time he receives the article, a person who takes any article in pawn (the pawnee) under a regulated agreement must give to the person from whom he receives it (the pawnor) a receipt in the prescribed form (a " pawn-ticket "). It is an offence to take any article in pawn from an individual known to be or appearing to be a minor. This does not apply to a pledge of documents of title or a non-commercial agreement (s. 114). Failure to give a pawn-receipt is an offence. So is failure to supply copies of any pledge agreement (s. 115). For penalties see s. 167, Sch. 1. A pawn is redeemable at any time within six months after it was taken. Subject to this the redemption period is fixed by agreement of the parties, a pawn remains redeemable until it is realised by sale or (in the case of a small credit (£15)) until the property passes automatically to the pawnee (ss. 116, 120). The imposition of special charges for redemption after the end of the redemption period and of higher rates of charge for safe keeping after the redemption period is prohibited (s. 116 (4)). On surrender of the pawn-receipt and payment of the amount owing, the pawnee must deliver the pawn to the bearer of the pawn-receipt unless the pawnee knows or has reasonable cause to suspect that the bearer of the pawn-receipt is neither the owner of the pawn nor authorised by the owner to redeem it. The pawnee is not liable to any person in tort for delivering the pawn to the bearer of the pawn-receipt or for refusing to deliver it in the circumstances stated above (s. 117). The procedure to be followed where the pawn-receipt has been lost, mislaid, destroyed, stolen, etc., is laid down in s. 118. Unreasonable refusal to allow a pawn to be redeemed is an offence (s. 119). For penalty see s. 167, Sch. 1. The burden of proving that he had reasonable cause to refuse to allow the pawn to be redeemed rests on the pawnee (s. 171 (6)). He may prove that the article has been honestly lost by him (*Allworthy* v. *Clayton* [1907] 2 K.B. 685). If the pawn is not redeemed, then, if the credit does not exceed £15, the property in the pawn passes to the pawnee. In all other cases the pawn may be sold (s. 120) after giving the pawnor notice. The result of the sale is to be communicated to the pawnor. The debt is *pro tanto* discharged. Any surplus is payable to the pawnor. Any shortfall is a debt to the pawnee. The pawnor may challenge the price realised on sale or the expenses of sale, and the burden is then on the pawnee to justify the price or expenses as the case may be.

The county court has power to reopen extortionate credit bargains (ss. 137–140, 189 (1)).

Pawnbrokers must be licensed by the Director of Fair Trading (ss. 1, 21 *et seq.*).

Restitution of stolen property which has been pawned may be ordered, see RESTITUTION; but if such order is not made on the application of the owner, he is not thereby prevented from bringing a common law action (*Leicester* v. *Cherryman* [1907] 2 K.B. 101).

Firearms and ammunition must not be taken in pawn (Firearms Act, 1968, s. 3 (6), Sch. 6 Pt. I).

As to the power of an executor to pledge the personal chattels of his testator, see *Solomon* v. *Attenborough* [1913] A.C. 76. As to the effect of bankruptcy upon goods in pawn, see the Bankruptcy

Act, 1914, ss. 154 (1) (15), (3); Bankruptcy (Amendment) Act, 1926, s. 5.

Pawnee, the person with whom a pawn is deposited. See PAWN.

Pawner, or **Pawnor,** the person depositing a pawn. See PAWN.

Pax regis, the king's peace, the verge of the court.

Pay Board. The Pay Board set up under the Counter-Inflation Act, 1973, was abolished under the Prices Act, 1974, s. 6; S.I. 1974 No. 1218.

Pay-as-you-earn, the name given to the system whereby income tax in respect of emoluments chargeable under Sched. E is deducted from time to time as the emoluments are earned and paid after allowing for reliefs in accordance with the employee's code number (Income and Corporation Taxes Act, 1970, ss. 204, 205; Finance Act, 1975, s. 37). The employer accounts to the Revenue for the amount so deducted.

Payable. A sum of money is said to be payable when a person is under an obligation to pay it. " Payable " may therefore signify an obligation to pay at a future time, but when used without qualification " payable " means that the debt is payable at once, as opposed to " owing " (*q.v.*).

Payee, one to whom a bill of exchange or promissory note or cheque is made payable; he must be named or otherwise indicated therein, with reasonable certainty. By the Bills of Exchange Act, 1882, s. 7, the bill, note or cheque may be made payable to one or more payees jointly, or in the alternative to one of two or one or some of several payees, or to the holder of an office for the time being; but where the payee is a fictitious or non-existing person, it may be treated as payable to bearer (*Bank of England* v. *Vagliano* [1891] A.C. 107). See BILL OF EXCHANGE; CHEQUE.

Paymaster-General, the officer who makes the various payments out of the public money required for the different departments of the State, by issuing drafts on the Bank of England.

The salary of the Paymaster-General is £7,500–£9,500 unless he is a member of the Cabinet when it is £13,000 (Ministerial and Other Salaries Act, 1975, s. 1, Sch. 1).

By the Chancery Funds Act, 1872, the duties of the Accountant-General of the Court of Chancery were transferred to the Paymaster-General. The Paymaster-General carried out the duties so transferred to him at the Office of the Paymaster-General for Chancery Business in the Royal Courts of Justice, London. The business transacted there included the issuing of directions for the payment and transfer into court of the moneys and securities belonging to suitors, the payment by drafts on the Bank of England of sums payable out of court, and of the interest on funds in court, the keeping of the necessary accounts, and the issuing of certificates and transcripts of the accounts. Under the Supreme Court of Judicature (Funds, etc.) Act, 1883, all the accounting departments of the various divisions were consolidated into the Pay Office of the Supreme Court, with the Paymaster-General as its head. These duties were transferred to the Accountant-General (*q.v.*) by the Judicature Act, 1925, s. 133.

See CERTIFICATE; PAYMENT INTO COURT.

Payment, a transfer of money from one person (the payer) to another (the payee). When made in pursuance of a debt or obligation it is sometimes called payment in satisfaction.

Payment in fact is an actual payment from the payer to the payee; payment in law is a transaction equivalent to actual payment; thus, payment in fact by a debtor to one of two or more joint creditors is payment in law to all; and retainer, set-off, allowance in account, acceptance of security, goods or other means of obtaining actual payment, and payment into court (*q.v.*), are said to be equivalent to payment, because they produce a satisfaction of the debt.

Payment in satisfaction is said to be absolute when the debt is completely discharged, as by payment of cash without stipulation; conditional payment is where the debt may afterwards revive if the mode of payment does not result in actual payment, as where a creditor is paid by a cheque or bill which is afterwards dishonoured (*Burden* v. *Halton* (1827) 4 Bing. 452; *Davis* v. *Reilly* [1898] 1 Q.B. 1); whether the acceptance by the creditor of a negotiable security operates as conditional or absolute payment is a question of fact in each case.

The payment of money before the day appointed is in law payment at the day; for it cannot, in presumption of law, be any prejudice to him to whom the payment is made to have his money before the time; and it appears by the party's receipt of it that it is for his own advantage to receive it then, otherwise he would not take it (5 Co.Rep. 117).

As to general and appropriated payments, see APPROPRIATION.

As to the effect of part payment, see PART PAYMENT.

In the law of bills of exchange, payment for honour is where a person pays a dishonoured bill for the honour of some one of the parties. The payer has the rights of a holder against the person for whose honour he has paid, and against all antecedent parties, but the subsequent parties are discharged. See ACCEPTANCE OF BILLS; HONOUR; PROTEST.

Payment into court, the deposit of money with the official of or banker to the court for the purpose of proceedings commenced in that court. Payment into court is not strictly a defence; it is rather an attempt at a compromise. No such plea was known to the common law; it is entirely the creature of statute.

By the Common Law Procedure Act, 1852, s. 70, the defendant in all actions (except for assault and battery, false imprisonment, libel, slander, malicious arrest or prosecution of seduction) might pay into court a sum of money by way of compensation or amends, and by the Libel Act, 1843, money might be paid into court in actions of libel, but this provision was repealed by the Statute Law Revision Act, 1879.

Payment into court is now regulated by R.S.C., Ord. 22, by which, where any action is brought to recover a debt or damages, any defendant may, at any time after he has entered an appearance in the action, pay into court a sum of money in satisfaction of the cause of action in respect of which the plaintiff claims (r. 1). Except in the case of a plea of tender (see Ord. 18, r. 16) or a plea under the Libel Act, 1843 (see Ord. 82, r. 4 (3)) a payment into court in

satisfaction must not be alleged or stated as a fact in any pleading and the fact that it has been made must not be communicated to the court at the trial or hearing until after determination of all questions of liability and quantum (R.S.C., Ord. 22, r. 7), but, of course, before the question of costs is dealt with. As to acceptance of money paid into court see Ord. 22, r. 3.

As to tender of amends and payment into court by justices of the peace and other persons acting in the performance of certain public functions for anything done in the execution of their offices, see PUBLIC AUTHORITIES, ETC.

Quite distinct from payment into court in an action is the Chancery practice of payment or transfer into court of money or funds in the hands of an executor or trustee who is unable to obtain a good discharge from the person beneficially entitled. This was formerly done under the Legacy Duty Act, 1796, s. 32, or the Trustee Relief Act, 1847, ss. 1, 2, and the Trustee Relief Act, 1849, replaced by the Trustee Act, 1893, s. 42, and is now regulated by the Trustee Act, 1925, s. 63, as amended by the Administration of Justice Act, 1965, s. 6. See R.S.C., Ord. 92, r. 2.

See ACCOUNTANT-GENERAL; DEPOSIT; PAYMASTER-GENERAL; TRANSFER.

Peace, a quiet behaviour towards the sovereign and his subjects. It is one of the prerogatives of the Crown to make war and peace (1 Bl.Comm. 257).

In international law it means the condition of inter-State relations in which the powers do not apply military pressure against each other, apart from reprisals (q.v.), and in which the law of peace applies.

In municipal as opposed to international law, " peace " or the " king's peace " refers to the law relating to public order. Hence, an indictment used formerly to conclude with a charge that the offence complained of was committed " against the peace of our lord the king." See ARTICLES OF THE PEACE; CONTRA PACEM; PLEAS OF THE CROWN.

Peace, Bill of, a remedy from needless litigation by establishing and perpetuating a right which the plaintiff claimed and which might be controverted at different times (*Sheffield Waterworks* v. *Yeoman* (1866) L.R. 2 Ch. 8). The results obtained by this bill would now generally be obtained by an action in the High Court for a declaration of title and an injunction (R.S.C., Ord. 15, r. 16). See BILL OF PEACE.

Peace, breach of the. See BREACH OF THE PEACE.

Peace, clerk of the. See CLERK OF THE PEACE.

Peace, Commission of the. See COMMISSION OF THE PEACE.

Peace, Justices of the. See JUSTICES, ETC.

Peace officer, a constable, coroner, justice or sheriff.

An ordinary person must act as a peace officer on occasion. He may use such force as is reasonable in the circumstances in the prevention of crime or in effecting or assisting in the lawful arrest of offenders or suspected offenders or of persons unlawfully at large (Criminal Law Act, 1967, s. 3).

Peace of God and the Church [*pax Dei et ecclesiae*], that cessation which all subjects had from trouble and suit of law between the terms, and on Sundays and holidays (Cowel).

Peace of the king [*pax regis*], that security for life and goods promised by the king to all his subjects, or others taken into his protection. See BREACH OF THE PEACE.

Peace, Sureties of. See SURETIES OF THE PEACE AND GOOD BEHAVIOUR.

Peccata contra naturam sunt gravissima (3 Co.Inst. 20). (Crimes against nature are the most heinous.) Cited as a comment on the crimes of patricide and matricide.

Peccatum peccato addit qui culpae quam facit patrocinium defensionis adjungit (5 Co.Rep. 49). (He adds one offence to another who, when he commits an offence, joins the protection of a defence.) This is quoted in connection with the practice as to a defendant on a writ of *Quibus, etc.* (*q.v.*), who had vexatiously defended the case. See PRUDENTER, ETC.

Pecia, a piece or small quantity of ground (Paroch.Antiq. 240).

Peck, a measure of capacity containing two imperial gallons (Weights and Measures Act, 1963, s. 10, Sch. 1 Pt. IV). The peck is no longer a unit of measurement (s. 10 (8)). Formerly the peck varied in different places and for different articles. It was never used for fluids.

Peculatus, embezzling public money.

Peculiar, a particular parish or church which has jurisdiction within itself, and exemption from that of the ordinary. There are several sorts: royal peculiars, which are the sovereign's free chapels, and are exempt from any jurisdiction but that of the sovereign; peculiars of the archbishops, exclusive of the bishops and archdeacons, which arose from a privilege they had to enjoy jurisdiction in such places where their seats and possessions were; peculiars of bishops, exclusive of the jurisdiction of the bishops of the diocese in which they are situate; peculiars of bishops in their own dioceses; exclusive of archidiaconal jurisdiction; and peculiars of deans, deans and chapters, prebendaries, and the like, which are places wherein, by ancient compositions, the bishops have parted with their jurisdiction as ordinaries to these corporations (*Parham* v. *Templer* (1820) 3 Phill. Ecc.Rep. 245). Formerly the peculiar jurisdictions in England amounted to nearly three hundred; but they have been practically abolished by legislation which was initiated by the Ecclesiastical Commissioners Act, 1836. See ORDINARY.

Peculiars, Court of. See COURT OF PECULIARS.

Peculium, the savings of a son or slave accumulated with the father's or master's consent (Civil Law).

Pecunia [Lat. *pecus*, cattle], properly money, but anciently cattle, and sometimes other goods as well as money.

Pecunia dicitur a pecus omnes enim veterum divitiae in animalibus consistebant (Co.Litt. 207). (Money (*pecunia*) is so called from cattle (*pecus*), because all the wealth of our ancestors consisted in cattle.) So chattels (cattle) means all tangible personalty.

Pecunia sepulchralis, money paid to a priest at the opening of a grave for the good of the deceased's soul. See MORTUARIES.

Pecuniary causes. In the terminology of the ecclesiastical courts, this expression meant such injuries to private persons as these courts could entertain for the purpose of making pecuniary satisfaction to those persons (3 Bl.Comm. 88).

Such causes related chiefly to the subtraction (*q.v.*) of tithe, and to the nonpayment of various clerical dues. They became obsolete after tithe was commuted into tithe rentcharge.

Pecuniary legacy. See LEGACY.

Pedage, toll paid for passing, whether on horse or on foot, through a town or other place (Spelman).

Pedestrian crossings. See the Road Traffic Regulation Act, 1967, ss. 21–23; Local Government Act, 1972, Sch. 19 Pt. II para. 11; Road Traffic Act, 1974, Sch. 5 Pt. II; *Gibbons* v. *Kahl* [1956] 1 Q.B. 59; *Lockie* v. *Lawton* (1959) 57 L.G.R. 329; *Neal* v. *Bedford* [1966] 1 Q.B. 505; *Burns* v. *Bidder* [1967] 2 Q.B. 227.

As to "zebra" crossings, see the "Zebra" Pedestrian Crossings Regulations, 1971 (S.I. 1971 No. 1524). At a "zebra" crossing a driver must accord precedence to a pedestrian who is on the carriageway within the limits of the striped area before any part of his vehicle comes on to such area (*Moulder* v. *Neville* [1974] R.T.R. 53).

"Pelican" crossings are pedestrian crossings with lights which can be operated by pedestrians. See S.I. 1969 No. 888. No notice of intended prosecution is required regarding an alleged infringement of the regulations (*Sulston* v. *Hammond* [1970] 1 W.L.R. 1164). See SCHOOL CROSSINGS.

Pedestrians. Pedestrians must comply with the directions of a constable in uniform (Road Traffic Act, 1972, s. 23). An offender is required to give his name and address to a constable (s. 165) or a traffic warden (S.I. 1970 No. 1958). For penalties see Sch. 4; Road Traffic Act, 1974, Sch. 5 Pt. III.

It is not necessarily negligent for a pedestrian to walk on the near side of a country road (*Kerley* v. *Downes* [1973] R.T.R. 189).

Pedigree [Fr. *per, degré*], genealogy; lineage; account of descent.

In proceedings with reference to the devolution of a deceased person's property, questions as to the relationship of the claimants are called questions of pedigree. They are subject to peculiar rules of evidence. Thus, declarations by deceased persons (see DECLARATION, ETC.; LIS MOTA), the general reputation of a family proved by a surviving member of it, entries contained in family Bibles or other books produced from the proper custody, inscriptions on tombstones, and charts of pedigrees made or adopted by deceased members of the family are admissible as evidence on questions of pedigree, by way of exception to the general rule against derivative evidence. See EVIDENCE; REPUTATION.

Falsifying a pedigree, upon which title does or may depend, was punishable under the Law of Property Amendment Act, 1859, s. 24, now the Law of Property Act, 1925, s. 183 (1) (*b*); and see the Forgery Act, 1913.

Pedis abscissio, the cutting off of a man's foot, a punishment at one time inflicted instead of the death penalty (Leg.Will. I, c. 7; 1 Fleta, c. 38; Bracton, c. 32).

Pedis possessio, an actual possession or foothold.

Pedlar, any hawker, pedlar, petty chapman, tinker, caster of metals, mender of chairs, or other person who, without any horse or other beast drawing or bearing burden, travels and trades on foot and goes from town to town or to other men's houses, carrying to sell or exposing for sale any goods, wares or merchandise or procuring orders for goods, wares or merchandise immediately to be delivered, or selling or offering for sale his skill in handicraft (Pedlars Act, 1871, s. 3). Every such person must hold a certificate, costing 25p and expiring one year after the date of issue (ss. 4, 5), unless he is a commercial traveller, a seller of fish, fruit or vegetables, or a seller at a fair or market (s. 23). The certificate is good for any part of the United Kingdom (Pedlars Act, 1881). The essential difference between a hawker (*q.v.*) and a pedlar is that a hawker employs, while a pedlar does not employ, a horse or other beast of burden, in the course of his business. A man who goes to a fixed point by car and then proceeds to go from house to house on foot "travels" within the meaning of the Pedlars Act, 1871, s. 3, and requires a certificate

(*Sample* v. *Hulme* [1956] 1 W.L.R. 1319).

Pedones, foot soldiers.

Peel's Acts, the statutes 1827, 7 & 8 Geo. 4, cc. 27, 29, 30 (all relating to the criminal law), the Sliding Scale Act, 1828 (a corn law), and the New Parishes Acts, 1843 and 1844, named after the first Sir Robert Peel.

Peer, an equal; one of the same rank; a member of the House of Lords, as duke, marquis, earl, viscount, or baron, or a Scots or, formerly, an Irish, representative peer. The sovereign cannot create a dignity with a mesne between baron and baronets (Co.Litt. 16 (b), Harg., n. 8).

A member of the House of Lords cannot become a member of the House of Commons, nor can he vote at an election to that House (*Beauchamp* v. *Madresfield* (1872) L.R. 8 C.P. 245), although he was an Irish non-representative peer (*Rendlesham* v. *Haward* (1873) L.R. 9 C.P. 252); but an Irish peer may be elected a member of the House of Commons. A peer cannot surrender his dignity to the Crown so as to affect the rights of his descendants therein (*Norfolk Earldom* [1907] A.C. 10) (Co.Litt. 160; Jacob). See also the Report of the Personal Bills Committee of the House of Lords dated February 28, 1955, on the petition for the Wedgwood Benn (Renunciation) Bill, 1955. But see the Peerage Act, 1963; PEERAGE.

A peer is disqualified from sitting in the House of Commons whether or not a writ of summons has been issued by the Crown (*Re Parliamentary Election for Bristol South East* [1964] 2 Q.B. 257).

Peers and peeresses entitled to receive a writ of summons to attend the House of Lords are excusable as of right from jury service. See JURY.

When an indictment for felony was found against a peer it was formerly removable by writ of certiorari into the Court of the Lord High Steward (*q.v.*), but this privilege of peerage was abolished by the Criminal Justice Act, 1948, s. 30. See PEERS.

Peerage. The peerage consists of dukes, marquises, earls, viscounts and barons. They are divided into peers of England created before the Union with Scotland in 1707; peers of Great Britain created after 1707 and before the Union with Ireland in 1800; peers of the United Kingdom created since 1800; peers of Scotland created before 1707; and peers of Ireland created at any time: as to the right of these five classes respectively to sit in the House of Lords, see HOUSE OF LORDS. The Life Peerages Act, 1958, makes provision for the creation of life peerages carrying the right to sit and vote in the House of Lords. A life peerage may be conferred upon a woman.

All peerages except baronies (*q.v.*) have always been created since 1387 by letters patent, except in the few cases in which they have been created by charter or by statute, and all, except baronies, have always been limited to the heirs male of the body of the original grantee. If the claim is by writ, actually sitting in Parliament is also essential, for until he sits the writ has no operation (Co.Litt. 9 (b), 16 (b)).

As to what will amount to a Parliament for this purpose, see *St. John Peerage Claim* [1915] A.C. 282.

The creation of a baron by writ of summons is now obsolete, except for the purpose of calling up the eldest son of a peer during such peer's life.

Where, on the death of a peer, doubts arise respecting the devolution of his dignity, and in all cases of long abeyance or other non-enjoyment of a peerage, the Lord Chancellor will not issue his writ of summons to a claimant without a previous investigation of his title, in order to which the claimant must present a petition to the Crown through the Home Secretary, which the Crown then refers to the Attorney-General, and in most cases the claim is subsequently referred to the Lords Committee for Privileges. For the practice and procedure in peerage claims, see *Shrewsbury Peerage* (1857) 7 H.L.C. 1.

A peerage may be disclaimed for the life of a person who succeeds to a peerage. The disclaimer does not accelerate the succession to the peerage nor affect its devolution on death. Where a peerage is disclaimed, no other hereditary peerage may be conferred upon the person by whom it is disclaimed and no writ of acceleration may be issued in respect of that peerage. The disclaimer does not affect property rights (Peerage Act, 1963, ss. 1–3).

The Honours (Prevention of Abuses) Act, 1925, prevents abuses in connection with the grant of honours.

The House of Commons had for centuries been in the habit of annually passing a resolution to the effect that the interference of any peer in a parliamentary election was a breach of the privileges of that House, but no such resolution has been passed since 1909.

The children of peers are in point of law commoners, although they bear courtesy titles ranging, according to the rank of the peer, from " Marquis " to " Honourable."

See *Reports on the Dignity of a Peer*; Palmer, *Peerage Law*.

Peeress, the wife or the unmarried widow of a peer (*q.v.*), or a woman upon whom a peerage has been conferred, or a woman holding a peerage descendible to the heirs general of the original grantee.

Women may acquire peerages by creation (as the Baroness Burdett Coutts), descent (as where a peerage goes in the female as well as in the male line, to which line it is usually confined), or marriage, but they have never had the legislative power, and it was decided in *Viscountess Rhondda's Claim* [1922] 2 A.C. 339, that a peeress of the United Kingdom in her own right was not entitled to receive a writ of summons to Parliament by virtue of the Sex Disqualification (Removal) Act, 1919. But this was reversed by the Peerage Act, 1963, s. 6. As to women life peers see PEERAGE.

Before the Criminal Justice Act, 1948, s. 30, a peeress was, under the statute 1442, 20 Hen. 6, c. 9, entitled to be tried by the House of Lords if charged with treason or felony.

Peers [Lat. *pares*]. In the old books it is laid down that *pares sunt qui de eodem domino feudam tenent* (those are peers, or equals, who hold of the same lord). These are the peers contemplated by the declaration in Magna Carta, 1215, s. 39, that no freeman was to be condemned *nisi per legale judicium parium suorum*

(except by the lawful judgment of his peers). See PARES; PEER.

Peers of fees, vassals or tenants of the same lord, who were obliged to serve and attend him in his courts, being equal in function; these were termed peers of fees, because holding fees of the lord, or because their business in court was to sit and judge, under their lords, of disputes arising upon fees; but if there were too many in one lordship, the lord usually chose twelve, who had the title of peers, by way of distinction; whence, it is said, we derive our common juries and other peers (Cowel).

Peine forte et dure (the strong and hard pain), the common law sequel to a refusal by one indicted for felony to plead guilty or not guilty. *Peine* (or penance) was probably a corrupted abbreviation of *prisone* (3 Bl.Comm. 325).

The judgment of the court, pronounced after a threefold admonition (*trina admonitio*), was " That you return from whence you came to a low dungeon into which no light can enter; that you be stripped naked save a cloth about your loins, and laid down, your back upon the ground; that there be set upon your body a weight of iron as great as you can bear, and greater; that you have no sustenance save on the first day three morsels of the coarsest bread, on the second day three draughts of stagnant water from the pool nearest the prison door, on the third day again three morsels of bread as before, and such bread and such water alternately from day to day, till you be pressed to death; your hands and feet tied to posts and a sharp stone under your back." The object of a prisoner in refusing to plead, or standing mute as it was called, was to obviate the attainder which resulted from a conviction of felony. Even this means of saving a family from ruin was not available to one indicted for treason: for him, as for one indicted for misdemeanour, refusal to plead was taken as being a plea of guilty (4 Bl.Comm. 324; Vin.Abr.tit. Mute).

The Felony and Piracy Act, 1772, made refusal to plead to a charge of felony equivalent to a plea of guilty, and so abolished the *peine forie et dure*.

By the Criminal Law Act, 1967, s. 6 (1), if a prisoner refuses to plead, the court may order a plea of not guilty to be entered. See MUTE.

Pela, a peel, pile, or fort.

Peles, issues arising from or out of a thing.

Pelf, Pelfe, Pelfre, booty; the personal effects of a felon convict; a perquisite of the serjeants of the peace (q.v.) who seized the goods of felons and outlaws.

" Pelican " crossings. See PEDESTRIAN CROSSINGS.

Pell. In addition to meaning a skin of parchment, pell also meant a skin which had not been converted into parchment. See CLERK OF THE PELLS; PELLAGE.

Pellage, a duty levied on skins exported out of the kingdom (Rot.Parl. 11 Hen. 4).

Pellicia, a pilch or surplice (Spelman).

Pelliparius, a leatherseller or skinner (Jacob).

Pellota, the ball of a foot (4 Co.Inst. 308).

Pells, Clerk of the. See CLERK OF THE PELLS; COMPTROLLER.

Pells of issue and receipt, records of daily payments and receipts by the Exchequer. They took the place of the earlier receipt rolls (q.v.). The pells of issue now in the Record Office cover the periods 1221–1470 and 1566–1797, while the pells of receipt preserved in the same office run from 1213 to 1782. See CLERK OF THE PELLS.

Pelt-wool, the wool pulled off the skin or pelt of dead sheep: see the statute 1429, 8 Hen. 6, c. 22.

Pembroke. This was anciently a county palatine, but the statute 1535, 27 Hen. 8, c. 26, s. 14, made it merely an ordinary county.

Pen [Wel.], a high mountain (Camd. Brit.).

Penal action, an action for a penalty imposed by some statute as a punishment. When the statute gave the penalty to any person who would sue for it, such an action was known as a popular action; and where the statute gave the penalty partly to the Crown and partly to the informer, the action was known as a *qui tam* action, because the action was described as being brought by one

qui tam pro domino rege quam pre se ipso in hac parte sequitur (who sues on behalf of our lord the king as well as for himself). Proceedings by common informers were abolished by the Common Informers Act, 1951. See PENAL STATUTES.

Penal laws, those laws which prohibit an act, and impose a penalty for its commission. For the penal laws *par excellence*, see ROMAN CATHOLICS.

Penal rent. See NOMINE POENAE.

Penal servitude, a punishment which consisted in keeping an offender in confinement and compelling him to labour. It was substituted for transportation by the Penal Servitude Act, 1853. The main distinction between penal servitude and imprisonment with hard labour was that the latter was carried out within the walls of a gaol, and could not be inflicted for more than two years as a rule, though in some cases it might be for three years, while penal servitude was carried out in any place appointed for the purpose by the proper authority, and might be for life or any period not less than three years. This minimum of three years was altered to five by the Penal Servitude Act, 1864, s. 2, but altered back to three by the Penal Servitude Act, 1891, s. 1.

By the Penal Servitude Act, 1926, the court was given power to inflict penal servitude in lieu of imprisonment in the case of certain crimes.

Penal servitude and imprisonment with hard labour were abolished by the Criminal Justice Act, 1948, s. 1, and ordinary imprisonment substituted.

See CONVICT; FORFEITURE; IMPRISONMENT; TICKET OF LEAVE.

Penal statutes, those which impose penalties or punishments for an offence committed; they are construed strictly in favour of the person charged with the offence.

The penalties or forfeitures under these statutes are generally made recoverable by the Crown, or the party aggrieved, or a common informer, as the case may be: see, *e.g.*, the statutes 1489, 4 Hen. 7, c. 20; 1575, 18 Eliz. 1, c. 5; 1588, 31 Eliz. 1, c. 3; 1623, 21 Jac. 1, c. 4. The remedy is generally designated a penal action; or, where one part of the forfeiture is given to the

Crown and the other part to the informer, a popular or *qui tam* (*q.v.*) action. Proceedings by common informers were abolished by the Common Informers Act, 1951.

Penal sum; Penalty. A penalty or penal sum is a sum of money payable as an equivalent or punishment for an injury.

Some penalties are imposed by law; thus, many statutes creating duties of a public nature contain provisions for the recovery of penalties against persons neglecting those duties. Some of these may be enforced by information (*q.v.*); others could, before the Common Informers Act, 1951, be enforced by an ordinary action brought by a common informer. See INFORMER.

The exemplary damages recoverable in certain actions for tort are in the nature of penalties. See DAMAGES.

Penalties may also be agreed on by the parties. Thus, in a bond with a condition, the penalty or penal sum is a nominal sum (*e.g.*, double the amount to be secured) which the obligor binds himself to pay if the condition is not complied with. When the obligee sues on it, he recovers only what is due to him under the terms of the condition. See BOND.

Where the parties to a contract agree that in the event of a breach of its provisions, the one shall pay to the other a specified sum of money as liquidated damages, and it appears on the true construction of the instrument, whatever the form of words used, that the sum so specified does not represent a genuine pre-estimate of the amount of damage likely to be caused by a breach of the contract if it should occur, but is merely a sum stipulated as *in terrorem* of the offending party, as in the case of a bond, then the sum so specified is called a penalty; and if the person injured sues on the contract, he cannot recover the penalty, but only damages for the injury which he has actually sustained (*Willson* v. *Love* [1896] 1 Q.B. 626; *Dunlop* v. *New Garage* [1915] A.C. 79; *Widnes Foundry* v. *Cellulose Acetate Co.* [1933] A.C. 20). See DAMAGES.

Formerly the Court of Chancery granted relief against penalties in many cases where the courts of common law allowed them to be enforced. But this distinction has been abolished since the Judicature Acts, 1873–75. See EQUITY.

Penance [*poenitentia*], an ecclesiastical punishment affecting the body of the penitent, by which he is obliged to give public satisfaction to the Church for the scandal which he has given by his evil example: see the *Articuli Cleri*, 1315, c. 2, and the introduction to the commination service in the Prayer Book. An open confession generally forms part of the penance, while in some cases the penance may be commuted for a sum of money to be applied for pious uses. But now this punishment is never enforced. See CENSURE.

Pendency. An action, arbitration or other proceeding is said to be pendent after it has been commenced and before the final judgment or award has been given. Pendency is the state of being pendent. See LIS ALIBI PENDENS.

Pendente lite, during litigation.

Administration *pendente lite* is sometimes granted when an action is commenced touching the validity of a will. See GRANT OF PROBATE.

An injunction may be granted to restrain a party from disposing of or dealing with property *pendente lite*. As to registration of a *lis pendens,* see LAND CHARGE.

Pendente lite, Alimony. See ALIMONY.

Pendente lite nihil innovetur (Co.Litt. 344). (Nothing should be altered during litigation.) Quoted in connection with the common law rule that, if, pending the decision of a *quare impedit* (*q.v.*), the defendant bishop instituted a clerk of his own, then the plaintiff in the *quare impedit* had a writ against the bishop for the removal of the bishop's clerk.

Pendentes, ungathered fruits (Civil Law).

Penerarius, an ensign-bearer (Cowel).

Penitentiary-houses, prisons where criminals were confined to hard labour: see the repealed statute, 1779, 19 Geo. 3, c. 74. See GAOL.

Pennon, a standard, banner, or ensign carried in war.

Penny. A penny, whether of copper or of silver, was worth one two-hundred and fortieth part of the pound for the time being: but the gold penny was in a class by itself. See COPPER COINS; GOLD COINS; SILVER COINS.

Penny bank. See SAVINGS BANK.

Penny post. This, in the modern sense, was instituted pursuant to the Post Office (Duties) Act, 1840. During the war of 1914–18 it became a three-halfpenny post; subsequently it became a two-penny post; in 1922 it again became a three-halfpenny post; during the war of 1939–45 it became a twopenny and then a twopence-halfpenny post; in 1957 it became a threepenny post. The rates are frequently revised in an upward direction and are now expressed in decimal currency (*q.v.*). There was an earlier penny post, but only for places within ten miles of the General Post Office, under the statute 1710, 9 Anne, c. 11.

Pennyweight. The pennyweight is no longer a unit of measurement (Weights and Measures Act, 1963, s. 10 (8)). It was formerly 24 grains (Sch. 1 Pt. V).

Pensa salis, a weight of salt: an old measure containing 256 pounds (Cowel).

Pensam, Ad. Payment *ad pensam* was payment by weight, as where payment of a pound was made in a pound weight of silver, instead of in twenty shillings. See LIBRA PENSA.

Pension, an annual allowance made to a person, usually in consideration of past services.

Crown pensioners were disqualified by the Succession to the Crown Act, 1707, and the Crown Pensioners Act 1716, from membership of the House of Commons but these disabilities were removed by the House of Commons Disqualification Act, 1957, ss. 9, 14, Sch. 4 Pt. I.

When a pension is granted by the Crown to one who, though not for the time engaged in any active duties, is still liable to be called to active service, and is therefore to be considered in the service of the Crown, as in the case of an officer on half-pay, the pension cannot be assigned, attached or otherwise made liable to his debts. But a pension granted entirely as a compensation for past services may be assigned by the grantee, or it may be taken in execution by his creditors. See CIVIL LIST PENSIONS; POLITICAL PENSION; SUPERANNUATION.

Pensions are payable under special statutory provisions to grantees from the Crown for political, naval and military, police, civil and other services and for services under local authorities.

The Old Age Pensions Act, 1908, which was not on a contributory basis, gave to every person the right to a pension who fulfilled certain conditions. This Act was replaced by the Old Age Pensions Act, 1936. A contributory old age pension under the Widows, Orphans and Old Age Contributory Pensions Act, 1936, was paid to persons between sixty-five and seventy, whereas non-contributory old age pensions were payable at seventy. These provisions are superseded by retirement pensions under the Social Security Act, 1975 (see ss. 12–13, 27–30, 39–40). For occupational pension schemes, see the Social Security Pensions Act, 1975, ss. 26, 30–41, 44–63; as to the reserve pension scheme, see the Social Security Act, 1973, ss. 73–83.

See Calvert, *Social Security Law*. See also the Pensions Increase Act, 1971 (as amended by S.I. 1974 No. 595 art. 3 (16)), the Parliamentary and Other Pensions Act, 1972, the Overseas Pensions Act, 1973, the Pensions (Increase) Act, 1974; Cmnd. 5904 (occupational pension schemes).

" Pension " also meant certain sums of money paid to the clergy in lieu of tithes. A clerk could sue in the ecclesiastical court for a pension originally granted and confirmed by the ordinary; but where it was granted by a temporal person to a clerk, he had to sue for it in the temporal courts. Pensions are payable to the clergy under the Clergy Pensions Measures, 1961 to 1972.

At the University of Cambridge " pension " means, and in the Inns of Court it formerly meant, certain fees payable to those bodies. It also means a consultative meeting of the Benchers of Gray's Inn; it would appear from Waterhouse's *Commentary upon Fortescue* (1663) that formerly all members of the Inn, except students, took part in it; and this seems to have applied to the Parliaments of the two Temples and to the Council of Lincoln's Inn, which are the meetings in those Inns corresponding to the Pension of Gray's Inn. Now, however, only the Benchers of the Inns attend the Pension, the Parliaments, or the Council.

Pension writ, an order which was issued against members of the several Inns of Court who were in arrear for commons (that is to say, dinners) or dues payable to their Inns. The order, which of course was without legal effect, precluded the member against whom it was made from coming to commons or being discharged from his Inn until the arrears were paid.

Pensioner, one who is supported by an allowance at the will of another; a dependant; he who receives an annuity from Government without filling any office; a member of a college at Cambridge who is not on the foundation; one of a band of gentlemen who attend as a guard on the royal person, instituted in 1539 and now called the Honourable Body of Gentlemen-at-Arms.

Pensions and National Insurance, Ministry of. The Ministry of Pensions was established by the Ministry of Pensions Act, 1916, to take over the powers and duties of the Admiralty with respect to the pensions and grants to persons who had served in the naval forces and their dependants, other than service pensions, so far as the pensions and grants were payable out of moneys provided by Parliament and not provided exclusively for Greenwich Hospital; of the Commissioners for the Royal Hospital for Soldiers at Chelsea with respect to the grant and administration of disability pensions and grants other than in-pensions; and of the Army Council and the Secretary of State for War with respect to the pensions and grants to persons who had served in any of the military forces and their dependants, and to persons who had served in the nursing services of these forces, other than service pensions. It was amalgamated with the Ministry of National Insurance in 1953. It is now a part of the Department of Health and Social Security.

Pensions appeal tribunals, tribunals appointed to hear appeals as to war pensions under the Pensions Appeal Tribunals Acts, 1943 and 1949. See also the Chronically Sick and Disabled Persons Act, 1970, s. 23; Tribunals and Inquiries Act, 1971, Sch. 1.

Pentecostals, oblations or offerings made by parishioners at Pentecost, or Whitsuntide, to their parish priest and sometimes by inferior churches or parishes to the principal mother-church. They were divided into four parts, of which one went to the priest, one to the poor, one to the bishop and one was for repair of the church. Pentecostals were also known as Whitsuntide Farthings, and as Smoke Farthings. These offerings were originally in kind; subsequently they were commuted to money payments (Stephen, *Procurations and Pentecostals*; Kennet, Glos.). See QUADRAGESIMALS.

Pentecostals were abolished by the Ecclesiastical Jurisdiction Measure, 1963, s. 82 (3).

People [Fr. *peuple*; It. *populo*; Sp. *pueblo*; Lat. *populus*], the many, the multitude, the inhabitants of a nation, state, town, etc.; the commonalty or common folk, as distinguished from the higher classes; men; individuals.

Peppercorn rent. When it is desired to reserve only a nominal rent for any period, a " peppercorn if demanded," is usually reserved. A writing showing that a peppercorn has been handed over is not a receipt for the last payment due for rent within the Conveyancing Act, 1881, s. 34, now the Law of Property Act, 1925, s. 45 (2) (3) (*Re Moody and Yates* (1885) 30 Ch.D. 344). These rents may be reserved in building leases by mortgagors and mortgagees (Law of Property Act, 1925, s. 99), and in building and and forestry leases by tenants for life (Settled Land Act, 1925, ss. 44, 48). See RENT.

Per and Post. To come in in the *per* was to claim by or through the person last entitled to an estate, as the heirs or assigns of the grantee: to come in in the *post* was to claim by a paramount and prior title, as the lord by escheat (Co.Litt. 271b, Harg., n. (1) II). See ENTRY SUR DISSEISIN, ETC.

Per annum, by the year.

Per auter vie. See TENANT FOR LIFE.

Per capita; Per stirpes (by heads; by stocks). When property is given to the descendants or relations of two or more persons, the question frequently arises whether the donees are to take *per stirpes*, that is, as representatives of their respective ancestors or relations, or *per capita*, that is, whether they together form one class each member of which is to take an equal share. The question chiefly arises in gifts to descendants. If a testator leaves property to his issue and dies leaving children who are living and grandchildren who are the issue of deceased children, then the property is divided *per capita*, that is, each child and grandchild takes an equal share of the whole (*Abrey* v. *Newman* (1853) 16 Beav. 431). But if there is a gift to two or more persons, with a substitutional gift to the children of such of them as shall die before the gift takes effect, then the distribution takes place *per stirpes*. Thus, if there were three original donees, A, B and C, and B has died leaving three children, and C has died leaving two children, the property is divided into three parts, one going to A, another to B's three children, and the third to C's two children. The expressions *per capita* and *per stirpes* are also used in the law of distribution on intestacy with reference to the rule of representation; see the Administration of Estates Act, 1925, s. 47, as amended by the Intestates' Estates Act, 1952. See DESCENT; DISTRIBUTION; NEXT-OF-KIN; REPRESENTATION.

Per cent., Per centum, by the hundred.

Per, Cui, and **Posts,** writs of entry. See PER AND POST.

Per curiam, Per cur., by the court.

Per diem, by the day.

Per eundem, by the same; by the same judge.

Per incuriam, through want of care. A decision or dictum of a judge which clearly is the result of some oversight is said to have been given *per incuriam*.

Per infortunium, by mischance. See HOMICIDE.

Per mensem, by the month.

Per minas, by menaces.

Per my et per tout, not of any part but of the whole. Joint tenants, by reason of the combination of entirety of interest with the power of transferring in equal shares, are said to be seised *per my et per tout*. Each is seised by every parcel and by the whole (Co.Litt. 186a).

Et sic totum tenet et nihil tenet, scil., totum conjunctim et nihil per se separatum (and so he holds all and he holds nothing, meaning all jointly and nothing separate by itself): See *Murray* v. *Hall* (1849) 7 C.B. 455).

If any joint tenant severs by alienating his share, he destroys the joint tenancy in that share and the grantee obtains no joint tenancy. See ENTIRETIES; JOINT TENANTS.

Per pais, Trial, trial by the country, *i.e.*, by jury. See COUNTRY; PATRIA.

Per pro., Per proc., P.P., by procuration. See PROCURATION.

Per quae servitia. Before the levying of fines (*q.v.*) was abolished in 1833, the writ *per quae servitia* was a judicial writ issuing on the note of a fine (*q.v.*) and lay for the cognisee (*q.v.*) of a manor, seignory, chief rent, or other services, to compel the tenants at the time of the fine being levied to attorn (*q.v.*) to him thereon (West, Symbol., 2, 126; Old Nat. Brev. 155).

Per quod, whereby. In the old common law system of pleading the *per quod* was that part of the declaration in which the plaintiff alleged the special damage which the wrongful act of the defendant had caused him. See DAMAGE.

Per quod consortium amisit (whereby he has lost the benefit of her society), the allegation which was used in an action against a person for injuring a man's wife. See CONSORTIUM; ENTICEMENT.

Per quod servitium amisit (whereby he has lost the benefit of his service), words used by a plaintiff in his claim for damages from a defendant who had deprived him of the services of his servant by a wrongful act (*Martinez* v. *Gerber* (1841) 3 M. & G. 88; *The Amerika* [1917] A.C. at p. 38). The action only lies when the servant can properly be regarded as a member of the master's household, that is, as part of his family: it does not lie at the instance of governments, companies or other employers who keep no household (*I.R.C.* v. *Hambrook* [1956] 2 Q.B. 641; *Metropolitan Police District Receiver* v. *Croydon Corporation* [1957] 2 Q.B. 154). See SEDUCTION.

Per se, by itself, taken alone.

Per stirpes, according to the stocks; by the right of representation. See PER CAPITA.

Per subsequens matrimonium, by the subsequent marriage. See LEGITIMATION.

Per totam curiam, by the voice or judgment of the whole court; a unanimous decision.

Per varios actus legem experientia fecit (4 Co.Inst. 50). (By various acts experience framed the law.)

Per verba de futuro, Per verba de praesenti, a contract of marriage by words. See VERBA, ETC.

Perambulation, the act of walking over the boundaries of a district or piece of land, either for the purpose of determining them or of preserving evidence of them. Thus, in many parishes it was the custom for the parishioners to perambulate the boundaries of the parish in Rogation Week of every year. Such a custom entitles them to enter any man's land and abate nuisances in their way. (*Godday* v. *Michel* (1525) Cro.Eliz. 441). See PARISH BOUNDARIES; PURLIEU.

Perambulatione facienda, De, a writ which formerly lay where encroachments were alleged to have been made between adjoining lordships. It commanded the sheriff to make due perambulation and to settle the boundaries (Jacob).

Perca, a perch of land, 16½ feet. See PERCH.

Percaptura, a part of a river which was embanked so as to be in the nature of a fish-pond (Paroch.Antiq. 120).

Perch. The perch, rod or pole was a measure of length containing five yards and a half (Weights and Measures Act, 1878, s. 11) but is no longer a unit of measurement as it is not included in the Weights and Measures Act, 1963, s. 10, Sch. 1. Even before the perch had a statutory meaning, it was in most cases taken as being of the statutory length; but in Staffordshire it was eight yards, while in Hereford it was seven yards as regards ditching, and only five and a half as

regards walling, and there were many similar local variations (Skene).

A square perch of land contained 30¼ square yards, being 5½ yards (or one perch) on each side, if it is an exact square.

Perdings, men of no substance (Leg. Hen. 1, c. 29).

Perdonatio utlagariae, a pardon for outlawry. This was available to a man who had been outlawed for not yielding obedience to the process of the king's court and who had afterwards of his own accord surrendered himself (Reg.Orig. Leg.Ed. Confess. cc. 18, 19).

Perdono, an original writ which released the king's claim to have certain moneys paid into the Exchequer.

Perduellio, treason (Civil Law).

Perdurable. As applied to an estate, this signifies lasting long or for ever: thus, a disseisor or tenant in fee simple upon condition had as high and great an estate as the rightful owner or tenant in fee simple absolute, but not so perdurable. The term is chiefly used with reference to the extinguishment of rights by unity of seisin, which does not take place unless both the right and the land out of which it issues are held for equally high and perdurable estates (Co.Litt. 313).

Peregrini, foreigners commorant or sojourning in Rome (Civil Law).

Perempt. In ecclesiastical procedure an appeal is said to be perempted when the appellant has by his own act waived or barred his right of appeal: as where he partially complies with or acquiesces in the sentence of the court (Ayliffe, *Parergon,* 82).

Peremption, a nonsuit; also a quashing or killing. See NONSUIT.

Peremptory [Lat. *perimere,* to cut off], final, determinate and, in statutes, obligatory, as opposed to permissive.

Peremptory challenge, an arbitrary species of challenge to a certain number of jurors without showing any cause. See CHALLENGE.

Peremptory mandamus, a second mandamus, which issues where the return which has been made to the first is found either insufficient in law or false in fact. To this no other return will be admitted but a certificate of perfect obedience and due execution. See MANDAMUS.

Peremptory pleas, or **Pleas in bar,** those which were founded on some matter tending to impeach the right of action.

Peremptory rule. Formerly a defendant might obtain a peremptory rule to declare within a certain time, absolute in the first instance. This was abolished by the Common Law Procedure Act, 1852, s. 53, and a four-day notice substituted. See STATEMENT OF DEFENCE.

Perengaria. See ANGARIA.

Perfecting bail. See BAIL.

Performance. With reference to a contract or condition, performance is the act of doing that which is required by the contract or condition. The effect of performance, in the case of a contract, is to discharge the person bound to do the act from liability, and, in the case of a condition, to create or establish the right dependent on the condition. Thus, where A contracts to supply goods to B, not only is he bound to supply them, but he cannot claim their price until he has done so, this being a condition precedent; if he performs the contract by supplying them, he discharges his liability, and at the same time entitles himself to claim the price.

Part performance is where a contract has been partly carried into effect; what is called the doctrine of part performance is the rule that where a contract for the sale or other disposition of land or any interest in land is not enforceable by action for want of written evidence as required by the Law of Property Act, 1925, s. 40, and it has been partly carried into effect by one of the parties, the other cannot set up the want of writing as a defence: as where possession had been taken under a contract for the sale of land. See PART PAYMENT.

Partial performance of an entire contract will, as a rule, give no right of action to the person who has partially performed it; but an action will lie on a *quantum meruit* for a reasonable sum against one who has accepted the benefit of the partial performance if the failure to complete the performance was due to his fault or if the parties have agreed to rescind the contract and substitute a new one; and where the contract has been substantially performed an action lies for the contract price less a deduction of a reasonable sum in respect of what has not been done or has not been done properly.

In equity, the doctrine of performance is applied to cases where A has covenanted to purchase and settle or leave by will property in favour of B, and B has obtained the benefit stipulated for, although the covenant has not been strictly performed. Thus, where A covenanted to purchase lands of £200 a year and to settle them on his wife and the children of the marriage, and purchased lands of that value, but did not settle them, it was held that this was a performance of his covenant, and that the eldest son was therefore not entitled to have both the benefit of the lands which had descended to him as heir-at-law and to have the covenant performed by the purchase of other land.

See DISCHARGE; ESSENCE OF THE CONTRACT; PAYMENT; SATISFACTION.

Performers. The Dramatic and Musical Performers' Protection Act, 1958, and the Performers' Protection Acts, 1963 and 1972, penalise the making, etc., without the consent of the performers, of records, cinematograph films and broadcasts.

Performing rights. See COPYRIGHT.

Perfumery. As to the standards of measurement, etc. on this sale of perfumery and toilet preparations see the Weights and Measures Act, 1963, s. 21, Sch. 7 Pt. V.

Periculosum est res novas et inusitatas inducere (Co.Litt. 379). (It is a dangerous thing to introduce innovations which have never been tried before.) See EVENTUS VARIOS, ETC.; MINIME MUTANDA, ETC.

Periculum rei venditae, nondum traditae, est emptoris. (A thing, sold but not yet delivered, is at the risk of the purchaser.) See DAMNUM SENTIT, ETC.; MORA, ETC.; RES PERIT, ETC.

Peril [Lat. *periculum*], the word peril, like *periculum*, is in itself ambiguous, and sometimes denotes the risk of inevitable mischance, and sometimes the danger arising from the want of due circumspection (Jones on *Bailments*, 98). See INSURANCE; RISK.

Perils of the seas, all kinds of marine casualties, such as shipwreck, foundering, stranding, etc.; as also every species of damage done to the ship or goods at sea by the fortuitous action of the wind and waves, as distinct from that included in the ordinary wear and tear of the voyage or directly referable to the acts and negligence of the assured as its proximate cause. No casualty can be included which is not due to a peril of the seas (Arnould, *Marine Insurance*).

They are strictly the natural accidents peculiar to the water, but the law has extended this phrase to comprehend events not attributable to natural causes, as captures by pirates, and losses by collision, where no blame is attachable to either ship, or at all events to the injured ship. In *Hamilton, Fraser & Co.* v. *Pandorf & Co.* (1887) 12 App.Cas. 518, where, under a charterparty or bills of lading which excepted dangers and accidents of the seas, rats gnawed a hole in a pipe on board ship, whereby sea-water escaped and damaged a cargo of rice, without neglect or default on the part of the shipowners or their servants, the damage was held to be due to a peril of the sea (as the proximate cause) and within the exception.

Perinde valere, the initial words of the dispensation given by the Pope to a clerk presented to a benefice for which he was disqualified. The power of granting such dispensations was transferred from the Pope to the Archbishop of Canterbury by the statute 1533, 25 Hen. 8, c. 21 (Gibson, 87).

Perindinare, to stay, remain, or abide in a place.

Periphrasis, circumlocution; use of many words to express the sense of one.

Perishable goods, goods which decay and lose their value if not consumed soon, as fish, fruit, and the like. By the Sale of Goods Act, 1893, s. 48 (3), if on the sale of goods of a perishable nature the buyer does not within a reasonable time pay or tender the price, the unpaid seller may resell and recover damages from the buyer. By R.S.C., Ord. 29, r. 4, perishable goods, when the subject of an action, may, by order of the court or a judge, be sold.

Perished goods. Where there is a contract for the sale of specific goods and the goods without the knowledge of the seller have perished at the time when the contract is made, the contract is void (Sale of Goods Act, 1893, s. 6). Where there is an agreement to sell specific goods and subsequently the goods, without any fault on the part of the seller or buyer, perish before the risk passes to the buyer, the agreement is thereby avoided (Sale of Goods Act, 1893, s. 7). See IMPOSSIBILITY.

Perjury, the offence committed when a lawful oath (*q.v.*) or affirmation (*q.v.*) is administered and the witness swears or affirms falsely in a matter material to the issue. It was a misdemeanour at common law, and is a misdemeanour under the Perjury Act, 1911. See FALSE SWEARING.

The Perjury Act, 1911, consolidates the law relating to perjury and kindred offences; it repeals the statutes 1562, 5 Eliz. 1, c. 9, and 1728, 2 Geo. 2, c. 25, and other statutes. The Act provides that if any person lawfully sworn as a witness or as an interpreter in a judicial proceeding wilfully makes a statement material in that proceeding which he knows to be false or does not believe to be true, he will be guilty of perjury; a judicial proceeding includes a proceeding before any court, tribunal, or person having by law power to hear, receive and examine evidence on oath, and the question whether a statement was material is a question of law to be determined by the court of trial (s. 1). S. 2 deals with false statements on oath otherwise than in a judicial proceeding, and s. 3 with false oaths, declarations, notices, etc., with reference to marriage. S. 4 deals with false answers, declarations, etc., as to births and deaths; s. 5 with false statutory declarations (*q.v.*) and other false statements without oath; and s. 6 with false or fraudulent declarations, certificates, or representations, made in order to obtain registration for the purpose of carrying on any vocation or calling. Every person who aids, abets, counsels, procures or suborns another to commit an offence against the Act is liable as a principal offender, and every person who incites or attempts to procure or suborn another to commit an offence is guilty of a misdemeanour (s. 7). See SUBORNATION.

No person can, however, be convicted of any offence against the Act, or of any offence declared by any other Act to be perjury or subornation of perjury or to be punishable as such, solely upon the evidence of one witness as to the falsity of any statement alleged to be false (s. 13); in other words, there must be corroboration on that issue.

S. 9 empowers judges and others to direct a prosecution for perjury and s. 14 deals with the proof of certain proceedings in which perjury can occur. See also the Criminal Justice Act, 1925, s. 28; Magistrates' Courts Act, 1952, s. 19, Sch. 1; Criminal Law Act, 1967, Sch. 3 Pt. III; Criminal Justice Act, 1967, Sch. 3 Pts. I, III; Courts Act, 1971, Sch. 11 Pt. IV.

False statements made in evidence in the Court of Justice of the European Communities constitute perjury (European Communities Act, 1972, s. 11).

Perjury merits a severe penalty (*R.* v. *Simmonds* (1969) 53 Cr.App.R. 488).

Perkins, John, of the Inner Temple, was the author of a *Profitable Book treating of the Laws of England.* It was first published in French in 1528, and was translated into English in 1642. It deals chiefly with conveyancing and was very popular in the sixteenth and seventeenth centuries. Altogether twenty-nine editions were published, the last, and best, edition in English was issued in 1827.

Permissions, negations of law, arising either from the law's silence, or its express declaration (1 Ruth.Nat. Law, c. 1).

Permissive use, a passive use which was resorted to before the Statute of Uses, 1535, in order to avoid a harsh law, as that of mortmain of a feudal forfeiture; it was a mere invention in order to evade the law by secrecy, as a conveyance to A to the use of B. A simply held the possession, and B enjoyed the profits of the estate.

Permissive waste, the neglect of necessary repairs. See WASTE.

Permit, a licence; an instrument granted by the officers of excise, certifying that the excise duties on certain goods have been paid, and permitting their removal from some specified place to another.

Permutation, barter, the exchange of one movable thing for another.

Permutatione archidiaconatus et ecclesiae eidem annexae cum ecclesia et prebenda, De, a writ addressed to the ordinary requiring him to admit to a benefice a clerk who had made an exchange with the incumbent (Reg. Orig. 307).

Pernancy [Fr. *prendre*, to take], the taking or receiving of anything, *e.g.*, tithes.

Pernor, he who received the profits of lands, etc.; the *cestui que use* (1 Co.Rep. 123; Co.Litt. 323b, 351a).

Perpars, a part of the inheritance.

Perpetua lex est, nullam legem humanam ac positivam perpetuam esse, et clausula quae abrogationem excludit, ab initio non valet (Bac.Max. 19). (It is an everlasting law that no positive and human law shall be perpetual, and a clause which excludes abrogation is invalid from its commencement.) See LEGES POSTERIORES, ETC.; NON IMPEDIT, ETC.; POTESTAS, ETC.

Perpetual commissioners. See COMMISSIONERS FOR TAKING ACKNOWLEDGMENTS, ETC.

Perpetual curate, a minister in holy orders, who is charged with the permanent care of a parochial church, which, although an appropriation, has no endowed vicar. He is entitled to emolument for his services.

See CHAPEL; CURATE.

Perpetual injunction, an injunction which finally disposes of the suit, and is indefinite in point of time; as opposed to an injunction *ad interim, i.e.,* until the trial or further order. See INJUNCTION.

Perpetuating testimony. When evidence is likely to be irrecoverably lost, by reason of a witness being old, or infirm, or going abroad before the matter to which is relates can be judicially investigated, equity will, by anticipation, preserve and perpetuate such evidence in order to prevent a failure of justice.

Under the Perpetuation of Testimony Act, 1842, which was repealed by the Statute Law Revision and Civil Procedure Act, 1883, s. 3, any person who would, in circumstances alleged by him to exist, become entitled, upon the happening of any future event, to any honour, title, dignity or office, or to any estate or interest in any property, real or personal, the right or claim to which he could not bring to trial before the happening of that event, might file a bill in Chancery to perpetuate any testimony material for establishing his claim; and where the Crown was affected by the claim, the Attorney-General was a necessary defendant. In a proper case, the court made an order that the witnesses whose testimony was required should be examined, cross-examined and re-examined in the usual way: and, when this had been done, the cause was at an end. This jurisdiction was transferred to the Chancery Division by the Judicature Acts, 1873–75, and under R.S.C., Ord. 39, r. 15, Ord. 77, r. 14, the procedure is similar, except that the commencement of an action is substituted for the filing of a bill in Chancery. A common case used to be that of a devisee establishing a will against the heir-at-law, by compelling him to litigate the question at once or not at all, and by perpetuating the evidence of the attesting witnesses. Bills to perpetuate testimony as to legitimacy were formerly of not infrequent occurrence. Declarations of legitimacy may now be sought under the Matrimonial Causes Act, 1973, s. 45. See LEGITIMACY; LEGITIMATE.

As to the taking and admissibility of evidence of persons dangerously ill, see DEPOSITION.

Perpetuity, unlimited duration; exemption from intermission or ceasing. It is odious in law, destructive to the commonwealth, and an impediment to commerce, by preventing the wholesome circulation of property.

The rule against perpetuities, or the doctrine of remoteness, is that the vesting of property cannot be postponed, or the alienation of it restricted, beyond any number of lives in being, whether interested or not, and twenty-one years from the death of the surviving life, allowance for gestation being made where it exists (*Duke of Norfolk's Case* (1681) 3 Ch.Ca. 1; *Stephens* v. *Stephens* (1736) Ca.temp.Talb. 228). If proof of the extinction of the lives mentioned is impracticable before the property can vest, the limitation is void (*Re Villar* [1929] 1 Ch. 243).

The rule requires that a limitation, whether of an absolute or partial interest, shall necessarily vest within the period prescribed, and not depend upon a mere possibility. Moreover, not only the person to take, but also the precise amount of his interest, must be ascertained within the prescribed period (*Blight* v. *Hartnoll* (1881) 19 Ch.D. 294; *Re Thompson* [1906] 2 Ch. 202).

Under the Perpetuities and Accumulations Act, 1964, a settlor or testator may specify a period of years not exceeding eighty as the perpetuity period (s. 1). For the purposes of the rule against perpetuities, males under fourteen and females under twelve and over fifty-five are presumed to be incapable of having children. Evidence is admissible to show that a living person will or will not be able to have a child (s. 2). The former rule that possible and not actual events are to be considered and that an interest which could conceivably vest too remotely is void even if it actually vests within the period is abolished. The new principle is " wait and see ": a disposition is to be treated as valid until events have shown that the interest must vest (if at all) after the end of the perpetuity period (s. 3). If the vesting age for unborn persons is specified at a greater age than twenty-one, and the " wait and see " provisions of s. 3 do not save the gift, the age is to be reduced, not to twenty-one as under the repealed s. 163 of the Law of Property Act, 1925, but to the age nearest the specified age which is consistent with the gift being valid (Perpetuities and Accumulations Act, 1964, s. 4; Children Act, 1975, Sch. 3 para. 43). The " trap of the unborn widow " (see Morris and Leach, pp. 72–73) is eliminated. Vesting is accelerated to the end of the perpetuity period (s. 5). The rule that ulterior interests expectant and dependent on prior interests that are too remote are also void, even if they are intrinsically valid (Morris and Leach, pp. 173–181) is abolished. The notion that the doctrine of acceleration does not apply in perpetuity cases is also abolished (s. 6).

The foregoing sections apply only in

relation to instruments taking effect after the commencement of the Act (s. 15 (5)).

The rule against perpetuities is excluded in relation to the trusts of or any disposition made under an occupational pension scheme (Social Security Act, 1973, s. 69).

The period presented by the rule is computed from the date of delivery of the deed creating the limitations, or from the testator's death when created by will, that being the period at which a will takes effect, while a power in favour of a special class or classes is considered to have been created by the instrument conferring the power and not by the instrument exercising it.

The following limitations are exempt from the perpetuity rule: a limitation expectant upon an entail, for it can be destroyed by barring the entail, but should the entail be preceded by a term of years, and its trusts be postponed until the failure of the issue in tail, they will be void, because limited to arise on an indefinite failure of issue; limitations the nature of the subject-matter of which is such as to render it necessary for them to take effect, if at all, within the period prescribed by the perpetuity rule; limitations to charitable uses; and perpetuities allowed or created by Act of Parliament, as in the case of Blenheim, settled upon the Duke of Marlborough and his posterity by the statutes 1704, 3 & 4 Anne, c. 4, and 1706, 6 Anne, c. 6 and Strathfieldsaye, settled on the Duke of Wellington and his posterity by the Wellington Estate Acts, 1812 to 1947. See also as to the effect of an Act of Parliament, *Manchester Ship Canal Co.* v. *Manchester Racecourse Co.* [1901] 2 Ch. 37.

Exceptions are also set out in the Law of Property Act, 1925, s. 162, relating to rents, rentcharges and rights to land or relating to land and certain rights or remedies connected therewith; see also s. 7 as to determinable fees.

Closely connected with the rule against perpetuities was another and independent rule, commonly known as the rule against double possibilities, or the rule in *Whitby* v. *Mitchell* (1890) 44 Ch.D. 85, *viz.*, that after an estate had been limited to an unborn person for life, a remainder could not be limited to any child of that unborn person; this rule applied to equitable as well as to legal estates (*Re Nash* [1901] 1 Ch. 1). This rule was abolished by the Law of Property Act, 1925, s. 161. See POSSIBILITY.

As to options to purchase in a lease, and restrictions on the creation of a lease *in futuro,* see LEASE; OPTION.

The Law of Property Act, 1922, s. 190 (iii), Sch. XV, and the Law of Property Act, 1925, s. 202, abolished perpetually renewable leases and converted them into leases for 2,000 years determinable by the lessee by ten days' notice before the renewal date. See Gray, *Rule against Perpetuities*; Morris and Leach, *Rule against Perpetuities*. See ACCUMULATION; APPOINTMENT, POWER OF; DRAIN; DRAINAGE; GESTATION; MORTMAIN; REMOTENESS.

Perquisite, anything acquired by perquisition (*q.v.*); anything acquired by the holder of a place or office over and above the wages or salary thereof; and, in connection with copyholds, such things as fines, escheats, heriots, reliefs, wards, etc., as distinguished from yearly profits or income. See FRINGE BENEFITS.

Perquisitio; Perquisition, the acquisition of anything otherwise than by inheritance.

Perquisitor, a searcher.

Perry, a drink made from the juice of pears fermented. The Customs and Excise Act, 1952, s. 307 (1), provides that any reference to cider shall include a reference to perry. See CIDER.

Persistent offenders. Where an offender is convicted on indictment of an offence punishable with imprisonment for a term of two years or more, the court, if satisfied, by reason of his previous conduct and of the likelihood of his committing further offences, that it is expedient to protect the public from him for a substantial time, may impose an extended term of imprisonment (Powers of Criminal Courts Act, 1973, ss. 28, 29). This supersedes the sentences of preventive detention and corrective training authorised by the Criminal Justice Act, 1948, s. 21. As to persistent shoplifters see *R.* v. *Anderson* (1972) 56 Cr.App.R. 863.

Person. In jurisprudence, a person is the object of rights and duties, that is, capable of having rights and of being liable to duties, while a thing is the subject of rights and duties.

Persons are of two kinds, natural and artificial. A natural person is a human being (see MONSTER). Artificial persons include a collection or succession of natural persons forming a corporation (*q.v.*); and, in some systems, a collection of property to which the law attributes the capacity of having rights and duties. The latter class of artificial persons is not recognised in English law, although the estate of a bankrupt or deceased person, and the assets of a company or partnership, have some of its characteristics. See STATUS.

As to the status of trade unions and employers' associations, see the Trade Union and Labour Relations Act, 1974, ss. 2, 3; *Bonsor* v. *Musicians' Union* [1956] A.C. 104. See TRADE UNION.

In the construction of an Act of Parliament, the word " person " includes a body corporate if the Act relates to an offence punishable summarily or on indictment, and includes any body of persons corporate or unincorporate if the Act relates to any other subject, unless in either case a contrary intention appears (Interpretation Act, 1889, ss. 3, 19).

A corporation, such as a limited company, may be a " respectable and responsible person " within the meaning of a covenant against assignment in a lease (*Willmott* v. *London Road Car Co.* [1910] 2 Ch. 525). A corporation was held not to be a person for the purpose of suing for penalties as a common informer (*q.v.*) in *St. Leonards* v. *Franklin* (1878) 3 C.P.D. 377. A limited company is not a person for the purposes of the Sunday Observance Act, 1677 (*Rolloswin Investments* v. *Chromolit Portugal Cutelarias* [1970] 1 W.L.R. 912).

Apart from the provisions of the Interpretation Act, 1889, a firm of partners is not a person, although partners may sue or be sued in the firm's name (R.S.C., Ord. 81, r. 1), and artificial persons are endowed only with the status or capacity conferred by the charter or statute of incorporation. See COMPANIES; CORPORATION; TRUST CORPORATION.

Person of full age. Under the Settled Land Act, 1925, this means a person not being an infant (*Re Earl of Carnarvon's Settled Estates* [1927] 1 Ch. 138), and therefore includes a corporation. An infant cannot be a tenant for life under s. 19 of the Act. See FULL AGE.

Person aggrieved. This expression may or may not include a local authority. See *R.* v. *Surrey Quarter Sessions, ex p. Lilley* [1951] 2 Q.B. 749, *R.* v. *Nottingham Quarter Sessions, ex p. Harlow* [1952] 2 Q.B. 601 and *Phillips* v. *Berkshire County Council* [1967] 2 Q.B. 991 for the affirmative and *R.* v. *London Quarter Sessions, ex p. Westminster Corporation* [1951] 2 K.B. 508 and *R.* v. *Dorset Sessions Appeal Committee, ex p. Weymouth Corporation* [1960] 2 Q.B. 230, for the negative.

The expression includes only persons with a legal grievance (*Buxton* v. *Minister of Housing and Local Government* [1961] 1 Q.B. 278).

Person of unsound mind. The Mental Treatment Act, 1930, s. 20, provided that the word " lunatic " should cease to be used and that the expression " person of unsound mind " should be used instead. The expression now used is " mentally disordered patient " or, more usually, simply " patient." See MENTAL HEALTH.

Persona, anybody capable of having and becoming subject to rights (Civil Law).

Persona conjuncta aequiparatur interesse proprio (Bac.Max. 18). (A connection is regarded as being on the same footing as a man himself.) Thus a deed is deemed to be executed under duress and is void as against anyone induced to execute it by threats of injury to his wife, parent or child.

Persona designata, a person pointed out or described as an individual, as opposed to a person ascertained as a member of a class, or as filling a particular character. Thus, if a testator bequeaths property to his children as a class, only those who fill that character at his death, that is, the survivors, can participate in the gift, while if he bequeaths it to them as *personae designatae*, the children of such of them as have died in his lifetime will take their parents' shares under the Wills Act, 1837, s. 33 (*Re*

Stansfield (1880) 15 Ch.D. 84). See LAPSE.

So property may be given to an illegitimate child as *persona designata*, but not, formerly, as a child simply (*Megson* v. *Hindle* (1880) 15 Ch.D. 198). See CHILD; NOMEN COLLECTIVUM.

Persona extranea, a person outside one's family (Civil Law).

Persona publica, a public officer; a notary (Civil Law).

Personable, having the status of a person (*q.v.*), and thus able to maintain an action in a court, as in the expression " the defendant was judged personable to maintain his action " (Old Nat.Brev. 142).

It also signified to be of capacity to take anything granted or given (Plowd. 27).

Personae ecclesiae, the parson or personation of the church. See PARSON.

Personal, that which has reference to the person of an individual, as in the case of a personal contract (see CONTRACT). A personal injury is an injury to the person of an individual, such as an assault, as opposed to an injury to his property. See ACTIO PERSONALIS MORITUR CUM PERSONA.

A system of law is said to be personal when its operation is limited to one of several races inhabiting a State.

Personal Act. See ACT OF PARLIAMENT.

Personal action. In the division of actions, a personal action originally meant one which was brought to enforce a remedy against a person, while in a real action the remedy was to recover a thing, the *res*, itself. Thus, an action on a contract or tort was a personal action, while an action to recover land was a real action, because the land itself could always be recovered. (See ACTION; IN PERSONAM; IN REM.) Hence also arose the distinction between real and personal property, for real property, *e.g.*, freehold land, was always specifically recoverable, whereas in the case of personal property, *e.g.*, leasehold land or chattels, formerly only a personal action for damages lay.

Personal Acts of Parliament, statutes confined to particular persons, *e.g.*, authorising a person to change his name, etc.

Personal chattels, goods, money, or movables; and see the definitions in the statutory forms of wills prescribed under the Law of Property Act, 1925, s. 179, and in the Administration of Estates Act, 1925, s. 55.

Personal injuries, Damages for. See DAMAGES.

Personal injuries scheme. The Personal Injuries (Civilians) Scheme, 1949, as amended, regulated the payment of compensation for war injuries to civilians under the Personal Injuries (Emergency Provisions) Act, 1939.

Personal property, money, goods, cattle, chattels, stocks, shares, securities, debts, etc., and also leaseholds. Personal property is either in possession or in action, *i.e.*, where a man has not the actual occupation of the thing, but only a right to it arising upon some contract, and recoverable by an action at law.

Any person may assign personal property, including chattels real, directly to himself and another person or other persons or corporation, by the like means as he might assign the same to another (Law of Property Amendment Act, 1859, s. 21). This was extended by the Conveyancing Act, 1881, to conveyances of freehold land or choses in action by a husband to a wife or *e contra.* Now, by the Law of Property Act, 1925, s. 72, a person may convey real or personal property to himself with others or alone.

In the case of real property there can be no such thing as an absolute ownership in the subject-matter, *i.e.*, land; the utmost that any one, even an owner in fee simple, can have is an estate. But in the case of personal property the primary rule is precisely the reverse; such property is essentially the subject of absolute ownership and cannot be held for any estate. This strict rule of the law, however, was not recognised in equity, and accordingly under a gift of personal property to A for life and after his death to B, the Court of Chancery, to carry out the obvious intention, would hold that A was entitled to a life interest merely, and that B had during the life of A a vested interest in remainder of which he could dispose at his pleasure; and if the property consisted of movable goods, A could be compelled to furnish and sign an inventory of them and an undertaking to take proper care of them (*Re Swan* [1915] 1 Ch. 829). The only exception was in the case of goods *quae ipso usu consumuntur*, *e.g.*, wines and household provisions, for in these a person to whom they are given for life takes the absolute interest. The proper and usual mode of creating limited interests in personal property is by means of the doctrine of trusts, *i.e.*, by vesting the property absolutely in trustees and declaring that they shall hold it upon trust for the beneficiaries either for life or otherwise as may be agreed. But even in equity personalty which was settled either by deed or will to follow the trusts of an equitable entailed estate in land vested absolutely in the first tenant in tail at his birth (*Re Lord Chesham* [1909] 2 Ch. 310). Joint tenancy and tenancy in common may subsist in the case of personal property, though tenancy in common of any legal estate in land, including leaseholds or other interests in land, has been abolished (Law of Property Act, 1925, s. 1). The Law of Property Act, 1925, s. 130, provides that personal property may be entailed like real estate, but only (in either case) by way of equitable interest. Before the Land Transfer Act, 1897, realty devolved directly on the heir or devisee upon the death of a person seised of the estate or inheritance. After that Act it devolved upon the personal representative in trust for the heir or devisee. Since the Administration of Estates Act, 1925, it devolves, as personal property and chattels real have always devolved, upon the personal representative, whose conveyance or assent is necessary and sufficient to confer title.

Mixed or impure personalty consists of leaseholds, estates at will, land directed to be converted into money (see CONVERSION), and money secured on land, *e.g.*, by mortgage. The term impure personalty was generally used to denote property which, though personalty, was not until the Mortmain and Charitable Uses Act, 1891, allowed to be given to charitable uses by will, etc. See CHARITABLE USES, ETC.; DEBENTURE; MORTMAIN.

Personal property is also divisible into corporeal personal property, which includes movable and tangible things, such as animals, ships, furniture, merchandise, etc.; and incorporeal personal property, which consists of such rights as personal annuities, stocks, shares, patents and copyrights.

Personal representatives, executors (*q.v.*) and administrators (*q.v.*), whether acting with regard to personal property (*q.v.*) or with regard to real property. See REAL REPRESENTATIVE.

Personal rights, the rights of personal security, comprising those of life, limb, body, health, reputation, and the right of personal liberty.

Personal tithes, those which were paid out of such profits as came by the labour of a man's person, as by buying and selling, gains of merchandise, handicrafts, etc.

Personal union, a composite State consisting of separate States which have only the head of the State in common, *e.g.*, formerly Denmark and Iceland.

Personality of laws. By the personality of laws, foreign jurists generally mean all laws concerning the condition, state, and capacity of persons; by the reality of laws all laws which concern property or things, *quae ad rem spectant*. Whenever they wish to express that the operation of a law is universal, they compendiously announce that it is a personal statute; and whenever, on the other hand, they wish to express that its operation is confined to the country of its origin, they simply declare it to be a real statute (Story, *Confl. of Laws,* 8th ed., p. 20).

Personalty, personal property, as distinguished from realty, or real property, *i.e.*, freehold land; also that which relates to the person. See PERSONAL PROPERTY.

Personation, the act of representing oneself to be someone else, whether living or dead, real or fictitious. At common law personation for the purpose of fraud is a misdemeanour.

Personation in order to obtain property amounts to the obtaining of property or a pecuniary advantage by deception, and is an offence under the Theft Act, 1968, ss. 15, 16. Personation of a voter is a corrupt practice (Representation of the People Act, 1949, ss. 47, 146; Criminal Law Act, 1967, Sch. 3 Pt. II; Representation of the People Act, 1969, Sch. 3 Pt. 1), and personation of a master for the purpose of giving a false character to a servant is a misdemeanour by the Servants' Characters Act, 1792. As to personation of an official entitled to wear uniform, see the Official Secrets Act, 1920, s. 1; of police, see the Police Act, 1964, s. 52; of a shareholder, see the Companies Act, 1948, s. 84. As to personating a husband, see RAPE.

Perspicua vera non sunt probanda (Co. Litt. 16). (Evident truths need not be proved.)

Persuasive authority, a decison or other source of law which depends on its intrinsic value for whatever force it may have and not on its binding character, *e.g.,* a decision of one of the inferior courts or a foreign court or a textbook.

Perticata terrae, the fourth part of an acre.

Perticulas, a pittance; a small portion of alms or victuals; also, certain poor scholars of the Isle of Man.

Perturbatrix, a woman who breaks the peace.

Perverse verdict, a verdict (*q.v.*) whereby the jury refuse to follow the direction of the judge on a point of law. See NEW TRIAL; TRIAL.

A perverse decision of justices is one in which they have taken into account matters which they ought not to have taken into account or shut their eyes to the obvious (*Gibbons* v. *Karl* [1956] 1 Q.B. 59).

Pervert practices. See LESBIANISM; SODOMY.

Pervise, the palace-yard at Westminster (Somner).

Pesa, a weight of 256 lb.

Pesage, Persage, a custom or duty paid for weighing merchandise or other goods (Seld.Hon.).

Pessimi exempli, of a very bad example.

Pessona, mast of oaks, etc., or money taken for mast, or feeding hogs (Cowel).

Pessurable, Pestarble, or **Pestarable wares,** merchandise which takes up a good deal of room in a ship.

Pests. See DESTRUCTIVE INSECTS.

Pet animals. See CRUELTY TO ANIMALS.

Peter ad Vincula, St. See GULE OF AUGUST; PETER PENCE.

Peter pence, a levy of one penny per house formerly made annually on August 1, that day being the feast of St. Peter

ad Vincula. The proceeds went to the Pope. It was abolished by the statute 1533, 25 Hen. 8, c. 21, s. 1, which was repealed by the statute 1554, 1 & 2 Phil. & Mar., c. 8, s. 3, and revived by the statute 1558, 1 Eliz. 1, c. 1, s. 4. See DENARII S. PETRI.

Petit assize. See ASSISE, PETTY.

Petit cape. See CAPE.

Petit jury, a jury in criminal cases who try the bills formerly found by the grand jury. See JURY.

Petit larceny, stealing of goods to the value of a shilling or under. The distinction between grand and petit larceny was abolished by the statute 1826, 7 & 8 Geo. 4, c. 29, s. 2.

Petit serjeanty, holding lands of the Crown by the service of rendering annually some small implement of war, as a bow, a sword, a lance, an arrow, flag, or the like (Litt. 159, 160; Co.Litt. 108a).

The statute 1660, 12 Car. 2, c. 24, took away the incidents of livery and primer seisin. The Law of Property Act, 1922, s. 136, provides that nothing in the Act affects the services incident to grand or petty serjeanty, which are not to be deemed manorial incidents, and the land is to be held in like manner as if before the commencement of the Act it had been held in free and common socage or had been copyhold as the case may require. See TENURE.

Petit treason, treason of a lesser kind, as if a servant killed his master, a wife her husband, a secular or religious man his prelate. But by the statute 1828, 9 Geo. 4, c. 31, s. 2, every offence which before the statute would have amounted to petit treason is deemed murder only.

Petitio, a count or declaration (Glanv.).

Petitio principii, begging the question; taking a thing in itself in dispute or not proved or false, for true or for granted, and drawing conclusions from it as such, when it is really dubious and perhaps false, or at least wants to be proved before any rational inference can be drawn from it.

Petition, a supplication made by an inferior to a superior having jurisdiction to grant redress.

The right of the subject to petition the sovereign or Parliament was denied by

PETITION

James II, but was affirmed by the court in 1688 in the Case of the Seven Bishops (see BISHOPS, CASE OF THE SEVEN), and all commitments and prosecutions for such petitioning are declared by the Bill of Rights, 1688, to be illegal. By the statute 1661, 13 Car. 2, st. 1, c. 5, which is directed against tumultuous petitioning, it is enacted that not more than twenty names shall be signed to a petition to the Crown or either House of Parliament for alteration of matters in Church or State, without the previous approval of the contents by three justices and that no petition shall be presented by a company of more than ten persons. This statute was put into force on the threatened presentation of the Chartist petition in 1848. There are several regulations respecting petitions to Parliament, which, if neglected in any one particular, will prevent their reception. For instance, signatures or marks must be original, not copies or signatures of agents on behalf of others; no chairman of a public meeting can sign for the whole meeting (though the common seal of a corporation is received as the petition of the whole corporate body).

A petition to the court is a written statement addressed to the court setting forth facts on which the petitioner bases a prayer for remedy or relief. Petitions are merely a peculiar mode of applying to a court, and do not necessarily indicate that the right sought to be maintained is different in its nature from ordinary rights. See ACTIONS AND MATTERS IN THE HIGH COURT; MOTION; SUMMONS.

The person by whom a petition is presented is called the petitioner, and the persons on whom it is served, in order that they may appear at the hearing and oppose or consent to the granting of the prayer, are called the respondents.

Petitions in the Chancery Division have been superseded to a large extent by summons or motion but it has not been possible to abolish them because in a few cases the use thereof is required by statute. See R.S.C., Ord. 9.

In the Family Division every matrimonial suit is commenced by a petition praying the relief sought, e.g., a decree of nullity or dissolution of marriage, etc.

In addition to these original petitions, subsidiary or incidental petitions of various kinds were sometimes required to be presented in a suit, e.g., to claim the custody of children, for maintenance, etc., but they are now dealt with on summons.

Formerly the pleadings in Admiralty actions commenced with a petition by the plaintiff in the nature of a declaration (q.v.) at common law. See PROTEST; STATEMENT OF CLAIM.

In bankruptcy, a petition is the mode by which proceedings to administer an insolvent's estate are commenced. It may be a petition presented by a creditor, or by the debtor himself. See ADJUDICATION; ARRANGEMENTS, ETC.; BANKRUPTCY; DECLARATION, ETC.

A winding up of a company by order of the court must be begun by petition (Companies Act, 1948, s. 224). See WINDING UP.

In the House of Lords and Privy Council, every appeal is commenced by a petition of appeal praying that the judgment appealed from may be reversed or varied. Interlocutory petitions are also sometimes required, e.g., to extend the time for lodging the cases or for leave to introduce fresh evidence.

Petitions and addresses to the Crown may be sent post free. Petitions to the Crown or Parliament may be sent to a member of either House post free if they do not exceed thirty-two ounces in weight and are sent without covers or covers open at the sides (Post Office Act, 1969, s. 84).

See COMMON PETITIONS; ELECTION PETITIONS; PETITION OF RIGHT.

Petition de droit, Petition of right, one of the common law methods of obtaining possession or restitution from the Crown of either real or personal property, or compensation in damages for breach of contract, the Crown formerly not being liable to an ordinary action at the suit of a subject. It is said to owe its origin to Edward I.

The petition was a document in which the petitioner set out his right, legal or equitable, to that which was demanded by him, and prayed the sovereign to do him right and justice, and, upon a due and lawful trial of his right and title, to make him restitution. The petitioner was

1358

called the suppliant, and the persons against whom relief was prayed (for any person in enjoyment of the property or right claimed was made a party) were called the respondents. The petition could be presented in any of the divisions of the High Court on the Home Secretary granting his fiat for that purpose (Petition of Right Act, 1860, s. 1; Naval Prize Act, 1864, s. 52). The Petition of Right Act, 1860, ss. 6, 7, provided that, if the petition was presented in Chancery, the subsequent proceedings up to judgment were to follow those in a suit in equity; and if in one of the common law courts, that they were to follow those in an action at law. As petitions of right were not affected by the Judicature Acts, 1873–75, the rules of the former common law and equity practice were still applicable to them. A judgment that the suppliant was entitled to the whole or some portion of the relief sought by his petition, or to such other relief as the court might think right, had the same effect as a judgment of *amoveas manus*. For the form of a Petition of Right see *Franklin* v. *The Queen* [1974] Q.B. 202. The Crown Proceedings Act, 1947, s. 1, provides that any claim which might have been enforced by a petition of right may be enforced by proceedings under that Act, which are similar in most respects to an ordinary action. See AMOVEAS MANUS, ETC.; FIAT; MONSTRANS DE DROIT; TRAVERSE.

Petition of Right, 1627, a parliamentary declaration of the liberties of the people, assented to by Charles I in the beginning of his reign.

In the first Parliament of Charles I, which met in 1626, the Commons refused to grant supplies until certain rights and privileges of the subject, which they alleged had been violated, should have been solemnly recognised by a legislative enactment. With this view they framed a petition to the king, in which, after reciting various statutes by which their rights and privileges were recognised, they prayed the king that no man should be compelled to make or yield any gift, loan, benevolence, tax, or suchlike charge, without common consent by Act of Parliament; that none should be called upon to make answer so to do; that freemen should be imprisoned or detained only by the law of the land, or by due process of law, and not by the king's special command, without any charge; that persons should not be compelled to receive soldiers and mariners into their houses against the laws and customs of the realm; and that commissions for proceeding by martial law should be revoked. To this petition the king at first sent an evasive answer, but at length gave his assent.

Petitioning creditor, one who applies for a receiving order in bankruptcy against his debtor. The Bankruptcy Act, 1914, s. 3, provides that the creditor's debt must be a liquidated one for £50 at least, and grounded upon an act of bankruptcy (*q.v.*) having occurred within three months before the presentation of the petition.

Petitum, the object of a claim.

Peto's Act, the Trustee Appointment Act, 1850, passed at the instance of Sir Samuel Peto, whereby property conveyed for religious or educational purposes vests in the trustees from time to time without any further conveyance; it was extended by the Trustees Appointment Act, 1890, to societies of associated congregations such as those of the Wesleyan Methodists, to which body the Act of 1850 had been held in *Re Hogton Chapel* (1854) 2 W.R. 631, not to apply. It was extended to burial grounds by the Trustee Appointment Act, 1869.

Petra, a stone (*q.v.*) weight (Cowel).

Petroleum. The landing, carriage, and storage of petroleum is regulated by the Petroleum (Consolidation) Act, 1928 (amended by the Petroleum (Transfer of Licences) Act, 1936), under which petroleum includes crude petroleum, oil made from petroleum or from coal, shale, peat or other bituminous substances, and other products of petroleum; and petroleum spirit means petroleum which when tested in the manner set out in the Schedule gives off an inflammable vapour at a temperature of less than 73° Fahrenheit. The Act also prohibits the keeping of petroleum without a licence (except a small amount in sealed cans for private use). Accidents causing loss of life by petroleum must be reported to the Home Secretary. The

Acts of 1928 and 1936 are amended by S.I. 1974 No. 1942, made under the Health and Safety at Work etc. Act, 1974, ss. 15, 82.

The Petroleum (Production) Act, 1934, replacing the Petroleum (Production) Act, 1918, vests in the Crown the property in petroleum and natural gas within Great Britain and makes provision with respect to searching and boring for petroleum. It prohibits boring for petroleum in the United Kingdom unless on behalf of or under licence from the Crown. Petroleum for the purposes of the Act includes any mineral oil or relative hydrocarbon and natural gas existing in its natural condition in strata, but does not include coal or bituminous shales or other stratified deposits from which oil can be extracted by destructive distillation.

Petroleum production licences are dealt with by the Petroleum Production Regulations, 1966 (No. 898) and 1971 (No. 814) and the Petroleum and Submarine Pipe Lines Act, 1975, ss. 17–19, Schs. 2, 3.

A new tax in respect of profits from substances won or capable of being won under the authority of licences granted under the Petroleum (Production) Act, 1934, is imposed under the Oil Taxation Act, 1975, amended by the Finance Act, 1976, s. 130.

Off-shore drilling for petroleum is dealt with by the Continental Shelf Act, 1964. See CONTINENTAL SHELF.

The Petroleum and Submarine Pipelines Act, 1975, established the British National Oil Corporation (ss. 1–16). The Act deals with submarine pipe-lines (ss. 20–33, Sch. 4) and refineries (ss. 34–39).

Customs and excise duties on hydrocarbon oil, petrol substitutes and power methylated spirits are levied under the Hydrocarbon Oil (Customs and Excise) Act, 1971.

As to the standards of measurement, etc., on the sale of liquid fuel and oil see the Weights and Measures Act, 1963, s. 21, Sch. 7 Pt. I.

See EXPLOSIVES; OIL IN NAVIGABLE WATERS; SOLUS AGREEMENT.

Pettifogger [Fr. *petit*, little; *vogueur*, a rower; Old Dut. *focker*, to cheat], a dishonest lawyer in a mean way of business.

Petty bag office, the principal office on what was formerly the common law side of the Court of Chancery; it was under the management of an officer called the Clerk of the Petty Bag (*q.v.*). Under the Judicature Act, 1873, s. 16, it became an office of the High Court. Out of it issued all original writs, certain kinds of writs of error and certiorari, commissions of charitable uses, idiocy, and lunacy, commissions to seize escheated and forfeited lands, etc., writs of *dedimus potestatem*, *congé d'élire*, *scire facias* to repeal letters patent and enforce recognisances, etc., and writs on the calling of a new Parliament. In it were filed traverses of inquisitions and returns to various commissions, including commissions for production of a *cestui que vie*. In it was also transacted business connected with the admission of solicitors, which in 1888 was transferred to the Law Society (*q.v.*). The practice of the office was regulated by the Petty Bag Act, 1849, and the general orders. By the Judicature (Officers) Act, 1879, s. 14, and the Great Seal Offices Act, 1884, s. 5, the office of Clerk of the Petty Bag was abolished as from the occurrence of the next vacancy, which in fact occurred in 1888; his powers and duties are now vested in the Senior Clerk of the Crown Office Department of the Central Office (*q.v.*). The Petty Bag Office was so called because in it the proceedings in which the Crown was concerned were preserved in a little sack or bag (*in parva baga*) instead of being enrolled on rolls as in the case of other proceedings (3 Bl.Comm. 49). See CHANCERY; HANAPER OFFICE.

Petty constables, inferior officers in every town and parish, subordinate to the high constable of the hundred. See CONSTABLES.

Petty jury. See PETIT JURY.

Petty larceny. See PETIT LARCENY.

Petty serjeanty. See PETIT SERJEANTY.

Petty sessional court, a court of summary jurisdiction consisting of two or more justices when sitting in a petty sessional court-house, and including the Lord Mayor or any alderman of the City of London, or any salaried magistrate (Interpretation Act, 1889, s. 13). It is now known as the magistrates' court (Magistrates' Courts Act, 1952, s. 124).

Petty sessions, a meeting of two or more justices of the peace. Petty sessions can lawfully be held periodically at more than one place within a petty sessional division, if such place has been appointed for the purpose. No meeting of justices in petty sessions may be held in licensed premises (Licensing Act, 1964, s. 190). As to petty sessional divisions, see the Justices of the Peace Act, 1949, s. 18.

The number of justices sitting in petty sessions is not to be greater than seven (Justices of the Peace (Size and Chairmanship of Bench) Rules, 1964, r. 2). See JUSTICES OF THE PEACE; SPECIAL SESSIONS.

Pew [Dut. *puye*; Fr. *appui*], an enclosed seat in a church. It is somewhat in the nature of an heirloom, and may descend by immemorial custom, without any ecclesiastical concurrence, from an ancestor to his heir.

The right to sit in a particular pew in the church arises either from prescription, as appurtenant to a messuage (*Morgan* v. *Curtis* (1829) 3 M. & Ry. 389), but not to land (*Philipps* v. *Halliday* [1891] A.C. 228), or from a faculty or grant from the ordinary, for he has the disposition of all pews which are not claimed by prescription. As to the proof of a right by prescription and the doing of repairs, see *Stileman-Gibbard* v. *Wilkinson* [1897] 1 Q.B. 749, and *Bathurst* (*Earl*) v. *Cirencester Parish* [1921] P. 381. All other pews and seats in the body of a church are the property of the parish, and the churchwardens, as the officers of the ordinary, and subject to his control, have authority to place the parishioners therein (*Corven's Case* (1612) 12 Co.Rep. 105); *Reynolds* v. *Monckton* (1841) 2 M. & Rob. 384).

A pew annexed by prescription to a messuage cannot be severed from it (*Re St. Columb* (1863) 8 L.T. 861).

As to the chief pew in the chancel, see CHANCEL.

In the case of churches erected under the Church Building Acts, the distribution of the pews and seats is vested in the Church Commissioners (*q.v.*) and the bishop of the diocese, and they have power to fix rents for pews, subject to the provisions of the Acts.

By the Church Seats Act, 1872, the Church Commissioners may accept a church site under a grant declaring that the pews or part of them shall not be let.

Pharaoh. See FARO.

Pharmacists. See CHEMISTS AND DRUGGISTS.

Pharmacopoeia, British. See BRITISH PHARMACOPOEIA.

Pharos, a watch-tower, or sea-mark, which cannot be erected without lawful warrant and authority (3 Co.Inst. 204).

Pheasant. As to theft of young hen-hatched pheasants, see *R.* v. *Corry* (1864) 10 Cox 23. See GAME.

Philosophers' stone, an imaginary substance reputed by the medieval alchemists to be efficacious for the multiplication (*q.v.*) of metals. Henry VI (notwithstanding a statute of Henry IV against multiplication) granted letters patent to various persons authorising them to find the philosophers' stone (Pat. 34 Hen. 6; 3 Co.Inst. 74).

Photograph. For the purposes of copyright (*q.v.*) photograph means any product of photography or of any process akin to photography, other than a part of a cinematograph film (Copyright Act, 1956, s. 48 (1)). The person who commissions a photograph is entitled to the copyright (s. 4); and such person can restrain the public sale of his photographic likeness (*Pollard* v. *Photographic Co.* (1888) 40 Ch.D. 345). The period for which copyright in a photograph subsists is fifty years from the end of the calendar year in which the photograph is first published (s. 3).

As to obscene and indecent photographs see OBSCENITY.

Photographing or sketching a judge, magistrate, coroner or any litigant, juror, etc., in a court or its precincts is an offence under the Criminal Justice Act, 1925, s. 41. As to prohibited places, see the Official Secrets Act, 1911 and 1920.

As to the use of photographs in identifying criminals, see Home Office circular No. 9/1969.

Photography in the streets may amount to "street trading" so as to be prohibited (*Dove* v. *Dyson* [1953] C.L.Y.

PHOTOGRAPH

2158; *Waite* v. *Marylebone Borough Council* (1953) 117 J.P. 447. Contrast *Newman* v. *Lipman* [1951] 1 K.B. 333). As to street trading in London, see HAWKER; PEDLAR.

Phylasist [φυλάσσω, to keep], a gaoler.

Physician, one who professes the art of healing.

The necessity of placing under supervision the practitioners of physic and surgery appears early in the statute-book; for by the statute 1511, 3 Hen. 8, c. 11, it was enacted that no person within London or seven miles thereof should practise as a physician or surgeon without examination and licence of the Bishop of London or the Dean of St. Paul's (duly assisted by the faculty), or beyond these limits without licence from the bishop of his diocese or his vicar-general similarly assisted, saving the privileges of the Universities of Cambridge and Oxford. The superintendence of the bishops was taken away by a royal charter, dated September 23, 1518, which incorporated the physicians. By the statute 1523, 14 & 15 Hen. 8, c. 5, this charter was confirmed, and a perpetual college of physicians established with a constitution of eight elects, etc. The Medical Act, 1956, s. 27, allows a physician to recover his fees by action unless he is a fellow of a college of physicians prohibited by by-law from so doing; by-law 170 of the Royal College of Physicians forbids such recovery. See MEDICAL PRACTITIONER.

Piacle [Lat. *piaculum*], an enormous crime.

Picard; Pickard; Piker, a large boat or barge propelled by sails and of from about fifteen to forty tons, which was used for coasting and river work: see the statutes 1357, 31 Edw. 3, stat. 2, c. 2, and 1542, 34 & 35 Hen. 8, c. 9, s. 1; also a fishing boat: see the statute 1571, 13 Eliz. 1, c. 11.

Picaroon [Ital. *picare*], a robber; a plunderer.

Piccage, Pickage [Law Lat. *picagium*], a duty payable to the owner of a fair for liberty to pick holes in the ground for the posts of stalls.

Pick of land, a narrow slip of land running into a corner.

Pickard, an instrument with iron spikes or teeth for raising a nap upon cloth,

the use of which was prohibited by the statute 1549, 3 & 4 Edw. 6, c. 2. See PICARD.

Picketing [Fr. *piquet*; *pique*, a pike], stationing men to watch and accost workmen passing between their homes and place of employment in order thereby to induce them to come out on strike, or to remain on strike.

The Trade Disputes Act, 1906, s. 2 (1), legalised peaceful picketing. It was repealed by the Industrial Relations Act, 1971, and replaced by s. 134. That Act was repealed by the Trade Union and Labour Relations Act, 1974, which provides that it shall be lawful for one or more persons in contemplation or furtherance of a trade dispute to attend at or near (a) a place where another person works or carries on business; or (b) any other place where a person happens to be, not being a place where he resides, for the purpose only of peacefully obtaining or communicating information or peacefully persuading any person to work or abstain from working (s. 15). Under the repealed s. 134 of the Industrial Relations Act, 1971, it was held that the powers of peaceful picketing were limited to oral and visual methods and did not authorise acts which would otherwise be illegal, such as the physical obstruction of a vehicle or person (*Broome* v. *D.P.P.* [1974] A.C. 587) and it was held that the section did not create rights capable of being infringed by police officers acting reasonably to prevent a breach of the peace (*Kavanagh* v. *Hiscock* [1974] Q.B. 600).

It was held in *Bird* v. *O'Neal* [1960] A.C. 908, that pickets employed by executives of a trade union are not the servants of the executives so as to make the executives vicariously liable for torts committed by the pickets. But a trade union may be held responsible for unlawful acts committed at the behest of its shop stewards who have implied authority to take industrial action (*Heaton's Transport (St. Helens)* v. *Transport and General Workers' Union* [1973] A.C. 15; *General Aviation Services (U.K.)* v. *Transport and General Workers' Union* [1974] I.R.C. 35).

Picketing on a highway otherwise than in contemplation or in furtherance of a trade dispute is unlawful and may be restrained by interlocutory injunction (*Hubbard* v. *Pitt* [1976] Q.B. 142). The Conspiracy and Protection of Property Act, 1875, provides penalties for intimidation, which includes violence, persistent following, and watching and besetting (s. 7, as amended by the Trade Disputes Act, 1906, s. 2). See BESET; INTIMIDATION; MOLESTATION; TRADE UNIONS.

Picking flowers, etc. A person who picks flowers, fruit or foliage from a plant growing wild on any land does not steal what he picks unless he does it for reward or for sale or other commercial purpose. " Plant " includes any shrub or tree (Theft Act, 1968, s. 4 (3)). See MUSHROOMS.

Pickle, Pycle, or Pightel [Ital. *piccolo*], a small parcel of land enclosed with a hedge, which in some counties is called a pingle.

Pick-lock, an instrument by which locks are opened without a key.

Picnics. Power to provide picnic sites and public conveniences on trunk and county roads is given by the Highways Act, 1971, ss. 26–29.

Pick-pocket, or **Pick-purse,** a thief who steals by putting his hand privately into the pocket or purse of another: an offence punishable with great severity in early times and now punishable as theft under the Theft Act, 1968, ss. 1, 7. In *R.* v. *Ring* (1892) 61 L.J.M.C. 116, it was held an offence to attempt to pick an empty pocket.

Picture. As to copyright (*q.v.*) in artistic works, see the Copyright Act, 1956, s. 3. As to the copyright in a picture not registered at the commencement of the Copyright Act, 1911, see *Savory* v. *World of Golf* [1914] 2 Ch. 566. See FINE ARTS.

Where framed pictures are sent by rail. the frames as well as the pictures are within the Carriers Act, 1830 (*Henderson* v. *London and N.W. Ry.* (1870) L.R. 5 Ex. 90). See CARRIERS ACT.

A picture may be libellous (5 Co.Rep. 125).

Piedpoudre, Court of; Piepowder court. See COURT OF PIE POUDRE.

Pierage, the duty for maintaining piers and harbours (Tomlin).

Now, when used at all, it means a toll for the use of a pier by a vessel.

Piers and harbours. See HARBOUR.

Pietantia, a pittance, a portion of victuals distributed to the members of a college. See PITTANCE.

Pietantiarius, the officer in a college who distributed the *pietantia* (*q.v.*).

Pigeon-house. Anciently it was held that none but the parson or the lord of the manor or a tenant by permission of the lord could have a pigeon-house or dovecot on his land: but by Coke's time it was established that any freeholder might have one on his land (3 Salk. 148; 5 Co.Rep. 104).

This restriction of the right to keep pigeons was due to the fact that pigeons kept by the lord of the manor and feeding on the lands of the tenants were of distinct value: and the right to keep a dovecot was one jealously insisted on by the French *seigneur* down to 1789.

Pigeons. As to the theft of pigeons see the Theft Act, 1968, ss. 1, 4.

Power to abate a nuisance from pigeons, doves, starlings or sparrows is given by the Public Health Act, 1961, s. 74; London Government Act, 1963, s. 40.

Piggot's Act, the statute 1740, 14 Geo. 2, c. 20, relating to common recoveries.

Pightel, a little enclosure.

Pignorative, Pignorary [Lat. *pignus*], pledging, pawning.

Pignus, a pledge or security for a debt or demand. Gaius says the word is derived from *pugnus: quia quae pignori dantur, manu traduntur* (Dig. 50, 16, 238). The element of *pignus* (*pig*) is however contained in the word *pa(n)go* and its cognate forms.

A pledge was called *pignus* when the possession of a thing was transferred to the pledgee, and *hypotheca*, when the pledgor retained it in his possession.

Pigs. See AGRICULTURAL MARKETING BOARDS; ANIMALS; CATTLE; LIVESTOCK.

Pigsty. Keeping a pigsty on a street may be an offence (Town Police Clauses Act, 1847, s. 28; Metropolitan Police Act, 1839, s. 60).

For damages for loss of amenity due to smell from a pig farm, see *Bone* v. *Seale* [1975] 1 W.L.R. 797.

Pila, that side of money which was called *pile*, because it was the side on which there was an impression of a church built on piles (1 Fleta, c. 39).

Pile ou face is French for " heads or tails."

Pileus supportationis, the cap of maintenance (*q.v*).

Pilferer, one who steals petty things.

Pillery, rapine; robbery.

Pillettus [Lat. *pila*, a ball], an arrow which had a round knob a little above the head, to hinder it from going into the mark.

Pillory, a wooden framework arranged in such a way that an offender was kept standing behind it, with his head and his hands protruding through holes. The instrument seems to have dated from very soon after the Conquest. It was used as a common-law punishment for offences involving fraud on the public, who frequently took a hand in the matter by pelting the culprit with missiles ranging from bad eggs to brickbats: this sometimes had fatal results, for which no one was ever made amenable. The pillory was also used during the seventeenth and eighteenth centuries as part of the common-law punishment of persons convicted of minor political offences, such as libel and sedition. It was, moreover, a statutory punishment for various offences. The statute 1562, 5 Eliz. 1, c. 9, s. 2, for instance, provided, not merely that one convicted of perjury should be put in the pillory, but also that his ears should be nailed to it. This enactment remained unrepealed until the Perjury Act, 1911; but the pillory had in the meantime been abolished by the Pillory Abolition Act, 1816, for all offences except perjury and cognate offences, and, by the statute 1837, 7 Will. 4 & 1 Vict. c. 23, for all offences. See HEALFANG; STOCKS.

Pilot, a person taken on board at any particular place for the purpose of conducting a ship through a river, road, or channel, or from or into a port. The Merchant Shipping Act, 1894, s. 742, defines a pilot as any person not belonging to a ship who has the conduct thereof. Pilots are established in various parts of the country, by ancient charters of incorporation or by particular statutes.

The most important of these in corporations are those of the Trinity House, Deptford Strond; the fellowship of the Pilots of the Dover, Deal, and the Isle of Thanet, commonly called the Cinque Port Pilots; and the Trinity Houses of Hull and Newcastle. A licensed pilot is one licensed for a particular district by a pilotage authority (Pilotage Act, 1913, s. 16). Pilotage is not, however, by any means exclusively in the hands of such persons. A pilotage authority may grant to the master or mate of a ship a pilotage certificate under which he can act as her pilot within the district of the authority (s. 23): and such a certificate is frequently held by an officer on board vessels trading regularly and at short intervals to or from certain ports. The chief pilotage authority is the Trinity House (*q.v.*).

Pilotage, the guidance of a pilot; the remuneration of a pilot. Pilotage dues are not payable by naval vessels (*Symons* v. *Baker* [1905] 2 K.B. 723), unless they are registered under the Merchant Shipping Act, 1906, s. 80. The law on the subject of pilots and pilotage is contained in the Pilotage Acts, 1913 to 1936.

By the Pilotage Act, 1913, s. 15 (reversing the common law rule), owners and masters of ships are made liable for damage caused by the ship at fault in navigation, in districts where the employment of a pilot is compulsory, even though the pilot was in charge of the ship. See COMPULSORY PILOTAGE.

Pimp tenure. In *Pla. Cor. apud Windesor* for 12 Edw. 1, rot. 28, there is this record: *Wilhelmus Hoppeshort tenet dimidiam virgatam terrae in eadem villa* [*Bokhampton*] *per servitium custodiendi sex damisellas, scil. meretrices, ad custum dominini regis* (William Hoppeshort holds half a virgate of land in the same vill [Bokhampton] by the service of keeping six damsels, that is to say, harlots, at the cost of our lord the king). This is noted under the head of pimp tenure by various writers, upon the strength of the substitution of *usum* for *custom*, which makes the last four words mean " for the use of our lord the king," instead of " at the cost of our lord the king." If *meretrix* is to be taken in its ordinary sense, the record merely shows that William Hoppeshort was bound to do what is now known as rescue work, the cost of which was defrayed by the king. Blount (*Tenures*, p. 3), indeed, notes that in those times *meretrices* meant "laundresses": but Du Cange does not show any such use of the word. See Jus PRIMAE NOCTIS.

Pin, a small barrel, containing four and a half gallons, used for beer. It is not a legal measure.

Pin money, an allowance made by a husband to a wife for her dress and personal expenses (*Howard* v. *Digby* (1834) 2 Cl. & F. 634). It may be secured by settlement, or it may be given voluntarily. When secured by settlement the wife cannot assign it; if she predeceases her husband, her representative cannot recover the arrears, if any; if she is living with her husband she generally cannot on his death claim arrears for more than one year (*Peacock* v. *Monk* (1748) 2 Ves. 190). A legacy by a husband satisfies *pro tanto* a claim for the allowance.

There was an ancient tax in France for providing the queen with pins.

Pinder, an officer of a manor or borough, whose duty it was to impound all stray cattle within the manor or borough. The village of Laxton in Nottinghamshire still has its pinder. See OPEN FIELDS; POINDING.

Pinfold, a pound for stray cattle in a manor.

Pinnage, poundage of cattle.

Pinner, a pounder of cattle, a pound-keeper.

Pint, a measure of capacity containing half a quart (Weights and Measures Act, 1963, s. 10, Sch. 1 Pt. IV). See BEER; GALLON; QUART.

Pipe, a roll in the Exchequer; otherwise called the Great Roll. The Pipe Rolls contained an account of the ancient revenues of the Crown, written out in process every year to the several sheriffs of England, who were the general receivers and collectors thereof, and by them levied and answered to the Crown upon their annual accounts, before the Clerk of the Pipe. The Pipe-office was abolished by the Fines Act, 1833. See CLERK OF THE PIPE; COMPTROLLER.

A pipe is also a measure of wine containing two hogsheads (*q.v.*): see the statute 1484, 1 Ric. 3, c. 13.

Pipelines. The construction and control of cross-country pipelines is regulated by the Pipe-lines Act, 1962, as amended. Pipe-line is defined generally as a pipe for the conveyance of any thing other than air, water, water vapour or steam (s. 65). See also S.I. 1974 No. 1986.

The construction and control of submarine pipe-lines is regulated by the Petroleum and Submarine Pipe-lines Act, 1975.

For powers of maintaining wartime government pipelines see the Requisitioned Land and War Works Act, 1948, ss. 12-17; Land Powers (Defence) Act, 1958, ss. 12–18.

Piracy [Lat. *pirata*], the commission of those acts of robbery and violence upon the sea which if committed upon land would amount to felony. Pirates hold no commission or delegated authority, from any sovereign or State, empowering them to attack others. They can, therefore, be only regarded in the light of robbers. They are, as Cicero has truly stated, the common enemies of all (*communes hostes omnium*); and the law of nations gives to everyone the right to pursue and exterminate them without any previous declaration of war (*Re Piracy Jure Gentium* [1934] A.C. 586), but it is not allowed to kill them without trial, except in battle. Those who surrender or are taken prisoners must be brought before the proper magistrates, and dealt with according to law. By the ancient common law, piracy, if committed by a subject, was held to be a species of treason, being contrary to his natural allegiance; if by an alien, to be felony only; but after the Treason Act, 1351, it was held to be only felony in a subject. Formerly this offence was only cognisable by the Admiralty Courts, which proceed by the rules of the civil law, but it being inconsistent with the liberties of the nation that any man's life should be taken away unless by the judgment of his peers, the Offences at Sea Act, 1536, established a new jurisdiction for this purpose, which proceeded according to the course of the common law.

Piracy *jure gentium* is defined in the Tokyo Convention Act, 1967, s. 4, Sch. arts 15–17. It extends to acts of piracy against an aircraft. The Act is supplementary to the common law (*Cameron* v. *H.M. Advocate*, 1971 S.C. 50).

Piracy with violence is an offence punishable with death (Piracy Act, 1837, s. 2). Other acts of piracy are punishable with imprisonment for life (Piracy Act, 1698, ss. 7, 8; Piracy Act, 1721; Piracy Act, 1837, s. 3).

The distinction between felony and misdemeanour having been abolished piracy is governed by the rules relating to misdemeanour (Criminal Law Act, 1967, s. 1).

As to the jurisdiction of the Admiralty Court (*q.v.*) in regard to the colonies, see the Admiralty Offences (Colonial) Act, 1849, and the Piracy Act, 1850. See also the Territorial Waters Jurisdiction Act, 1878, s. 6. See SLAVE TRADING.

As to the meaning of piracy in a policy of marine insurance, see *Bolivia Republic* v. *Indemnity Mutual Insurance Co.* [1909] 1 K.B. 785.

In private or civil law, piracy is the infringement of copyright (*q.v.*). Where a person reproduces the whole or part of a work which is the subject of copyright, so as to interfere with the profit of the owner, he commits a piracy, unless the new work is a bona fide abridgment of the other, and unless such abridgement is something more than a mere concatenation of extracts. An author's right to his works consists in an exclusive right to the sequence of the words as they stand; and if anyone else reprints these without addition, subtraction, or transposition, it is an inroad on the author's right. But, on the one hand, the sentences and words may be so rearranged that, although nothing be added to or taken from them, they give a substantially new idea to the public, and are therefore no infringement of the law; and, on the other hand, although parts may be omitted and new passages introduced, yet, if these alterations are merely colourable, and it is really an attempt to profit by taking the ideas of another, the publication is a piracy. An author who has been led by a former author to refer to older writers may, without committing piracy, use the same passages in the older writers which were used by the former author (*Pike* v. *Nicholas* (1869) L.R. 5 Ch. 251); as to pirating news from another newspaper,

see *Walter* v. *Skeinkopff* [1892] 3 Ch. 489. The importation of pirated copies from abroad is an infringement of copyright. The remedy for a threatened piracy or for continued infringement is by injunction; for a past infringement the remedy is damages, and in certain cases a penalty is imposed by statute (Copyright Act, 1956, s. 21).

Piracy ex jure gentium, piracy according to the law of nations, as opposed to offences made piracy by statute. See PIRACY.

Pirata est hostis humani generis (3 Co. Inst. 113). (A pirate is an enemy of the human race.) See PIRACY.

Pirate radio stations. See the Marine etc., Broadcasting (Offences) Act, 1967.

Piscary, a right or liberty of fishing in the waters of another person (*Ecroyd* v. *Coulthard* [1898] 2 Ch. 358; *Chesterfield* v. *Harris* [1911] A.C. 623; *Staffordshire, etc., Navigation* v. *Bradley* [1912] 1 Ch. 91). See FISHERY.

Pistol. See FIREARMS.

Pit and gallows. See FURCA ET FOSSA.

Pitching, Pitching-pence, money (commonly a penny) paid for pitching or setting down every bag of corn or pack of goods in a fair or market (Jacob; Tomlin).

Pittance, a slight repast or refection of fish or flesh more than the common allowance; the pittancer was the officer who distributed this at certain appointed festivals (Jacob).

Pitt Lewis's Act, the Forged Transfers Act, 1891.

Pitt Press, the University Press at Cambridge.

Pitt's Act, the statute 1784, 24 Geo. 3, sess. 2, c. 25, relating to India.

Pix, See PYX.

Pl., abbreviation for *placitum* (*q.v.*).

Placard, or **Placart** [Fr. *placard*; *plaque*, a flat piece of metal, stone, or wood], an edict, a declaration, a manifesto; an advertisement or public notification; a licence to use certain games: see the statutes 1541, 33 Hen. 8, c. 6, and 1555, 2 & 3 Ph. & Mar., c. 9.

Place. See PUBLIC PLACE.

Place of abode. The meaning of this expression varies for the purposes of different statutes. As used in the Municipal Corporations Act, 1835, s. 32 (providing that voting papers should set out, amongst other things, the "places of abode" of the persons voted for), and as used in the Summary Jurisdiction Act, 1848, s. 1, replaced by the Magistrates' Courts Rules, 1968, r. 82 (1) (providing that a summons may be served by leaving it with some person at the last or usual place of abode of the defendant), it was held to mean "place of residence," as distinguished from place of business. But it was decided that there was a sufficient compliance with the Constables Protection Act, 1751, s. 1 (which required notice of an intended action against a justice to be indorsed with the name of the attorney proposing to issue the writ and with "the place of his abode"), where the notice was indorsed with the attorney's place of business, although he slept and resided elsewhere (*Roberts* v. *Williams* (1835) 2 C.M. & R. 561). See ABODE.

Place of trial. See VENUE.

Placeman, one who exercises a public employment, or fills a public station; one who lays himself out for the obtaining of public appointments.

Placit, or **Placitum,** decree, determination.

Placita, the public assemblies of all degrees of men where the sovereign presided, who usually consulted upon the great affairs of the kingdom; pleas, pleadings, or debates, and trials at law; penalties, fines, mulcts, or emendations; the style of the court at the beginning of the record at *nisi prius* (Jacob). See PLEA.

Placita coronae, pleas of the Crown. See PLEA.

Placitare, to plead.

Placitator, a pleader.

Placitory, relating to pleas or pleading.

Placitum, any of the points decided in a judgment put concisely by the reporter, abbreviated *pl.* See PLACITA.

Placitum aliud personale, aliud reale, aliud mixtum (Co.Litt. 284). (Pleas are personal, real, and mixed.)

Placitum nominatum, the day appointed for a criminal to appear and plead and make his defence (Leg.Hen. 1, c. 29). *Placitum fractum* was when the day was past.

Plagiarist, or **Plagiary,** one who publishes the thoughts and writings of another as his own; if thoughts only, not expressed in the same or substantially the same words, there is no breach of copyright. See PIRACY.

Plagiarius, one who knowingly kept in irons, or confined, sold, gave, or bought a citizen (whether freeborn or a freedman), or the slave of another, the offence being called *plagium* (Civil Law).

Plagiary [Lat. *plagiarius*], a manstealer.

Plagii-crimen, or **Plagium,** the stealing and retaining of children of freemen and slaves (Civil Law).

Plague [πληγη, a wound], pestilence; a contagious and malignant fever.

By the statute 1604, 1 Jac. 1, c. 31, it was a capital offence for anyone infected with the plague, after having been commanded by the mayor or constable, etc., to keep house, to go abroad and in company. This Act was repealed by the Punishment of Offences Act, 1837. See PUBLIC HEALTH; QUARANTINE.

Plaideur [Fr.], an attorney who pleaded the cause of his client; an advocate.

Plainant, a plaintiff.

Plaint [Fr. *plainte*; Lat. *querela*], the statement in writing of a cause of action. It is the first process in an inferior court in the nature of an original writ, because there is briefly set forth the plaintiff's cause of action: and the judge is bound, of common right, to administer justice therein without a special mandate from the Crown.

Actions in the county court are commenced by the registrar entering, in a book kept for the purpose, at the request of the intended plaintiff, a plaint in writing, stating the names and the addresses of the parties, and the substance of the action: on this a summons (*q.v.*) is issued. The registrar gives the plaintiff a note called a plaint note, containing the date of the entry, the date fixed for the trial, and some notes for the guidance of the plaintiff.

Before the abolition of real actions (see ACTIONS) a copyholder could only plead and be impleaded in respect of his copyhold land in the court of the manor, by what were called customary plaints, which were analogous to the common law writs in real actions, and called after them, *e.g.*, plaints in the nature of writs

1367

of entry, plaints in the nature of writs of right, etc.

Formerly " plaint " meant, in the superior courts, the cause for which the plaintiff complained against the defendant and for which he obtained the king's writ.

Plaintiff [Fr. *plaintif*], a person who brings an action. See PARTIES.

Plan. Under various Acts, plans have to be deposited with local authorities for various purposes. If the local authority neglect to pass the plans the remedy is by mandamus (*Davis* v. *Bromley Corporation* [1908] 1 K.B. 170; *R.* v. *Cambridge Corporation* [1922] 1 K.B. 250).

As to a purchaser's right to have the property conveyed to him by reference to a plan on his conveyance, see *Re Sansom* [1910] 1 Ch. 741; *Re Sparrow* [1910] 2 Ch. 60. As to maps as evidence, see *Storey* v. *Eastbourne R.D.C.* [1927] 1 Ch. 367.

Under the Land Registration Act, 1925, s. 76, land may be identified by description and a map or plan.

As to property in plans, see ARCHITECT.

As to wrongful communication of plans, see OFFICIAL SECRETS.

Planning. See DEVELOPMENT; PLANNING PERMISSION.

Planning and Local Government, Ministry of. This Ministry is part of the Department of the Environment. See SECRETARY OF STATE FOR THE ENVIRONMENT.

Planning appeals. See DEVELOPMENT.

Planning blight. The effect of a development plan (see TOWN AND COUNTRY PLANNING) may be such as to give owner-occupiers and mortgagees of land affected by it the right to serve a blight notice requiring the acquisition of their interests by the appropriate authority. The authority may challenge the grounds on which the blight notice rests by means of a counter-notice and the dispute is decided by the Lands Tribunal. The onus of proving blight lies upon the claimant. When a blight notice becomes effective the appropriate authority is required to acquire the land on the basis of compulsory purchase (Town and Country Planning Act, 1971, ss. 192–208; Local Government Act, 1972, s. 182 (3), Sch. 16 paras. 45, 52;

Land Compensation Act, 1961, s. 9; Land Compensation Act, 1973, ss. 68–82).

Planning inquiries. Planning inquiries which, under Sch. 9 of the Town and Country Planning Act, 1971, are to be determined by an Inspector of the Department of the Environment are conducted in accordance with the Town and Country Planning Appeals (Determination by Appointed Persons) (Inquiries Procedure) Rules, 1968.

Planning inquiries in respect of matters where the decision lies with the Secretary of State for the Environment are conducted in accordance with the Town and Country Planning (Inquiries Procedure) Rules, 1969. The hearing is by an Inspector of the Department of the Environment who makes a report to the Secretary of State for his decision.

Planning permission, permission by the local planning authority, or on appeal, the Secretary of State for the Environment, to carry out development on land, under the Town and Country Planning Act, 1971. See DEVELOPMENT.

Plant. Theft of any plant is an offence under the Theft Act, 1968, ss. 1, 4, except that a person who picks mushrooms (including any fungus) growing wild on any land or who picks flowers, fruit or foliage from a plant (including a shrub or tree) growing wild on any land does not steal what he picks unless he does it for reward or for sale or other commercial purpose (s. 4 (3)). Destroying or damaging plants is an offence under the Criminal Damage Act, 1971, ss. 1, 10. Mushrooms (including fungus) growing wild and flowers, fruit or the foliage of a plant (including a shrub or tree) growing wild are excluded from the Act (s. 10 (1)).

Breeders and discoverers of new varieties of plants are granted limited monopoly rights by the Plant Varieties and Seeds Act, 1964, ss. 1–15, as amended by the Agriculture (Miscellaneous Provisions) Act, 1968, s. 43, Sch. 7; Tribunals and Inquiries Act, 1971, s. 18, Schs. 3, 4; European Communities Act, 1972, c. 68, s. 4, Sch. 3 Pt. III, Sch. 4 para. 5 (5).

Uprooting wild plants is an offence. Certain rare plants are protected. These are Alpine Gentian, Alpine Sow-thistle,

Alpine Woodsia, Blue Heath, Cheddar Pink, Diapensia, Drooping Saxifrage, Ghost Orchid, Killarney Fern, Lady's-slipper, Mezereon, Military Orchid, Monkey Orchid, Oblong Woodsia, Red Helleborine, Snowdon Lily, Spiked Speedwell, Spring Gentian, Teesdale Sandwort, Tufted Saxifrage, Wild Gladiolus (Conservation of Wild Creatures and Wild Plants Act, 1975).

Plant and machinery, the fixtures, tools, machinery, and apparatus necessary to carry on a trade or business. In *Yarmouth* v. *France* (1887) 19 Q.B.D. 647, a horse was held to be "plant" within the meaning of the Employers' Liability Act, 1880; and see *National Provincial Bank* v. *Charnley* [1924] 1 K.B. 431, and *Daphne* v. *Shaw* (1926) 53 T.L.R. 45.

"Plant" was held not to include a lawyer's books under the Finance Act, 1925, s. 16, in *Daphne* v. *Shaw* (1926) 11 T.C. 256. This decision was reluctantly followed by Fox J. in *Mumby* v. *Furlong* (1975) *The Times*, December 20.

As to rating, see the General Rate Act, 1967, ss. 21, 22, Sch. 3. As to plant and machinery for income tax purposes see the Income and Corporation Taxes Act, 1970, ss. 60, 78, 306.

Plant health. See Destructive Insects and Pests.

Plantation. This was the term applied to the steps taken in the reign of James I for the division between English settlers, or planters, of the forfeited lands which had been held in Ulster by the Earls of Tyrconnell and Tyrone.

Plantations, colonies. With respect to their internal policy they were of three sorts: provincial establishments; proprietary governments; charter governments.

The Plantations was the name applied to the English settlements in North America and in the adjacent West Indian Islands. These were the Plantations of Jamaica, Barbados, the Bermudas, the Leeward Islands, etc., later British colonies; and there were also on the mainland the Plantations of Virginia, Maryland, Carolina, Georgia, New England, and New York, which now are included in the United States of America. The term "plantations" fell into disuse during the second half of the eighteenth century: it was never applied to the British settlements in the Antipodes.

See Board of Trade; Colonies; Transportation.

Plate, of gold and silver.

The standard and marking of gold and silver plate have been regulated from early times (see Safford, *Law and Merchandise Marks*, pp. 204 *et seq.*).

The Hallmarking Act, 1973, provides for the composition, assaying, marking and description of articles of precious metal, *i.e.*, gold, silver or platinum and any other metal to which, by order, the Act may be applied. The approved marks are the sponsor's mark indicating the manufacturer or sponsor of the article, the assay mark denoting the standard of fineness and place where the assay took place and a letter of the alphabet denoting the year in which the article was marked. Approved hallmarks are marks struck by an assay office in the United Kingdom, whether before or after the commencement of the Act under the law for the time being in force or marks struck by the Wardens and Commonalty of Goldsmiths of the City of Dublin before April 1, 1923, or "convention hallmarks" which are marks struck by an assay office outside the United Kingdom and recognised by the Government of the United Kingdom. The Act also regulates the permitted description of unhallmarked articles. The Act consolidates more than thirty statutes dealing with the subject. The Sovereign's head is not necessary since the duty on plate was abolished by the Customs and Inland Revenue Act, 1890, s. 10.

The Act of 1973 created the British Hallmarking Council (s. 13). See also Carat.

Platform. He who causes a platform to be erected for viewing a public exhibition, and admits the public for payment thereto, impliedly warrants, to those so admitted that the platform is as safe as reasonable skill and care can make it (*Francis* v. *Cockerell* (1870) L.R. 5 Q.B. 591); the extent to which he can restrict his liability by contract is limited by the Occupiers' Liability Act, 1957, s. 3.

Platinum is sold by troy weight (Weights and Measures Act, 1963, s. 10 (2)). As to hallmarking, see PLATE.

Play-grounds. See RECREATION GROUNDS.

Playing cards. See CARDS.

Playing fields. See RECREATION GROUNDS.

Plays. See THEATRE.

Plea [Fr. *plée*], the defendant's answer of fact to the plaintiff's declaration; also a suit or action.

A plea is a mode of putting forward a defence to certain proceedings. Thus, if a writ of *scire facias* is issued against a person, and he wishes to put forward facts in answer to the writ, he does so by plea: or, if a return is made to such a writ, and the person at whose instance the writ was issued wishes to contest it, he puts in a plea to the return. (See TRAVERSE.) This formerly applied also to prohibition (*q.v.*) in which now, however, the proceedings are the same as in an ordinary action.

In a criminal prosecution, the prisoner has to plead to the indictment, which he may do by pleading to the jurisdiction, that is, alleging that the court has no jurisdiction to try him; or by demurring (see DEMURRER); or by pleading some plea in bar, namely, either a general plea of guilty or not guilty, or a special plea, such as *autrefois acquit, autrefois convict*, or pardon.

A person arraigned on indictment may make a plea of not guilty in addition to any demurrer or special plea (Criminal Law Act, 1967, s. 6 (1) (*a*)). He may plead not guilty of the offence charged in the indictment but guilty of another offence of which he might be found guilty on that indictment (s. 6 (1) (*b*)). As formal defects are now always capable of amendment, pleas in abatement (*q.v.*) are obsolete.

The practice of plea bargaining is improper since it tends to restrict the accused's freedom of choice as to his plea (*R.* v. *Turner* [1970] 2 Q.B. 321). See Practice Direction, July 26, 1976 [1976] 7 C.L. 45c.

The word " plea " is used colloquially to mean a plea of guilty.

In the ecclesiastical courts, all the pleadings are called pleas. The first plea is either articles or a libel, and every subsequent plea is an allegation.

Formerly a plea was the principal mode of putting forward a defence to a civil action or suit. In an action at common law, the plea was similar to the statement of defence under the present practice in that it stated facts as an answer to the declaration, as opposed to a demurrer (*q.v.*); but it differed from a statement of defence in stating the facts vaguely and in a peculiar form. Pleas were of two kinds, dilatory and peremptory. The first class included pleas to the jurisdiction, that is, pleas denying the jurisdiction of the court, pleas in suspension, and pleas in abatement; the second class consisted of pleas in bar. A plea in suspension was one which alleged grounds for not proceeding with the action at present: where it was grounded on infancy it was also known as demurrer of the parol (see DEMUR). A plea in abatement did not give an answer to the plaintiff's case, but showed that he had committed some informality, *e.g.*, that he had not joined the proper parties to the action. A plea in bar showed a substantial defence to the action, either by traverse or by confession and avoidance (*q.v.*). Formerly pleas were distinguished as general issues, in which the defendant simply traversed the plaintiff's allegations, and special pleas, in which the defendant stated the grounds of his defence; from the latter term arose the expression special pleading (see ISSUE; PLEADER). A plea *puis darrein continuance* (after the last continuance) was a plea setting up a ground of defence which had arisen after the defendant had pleaded in the ordinary course: thus if, after the defendant had delivered his plea, the plaintiff gave him a release, the defendant could set up the release by plea *puis darrein continuance*. After continuances (*q.v.*) had been abolished the defendant could, after defence, plead new matter of defence which had arisen since the writ or since his defence by a pleading which was said to be to the further maintenance of the action; and this pleading was in substitution for the original defence.

In equity, pleas were very rare in practice, and were only used in cases where the defendant was in a position to state one or more facts, which if inserted in the bill would make it demurrable; in such a case the defendant by filing a plea (which generally had to be sworn to by him) might avoid putting in an answer, and bring the suit to an end at once. Pleas in equity were of various kinds, of which pleas to the jurisdiction and pleas in bar were the principal.

A defendant now raises his defence in all actions in the High Court by a statement of defence (q.v.).

In its original sense, "plea" meant any legal proceeding. Pleas of the Crown were criminal proceedings, while civil actions were called common pleas, or pleas simply (Co.Litt. 287a).

The Court of Queen's Bench was said to have a Crown side and a plea side, the former being its jurisdiction in Crown business, and the latter its jurisdiction in ordinary actions: so the jurisdiction of the Court of Exchequer in ordinary actions was called its plea side, as opposed to its jurisdiction in revenue matters. See FOREIGN PLEA; PLEADING.

Plea rolls. See ROLL.

Plea to the action, a pleading in which the plaintiff's cause of action was attacked; it is to be distinguished from an action of a writ which attacked only the form of the plaintiff's action. See ACTION OF A WRIT.

Plead, to make an allegation in a cause; also to argue a cause in court.

In its general sense, to plead is to answer the previous pleading of the opposite party in an action or other proceeding by denying the facts therein stated, or by alleging some fresh facts; pleading was formerly opposed to demurring: the former raised a question of fact, the latter a question of law. Thus, if a plaintiff delivered a statement of claim which was not only demurrable but also failed to state the facts correctly, the defendant might apply for leave to plead and demur, and, if he obtained leave to do so, he delivered a statement of defence and a demurrer.

To plead also signifies to plead a plea: thus, in a criminal prosecution the prisoner pleads guilty or not guilty, etc.; and under the old common law practice, a defendant was said to plead to the juris-

diction, to plead in bar, etc., according to the nature of his plea. To plead issuably, was to demur or plead some substantial defence to the action, so that it might be determined on its merits.

In criminal practice, a prisoner charged with treason or felony is said to plead over when in addition to, or after, pleading specially, he pleads not guilty. As to a further use of the term "pleading over," see AID BY VERDICT.

The word "plead" is used colloquially to mean plead guilty.

As to unfitness to plead see MENTAL HEALTH.

See PLEA; RESPONDEAT OUSTER.

Pleader [Lat. *narrator*], one who draws pleadings.

Formerly, when pleading at common law was a highly technical and difficult art, there was a class of men known as special pleaders not at the bar, who held a position intermediate between counsel and attorneys. The class is now extinct. See COMMON PLEADER, ETC.; DRAFTSMAN; SPECIAL PLEADER.

Pleading. The science of pleading was no doubt derived from Normandy. The use of stated forms of pleading is not to be traced among the Anglo-Saxons. Pleading was cultivated as a science in the reign of Edward I. The object of pleading is to ascertain, by the production of an issue, the subject for decision.

The pleadings in an action in the High Court are written statements delivered alternately by the parties to one another, until the questions of facts and law to be decided in the action have been ascertained. Each pleading commences with the title of the action, and states concisely the material facts on which the party pleading relies, but not the evidence by which they are to be proved (R.S.C., Ord. 18, r. 7). The first pleading is the plaintiff's statement of claim (q.v.), unless the writ of summons itself is endorsed with the statement of claim (Ord. 6, r. 2). The next pleading is delivered by the defendant, and is a statement of defence or a statement of defence and counter-claim (q.v.) combined. The next pleading is a reply (q.v.). If the reply is not merely a joinder of issue (q.v.), the next pleading is delivered by the defendant. This and the subsequent pleadings, if any, follow the names of the old pleadings at common law, *viz.*, rejoinder, surrejoinder, rebutter and surrebutter (*q.v.*); but the general rule that no pleading subsequent to reply shall be served without leave of the court (Ord. 18, r. 4), coupled with the power of the judge to order issues to be settled (see ISSUE), and the power of amendment (*q.v.*), will in general prevent the pleadings from going so far. In any case, however, unless either party makes default in pleading, or unless issues are settled, the ultimate result must be that one party joins issue upon the preceding pleading of his adversary (Ord. 18, r. 14), the pleadings in an action are deemed to be closed (a) at the expiration of fourteen days after service of the reply or, if there is no reply but only a defence to counterclaim, after service of the defence to counterclaim or (b) if neither a reply nor a defence to counterclaim is served, at the expiration of fourteen days after service of the defence (Ord. 18, r. 20). As to judgment by default, see JUDGMENT.

Pleadings are by no means so essential a part of an action as they once were. The necessity for the leave of a master before a pleading subsequent to reply can be served (see above), the control exercised by the court (see DIRECTIONS, SUMMONS FOR) and the provision made by Ord. 18, r. 21, have materially altered the old practice. See COMMERCIAL CAUSES; INDICTMENT; INFORMATION; PLEA.

Formerly different systems of pleadings, except as to demurrers, prevailed in the common law and equity courts. In a common law action the pleadings consisted of the declaration, plea, replication, rejoinder, surrejoinder, rebutter, surrebutter (Co.Litt. 303b).

In a suit in equity the pleadings consisted of the bill of complaint; a demurrer, plea, answer or disclaimer or a combination of these; and a replication. Formerly re-rejoinders were also used in Chancery pleadings, but they had been disused long before the Judicature Act, 1873. According to the later practice of the Court of Chancery, if the plaintiff required to state fresh facts after the defendant had filed his answer or plea, he amended his bill.

In the early ages of the common law the pleadings were oral statements, or arguments by the parties or their counsel, made alternately until the question in dispute was ascertained.

Plead over, to follow up an opponent's pleading by replying, etc., and so overlooking some defect to which exception might have been taken. See AID BY VERDICT.

Pleas of the Crown, the criminal law department of our jurisprudence; so called because the sovereign, in whom centres the majesty of the whole community, is supposed by the law to be the person injured by every wrong done to that community, and is, therefore, in all cases, the proper prosecutor for every such offence.

Originally pleas of the Crown meant offences which were triable only in the king's courts, as distinguished from offences which could be dealt with in the old county court (known as pleas of the sheriff), and those cognisable in manor and borough courts. After justices of the peace had been established all offences were included in the expression pleas of the Crown: and in proceedings relating to them they were averred to have been committed *contra pacem domini regis, coronam et dignitatem suam* (against the peace of our lord the king, his crown and dignity). In the form used in pleas of the sword (*q.v.*), *gladius* was substituted for *corona*. See Hale, *Historia Placitorum Coronae*: Hawkins, Pl.Cr.; East, Pl.Cr.

The term pleas of the Crown was also applied to the various interrogatories which collectively made up the articles of the eyre (*q.v.*).

Pleas of the sword. When William the Conqueror granted the earldom of Chester (*q.v.*) to Hugh Lupus, the grant carried with it *jura regalia* (*q.v.*), including the right to hold courts corresponding to the king's courts elsewhere than in a county palatine. In proceedings before a court of the earldom with regard to what were known in England generally as pleas of the Crown, it was averred that any given offence had been committed *contra pacem domini comitis gladium et dignitatem* (against the peace of our lord the earl, his sword and dignity). In a later grant by Henry III of the earldom of Chester, pleas of the sword or *placita* *gladii* were expressly excepted from the grant. See SPATAE PLACITUM.

Pleasure boats. A local authority may themselves provide and let for hire or may license any person to let for hire pleasure boats on any lake or piece of water in any park or pleasure ground provided by them; and may make by-laws in connection with them (Public Health Acts Amendment Act, 1890, s. 44 (2); Local Government Act, 1972, Sch. 14 para. 27 (2)). Licences for pleasure boats may be granted under the Public Health Acts Amendment Act, 1907, s. 94 (as amended by the Criminal Justice Act, 1967, Sch. 3 Pt. I; Local Government Act, 1974, s. 35, Sch. 6 para. 1; S.I. 1968 No. 170). A local authority's power to suspend or revoke pleasure boat licences under the Public Health Act (Amendment) Act, 1907, s. 94 (2), is not given for the purpose of punishment and should not be so used (*Weymouth Corporation* v. *Cook* (1973) 71 L.G.R. 458).

A local authority may provide boating pools and lakes together with boathouses and boats under the Public Health Act, 1961, s. 54; Local Government Act, 1972, Sch. 14 para. 42, Sch. 30. See also the London Government Act, 1963, s. 58 (1).

A local authority may make by-laws as to seaside pleasure boats (Public Health Act, 1961, s. 76). As to London see the London County Council (General Powers) Act, 1935, ss. 42, 53.

Pleasure-grounds. These may be provided by local authorities under the Public Health Act, 1875, s. 164 (as amended by the Local Government Act, 1972, Sch. 14 para. 27). Rules prescribing restrictions and conditions can be made. See RECREATION GROUNDS.

A local authority may make by-laws regulating pleasure fairs and roller-skating rinks (Public Health Act, 1961, s. 75).

As to the powers of a local authority to provide car parks, see *Att.-Gen.* v. *Southampton Corporation* (1970) 21 P. & C.R. 281.

The words " pleasure-ground " in the Electricity (Supply) Act, 1919, s. 22 (1), import the conception that it is the ground which gives pleasure to people: it does not mean ground upon which a person carries on an activity (in this case gliding) which is pleasurable to him or her (*Central Electricity Generating Board* v. *Dunning* [1970] 1 Ch. 643). The words " pleasure fair " in the Betting, Gaming and Lotteries Act, 1963, Sch. 6 para. 4 (as substituted by the Gaming Act, 1968, Sch. 11 Pt. II) mean a place containing roundabouts, dodgems and hoopla and not bingo (*q.v.*) and one-armed bandits (*q.v.*) (*R.* v. *Herrod, ex p. Leeds City District Council* [1974] 1 W.L.R. 1275).

Plebanus, a rural dean.

Plebeity, or Plebity, the common or meaner sort of people; the plebeians.

Plebiana, a mother church.

Plebiscite, or Plebiscitum, a law enacted by the common people at the request of the tribune or some other plebian magistrate, without the intervention of the senate; more particularly applied to the law which the people made, when upon some misunderstanding with the senate they retired to the Aventine mount (Civil Law).

Pledge, anything put to pawn or given by way of warrant or security; also a surety, bail, or hostage. See PAWN; PIGNUS.

A pledge is where the owner of a chattel agrees with another person that it shall be held by the latter (the pledgee) as security for the payment of a debt or performance of an obligation. This entitles the pledgee to hold the chattel until payment or performance, and, upon failure of payment or performance at the proper time, to sell it; but until he does so, the pledgor may redeem it by payment or performance. Specific appropriation is sometimes called an equitable pledge. See APPROPRIATION; BAILMENT; CHARGE; MORTGAGE.

Pledgee, one who receives pledges; a pawnee. See PAWNBROKER.

Pledgery, suretyship; an undertaking or answering for another.

Pledges to restore. Before the plaintiff in foreign attachment could issue execution against the property in the hands of the garnishee, he had to find " pledges to restore," consisting of two householders, who entered into a recognisance for the restoration of the property, as a security for the protection of the defendant; for, as the plaintiff's debt was not proved in any stage of the proceedings, the court guarded the rights of the absent defendant by taking security on his behalf, so that if he should afterwards disprove the plaintiff's claim he might obtain restitution of the property attached. See FOREIGN ATTACHMENT.

Pledgor, one who offers a pledge; a pawner.

Plegii de prosequendo, pledges to prosecute with effect an action of replevin.

Plegii de retorno habendo, pledges to return the subject of distress, should the right be determined against the party bringing the action of replevin.

Plegiis acquietandis, a writ which lay for a surety against him for whom he was surety, if he did not pay the money on the due day (Fitz.N.B. 173).

Pleins pouvoirs. See PLENIPOTENTIARY.

Plena forisfactura, a forfeiture of all a person's possessions.

Plena probatio, testimony by two witnesses (Civil Law).

Plenarty [Lat. *plenus*, full]. Under the old practice, when a defendant in an action of *quare impedit* pleaded that the church was full (that is, that a clerk had been previously presented and instituted), he was said to plead plenarty. (See VACATION.) This plea, if proved, was at common law a good defence to the action; but the Statute of Westminster II, 1285, c. 5, enacted that it should not be a defence to an action brought by the rightful patron within six months; and it is no defence to an action at any time by the Crown (2 Co.Inst. 361).

Plenary, full, complete; an ordinary proceeding through all its gradations and formal steps as opposed to summary.

An admission or confession, whether in civil or in criminal law, is said to be plenary when it is, if believed, conclusive against the person making it.

Plenary causes in the ecclesiastical courts are suits for ecclesiastical dilapidations, suits relating to seats or sitting-places in churches, and formerly suits for tithes. See CAUSE.

Plene administravit (he has fully administered), a defence by an executor or administrator that he has fully administered all the assets which have come to his hands. If the defendant simply pleads *plene administravit* without any other defence, the plaintiff may apply to have judgment for his debt and costs of future assets *quando acciderint* (when they shall happen) (R.S.C., Ord. 14, rr. 3, 4, note 17); or he may take issue on the defence, and if successful obtain judgment to the· extent of the existing assets against the defendant and of future assets *quando acciderint* for the residue of his debt.

Plene administravit praeter (he has fully administered, except), a defence by an executor or administrator that he has fully administered the assets which have come to his hands, except, etc. The plaintiff may go to trial upon this defence, or may apply under R.S.C., Ord. 32, r. 6, for leave to sign judgment to the extent of the assets admitted and of future assets *quando acciderint* for the residue of his debt and costs (R.S.C., Ord. 14, rr. 3, 4, note 17).

Plenipotentiary, a person who has full powers (*pleins pouvoirs*) and commission to do anything, generally used in connection with ambassadors and delegates of States.

Pleno lumine, In, in broad daylight. See IN PLENO LUMINE.

Plenum dominium, a title combining the right and the corporal possession of property, which possession could not be acquired without both an actual intention to possess, and an actual seisin or entry into the premises, or part of them, in the name of the whole (Civil Law).

Plevin [Low Lat., *plevina*], a warrant or assurance; now obsolete except in the compound form replevin (*q.v.*).

Plight, an estate, with the habit and quality of the land; it extended to a rent-charge and to a possibility of dower (Co.Litt. 221b).

Plight and condition, Affidavit of, an affidavit that a will is in the same condition as when it was found, which is required when probate is sought of a will bearing any unusual marks, etc.

Plight, Schedule of, a list of defects attached to a lease or tenancy agreement when the premises are not in good repair at the time of the letting and the tenant undertakes to deliver up the premises at the end of the term only in as good a state of repair as they were in at the commencement.

Plimsoll mark, the load line or mark along a ship's side to mark the depth to which her proper cargo causes her to sink. Overloading is punishable with a fine of £400 plus a further £400 for every inch the load line is submerged (Merchant Shipping (Load Lines) Act, 1967, ss. 2–4). As to the effect of overloading on a contract of carriage, see *St. John Shipping Corporation* v. *Joseph Rank* [1957] 1 Q.B. 267.

Plough, plough-land (*q.v.*).

Plough-alms [*eleemosynae aratrales*], a payment of a penny to the Church from every plough-land (1 Dugd.Mon. 256).

Plough-bote, the right to take wood for the repair of ploughs, carts and harrows, and for making rakes, forks, etc. See ESTOVERS.

Plough-land, a hide of land, a carucate; a quantity of land not of any certain extent, but as much as a plough can by course of husbandry plough in a year (Co. Litt. 69a, 86b).

It was probably about 120 acres, and was divided into acres (*q.v.*) and virgates, a virgate being one fourth of a hide (2 Holds.H.E.L. 66).

In Anglo-Saxon times a plough, or plough-land, in the northern and eastern counties, meant as much land as could be tilled in a year by one team of eight oxen; and it seems also to have included originally the meadow and pasture land of the holding. The corresponding term in the other counties was the hide of land. Both terms seem to be represented in Domesday and other Latin records by *carrucata.* See CARUCATE; OXGANG; SULUNG; YARDLAND.

Plough-Monday, the Monday after Twelfth-Day or Epiphany (*q.v.*).

Ploughing grants, contributions made by the Government towards the cost of ploughing up land under the Agriculture (Ploughing Grants) Act, 1952, as amended by the Agriculture Act, 1970, s. 36 and extended by the Agriculture (Small Farmers) Act, 1959, s. 2 (2) (*a*).

Plow alms. See PLOUGH-ALMS.

Plowden, Edmund. He was born in 1518, entered the Middle Temple in 1538,

and was subsequently called to the Bar; he died in 1585. He is best known by his Commentaries, or Reports, covering the period 1550–78. On the title-page of the portion published in 1571 he describes himself as *un apprentice de la comen ley*, which indicated that, although a barrister, he was not a serjeant-at-law, as he would have been but for his refusal to conform to the established church. See APPRENTICII AD LEGEM.

Plumage. See the Importation of Plumage (Prohibition) Act, 1921.

Plunderage, embezzling goods on shipboard.

Plural. See SINGULAR.

Pluralist, one who holds more than one ecclesiastical benefice with cure of souls.

Plurality, majority; in greater number than one. Pluralities, that is the holding of more than one ecclesiastical benefice at a time, or in plurality, are restricted.

A pastoral scheme may provide for the holding in plurality of any two or more benefices (Pastoral Measure 1968, s. 17). See further s. 88 and the Clergy (Ordination and Miscellaneous Provisions) Measure, 1964, s. 11.

Plures cohaeredes sunt quasi unum corpus propter unitatem juris quod habent (Co.Litt. 163). (Several co-heirs are, as it were, one body, by reason of the unity of right which they possess.)

Plures participes sunt quasi unum corpus, in eo quod unum jus habent. (Co. Litt. 164). (Several sharers are as one body, in that they have one right.) This is a quotation from Fleta which Coke uses to illustrate the law as to coparceners.

Pluries (as often), a writ which issued in the third instance, after the first and the *alias* had been ineffectual. See ALIAS WRIT; EXECUTION.

Plus petitio, or **Pluris petitio,** when a demandant included in his demand (in the *intentio* of the formula) more than his due (Just.Inst. 4.6.33).

Plus valet quod agitur quam quod simulate concipitur. (What is done more avails than what is pretended to be done.)

Plus valet unus oculatus testis quam auriti decem (4 Co.Inst. 279). (One eyewitness is worth more than ten witnesses who can speak only from hearsay.) Hearsay evidence is inadmissible except in certain cases. See HEARSAY.

Plus valet vulgaris consuetudo quam regalis concessio (Co.Copyh. 31). (Common custom has more power than royal grant.) No royal grant could create the immemorial custom essential to a manor.

Plutonium. For powers of searching for uranium, thorium, plutonium, neptunium and other substances useful for the production of atomic energy see the Atomic Energy Act, 1946, ss. 6, 18 (1).

Pluvius policy, a rain insurance policy; a policy providing that if rain up to a given amount should fall during certain stated hours a certain sum will be paid; used to insure open-air functions against loss through a wet day.

Pneumoconiosis. See BYSSINOSIS.

Poaching, the popular name for the offence of unlawfully taking or destroying game (*q.v.*) on another man's land; it is part of the title of the Poaching Prevention Act, 1862, though the offences dealt with in that Act are not described in it as poaching. It also means taking fish, *e.g.*, salmon and trout, by illegal methods.

Trespassing in the daytime in pursuit of game (*i.e.*, hares, pheasants, partridges, grouse, heath or moor game, black game, or bustards), or woodcock, snipe, quails, landrail, or rabbits, is punishable summarily by a fine up to £20, and, in the case of a trespass by five or more, up to £50; the leave of the occupier is no defence if the landlord or other person has by reservation the right to kill the game (Game Act, 1831, ss. 2, 20; Game Laws (Amendment) Act, 1960, s. 4). Occupiers of land and certain other persons (*e.g.*, gamekeepers) may require any person found in pursuit of game in the daytime to quit the land and give his name and address, and if he fails to do so may apprehend him. These powers are exercisable by a police constable (Game Act, 1831, s. 31; Game Laws (Amendment) Act, 1960, s. 1 (2)). A constable has powers of entry (Act of 1960, s. 2). A police constable by or in whose presence a person was apprehended may search him and seize and detain any game or rabbits or any gun, part of a gun, or cartridges or other ammunition or any nets, traps, snares or other devices

of a kind used for the killing or taking of game or rabbits which are found in his possession. If he is convicted these articles may be forfeited. If no conviction takes place the articles or the value thereof must be restored (Game Laws (Amendment) Act, 1960, s. 4).

Unlawfully taking game in the night, *i.e.*, between the expiration of the first hour after sunset and the commencement of the first hour before sunrise, is punishable summarily by imprisonment; and any persons, to the number of three or more, by night unlawfully entering lands for the purpose of taking or destroying game or rabbits (any of them being armed with any gun or other offensive weapon) are each guilty of a misdemeanour, and liable to seven years' imprisonment (Night Poaching Act, 1828). A police constable may arrest persons trespassing in pursuit of game by night (Game Laws (Amendment) Act, 1960, s. 1 (1)), and has powers of entry for this purpose (s. 2). For powers of search and forfeiture see s. 4, noted above.

Any constable in any highway or public place may search any person whom he may have good cause to suspect of coming from any land where he has been unlawfully in search of game (which means for the purpose of the Act, hares, pheasants, partridges, eggs of pheasants or partridges, woodcock, snipe, rabbits, grouse, black or moor game, or eggs of grouse, black or moor game) and having in his possession any game unlawfully obtained, or any gun, or part of a gun or cartridges and other ammunition and nets, traps, snares and other devices of a kind used for the killing or taking of game, and may stop and search any cart or other conveyance in which such constable shall have good cause to suspect that any such game, etc., is being carried by any such person, and should there be found any game, etc., upon such person, cart or conveyance, may seize such game, etc. (*Stone* v. *Benstead* [1909] 2 K.B. 415); the constable must in such case apply to a justice for a summons citing such person to appear before two justices who may impose a fine of £50 and order that any game, gun or other article seized be forfeited. If no conviction takes place the game or other thing seized or the value thereof must be restored (Poaching Prevention Act, 1862, ss. 1, 2; Game Laws (Amendment) Act, 1960, ss. 3, 5 (3)).

As to unlawfully taking fish in private water, see FISHERY.

Carrying a shotgun on a poaching expedition may result in the revocation of a firearms licence (*Ackers* v. *Taylor* [1974] 1 W.L.R. 405).

Pocket judgment, a colloquial equivalent for a statute merchant (*q.v.*), the holder of which had, so to speak, a judgment in his pocket, inasmuch as he could, upon non-payment on the date fixed, levy execution as if he had recovered a judgment.

Pocket-sheriff. If the Crown appointed as sheriff a person who was not one of the three persons nominated for the office in the Exchequer, the person so appointed was known as a pocket-sheriff (1 Bl.Comm. 342). See PRICKING FOR SHERIFFS.

Poena, a penalty, the punishment of an offence; generally inflicted for delicts. It was not confined to a money payment, as was *multa*, a fine, but might extend to the *caput*, or status, of the offender, and was not left to the discretion of the judge, but was attached to or appointed for each particular delict (Civil Law).

Poena ex delicto defuncti, haeres teneri non debet (2 Co.Inst. 198). (The heir ought not to be bound in a penalty for the wrong done by the defunct.) See IN RESTITUTIONEM, ETC.

Poenae potius molliendae quam exasperandae sunt (3 Co.Inst. 220). (Punishments should rather be softened than aggravated.)

Poet laureate. It is stated to have been the custom of the medieval universities to invest with a wreath of laurel anyone who had taken the degree of grammar, which included rhetoric and the making of verses; and this gave him the title of *poeta laureatus*, or poet laureate. John Kay (or Caius), in dedicating to Edward IV a translation of a Latin poem, described himself as the king's humble poet laureate; but this did not necessarily mean that he held any position analogous to that of the earlier *versificator* (*q.v.*). A succession of poets

from Chaucer, who died in 1400, to Spenser, who died in 1599, acted occasionally as informal poets laureate, or court poets: and the academic use of the title *poeta laureatus* ceased. The first actual appointment as poet laureate was that of Ben Jonson in 1617. Since then the office has been conferred by letters patent on various poets, of whom Dryden, Southey, Wordsworth and Tennyson were the most notable. From 1670 the laureate got annually a butt of canary (commuted in 1813 for £27 a year): and there has always been also a small stipend. Down to 1813 the laureate wrote, or was supposed to write, an ode on each birthday of the sovereign. Now he has no definite duties. See LAUREATE.

Points of claim; Points of defence. See STATEMENT OF CLAIM; STATEMENT OF DEFENCE.

Poison [Fr. *poison*; Lat. *potio*, a drink, applied originally to a medicated drink or draught].

On a trial for murder by poisoning, evidence of a subsequent poisoning of other persons is admissible against the prisoner (*R.* v. *Geering* (1849) 18 L.J.M.C. 215; *R.* v. *Armstrong* (1922) 38 T.L.R. 631); as also of antecedent poisoning (*R.* v. *Garner* (1863) 3 F. & F. 681).

The unlawful and malicious administering of poison so as to endanger life or to inflict grievous bodily harm is punishable with ten years' imprisonment; and such administration with intent to injure, aggrieve, or annoy is punishable with up to five years' imprisonment (Offences against the Person Act, 1861, ss. 23, 24; Criminal Justice Act, 1948, s. 1 (1)). As to poisoning to procure miscarriage of a woman, see ABORTION.

The Pharmacy and Poisons Act, 1933, set up an advisory committee, called the Poisons Board, to prepare a list of substances to be treated as poisonous for the approval of the Home Secretary. The Poisons Board is continued by the Poisons Act, 1972, s. 1, Sch. 1. The list, known as the Poisons List, continues to have effect. It is divided into two parts, Part I consisting of substances which, where they are non-medicinal poisons are to be sold only by a person lawfully conducting a retail pharmacy business and Part II consisting of substances which, when they are non-medicinal poisons, are to be sold only by a person lawfully conducting a retail pharmacy business or by a person whose name is entered in a local authority's list (Act of 1972, ss. 2, 5, 6) the sale of poisons is regulated (s. 3) and Poisons Rules may be made by the Home Secretary (s. 7). As to fees payable by authorised sellers of poisons, see the Pharmacy and Poisons (Amendment) Act, 1964. See the Poisons Rules, 1972 (No. 1939); Local Authorities, etc. (Miscellaneous Provisions) (No. 2) Order, 1974 (No. 595) art. 4 (11).

As to dangerous drugs, see DRUGS, DANGEROUS. As to medicinal poisons, see the Medicines Acts, 1968 and 1971.

Penalties are imposed upon persons placing poisoned fluid or edible matter upon land, and upon persons selling or exposing for sale poisoned grain or seed, unless for bona fide use in agriculture (Protection of Animals Act, 1911, s. 8; Protection of Animals (Amendment) Act, 1927, s. 1), but poisonous gas may be used to destroy rabbits in holes (Prevention of Damage by Rabbits Act, 1939, s. 4); and hares and other rodents, deer, foxes and moles and wild birds other than protected birds (Agriculture Act, 1947, s. 98 (3) (4); Protection of Birds Act, 1954, s. 15 (1), Sch. 5). The use of poison for the purpose of destroying grey squirrels or coypus may be authorised (Agriculture (Miscellaneous Provisions) Act, 1972, s. 19).

The Protection of Animals Act, 1911, s. 1 (1) (d), restricts the administering of poisonous drugs to animals.

The Agriculture (Poisonous Substances) Act, 1952, provided for the protection of employees against risk of poisoning by substances used in agriculture. See now the Health and Safety at Work, etc., Act, 1974; S.I. 1975 Nos. 45, 46, 282.

Poison gas, the making, sale or possession of weapons or ammunition for discharge of noxious liquids or gas is prohibited by the Firearms Act, 1968, s. 5.

Pole, a measure of five and a half yards. See PERCH.

Police [πόλις, a city], the regulation and government of a country or city; the constabulary of a locality. The police forces now consist of county, Metropolitan and City of London police.

The control and administration of county police forces is provided for in the Police Act, 1964, as amended. The chief constable is vicariously liable for torts committed by the police under his command (Police Act, 1964, s. 48). See also the Police Act, 1969; the Local Government Act, 1972, ss. 107, 196, Sch. 30; the Police Pensions Act, 1976; the Police Act, 1976.

As to whether a local authority is liable for a tort committed by a member of its police force, see *Stanbury* v. *Exeter Corporation* [1905] 2 K.B. 838. Police authorities are not entitled to claim for loss of the services of police officers against persons who injure them (*Metropolitan Police District Receiver* v. *Croydon Corporation* [1957] 2 Q.B. 154). It is an offence to wear uniform which is likely to deceive persons into thinking that one is a police officer, even if that deception is not intended (*Turner* v. *Shearer* [1972] 1 W.L.R. 1387). As to wasting the time of the police, see PUBLIC MISCHIEF. As to airports, see the Policing of Airports Act, 1974. See AERODROMES; AIR NAVIGATION. Police officers are ineligible for jury service. See JURY. As to sex discrimination, see the Sex Discrimination Act, 1975, s. 17. See CONSTABLES; METROPOLITAN POLICE DISTRICT.

Police court, a magistrates' court; a petty sessional court (*q.v.*), held before the justices of the peace or in London and in a number of the large provincial cities, as well as in some thickly populated semi-urban areas, by a barrister who is known in London as a metropolitan stipendiary magistrate (*q.v.*), and elsewhere as a stipendiary magistrate (*q.v.*). The expression " police court " has been replaced by " magistrates' court " (Justices of the Peace Act, 1949, s. 44 (1)).

Police magistrate. See METROPOLITAN STIPENDIARY MAGISTRATE; STIPENDIARY MAGISTRATES.

Policies of Insurance, Court of. The preamble to the statute 1601, 43 Eliz. 1, c. 12, recited that it had long been the custom of merchants to take out policies of insurance for goods, merchandise, ships, and things adventured with bodies of insurers and that controversies which had arisen had been settled by grave and discreet merchants appointed by the Lord Mayor of London, until of late years divers persons had sought to compel the parties insured to obtain payment from each of the insurers by means of separate suits in the superior courts; and the statute then proceeded to enact that the Lord Chancellor should constitute and keep constituted a court consisting of the judge of the Admiralty, the recorder of London, two doctors of the civil law, two common lawyers and eight grave and discreet merchants, for the summary decision, subject to appeal to the Court of Chancery, of all disputes as to policies of insurance entered at the office of insurance in the City of London. This enactment was amended by the statute 1662, 14 Car. 2, c. 23. The court fell into disuse during the eighteenth century, and both the statutes above referred to were repealed by the Statute Law Revision Act, 1863.

Policy [πολιτεια, πόλις, a city or state; Med. Lat., *politia,* government of a state], the general principles by which a government is guided in its management of public affairs, or the legislature in its measures. Policy, as applied to a statute, regulation, rule of law, course of action, or the like, refers to its probable effect, tendency or object, considered with reference to the social or political well-being of the State.

Thus certain classes of acts are said to be against public policy (*q.v.*) when the law refuses to enforce or recognise them on the ground that they have a mischievous tendency so as to be injurious to the interests of the State, apart from illegality (*q.v.*) or immorality (*q.v.*). Thus, trading with an enemy without licence from the Crown, marriage-brokage contracts, and agreements in general restraint of marriage or trade (*q.v.*), are instances of acts against public policy. The policy of the law seems to be the same thing as public policy (*q.v.*).

The policy of a statute, or of the legislature as applied to a statute, means the intention with which a statute was passed or by which Parliament was actuated.

Policy of insurance [Ital. *polizza,* an instrument under seal; Lat. *pollex,* a seal], a contract between A and B that, upon A's paying a premium equivalent to the hazard run, B will indemnify or insure him against a particular event. A policy is an instrument containing a contract of insurance, and is called a maritime (or marine), fire, life or accident policy, according to the nature of the insurance. See INSURANCE.

Maritime policies are either unvalued (or open) or valued (Marine Insurance Act, 1906, s. 27 (1)). An unvalued policy is where the value of the thing insured is not stated in the policy (s. 28), and must therefore be proved if a loss happens. A valued policy is where the value of the thing is settled by agreement between the parties and inserted in the policy (s. 27 (2)). An insurance may be effected either for a voyage or for a number of voyages, in either of which cases the policy is called a voyage policy; or the insurance may be for a particular period, not exceeding twelve months, irrespective of the voyage or voyages upon which the vessel may be engaged during that period, and the policy is then called a time policy; in addition to the two last-mentioned kinds of policy, there is a third, which is usually called a mixed policy, as, for instance, where a ship is insured from one port to another for a year, this being in effect a time policy with the voyage specified. Voyage policies, time policies, and mixed policies are all sanctioned by s. 25 of the Act.

Before the Acts forbidding insurances by persons having no interest in the subject-matter of insurance, it was sometimes provided in the policy that it should be valid whether the insurer had any interest or not, in order to dispense with proof of interest in case of loss; these were called " interest or no interest policies " or " wager policies." See INTEREST; POLICY PROOF OF INTEREST.

Life policies for the whole life of the *cestui que vie, i.e.,* payable whenever the death happens are called whole life policies; a policy for a term of years gives no right to the sum insured unless the life drops within the period.

When a fire insurance is made for a limited period (*e.g.*, a year) it is called a time policy. When it is made to insure not any specific goods, but the goods which may at the time of the fire be in a certain building, it is called a floating policy.

The Policies of Assurance Act, 1867, enabled assignees of life policies to sue thereon in their own names. The Marine Insurance Act, 1906, s. 50 (2), makes like provision in regard to marine policies. See ASSIGN; ASSURANCE; CHOSE; LOST OR NOT LOST; MEMORANDUM; UNDERWRITER.

Policy proof of interest; P.P.I., a policy of marine insurance purported to be made valid by its terms although the insurer had no insurable interest. Such a policy in the absence of an insurable interest is made void by the Gaming Act, 1845, s. 18. The Marine Insurance Act, 1906, s. 4, declares such policies void. The Marine Insurance (Gambling Policies) Act, 1909, makes it an offence to effect a contract of marine insurance without an insurable interest.

Politiae legibus non leges politiis adaptandae (Hob. 154). (Politics are to be adapted to the laws, and not the laws to politics.)

Political fund, the separate fund out of which a trade union may apply money in furtherance of political objects (Trade Union Act, 1913, s. 3; *Birch* v. *National Union of Railwaymen* [1950] Ch. 602).

Political offence. For the purposes of the laws under which various offences are punishable within the United Kingdom, there is not, and there never has been, such a thing as a political offence. A person committing any given offence is liable to the one punishment whether he commits it from political motives or from motives which are not political. But, as regards offenders whose extradition to or from this country is sought, there is a distinction between political and other offences. Offences of a political character are invariably excepted in extradition treaties from the list of offences for which extradition may be obtained; and the Extradition Act, 1870, s. 3, provides that a fugitive offender shall not be surrendered by this country if the offence for which his extradition is demanded is of a political character. In this country, an offence of a political character is held to mean any offence committed in connection with or as part of political disturbances (*Re Castioni* [1891] 1 Q.B. 149; *Re Meunier* [1894] 2 Q.B. 415). Genocide is not an offence of a political character (Genocide Act, 1969, s. 2 (2)). See EXTRADITION.

Political uniforms. See PUBLIC ORDER.

Polity [πολιτεία, the government of a city], the form of government; civil constitution.

Poll, to give a vote at an election; also to receive a vote; also a taking of votes of all persons entitled to vote present, by proxy, or otherwise, as opposed to counting the votes of voters present at a meeting.

As to taking a poll at parliamentary and local government elections by secret voting, see the Representation of the People Act, 1949, s. 53. As to the countermand or abandonment of a poll on the death of a candidate see the Representation of the People Act, 1969, s. 13.

Wherever a person has to be chosen, or a thing may be ordered to be done, by the majority of persons entitled to vote, there is a common law right to demand a poll, so that all entitled to vote may have a second opportunity of voting (*R.* v. *Wimbledon Local Board* (1881) 8 Q.B.D. 459). Voting papers are allowed if the articles of association or other regulations so provide (*McMillan* v. *Le Roi Mining Co.* [1906] 1 Ch. 331). As to the power of the chairman to direct a poll to be taken forthwith, *i.e.,* at the meeting, see *Re Chillington Iron Co.* (1885) 29 Ch.D. 159; *Re British Flax Co.* (1889) 60 L.T. 215. The taking of a poll is not a meeting (*Shaw* v. *Tati Concessions* [1913] 1 Ch. 292). For the purposes of the Companies Act, 1948, s. 182, a person is not elected a director of a company where a poll has been demanded until the result of the poll has been ascertained (*Holmes* v. *Keyes* [1959] Ch. 199).

See CHALLENGE; DEED-POLL.

Pollards, or **Pollengers,** trees which have been lopped, distinguished from timber-trees (Plowd. 649).

Pollicitation, a promise before it is accepted (Civil Law).

Pollock's Act, the Limitation of Actions and Costs Act, 1842.

Polls, Challenge to the. See CHALLENGE.

Poll-tax; Poll-money; Poll-silver, a tax upon every poll or head, that is to say, upon every person. Sometimes the tax was levied equally on all persons, as in the case of the poll-tax, which led to the rebellion of Wat Tyler; at other times it was graduated according to the rank of the payer, as in the case of the poll-tax imposed by the statute 1666, 18 & 19 Car. 2, c. 1, s. 10, which ran from £100 in the case of a duke to £5 in the case of an esquire, and from £50 in the case of an archbishop to £5 in the case of a doctor of divinity.

Pollution. The Prevention of Oil Pollution Act, 1971, consolidated the Navigable Waters Acts, 1955, 1963 and 1971, and some other enactments. It prohibits pollution by oil within and without the territorial waters of the United Kingdom by ships, hovercraft and pipe-lines or as the result of exploration for oil. A fine may be imposed on summary conviction of an offence of oil pollution not exceeding £50,000. On conviction on indictment there is no prescribed limit to a fine. In the case of shipping casualties liable to cause oil pollution in the United Kingdom or in territorial waters, the Secretary of State has unlimited powers for dealing with the emergency. The Merchant Shipping (Oil Pollution) Act, 1971, makes provision with respect to civil liability for oil pollution by merchant ships and hovercraft.

The Merchant Shipping Act, 1974, sets up the International Oil Pollution Compensation Fund (ss. 1–9). As to restrictions on oil tankers see ss. 10–13. Pollution of rivers can also be dealt with by injunction (*Pride of Derby and Derbyshire Angling Association* v. *British Celanese* [1953] Ch. 149). An action for an injunction may be supported by an association of riparian owners without committing champerty (*Martell* v. *Consett Iron Co.* [1955] Ch. 363).

The dumping of articles in the sea is controlled by the Dumping at Sea Act, 1974.

The Control of Pollution Act, 1974, makes further provision with respect to waste disposal, water pollution, noise, atmospheric pollution and public health. Part I (ss. 1–25) makes arrangements for waste disposal (see WASTE DISPOSAL). Part II (ss. 26–51) deals with the pollution of water (see WATER). Part III (ss. 52–69) deals with noise (see NOISE). Part IV (ss. 70–78) deals with pollution of the atmosphere (see AIR).

An appeal against any decision of a magistrates' court (other than a decision made in criminal proceedings) lies to the Crown Court (s. 85). As to the liability of officers of corporations, see s. 87 (1). Where the commission by any person of an offence under the Act is due to the act or default of some other person, that other person is guilty of the offence and may be convicted thereof whether or not any proceedings are taken against any other person (s. 87 (2)). An information may be laid within one year of the commission of an offence (s. 87 (3)). A judge or a justice of the peace is not disqualified from acting by being a ratepayer (s. 87 (6)). Any person may be required by notice to furnish information required under the Act (s. 93). Disclosure of information is an offence under s. 94. See also the Border Rivers (Prevention of Pollution) Act, 1951, the Rivers Prevention of Pollution Act, 1961, s. 12; the Water Act, 1973, Sch. 9, Sch. 13 para. 15, Sch. 14 Pt. I; the Control of Pollution Act, 1974, Sch. 3 para. 17; Salmon and Freshwater Fisheries Act, 1975, s. 4. The importation and use, etc., of injurious substances may be prohibited (Act of 1974, s. 100). For the Final Act of the International Conference of Marine Pollution, 1973, see Cmnd. 5748. For the Convention for the prevention of marine pollution from land-based sources (Paris, June 4, 1974), see Cmnd. 5803.

Polyandry, the state of a woman who has several husbands. See BIGAMY.

Polygamy [πολύς, many; ἀρχή, marriage], plurality of wives or husbands. It is prohibited by the Christian religion, but permitted by some others. See BIGAMY.

As to the rights of succession of the issue of a polygamous marriage to personal property in England, see *Bamgbose* v. *Daniel* [1955] A.C. 107.

Matrimonial relief may be granted in

respect of a polygamous marriage (Matrimonial Causes Act, 1973, ss. 11, 47).

Polygarchy [πολύς, many; αρχή, government], that kind of government which is in the hands of many.

Pond. As to the powers of a local authority to deal with ponds, ditches and watercourses, see the Public Health Act, 1936, ss. 259 *et seq.*, and the London Government Act, 1963, s. 40, Sch. 11 Pt. II para. 1.

Pondus, poundage, *i.e.*, a duty paid to the Crown according to the weight of merchandise.

Pondus regis, the king's weight. This was anciently a synonym for troy weight (*q.v.*). There seems to have been an idea that troy weight was a corruption of *le roy* weight (though it was actually derived from Troyes, the town at which it first came into use), and this led someone to invent the *pondus regis* as being the true and original form of *le roy* weight (Cowel).

Pone. If goods had been replevied by virtue of a *replegiari facias*, the plaint in county court was removed into the King's Bench or Common Pleas by writ of *pone*. It was an original writ obtained from the cursitor, bearing *teste* after the entry of the plaint in the county court, and returnable on a general day in term. It was also the proper writ to remove all suits which were before the sheriff by writ of *justicies* (Fitz.Nat.Brev. 4, 69; 2 Co. Inst. 339).

Pone per vadium, a writ to the sheriff to summon the defendant to appear and answer the plaintiff's suit, on his putting in sureties to prosecute: it was so called from the words of the writ, *pone per vadium et salvos plegios* (put by gage and safe pledges) A. B., the defendant (Finch, 345). See TOLT.

Ponendis in assisis, a writ granted by the Statute of Westminster II, 1285, c. 38. It related to the impanelling of assizes (Reg.Orig. 175: Fitz.Nat.Brev. 165).

Ponendum in ballium, a writ which ordered a prisoner to be bailed in cases bailable (Reg.Brev. 133).

Ponendum sigillum ad exceptionem, a writ by which judges were required to put their seals to exceptions exhibited by a defendant against a plaintiff's evidence, verdict, or other proceedings before them, according to the Statute of Westminster II, 1285, c. 31. See BILL OF EXCEPTIONS.

Pontage [Lat. *pons*, a bridge], a duty paid for the reparation of bridges; also, a due to the lord of the fee for persons or merchandise passing over rivers, bridges, etc. (Tomlin). See TRINODA NECESSITAS.

Pontibus reparandis, a writ which was directed to the sheriff commanding him to cause the owner of a bridge to repair it (Reg.Orig. 153).

Pool, a small lake of standing water. By the grant of a pool, both the land and water will pass (Co.Litt. 5).

Pools, Football. See BETTING.

Poor knights, the Knights of Windsor (*q.v.*).

Poor law, the law which related to the public or compulsory relief of the indigent poor. The subject was first dealt with by the statute 1535, 27 Hen. 8, c. 25. By the Poor Relief Act, 1601, overseers of the poor were appointed in every parish, to provide for the relief of paupers settled in their parish (see SETTLEMENT OF PAUPERS), the necessary funds being produced by a poor rate levied on property within the parish (see RATE). The system of overseers being unsatisfactory, the statute 1782, 22 Geo. 3, c. 83, authorised a parish to appoint guardians in lieu of overseers, and also to enter into a voluntary union with one or more other parishes for the more convenient accommodation, maintenance and employment of their paupers in common (see GUARDIANS OF THE POOR; OVERSEERS; VESTRY). By the Poor Law Amendment Act, 1834, the general management of the poor, and of the funds for their relief, was placed under the superintendence and control of a body called the Poor Law Commissioners, whose functions were transferred by the Poor Law Board Act, 1847, and the Poor Law Amendment Acts, 1849 and 1867, to the Poor Law Board and by the Local Government Board Act, 1871, to the Local Government Board, which by the Ministry of Health Act, 1919, became the Ministry of Health, which had the power of making general poor law rules (Poor Law Amendment Act, 1834, s. 15), and of compulsorily consolidating any two or more parishes into one union for the relief and management of their paupers, or of constituting separate parishes out of divided parishes or amalgamating parts of divided parishes with other parishes (Divided Parishes and Poor Law Amendment Act, 1876, ss. 1–9).

By the Poor Relief Act, 1601, overseers of the poor were annually appointed in every parish, the churchwardens of every parish being *ex-officio* overseers, except in rural parishes, in which the churchwardens ceased to be overseers by virtue of the Local Government Act, 1894.

Overseers of the poor and boards of guardians were abolished by the Rating and Valuation Act, 1925, and their powers, duties and property were transferred to local authorities.

The Poor Law Act, 1930, consolidated the enactments relating to the relief of the poor, and repealed the greater part of the Poor Law Act, 1927, but did not provide for all the powers and duties which had been conferred on overseers of the poor and boards of guardians by various statutes relating to vaccination, bastardy, and lunacy, the functions of boards of guardians in connection with which were transferred to local authorities by the Local Government Act, 1929. The Poor Law Act, 1934, amended the Poor Law Act, 1930, so as to secure uniformity throughout Great Britain in the provisions relating to the disregarding of sick pay, maternity benefit, and wounds or disability pensions in connection with relief.

The duty of making and levying the poor-rate or parochial fund, out of which the relief was to be afforded, belonged to the churchwardens and overseers; and the concurrence of the inhabitants was not necessary. But for the better execution of these duties, the appointment of collectors and assistant overseers was authorised. They were abolished by the Rating and Valuation Act, 1925. The rate was raised prospectively for some given portion of the year, and upon a scale adapted to the probable exigencies of the parish; and the Poor Relief Act, 1601, directed that it should be raised by taxation of every inhabitant,

parson, vicar, etc., and of every occupier of lands, houses, tithes impropriate, appropriations of tithes, coal mines, or saleable underwoods in the parish. By the Rating Act, 1874, the liability to rates was extended to land used for a plantation or wood, or for the growth of saleable underwood, and not subject to any right of common, to rights of fowling, shooting, taking, or killing game or rabbits, and fishing, when severed from the occupation of the land; and to mines of every kind not mentioned in the Poor Relief Act, 1601. As an occupier, a man was rateable for all lands which he occupied in the parish, whether resident or not; but the tenant and not the landlord was considered as the occupier.

The poor rate became part of the general rate under the Rating and Valuation Act, 1925, which consolidated the rates levied by different authorities and enlarged the unit of administration so as to secure uniformity, the power to make rates being conferred on the rating authority, with special provisions for representation of every parish in rural areas.

All those in need of relief were entitled to be relieved in the parish (or union) in which they happened to be, whether they were settled or casual poor (see IRREMOVABILITY; REMOVAL; SETTLEMENT). Aliens had the same right to relief as natural-born subjects. In many cases there was a person bound to maintain a pauper in exoneration of the guardians: as where the pauper had a wife, husband, child, parent, or grandparent, able to maintain him or her.

Penalties were imposed on persons who refused or neglected to work to maintain their families, or deserted them, leaving them chargeable to the parish (Nicholls, *History of the English Poor Law*; Webb, *English Poor Law History*).

The poor law was abolished by the National Assistance Act, 1948, and national assistance (*q.v.*), administered by branch offices of the National Assistance Board, substituted.

Poor law union, any parish or union of parishes for which there was a separate board of guardians (Interpretation Act, 1889, s. 16).

Poor persons. A person might be admitted to take or defend or be a party to legal proceedings in the High Court as a poor person, if he was not worth a sum exceeding £50 excluding wearing apparel, tools of trade, and the subject-matter of the proceedings) or exceptionally £100, and if his income did not exceed £2 a week or exceptionally £4 a week. The poor person had a solicitor and counsel assigned to him free of cost; he paid no costs to the other side except as specially ordered, and his own costs were limited to out-of-pocket expenses, unless he recovered money in the case; and he made no deposit except in matrimonial cases, in which he had to deposit at the least £5 in ordinary cases and £20 at the least in nullity cases involving medical examination.

The provision of free legal assistance to poor persons by counsel and solicitors on the panel of persons willing to give such assistance was superseded by legal aid under the Legal Aid and Advice Acts, 1949 to 1972, which were consolidated by the Legal Aid Act, 1974. See LEGAL AID.

Poor prisoners. See COSTS IN CRIMINAL PROCEEDINGS.

Popery. See PAPIST.

Popular action, an action brought by a member of the public to recover a penalty given by statute to any person who chose to sue for it. Proceedings by common informers (q.v.) were abolished by the Common Informers Act, 1951. See PENAL ACTION; QUI TAM.

Population. The Population (Statistics) Act, 1938, s. 1, requires information to be furnished on the registration of births and deaths for the purpose of providing statistical information as to the population. The Act was amended by the Registration Service Act, 1953, Sch. 2, and the Population (Statistics) Act, 1960, which made the Act of 1938 permanent.

Porrect. In the procedure of the ecclesiastical courts this means to submit for examination or approval. Porrecting means producing for examination or taxation, as porrecting a bill of costs, by a proctor, or putting in a draft sentence for the Court of Chivalry to pronounce (*Manchester Corporation* v. *Manchester Palace of Varieties* [1955] P. 133).

Port, a place for the lading or unlading of ships, created by royal charter or lawful prescription (*Foreman* v. *Free Fishers and Dredgers of Whitstable* (1869) L.R. 4 H.L., at p. 285). *Portus est locus in quo exportantur et importantur merces* (a port is a place where goods are exported and imported) (2 Co.Inst. 148).

A port is a harbour where customs officers are established, and where goods are either imported or exported to foreign countries, as distinguished from a mere harbour (q.v.) or haven (q.v.), which is simply a place, natural or artificial, for the safe riding of ships. It is said that every port comprehends a city or borough (sometimes called *caput portus*), with a market and accommodation for sailors (*Hunter* v. *Northern Marine Insurance Co.* (1888) 13 App.Cas. 722). No person may land customable goods on his own land or elsewhere than at a port. The privilege of erecting ports and taking dues and tolls as incident thereto is part of the royal prerogative, and can belong to a subject as a franchise only by grant or prescription from the Crown, or by Act of Parliament. The owner of the port is bound to keep it in repair (Moore, *Foreshore*, 322). See TOLL.

In other respects a port is the same thing as a harbour (q.v.).

Port also in Saxon times meant a city or town. See PORTMEN; PORTMOTE; PORTGREVE; PORTSALE; PORTSOKEN.

As to airports, see AERODROMES.

Port health authority. See QUARANTINE; SANITARY AUTHORITY.

Port wine. The use of the word " port " is confined to wine the produce of Portugal (Anglo-Portuguese Commercial Treaty Acts, 1914 and 1916). An offence is committed by using the word " port " in conjunction with another word, such as " Tarragona port " (*Sandeman* v. *Gold* [1924] 1 K.B. 107).

Portatica, port-duties charged on ships.
Portcullis. See HERALD.
Porteous mob, an extraordinary riot and conspiracy which occurred in Edinburgh in 1736. On the occasion of the execution of a man named Wilson, Porteous, the Captain of the City Guard, fearing a riot, had given orders to fire on the crowd who had assembled to witness the spectacle, and several persons were killed. For this he was tried and sen-

tenced to death, but on the eve of his execution he was respited by orders from London. This enraged the mob, with whom Porteous was very unpopular, with the result that they rose, stormed the Tolbooth in which Porteous was confined, and themselves hanged him in the Grassmarket. See Scott, *Heart of Midlothian.*

Porter, an officer who carried a white rod before the justices in eyre, so called *a portando virgam*: see the statute 1285, 13 Edw. 1, c. 41. There was also a porter who bore a verge before the justices of either bench (Cowel).

Porters in the City of London are regulated by the Corporation. See PORTERS, COMPANY OF.

Porter is also a form of beer (Customs and Excise Act, 1952, s. 307 (1)).

Porterage, a duty paid at the customhouse to those who attended the waterside, which belonged to the packageoffice; also, the charge made for sending parcels. See PACKAGE.

Porters, Company of. The metage (*q.v.*) rights of the City of London were exercised through the Company of Porters. The abolition of those rights led in 1894 to the abolition of the Company by an act of the Court of Common Council.

Porteus's Act, the Sunday Observance Act, 1780.

Portgreve; Portreeve. In the time of the Conqueror the authorities of the City of London were the bishop, the portgreve, and the burgesses. The portgreve was in fact the predecessor of the mayor, or Lord Mayor (see LONDON). The portreeve was everywhere the chief municipal magistrate at the time of the Conquest. In most places he was replaced by the mayor, but in many small towns he survived until modern times, as at Crediton, Holsworthy and Tavistock.

Portion, property settled or provided in favour of children or their issue. In settlements by deed or will of personal property, portions are usually effected by direct trusts in favour of the children or issue, either immediately or after the death of the parent or parents. When land is settled in strict settlement, that is to say, on the husband for life with remainder in tail to the eldest son, it is usual to provide for the payment to the younger children (that is, all except the one who takes the estate) of gross sums of money, on their attaining twenty-one, or, in the case of daughters, marrying. To enable these portions to be raised, the land is generally limited to trustees for a long term of years with power to mortgage it. (See ATTENDANT TERM; OUTSTANDING TERM; SETTLEMENT; TERM.) This term preceded the settlement of the estate for life or in tail according to the intention of the settlor. This method is still available although the term is not a legal estate and will not affect a purchaser even with notice who takes his title from an estate owner who is entitled to sell the estate unaffected by the term, but the trustees entitled to the term may require to have the term secured by a legal mortgage (Law of Property Act, s. 3 (1); Settled Land Act, s. 16, Sch. 1 Form 3). Settlements of portions usually contain a provision for hotchpot and maintenance of infants and advancement of capital before the period of vesting or distribution. Interest is payable on portions from the time they become due. All causes and matters connected with the raising of portions or other charges on lands are assigned to the Chancery Division (Judicature Act, 1925, s. 56).

As to the operation of the rule against double portions, by which a child is prevented from taking both a sum paid to him as a portion and a legacy bequeathed to him as a portion, see SATISFACTION.

Portioner, a minister who serves a benefice together with others, so called because he had only a portion of the tithes or profits of the living; also an allowance which a vicar commonly has out of a rectory or impropriation.

Portjoye, an early officer of the Chancery whose principal duty was to keep the sumpter-horse which carried the hanapers (*q.v.*) when the Chancery went into the provinces.

Portman-mote, the assembly of the portmen (*q.v.*) or citizens of a town.

Portmen. In Old English this meant the inhabitants of towns generally, and later it meant the inhabitants of the Cinque Ports in particular. In a narrower sense it meant citizens having authority within a town; thus formerly the municipal authority at Ipswich was the Mayor, the Portmen and the Common Council, while at Oxford it was the Mayor, eight Portmen, and twelve Capital Burgesses (Camd.Brit.).

Portmote, a court held in haven towns or ports, and sometimes in inland counties. It meant either the portman-mote (*q.v.*) or (more especially in the county palatine of Chester and in the Cinque Ports) the court of a town: see the statute 1601, 43 Eliz. 1, c. 15.

Portoria, duties paid in ports on merchandise (Civil Law).

Portrait. Where a portrait is ordered and made for valuable consideration, the person who gave the order is owner of the copyright (Copyright Act, 1956, s. 4).

Portsale, a sale in the town; a public sale of goods, more especially a public sale of fish at the place where they were landed: see the statute 1533, 25 Hen. 8, c. 4. See PORT.

Portsoka, Portsoken, Portsokne [Old Eng. *port*, town; *soca*, jurisdiction], the suburbs of a city, or any place within its jurisdiction; the liberties of the City of London which were granted to the City by Henry III. They were outside the walls of the City. In the pleas of the time of Edward I there is reference to steps for the putting down of murder within the City and in Portsokne. They now form the Ward of Portsoken.

Portuas, a breviary.

Positio, a claim.

Positive evidence, proof of the very fact; opposed to negative evidence.

Positive law, rules of conduct laid down and enforced by sovereign sanctions as distinguished from such entities as the " law of nature," which is merely a series of propositions as to what the law ought to be. See LAW; MALA PROHIBITA.

Positivism. In international law, this means the method which attemps to present law as actually applied in State practice.

Posse, a possibility. A thing is said to be *in posse* when it may possibly be; *in esse* when it actually is.

Posse comitatus, the power of the county; an assemblage of the able-bodied male inhabitants above the age of fifteen of a county, except peers and clergymen. The sheriff of the county may summon the *posse comitatus* to defend the county against the enemies of the Crown, or to keep the peace, or to pursue felons, or to enforce the royal writ. Persons failing to obey the summons are liable to fine and imprisonment. The use of the *posse* fell into disuse as the result of the establishment of the police forces during the last century: but the power to call out the *posse* remained in law until the repeal of the Sheriffs Act, 1887, s. 8 (1) by the Criminal Law Act, 1967, Sch. 3.

Possessio, possession. In the civil law *possessio* is the condition or power by virtue of which a man has such a mastery over a corporeal thing as to be able to deal with it as his pleasure, and to exclude other persons from meddling with it. This condition or power is detention; and it lies at the bottom of all legal senses of the word " possession." This possession is no legal state or condition, but it may be the source of rights, and it then becomes *possessio* in a juristical or legal sense. Still, even in this sense it is not to be confounded with property (*proprietas*). A man may have the juristical possession of a thing without being the proprietor, and a man may be the proprietor of a thing without having the juristical possession of it, and consequently without having the detention of it (Dig. 41, 2, 12).

Ownership is the legal capacity to operate on a thing according to a man's pleasure, and to exclude everybody else from doing so. Possession, in the sense of detention, is the actual exercise of such a power as the owner has a right to exercise. The term *possessio* occurs in the Roman jurists in various senses. There is *possessio* generally, *possessio civilis*, and *possessio naturalis*. *Possessio* denoted, originally, bare detention; but this detention, under certain conditions, becomes a legal state inasmuch as it leads to ownership through *usucapio*. Accordingly the word *possessio*, which required no qualification so long as there was no other notion attached to *possessio*, requires such qualification when detention becomes a legal state. This detention, when it has the conditions necessary to *usucapio* (*i.e.*, when free from *vitium*, and held *ex justa causa* and *bona fide*) is called *possessio civilis,* and all other *possessio* as opposed to *civilis* is *naturalis.*

See POSSESSION.

Possessio fratris, possession of a brother. Under the old law of descent, where A had a son and a daughter by one marriage, and another son by a subsequent marriage, and died intestate seised of land in fee simple, then if the eldest son entered on the land and died without issue, the daughter took the land, because the descent was traced from the person last seised; and in this case the younger son, being of the half-blood to his brother, could not inherit from him. This was called *possessio fratris,* the rule being *possessio fratris de feodo simplici facit sororem esse haeredem* (the possession of the brother makes the sister heir) (Co.Litt. 14b; 3 Co.Rep. 41).

The Inheritance Act, 1833, provided that descent should be traced from the purchaser and not from the person last seised, so that *possessio fratris* disappeared. See DESCENT.

Possession, the visible possibility of exercising physical control over a thing, coupled with the intention of doing so, either against all the world, or against all the world except certain persons. There are, therefore, three requisites of possession. First, there must be actual or potential physical control. Secondly, physical control is not possession, unless accompanied by intention; hence, if a thing is put into the hand of a sleeping person, he has not possession of it. Thirdly, the possibility and intention must be visible or evidenced by external signs, for if the thing shows no signs of being under the control of anyone, it is not possessed; hence, if a piece of land is deserted and left without fences or other signs of occupation, it is not in the possession of anyone, and the possession is said to be vacant. The question whether possession of land is vacant is of importance in actions for recovering possession, as in such cases service of the writ is effected (under R.S.C., Ord. 10, r. 4) by posting a copy of it on part of the land. See SERVICE OF PROCESS.

Possession is actual, where a person enters into lands or tenements conveyed to him; apparent, which is a species of presumptive title, as where land descended to the heir of an abator, intruder, or disseisor, who died seised; in law, when lands had descended to a man and he had not actually entered into them; or naked, that is, mere possession, without colour of right.

The primary meaning is physical control. A secondary meaning is physical control by an agent or servant, or by relation back, *e.g.,* by the owner having entered without remaining in physical possession (*Ocean Accident etc., Corporation* v. *Ilford Gas Co.* [1905] 2 K.B. 493).

Possession may also extend over a thing in itself uncontrolled within an inclosure which is controlled, such as horses, sheep or cattle within a fenced field. See ANIMALS FERAE NATURAE.

Possession may connote different kinds of control according to the nature of the thing or right over which it is being exercised. A man may possess an estate of land; if he leases it he will be in possession of the rents and profits and the reversion, but not of the land which is in the lessee who may bring an action of trespass against the lessor. In regard to real property a mere right without possession is not sufficient to found an action of trespass; for instance, until 1926 a lessee before entry having a mere *interesse termini* could not bring an action for trespass on the land demised (*Wallis* v. *Hands* [1893] 2 Ch. 75). See POSSESSIO FRATRIS.

In regard to chattels it may be subject to a temporary interest of another, such as a bailee, if his possession is inconsistent with the owner's right to possession at the same time. The bailee is the only person who can bring an action for trespass, detinue or conversion if and so long as his contract of bailment has not been exceeded (*Donald* v. *Suckling* (1866) L.R. 1 Q.B. 585). If the owner, reversioner or person entitled, subject to the bailee's interest has suffered damage by the same acts, he may sue for the damage done to his interest, but not on the causes of action referred to.

Under the Law of Property Act, 1925, s. 205 (1) (xix), possession includes the receipt of rents and profits or the right to receive the same.

The adage, possession is nine parts of the law, means that the person in possession can only be ousted by one whose title is better than his; every claimant must succeed by the strength of his own title and not by the weakness of his antagonist's; *beati possidentes,* blessed are those in possession. For instance, if the claimant was able to show descent (*q.v.*) under the old law from the grantor of the estate, perfect except in one link of the chain, and the man in possession was a stranger, the stranger kept the estate; and so, also, if the claimant was an illegitimate son of the last owner and adopted by him, and declared by him to be designed as his heir, yet if he died without making a will in his favour, a stranger in possession had a better title.

The Statute of Forcible Entry, 1381, makes a forcible entry an indictable offence. The effect of the statute is that when a man is in possession he may use force to keep out a trespasser; but if a trespasser has gained possession, the rightful owner cannot use force to put him out, but must appeal to the law for assistance (*Beddall* v. *Maitland* (1881) 17 Ch.D. 183; *Lows* v. *Telford* (1876) 1 App.Cas. 414). But although forcible entry is a criminal offence, the person entitled to possession will not be liable in damages if he uses no more force than necessary (*Hemmings* v. *Stoke Poges Golf Club* [1920] 1 K.B. 720). See Forcible Entry; Potior est Conditio Defendentis; Potior est Conditio Possidentis.

Possession does not necessarily imply use or enjoyment; thus a warehouseman has possession of the goods entrusted to him, without having the use of them. But, inasmuch as the use of property cannot be had without possession, the term possession is frequently used as implying use and enjoyment, and in this sense is opposed to reversion, remainder, expectancy, action, etc.; thus a tenant for life in possession is one who has the immediate benefit of the property (*e.g.*, by occupation, receipt of the rents or income, etc.), as opposed to a tenant in remainder, whose right to the enjoyment of the property is deferred; a chose in possession is a chattel which can be immediately used, such as a book, while a chose in action is merely the right to obtain possession of a chattel, as in the case of a debt (2 Bl.Comm. 396). See Chose; Reduction into Possession.

Possession gives rise to peculiar rights and consequences. The principal is that a possessor has a presumptive title, that is to say, is presumed to be absolute owner until the contrary is shown, and is protected by law in his possession against all who cannot show a better title to the possession than he has (*Asher* v. *Whitlock* (1866) L.R. 1 Q.B. 1). Thus, if a person takes possession of a piece of deserted land no one can eject him from it except the rightful owner, and even he only by taking legal proceedings to prove his title. This is called the right of possession. Ordinarily, possession (unless combined with other elements) does not affect the question of ownership; and therefore if A, being wrongfully in possession of a thing, conveys it to B, B cannot retain it against the true owner, even though he may have believed A to be the true owner and paid him the value of the thing. But in a few cases possession is sufficient to enable a person without title to give a perfect title to a bona fide acquirer: thus if A steals money or a negotiable instrument from B and transfers it for value to C, who has no notice of the theft, B cannot claim it from C (see Earmark; Market Overt; Negotiable Instruments). So under the Factors Act, 1889, a person in possession of goods belonging to another may, in certain cases, sell or pledge them, so as to give a good title to the purchaser or pledgee.

In criminal law, possession frequently gives rise to a presumption against the possessor, so as to shift the burden of proof on to him. Thus the possession of stolen goods, where recent and exclusive, is, in many cases, sufficient to raise a presumption of theft (*q.v.*) or of handling stolen goods (*q.v.*) against the possessor, which he must rebut by showing that he came honestly by them; but to prove possession there must be something more than the fact that goods were found on the defendant's premises (*R.* v. *Cavendish* [1961] 1 W.L.R. 1083).

With reference to its origin, possession is either with or without right.

Rightful possession is where a person has the right to the possession of (that is, the right to possess) property, and is in the possession of it with the intention of exercising his right. This kind of possession necessarily varies with the nature of the right from which it arises; a person may be in possession of a thing by virtue of his right of ownership, or as lessee, bailee, etc.; or his possession may be merely permissive, as in the case of a licensee; or it may be a possession coupled with an interest, as in the case of an auctioneer (*Woolfe* v. *Horne* (1867) 2 Q.B.D. 358). So the right may be absolute, that is, good against all persons: or relative, that is, good against all with certain exceptions; thus a carrier or borrower of goods has a right to their possession against all the world except the owner.

In jurisprudence, the possession of a lessee, bailee, licensee, etc., is sometimes called derivative possession, while in English law the possessory interest of such a person, considered with reference to his rights against third persons who interfere with his possession, is usually called a special or qualified property, meaning a limited right of ownership. See PROPERTY.

Possession without right is called wrongful or adverse, according as the rights of the owner or those of the possessor are considered. Wrongful possession is where a person takes possession of property to which he is not entitled, so that the possession and the right of possession are in one person, and the right to possession in another. Where an owner is wrongfully dispossessed, he has a right of action to recover his property, or, if he has an opportunity, he can exercise the remedy of recaption in the case of goods, or of entry in the case of land (see ENTRY; RECAPTION). Formerly the doctrine of wrongful possession was of more importance than now, owing to the peculiar rules applicable to disseisin, intrusion, feoffments, etc. See ADVERSE POSSESSION.

A person has actual possession (*de facto* possession, possession in fact) of a thing when he exercises physical control over it. Thus a person who holds a thing in his hand has actual possession of it, and the lessee of a house is in actual possession of it while he occupies it.

A person has constructive possession (or possession in law) when someone representing him has actual possession of the thing. Thus if A, the owner of the land, leases it to B, A has constructive possession by B, and if A dies intestate leaving C his executor, C is immediately in constructive possession of the land by B, although he has never had actual possession. A person may have constructive possession of one thing because he has actual possession of another; thus if a person is in legal possession of a house he is ordinarily in constructive possession of the goods in it, or if he is in legal possession of a portion of an estate or farm he is in constructive possession of the whole of it.

Joint or concurrent possession is where two or more persons have possession of the same thing at the same time.

Under the Bills of Sale Acts, the validity of an unregistered bill of sale frequently depended upon whether the owner of the goods remained in apparent possession of them, having merely given formal possession to the creditor. Thus where the holder of an unregistered bill of sale of furniture put a man into the house, but did not interfere with the furniture in such a manner as to show that it had been taken out of the debtor's control, it was held that the possession so taken was merely formal, and that the goods remained in the apparent possession of the debtor. This doctrine of apparent possession now applies only to bills of sale to which the Bills of Sale Act (1878) Amendment Act, 1882, does not apply. See BILL OF SALE.

As to possession in the law of bankruptcy, see ORDER AND DISPOSITION; REPUTED OWNER.

In criminal law, possession is sometimes distinguished from custody. Thus if the owner of a chattel gives it to his servant to keep for him for a specific purpose or until he requires it again, the chattel is in the custody of the servant and in the possession of the master; if, however, the servant receives anything for his master from a third person (not being a fellow-servant), *e.g.*, a tradesman, he has the possession and not merely the custody of it until he places it in his master's possession by putting it into a place or thing belonging to his master, or by some similar act. The former importance of the distinction was with reference to the difference between larceny and embezzlement. See CUSTODY.

Possession is sometimes used in the old books in the technical sense of seisin or feudal possession of land. There was *jus proprietatis,* a right of ownership, *jus possessionis,* a right of seisin or possession, and *jus proprietatis et possessionis,* a right both of property and possession; and this was called *jus duplicatum,* or *droit droit.* For example, if a man was disseised of an acre of land, the disseisee had *jus proprietatis,* the disseisor had *jus possessionis,* and if the disseisee released to the disseisor, he had *jus proprietatis et possessionis* (Co.Litt. 266a; 2 Bl.Comm. 195). See DROIT; POSSESSIO FRATRIS; SEISIN.

Possession is also sometimes opposed to seisin. A lessee is possessed, and yet the lessor is still seised (Noy, Max. 64; Pollock and Wright, *Possession*).

See ENJOYMENT; POSSESSIO; QUASI-POSSESSION; SQUATTER.

Possession money, the fee to which a sheriff's officer or bailiff is entitled for keeping possession of property under a writ or warrant of execution.

Possession of ships. The Admiralty Court Act, 1840, s. 4, gave, for the first time, the Admiralty Court jurisdiction to decide all questions as to the title to or ownership of ships. See now the Administration of Justice Act, 1956, s. 1.

Possession, Writ of, the writ of execution employed to enforce a judgment to recover the possession of land. It commands the sheriff to enter the land and give possession of it to the person entitled under the judgment. It is issued under R.S.C., Ord. 45, r. 3. See EXECUTION; HABERE FACIAS POSSESSIONEM; DELIVERY, WRIT OF.

Possessory, that which arises out of or is concerned with possession. Thus a possessory action, in the days of real actions, was an action to recover the possession of land. See DROIT.

Possessory lien. A possessory lien arises at common law from an agreement express or implied. As a rule it is immaterial how possession is obtained (*Robbins v. Gray* [1895] 2 Q.B. 501; *Keene v. Thomas* [1905] 1 K.B. 136). The lien can be extinguished by tender of the amount due and may be lost by waiver express or implied, and continues only so long as actual possession is retained. See LIEN.

Possessory title, a squatter's title (*q.v.*); the title acquired by occupying land for twelve years without paying rent or otherwise acknowledging the title of the true owner (Limitation Act, 1939, s. 4). If the true owner is the Crown or a spiritual or eleemosynary corporation sole the period is thirty years. Land is usually registered under the Land Registration Act, 1925, with an absolute title on production to the registrar of such deeds and documents and other evidence showing title for the same period as would be required in the case of unregistered land. Land may be registered with a possessory title on production to the registrar of such evidence and on service of such notices as may for the time being be prescribed by rules made under the Act, but the registrar may register the title as absolute even though the application is only for registration with a possessory title (s. 4).

Possibility, a future event the happening of which is uncertain. In the law of real property, the term also signifies an interest in land which depends on the happening of such an event. In this sense, a possibility is said to be either bare or coupled with an interest. Thus, the expectation of an eldest son of succeeding to his father's land was a bare possibility, which was not recognised by law as being capable of transfer, though it might form the subject of a covenant to settle after-acquired property. If land is conveyed to A for life, and if C should be living at his death, then to B in fee, B's contingent remainder is a possibility coupled with an interest: such a possibility may be devised by will or conveyed by deed (Law of Property Act, 1925, s. 4 (2), replacing the Real Property Act, 1845, s. 6).

In the old books a distinction is drawn

between a common or near possibility, and a double or remote possibility, or possibility on a possibility. Thus, the chance that a man and a woman, both married to different persons, shall themselves marry one another, is a common possibility, and therefore a gift to two such persons, and the heirs of their two bodies, gives them an entailed interest; but if land was given to a man and two women and the heirs of their bodies, they had a joint estate for life and each of them a several inheritance, because they could not have one issue of their bodies, for there could not be a possibility upon a possibility, *viz.*, that he should marry the one first and then the other (Co.Litt. 25b, 184a; 10 Co.Rep. 50b).

The idea that there could not be a possibility on a possibility seems to have been a conceit invented by Popham C.J., but it was never really intelligible (*Whitby* v. *Mitchell* (1890) 44 Ch.D. at p. 92); it never applied to trusts of personal estate (*Re Bowles* [1902] 2 Ch. 650). It gave rise to the rule, abolished by the Law of Property Act, 1925, s. 161, that if land was limited to an unborn person for life, a remainder could not be limited so as to confer an estate by purchase on that person's issue (*Whitby* v. *Mitchell* (1890) 44 Ch.D. 85), which applied to equitable as well as to legal limitations (*Re Nash* [1910] 1 Ch. 1; *Re Park's Settlement* [1914] 1 Ch. 595). See PERPETUITY.

When an estate in fee simple conditional at common law is created, the donor has what is called a possibility of reverter (*q.v.*).

See TENANT IN TAIL AFTER POSSIBILITY OF ISSUE EXTINCT.

Possidere pro herede, to possess in the belief that one is heir (Civil Law).

Possidere pro possessore, to possess without any right and with knowledge that one is not the owner (Civil Law).

Post, after; occurring in a report or a textbook, it is used to direct the reader to a subsequent part of the book.

Post also means a conveyance for letters or dispatches, the word being derived from *positi,* the horses carrying the letters or dispatches being kept or placed at fixed stations. The word is also applied to the person who conveys the letters to the houses where he takes up and lays down his charge, and to the stages or distances between house and house; hence the phrases, post-boy, post-horse, post-house, etc.

A letter of acceptance posted, though not received, if the post has been expressly or impliedly authorised as a means of communication, creates a binding contract between the party offering and the party accepting as soon as it is posted (*Household Fire Insurance Co.* v. *Grant* (1879) 4 Ex.D. 216), but a revocation of an offer is of no effect until brought to the mind of the person to whom the offer was made, and therefore a revocation sent by post does not operate from the time of posting it (*Henthorn* v. *Fraser* [1892] 2 Ch. 27). See LETTER.

As to service by post, see SERVICE OF PROCESS.

Post and per. See PER AND POST.

Post conquestum, after the Conquest.

Post diem, after the day. Where a writ was returned after the day assigned, the *custos brevium* (*q.v.*) received a fee of fourpence (Tomlin).

Post disseisin, a writ which lay for a person who, having recovered lands by *praecipe quod reddat,* on default or reddition, was again disseised by the former disseisor; under it, the party suing it out got double damages and the disseisor was imprisoned. See ASSISE OF NOVEL DISSEISIN; PRAECIPE.

Post entry, a corrective entry (*q.v.*) made to the customs authorities by an importer whose original entry is found to be erroneous.

Post fine, a duty otherwise called the king's silver, formerly paid to the king for the *licentia concordandi,* or leave to agree the suit on the levying of a fine (2 Bl. Comm. 350). See FINE.

Post glossators, an Italian law school in the fourteenth and fifteenth centuries.

Post litem motam, after the commencement of litigation. Statements made by deceased persons, though sometimes admissible if made *ante litem motam* (before the commencement of litigation), are not admissible as a rule when made after the litigation has commenced.

Post Office. The Post Office was established in 1643 as a government service for the carriage of letters. It was reorganised under the Post Office Act, 1969, as a public authority with a chairman and six other members appointed by the Secretary of State for Industry as successor to the Minister of Posts and Telecommunications (*q.v.*). It is not to be regarded as a servant or agent of the Crown or as enjoying any status, immunity or privilege of the Crown. Its property is not to be regarded as Crown property (s. 6). The functions of the Post Office are to provide postal services (including cash on delivery services); telecommunication (*q.v.*) services, a banking service (Post Office (Banking Services) Act, 1976); other services by means of which money may be transmitted in the form of money orders, postal orders, etc.; data processing services, and other services for the government or for local or national health service authorities (Act of 1969, s. 7). The Secretary of State may direct the Post Office to do work for the government such as payment of old age and retirement pensions and family allowances. The Post Office may also be directed to do work for local authorities in the issue of dog licences (see DOG) and licences for dealing in or killing game (see GAME LICENCE) (s. 12). The Post Office has a monopoly in the transmission of all letters and, with certain exceptions, of telecommunications (ss. 23–27). In general no action in tort lies against the Post Office in respect of loss or damage suffered from failure to collect or deliver letters, failure in respect of telecommunication services or error in telephone etc. directories (s. 29). The Post Office is subject to a limited liability in respect of registered letters (s. 30).

In the case of sub-postmasters engaged prior to the creation of the Post Office as a public authority separate from the Crown, the Post Office must be deemed to have inherited the Crown's right to terminate at pleasure or at least on reasonable notice (*Malins* v. *Post Office* [1975] I.C.R. 60).

Certiori does not lie when a post office employee is suspended by a general manager acting under Post Office disciplinary procedure (*R.* v. *Post Office, ex p. Byrne* [1975] I.C.R. 221).

As to compensation payable for lost registered postal packets, see *Building and Civil Engineering Holidays Scheme Management* v. *Post Office* [1966] 1 Q.B. 247. Postal packets in the post are inviolate (s. 64).

As to the rating of hereditaments occupied by the Post Office, see the Local Government Act, 1974, s. 19, Sch. 3 para. 5.

Thefts by post office employees are likely to attract a substantial sentence of imprisonment (*R.* v. *Rendall* (1973) 57 Cr.App.R. 714).

See PENNY POST.

Post Office Users' Councils. See the Post Office Act, 1969, ss. 14, 15; Chronically Sick and Disabled Persons Act, 1970, s. 14.

Post terminum, the return of a writ, not merely after the day assigned (see POST DIEM), but after the end of the term in which that day fell. In that case the *custos brevium* (*q.v.*) received a fine of twenty pence, and the fine was also known as a *post terminum*.

Post-dating. A bill or note or cheque may be post-dated (Bills of Exchange Act, 1882, s. 13 (2)).

Post-mortem examination, a medical examination of a corpse in order to discover the cause of death. It may be ordered by a coroner (*q.v.*) under the Coroners Act, 1887, s. 21. It may be made without an inquest (Coroners (Amendment) Act, 1926, s. 21).

No post-mortem examination is to be carried out otherwise than by or in accordance with the instructions of a fully registered medical practitioner (*q.v.*), and no post-mortem examination which is not directed or requested by the coroner or any other competent legal authority may be carried out without the authority of the person lawfully in possession of the body (Human Tissue Act, 1961, s. 2).

Post-natus, the second son; also one born in Scotland after the accession of James I, and therefore not an alien in England (*Calvin's Case* (1608) 7 Co.Rep. 1). See CALVIN'S CASE.

Post-note, a species of bank-note, intended for transmission by post, which is payable to order on a future specified date instead of to bearer on sight, as in the case of the ordinary bank-note. The term seems to be confined to the United States. The British equivalent is a bank post-bill.

Post-nuptial settlement, a settlement made after marriage; it is generally deemed voluntary unless made pursuant to written articles entered into before marriage. See VOLUNTARY CONVEYANCE.

Post-obit, a money bond conditioned for payment at or after the death of some person other than the giver of the bond. It is a form of quasi-security not infrequently given to moneylenders by expectant heirs (*q.v.*). See BOND; CATCHING BARGAIN.

Post-war credits, the amounts to be credited to income tax payers, at a date to be fixed by the Treasury, in respect of the additional tax paid by reason of the reductions of reliefs and allowances enacted by the Finance Act, 1941. Certificates were issued stating the amount of the post-war credit for the years 1941–42 to 1945–46.

Post-war credits became payable under the Finance Act, 1946, s. 26; Finance Act, 1947, s. 16; Income Tax (Repayment of Post-War Credits) Act, 1959; S.I. 1959 No. 876; 1960 No. 769; 1962 No. 2455; 1972 Nos. 374, 1840; Income and Corporation Taxes Act, 1970, s. 537 (2); Finance Acts, 1972, s. 131; 1976, s. 59.

Post, Writ of entry in the, a writ given by the Statute of Marlbridge, 1267, which provided that when the number of alienations or descents exceeded the usual degrees, a new writ should be allowed, without any mention of degrees at all.

Postage, the duty or charge imposed on letters or parcels conveyed by post. See POST OFFICE.

Postal convention, a treaty made at Berne in October, 1874, for the regulation of rates of postage and matters connected with the Post Office, between England and various other countries.

Postea, afterwards. In the common law practice before the Judicature Acts, 1873–75, this was a formal statement, indorsed on the *nisi prius* record, which gave an account of the proceedings at the trial of the action (2 Lil.Abr.337; 16 Vin. Abr. 465).

Under the present practice, the associate makes an entry of the findings of the jury, and of the directions and certificates given by the judge at the trial, in a book kept for that purpose. See CERTIFICATE.

Posteriority, a word of comparison and relation in tenure, the correlative of priority. A man holding lands of two lords, held of his more ancient lord by priority, and of his later lord by posteriority, and when he died his more ancient lord had the wardship of the heir (Cowel).

Posterity, succeeding generations; descendants, as opposed to ancestors.

Posthumous child, a child born after his father's death. By the statute 1698, 10 & 11 Wm. 3, c. 22, such child might take an estate as if born in his father's lifetime, although there were no limitation to trustees to preserve the contingent remainder to such child. See EN VENTRE SA MERE.

As to the nationality and status of a posthumous child, see the British Nationality Act, 1948, s. 24.

Posthumous works. Provision is made for the copyright in posthumous literary, dramatic and musical works by the Copyright Act, 1956, s. 2.

Postliminium, the return of a person to his own country, after having sojourned abroad. The right of postliminy (*jus posliminii*) is that by virtue of which persons and things taken by an enemy in war are restored to their former state, upon coming again under the power of the nation to which they belonged. To what cases the rule is applicable depends to a great extent on the practice of each particular nation, for it properly belongs to private international law, though the term *postliminium* is also said to apply to those cases where captured property has come into the hands of neutrals, and is reclaimed by the belligerent from whom it was taken. As to the English law on the subject, see RECAPTURE.

It also means the return of territory under occupation of an enemy to its position prior to the occupation.

Postman, a junior barrister in the Court of Exchequer who, except in

Crown business, had precedence in motions (3 Bl.Comm. 28).

The office ceased to exist when the Court of Exchequer, as the result of the Judicature Acts, 1873–75, was merged in the Queen's Bench Division, but the judges intimated that whenever a Divisional Court sat in what had been the Court of Exchequer, the barrister who had held the post was to have his old precedence. The last postman was Sir Charles Hall, Recorder of London, 1892–1900. The postman took his name from the fact that his place in the Court of Exchequer was by the post anciently used as a measure of length in exise cases. See TUBMAN.

A postman is also an official of the post office employed to deliver letters. Although a letter of acceptance takes effect from the time it is put into the pillar-box, delivery of a letter to a postman not authorised to receive letters does not take effect from the time it is handed to him (*Re Northern and London Bank* [1900] 1 Ch. 220).

Postmaster-General. The Postmaster-General was the successor of the Master of the Posts (*q.v.*) and the head of the Post Office. The office was abolished by the Post Office Act, 1969, s. 1, and the functions of the Postmaster-General were distributed. See POST OFFICE; POSTS AND TELECOMMUNICATIONS, MINISTER OF; SAVINGS, DIRECTOR OF.

Postremo-geniture, borough - English (*q.v.*).

Posts and Telecommunications, Ministry of. This ministry was created under the Post Office Act, 1969, s. 2, on the abolition of the office of Postmaster-General (*q.v.*). It was dissolved and its functions transferred to the Secretary of State for Industry (S.I. 1974 No. 691).

Postulatio, the first act in a criminal proceeding (Civil Law).

Postulation, a petition.

Postumus, a child of a testator born after his death who, if born in his lifetime, would have been under his *potestas* and entitled to succeed him if he had died intestate; also a child of a testator conceived before the date of the will but born a *suus heres* after the date of the will and before the testator's death, called a *posthumus Vellaeanus*, from the *lex*

Julia Vellaea, which provided that the testator might institute or exclude such a child (Civil Law).

Postumusalienus, a posthumous stranger; a posthumous child who would not have been under the testator's *potestas* if born in his lifetime (Civil Law).

Potentia propinqua, a common possibility which may be expected to happen.

Potentia remota, a remote possibility which is not likely to happen.

Potestas suprema seipsam dissolvere potest, ligare non potest (Bac.Max. 19). (The supreme power may loose, but cannot bind, itself.) See PERPETUA, ETC.

Pothier. Robert Joseph Pothier was born on January 9, 1699, at Orleans, where he afterwards became professor; he died on March 2, 1772. He wrote *Pandectae Justinianeae in novum ordinem digestae*, and treatises on other branches of law, including *Traité des Obligations*, translated by W. D. Evans. Complete editions of his works were published in 1820–22, 1825, 1845 and 1861.

Potior est conditio defendentis. (The condition of a defendant is better.) Where a plaintiff can succeed only as the result of either an illegal or a disgraceful course of conduct, the court will not decide in his favour, even though the conduct of the defendant be equally discreditable. *In pari delicto melior est conditio possidentis* (where both paries are in the wrong, the position of the possessor is the better). See EX TURPI CAUSA; POTIOR EST CONDITIO POSSIDENTIS.

Potior est conditio possidentis. (The condition of one in possession is the better.) See POSSESSION.

Potwaller; Potwalloper, one, either a householder or a lodger, who provided his own food and cooked it at his fireplace. Such persons were entitled to the parliamentary electoral franchise in some boroughs. The rights of existing potwallers were preserved by the Representation of the People Act, 1832, s. 33. See ELECTORAL FRANCHISE; FAGGOT VOTE.

Poultry. The protection of live poultry from unnecessary suffering was provided for by the Poultry Act, 1911. Orders for that purpose are now made under the Diseases of Animals Act, 1950. See ANIMALS, DISEASES OF.

The humane slaughter for commercial purposes of poultry is provided for by the Slaughter of Poultry Act, 1967.

As to the standards of measurement etc. on the sale of poultry, see the Weights and Measures Act, 1963, s. 21, Sch. 4 Pt. II.

Pheasants are not poultry (*Hardwicke Game Farm* v. *Suffolk Agricultural Poultry Producers Association* [1966] 1 W.L.R. 287).

Pound [Sax. *pund*; Lat. *pondo*] as a measure of mass or weight is 0·45359237 of a kilogramme (Weights and Measures Act, 1963, s. 10, Sch. 1 Pt. V). See KILO-GRAMME.

Up to the reign of Edward III the pound of 5,760 grains, made up of twelve ounces each containing 480 grains, was in general use. After that period this ounce was reserved for precious metals, and the pound of 7,000 grains came into use for other substances. See FORMELLA.

The pound sterling now consists of 100 new pence (Decimal Currency Act, 1967, s. 1). Formerly the pound meant the sum of 20 shillings, said to be so called because in Saxon times 240 pence weighed a pound (Lambard 219).

A pound, or penfold, or pinfold, so called from the Saxon *pindan*, meaning to shut in, is an inclosure, building or piece of land where goods which have been seized as distress are placed by the distrainor; as soon as this has been done, the goods are in the custody of the law. See POUND-BREACH; RESCUE.

A pound is either overt (open) or covert (close). A pound overt is practically only used for cattle, and may be either a common pound overt, which is a pinfold or structure of wood made for such purposes on a public piece of land: or a special pound overt, which is where the cattle are impounded (under the Distress for Rent Act, 1737, s. 10) on the land where the distress was made, or on that of the distrainor, or of some other person by his consent, in which two latter cases the distrainor must give notice to the owner of the cattle, because where cattle were impounded in a pound overt it was, formerly, their owner who had to supply them with food and drink. A pound overt is so called, either because it is open overhead, or because the owner of the

cattle may go to it wherever it is, without being liable for a trespass. A pound covert or close is where the distrainor impounds the cattle or goods in some part of a house (*e.g.*, a stable), and then he is bound to supply the cattle with food and drink. Goods which are liable to be damaged by the weather or stolen must always be impounded in a pound covert (Co.Litt. 47b; 3 Bl.Comm. 12).

The lord's pound was a pound on the waste of the manor.

Formerly a distrainor could not impound the distress on the land of the tenant, but had to remove it. Now, however, the distrainor may convert any part of the premises upon which a distress is taken into a pound *pro hac vice* (Distress for Rent Act, 1737, s. 10).

Pounds may be used for the confinement of cattle found trespassing, for stray cattle on highways, and also for stray cattle found by the police in any place to which the Town Police Clauses Act, 1847, applies.

At common law neither the person impounding an animal nor the pound-keeper was obliged to feed it, and no charge could be made for its keep. Now any person who impounds an animal is bound to supply it with food and water; on his default, anyone can enter the pound and feed the animal, and the cost of the food can in either case be recovered from the owner (Protection of Animals Act, 1911, s. 7).

See PARCO FRACTO, DE.

Pound of land, an uncertain quantity of land, said to be about fifty-two acres.

Poundage, a fee payable to an officer of a court, or to the public revenue, in respect of services performed by the officer: it is so called because it is calculated at so much for every pound sterling of the amount with which he has to deal. Thus, a sheriff is entitled to poundage on executing a *fieri facias* (Sheriffs Act, 1887, s. 20 (2)).

Poundage was also a duty at the rate of so much (usually twelve pence) per pound sterling upon the value of merchandise (other than wine) imported into the kingdom. The statutes which granted it also invariably granted tonnage (*q.v.*) as well, the two being known as tonnage and poundage.

Poundagium, the liberty (or right) of impounding cattle.

Pound-breach, the act of taking goods out of a pound before the distrainor's claim has been satisfied, and that whether the distress was lawfully made or not, because impounded goods are in the custody of the law. The distrainor's remedy is either by action for treble damages under the Distress for Rent Act, 1689, s. 4; Administration of Justice Act, 1965, Sch. 2 or by proceedings for a penalty before justices under the Pound-Breach Act, 1843; Justices of the Peace Act, 1949, Sch. 7 Pt. III; Criminal Justice Act, 1967, Sch. 3 Pt. I. See DOUBLE DAMAGES; PARCO FRACTO, DE; RESCUE.

Pound breach is a misdemeanour at common law.

Where the cattle are impounded under the Town Police Clauses Act, 1847, s. 24, pound-breach is punishable summarily under s. 25 of that Act; and where they have been found straying on the highway and have been impounded under the Highways Act, 1959, s. 135. The penalties are increased by the Criminal Justice Act, 1967, s. 92, Sch. 3 Pt. I.

Pour fair proclaimer que null inject fimes ou ordures en fosses ou rivers pres cities (to make proclamation that none should throw filth or ordure into ditches or rivers near cities), a writ directed to the mayor or bailiff of a city or town founded on the statute 1388, 12 Ric. 2, c. 13, and now replaced by an indictment for nuisance (Fitz.Nat.Brev. 176).

Pour seisir terres la femme qui tient in dower (to seize the lands held by the wife in dower), a writ which lay for the king when the widow of a tenant *in capite* had remarried without the king's leave (Fitz. Nat.Brev. 174).

It was abolished by the statute 1660, 12 Car. 2, c. 24.

Pourallee. See PURLIEU.

Pourparty, to divide the lands which fall to parceners (Old N.B. 11).

Pourpresture or **Purpresture** [Fr. *purprendre*, to encroach or enclose; *pourpris*, an inclosure], anything done to the nuisance or hurt of the Crown's demesnes, or the highways, etc., by enclosure or building, endeavouring to make that private which ought to be public (Co.Litt. 277b).

The difference between a purpresture and a public nuisance was that purpresture was an invasion of the *jus privatum* of the Crown; but where the *jus publicum* was violated it was a nuisance.

There were three sorts of this offence: against the Crown; against the lord of the fee; against a neighbour (2 Co.Inst. 38; Skene).

Purpresture within a forest was where any man made any manner of encroachment upon the forest either by building or inclosure or by using of any liberty or privilege without lawful warrant so to do (Glanv. i. 9, c. 11; Williams, *Common* 231).

Purpresture, or purpresture land, was also used as meaning the enclosed land itself.

See USURPATION.

Poursuivant, a king's messenger; those employed in martial causes were called poursuivants-at-arms.

There are in the Heralds' Office four poursuivants. *Rouge Croix* was instituted at an uncertain period, but is generally considered to be the most ancient; the title is doubtless derived from the cross of St. George. *Bluemantle* was instituted by Edward III or Henry V, and named either in allusion to the colour of the arms of France or to that of the robes of the Order of the Garter. *Rouge Dragon* was instituted by Henry VII on the day before his coronation, the name being derived from the ensign of his ancestor, Cadwaladyr; he assumed a red dragon as the dexter supporter of his arms. *Portcullis* was also instituted by Henry VII, from one of whose badges the title was derived. See HERALDS.

As to the office of poursuivant of the Great Seal, see the Great Seal Offices Act, 1874.

Pourveyance, or **Purveyance,** the providing of necessaries for the sovereign, by buying them at an appraised valuation in preference to all others, and even without the owner's consent. See PURVEYANCE.

Pourveyor, or **Purveyor,** a buyer; one who provided for the royal household.

Powdike. In Norfolk, west of the Great Ouse, there were three embankments built to keep the waters of the fens out of the tract in the Isle of Ely known as Marshland. There was the Old Powdike, built about 1225; the New Powdike, built about 1425; and the Little Powdike, adjoining the Old Powdike. The statute 1530, 22 Hen. 8, c. 11, made it felony maliciously to injure them.

Power is sometimes used in the same sense as " right," as when we speak of the powers of user and disposition which the owner of property has over it; but strictly speaking a power is that which creates a special or exceptional right, or enables a person to do something which he could not otherwise do. Powers are either public or private.

Public powers are those conferred by the Crown, by the legislature (parliamentary powers), or by a delegate of the Crown or legislature, such as the Privy Council or Department of Trade, for a public purpose, e.g., making a railway. When a parliamentary power authorises acts by which the rights of private persons may be affected against their will, it is called a compulsory power; such are the powers given to statutory undertakers for the compulsory purchase of land required for their undertakings. See ACT OF PARLIAMENT.

Private powers are those conferred on private persons. Some are created by the parties themselves, in which case the person conferring the power is called the donor, and the person to whom it is given the donee; others are statutory, that is, conferred by statute.

Powers must be distinguished from trusts: powers are never imperative—they leave the act to be done at the will of the party to whom they are given. Trusts are always imperative. Powers are, however, sometimes divided into (1) mere, bare or naked powers (or powers in the proper sense of the word), and (2) powers coupled with a trust, or powers in the nature of trusts, which the donees are bound to exercise; they are, therefore, really trusts, and are powers only in form (*Brown* v. *Higgs* (1799) 8 Ves. 570).

Powers are of two principal kinds, viz., those which are by law incident to an office, such as the ordinary powers of directors, solicitors, guardians, executors, trustees, etc.; and those conferred specially, such as a power of sale or leasing, or an authority conferred, e.g., by a power of attorney. The latter class may be divided into those which enable the donee to create or modify estates or interests in property (called in conveyancing " powers " *par excellence*), and those conferred for other purposes.

Powers which enable the donee to create or modify estates or interests in property confer the right of alienation as opposed to that of enjoyment; that is, the power enables the donee to declare in whom and in what manner the property is to vest, but gives him (*qua* donee) no right of ownership over it. Such a power is said to be legal when it operates upon or passes the legal estate in the property, and equitable when it only operates on or passes a beneficial or equitable interest.

Legal powers formerly operated under the Statute of Uses, 1535, or under the Wills Act, 1837, or by custom. Powers under the Statute of Uses, 1535, operated in the following manner: if land was conveyed to A and his heirs to such uses as B should appoint, and B appointed or declared the uses to C for life, and after C's death to himself in fee, then the legal estate passed to C for his life with remainder to B, as if the estates had been originally so conveyed to them. (See APPOINTMENT, POWER OF; USE.) Powers operating under the Wills Act, 1837, were similar to those operating by way of use, except that they could be created and take effect with greater freedom. Powers operating by virtue of a custom (*e.g.,* a custom applicable to copyholds) resembled those under the Statute of Uses, 1535, in their effect, but were less flexible in their application.

By the Law of Property Act, 1925, s. 1 (7), all powers of appointment over, or powers to convey or charge land or any interest therein, whether created by statute or other instrument or implied by law, operate only in equity and are termed equitable powers. The only exceptions are legal powers, *i.e.*, the powers vested in a legal mortgagee, the powers vested in an estate owner and exercisable by him or on his behalf, and certain statutory powers (ss. 7, 8). The Act having abolished the Statute of Uses, 1535, powers deriving their effect by way of a declaration to uses only take effect as equitable powers. By s. 205 (1) (xi), legal powers include the powers vested in a chargee by way of legal mortgage or in an estate owner under which a legal estate can be transferred or created, and equitable powers mean all the powers in or over land under which equitable interests or powers only can be transferred or created.

Legal powers are appendant or appurtenant, when the donee has an estate in the land and the power is to take effect wholly or in part out of that estate, as in the case of a tenant for life having a power of leasing, or a mortgagee having a power of sale; in gross either where the donee has an estate in the land, but the power does not take effect out of it, as where a tenant for life has power to appoint an estate to commence after his death, or where the donee has no present estate, but may exercise the power for his own benefit; merely collateral or naked, where the donee neither has an estate nor can exercise the power for his own benefit, as in the case of executors having a mere power of sale. If lands are devised to an executor with a trust or power of sale, this is sometimes called a power coupled with an interest, to distinguish it from a bare or naked power (Co.Litt. 113a).

This classification of powers was of importance with reference to the ability of the donee to release, suspend or extinguish the power. Thus, executors who had a merely collateral power to sell land could not release or extinguish it.

By the Law of Property Act, 1925, s. 155, replacing the Conveyancing Act, 1881, s. 52, a person to whom any power, whether coupled with an interest or not, is given, may by deed release or contract not to exercise the power, see *Re Wills' Trust Deeds* [1964] Ch. 219; and by the Law of Property Act, 1925, s. 156, replacing the Conveyancing Act, 1881, s. 6, a person to whom any power, whether coupled with an interest or not, is given, may by deed disclaim the power, and after disclaimer is not capable of exercising or joining in the exercise of the power, though it may be exercised by the other or others of the persons to whom the power is given unless the con-

trary is expressed in the instrument creating the power. A power given to two or more jointly annexed to an office, *e.g.*, a trust, survives to the other or others after the death of one of the donees (Trustee Act, 1925, s. 18), but a bare power to two or more by name will not survive.

Equitable powers are analogous to legal powers. Thus, if land or stock is vested in trustees upon such trusts as B shall appoint, and B appoints it to C, the legal ownership of the land or stock remains in the trustees, but the equitable ownership passes to C, and he can compel the trustees to convey the land or transfer the stock to him.

Powers are also divisible into powers of revocation, which give only the right of revoking existing estates, and powers of appointment, which enable the donee to create or appoint new estates. When a power of appointment is not preceded by an existing estate, it is sometimes called a primary power; when it is preceded by an existing estate which the donee may revoke, it is called a power of revocation and new appointment, or a subsidiary power. As to the operation of appointments with reference to the rule against perpetuities, see APPOINTMENT, POWER OF.

Powers are either general (that is to say, absolute) or limited. A general power enables the donee to appoint the property to any person or persons (including himself), for any estate, and on any conditions, and is therefore equivalent to ownership. If he dies having exercised it by will in favour of a volunteer or if he becomes bankrupt, the power forms part of his assets (*q.v.*) for payments of his debts.

A limited power is either special or particular. A special power is one which is restricted as to the nature or duration of the estates or interests to be created under it, as in the case of the power to grant leases for terms in excess of those permitted by the Settled Land Act, 1925, which are frequently given to the tenant for life under a settlement. A particular power is one which is restricted as to its objects or the persons in whose favour it may be exercised, as in the case of a power to appoint property among a certain class only (*e.g.*, the children of the donee); but the term "special" is now usually applied to this last type of power, and the term "particular" is seldom used. The main division of powers is into general and special powers, but there is a third type, *viz.*, a power to appoint to anyone except a certain person (*Re Jones* [1945] Ch. 105; *Re Harvey* [1950] 1 All E.R. 491). When a power of appointment among a class requires that each shall have a share, it is called a distributive or non-exclusive power; when it authorises, but does not direct, a selection of one or more to the exclusion of the others, it is called an exclusive power and is also distributive; when it gives the power of appointing to a certain number of the class, but not to all, it is exclusive only, and not distributive. A power authorising the donee either to give the whole to one of a class, or to give it equally amongst such of them as he may select (but not to give one a larger share than the others), is called a mixed power. Formerly, if the donee of a non-exclusive power excluded one of the objects from his appointment, or only gave him an illusory share, the appointment was held void; but this rule was abolished by the Illusory Appointments Act, 1830, and the Powers of Appointment Act, 1874, known as Lord Selborne's Act, now the Law of Property Act, 1925, s. 158 (see APPOINTMENT, POWER OF). As to frauds on powers, see FRAUD.

Wills in execution of powers of appointment by will must be executed like other wills, and are then valid although other solemnities required by the will are not observed (Wills Act, 1837, s. 10); and a deed attested by two witnesses is a valid execution of a power of appointment by deed or by any instrument in writing not testamentary, notwithstanding that it was expressly required that a deed or instrument in writing made in exercise of such power should be executed or attested with some additional or other form of execution, or attestation or solemnity (Law of Property Act, 1925, s. 159, replacing the Law of Property Amendment Act, 1859, s. 12). Equity will aid defective execution in certain cases.

For ascertaining the date for the purpose of the rule against perpetuities, the date from which the period is taken is the date of the instrument conferring the power unless the power is exercisable by an owner or person having a general power equivalent to that of ownership.

Powers not given for the purpose of creating or modifying estates or interests in property are of great variety. Thus, a power of appointing new trustees is incident to every settlement created by will or deed, either by express provision or by statutory enactment. So a power of distress and entry may be inserted in a deed to enable the donee to enter and distrain on certain land of the donor, to enforce the performance of some covenant, *e.g.*, the payment of an annuity. See DISTRESS.

Power, Minister of. The Minister of Fuel and Power became the Minister of Power (S.I. 1957 No. 48). The Ministry of Power was dissolved and the functions of the Minister were transferred to the Minister of Technology (S.I. 1969 No. 1498). These functions are now vested in the Secretary of State for Energy. See TECHNOLOGY, MINISTRY OF.

Power of appointment, a power given by deed or will by which a nominated person may direct an interest in property to devolve on anyone (including himself) if it is a general power, or on a specified person or persons or on a member or members of a specified class if it is a special power. See APPOINTMENT, POWER OF; POWER.

Power of attorney, a formal instrument by which one person empowers another to represent him, or act in his stead for certain purposes. A power of attorney is usually a special instrument in the form of a deed poll, but it may form part of a deed containing other matter; thus a deed of dissolution of partnership often contains a power of attorney from the retiring to the continuing partner, to enable the latter to wind up the business and collect the assets. A power which authorises the execution of a deed or the transfer of stock at the Bank of England must itself be conferred by deed. It is always well that the execution of the power of attorney should be attested by two witnesses; and, for the transfer of stock at the Bank of England, the power of attorney must be so attested.

The donor of the power is called the principal or constituent; the donee is called the attorney. As a general rule, an infant may be an attorney.

A power of attorney which authorises the attorney to do all acts of a certain class from time to time, such as to carry on a business, collect debts, etc., is sometimes called a general power, as opposed to a special or particular power, or one which is confined to a specified act or acts. A limited power is one containing precise instructions as to the mode of executing it, while an unlimited power leaves this to the discretion of the attorney.

As to the persons who can empower others to act for them by power of attorney, see AGENT; AUTHORITY; DELEGATUS NON POTEST DELEGARE.

An instrument creating a power of attorney must be signed and sealed by the donor of the power. Alternatively, it may be signed and sealed by direction of and in the presence of the donor provided that two other persons are present as witnesses and attest the instrument. This is without prejudice to any other statutory requirement and to the rules relating to the execution of instruments by bodies corporate (Powers of Attorney Act, 1971, s. 1). Formerly a power of attorney relating to land had to be filed at the central office of the Supreme Court or at the Land Registry. This requirement is abolished but the right to search for or obtain copies of documents filed is preserved (s. 2).

The contents of a power of attorney may be proved by means of a photographic copy certified by the donor or his solicitor or stockbroker (s. 3).

Powers of attorney given as security are irrevocable (ss. 4, 5). The donee of a revocable power is not liable for acts done after the revocation of the power if he did not know that the power had been revoked and a person dealing with the donee is protected (s. 5). Additional protection for transferees under stock exchange transactions is conferred by s. 6.

The donee of a power of attorney may execute any instrument with his own signature and seal it with his own seal and do any other act in his own name (s. 7).

Power to delegate trusts during the absence abroad of a trustee, personal representative, tenant for life or statutory owner is conferred by the Trustee Act, 1925, s. 25, and the Powers of Attorney Act, 1971, s. 9.

A general power of attorney in the prescribed form or in a like form expressed to be made under the Act operates to confer on the donee of the power or, if there is more than one donee, on the donees acting jointly or acting jointly or severally as the case may be authority to do on behalf of the donor anything which he can lawfully do by an attorney. This does not apply to functions which the donor has as a trustee or personal representative or as a tenant for life or statutory owner (Act of 1971, s. 10). A company can give a power of attorney under the Companies Act, 1948, s. 34, to execute deeds on its behalf outside the United Kingdom.

Power of the county. See POSSE COMITATUS.

Poynding. See POINDING.

Poynings' Act, or **Statute of Drogheda,** the statute, 1495, 10 Hen. 7, c. 22, made in Ireland, so called because Sir Edward Poynings was lieutenant there when it was made, whereby all general statutes before then made in England were declared of force in Ireland, which, before that time, they were not (12 Co. Rep. 109).

Practical joke. An employer may be liable in damages for a practical joke played by one of his employees on another (*Hudson* v. *Ridge Manufacturing Co.* [1957] 2 Q.B. 348).

Practice, the form and manner of conducting and carrying on suits, actions, or prosecutions at law or in equity, civil or criminal, through their various stages, from the commencement to final judgment and execution, according to principles and rules laid down by the several courts. As to the precise meaning of " practice," see *Att.-Gen.* v. *Sillem* (1864) 10 Jur.(N.S.) 457.

The law of practice or procedure is that which regulates the formal steps in an action or other judicial proceeding. It therefore deals with writs of summons, pleadings, affidavits, notices, summonses, motions, petitions, orders, trial, judgment, appeals, costs and execution. In jurisprudence it forms part of adjective law. See LAW.

Multa exercitatione multo facilius quam regulis percipies (you will perceive many things much more easily by practice than by rules) (4 Co.Inst. 50).

Practice Court, the Bail Court (*q.v.*).

Practice Master. R.S.C., Ord. 63, r. 2 provides that one of the Masters of the Queen's Bench Division shall be present at the Central Office on every day on which the office is open for the purpose of superintending the business performed there and giving any directions which may be required on questions of practice and procedure. The Masters' Practice Directions are published in the Supreme Court Practice, Vol. 2 Pt. 4. They have no statutory authority (*Hume* v. *Somerton* (1890) 25 Q.B.D. at p. 243; *Re Langton, Langton* v. *Lloyds Bank* [1960] 1 W.L.R. 246). They must be followed in district registries (R.S.C., Ord. 63, r. 11).

Practising certificate, the certificate taken out annually by a solicitor from the Law Society which entitles him to practise as a solicitor.

Practitioner, one who is engaged in the exercise or employment of any art or profession.

Praebendam, In. See PREBEND.

Praecaria bedrepium, bedrip (*q.v.*).

Praeceptories, a kind of benefices, so called because they were possessed by the more eminent Templars, whom the Chief Master by his authority created and called *praeceptores Templi* (2 Dugd.Mon. 543).

Praeceptors. Masters in Chancery (*q.v.*) were called *praeceptors*, as having the direction of making out remedial writs.

Praecipe (command), a slip of paper on which a party to a proceeding writes the particulars of a document which he wishes to have prepared or issued; he then hands it to the officer of the court whose duty it is to prepare or issue the document. Thus, when a party wishes to issue a writ of execution, he must file a *praecipe* as required by R.S.C., Ord. 46, r. 6 and Masters' Practice Directions 23. For procedure in Admiralty actions see Ord. 75, r. 4.

The instructions for issuing an original writ consisted of a copy of the writ required, and therefore began with the word *praecipe*; hence probably the use of the word in its modern sense.

Formerly a *praecipe* was a species of original writ, so called because it required the sheriff to command the defendant either to do a certain thing or to show cause why he had not done it; *e.g.,* the *praecipe quod reddat,* commanding the defendant to give up land to the demandant, which was the writ by which a common recovery was commenced against the tenant of the freehold (Co. Litt. 101a; 3 Bl.Comm. 274).

In order to have a recovery with double voucher to bar an entail, it was usual for the tenant in tail to convey an estate of freehold to a friend against whom the *praecipe* was brought; this was called making a tenant to the *praecipe* (*q.v.*). See ONE HUNDRED THOUSAND POUND CLAUSE; RECOVERY; VOUCH.

Praecipe in capite, a writ issuing out of the Chancery for a tenant *in capite* who had been dispossessed of his lands (Magna Carta, 1215, c. 24). See NON INTROMITTENDO, ETC.

Praecipe quod reddat, an original writ, commanding the person to whom it was directed either to do some act or to show cause why he had not done it (3 Bl.Comm. 274; Old Nat.Brev. 13).

Praecipitium, the punishment of casting headlong from some high place.

Praecognita, things which must be previously known in order that something which follows may be understood.

Praeda belli, booty, property seized in war.

Praedia stipendiaria, provincial lands belonging to the people (Civil Law).

Praedia tributaria, provincial lands belonging to the emperor (Civil Law).

Praedia volantia. In the duchy of Brabant, certain things movable, such as beds, tables, and other heavy articles of furniture, were ranked amongst immovables, and were called *praedia volantia,* or volatile estates (2 Bl.Comm. 428).

Praedial servitude, a servitude affecting land.

Praedial tithes [Lat. *praedium,* ground], tithes which arose merely and immediately from the ground; as grain of all sorts, hops, hay, wood, fruit, herbs.

Praedict, aforesaid.

Praedium dominans, an estate to which a servitude is due; the ruling estate (Civil Law).

Praedium rusticum, heritage which is not destined for the use of man's habitation; such, for example, as lands, meadows, orchards, gardens, woods, even though they should be within the boundaries of a city (Civil Law).

Praedium serviens, an estate which suffers or yields a service to another estate (Civil Law).

Praedium urbanum, a building or edifice intended for the habitation and use of man, whether built in the city or the country (Civil Law).

Praefectus. See PRAEPOSITUS.

Praefectus urbi, from the time of Augustus, an officer who had the superintendence of the city and its police, with jurisdiction extending one hundred miles from Rome, and power to decide both civil and criminal cases. As he was considered the direct representative of the emperor, much that previously belonged to the *praetor urbanus* fell gradually into his hands (Civil Law).

Praefectus vigilum, the chief officer of the night-watch. His jurisdiction extended to certain offences affecting the public peace, and even to larcenies. But he could inflict only slight punishments (Civil Law).

Praefectus villae, the mayor of a town.

Praefine; Prefine, a fee payable on the issue of the writ which formed the first part of a fine (*q.v.*). It was usually about one-tenth of the annual value of the lands sued for. It was known also as *primer fine* (2 Bl.Comm. 350).

Praejuramentum. See ANTEJURAMENTUM.

Praemium pudicitiae, the consideration given by the seducer of a chaste woman for her defilement (*Annandale* v. *Harris* (1727) 2 P.Wms. 432).

Praemunire [Lat. *praemoneri*, to be forewarned], an offence so called from the words of the writ preparatory to the prosecution thereof: *praemunire facias* A. B. (cause A. B. to be forewarned) that he appear before us to answer the contempt wherewith he stands charged; which contempt is particularly recited in the preamble to the writ. The offence of *praemunire* is introducing a foreign power into the land, and creating *imperium in imperio,* by paying that obedience to alien process which constitutionally belongs to the sovereign alone (4 Bl.Comm. 103).

Praemunire is the offence of directly or indirectly asserting the supremacy of the Pope over the Crown of England, as by procuring excommunications or bulls from Rome.

The statutes relating to *praemunire* were framed to encounter papal usurpation by presentation of aliens to English benefices. The Statute of Provisors, 1352, was the foundation of all the subsequent statutes of *praemunire*. The Statute of Praemunire, 1392, is incorporated by reference in many subsequent statutes; *e.g.*, in the statutes 1533, 25 Hen. 8, c. 20, s. 6, whereby an archbishop or bishop refusing to confirm and consecrate a person elected bishop incurs a *praemunire,* and 1661, 13 Car. 2, c. 1, whereby to assert maliciously and advisedly, by speaking or writing, that both Houses or either House of Parliament have or has a legislative authority without the sovereign, is a *praemunire,* and the Habeas Corpus Act, 1679, s. 11, whereby it is a *praemunire* to send any subject of the realm a prisoner, under certain exceptions in the Act specified, into parts beyond the seas.

The punishment of the offence is that, from the conviction, the defendant is out of the Crown's protection, and his lands and goods are forfeited to the Crown (Statute of Provisors, 1352; Statute of Praemunire, 1392). Until the Act of Supremacy, 1562, it was perhaps lawful to kill the defendant (Co.Litt. 391a).

Praenomen, the name of a person, distinguishing him from others of the same family (Civil Law).

Praepositus (one put in front), an officer next in authority to the alderman of a hundred, called *praepositus regius*; or a steward or bailiff of an estate, answering to the *wicnere* (Anc.Inst.Eng.).

It also meant the person from whom descents were traced under the old canons of descent.

Praepositus ecclesiae, a church-reeve or churchwarden.

Praepositus villae, a constable of a town, or petty constable.

Praerogitava. See PREROGATIVA REGIS.

Praescriptio est titlulus ex usu et tempore substantiam capiens ab authoritate legis (Co.Litt. 113a, b). (Prescription is a title from use and time taking its substance from the authority of the law.)

Praesentia corporis tollit errorem nominis; et veritas nominis tollit errorem demonstrationis (Bac.Max. 25). (The presence of the body cures error in the name; the truth of the name cures error of description.) If you have the right man it does not matter that you have called him by a wrong name, and if you mention the right thing it does not matter that you have made an error in describing it. Thus, where one on the jury panel is erroneously called and sworn in the name of another who is also on the panel, the error is immaterial; and a legacy of something which can be clearly identified is not invalidated by error in description of details. See FALSA DEMONSTRATIO, ETC.

Praeses, the president or governor of a province, a *legatus Caesaris* being the governor of a province reserved by the emperor (Civil Law).

Praestat cautela quam medela (Co. Litt. 304). (Caution is better than cure.)

Praestita rolls, rolls in the Record Office containing lists of payments made by the Exchequer to royal officials between 1199 and 1603.

Praesumitur pro negante (it is presumed for the negative), the rule of the House of Lords when the numbers are equal on a motion. See SEMPER PRAESUMITUR PRO NEGANTE.

Praesumptio, intrusion, or the unlawful taking of anything (Leg.Hen. 1, c. 11).

Praesumptio violenta valet in lege (Jenk.Cent. 56). (Strong presumption avails in law.) See PRESUMPTION.

Praetor, the consul whose special function was to administer justice in Rome (*praetor urbanus*). A second *praetor* was appointed to deal with cases between citizens and aliens, or between aliens alone (*praetor peregrinus*).

Although theoretically the *praetor* merely administered the law, his powers of interpretation and amendment developed the law. He applied as far as possible the rules of natural justice (*naturalis aequitas*). On taking office he issued an edict stating the rules by which he would be guided. The *praetors* achieved the admission of aliens to the *jus civile*, the supersession of formalism by rules giving effect to the intention of the parties, and the change of the law of intestate succession from the basis of *potestas* to blood.

Praetor fidei-commissarius, the judge at Rome who enforced the performance of all fiduciary obligations and confidence.

Pragmatic sanction, a rescript or answer of the sovereign, delivered by advice of his council to some college, order, or body of people, who consulted him in relation to the affairs of the community. A similar answer given to an individual was called a rescript (Civil Law).

It also means the instrument by which the Emperor Charles VI endeavoured to secure the succession of his daughter Maria Theresa to the Austrian dominions after his death.

Pratique [Ital. *practica*], a licence for the master of a ship to traffic in the ports of Italy upon a certificate that the place whence he came was not annoyed with any infectious disease.

Pratum bovis, or **Carucae,** a meadow for oxen employed in tillage.

Praxis, use, practice.

Pray in aid, to petition in a court of justice for the calling in of help from another who has an interest in the cause in question. See AID PRAYER.

Prayer Book. The Sarum Missal and Breviary was drawn up in 1085 for the cathedral church at Salisbury. This was in most general use throughout England at the time of the Reformation. It formed the basis of the Prayer Book of Edward VI, published in 1548; and the Book of Common Prayer Act, 1548, enacted that only the services mentioned in this Prayer Book should be used. The Prayer Book was suppressed by Mary; Elizabeth I revived it, with alterations, by the Act of Uniformity, 1558. Under that Act Elizabeth I made alterations in 1561, and James I made some more in 1604. The Puritans suppressed the book, but after the Restoration it was revived, in substantially the modern form, by the Act of Uniformity, 1662. Modern enactments on the subject are the Prayer Book (Table of Lessons) Act, 1871; the Act of Uniformity Amendment Act, 1872; the Revised Table of Lessons Measure, 1922; the Prayer Book (Alternative and Other Services) Measure, 1965; the Prayer Book (Miscellaneous Provisions) Measure, 1965; the Prayer Book (Versions of the Bible) Measure, 1965; the Prayer Book (Further Provisions) Measure, 1968; the Synodical Government Measure, 1969, s. 3. See COPYRIGHT; QUEEN'S PRINTER; UNIFORMITY, ACTS OF.

Prayers for the dead. A bequest for masses for the dead is not void as a gift to superstitious uses (*Bourne* v. *Keane* [1919] A.C. 815, overruling *West* v. *Shuttleworth* (1835) 2 My. & K. 684).

Prayers for the dead are not expressly prohibited by the Church of England. They are discouraged but are not contrary to law unless they necessarily involve the doctrine of purgatory, which is expressly forbidden by the Church of England (*Re South Creake Parish* [1959] 1 W.L.R. 427; *Re St. Mary the Virgin, Ilmington* [1962] P. 147). Mortuary celebrations of the Holy Communion for the repose of the departed were condemned in *Elphinstone* v. *Purchas* (1870) L.R. 3 A. & E. 66, and in *Pearson* v. *Capel* [1903] P. 66, the ecclesiastical court authorised the removal of a tombstone inscribed with a request for prayers for the soul of the departed. In *Breeks* v. *Woolfrey* (1838) 1 Curt. 880, however, the ecclesiastical court had refused authority for the removal of such a tombstone and in *Egerton* v. *All Saints* [1894] P. 13, a compromise was effected by permission being given for the substitution of the inscription *requiescat in pace*.

Preamble, introduction, preface. The preamble of an Act of Parliament is that part which contains the recitals showing the necessity for it. It, unlike the marginal notes (*q.v.*), is part of the statute and may be used in order to ascertain the meaning (*West Ham* v. *Iles* (1883) 8 App.Cas. 388), but only when the preamble is clear and definite in comparison with obscure and indefinite enacting words (*Att.-Gen.* v. *Prince Ernest of Hanover* [1957] A.C. 436). Preambles are now the exception rather than the rule. Formerly they were often of great length, and those in early statutes are frequently of historical value. Their function is now-

adays performed to some extent by the explanatory and financial memoranda which are printed in front of Bills of any complexity, but which are omitted when the Bill becomes an Act.

The preamble serves to portray the interests of its framers, and the mischiefs to be remedied, and is a good means to find out the meaning of the statute (1 Co. Inst. 79a).

In *Sussex Peerage Case* (1844) 11 Cl. & F. 143, and *Winn* v. *Mossman* (1869) L.R. 4 Ex. 299, it was said that as a general rule the preamble is to be resorted to only in case of ambiguity in the statute itself.

In Statute Law Revision Acts passed since 1888, Parliament has repealed many preambles of statutes still in force, but in *Powell* v. *Kempton Park Race Course* [1899] A.C. 143, it was said that the repeal of a preamble by a Statute Law Revision Act would in no way affect the future construction of the Act.

When a private Bill is referred to a Select Committee, and is opposed on the question of its general expediency, the promoters have to adduce arguments and evidence in support of it; this is called proving the preamble. If it is not proved, the Bill is generally rejected by the House.

Pre-audience. The right of pre-audience in a court of law is the right which one person has of being heard before another, in business which is not set down to be heard in a particular order, *e.g.*, motions. Thus the Attorney-General and Solicitor-General have precedence of other counsel in most matters, Queen's Counsel over junior barristers, and junior barristers generally in the order of their call. See POSTMAN; TUBMAN.

Prebend; Prebendary. A prebend is an endowment of land or money held by a cathedral or collegiate church *in praebendam*, that is to say, for the maintenance of a canon known as a prebendary. The word prebend came to mean also both the prebendary and the annual payment which he received from the endowment; but the word is properly and usually applied to the endowment. There are simple prebendaries, being those who have no cures of souls and no clerical incomes except such as are received by them as prebendaries, and dignitary prebendaries, being those who have cures of souls as well as prebends.

The term "prebend" is sometimes confounded with canonicate; but there is a difference between them. A prebend is the stipend granted to an ecclesiastic in consideration of his officiating and serving in the church; whereas a canonicate is a mere title or spiritual quality which may exist independently of any stipend.

Prebenda, or **Probanda,** provisions.

Precariae, or **Preces,** days which the tenants of certain manors were bound to give their lords in harvest time, also known as bind days. *Magna precaria* was a great or general reaping day.

Precarium, a contract by which the owner of a thing, at another's request gave him the thing to use as long as the owner pleased. It was distinguished from an ordinary gratuitous loan, and gave rise to different obligations on the part of the borrower (Civil Law).

Precatory words, expressions in a will praying or recommending that a thing be done, *e.g.,* that property bequeathed to a legatee be disposed of by him for the benefit of other persons, the question then arising whether the legatee was meant to take absolutely or merely as a trustee for such other persons. The general rule is that such words will create a trust only if they are capable of being construed as imperative. In former times the court was very apt to construe words of recommendation as imperative, but of late years the tendency has been the other way (*Hill* v. *Hill* [1897] 1 Q.B. 483; *Williams* v. *Williams* [1897] 2 Ch. 12; *Re Oldfield* [1904] 1 Ch. 549; *Comiskey* v. *Bowring-Hanbury* [1905] A.C. 84). See TRUST.

Precedence, or **Precedency,** the act or state of going before; adjustment of place.

For the order of precedence in England see Whitaker's *Almanac*.

Precedence, Patent of. Letters patent of precedence are grants whereby the Crown occasionally assigns to some person a rank higher than that to which he is otherwise entitled (3 Bl.Comm. 97).

Patents of precedence were sometimes granted by the Crown to such barristers as it thought proper to honour with that rank of distinction, whereby they were entitled to such rank and pre-audience as were assigned in their respective patents. See QUEEN'S COUNSEL; SERJEANTS-AT-LAW.

Precedent. A judicial precedent is a judgment or decision of a court of law cited as an authority for deciding a similar state of facts in the same manner, or on the same principle, or by analogy. The rules of common law and equity are contained in precedents established by the courts, that is, they have to be arrived at by ascertaining the principle on which those cases were decided. See LAW; REPORT, LAW; STARE DECISIS.

Each of the three superior courts of common law was by the practice of the law bound to follow a decision of its own or of either of the others on a point of law, and a decision of its own on a point of practice; but it was not bound to follow the decisions of another co-ordinate court on a point of practice. The same rules prevailed in the courts of equity. The Divisions of the High Court being parts of one and the same court, each Division ordinarily considers itself bound by the decisions of the other Divisions upon points of practice as well as of law; and so of each Divisional Court; but in more than one case where there was no appeal, a Divisional Court, inclined to disagree with a prior judgment of another Divisional Court upon the same point, has been strengthened in number, and so strengthened, has declined to follow such prior judgment (*Winyard* v. *Toogood* (1882) 52 L.J.M.C. 25).

The House of Lords was formerly absolutely bound by its own prior decisions, although decided, on an equality of votes, in the negative (*London Tramways Co.* v. *London County Council* [1898] A.C. 75; *London Transport Executive* v. *Betts* [1959] A.C. 213). This rule has been modified and the House will depart from a previous decision when it appears right to do so (Practice Statement (H.L.) (Judicial Precedent) [1966] 1 W.L.R. 1234).

In *White* v. *Bristol Aeroplane Co.* [1944] K.B. 718, it was held that the Court of Appeal is bound by its own decisions except where they are conflicting, or are inconsistent with a decision of the House of Lords or were given *per incuriam*. But in *Gallie* v. *Lee* [1969] 2 Ch. 17, Lord Denning M.R. said that the Court of Appeal is not absolutely bound by its own prior decision and Salmon L.J. said that the Court of Appeal could, by a decision of a full court abandon its practice of rigid adherence to its own precedents.

In its criminal jurisdiction the Court of Appeal does not apply the doctrine of *stare decisis* as rigidly as in its civil jurisdiction (*R.* v. *Gould* [1968] 2 Q.B. 65).

The decisions of the Judicial Committee of the Privy Council are not binding on the High Court, though of course treated with great respect.

Scottish (*Hoyle* v. *Hitchman* (1879) 4 Q.B.D. 423) and Irish (*London and North Western Ry.* v. *Skerton* (1864) 33 L.J.M.C. 158) decisions are treated with respect in the English courts and differed from with reluctance.

A decision of a judge on circuit is less authoritative than a decision given by him when sitting in the High Court in London.

As to the extent to which judgments of the European Court are binding, see *Da Costa en Schaake N.V.* v. *Nederlandse Belastingadministratie* (Nos. 28–30/62) [1963] C.M.L.R. 224; *Association Générale des Fabricants Belges de Ciment Portland Artificial S.A.* v. *Carrière Dufour S.A.* [1967] C.M.L.R. 250; *Re Import of Powdered Milk (No. 3)* (No. VII 156/65) [1967] C.M.L.R. 326.

In conveyancing, a precedent is a copy of an instrument used as a guide in preparing another instrument of a similar description.

Precedent condition, such as must happen or be performed before an interest can vest or be enlarged, or an obligation be performed. See CONDITION.

Prece partium, at the request of the parties; used in the statute 1285, 13 Edw. 1, c. 27.

Precept, an order or direction given by one official person or body to another requiring him to do some act within his province; a rule authoritatively given; a mandate; a command in writing by a justice of the peace or other officer for bringing a person or record before him; the direction of the sheriff to the proper officer to proceed to the election of mem-bers of parliament; a provocation whereby one incites another to commit a felony.

A county council and the Greater London Council may issue precepts to the appropriate rating authorities for the levying of rates (Local Government Act, 1972, s. 149). A parish (*q.v.*) or (in Wales) community council (see COMMUNITIES) may issue precepts to the district (*q.v.*) council (s. 150).

Précepte d'Assize, the title of an ancient collection of records which, as from a date soon after 1205, set out a series of decisions or statements of the Royal Court of Guernsey as to the customary laws of that island. It was sometimes supposed that these statements were approved by officials sent to the island in 1340 under a *Précepte d'Assize* of Edward III and afterwards by various justices in eyre. The *Précepte* is a record of the customary law of the island from an early date and, together with the *Approbation des Loix* (*q.v.*), is one of the sources of the laws of Guernsey. See GRAND COUSTUMIER, ETC.

Preces primariae or **primae.** In the Holy Roman Empire the emperor had the right, known as *preces primariae*, of presentation to the first prebend in every cathedral which fell vacant after his accession. Edward I is said to have exercised a similar right in England; and this is stated to have been the origin of the Crown's right of corody (*q.v.*).

Precinct, a constable's district; the immediate neighbourhood of a palace, court or cathedral.

Precipe. See PRAECIPE.

Precludi non (not to be barred), the name of the commencement of a replication to a plea in bar; it was abolished by the Common Law Procedure Act, 1852, s. 66.

Precognitors. See ASSISE, GRAND.

Preconisation [Lat. *praeconium*, the office of a crier], proclamation.

Pre-contract, a contract preceding another. The term was used in the ecclesiastical law which made an existing contract of marriage a bar to the marriage of either of the parties to anyone except the other party (Co.Litt. 79b).

The ecclesiastical courts could formerly enforce this agreement, by compelling the parties to a public marriage, and if one of them had already married, such marriage would be void *ab initio*; but until thus avoided it was good: see the statutes 1540, 32 Hen. 8, c. 38, and 1548, 2 & 3 Edw. 6, c. 23, s. 2. But pre-contract is no longer a cause for dissolving a marriage in England (*Beachey* v. *Brown* (1858) E.B. & E. 796): see the statute 1753, 26 Geo. 2, c. 33. See BREACH OF PROMISE.

Predecessor, one who has preceded another. When a person who is a corporation sole, such as a bishop or parson, dies, and the land held by him in his corporate capacity passes to his successor, the person so dying is called the predecessor, just as a natural person from whom land descended to his heir was called the ancestor (Co.Litt. 78b). See SUCCESSOR.

The term predecessor was used as the correlative of successor in the Succession Duty Act, 1853.

A predecessor in title is a person through whom another traces his title to property.

Under the Landlord and Tenant Act, 1927, s. 25, a predecessor in title is defined in relation to a tenant or landlord, as any person through whom either respectively has derived title by assignment, will, intestacy or operation of law.

Predial. See PRAEDIAL.

Predicament, the condition of things concerning which a logical proposition may be stated.

Predicate, that which is said concerning the subject in a logical proposition, as, " The law is the perfection of common sense "; " perfection of common sense," being affirmed concerning the law (the subject, is the predicate or thing predicated).

To predicate means to affirm logically.

Pre-emption. The right of pre-emption is the right of purchasing property before or in preference to other persons. Thus, under the Lands Clauses Consolidation Act, 1845, s. 128, where a body has, under its compulsory powers, purchased land which is not required for the purposes of its undertaking and is not situate in a town or used for building purposes, the body must first offer it for sale to the person owning the lands from which it

was originally severed. This is commonly called the right of pre-emption.

A landlord has a right of pre-emption in respect of fixtures removable by a tenant under the Agricultural Holdings Act, 1948, s. 13.

A contract giving a right of pre-emption in respect of a legal estate in land must be registered as an estate contract under the Land Charges Act, 1972, s. 2 (4). See OPTION.

Pre-emption was formerly part of the royal prerogative allowed to the royal purveyor, and consisted in the right of buying up provisions and other necessaries for the use of the royal household, at an appraised value, in preference to all others, and without the consent of the owner. This right was surrendered by Charles II at his restoration, and was abolished by the statute 1660, 12 Car. 2, c. 24.

In international law, pre-emption is the right of a government to purchase, for its own use, the property of the subjects of another State *in transitu*, instead of allowing it to reach its destination. Formerly the right appears to have been exercised in times of peace on any cargoes which entered the ports of the purchasing State, but this practice has long fallen into disuse, and at the present day pre-emption is confined to time of war, and to cases where the goods are of such a description that their transport to the enemy of the pre-empting State would be manifestly to the disadvantage of the latter, while on the other hand the law of contraband does not justify their confiscation. This right of pre-emption is to be distinguished from the *droit d'angarie* (*q.v.*).

Prefer, to apply, to move for; to prefer for costs meant to apply for costs.

Preference, Fraudulent. See FRAUDULENT PREFERENCE.

Preference shares, shares in respect of which the memorandum and articles of a company confer on the holders some preference over other classes in respect of dividend or of repayment of capital or of both. Preference shareholders sometimes have the right to participate with other shareholders after their preferential rights have been satisfied.

Preferential or **Preference shares** or **stock,** shares or stock in a company having priority as to payment of dividends of a fixed amount, and, in some cases of capital upon a winding up, over the ordinary shares. The dividends are usually contingent upon the profits of each year or half-year. In some cases, however, the arrears of dividend form an accumulating debt by the ordinary to the preference shareholders, the preference being in that case described as a non-contingent or a cumulative preference. See DEFERRED STOCK.

Preferential payments. In bankruptcy, administration of estates of persons dying insolvent, and winding up of companies, one year's rates and taxes, four months' salaries of clerks and workmen up to £200, and a number of other items are payable in preference to other debts. See the Bankruptcy Act, 1914, s. 33 as amended and extended; Administration of Estates Act, 1925, Sch. 1 Pt. I para. 2; Companies Act, 1947, ss. 91, 115; Companies Act, 1948, ss. 317, 319; Employment Protection Act 1975, s. 63; Social Security Pensions Act, 1975, Sch. 3, Sch. 4 paras. 2, 3; Development Land Tax Act, 1976, s. 42; Finance Acts, 1972, s. 41; 1976, s. 22; Social Security Act, 1975, s. 153, Sch. 18. These debts rank equally between them unless the assets are insufficient, in which case they abate in equal proportions. By the Companies Act, 1948, s. 319 (5), these debts have priority over the claims of holders of debentures or debenture stock under any floating charge created by a company. The debts are a first charge on goods or proceeds distrained upon within three months of the date of the receiving order or winding-up order, but if the landlord pays the debts he has a first charge for the debts on the goods or proceeds (Bankruptcy Act, 1914, s. 35; Companies Act, 1948, s. 319 (7)): see *Cairney* v. *Back* [1906] 2 K.B. 746; *Re Beeton* [1913] 2 Ch. 279; *Re Havana Co.* [1916] 1 Ch. 8; *Re Lewis Merthyr Colleries* [1929] 1 Ch. 498.

The right of a personal representative to prefer creditors was abolished by the Administration of Estates Act, 1971, s. 10.

See FRAUDULENT PREFERENCE.

Prefine. See PRAEFINE.

Pregnancy, the state of being with child. It may be an " illness " preventing the attendance of a witness (*R.* v. *Wellings* (1878) 3 Q.B.D. 426).

See JURY OF MATRONS; VENTRE INSPICIENDO, DE.

Prejudice, injury. An offer which is made " without prejudice " for the purpose of settling an existing dispute cannot be construed as an admission of liability, or given in evidence at all. The term is given to overtures and communications between parties in the course of negotiation, or between litigants before action, or after action, but before trial or verdict. The words import an understanding that if the negotiation fails, nothing that has passed shall be taken advantage of thereafter; so, if a defendant offers, " without prejudice," to pay half the claim, the plaintiff may not rely on the offer as an admission of his having a right to some payment.

The rule is that nothing written or said " without prejudice " can be considered at the trial without the consent of both parties—not even by a judge in determining whether or not there is good cause for depriving a successful litigant of costs (*Walker* v. *Wilsher* (1889) 23 Q.B.D. 335; *Hulton* v. *Chadwick* (1919) 35 T.L.R. 620; *Rabin* v. *Mendoza & Co.* [1954] 1 W.L.R. 271). The offer will be deemed to be without prejudice if on its face it was made for the purpose of effecting a settlement (*Waldridge* v. *Kennison* (1794) 1 Esp. 142). But the existence of a dispute is indispensable; thus a notice to creditors of intention to suspend payment issued " without prejudice " may be used as evidence in bankruptcy proceedings (*Re Daintree* [1893] 2 Q.B. 116); and where letters expressed or intended to be " without prejudice " result in an agreement between the parties settling the issue between them they are admissible in evidence (*Att.-Gen.* v. *Dyer* [1947] Ch. 67).

The word is also frequently used without the foregoing implications in statutes and *inter partes* to exclude or save transactions, acts and rights from the consequences of a stated proposition and so as to mean " not affecting," " saving," or " excepting."

Prelate, an archbishop or bishop.

Prelector, a public reader or lecturer. It was used as a translation of the title Reader (*q.v.*) in the Inns of Court. At Oxford it was formerly used as interchangeable with professor, except in the case of the Regius Professors. At Cambridge it meant either a college tutor or a lecturer on some subject. In the cathedral church of Hereford one of the prebendaries is elected prelector and has to preach on certain days; he vacates his prelectorship on becoming a canon resident.

Preliminary accounts. The Court of Chancery could direct preliminary accounts and inquiries at any time after the appearance of the defendant. The present rules as to accounts and inquiries do not specifically refer to preliminary accounts. See ACCOUNTS AND INQUIRIES.

Preliminary act. In actions for damage by collision between vessels, unless the court otherwise orders, the solicitor for each party, before any pleading is delivered, must file a sealed-up document, called a preliminary act, which is not opened until ordered by the court. It contains a statement as to the names of the ships which came into collision and their ports of registry, the date, time and place of collision, the state of the wind, weather and tide, the course, speed and lights of each vessel, and other particulars tending to show how the collision happened; and the court may order the preliminary acts to be opened and the evidence to be taken thereon without any pleadings being delivered (R.S.C., Ord. 75, r. 18). The object of the rule requiring preliminary acts is to obtain a statement of the facts while they are still fresh in the recollection of the witnesses, and to prevent either party varying his version of facts so as to meet the allegations of his opponent. A statement of fact in a preliminary act is a formal admission, binding the party making it, and can only be departed from by special leave. As a rule, therefore, the court will not allow either party to alter any allegation contained in his preliminary act, not even to correct a clerical error, but a party who has filed a defective preliminary act which does not give the information required by the rule, may be ordered to amend it.

Preliminary examination, a private examination by the official receiver of a person against whom a receiving order has been made, with a view to ascertaining his assets and liabilities. The debtor's answers are taken down in writing and filed in the court.

Preliminary expenses, expenditure in connection with the promotion, formation, establishment and registration of a company. It is usually written off over a period of years and the amount not written off must be shown under a separate heading in the balance sheet (Companies Act, 1948, Sch. 8 para. 3).

Premier, the Prime Minister (*q.v.*). It is an abbreviated form of " premier minister," and has been in use for over two hundred years.

Premises [Lat. *praemissa*], in logic propositions antecedently supposed or proved.

In the primary sense of the word, " premises " signifies that which has been before " premised " or mentioned. Thus, after a recital of various facts in a deed, it frequently proceeds to recite that in consideration of the premises, meaning the facts recited, the parties have agreed to the transaction embodied in the deed. See DEED.

In a conveyance, when the property to be dealt with has been fully described, it is often referred to in the subsequent parts of the deed, as " the premises hereinbefore described and intended to be hereby assured," or similar words. From this use of the word, " premises " has gradually acquired the popular sense of land or buildings. Originally, it was only used in this sense by laymen, and it was never so used in well-drawn instruments, but it is now frequently found in instruments and in Acts of Parliament as meaning land or houses, *e.g.* the Public Health Act, 1875, s. 4, where " premises " includes messuages, buildings, lands, easements, tenements and hereditaments of any tenure.

In its technical sense, the " premises " is that part of a deed which precedes the *habendum*, and therefore includes the introduction, the date, and (in deeds between parties the parties or (in deeds poll) the name of the person executing the instrument, the recitals, the consideration and the grant, release or other operative part (Shep.Touch. 74).

Premium, a consideration; something given to invite a loan or a bargain; the consideration paid to the assignor by the assignee of a lease, or to the transferor by the transferee of shares or stock; the annual or other payment for renewal of a policy of insurance; the excess over par value of shares and other securities.

In granting a lease, part of the rent is sometimes capitalised and paid in a lump sum at the time the lease is granted. This is called a fine or premium. Formerly, a limited owner, such as a tenant for life, could not as a rule take a premium on granting a lease under a power, as the power generally forbade him to do so, but now he can take a fine or premium which, however, is to be treated as capital money (Settled Land Act, 1925, s. 42, replacing the Settled Land Act, 1882, s. 6, and the Settled Land Act, 1884, s. 4).

It is an offence punishable with a fine of £100 to take a premium on a grant or assignment of a tenancy to which the Rent Acts apply and unlawful premiums may be recovered by action (Rent Act 1968, ss. 85–92).

Premunire. See Praemunire.

Prender [Fr. *prendre*], to take anything as of right before it is offered. It was opposed to " render." Thus heriots were in prender, it being the right of the lord to take them; rents were in render, it being the duty of the tenant to pay them. See Profit; Render.

Prender de baron, to take a husband (see Baron and Feme). Upon a woman making an appeal of felony (*q.v.*) against a person who had murdered her husband, *prender de baron* was an exception (or objection) taken on the ground that she had remarried (3 St.P.C. c. 59).

Prepense, aforethought, preconceived, contrived beforehand. Malice prepense or prepensed malice (*malitia praecognita*) is the same as malice aforethought, that is to say, the malice necessary to constitute the offence of murder (*q.v.*). See Malice.

Prerogativa regis, the king's prerogative. An enactment is printed under this title in the *Statutes of the Realm* amongst the *Statutes of Uncertain Date*, and in the *Statutes at Large* as 1324, 17 Edw. 2, st. 1, cc. 4–6, 7-16.

Prerogative, those exceptional powers, pre-eminences and privileges which the law gives to the Crown (Co.Litt. 90b; 1 Bl.Comm. 239).

Prerogatives are either direct or by way of exception. Those by way of exception are such as exempt the Crown from some general rule binding on the rest of the community, as that lapse of time is no bar to a claim by the Crown, though this rule has been modified by statute. See Nullum Tempus Aut Locus Occurrit Regi; Regalia.

The direct prerogatives may be divided into three kinds, as they regard the royal character, the royal authority and the royal income. To the first class is generally referred the rule that the king can do no wrong, in other words, that he is not liable to be sued or punished for any act or default (see Petition of Right). The second class includes the right of sending and receiving ambassadors, making treaties declaring war and peace, assembling, proroguing and dissolving Parliament, raising and regulating fleets and armies (see Mutiny Act), appointing ports and harbours (*q.v.*), appointing judges and magistrates, creating titles and offices, pardoning convicted criminals. (see Pardon), and coining money (1 Bl.Comm. 252).

The third class, or fiscal prerogatives, are the sources of the royal revenue; these, however, though nominally belonging to the Crown, have for long past been surrendered to the public use, and now form part of the public income known as the Consolidated Fund (*q.v.*), out of which the Crown receives an annual sum, called the Civil List (*q.v.*) for the expenses of the royal household and establishment. The ancient fiscal prerogatives included the profits of the demesne lands of the Crown, the right to royal fish, wrecks treasure-trove, waifs and estrays, escheats, etc. The rest of the public income consists chiefly of taxes, duties and other imposts voted by Parliament (1 Bl.Comm. 282).

The Crown also has certain protective prerogatives, such as its prerogatives in connection with charities, and the foreshore of lands adjoining the sea.

The prerogative of the Crown cannot be taken away even by an Act of Parliament unless the Act contains express words to that effect (*Re Wi Matua's Will* [1908] A.C. 448; *Att.-Gen.* v. *De Keyser's Royal Hotel* [1920] A.C. 508; *British Coal Corporation* v. *R.* [1935] A.C. 500; *Moore* v. *Att.-Gen. for Irish Free State* [1935] A.C. 484). See QUEEN; REGALIA.

Prerogative courts. Before the Probate Court (*q.v.*) was established, there was an ecclesiastical court held in each province, before a judge appointed by the archbishop, for granting probates and administrations in cases where the deceased left *bona notabilia* (*q.v.*) in different dioceses. It was called a prerogative court because the archbishop claimed the jurisdiction by way of special prerogative (3 Bl. Comm. 65; Cowel; Tomlin).

Appeals lay to the Privy Council (Privy Council Appeals Act, 1832). The Judicature Act, 1925, ss. 20 (*a*), 107, replacing the Court of Probate Act, 1857, s. 4, took away their jurisdiction in testamentary matters.

Prerogative of mercy. In early times the operation of the royal prerogative of mercy was far wider than at the present day as it was not only extended to some persons who in later ages would not be considered to have incurred any criminal responsibility, *e.g.*, persons who had committed homicide by misadventure or in self-defence, but was even extended to jurors who had been attainted for an oath that, though not false, was fatuous (2 P. & M.H.E.L. 476, 661).

In early times, there were fewer offences that did not admit of being pardoned. In appeals (*i.e.* private accusations of felony) which were not the suit of the king, but of the party injured, the prosecutor might release, but the king could not pardon (3 Co.Inst. 237). Appeals by wager of battel (*q.v.*) were abolished by the statute 1819, 56 Geo. 3, c. 46, in consequence of *Ashford* v. *Thornton* (1818) 1 B. & A. 405. The Crown cannot pardon a common

nuisance while it remains unredressed, or so as to prevent an abatement of it; though afterwards the fine may be remitted because, though the prosecution is vested in the Crown to avoid multiplicity of suits, yet (during its continuance) this offence savours more of the nature of a private injury to each individual in the neighbourhood than of a public wrong. The Crown could pardon some offences against a popular or penal statute, after information brought (3 Co. Inst. 238; 4 Bl.Comm. 397). See PENAL ACTION.

The Habeas Corpus Act, 1679, s. 12, makes the offence of sending a subject to a foreign prison unpardonable by the Crown.

The prerogative of mercy was frequently invoked to alter the sentence, either to obviate the necessity for the literal execution of the sentence in cases of high treason, or to change the sentence of death by hanging for felony into one of decapitation: see, *e.g.*, the advice given by the judges to James II in *Lady Lisle's Case* (1685) 11 How.St.Tr. 297, 378. In the eighteenth century conditional pardons for felony were regularly granted in order that the offender might transport himself for a term of years. Formerly free pardons were only grantable under the Great Seal, but by the Criminal Law Act, 1827, s. 13 (repealed) the Crown was enabled to grant a free pardon for felony by sign manual. The practice of obtaining a free pardon before 1848 was explained in a letter to the Home Secretary by the judges who formed the Special Commission before whom Frost and others were tried for treason in 1839 (*R.* v. *Frost* (1839) 4 St.Tr.(N.S.) 85, 479 480).

The anomaly of pardoning either an innocent or a guilty man on the ground of his innocence, protested against by the judges before a Select Committee of the House of Lords in 1848 and by the Beck Commission in 1904, may if the Home Secretary thinks fit be avoided under the provision in the Criminal Appeal Act, 1968, s. 17, by which he may, if he thinks fit, refer the case to the Court of Appeal (as upon an appeal) or refer any point to that court. The prerogative of mercy is not affected by the Act (s. 49). See PARDON.

Prerogative writs and orders, processes issued upon extraordinary occasions on proper cause shown. They are the writs or orders of *procedendo*, mandamus, prohibition, *quo warranto*, habeas corpus, and certiorari.

By the Administration of Justice (Miscellaneous Provisions) Act, 1938, s. 7, orders of mandamus, prohibition and certiorari were substituted for the corresponding writs.

Presbyter, a priest, elder, or honourable person.

Presbyterian, a presbytery; that part of the church where divine offices are performed; it was applied to the choir or chancel because it was the place appropriated to the bishop, priest, and other clergy, while the laity were confined to the body of the church (1 Dugd. Mon. 243.

Presbyterian Church of England, a Protestant church constituted under the Book or Order of that church.

Presbyterian Church of Scotland. The established church of Scotland. See the Scottish statute, 1690, c. 5, the Union with Scotland Act, 1706, and *Free Church of Scotland* v. *Overtoun* [1904] A.C. 515.

Presbyterians, a sect of Christians chiefly to be found in Scotland and Northern Ireland (Irish Presbyterian Church Act, 1870), who do not acknowledge the authority of bishops. In England the term Presbyterian originally designated a distinct body of Protestant dissenters. The Presbyterian form of worship was established in England during the Commonwealth, and when the Presbyterian ministers who filled the churches were ejected by the Act of Uniformity, 1662, they spread over the country and founded Presbyterian churches in almost every part of it. In process of time, however, many of these Presbyterian congregations gradually changed their views, some becoming Independents, others Baptists, and others Unitarians (*Att.-Gen.* v. *Bunce* (1868) L.R. 6 Eq. 563).

Presbytery, a church court in Scotland next above the kirk session, consisting of a minister and an elder from each church within a certain district.

Prescribe [*praescribere*], to claim a right by prescription. As to the meaning of the expression " to prescribe in a *que* estate " see PRESCRIPTION.

In modern Acts of Parliament relating to matters of an administrative nature, it is common to indicate in general terms the nature of the proceedings to be adopted, and to leave the details to be " prescribed " or regulated by rules or orders to be made for that purpose in pursuance of an authority contained in the Act. See ORDER; RULE.

Prescription, where a right, immunity or obligation exists by reason of lapse of time. Thus, where a number of persons in succession have acted and been treated as a corporation from time immemorial without being able to show any express creation, they constitute a corporation by prescription (*Mellor* v. *Spateman* (1669) 1 Wms.Saund. 339).

Corporations by prescription are those which have existed beyond the memory of man, and therefore are looked upon in law to be well created, such as the City of London and many others (1 Bl.Comm. 473).

More commonly, however, prescription is applied to incorporeal hereditaments and rights or obligations connected with the use of land, to signify that they have been enjoyed as of right, and without interruption for a certain period. Thus, prescription is one of the principal modes by which easements, profits *à prendre*, franchises and other incorporeal hereditaments are created or evidenced. So, also, a privilege or exemption may be prescriptive, *e.g.*, a *modus decimandi*, a *de non decimando* and an exemption from toll or stallage (*q.v.*).

Prescription differs from custom in being personal: that is, when a person claims a right by prescription, he must allege that it has been enjoyed by him and his ancestors or predecessors in title (See CUSTOM). Prescription differs from limitation in its application to incorporeal hereditaments and similar rights, and not to land or other corporeal hereditaments (*Wilkinson* v. *Proud* (1843) 11 M. & W. 33). Villeinage was capable of existing by prescription; and it would appear that two persons may be tenants in common of lands by title of prescription (Co.Litt. 195b).

Title by prescription, known in the civil law as *usucapio*, arises from a long-continued and uninterrupted possession of property. *Praescriptio est titulus ex usa et tempore substantiam capiens ab authoritate legis* (prescription is a title from use and time taking its substance from the authority of the law) (Co.Litt. 113b).

Every species of prescription, by which property is acquired or lost, is founded on the presumption that he who has had a quiet and uninterrupted possession of anything for a long period of years is supposed to have a just right, without which he would not have been suffered to continue in the enjoyment of it. For a long possession may be considered as a better title than can commonly be produced, as it supposes an acquiescence in all other claimants; and that acquiescence also supposes some reason for which the claim was forborne.

There are two kinds of prescription, *viz.*, negative, which relates to realty or corporeal hereditaments, whereby an uninterrupted possession for a given time gives the occupier a valid and unassailable title, by depriving all claimants of every stale right and deferred litigation, now mainly governed by the Limitation Act, 1939, and positive which relates to incorporeal hereditaments, and originated at the common law from time immemorial or long usage only.

The most important rules of the common law concerning positive prescription are as follows: the only property claimable by positive prescription is an incorporeal hereditament; it must be founded on actual usage or enjoyment, for a mere claim will not establish the right; the use or enjoyment must have been continuous and peaceable, although an interruption of comparatively short duration will not destroy it; the usage must have been from time immemorial, or from time whereof the memory of man runneth not to the contrary, which is held to be from the beginning of the reign of Richard I; and the prescription must be certain and reasonable (2 Bl. Comm. 263).

At common law, a title by prescription is where a right has been enjoyed from time immemorial, or time out of mind. By analogy to the old statutes of limitation, " time out of mind " was held to mean the first year of Richard I's reign but when this period became inconveniently long, it was held to be sufficient if evidence of the enjoyment of the right was carried back as far as living memory would go. And when the Limitation Act, 1623, limited the time for bringing a possessory action to twenty years, the courts held by analogy that if a right had been enjoyed for twenty years, it should be presumed to have been enjoyed from time immemorial, the presumption being based, according to some, on the fiction of a lost grant (see LOST GRANT), and, according to others on the analogy between prescription and limitation. According to some of the older writers, however, the real common law prescription was when a right had been enjoyed " from time whereof the memory of man runneth not to the contrary, that is as much as to say, when such a matter is pleaded, that no man then alive hath heard any proof of the contrary, nor hath no knowledge to the contrary "; but subsequently the two expressions " time out of mind," and " time whereof the memory of man runneth not to the contrary," became synonymous (Litt. 170; Co.Litt. 114b). See MEMORY.

The Prescription Act, 1832, also known as Lord Tenterden's Act, shortens the time of prescription. Claims to right of common and other profits *à prendre* (except tithes and rent) are prima facie indefeasible after thirty years' uninterrupted enjoyment (*q.v.*), and absolutely indefeasible after sixty years, except by showing that the enjoyment was by some agreement in writing. Claims to ways or other easements or use of water are prima facie indefeasible after twenty years' uninterrupted enjoyment, and absolutely indefeasible after forty years, except by showing that the enjoyment was by some agreement in writing. Claims to light for a building uninterruptedly enjoyed for twenty years are absolutely indefeasible after twenty years' enjoyment, except by showing that the enjoyment was by some agreement in

PRESCRIPTION

writing (*Richardson* v. *Graham* [1908] 1 K.B. 39. See ANCIENT LIGHTS.

By the Prescription Act, 1832, s. 4 the periods are to be taken to be the period next before some suit or action relating to the right in dispute, and no act or matter is deemed to be an interruption (*q.v.*) within the meaning of the statute unless the same has been submitted to or acquiesced in for one year (*Reilly* v. *Orange* [1955] 2 Q.B. 112).

The registration of a notice as a local land charge (*q.v.*) operates in lieu of an obstruction of light. See the Rights of Light Act, 1959; ANCIENT LIGHTS.

With reference to the manner in which a prescriptive right is claimed, prescription is of three kinds, namely: (1) where the person claiming the right proves that it has been enjoyed by him and his ancestors during the time required by law, as in the case of an advowson or common in gross; (2) where the members of a corporation and their predecessors have enjoyed the right for the period required by law; and (3) where the person claiming the right proves that it has been enjoyed by him and his predecessors in title; or, as the old writers say, he must claim that the right is *en luy et en ceux que estate il ad* (in him and in those whose estate he has): hence this is called prescribing in a *que* estate (Litt. 183; Co. Litt. 121a; 2 Bl.Comm. 266.

A prescription in a *que* estate is simply a right annexed to and going along with certain lands, as where a man claims a right of advowson as appendant to a manor belonging to him. The rule of common law pleading used to be that a prescription in a *que* estate could only be claimed by a tenant in fee, and that if a tenant for a less estate wished to claim such a right, he was obliged to allege it as belonging to the tenant in fee. The most important practical result of this rule was that copyholders, being in theory mere tenants at will, were obliged to prescribe in the name of the lord of the manor, in whom the fee was vested; hence they were allowed to claim rights of common against the lord by custom (*q.v.*) instead of prescription. This rule was abolished by the Prescription Act, 1832, s. 5.

In the civil law the *praescriptio* was a clause placed at the head of the pleadings (*prae*, before, and *scribere*, to write), in order to raise a kind of preliminary objection or reservation. One of the cases in which a defendant could make use of a *praescriptio* was where he wanted to raise the defence that the plaintiff's claim was barred by what corresponded to a statute of limitations: hence the modern sense of the word (Ortolan, Inst. iii. 532).

See Herbert, *History of Prescription*; Carson, *Prescription and Custom*.

Prescription de modo decimandi. See MODUS DECIMANDI.

Present, to tender or offer. Thus, to present a bill of exchange for acceptance or payment is to exhibit it to the drawee or acceptor (or his authorised agent) with an express or implied demand for acceptance or payment. See BILL OF EXCHANGE; HONOUR.

Present use, one which had an immediate existence and was at once operated upon by the Statute of Uses, 1535.

Presentation, the offering by the patron of a benefice to the ordinary of a person to be instituted to the benefice (1 Bl.Comm. 384).

The Statute of Frauds, 1677, required a presentation to be in writing. It is in the nature of letters-missive to the ordinary.

The sovereign, as *protector ecclesiae*, is the patron paramount of all benefices which do not belong to other patrons, and usually presents by letters patent (Acts of Supremacy, 1534 and 1558).

As to other patrons, the right of presentation is sometimes confounded with that of nomination; but presentation is the offering a person to the bishop, while nomination is the offering such a person to the patron. These two rights may co-exist in different persons; thus where an advowson is vested in trustees or mortgagees they have the right of presentation, while the right of nomination is in the *cestui que trust* or the mortgagor, but the trustees or the mortgagees must judge of the qualifications of the nominee (Mirehouse, *Advowsons*, 136).

A bishop has, by Canon 95 (which abridged the period from two months), 28 days for inquiry before instituting the clergyman presented by the patron. See INSTITUTION.

All persons seised in fee, in tail, or for life, or possessed of a term for years of a manor to which an advowson is appendant, or of an advowson in gross, may present; the right descended by course of inheritance, from heir to heir, and it passes to a devisee or purchaser, unless the benefice becomes vacant in the lifetime of the patron, when the void turn devolves upon the personal representatives (*Mirehouse* v. *Rennell* (1833) 7 Bli. 241), being, indeed, a personal right or interest dis-annexed from the estate in the advowson, and vested in the patron simply as an individual. And where the incumbent was also a patron, if he died seised of the advowson, without having devised it, his heir, not his executor, was entitled to present, because the descent of heir and the fall of the avoidance to the executor happening at the same time, the elder right prevailed. If a bishop dies, a church being vacant in his lifetime, the Crown exercises its prerogative to present (Co.Litt. 388a).

Joint tenants and tenants in common should present jointly; and if coparceners cannot agree, the eldest sister is entitled to the first turn, the second sister the second turn, *et sic de caeteris*, every one in turn according to seniority, and this part which the oldest thus takes by virtue of her priority of age is called the *enitia pars* (*q.v.*).

An infant at any age could nominate or present (*Hearle* v. *Greenbank* (1749) 3 Atk. at p. 710; *Arthington* v. *Coverly* (1733) 2 Abr.Cas.Eq. 518). The position now appears to be doubtful; an advowson or right to fill a church and benefice is now " land " (Law of Property Act, 1925, s. 205), and previously was an incorporeal hereditament, but if the benefice has become vacant, the nature of the right of presentation is altered: it becomes a personal right or chattel. In the latter case an infant is not incapacitated from owning or exercising the right.

A corporation aggregate presents by the corporate name under its common seal.

A patron may present himself (*Walsh* v. *Bishop of Lincoln* (1875) L.R. 10 C.P. 518).

The sale of the right of next presentation in invalidated by the Benefices Act, 1898, which Act also enlarges the powers of the bishop to refuse to institute. See BENEFICE.

A presentation may be revoked or varied before admission and institution, since it does not vest any right, and does not confer, before institution, any interest whatever.

The right of a Roman Catholic to present devolves upon the Universities of Oxford or Cambridge: see the statutes 1605, 3 Jac. 1, c. 5, and 1688, 1 W. & M. c. 26, the Presentation of Benefices Act, 1713, and the Church Patronage Act, 1737. The mode of exercising this devolved right is regulated by the Benefices Act, 1898, s. 7. The right of presentation of a person professing the Jewish religion, in right of any office held by him in the gift of the Crown, devolves on the Archbishop of Canterbury (Jews Relief Act, 1858, s. 4).

See ADVOWSON; INSTITUTION; NEXT PRESENTATION; SIMONY.

Presentation Office, the office of the Lord Chancellor's official, the Secretary of Presentations, who conducted all correspondence having reference to the twelve canonries and 650 livings in the gift of the Lord Chancellor, and drew and issued the *fiats* of appointment. The office was abolished by the Lord Chancellor's Pension Act, 1832, and the duties are now performed by the official in the Lord Chancellor's office who is known as the Secretary for Ecclesiastical Patronage.

Presentative advowson. See ADVOWSON.

Presentee, the clerk presented to a benefice: see the statute 1389, 13 Ric. 2, st. 1, c. 1.

Presenter, one who presents a presentee to a benefice.

Presentment, a kind of report by a jury or other body of men. Thus, formerly, at every customary court of a manor, all events relating to the alienation of the copyhold lands of the manor were presented by the homage for the information of the lord. In order to give effect to a surrender out of court it was formerly necessary that due mention or presentment of the transaction should be made at some subsequent court.

The surrender, and every other document relating to the title, on being presented in court, had to be endorsed that it had been presented and enrolled at a court held for the manor and then undersigned by at least two of the homage. By the Copyhold Act, 1841, s. 89, a presentment was made unnecessary for the alienation of copyholds.

Most commonly, however, presentment signified one made by a jury acting in a judicial capacity; and, in its general sense, it included inquisitions of office (*q.v.*), and indictments by a grand jury. But in the narrower sense of the word a presentment was the notice taken by a grand jury of any matter or offence from their own knowledge or observation, without any bill of indictment laid before them at the suit of the Crown; such as the presentment by them of a nuisance, a libel, or the like, upon which the officer of the court had afterwards to frame an indictment (4 Bl.Comm. 301).

Presentment of a bill of exchange, the presenting of a bill by the holder to the drawee for acceptance, or to the acceptor or an indorser for payment, of a cheque to the banker for payment, and of a note to the maker or indorser for payment.

The law on this subject is regulated by the Bills of Exchange Act, 1882. Presentment is necessary if the bill is payable after sight or if it is expressly stipulated for by the bill, or if it is drawn payable elsewhere than at the residence or place of business of the drawee, but in no other case (s. 39). When a bill payable after sight is negotiated the holder must either present or negotiate it within a reasonable time (s. 40).

The presentment must be made by or on behalf of the holder to the drawee or to some person authorised to accept or refuse acceptance on his behalf at a reasonable hour on a business day and before the bill is overdue. Presentment must be made to each of several drawees, not being partners or having authorised one to accept for all. Where authorised by agreement or usage, a presentment through the post is sufficient. Presentment is excused by the death or bankruptcy of the drawee, or where, after the exercise of reasonable diligence, such presentment cannot be effected, but the fact that the owner has reason to believe that the bill, on presentment, will be dishonoured, does not excuse presentment (s. 42).

Unless a bill is duly presented for payment, or presentment for payment is dispensed with by the drawee being a fictitious person, or by waiver or impracticability of presentment, the drawer and indorsers are discharged.

Where the bill is not payable on demand, presentment must be made on the day it falls due. A bill payable on demand must be presented within a reasonable time after its issue in order to render the drawer liable, and within a reasonable time after its indorsement in order to render the indorser liable. Presentment must be made at the proper place at a reasonable hour on a business day. Where authorised by agreement or usage, presentment through the post is sufficient (ss. 45, 46).

A cheque must be presented within a reasonable time after its issue in order to render the drawer liable, and within a reasonable time after its indorsement in order to render the indorser liable (ss. 45, 46, 73); and all the provisions of the Bills of Exchange Act, 1882, applicable to a bill of exchange payable on demand apply to a cheque also (s. 73). A reasonable time, is, in general, if customer and banker reside in the same place, the day after the cheque is received (*Alexander v. Burchfield* (1842) 7 M. & G. 1061).

Presentment within a reasonable time of indorsement is necessary in order to render an indorser liable but not in order to render the maker liable, unless the note is made payable at a particular place (ss. 86, 87).

Presents. " These presents " is the phrase by which reference is made in a deed to the deed itself; *e.g.,* " And whereas the parties to these presents have agreed, etc."

Preservation orders may be made in respect of historic buildings. See HISTORIC BUILDINGS.

Preservatives in foods. See the Food and Drugs Act, 1955, s. 4.

President, one placed in authority over others; one at the head of others; a governor; a chairman.

President of the Council, a great officer of state; a member of the Cabinet. He attends on the sovereign, proposes business at the council-table, and reports to the sovereign the transactions there (1 Bl.Comm. 230). See LORD PRESIDENT, ETC.

Press. Upon the art of printing becoming general, the press was subjected to a rigorous censorship, first on the part of the Church, and afterwards on the part of the State. Thus, in the reign of Elizabeth I, printing was interdicted, save in London, Oxford, and Cambridge. In the reign of James I the first newspapers were printed, but that king and his successor endeavoured to silence them by means of the Star Chamber jurisdiction. In 1641, when the Star Chamber was abolished, newspapers promised to become more abundant, especially as the mind of the nation was at that time in a very active and even excited state; but the Long Parliament by various ordinances endeavoured to restrain printing, at least on the part of the royalist and prelatical party. This conduct on the part of the Long Parliament was the occasion of Milton's treatise, entitled " Areopagitica, A Speech for Liberty of Unlicensed Printing." The statute 1660, 13 & 14 Car. 2, c. 33, placed printing under the control of the government, and confined the trade to London, York, Oxford, and Cambridge, limiting also the number of master printers to twenty. This statute expired in 1695, after various periods of renewal, and was not again re-enacted, it having been the opinion of Scroggs C.J. and of twelve other common law judges, that the common law was sufficient of itself, and without any statute, to repress the publication of any matter without the king's licence, and the liberal opinions which sprang up after the Revolution of 1688, preferring to entrust the control of the press to the ordinary jurisdictions at common law.

From this date newspapers rapidly increased, and in the reign of Anne began to be published regularly, and some even daily; and in that reign they began for the first time to combine political discussion with matters of intelligence, and were subject only to the two following restraints, the stamp duty on newspapers, which was imposed for the first time in 1712, and the law of libel.

The tax upon newspapers, which was 4d. in the reign of Anne, was reduced to 1d. in 1836, and was repealed altogether in 1855, and ultimately, in 1861, the duty upon paper also was repealed.

The law of libel was at first extremely severe, any reflection upon the government, or upon ministers, being construed into a reflection upon the king himself, and therefore as a seditious libel. This state of the law of libel was rendered all the worse by reason of the then doctrine of the common law, that the jury could only find the particular fact of publication, and not a general verdict of libel or no libel, that matter being left to the judges, who (as being the servants of the Crown) were naturally suspected of being disposed towards the Crown. And although in the *Case of the Seven Bishops* (1688) 12 St.Tr. 183, the jury brought in a general verdict of no libel, yet that precedent was insufficient of itself to change the law, more especially as it was given in bad times. It was left to Erskine, in *R.* v. *Shipley* (1784) 4 Dougl. 73, at p. 91, to advocate the right of the jury in actions of libel to find a general verdict, and to Fox, in his Libel Act, 1792, to confer that right upon the jury. By the Libel Act, 1843, s. 6, a defendant, in a criminal information, was for the first time enabled to plead in defence or justification the truth of the matters published, and that the same were so published for the public good.

The right of the press to attend meetings of local authorities is regulated by statute. See LOCAL AUTHORITY.

Where the public are excluded from court during the showing of allegedly indecent films, representatives of the press should be allowed to attend (*R.* v. *Waterfield* [1975] 1 W.L.R. 711).

There is no longer any censorship of the press in this country, and any man may write and publish whatever he pleases concerning another, subject only to this—that he must take the consequences if a jury should deem his words defamatory. The liberty of the press consists in printing without any previous licence, subject to the consequences of law.

The case of *Stockdale* v. *Hansard* (1839) 9 A. & E. 1, led to the passing of the Parliamentary Papers Act, 1840, which Act made reports published by order of Parliament absolutely privileged, and the printing of any extract or abstract of such report subject to qualified privilege; if found published bona fide and without malice, a verdict of not guilty is to be entered.

The Newspaper Libel and Registration Act, 1881, s. 4, enables a court of summary jurisdiction to make inquiry as to a newspaper libel being for the public benefit or being true. The Law of Libel Amendment Act, 1888, extended the privilege to reports of proceedings in court, public meetings, etc., and requires the leave of a judge before criminal proceedings can be brought against the press. The Defamation Act, 1952, s. 7, gives qualified privilege to statements in newspapers in the cases set out in the Schedule to the Act. See APOLOGY; CONFIDENTIAL COMMUNICATION; CONTEMPT OF COURT; FOX'S LIBEL ACT; JUSTIFICATION; LIBEL; LIBERTY OF THE PRESS; LOCAL AUTHORITY; NEWSPAPERS; PRINTERS; PRIVILEGE. As to the " Charter of the Freedom of the Press," see the Trade Union and Labour Relations (Amendment) Act, 1976, s. 2.

Press-gang. See IMPRESSMENT.

Pressing seamen. See IMPRESSMENT.

Pressing to death. See PEINE FORTE ET DURE.

Prest, a duty in money which was to be paid by the sheriff on his account in the Exchequer, or for money left or remaining in his hands, abolished by the statute 1548, 2 & 3 Edw. 6, c. 4; a forced loan levied by the king; an impost, and more especially a deduction from any payment; the money paid to a soldier on enlistment. Absconding after receiving prest-money, in its last-mentioned sense, was felony without benefit of clergy under the statute 1491, 7 Hen. 7, c. 1.

Prestation money, money payable by an archdeacon to his bishop *pro exteriore jurisdictione,* that is, for being allowed to exercise a jurisdiction which originally appertained to the bishop. The term was formerly also used as meaning purveyance (*q.v.*).

Prestimony, or **Praestimonia,** a fund or revenue appropriated by the founder for the subsistence of a priest, without being erected into any title or benefice, chapel, prebend or priory. It is not subject to the ordinary; but of it the patron, and those who have a right from him, are the collators (Canon Law).

No such thing would appear to be known to the present ecclesiastical law.

Prest-money, a payment which binds those who receive it. See PREST.

Presumptio juris et de jure. See PRESUMPTION.

Presumption. In the law of evidence, a presumption is a conclusion or inference as to the truth of some fact in question, drawn from some other fact judicially noticed, or proved or admitted to be true.

Presumptions are of three kinds. Irrebuttable or conclusive presumptions (*praesumptiones juris et de jure*) are absolute inferences established by law; they are called irrebuttable because evidence is not admissible to contradict them. Thus, by the Children and Young Persons Act, 1933, s. 50 (as amended by the Children and Young Persons Act, 1963, s. 16 (1)), there is a conclusive presumption that no child under the age of ten years can be guilty of any offence, and the presumption cannot be rebutted by the clearest evidence of a criminal intention. Irrebuttable presumptions are more properly called rules of law or fictions of law, according as the fact presumed is probably true, or is known to be false. See AGE; FICTION.

Inconclusive or rebuttable presumptions of law (*praesumptiones juristantum*) are inferences which the law requires to be drawn from given facts, and which are conclusive until disproved by evidence to the contrary; thus a child between ten and fourteen is presumed to be incapable of committing an offence, but evidence may be given to prove a criminal intention.

Presumptions of fact (*praesumptiones hominis vel facti*) are inferences which the tribunal (*e.g.*, a jury) is at liberty, but not compelled, to draw from the facts before it; if the tribunal thinks that the facts do not support the inference suggested, the presumption fails from its own weakness. This class is divisible into strong presumptions, or those which shift the burden of proof, and slight presumptions, which do not. Thus, possession is a strong presumption or prima facie evidence of ownership (see POSSESSION), while the presumption of guilt arising from the fact of a person having a pecuniary interest in the death of a murdered person is too slight to put him on his defence. Mixed presumptions, or presumptions of facts recognised by law, or presumptions of mixed law and fact, are certain presumptive inferences which, from their strength, importance, or frequent occurrence, attract as it were the observation of the law. The presumption of a " lost grant " (q.v.) falls within this class.

As to presumptive evidence, see EVIDENCE.

Presumption against a wrongdoer. See OMNIA PRAESUMUNTUR CONTRA SPOLIATOREM.

Presumption of advancement. See ADVANCEMENT.

Presumption of age of child bearing. See AGE.

Presumption of agency. See AGENCY.

Presumption of correctness. See OMNIA PRAESUMUNTUR RITE ET SOLEMNITER ESSE ACTA.

Presumption of innocence. Generally in criminal cases (unless otherwise directed by statute) the presumption of innocence casts on the prosecution the burden of proving the guilt of the prisoner beyond reasonable doubt (*Woolmington* v. *D.P.P.* [1935] A.C. 462).

Presumption of life or death. Where a person is once shown to have been living, the law will in general presume that he is still alive, unless after a lapse of time considerably exceeding the ordinary duration of human life; but if there is evidence of his continued unexplained absence from home and of the non-receipt of intelligence concerning him for a period of seven years, the presumption of life ceases and he is presumed to be dead at the end of the seven years. But the law raises no presumption as to the time of his death, and, therefore, if anyone has to establish the precise time during those seven years at which such person died, he must do so by evidence (*Nepean* v. *Doe* (1837) 2 M. & W. 894; *Re Rhodes* (1887) 36 Ch.D. 586). By the Cestui que Vie Act,

1666, a person on whose life a lease for lives depends is accounted dead if not proved alive after an absence of seven years, and the lessee may be ejected, with the proviso, however, that if he should turn out to be alive, the lessee may be reinstated.

The Family Division (q.v.) of the High Court may on petition by a married person alleging reasonable grounds for supposing that the other party to the marriage is dead grant a decree of presumption of death and dissolution of the marriage. The fact that for a period of seven years or more the other party to the marriage has been continually absent from the petitioner and the petitioner has no reason to believe that the other party has been living within that time is evidence that the other party is dead until the contrary is proved (Matrimonial Causes Act, 1973, s. 19 (1) (3)). The decree is a decree nisi in the first instance as in the case of a decree of divorce (s. 19 (4)). See DIVORCE.

The court has jurisdiction to entertain proceedings for death to be presumed and a marriage to be dissolved if (and only if) the petitioner (a) is domiciled in England and Wales on the date when the proceedings are begun, or (b) was habitually resident in England and Wales throughout the period of one year ending with that date (Domicile and Matrimonial Proceedings Act, 1973, s. 5). And see DOMICILE.

Proceedings for a decree of presumption of death and dissolution of marriage are assigned to the Family Division (q.v.) of the High Court (Administration of Justice Act, 1970, s. 1, Sch. 1). See ABSENCE FOR SEVEN YEARS; COMMORIENTES; LIFE.

Presumption of ownership. See FINDER OF LOST PROPERTY.

Presumption of survivorship. Where two or more persons perish by the same calamity, by the Law of Property Act, 1925, s. 184, in all questions affecting title to property the younger is presumed to have survived, subject to any order of the court; but as regards estate duty, they are presumed to have died at the same instant (Finance Act, 1958, s. 29; Finance Act, 1969, Sch. 17 Pt. III para. 24). See COMMORIENTES.

Presumptive heir, one who, if the ancestor had died immediately, would have been his heir, but whose right of inheritance might be defeated by the contingency of some nearer heir being born.

Presumptive title. A barely presumptive title, which is of the very lowest order, arises out of the mere occupation or simple possession of property (*jus possessionis*), without any apparent right, or any pretence of right, to hold and continue such possession. This may happen when one man disseises another; or where after the death of the ancestor, and before the entry of the heir, a stranger abated and kept out the heir. The law assumes that the actual occupant of land has the fee simple in it, unless there is evidence rebutting such presumption, or his possession is properly explained and shown to be consonant with the right of the true owner. Such a presumption, in the absence of any satisfactory proof to the contrary, will sustain an action for a trespass by a wrongdoer, and will indeed be strengthened, by lapse of time, into a title complete and indefeasible. This assumption is based on the feudal maxim that seisin was the basis or standpoint in the deduction of every title except in the case of descent. See POSSESSION.

Prêt à usage [Fr.], loan for use.

Pretenced right or title. Where one is in possession of land and another claims and sues for it, there is said to be a "pretenced title" in the latter person. The sale of any pretenced title was void at common law and was prohibited by the Bill of Bracery and Buying of Titles, 1540, s. 2, which provided that no one might sell or purchase any title to land unless the vendor had received the profits, or been in possession of the land, or of the reversion or remainder, for one whole year, on pain that both purchaser and vendor should each forfeit the value of such land to the king and the prosecutor. The Real Property Act, 1845, s. 6, made a right of entry or pretenced title transferable by deed; but the Act of 1845 did not repeal the Act of 1540, which, however, was repealed by the Land Transfer Act, 1897, s. 11, now the Law of Property Act, 1925, s. 4 (2). To recover under the Act of 1540 it had to be shown that the buyer knew the title to be bad (*Kennedy* v. *Lyell* (1885) 15 Q.B.D. 491).

Preterition, the entire omission of a child's name in the father's will, which rendered it null, exheredation being allowed but not preterition (Civil Law).

Pretium sepulchri, mortuary (*q.v.*).

Pretium succedit in loco rei (2 Buls. 321). (The price succeeds in the place of the thing.)

Prevarication, a collusion between an informer and a defendant, in order to a feigned prosecution; also, any secret abuse committed in a public office or private commission; also, the wilful concealment or misrepresentation of truth, by giving evasive or equivocating evidence.

Prevention [Lat. *praevenio*], the right which a superior person or officer has to lay hold of, claim, or transact, an affair prior to an inferior one, to whom otherwise it more immediately belongs (Canon Law).

Prevention of crimes. The Prevention of Crimes Acts, 1879 to 1908, which replaced the Habitual Criminals Act, 1869, provided for the keeping of a register of criminals, and the photographing of all persons convicted of crime with a view to their identification, and for subjecting to the supervision of the police persons twice convicted of crime. The Acts were replaced by the Criminal Justice Act, 1948, ss. 21–23, repealed by the Criminal Justice Act, 1967. See now the Powers of Criminal Courts Act, 1973.

A person may use such force as is reasonable in the circumstances in the prevention of crime, or in effecting or assisting in the lawful arrest of offenders or suspected offenders or of persons unlawfully at large (Criminal Law Act, 1967, s. 3). See BORSTAL INSTITUTION; PENAL SERVITUDE; PERSISTENT OFFENDERS.

Prevention of frauds. See SHARE-PUSHING.

Preventive detention. See PERSISTENT OFFENDERS.

Preventive service, the coastguard (*q.v.*). See the Coastguard Act, 1925, replacing the Coastguard Service Act, 1856.

Previous conviction. Persons convicted of offences after a previous conviction are usually punished more severely than first offenders. *Multiplicata transgressione crescat poenae inflictio* (with repeated transgression the infliction of punishment increases) (2 Co.Inst. 479).

The mode of arraigning a defendant for any offence committed after a previous conviction is, in the first instance, to arraign him upon so much only of the indictment as charges the subsequent offence, and, if he pleads not guilty or the court orders a plea of not guilty to be entered, to charge the jury in the first instance to inquire only concerning the first offence.

The following statements are to be read subject to the statutory provisions relating to spent convictions. See RE-HABILITATION OF OFFENDERS.

It is now the practice, after verdict, to hear evidence of character generally, and of previous convictions not included in the indictment. The practice is regulated by Practice Direction (C.C.A.) (Crime: Antecedents) [1966] 1 W.L.R. 1184. No evidence of previous convictions under the age of fourteen is admissible on the trial of a person over the age of twenty-one (Children and Young Persons Act, 1963, s. 16 (2)).

A witness, other than the defendant, may be questioned about previous convictions (Criminal Procedure Act, 1865, s. 6).

A previous conviction may conveniently be proved by extract from the record together with proof of identity (Prevention of Crimes Act, 1871, s. 18). It may also be proved by a certificate of the clerk of the court (Evidence Act, 1851, s. 13; Criminal Procedure Act, 1865, ss. 1, 6), by proof of finger-prints or palm-prints (Criminal Justice Act, 1948, s. 39; Criminal Justice Act, 1967, s. 33). Proof of summary conviction is by production of the register of the magistrates' court or an extract certified by the clerk to the justices (Magistrates' Courts Rules, 1968, r. 56). Evidence of previous convictions may be given in handling cases (Theft Act, 1968, s. 27 (3) (b)).

A prisoner giving evidence on his own behalf may not be questioned as to whether he has committed or been convicted of any offence other than that charged unless evidence of a previous conviction is admissible to show whether he is or is not guilty of the offence charged, or unless in the course of the case he has sought to prove his own good character or the bad character of the prosecutor or the prosecutor's witnesses, or unless he has given evidence against anyone charged with the same offence (Criminal Evidence Act, 1898, s. 1 (f)).

Price control, the fixing of prices in order to maintain economic stability in spite of abnormal conditions. See the Counter-Inflation Act, 1973, and the Prices Acts, 1974 and 1975. The Secretary of State for Prices and Consumer Protection is the central authority. See also the Remuneration, Charges and Grants Act, 1975. See S.I. 1976 Nos. 1170, 1171.

Price maintenance agreements, agreements between manufacturers and retailers by which the retailers contract not to sell the manufacturers' goods at less than a stated price. See RESALE.

Prices and Consumer Protection, Secretary of State for. The Department of Prices and Consumer Protection is responsible for consumer protection, consumer credit and standards, and weights and measures. It supervises the work of the Price Commission and deals with prices in shops including food prices. It is responsible for monopolies, mergers, restrictive practices and the office of the Director of Fair Trading.

Certain miscellaneous powers were transferred to the Department by S.I. 1974 No. 692, Sch. 1 Pt. IV.

Pricking for sheriffs. When the yearly list of persons nominated for the office of sheriff (q.v.) in each county is submitted to the King or Queen in Council, he or she takes a silver bodkin, and, to ensure impartiality, lets the point of it fall upon one of the three names nominated for each county, etc., and the person upon whose name it chances to fall is sheriff for the ensuing year. This is called pricking for sheriffs. In practice, persons whose names are pricked have been decided on beforehand, and there is really no element of chance in the matter. See POCKET-SHERIFF.

Pricking does not apply to Cornwall (the sheriff of which is appointed by the Prince of Wales as Duke of Cornwall), or to Lancashire (the sheriff of which is appointed by the Crown in right of the Duchy of Lancaster).

Pride; Pride-gavel. The pride was the lamprey; and pride-gavel was a rent paid until modern times by the tenants of the manor of Rodeley, in Gloucestershire, for the privilege of fishing for lampreys in the Severn (Tayl.Hist.Gavelk. 112).

Priest, one in priest's orders of the Church of England or of the Roman Catholic Church, or, it would seem, of the Greek Church. In the Church of England deacon's orders are a necessary preliminary to priest's orders. As to the age at which a person may receive priest's orders see ORDINATION.

As to sex discrimination see the Sex Discrimination Act, 1975, s. 19.

No one, other than a priest—every bishop is of necessity a priest—can consecrate the Holy Communion or pronounce the Absolution. See DEACON; HOLY ORDERS.

Prima facie, at first sight; on the face of it.

Prima facie evidence, that which, not being inconsistent with the falsity of the hypothesis, nevertheless raises such a degree of probability in its favour that it must prevail if believed by the jury unless rebutted or the contrary proved; conclusive evidence, on the other hand, is that which excludes or at least tends to exclude, the possibility of the truth of any other hypothesis than the one attempted to be established.

Prima tonsura, a grant of a right to have the first crop of grass (1 Chit.Pr. 181).

Primacy, the office or authority of a primate (q.v.).

Primae (or Primariae) preces. See PRECES PRIMARIAE.

Primae impressionis, of first impression. A case *primae impressionis* is a case of a new kind, to which no established principle of law directly applies, and which must be decided entirely by reason as distinguished from authority (*Mirehouse* v. *Rennell* (1832) 8 Bing. at p. 515). See COMMON LAW; FIRST IMPRESSION.

Primage, a small payment, also known as hat-money (q.v.), made by the owner or consignee of goods to the master of the vessel in which they are shipped for his care and trouble, varying in amount according to the particular trade in which the ship is engaged or to the custom of the place (*Best* v. *Saunders* (1828) M. & M. 208; *Charleton* v. *Cotesworth* (1826) R. & M. 175; *Caughey* v. *Gordon & Co.* (1878) 3 C.P.D. 419). The payment of this sum is generally stipulated for in the bill of lading (q.v.). See AVERAGE.

Primaria ecclesia, the mother church.

Primary conveyances. Original conveyances, sometimes opposed to secondary conveyances, such as releases, surrenders, etc. (see DERIVATIVE DEED), are or were feoffments, grants, gifts, leases, exchanges and partitions. See CONVEYANCE.

Primary education. See EDUCATION.

Primary evidence, the best evidence, as distinguished from secondary evidence. See EVIDENCE.

Primate, a chief ecclesiastic; part of the style and title of an archbishop; thus the Archbishop of Canterbury is styled Primate of All England; the Archbishop of York is Primate of England.

Prime election, first choice.

Prime Minister, the statesman who in response to a summons from the sovereign accepts the commission to form a Ministry; the Premier (q.v.). The expression is of comparatively recent origin, dating from about the end of the eighteenth century. In point of law, as distinguished from constitutional law, there is no such office as that of Prime Minister though his existence is recognised by statute for certain purposes, such as salary and pension. He is simply the particular member of one House of Parliament or the other to whom the sovereign deputes the function of selecting other members of those Houses as the persons to form the Cabinet. The Prime Minister is also First Lord of the Treasury, and he receives a salary of £20,000 a year (Ministerial and other Salaries Act, 1975, s. 1, Sch. 1). As to pension, see the Ministerial Salaries Consolidation Act, 1965, the Pensions (Increase) Act, 1969, s. 1 (1), Sch. 1 Pts. I, IV, the Parliamentary and other Pensions Act, 1972, ss. 26, 29, 31, 36, Sch. 4.

Although the Prime Minister, as such, has no legal status, he is the head of the government for the time being. Other members of the Cabinet hold office only at his pleasure: he remains the predominant member of the Cabinet so long as he commands a majority in the House of Commons, and he, for that reason, is always the leader of the political party which, for the time being, is the strongest. See PREMIER.

By Royal Warrant dated December 2, 1905, the Prime Minister takes precedence next after the Archbishop of Canterbury (who ranks next after the princes of the blood royal), the Lord Chancellor and the Archbishop of York.

In the Chequers Estate Acts, 1917, and 1958, the Prime Minister is referred to *eo nomine*: but this is a statutory recognition merely of the fact that a particular person bears a particular label for the time being.

Primer, first.

Primer election, first choice.

Primer fine. On suing out the writ or *praecipe* called a writ of covenant, there was due to the Crown, by ancient prerogative, a *primer fine,* or a noble for every five marks of land sued for, *i.e.,* one-tenth of the annual value. See PRAEFINE.

Primer seisin, a payment due by a tenant of land held of the Crown *in capite ut de corona* if he succeeded to it by descent when of full age. The payment consisted of one year's profits of the land if it was in possession, and half a year's profits if it was in reversion (Co. Litt. 77a).

Primer seisin was abolished by the statute 1660, 12 Car. 2, c. 24.

See CAPITE, TENURE IN; LIVERY; OUSTERLEMAIN.

Primicerius, the first of any degree of men (1 Dugd.Mon. 838).

Primitiae, the first fruits which were presented to the gods by the ancients; also, the profits of a living during the first year after avoidance, formerly taken by the Crown. See ANNATES.

Primo beneficio, a writ which, upon occasion, was formerly addressed to the Chancellor or the Keeper directing him to bestow upon such and such a clerk the first benefice in the royal gift, and over a certain value, which became vacant (Cowel). See BENEFICIO, ETC.

Primo excutienda est verbi vis, ne sermonis vitio obstruetur oratio, sive lex sine argumentis (Co.Litt. 68). (The meaning of the word must be first examined in order that the meaning of the sentence may not be obscured by a verbal error, and that the law may not be left obscure for want of its being argued.) Words are to be construed according to their natural meaning, unless such a construction would either render them senseless or would be opposed to the general scope and intent of the instrument, or unless there is some very cogent reason of convenience in favour of a different interpretation.

Primo loco, in the first place.

Primogeniture [Lat. *primo-genitus,* first-born], seniority, eldership, the state of being first-born; the rule of inheritance according to which the eldest of two or more males in the same degree succeeded to the ancestor's land to the exclusion of the others.

The right of primogeniture obtaining in England was that right whereby the eldest son succeeded to all the real estate of an intestate parent. An analogous right of succession is frequently given by will, and even more frequently given and preserved by marriage or other settlements. The right was not acknowledged by the Romans, among whom sons and daughters all shared equally the property of their parents, and in continental countries exists in a modified form only, if at all. In England the customs of gavelkind and borough-English were almost the only exceptions to this Norman rule of inheritance.

The right, which was a corner-stone of the social structure in England, was swept away by the land legislation of 1925, but hereditary dignities and titles of honour are not affected (Law of Property Act, 1925, s. 201 (2)).

See DESCENT; ENTAIL; SETTLEMENT.

Primum decretum, a provisional decree.

Primus actus judicii est judicis approbatorius. (The first step which a party to an action takes in the action is a concession that the court has jurisdiction.) This does not apply if his plea is to the jurisdiction.

1423

Prince [Lat. *princeps*], a sovereign; a chief ruler of either sex. Thus Elizabeth I was said to be a prince admirable above her sex for her princely virtues (Camden).

Prince Consort. This title was bestowed by patent in 1857 upon Prince Albert of Saxe-Coburg, the husband of Queen Victoria. Until then he had been merely "Prince Albert" with, however, a patent of precedence next after the Queen. The title of Prince Consort was merely honorific, and made no substantial difference in the position of the Prince.

Prince of Scotland, the title borne by the eldest son of the King of Scots. The principality of Scotland consisted of lands in Ayr, Renfrew and Ross.

Prince of Wales, the eldest son of the reigning sovereign, if so created. He is the heir apparent to the Crown; he is created Earl of Chester, and is Duke of Cornwall by inheritance (during the life of the sovereign), without any new creation. The eldest son of the reigning sovereign is always created Prince of Wales and Earl of Chester by patent. George III, when he became heir apparent to George II upon the death of Frederick, Prince of Wales, was also created Prince of Wales and Earl of Chester; but he was never Duke of Cornwall. Since the accession of James I, the heir apparent has been by inheritance Duke of Rothesay, Earl of Carrick, Baron Renfrew in the peerage of Scotland, and Lord of the Isles and Great Steward of Scotland, these titles being inherited under an Act of the Scottish Parliament passed on November 27, 1469. As to rights of the heir apparent to submarine mines and minerals in Cornwall, see the Cornwall Submarine Mines Act, 1858. See CIVIL LIST; CORNWALL; HEIR APPARENT.

Prince of Wales Island, Singapore and Malacca, territories administered together as a British colony under the Straits Settlements Act, 1866, repealed by the Straits Settlements (Repeal) Act, 1946.

Princes of the royal blood, the younger sons and daughters of the sovereign and other branches of the royal family who are not in the immediate line of succession.

Princes, rulers and peoples. "Arrests, restraints and detainments of princes, rulers and peoples," are almost always provided against in contracts of affreightment and policies of marine insurance. The expression virtually means interference of a lawful authority.

Princess Royal, the title borne by the eldest daughter of the sovereign, if and when it is conferred on her by the sovereign. No grant by letters patent is necessary. The question as to what happens when the title is borne by the eldest daughter of a deceased sovereign and there is an eldest daughter of a subsequent sovereign had never arisen until after the death of Edward VII. It would seem that the title may not be held by more than one person at the same time.

Principal, a head, a chief; also, a capital sum of money placed out at interest; also, an heirloom, mortuary, or corsepresent.

Principal and accessory. Principals in offences are of two degrees: of the first degree, *i.e.*, the actual perpetrators of the crime; of the second degree, *i.e.*, those who are present, aiding and abetting the act to be done. See DEGREE.

Accessories are not the chief actors in the offence, nor present at its performance, but are in some way concerned therein, either before or after the fact is committed. See ACCESSORY.

The abolition of the distinction between felony (*q.v.*) and misdemeanour (*q.v.*) has the result that principals of either degree and accessories before the fact are treated alike as principal offenders (Criminal Law Act, 1967, s. 1).

Principal and agent. He who, being *sui juris* and competent to do any act for his own benefit on his own account, employs another person to do it, is called the principal, constituent or employer, and he who is thus employed is called the agent, attorney, proxy or delegate of the principal, constituent or employer. The relation thus created between the parties is termed an agency. The power thus delegated is called in law an authority, and the act, when performed, is often designated as an act of agency or procuration.

A person who authorises another to act on his behalf is generally called the principal, and the person so authorised is called the agent. The law of principal and agent deals both with the rights and duties of the principal and agent *inter se,* and with those of each of them towards third persons. See AGENCY; AUTHORITY; POWER OF ATTORNEY; VICARIOUS RESPONSIBILITY.

When an authorised agent does an act in his own name and professedly on his own behalf, though really on behalf of his principal, the latter is said to be undisclosed; the general rule is that an agent contracting for an undisclosed principal is himself liable to the person contracting with him, and that the latter also has the option of suing the principal as soon as he discovers his existence, unless in the meantime the principal has bona fide paid the agent, in which case the principal is discharged from liability (*Irvine* v. *Watson* (1879) 5 Q.B.D. 102).

Principal and surety. A person who owes a debt for which another person is liable in case of his default in paying it, is called the principal or principal debtor, the other being his surety (*q.v.*). See GUARANTEE; INDEMNITY.

Principal challenge, a species of challenge to the array made on account of partiality or some default in the officer who arrayed the panel. See CHALLENGE.

Principal debtor, the person whose liability is guaranteed by a surety.

Principal mansion-house. The Settled Land Act, 1925, s. 65, replacing the Settled Land Act, 1890, s. 10, enacts that the principal mansion-house, and the pleasure grounds and parks usually occupied therewith, cannot be sold, exchanged or leased without the consent of the trustees of the settlement or an order of the court; a house usually occupied as a farmhouse, or occupying with its park and grounds less than twenty-five acres, is not within the section. Where there are more mansion-houses than one upon the same estate the question as to which is the principal mansion-house depends upon the facts. Where there is only one mansion-house on settled land it is a " principal mansion-house " unless it is such house as is specified in the section.

Principal moneys, the sum lent, as distinct from interest and other moneys covenanted to be paid in a mortgage.

Principiorum non est ratio (2 Buls. 239). (First principles do not require proof.) See NON OMNIUM, ETC.

Principum placita, the enactments or constitutions of the emperor. What the emperor determined had the force of a statute (Civil Law).

Printers. The Newspapers, Printers, and Reading Rooms Repeal Act, 1869, repeals a number of earlier Acts except as regards certain parts set out in the second Schedule. These unrepealed parts of the earlier Acts provide that a printer shall incur a penalty of £20 in respect of anything (other than parliamentary papers, bank notes, bills of exchange and various documents used in the course of law or business, or papers for public departments) which he prints for hire, unless he keeps a copy bearing the name and address of his employer; that he shall incur a penalty of £5 for every copy of anything intended for publication which does not bear his name and address, unless it was, and is declared to have been, printed at the University Press, Oxford, or the Pitt Press, Cambridge; and that no such penalty can be sued for except in the name of a law officer (*q.v.*). Greeting and picture cards are exempt (Printer's Imprint Act, 1961).

As to compelling discovery of the printer of a newspaper, see *Dixon* v. *Enoch* (1872) L.R. 13 Eq. 394.

A print works is a factory for the purpose of the Factories Act, 1961, s. 175 (2) (g).

Printing of pleadings. This is regulated by R.S.C., Ord. 66.

Prior, chief of a priory, next in dignity to an abbot.

Prior petens, the person first applying. As to the order of priority for a grant where the deceased left a will see the Non-Contentious Probate Rules, 1954, r. 19. As to the order of priority for a grant in case of intestacy, see r. 21.

Prior tempore potior jure. See QUI PRIOR, ETC.

Priores leges ad posteriores trahantur (D. 1, 3, 26). This literally is: " Earlier laws are drawn to those of later date." It practically means the same as *lex posterior derogat priori* (*q.v.*).

Priority, an antiquity of tenure in comparison with another less ancient;

also that which is before another in order of time. See POSTERIORITY.

When two persons have similar rights in respect of the same subject-matter, but one is entitled to exercise his right to the exclusion of the other, he is said to have priority. The question is chiefly of importance with reference to securities on property; thus, if A mortgages his land first to B by deposit of title-deeds, then to C by formal deed of mortgage, and then to D by an equitable charge, the question arises who is entitled to realise his security in priority to the others. The general rule is that he who has the first mortgage and has a legal estate has priority over all other incumbrancers unless he has been guilty of gross negligence, *e.g.,* in omitting to inquire as to the deeds (*Hewitt* v. *Loosemore* (1851) 9 Hare 449).

The priority of legal and equitable assignments of equitable choses in action is determined according to the date of receipt of notice by the persons who are for the time being owners of the legal interest in the property assigned. The notice must, for the purposes of establishing priority among competing claims, be in writing (Law of Property Act, 1925, s. 137). See DEARLE *v.* HALL, RULE IN.

Subject to the Land Charges Act, 1972, the assignee of an equitable interest in land having notice will himself be bound to give effect to prior equitable claims of which he has notice, whether verbal or written, or actual or constructive (*Torkington* v. *Magee* [1902] 2 K.B. 427). The notice does not, under the rule in *Dearle* v. *Hall* (1823) 3 Russ. 1, affect the validity of the assignment (*Ward* v. *Duncombe* [1893] A.C. 369); it merely establishes priority. Under the Law of Property Act, 1925, s. 137, all equitable interests in land (*i.e.,* all estates for less than a fee simple absolute in possession or a term of years absolute) and corresponding incorporeal hereditaments, as well as all equitable interests in capital money and securities representing capital money, were brought within this rule. Before 1926 the priorities in regard to these were determined by the date and time of creation of the equitable interest and subject to the

formalities required for the transfer. Special rules as to the persons, if any, to whom notice must be given and, in their absence, for the indorsement of a memorandum on the trust instrument, are provided by the section.

In regard to mortgages, before 1926, puisne mortgagees to whom the equity of redemption was conveyed in succession obtained priority by the order in date of their mortgages, subject to the application of the doctrine of tacking or to equitable reasons (if any) for the postponement of their mortgages.

After 1926 subsisting and future mortgages of the equity of redemption of a legal estate, *i.e.,* a fee simple or a term of years absolute, but not mortgages of life interests or of an undivided share or of an estate in remainder or reversion, were transformed into legal mortgages. Consequently the former rules of equity, based on the rule of equity *qui prior in tempore potior est in jure* ceased to apply. Priority among all mortgages, both legal and equitable, of a legal estate is now ascertained by possession of the documents of title subject to notice, actual or constructive, of equities affecting the security, and by date of registration under the Land Charges Act, 1972, s. 2, Class C (Law of Property Act, 1925, s. 97). If the mortgage is by trustees for sale, or a tenant for life as estate owner, or personal representatives or other persons referred to in the Law of Property Act, 1925, s. 2, and is made in accordance with the statutory requirements, the mortgagees as purchasers, whether registered or not, will not be affected by equities which can be overreached.

Mortgages of registered land have priority according to the date of registration (Land Registration Act, 1925, s. 29). See REGISTRATION OF TITLE TO LAND.

Priorities are subject to the provisions of the Land Registration Act, 1925, s. 144, and the Land Charges Act, 1972, s. 11, relating to priority notices (*q.v.*).

Priorities in respect of equitable charges by a tenant for life or statutory owner for death duties and other estate liabilities discharged by him, subject to those equitable charges which are not protected by possession of the documents of title or which do not affect interests under a trust for sale or settlement, are determined by the date of their registration under the Land Charges Act, 1972, s. 2, Class C.

In regard to equitable mortgages and other charges upon land, or any interest therein created before 1926, which have not been transferred or conveyed after 1925, the rule *qui prior est tempore potior in jure* prevails if the equities are equal, and a purchaser is still affected with notice of these and cannot gain priority by registration, but registration, if available, amounts to notice. See ASSETS; PREFERENTIAL PAYMENTS.

Priority may arise by the doctrines of tacking (*q.v.*), of consolidation (*q.v.*), or of salvage (*q.v.*).

As to priority among creditors, the Administration of Estates Act, 1869, reproduced by the Administration of Estates Act, 1925, ss. 32–34, Sch. 1, provides that in the administration of the estate of a deceased person, no debt or liability shall be entitled to any priority or preference by reason merely that it is secured by or arises under a bond, deed or other instrument under seal, or is otherwise made or constituted a specialty debt. See ASSETS; LEGACY; PREFERENTIAL PAYMENTS.

Priority caution, a form of caution at the Land Registry for the protection of persons entitled to minor interests; it does not affect a purchaser for value.

Priority notice. Any person intending to make an application for the registration of any contemplated charge, instrument or other matter in pursuance of the Land Charges Act, 1972, or any rule made under the Act may give a priority notice in the prescribed form at least fifteen days before the registration is to take effect (ss. 11 (1), 6 (*a*)). If the application is presented within thirty days thereafter and refers in the prescribed manner to the notice, the registration takes effect as if the registration had been made at the time when the charge etc. was created (s. 11 (3), 6 (*b*)). Where a purchaser has obtained an official certificate of search under s. 10 of the Act, any entry made in the register after the date of the certificate and before the completion of the purchase and is not made pursuant to a priority notice

entered on the register on or before the date of the certificate, will not affect the purchaser if the purchase is completed before the expiration of fifteen days after the date of the certificate (s. 11 (5), 6 (*a*)).

The numbers of days referred to above may be altered by rules. In reckoning the number of days, any days when the registry is not open to the public are excluded (s. 11 (6)).

In regard to registered land, a priority notice is a form of notice providing temporary protection for an application about to be made for first registration of land at the Land Registry; also a notice protecting the priority of an intended dealing in registered land; the notice must be accompanied by the land certificate or charge certificate, and is usually effective for fourteen days after lodgment (Land Registration Act, 1925, s. 144).

Priority neighbourhood. If an area cannot be declared a "housing action area" (*q.v.*) or a general improvement area (see IMPROVEMENT AREAS) it may be declared a priority neighbourhood (Housing Act, 1974, ss. 52–55).

Prisage, an ancient hereditary revenue of the Crown, consisting in the right to take a certain quantity from cargoes of wine imported into England. In Edward I's reign it was converted into a pecuniary duty called butlerage. All prisage and butlerage on wines were abolished as regards England, except the Duchy of Lancaster, by the statute 1809, 49 Geo. 3, c. 98, ss. 35, 36, and, as regards the Duchy, by the statute 1832, 2 & 3 Will. 4, c. 84, s 40. The present duties on wines are regulated by the Customs and Excise Act, 1952. See BOTILER OF THE KING; CIVIL LIST; CONSOLIDATED FUND; CUSTOMS.

Prisage is also said to have been the share of the king or the Lord High Admiral in ships lawfully taken in prize (Cowel).

Priso, a prisoner taken in war (Hovenden, 541).

Prisonam frangentibus, Statutum de, the statute 1295, 23 Edw. 1. It is taken as the foundation of the doctrine that prison-breach was felony in the case of one confined on a charge of felony, and misdemeanour in the case of one confined on a charge of any lesser offence (1 Hale P.C. 612).

Prison-breach, or prison-breaking, is where a person, being lawfully detained on a charge of or under sentence for an offence, breaks out of the place where he is detained; that is, escapes with force. The degree of the offence and its punishment varies at common law with that of the offence for which he was detained.

Prisoner, one who is confined in a prison. As to the forcible feeding of a prisoner, see *Leigh* v. *Gladstone* (1909) 26 T.L.R. 139. As to the temporary discharge of prisoners on account of the condition of their health, see the Prison Act, 1952, s. 28, replacing the Prisoners (Temporary Discharge for Ill-health) Act, 1913. As to legal aid, see COSTS IN CRIMINAL PROCEEDING.

Natural justice does not require that a prisoner be entitled to legal representation at the hearing of a prison disciplinary offence; such offences must be heard and decided promptly (*Fraser* v. *Mudge* [1975] 1 W.L.R. 1132).

Prisoners of war. The treatment and rights of these are provided for by the Hague Convention, 1899, and the Geneva Conventions, 1949: see GENEVA CONVENTIONS. See Draper, *Red Cross Conventions.*

The Limitation (Enemies and War Prisoners) Act, 1945 (as amended), grants an extension of time for bringing actions where either party has been a prisoner of war.

Prisons, places in which persons are kept either for safe custody until they have been tried for an offence of which they stand charged, or for punishment after being tried and convicted. See FLEET; FRANCHISE PRISONS; HOLLOWAY; MARSHALSEA; MILLBANK PENITENTIARY; NEWGATE; PENTONVILLE; QUEEN'S PRISON; WHITECROSS STREET PRISON.

The general administration of prisons is vested in the Home Secretary, assisted by Prison Commissioners appointed by the Crown, and each prison is further under the more immediate jurisdiction of boards of visitors appointed by the Home Secretary. See BORSTAL INSTITUTIONS; HABEAS CORPUS; IMPRISONMENT; PENAL SERVITUDE.

The Prison Act, 1877, transferred the management of prisons from counties and boroughs to the government, and put an end to the obligation theretofore existing on the part of the counties and boroughs to maintain prisons of their own, and the Prison Act, 1898, constituted the Prison Commissioners, established three divisions of prisoners not sentenced to penal servitude or hard labour, and restricted the authorisation of corporal punishment. Prisons are now regulated by the Prison Act, 1952.

Prison governors and officials are ineligible for jury service. See JURY.

As to sex discrimination of prison officers see the Sex Discrimination Act, 1975, s. 18.

Private Acts of Parliament, Acts operating upon particular persons and private concerns, as Naturalisation Acts, Divorce Acts and Change of Name Acts. They are generally not printed, but copies of them can be obtained at the Copyists' Office, House of Lords, on payment of fees. See ACT OF PARLIAMENT.

Private Bill Office, an office of Parliament where the business of obtaining private Acts of Parliament is conducted. See BILL.

Private chapels. By the Private Chapels Act, 1871, the bishop may license a clergyman to serve the chapel of any college, school, hospital, etc., whether consecrated or unconsecrated, but not to solemnise marriages therein. The Act was repealed by the Extra-Parochial Ministry Measure, 1967, with a saving for licences granted under the Act (s. 4).

Private chattels scheme, a scheme for compensation for war damage to chattels made under the War Damage Act, 1943.

Private company, a company which by its articles restricts the right to transfer its shares, and limits the number of its members to 50, not including persons who are in the employment of the company and persons who, having been formerly in the employment of the company, were, while in that employment, and have continued after the determination of such employment to be, members of the company, and prohibits any invitation to the public to subscribe for any shares or debentures of the company (Companies Act, 1948, s. 28 (1)). Where two or more persons hold one or more shares in a company jointly they are treated as a single member (s. 28 (2)). S. 27 provides that if a company alters its articles so that the provisions of s. 28 for the constitution of a private company are not included, the company ceases upon such alteration to be a private company and must deliver to the registrar of companies a prospectus or statement in lieu of prospectus within fourteen days, and if the company makes default in complying with those provisions, although contained in its articles, it loses the privileges and exemptions of private companies to be found in, *e.g.,* ss. 31, 222, 224 (reduction of number of members below the legal minimum), s. 48 (statement in lieu of prospectus and allotment of shares), s. 109 (commencement of business), s. 130 (statutory meeting and report), and s. 176 (number of directors), which do not apply to private companies.

All private companies except certain unlimited companies must now file accounts. See EXEMPT PRIVATE COMPANY.

Private international law, conflict of laws (*q.v.*). See INTERNATIONAL LAW.

Private law. See LAW.

Private nuisance. See NUISANCE.

Private streets. A private street is a street not being a highway maintainable at the public expense (Highways Act, 1959, s. 213 (1); Public Health Act, 1961, Sch. 1 Pt. III; Local Government Act, 1972, Sch. 30).

In proceedings under s. 213 of the Highways Act, 1959, the highway authority discharges the onus of proving that the street in question is a private street (unless something in the circumstances suggests that it might have become repairable by the inhabitants at large in some special way) by showing that the highway did not exist before 1835 and that the procedure established by the Highway Act, 1835, s. 23 had not been followed (*Alsager U.D.C.* v. *Barratt* [1965] 2 Q.B. 343). The execution of street works in private streets is regulated by the Highways Act, 1959, ss. 173–188 (" The Code of 1892 "). Outside Greater London the local authority is the county council (Local Government Act, 1972, s. 188 (5)). As to guard rails in private streets see the Public Health Act, 1961, s. 43; London Government Act, 1963, Sch. 11 Pt. I

para. 37). As to urgent repairs see the Public Health Act, 1961, s. 47; Local Government Act, 1972, s. 187 (2) (*b*).

A private street may be declared a highway under the Highways Act, 1959, s. 37; London Government Act, 1963, s. 16 (2), Sch. 6 para. 12; Local Government Act, 1972, s. 188 (7) (*a*), Sch. 21 para. 14.

Privateers, ships commissioned by letters of marque (*q.v.*) to exercise general reprisals (see REPRISALS). Privateering, properly so called, was abolished as between European nations by the Declaration of Paris, 1856. But during the Franco-Prussian War the Prussian Government incorporated all its merchant ships into its navy, and used them for ordinary naval operations: during the Russo-Japanese War the Russian Government used armed merchantmen as cruisers; and the same practice was followed by the belligerents on both sides in the wars of 1914–18 and 1939–45. There is, however, a clear distinction between the new quasi-privateer and the old privateer. In the old privateering, the privateer was for all purposes a private ship except that her master had letters of marque: now when a private ship is used for warlike purposes she is under naval discipline, and is precisely the same as a regular warship, except that she was not originally built as one. See Navy Records Soc., vols. 49, 50.

Privation, an abbreviation, by aphaeresis, of the word deprivation (*q.v.*), a taking away or withdrawing (Co.Litt. 239).

Privatis pactionibus non dubium est non laedi jus caeterorum (D. 2, 15, 3). (It is clear that the rights of others are not prejudiced by private agreements.) See DEBITORUM, ETC.; PACTA PRIVATA, ETC.

Privatorum conventio juri publico non derogat (9 Co.Rep. 141). (An agreement between private persons does not derogate from the public right.) See PACTA PRIVATA, ETC.

Privatum commodum publico cedit (Jenk.Cent. 223). (Private good yields to public good.) See SALUS POPULI, ETC.

Privatum incommodum publico bono pensatur (Jenk.Cent. 85). (Private loss is compensated by public good.)

Privement ensient, pregnant but not yet quick with child (Wood, Inst. 662).

Privies, those who are partakers or have an interest in any action or thing, or any relation to another. They are said to be of six kinds: privies in blood, such as the heir to his ancestor, or between coparceners; privies in representation, as executors or administrators to their deceased testator or intestate; privies in estate, as grantor and grantee, lessor and lessee, assignor and assignee, etc.; privies in respect of contract, such privities being personal privities extending only to the persons of the lessor and lessee, or the parties to the contract or assignees upon a fresh contract or novation with the assignee; privies in respect of estate and contract together, as where the lessee assigns his interest, but the contract between lessor and lessee continues, the lessor not having accepted the assignee in substitution; and privies in law, as the lord by escheat, a tenant by the curtesy, or in dower, the incumbent of a benefice, a husband suing or defending in right of his wife, etc. (Co.Litt. 271a; Jacob). See PRIVITY; PRIVY.

Privilege, an exceptional right of advantage; an exemption from some duty, burden, or attendance, to which certain persons are entitled, from a supposition of law that the stations they fill or the offices they are engaged in are such as require all their care, and that, therefore, without this indulgence, it would be impracticable to execute such offices so advantageously as the public good requires.

With reference to the persons who enjoy them, personal privileges are of various kinds: the principal are those belonging to the royal family, the Houses of Parliament, peers, ambassadors, barristers, solicitors and clergymen. With reference to the nature of the right or exemption, the principal privileges are the freedom from arrest enjoyed by ambassadors (*q.v.*) and peers; the exemption from serving on juries enjoyed by peers, members of Parliament, ministers, barristers, solicitors, medical practitioners, etc.; the privileges exempting barristers, solicitors and patent agents from giving discovery or evidence of matters communicated to them by their clients in professional confidence, etc. See CONFIDENTIAL COMMUNICATIONS.

With reference to their duration, privileges are either permanent or temporary: thus, a member of Parliament is privileged from arrest on civil process during the sitting of the House, and for forty days before and after a prorogation: a barrister has a similar privilege while he is on circuit, and a peer always possesses a similar privilege.

The privileges of either House of Parliament are extensive, but they are at the same time uncertain and indefinite. Amongst those privileges are the power of committing persons to prison; the power of publishing matters which, if not issuing from such high authority, might become the subject of proceedings in a court of law; the power of directing the Attorney-General to prosecute persons accused of offences against the law or affecting the privilege of Parliament; and the power vested in each House, respectively, of doing anything not directly contravening an Act of Parliament which may be necessary for the vindication or protection of itself in the exercise of its own constitutional functions. In the daily proceedings of Parliament questions of privilege take precedence of all other business.

The privileges of individual members of Parliament are freedom of speech (*Re Parliamentary Privilege Act, 1770* [1958] A.C. 331) and person, including freedom from arrest and seizure under process of the courts of justice; this, however, does not extend to indictable offences, to actual contempts of the courts of justice, or to proceedings in bankruptcy. Members of Parliament are exempt from serving the office of sheriff, from obeying a subpoena, and from serving on a jury. Privilege of Parliament continues to peers at all times (*Dingle* v. *Associated Newspapers* [1961] 2 Q.B. 162; *Stourton* v. *Stourton* [1963] P. 302), and to commoners for a convenient time after prorogation and dissolution. When arraigned for any criminal offence peers were, before the Criminal Justice Act, 1948, s. 30, tried by their fellow-peers who returned a verdict, not upon oath, but upon honour; they have the privilege of sitting covered in courts of justice.

Barristers are privileged from arrest *eundo, morando et redeundo,* going to, coming from, and abiding in court, including judges' chambers; so clergymen as to divine service. As to the immunity from arrest of a litigant, see *Re Hunt* [1959] 2 Q.B. 69.

A statement is said to be privileged when it is made in such circumstances. that it does not render the person making it liable to proceedings for slander or libel, although it would have that effect in the absence of those circumstances. The principal instances of privileged statements are those made between a solicitor or counsel and the client; by a witness in the course of his examination (*Seaman* v. *Netherclift* (1876) 1 C.P.D. 540), or counsel in his speech; those made where it is the duty of the person making it to do so, *e.g.,* where a master is giving the character of a servant (*Waller* v. *Loch* (1881) 7 Q.B.D. 622), or where the matter is of public interest (*Davies* v. *Snead* (1870) L.R. 5 Q.B. 611); this last is sometimes called privilege by reason of the occasion: thus, statements made in the course of legal proceedings and parliamentary debates are privileged, as are also fair reports or comments on such proceedings (*Purcell* v. *Towler* (1877) 2 C.P.D. 215), and fair criticisms on literary publications and works of art. Findings and orders of the disciplinary committee set up under the Solicitors Act, 1957, are privileged (now the Solicitors Disciplinary Tribunal (Solicitors Act, 1974, s. 46)) (*Addis* v. *Crocker* [1961] 1 Q.B. 11). The privilege is said to be absolute where the intention of the speaker or writer is immaterial (as in the case of judges, members of Parliament, etc.), or qualified, when it does not excuse malice in fact, as in the case of statements made by persons in the discharge of some public or private duty, or in the conduct of his own affairs (*Clark* v. *Molyneux* (1878) 3 Q.B.D. 237). See LIBEL; MALICE.

A communication by a Member of Parliament of a substantial complaint by a constituent to the appropriate body is the subject of qualified privilege (*Beach* v. *Freeson* [1972] 1 Q.B. 14).

Absolute privilege is given to communications arising out of complaints of local maladministration made to a Local Commissioner (*q.v.*) (Local Government Act, 1974, s. 32).

Privilege may exist in respect of things. Some chattels are privileged from distress (*q.v.*), and some from being taken in execution (*q.v.*) (see GOODS). A document is privileged from production when its production cannot be compelled under the ordinary order for production in an action (see PRODUCTION); the principal instances of privileged documents are documents of title and confidential communications (*q.v.*) (*Webb* v. *East* (1880) 5 Ex.D. 108). No order can be made for disclosure of a party's medical reports unless he has agreed to waive his privilege regarding them (*Causton* v. *Mann Egerton* (*Johnsons*) [1974] 1 W.L.R. 162). See DISCOVERY.

As regards the Court of Common Pleas, privilege meant the right of all belonging to that court, whether attorneys or their clerks, to sue or be sued only therein. See CLERK OF THE PLEAS.

See CROWN PRIVILEGE.

Privilege, Writ of, a process to enforce or maintain a privilege.

Privileged communication, a communication which a witness cannot be compelled to divulge, secrets of State, etc.; also a communication which cannot be made the ground of an action for defamation. See CONFIDENTIAL COMMUNICATIONS; LIBEL; PRIVILEGE.

Privileged copyholds, customary freeholds (*q.v.*).

Privileged debts, preferential debts, debts which an executor may pay in preference to all others, such as funeral expenses, etc. See DEBT; PREFERENTIAL PAYMENTS.

Privileged places. These were places in or near the City of London in which a pretended right of sanctuary (*q.v.*) existed. They were Whitefriars, the Savoy, Salisbury Court, Ram Alley, Mitre Court, Fuller's Rents, Mintage Close, the Minories, the Mint, and Clink or Deadman's Place. This pretended right was taken away by the statute 1697, 8 & 9 Will. 3, c. 27, which provided for the execution of process within these places and for the punishment of anyone resisting. The statute 1723, 9 Geo. 1, c. 28, dealt further with the Mint (*q.v.*).

Privileged villeinage, ancient demesne (*q.v.*).

Privileged wills, wills of soldiers, sailors and airmen, which may be valid although they do not comply with the Wills Act, 1837. See NUNCUPATIVE WILL.

Privileges, Committee for, a Committee of the House of Lords appointed every session. Any Lord may sit as a member of it. In any claim of peerage three Lords of Appeal must be present. The House refers to this committee all questions concerning its orders, customs and privileges, claims of peerage and precedence. (Erskine May, *Parliamentary Practice.*)

Privileges, Committee of. Since the seventeenth century it has been the practice of the House of Commons to appoint a Committee of Privileges at the beginning of every session. The committee is nominated at an early date in the session; the number of members is usually ten, the quorum being fixed at five. The scope of any inquiry comprises all matter relevant to the complaint (Erskine May, *Parliamentary Privilege*).

Privilegia, laws *ex post facto,* laws enacted after an act is committed declaring it for the first time to have been a crime, and inflicting a punishment upon the person who has committed it (*Cicero Pro Domo,* 17).

Privilegium clericale, the benefit of clergy, abolished by the Criminal Law Act, 1826. See BENEFIT OF CLERGY.

Privilegium est beneficium personale, et extinguitur cum persona (3 Buls. 8). (A privilege is a personal benefit, and dies with the person.)

Privilegium est quasi privata lex (2 Buls. 189). (Privilege is, as it were, a private law.)

Privilegium non valet contra rempublicam (Bac.Max. 5). (A privilege avails not against the State.) For this reason the husband's coercion does not excuse the wife if she joins him in committing treason. See NECESSITAS INDUCIT, ETC.

Privilegium, propter. Property *propter privilegium* is a qualified property in animals *ferae naturae, i.e.,* a privilege of hunting, taking, and killing them, in exclusion of others (2 Bl.Comm. 394).

Privity, participation in interest or knowledge.

Originally "privy" signified a friend or acquaintance, as opposed to a stranger; and hence privity means knowledge: thus, the rule is that when any deed is altered in a material point by the plaintiff himself, or by any stranger without the privity of the obligee, the deed thereby becomes void (11 Co.Rep. 27). See ALTERATION.

In its secondary sense, privity denotes a peculiar relation in which a person stands either to a transaction or to some other person. The persons standing in such a relation are called privies (*q.v.*). Thus, in the law of fines, the heirs and successors of the parties to a fine were said to be privies to it, and were bound by it as if they had been parties, as opposed to strangers, that is, persons who were neither parties nor privies (2 Co.Inst. 516; Shep.Touch. 21).

Privity of contract is the relation which exists between the immediate parties to a contract, as where A agrees with B to pay him £100. Privity of contract is necessary to enable one person to sue another on a contract. Thus, if A agrees with B that he will pay C £100, C, for want of privity between them, cannot bring an action against A on the contract (*Moore* v. *Bushell* (1858) 27 L.J.Ex. 3).

Privity of estate is that which exists between lessor and lessee, tenant for life and remainderman or reversioner, etc., and their respective assignees, and between joint tenants and coparceners. Privity of estate is required for a release by enlargement. Thus, if A grants land to B for life, and B grants a lease to C, and then A executes a release to C, this is void as a release, because there is no privity between A and C; but the assignee of a lease is liable to the rent and covenants contained in it, although there is no privity of contract between him and the lessor (Co.Litt. 272b).

Privity of blood exists between an heir and his ancestor (privity in blood inheritable), and between coparceners. This privity was formerly of importance in the law of descent cast (*q.v.*) (Co.Litt. 271a, 242a; 8 Co.Rep. 42b).

Privity in representation exists between a testator and his executors; and privity in succession exists between a predecessor and a successor, in the case of a corporation sole. Either kind is also called privity in right (Perkins, *Prof.Book*, 833).

Privity in tenure is that which exists between a lord and a tenant who holds of him by a service (*Termes de la Ley*). See TENURE.

In the old books, privity of person is said to exist between trustee and *cestui que trust*; between husband and wife; and between coparceners (Litt. 462; Co. Litt. 354b, 169a).

Privity of possession exists between joint tenants, tenants in common and coparceners.

Privity in deed is a privity created by the act or consent of the party, as opposed to privity in law, which is one created by the law (Co.Litt. 46b, 90b, 172a, 209a; Perkins, *Prof.Book*, 831, 832).

Privy [Fr. *privé*], having a participation in some act, so as to be bound thereby (*Woodhouse* v. *Jenkins* (1832) 9 Bing. 441): see the word in this sense in the statutory implied covenant in the Law of Property Act, 1925, Sch. 2 Pt. VI; also a participation in interest or knowledge. See PRIVIES; PRIVITY.

The word also means sanitary accommodation. It is the duty of a district council (*q.v.*) and of a London borough council to empty without charge privies serving one or more private dwellings in its area. Privy means a latrine which has a movable receptacle for faecal matter. Any other privy may be emptied on payment if demanded (Control of Pollution Act, 1974, ss. 12 (5), 30 (1)). See PUBLIC HEALTH.

Privy Council, a great council of State held by the sovereign with his councillors, to concert matters for the public service, and for the honour and safety of the realm.

The sovereign nominates privy councillors, and no patent or grant is necessary. The number of the council is indefinite, and is dependent upon the royal will. It is summoned on a warning of forty-four hours, and never held without the presence of a Secretary of State; the junior delivers his opinion first, and the sovereign, if present, last; it is dissolved six months after the demise of the Crown, unless sooner determined by the successor.

Privy councillors, on taking the necessary oaths, become immediately privy councillors, with the title of " Right Honourable," during the life of the sovereign who chooses them, but subject to removal at the royal discretion (*R.* v. *Speyer* [1916] 1 K.B. 595).

The Privy Council is, in theory, the principal council of the Crown, and consists of such persons as are nominated by the Crown to the office. Nominally the council is supposed to advise the Crown on affairs of State, but practically that duty is fulfilled by a select body called the Cabinet, who are members of either House of Parliament and hold the principal offices of State. The only members of the Privy Council (other than the Cabinet) who perform active duties are those constituting the Judicial Committee (*q.v.*). In the case of a large number of privy councillors the office is, therefore, purely nominal.

See FORMA JURAMENTI, ETC.; GREAT COUNCIL; KING'S COUNCIL; LORD PRESIDENT OF THE COUNCIL.

Privy purse, the only part of the Civil List (*q.v.*) which the sovereign can spend as he pleases.

Privy seal [*privatum sigillum*], a seal of the sovereign under which charters, pardons, etc. signed by the sovereign, passed before they came to the great seal; it was also used for some documents of less consequence which did not pass the great seal at all, such as discharges of recognisances, debts, etc. It was a seal, intermediate between the signet (*q.v.*) and the great seal (*q.v.*), employed by the Crown, chiefly as an authority to the Lord Chancellor to affix the great seal to certain documents, *e.g.*, letters patent (2 Co.Inst. 554).

The privy seal was affixed either to the bill (*q.v.*) or draft of the letters patent, or to a warrant which set them forth and directed the Lord Chancellor to have them passed under the great seal. It was abolished in 1884. See CLERKS OF THE

PRIVY SEAL; LORD PRIVY SEAL; PRIVY SIGNET.

Privy signet. The privy signet is one of the sovereign's seals, used in sealing his private letters, and all such grants as pass his hand by bill signed, which seal is always in the custody of the royal secretaries. There were formerly four clerks of the Signet Office, but by the Great Seal Act, 1851, s. 3, the offices of the clerks of the signet and of the privy seal were abolished. See SEAL; SIGNET.

Privy tithes, small tithes.

Prize bounty. Under the Naval Prize Act, 1864, s. 42, the Crown granted prize bounty for distribution amongst the officers and men of naval vessels which were present at the capture or destruction of any armed enemy ship, such bounty being at the rate of £5 for each of the crew of such enemy ship. At the Battle of Jutland on June 1, 1916, eleven German ships, with crews numbering in the aggregate 4,537, were destroyed: and it was held that the sum of £22,685 was divisible amongst the 151 vessels which formed the British fleet (*Re Battle of Jutland* [1920] P. 408).

Prize bounty is a purely naval award and is, therefore, not payable in respect of any capture or destruction effectuated otherwise than by or with the assistance of the naval forces of the Crown (*Schiffahrt-Treuhand* v. *Procurator-General* [1953] A.C. 232).

The Prize Act, 1939, applied prize law to aircraft (s. 1).

The Prize Act, 1948, made provision for the payment of prize money in respect of the war of 1939–45 but extinguished for the future the prerogative right to make grants of prize money to captors and to grant prize bounty.

Prize court, a tribunal existing only by virtue of a special commission under the great seal, during war or until litigations incident to war have been brought to a conclusion. It is frequently confounded with the Court of Admiralty, in consequence, perhaps, of the same judge having usually presided in both courts; but this is a mistake, for the whole system of litigation and jurisprudence in the prize court is peculiar to itself, and is governed by rules not applying to the instance court of the Admiralty (now part of the High Court), which is a mere civil tribunal.

The old Court of Admiralty had from ancient times two separate and distinct jurisdictions, the instance jurisdiction and the prize jurisdiction. When the High Court of Admiralty became merged in the High Court, the Judicature Act, 1891, s. 4, replaced by the Judicature Act, 1925, s. 23, provided that the High Court should be a prize court within the meaning of the Naval Prize Acts, 1864 to 1916, and should have all such jurisdiction on the high seas and in every place where the Crown had jurisdiction as the High Court of Admiralty possessed when acting as a prize court. This is restricted by the Statute of Westminister, 1931, ss. 1, 6, 10. Jurisdiction as a prize court was assigned to the Probate, Divorce and Admiralty Division (Judicature Act, 1925, s. 56 (3)). The jurisdiction of the Probate, Divorce and Admiralty Division of the High Court as a prize court is now exercised by the Admiralty Court (*q.v.*). The procedure and practice in the prize court are regulated by rules made under Prize Courts (Procedure) Act, 1914, which repealed those sections of the Naval Prize Act, 1864, which dealt with the practice and procedure of prize courts; and see the Naval Prize (Procedure) Act, 1916. The Act of 1914 excepted ships of war. See also the Prize Courts Acts, 1894 and 1915, and, as to vice-Admiralty Courts in the colonies, the Colonial Courts of Admiralty Act, 1890. The Prize Acts were extended to aircraft by the Prize Act, 1939.

The law administered in the prize court is the course of Admiralty and the law of nations, the questions arising being those relating to captures, prize, and booty (see BOOTY OF WAR). There is an appeal from this court to the Privy Council.

See Roscoe, *History of the Prize Court*; Colombos, *Law of Prize* 40.

See PRIZE BOUNTY.

Prize fight. If two men fight with ungloved fists until one of them can fight no more, each of them is guilty of assault: so also, it would seem, are those promoting or assisting at the fight; and they all are guilty of unlawful assembly (*R.* v. *Billingham* (1826) 2 C. & P. 234). The same is the case if gloves are worn but the contest is decided not upon the skill of the competitors but by one or the other being rendered incapable of fighting any longer (*R.* v. *Orton* (1879) 14 Cox C.C. 226). If death ensues, the surviving combatant is guilty of manslaughter. Public prize-fighting is an affray and an indictable misdemeanour on the part of both combatants and backers, but in *R.* v. *Coney* (1882) 8 Q.B.D. 534, it was held that the mere presence of persons at a prize fight was not enough to sustain a conviction against them for assault.

Prize money, prize bounty (*q.v.*).

Prize of war. See BOOTY OF WAR; PRIZE BOUNTY; PRIZE COURT.

Prize salvage. Under the Naval Prize Act, 1864, s. 40, where a ship or cargo belonging to a British subject, after being taken as prize by an enemy, is recaptured by a naval vessel and restored to the owners, the crew of the naval vessel are entitled to salvage at the rate of not less than one-eighth or more than one-fourth of what they have recaptured: this is termed marine salvage. Under the law of nations, a naval vessel is entitled to receive analogous payments in respect of the recapture of a neutral ship, captured by the enemy, which, but for the recapture, would have been confiscated or destroyed. See also the Prize Act, 1939, s. 1 (2), Sch. Pt. I (application to aircraft).

Pro, for, in respect of. In the grant of an annuity, *pro consilio,* showing the cause of a grant, amounted to a condition; but in a feoffment or lease for life, etc., it was the consideration, and did not amount to a condition; for the state of the land by the feoffment was executed, and the grant of the annuity was executory (Plowd. 412).

Pro confesso, as if confessed. Under the old practice in Chancery, when it appeared that a defendant in a suit had absconded to avoid being served with the bill, or absconded after being served and without putting in an answer, the court might order the bill to be taken *pro confesso* (as if the defendant had confessed or admitted the truth of it), either immediately or at some future time. The cause was accordingly set down for hearing, and such decree was made as the court thought just (Contempt of Court Act, 1830, s. 3). See DEFAULT.

Pro eo quo, for this which.

Pro falso clamore suo (for his false claim), a nominal amercement of a plaintiff for his false claim, which used to be inserted in a judgment for the defendant. See AMERCIAMENT.

Pro forma, as a matter of form.

Pro hac vice, for this occasion, as when a Lord High Steward (*q.v.*) was appointed for the trial of a peer.

Pro indiviso (as undivided), the possession or occupation of lands or tenements belonging to two or more persons, whereof none knows his several portion; as coparceners before partition (Cowel).

Pro interesse suo, in respect of his interest.

Where sequestrators acting under a writ of sequestration have seized property apparently belonging to the party in default, any person claiming that it belongs to him must make an application to the court for an inquiry as to the nature of his interest therein. This is called an inquiry *pro interesse suo.* In the Chancery Division the inquiry is conducted in the usual way before the master, and he makes his certificate of the result. If it is in favour of the claimant, the court directs the sequestrators to deliver up the property to him. The same rule applies where property is taken possession of by a receiver. See CERTIFICATE; INQUIRY.

Pro laesione fidei. See LAESIO FIDEI.

Pro partibus liberandis, a writ for partition of lands between co-heirs (Reg. Brev. 316).

Pro querente; Pro quer., for the plaintiff.

Pro rata: Pro rata parte, in proportion.

Pro re nata, to meet the emergency, as the occasion arises.

Pro salute animae, for the good of his soul. All prosecutions in the ecclesiastical courts are *pro salute animae.*

Pro tanto, for so much; to that extent.

Pro tempore; Pro tem., for the time being, temporarily.

Proamita, a great paternal aunt, the sister of one's grandfather.

Proamita magna, a great great-aunt.

Proavia, a great-grandmother.

Proavunculus, a great-uncle.

Proavus, a great-grandfather.

Probable cause, reasonable grounds.

Probandi necessitas incumbit illi qui agit (Just.Inst. 2, 20, 4). (The necessity of proving lies upon him who commences proceedings.) See EI QUI, ETC.

Probate. This is a certificate granted by the Family Division of the High Court to the effect that the will of a certain person has been proved and registered in the court and that administration of his effects has been granted to the executor proving the will, he having first sworn faithfully to administer them and to exhibit a true inventory and render a just account when called on. This certificate was formerly on a piece of parchment annexed to a copy of the will and codicils or other testamentary papers, if any, engrossed on parchment: but since January 1, 1901, paper of a special kind and size has been substituted for the parchment. The whole is commonly referred to as the probate, but inaccurately, the certificate being the probate, and the copy of the will being the probate copy.

When a grant of probate has been made, the Clerk of the Seat (q.v.) makes an entry or memorandum of the fact; this (or a copy of it) is called the probate act.

Probate may be granted either in solemn form or in common form. Probate in solemn form, or *per testes,* is only employed when there is or is likely to be a dispute as to the validity of the will, and in such a case the person who wishes its validity to be established commences an action against the person who disputes it. The action proceeds as to pleadings, trial, etc., in the same way as an ordinary action; if the plaintiff makes out his case, the court pronounces for the validity of the will and the executor may then take probate of it as if it had not been disputed. As a general rule, probate in solemn form is conclusive on all who are parties to the proceedings or cognisant of them. For practice see R.S.C., Ord. 76. As to capital transfer tax, see the Finance Act, 1975, Sch. 4 para. 38. See ESTABLISHMENT OF WILLS.

Probate in common form is granted in ordinary cases as a matter of course on the executor swearing and filing an affidavit called the oath of executor or oath of office, by which he swears that the will annexed to the affidavit is the true and original last will and testament of the testator and that he will faithfully administer the estate, and an affidavit for Inland Revenue. For practice see the Non-Contentious Probate Rules, 1954; *Supreme Court Practice,* Vol. 2.

As to limited grants of probate, see GRANT, ETC.

" Probate business " is used as a general term to include all business relating to the granting and revoking of probates and letters of administration both in contested and uncontested cases. The non-contentious business is transacted in the Principal Registry of the Family Division (Administration of Justice Act, 1970, s. 1) or in the district probate registries (Judicature Act, 1925, ss. 107, 108) (see DISTRICT REGISTRIES). Contentious probate business is assigned to the Chancery Division (Judicature Act, 1925, s. 56 (1) (*bb*); Administration of Justice Act, 1970, s. 1 (6), Sch. 2 para. 8), but proceedings may be brought in the county court where the value of the estate is less than £1,000 (County Courts Act, 1959, s. 62).

The Probate Registrar and district probate registrars are appointed by the Lord Chancellor with the concurrence of the Minister for the Civil Service as to numbers and salaries (Courts Act, 1971, s. 26).

Probate, Court of, a tribunal established by the Court of Probate Act, 1857, to which the former jurisdiction of the ecclesiastical courts in testamentary matters was transferred. By Judicature Acts, 1873–75, it was merged in the Supreme Court (q.v.). See COURT OF PROBATE; WILL.

Probate, Divorce and Admiralty Division. This division of the High Court exercised jurisdiction in matters formerly within the exclusive cognisance of the Court of Probate, the Court for Divorce and Matrimonial Causes, and the High Court of Admiralty. It has been renamed the Family Division (q.v.). Admiralty and prize jurisdiction has been transferred to the Admiralty Court, which is part of the Queen's Bench Division. Probate (other than non-contentious or common form probate business) has been transferred to the Chancery Division (Administration of Justice Act, 1970, ss. 1, 2).

Probate duty, a tax (merged in estate duty) on the gross value of the personal property of the deceased testator, first introduced in 1694. It was payable under the Stamp Act, 1815, the Customs and Inland Revenue Act, 1880, and the Customs and Inland Revenue Act, 1881. By the Stamp Act, 1815, s. 37, a penalty of £100 and 10 per cent. additional duty were payable by a person acting as executor and not obtaining probate within six months. The Finance Act, 1894, substituted estate duty, to which both real property and personal property were liable, for probate duty. See ESTATE DUTY.

Probate value. For the purpose of probate, investments are valued so as to include dividends and interest accrued up to the date of the death of the deceased. Where shares are quoted at two prices, a selling price and a purchasing price, the lower price plus one-fourth of the difference is accepted for valuation.

Probation, proof; suspension of a final appointment to an office until a person temporarily appointed (who is called a probationer) has by his conduct proved himself to be fit to fill it.

Probation of offenders. A court by or before which a person of or over seventeen years of age is convicted of an offence (not being an offence the sentence for which is fixed by law) may, instead of sentencing him, make a probation order, that is to say, an order requiring him to be under the supervision of a probation officer for a period to be specified in the order of not less than one year nor more than three years. The age of a person is deemed to be what the court thinks it is. Before making the order, the court must explain to the offender in ordinary language the effect of the order and that if he fails to comply with it or commits another offence he will be liable to be sentenced for the original offence. The court is not to make a probation order unless the offender expresses his willingness to comply with its requirements (Powers of Criminal Courts Act, 1973, ss. 2, 12, 13; *R.* v. *Marquis* [1974] 1 W.L.R. 1087). Probation orders may require treatment for mental condition (s. 3) or attendance at a day training centre (s. 4). As to the discharge and amendment of probation orders see s. 5, Sch. 1. On breach of a probation order a justice of the peace may issue a summons requiring the probationer to appear before him and may issue a warrant for his arrest (s. 6).

Where a person is brought before the court for breach of a probation order the breach alleged should be put to him in the clearest possible terms and he should be asked to say whether he admits it or not (*R.* v. *Devine* [1956] 1 W.L.R. 236; *R.* v. *Long* [1960] 1 Q.B. 681. Breach of a probation order may be dealt with under s. 6, by, *inter alia,* fine, community service (*q.v.*) order or requirement to attend at an attendance centre. As to further offences, see s. 8. Conditional discharge may be substituted for probation (s. 11).

As to the probation and after-care service and its functions, see s. 47. As to probation hostels and homes, see ss. 49, 50, 57.

Although a probation order is a " sentence " it does not amount to conviction of an offence and accordingly no appeal against sentence lies therefrom (*R.* v. *Tucker* [1974] 1 W.L.R. 615). The Crown Court to whom an incorrigible rogue has been committed by justices is not the convicting court and has no power to make a probation order (*R.* v. *Jackson* [1974] Q.B. 517).

Probation officers are ineligible for jury service. See JURY.

Probatis extremis praesumuntur media. (The extremes being proved, the mean is presumed.) See OMNE MAJUS, ETC.

Probator, an examiner; an accuser or approver, or one who undertakes to prove a crime charged upon another. See QUEEN'S EVIDENCE.

Probatory term, a term for taking testimony.

Probatum est, it is tried or proved.

Probi et legales homines, good and lawful men.

Proc., short for procuration (*q.v.*).

Procedendo, a writ which issued out of the common law jurisdiction of the Court of Chancery when judges of any subordinate court delayed the parties by not giving judgment on the one side or on the other. In such a case either a writ of mandamus or a writ of *procedendo ad judicium* was awarded, commanding the inferior court to proceed to judgment, but without specifying any particular judgment; for that, if erroneous, might be set aside by proceedings in error, or by writ of false judgment; and upon further neglect or refusal, the judges of the inferior court might be punished for their contempt by writ of attachment (3 Bl.Comm. 109).

It also lay where an action had been removed from an inferior to a superior court by habeas corpus, certiorari, or any like writ, and it appeared to the superior court that it was removed on insufficient grounds. A suit once so remanded could not afterwards be removed before judgment in any court whatever: see the statute 1624, 21 Jac. 1, c. 23.

Procedendo on aid prayer. If one prayed in aid of the Crown, and aid was granted, it was awarded that he applied to the sovereign in Chancery, and proceedings were stayed until the court had received a writ *procedendo de loquela* (to proceed to deliver judgment) (New N.B. 154).

Procedure, the mode in which the successive steps in litigation are taken. The procedure of the common law courts was regulated by the Common Law Procedure Acts, 1852, 1854, and 1860. The procedure in actions in the High Court and the Court of Appeal is now governed under the Judicature Act, 1925, for the most part by the Rules of the Supreme Court, based on the rules in the Schedule to the Judicature Act, 1875; but where no other provision is made by the Acts or the rules, the former procedure remains in force. See PRACTICE.

Proceeding. See ACTIONS AND MATTERS, ETC.

Proceeds, the sum, amount, or value of land, investments, or goods, etc., sold, or converted into money.

Proceres, chief magistrates. *Domus Procerum, Dom. Proc.,* meant the House of Lords.

Procès verbal [Fr.], an authentic minute of an official act, or statement of acts.

Process, the proceedings in any action or prosecution, real or personal, civil or criminal, from the beginning to the end; strictly, the summons by which one is cited into a court, because it is the beginning or principal part thereof, by which the rest is directed (Britt. 138).

At common law the three superior courts at Westminster, in personal actions, differed greatly, before the Uniformity of Process Act, 1832, in their modes of process, and even the same court admitted a considerable variety of methods, according to the circumstances of the case. The ordinary process in Chancery suits was service of a copy of the bill or claim, with an endorsed citation, which required the defendant to appear on a certain day.

The process now for the commencement of all actions is the same in all the Divisions of the High Court, and is called a writ of summons. The process consists of writs (*q.v.*) and originating summonses (*q.v.*). See SUMMONS.

In civil actions process is of two kinds, *viz.,* process against a defendant, being either process to compel him to appear, now consisting of a writ of summons or originating summons, or process of execution, by which the judgment, decree, etc., is executed or carried into effect (see EXECUTION); and process against persons not parties to the action, *e.g.,* process to summon jurors, witnesses, etc. (Co.Litt. 289a; Finch, *Law,* 436).

Process in a proceeding in foreign attachment (*q.v.*) denoted the attachment paper served upon the garnishee.

In the practice of the Privy Council in ecclesiastical appeals, process means an official copy of the whole proceedings and proofs of the court below, which is transmitted to the registry of the appellate court, by the registrar of the court below in obedience to an order or requisition requiring him so to do, called a monition for process, issued by the appellate court. See MONITION.

In criminal proceedings, process means proceedings issued to bring in a person to answer an indictment which has been found against him. Summary process consisted of the writs of *venire facias, distringas* and *capias ad respondendum* (*q.v.*), though a justice's warrant is now commonly used (see WARRANT). If summary process was ineffectual, process of outlawry (*q.v.*) might formerly be issued.

Formerly process in common law actions was much more complicated and important than now. It was either original or judicial. The former (which was so called because at one time it commenced with the original writ issued out of Chancery) had for its object to compel the defendant to appear (see WRIT). Original process against either the person or the property of the defendant was called single process; when it was against both it was called mixed. Judicial process was that which issued out of the common law courts, either when the original writ was returned or without an original being issued at all. When original writs fell into disuse, an action was commenced by process issued out of the common law court to compel the defendant's appearance, to compel him to give bail, etc., and this was called mesne process; the term also included other kinds of process, *e.g.*, jury process, or writs to compel the attendance of jurors. Writs used to revive an action or remove it into another court, or the like, were called judicial process in the nature of new originals (Finch, *Law*, 343). Process of execution or final process was much the same as at present, except that imprisonment for debt has been abolished in most cases (see ARREST).

Processions. Powers to prevent obstructions in the streets during public processions and other occasions when the streets are thronged are given by the Town Police Clauses Act, 1847, s. 21 (as amended by the Criminal Justice Act, 1967, Sch. 3) and the Metropolitan Police Act, 1839, s. 52 (as amended by the Road Traffic Regulation Act, 1967, s. 81 (4A)).

Barriers may be erected in streets to control processions (Public Health Act, 1961, s. 44; Criminal Damage Act, 1971; London Government Act, 1963, s. 40, Sch. 11 para. 37).

Stands to view processions must be made safe (Public Health Acts Amendment Act, 1890, s. 37).

Powers to regulate processions are conferred by the Public Order Act, 1936. See PUBLIC ORDER.

Processum continuando, a writ for the continuance of process after the death of the chief justice or other justices in the commission of *oyer* and *terminer* (Reg. Brev. 128).

Prochein amy [*proximus amicus*], the next friend or next-of-kin to a child in his nonage, who in that respect was allowed to deal for the infant in the management of his affairs, as to be his guardian if he held land in socage, and in the redress of any wrong done to him (Jacob). See NEXT FRIEND.

Prochein avoidance, a power to appoint a minister to a church when it shall next become void. See AVOIDANCE.

Prochronism [πρόχρονος, anterior], an error in chronology; dating a thing before it happened.

Proclamation, publication by authority; a notice publicly given of anything whereof the sovereign thinks fit to advertise his subjects. Proclamation is used particularly in the beginning or calling of a court, and at the discharge or adjourning thereof, for the attendance of persons and dispatch of business (Jacob).

Proclamation, Fine with. To render a fine (*q.v.*) more universally public and less liable to be levied by fraud or covin, it was directed by the statute 1489, 4 Hen. 7, c. 24 (in confirmation of a previous statute), that a fine after engrossing should be openly and solemnly read and proclaimed in court (during which all pleas should cease), sixteen times, *viz.*, four times in the term in which it was made, and four times in each of the three succeeding terms, which was reduced to once in each term by the statute 1588, 31 Eliz. 1, c. 2, and these proclamations were endorsed on the record. This procedure was abolished by the Fines and Recoveries Act, 1833.

Proclamation, Writ of. See COMMISSION OF REBELLION; OUTLAWRY.

Proclamations, Royal. The Statute of Proclamations, 1539, gave royal proclamations the force of Acts of Parliament; but this enactment was repealed by the statute 1547, 1 Edw. 6, c. 12, s. 4. The Statute of Proclamations, 1539, had legalised for the time being the practice of legislating by way of proclamation which the Crown had from time to time pursued. The practice was not abandoned after the enactment of the statute 1547 but it was decided in the *Case of Proclamations* (1610) 12 Co.Rep. 74 (see DELIBERANDUM EST, ETC.), that the practice was without legal warrant: and it ceased when the Star Chamber (*q.v.*) was abolished.

If martial law (*q.v.*) became necessary, a royal proclamation would be one of the means by which it could be set up: but such a proclamation would not involve a claim by the Crown of any right to legislate, for the proclamation, like martial law itself, would be entirely extra-legal.

No question of law-making arises in connection with the issue of royal proclamations for the usual purposes, that is to say, to assemble or dissolve Parliament, to appoint days of public thanksgiving (see FAST DAY), to declare peace or war, to annex new territories, to constitute new colonies, etc.

A royal proclamation is valid in law, that is to say, has such force as the law allows, if published in the *London Gazette* (Crown Office Act, 1877, s. 3 (3)). It can be proved by a copy purporting to be printed by the Queen's Printer (Evidence Act, 1845, s. 3).

Proclamations, Statutory. These, as distinguished from royal proclamations, which are issued under the prerogative, are issued by the Crown under statutory powers, which give them the force of law. A recent example is the power by proclamation to appoint a day to be a bank holiday given by the Banking and Financial Dealings Act, 1971, s. 1. January 1, has been so proclaimed. Most statutes now, however, authorise the issue of Orders in Council (*q.v.*) or ministerial regulations rather than proclamations.

Proclamator, an officer of the Court of Common Pleas.

Proconsules, justices in eyre.

Proctor [Lat. *procurator*], a manager of another person's affairs.

In the ecclesiastical and admiralty courts proctors discharged duties similar to those of solicitors and attorneys in other courts. They were empowered to institute or withdraw proceedings by an instrument called a proxy, signed by the litigant, attested, and deposited in the registry of the court.

Owing to the abolition of the jurisdiction of the ecclesiastical courts in causes matrimonial and testamentary, the Court of Probate Act, 1857, ss. 43, 105, 106, and the Matrimonial Causes Act, 1857, s. 69, awarded compensation to the proctors, and admitted them to practise, not only in the probate and divorce courts, but also in the courts of equity and common law.

By the Attorneys and Solicitors Act, 1870, s. 20, attorneys and solicitors were empowered to practise in the ecclesiastical courts, except the provincial courts of York and Canterbury, and the diocesan court of London; and they were admitted to these excepted courts by the Solicitors Act, 1877, s. 17, which also allowed solicitors to practise as proctors; the Judicature Act, 1925, s. 256 (1), replacing the Judicature Act, 1873, s. 87, gave them the title of solicitors of the Supreme Court. The Solicitors Act, 1974, ss. 19, 89 (6), allows solicitors to appear in ecclesiastical courts.

At Oxford and Cambridge, proctors are university officials who have disciplinary power over members of the universities. Solicitors appointed to practise in the Chancellor's Court at Oxford who are sworn in before the Vice-Chancellor, are called proctors.

In Convocation (*q.v.*), proctors are the representatives of the chapters of cathedrals and of the beneficed clergy of each diocese.

In certain colonies, a solicitor is called a proctor.

See COURT OF ARCHES; QUEEN'S PROCTOR; QUOD CLERICI BENEFICIATI DE CANCELLARIA.

Procuratio est exhibitio sumptuum necessariorum facta praelatis, qui dioceses peragrando, ecclesias subjectas visitant (Dav. 1). (Procuration is the providing necessaries for the bishops, who, in travelling through their dioceses, visit the churches subject to them.)

Procuration, an agency, the administration of the business of another. See PROCURATIONS.

Bills of exchange may be drawn, accepted, or indorsed by procuration, *i.e.*, by an agent who has an authority for such a purpose, and a signature by procuration operates as notice that the agent has but a limited authority to sign, and the principal is only bound by such signature if the agent so signing was acting within the actual limits of his authority (Bills of Exchange Act, 1882, s. 25). The abbreviation per pro. or p.p. (by procuration) usually follows the signature of an agent, and by the Bills of Exchange Act, 1882, s. 26, a person signing a bill and adding words indicating that he signs in a representative capacity is not personally liable on the bill.

Procuration fee, a commission taken by scriveners, brokers, etc., for procuring loans of money. This was limited to five shillings per cent. per annum by the statute 1713, 13 Anne, c. 15, repealed by the Usury Laws Repeal Act, 1854.

Procuration of women, the providing of women for the purposes of illicit intercourse. It is an offence punishable with two years' imprisonment (Sexual Offences Act, 1956, ss. 2, 3, 4, 22, 23, Sch. 2). Conspiring to procure is a misdemeanour at common law (*R.* v. *Mears* (1851) 20 L.J.M.C. 59). See CARNAL KNOWLEDGE; CORROBORATION.

Procurationem adversus nulla est praescriptio (Dav. 6). (There is no prescription against procuration.)

Procurations; Procurationes. These were contributions of provisions made by parish priests for the sustenance of the bishop or archdeacon when upon visitation, *ratione visitationis*; they were also called proxies, and it is said that there were three sorts, *ratione visitationis, consuetudinis, et pacti* (Hardr. 180).

They were subsequently commuted to payments in money. Procurations were abolished by the Ecclesiastical Jurisdiction Measure, 1963, s. 82 (3).

Procurator, one who has a charge committed to him by any person; an agent. In the old law books the proxies (*q.v.*) of peers were sometimes termed *procuratores,* and the bishops, as members of the House of Lords, were sometimes described as the *procuratores ecclesiarum.* In 1327, Trussel, Speaker of the House of Commons, acting as *procurator* of both Houses, renounced allegiance to Edward II. *Procurator* was

also an early form of proctor (*q.v.*) (Tomlin).

Procurator fiscal, the procurator for the fiscal or treasury. Each of the sheriff courts in Scotland had its procurator fiscal, who acts, with deputies if necessary, as public prosecutor, and also makes inquiry into suspected offences in his area. There are no coroners in Scotland.

Procuratores ecclesiae parochialis, churchwardens (Paroch.Antiq. 562).

Procurator-General and Treasury Solicitor. See TREASURY SOLICITOR.

Procuratorium, the instrument by which any person or community constituted or delegated their proctor to represent them in any court or cause.

Prodes hommes, the barons or other tenants *in capite* who were summoned to the king's council (Tomlin).

Prodition, treason, treachery.

Proditor, a traitor.

Proditorie, treasonably; formerly, when indictments were in Latin, the technical word in an indictment for treason (Tomlin).

Producent, the party calling a witness under the old system of the ecclesiastical courts.

Production. The High Court may make an order for production of documents and business books for inspection (R.S.C., Ord. 24, rr. 11–17). See AFFIDAVIT; DISCOVERY; INSPECTION; NOTICE TO PRODUCE; PRIVILEGE.

Where a person is entitled to property in reversion or remainder expectant on the death of another person, and has reason to believe that that person (called the *cestui que vie* (*q.v.*)) is dead, and that his death is concealed, he may apply to the Chancery Division for an order directing the person in possession of the property to produce the *cestui que vie* to persons named by himself, and in case of non-production to them the *cestui que vie* is ordered to be produced in open court or to commissioners appointed by the court, and on failure of production the applicant may take possession of the property as if the *cestui que vie* were actually dead (Cestui que Vie Act, 1707, s. 1).

Production, Census of. See CENSUS OF PRODUCTION.

Profane swearing. See SWEARING.

Profaneness. See BLASPHEMY.

Profer [Fr. *proférer*], to produce; an offer to endeavour to proceed in an action.

Profert, he produces. Formerly the general rule was that where a party to an action relied in his pleading on a document under seal, to which he was party or privy, the deed had to be shown forth or produced to the court. Hence the party in his pleading used to allege that he brought the deed into court, although it was not actually done. This was called *profert in curia,* and entitled the opposite party to *oyer* (*q.v.*) of the deed (Shep.Touch. 73; 3 Bl.Comm.App.).

Profert and *oyer* were abolished by the Common Law Procedure Act, 1852, s. 55.

Professed. Formerly a man was said to be professed or " entered and professed in religion " when he had entered a religious order, taken the habit of religion and vowed three things, obedience, wilful poverty, and perpetual chastity. A nun was, in similar circumstances, also said to be professed. Profession operated as a civil death. Since the Reformation, however, religious profession is not recognised by the law (Litt. 200; Co.Litt. 132a; 1 Bl.Comm. 133).

Profession, calling, vocation, known employment; divinity, medicine, and law are called the learned professions.

Professional privilege, the privilege which exempts barristers and solicitors from disclosing matters confided to them in their professional capacity by clients. See CONFIDENTIAL COMMUNICATIONS; PRIVILEGE.

Profit, advantage or gain in money or in money's worth. Thus, in an action in the Chancery Division for infringement of a patent or copyright, the plaintiff generally has his election whether the defendant shall be ordered to pay him the damages caused to him by the infringement, or the profits which the defendant has made by the wrongful use of the patent or copyright (*Neilson* v. *Betts* (1871) L.R. 5 H.L. 1). See INQUIRY.

In the law of real property " profit " is used in a special sense to denote a produce or part of the soil of land. Therefore, if a man seised of lands in fee by his deed granted to another the profit of those lands, to hold to him and his heirs, and made livery *secundum formam chartae,* the whole land itself passed; for the land is but the profits thereof, for thereby vesture, herbage, trees, mines, etc., all pass (Co.Litt. 4b).

In the old books, an easement is defined to be a privilege, without profit, which one neighbour has of another (*Termes de la Ley*).

Profits in this sense are of three classes. Profits lying in render consist of rents, dues and services rendered to a lord by his tenant. They are so called because it is the duty of the tenant to pay or render them to the lord, as opposed to profits *à prendre,* which are rights of taking the produce or part of the soil from the land of another person, and the casual profits which accrue to a lord from his tenants by chance and unlooked for, such as escheats (Co.Litt. 92b). See PROFIT À PRENDRE.

Profit à prendre, a right for a man, in respect of his tenement, to take some profit out of the tenement of another man. It may be claimed by grant or prescription (*q.v.*) but except formerly in the case of a copyholder no claim of a profit *à prendre in alieno solo* can be made by custom, nor can it be claimed by a fluctuating body such as the inhabitants of a place (see LAMMAS LANDS). A prescription in a *que estate* for a profit *à prendre in alieno solo* without stint and for commercial purposes is unknown to the law (*Harris* v. *Chesterfield* [1911] A.C. 623). As to a demise of a profit *à prendre,* see *Radcliff* v. *Hayes* [1907] 1 Ir.R. 101. A profit *à prendre* in gross is a right of property which may be dealt with and transferred in the manner appropriate to the right (*Welcome* v. *Upton* (1840) 6 M. & W. 536).

Profits *à prendre* consist of rights of common (see COMMON), and rights of sole or several pasture, vesture and herbage (see PASTURE; VESTURE). The custom of tinbounding (*q.v.*) is also sometimes treated as a profit *à prendre.* The right of taking water from a well or stream on another's land is not a profit *à prendre,* but an easement (*Race* v. *Ward* (1855) 4 E. & B. 702).

See MESNE PROFITS.

Profit and loss, the gain or loss arising from goods bought or sold, or from carrying on any other business, the former of which, in book-keeping, is placed on the creditor's side, the latter on the debtor's side. Net profit is the gain made by selling goods at a price beyond what they cost the seller, and beyond all costs and charges.

Profit sharing, an arrangement whereby an employer agrees that his employees shall receive a share, fixed beforehand, in the profits of the undertaking. See Harper, *Profit Sharing.*

Profits tax, a tax originally imposed by the Finance Act, 1937, and known as national defence contribution (*q.v.*), on the profits of bodies corporate and unincorporated societies (Profits Tax Act, 1949).

Progressive rent, a rent which automatically rises during the continuance of a tenancy either by reference to fixed and ascertained periods or by reference to the happening of contingencies.

Prohibited degrees. See AFFINITY; LYNDHURST'S (LORD) ACT.

Prohibited place. See OFFICIAL SECRETS.

Prohibitio de vasto directa parti, a judicial writ addressed to the tenant of lands which were in controversy, prohibiting him from making waste upon the lands during the suit (Reg.Judic. 21). It might also be issued against anyone committing waste in the house or building of an incumbent or on the glebe (Moor 917).

Prohibitio formata de statuto articuli cleri. (Prohibition made upon the Articles of the Clergy.) An enactment is printed under this title in the *Statutes of the Realm* amongst the *Statutes of Uncertain Date,* and is printed also in the *Statutes at Large* as of uncertain date. It appears to have been framed on certain *Articuli Cleri* of 1266 (2 Co.Inst. 600).

Prohibition, an order issuing out of the High Court to restrain an inferior court within the limits of its jurisdiction. It is granted in all cases where an inferior court exceeds its powers, either by acting where it has no jurisdiction, or where, having a primary jurisdiction, it takes upon itself the decision of something not included within its jurisdiction.

An absolute prohibition is peremptory, and wholly ties up the inferior jurisdiction, but if the superior court afterwards comes to the conclusion that the matter relied on is not a sufficient ground for prohibition, a writ of consultation (*q.v.*) may be awarded, by which the cause is remanded to the inferior court; this latter writ seems in practice to be awarded only in ecclesiastical cases (3 Bl.Comm. 114).

A temporary prohibition (sometimes called a prohibition *quousque*) is operative only until a particular act is done, and is *ipso facto* discharged on the act being done.

A limited or partial prohibition (sometimes called a prohibition *quoad*) extends only to that part of the proceeding which exceeds the jurisdiction of the inferior court, allowing it to proceed as to the residue.

Prohibition issued not only out of the Queen's Bench, but also out of the Courts of Chancery, Exchequer, and Common Pleas. If either the judge or a party proceeds after prohibition, an attachment may be had against him for contempt, at the discretion of the court which awarded it; and an action for damages will lie against him by the party injured.

Orders of prohibition were substituted for writs of prohibition by the Administration of Justice (Miscellaneous Provisions) Act, 1938, s. 7.

The High Court has jurisdiction to make an order of prohibition to the Crown Court (*q.v.*) except in relation to its jurisdiction in matters relating to trial on indictment (Courts Act, 1971, s. 10 (5)).

Applications for an order of prohibition are regulated by R.S.C., Ord. 53, modified by Ord. 53, r. 7, in the case of prohibition to a county court.

Where a want of jurisdiction is apparent on the face of the proceedings in an inferior court, the High Court is bound to grant a prohibition, although the applicant has acquiesced in the proceedings of the inferior court (*Farquharson* v. *Morgan* [1894] 1 Q.B. 552). Prohibition may issue even though there is an alternative remedy (*Channel Coaling Co.* v. *Ross* [1907] 1 K.B. 145).

See PLEA.

Project, the draft of a proposed treaty or convention.

Prolem ante matrimonium natam, ita ut post legitimam, lex civilis succedere facit in haereditate parentum; sed prolem, quam matrimonium non parit, succedere non sinit lex Anglorum (Fort. c. 39). (The civil law permits the offspring born before marriage, provided such offspring be afterwards legitimised, to be the heirs of their parents; but the law of the English does not suffer the offspring not produced by the marriage to succeed.) This was the law until the Legitimacy Act, 1926. See LEGITIMATION; MERTON, STATUTE OF.

Proles, progeny. See S.P.

Proletarius, a person who had no property to be taxed, but paid a tax only on account of his children (Civil Law).

Prolicide [Lat. *proles,* offspring; *caedere,* to kill], the destruction of human offspring, either foeticide or infanticide (*q.v.*).

Prolixity, the allegation of facts at unnecessary length in a pleading or affidavit. The party offending may be ordered to pay the costs thereby occasioned, or the affidavit may, by virtue of the inherent power of the court, be ordered to be taken off the file (R.S.C., Ord. 41, r. 6, notes).

Prolocutor. One of the members of the Lower House of Convocation (*q.v.*) is selected by the members of that House to represent their resolutions and opinions to the Upper House. He is known as the *prolocutor* and sometimes also as the *referendarius.* The office is always filled at the beginning of each sitting of Convocation; the *prolocutor* has the power of appointing a deputy; and if a vacancy occurs during the sitting there must be a new election. The appointment of the *prolocutor* or of a deputy requires confirmation by the archbishop.

One of the members of the Upper House is *prolocutor* thereof and presides over its sittings.

The Keeper of the Great Seal (see LORD KEEPER) was called the *prolocutor* or mouth of the Higher House of Parliament, that is to say, was the Speaker of the House of Lords (Lambarde). See CHANCELLOR, LORD.

Prolytae, students of the civil law during the first and last year of their studies.

Promatertera, a maternal great-aunt; the sister of one's grandmother.

Promatertera magna, a great-great-aunt.

Promise, an engagement for the performance or non-performance of some particular thing, which may be made either by deed, or without deed, when it is said to be by parol; " promise " is usually applied when the engagement is by parol only, for a promise by deed is technically called a covenant. See CONTRACT.

A promise, not under seal, made voluntarily and without valuable consideration, is not binding either at law or in equity (*Re Whitaker* (1889) 42 Ch.D. 119; *Tweddle* v. *Atkinson* (1861) 1 B. & S. 393).

Promises are of two kinds. A true promise is the expression of an intention to do or forbear from some act, made by one person (the promisor) to another (the promisee). Expressions in the form of promises, but reserving an option as to their performance, and illusory promises (*e.g.,* a promise by A to pay B such a sum as A thinks proper), are not true promises (*Taylor* v. *Brewer* (1813) 1 M. & S. 290).

Promises are either express or implied; thus, if A requests B to lend him £50, and he does so, a promise by A to repay it is implied. See EXPRESS.

To have legal effect, a promise must either be under seal, when it forms a covenant (*q.v.*), or must form part of a contract, that is, be made in consideration of something done or to be done in return by the promisee see (CONSIDERATION; CONTRACT). When that consideration consists of another promise, each party is both a promisor and a promisee, and the contract consists of mutual promises; thus, in an ordinary contract of sale the seller's promise to deliver the goods is in consideration of the buyer's promise to pay for them, and vice versa. Mutual promises are said to be independent, where either party may sue the other for the breach of his promise and where it is no excuse for the party sued to allege a breach by the plaintiff of his own promise (see APPORTIONMENT OF

CONTRACT); dependent, when the performance of one promise depends on the performance of the other and therefore, until the prior condition is performed, the other party is not liable on his promise, as where A promises B to keep some buildings in repair on condition of their being first put into repair by B; concurrent, where both promises are mutually dependent, as where A agrees to sell property to B, when neither can sue the other without showing that he has performed or is ready to perform his part of the contract (*Jones* v. *Barkley* (1781) 2 Doug. 684).

Fictitious promises, sometimes called implied promises, or promises implied in law, occur in the case of those contracts which were invented for the purpose mentioned under CONTRACT.

Promise of marriage. See BREACH, ETC.

Promisee, one to whom a promise has been made.

Promisor, one who makes a promise.

Promissory note, an unconditional promise in writing made by one person to another signed by the maker, engaging to pay on demand or at a fixed or determinable future time, a sum certain in money to, or to the order of, a specified person or to bearer (Bills of Exchange Act, 1882, s. 83 (1)). It may contain also a pledge of collateral security (s. 83 (3)) but it may not contain anything else. It may be made by two or more persons, who may make themselves liable jointly or jointly and severally (s. 85).

The note can require payment at a particular place (*Josolyne* v. *Roberts* [1908] 2 K.B. 349). The person who makes the note is called the maker, and the person to whom it is payable is called the payee: when it is negotiated by the indorsement of the payee, he is called the indorser, and the person to whom the note is transferred is called the indorsee. Promissory notes are negotiable or transferable in the same manner as bills of exchange.

The legal effect of making a note is that the maker contracts to pay the note according to its tenour (s. 88 (1)). As to the effect of an indorsement, see BILL OF EXCHANGE.

The rules are the same in both cases, the maker of a note being in the same position as the acceptor of a bill (s. 89 (1)) save as regards the exception set out in s. 89 (3).

A promissory note is invalid if the sum payable is wholly or partly in shillings and pence (Decimal Currency Act, 1969, s. 2).

Promissory oaths, oaths taken by persons entering upon certain offices. The subject is regulated by the Promissory Oaths Act, 1868. See OATH.

Promoter. Anciently this meant the persons who laid themselves out to bring, as common informers, penal (*q.v.*) and popular (*q.v.*) actions. They were not in good repute: Coke calls them *turbidum hominum genus* (3 Co.Inst. 191).

Now it generally means either a person who procures the passing of a private Act of Parliament or a person who "floats" a company, in which latter case it means, for the purposes of the Companies Act, 1948, s. 43, which relates to liability for misstatements in a prospectus, a person who was a party to the preparation of the prospectus or of the portion thereof containing the untrue statement but does not include any person by reason of his acting in a professional capacity for persons engaged in procuring the formation of a company. In many respects promoters stand in a fiduciary capacity towards the company which they are engaged in forming (*Twycross* v. *Grant* (1877) 2 C.P.D. 469; *Lagunas Nitrate Co.* v. *Lagunas Syndicate* [1899] 2 Ch. 392; *Electric Palace* v. *Baines* [1914] 1 Ch. 532). The promoters usually pay the registration fees, and the company is under no liability to repay them (*Re National Motor Co.* [1908] 2 Ch. 515). See DIRECTOR; MISFEASANCE; PROSPECTUS.

In the Lands Clauses Consolidation Act, 1845, "promoters of the undertaking" means the company, commissioners, etc., or private persons who are empowered to execute the works or undertaking authorised by the special Act (Lands Clauses Consolidation Act, 1845, s. 2). See ACT OF PARLIAMENT.

In the practice of the Privy Council in ecclesiastical appeals, a promoter is a person who brings an appeal from the judgment of an inferior court (*Combe* v.

Edwards (1878) 3 P.D. 103). See OFFICE OF THE JUDGE.

Promovent, the plaintiff in a suit of *duplex querela* (*q.v.*).

Promulgation, publication; open exhibition.

Promutuum, a *quasi*-contract, by which he who receives a certain sum of money, or a certain quantity of fungible (*q.v.*) things, delivered to him through mistake, contracts the obligation of restoring as much. It resembles the contract of *mutuum,* in that in both a sum of money or some fungible things are required, there must be a transfer of the property in the thing, and there must be returned the same amount or quantity of the thing received (Civil Law).

Pronepos, a great-grandson.

Pronotary, first notary. See PROTHO-NOTARY.

Pronurus, the wife of a great-grandson.

Proof, evidence, testimony, convincing token, means of conviction.

In the law of evidence, an allegation of fact is said to be proved when the tribunal is convinced of its truth, and the evidence by which that result is produced is called proof. Where a person who makes an allegation is bound to prove it, the burden or onus of proof (*onus probandi*) is said to rest on him. The general rule is that the burden of proof lies on the party who asserts the affirmative of the issue or question in dispute. See EI INCUMBIT PROBATIO, ETC.

Where a person on whom the burden of proof lies adduces evidence sufficient to raise a presumption that what he asserts is true, he is said to shift the burden of proof: that is, his allegation is taken to be true, unless his opponent adduces evidence to rebut the presumption. See EVIDENCE; PRESUMPTION.

When evidence is to be given viva voce, *e.g.,* at the trial of an action, the solicitor of the party on whose behalf a witness is to be called usually sees the witness beforehand, and takes down a statement of the facts on which he is able to give evidence. The statement is called the "proof" of the witness. A copy of it is furnished to counsel for the party for his guidance in examining the witness.

In Admiralty practice, "proof" was equivalent to evidence, and was divided into three kinds—proofs by affidavit, by written depositions and by oral examination of witnesses in open court. The rules as to evidence in Admiralty actions are now the same as in other actions.

In bankruptcy, "proof" denotes not only the operation of proving the existence of a debt owing from the bankrupt's estate, but also the affidavit, declaration, etc., by which debts are usually proved: and hence to "prove against the estate" means to bring forward a claim in that way. An ordinary proof is an affidavit by the creditor to the effect that the bankrupt was at the date of the order of adjudication, and still is, justly and truly indebted to the creditor, stating the amount and the consideration for the debt, and whether the creditor holds any security for it. See CREDITOR; DEBT; SECURITY.

It was formerly the rule that if a person was liable in respect of distinct contracts, either as member of two or more distinct firms, composed in whole or in part of the same individuals, or as a sole contractor and also as member of a firm, then the creditors under those contracts could not prove against the estates of the two firms in the one case, or against the several estate of the sole contractor and the joint estate of his firm in the other case, but could only prove against one estate. This rule against double proof was abolished by the Bankruptcy Act, 1869, s. 37. Now the Bankruptcy Act, 1914, Sch. 2, r. 19, also provides against the operation of the rule. But if a firm is carrying on business in England and abroad, and its property abroad is divided among its creditors, those of them who prove against the estate in England must give credit for what they have received abroad.

When a proof has been admitted by the trustee, it may afterwards happen that circumstances are disclosed which, if known at the time of proof, would have excluded the creditor from the right to prove, wholly or in part, or circumstances may arise after proof so as materially to change the state of the debt, and in these cases it becomes necessary either to expunge the proof, that is, to reject it retrospectively, as if it had never been made, or to reduce it, that is, reduce the amount on which the creditor is to receive dividends, as if he had originally proved for the smaller amount (Bankruptcy Act, 1914, Sch. 2, rr. 24–27).

An executor is said to prove a will when he obtains probate of it, either in common or in solemn form. See PROBATE.

" Proof " also means the standard of strength of spirituous liquids (see the Customs and Excise Act, 1952, s. 172).

Propatruus magnus, a great-great-uncle.

Proper feuds, the original and genuine feuds held by pure military service.

Property [Norm.Fr. *propreté*; Lat. *proprietas*; *proprius*, one's own], the highest right a man can have to anything, being that right which one has to lands or tenements, goods or chattels which does not depend on another's courtesy.

In its largest sense property signifies things and rights considered as having a money value, especially with reference to transfer or succession, and to their capacity of being injured. Property includes not only ownership, estates, and interests in corporeal things, but also rights such as trade marks, copyrights, patents, and rights *in personam* capable of transfer or transmission, such as debts.

Property is of two kinds, real property (*q.v.*) and personal property (*q.v.*).

Property in realty is acquired by entry, conveyance, or devise; and in personalty, by many ways, but most usually by gift, bequest, or sale. Under the Law of Property Act, 1925, s. 205, " property " includes any thing in action and any interest in real or personal property. There must be a definite interest; a mere expectancy as distinguished from a conditional interest is not a subject of property.

" Property " also signifies a beneficial right in or to a thing. Sometimes the term is used as equivalent to ownership; as where we speak of the right of property as opposed to the right of possession (*q.v.*), or where we speak of the property in the goods of a deceased person being vested in his executor. The term was chiefly used in this sense with reference to chattels (Finch, *Law* 176).

Property in this sense is divided into general and special or qualified.

General property is that which every absolute owner has (Co.Litt. 145b). See OWNERSHIP.

" Special property " has two meanings. First, it may mean that the subject-matter is incapable of being in the absolute ownership of any person. Thus a man may have a property in deer in a park, hares or rabbits in a warren, fish in a pond, etc.; but it is only a special or qualified property, for if at any time they regain their natural liberty his property instantly ceases, unless they have *animus revertendi* (2 Bl.Comm. 391). See ANIMALS FERAE NATURAE.

Secondly, a person may have a special property in a thing in the sense that he can only put it to a particular use. Thus, in the case of a bailment (*q.v.*), the bailee has a special property in the thing bailed, for he is only entitled to deal with it in accordance with the contract of bailment; but he can maintain an action in respect of it against a wrongdoer. So possession is said to confer a special property, by which is meant that the possessor of a thing is deemed to be owner of it as against everyone who cannot show a better title. See MELIOR, EST, ETC.

See Lavaleye, *Propriété*; Maine, *Anc. Law,* c. viii; Block, *Dict. de la Politique*; Markby, *Elements of Law,* 464.

Property qualification. The enactments requiring candidates to be possessed of certain real or personal property as a qualification for election were abolished as regards Parliament by the statute 1858, 21 & 22 Vict. c. 26, and as regards municipal corporations and local government bodies by the Town Councils and Local Boards Act, 1880. See QUALIFICATION.

Property tax, income tax (*q.v.*) payable in respect of landed property under the Income Tax Act, 1952, s. 83, known as Sch. A tax, the rules relating to it having formerly been contained in Sch. A to the Income Tax Acts, 1853 and 1918.

The Finance Act, 1963, introduced a new code for the taxation of income from land. Sch. A in its original form ceased to have effect. A new Case VIII of Sch. D was introduced to tax income from land (ss. 14–18). Case VIII of Sch.

PROPERTY

D was renamed Sch. A by the Finance Act, 1969, s. 60, Sch. 20 para. 1. See now the Income and Corporation Taxes Act, 1970, ss. 67–79.

Prophecies. See FALSE PROPHECIES.

Propinqui et consanguinei, the nearest of kin to a deceased person.

Propinquity, kindred, parentage.

Proponent, the propounder of a thing, in the ecclesiastical courts.

Proportional representation. As to this system of voting, see *Re McDougall Fund Trusts* [1957] 1 W.L.R. 81.

Proportum, intent or meaning.

Proposal. An offer to insurers by a person desiring insurance is called a proposal. Non-disclosure of any material fact makes the policy voidable at the option of the insurance company.

Proposition, a single logical sentence.

Propositus, the person proposed; the person from whom a descent is traced; also the name by which a testator is referred to on propounding his will.

Propound, to produce (*e.g.,* a will) as authentic.

An executor or other person is said to propound a will or other testamentary paper when he institutes an action for obtaining probate in solemn form. (See PROBATE.) The term was formerly also used technically as meaning to make the allegations in the statement of claim, by which the plaintiff alleges that the testator executed the will with proper formalities, and that he was of sound mind at the time.

Proprietary, he who has a property in anything.

Proprietary chapels, chapels erected by and belonging to private persons, and not consecrated for divine service. Such a chapel has no parochial rights, unless acquired by a composition with the patron, incumbent and ordinary of the parish church, nor can public divine service be celebrated in it except with the consent of the incumbent and the licence of the bishop (*Hodgson* v. *Dillon* (1840) 2 Curt. 388). The bishop, on the other hand, has no authority over such a chapel (*Richards* v. *Fincher* (1874) L.R. 4 A. & E. 255). Such chapels were formerly sometimes erected as commercial speculations; but, in view of the facilities for forming new parishes (*q.v.*)

since the Church Building Act, 1818, proprietary chapels are now rare. Some unconsecrated private chapels have been converted to secular uses.

The Private Chapels Act, 1871, dealt only with the chapels, whether consecrated or unconsecrated, of colleges, schools, hospitals, asylums, or public or charitable institutions. The Act has been repealed. See now the Extra-Parochial Ministry Measure, 1967, ss. 2, 4; Education Act, 1973, Sch. 2 Pt. II.

Proprietary medicines. These were defined by the Medicine Stamp Act, 1812, repealed by the Pharmacy and Medicines Act, 1941, as preparations intended to be used medicinally by human beings, when the seller claimed that they were made by a secret process, or that he had the exclusive right of manufacture, or which were protected by letters patent, or which had been advertised as beneficial. See PATENT MEDICINES.

Proprietary rights, those rights which an owner of property has by virtue of his ownership. When proprietary rights are opposed to acquired rights, such as easements, franchises, etc., they are sometimes called natural rights (*q.v.*). See OWNERSHIP.

Proprietas nuda; Proprietas deducta usufructu, bare ownership, ownership without usufruct (Civil Law).

Proprietas verborum est salus proprietatum (Jenk.Cent. 16). (Propriety of words is the salvation of property.)

Proprietate probanda, De, a writ commanding the sheriff to inquire whether goods distrained were the property of the person who had sued out a writ of replevin (*q.v.*). It issued when the sheriff returned as his reason for not executing the writ of replevin that some third person claimed a property in the goods distrained (Finch, *Law,* 316).

The modern equivalent is a summons to interplead. See INTERPLEADER.

Proprietor, owner (*q.v.*), as in the phrase " riparian proprietor " (see RIPARIAN). A person entitled to a trade mark or design is called the proprietor of the trade mark or design (Trade Marks Act, 1938, s. 1; Registered Designs Act, 1949, s. 2).

Proprio vigore, by its own force.

Propter, because of. See CHALLENGE.

Prorogation, prolonging or putting off to another day; the bringing of a session of Parliament (*q.v.*) to an end. This, like dissolution (which brings the Parliament to an end) can be effected only by an exercise of the royal prerogative. Adjournment to a future hour on the same day, or to a future day, can be effected by either House of its own motion.

The House of Lords can at all times sit as a court of appeal without regard to the prorogation or dissolution of Parliament: and an impeachment is carried on from one session to another or from one Parliament to another: but all other business lapses upon prorogation and, *a fortiori,* upon dissolution, and must be reintroduced in the new session or the new Parliament.

Prosecution, a proceeding by way of indictment in the criminal courts, in order to put an offender upon his trial. In all criminal prosecutions the Crown is nominally the prosecutor.

Prosecutor, a person who takes proceedings against another in the name of the Crown. The commonest instance of a prosecutor is in criminal matters. The prosecutor may be a private person, in which case he is generally the person specially injured by the crime. When the crime is of a heinous nature or likely to go unpunished for want of a prosecutor, the proceedings are conducted by the Director of Public Prosecutions (*q.v.*), in the name of the Attorney-General. See ADVOCATE, LORD; PUBLIC PROSECUTOR.

A person who sets in motion proceedings by *scire facias* to revoke a Crown grant (see SCIRE FACIAS), or the prerogative process of mandamus, or, formerly, information (*q.v.*), or similar proceedings, is sometimes called the prosecutor, as is also a person who institutes proceedings for attachment (*q.v.*). See INFORMER.

Prospectus. The Companies Act, 1948, s. 455, defines a prospectus as any prospectus, notice, circular, advertisement, or other invitation, offering to the public for subscription or purchase any shares or debentures of a company. By s. 38 of the Act every prospectus issued by or on behalf of a company or any person engaged or interested in its formation, must state the matters specified in Sch.

4 Pt. I and set out the reports specified in Pt. II of that Schedule, subject as to both parts to the provisions of Pt. III, and otherwise comply with the requirements of the Act. Any condition waiving compliance with this provision is void. The issue of any form of application for shares or debentures of a company unaccompanied by a prospectus is prohibited except in an offer to underwriters or not to the public, or to existing members or debenture holders of the company. By s. 42, contracts referred to in a prospectus are not to be varied without the approval of the statutory meeting (*q.v.*). As to the liability of directors and others for statements in the prospectus, see s. 43 (see DECEIT; DIRECTORS). These requirements extend to offers by the purchasers of shares or debentures offered by the company to them with a view to sale by them to the public under s. 45. The statutory requirements as to registering the prospectus are set out in s. 41. Under Sch. 4 Pt. III, certain particulars may be omitted from a prospectus which is issued more than two years after the company is entitled to commence business. As to prospectuses by companies incorporated outside Great Britain, see s. 417.

If a prospectus is made the vehicle of misrepresentation, persons induced to subscribe on the faith of the statements contained in it acquire a right of action for damages or rescission of the contract. This right, however, is limited, as a rule, to those who subscribe to the issue, and does not extend to persons who may have bought shares or bonds on the market after seeing a prospectus inviting subscriptions (*Peek* v. *Gurney* (1873) L.R. 6 H.L. 377): but if the prospectus is part of a scheme to induce persons to purchase in the market, then persons who have so bought may have a good cause of action for damages.

See COMPANIES.

Prostitute, a woman who indiscriminately consorts with men for hire. Solicitation by prostitutes is punishable under the Street Offences Act, 1959. See LOITERING.

A licensed retailer of intoxicating liquor permitting his premises to be the habitual resort of reputed prostitutes, whether their object be prostitution or not, is, if he allows them to remain longer than is necessary for the purpose of obtaining reasonable refreshment, liable to a penalty under the Licensing Act, 1964, s. 175.

A man who lives on the earnings of prostitution is liable to seven years' imprisonment (Sexual Offences Act, 1956, s. 30, Sch. 2, as amended by the Street Offences Act, 1959, s. 4). A person lives on the earnings of prostitution if he is paid by prostitutes for goods or services which he would not supply if they were not prostitutes (*Shaw* v. *D.P.P.* [1962] A.C. 220). It is an offence for a woman for purposes of gain to exercise control over a prostitute (Sexual Offences Act, 1956, s. 31). Causing the prostitution of a woman is an offence under the Sexual Offences Act, 1956, s. 22. Causing or encouraging the prostitution of or intercourse with or indecent assault on a girl under sixteen is an offence under s. 28. Causing or encouraging the prostitution of a defective is an offence under s. 29.

A conspiracy to corrupt public morals by publishing advertisements of prostitutes is punishable as such in spite of s. 2 (4) of the Obscene Publications Act, 1959. A person who publishes such advertisements for gain is guilty of living on the earnings of prostitutes contrary to s. 30 (1) of the Sexual Offences Act, 1956 (*Shaw* v. *D.P.P.* [1962] A.C. 220). See OBSCENITY.

Prostitute and prostitution are not confined to cases of ordinary sexual intercourse (*R.* v. *Webb* [1964] 1 Q.B. 357). A matrimonial order may be made on the complaint of a wife that she has been forced to submit to prostitution. See MATRIMONIAL PROCEEDINGS IN MAGISTRATES' COURTS.

Words imputing that a woman or girl is a prostitute are actionable without proof of special damage (Slander of Women Act, 1891).

The use of premises for the purposes of prostitution may amount to a nuisance (*Thompson-Schwab* v. *Costaki* [1956] 1 W.L.R. 335).

See CONTAGIOUS DISEASES PREVENTION ACTS, ETC.; PROCURATION OF WOMEN.

Protected states. See PROTECTORATE.

Protected transactions. Every bankruptcy is deemed to commence from, at latest, the act of bankruptcy upon which the receiving order was made, and sometimes from three months before the presentation of the petition (Bankruptcy Act, 1914, s. 37 (1)). The effect of this is to invalidate alienations and dispositions of property by the debtor, and judgments against him made or obtained since the commencement of his bankruptcy; the object is to protect the general creditors against fraudulent and collusive arrangements for the benefit of particular creditors. But to prevent the rule from bearing hardly on honest creditors, the bankruptcy law excludes from its operation payments, transfers, contracts, and dealings, when made or obtained before the date of the receiving order and for valuable consideration by persons not having notice of an act of bankruptcy (s. 45); and it also excludes executions and attachments completed before the date of the receiving order without notice of the petition or of an act of bankruptcy (s. 40). These are known as protected transactions. See SETTLEMENT.

Protecting power, a neutral power charged with the protection of the interests of a belligerent power and its nationals in an enemy country.

Protectio trahit subjectionem, et subjectio protectionem (Co.Litt. 65). (Protection involves subjection; subjection, protection.) While an alien is within the British dominions he is subject, in many respects, to British law, but, on the other hand, he is within the protection of our law even though he may be the subject of an enemy State.

Protection, Court of. See COURT OF PROTECTION.

Protection of animals. See CRUELTY TO ANIMALS.

Protection order. As regards licensed premises this means an order which may be made by justices when a transfer of a justices' licence has been authorised: it authorises the transferee to carry on business until the next transfer sessions or any adjournment thereof (Licensing Act, 1964, s. 10; Finance Act, 1967, ss. 5 (1) (*a*), 45 (8), Sch. 16 Pt. I.

Under the Matrimonial Causes Act, 1858, s. 21, a deserted wife could obtain from either the High Court or a petty sessional court an order protecting her property and earnings from her husband and those claiming through him. The Married Women's Property Acts and the Summary Jurisdiction (Married Women) Act, 1895, made applications for such orders of rare occurrence. See DESERTION.

Protection, Writ of, a writ which, from a very early period, issued out of the Chancery to subjects absent overseas on the king's service. It made them free of all suits except some few such as the assize of novel disseisin, the assize of darrein presentment, attaints, etc. It could not, as a rule, be pleaded to a charge of felony nor to any suit instituted before it was issued: see the statute 1389, 13 Ric. 2, st. 1, c. 16. The last instance of its issue was in *Barrudale* v. *Cutts* (1690) 3 Lev. 332.

The writ was also issued to Crown debtors in order to prevent private creditors from getting priority of the Crown (Fitz.N.B. 65). See NON MOLESTANDO.

Protectionibus, Statutum de. An enactment is printed under this title in the *Statutes of the Realm* amongst the *Statutes of Uncertain Date* and in the *Statutes at Large* as 1305, 33 Edw. 1, st. 1. Under it the validity of a writ of protection (*q.v.*) could be challenged and investigated.

Protective trust, a trust for the life of the beneficiary, or any less period, which is to be determined in certain events, such as the bankruptcy of the beneficiary, whereupon the trust income is to be applied for the maintenance, etc., of the beneficiary and his family at the absolute discretion of the trustees (Trustee Act, 1925, s. 33). Illegitimate children may benefit (Family Law Reform Act, 1969, s. 15 (3)).

As to capital transfer tax, see the Finance Act, 1975, Sch. 5 para. 18. A person may not make a settlement of his own property on himself defeasible in the event of his bankruptcy (*Merry* v. *Pownall* [1898] 1 Ch. 306). As to variation, see the Variation of Trusts Act, 1958. See DISCRETIONARY TRUST.

Protector of the settlement, the person whose consent is required to enable a remainderman in tail to bar the entail. In the absence of such consent the remainderman can only bar his own issue and

create a base fee (*q.v.*). Under the Fines and Recoveries Act, 1833, s. 32, the settlor might appoint a special protector. In the absence of this special protector, the owner of the first (sufficient) estate in possession, *e.g.,* the tenant for life under the same settlement, was and is a statutory protector. The special protector was to be appointed as stated in substitution for the old tenant to the *praecipe,* whose concurrence in barring estates tail in remainder was required in order to preserve the control of the tenant for life over the remainderman. The statutory protector might be excluded by the settlor, who by the settlement creating the entail might appoint not more than three persons *in esse,* not being aliens, to be special protectors, in which case the office survived and the last surviving protector could exercise it (*Cohen* v. *Bayley-Worthington* [1908] A.C. 97). Under the Law of Property Act, 1925, Sch. 7, repealing the Fines and Recoveries Act, 1833, s. 32, special protectors are abolished. As to married women acting alone as protectors of a settlement, see the Married Women's Property Act, 1907, s. 3, as amended by the Law Reform (Married Women and Tortfeasors) Act, 1935.

The office of protector is not assignable, and if the protector is tenant for life under the settlement he may by the Fines and Recoveries Act, 1833, ss. 36, 37, make terms in consideration of his consent (*Banks* v. *Le Despencer* (1843) 11 Sim. 508).

See DISENTAILING DEED; ENTAIL; TENANT TO THE PRAECIPE.

Protectorate, the period during which Oliver Cromwell ruled in this country under the title of Lord Protector of the Commonwealth of England, Scotland and Ireland and of the dominions and territories thereunto belonging; the office of protector.

Territories placed under the protection of the British sovereign, generally by treaty with the native ruler or chiefs, and administered on the same lines as Crown colonies are protectorates or protected States (British Nationality Act, 1948, s. 30).

Protest, a solemn declaration of opinion, generally of dissent; an express declaration by a person doing an act that the act is not to give rise to an implication which it might otherwise cause (Savigny; Syst. iii. 246).

Thus, the payment of a sum of money by A in answer to a demand by B would in general give rise to the presumption that the money was owing by him to B, and if A wishes to prevent it from doing so, he pays the money under protest. As a general rule, a protest is not effectual unless the payment or other act takes place under compulsion: thus, if A wrongfully distrains goods belonging to B, and B pays the sum claimed for rent under protest in order to regain his goods, he may afterwards sue A to recover the amount.

Upon a payment under protest or under duress (*q.v.*) of more than is legally due, the excess can be recovered (*Baxendale* v. *London and South Western Ry.* (1866) L.R. 1 Exch. 137).

Each peer has a right, when he disapproves of the vote of the majority of the House of Lords, to enter his dissent on the Journals of the House, with his reasons for such dissent, which is usually styled his protest.

In the law of bills of exchange, a protest is a solemn declaration by a notary stating that he has demanded acceptance or payment of a bill, and that it has been refused, with the reasons, if any, given by the drawee or acceptor for the dishonour. The object of a protest is to give satisfactory evidence of the dishonour to the drawer or other antecedent party; but it is not necessary except in the case of a foreign bill (see BILL OF EXCHANGE; NOTING). Where the acceptor of a bill becomes bankrupt or suspends payment before it matures, the holder may cause the bill to be protested for better security against the drawer and indorsers (Bills of Exchange Act, 1882, s. 55 (5)). The advantage of a protest is that there may be an acceptance (*q.v.*) for honour. The expenses of the protest are recoverable where it is for non-acceptance or non-payment (s. 57 (1) (*c*)); but not where it is for better security. By the Bills of Exchange Act, 1882, s. 51 (amended by the Bills of Exchange (Time of Noting) Act, 1917, s. 1), a foreign bill dishonoured by non-acceptance or non-payment must be duly protested, otherwise the drawer and indorsers are discharged. There may be a protest by a householder when the services of a notary cannot be obtained. The stamp duty on protests was abolished by the Finance Act, 1949, Sch. 10.

A protest is also a writing attested by a justice of the peace or consul, drawn up by a master of a ship, stating the circumstances under which an injury has happened to the ship, or to the cargo, or other circumstances calculated to affect the liability of the shipowner or the charterer, etc.

A protest is also an objection made to a proceeding in which the person protesting is by force of circumstances obliged to take part against his will (*Vionet* v. *Barrett* (1885) 55 L.J. 39).

A defendant to an action may with the leave of the court enter a conditional appearance in the action. He is entitled to object to any irregularity in the issue or service of the writ or to the jurisdiction of the court (R.S.C. Ord. 12, r. 7). There is no real distinction between conditional appearance and appearance under protest.

Protestando, a word made use of to avoid double pleading in actions; it prevented the party who made it from being concluded, by the plea he was about to make, that issue could not be joined upon it; and it was also a form of pleading where one would not directly affirm or deny anything alleged by another or himself. It was abolished by rules of court in 1834, whereby it was rendered unnecessary. See PROTESTATION.

Protestant. This term does not occur in the Canons of 1603, or the Thirty-nine Articles, or in the Acts of Uniformity, but appears in many statutes of later date, notably in the Act of Settlement, 1700, in which, by way of making further provision (in addition to that made by the Bill of Rights, 1688) for the succession of the Crown in the Protestant line, the Crown was settled, in default of issue of Princess Anne of Denmark (afterwards Queen Anne) and William III, on the Princess Sophia and the heirs of her body, being Protestants; it being added that whosoever should thereafter come to the possession of the Crown should join in communion with the Church of England as by law established.

The Bill of Rights, 1688, after reciting that it had been found by experience that it was inconsistent with the safety and welfare of this Protestant kingdom to be governed by a popish prince or by any king or queen marrying a papist, debars such from succession to the Crown, and entails the succession on such person or persons being Protestants as would have succeeded in case the person reconciled to or holding communion with the Church of Rome or professing the popish religion or marrying a papist were dead, and also required every sovereign on the first day of the meeting of his first parliament or on coronation, which should first happen, to make a declaration taken from the statute 1678, 30 Car. 2, st. 2 (repealed by the Parliamentary Oaths Act, 1866), and expressed therein to be in the plain and ordinary sense of the words as they are commonly understood by English Protestants, against transubstantiation, invocation of saints, and the sacrifice of the Mass as used in the Church of Rome. For the declaration which now has to be made by the sovereign, see BILL OF RIGHTS.

The Union with Scotland Act, 1706, confirms the English succession to the Crown of the heirs of the body of the Electress Sophia, being Protestants, and so did the Union with Ireland Act, 1800, though not in express terms; art. 5 of that Union, however, provided for the union of the churches of England and Ireland into one Protestant Episcopal Church, a union dissolved by the Irish Church Act, 1869.

The term was originally applied to those who " protested " against a decree of the Emperor Charles V and the Diet held at Spires in 1529. See ROMAN CATHOLICS.

Protestation. Protestation was once used in pleadings at common law when a party wished to prevent an admission of a fact by him in one action from being afterwards used against him in another action as an estoppel or conclusion of the truth of the fact. The use of the word *protestando* (*q.v.*) was necessary to such a pleading; and the pleading itself was

known as a *protestando*. Protestation was abolished by rules of court in 1834.

Prothonotary, a principal notary, that is to say, a chief clerk. In the Middle Ages he drew pleas or put them into formal shape (3 Holds. H.E.L. 645).

The title was borne by three officers of the Common Pleas, by one officer of the Kings' Bench and by one officer of the Chancery. The Prothonotary of the King's Bench recorded all civil actions; all criminal matters in that court were recorded by the Clerk of the Crown Office (*q.v.*). The prothonotaries of the Common Pleas, in conjunction with the filacers (*q.v.*), performed functions analogous to those of the modern Master. Both prothonotaries and filacers were abolished by the Superior Courts (Officers) Act, 1837, which replaced them by the Masters of the Common Pleas. The last prothonotary of the Chancery was appointed in 1792 and survived until 1874, drawing his salary for a sinecure office for more than 82 years (Maxwell-Lyte, *Great Seal*). See MASTERS OF THE QUEEN'S BENCH, ETC.

A prothonotary is the principal registrar and chief administrative officer in the Supreme Courts of New South Wales, Queensland, Victoria and Western Australia.

See DISTRICT REGISTRIES.

Protocols [$\pi\rho\tilde{\omega}\tau\sigma\varsigma$, $\kappa\acute{o}\lambda\lambda\eta$, the things first glued together], the original drafts, the original copy of any writing. An original is styled the protocol or *scriptura matrix* (Encyc.Londin.).

The original acts and proceedings in an ecclesiastical cause taken down by a notary are called protocols.

Since the Congress of Vienna, it has also meant the minutes of a deliberative assembly of the representatives of nations (Calvo, *Dict. de Droit International*).

It is also used as meaning the rules of ceremonial followed in the official relations between States and their representatives.

Protonotary. See PROTHONOTARY.

Protutor, a quasi tutor (Civil Law).

Prout patet per recordum (even as it appears by the record). The omission of the words *per recordum* was but form (*Hancocke* v. *Prowd* (1679) 1 Saund. 336; *Clegat* v. *Bambury* (1657) 1 Saund.

337b, n (4) *sub nom. Claggett* v. *Compton*, 2 Sid, 16). It was rendered unnecessary by the Criminal Procedure Act, 1851, s. 24.

Prove. See PROOF; PROBATE.

Prover, an approver (*q.v.*).

Provided school, a council school (*q.v.*).

Provident societies. See INDUSTRIAL AND PROVIDENT SOCIETIES.

Province, the district over which the jurisdiction of an archbishop extends. England is divided into two provinces, Canterbury and York; the province of York comprises all north of the Humber, *i.e.,* Yorkshire and Lancashire, etc., and Cheshire; all the rest of the country is in the province of Canterbury. See ARCHBISHOP; BISHOPRICS; DIOCESE; PROVINCIAL COURTS.

Metaphorically it means sphere of duty, as the province of the judge and the province of the jury.

Provincial constitutions, the decrees of provincial synods held under divers archbishops of Canterbury, from Stephen Langton, in the reign of Henry III, to Henry Chichele, in the reign of Henry V, and adopted also by the province of York in the reign of Henry VI (Lynd.*Provinciale*). See CANON LAW.

Provincial courts, ecclesiastical courts within the provinces of the two primates, hence also called the courts of the primates. In the province of Canterbury, they are the Court of Arches (*q.v.*); the Court of the Vicar-General, wherein bishops of the province are confirmed; the Court of the Master of the Faculties, wherein matters relating to notaries public are dealt with (see FACULTY; NOTARY); the Court of Audience (now obsolete); the Court of Peculiars (now obsolete); and the Court of the Commissary (*q.v.*) of the Archbishop. In the province of York they are the Supreme Court or Chancery Court (see CHANCERY); the Consistory Court (*q.v.*); and the Court of Audience (now obsolete). See DIOCESAN COURTS.

Provinciale, a work on ecclesiastical law, by William Lyndwode, official principal to Archbishop Chichele in the reign of Edward IV (4 Reeves, c. xxv, 117).

Proving a will, obtaining probate (*q.v.*).

Provision, a nomination by the Pope to an English benefice before it became void; the term was afterwards indiscriminately applied to any right of patronage exerted or claimed by the Pope. The statute 1307, 35 Edw. 1, was the first statute against provisions. Persons who attempted to take the benefit of provisions were called provisors (*q.v.*).

A provision also means a clause in a legal document.

Provisional assignees, those who under a former system of the bankruptcy law were appointed under fiats in bankruptcy in the country to take charge of bankrupts' estates, etc., until the creditors' assignees were appointed.

Provisional committee, a committee appointed for a temporary occasion.

Provisional order. Under various Acts of Parliament public bodies and departments of the government are authorised to inquire into matters which, in the ordinary course, could only be dealt with by a private Act of Parliament, and to make orders for their regulation. These orders have no effect unless they are confirmed by an Act of Parliament, and are hence called provisional orders. Several orders may be confirmed by one Act. The object of this mode of proceeding is to save the trouble and expense of promoting a number of private Bills. See the Local Government Act, 1972, s. 240 and S.I. 1974 No. 487, Art. 21.

Provisional specification. See SPECIFICATION.

Provisiones, those Acts of Parliament which were passed to curb the arbitrary power of the Crown (Mat.Paris.).

Provisions of Oxford. See PARLIAMENTUM INSANUM.

Proviso, a clause in a deed or other instrument beginning " provided always that, etc."; in Latin, *proviso semper.* It operates as a condition, limitation, qualification or covenant, according to its tenor (Co.Litt. 203b).

A common instance of a proviso is that for re-entry contained in every well-drawn lease; another is the proviso for redemption contained in a mortgage (*q.v.*). See CONDITION; FORFEITURE; PROVISO FOR REDEMPTION; RIGHT OF ENTRY; USUAL COVENANTS.

The terms proviso and condition are synonymous, and signify some quality annexed to a grant by virtue of which it may be defeated, enlarged, or created upon an uncertain event. Such qualities annexed to personal contracts and agreements are generally called conditions. A proviso or condition differs from a covenant in that the former is in the words of, and binding upon, both parties, whereas the latter is in the words of the covenantor only. At the same time a proviso or condition may be construed as a covenant or agreement if the proviso involves the consideration upon which the benefit is obtained; *a fortiori,* where words such as " provided that, and it is hereby agreed " are used. But if no intention that the proviso was intended to be obligatory can be gathered from the deed or contract, the proviso merely amounts to a qualification of the grant or promise.

Provisos are frequently inserted in statutes, *e.g.,* for the purpose of saving existing rights, or rights of the Crown, or generally for exemptions from the operation of the particular Act.

Proviso est providere praesentia et futura non praeterita (Co.Inst. 72). (A proviso is to provide for the present or future, not the past.)

Proviso for redemption, the condition in a mortgage whereby, if the mortgagor pays to the mortgagee the principal, interest, and any other moneys secured by the mortgage on a specified day, the mortgagee becomes bound to reconvey the mortgaged property to the mortgagor at any time at his request and cost. By the Law of Property Act, 1925, s. 115, a receipt of the person entitled to give a receipt for the moneys secured by the mortgage endorsed on or written at the foot of, or annexed to the mortgage operates as a surrender or release of the mortgagee's term or as a reconveyance of all the mortgaged interest or property, and in either case a discharge of all the moneys secured by the mortgage without any other reconveyance, surrender or release. See MORTGAGE.

Proviso, Trial by. Where the plaintiff in an action desisted from prosecuting his suit and did not bring it to trial in convenient time, the defendant might formerly take out a *venire facias (q.v.)* to the sheriff (containing the words *proviso quod*) upon which the case was set down for trial. This was called trial by proviso (Old Nat.Brev. 159).

An alternative course was permitted to the defendant under the Common Law Procedure Act, 1852, s. 101, but s. 116 of that Act preserved the right to trial by proviso. Since the Judicature Acts, 1873–75, the defendant's remedy has been to apply for dismissal for want of prosecution (R.S.C., Ord. 19).

Provisor, a purveyor; also one who sued to the court of Rome for a provision or pre-arrangement that a particular benefice when it should fall vacant should be bestowed, for an immediate payment by the provisor, on a particular person.

Various statutes, called generally Statutes of Provisors, were passed to suppress such practices. In the statute 1533, 25 Hen. 8, c. 20, s. 7, the most important of them, 1351, 25 Edw. 3, st. 5, c. 22, is called the Statute of the Provision and Praemunire. See PRAEMUNIRE.

Provisor victualium. Before the abolition of the right of purveyance (*q.v.*), this was the officer of the royal household who exercised the right (Cowel).

Provisors, Statute of, the statute 1351, 25 Edw. 3, st. 4, one of a series directed against provision (*q.v.*). See PROVISOR.

Provocation. In law no provocation whatever can render homicide justifiable, but it may reduce the offence to manslaughter (*q.v.*). To reduce homicide upon provocation to manslaughter, the wounding, etc., must have been inflicted immediately upon the provocation being given and before anger has had time to subside, and the provocation must be of a kind which would deprive an ordinary man of self-control. See ASSAULT.

Where on a charge of murder there is evidence on which the jury can find that the person charged was provoked (whether by things done or by things said or by both together) to lose his self-control, the question whether the provocation was enough to make a reasonable man do as he did must be left to the jury who must take into account everything both done and said according to the effect which, in their opinion, it would have on a reasonable man (Homicide Act, 1957, s. 3). See *R.* v. *Martindale*

[1966] 1 W.L.R. 1564; *R.* v. *Ives* [1970] 1 Q.B. 208; *R.* v. *Walker* [1969] 1 W.L.R. 311.

When considering the defence of provocation, a jury should be directed to consider first whether the accused was in fact provoked, and second whether the provocation was enough to make a reasonable man do as the accused did (*R.* v. *Brown* (*Egbert Nathaniel*) [1972] 2 Q.B. 229).

The jury may find a verdict of manslaughter on the ground of provocation even though provocation has not been pleaded (*R.* v. *Porritt* [1961] 1 W.L.R. 1372).

Acts or words emanating from a person other than the victim are capable of amounting to provocation as a defence to a charge of murder (*R.* v. *Davies* (*Peter*) [1975] Q.B. 691).

Provocation is not a defence on a charge of malicious wounding (*R.* v. *Cunningham* [1959] 1 Q.B. 288).

Provost, a governing officer of a university or college.

Provost-marshal, an officer of the royal forces who has the charge of military prisoners: see the statute 1661, 13 Car. 2, c. 9.

Provost-marshals arrest and detain for trial persons subject to military law committing offences, and execute punishments ordered by courts-martial.

In the navy, a senior member of the ship's police is appointed provost-marshal when a court-martial is to be held. He arrests the accused and produces him to the court.

Proxenta; Proxeneta, a marriage broker.

All contracts for marriage (commonly called marriage-brokage contracts), by which a party engages to give another a compensation if he will negotiate an advantageous marriage for him, are void, as being injurious to or subversive of the public interest (*Hermann* v. *Charlesworth* [1905] 2 K.B. 123).

The civil law allowed *proxenetae,* or match-makers, to receive a reward for their services to a limited extent. See MARRIAGE BROKAGE.

Proxies, annual payments by the parochial clergy to the bishop, etc., on visitation; procurations (*q.v.*). See PROXY.

Proximate cause. See CAUSA CAUSANS.

Proximo, Prox., next month.

Proxy, a person appointed, usually by written authority, by a person entitled to vote personally, to vote at the discretion of the proxy (*Harben* v. *Phillips* (1883) 23 Ch.D. 35).

A member of a company may appoint another person to attend a meeting and vote under the Companies Act, 1948, s. 136.

As to voting by proxy under the Companies Clauses Consolidation Act, 1845, see ss. 76, 77 of that Act, as amended, in the case of a company being a shareholder, by the Companies Clauses Consolidation Act, 1888.

A letter for the sole purpose of appointing or authorising a proxy to vote at any one meeting at which votes might be given by proxy, whether the number of persons named in such instrument was one or more, had formerly to bear a penny stamp, and to specify the day on which the meeting was to be held, and was available only at the meeting so specified, and any adjournment thereof (Stamp Act, 1891). The standing orders of Parliament prohibited the sending out of stamped proxies in connection with extension Bills. The stamp duty on proxies was abolished by the Finance Act, 1949, Sch. 10.

Directors, acting in good faith in the interests of the company, may do what they think advisable to get shareholders to vote either in favour of or against a resolution, *e.g.,* they may send out proxies at the company's expense (*Peel* v. *L. & N.W. Ry.* [1907] 1 Ch. 5, overruling *Studdert* v. *Grosvenor* (1886) 33 Ch.D. 528).

On a show of hands, a proxy has only one vote, however many persons he may represent: see *Ernest* v. *Loma Gold Mines* [1897] 1 Ch. 1, in which it was also held that a blank date of the meeting in the proxy paper might be filled up by the secretary of the company before the paper was lodged.

Voting by proxy at the meetings of the creditors of a bankrupt is regulated by the Bankruptcy Act, 1914, s. 13, Sch. 1, and at the meetings of the creditors and contributories of a company being wound up, by the Companies (Winding-up) Rules, 1949, rr. 146–156.

Voting by proxy at parliamentary and local government elections is regulated by the Representation of the People Act, 1949, ss. 12–15, 23–25; Representation of the People Act, 1969, ss. 5, 6; Representation of the People (Armed Forces) Act, 1976.

From an early date, peers had exercised the right of voting in the House of Lords by proxy entrusted to another peer. At first this was done only by permission of the Crown in each case. Then the permission was dispensed with and votes were given by proxy as of right, many proxies being sometimes held by the one peer. In 1868 the orders of the House on the subject were to the effect that no peer should hold more proxies than two, and that proxies should not be used at all in committees or when the House was sitting as a court of appeal. In 1868 it was unanimously resolved by the House that the use of proxies should be discontinued.

A marriage by proxy which is valid by the law of the country in which it is celebrated is a valid marriage in English law (*Apt* v. *Apt* [1948] P. 83).

Prudenter facit qui praecepto legis obtemperat (5 Co.Rep. 49). (He acts prudently who complies with the command of the law.) This is quoted in connection with the observation that he who commits a wrong and at the first confesses it and obeys the king's command by his writ, shall not be amerced. As to one who took the opposite course, see PECCATUM PECCATO, ETC.

Pryk. In the reign of Richard II certain land was held *per servitum unum equum unum saccum et unum pryk in guerra Walliae* (subject to supplying one horse, one sack and one pryk for the Welsh war). The *pryk* was a spur with one point only. In the time of Henry VIII, light horsemen were called *prickers* from their use of such spurs (Blount; Tomlin).

Psalter, the table of Psalms. The Prayer Book (Table of Lessons) Act, 1871, amends the law relating to the Tables of Lessons and Psalter contained in the Prayer-book. See also the Revised Tables of Lessons Measure, 1922.

Pseudograph, false writing.

Pseudonym. Copyright in anonymous and pseudonymous work is protected by the Copyright Act, 1956, ss. 11, 20 (6), Sch. 2.

Psychopath. Psychopathic disorder is a persistent disorder or disability of mind (whether or not including a state of arrested or incomplete development of mind) which results in abnormally aggressive or seriously irresponsible conduct and requires or is susceptible to medical treatment (Mental Health Act, 1959, s. 4).

Pubertas, puberty (*q.v.*). See AGE.

Pubertas, Plena (full puberty), was the age of eighteen (Civil Law).

Pubertati proxime, children in the stage prior to puberty (*q.v.*) (Civil Law).

Puberty [Lat. *pubertas*], the age of fourteen in males and twelve in females, when they were held fit for and capable of contracting marriage (Civil Law).

Public accounts, the accounts of the expenditure of the nation. They are rendered to the Comptroller and Auditor-General under the Exchequer and Audit Department Acts, 1866 to 1957.

Public Act. See ACT OF PARLIAMENT.

Public agent. See PUBLIC OFFICER.

Public analyst, an analyst appointed by a local authority under the Food and Drugs Act, 1955, s. 89; Local Government Act, 1972, s. 199 (7), Sch. 30. See ANALYSIS.

Public appointments. The sale of public appointments is contrary to the policy of the law. See OFFICE.

Public assistance. See NATIONAL ASSISTANCE.

Public authorities, Protection of. Numerous Acts have from time to time protected justices of the peace, constables, surveyors of highways, local boards and other public authorities from vexatious actions for things done in pursuance of the Acts. This protection was afforded by requiring the plaintiff to give notice of action, by compelling him to bring the action in the place where the cause of action arose, by requiring him to bring his action within a short limit of time, by enabling the defendant to plead the general issue (*q.v.*) and to tender amends, and by enacting that the plaintiff if unsuccessful should pay double or treble costs. These various enactments were reduced into one by the Public Authorities Protection Act, 1893, which applied to common law as well as to statutory duties, to individuals as well as to public authorities, and to acts of omission as well as to acts of commission. This Act provided six months (increased to twelve months by the Limitation Act, 1939, s. 21) as the limit of time for the action; it did not apply to an action *in rem* (*The Burns* [1907] P. 137), or if the cause of action alleged was fraud (*Pearson* v. *Dublin Corporation* [1907] A.C. 351), or if there was a continuance of the injury or damage (*Hague* v. *Doncaster Rural Council* (1909) 100 L.T. 121; *Brownlie* v. *Barrhead Magistrates,* 1923 S.C. 915). It also provided for costs as between solicitor and client if judgment was given for the defendant. It only applied to an action, prosecution or other proceeding against a person for an act done in pursuance or execution or intended execution of an Act of Parliament or a public duty or authority or in respect of an alleged neglect or default in the execution of such act, duty or authority (*Bradford Corporation* v. *Myers* [1916] 1 A.C. 242; *Betts* v. *Metropolitan District Receiver* [1932] 2 K.B. 595).

The Public Authorities Protection Act, 1893, was repealed by the Law Reform (Limitation of Actions, etc.) Act, 1954, s. 1, which assimilated the law applicable to proceedings against public authorities to that applicable in other cases.

Public body. The Public Bodies Corrupt Practices Act, 1889, s. 7, defines this expression for the purposes of that Act. See also the Prevention of Corruption Act, 1916, s. 4 (2); Representation of the People Act, 1949, s. 99; Race Relations Act, 1968, s. 27 (12); Local Government Act, 1972, s. 270 (1). For the purposes of s. 2 of the Act of 1916, a public body is one, whether elected or created by statute, which functions and performs its duties for the benefit of the public, as opposed to private gain (*R.* v. *Joy and Emmony* (1975) 60 Cr.App.R. 132).

As to meetings of public bodies see LOCAL AUTHORITY.

Public building. See the London Building Act, 1930, s. 5; London Building Acts (Amendment) Act, 1939, s. 4.

Public Buildings and Works, Ministry of. This Ministry was dissolved and its functions transferred to the Secretary of State for the Environment by S.I. 1970 No. 1681. For earlier order see S.I. 1964 No. 263. The responsible minister is the Minister for Housing and Construction. See ENVIRONMENT, SECRETARY OF STATE FOR.

Public chapels, chapels founded at some period later than the church itself, and designed for the accommodation of such of the parishioners as in course of time had begun to fix their residence at a distance from its site; chapels so circumstanced were described as chapels of ease, because built in aid of the original church. See CHAPEL.

Public companies. See COMPANIES.

Public document, a document made for the purpose of the public making use of it, *e.g.*, registers kept by public officials, judicial records, etc. A record kept for the information of the Crown and the executive, however, is not a public document, and production of it in court can be refused if it is considered contrary to the public interest to produce it.

The contents of a public document are proved by producing the document itself for inspection from the proper custody and identifying it as what it purports to be, or by an examined copy. An entry by a public officer in a public document is presumed to be true when made and is receivable accordingly.

Public elementary school. See EDUCATION.

Public funds. See FUNDS, PUBLIC.

Public health. The first Public Health Act was passed in 1848; this was an adoptive Act not applying to London, and forms the foundation of modern sanitary legislation. It was followed by some twenty-nine amending Acts which were repealed and consolidated by the Public Health Act, 1875. The Local Government Act, 1933, repealed certain sections of this Act, re-enacting them with amendments. The Public Health Act, 1936, consolidates many of the provisions of earlier legislation, without, however, repealing parts of the Public Health Acts, 1875, 1890, 1907 and 1925. The Act repeals and replaces among other enactments the Baths and Washhouses Acts, 1846 to 1899, the Public Health Act, 1925, Part IX, and parts of the Local Government Acts, 1871 and 1894, relating to the same subject, and the greater part of the previous legislation relating to infectious diseases. The Act is directed to promoting healthy and sanitary surroundings and sanitation for the general population under the following heads: port health authorities, building from the sanitary point of view, sewage and sewers, drains and cesspools, filthy or verminous premises or persons, public conveniences, nuisances, offensive trades, smoke, water supply (works, wells, charges, supply, waste); prevention, notification and treatment of diseases; preventing the spread of infection, disinfection of premises and removal of infected persons, tuberculosis, blindness, medicine, medical assistance and instruction, hospital and nursing cases, laboratories, ambulances and mortuaries; notification of births, child welfare and life protection, baths, wash-houses, bathing places, lodging-houses, canal boats, watercourses, ditches, ponds, ships and boats, tents, vans and sheds, and hop-pickers. The Ministry of Health Act, 1919, established a Ministry of Health to exercise powers with respect to health and local government; the Ministry superseded the Local Government Board. The central authority for the purpose of public health is the Department of Health and Social Security which was created on November 1, 1968, from the Ministry of Health and the Ministry of Social Security. See S.I. 1968 No. 1699.

The Public Health Act, 1961 (as amended), makes miscellaneous amendments of the Act of 1936, and contains substantive provisions relating to building regulations (ss. 4–11) and trade effluents (ss. 55–71). For other Acts, see the Public Health Laboratory Service Act, 1960, the Public Health (Notification of Births) Act, 1965, and the Public Health (Recurring Nuisances) Act, 1969.

The law relating to public health in London was assimilated to the law elsewhere by the London Government Act, 1933, s. 40, Sch. 11.

The microbiological service provided under the National Health Service Act, 1946, s. 17, is administered under the Public Health Laboratory Service Act, 1960; National Health Service Reorganisation Act, 1973, Sch. 4 paras. 97, 98.

For an early instance of a Public Health Act, see SUPER STATUTO QUE NUL JECT DUNG.

Public house, premises on which excisable liquors are sold, for consumption thereon, to the public at large. The use of premises as a club in which such liquors are sold to members only is not a breach of a covenant against use as a public house; but the Refreshment Houses Act, 1860, s. 44, provides that the sale of wine, to be consumed on the premises, under a licence for such sale and consumption, is a breach of such a covenant.

The Public House Closing Act, 1864, was an adoptive Act whereby public houses and refreshment houses, till then allowed to be open all night, were closed in boroughs and certain other districts between 1 and 4 a.m. The matter is now dealt with by the Licensing Act, 1964. See INTOXICATING LIQUORS; PUBLICAN; REFRESHMENT HOUSES; VINTNERS COMPANY.

Public international law. See INTERNATIONAL LAW.

Public law. See POSITIVE LAW.

Public libraries. See LIBRARIES.

Public local inquiries. A general power to order the holding of a local inquiry is given by the Local Government Act, 1972, s. 250. Inquiries are held on appeals against decisions of local planning authorities. See DEVELOPMENT. As to the holding of local inquiries in relation to the compulsory purchase of land, see the Acquisition of Land (Authorisation Procedure) Act, 1946, s. 5.

Public meeting, a meeting which any person may attend. Any number of persons may meet in any place for any lawful purpose with the consent of the owner of that place; but without such consent, and in any case in the public streets, which may be lawfully used for the purpose of passing and repassing only and for purposes incidental thereto (*Ex p. Lewis* (1888) 21 Q.B.D. 191), there is no right of public meeting known to the law.

Political meetings within a mile of

Westminster Hall during a session of Parliament are prohibited by the Seditious Meetings Act, 1817, s. 23.

Under the Public Meeting Act, 1908, any person who at a lawful public meeting acts in a disorderly manner for the purpose of preventing the transaction of the business for which the meeting was called together is guilty of an offence and is liable on summary conviction to imprisonment for three months or a fine of £100 or both and on conviction on indictment to imprisonment for twelve months or a fine of £500 or both (s. 1 (1), as amended by the Representation of the People Act, 1949, Sch. 9, and the Public Order Act, 1963, s. 1). Any person who incites others to commit the offence is guilty of a like offence (Act of 1908, s. 1 (2)). If a constable reasonably suspects a person of committing an offence under the section, he may if requested so to do by the chairman of the meeting, require that person to declare to him immediately his name and address and, if that person refuses or fails so to declare his name and address or gives a false name and address he shall be guilty of an offence and liable on summary conviction to a fine not exceeding two pounds, and if he refuses or fails to declare his name and address or if the constable reasonably suspects him of giving a false name and address, the constable may without warrant arrest him (Act of 1908, s. 1 (3), inserted by the Public Order Act, 1936, s. 6).

As to provoking a breach of the peace in any public place or at a public meeting, see BREACH OF THE PEACE.

Any person who while present at any public meeting or on the occasion of any procession has with him any offensive weapon (*q.v.*) otherwise than in pursuance of lawful authority is guilty of an offence (Public Order Act, 1936, s. 4; S.I. 1965 No. 1536, art. 12 (2), Sch. 3), punishable on summary conviction with imprisonment for three months or a fine of £50 or both (Public Order Act, 1936, s. 7 (2); Public Order Act, 1963, s. 1 (2)).

A person is guilty of an offence if with intent to stir up hatred against any section of the public in Great Britain distinguished by colour, race, or ethnic or national origins (a) he publishes or distributes written matter which is threatening, abusive or insulting, or uses in any public place or at any public meeting words which are threatening, abusive or insulting being matter or words likely to stir up hatred against that section on grounds of colour, race or ethnic or national origins (Race Relations Act, 1965, s. 6 (1)). The offence is punishable on summary conviction with imprisonment for six months or a fine of £200 or both and on conviction on indictment with imprisonment for two years or a fine of £1,000 or both but no prosecution for such an offence may be instituted except by or with the consent of the Attorney-General (s. 6 (3)). See *Brutus* v. *Cozens* [1973] A.C. 854.

A public meeting held on a highway constitutes an obstruction under the Highways Act, 1959, s. 121 (*Arrowsmith* v. *Jenkins* [1963] 2 Q.B. 561).

A fair and accurate newspaper report of the proceedings at any public meeting (that is to say a meeting bona fide and lawfully held for a lawful purpose and for the furtherance or discussion of any matter of public concern, whether the admission to the meeting is general or restricted) is privileged unless the publication is proved to be made with malice (Defamation Act, 1952, s. 7 (1), Sch. Pt. II para. 9). The newspaper must if requested publish in an adequate and reasonable manner a reasonable letter or statement by way of explanation or contradiction (s. 7 (2)).

As to meetings of public bodies see LOCAL AUTHORITY.

See LIBEL; MEETING; NEWSPAPERS; TRAFALGAR SQUARE.

Public mischief. A conspiracy to effect a public mischief is a crime, but actions of an individual not committed in combination with others are indictable only if they constitute common law or statutory offences (*R.* v. *Newland* [1954] 1 Q.B. 158, overruling *R.* v. *Manley* [1932] 1 K.B. 529). But where a person causes any wasteful employment of the police by knowingly making to any person a false report tending to show that an offence has been committed, or to give rise to apprehension for the safety of any persons or property, or tending to show that he has information material to any police inquiry, he is liable on summary conviction to imprisonment for not more than six months or to a fine of not more than £200 or to both (Criminal Law Act, 1967, s. 5 (2)). No proceedings are to be instituted except by or with the consent of the Director of Public Prosecutions (s. 5 (3)).

Conspiracy to indemnify a person of his bail is a public mischief (*R.* v. *Foy*; *R.* v. *Noe*; *R.* v. *Keily* [1972] Crim.L.R. 504). An agreement to use dishonest means to induce officials of banks, building societies, etc. and officers of government and local government to disclose confidential information is not a conspiracy to effect a public mischief by defrauding the public (*D.P.P.* v. *Withers* [1975] A.C. 842).

Public morals. A conspiracy to corrupt public morals is a crime at common law (*Shaw* v. *D.P.P.* [1962] A.C. 220 (publishing advertisements by prostitutes)). See PROSTITUTE.

Public officer. This sometimes means the holder of a public office under the Crown, but it is also used to denote an officer of a joint stock company or corporation.

The term " public officer " in the latter sense seems to be derived from the Country Bankers Act, 1826, which provided for the appointment of public officers of banking companies, and empowered such companies to sue and be sued in the name of any such officer, although the companies themselves were not incorporated. A similar provision was frequently contained in private Acts authorising the formation of unincorporated companies. Companies formed under modern Acts are always incorporated.

A public officer in the former sense is sometimes called a public agent. A public agent cannot sue in his own name in respect of any contract made by him in his public capacity (*Bowen* v. *Morris* (1810) 2 Taun. 374), nor can he be sued thereon unless he pledged his personal credit (*Prosser* v. *Allen* (1818) Gow 117); he is accountable only to the Crown for moneys received by him in his official capacity (*R.* v. *Treasury* (1872) L.R. 7 Q.B. 387); no action lies against him for acts done by his subordinates unless he was party or privy thereto (*Nicholson* v. *Mounsey* (1812) 15 East 384); and, while he is personally liable for his own wrongful acts or omissions, no action lies against the Crown in respect of anything wrongfully done or left undone by him (*Tobin* v. *R.* (1864) 16 C.B.(N.S.) 310), except as provided by the Crown Proceedings Act, 1947.

Public offices, Sale of. The Sale of Offices Act, 1551, prohibited the sale of certain offices. The Sale of Offices Act, 1809, extended the Act of 1551 to all offices under the Crown whether civil, naval or military, except in so far as the sale of commissions in the army was permitted. Now only such payments as are specified in the Regimental Exchange Act, 1875, can be made in connection with the exchange of commissions.

Public order. The Public Order Act, 1936, prohibits the wearing of uniforms in connection with political objects and the maintenance by private persons of associations of military or similar character, and makes provision for the preservation of public order on the occasion of public processions and meetings and in public places (ss. 1–3; Criminal Jurisdiction Act, 1975, Sch. 5). Where an article such as a beret is worn to show that a group of men are in association, that article can be regarded as " uniform " without proof of its previous use as such (*O'Moran* v. *D.P.P.* [1975] Q.B. 864). See BREACH OF THE PEACE; PUBLIC MEETING; PUBLIC PLACE.

Public parks. See OPEN SPACE; PARK; PLEASURE-GROUNDS.

Public place. This expression occurs in many Acts of Parliament, which declare such and such a thing to be an offence if done in a " public place." In each case the meaning depends upon the context and upon the object of a statute. A place may be a public place at one time and not at other times. Thus a railway carriage is a public place while being used for the reception and conveyance of passengers, but not while it lies empty in a siding (*Langrish* v. *Archer* (1882) 10 Q.B.D. 44).

A public place would seem to include a place to which the public are accustomed to resort without being interfered with, though there is no legal right to do so (*R. v. Wellard* (1884) 14 Q.B.D. at p. 66). But for criminal purposes the attribute " public " will apply to many other places, *e.g.*, the roof of a private house within the view of many persons (*R. v. Thallman* (1863) 33 L.J.M.C. 58).

In the Public Order Act, 1936, s. 9, as amended by the Criminal Justice Act, 1972, s. 33, public place includes any highway and any other premises to which at the material time the public have or are permitted to have access, whether on payment or otherwise.

Unless a licensee's invitation to the public continues after an inn is closed, the inn car-park is not a public place after licensing hours for the purposes of the Road Traffic Act, 1972, s. 6 (2) (*Sandy v. Martin* [1974] R.T.R. 263). See also *R. v. Shaw* [1974] R.T.R. 225.

Public policy, the principles under which freedom of contract or private dealings is restricted by law for the good of the community. See CHAMPERTY; MORTMAIN; POLICY; RESTRAINT OF MARRIAGE; RESTRAINT OF TRADE.

Public policy, however, is "a very unruly horse" (*Richardson v. Mellish* (1824) 2 Bing. 252). The term does not admit of any precise definition (*Davies v. Davies* (1887) 36 Ch.D. 364; *Besant v. Wood* (1879) 12 Ch.D. 620; *Egerton v. Brownlow* (1853) 4 H.L.C. 1).

A disposition in favour of illegitimate children not in being when the disposition takes effect is not against public policy (Family Law Reform Act, 1969, s. 15 (7)).

Public prosecutor. See DIRECTOR OF PUBLIC PROSECUTIONS.

Public records, the general records of the realm which are kept at the Record Office (*q.v.*).

Copies purporting to be sealed with the seal of the Record Office are admissible as evidence (Public Records Act, 1958, s. 9). The Act transfers the responsibility for public records from the Master of the Rolls to the Lord Chancellor (s. 1). Public records in the Public Record Office are not available for public inspection until the expiration of thirty years beginning with January 1, in the year next after that in which they were

created or of such other period as the Lord Chancellor may prescribe (Public Records Act, 1958, s. 5; Public Records Act, 1967). See Giuseppi, *Guide to Public Records.*

See JOURNALS OF PARLIAMENT; RECORD.

Public right, a right enjoyed by the public as distinguished from a private or personal right attached to the personalty of an individual. Public rights exist at common law, such as the right of the public to pass along a highway, or they may be conferred by statute. In either case if the statute does not provide a remedy, the remedy for infringement is by indictment or by an action for an injunction brought by the Attorney-General either directly or upon the relation of an individual (called a relator) who becomes liable for the costs, but if the individual has suffered special damage peculiar to himself or some private right has been interfered with specially, the Attorney-General is not an essential party to the action though he is often joined as a party (*Boyer v. Paddington Borough Council* [1903] 1 Ch. 109; *David v. Britannic Merthyr Coal Co.* [1909] 2 K.B. 146; *Att.-Gen. v. P.Y.A. Quarries* [1957] 2 Q.B. 169). See NEGLIGENCE; NUISANCE.

Public schools, schools open to all, subject to the terms of their foundation and the regulations of some governing body, private schools being only open to such pupils as the proprietor or head-master chooses to admit. The term has in some modern statutes been confined to the larger public schools the governing bodies of which were, by the Public Schools Act, 1868, empowered to make regulations for their constitution and management, requiring confirmation by Order in Council (*Birkenhead School v. Dring* (1926) 43 T.L.R. 48).

In the narrower sense it means the seven schools, Eton, Winchester, Westminster, Charterhouse, Harrow, Rugby and Shrewsbury, mentioned in the Public Schools Act, 1868, s. 3. These seven schools were declared by the Endowed Schools Act, 1869, s. 8, not to be "endowed" for the purposes of that Act. They are carried on subject to the Public Schools Acts, 1868 to 1873.

St. Paul's School, the Merchant Taylors'

School, Marlborough, Wellington, Bradfield, Haileybury, Clifton, Cheltenham and others are colloquially spoken of as public schools, but they are not affected by the Public Schools Acts.

The term is also sometimes applied to schools which are represented at the Headmasters' Conference.

Public service vehicle, a motor vehicle used for carrying passengers for hire or reward which either (a) is carrying passengers or (b) is not carrying passengers at separate fares but is adapted to carry eight or more passengers, not being a tramcar or trolley vehicle (Road Traffic Act, 1960, ss. 117 (1), 118). Part III of that Act deals with the regulation of public service vehicles. See CONTRACT CARRIAGE; EXPRESS CARRIAGE; STAGE CARRIAGE.

No person may use a motor vehicle on a road as a stage carriage (*q.v.*), an express carriage (*q.v.*) or a contract carriage (*q.v.*) unless he holds a public service vehicle licence (Road Traffic Act, 1960, ss. 127–133; Road Traffic Act, 1962, Sch. 4 Pt. I; Transport Act, 1968, s. 35; Transport (London) Act, 1969, s. 34; Road Traffic Act, 1974, Sch. 2 Pt. I, Sch. 7). Drivers and conductors require to be licensed (Road Traffic Act, 1960, ss. 144–146). As to regulations governing the conduct and number of passengers, see ss. 147, 148; Criminal Justice Act, 1967, Sch. 3 Pt. I; Road Traffic Act, 1974, Sch. 7. As to penalties, see the Road Traffic Act, 1974, Sch. 5 Pt. I.

Powers of arrest without warrant of passengers misconducting themselves are given by the Public Service Vehicles (Arrest of Offenders) Act, 1975.

Public sewer. Sewers which become vested in a water authority are known as public sewers. See the Public Health Act, 1936, s. 20, as substituted by the Water Act, 1973, Sch. 8 para. 33.

Public statues. The Public Statues (Metropolis) Act, 1854, placed public statues in the metropolitan police district under the control of the Commissioners of Works and Public Buildings, now the Ministry of Housing and Construction.

Public stores. By the Public Stores Act, 1875, provision is made for the protection of public stores and the punishment of persons improperly obtaining the same or obliterating the marks thereon. S. 3 declares that the Act shall apply to all stores under the care, superintendence or control of a Secretary of State or the Admiralty or any public department or office or of any person in the service of Her Majesty (for adaptations to the Ministry ·of Defence, see S.I. 1964 No. 488), and such stores are in the Act referred to as Her Majesty's stores. S. 2 enacts that the term "stores" includes all goods and chattels and any single store or article.

Public, true, and notorious, the old form by which charges in the allegations in the ecclesiastical courts were described at the end of each particular.

Public Trustee. The office of Public Trustee was established by the Public Trustee Act, 1906. The Public Trustee is a corporation sole, and may if he thinks fit act in the administration of estates of deceased persons if under one thousand pounds; act as custodian trustee (*q.v.*) (*Re Cherry's Trusts* [1914] 1 Ch. 83); act as an ordinary trustee; be appointed a judicial trustee (*q.v.*); and be appointed an executor and obtain a grant of probate (s. 5). He may be appointed an original trustee or a new trustee or an additional trustee, in the same cases and manner and by the same persons or court as if he were a private trustee; he may be appointed sole trustee although the trustees originally appointed were two or more; but he cannot be appointed a new or additional trustee when the trust instrument directs the contrary unless the court otherwise orders and notice of any proposed appointment must be given to the beneficiaries. The Public Trustee may decline to accept any trust, but not on the ground only of the small value of the trust property; and he cannot, except under certain conditions, accept a trust which involves the carrying on of any business, nor a trust under a deed of arrangement, nor the administration of an insolvent estate, nor a trust exclusively for religious or charitable purposes (s. 2). The Consolidated Fund is liable to make good all sums required to discharge any liability which the Public Trustee, if he were a private trustee, would be personally liable to discharge (s. 7). By s. 13 an investigation and audit of trust accounts may be made at the instance of any trustee or beneficiary, by some agreed solicitor or accountant, and in default of agreement, by the Public Trustee or some person appointed by him; under s. 3 (4), the Public Trustee can take the opinion of the court on any question arising in the course of his administration of an estate. The Public Trustee cannot accept the trusteeship of any settlement other than an English one (*Re Hewitt's Settlement* [1915] 1 Ch. 228). For modifications of the Act of 1906 in relation to common investment funds, see the Administration of Justice Act, 1965, s. 2.

See the Public Trustee Rules, 1912 (No. 348), the Public Trustee (Custodian Trustee) Rules, 1971 (No. 1894), the Local Authorities etc. (Miscellaneous Provisions) (No. 2) Order, 1974 (No. 595), art. 4.

The Public Trustee is the person in whom the legal estate vested in certain cases of undivided shares in land, and of infancy subsisting on January 1, 1926, under the transitional provisions of the Law of Property Act, 1925, s. 39, Sch. 1.

As to the fees chargeable by the Public Trustee, see the Public Trustee (Fees) Act, 1957; Public Trustee (Fees) Orders, 1957 and 1959 (S.I. 1957 No. 485; 1959 No. 2984).

See CUSTODIAN TRUSTEE; TRUST CORPORATION; TRUSTEE.

Public utility undertaking was defined in the Emergency Laws (Repeal) Act, 1959, Sch. 2 Pt. I para. 100, as any of the following undertakings the carrying on of which is authorised by any Act or by order: (a) any undertaking for the supply of electricity, gas or water; (b) any railway, light railway, tramway, road transport, water transport, canal, inland navigation, dock, harbour, pier or lighthouse undertaking; (c) any sewerage or sewage disposal undertaking, or any undertaking for the collection or disposal of refuse; (d) any undertaking of a drainage authority. It includes any such undertaking which is carried on by a local authority. This paragraph was repealed by the Emergency Laws (Re-enactments and Repeals) Act, 1964, Sch. 2. See also the Trade Facilities Act, 1924, s. 2 (6),

the Bridges Act, 1929, s. 16, and the War Damage (Public Utility Undertakings) Act, 1949, Sch. 1.

Public way, a highway (*q.v.*).

Public Works Loan Commissioners, a body which makes advances of public funds to public bodies for public works. It was established by the Public Works Loans Act, 1875, which repealed earlier statutes on the same subject. See also the Public Works Loans Acts, 1881, 1882, 1887, 1892, 1911, 1944, 1946, 1952, 1964, 1965 and 1967, and the Public Works Loans (Money) Act, 1876.

See LOAN COMMISSIONERS.

Publican, one who keeps a public house (*q.v.*) and is authorised by licence to retail therein, for consumption on or off the premises, intoxicating liquors (*q.v.*) of all kinds; a licensed victualler.

Publicatio, confiscation (Civil Law).

Publication, divulgation; proclamation; communication of defamatory words to some person or persons other than the person defamed.

The publication of fair reports of legal proceedings in court (other than *ex parte* proceedings) is a common law right exempt from proceedings for libel.

As to the publication of an apology for libel in a newspaper, see APOLOGY.

It is essential in an action of defamation that the publication be to a third person, though the law is otherwise in Scotland. There can be no publication as between husband and wife (*Wennhak* v. *Morgan* (1888) 20 Q.B.D. 635); but publication can be made to either husband or wife respecting the other (*Jones* v. *Williams* (1885) 1 T.L.R. 572; *Theaker* v. *Richardson* [1962] 1 W.L.R. 151). The third party to whom the matter is published may be in the position of a servant or clerk (*Edmondson* v. *Birch & Co.* [1907] 1 K.B. 371; *Osborn* v. *Boulter & Son* [1930] 2 K.B. 226). He must be able to understand the defamatory character of the matter (*Sadgrove* v. *Hole* [1901] 2 K.B. 1). It is no defence that the publication was unintentional unless without negligence the person charged with publishing was in fact ignorant of the contents of the document (*M'Leod* v. *St. Aubyn* [1899] A.C. 549); the onus of proving this lies on the defendant (*Vizetelly* v. *Mudie's Library* [1900] 2 Q.B. 170). In criminal libel, publication to the prosecutor is sufficient.

As only a new and original invention can be patented, publication before protection defeats the inventor's right to protection by patent, unless the publication was without the knowledge or consent of an inventor who has not been guilty of unreasonable delay in obtaining protection. An invention covered by a patent is not deemed to have been anticipated by reason only of publication in a specification left pursuant to an application made not less than fifty years before the patent, or of publication in a provisional specification of any date not followed by a complete specification (Patents Act, 1949, ss. 50, 52). Similarly, prior publication of a design (*q.v.*) prevents registration, but publication by exhibition at industrial and international exhibitions and exhibition elsewhere without the proprietor's privity or consent does not operate as publication (Registered Designs Act, 1949, s. 6). As to the meaning of publication in relation to copyright, see the Copyright Act, 1956, s. 49.

For the validity of a will it was formerly necessary that, it should be proved to have been " published " by the testator, that is to say, declared by him, in the presence of witnesses, to be his will; but proof of " publication " was not insisted on in the case of a holograph will. Now under the Wills Act, 1837, s. 13, no proof of publication is required other than such as is implied by properly attested execution.

In the practice of the Court of Chancery, it was at one time customary to pass a rule (or order) for the " publication " of the depositions of witnesses, that is to say, to authorise the giving out of copies, but this ceased to be the practice after all parties were permitted to attend the examination of witnesses.

Publici juris, of public right. As applied to a thing or right, this means that it is open to or exercisable by all persons.

When a thing is common property, so that any one can make use of it, it is said to be *publici juris,* as in the case of light, air and public water. (See AIR; LIGHT; NATURAL RIGHTS; WATER.) So when a

copyright or patent has expired, or a trade mark or trade name becomes common property, the book, process, trade mark, or trade name is said to be *publici juris,* that is, any person can print or use it.

As applied to the case of water flowing through private land, *publici juris* means that the water flows in such a defined channel as to give the owner of each piece of land through which it passes what are called rights of water in respect of it, as opposed to water which is either confined to one piece of land, as in a pond, or percolates or flows in no defined course.

Publicist, a writer on the law of nations.

Publicity. See ADVERTISEMENT.

Publisher. A publisher of libellous matter is liable both civilly and criminally in respect of any such matter he may publish, and his civil liability exists even though the publication takes place without his knowledge. Not only the party who originally prints, but every party who sells, who gives, or who lends a copy of an offensive publication is liable to be prosecuted as a publisher (*R.* v. *Carlile* (1819) 3 B. & Ald. 169).

If the publisher of a book becomes bankrupt, an author to whom royalties are due is not in any more favourable position than other creditors, and can only prove for the damages he has sustained by the breach of contract (*Re Grant Richards* [1907] 2 K.B. 33).

As to the duty of publishers to send a copy of every book published in the United Kingdom to the British Library and other libraries see COPYRIGHT; LIBRARY.

Puchta. Georg Friedrich Puchta was born on August 31, 1798, became professor at Erlangen, Munich, Marburg, Leipzig and Berlin, and died on January 8, 1846. He wrote numerous works on the civil law, especially the *Cursus der Institutionen* and the *Lehrbuch der Pandecten.*

Pudzeld, to be free from the payment of money for taking wood in a forest (Co.Litt. 233a). See WOODGILD.

Pueritia, the age from seven to fourteen.

Pufendorf. Samuel (Freiherr) von Pufendorf was born on January 8, 1632, became professor at Heidelberg, and died on October 16, 1694. He wrote *De jure naturae et gentium* and other works.

Puffer, one who attends a sale by auction, to bid on the part of the owner, for the purpose of raising the price and exciting the eagerness of the bidders.

The Sale of Land by Auction Act, 1867, regulates the employments of puffers at an auction for the sale of land, and enacts that all sales of land where a puffer had bid shall be illegal unless a right of bidding on behalf of the owner has been reserved; that the conditions of sale shall state whether the sale is to be without reserve, or subject to a reserve price, or whether a right to bid is reserved; that if it is stated that the sale is to be without reserve, a puffer is not to be employed; that if a right to bid is reserved, the seller or one puffer may bid; and that the practice of opening biddings (*q.v.*), formerly sanctioned by courts of equity, shall be discontinued. As to sale of goods by auction, see the Sale of Goods Act, 1893, s. 58. See AUCTION.

Pugilism. See PRIZE FIGHT.

Puis darrein continuance, since the last continuance. When the pleadings were each entered separately on the record, every entry after the first was called a continuance (*q.v.*). When the matter of defence arose after writ, but before plea or continuance, it was said to be pleaded " to the further maintenance " of the action. When it arose after plea or continuance it was called a plea of *puis darrein continuance,* since the last continuance. A plea *puis darrein continuance* was one in which the defendant pleaded some matter of defence which had arisen since the last continuance or adjournment. After the abolition of continuances, the same name was given to pleas of defences which arose after the defendant had put in his plea (*q.v.*). Under R.S.C., Ord. 18, r. 9, matter may be pleaded whenever arising.

Puisne [Fr. *puisné*], later born, junior, inferior, lower in rank. The judges and barons of the former common law courts at Westminster, other than the Chief Justices, were called puisne.

Under the Judicature Act, 1925, s. 2 (4), the puisne judges of the High Court are styled justices of the High Court.

The term is also used as meaning later or subsequent with reference to mortgagees and the like, *e.g.,* puisne mortgages (*q.v.*).

See MULIER.

Puisne mortgage. Before 1926 this meant a mortgage subsequent to the mortgage of a legal estate, but for the purposes of the Land Charges Act, 1972, s. 2 (4), Class C, it means any legal mortgage (including the first) of a legal estate not being a mortgage protected by a deposit of documents relating to the legal estate affected. These mortgages must be registered at the Land Charges Registry, or they will lose priority. This amounts to notice, but even this notice may not prevent tacking of further advances by a prior mortgagee. See TACKING.

Under the transitional provisions of the Law of Property Act, 1925, Sch. 1, puisne mortgages not protected by deposit of documents or registered as land charges became mortgages of a legal estate, but as against a purchaser in good faith without notice, the mortgages remain equitable interests. See LAND CHARGE; MORTGAGE; NOTICE.

Pulsare, to accuse or make complaint against (Leg.Hen.I. c. 26).

Pulsator [Lat. *pulsare,* to accuse], the plaintiff or actor; the complainant or prosecutor.

Punctually. Payment " punctually " means payment on the day fixed for payment (*Leeds and Hanley Theatre of Varieties* v. *Broadbent* [1898] 1 Ch. 343). Payment " duly " does not necessarily mean " punctually " (*Starkey* v. *Barton* [1909] 1 Ch. 284).

Punctuation. Properly drawn deeds are never punctuated, and must be so drawn that their meaning is clear without any marks of punctuation. Punctuation in deeds, if it does occur, is disregarded. Even in Acts of Parliament it is of little importance (*Piper* v. *Harvey* [1958] 1 Q.B. 439). Even if punctuation in modern Acts can be looked at (which is very doubtful) one cannot have any regard to punctuation in older Acts (*I.R.C.* v. *Hinchy* [1960] A.C. 748, *per* Lord Reid).

Pund-brech, pound-breach.

Punishment, the penalty for transgressing the law: in England it is usually left within wide limits to the discretion of the court. Too great severity has frequently led to refusals of juries to convict, especially where the punishment is death, as it was down to 1810 for the offence of stealing goods to the value of forty shillings from a dwelling-house, and down to 1832 for forgery. In the former case the jury would falsely find the value of the goods stolen to be thirty-nine shillings; in the latter, a petition of bankers hastened the mitigation of a punishment which failed to protect them. See Crime; Death; Imprisonment; Penal Servitude; Penalty; Probation of Offenders; Rehabilitation of Offenders; Whipping.

Punitive damages, damages given, on the principle of punishing the defendant, over and above compensation to the plaintiff. See Exemplary Damages.

Pupil, a ward, one under the care of a guardian. The word minor (q.v.) is sometimes loosely used to include a pupil.

Pupillus, a person *sui juris,* under the age of puberty (q.v.), whose affairs were managed and whose want of legal capacity supplied by a tutor (Civil Law).

Pur autre vie. See Autre Vie, Estate pur; Tenant for Life.

Pur cause de vicinage. See Common.

Purchase [Lat. *perquisitio, conquaestus*]. In its poular sense " purchase " means an acquisition of land, obtained by way of sale, for money or some other valuable consideration. In its strict legal acceptation, however, it means an acquisition of land in any lawful manner other than by descent or the mere act of law, and includes escheat, occupancy, prescription, forfeiture and alienation. Generally, it is possession to which a man comes not by title of descent (Co.Litt. 18b).

Purchase is used in law not only in the popular sense of buying (see Vendor and Purchaser), but also in a technical sense to denote that a person has acquired land by the lawful act of himself or another, e.g., by conveyance, gift or devise, as opposed to title by act of the law, such as descent, dower, curtesy, etc., and to title by wrong, as in the case of disseisin (Co. Litt. 3b, 18b). See Purchaser; Title.

Anciently the word " purchase " meant to acquire or seek for. Hence the old writers speak of " purchasing " land by accretion, and of purchasing writs, charters of pardon, etc. (Britton 86b; Co.Litt. 128b).

Purchase notices. On the refusal of planning permission for the development (q.v.) of land or on the grant of a permission subject to unacceptable conditions, the owner of the land may have the right to require the land to be purchased by the local authority. The requirement takes the form of a purchase notice given within twelve months of the planning decision on which it is founded. A purchase notice requires confirmation by the Secretary of State for the Environment in order to become effective. Instead of confirming a purchase notice the Secretary of State may grant planning permission for the development sought or for some other development. In the latter case compensation may become payable. The decision of the Secretary of State in relation to the purchase notice may be challenged within six weeks on a point of law by application to the High Court. The ground for confirming a purchase notice is that the land is rendered incapable of reasonably beneficial use by reason of the planning control. The confirmation of a purchase notice operates as an irrevocable notice to treat to acquire the land compulsorily. If the Secretary of State does not act within six months the purchase notice is deemed to be confirmed. A purchase notice may also be served when an existing planning permission is revoked or modified, or an existing use is interfered with or existing buildings or works are required to be removed or altered, in relation to a Tree Preservation Order (see Tree), or the control of advertisements (see Advertisements), or in certain cases in relation to the refusal of planning permission for industrial development (Town and Country Planning Act, 1971, ss. 180, 191, 208; Local Government Act, 1972, Sch. 30; Town and Country Planning General Regulations, 1969, reg. 19).

Purchase tax, a tax levied on the

wholesale value of goods transferred by a registered person to an unregistered person or by appropriation to any other taxable purpose. It was introduced by the Finance (No. 2) Act, 1940, s. 18. The legislation on the subject was consolidated by the Purchase Tax Act, 1963. Purchase tax was abolished by the Finance Act, 1972, s. 54, on the introduction of value added tax (*q.v.*).

Purchase, Words of, words by which, taken absolutely without reference to or connection with any other words, an estate first attaches, or is considered as commencing in point of title, in the person described by them. By the rule of law known as the rule in *Shelley's Case* (1551) 1 Co.Rep. 104a, when the ancestor by any gift or conveyance took an estate of freehold, and in the same gift or conveyance an estate was limited either mediately or immediately to his heirs in fee or in tail, in such cases " the heirs " were words of limitation of the estate and not words of purchase (*Van Grutten* v. *Foxwell* [1897] A.C. 658). The rule was abolished by the Law of Property Act, 1925, s. 131, and in a limitation to an ancestor for life and then to his heir or any class of heirs or issue, the words heirs or issue are now words of purchase and not of limitation. At the same time, a grant to A and his heirs may still be used to limit an estate in fee simple in law, but any words of limitation other than the conveyance to the grantee are unnecessary for that purpose (Law of Property Act, 1925, s. 60). See WORDS OF LIMITATION, ETC.

Purchaser, a person who buys property (see VENDOR AND PURCHASER); a person who acquires land by purchase in the technical sense of the word (see PURCHASE); a person who acquires land otherwise than by descent. It is in the last sense that the term is used in the Inheritance Act, 1833. See DESCENT.

As to a limitation to the heir taking effect as purchase, see the Law of Property Act, 1925, s. 132.

The Inheritance Act, 1833, enacted that descent should be traced from the purchaser, meaning the person last entitled to the land otherwise than by inheritance.

For various meanings of the word " purchaser," see *I.R.C.* v. *Gribble* [1913] 3 K.B. 218, in which the word " purchase " in the Finance (1909–10) Act, 1910, s. 14 (1), was held to mean " buy " in the ordinary commercial sense; and the same meaning was attributed to it in the Law of Property Amendment Act, 1859, s. 27 (*Re Lawley* [1911] 2 Ch. 530).

Under the Law of Property Act, 1925, s. 205, " purchaser " means a purchaser in good faith for valuable consideration and includes a lessee, mortgagee or other person who for valuable consideration acquires an interest in property except that in Part I (ss. 1 to 39) of the Act, ' purchaser " only means a person who acquires an interest in or charge on property for money or money's worth. Valuable consideration includes marriage but does not include a nominal consideration in money. In the Land Charges Act, 1972, ss. 4, 17 (1) a purchaser means any person (including a mortgagee or lessee) who, for valuable consideration, takes any interest in land or in a charge on land.

Purchaser for value without notice, one who has purchased property bona fide for valuable consideration (even though inadequate) without notice (*q.v.*) of any prior right or title which, if upheld, would derogate from the title which he has purported to acquire. Such a purchaser, if he has got in the legal estate, will usually take priority of equitable claims ranking before him as to time; and, if he has not got in the legal estate, he will usually take priority of mere equities as distinguished from equitable interests. As to the position of such a purchaser, see *Phillips* v. *Phillips* (1862) 4 De G.F. & J. 208. See LAND CHARGE; NOTICE.

Purgation, the clearing a man's self of a crime of which he was publicly suspected, and accused before a judge. It was either canonical, which was prescribed by the canon law, the form whereof, used in the spiritual court, was that the person suspected took his oath that he was clear of the fact objected against him, and brought his honest neighbours with him to make oath that they believed he swore truly; or vulgar, which was by fire or water ordeal, or by combat (3 Bl. Comm. 100; Jacob). See COMPURGATION.

Purgatory. See PRAYERS FOR THE DEAD.

Purging contempt, atoning for, or clearing oneself from contempt of court. See CONTEMPT OF COURT.

Purification, Feast of the, the Purification of the Blessed Virgin, which falls on February 2. It is also known as Candlemas. In the statute 1540, 32 Hen. 8, c. 21, it is mentioned under its full title of *Purificatio Beatae Mariae Virginis.* See FAST DAY; FEASTS.

Puritans. See DISSENTERS.

Purlieu [Norm. Fr. *puralé, pourallee,* a perambulation; Lat. *perambulatio*; Fr. *poirallée*], land formerly added to an ancient forest by unlawful encroachment, and disafforested by the Carta de Foresta (4 Co.Inst. 303).

It was adjoining a forest, bounded with immovable boundaries known by matter of record only, which land was once forest and was afterwards disafforested by the perambulations made for the severing of the new forests from the old, in accordance with the Carta de Foresta (*q.v.*) (Manwood, c. 20, s. 8). See FOREST.

Purlieu-man, one who had, within the purlieu (*q.v.*), freehold land of the annual value of forty shillings. He could keep greyhounds on his land, and had certain privileges as regards hunting deer (Manwood, 151, 157, 180, 186).

Purparty, share or portion; to hold land in purparty with a person was to hold it jointly with him (Britton, 184a; Litt. 262).

Purpresture, an inclosure; where an erection or inclosure is made on any part of the royal demesnes, or on a highway, or a common street or public water, or the like, the offence being more usually called a common nuisance (*q.v.*). See POURPRESTURE.

Purprise [Law Lat. *purprisum*], a close or inclosure; the whole compass of a manor.

Purpure, or **Porprin,** the colour commonly called purple, expressed in engravings by lines in bend sinister. In the arms of princes it was formerly called mercury, and in those of peers, amethyst.

Pursebearer to the Lord Chancellor. The Great Seal (Offices) Act, 1874, s. 7, made provision for the abolition of this office.

Pursuance, prosecution, process.

Pursue. To pursue a warrant or authority, in the old books, is to execute it or carry it out (Co.Litt. 52a). See EXECUTE.

Pursuivant. See POURSUIVANT.

Purus idiota, a congenital idiot.

Purveyance, the Crown's prerogative right to buy up provisions and other necessaries for the royal household at an appraised price, and of impressing horses and vehicles at an appraised price for the royal use. Various statutes, beginning with the statute 1300, 28 Edw. 1, c. 2, were directed against the abuse of the right; and it was abolished by the statute 1660, 12 Car. 2, c. 24, which provided for the indictment of any officials purporting to exercise it. The right of impressing carriages, etc., but only by officers of the navy, was revived by the statute 1662, 14 Car. 2, c. 20; and the right now exists for all branches of the armed forces (see IMPRESSMENT). The right of the king to take carriages, etc., for his personal use on royal progresses was revived by the statute 1685, 1 Jac. 2, c. 10, but this revived right had been obsolete since 1688, and the statute was formally repealed in 1863. See BOARD OF GREEN CLOTH; PROVISOR VICTUALIUM.

Purview [Norm. Fr. *purveu est*; Lat. *provisum est,* it is provided], that part of a statute which provides or enacts, as opposed to the preamble, which recites the reason or occasion for the statute (12 Co.Rep. 20; 2 Co.Inst. 403).

The word is now, however, more generally used as meaning scope or policy. Hence a case was formerly said to be within the purview of an Act when it was expressly covered by the provisions of the Act: now, the same expression would rather mean that the case was impliedly covered by the Act.

Purveu est or *provisum est* are the words used in the enacting part of old statutes.

Putage, Putagium, incontinence (Spelman).

Putative, supposed, reputed; used of a man adjudged under the Affiliation Proceedings Act, 1957, s. 4, to be the father of an illegitimate child.

The putative father should be allowed to appear in adoption proceedings (*Re Adoption Application* (*No. 41 of* 1961) [1963] Ch. 315), but his consent to an adoption is not required (*Re Adoption Application* (*No. 41 of* 1961) (*No. 2*) [1964] Ch. 48; *Re O.* (*an infant*) [1965] Ch. 23).

Putts and refusals, time-bargains or contracts for the sale of supposed stock on a future day. They were forbidden by the Stock Jobbing Act, 1733, s. 1, repealed by the statute 1860, 23 & 24 Vict. c. 28. See GAMING; STOCK JOBBING.

Puture, a custom claimed by serjeants of the peace, keepers in forests, and sometimes by bailiffs of hundreds, to get without payment provisions for themselves, and their horses and dogs, from the tenants and inhabitants within the perambulation of the forest, hundred, etc. The land subject to this custom was called *terra putura.* Others, who call it *pulture,* explain it as a demand in general; and derive it from the monks, who before they were admitted, *pulsabant,* knocked at the gates for several days together (4 Co.Inst. 307).

Before the time of Edward III, this right had been commuted for a small payment (generally fourpence) from each tenant; and the statute 1351, 25 Edw. 3, st. 5, c. 7, prohibited the taking of anything (under colour of puture) except the accustomed payments. It was also called serjeants' food or fold.

Pyramid selling. The Fair Trading Act, 1973, regulates the activities of promoters of trading schemes for the supply of goods and services otherwise than through retail outlets. A common example of such a scheme is one where a participant receives benefits for the introduction of other participants in the scheme. Regulations made by the Secretary of State restrict the operation of the Act to cases which are socially objectionable (ss. 118–123). See S.I. 1973 No. 1740.

Pyx [$\pi v \xi \iota \varsigma$, a box], the box in which sample coins are kept. For the purpose of ascertaining that coins issued from the Mint have been coined in accordance with law, a trial of the pyx is held once at least in every year in which coins have been issued (Coinage Act, 1971, s. 8). The trial takes place before the Queen's Remembrancer and a jury of six members of the Goldsmiths' Company, summoned by the officials of that company, who are known as the Prime Warden and the Wardens; there is a weighing, melting and assaying of the coins in order to ascertain whether they are of proper weight and fineness, and the verdict of the jury, which must be signed by each of them, contains various averments as to these matters. A member of the jury is not entitled to payment of his expenses (Juries Act, 1974, s. 19 (6)).

A pyx hanging from a baldachino is an ornament but if the sacrament is reserved from it, its use is subsidiary to the services of the church and it is not unlawful (*Re St. Nicholas, Plumstead* [1961] 1 W.L.R. 916). See COIN; MAUNDY THURSDAY; TENDER.

Q

Q.B., Q.B.D. Queen's Bench; Queen's Bench Division.

Q.C., Queen's Counsel. See QUEEN'S COUNSEL.

Q.v. [*quod vide,* which see], used to refer a reader to the word, chapter, etc., the name of which it immediately follows.

Qua, in the character of, in virtue of being; used in such phrases as "*qua* trustee."

Quacunque via data, whichever way you take it.

Quadragesima, the time of Lent, because it consists of forty days.

Quadragesima Sunday, the first Sunday in Lent.

Quadragesimals. On Mid-Lent Sunday

(the fourth Sunday in Lent), it was the custom to make certain offerings, in kind, on the high altar of the church; subsequently these offerings were commuted to money payments known as *Quadragesimalia, Chrismatis Denarii, Denarii Quadragesimales,* Easter Pence, *Letare Jerusalem,* Paschals or Paschal Rents. These offerings seem to have gone to the bishop or his suffragan. See PENTECOSTALS.

Quadragesms, the third part of the yearbooks of Edward III, commencing with the year 1366 (2 Reeves, c. xvi, p. 436).

Quadrans, the fourth of a whole (Civil Law).

Quadrant, an angular measure of 90 degrees; an instrument used in astronomy and navigation for taking altitudes and angles.

Quadrantata terrae, a quarter of an acre, now called a rood. See FARDINGDEAL.

Quadripartite, having four parties; divided into four parts.

Quadripartitus. See LIBER QUADRIPARTITUS.

Quadruplatores, informers among the Romans, who, if their information was followed by conviction, had the fourth part of the confiscated goods for their trouble.

Quadruplicatio, a surrebutter (Civil Law).

Quae ab initio inutilis fuit institutio, ex post facto convalescere non potest (D. 50, 17, 210). (That which was a useless institution from the commencement cannot be strengthened by anything subsequent.) See QUOD AB INITIO, ETC.

Quae accessionum locum obtinent extinguuntur cum principales res peremptae fuerint (2 Pothier, Oblig. 202). (Things which are incidents are extinguished when the things to which they are incidental are extinguished.) See ACCESSORIUM NON DUCIT, ETC.; QUUM PRINCIPALIS, ETC.

Quae ad unum finem loquuta sunt, non debent ad alium detorqueri (4 Co.Rep. 14). (Those things which are spoken for one purpose ought not to be perverted to another.)

Quae communi legi derogant stricte interpretantur (Jenk., Cent. 221). (Things derogating from the common law are to be interpreted in a narrow sense.)

Quae contra rationem juris introducta sunt, non debent trahi in consequentiam (12 Co.Rep. 75). (Things introduced contrary to a rule of law ought not to be drawn into a precedent.) Used by Coke, where he says, "we do find divers precedents of proclamations which are utterly against law and reason." See PROCLAMATIONS, ROYAL.

Quae dubitationis tollendae causa inseruntur, communem legem non laedunt (Co.Ltt. 205). (Things which are inserted for the purpose of removing doubt do not injure the common law.) Coke is here speaking of words inserted for greater clearness in a deed where the effect would be the same if the words were omitted. See SURPLUSAGIUM, ETC.

Quae est eadem (which is the same thing). This was formerly used in pleadings to supply the place of a traverse (*q.v.*) in certain actions, more especially the action of trespass. Thus in a *clausum fregit* (see CLOSE), where the declaration (*q.v.*) alleged the trespass to have been on November 1, and the defendant justified in respect of November 2, a plea (*q.v.*) averring *quae est eadem* was good if the date was immaterial, but if the date was material, then a traverse was necessary. If, however, the defendant justified in respect of the date averred, then neither a *quae est eadem* nor a traverse was required.

Quae in curia regis acta sunt rite agi praesumuntur (3 Bulst. 43). (Things which are done in the king's court are presumed to be done in the right way). See OMNIA PRAESUMUNTUR RITE, ETC.

Quae in testamento ita sunt scripta, ut intelligi non possint, perinde sunt ac si scripta non essent (D. 50, 17, 73). (Those things which in a will are so written that they are not capable of being understood are as if they had not been written at all.) See AMBIGUITY.

Quae mala sunt inchoata in principio vix est ut bono perangantur exitu (4 Co. Rep. 2). (Things bad in the commencement can scarcely be carried through to a good ending.) See QUOD AB INITIO, ETC.

Quae non valeant singula juncta juvant (2 Bulst. 132). (Words which are of no effect by themselves may be effective when combined.) See NOSCITUR, ETC.

Quae plura (of what more). Where an *inquisitio post mortem* (*q.v.*) had been held and there was reason to believe that the deceased had died seised of lands other than those disclosed at the inquest, then the escheator, etc., who held the inquest, could sue out the writ of *quae plura* to inquire of what more (*quae plura*) the deceased had been seised (Reg.Brev. 293).

The writ was virtually abolished by the abolition of the Court of Wards and Liveries in 1660.

Quae servitia. See PER QUAE SERVITIA.

Quaelibet concessio fortissime contra donatorem interpretanda est (Co.Litt. 183a). (Every grant is to be construed as strongly as possible against the grantor.) See VERBA CARTARUM, ETC.

Quaelibet poena corporalis, quamvis minima, major est qualibet poena pecuniaria (3 Brac. 105a; 3 Co.Inst. 220). (Corporal punishment, however slight, is more efficacious than a fine.)

Quaerens non invenit plegium (the plaintiff has not found pledge), a return made by a sheriff upon certain writs directed to him with the clause *si A fecerit B securum de clamore suo prosequendo, etc.* (Fitz.N.B. 38). See QUERENS, ETC.

Quaesta, an indulgence or remission of penance, sold by the Pope.

Quaestio, a commission to inquire into a criminal matter (Civil Law).

Quaestionarii, those who carried *quaesta* (*q.v.*) about from door to door.

Quaestor, or **Questor,** a Roman magistrate.

Quaestum. See HEREDITAS.

Quaestus, that estate which a man had by acquisition or purchase, in contradistinction to *haereditas,* which is what he had by descent (7 Glanvil, c. 1).

Quaker, a member of the Society of Friends. They have never formally adopted the title, but it has received statutory recognition (Quakers and Moravians Act, 1833).

The society was founded by George Fox about the middle of the seventeeth century, and gained many adherents owing to the discontent with the existing priestcraft of the day. There is no ad-

herence to any definite or formal creed, and the tenets of the society are chiefly distinguishable from those of other Christian bodies in that the members disclaim any necessity for the outward observance of baptism or partaking of the Sacrament, and further believe that all war is contrary to Christian principles. Men and women alike share in the ministry and government of the religious body.

As to affirmations by Quakers instead of oaths, see AFFIRMATION. As to their marriages, see MARRIAGE.

Quale jus (what right), a judicial writ framed after the enactment of the Statute of Westminster II, 1285, c. 32. It was designed to enforce the provisions of that statute which were directed against the alienation of lands in mortmain (*q.v.*). Where an abbot or other religious person had recovered lands by a judgment in default, then the abbot, etc., had to sue out this writ in order to have it decided whether he really had a right to the lands or whether the judgment was collusive; and execution was stayed pending a decision on the point (Reg. Judic. 8, 16, 46).

Qualification, that which makes any person fit to do a certain act; also, abatement, diminution.

Qualification is a quality which makes a person eligible for an office or profession. As to the qualification for jury service, see JURY.

A director of a company is generally required to be the holder of a certain number of shares.

An annual Act used to be passed indemnifying persons who had omitted to qualify themselves for certain offices and employments, and to extend the time limited for those purposes: see the statute 1863, 26 & 27 Vict. c. 107. But by the statute 1866, 29 & 30 Vict. c. 22, it was rendered unnecessary to make and subscribe declarations theretofore required as a qualification for offices and employments.

The Qualification Act, 1671, by which any person not having freehold land of the yearly value of £100, or for his life or for 99 years or more of the yearly value of £150, other than the son and heir of an esquire or person of higher degree or the owner of a park or warren, was prohibited from having guns, bows, greyhounds, setting-dogs, ferrets, coney-dogs, lurchers, bags, nets, loubels, hare-pipes, gins, snares, or other engines, for taking game, was repealed by the Game Act, 1831. See GAME.

Various statutes had from time to time made certain property qualifications necessary for the office of justices of the peace, but they were repealed by the Justices of the Peace Act, 1906, s. 5, Sch.

See PROPERTY QUALIFICATION.

Qualified, a term applied to a person enabled to hold two benefices. See PLURALITY.

Qualified acceptance, an acceptance with some variation of the effect of a bill as drawn (Bills of Exchange Act, 1882, s. 19).

Qualified fee. See BASE FEE; FEE.

Qualified indorsement, an indorsement *sans recours, i.e.,* without recourse to the indorser for payment. See INDORSEMENT.

Qualified privilege. See LIBEL; PRIVILEGE; PRIVILEGED COMMUNICATION.

Qualified property, an ownership of a special and limited kind. It may arise either from the peculiar circumstances of the subject-matter, which render it incapable of being under the absolute dominion of any proprietor, as in the case of animals *ferae naturae,* or from the peculiar circumstances of the possessor, as in the case of a bailment. See BAILMENT; POSSESSION.

Qualified title, a title registered subject to an excepted estate, right or interest arising before a specified date or under a specified instrument, or otherwise particularly described in the register (Land Registration Act, 1925, s. 7).

Qualify, to become qualified.

Quality of estate, the period when, and the manner in which, the right of enjoying an estate or interest is exercised. It is of two kinds: the period when the right of enjoying an estate or interest is conferred upon the owner, whether at present or in the future; and the manner in which the owner's right of enjoyment is to be exercised, whether solely, jointly, in common, or in coparcenary. See ESTATE.

Quality or fitness. As to implied undertakings of quality or fitness on a sale of goods see the Sale of Goods Act, 1893, s. 14; Supply of Goods (Implied Terms) Act, 1973, ss. 3, 7 (2); in a hire-purchase agreement, see the Act of 1973, s. 10; Consumer Credit Act, 1974, Sch. 4 para. 35.

Quam longum debet esse rationabile tempus, non definitur in lege, sed pendet ex discretione justiciariorum (Co.Litt. 56). (How long reasonable time ought to be is not defined by law, but depends upon the discretion of the judges.) But where a case is being tried by a judge with a jury, the question of reasonable time is usually for the jury.

Quamdiu se bene gesserit (as long as he shall behave himself well), a clause frequent in letters patent or grants of certain offices, as that of judge or recorder, to secure them so long as the persons to whom they are granted shall not be guilty of abusing them. The opposite clause is *durante bene placito* (during the pleasure of the grantor). See AD VITAM AUT CULPAM; OFFICE.

Quando abest provisio partis, adest provisio legis. (When provision of party is wanting, provision of law is there.) That is to say, a point not expressly covered by contract is decided according to general rules of law.

Quando acciderint (when they shall fall in). See JUDGMENT; PLENE ADMINISTRAVIT.

Quando aliquid mandatur, mandatur et omne per quod pervenitur ad illud (5 Co.Rep. 115b; Broome 313). (When anything is commanded, everything by which it can be accomplished is also commanded.) And so a master employed to navigate a ship is impliedly authorised to do all things necessary for the voyage, such as the giving of bottomry bonds in case of need.

Quando aliquid prohibetur fieri, prohibetur ex directo et per obliquum (Co. Litt. 223). (When the doing of anything is forbidden, then the doing of it either directly or indirectly is forbidden.) The law will not uphold anything which is a mere device for carrying into effect that which the legislature has said shall not be done.

QUANDO

Quando aliquid prohibetur, prohibetur et omne per quod devenitur ad illud (2 Co.Inst. 48). (When anything is prohibited, everything also is prohibited by which the same thing is arrived at.)

Quando duo jura in una persona concurrunt, aequum est ac si essent diversis (2 Prest.Abs.Tit. 449). (When two titles concur in one person, it is the same as if they were in different persons.) The *jura* here spoken of are titles to property. Thus, what A cannot take as half-brother to B, he may take as cousin of B, if such in fact he is, and in each capacity he is dealt with by the law as a separate person.

Quando jus domini regis et subditi concurrunt jus regis praeferri debet (9 Co.Rep. 129; Broome 35). (When the titles of the king and of a subject concur, that of the king is to be preferred.) The Crown cannot have a joint property with any person in one entire chattel; where the titles of the Crown and of a subject concur, the Crown takes the whole. The Crown's debts, in suing out execution, are preferred to that of every other creditor who had not obtained judgment before the Crown commenced suit. As to the priority of the Crown in bankruptcy and in the winding up of a company, see the Bankruptcy Act, 1914, s. 33 (1), as amended by the Companies Act, 1947, s. 115, and the Companies Act, 1948, s. 319.

Quando lex aliquid alicui concedit, concedere videtur id sine quo res ipsa esse non potest (5 Co.Rep. 47). (When the law gives anything to anyone, it gives also all those things without which the thing itself could not exist.) A person who has a right to expose goods for sale in a public market has also a right to occupy the soil with baskets necessary and proper for containing the goods; and that as against one to whom the owner of the fee simple of the soil has made a devise. See CUICUNQUE ALIQUIS, ETC.

Quando lex est specialis, ratio autem generalis, generaliter lex est intelligenda (2 Co.Inst. 83). (Where a law is special, but its reason general, the law is to be understood generally.) Coke applies this maxim to illustrate the practice under which the assize of novel disseisin referred to in the Statute of Merton,

1235, c. 3, might be taken, not merely before the itinerant justices there mentioned, but also before the King's Bench or the Common Pleas, or the justices of assize who had taken the place of the itinerant justices.

Quando mulier nobilis nupserit ignobili desinit esse nobilis nisi nobilitas nata fuit (4 Co.Rep. 118). (When a noble woman marries a man not noble, she ceases to be noble, unless her nobility was born with her.) That is to say, she ceases to be noble unless she is a peeress in her own right.

Quando plus fit quam fieri debet, videtur etiam illud fieri quod faciendum est (5 Co.Rep. 115a). (When more is done than ought to be done, then that is considered to have been done which ought to have been done.) The act is void *quoad* the excess only. Thus, if a man has power to lease for ten years, and he leases for twenty, the lease for the twenty years is good for ten years of the twenty (*Bartlett* v. *Rendle* (1814) 3 M. & S. 99). See OMNE MAJUS, ETC.

Quando res non valet ut ago, valeat quantum valere potest (Cowp. 600). (When anything does not operate in the way I intend, let it operate as far as it can.) If a deed cannot operate precisely as the parties intend, the law will nevertheless give effect to their intention so far as is possible.

Quando verba statuti sunt specialia, ratio autem generalis, generaliter statutum est intelligendum (10 Co.Rep. 101). (When the words of a statute are special, but the reason is general, the statute is to be understood generally.) See QUANDO LEX, ETC.

Quantity of estate, the time of continuance of an estate or interest, or its degree, as in fee, during life, or for years. See ESTATE; QUALITY OF ESTATE.

Quantity surveyor, a person whose business consists in taking out in detail the measurements and quantities from plans prepared by an architect for the purpose of enabling builders to calculate the amount for which they would execute the plans.

A person may be restrained from describing himself as a chartered quantity surveyor if he is not a member of the Royal Institute of Chartered Surveyors

(Royal Institute of Chartered Surveyors v. *Shepherd* (1947) 149 E.G. 370).

Quantum damnificatus, the amount of damage suffered. The issue *quantum damnificatus* was one which the Court of Chancery used to have tried in a court of law when it appeared that a party was entitled to damages as well as to an injunction. The Chancery Amendment Act, 1858, empowered the Court of Chancery itself to take the verdict of a jury as to the amount: there was no such power previously.

Quantum meruit, as much as he has earned. If a person enters into a contract to perform services for another, and either the contract is put an end to before they are completed, or they are not rendered in the manner provided by the contract, the contractor is obviously not entitled to be paid his contract price, but in some cases he is entitled to be paid the actual value of his services; and if he brings an action to recover it, he is said to sue on a *quantum meruit*. Thus, where the failure to complete performance of the contract is due to the fault of the other party, the party not in default has the right to sue on a *quantum meruit* for the services which he has done under it.

In its early history the action for *quantum meruit* was, no doubt, a genuine action in contract, based on a real promise to pay, although the promise had not been expressed in words and the amount of the payment had not been agreed. Subsequent developments have, however, considerably widened the scope of this form of action, and in many cases the action is now founded on what is known as " quasi-contract " (*q.v.*), similar in some ways to the action for money had and received (*q.v.*). In these quasi-contractual cases the court looks at the true facts and ascertains from them whether or not a promise to pay should be implied, irrespective of the actual views or instructions of the parties at the time when the work was done or the services rendered: (*Lacey* v. *Davies* [1957] 1 W.L.R. 932).

A claim on a *quantum meruit* may be indorsed on a writ as a debt or liquidated demand under R.S.C., Ord. 6, r. 2.

See QUANTUM VALEBANT.

Quantum tenens domino ex homagio, tantum dominus tenenti ex dominio debet praeter solam reverentiam; mutua debet esse dominii et homagii fidelitatis connexio (Co.Litt. 64). (As much as the tenant by his homage owes to his lord, so much is the lord, by his lordship, indebted to the tenant, except reverence alone; the tie of dominion and of homage ought to be mutual.)

Quantum valebant, as much as they were worth. If a person contracts to supply goods of a certain kind, and supplies goods of a different kind, and the other party does not avail himself of the right of rejecting them, the former, although he cannot claim the price payable under the contract (for it has not been performed), can claim the actual value of the goods supplied; and if he brings an action for it, he is said to sue on a *quantum valebant*. See QUANTUM MERUIT.

Quarantine, Quarentine, Quarentaine [Ital. *quaranta,* forty], a period of forty days. The expression was used to denote the period (whether forty days or not) which persons coming from a country or ship in which an infectious disease was prevalent were obliged to wait before they were permitted to land in England, it being supposed that if no infectious disease broke out within forty days or six weeks, no further danger need be apprehended.

Quarantine regulations were embodied in the Quarantine Act, 1825, and kept up by the Public Health Act, 1875, but the Public Health Act, 1896, repealed the Act of 1825, and was amended by the Public Health Act, 1904, to enable regulations to be made.

The Public Health Act, 1936, Pt. I constituted port health authorities and districts. These are gradually superseded under the provisions of the Local Government Act, 1972, s. 263, Sch. 30.

Cattle, etc., imported and not slaughtered at the port of landing are required to be kept in quarantine (Diseases of Animals Act, 1950, ss. 25–32, Schs. 1, 2).

Dogs and cats imported into this country from abroad must be kept in quarantine for nine months (Importation of Dogs and Cats Orders, 1928 (No.

922); 1970 (Nos. 358, 441, 1271). Orders may be made under the Rabies Act, 1974, for the quarantine of any mammals which may be carriers of rabies.

By Magna Carta, 1215, it was provided that a widow should not be compelled to marry afresh if she chose to live without a husband, but she could not, however, marry without the consent of the lord; and nothing could be taken for assignment of her dower, but she was to be allowed to remain in her husband's capital mansion-house for forty days after his death, during which time her dower was to be assigned. These forty days were called the widow's quarantine. Marriage during these forty days forfeited the dower. This right was enforced by writ of *quarentina habenda* (*q.v.*).

Quarantine also meant a quantity of land containing forty perches (Leg.Hen. 1, c. 16).

Quare clausum fregit (wherefore he broke the close). Trespass is of three kinds: to the person, to the goods, and to the lands of the plaintiff. The action for the third kind of trespass was termed trespass *quare clausum fregit,* from the language of the writ, which commanded the defendant to show *quare clausum querentis fregit* why he broke the close of the plaintiff. This was followed by the *ac etiam* (*q.v.*).

Quare ejecit infra terminum (wherefore he ejected within the term), a writ which lay where the wrongdoer or ejector was not himself in possession of the lands, but another who claimed under him. The writ fell into disuse after the introduction of fictitious ousters, whereby the title could be tried against any person in possession of the land, without regard to the means by which he acquired it, and the subsequent recovery of damages by action of trespass for mesne profits. It was abolished by the Real Property Limitation Act, 1833, s. 36.

Quare impedit (wherefore he hindered), a real possessory action, which could formerly be brought only in the Court of Common Pleas. It lies to recover a presentation, when the patron's right is disturbed, or to try a disputed title to an advowson.

Prior to the passing of the Common Law Procedure Act, 1860, the action was commenced by an original writ issuing out of Chancery, but s. 26 of that Act did away with this procedure, which is now the same as in other actions in the High Court. If, on a living becoming vacant, two persons present clerks to the bishop, the action of *quare impedit* may be instituted, upon the ordinary writ of summons, by either of the alleged patrons, the bishop and the other alleged patron and his clerk being the defendants.

The judgment is that the successful party recover his presentation, and a writ issues to the bishop, commanding him to admit his presentee.

The action of *quare impedit* also lay against a bishop who had refused to admit on the ground of unfitness: but, under the Benefices Act, 1898, s. 3 (5), no proceeding in the nature of *quare impedit* lies against a bishop who has refused to admit on that ground, and the remedy is by appeal to the archbishop.

See GRAND DISTRESS; NE ADMITTAS; USURPATION.

Quare incumbravit (wherefore he has incumbered), a writ which lay against a bishop who, within six months after the vacation of a benefice, and while two other persons were prosecuting a claim to the right of presentation, conferred it on a clerk, to show why he had incumbered the church (Reg.Orig. 32).

It also lay after a recovery in *quare impedit* (*q.v.*) or assize of *darrein presentment,* against a bishop who had thus admitted a clerk notwithstanding a writ *ne admittas.* The writ was abolished by the Real Property Limitation Act, 1833, s. 36.

Quare intrusit, a writ, impliedly abolished by the statute 1660, 12 Car. 2, c. 24 (abolishing the Court of Wards and Liveries), which lay for a lord who had offered a suitable marriage to his ward, who rejected it and married another, so that the lord's right to the value of the marriage was not satisfied.

Quare non admisit, a writ directed to a bishop who had refused to admit a clerk to a benefice. See QUARE IMPEDIT.

Quare non permittit, a writ which lay for one who had a right to present to a church for a turn against the proprietary (5 Fleta, c. 6).

Quare obstruxit, a writ which lay for him who, having a liberty to pass though his neighbour's ground, could not enjoy his right because the owner had obstructed it (4 Fleta, c. 26).

Quarentene. See QUARANTINE.

Quarentene terrae, a furlong (Co.Litt. 5b).

Quarentina habenda, De, a writ which lay for a widow to enforce her right of quarantine (*q.v.*).

Quarrel, a dispute, contest; also, an action real or personal.

Actions, whether real or personal, and all causes of actions and suits, are released by a release of " all quarrels " (8 Co.Rep. 153).

Quarry. A quarry, as opposed to a mine (*q.v.*), implies surface workings of stone or slate, having no roof overhead. A quarry is worked by taking away the surface, not by sinking a shaft. The Mines and Quarries Act, 1954, s. 180, defines a quarry as an excavation or system of excavations made for the purpose of, or in connection with, the getting of minerals (whether in their natural state or in solution or suspension) or products of minerals, being neither a mine (*q.v.*) nor merely a well or borehole or a well and borehole combined. Adjoining land and works, dumps, railway lines and conveyor or aerial ropeways may form part of the quarry. A general duty to comply with the Act is imposed on owners of mines and quarries by s. 1. Management and control of quarries are regulated by ss. 98–107, and safety, health and welfare by ss. 108–115, notification and investigation of accidents by ss. 116–122, inspection by workmen by s. 123, employment of women and young persons by ss. 124–132, records, returns and information by ss. 133–140, regulations by ss. 141–143, inspectors by ss. 144–146, certificates by ss. 147–150, fencing of abandoned and unused mines and quarries by s. 151, and offences, penalties and legal proceedings by ss. 152–167.

As to tips, see MINES. As to the rating of quarries see the Local Government Act, 1974, s. 19, Sch. 3 para. 7.

Quarries come under the supervision of the Secretary of State for Energy.

Quart, one fourth part of a gallon (Weights and Measures Act, 1963, s. 10, Sch. 1 Pt. IV). See GALLON. The " reputed quart " in the Customs and Excise Act, 1952, ss. 146 (6), 148 (4) is abolished (Act of 1963, s. 59).

Quarta Antoninia, Quarta D. Pii. An arrogated son under puberty if disinherited, or emancipated without lawful cause, received back all the property he had brought to the arrogator or acquired for him, and also one-fourth of the arrogator's property, as enacted by Antoninus Pius (Civil Law).

Quarter, a measure of mass or weight consisting of twenty-eight pounds (Weights and Measures Act, 1963, s. 10, Sch. 1 Pt. V). See POUND.

Quarter also means a length of four inches; also a quarter of a year (Co. Litt. 135b).

Quarter sessions. Courts of quarter sessions were abolished on January 1, 1972 (Courts Act, 1971, s. 3) and the offices of chairman and deputy chairman (Courts Act, 1971, s. 44). The appellate and other jurisdiction of quarter sessions, except certain administrative functions, have been transferred to the Crown Court (Courts Act, 1971, ss. 8, 56, Schs. 1, 8–10). The administrative functions have been transferred to local authorities (Sch. 8 para. 1). References to a court of quarter sessions are to be construed as references to the Crown Court (Sch. 8).

Formerly quarter sessions were the sittings of the whole body of the justices of the peace in a county, and of a recorder in a borough having a separate court of quarter sessions, four times in each year, or oftener, to try certain indictable offences and hear appeals from petty sessions.

A court of quarter sessions was a court of record held before two or more justices of the peace once in every quarter of the year for execution of the authority given them by the commission of the peace and certain statutes. They had met four times a year by statute since 1363. Formerly, their jurisdiction, in theory, extended to trying all misdemeanours and felonies other than forgery or perjury, though in practice they sent the more serious cases to the assizes. Their jurisdiction to try cases of treason, murder, manslaughter, rape, incest, frauds by agents, and numerous other serious offences, was taken away altogether, chiefly by the Quarter Sessions Act, 1842, so that in those cases their jurisdiction ceased as soon as the indictment had been found. See GENERAL SESSIONS.

There were over a hundred boroughs with separate courts of quarter sessions, granted under the Municipal Corporations Act, 1835, s. 103, or under the Municipal Corporations Act, 1882, s. 162. These sessions were known as borough sessions: the borough justices could not act as justices of any gaol delivery or quarter sessions (Act of 1882, s. 158 (1)), and the recorder was the sole judge (s. 165 (2)). The Justices of the Peace Act, 1949, s. 10, set out the conditions to be satisfied by non-county boroughs in order that they might have a separate commission of the peace.

Proceedings at quarter sessions consisted of the trial of indictments of business falling within the original jurisdiction of quarter sessions, chiefly in matters relating to the preservation of the peace and the punishment of rogues and vagabonds; of business within the appellate jurisdiction, which included appeals from petty and special sessions in bastardy, highway, rating, and licensing cases, under various statutes relating to those matters, and appeals from any conviction by a court of summary jurisdiction for any offence other than an offence to which the defendant had pleaded guilty (Criminal Justice Administration Act, 1914, s. 37 (1)). The appellate jurisdiction in bastardy was extended by the Criminal Justice Administration Act, 1914, s. 37 (2).

The Assizes and Quarter Sessions Act 1908, contained provisions under which the holding of assizes or quarter sessions and the attendance of jurors thereat could be dispensed with when there was no business to be transacted; it also amended the law as to the dates for quarter sessions.

See CUSTOS ROTULORUM.

Quarter-days, the days which be in the four quarters of the year, *viz.*, March 25, or Lady Day; June 24, or Midsummer Day; September 29, or Michaelmas Day; and December 25, or Christmas Day. The half-quarter days are February 8, May 9, August 11, and November 11. The Scottish quarter-days are February 2, May 15, August 1, and November 11. In Northern Ireland the quarter-days are the same as for England. There are, however, some local variations: thus, in Bristol the customary December quarter-day is or was December 21 instead of Christmas Day.

Quartering traitors. The judgment for high treason, as prescribed by the Treason Act, 1814, s. 1, was that the head of the person after death by hanging should be severed from his body, and that the body, divided into four quarters, should be disposed of as the sovereign should think fit; but this portion of the Act was repealed by the Forfeiture Act, 1870, s. 31.

Quarto die post, the fourth day inclusive after a return of a writ, and if a defendant appeared then it was sufficient; but this practice was afterwards altered (1 Tidd's Pr. 107).

Quash [Lat. *cassum facere*; Fr. *casser*], to discharge or set aside an order of an inferior court; to overthrow or annul, as to quash an indictment, or order of justices, or a rate or a sentence (*Hancock v. Prison Commissioners* [1960] 1 Q.B. 117). See CERTIORARI.

Quasi. This word prefixed to a noun means that although the thing signified by the combination of " quasi " with the noun does not comply in strictness with the definition of the noun, it shares its qualities, falls under the same head, and is best marked by its approximation thereto.

Quasi-contract, liability, not exclusively referable to any other head of law, imposed upon a particular person to pay money to another particular person on the ground that non-payment of it would confer on the former an unjust benefit (Winfield, *Quasi-Contracts*).

The main heads of quasi-contractual liability are: (1) money paid by the plaintiff at the request of the defendant, including payment by sureties and contribution between joint contractors; (2) money had and received by the defendant for the use of the plaintiff, including cases (i) where the plaintiff may waive a tort committed by the defendant where by conversion he has received money belonging to the plaintiff or a bribe, (ii) of recovery from a stakeholder, (iii) of failure of consideration, (iv) of payment under a mistake of fact (but not of law), (v) of money obtained by fraud or extortion, (vi) of money paid under an illegal contract, (vii) of money paid under a void judgment or compulsion of law; (3) salvage; (4) *quantum meruit (q.v.)*; (5) account stated; (6) necessaries.

In the civil law, if a person left his property without anyone to look after it, a stranger might undertake the care of it, and had a right of action against the owner for his expenses (*actio negotiorum gestorum*); and this was for the sake of utility, lest the affairs of persons suddenly called away without being able to arrange for their management should be neglected, for no one would look after them if he had not a right of action for his expenses (3 Junst.Inst. 27, 1).

Quasi-corporation. See CORPORATION.

Quasi-delict, a delict not falling under one of the recognised heads of delictal liability in the civil law.

Quasi-easement. An easement can exist only in respect of two pieces of land occupied by different persons. However, an owner may exercise over a portion of his own land rights analogous to easements and these may pass to a purchaser of the portion of the land benefiting from the exercise of the rights; such rights are sometimes called quasi-easements.

Quasi-entail. An interest *pur autre vie* may be granted, not only to a man and his heirs, but to a man and the heirs of his body, which is termed a quasi-entail, the interest so granted not being properly an entailed interest (for the statute *De Donis*, 1285, applied only where the subject of the entail was an estate of inheritance), but yet so far in the nature of entailed interest that it went to the heir of the body as special occupant during the life of the *cestui que vie,* in the same manner as an estate of inheritance would have descended if limited to the grantee and the heirs of his body. Such an interest may also be granted with a remainder thereon during the life of the *cestui que*

vie; and the alienation of the quasi-tenant-in-tail will bar not only his issue but those in remainder. The alienation, however, for that purpose (unlike that of an entailed interest, properly so called), might, before 1926, have been effected by any method of conveyance, except a will; after 1926, these interests became equitable interests only and may be devised or barred by will. See AUTRE VIE.

Quasi-fee, an estate gained by wrong.

Quasi-international law, relations on a footing of equality similar to those of independent States.

Quasi-judicial functions, functions akin to those of a judge, as those exercised by an arbitrator or an administrative tribunal.

An inspector holding a public local inquiry must act judicially (*Steele* v. *Minister of Housing and Local Government* (1956) 6 P. & C.R. 386), but a Minister acting in his administrative capacity is not bound to act judicially (*Miller* v. *Minister of Health* [1946] K.B. 626; *Price* v. *Minister of Health* [1947] 1 All E.R. 47; *B. Johnson & Co. (Builders)* v. *Minister of Health* [1947] 2 All E.R. 395). See INQUIRY.

Quasi-legislative international institutions, international institutions, such as the International Labour Organisation, the competence of which falls short of that of legislative institutions within a State.

Quasi-personalty, things which are movable in point of law, though fixed to things real, either actually, as emblements (*fructus industriales*), fixtures, etc., or fictitiously, as chattels-real, leases for years, etc.

Quasi-possession. This is to a right what possession is to a thing—it is the exercise or enjoyment of the right, not necessarily the continuous exercise, but such an exercise as shows an intention to exercise it at any time when desired. When the right itself is exercised by means of possession of the thing which is the subject of the right, as in the case of ownership, the idea of quasi-possession does not arise, and hence the term is confined to those rights which merely give a limited power of using the thing, as in the case of easements and profits *à prendre*; it is, however, not much used in English law, the word "enjoyment" (*q.v.*) being more frequently employed.

Quasi-realty, things which are fixed in contemplation of law to realty, but movable in themselves, as heirlooms (or limbs of the inheritance), title-deeds, court rolls, etc.

Quasi-tenant at sufferance, an underlessee who continues in possession, after the termination both of his own and of his lessor's leases, without the reversioner either assenting or dissenting.

Quasi-tort. This, though not a recognised term of English law, has sometimes been used in those cases where a man who has not committed a tort is liable as if he had. Thus, a master is liable for wrongful acts done by his servant in the course of his employment. The ground of the liability is expressed by the maxims *qui facit per alium facit per se* and *respondeat superior* (*R.* v. *Holbrook* (1879) 4 Q.B.D. at pp. 46, 51). See QUASI-CONTRACT.

Quasi-trustee, a person who reaps a benefit from a breach of trust, and so becomes answerable as a trustee.

Quatuor maria, the four seas (*q.v.*).

Quatuorviri, magistrates who had the care and inspection of roads among the Romans (Civil Law).

Quays. See HARBOUR.

Que est le mesme [Lat. *quae est eadem,* which is the same], a term used in actions of trespass, etc., for a direct justification of the very act complained of by the plaintiff as a wrong. See QUAE EST EADEM.

Que estate [Lat. *quorum statum,* whose estate he has]. Where prescriptive rights are claimed by reason of the continuous and immemorial enjoyment thereof by the claimant, a person seised in fee, and by all those whose estate he has, this is called a prescription in a *que estate.* The phrase is taken from the Norman-French: that he, and all those whose estate he has, *tous ceux que estate il ad,* have from time immemorial enjoyed the right (Co.Litt.121a; 2 Bl.Comm. 264; 2 Br. & Had.Com. 419; Williams, Common 16).

A prescription in a *que estate* for a profit *à prendre in alieno solo* without stint and for commercial purposes is unknown to the law (*Harris* v. *Chesterfield* [1911] A.C. 623). See PRESCRIPTION.

Queck board. See CLOSH.

Queen [Sax. *cwen,* a wife], a woman who is sovereign of a kingdom. The queen regent, regnant, or sovereign is she who holds the Crown in her own right, and such queen of England has the same powers, prerogatives, rights, dignities, and duties as if she had been a king; see the statute 1554, 1 Mar. sess. 3, c. 1.

The Queen's style and title was proclaimed under the Royal Titles Act, 1953, Elizabeth II, by the Grace of God of the United Kingdom of Great Britain and Northern Ireland and of her other Realms and Territories Queen, Head of the Commonwealth, Defender of the Faith. Corresponding forms were adopted by other member States of the Commonwealth (see ROYAL TITLE). She derives her title from the Act of Settlement, 1700, by which the Crown " of England, France and Ireland " was settled, after the death of William III and Princess Anne without issue, on the Electress Sophia of Hanover and the heirs of her body being Protestants; the Union with Scotland Act, 1706, which constituted one kingdom of Great Britain; and the Union with Ireland Act, 1800, as varied by the Government of Ireland Act, 1920, and the Royal and Parliamentary Titles Act, 1927, whereby the United Kingdom means Great Britain and Northern Ireland, Southern Ireland having ceased to be part of the United Kingdom.

The Queen has all spiritual and ecclesiastical jurisdiction by virtue of the Act of Supremacy, 1558, s. 8, though the Act of Supremacy, 1534, declaring Henry VIII to be supreme head on earth of the Church of England, repealed by the statute 1554, 1 & 2 Ph. & Mar. c. 8, continued repealed by the Act of Supremacy, 1558, and her supremacy over the Church of England is also declared by the first of the Canons of 1603.

The Queen is also head of the armed forces. She appoints archbishops and bishops by virtue of the statute 1533, 25 Hen. 8, c. 20, and judges of the Supreme Court by virtue of the Judicature Act, 1925, s. 11.

There is no legislative power in either or both Houses of Parliament without the Queen: see the statute 1661, 13 Car. 2, st. 1, c. 1, s. 3

A queen may be a queen regnant, who is for every purpose the same as a king; a queen consort (or wife of a reigning king), who has no political power whatever; or a queen dowager (or widow of a deceased king), who likewise has no political position.

A queen consort was anciently entitled to queen gold (*q.v.*). Her person and her chastity are specially protected by the Treason Act, 1351. She is not subject to any toll, fine or amerciament. She is entitled to appoint her own attorney-general and solicitor-general.

A queen dowager retains her rank in the event of her remarriage and retains most of the privileges of a queen consort.

See BILL OF RIGHTS; CIVIL LIST; CROWN; NULLUM TEMPUS; SIGN MANUAL.

Queen Anne's Bounty. By the statute 1534, 26 Hen. 8, c. 3, certain duties called first fruits and tenths, which had up to that time been paid by the incumbents of ecclesiastical benefices to the Pope, were made part of the revenues of the Crown. Queen Anne determined to apply them to the augmentation of the livings of the poorer clergy, and under the provisions of the statute 1703, 2 & 3 Anne, c. 20, she appointed certain persons to be a corporation to receive and apply for this purpose the first fruits and tenths, and also any gifts and benevolences given to them for the same purpose; they were called the Governors of the Bounty of Queen Anne for the Augmentation of the Maintenance of the Poor Clergy. They were united with the Ecclesiastical Commissioners for England under the name of the Church Commissioners by the Church Commissioners Measure, 1947. See ANNATES; BOUNTY OF QUEEN ANNE; FIRST FRUITS; RECEIVER, ETC.; TENTHS. See also the Queen Anne's Bounty (Powers) Measures, 1937 and 1939.

Queen consort, the wife of a reigning king. See QUEEN.

Queen dowager, the widow of a deceased king. See QUEEN.

Queen gold, a revenue payable to a queen consort for the duration of her marriage to the king. It consisted of the amounts payable to the king for privileges, dispensations, pardons, and similar exercises of the royal prerogative, and of an additional ten per cent. upon every such amount. It ceased to be paid after the restoration of Charles II (Tomlin). See AURUM REGINAE.

Queen's Bench. The Court of Queen's Bench or King's Bench was one of the superior courts of common law, having in ordinary civil actions concurrent jurisdiction with the Courts of Common Pleas and Exchequer; it was, however, considered superior to them in dignity and power, its principal judge being styled the Lord Chief Justice of England, and taking precedence over the other common law judges, and there being formerly an appeal to it from the Exchequer and the Common Pleas. It also had special jurisdiction over inferior courts, magistrates and civil corporations by the prerogative writ of mandamus, and (concurrently with the two other courts) by prohibition and certiorari (*q.v.*), and in proceedings by *quo warranto* and habeas corpus. It was also the principal court of criminal jurisdiction: informations might be filed and indictments preferred in it in the first instance, and indictments from inferior courts might be removed into it by certiorari, subject to certain limitations. See CERTIORARI; INDICTMENT; INFORMATION.

The court accordingly had two " sides " or sets of offices, namely, the " plea side," in which civil business was transacted; and the " Crown side," or " Crown Office," in which matters within the criminal and extraordinary jurisdiction of the court were transacted. See CROWN OFFICE.

It is said to have been called the King's Bench or Queen's Bench, both because its records ran in the name of the king or queen (*coram rege,* or *regina*), and because the sovereign in former times often personally sat there.

The court, which was the remnant of the *aula regia,* was not, nor could be, from the very nature and constitution of it, fixed to any certain place, but might follow the king's person wherever he went, for which reason all process issuing out of the court in the king's name was returnable *ubicunque fuerimus in Anglia.*

For some centuries, and until the opening of the royal courts, the court usually sat at Westminster, being an ancient palace of the Crown, but might remove with the king as he thought proper to command.

On the plea side the court exercised a general jurisdiction over all actions between subject and subject, with the exception of real actions and suits concerning the revenue. Its jurisdiction in civil actions was formerly limited to trespass or injuries said to have been committed *vi et armis,* but by means of fictitious proceedings called Bill of Middlesex (*q.v.*) and *latitat* it usurped jurisdiction over all personal actions; direct jurisdiction in all such actions was given by the statute 1832, 2 & 3 Wm. 4, c. 39, which abolished these fictitious proceedings. Error lay from this court to the Exchequer Chamber.

By the Judicature Acts, 1873–75, the jurisdiction of the court was transferred to the High Court. Its judges (namely, the Lord Chief Justice and the five puisne justices) formed a separate division of the High Court, called the Queen's Bench Division, to which was assigned all business (civil and criminal) which was formerly within the exclusive cognisance of the Court of Queen's Bench. In 1881, however, the Common Pleas and Exchequer Divisions were consolidated with it into one division called the Queen's Bench Division.

See SUPREME COURT, ETC.

Queen's Bench Division. The jurisdiction of the Court of Queen's Bench was assigned by the Judicature Act, 1873, s. 34, to the Queen's Bench Division of the High Court; and by Order in Council under s. 32 of the Act, the Common Pleas and Exchequer Divisions were, in February, 1881, merged in the Queen's Bench Division, which was styled from the death of Queen Victoria in January, 1901, until the death of George VI in February, 1952, the King's Bench Division. As to assignment of business to the Queen's Bench Division, see the Judicature Act, 1925, s. 56 (2).

Queen's Bench Prison, a debtors' prison in Southwark, which was replaced by the Queen's Prison (*q.v.*) in 1842.

Queen's chambers, those portions of

the seas, adjacent to the coasts of Great Britain, which are inclosed within headlands so as to be cut off from the open sea by imaginary straight lines drawn from one promontory to another. They appear to have always formed part of the territorial waters of the Crown. See HIGH SEAS; TERRITORIAL.

Queen's Coroner and Attorney, an officer on the Crown side of the Queen's Bench (see the statute 1843, 6 & 7 Vict. c. 20), who by the Judicature (Officers) Act, 1879, became a Master of the Supreme Court. This official is distinct from the Coroner of the Queen's Household or Coroner of the Verge. See CORONER.

The Queen's Coroner and Attorney was formerly appointed by letters patent. He is now appointed by the Lord Chancellor with the concurrence of the Minister for the Civil Service as to salary (Courts Act, 1971, s. 26). The only inquests (*q.v.*) with which he ever was concerned were those held upon persons dying within the now-abolished Queen's Bench Prison or the rules (*q.v.*) thereof. His further duty was to write out and extract all " amerciaments, fines, issues and forfeitures to the Crown." He now, in so far as he exists at all, is an officer of the Crown Office. The last Queen's Coroner who had held only that office died in 1892, and the Master of the Crown Office was thereupon appointed, without additional salary, to the office, and is now entitled the Queen's Coroner and Attorney and Master of the Crown Office. The person appointed to the office of Queen's Coroner and Attorney is, by virtue of his appointment, a master of the Supreme Court (Queen's Bench Division) (Courts Act, 1971, s. 26 (2)). The office must be held by one of the Masters of the Supreme Court (Queen's Bench Division) (Judicature Act, 1925, s. 106 (2)). See Wellington, *King's Coroner.*

Queen's Counsel, barristers who have obtained the appointment of counsel to the Crown by reason, as old writers put it, of their learning and talent. They wear silk gowns, sit within the bar and take precedence in court over utter barristers, that is to say, the ordinary barristers, who sit outside the bar. They have no active duties to the Crown to perform, but they could not formerly be employed in any cause against the Crown (*e.g.*, in defending a prisoner) without special licence. Now, however, by a general dispensation granted in 1920, they can appear against the Crown without such licence. There used to be also Queen's Counsel in the County Palatine of Lancaster (Judicature Act, 1873, s. 78), who took precedence of other barristers in the Palatine Courts. All Queen's Counsel at the death of Queen Victoria became King's Counsel, and all King's Counsel at the death of George VI became Queen's Counsel without any new appointment. See BAR; BARRISTER; INNS OF COURT; SERJEANTS-AT-LAW.

Queen's evidence. A prisoner who, instead of being put upon his trial, is permitted by the Crown to give evidence against those associated with him in crime, is said to turn Queen's evidence. See ACCOMPLICE; APPROVER.

Queen's Printer, the person to whom is delegated the right possessed by the Crown of publishing under authority Acts of Parliament, royal proclamations, and other such public documents. As to the admissibility in evidence of copies of public documents purporting to be printed by the Queen's Printer, see the Evidence Act, 1845, s. 3.

Acts of Parliament, royal proclamations and other such public documents are now printed by the Stationery Office (*q.v.*). The right to print the Authorised Version of the Bible and the Prayer Book remains with the Queen's Printer. The right is shared with the Universities of Oxford and Cambridge. See BIBLE.

Queen's Prison, a debtor's prison in Southwark which was established by the Queen's Prison Act, 1842, to take the place of the Queen's Bench, Fleet, and Marshalsea Prisons (*q.v.*). It was abolished by the Queen's Prison Discontinuance Act, 1862, which provided for the transfer of prisoners to Whitecross Street Prison (*q.v.*). By s. 12, if the City of London should provide proper accommodation in another prison, that other prison was to be substituted for Whitecross Street Prison. In accordance with this provision, all the prisoners in White-cross Street were removed in 1870 to the City Prison at Holloway.

Queen's Proctor, the solicitor or proctor representing the Crown in the Family Division. His function is, in a proper case, to intervene (*q.v.*) to show cause why a decree nisi (*q.v.*) of divorce or nullity should not be made absolute because material facts were not brought before the court. The Queen's Proctor may intervene when the papers in the case have been sent to him by the court or on receipt of information by a member of the public (Matrimonial Causes Act, 1973, ss. 8, 9, 15).

Queen's Regulations. The Queen's Regulations and Orders for the Army are issued by the Crown, through the Army Council (*q.v.*), for the government of the army. Their legal force depends upon the constitutional principle that the Crown commands the army subject to statutory regulation. See ARTICLES OF WAR.

The Queen's Regulations and Admiralty Instructions are made by Order in Council countersigned by the Lords of the Admiralty (*q.v.*), and they, along with the Articles of War, constitute the code under which the navy is governed.

Queen's Remembrancer, an officer on the revenue side of the Court of Exchequer (Queen's Remembrancer Act, 1859; Crown Suits Act, 1865). He became an officer of the Supreme Court by the Judicature Act, 1873, s. 77.

The senior master of the Supreme Court (Queen's Bench Division) holds the office of Queen's Remembrancer (Judicature Act, 1925, s. 122; Courts Act, 1971, s. 26 (3)).

The Transfer of Functions (Treasury and Secretary of State) Order, 1974, No. 1274, transferred to the Secretary of State certain specified functions of the Treasury formerly carried out by its officer, the Queen's and Lord Treasurer's Remembrancer.

See REMEMBRANCERS.

Queen's warehouses, places provided by the Crown and approved by the Commissioners of Customs and Excise for the deposit of goods for the security thereof and of the duties thereon, including unclaimed goods or seized goods, *e.g.*, contraband.

Quem redditum reddit, a real action by which the grantee of a rent could compel the tenants of the land out of which the rent issued to attorn to him and pay the rent which he rendered (Old Nat.Br. 126).

It was abolished by the Real Property Limitation Act, 1833, s. 36. See ATTORNMENT.

Querela, any civil proceeding in any court. See AUDITA QUERELA; DUPLEX QUERELA.

Querela coram rege et concilio, a writ whereby one was called to justify a complaint of trespass made to the king himself before the king and his council (Reg.Orig. 124).

Querela frescae fortiae, a writ of fresh force (*q.v.*).

Querele, a complaint to a court.

Querens, plaintiff or complainant.

Querens non invenit plegium (the plaintiff has not found security), a return made by a sheriff to a writ commanding him to do such and such a thing, *si A fecerit B securum de clamore suo prosequendo* (if A shall give B security for the prosecution of the complaint (Fitz. N.B. 38).

Querent [Lat. *querens*], a plaintiff, complainant, inquirer.

Quest, inquest, inquisition, or inquiry; an inquest or inquisition held upon the oaths of a jury duly impanelled (Cowel).

The word now survives only in "crowner's quest" sometimes colloquially used as a provincial equivalent for coroner's inquest. See QUESTMAN.

Question, interrogatory; anything inquired. Putting to the question meant torture.

Questions of fact. These might be stated in an issue without pleadings by consent, under the Common Law Procedure Act, 1852, s. 42, and may now be so stated under R.S.C., Ord. 34, r. 9. See FACT.

In general when a jury is sworn it decides all the issues of fact; but if there arises in the course of the trial a question of fact preliminary to the decision of a point of law, *e.g.*, the genuineness of a document as necessary to its being admitted in evidence, that question of fact must be decided by the judge; so also in questions as to the competence of a witness to be sworn. See OATH; VOIRE DIRE; WITNESS.

The law of a foreign country is a question of fact but it is decided by the judge. See FOREIGN LAW.

Questions of law. Questions of law or of fact or partly of fact and partly of law may be stated for the opinion of the court in the form of a special case (*q.v.*) under R.S.C., Ord. 33, r. 3. See CASE STATED; COURT FOR CROWN CASES RESERVED; FACT.

Questman, or **Questmonger,** a starter of law-suits or prosecutions; also a person chosen to inquire into abuses, especially such as relate to weights and measures; also a churchwarden or sidesman. Two persons were formerly elected by the parishioners of every parish as questmen whose duty it was to make quest (*q.v.*) as to ecclesiastical offences and to present the offenders to the ecclesiastical courts. They were called questmen or synod's men, which last appellation has been converted into sidesmen (*q.v.*). By the end of the sixteenth century a great part of these duties had devolved upon the churchwardens, who were sometimes called questmen.

Questum. See HEREDITAS.

Questus, land which did not descend by hereditary right, but was acquired by one's own labour and industry. See PURCHASE.

Questus est nobis. The statute 1285, 13 Edw. 1, c. 24, provided that the writ *questus est nobis* (hath complained to us), a form of the writ of nuisance (*q.v.*), should lie against a person to whom had been sold a house, wall, etc., which had been erected so as to cause a nuisance (Cowel).

Qui aliquid statuerit parte inaudita altera, aequum licet statuerit, haud aequus fuerit (6 Co.Rep. 52). (He who shall decide anything, one party being unheard, though he shall decide rightly, will not be just.) See AUDI, ETC.

Qui alterius jure utitur eodem jure uti debet (Pothier, Tr. de Change, pt. 1, c. 4, art. 5, s. 114; Broom). (He who is clothed with the right of another ought to be clothed with the very same right.)

Qui concedit aliquid, concedere videtur et id sine quo concessio est irrita, sine quo res ispsa esse non potuit (11 Co.Rep. 52).

(He who concedes anything is considered as conceding that without which his concession would be void, without which the thing itself could not exist.)

Qui cum alio contrahit, vel est, vel debet esse, non ignarus conditionis ejus (D. 50, 17, 19). (He who contracts with another, either is, or ought to be, acquainted with the condition of that other.)

Qui exdamnato coitu nascuntur inter liberos non computentur (1 Bract. c. 6, s. 7; Co.Litt. 8a). (Those who are born from unlawful intercourse are not counted among the children.) See BASTARD.

Qui facit per alium facit per se (Co. Litt. 258). (He who acts through another is deemed to act in person.) A principal is liable for the acts of his agent within the scope of his authority. See AGENT; MASTER AND SERVANT; RESPONDEAT SUPERIOR.

Qui fraudem agit, frustra agit (2 Rolle 17). (He who works a fraud is labouring in vain.) He can thereby acquire no right of action. See EX DOLO, ETC.

Qui haeret in litera haeret in cortice (Co.Litt. 283b; Broom 466). (He who sticks in the letter sticks in the bark.) That is to say, he who considers merely the letter of an instrument cannot comprehend its meaning; he never gets at its true inwardness. The law on the other hand, concerns itself with the substance, as distinguished from the form, of any matter. See FALSA DEMONSTRATIO, ETC.

Qui in jus dominiumve alterius succedit jure ejus uti debet (D. 50, 17, 177). (He who succeeds to the right or property of another ought to be clothed with his right.) If he takes over the rights he does not escape the liabilities. See ASSIGNATUS, ETC.

Qui jure suo utitur neminem laedit (D. 50, 17, 151). (He who exercises his legal right inflicts upon no one any injury.) For here there is *damnum sine injuria* (*q.v.*).

Qui jussu judicis aliquod fecerit non videtur dolo malo fecisse quia parere necesse est (10 Co.Rep. 76). (He who does anything by command of a judge will not be supposed to have acted from an improper motive; because there is an obligation to obey.) The maxim is cited by Coke in support of the rule that no action will lie against anyone executing

the order of a court, given in a matter within its jurisdiction, even though given erroneously or irregularly. See JUDICIUM A NON, ETC.

Qui non habet in aere, luet in corpore (2 Co.Inst. 173). (Let him who has not the money, pay with his person.) Quoted by Coke in connection with the provision contained in the Statute of Westminster I, 1275, c. 9, for the imprisonment (in default of payment of a penalty) of officials who had failed to apprehend felons.

Qui non improbat, approbat (3 Co.Inst. 27). (He who does not disapprove, approves.) Provided, of course, that he would naturally express disapproval unless he in fact approves.

Qui non obstat quod obstare potest facere videtur (2 Co.Inst. 146). (He who does not prevent what he can prevent is regarded as doing the thing.) See IDEM EST FACERE, ETC.

Qui non prohibet quod prohibere potest assentire videtur (2 Co.Inst. 305). (He is deemed to consent who does not prohibit a thing which he has power to forbid.) See IDEM EST FACERE, ETC.

Qui omne dicit nihil excludit (2 Co. Inst. 81; 11 Co.Rep. 29b). (He who says all excludes nothing.) Cited in connection with the statement that a provision as to *omnes viduae* in the Statute of Merton, 1235, related to every tenant in dower whether she took under one or the other of the five kinds of dower known to the law; and cited also as showing that, where it was provided that all penalties went to the Crown, then no one else got any part of them. See GENERALE TANTUM, ETC.

Qui peccat ebrius, luat sobrius (Cary, 133). (Let him who sins when drunk be punished when sober.) Said of one who while drunk had slandered his neighbour. See DRUNKENNESS.

Qui per alium facit, per seipsum facere videtur (Co.Litt. 258a). (He who does anything by another is deemed to have done it himself.) See QUI FACIT, ETC.

Qui prior est tempore potior est jure (Co.Litt. 14a; Broom). (He who is first in time is better in law.) Equitable incumbrances rank as a rule according to their dates; the first grantee is *potior*, that is, *potentior*; he has a better and superior, because a prior, equity (*Phillips* v.

Phillips (1862) 4 De G.F. & J. 215). But the acquisition of the legal estate may make a material alteration in the rights of the parties (*Bailey* v. *Barnes* [1894] 1 Ch. 25), and the application of the rule in *Dearle* v. *Hall* (1823) 3 Russ. 1, to land by the Law of Property Act, 1925, s. 137, has lessened the importance of the maxim. See PRIORITY.

The principle embodied in this maxim also governs the law as to lost property, wreck, derelicts, and waifs. See MELIOR EST CONDITIO, ETC.

Qui rationem in omnibus quaerunt rationem subvertunt (2 Co.Rep. 75a). (They who search for reason in all things subvert reason.) See CONTRA NEGANTEM, ETC.; NON OMNIUM, ETC.; PRINCIPIORUM, ETC.

Qui sentit commodum sentire debet et onus; et e contra (1 Co.Rep. 99; Broom 482). (He who enjoys the benefit ought also to bear the burden; and vice versa.) This rule applies precisely in the case of a covenant running with the land and in the case of a contract which is made on behalf of or is assigned to another. Similarly, *secundum naturam est, commoda cujusque rei eum sequi, quem sequuntur incommoda* (it is natural that the advantages of anything should follow him whom the disadvantages follow) (D. 50, 7, 10).

Qui tacet consentire videtur (Jenk., Cent. 32). (He who is silent is deemed to consent.) Provided that the circumstances are such that it would have been natural for him to express dissent unless he actually consents. See QUI NON IMPROBAT, ETC.

Qui tam (who as well), a popular action (*i.e.*, one which anyone may bring) on a penal statute (*q.v.*) which was partly at the suit of the Crown and partly at that of an informer; so called from the words *qui tam pro domino rege, quam pro se ipso, sequitur* (who as well for our lord the king, as for himself, sues).

As to the power of the Crown to remit these penalties, see the Remission of Penalties Act, 1859. Proceedings by common informers were abolished by the Common Informers Act, 1951. See PENAL ACTION.

Qui vult decipi decipiatur. (If a man wants to be deceived, then let him be deceived.) That is to say, if a man enters into an agreement with express knowledge of the falsehood of representations upon the faith of which the agreement is made, he cannot afterwards be heard to plead such false representations; but the case is otherwise if he has only the means of knowledge, as distinguished from express knowledge, and has negligently failed to avail himself of such means.

Quia Emptores, the statute 1289, 18 Edw. 1, st. 1, c. 1, passed in the third notable parliament held at Westminster and therefore also called the Statute of Westminster III. It is entitled in the Parliament-roll, from the subject of it, *statutum regis de terris vendendis et emendis.* After reciting that purchasers of lands (*quia emptores terrarum*) of great men and other lords had many times theretofore entered into their fees, to the prejudice of the lords to whom the freeholders of such great men had sold their lands, whereby the latter lost the feudal fruits of tenure, it enacted that every freeman should be at liberty to sell his lands, but that the purchaser should hold them of the chief lord, so as to take the place of the vendor. Prior to this statute any person might, by a grant of land, have created a tenure as of his person; but if no such tenure was reserved, the feoffee held of the feoffor by the same services as the feoffor held by of his superior lord. The consequence was that all the fruits of tenure fell into the hands of the feoffor or mesne lord, to the prejudice of the superior lord of the fee; for remedy whereof it was enacted that thenceforth it should be lawful to every freeman to sell at his own pleasure his lands and tenements, or part of them, so that the feoffee should hold the same lands or tenements of the chief lord of the same fee by such service and customs as his feoffor held before. The statute, therefore, abolished subinfeudation (*q.v.*), and thus made the future creation of seignories, manors, honours, etc., impossible. It also first authorised conveyances of feudal lands, which had previously been considered inoperative as against the lord (2 Bl.Comm. 91; 2 Co.Inst. 500).

Quia forma non observata, infertur adnullatio actus (12 Co.Rep. 7). (Because the prescribed procedure has not been observed, the proceedings are void.) This was said in connection with an alleged irregularity in the procedure of the ecclesiastical courts.

Quia improvide, a *supersedeas* (*q.v.*) which was granted in the case of a clerk of the Chancery who had, in contravention of the privilege of that court, been sued in the Common Pleas. The term *quia improvide* was also used as meaning a *supersedeas* generally in the case of writs erroneously or improvidently sued out (Dyer 33, n. 18).

Quia improvide emanavit (because it issued mistakenly), a *supersedeas* to quash and nullify a writ erroneously issued.

Quia profecturus. The writ of protection (*q.v.*) used to contain a clause commencing with the words *quia profecturus est* (because he is about to set out). This was known as the *quia profecturus*: see the statute 1390, 13 Ric. 2, st. 1, c. 16.

Quia timet (because he fears), an action for the purpose of quieting a present apprehension of a probable future injury to property. In order to succeed in a *quia timet* action the plaintiff must prove imminent danger of a substantial kind, or that the apprehended injury, if it does come, will be irreparable (*Fletcher* v. *Bealey* (1885) 28 Ch.D. 688; *Colls* v. *Home and Colonial Stores* [1904] A.C. 179). A mandatory injunction *quia timet* (or damages in lieu thereof) may be granted where a real probability of future damage is established. It is not essential that such damage should be " imminent " except in the sense that the relief is not in all the circumstances sought prematurely (*Hooper* v. *Rogers* [1975] Ch. 43).

The court will not grant an injunction compelling the defendant to do something he is willing to do and has undertaken to do (*Bridlington Relay* v. *Yorkshire Electricity Board* [1965] Ch. 436). See BILL QUIA TIMET.

Quibus sur disseisin, De. A writ of *De quibus* was brought in the place of an assize where a man was disseised of any lands, tenements or rents, whereof he had an estate in fee (Fitz.N.B. 191).

Quibusdam de certis causis, a writ by which a defendant was summoned to

appear before the king's council (1 Holds. H.E.L. 485).

Quick successions. See ESTATE DUTY.

Quicquid demonstratae rei additur satis demonstratae frustra est (D. 33, 4, 1). (Whatever is added to describe anything already sufficiently described, is without effect.) See FALSA DEMONSTRATIO, ETC.; SURPLUSAGIUM, ETC.

Quicquid necessitas cogit, defendit (Hale, P.C. 54). (When anything is done of necessity, then necessity can be pleaded as a defence.) See NECESSITAS EST, ETC.

Quicquid plantatur solo, solo cedit (Went.Off. of Exec. 58). (Whatever is affixed to the soil belongs to the soil.) See AEDIFICATIO, ETC.; FIXTURES.

Quicquid recipitur, recipitur secundum modum recipientis (Halk. 149). (Whatever is received, is received according to the intention of the party receiving it.) See APPROPRIATION.

Quicquid solvitur, solvitur secundum modum solventis (2 Vern. 606). (Whatever is paid is paid according to the direction of the payer.) See APPROPRIATION.

Quid juris clamat, a judicial writ issued out of the record of a fine, which remained with the *custos brevium* of the Common Pleas before it was engrossed. It was a real action by which the grantee of a reversion or remainder expectant on an estate for life could compel the tenant for life to attorn to him (Reg.Jud. 571; Shep.Touch. 254).

It was abolished by the Real Property Limitation Act, 1833, s. 36. See ATTORNMENT.

Quid pro quo (something for something), consideration (*q.v.*). In every simple contract there must be *quid pro quo* (Co.Litt. 47b).

Quiet enjoyment. A qualified covenant for quiet enjoyment is usually inserted in leases and excludes the implied covenant, which is more extensive, for the implied covenant may protect the lessee against any lawful entry whatever, whereas the express covenant, as usually worded, guarantees the lessee only against entry by the lessor or persons claiming through or under him, so that a lessor having no title to the demised premises may safely enter into the qualified covenant for quiet enjoyment, for an ejectment of the lessee by the real owner would not be an ejectment by a person claiming through the lessor, but against him (*Baynes* v. *Lloyd* [1895] 2 Q.B. 610; *Jones* v. *Lavington* [1903] 1 K.B. 253).

A covenant for quiet enjoyment is implied by virtue of the Conveyancing Act, 1881, s. 7, reproduced in the Law of Property Act, 1925, ss. 76, 77, Sch. 2 Pts. I, II, in any conveyance for value by a person conveying and expressed to convey as beneficial owner. The section is to the effect that notwithstanding anything by the person who so conveys or anyone through whom he derives title otherwise than by purchase for value made, done, executed or omitted or knowingly suffered, the subject-matter of the conveyance shall remain to and be quietly entered upon, received and held, occupied, enjoyed, and taken by the person to whom the conveyance is expressed to be made, and any person deriving title under him and the benefit thereof shall be received and taken accordingly, without any lawful interruption or disturbance by the person who so conveys or any person conveying by his direction, or by, through, or under any one not being a person claiming in respect of an estate or interest subject whereto the conveyance is expressly made, through whom the person who so conveys derives title, otherwise than by purchase for value (*David* v. *Sabin* [1893] 1 Ch. 523). See COVENANT; LEASE.

Quieta non movere. (A settled state of affairs should not be disturbed.)

Quietare, to quit, discharge or save harmless: often found in deeds of dates during the seventeenth century and earlier.

Quiete clamare, to quit claim, that is to say, to renounce all claim to.

Quietus, freed or acquitted; discharged of all further liability (*Ex p. Pullman* (1890) 45 Ch.D. 466). *Quietus* was a discharge granted by the Crown or its officer to a person indebted to the Crown, *e.g.,* an accountant, and more especially a sheriff. It was a defence to a writ of extent, and might be entered on the register of judgments in discharge of an execution already issued. It seems to have been originally a writ addressed to the barons of the Exchequer, directing that the debtor should be discharged (*quietus sit*) of all claims. Afterwards it was the term made use of by the Clerk of the Pipe in the certificate *quietus est* (he is quit) which he gave to a sheriff when the sheriff had paid any balance due after the sheriff's bill of cravings (*q.v.*) had been allowed in whole or in part.

The term *quietus* was in use down to a recent period: see, *e.g.,* the Judgments Act, 1839, s. 9, repealed by the Land Charges Act, 1900, s. 5, Sch.

See SURPLUSAGE.

Quietus redditus, quit-rent. See RENT.

Quilibet potest renunciare juri pro se introducto (2 Co.Inst. 183; Co.Litt. 99a; Broom 480). (Every man is entitled to renounce a right introduced in his favour.) And so a defendant may, as a rule, decline to avail himself of a defence which would be a sufficient answer to the plaintiff's claim, and waive his right to insist on that defence. See OMNES LICENTIAM, ETC; WAIVER.

Quillet, a quibble.

Quinque portus. See CINQUE PORTS.

Quinquepartite, consisting of five parts.

Quinsime, Quinsteme, Quinzime, a tax of one fifteenth part or *quinzième*: see the statute 1352, 25 Edw. 3, st. 7. The word was also used as meaning the fifteenth day after any feast, as the *quinsime* of St. John the Baptist: see the statute 1285, 13 Edw. 1, in the preamble. See FIFTEENTHS.

Quintal. See KILOGRAMME.

Quint-exact; Quinto exactus, called for the fifth time; used as meaning the fifth or last call in the old process of outlawry (*q.v.*): see the statute 1588, 31 Eliz. 1, c. 3 (Cowel).

Quit claim [*charta de quieta clamantia*], a release or acquitting of a man for any action that the releasor had or might have against him (*Termes de la Ley*; Co.Litt. 264b).

The expression is used in old-fashioned releases as an operative word equivalent to release. See QUIETE CLAMARE.

Quit rent [*quietus redditus*], a rent payable to the lord by a freeholder or ancient copyholder of a manor, so called because thereby the tenant goes quit and free of all other services (2 Bl. Comm. 42).

As no manor has been created since

the statute *Quia Emptores,* 1289 (see MANOR; QUIA EMPTORES), every quit rent must have become first payable at a date prior to that statute.

A quit rent may be redeemed by the owner of the land subject thereto, under the Law of Property Act, 1925, s. 191, reproducing the Conveyancing Act, 1881, s. 45. As to the remedies for non-payment, see the Law of Property Act, 1925, s. 121. See RENT.

Quittance, an acquittance (*q.v.*), a release (*q.v.*) (*Re Northumberland (Duke) and Tynemouth Corporation* [1909] 2 K.B. 374).

Quo animo, with what mind.

Quo jure, a species of writ of right which compelled claimants to common in the land of another to show their title (Fitz.N.B. 128).

It was abolished by the Real Property Limitation Act, 1833, s. 36.

Quo ligatur, eo dissolvitur (2 Rolle 21). (Whatsoever binds can also release.) See EODEM LIGAMINE, ETC.

Quo minus (by which the less), a writ which lay for him who had a grant of house-bote and hay-bote in another's woods against the grantor making waste whereby the grantee could the less enjoy his grant (Old N.B. 148).

It also lay for the king's accountant in the Exchequer against any person against whom he had a right of action, and was called a *quo minus* because in it the plaintiff suggested that he was the king's farmer or debtor, and that the defendant had done him the injury or damage complained of, *quo minus sufficiens existit,* by which he was less able to pay the king his debt or rent (3 Bl.Comm. 45).

Afterwards this suggestion of being debtor to the king was allowed to be inserted by any plaintiff who wished to proceed in that court against any defendant, as a mere matter of form, and in this way the Court of Exchequer obtained a jurisdiction co-extensive with that of the Common Pleas in actions personal. The writ was impliedly abolished by the Uniformity of Process Act, 1832, s. 1, which substituted the writ of summons in all personal actions in all the common law courts. See COMMUNIA PLACITA, ETC.; FICTION.

Quo warranto (by what authority), a high prerogative writ by the Crown against one who claimed or usurped any office, franchise or liberty, to inquire by what authority he supported his claim. It lay also in cases of non-user, or mis-user, of a franchise whereby it was forfeited, or where any public trust was executed without authority, though it might be no usurpation of a franchise of the Crown (Chit.Prerog. 336).

The prerogative writ of *quo warranto* fell into disuse, having been supplanted by what was called an information in the nature of a writ of *quo warranto,* wherein the process was speedier, and the judgment not so inconveniently decisive, as on the ancient writ.

Informations in the nature of *quo warranto* were abolished by the Administration of Justice (Miscellaneous Provisions) Act, 1938, s. 9, and proceedings for an injunction substituted. See R.S.C., Ord. 53, r. 9.

The Municipal Offices Act, 1710, s. 4, permitted an information in the nature of a *quo warranto* to be brought with leave of the court, at the relation of any person desiring to prosecute the same (who was styled the relator) against any person usurping, intruding into, or unlawfully holding any franchise or office in any city borough or town corporate. A private relator could only challenge the right of an individual to act as a member of a corporation; the right of a corporation as an aggregate to act could be challenged only by the Attorney-General. Such application as a private relator could make had to be made within twelve months after the alleged disqualification arose (Municipal Corporations Act, 1882, s. 225; Local Government Act, 1888, s. 75).

This proceeding was the one generally adopted for the purpose of trying the right to be elected to municipal offices, but the Corrupt Practices (Municipal Elections) Act, 1872, s. 12 (replaced by the Municipal Corporations Act, 1882, s. 87, the Local Government Act, 1894, s. 48, the Local Government Act, 1933, s. 71, and the Representation of the People Act, 1949, s. 112), substituted an election petition in cases where an election is sought to be questioned on the ground of bribery, etc., disqualification, or undue return.

If the defendant was adjudged guilty of an intrusion or usurpation, the court might give judgment of *ouster* against him, fine him, and order him to pay costs to the relator.

An application in the nature of *quo warranto* must be made by counsel; it cannot be made by an applicant in person (*Re A Solicitor* [1903] 2 K.B. 205).

The statute 1289, 18 Edw. 1, contains two statutes each known as the *Statutum de Quo Warranto.*

Quoad, regarding; as to.

Quoad hoc, as to that.

Quoad ultra, as to the rest.

Quod ab initio non valet in tractu temporis non convalescit (Noy, Max., 16). (That which is bad from the beginning does not improve by length of time.) Cited in the *Case of Tanistry* (1608) Dav. 32, as showing that where a custom was bad at its inception, it could never become good through lapse of time.

Quod aedificatur in area legata cedit legato. (That which is built on ground that is devised passes to the devisee.) The general rule is that the devisee is entitled to everything which is affixed to the land. See FIXTURES; QUICQUID PLANTATUR, ETC.

Quod approbo non reprobo. (What I approbate I do not reprobate.) That is to say, I cannot blow hot and cold. And so where a condition is annexed to a bequest, the legatee cannot usually accept the bequest and reject the condition. See QUI SENTIT, ETC.

Quod clerici beneficiati de cancellaria, a writ which lay for a clerk of the Chancery to exempt him from contributions in respect of the proctors (*q.v.*) of the clergy (Reg.Orig. 261).

Quod clerici non eligantur in officio ballivi, etc., a writ which lay for a clerk who, by reason of some land he had, was made, or was about to be made, bailiff, beadle, reeve, or some such officer, to obtain exemption from serving the office (Reg.Orig. 117; Fitz.N.B. 261).

Quod computet, an interlocutory judgment or decree in a matter of account. In the action of accompt, one of the steps was a judgment of *quod computet*, by which auditors, or persons to take the account, were appointed. See ACCOUNT, ACTION OF.

Quod constat curiae opere testium non indiget (2 Co.Inst. 662). (What is well known to the court needs not the help of witnesses.) Coke is speaking of propositions of law. See JUDICIAL NOTICE.

Quod contra legem fit, pro infecto habetur (*Grounds of Law*, 405). (What is done contrary to law is deemed not to have been done at all.) See QUOD AB, ETC.

Quod contra rationem juris receptum, non est producendum ad consequentias (D. 50, 17, 141). (That which is received against the reason of the law is not to be advanced to a precedent.) For the corresponding maxim of English law, see QUAE CONTRA, ETC.

Quod cum, for that whereas: formerly used in pleadings and indictments.

Quod dubitas ne feceris (Hale P.C. 300). (Do nothing about which you feel doubtful.)

Quod ei deforceat, a writ or action which lay for the recovery of land where a tenant for life, in tail, or the like, had lost the right of possession through his default or non-appearance in a possessory action (Co.Litt. 331b; Bl.Comm. 193).

It was abolished by the Real Property Limitation Act, 1833, s. 36.

Quod est inconveniens, aut contra rationem, non permissum est in lege (Co. Litt. 178). (What is inconvenient, or contrary to reason, is not permitted in law.) See NIHIL QUOD EST INCONVENIENS, ETC.

Quod fieri debet facile praesumitur (Halk. 153). (What ought to be done is easily presumed to have been done.) See OMNIA PRAESUMUNTUR RITE, ETC.

Quod fieri non debet factum valet (5 Co.Rep. 38). (What ought not to be done is valid if it has been done.) This principle is more accurately expressed, *fieri non debuit sed factum valeat* (it ought not to have been done, but, since it has been done, it will be regarded as valid), which was acted on in a case where the court declined to go into the question of the legality of payments made to special constables who had been irregularly appointed and where the payments had not been regularly sanctioned.

Quod in minori valet valebit in majori; et quod in majori non valet nec valebit in minori (Co.Litt. 260). (What avails in the lesser will avail in the greater; and what does not avail in the greater will not avail in the lesser.) See ARGUMENTUM A MAJORI, ETC.; OMNE MAJUS, ETC.

Quod meum est sine facto meo vel defectu meo amitti vel in alium transferri non potest (Prest.Abs. 147, 318). (That which is mine cannot be lost or transferred to another without my act or default.) See QUOD NOSTRUM, ETC.

Quod necessarie intelligitur id non deest (1 Bulst. 71). (There is no omission of a thing which is necessarily understood.)

Quod necessarium est est licitum (Jenk., Cent. 85). (Anything which is necessary is also lawful.) See NECESSITAS, ETC.

Quod non apparet non est (2 Co.Inst. 479). (That which does not appear does not exist.) That is to say, the court knows nothing except what is proved in the case. See DE NON APPARENTIBUS, ETC.; INCERTA PRO, ETC.; JUDICIAL NOTICE.

Quod non habet principium non habet finem (Co.Litt. 345a; Broom). (That which has not a beginning has not an end.) No structure can exist without a foundation. See DEBILE, ETC.

Quod non legitur non creditur (4 Co. Inst. 304). (What is not read is not believed.)

Quod nostrum est, sine facto sive defectu nostro, amitti seu in alium transferri non potest (8 Co.Rep. 92). (That which is ours cannot be lost or transferred to another without our own act, or our own fault): except, of course, by force of a statute.

Quod nullius est, est domini regis (Fleta 3). (That which is the property of nobody, belongs to our lord the king.) Thus, in default of any person taking an absolute interest therein, the residuary estate of a person dying intestate belongs to the Crown, or the Duchy of Lancaster, or the Duke of Cornwall as *bona vacantia* (Administration of Estates Act, 1925, s. 45). See ESCHEAT.

Quod nullius est id ratione naturali occupanti conceditur (Dig. 41, 1, 3; Just. Inst. 2, 1, 12). (That which is no one's is granted to the occupant by natural right.) See FINDER OF LOST PROPERTY; POTIOR EST CONDITIO POSSIDENTIS.

Quod per me non possum, nec per alium (4 Co.Rep. 24). (What I cannot do in person, I cannot do by proxy.) See NEMO POTEST PLUS, ETC.

Quod per recordum probatum, non debet esse negatum. (What is proved by record ought not to be denied.) See RECORD.

Quod permittat, a writ which lay against one who built a house, wall, etc., which was a nuisance to his neighbour's land; also a writ which lay for the heir of one disseised of common of pasture (2 Lill. Abr. 413; New Nat.Brev. 272; *Termes de la Ley* 479).

All writs of *quod permittat* were abolished by the Real Property Limitation Act, 1833, s. 36.

Quod permittat prosternere, a writ in the nature of a writ of right to abate a nuisance (Fitz.N.B. 104).

Quod persona nec prebendarii, etc., a writ which lay for spiritual persons distrained in their spiritual possessions for payment of a fifteenth with the rest of the parish (Fitz.N.B. 175). See FIFTEENTHS.

Quod prius est verius; et quod prius est tempore potius est jure (Co. Litt. 347). (What is first is truer, and what is first in time is better in law.) The law prefers a sure and constant right, though it be little, before a great estate by wrong and defeasible.

Quod recuperet (that he do recover), a final judgment for a plaintiff in a personal action.

Quod remedio destituitur ipsa re valet si culpa absit (Bac.Max. 9.) (That which is without remedy avails of itself if there is no fault in the party seeking to enforce it.) When the law deprives a man of his remedy without his own fault, it sometimes gives him the thing itself by operation of law without any act of his own. The maxim applied in the case of retainer, that is, where a creditor was made executor or administrator to his debtor, for he cannot sue himself.

Quod semel aut bis existit praetereunt legislatores (Dig. 1, 3, 6). (Legislators pass over that which happens only once or twice.) See AD EA, ETC.

Quod semel meum est amplius meum esse non potest (Co.Litt. 49b). (What is once mine cannot be more fully mine.) Coke cites this maxim as illustrating the old law that livery of seisin could not be made to one in actual possession of lands.

QUOD

Quod semel placuit in electione, amplius displicere non potest (Co.Litt. 146). (Where choice is once made it cannot be altered.) Coke cites this maxim in support of the old law that, where a rent-charge was in arrear, the grantee of the charge might either sue out the writ of annuity against the grantor, or distrain the lands; but that if the grantee took the latter course and in an action of replevin (*q.v.*) made avowry, the action of annuity was thereby barred. The maxim may also be quoted in support of the rule that, where a contract is induced by fraud, the person defrauded may within a reasonable time elect either to treat the contract as valid or to rescind it, and that he must abide by such election as he makes. See ELECTIO SEMEL, ETC.

Quod subintelligitur non deest (Ld. Raym. 832). (What is understood is not lacking.) See QUOD NECESSARIE, ETC.

Quod vanum et inutile est, lex non requirit (Co.Litt. 319). (The law requires not what is vain and useless.) See LEX EST RATIO, ETC.; LEX NON COGIT, ETC.; LEX NON PRAECIPIT, ETC.

Quodcunque aliquis ob tutelam corporis sui fecerit, jure id fecisse videtur (2 Co.Inst. 590). (Whatsoever anyone shall do in defence of his person, that he is considered to have done legally.) But there must be *inevitabilis necessitas,* as where a prisoner breaks out of his prison in order to save his life when it has been set on fire, otherwise than by his privity.

Quoits. See CLOSH.

Quomodo quid constituitur eodem modo dissolvitur (*Doctor and Student,* dia. 2; Jenk., Cent. 74). (In the manner by which anything is constituted, so also is it dissolved.) See QUO LIGATUR, ETC.

Quorum (of whom). When a committee, board of directors, meeting of shareholders, or other body of persons, cannot act unless a certain number at least of them are present, that number is called a quorum. Thus, a first meeting of creditors in bankruptcy cannot act for any purpose, except the election of a chairman, the proving of debts, and the adjournment of the meeting, unless a quorum of three creditors (or all the creditors if the number is less than three) are present (Bankruptcy Act, 1914, s. 13, Sch. 1). As to company meetings, see the Companies Act, 1948, s. 134.

The expression quorum is derived from the use of the word in the form of commission (*q.v.*) of the peace, which was issued up to 1878. The justices *quorum aliquem vestrum A. B. C. D. unum esse volumus* were known as " justices of the quorum " until such time as every justice was named as of the quorum, so as to put all on the same footing.

It may be sufficient if there is a quorum present at the beginning of a meeting (*Re Hartley Baird* [1955] Ch. 143).

Quorum nomina, a form of writ framed in the reign of Henry VI for the purpose of enabling accountants to the king to obtain their *quietus* (*q.v.*) at less expense than had previously been necessary (Chron. Angl.).

Quota, the proportion of a contribution. See, *e.g.,* Militia Act, 1882, s. 37; Land Tax Act, 1797, s. 2.

Quotiens dubia interpretatio libertatis est secundum libertatem respondendum est (D. 50, 17, 20). (Whenever it is possible to decide either for liberty or against it, then the decision in favour of liberty should be given.)

Quotiens idem sermo duas sententias exprimit: ea potissimum excipiatur, quae rei generandae aptior est (D. 50, 17, 67). (Whenever the same language is capable of two meanings, that is to be taken which is the better fitted for effecting the proposed end.)

Quoties in verbis nulla est ambiguitas ibi nulla expositio contra verba expressa fienda est (Co.Litt. 147). (When in the words there is no ambiguity, then no interpretation contrary to the actual words is to be adopted.) See A VERBIS, ETC.; AMBIGUITY; MALEDICTA, ETC.

Quousque. See PROHIBITION; SEIZURE.

Quum principalis causa non consistit, ne ea quidem quae sequuntur locum habent (D. 50, 17, 129). (When the principal cause does not hold its ground, then the things which arise thereout have no place.) See ACCESSORIUM NON DUCIT, ETC.; QUAE ACCESSIONUM, ETC.

R

R., the king (**rex**) or queen (**regina**); rule. See BRANDING.

R.S.C., Rules of the Supreme Court (*q.v.*). See RULES OF COURT.

Rabbits, also termed " coneys " in the Game Act, 1831, which renders trespass in the daytime in pursuit of coneys punishable on summary conviction by a fine up to £20; trespassers may be required to quit the land and to tell their names and abodes on pain of arrest on refusal, and similar trespass with violence by five or more armed persons is punishable by fine up to £50 (ss. 30–32; Game Laws (Amendment) Act, 1960, s. 5 (1)). By the Night Poaching Act, 1828, s. 1, unlawfully taking or destroying game or rabbits by night is punishable on summary conviction by imprisonment up to three months with increased punishments for second or third offences; and by s. 9 of the same Act, armed persons to the number of three or more unlawfully entering land for the purpose of destroying game or rabbits are punishable after conviction on indictment by up to ten years imprisonment. For powers of the police see the Game Laws (Amendment) Act, 1960, ss. 1 (1), 2, 4.

A tenant may shoot rabbits on his farm, although the right of sporting is reserved to the landlord (Ground Game Act, 1880). The Forestry Act, 1967, s. 7, empowers the Commissioners to enter land and to destroy rabbits, hares, or vermin in order to protect trees or tree plants after notice to the occupier of the land and his failure to prevent such damage.

The destruction and control of rabbits are provided for by the Pests Act, 1954, under which rabbit clearance areas may be established.

See AGRICULTURAL HOLDING; ANIMALS, LIABILITY FOR; DESTRUCTIVE INSECTS AND PESTS; GAME; GROUND GAME; MYXOMATOSIS; POACHING; POISON.

Rabies, madness. Under the Metropolitan Police Act, 1839, s. 61, the metropolitan police may destroy any dog or animal reasonably suspected to be in a rabid state or to have been bitten by a dog or animal in a rabid state. As to muzzling orders, see ANIMALS, DISEASES OF. As to imported dogs, see QUARANTINE.

Foxes and other wild animals may be destroyed in an area declared to be infected with rabies (Rabies Act, 1974, s. 1). Further powers including those of vaccination are conferred by s. 2, and quarantine by s. 3. Notice of rabies or suspected rabies must be given to a constable (s. 4). Ss. 5, 6 deal with imported animals.

Rabula [Lat.], a wrangling advocate, a pettifogger (*q.v.*) (30 L.Q.R. 167).

Racecourse Betting Control Board. See TOTALISATOR BOARD.

Rachetum [Lat. *redimo*], the compensation or redemption of a thief.

Racial relations. Discrimination on grounds of colour, race or ethnic or national origins is declared to be unlawful by the Race Relations Act, 1968. The provisions of the Act are administered by the Race Relations Board assisted by local conciliation committees. There is also a Community Relations Commission.

A working men's club which provides facilities for duly elected members, their guests and members of associated clubs is not concerned with providing facilities to " the public or a section of the public " within the meaning of s. 2 (1) of the Race Relations Act, 1968. (*Dockers' Labour Club and Institute* v. *Race Relations Board* [1974] 3 W.L.R. 533.)

See also the Employment and Training Act, 1973, Sch. 3 para. 10; Trade Union and Labour Relations Act, 1974, Sch. 1 para. 28; CLUB; LICENCE TO ASSIGN; PUBLIC ORDER.

The Race Relations Board, though not a judicial body, is an administrative or investigating body, and is under a duty to act fairly. A hearing need not be held nor need parties be present, though a person adversely affected by proceedings should be told the case against him and afforded a fair opportunity of answering it (*R.* v. *Race Relations Board, ex p. Selvarajan* [1975] 1 W.L.R. 1686). Incitement to racial hatred by means of the public performance of a play is an offence (Theatres Act, 1968, ss. 5, 7–10).

See BREACH OF THE PEACE; LICENCE TO
ASSIGN; PUBLIC MEETING.

Racing tips. Neither the giving nor the
publication of advertisements offering to
give racing tips (or prophecies as to the
winning of horse-races) is illegal (*Hawke*
v. *M'Kenzie* [1902] 2 K.B. 225).

Rack, an engine of torture, said not to
have been used in England since 1640.
See TORTURE.

Rack-rent, rent raised to the uttermost;
the full annual benefit of the property. In
the Public Health Act, 1936, s. 343, rack-
rent means a rent which is not less than
two-thirds of the rent at which a house
or other property might reasonably be
expected to let from year to year, free
from all usual tenant's rates and taxes and
tithe rentcharge (if any), and deducting
therefrom the probable average annual
cost of the repairs, insurance and other
expenses (if any) necessary to maintain
the same in a state to command such rent.
See *Rawlance* v. *Croydon Corporation*
[1952] 2 Q.B. 803 (effect of Rent Acts
to be considered); *R.* v. *Minister of Housing and Local Government* [1954] 1
Q.B. 140 (whether ground rent can become a rack rent); *London Corporation*
v. *Cusack-Smith* [1955] A.C. 337 (rack
rent at time of grant of lease). See also
the Housing Act, 1957, s. 39 (2); Highways Act, 1959, s. 295. See RENT.

Rack-vintage, a second vintage, wines
drawn from the lees.

Radio. See WIRELESS TELEGRAPHY.

Radio-active substances. See ATOMIC
ENERGY AUTHORITY.

Radiological protection. See ATOMIC
ENERGY.

Radium. The National Radium Trust
is a body incorporated by royal charter
(Cancer Act, 1939, s. 5).

Radknight; Radman, a rodknight (*q.v.*).

Radour [Fr.], a term including the repairs made to a ship, and a fresh supply
of furniture and victuals, munitions, and
other provisions, required for the voyage.

Raffles. See LOTTERY.

Rag dealer. See the Public Health Act,
1936, s. 154, amended by the Criminal
Justice Act, 1967, Sch. 3; London Government Act, 1963, s. 40.

Rag flock. The Rag Flock and Other
Filling Materials Act, 1951 (replacing the
Rag Flock Acts, 1911 and 1928), sets up
a system of control to ensure that the

filling materials used in upholstery are
clean. See also the Consumer Credit Act,
1974, Sch. 4 para. 11.

Rageman [Lat. *regimen*], a rule, form
or precedent.

Rageman, Statute of, the statute 1276,
4 Edw. 1, under which justices were
appointed to hear and determine complaints which had arisen throughout the
kingdom during the twenty-five years preceding the Michaelmas of that year.
These justices were sometimes described
as *juratores de rageman.* The commission
of trailbaston (*q.v.*) dated from this
statute.

Ragged school. The Sunday and Ragged
Schools (Exemption from Rating) Act,
1869, s. 1, provided that any rating
authority might exempt from any rate any
building used exclusively as a Sunday
school or a ragged school. A ragged
school means any school used for the
gratuitous education of children and
young persons of the poorest classes, and
for the holding of classes and meetings
in furtherance of the same object, and
without any pecuniary benefit being
derived therefrom except to the teacher
or teachers employed. The Act also gave
the same advantage to Sunday schools.
The Act defined a Sunday school as any
school used for giving religious instruction to children and young persons on
Sundays and on weekdays for the holding
of classes and meetings in furtherance
of the same object and without pecuniary
profit being derived therefrom. Ragged
schools became obsolete with the establishment of free education by the State.

Ragler; Raglor, the sheriff or constable
or other chief officer of a Welsh commote
(*q.v.*).

Raglorious, a steward (Seld., Tit. of
Hon. 597).

Ragman. See RAGEMAN, STATUTE OF.

Ragman's roll, or **Ragimund's-roll,** a
roll, called from one Ragimund, or
Ragimont, a legate in Scotland, who,
summoning all the beneficed clergymen in
that kingdom, caused them on oath to
give in the true value of their benefices,
according to which they were afterwards
taxed by the court of Rome.

The term Ragman's-toll also means the
list of the barons and men of note who
subscribed the submission to Edward I in

1296, and which was delivered up to the Scots in 1328 (1 Scott, Hist.Scot. 162).

Railway, a road owned by a private person or a public company or the State on which carriages run over iron rails; if the road is a public highway, that part of it on which the rails are laid is called a tramway. Every railway in this country (except a few private railways running through land owned by the owner of the railway) was constructed and managed under a local and personal Act and the Companies Clauses Consolidation Act, 1845, the Lands Clauses Consolidation Act, 1845, and the Railways Clauses Consolidation Act, 1845, and under the general Acts relating to railways. The Railways Act, 1921, provided for the reorganisation of almost all the railways in England, and the Transport Act, 1947, for their nationalisation under the British Transport Commission. The British Railways Board was created by the Transport Act, 1962, to take over the railway functions of the British Transport Commission. The duty and powers of the Railways Board are specified in s. 3 as amended by the Transport Act, 1968, s. 50 (1). The Railways Board has power to provide road services (Act of 1962, s. 4 (1)), shipping and air services (Act of 1962, s. 5)) and hotels (Act of 1968, s. 50 (2)). The Railways Board is freed from statutory duties to afford reasonable services and facilities, liability for negligence in the carriage of goods or obligation to revise their freight charges on complaint by competitors or traders (Act of 1962, s. 43 (4)) and may make such charges as they think fit (Act of 1962, s. 43 (3); Act of 1968, s. 50 (10)). The Railways Board is not a common carrier by rail or inland waterway (Act of 1962, s. 43 (6)). The Railways Board is liable in respect of the death or injury to a passenger other than a passenger travelling on a free pass (Act of 1962, s. 43 (7)). The liability is regulated by the International Convention set out in the Schedule to the Carriage by Railway Act, 1972. See S.I. 1974 No. 1250. The National Freight Corporation was established by the Transport Act, 1968, ss. 1–8. See further the Railways Act, 1974.

Powers as carriers were given by the Railways Clauses Consolidation Act, 1845, s. 86, the Railway and Canal Traffic Acts, 1854 to 1894, and the Road and Rail Traffic Act, 1933.

As to passenger transport areas, see the Transport Act, 1968, ss. 9–23.

As to the rating of railway and canal premises, see the General Rate Act, 1967, s. 32; Transport Act, 1968, s. 162 (5); Transport (London) Act, 1969, Sch. 3 para. 1; Town and Country Planning Act, 1971, Sch. 23 Pt. II; Local Government Act, 1974, s. 19, Sch. 3 para. 2.

As to standards of health, welfare and safety in railway premises, see OFFICES.

The relation of master and servant exists in the case of railway special constables (*Lambert* v. *G.E. Ry.* [1909] 2 K.B. 776).

Railway and Canal Commission, a court established by the Railway and Canal Traffic Act, 1888, s. 1. It was abolished by the Railway and Canal Commission (Abolition) Act, 1949, and its principal functions transferred to the High Court and the Court of Session. Other powers were transferred to the Railway Rates Tribunal (*q.v.*).

Railway Commission, a body of three commissioners appointed under the Regulation of Railways Act, 1873. They were replaced by the Railway and Canal Commission (*q.v.*).

Railway fires. See ENGINE.

Railway Rates Tribunal, a tribunal established by the Railways Act, 1921, s. 20. To it were transferred some of the powers exercised by the Railway and Canal Commission (*q.v.*), and further powers were granted by the Road and Rail Traffic Act, 1933. It became the Transport Tribunal under the Transport Act, 1947, s. 72. See also the Transport Act, 1962, s. 57, Sch. 10. The Act of 1921, s. 20, and the Act of 1962, s. 72, were repealed by the Act of 1962, Sch. 12 Pt. I.

Railway rolling stock. The Railway Rolling Stock Protection Act, 1872, protects from distress by a landlord rolling stock not being the property of the tenant. The Railway Companies Act, 1867, s. 4, and the Railway Companies (Scotland) Act, 1867, s. 4, protect all rolling stock from execution. See also the Carriage by Railway Act, 1972, s. 6 (3).

Rain insurance. See PLUVIUS POLICY.

Raise, to create, *e.g.*, a use (*q.v.*).

Ram Alley. See PRIVILEGED PLACES.

Rams. Regulations may be made for the control of rams under the Hill Farming Act, 1946, s. 18, and the Livestock Rearing Act, 1951, s. 7.

Ran, open or public theft; evident rape which cannot be denied (Leg. Will. 1).

Ranger, a sworn officer of the forest, appointed by royal letters patent. His duties were to walk daily through his charge, and see, hear, and inquire of trespasses in his bailiwick; to drive the beasts of the forest, both of venery and chase, out of the disafforested into the forested lands; and to present all trespasses of the forest at the next court holden for the forest. A ranger also means an official in control of royal parks.

Rank. A claim to a prescriptive payment, such as a *modus*, was said to be rank when it was excessive, and therefore void. Thus if a *modus* set up was so large that it exceeded what would have been, in the time of Richard I, the value of the tithes in lieu of which it was claimed, the *modus* was rank and destroyed itself. See MODUS DECIMANDI.

Ransom [Fr. *rançon*], the price of redemption of a captive or prisoner of war, or for the pardon of some great offence. It differs from amerciament, because it excuses from corporal punishment.

Anciently those who held by knight's tenure were under obligation to ransom, or pay money for the release of, their lord when he was captured in war.

A ransom bill is given by the master of a captured vessel, together with a hostage, to the captor, who in exchange gives a safe conduct, so that the ship may continue her voyage. If the captor is taken with the ransom bill on board he loses his rights. Under the Naval Prize Act, 1864, s. 45, Orders in Council may be made prohibiting, allowing or regulating the ransoming of ships or goods captured by an enemy. Nothing was heard of ransom during the wars of 1914–18 or 1939–45. See Holland, Lectures Int. Law, p. 375.

Rape, a division of the county of Sussex. The rapes are Chichester, Arundel, Bramber, Lewes, Pevensey and Hastings; they appear to have been military governments in early Norman times. The equivalent in Kent is the lathe (*q.v.*), and in Yorkshire, the wapentake (Tomlin).

In criminal law, rape is the act of having sexual intercourse with a woman against her will or without her conscious permission, or where her permission has been extorted by force or fear of immediate bodily harm. A person cannot be convicted of rape if he believed, albeit mistakenly, that the woman consented, even though he had no reasonable grounds for that belief (*D.P.P.* v. *Morgan* [1975] 2 W.L.R. 913). Rape is an indictable offence, punishable with imprisonment for life. Connection with a married woman by personation of her husband is rape. Upon an indictment for rape the jury may convict for indecent assault (Sexual Offences Act, 1956, ss. 1, 37, Sch. 2). If a person at the time of committing rape has unlawful possession of a firearm or imitation firearm he is guilty of an offence under the Firearms Act, 1968, see s. 17 (2), Sch. 1 para. 6.

On an indictment for rape, indecent assault (*q.v.*) is an alternative verdict but unlawful sexual intercourse is not (*R.* v. *Mochan* [1969] 1 W.L.R. 1331; *R.* v. *Fisher* [1969] 2 Q.B. 114; *R.* v. *Hodgson* [1973] 1 Q.B. 565).

Evidence that the complainant is of notoriously bad character for chastity or is a common prostitute is admissible (*R.* v. *Bashir* [1969] 1 W.L.R. 1303). Rape was for a long period punished as a capital crime in this country.

The complaint of the woman shortly after the occurrence, and its particulars, may be given in evidence for the prosecution, not as evidence of the facts complained of, but of the consistency of the conduct of the woman with the story told by her in the witness-box, and as negativing consent on her part (*R.* v. *Lillyman* [1896] 2 Q.B. 167). It is the universal practice to require corroboration of the woman's accusation (*R.* v. *Osborne* [1905] 1 K.B. 551).

Sexual intercourse is complete on proof of penetration with proof of completion of the intercourse by the emission of semen (Sexual Offences Act, 1956, s. 44; *R.* v. *Marsden* [1891] 2 Q.B. 149). Where rape is alleged a person may be found guilty of aiding and abetting that alleged rape even though the principal may be found not guilty of the offence (*R.* v. *Cogan* [1976] Q.B. 217). See ABUSING CHILDREN; AGE; CORROBORATION; HUSBAND AND WIFE; INDECENT ASSAULT.

Rape of the forest, trespass, with violence, on the forest. It was one of the crimes of which only the king had cognisance (Leg.Hen. 1, c. 10).

Rape-reeve, an officer who used to act in subordination to the shire-reeve.

Rapine [Lat. *rapina*], the taking a thing against the owner's will, openly or by violence; robbery. The word occurs in the title of the statute 1662, 14 Car. 2, c. 22, which was directed to the prevention of theft and rapine upon the northern borders of England, but neither in that statute nor elsewhere is it used as a legal description of an offence.

Raptu haeredis, a writ for taking away an heir holding in socage; there were two sorts, one when the heir was married, the other when he was not (Reg.Brev. 163).

It was subsequently known as the writ of *ravishment de gard* (*q.v.*).

Rastell. John Rastell and William Rastell, his son, were lawyers and printers in the time of Henry VIII. John Rastell translated from the French the " Abridgement of the Statutes prior to the time of Henry VII." He also abridged those of Henry VII, and down to 1532 of Henry VIII, which were printed together by the son William Rastell in 1533. This was the first abridgment in the English language.

The performances which most distinguish William Rastell belong to a later period than the reign of Henry VIII. These are his collection of English statutes printed in 1559, and his "Entries," printed long after his death in 1596 (4 Reeves 418).

Rasure, the act of scraping or shaving; erasure.

Rasure of a deed, so as to alter it in a material part, without the consent of the party bound by it makes it void. Where a deed by rasure, addition, or alteration becomes no deed, the defendant may plead *non est factum* (5 Co.Rep. 23, 119).

A rasure or interlineation in a deed is presumed, in the absence of rebutting evidence, to have been made at or before its execution, but in a will it is presumed to have been made after its execution. See INTERLINEATION.

Rate, a sum assessed or made payable by a body having local jurisdiction over the district in which the person on whom the rate is assessed dwells or has property. See TAX.

Rates are almost always, if not invariably, assessed in respect of the enjoyment or occupation of real property in proportion to its value (*pro rata,* whence the term " rate "); and when a person has such an occupation of property as to be liable to payment of rates, his occupation is said to be rateable. The oldest rate appears to be that imposed for the relief of the poor, and the principles on which it is assessed and levied have been followed (with certain modifications) in the case of other rates.

It is only the beneficial occupation of property which is rateable, and therefore, in arriving at the value of it, repairs, insurance and other necessary outgoings are allowed to be deducted. On the other hand, the fact that the occupation of property is in effect unprofitable, because the occupier has a heavy rent or other outgoings to bear, does not affect his liability to be rated. The test for beneficial occupation is not whether a profit could be made but whether the occupation is of value (*Kingston-upon-Hull Corporation* v. *Clayton* [1963] A.C. 28, *per* Lord Guest).

As to the rating of owners instead of occupiers, see the General Rate Act, 1967, ss. 55–57; S.I. 1972, no. 1983.

Unoccupied property is not in beneficial occupation and was formerly not rateable but liability in respect of unoccupied property is imposed by the General Rate Act, 1967, ss. 17, 17A, 17B, Sch. 1, as amended by the Local Government Act, 1974, ss. 15, 16.

The poor rate was levied under the Poor Relief Act, 1601, on the occupiers in each parish of lands, houses, tithes, coal mines, or saleable underwoods. The Rating Act, 1874, extended the liability to rates to land used for a plantation or a wood, or for the growth of saleable underwood, and not subject to any right of common; rights of fowling, shooting, taking, or killing game, or rabbits, and of fishing when severed from the occupation of the land; and mines of every kind (*e.g.*, iron mines) not mentioned in the Poor Relief Act, 1601.

Personal property is not rateable, and stock in trade was expressly excepted by the Poor Rate Exemption Act, 1840.

The multiplicity of rates leviable by public bodies for public purposes was simplified by the Rating and Valuation Act, 1925. By this Act one general rate replaced almost all the rates formerly made by the respective authorities having power to raise money by a public rate. The law was consolidated by the General Rate Act, 1967, as subsequently amended.

The rating authorities are the district councils (*q.v.*), in the City of London the Common Council; in the Inner Temple the Sub-Treasurer, and in the Middle Temple the Under-Treasurer (General Rate Act, 1967, s. 1; Local Government Act, 1972, s. 179). The general rate is raised on so much in the pound on the rateable value of each hereditament in rateable occupation according to the valuation list (General Rate Act, 1967, s. 2; Local Government Act, 1972, Schs. 13, 30). As to rebates see the Rating Act, 1966, s. 9, the General Rate Act, 1967, Sch. 9; Rate Rebate Act, 1973; S.I. 1968 No. 1066; 1970 No. 847. Contributions required by bodies such as the county council entitled out of the general rate are obtained by precepts to the rating authority requiring a levy of a specified amount in the pound calculated on the authority's estimate of the produce of a penny rate in its area. (General Rate Act, 1967, ss. 11, 12; Decimal Currency Act, 1969, s. 10 (3), Sch. 2 para. 28). See QUARTER-RATING.

Valuation for rating is now in the hands of the Inland Revenue under the General Rate Act, 1967, Pt. V as amended by the Local Government Act, 1972, Schs. 13, 30.

The Local Government Act, 1974, contains provisions as to "rate support grants" (ss. 1–5); grants for particular purposes; rate rebates, ss. 11–14; rating of unoccupied property, ss. 15, 16; increases in statutory deduction from gross value, s. 17; rating of plant and machinery, s. 18; rating of public utilities etc., s. 19; relief for disabled persons, s. 20; restriction on raising the gross rateable value on account of minor alterations to dwellings, s. 21. See also s. 42, Sch. 7 paras. 3–10 amending the General Rate Act, 1967.

Liability and valuation in some special cases are dealt with by the General Rate Act, 1967: agricultural premises (s. 26, as amended by the Rating Act, 1971, s. 1); land used as plantations (s. 27), advertising stations (s. 28), sporting rights (s. 29), school premises (s. 30), railways (see RAILWAY). The rating of hereditaments of certain public utility undertakings is regulated by order made under the Local Government Act, 1974, s. 19. These are: water hereditaments, railway and canal premises, hereditaments occupied by the British Gas Corporation, an Electricity Board, and the Post Office, mines and quarries, hereditaments occupied by a dock or harbour undertaking or an undertaking for rediffusion (Act of 1974, Sch. 3). As to water rates, see WATER. As to rates in respect of the matrimonial home, see MATRIMONIAL HOME.

Rate of exchange. Where the consideration for a contract is expressed in a foreign currency, but damages have to be awarded in an English court, the conversion of the foreign currency into sterling is made at the rate of exchange ruling when payment was due or the breach took place (*Di Fernando* v. *Smits* [1920] 3 K.B. 409).

Rate-tithe. When any sheep or other cattle were kept in a parish for less time than a year, the owner had to pay tithe for them *pro rata* according to the custom of the place (Fitz.N.B. 51).

Ratification, confirmation. Agency may be created by ratification. Where A purports to act as agent for B, either having no authority at all or having no authority to do that particular act, the subsequent adoption by B of A's act has the same legal consequences as if B had originally authorised the act. But there can be no ratification unless A purported to act as agent, and to act for B; and in such a case B alone can ratify. Nor can there be any binding ratification of any agreement which was void or where the principal was not in existence at the time of the act, either in fact or in the contemplation of law as in the case of persons such as trustees in bankruptcy or personal representatives who acquire title by relation (*Kelner* v. *Baxter* (1867) L.R. 2 C.P. 174). The doctrine of ratification is also applied to torts.

See ADOPT; AUTHORITY; INFANT; OMNIS RATIHABITIO RETROTRAHITUR, ETC.; REPUDIATION; ULTRA VIRES.

Ratihabitio mandato comparatur (D. 50, 17, 60). (Ratification is equivalent to a command.) See RATIFICATION.

Ratio, an account, a rule of proportion; also, a cause, or giving judgment therein. *Ponere ad rationem* meant to cite one to appear in judgment (Wals. 88).

Ratio means also a reason, as in the phrase *ratio decidendi*, the reason or ground of a decision as opposed to an *obiter dictum* (*q.v.*). It also meant an account, as in *reddere rationem*, to render an account (Tomlin).

Ratio legis est anima legis Jenk. Cent. 45). (The reason for the law is the soul of the law.) That is to say, for the proper understanding of a statute or rule of the law, one must understand why the statute or rule came into existence. See CESSANTE RATIONE, ETC.

Rationabili estoverium, alimony (q.v.) (Tomlin).

Rationabili parte, De, a writ which lay for brothers in gavelkind and sisters and other coparceners. The writ claimed a certain portion of the land to be held in severalty or, in modern parlance, partition (*q.v.*). It was abolished by the Real Property Limitation Act 1833, s. 36.

Rationabili parte bonorum, De. Where a custom existed that one-third of a man's chattels should go to his wife, another third to his children, and the remaining third as he directed by his will, the writ *de rationabili parte bonorum* might be brought by the wife or the children to enforce their rights. This custom existed in some places down to a late period. The statute 1692, 4 Will. & Mar. c. 2, enabled the inhabitants of the province of York to dispose of their personal estates by their wills, notwithstanding the custom of that province, that is to say the archbishopric of York. The statute 1696, 7 & 8 Will. 3, c. 38,

took away the custom of Wales which hindered persons from disposing of their personal estates by their wills.

Before the statute 1725, 11 Geo. 1, c. 18, freemen of the City of London were unable to dispose by will of their personal estates. This deterred citizens of the better class from becoming freemen; and the local and parliamentary franchises were thus largely in the hands of an undesirable class. See COMPANIES, CITY; CUSTOM OF LONDON; REASONABLE PARTS.

Rationabilis dos, a widow's third, or reasonable dower (*q.v.*).

Rationalibus (or Rationabilibus) divisis, De, a writ which commanded the sheriff to delimit the boundaries of the lands of adjoining tenants for life or in fee simple (Fitz.N.B. 128; Reg.Orig. 157).

Ratione soli, by reason only.

Ratione tenurae, by reason, or in respect, of his tenure. Thus, when a person is liable to repair a highway (*q.v.*) by reason of his having the tenure or occupation of the adjoining lands, his obligation is said to be *ratione tenurae*.

Rationes [M. Lat.], the pleadings in a suit.

Rationes exercere, or **Ad rationes stare,** to plead.

Rationing, the fixing of a periodical allowance, *e.g.*, of food, clothing, motor spirit, etc. Rationing was imposed during the war of 1914–18 under the Defence of the Realm Regulations, made under the Defence of the Realm Acts, 1914 to 1918, and during the war of 1939–45 under the Defence (General) Regulations, 1939, made under the Emergency Powers (Defence) Act, 1939.

Rats and mice. See DESTRUCTIVE INSECTS AND PESTS.

Rattening, where the members of a trade union cause the tools, clothes or other property of a workman to be taken away or hidden, in order to compel him to join the union or cease working. Under the Conspiracy and Protection of Property Act, 1875, s. 7, it is an offence punishable by fine or imprisonment. See MOLESTATION.

Ravishment, the tortious act of taking away a wife from her husband or a ward from his guardian (Co.Litt. 136b; 3 Bl. Comm. 139). See ABDUCTION; RAPE.

Ravishment de gard, a writ which lay for a guardian by knight service or in socage against one who deprived him of the custody of his ward or *gard* (Statute of Westminster II, 1285, c. 35). It was abolished by the statute 1660, 12 Car. 2, c. 24, along with the Court of Wards and Liveries (*q.v.*). It was also known as the writ *de haerede rapto* (*q.v.*).

Re, in the matter of.

Re. fa. lo., an abbreviation of the name of the writ *recordari facias loquelam* (*q.v.*).

Readers, ancients or benchers of the Inns of Court who were selected to give " readings " or dissertations in their Inns. A " double reader " was one who had been already a reader eight or nine years before. Election as a double reader was a mark of distinction and, down to 1664, gave the right of calling at first four, and then eight, students to the Bar.

At the Temple Church there is an official, known as the Reader, who reads the lessons and preaches on Sunday afternoons. He is elected alternately by the benchers of the Inner and Middle Temple, and his salary is paid by the two societies in equal proportion. See MASTER OF THE TEMPLE.

Reading in. Every clergyman of the Church of England who is instituted or collated to any benefice or preachership must, on the first Sunday that he officiates in his church, publicly read the Thirty-nine Articles and then make a declaration in which he assents to the Articles and undertakes to use the forms in the Book of Common Prayer, and none other except so far as shall be ordered by lawful authority (Clerical Subscription Act, 1865, ss. 1, 7). If he does not go through these formalities (popularly known as " reading in") his institution or collation becomes void (s. 7).

Reading rooms. See LIBRARIES.

Reafforest, to turn again into forest land which had been disafforested: the Dean Forest Act, 1968, did so as regards the Forest of Dean.

Real. See COVENANT; EVIDENCE; IN PERSONAM; IN REM; PERSONAL; SECURITY.

Real accounts. See IMPERSONAL ACCOUNTS.

Real action, the proceedings at common law by means of which a freeholder could recover his land, *viz.,* (1) actions commenced by writ of right (*q.v.*) to decide the question of title to land; actions were delayed by dilatory pleas (essoins) (see ESSOIN) and trial by battle (see BATTLE, TRIAL BY) was possible; (2) possessory assizes, to decide questions of disseisin (*q.v.*) and (3) writs of entry (see ENTRY AD COMMUNEM LEGEM). The real actions were displaced by the action of ejectment (*q.v.*).

By the Real Property Limitation Act, 1833, s. 37, all real and mixed actions, except the writ of right of dower, or writ of dower *unde nihil habet, quare impedit,* and ejectment, were abolished. By the Common Law Procedure Act, 1860, s. 26, the procedure in the excepted actions of dower, etc., except ejectment, was assimilated to that of ordinary actions, and by the rules of court under the Judicature Acts, 1873–75, all remaining distinction between ejectment and other actions was abolished. See ACTION.

Among the civilians, real actions, otherwise called vindications, were those in which a man demanded something that was his own. They were founded on dominion, or *jus in re.*

The real actions of the civil law were not, like the real actions of the common law, confined to real estate, but included personal as well as real property. But the same distinction as to classes of remedies and actions pervaded the common and the civil law. Thus there were in the common law the distinct classes of real actions, personal actions, and mixed actions, the first embracing those which concerned real estate where the proceeding was purely *in rem*; the next embracing all suits *in personam* for contracts and torts; and the last embracing those mixed suits where a person was liable by reason of and in connection with property.

Real chattels. See CHATTELS.

Real composition, an agreement made between the owner of land and the incumbent of a parish, with the consent of the ordinary and the patron of the living, that the land should for the future be discharged from payment of tithes, by reason of some land or other real recompense given in lieu and satisfaction thereof. But after the statute 1571, 13 Eliz. 1, c. 10, no real composition could be made for any longer term than three lives or twenty-one years (2 Bl.Comm. 28). See TITHES.

Real estate. Before 1926 this meant land (with all houses, etc., built thereon) including all estates and interests in lands held for life (but not for years, however many) or for some greater estate, and whether such lands were of freehold or copyhold tenure. For the purposes of devolution upon deaths after 1925, the Administration of Estates Act, 1925, s. 3, defines real estate as including chattels real and land in possession, remainder or reversion and every interest in or over land to which the deceased was entitled at his death and real estate held on trust (including settled land) or by way of mortgage or security, but not money to arise under a trust for sale of land nor money secured or charged on land. See TRUST.

Real property, property which, on the death of the owner intestate before 1926, passed to his heir through the real representative (*q.v.*). See REAL ESTATE.

Real representative, a personal representative on whom real estate devolved on the death of a person under the Land Transfer Act, 1897.

Prior to the Land Transfer Act, 1897, the real estate of a deceased person vested in his heir or devisee, and his personal estate in his executors or administrators. The Land Transfer Act, 1897, reproduced and extended by the Administration of Estates Act, 1925, established a real representative in the person of the executor or administrator in whom all the real estate except copyhold was vested notwithstanding the will, unless, as in a joint tenancy, any other person had a right to take by survivorship, so that one and the same person had the legal title to both the real estate and the personal estate of the deceased.

These provisions, and the Conveyancing Act, 1881, s. 30 (relating to the devolution upon the personal representative of trust and mortgage estates belonging to the deceased), were consolidated and extended by the Administration of Estates Act, 1925, with the object of assimilating the law of succession to real and personal property. The Administration of Estates Act, 1925, s. 1, provides that real estate to which a deceased person was entitled for an interest not ceasing on his death shall, on his death and notwithstanding any testamentary disposition thereof, devolve on the personal representative in like manner as, before the commencement of the Act, chattels real devolved on the personal representative.

The personal representatives for the time being of a deceased person are deemed in law his heirs and assigns within the meaning of all trusts and powers.

The personal representatives are the representatives of the deceased in regard to his real estate to which he was entitled for an interest not ceasing on his death as well as in regard to his personal estate. The Administration of Estates Act, 1925, s. 2, applies the law relating to chattels real to real estate except that (reproducing and amending the Land Transfer Act, 1897, s. 2, and the Conveyancing Act, 1911, s. 12) all the personal representatives or all the proving executors are to join in a conveyance either of realty or of chattels real, and, without prejudice to the rights and powers of a personal representative, preserves the order of administration and rights of property and action relating to real estate in favour of the persons entitled.

Real estate over which a person exercises a general power of appointment by his will and an entailed interest disposed of by will under the statutory power devolve upon the personal representative (Law of Property Act, 1925, s. 176). An entailed interest or a reversion or remainder thereto which was not disposed of by will does not devolve upon them, nor does the interest in a joint estate passing by survivorship or the interest of a corporation sole. The trustees of settled land vested in the testator and not settled by his will may be appointed by the testator (and if not so appointed, will be deemed to have been appointed) as the special representatives of the settled land without prejudice to the appointment of general representatives (Administration of Estates Act, 1925, s. 22); see *Re*

Bridgett and Hayes' Contract [1928] Ch. 163.

Pending the effective creation of a personal representative the real estate of an intestate formerly devolved on the heir-at-law (*Re Griggs* [1914] 2 Ch. 547); it now vests in the President of the Family Division (Administration of Estates Act, 1925, ss. 9, 55; Administration of Justice Act, 1970, s. 1 (6)). As to the powers of an administrator over the real estate prior to the grant to him, see *Re Pryse* [1904] P. 301.

The real representative, by the Land Transfer Act, 1897, s. 2, held the real estate as trustee for the person by law beneficially entitled thereto, *e.g.*, for the devisee, and might at any time after the death assent to a devise or convey the real estate to such person, but after 1925 a will cannot pass a legal estate except to the personal representatives, and testamentary dispositions are only equitable. The legal estate or property passes to the beneficiary only upon assent or conveyance by the personal representatives. See ASSENT, ETC.

Real right, the right of property, *jus in re.* The person having such right may sue for the subject itself. A personal right, *jus ad rem,* entitles the party only to an action for performance of the obligation.

Real securities, mortgages of land and ground rents.

Real things, things substantial and immovable, and the rights and profits annexed to or issuing out of them.

Real union, a composite State, the components of which remain distinct units but which have some institutions in common, *e.g.*, the former Austro-Hungarian empire. See PERSONAL UNION.

Realisation account, an account prepared when a partnership or company is dissolved showing the book value of the assets and the amount realised by their sale; also showing, usually, the net result of the winding up.

Reality of laws. See PERSONALITY OF LAWS.

Realm, a kingdom or country.

Realty, real property. In the old books, an " action in the realty " means a real action.

Reapsilver, a yearly payment made by tenants to a lord for exemption from the duty of reaping for him.

Reason, the very life of law, for when the reason of law once ceases the law itself generally ceases, because reason is the foundation of all our laws (Co.Litt. 97b, 183b).

Reasonable. If there is a contract to do a thing or to buy goods, and no time or price is mentioned, the law implies that the thing is to be done in a reasonable time, and that a reasonable price is to be paid. See REASONABLE TIME.

Reasonable aid, a duty claimed by the lord of the fee of his tenants holding by knight service, to marry his daughter, etc.

Reasonable and probable cause, such grounds as justify anyone in suspecting another of a crime and giving him in custody thereon. Its absence is one of the causes of action in an action for malicious prosecution and its existence is a defence to an action for false imprisonment. After the jury have found the facts, the question whether the facts show a reasonable and probable cause is a question of law, not fact, but the judge may leave that finding to the jury in some cases (*McDonald* v. *Rooke* (1835) 2 Bing.N.C. 217). See FALSE IMPRISONMENT; MALICIOUS PROSECUTION.

Reasonable parts, the two-thirds of a man's personal property, one of which went on his death to his widow, and the other to his children, the remaining third going in accordance with his will. This right of the widow and children was saved to them by Magna Carta, 1215, but became lost by degrees. The Wills Act, 1837, is inconsistent with, but does not expressly repeal, the saving of Magna Carta, 1215, for the reasonable parts, but the Wills Act, 1837, does not apply to Scotland, where, as generally throughout Europe, except in England and Ireland, the rights of the widow and children are in full force. See HEREDITAS; LEGITIM; RATIONABILI PARTE BONORUM.

Provision is made for maintenance of a spouse and children by the Inheritance (Provision for Family and Dependants) Act, 1975. See FAMILY PROVISION.

Reasonable time. By the Sale of Goods Act, 1893, ss. 11 (2), 18 (4), 29 (4), 35, 37, 56, what is a reasonable time in connection with the sale of goods is a question of fact. What is a reasonable time for giving notice of dishonour of a bill of exchange is, however, a question of law to be determined in accordance with the Bills of Exchange Act, 1882, s. 49. Where a contract is silent as to time the law implies a contract to do the stipulated act within a reasonable time (*Ford* v. *Cotesworth* (1868) L.R. 4 Q.B. 132).

Re-assurance, a contract which a first insurer enters into to release himself wholly or in part from a risk which he has undertaken by throwing it upon some other insurer. See RE-INSURANCE.

Re-attachment, a second attachment of one who had formerly been attached and had been dismissed the court without day by reason of the non-coming of the judges or some such casualty. A cause discontinued or put without delay could be revived only by re-attachment or re-summons (*q.v.*) (Broke Reg.Orig. 35; 2 Hawk.P.C. c. 27, 105; Jacob).

Rebate, discount; reducing the interest of money in consideration of prompt payment or otherwise; a deduction made from a payment. In bankruptcy a creditor who has proved for a debt payable *in futuro* does not receive the full amount of the dividends with the other creditors, but must deduct from each dividend a rebate of interest at five per cent. in respect of the period from the declaration of the dividend to the time when the debt becomes payable (Bankruptcy Act, 1914, Sch. 2 r. 22).

Rebellion, the taking up of arms traitorously against the Crown, whether by natural subjects or others when once subdued. It also meant disobedience to the process of the courts.

Rebellion, Commission of, one of the processes of contempt in the Court of Chancery. See COMMISSION, ETC.

Rebinare, to plough for the second or third time arable land lying fallow (2 Fleta, c. 73).

Rebouter, to repel or bar.

Rebus sic stantibus, things standing so; under the circumstances.

Rebut [Lat. *repellere*], to bar, reply, or contradict; to defeat or take away the effect of something. Thus, when a plaintiff in an action produces evidence which raises a presumption (*q.v.*) of the defendant's liability, and the defendant adduces evidence which shows that the presumption is ill-founded, he is said to rebut it. So, on a trial, when a fresh case (that is, a case not merely answering the case of the party who began) is set up by the responding party, and evidence is adduced in support of such fresh case, the party who began may give evidence to rebut it, called rebutting evidence, or proof of a rebutting case.

Rebutter. Under the practice before the Judicature Acts, 1873–75, both at common law and in Chancery, the rebutter was the pleading which followed the surrejoinder (Steph.Pl. 5, 64; Mitford Pl. 321). See PLEADING; REJOINDER.

In the old law of real property, to rebut was to repel or bar a claim. Thus, when a person was sued for land which had been warranted to him by the plaintiff or his ancestor, and he pleaded the warranty as a defence to the action, this was called a rebutter (Co.Litt. 365a; *Termes de la Ley*).

Rebutting evidence, that which is given by one party in a cause to explain, repel, counteract, or disprove evidence produced by the other party.

Recall, to supersede a minister, or deprive him of his office; also to revoke a judgment on a matter of fact.

Recaption, a species of remedy by act of the party which may be resorted to when a man has deprived another of his goods, or wrongfully detains his wife, child or servant; in such a case, the person injured may lawfully claim and retake them, provided he does not do so in a riotous manner, or so as to occasion a breach of the peace (3 Bl.Comm. 4). A request for the return of the property is not essential (*Whatford* v. *Carty* (1960) *The Times,* October 29).

Recaption, Writ of. If pending an action of replevin (*q.v.*) for a distress, the defendant distrained again for the same rent or service, the owner of the goods was not driven to another action of replevin, but was allowed a writ of recaption, by which he recovered the goods and damages for the defendant's contempt of the process of the law in making a second distress while the matter was *sub judice* (Fitz.N.B. 71).

The remedy would now be an application for an injunction or to have the defendant committed for contempt of court.

Recapture. By the doctrine of *postliminium* (*q.v.*) property which has been captured by an enemy and recaptured within twenty-four hours, or before being taken to a place of safety, reverts to its original owner; the rule, however, varies with different nations. Under the Naval Prize Act, 1864, s. 40 (amended by the Prize Act, 1939, s. 1 (2), Sch. Pt. I), British property captured at sea and recaptured at any time afterwards by a British ship or aircraft is to be restored to the owner on his paying to the recaptor prize-salvage (*q.v.*) at a rate to be fixed by the Prize Court (*q.v.*).

Receditur a placitis juris potius quam injuriae et delicta maneant impunita (Bac.Max. 12). (We dispense with the forms of law rather than that crimes and wrongs should be unpunished.) But this maxim cannot be applied generally except where the maxim *inter arma leges silent* (*q.v.*) comes into operation. Bacon quotes it as illustrating various propositions of law such as that if a man recovered by erroneous judgment and had issue two daughters, and one of them was attainted, the writ of error should be brought against both parceners notwithstanding the privity failed in the one.

Receipt, an acknowledgment in writing of having received a sum of money, which is prima facie but not conclusive evidence of payment (*Skaife* v. *Jackson* (1824) 3 B. & C. 421).

A receipt under seal amounts to an estoppel, and is conclusive.

Forgery of a receipt is punishable on indictment under the Forgery Act, 1913, s. 4; Criminal Law Act, 1967, Sch. 3 Pt. III. The offence is triable summarily with the consent of the defendant (Criminal Justice Act, 1967, s. 27).

A stamp duty first imposed in 1783 was progressively *ad valorem,* until 1853, when a uniform 1d. rate was imposed; this was increased to 2d. by the Finance Act, 1920. It was abolished by the Finance Act, 1970, s. 32, Sch. 7 para. 2.

An indorsed cheque is evidence of the receipt of the sum payable by the cheque (*Egg* v. *Barnett* (1800) 3 Esp. 196); so too is an unindorsed cheque (Cheques Act, 1957, s. 3).

In certain real and mixed actions, if a man seised of land in right of his wife was sued in respect of the land and made default, the wife might be received or admitted as a *feme sole* to defend her right. This was called receipt or *defensio juris* (Co.Litt. 352b).

See ACCOUNTABLE RECEIPT.

Receipt of the Exchequer, the legal description of the Exchequer (on its revenue side) before it was reorganised on modern lines: see, *e.g.,* the statutes 1817, 57 Geo. 3, c. 84, and 1834, 4 & 5 Will. 4, c. 15.

Receipt rolls, rolls in the Record Office on which the moneys received by the Exchequer were entered during the reigns of Henry II, Richard I, John, and Henry III. See PELLS OF ISSUE.

Receiver. In an action in the High Court, a receiver is a person appointed by the court, on an interlocutory application, to receive the rents and profits of real estate, or to get in and collect personal property affected by the proceedings, where it appears desirable that he should do so in lieu of the person then having the control of the property, or where the latter is incompetent to do so. The object is to protect the property until the rights of the parties have been ascertained; thus, in an action for the dissolution of a partnership, a receiver is frequently appointed to get in or realise the partnership assets; and under the Partnership Act, 1890, s. 23, a receiver may be appointed over the share of an individual partner (R.S.C., Ord. 30, r. 1). A receiver is an officer of the court, and generally has to give security for the due performance of his duties (Ord. 30, r. 2). See MANAGER.

In bankruptcy the official receiver may be appointed interim receiver, at any time after the presentation of the petition, if that course is necessary for the preservation of the estate (Bankruptcy Act, 1914, s. 8), and it is his duty to act as interim receiver after adjudication until a trustee is appointed (s. 74).

A mortgagee may appoint a receiver of the mortgaged property, if empowered so to do by the mortgage deed or by separate instrument, without having to apply to the court; and by the Law of Property Act, 1925, s. 101, the mortgagee, when the mortgage money has become due, may appoint a receiver of the income of the mortgaged property, or of any part thereof, with certain leasing powers conferred by the Law of Property Act, 1925, s. 99, but such power cannot (s. 109 of the Act of 1925) be exercised until the mortgagee is entitled to exercise the power of sale under the Act (*i.e.,* by s. 103 of the Act of 1925) unless default has been made in payment of the principal, after notice, or interest is in arrear for two months, or there has been other default on the part of the mortgagor. A receiver so appointed is the agent of the mortgagor. A practising barrister may be a receiver; a solicitor in the cause cannot be a receiver unless by consent, and without salary; nor can next friends of infant plaintiffs; nor trustees.

A receiver may be appointed by an interlocutory order of the court in all cases in which it appears to the court to be just or convenient that such order should be made (Judicature Act, 1925, s. 45).

" Receiver " includes consignee or manager appointed by the court (R.S.C., Ord. 1, r. 4) (*Re Newdegate Colliery Co.* [1912] 1 Ch. 468).

A receiver may be appointed by way of equitable execution where the property of a litigant against whom judgment has been obtained cannot be made available by *fi. fa.* or other ordinary process of execution (R.S.C., Ord. 51); as to the appointment of such a receiver, see *Harris* v. *Beauchamp Bros.* [1894] 1 Q.B. 801; *Morgan* v. *Hart* [1914] 2 K.B. 183. As to debenture holders, see the Companies Act, 1948, ss. 102, 366–376.

Receiver and manager, a person appointed to carry on or superintend a trade, business or undertaking in addition to receiving rents and profits, or to get in outstanding property. He has power to deal with the property and to appropriate the proceeds in a proper manner.

Receiver of the Metropolitan Police, a corporation sole in whom all the police property is vested (Metropolitan Police Act, 1829, s. 10; Metropolitan Police (Receiver) Act, 1861). The Receiver is not entitled to recover damages for loss of services of a police constable (*Metropolitan Police Receiver* v. *Croydon Corporation* [1957] 2 Q.B. 154).

Receiver of the Fines, an officer who received the money of all such as compounded with the king upon original writs (1 P. & M. 174).

Receiver of the First Fruits. In 1798, this was an officer of the Court of Exchequer (nominated by the Governors of Queen Anne's Bounty and appointed by the Treasury) whose office was worth about £50 a year after payment of expenses (*Commons Committees' Reports* (1803), Vol. 13, pp. 201, 319). It seems to have been a sinecure.

Receiver-General, an officer of the Duchy Court of Lancaster who receives the revenue of the Duchy.

Receiver-General of Inland Revenue, an officer of the Inland Revenue whose office was abolished by the Public Accounts and Charges Act, 1891, s. 1; moneys formerly receivable by him are now paid direct into the Bank of England.

Receiver-General of the Muster Rolls, an officer mentioned in the statute 1588, 35 Eliz. 1, c. 4.

Receivers of wreck, officers appointed by the Department of Trade, under the Merchant Shipping Act, 1894, ss. 5, 6, for the preservation of wreck, etc. The duties of a receiver of wreck are to take steps for the preservation of any vessel stranded or in distress within his district (ss. 511–513); to receive and take possession of all articles washed on shore from the vessel (s. 519); to suppress plunder and disorder (s. 514); to institute an examination on oath with respect to the vessel (s. 517); and, if necessary, to sell the vessel, cargo or wreck (s. 522). See WRECK.

Receiving order, an order of the court, on the petition of a creditor, or of the debtor himself, granted for the protection of the estate on an act of bankruptcy being established. The order constitutes the official receiver the receiver of the debtor's property. Legal proceedings against the person or property of the debtor in respect of debts provable in bankruptcy can thenceforth be restrained by the official receiver. The effect of the order is that unless a scheme or composition is accepted by the creditors the debtor may be adjudged bankrupt (Bankruptcy Act, 1914, ss. 3, 7, 37 (2), 107 (4)). Receiving orders in bankruptcy, whether or not known to affect land, must be registered at the Land Registry every five years or else the title of the trustee in bankruptcy will be void against a purchaser of a legal estate in good faith for money or money's worth without notice of an available act of bankruptcy under a conveyance made after the date of registration of the bankruptcy petition as a pending action, unless at the date of the conveyance either the registration of the pending action is in force or the receiving order is registered (Land Charges Act, 1972, ss. 6, 8). See BANKRUPTCY NOTICE.

Receiving stolen goods. See HANDLING STOLEN GOODS.

Recent possession. See POSSESSION.

Receptus, an arbitrator (Civil Law).

Recession, a re-grant.

Recidive [Fr.], a relapse; the commission of a second offence.

Recipitur in modum recipientis (5 Bing. N.C. 461). See QUICQUID SOLVITUR, ETC.

Reciprocity, mutuality (*q.v.*). The term is used in international law to denote the relation existing between two States when each of them gives the subjects of the other certain privileges, on condition that its own subjects shall enjoy similar privileges at the hands of the other State. See, for example, the Maintenance Orders (Reciprocal Enforcement) Act, 1972.

Recitals, statements in a deed, agreement or other formal instrument, introduced to explain or lead up to the operative part of the instrument. They are generally divided into narrative recitals, which set forth the facts on which the instrument is based; and introductory recitals, which explain the motive for the operative part. Thus, in an assignment of leasehold property, the deed commences by reciting the lease, that is, by stating that by a lease of such and such a date made between such and such parties the property was demised to the lessee for a certain term: this is a narrative recital; the deed then recites that the assignee has agreed with the assignor (the original lessee) for the purchase of the property for the residue of the term: this is an introductory recital, being followed immediately by the operative part or assignment. A formal recital always commences with the word " whereas."

A recital is evidence as against the parties to the instrument and those claiming under them; and in an action on the instrument itself (though not on a collateral matter) the recitals operate as an estoppel (*q.v.*). By the Law of Property Act, 1925, s. 45 (6), on the sale of land, recitals, statements, and description of facts, matters, and parties contained in deeds, instruments, Acts of Parliament, or statutory declarations twenty years old at the date of the contract are made prima facie evidence of the truth of such facts, etc.

If the recitals in a deed are clear and the operative part is ambiguous, the recitals govern the construction. If the recitals are ambiguous, and the operative part is clear, the operative part must prevail. If both the recitals and the operative part are clear, but they are inconsistent with each other, the operative part is to be preferred (*Ex p. Dawes* (1886) 17 Q.B.D. at p. 286).

Reclaimed animals, animals made tame by art, industry, or education, whereby a qualified property may be acquired in them. See ANIMALS FERAE NATURAE.

Reclaiming, the action of a lord pursuing, prosecuting, and recalling his vassal, who had gone to live in another place without his permission; also the demanding of a thing or person to be delivered up or surrendered to the prince or State it properly belongs to, when by some irregular means it has come into the possession of another.

Recognisance. At common law a recognisance is an obligation or bond acknowledged before some court of record or magistrate duly authorised, or before special commissioners appointed by the Crown, and afterwards entered of record, that is, enrolled in some court of record (*q.v.*). The person acknowledging it, that is, the person bound by it, is called the conusor (or cognisor), and the person in whose favour it is made, the conusee (or cognisee). The object of a recognisance is to secure the performance of some act by the conusor, such as to appear before the Crown Court (Courts Act, 1971, s. 13 (1)), to keep the peace, to pay a debt, to pay costs, etc. See ENROLMENT; PETTY BAG OFFICE.

Any reference in any enactment to a recognisance includes, unless the context otherwise requires, a reference to any other description of security given instead of a recognisance (Courts Act, 1941, s. 13 (5)).

Magistrates may make an attachment of earnings order to secure the payment of a forfeited recognisance. See ATTACHMENT.

Recognisances are not to operate as a charge on land or the unpaid purchase-money of any land unless a writ or order for the purpose of enforcing the recognisance is registered at the Land Registry (Law of Property Act, 1925, s. 195 (4); Land Charges Act, 1972, s. 6).

Formerly, a recognisance, like a judgment, bound the lands of the conusor. (See JUDGMENT.) A recognisance, however, still has priority over the ordinary debts of the conusor on his death. (See ASSETS.) The most usual way of enforcing a recognisance is by estreat (*q.v.*): procedure by way of *scire facias* (*q.v.*) no longer applies.

Recognisances by statute were those created under the statute 1531, 23 Hen. 8, c. 6, and called recognisances in the nature of statute staples, because they had the same formalities and effects as statute staples, except that they were acknowledged before judges instead of mayors. See STAPLE; STATUTE MERCHANT.

In criminal law, a person who has been found guilty of an offence may in many cases be required to enter into a recognisance by which he binds himself to keep the peace and be of good behaviour for a certain period. As to recognisances given in courts of summary jurisdiction, and the mode of their enforcement, see the Magistrates' Courts Act, 1952, ss. 91–97; Criminal Justice Act, 1967, Sch. 6; Local Government Act, 1972, Sch. 30. Recognisances are given orally in courts of record. See BAIL; BIND OVER; ESTREAT.

For the powers of the court in relation to forfeited recognisances see the Powers of Criminal Courts Act, 1973, ss. 31, 32.

Recognisee, the conusee in a recognisance (*q.v.*).

Recognisor, the conusor in a recognisance (*q.v.*).

Recognition, an acknowledgment. In early times it meant the inquiry held by recognitors (*q.v.*).

It is the title of the statute 1603, 1 Jac.

1, c. 1, whereby Parliament acknowledged the Crown of England rightfully to have descended to James I on the death of Elizabeth I.

Recognitione adnullanda per vim et duritiem facta, De, a writ which lay to the justices of the Common Bench directing them to send a record (*q.v.*) as to a recognisance which the recognisor alleged to have been acknowledged by force and duress, in order that, if such should appear to have been the case, the recognisance might be annulled (Reg. Orig. 183).

Recognitors, the jurors in an assize of novel disseisin or the like, because they acknowledged a disseisin by their verdict (5 Bract.; Co.Litt. 227b). See ASSISE.

Récolement [Fr.], re-examination.

Recommendation to mercy. See MERCY, ETC.

Reconduction, a relocation; a renewal of a lease (Civil Law).

Reconstruction of a company. Upon a voluntary winding up the company may sell its undertaking for property of (including profits in) the purchasing company (Companies Act, 1948, s. 287).

A company which is being wound up may be reconstructed by arrangement with its creditors under ss. 206–209.

Recontinuance. This signified that a person had recovered an incorporeal hereditament of which he had been wrongfully deprived. Thus, where A was disseised of a manor, whereunto an advowson was appendant, and a stranger (*i.e.*, neither A nor the disseisor) usurped the advowson, if the disseisee A entered into the manor, the advowson which was severed by the usurpation was recontinued. Recontinuance differed from a remitter, for there could not be a remitter unless there were two titles, but there might be a recontinuance where there was but one (Co.Litt. 363b). See DISCONTINUANCE; REMITTER.

Reconvention, an action by a defendant against a plaintiff in a former action; a cross-bill or litigation (Civil Law).

Reconversion, that imaginary process by which a prior constructive conversion is annulled and the converted property restored in contemplation of law to its original state. Thus, if real estate is devised to A upon trust to sell and to pay the proceeds to B, the realty, by virtue of this absolute trust, is constructively converted into personal estate; but if B, before the property is sold, elects to take it as land, it is then said to be reconverted, and A is bound to convey the land to him accordingly. This is called reconversion by act of the party. The right of reconversion cannot be exercised to the prejudice of other persons (*e.g.*, joint owners or remaindermen). Reconversion by operation of law is where the property originally directed to be converted comes into the possession of a person absolutely entitled to dispose of it, and is left by him in its original condition, without any declaration of his intention regarding it. See RESULT.

Reconveyance. This takes place where a mortgage debt is paid off, and the mortgaged property is conveyed again to the mortgagor or his representatives free from the mortgage debt. The operative words used in a reconveyance are the same as those which would be used if it were an ordinary conveyance between the parties, the *habendum* expressing that the property is discharged from the debt. The reconveyance is usually endorsed on the mortgage. Reconveyances are now seldom executed as the Law of Property Act, 1925, s. 115, provides that a receipt endorsed on a mortgage has the same effect without any formal reconveyance. See MORTGAGE; PROVISO FOR REDEMPTION; REDEMPTION.

Record. Records are the memorials of the legislature, and of the courts of justice, which are authentic beyond all matter of contradiction (Gilb. Ev. 5).

But legally records are restricted to the rolls of such courts as are courts of record, and do not include the rolls of inferior courts nor of any other courts which proceed not *secundum legem et consuetudinem Angliae*. The rolls being the records or memorials of the judges of the courts of record import in them such credit and verity as to admit no averment, plea, or proof to the contrary. If such a record is alleged, and it is pleaded that there is no such record, it is to be tried only by itself (Co.Litt. 260a). See NUL TIEL RECORD, ETC., RES JUDICATA; TRIAL.

Records are of the following principal kinds: Acts of Parliament, attainders and other parliamentary proceedings; judgments, fines, inquisitions, extents, returns to writs and other proceedings of courts of record; and proceedings on the revenue side of the Exchequer, recognisances, Crown grants, letters patent, and other instruments of an extrajudicial nature which have been enrolled. See PUBLIC RECORDS; RECORD OFFICE.

Another division is into judicial, as an attainder; ministerial, on oath, being an office or inquisition found; and by way of conveyance, as a deed enrolled.

Under the old common law practice, the *nisi prius* record was a copy of the issue (*q.v.*) as delivered in the action, engrossed on parchment. It was the official statement of the writ and pleadings for the use of the judge at *nisi prius*; to it were annexed the particulars of demand and set-off, if any (see PARTICULARS); and on it were subsequently entered the *postea* (*q.v.*) and judgment. The record was delivered to the proper officer of the court (generally the associate), which was commonly called entering the record, and it was retained by him until the case was disposed of, unless the plaintiff was not prepared to proceed with the trial, in which case he could withdraw the record, so as to prevent the trial from going on (Chitty, Pr. 361, 381). Now, in lieu of making up the record, the party entering the action for trial delivers to the officer two copies of the pleadings, one of which is for the use of the judge (R.S.C., Ord. 36, r. 30), and is sometimes referred to as the record. The practice of withdrawing the record has been abolished; but the court may order the action to be discontinued, on terms. See DISCONTINUANCE.

The Record Offices of the Supreme Court are now merged in the Central Office (R.S.C., Ord. 61).

The volume containing the case, evidence and transcripts of appellants and respondents on appeal to the House of Lords or Privy Council is also called the record.

As to local government records, see the Local Government (Records) Act, 1962; London Government Act, 1963, ss. 83, 93, Sch. 17 para. 27, Sch. 18 Pt. II;

Local Government Act, 1972, s. 272 (1), Sch. 30.

Record and writ clerks, three officers of the Court of Chancery, appointed under the Court of Chancery Act, 1842. As to their duties, see that Act and the Court of Chancery Act, 1852, s. 46, and the Charitable Trusts Amendment Act, 1855, s. 11. They were attached to the Supreme Court by the Judicature Act, 1873, s. 77, and made masters by the Judicature (Officers) Act, 1879; see now the Judicature Act, 1925, ss. 104–106. See CLERKS OF RECORDS AND WRITS.

Record, Conveyances by. Acts of Parliament under which land passes, royal grants, fines and common recoveries are all matters of record.

Record, Courts of, courts whose judicial acts and proceedings are enrolled for perpetual memorial and testimony, which rolls are called the records of the court, and are of such high and supereminent authority that their truth is not to be called in question. Courts of record are of two classes, superior and inferior. Superior courts of record include the House of Lords, the Judicial Committee, the Court of Appeal, the High Court, and the Crown Court. The county courts, coroners' courts and others are inferior courts of record. Every superior court of record has authority to fine and imprison for contempt of its authority; an inferior court of record can only commit for contempts committed in open court, *in facie curiae* (Co.Litt. 117b, 260a). See COURT.

Record, Debts of, those which appear to be due by the evidence of a court of record, such as a judgment, recognisance, etc. Since the Administration of Estates Act, 1869, all specialty and simple contract debts of deceased persons stand in equal degree. See DEBT.

Record Office. This office was established by the Public Record Office Act, 1838, which placed it under the superintendence of the Master of the Rolls (*q.v.*) whose responsibilities were transferred to the Lord Chancellor by the Public Records Act, 1958. The Keeper of the Records is, for practical purposes, the head of the office. The office, the full title of which is the Public Record Office, is accommodated in a building in Chancery Lane, London. Its museum was opened in 1902. The Record Office is sometimes called the Rolls Office (*q.v.*).

Record, Trial by. Before the Judicature Acts, 1873–75, where it appeared on the pleadings in an action that one party alleged and the other party denied the existence of a record (such as a judgment) this raised the issue known as *nul tiel record* (*q.v.*), and the court would thereupon order a trial by inspection and examination of the record. This was called a trial by record. Failing proof of the record, judgment was given for the party who had denied its existence. See FAILURE OF RECORD.

Recordari facias loquelam (abbreviated *re. fa. lo.*), a writ used to remove a suit from an inferior court not of record into one of the superior courts of common law: *e.g.*, a suit of replevin in the sheriff's county court, so called because it commanded the sheriff to make a record of the plaint and other proceedings in the county court and then to send up the cause (Fitz.N.B. 70). See CERTIORARI.

Recorded delivery. See the Recorded Delivery Service Act, 1962; Post Office Act, 1969, s. 5.

Recorder, prior to 1972, a barrister appointed by the Crown under the Municipal Corporations Act, 1882, to act as a justice of the peace in a borough having a separate court of quarter sessions. By virtue of his office he was the sole judge of the court of quarter sessions and of any civil court of record in the borough (other than the county court). Recorders also existed in the places listed in the Municipal Corporations Act, 1883, not subject to the Municipal Corporations Act, 1882.

Courts of quarter sessions were abolished by the Courts Act, 1971, s. 3, and their jurisdiction transferred to the Crown Court (*q.v.*). The Recorders of London, Liverpool and Manchester became circuit judges (Courts Act, 1971, s. 16, Sch. 2). The offices of recorder and deputy, assisstant or temporary recorder (except that of the Recorder of London) were also abolished (Courts Act, 1971, s. 44).

The Crown may now appoint paid recorders to act as part-time judges of the Crown Court and to carry out such other judicial functions as may be conferred on them by statute. A recorder so appointed must be a barrister or solicitor of at least ten years' standing. The retirement age of a recorder is seventy-two (Courts Act, 1971, ss. 4, 21). A recorder may, on the request of the Lord Chancellor, sit as a High Court judge (s. 23) and is capable of sitting as a judge of any county court (s. 20 (3)). A recorder must take the oath of allegiance and the judicial oath (s. 22). Honorary recorders may be appointed under s. 54.

Any judge who on December 31, 1971, held the office of Recorder of Liverpool or Recorder of Manchester should continue to be addressed as "My Lord" when sitting in the Crown Court either at Liverpool or Manchester (Practice Direction dated December 21, 1971 [1972] 1 W.L.R. 117). Any recorder appointed under s. 21 of the Courts Act, 1971, when sitting as such should be addressed in court as " sir " (Practice Direction dated December 21, 1971 [1972] 1 W.L.R. 117).

Limitations are placed on a recorder practising at a court where he also sits. See *Annual Statement of the Senate of the Inns of Court and the Bar, 1974–75*, p. 41.

Recorder of London, one of the justices of oyer and terminer, and a justice of the peace of the *quorum* for putting the laws in execution for the preservation of the peace and government of the City of London. Being the mouth of the City, he delivers the sentences and judgments of the court therein, and also certifies and records the City customs, etc. He is chosen by the Lord Mayor and aldermen, and attends the business of the City when summoned by the Lord Mayor, etc.; but by the Local Government Act, 1888, s. 42 (14), no recorder may exercise any judicial functions unless appointed by the sovereign to exercise such functions.

The Courts Act, 1971, which, in effect abolished the office of recorder (*q.v.*), preserved that of the Recorder of London (s. 44). On January 1, 1972, he became by virtue of his office a circuit judge (Courts Act, 1971, s. 16, Sch. 2) and

thereby of the Central Criminal Court (s. 4 (7)).

He was formerly not disqualified by office from being a member of the House of Commons; but he is now disqualified by the House of Commons Disqualification Act, 1975, Sch. 1.

Recorder's Act, the Larceny Act, 1868, which was passed at the instance of Mr. Russell Gurney, recorder of the City of London, 1857–78. In 1865 he had been elected to the House of Commons, of which he was a member until his death in 1878: and no Lord Chancellor protested.

Records, Gramophone. These are subject to the Copyright Act, 1956, s. 12; as to reproducing broadcast music, see the Copyright Act, 1956, s. 40, the Dramatic and Musical Performers' Protection Act, 1958, and the Performers' Protection Acts, 1963 and 1972.

Recoup, to keep back something due; to recompense.

Recourse. See WITHOUT RECOURSE, ETC.

Recoverer, the demandant in a common recovery after judgment. It was used in the fifteenth century as a synonym of recovery (*q.v.*) in the sense of common recovery.

Recovery, where a person obtains something which has been wrongfully taken or withheld from him, or to which he is otherwise entitled. See REMEDY.

Proceedings for the recovery of land from a person wrongfully in possession of it are taken in the High Court, or in the county courts, or before the justices. In the High Court the proceedings are of two kinds. The ordinary action for the recovery of land follows the same course as any other action, except in some cases as regards service of the writ (see SERVICE OF PROCESS) and appearance (*q.v.*) (see JOINDER). It is a substitute for the old action of ejectment (*q.v.*).

Under the Common Law Procedure Act, 1852, ss. 213 *et seq.*, an action for recovery of land could be brought where there was a contract of tenancy in writing, and the tenant held over after the determination of the tenancy; the tenant could be ordered to give bail by recognisance with two sureties, in default of which judgment was given for the plaintiff. See BAIL.

An action may be brought in a county court for the recovery of land where the net annual value for rating does not exceed £400 (County Courts Act, 1959, s. 48). See EJECTMENT.

As to the recovery of deserted premises, see DESERTED PREMISES.

A recovery or common recovery was a common assurance by matter of record, in fraud of the statute *De Donis*, 1285, whereby a tenant in tail in possession enlarged his estate tail into a fee simple and so barred the entail, and all remainders and reversions expectant thereon, with all conditions and collateral limitations annexed to them, and subsequent charges subordinate to the entail. But incumbrances on the estate tail equally affected such fee simple, and any estate or interest prior to the entail remained undisturbed.

This assurance consisted of two parts: the recovery itself, which was a fictitious real action in the Court of Common Pleas, carried on to judgment, and founded on the supposition of an adverse claim; and the recovery-deed, which was partly a preparatory step to suffering the recovery, and partly a declaration of the uses when suffered.

This method of barring an estate tail by a fictitious real action was based upon the doctrine that the tenant in tail could sell the entailed lands for an estate in fee simple, provided that judgment was obtained in favour of the tenant in tail and his heirs against someone for lands of equal value, and the law of warranty as applied in actions for recovery of land.

To bar the entail a tenant in tail adopted this procedure by means of a fictitious and collusive action. A, the tenant in tail, procured a friend D (the demandant) to bring an action for recovery of land against him. A pretended that he had bought the land from C and vouched C to warranty. C was a man of no substance (generally the crier of the court), who was willing to allow a judgment to be given against him. C admitted, contrary to the fact, that he had sold the land to A and craved leave to imparl with him, *i.e.*, to

consult with him outside the court. C failed to return, and judgment was therefore given in favour of D against A and in favour of A and his issue for land of equal value against C. D, becoming thus possessed of the fee simple, conveyed the land in fee simple to A or dealt with it as directed by him. This right to suffer a common recovery was considered as an incident of an estate tail. In later times the proceedings became more complicated; it was found inexpedient that the action should be brought against the tenant in tail himself, and so another person was brought into the action. The land was first conveyed by the tenant in tail to a friend, the tenant to the *praecipe* (so called because he was to be served with the *praecipe* or writ). The demandant then brought the action against the tenant to the *praecipe*; the latter vouched the tenant in tail to warranty; he in his turn vouched the court crier (the common vouchee) to warranty. The court crier admitted (untruly) that he had sold the land to the tenant in tail and craved leave to imparl with him outside the court. In his absence judgment was given by default that the lands belonged to the demandant in fee simple and that the common vouchee must give lands of equal value to the tenant in tail and his heirs (*Taltarum's Case* (1472) Y.B. 12 Edw. 4, 19). See PRAECIPE

This was called a recovery with double voucher, and effectually barred the entail, with every latent interest and all reversions and remainders expectant thereon. The only possible case in which a remainder with treble voucher was necessary was in the instance in which a tenant in tail created an entail derived out of his own, and the two entails were, in point of estate or of right, existing at one time in distinct persons, and both entails were to be barred.

To perfect the legal title, and to give a seisin to the demandant, a writ of *habere facias seisinam* must have been issued after judgment, and seisin duly delivered to him, whereupon the uses arose. This writ was returned by the sheriff, and the proceedings exemplified by the clerk of the court for the purpose of proving the suffering of the recovery. In a recovery deed the proper parties, either alone or jointly with other persons, were the person who had the immediate freehold, the intended vouchee, the intended tenant and the intended demandant (1 Shep.Touch. c. 3; 2 Bl. Comm. 357; 1 Prest.Conv. c. 1; 1 Hall. Cons.Hist. c. i. 12).

An estate tail might also be barred by a fine (*q.v.*). A friend brought an action of recovery against the tenant in tail. The action was then settled upon the terms that the friend should have the lands in fee simple and that the tenant in tail should be paid a sum of money as consideration. This compromise was entered on the rolls of the court. The effect of a fine varied from time to time, but eventually it became conclusive not only against the tenant in tail but against his issue, but inoperative as to remainders and reversions. See FINE.

These fictions were abolished by the Fines and Recoveries Act, 1833, which substituted a short deed, duly enrolled, as the mode of barring an estate tail. See TAIL.

In some manors estates tail in copyholds were barred by customary recoveries.

Recreant, yielding. See CRAVEN.

Recreation. Every water authority (see WATER) and statutory water undertaker may take steps to allow the use of water and land under their control for purposes of recreation (Water Act, 1973, ss. 20, 21).

Recreation grounds. The village green was the primitive recreation ground: on it the villagers had a limited right of recreation (see JUS SPATIANDI). Provision was made by Inclosure Acts for the appropriation of commons or parts of commons as places of recreation for the inhabitants of the vicinity: see for instance, the Inclosure Act, 1845, ss. 30, 73, and the Inclosure Act, 1846, s. 4, as extended by the Commons Act, 1876, ss. 22, 23. For the power of local authorities to provide recreation grounds see PLEASURE-GROUNDS.

Facilities for recreation may be afforded under the Countryside Act, 1968.

The Town Gardens Protection Act 1863, contains provisions for turning into public gardens derelict squares, etc., in cities and boroughs. See NATIONAL TRUST; OPEN SPACE.

Recrimination, a charge made by an accused person against the accuser.

Recta prisa regis (the lawful due of the king), the king's right to prisage, or taking of one butt or pipe of wine before, and another behind, the mast, as a custom for every ship laden with wines. See PRISAGE.

Rectification; Rectify. To rectify is to correct or define something which is erroneous or doubtful. Thus, where the parties to an agreement have determined to embody its terms in the appropriate and conclusive form, but the instrument meant to effect this purpose (*e.g.,* a conveyance, settlement, etc.) is by mutual mistake so framed as not to express the real intention of the parties, an action may be brought in the Chancery Division to have it rectified (Judicature Act, 1925, s. 56); but every Division can give effect to a claim for rectification in any action before it. The rectification is generally effected by endorsing on the instrument a copy of the judgment or order, declaring in what respects the instrument requires to be rectified. (See MISTAKE; RESCISSION.) County courts have a like jurisdiction where the relief sought does not exceed £5,000 in value (County Courts Act, 1959, s. 52; Administration of Justice Act, 1969, s. 5).

The power to rectify a written document which, as drawn, does not express the mutual and concurrent intention of the parties is a power which the courts of equity always possessed; but such jurisdiction is exercised with the greatest care and caution, and only on evidence of the clearest and most satisfactory description. But the power of rectification is not strictly confined to a case of common mistake (*A. Roberts & Co.* v. *Leicestershire C.C.* [1961] Ch. 555). That a tax benefit is obtained by rectification is no bar to an order (*Re Colebrook's Conveyances* [1972] 1 W.L.R. 1397).

Rectification has been made in almost every kind of instrument, *e.g.,* in marriage settlements (*Cogan* v. *Duffield* (1876) 2 Ch.D. 46), in agreements concerning land (*Olley* v. *Fisher* (1886) 34 Ch.D. 367), in conveyances (*White* v. *White* (1872) L.R. 15 Eq. 247), and in leases (*Cowan* v.

Truefitt [1899] 2 Ch. 309). As to wills, see *Vaughan* v. *Clerk* (1902) 87 L.T. 144; *Re Schott* [1901] P. 190.

Rectification also means an alteration correcting an entry in a register, *e.g.,* company, patents, trade marks, etc.

An action to rectify or ascertain the boundaries of two adjoining pieces of land may be brought in the Chancery Division. The Minister of Agriculture, Fisheries and Food has power, under the Inclosure Acts, 1845 to 1878, to settle confused boundaries in certain cases. See BOUNDARY.

Rectitudo, right or justice; legal dues; tribute or payment.

Recto, Breve de, a writ of right, which was of so high a nature that, as other writs in real actions were only to recover the possession of the land, etc., in question, this aimed to recover the seisin and the property, and thereby both the rights of possession and property were tried together.

There were two species: (1) writ of right patent, so called because it was sent open, and was the highest writ lying for him who had a fee simple in the lands or tenements sued for, against the tenant of the freehold at least, and in no other case; this writ was likewise called *breve magnum de recto*; (2) writ of right close, which was brought where one held lands and tenements by charter in ancient demesne in fee simple, fee tail, or for term of life, or in dower, and was disseised (Co.Litt. 158b; Jacob).

All writs of right except those relating to dower (*q.v.*) were abolished by the Real Property Limitation Act, 1833, s. 36. See ACTION, POSSESSORY; RIGHT CLOSE, ETC.

Recto de advocatione ecclesiae, a writ which lay at common law for the owner in fee of an advowson, where the clerk of the church died and a stranger presented a clerk to the church (Fitz.N.B. 30).

Recto de custodiae terrae et haeredis, a writ which lay for the lord of a tenant holding of him in chivalry, where the tenant died and a stranger both entered the land and took the body of the heir (Fitz.N.B. 139; Reg.Orig. 161).

It disappeared in 1660 with the Court of Wards and Liveries.

Recto de dote, a writ of right of dower which lay for a widow who alleged that she had received only part of her dower and claimed the residue against the heir of her husband (Fitz.N.B. 7, 8, 147; Co. Litt. 32, 38).

It was abolished by the Common Law Procedure Act, 1860, s. 26, which substituted a writ of summons. See DOWER.

Recto de dote unde nihil habet, a writ which lay for a widow who had received no part of her dower (Old Nat.Br. 6; Reg.Orig. 170).

It was abolished by the Common Law Procedure Act, 1860.

Recto de rationabili parte, a writ of right, of the reasonable part, which lay between privies in blood, as brothers of gavelkind, sisters, and other coparceners, for land in fee simple (Fitz.N.B. 9). See RATIONABILI PARTE.

Recto quando (or quia) dominus remisit curiam, a writ of right when (or because) the lord had remitted his court, which lay where lands or tenements in the seigniory of any land were in demand by a writ of right (Fitz.N.B. 16).

Recto sur disclaimer, a writ which lay in the Common Pleas for a lord whose tenant disclaimed to hold of him, that is to say, alleged that he did not hold of him. The question of title was tried upon this writ (Old Nat.Br. 150).

Rector, a governor; in ecclesiastical law, either a layman, sometimes called a lay rector or lay impropriator, who has that part of the revenues of a church which before the dissolution of the monasteries by Henry VIII was appropriated to a monastery, the incumbent generally being a vicar; or, in cases where the living had not been so impropriated, a spiritual person, the parson, who has the whole revenues together with the cure of souls (1 Bl.Comm. 384).

A rector is an officer of the church, having a benefice with cure of souls, that is, spiritual charge of his parishioners, with the right and duty of celebrating services and sacraments in the church. He obtains his benefice by ordination, presentation, institution, and induction (*q.v.*). He has an exclusive title to all the emoluments of the living, that is, the parsonage house and glebe, etc. An impropriator (*q.v.*) is sometimes called a lay rector; and an appropriator can properly be described as an appropriate rector. *Rector ecclesiae* meant a clerk having the parsonage of a vicarage which was endowed, while *rector ecclesiae parochialis* meant one having care and charge of a parish church. *Rector sinecure* was one without cure of souls. See ADVOWSON; APPROPRIATION; BENEFICE; PROPRIETARY CHAPELS.

Rectorial tithes, great or predial tithes. See TITHES.

Rectory, a spiritual non-impropriated living, composed of land, and formerly tithes and other oblations of the people, separate or dedicate to God, in any congregation for the service of the church there, and for the maintenance of the governor or the minister thereof, to whose charge the same is committed (Spelman).

It also means the house in which the rector resides. By the grant of a rectory or parsonage will pass the house and glebe and offerings belonging to it (Shep. Touch. 93).

A rectory is a certain portion of land and offerings established by law for the maintenance of an incumbent having the cure of souls within the parish of which he is rector. It is not essential that there should be a house, but the term is popularly applied only to the house which almost invariably is upon the land or glebe.

A sinecure rectory was one in which there were both a rector and vicar, the latter being entrusted with the cure of souls. Such rectories were practically abolished by the Ecclesiastical Commissioners Act, 1840, ss. 48, 54, 55, 71.

Rectum, right; also a trial or accusation.

Esse ad rectum in curia meant the same as *stare ad rectum,* to stand one's trial or to abide by the decision of a court.

Rectum esse, to be right in court.

Rectum rogare, to ask for right; to petition the judge to do right (Leg.Inae. c. 9).

Rectum, Stare ad, to stand trial, or abide by the sentence of the court (Hoved. 655).

Rectus in curia (right in the law), one who stood at the bar of a court and no

accusation was made against him (2 Smith, De Repub.Angl., c. 3). It also meant one whose outlawry had been reversed.

Recuperatores, judges to whom the praetor referred a question (Civil Law).

Recusants, a generic term applied after the Reformation to those who denied the supremacy of the king in matters ecclesiastical and refused to attend the services of the Church of England. At first there was no clear distinction made between various kinds of recusants. Thus, the Act of Uniformity, 1558, s. 4, imposed penalties of small amount upon all persons failing to attend the parish church. The statute 1592, 35 Eliz. 1, c. 2, entitled an Act against Popish Recusants, was however, specially directed against Roman Catholics, to whom the title of recusant came more especially to be applied. That statute, together with the statute 1605, 3 Jac. 1, c. 4, imposed heavy penalties on Roman Catholics who failed to receive the communion of the established church and to attend its services. An oath against transubstantiation was required by the statute 1672, 25 Car. 2, c. 2, entitled an Act for preventing dangers which may happen from Popish Recusants; and from this time other recusants came to be known distinctively as Protestant Dissenters. See NONCONFORMIST; NONJUROR; PAPIST; ROMAN CATHOLICS; TEST ACT.

By Canons 65, 66, ministers are enjoined to denounce recusants, and ministers being preachers are enjoined to labour diligently with them from time to time thereby to reclaim them from their errors.

Recusatio judicis, a refusal of, or exception to a judge upon any suspicion of partiality (Civil Law).

Red or **Rede** [Sax. *raed*], advice.

Red Book of the Exchequer [*liber rubens scaccarii*], an ancient record, wherein are registered the names of those who held lands *per baroniam* in the time of Henry II (Ryley, 667; Co.Litt. 68b, n. 7).

It is believed to have been compiled before 1234 by Alexander de Swereford, who before that year was an official in the Exchequer, and from 1234 to his death in 1246 was a baron of the Exchequer (*q.v.*). He compiled it in order that there might be a permanent record of the liability of Crown tenants for the various incidents of their tenure. But it was much more than that. It is a veritable encyclopedia of everything which might be useful to the officers of the Exchequer. It contained a register of documents relating to Crown property; forms of writs; directions as to procedure; and oaths to be taken by the officers of State, which were actually in use till quite recent times. Down to about 1375 numerous additions were made to the book, and during the subsequent two centuries some more were made.

The book was always of great authority, and was second only to Domesday in importance as a register. It was in the custody of the King's Remembrancer from the earliest times down to 1870, when it was transferred to the Master of the Rolls. It was edited (as No. 99 of the Rolls Series) by Hubert Hall in 1896.

Red Cross. See GENEVA CONVENTIONS.

Red ensign. See FLAG.

Red game, grouse (*q.v.*) as distinguished from black game (*q.v.*).

Reddendo singula singulis. A clause in an instrument is said to be read *reddendo singula singulis* (by giving each to each) when one of two provisions in one sentence is appropriated to one of two objects in another sentence, and the other provision is similarly appropriated to the other object. Thus, if a testator makes a will in these terms: "I devise and bequeath all my real and personal property to A," it will be construed *reddendo singula singulis* by applying "devise" to "real property," and "bequeath" to "personal property." Similarly, in such a phrase as "If anyone shall draw or load a sword or gun," the word "draw" is applied to "sword" only, and the word "load" to "gun" only, the former verb to the former noun, and the latter to the latter, because it is impossible to load a sword or draw a gun.

Reddendum (that which is to be paid or rendered), the clause in a lease which specifies the amount of the rent and the time at which it is payable. It commonly and properly succeeds the *habendum* and is usually made by the words "yielding and paying," or similiar expressions im-

porting a covenant if executed by the lessee. See DEED.

Reddidit se (he gave himself up). In connection with the old law of bail, under which a defendant in a pending civil action was arrested in default of finding bail, the term was used where a defendant who had found bail afterwards surrendered himself so as to discharge his bailsmen (2 Lill.Abr. 430).

Redditarium, a rental of an estate or manor.

Redditarius, a renter or tenant (Cowel).

Reddition, a surrendering or restoring; a formal admission in the course of legal proceedings that lands were the property, not of the person making the admission, but of him who sought to recover them (Tomlin).

Redditus, rent. The more correct form of the word is *reditus,* but the form *redditus* is generally used in the old books.

Redditus alibi. See ALBA FIRMA.

Redditus assisus, a set or standing rent. See ASSIZE RENT.

Redditus capitales, chief-rents. See RENT.

Redditus nigri. See ALBA FIRMA.

Redditus quieti, quit-rents. See RENT.

Redditus siccus, rent-seck. See RENT.

Redeem, to buy back. See REDEMPTION.

Redeemable dead rent, a rent payable under a mining lease on the terms that where the minimum rent is in excess of a royalty that excess may be redeemed out of subsequent periods when the royalties exceed the minimum rent.

Redeemable preference shares, preference shares issued on the terms that they may be redeemed out of profits or out of the proceeds of a fresh issue of shares (Companies Act, 1948, s. 58).

Redeemable rights, rights which return to the conveyer or disposer of land, etc., upon payment of the sum for which such rights are granted.

Re-delivery, a yielding and delivering back of a thing.

Re-demise, a re-granting of land demised or released. See DEMISE AND REDEMISE.

Redemption [Lat. *redimere,* to buy back], where a person having the right to do so pays off a mortgage debt or charge upon property, and thus buys back the property; he thereupon becomes entitled to have it reconveyed to him by the mortgagee or creditor. An action or suit for redemption is one brought to compel the mortgagee to reconvey the property on payment of the debt and interest. See EQUITY OF REDEMPTION; PROVISO FOR REDEMPTION; RECONVEYANCE.

By the Law of Property Act, 1925, s. 95, where a mortgagor is entitled to redeem, he may require the mortgagee, instead of reconveying to assign the mortgage debt and convey the mortgaged property to any third person, as the mortgagor directs. This provision does not apply where the mortgagee is or has been in possession; but in all other cases it applies notwithstanding any stipulation by the parties to the contrary.

Redemption also means the commutation or substitution of one lump payment for a succession of annual ones, *e.g.,* in case of land tax and tithe redemption annuities.

As to the redemption of quit-rents, etc., see RENT.

Red-handed, with the marks of crime fresh on him.

Redhibition, an action allowed to a buyer by which to annul the sale of some movable, and to oblige the seller to take it back again upon the buyer finding it damaged, or that there was some deceit (Civil Law).

Rediffusion. As to the rating of rediffusion undertakings, see the Local Government Act, 1974, s. 19, Sch. 3.

Redisseisin. Where a person, having been disseised, recovered seisin of his freehold and possession had been delivered by the sheriff, but he was again disseised by the same disseisor, this was a redisseisin, for which, under the Statute of Merton, 1235, the redisseisor was liable to imprisonment. Proceedings were taken by way of the writ of redisseisin (Old Nat.Br. 106; Fitz.N.B. 188).

Redisseisin was also known as *disseisina facta super disseisinam* (one disseisin after another).

Redistribution of seats. See HOUSE OF COMMONS.

Reditus, rent. See REDDITUS.

Reditus albi (white rents), quit-rents by freeholders or ancient copyholders of a manor, reserved in silver or white money (2 Bl.Comm. 42). See ALBA FIRMA.

Reditus assisus, a set or standing rent. See ASSISE RENT.

Reditus capitales, chief-rents paid by freeholders to go quit of all other services. See RENT.

Reditus nigri, black-mail, quit-rents paid in work, grain, or base money, as distinguished from *reditus albi,* or rents paid in silver (2 Bl.Comm. 43). See ALBA FIRMA.

Reditus quieti, quit-rents (*q.v.*). See RENT.

Reditus siccus, a rent-seck, or barren rent, the owner of which has neither seigniory nor reversion, nor any express power of distress reserved to him. See RENT.

Redmans, or **Radmans,** men who, by the tenure of custom of their lands, were to ride with or for the lord of the manor about his business (*Domesday*).

Re-draft, a second bill of exchange.

Redubbers, persons who bought stolen cloth and turned it into some other colour or fashion, that it might not be known again (3 Co.Inst. 134).

Reductio ad absurdam, the method of disproving an argument by showing that it leads to an absurd consequence.

Reduction into possession, the act of exercising the right conferred by a chose in action, so as to convert it into a chose in possession; thus a debt is reduced into possession by obtaining payment.

The term was chiefly used with reference to the exercise by a husband of the right to reduce into possession choses in action belonging to his wife; and the question whether he had done so was of importance from the rule that his wife's choses in action did not vest in him, as her other chattels did, unless he had reduced them into possession during the coverture. Thus, if C owed a debt of £500 to A, a *feme sole,* and A married B, B had the right to receive the £500 from C, or to sue him for it: and if he did so, and obtained payment or judgment against C, he had reduced the chose in action into possession, and the £500 belonged to him; if, however, B died without having enforced his right to the £500, it survived to A as if she had never been married. Choses in action falling within this rule included debts, arrears of rent, legacies, residuary personal estate, money in the funds, shares, etc., but not chattels personal which at the time of the marriage were in the possession of third persons. In order that the act of the husband might operate as a reduction into possession, there had to be an intention to that end, coupled with some act giving effect to the intention. As a general rule, any act by which the property was brought into the exclusive control of the husband (in his character of husband, and not as trustee, or executor, etc.), was a reduction into possession. Thus, if a debt due to the wife was received by the husband, or he brought an action for the debt in his sole name and recovered judgment, the debt was reduced into possession. And although an assignment by the husband of a debt due to the wife did not defeat her right by survivorship, unless the assignee reduced it into possession during the husband's lifetime, yet if a bill of exchange or promissory note was made or indorsed to a married woman during coverture, and the husband indorsed it to a stranger, or if he caused stock belonging to his wife to be transferred into his sole name, this operated as a reduction into possession. But if he transferred the stock into the joint names of himself and his wife, this did not operate as a reduction into possession. See MARRIED WOMEN'S PROPERTY.

Reduction of capital. By the Companies Act, 1948, ss. 66–71, any company limited by shares may pass a special resolution to reduce its capital. The resolution is inoperative until the company has applied to the court to confirm the reduction; and the court, if satisfied that the creditors of the company consent to the reduction, or that their claims have been discharged or secured, may make an order confirming the reduction. The court may order the words " and reduced " to be added to the name of the company.

Without the sanction of the court, a company limited by shares or guarantee may, if so authorised by its articles, reduce its capital by cancelling unissued shares (s. 61).

Redundancy, unnecessary or foreign matter inserted in a pleading.

Redundancy payments. The Redundancy Payments Act, 1965, places an obligation on employers to make redundancy payments to employees who have been dismissed by reason of redundancy, laid off or kept on short time (s. 1). Certain categories of employees are excluded from the provisions of the Act (ss. 15, 16, 17). So too are employees over 65, if male, 60, if female (ss. 3 (4), 4 (2), 6 (2)). Similarly excluded are employees dismissed justifiably (s. 2 (2)) except when the dismissal is as a result of a strike or lock-out (s. 10). Domestic servants come within the scope of the Act (s. 19). Written particulars of redundancy payments must be given (s. 18). No payment may be made unless it has been agreed or claimed in writing or determined by an industrial tribunal (ss. 7, 9, 21) or a complaint of his dismissal has been made to an industrial tribunal (Trade Union and Labour Relations Act, 1974, Sch. 1 para. 29).

Redundancy payments are exempt from income tax under Sch. E (Income and Corporation Taxes Act, 1970, s. 412).

The procedure for handling redundancies etc. is laid down by the Employment Protection Act, 1975, ss. 99–107, 125, Sch. 16. As to Crown employment see s. 120. See also the Redundancy Rebates Act, 1969.

Redundant churches. See the Pastoral Measure 1968, the Redundant Churches and Other Religious Buildings Act, 1969, and the Town and Country Planning Act, 1971, Sch. 23 Pt. II.

Re-entry. A proviso for re-entry, is inserted in every properly drawn lease, empowering the lessor to re-enter upon the demised premises if the rent is in arrear for a certain period, *e.g.,* twenty-one days, or if there is any breach of the lessee's covenants. A proviso for re-entry, strictly speaking, is only applicable to corporeal hereditaments (*Sitwell* v. *Londesborough* [1905] 1 Ch. at p. 465). A proviso for re-entry for breach of covenant was denounced as a most odious stipulation in *Hodgkinson* v. *Crowe* (1875) L.R. 10 Ch. at p. 626, but in practice is common enough. A proviso confined to the case of non-payment of rent is a usual stipulation (*Re Anderton* (1890) 45 Ch.D. 476). A lease of settled land must contain a condition of re-entry on the rent not being paid within a specified time not exceeding thirty days (Settled Land Act, 1925, s. 42; see also the Law of Property Act, 1925, s. 99). Waiver of a right of re-entry for non-payment of rent is a waiver for ever (*London and County (A. & D.)* v. *Wilfred Sportsman* [1969] 1 W.L.R. 1215). A right of re-entry is not registrable as a land charge (*Shiloh Spinners* v. *Harding* [1973] A.C. 691). See ENTRY; FORFEITURE; PROVISO; RIGHT OF ENTRY.

Reeve; Reve [Sax. *gerefa*], a steward or bailiff. In Anglo-Saxon times it meant an official holding high office under the king, but then and later it was also applied to many minor officials, such as the *praepositus ecclesiae,* who was later known as the church-reeve and was still later represented by the churchwarden. See DYKE-REEVE; FIELD-REEVE.

The word came to mean the bailiff of a franchise or manor; hence shire-reeve, a sheriff (*q.v.*) (Kitchin, 43).

Before the Municipal Corporations Act, 1835, the borough reeve was the principal officer of many towns. See PRAEPOSITUS; REVELAND.

Re-examination, the examination of a witness after cross-examination, upon matters arising out of such cross-examination. If the re-examination discloses new matter which the cross-examining party could not anticipate, the court in its discretion may permit him to cross-examine upon it. See EXAMINATION.

Re-exchange, the damages which the holder of a bill of exchange sustains by its being dishonoured in a foreign country where it was made payable (*Williams* v. *Ayers* (1878) 3 App.Cas. at p. 146). The theory of the transaction is as follows: A merchant in London indorses a bill for a certain number of Austrian schillings, payable at a future date in Vienna. The holder is entitled to receive in Vienna, on the day of the maturity of the bill, a certain number of Austrian schillings. Suppose the bill to be dishonoured. The holder is now, by the custom of merchants, entitled to immediate and specific redress, by his own act, in this way. He is entitled, being in Vienna, then and there to raise the exact number of Austrian schillings, by drawing and negotiating a cross bill, payable at sight, on his indorser in London, for as much English money as will purchase in Vienna the exact number of Austrian schillings, at the rate of exchange on the day of dishonour; and to include in the amount of that bill the interest and necessary expenses of the transaction. This cross bill is called in English a redraft, in French *retraite,* in German *Rückwechsel,* and in Italian *rivalsa.* The amount for which it is drawn is called in English re-exchange, in French *rechange*, and in Italian *ricambio.* If the indorser pays the redraft or cross bill, he has fulfilled the engagement of indemnity. If not, the holder of the original bill may sue him on it, and will be entitled to recover in that action the amount of the redraft or cross bill, with the interest and expenses thereon. The amount of the verdict will thus be an exact indemnity for the non-payment of the Austrian schillings in Vienna on the day of the maturity of the original bill. According to English practice, the redraft or cross bill is now seldom drawn, but the right of the holder to draw it is settled by the law merchant of all nations, and it is only by a reference to this supposed bill that the re-exchange, in other words, the true damages in an action on the original bill can be understood and computed (Byles, *Bills of Exchange,* 352, 353). See CAMBIUM.

The Bills of Exchange Act, 1882, s. 57 (2), is declaratory of the law as above stated; s. 89 of the same Act makes re-exchange recoverable in respect of a promissory note.

Re-extent, a second execution by extent in respect of the same debt. See EXTENT.

Refare, to rob or steal (Leg. Hen. 1, c. 83).

Refer; Reference. To refer a question is to have it decided by a person nominated for the purpose, in lieu of the ordinary procedure by action, trial or other judicial proceedings. The person to whom the question is referred is sometimes called the referee, and the proceedings before him constitute the reference; these proceedings to a great extent resemble those on an ordinary trial, except that they are private; witnesses are examined, and the referee is addressed on behalf of each of the parties, and he makes an award or report containing his decision. See ARBITRATION.

Sometimes a petition, instead of being disposed of in court, is referred to chambers to be dealt with by the judge in private; *e.g.*, a petition for leave to marry a ward of court.

Every appeal to the Privy Council is theoretically supposed to be first submitted to the Crown in Council, and then referred to the Judicial Committee, who report their opinion.

Referee, a person to whom a question is referred for his decision or opinion. See BOARD OF REFEREES; OFFICIAL REFEREE; REFER; TRIAL.

In parliamentary practice, referees on private bills are members who were appointed in 1864 by the House of Commons to report on engineering questions and questions of *locus standi* arising on private bills, but since 1868 they decide only questions of *locus standi* (*q.v.*). They are the Chairman and the Deputy Chairman of the Committee of Ways and Means, and the Counsel to Mr. Speaker, and not less than seven other members: collectively they are known as the Court of Referees; and three of them are necessary to constitute the court.

Reference in case of need. When a person draws or indorses a bill of exchange, he sometimes adds the name of a person to whom it may be presented " in case of need," that is, in case it is dishonoured by the original drawee or acceptor (Bills of Exchange Act, 1882, s. 15). See ACCEPTANCE OF BILLS.

Reference, Incorporation by, of an earlier statute by a later one was judicially stigmatised in *Knill* v. *Towse* (1889) 24 Q.B.D. 186, and *Chislett* v. *Macbeth & Co.* [1909] 2 K.B. at p. 815. See ACT OF PARLIAMENT.

Reference of action. See ARBITRATION.

Reference to the record. When an action is commenced, an entry of it is made in the cause book according to the year, the initial letter of the surname of the first plaintiff, and the place of the action in numerical order among those commenced in the same year; *e.g.,* "1958,

A. No. 26 "; and all subsequent documents in the action (such as pleadings and affidavits) bear this mark, which is called the reference to the record. See CAUSE BOOKS; TITLE.

Referendarius. See PROLOCUTOR.

Referendary, one to whose decision anything is referred (Cowel; Spelman).

Referendum [Fr. *plébiscite*], a direct vote of electors upon a particular matter or measure (see, *e.g.,* Referendum Act, 1975); also a note addressed by an ambassador to his own government touching a proposition as to which he is without power and instructions.

Reform. To reform an instrument is to rectify it. See RECTIFICATION.

Reform Acts, the Representation of the People Acts, 1832, 1867 and 1884, which extended the parliamentary franchise. The Acts of 1832 and 1867 applied to England and Wales only, there being separate Acts for Scotland and Ireland at the same period; the Act of 1884 applied to Scotland and Ireland as well. See now the Representation of the People Act, 1949, replacing the Representation of the People Acts, 1918 and 1948. See ELECTORAL FRANCHISE.

Refraction, reparation of a building (Civil Law).

Refresher, a fee paid to counsel on the trial of an action in addition to the fee originally paid to him with his brief. It is paid either for each period of five hours (or part thereof) after the first, during which a trial or hearing is proceeding or, at the discretion of the taxing officer, in respect of any day, after the first day on which the attendance of counsel at the place of trial is necessary. The amount is in the discretion of the taxing officer (R.S.C., Ord. 62, App. 2, Pt. X, 2 (4)).

As to refreshers to junior counsel for the prosecution see the *Annual Statement of the Bar Council 1971–72,* Tables I and II.

Refreshing memory. A witness is in some cases allowed to refresh his memory, while under examination, by referring to a document which is not itself admissible as evidence. Thus, a witness who has made a memorandum of a transaction may in many cases use it to refresh his memory. Many documents, however, which formerly could be used only to refresh memory are now admissible under the Evidence Act, 1938. A witness may not refresh his memory from records for which the Crown has successfully claimed privilege (*Gain* v. *Gain* [1961] 1 W.L.R. 1469). A witness may refresh his memory from a note written by someone else so long as he adopts it as his own particularly if he does so by signing it (*Groves* v. *Redbart* [1975] R.T.R. 268). Where a prosecution witness refreshes his memory from his statement before giving evidence, it is desirable but not essential that the defence be informed (*Worley* v. *Bentley* [1976] 2 All E.R. 449).

Refreshment houses. A licence is required to keep a house, room, shop or building (other than one licensed for the sale of beer, cider, wine or spirits) open for public refreshment, resort or entertainment between 10 p.m. and 5 a.m. (Late Night Refreshment Houses Act, 1969, ss. 1, 2). The licensing authorities are district councils, and, in London, the London boroughs and the Common Council of the City of London (s. 2; Local Government Act, 1972, s. 204 (9)). As to duties payable and duration of licences see the Act of 1969, ss. 3–5; Local Government Act, 1974, s. 35, Sch. 6 para. 24, Sch. 8). If intoxicating liquor is sold a justices' licence is required, see INTOXICATING LIQUORS, which obviates the need for a late night refreshment house licence (*Portsmouth Corporation* v. *Nishar Ali* [1973] 1 All E.R. 236). A local register of licences is kept (Act of 1969, s. 6). Conditions may be imposed as to opening after 11 p.m. A person aggrieved by a condition imposed may appeal to a magistrates' court. Appeal lies thence to the Crown Court (s. 7; Courts Act, 1971, Sch. 9 Pt. I). As to charges and touting, see s. 8. As to illegal and disorderly conduct, see ss. 9, 10. As to punishment of offences, see s. 11.

A coffee stall is not a late night refreshment house (*Frank Bucknell & Son* v. *Croydon London Borough Council* [1973] 1 W.L.R. 534).

As to non-payment for a meal, see *Ray* v. *Sempers* [1973] 1 W.L.R. 317.

Refusal, where one has, by law, a right and power of having or doing something of advantage, and declines it.

Refuse disposal. A local authority must provide dumps where residents may deposit their refuse free of charge (Civic Amenities Act, 1967, ss. 18–23; Local Government Act, 1972, Sch. 14 para. 45, Sch. 19 paras. 33–35, Sch. 30; Control of Pollution Act, 1974, Sch. 3 para. 25). Interference with refuse dumps is an offence under the Control of Pollution Act, 1974, s. 27.

A local authority has, in the interests of amenity, power to remove accumulations of rubbish from any vacant site in a built-up area (Public Health Act, 1961, s. 34; Civic Amenities Act, 1967, s. 26; Local Government Act, 1972, Sch. 14 para. 37; Control of Pollution Act, 1974, Sch. 3, para. 18).

See DUSTBINS; WASTE.

Reg., abbreviation for *Regina,* the Queen; also for regulation.

Regale episcoporum, the temporal rights and privileges of a bishop (Brady).

Regalia, the royal rights of a sovereign, which the civilians reckon to be six, *viz.*, power of judicature, of life and death, of war and peace, masterless goods, as waifs, estrays, etc., assessments, and minting of money. The word seems to be an abbreviation of *jura regalia* (*q.v.*). Some old writers divide the royal prerogative into *majora* and *minora regalia,* the former including the regal dignity and power, the latter the revenue or fiscal prerogatives of the Crown (1 Bl.Comm. 117).

The crown, sceptre and other articles used at a coronation are also commonly called the regalia. For an account of the extraordinary attempt made by Col. Blood in 1673 to steal them from the Tower, see Scott's *Peveril of the Peak,* Centen. ed., note BB.

Regalia facere, to do homage or fealty to the sovereign by a bishop when he is invested with the regalia.

Regalities. Used by certain modern writers as a synonym for regalia (*q.v.*); but the word seems to belong rather to Scottish law (see the Heritable Jurisdiction (Scotland) Act, 1746) than to English law. Regality means a territorial jurisdiction in Scotland conferred by the Crown. The lands were said to be given *in liberam regalitatem,* and the persons receiving the right were termed lords of regality.

Regard, money paid to a serjeant at law on his elevation to his degree. In 1495 it amounted to 12d. placed in a pair of gloves. Later it seems to have increased to £6 13s. 4d. and a pair of gloves (*Black Books of Lincoln's Inn*).

Regard, Court of, a forest court, held every third year to inquire into waste, purprestures and other matters affecting the forest. It also dealt with the lawing or expedition of dogs, to prevent them from chasing deer.

Regard of the forest, the area which constituted the forest and which was therefore inspected by the regarder (*q.v.*); the inspection made by the regarder (Cromp.Jurisd. 175, 199; Manwood, Pt. 1, 194, 198).

Regardant, appendant (*q.v.*). By Littleton's time it was only applied to villeins (*q.v.*) (Litt. 184; Co.Litt. 120).

Regardant, Villein, or **Regardant to the manor,** a servant or retainer annexed to a manor, who did the base services within the manor (Co.Litt. 120).

Regarder, a forest officer whose duty it was to exercise supervision over the forest, and to make a triennial inspection with a view to enforcing the forest laws (Cromp.Jurisd. 153; Manwood).

Rege inconsulto, a writ which issued from the king to the judges commanding them, in order to prevent prejudice to him, not to proceed with a cause until he had been advised (Jenk.Cent. 97; Moore 842).

Regency, a delegation, to one known as a regent, of the powers, or some of the powers, of the sovereign during his youth, incapacity or absence from the kingdom. Such delegation is unusual, though not unknown, during the absence of the sovereign overseas; in that case, the more usual course after the accession of William III was the appointment of Lords Justices. Lords Justices were frequently appointed between 1688 and 1760. There were no such appointments between 1760 and 1820, as neither George III nor the Prince Regent ever left the kingdom. Between 1820 and 1837 such appointments were sometimes made. During the reign of Queen Victoria there were no Lords Justices, it being held that the Queen, who never left Europe, could, under modern conditions, exercise the royal functions in person while, for instance, on a short visit to France. But the necessity for the appointment of some equivalent for a regent or Lords Justices is still recognised when the sovereign is absent for a long period at a remote place; and so, before George V went to India in 1911, he held a meeting of the Privy Council at which four Counsellors of State were nominated to transact business during his absence.

The Regency Act, 1937, provides that if the sovereign is, at his accession, under the age of 18 years, a regent is to be appointed (s. 1). So also if the sovereign is totally incapacitated (s. 2). The regent is, subject as stated below, the person next in line of succession to the Crown (s. 3). Power is given to delegate the royal functions to Counsellors of State in the case of illness or absence of the sovereign from the United Kingdom. The persons to be counsellors of State are to be the wife or husband of the sovereign, Her Majesty Queen Elizabeth the Queen Mother and the four persons next in the line of succession to the throne (s. 6; Regency Act, 1943; Regency Act, 1953, s. 3). If a regency becomes necessary on the succession to the Crown of a child of Her Majesty Queen Elizabeth II and H.R.H. the Duke of Edinburgh while under the age of 18 years, the Duke of Edinburgh is to be regent (Act of 1953, s. 1).

A Roman Catholic may not be regent (Roman Catholic Relief Act, 1829, s. 12).

Regest [Lat. *registum*], a register (Milton).

Regiam majestatem, a collection of the ancient laws of Scotland, said to have been compiled by order of David I, who reigned from 1124 to 1153 (Hale's Hist. 271).

Regicide, the murder of a sovereign; also the murderer.

Regimental debts. The Regimental Debts Act, 1893, s. 1, provides that on the death, desertion or insanity of anyone subject to military law, the Committee of Adjustment shall secure such of his property as is in camp or quarters, or, if the death takes place abroad, within a larger prescribed area, and ascertain and pay the preferential charges thereon.

Regio assensu, the writ by which the king assented to the election of a bishop (Reg.Orig. 294).

Register [Fr. *gîter*, to lodge], a public book serving to enter and record memoirs, Acts and minutes, to be had recourse to for the establishing matters of fact; as the register of companies under the Companies Act, 1948; of bills of sale under the Bills of Sale Acts, 1878 and 1882, and the Administration of Justice Act, 1925, s. 23; of births, deaths and marriages, and of baptisms; and of parliamentary and local government electors.

Register of charges. A company must keep a register of all charges and mortgages affecting its undertaking or property (Companies Act, 1948, s. 104).

Register of directors and secretaries. A company must keep a register of its directors and secretaries (Companies Act, 1948, s. 200) and of its directors' shareholdings (Companies Act, 1967, ss. 27–29).

Register of members. A company must keep a register of its members (Companies Act, 1948, ss. 110–118; Companies Act, 1967, s. 52 (2)).

Register of writs, a book in which new forms of original writs were entered. The *Register of Writs* is said to be the oldest book in the law. It was first printed in 1531. Other editions appeared in 1553, 1595, 1634 and 1687. The forms of writs were settled in their substance and language very nearly in the manner in which they were drawn ever after. However, this uniformity was not so exact as that the writs published and used in the reign of Henry VIII were all of them identically the same with those used at the first origin of this invention, in the reign of Henry II (Co.Litt. 16b, 37b, 159a; Maitland, *Select Essays in Anglo-American Legal History*). See ACTION ON THE CASE.

Register of writs and orders. Under the Land Charges Registration and Searches Act, 1888, s. 5, there was established at the Land Registry (*q.v.*) a register of writs and orders of any court which affected land; and any such writ or order was made void as against a purchaser for value unless registered in this register.

They are now registered under the Land Charges Act, 1972, s. 6. See LAND CHARGE.

Registered designs. See DESIGNS.

Registered land. See REGISTRATION OF TITLE TO LAND.

Registered office. A company must have a registered office to which communications and notices may be addressed, notice of the situation of which, and of any change therein, must be given to the Registrar of Companies (Companies Act, 1948, s. 107). Service of a writ or other process on a company is effected by leaving it or sending it by post to the company's registered office (s. 437).

Registered post. See the Post Office Act, 1969, s. 30.

Registrar, or **Registrary,** an officer whose business is to write and keep a register: as the registrars of the Chancery Division, who draw up the orders of the court (R.S.C., Ord. 42, r. 6), the Registrar of the Admiralty Court (Ord. 1, r. 4A, Ord. 32, r. 11), the registrars of the Family Division (Ord. 32, r. 11), the registrar of a county court (County Courts Act, 1959, s. 18); of solicitors, of which the Law Society performs the duties (Solicitors Act, 1974, ss. 6, 9); of friendly societies (Friendly Societies Act, 1974, s. 2); and many other statutes. See COMPANIES; REGISTRATION OF TITLE TO LAND.

Registrar and merchants. In Admiralty actions, the court itself does not enter into details relating to the assessment of damages or matters of account, unless the amount in dispute is small or unless the matter can easily be settled by the court, and whenever in the course of a cause it becomes necessary that the court should be informed upon such questions, it is usual to direct a reference to the registrar. In modern practice the Admiralty Registrar decides questions without the assistance of merchants in the great majority of cases. Nautical and other assessors, however, are not infrequently appointed by the registrar to assist him.

Registrar, District. See DISTRICT REGISTRIES.

Registrar in Bankruptcy. See BANKRUPTCY COURTS.

Registrar of Affidavits. This was an office in the Court of Chancery which was held in 1798 by the two daughters and co-heiresses of the second Earl of Northington, who between them received about £410 a year, out of which they paid £90 a year to a deputy for the actual performance of their duties. The duties consisted in filing and registering affidavits and making office copies thereof (*Commons Committees Reports*, Vol. 13, p. 233). The office was abolished by the Lord Chancellor's Pension Act, 1832, s. 1.

Registrar-General, the officer at the head of the system under which all births, deaths and marriages in the country are registered (Registration Service Act, 1953, s. 1). His office was established by the Births and Deaths Registration Act, 1836, s. 2.

Registrar-General of Shipping and Seamen. To secure the object of affording general information from time to time as to the state of the mercantile marine it is provided that there shall be a General Register and Record Office for Seamen, under the management of this officer (Merchant Shipping Act, 1970, s. 80).

Registrarius, a notary or registrar.

Registration of births. This is now governed by the Births and Deaths Registration Act, 1953, ss. 1–14, as amended. Where any child is born, the father (unless the child is a bastard (s. 10)), or mother, or the occupier of the house in which the child is born, or any person present at the birth, or the person having charge of the child, must, within forty-two days after the birth, give the specified particulars as to the birth to the registrar of births, deaths and marriages, and sign the register (ss. 1, 2). If default is made by all such persons, any of them must, on receipt of a written requisition from the registrar, attend and give the required particulars as to the birth (s. 4).

Any person finding or having charge of a new-born child who has been exposed must, within forty-two days of the child being found, give to the registrar any particulars known to him concerning the birth of the child (s. 3). Failure to comply with any of the above-mentioned sections is an offence punishable on summary conviction (s. 36; Legitimation (Re-registration of Birth) Act, 1957, s. 1 (2); Criminal Justice Act, 1967, Sch. 3 Pt. I. The birth of a child who has been abandoned may be registered under the 1953

Act, s. 3A, added by the Children Act, 1975, s. 92). No fee is to be charged for registration unless the registrar attends at a private residence to register the birth (Act of 1953, s. 5: S.I. 1968 Nos. 1242, 2049). The making to the registrar of false statements regarding the required particulars as to birth is an offence punishable either summarily or on indictment (Perjury Act, 1911, s. 4; Criminal Justice Act, 1925, s. 28; Criminal Justice Act, 1967, Sch. 3 Pt. I). Forgery in connection with the registration of births is dealt with in the Forgery Act, 1913, s. 3 (2); and also in s. 37 of the Act of 1953.

In the case of an illegitimate child the name of a person is not to be entered in the register as being the father, unless (a) such person acknowledges himself to be, and unless both he and the mother request that he be entered as, the father, and unless both he and the mother sign the register or (b) at the request of the mother on production of (i) a declaration by the mother stating who is the father of the child and (ii) a statutory declaration by the father acknowledging himself to be the father of the child (Act of 1953, s. 10; Family Law Reform Act, 1969, s. 27 (1)) or (c) at the request of the mother, in writing, on production of (i) a certified copy of an affiliation order naming that person as the putative father of the child and (ii) if the child has attained the age of sixteen years, the written consent of the child to the registration of that person as the father (Act of 1953, s. 10; Family Law Reform Act, 1969, s. 27 (1); Children Act, 1975, s. 93 (1). The birth of an illegitimate child may be re-registered under the 1953 Act, s. 10A added by the 1975 Act, s. 93 (2). See also LEGITIMATION.

Births on British ships at sea are dealt with in the Merchant Shipping Act, 1894, s. 245.

Parochial registers of birth are evidence. So also, under the Non-Parochial Registers Act, 1840, s. 6, except as stated in that Act, are non-parochial registers deposited in the General Register Office. See also the Births and Deaths Registration Act, 1858, s. 3.

Registration of burials. The effect of the Burial Act, 1853, s. 8, the Cemeteries

Clauses Act, 1847, s. 32, the Registration of Burials Act, 1864, ss. 1, 7, the Burial Laws Amendment Act, 1880, ss. 10, 11, Sch., the Burial and Registration Acts (Doubts Removal) Act, 1881, s. 2, and the Burial Act, 1900, s. 9, is that every burial in every cemetery or burial ground must be registered in the register to be kept by the person or body having control of each cemetery or burial ground. Such registers are evidence (Act of 1853, s. 8; Act of 1847, ss. 32, 33; Act of 1864, s. 5). Forgery of, or of copies of, any such register is an indictable offence (Forgery Act, 1913, s. 3 (2)).

Registration of business names. See BUSINESS NAMES, ETC.

Registration of charges on land. The Land Charges Act, 1972, provides for the registration of charges affecting land, and for the protection of purchasers for value of the land in case of non-registration, and for allowing searches of the registers on payment of fees. See LAND CHARGE.

Registration of companies. See COMPANIES.

Registration of copyright. The Copyright Act, 1842, authorised the registration of the title of the proprietor of copyright at Stationers' Hall, and providing that, without previous registration, no action should be commenced. This Act was repealed by the Copyright Act, 1911, and no such registration is now necessary.

Registration of deaths. Every death, and the cause thereof, must be registered (Births and Deaths Registration Act, 1953, s. 15). Where the death occurs in a house, the nearest relatives present at the death or in attendance during the last illness, and, in default of such relatives, the nearest relatives in the sub-district, and, failing them, the persons present at the death and the occupier of the house, and, failing them, all inmates of the house and the persons causing the body to be buried, are bound to give the required particulars to the local registrar within five days of the death, and to sign the register (s. 16). Where the death occurs or a body is found elsewhere than in a house, all relatives having knowledge of the required particulars, and, failing them, every person present at the death or finding or taking charge of or burying the body, is bound, within five days after the death or finding, to give the particulars to the registrar and to sign the register (s. 17). If a person bound to inform the registrar sends to him within the five days a written notice of the death and a medical certificate of its causes, then the specified particulars may be furnished within fourteen days instead of five days after the death (s. 18). After fourteen days and within twelve months from the death, the registrar may, if the death has not been registered, serve a written notice to register upon any person who is under an obligation so to do (s. 19). No fee is payable upon registration, unless the registrar has to attend at a house other than a public institution (s. 20). No death can be registered after twelve months without the written authority of the Registrar-General (s. 21). Where an inquest is held, the coroner must report the result to the registrar (s. 23). Where a registered medical practitioner has attended the deceased, he is bound to deliver to the registrar a certificate of the cause of death and to give notice of the signing of the certificate to some person bound to register, and such person is bound to deliver it to the registrar (s. 22). See also S.I. 1968 Nos. 1242, 2049. The making of false statements to the registrar concerning death is a misdemeanour (Perjury Act, 1911, s. 4; Criminal Justice Act, 1925, s. 28; Criminal Justice Act, 1967, Sch. 3 Pt. I); and forgery in connection with such registration is an indictable offence (Forgery Act, 1913, s. 3 (2)).

Deaths occurring on merchant vessels are registered pursuant to the Merchant Shipping Act, 1894, s. 254.

Entries in parochial registers and non-parochial registers (Non-Parochial Registers Act, 1840) are evidence of burial and, inferentially of death.

Registration of designs. This is governed by the Registered Designs Act, 1949, ss. 17–24. See DESIGNS.

Registration of electors. The Representation of the People Act, 1949, s. 7, provided for the preparation of a spring and an autumn register in each year by the registration officer for each parliamentary borough or county. Autumn registers were abolished by the Electoral

Registers Act, 1949, as amended by the Electoral Registers Act, 1953.

The council of every district (*q.v.*) and London borough (*q.v.*) appoints an officer of the council to be registration officer (Local Government Act, 1972, s. 39).

Registration of judgments. See REGISTER OF WRITS AND ORDERS.

Registration of marriages. Canon 70 of 1603 directs that in every church and chapel there shall be kept a parchment book in which the minister is to enter particulars of christenings, weddings and burials, and that the minister shall annually send copies of each year's entries to the ecclesiastical officer of each diocese who is known as the registrar. The Parochial Registers Act, 1812, imposed on the minister the statutory duty of keeping three separate registers of the like events in an iron chest and of sending copies annually to the registrar of the diocese. All the foregoing registers are evidence under the Non-Parochial Registers Act, 1840, s. 6, when deposited in the General Register Office.

The minister remains in some cases the registering officer, but the registrar of the diocese is not now concerned and the official to whom the registering officer is responsible is the Registrar-General

Every marriage must be registered, in the case of a marriage according to the rites of the Church of England, by the clergyman who solemnised it; in the case of a marriage according to the usages of the Society of Friends, by the local registering officer of that Society; in the case of a marriage according to Jewish usage, by the secretary of the husband's synagogue; in the case of a marriage in a registered building, by the registrar, if present, or, if absent, by the authorised person in whose presence the marriage is solemnised; and in the case of a marriage in the office of a superintendent registrar, by the registrar in whose presence it is solemnised (Marriage Act, 1949, s. 53).

Marriages solemnised abroad are to be forthwith registered by the marriage officer (*q.v.*) by or before whom they are celebrated (Foreign Marriage Act, 1892, s. 9). The master of every Brtish ship required to keep an official log must register therein the particulars of any marriage taking place on board (Merchant Shipping Act, 1894, ss. 240 (6), 253 (1) (viii)).

Anyone who makes any false statement as to the particulars to be registered in connection with a marriage in order to have it entered in a register is guilty of an offence punishable on indictment or summarily (Perjury Act, 1911, s. 3 (1); Criminal Justice Act, 1925, s. 28; Criminal Justice Act, 1967, Sch. 3 Pt. I). Forgery of any marriage register or of any certified copy thereof is an indictable offence (Forgery Act, 1913, s. 3 (2)).

Registration of road vehicles. The registration and licensing of road vehicles is effected under the Vehicles (Excise) Act, 1971, s. 19. The registration book is not a document of title and a person who buys a motor-car on the faith of the registration book may be liable to return it to its true owner (*Central Newbury Car Auctions* v. *Unity Finance*, [1957] 1 Q.B. 371).

Registration of title to land. The Land Registration Act, 1925, replacing the Land Transfer Acts, 1875 and 1897, provides for entry of the indicia of land ownership and transfer in a register. The advantages which are claimed for the system are that purchasers for value of an absolute or good leasehold title are absolved from any inquiry into the title other than as shown on the register; that certain equitable claims which would be binding on the land under the general law and cannot be removed or over-reached without onerous formalities do not affect such purchasers; that the method of conveyance or charge is simple; and that, subject to the statutory provisions, registration guarantees the title to purchasers for value and mortgagees. Mines and minerals which have been excepted from a grant of land are not guaranteed unless separately registered. All registered land, irrespective of the nature of title, remains subject to overriding interests, notwithstanding registration.

All estates and interests in land which come under the description of legal estates in the Land Registration Act, 1925, s. 3, and the Law of Property Act, 1925, s. 205, may, and in districts where registration is compulsory must, as a rule be registered except leaseholds having not more than 21 years unexpired, and except

REGISTRATION

mortgage terms where there is a subsisting right of redemption (Land Registration Act, 1925, s. 8). But the latter exception has little practical importance, for the reason that charges, which for all practical purposes are equivalent to mortgages, may be registered under the Land Registration Act, 1925, ss. 25, 27 (and see the Law of Property Act, 1925, ss. 86, 87).

Compulsory registration may be introduced in any county or part of a county by Order in Council (Land Registration Act, 1925, ss. 120 *et seq.*). Registration is compulsory on sale in the following counties or districts of counties: AVON (Bath, Bristol and Kingswood); BEDFORD-SHIRE (Bedford, Luton and South Bedfordshire); BERKSHIRE; BUCKINGHAM-SHIRE (Beaconsfield); CAMBRIDGESHIRE (Cambridge); CHESHIRE (Chester, Crewe, Nantwich, and Warrington); CLEVELAND; DERBYSHIRE (Derby and Erewash); DEVON (Exeter, Plymouth and Torbay); DORSET (Poole); DURHAM (Chester-le-Street, Darlington, Durham, Easington and Sedgfield); ESSEX (Brentwood, Southend-on-Sea and Thurrock); GLA-MORGAN, MID (Ogwr); GLAMORGAN, SOUTH; GLAMORGAN, WEST; GLOUCES-TERSHIRE (Gloucester); GWENT (Newport); HAMPSHIRE (Portsmouth and Southampton); HERTFORDSHIRE (Hertsmere, Stevenage, Three Rivers, and Watford); HUMBERSIDE (Grimsby, Kingston upon Hull, North Wolds and Scunthorpe); KENT; LANCASHIRE (Blackburn, Burnley and Preston); LEICESTERSHIRE (Leicester); LINCOLNSHIRE (Lincoln); LONDON, GREATER; MANCHESTER, GREATER; MERSEYSIDE; NORFOLK (Norwich); MIDLANDS, WEST; NORTHAMPTON-SHIRE (Northampton); NORTHUMBER-LAND (Blyth Valley); NOTTINGHAMSHIRE (Ashfield, Broxtowe, Gedling, Mansfield, Nottingham and Rushcliffe); OXFORD-SHIRE (Oxford, South Oxfordshire and Vale of White Horse); STAFFORDSHIRE (Stoke-on-Trent); SUFFOLK (Ipswich); SUSSEX, EAST (Brighton, Eastbourne, Hastings, Hove, Lewes and Rother); SUSSEX, WEST (Crawley and Mid Sussex); SURREY; TYNE AND WEAR; WARWICK-SHIRE (Nuneaton, Rugby and Warwick); YORKSHIRE, SOUTH; YORKSHIRE, WEST. In a compulsory area land may but need

not be registered until, in the case of freehold land, a sale takes place, and in the case of leasehold land, a grant or sale of a term thereout having not less than forty years to run is effected. The penalty for not registering land in a compulsory area within two months from the date of conveyance is that the purchaser will not acquire the legal estate, and until that takes place the purchaser is open to the risk of the vendor establishing or perfecting equities against him and even fraudulently conveying the land to another purchaser, who may obtain a perfect title if he registers his conveyance before the prior purchaser.

Freehold land may be registered with absolute, qualified, or possessory title. Leaseholds of which more than twenty-one years are still unexpired may be registered with absolute, qualified, good leasehold, or possessory title. Registration with absolute title, of either tenure, confers on purchasers for value the advantages referred to above. Registration with qualified title is granted where it appears to the registrar that the title can only be established for a limited period or subject to reservations; registration in this form is seldom effected. Registration with possessory title gives the registered proprietor no guarantee of title other than the registered title for what that may be worth, nor does it absolve a purchaser from inquiring into the vendor's title under the general law prior to registration (Land Registration Act, 1925, ss. 6, 20 (3)). But a possessory registered title confers on the registered proprietor and purchasers from him all the advantages of registration in respect of matters arising subsequently to registration, and further, under s. 77 of the Act, the registrar may change the possessory into absolute title under the statutory conditions if the land was registered before 1926, or if the title has been possessory for fifteen years.

The same incidents, according to the quality of the title, attach to registered leaseholds to the extent of the term and estate which has been registered.

Registration with good leasehold title confers the same privileges and is subject to the same incumbrances and interests (if any) as registration with absolute title, except that good leasehold title does not include a guarantee of the lease itself. Registration with qualified title is the same as absolute title but without prejudice to any excepted rights appearing on the register. Registration with possessory title gives such privileges as are conferred on possessory titles of freeholds to the extent of the registered leasehold estate.

A purchaser for value of registered land with any title but possessory is not affected by trusts, express, implied, or constructive (Land Registration Act, 1925, s. 74). A possessory title is affected by trusts arising prior to the first registration, of which the purchaser has actual or constructive notice either upon investigation of title or otherwise if these trusts have not been overreached upon conveyance under the Law of Property Act, 1925, or the Settled Land Act, 1925.

The incumbrances and other liabilities to which all registered land is subject are (a) all those entered on the register at the time of first registration, and (b) those entered subsequently to the first registration, viz., charges (s. 25), notices of leases (s. 48), annuities and rent-charges (s. 49), severance of mines and minerals (s. 49), land charges (ss. 3, 49, 59), widow's rights, notices by creditors and others (ss. 49, 59, 61), restrictive covenants (s. 50), (as amended by the Law of Property Act, 1969, s. 28 (7)), manorial incidents (s. 51), over-riding incidents (s. 70 (3)), notices of lien by deposit of certificate (s. 66), priority notices (s. 88), and notices as to a sole trustee of registered land (s. 99).

The priority of these incumbrances is regulated by the date of entry on the register. Registration under the Land Charges Act, 1972, does not affect registered land (Land Registration Act, 1925, s. 110 (7); Land Charges Act, 1972, s. 14 (1)), except local land charges, which obtain priority according to the date of registration in the local register. Under the Land Charges Act, 1925, s. 15 (8) (as set out in the Land Charges Act, 1972, Sch. 4), incumbrances are protected (1) by means of caution or restriction against the registered proprietor (Land Registration Act, 1925, ss. 54, 58); strictly speaking, cautions and restrictions are not incumbrances on the

land, but they serve to give the persons entitled time to assert their rights, if any; and (2) by entry or notice of the incumbrance (Land Registration Act, 1925, s. 25); and in addition to these the Land Registration Act, 1925, s. 57, confers a remedy styled inhibition, which is analogous to an injunction. The Land Registration Act, 1925, s. 61, provides for bankruptcy and priority inhibitions.

A number of incumbrances are not affected by registration of the land under the Land Registration Act, 1925. Such incumbrances are included among over-riding interests, a list of which is given in s. 70. Rights to mines and minerals are over-riding interests on land registered before 1898, and so are all such rights if created before first registration of the land after 1898 and before 1926. Mines and minerals in respect of land registered after 1925 are included in the word " land " by the Act. Persons interested in the transfer or charge of registered land should make inquiries outside the Land Registry in regard to the incumbrances, claims, charges and other matters included in the list contained in s. 70.

Claims by beneficiaries and others which would be over-reached upon sale by trustees for sale or under the Settled Land Act, 1925, or otherwise as provided by the Law of Property Act, 1925, s. 2, are not over-riding interests and are classed among minor interests (Land Registration Act, 1925, ss. 3 (xv), 101–103, 105), and being equitable will be over-ridden by a registered disposition for value subject to the entries on the register. A purchaser for value is not concerned with anything not appearing on the register, but, as between minor interests, those interests, which, if the Law of Property Acts, 1922 and 1925, had not been passed, would have been legal estates, have priority over other minor interests, and as regards dealings effected after 1925 between assignees and incumbrancers of life interests, remainders, reversions and executory interests, priority is established by order of special priority cautions or inhibitions, noted in the Minor Interests Index, which does not concern a purchaser of the land from a registered proprietor. Death duties after 1925, even if registered, do not affect a purchaser for money or money's worth of registered land, but with that exception they affect the registered proprietor and the land if entered on the register (Land Registration Act, 1925, s. 73).

On first registration the first registered proprietor of any land is affected by all minor interests of which he has notice, and subsequent registered proprietors not being purchasers for value are under the same liability in regard to minor interests which affected the registered proprietor at the time of transfer to them (s. 20 (4)).

Upon registration the proprietor becomes entitled to the issue to him of a certificate called the land certificate or charge certificate, as the case may be, which is evidence of the matters appearing therein (s. 58). The land certificate is conclusive evidence of the state of the register up to the time but not later than the date of its last issue from the registry. Subsequent entries (if any) are ascertained by inquiry at the Land Registry. The plan on the land certificate is not however conclusive evidence of the correctness of the boundaries where it differs from the plan on the transfer (*Lee* v. *Barrey* [1957] Ch. 251). The certificate must, as a rule, be produced by any person requiring an entry or notice on the register, and must be produced at the registry and indorsed on every dealing by the proprietor (s. 64). The register is in three parts, *viz.,* (1) the property register, or parcels by reference to the Land Registry General Map or to a filed plan; (2) the proprietorship register, stating the nature of the title, *e.g.,* absolute, good leasehold, possessory, etc., and the name and description of the registered proprietor; and (3) the charges register, notifying incumbrances, *e.g.,* registrable leases, and charges, mortgages, restrictive covenants, etc.

As a rule, no one but the proprietor of the land or of any charge or incumbrance thereon may inspect any entry on the register or any document in the custody of the registrar without authority of the proprietor of the land or any such charge or incumbrance. Any person authorised to inspect may apply for an official search against the title, charge or incumbrance, and obtain a certificate of the result from the registrar. The certificate is conclusive and comprehensive of all registered matters affecting the title or object of search. The search at the Land Registry is more conveniently practical for intending purchasers or incumbrancers than a search under the Land Charges Act, 1972, which must be made by reference to the names of proprietors and incumbrancers, who may be numerous and not easily identified. The search at the Land Registry is made by reference to the land registered and is made possible by the system of mapping and indexing. See LAND REGISTRIES.

Registration of trade marks. See TRADE MARKS.

Registrum brevium, a register of writs. See REGISTER OF WRITS, ETC.; WRIT.

Registry, District. See DISTRICT REGISTRIES.

Registry of ships. The registry of ships was introduced by the Navigation Act, 1660; provisions were made with respect to it by the statute 1696, 7 & 8 Wm. 3, c. 22, and the whole was reduced into a system by the statute 1787, 27 Geo. 3, c. 19. It is now provided for by the Merchant Shipping Act, 1894, s. 2, by which every British ship must be registered under the Act, except ships not exceeding fifteen tons burden employed solely in navigation on the rivers or coasts of the United Kingdom, or on the rivers or coasts of some British possession within which the managing owners of the ships are resident, and ships not exceeding thirty tons burden, and not having a whole or fixed deck and employed solely in fishing or trading coastwise on the shores of Newfoundland or parts adjacent thereto, or in the Gulf of St. Lawrence, or on such portions of the coasts of Canada as lie bordering on that gulf (s. 3).

Regius professor, a royal professor, or reader of lectures, founded in the universities by the king. In 1540, Henry VIII founded in each of the universities of Oxford and Cambridge five professorships, *viz.,* of divinity, Greek, Hebrew, law and physic.

Regnal year, the year as calculated from the sovereign's accession to the throne; *e.g.,* 6 Eliz. 2 means the sixth year since the accession of Elizabeth II on February 6, 1952, *i.e.*, February 6, 1957, to February 5, 1958. See ACT OF PARLIAMENT.

Regnant, reigning, having regal authority. See KING.

Regni populi, a name given to the people of Surrey and Sussex, and on the sea-coasts of Hampshire (Blount).

Regnum ecclesiasticum, the ecclesiastical kingdom (2 Hale, Hist.P.C. 324).

Regnum non est divisible (Co.Litt. 165). (The kingdom is not divisible.) Quoted in connection with the rule that the king's daughters do not take as coparceners, and that the eldest succeeds in default of issue male.

Re-grant. In the law of real property, when, after a person has made a grant, the property granted comes back to him (*e.g.*, by forfeiture) and he grants it again, he is said to re-grant it. Thus, before the Fines and Recoveries Act, 1833, one mode of barring an entail in copyholds was a preconcerted forfeiture of the lands by the tenant, followed by a re-grant from the lord to him in fee simple.

Regrating, the offence of buying corn, etc., in any market and selling it again in the same place, so as to raise the price: the statute 1843, 7 & 8 Vict. c. 24, made this no longer an offence (Illingworth, *Inquiry into the Laws respecting Forestalling, etc.*). See ENGROS; FORESTALL; JOURNEY-CHOPPER.

Regress, re-entry; used principally in the phrase " free entry, egress and regress " (*q.v.*); it was also used to signify the re-entry of a person who had been disseised of land (Co.Litt. 318b). See RIGHT OF ENTRY.

Regula est, juris quidem ignorantiam cuique nocere facti vero ignorantiam non nocere (D. 22, 6, 9). (It is the rule, that every man is prejudiced by ignorance of law, but is not prejudiced by ignorance of fact.) See IGNORANTIA FACTI, ETC.

Regulae generales (general rules), rules which the courts promulgated from time to time for the regulation of their practice. Before the Judicature Acts, 1873–75, the more important of these were those promulgated in Hilary term, 1853. Since the Acts the description is Rules of the Supreme Court, abbreviated as R.S.C.

Regular clergy, the monks, who lived *secundum regulas* of their respective houses or societies.

Regulars, those who profess and follow a certain rule of life (*regula*) belonging to a religious order, and observe the three approved vows of poverty, chastity, and obedience.

Regulations, subordinate legislation by government departments under the authority of Acts of Parliament. See STATUTORY INSTRUMENTS.

Rehabere facias seisinam (that you cause him to have seisin again), a judicial writ which issued when the sheriff, upon the *habere facias seisinam* (*q.v.*), had delivered more than he ought (Reg.Judic. 13, 51, 54).

Rehabilitate, to restore a delinquent to former rank, privilege, or right; to qualify again; to restore a forfeited right.

Rehabilitation, the re-enabling of a spiritual person to exercise his functions when he had incurred a disability. This was effected by a brief or other instrument from the Pope until the obtaining from Rome of any such instrument was prohibited by the statute 1533, 25 Hen. 8, c. 21.

Rehabilitation of offenders. The Rehabilitation of Offenders Act, 1974, is designed to rehabilitate an offender who has not been reconvicted of any serious offence for a period of years varying with the severity of the sentence to which it relates. The rehabilitation periods are from ten to five years (half those for persons under seventeen) and from seven to three years in the case of certain sentences of young offenders (s. 5 (2)). Excluded from the Act are cases in which a person has been sentenced to imprisonment for life, or sentenced to imprisonment or corrective training (*q.v.*) for a term exceeding thirty months, or sentenced to preventive detention (*q.v.*) or sentenced to detention during Her Majesty's pleasure or for life under the Children and Young Persons Act, 1933, s. 53 (Act of 1974, s. 5 (1)). See also s. 6. At the expiry of the relevant period the convicted person becomes a " rehabilitated person " and his conviction becomes a " spent conviction " (s. 1). A rehabilitated person is to be treated in law as if he had not committed or been charged with or prosecuted for or convicted of or sentenced for the offence for which he was convicted. No evidence of a spent conviction is admissible in judicial proceedings. He is not to be asked, and if asked is not required to answer any question about an offence which was the subject of a spent conviction. In any inquiry not in judicial proceedings a rehabilitated person is entitled to ignore a spent conviction. A spent conviction is not a proper ground for dismissing or excluding any person from any office, profession, occupation or employment, or for prejudicing him in any way in any occupation or employment. Judicial proceedings include arbitrations and any proceedings under the rules governing any association, institution, profession, occupation or employment (s. 4). The Act is applied to service disciplinary proceedings (s. 2). For limitations on the effect of rehabilitation, see s. 7. Unauthorised disclosure of spent convictions is an offence (s. 9).

A rehabilitated person may bring an action for libel (q.v.) or slander (q.v.) founded upon the publication of any matter imputing that he has committed or been charged with or prosecuted for or convicted of or sentenced for an offence which was the subject of a spent conviction. In such an action the defendant can rely on any defence of justification (q.v.) or fair comment (q.v.) or absolute or qualified privilege (q.v.). Where malice (q.v.) is alleged against a defendant who is relying on a defence of qualified privilege he may establish any matters in rebuttal of the allegation of malice. A defendant cannot rely on a defence of justification if the publication is proved to have been made with malice. The defendant may not set up the defence that the matter published constituted a fair and accurate report of judicial proceedings if it contained a reference to evidence which was ruled to be inadmissible under the Act. The defences of justification or fair comment or of absolute or qualified privilege are available without qualification in an action alleging defamation in any report of judicial proceedings contained in any bona fide series of law reports which does not form part of any other publication and consists solely of reports of proceedings in courts of law. So also of any report or account of judicial proceedings published for bona fide educational, scientific or professional purposes, or given in the course of any lecture, class or discussion given or held for any of those purposes (s. 8).

For exceptions, see the Rehabilitation of Offenders Act, 1974 (Exceptions) Order, 1975 (No. 1023).

See also Practice Direction dated June 30, 1975 [1975] 1 W.L.R. 1065.

Re-hearing, where a cause or matter which has been already adjudicated upon is re-argued and a second judgment pronounced. The term is derived from the practice of the Court of Chancery, in which an appeal from a vice-chancellor or the Master of the Rolls to the Lord Chancellor was looked upon as a re-hearing, because they were the delegates of the Chancellor and members of the same court; the same practice was kept up when the Court of Appeal in Chancery (q.v.) was created.

Since the Judicature Acts, 1873–75, every appeal to the Court of Appeal is by way of re-hearing (R.S.C., Ord. 59, r. 3). This means that the Court of Appeal is in the same position as if the re-hearing were the original hearing, and hence it may receive evidence in addition to that before the court below, and it may review the whole case and not merely the points as to which the appeal is brought; but evidence that was not given before the court below is not commonly received. The appeal is, as a rule, a re-hearing on the documents (including the judge's notes and the transcript, if any, of the shorthand notes of the evidence). See APPEAL.

If there has to be a re-hearing in a court of first instance because of the illness of the judge, the evidence taken before can, unless there is a jury, be used, the judge simply reading the transcript even though there are disputes of fact. This is so at any rate in an Admiralty case (*The Forest Lake* [1968] P. 270).

Reif [Sax. *refian*], a robbery.

Re-instatement in civil employment. See CIVIL EMPLOYMENT, ETC.

Re-insurance, where an insurer procures the whole or part of the sum which he has insured (*i.e.*, contracted to pay in case of loss, death, etc.) to be insured again to him by another person. See INSURANCE.

Under the statute 1746, 19 Geo. 2, c. 37, s. 4, re-insurance was illegal except in certain cases but contracts of re-insurance were legalised by the Inland Revenue (Stamp Duties) Act, 1864, s. 1; and the Marine Insurance Act, 1906, s. 9 (1), provides that an insurance may be effected in respect of the interest of an insurer under a contract of marine insurance.

Re-insurance is most common in the case of maritime risks, but fire insurance companies can and do re-insure against the risks run under their policies.

Rejoinder, a defendant's answer to a plaintiff's reply, which must have been delivered within four days after notice, unless the defendant was under any terms of rejoining gratis, which meant rejoining within four days from the delivery of the replication without a notice to rejoin, or a demand of a rejoinder. It could not be delivered without leave.

Until 1933, this was expressly provided by R.S.C., Ord. 23, but in that year, Ord. 23 was revoked and replaced by two rules which deal with reply (*q.v.*) only, and there is now no rule specifically enabling the court to order delivery of any pleadings subsequent to reply. Ord. 18, r. 4, however appears to assume that the court has inherent power to order a rejoinder or any subsequent pleading.

The pleadings subsequent to reply were rejoinder, surrejoinder, rebutter and surrebutter.

Relation, where two different times or other things are accounted as one, and by some act done the thing subsequent is said to take effect " by relation " from the time preceding. Thus letters of administration relate back to the intestate's death, and not to the time when they were granted (*Re Pryse* [1904] P. 301; *Foster* v. *Bates* (1843) 12 M. & W. 226). See BANKRUPTCY; FORFEITURE; TRESPASS.

The doctrine of relation is that by which an act is made to produce the same effect as if it had occurred at an earlier time. Thus, an adjudication in bankruptcy relates back to the act of bankruptcy on which the receiving order (*q.v.*) was made, or, if more acts of bankruptcy than one are proved, to the first act of bankruptcy

committed within three months before the presentation of the petition (Bankruptcy Act, 1914, s. 37 (1)) so as to invalidate all alienations, executions, etc., made or suffered during that period fraudulently or in favour of any person having notice of the act of bankruptcy. So also, if a person has an authority by law to enter on land, and after entering he abuses the authority by committing some positive misfeasance, he becomes a trespasser *ab initio,* because his wrongful act relates back to the time of his entry (*Six Carpenters' Case* (1610) 8 Co.Rep. 146a). See AB INITIO; OMNIS RATIHABITIO, ETC.; PROTECTED TRANSACTIONS.

Relations, a general word meaning, prima facie, next-of-kin of any degree or, colloquially, kindred of all degrees.

Relator, a rehearser, teller, or informer. It was the name given to a plaintiff in an information in Chancery, where the rights of the Crown were not immediately concerned, who was responsible for costs; he must have given the solicitor a written authority to file the information: see the statute 1852, 15 & 16 Vict. c. 86, s. 11. The term " relator " is still in use as meaning the person responsible for costs at whose suggestion (*ex relatione, ex rel.*) an action is commenced by the Attorney-General. A private citizen who has suffered no special damage cannot sue to enforce the performance of statutory duties by public bodies but must obtain the consent of the Attorney-General to relator proceedings. It may be that if it were ever to be shown that the Attorney-General had improperly refused his consent the courts would not be powerless to act (*Att.-Gen., ex rel. McWhirter* v. *Independent Television Authority* [1973] Q.B. 629).

It also meant a person who brought an information in the nature of a *quo warranto,* or a criminal information.

See EX RELATIONE.

Relativorum, cognito uno, cognoscitur et alterum (Cro.Jac. 539). (Of things relating to each other, one being known, the other is also known.) Thus when you know the cause you also know the inevitable result.

Release [Lat. *relaxatio*], a gift, discharge, or renunciation of a right of action; also a common law conveyance of a larger estate, or a remainder or reversion, to one already in possession, the operative verb in which is "release"; hence the name. It operates or inures in five modes:

(*a*) By passing an estate to one or more already in possession (*mitter l'estate*), as where a coparcener conveys his interest to his coparcener, or where one of more than two joint tenants conveys his interest to one or more but not all of the others so as to sever that share. It also operates without *mitter l'estate* where one joint tenant releases his estate to the other or all the other joint tenants so as not to create a severance. In consequence of the privity between such parties, a fee simple would pass without any words of limitation. Tenants in common, however, could not thus release to one another, since they had distinct interests in the property. They now are equitably interested only in the proceeds of sale, and the question of the release of a legal estate does not arise, but the interest can be released.

(*b*) By transferring a right (*mitter le droit*), as in the case of a disseisee discharging his right to a disseisor, his heir, or grantee. Words of limitation have never been necessary, since the subject of transfer is a simple right, which once discharged is for ever extinguished, and not an estate which may be qualified or restricted. The difference between this and the previous mode is, that the former passes an estate, where privity exists between the parties; this passes only a right in the absence of privity.

(*c*) By extinguishment, as the lord releasing his seigniorial rights to his tenant, or a life tenant having conveyed a greater estate than he owns, the expectant releasing his right to the tenant's grantee. A release of all demands extinguishes all actions and titles, and is the amplest discharge that can be given.

(*d*) By enlarging a particular estate into an estate commensurate with that of the person releasing; but privity of estate must at the time exist between the releasor and the releasee, who must have an estate actually vested in him susceptible of enlargement.

(*e*) By entry and feoffment, as a disseisee releasing to one of two disseisors, who then became as solely seised as if the disseisee had entered upon the property, put an end to the disseisin, and then enfeoffed such disseisor (Litt. 304, 465, 478; Shep.Touch. 320; Jacob). See LEASE AND RELEASE.

In modern practice a release generally means a discharge (*q.v.*) under seal of a right of action, or of some claim or demand upon another person, most commonly, perhaps, the formal discharge given by beneficiaries to trustees on the winding up of a trust. A trustee cannot ordinarily insist on a release under seal; he is only entitled (in the absence of special circumstances) to a simple receipt for the funds he hands over, but in practice a release is often given him. A release, however wide its terms, does not extend beyond the matters expressly in the contemplation of the parties, and every claim intended to be released should therefore be mentioned in the recitals. A release in general terms upon surrender of a lease does not impliedly release from past breaches of covenant but only future (*Richmond* v. *Savill* [1926] 2 K.B. 530).

When two persons have had several dealings, from which demands and rights of action, whether mutual or not, have arisen or may in future arise, a release of all such demands and rights of action is called a general release.

A release sometimes takes place by operation of law. Thus, if A covenants not to sue B for a debt which he owes him, this operates as a release, because otherwise A might sue B for the debt, and then B might sue A for breach of his covenant, which would cause a circuity of action. But if A has a right of action against two or more persons, and covenants with one of them not to sue him, this does not operate as a release of the others, though an express release to him would have that effect (*Green* v. *Wynn* (1869) 4 Ch. 204) (see JOINT). For the same reason, although a bankrupt who obtains his discharge, or a debtor who effects an arrangement with his creditors, is thereby released by operation of law from all his debts, with certain exceptions (see DISCHARGE), this does not release persons with whom he is jointly liable for any debt (*Megrath* v. *Gray* (1874) L.R. 9 C.P. 216).

In Admiralty actions, when a ship, cargo or other property has been arrested, the owner may obtain its release by giving bail or paying the value of the property into court; upon this being done he obtains a release, which is a kind of writ under the seal of the court, addressed to the marshal, commanding him to release the property. See ADMIRALTY ACTION; BAIL (ADMIRALTY).

Releasee, the person to whom a release is made.

Releaser or **Releasor,** the maker of a release.

Relegation, exile by special Act of Parliament; judicial banishment.

Abjuration, *i.e.*, a deportation for ever into a foreign land, was a civil death; relegation was banishment for a time only (Co.Litt. 133a).

In Rome, relegation was a less severe punishment than deportation, in that the relegated person did not thereby lose the rights of a Roman citizen, nor those of his family, as the authority of a father over his children, etc.

Relevant, applying to the matter in question; affording something to the purpose; especially of evidence as meaning supporting the contention of a party to a suit. A fact is said to be relevant when it is so connected, directly or indirectly, with a fact in issue in an action or other proceeding, that evidence given respecting it may reasonably be expected to assist in proving or disproving the fact in issue. Thus, if A is tried for the murder of B by poison, the fact that he had previously been guilty of other crimes would generally be irrelevant; but the fact that, before B's death, A procured poison similar to that by which B died would be relevant, and so also would the fact that A had administered to G poison of the same kind as that alleged to have been administered to B; and where the question is whether C murdered his wife D, the fact that E and F, to whom also he had been married, had each, like D, been found drowned in a bath in circumstances similar to those proved in the case of D, has been held relevant as tending to disprove the theory of accident. So if the question in an action is whether A, the owner of land adjoining a river, owns the entire bed of it or only half the bed at a particular spot, the fact that he owns the entire bed a little down the river is relevant.

The question of the relevancy of a fact to a given inquiry is of importance, because evidence is not admissible to prove an irrelevant fact.

Relict, a widow.

Relicta verificatione. Where a judgment was confessed by *cognovit actionem* after plea pleaded, and the plea was withdrawn, it was called a confession or *cognovit actionem relicta verificatione.*

Formerly, a defendant who had pleaded a bad plea which was demurred to, could withdraw it by entering a *relicta verificatione,* upon which he would not have to pay costs until the plaintiff obtained judgment in the action; but by rules of court made in 1856, a defendant was prohibited from waiving his plea, or entering a *relicta verificatione* after a demurrer, without leave of the court or the consent of the plaintiff.

Reliction, the sudden recession of the sea from land. See DERELICTION.

Relief [Norm.Fr. *relef, reliefve*; Late Lat. *relevium, relevatio*; *relevare*, to take up], a payment which a tenant of full age was bound to pay to the feudal lord on succeeding to the land by descent; it was an incident to the service of every free tenure, and hence was sometimes called relief-service (Bract. 86a; Brit. 177b; Co.Litt. 83a).

Reliefs incident to knight's service were abolished by the statute 1660, 12 Car. 2, s. 24. A relief lay in render (*q.v.*) and might be distrained for. See INGRESSUS.

Improper reliefs differed from ordinary reliefs in being derived from custom, prescription or express reservation. A prescriptive relief was one which was presumed to have been reserved by a deed which had been lost (see LOST GRANT; PRESCRIPTION). A customary relief (or relief-custom) was due by the special custom of some manors on every descent, and in some cases on every purchase, or freehold tenements held of the manor, and in some manors the customary fines in respect of copyholds were called reliefs (see FINE). Reliefs due by custom and prescription were not recoverable by distress unless the custom or prescription warranted it.

A relief, like a heriot (*q.v.*), might be extinguished, at the instance of either the lord or the tenant, under the Copyhold Act, 1894, s. 2. See COPYHOLD.

Every action (except actions for discovery and a few others) is instituted for the purpose of obtaining relief, that is, satisfaction for a past injury, or the prevention of a threatened injury, or the enforcement or protection of a right. Thus on the Chancery side a plaintiff usually claims not only a particular kind of relief (specific relief), but also general relief, by asking for such further or other relief as the nature of the case may require, and he may ask for alternative relief: that is, he may mention two kinds of relief, and ask for one of them, *e.g.,* either specific performance or damages.

Under the Income and Corporation Taxes Act, 1970, reliefs are allowed from an individual's total income before computing the tax payable (ss. 5–27, as amended). Relief is also given against double taxation of income arising abroad in cases where arrangements have been made with the government of the country concerned.

If a candidate at a parliamentary or local government election has become responsible in respect of an election offence committed innocently, he can apply to the court for relief under the Representation of the People Act, 1949, s. 145; Representation of the People Act, 1969, s. 24 (4), Sch. 3 Pt. I (*Shaw* v. *Reckitt* [1893] 2 Q.B. 59; *Nichol* v. *Fearby* [1923] 1 K.B. 480).

See FORFEITURE; POOR LAW; TRUST.

Relieve, to depend: thus the seignory of a tenant *in capite* was said to relieve of the Crown, which meant that the tenant held of the Crown.

Religion. The uniformity of religious worship in the Church of England is enjoined by the Act of Uniformity, 1662; but restrictions on religious worship by Nonconformists are removed by the Toleration Act, 1688, and other Acts. The Roman Catholic Relief Act, 1829, ss. 28–36, however, subjected Jesuits and members of other religious orders in the Church of Rome (except nuns) to banishment for life (*R.* v. *Kennedy* (1902) 86 L.T. 753; *Re Smith* [1914] 1 Ch. 937); these sections were repealed by the Roman Catholic Relief Act, 1926. See JESUITS; ROMAN CATHOLICS.

As to conditions as to religion, see *Re Allen* [1953] Ch. 810; *Re Wolffe* [1953] 1 W.L.R. 1211; *Re Allen (No. 2)* [1954] Ch. 259.

Religious charities. See CHARITY.

Religious education. As to religious education in primary and secondary schools, see the Education Act, 1944, ss. 9 (2), 25–30; in special schools, s. 33; Education (Miscellaneous Provisions) Act, 1953, s. 17, Sch. 1.

Religious men, men who entered into some monastery or convent, there to live devoutly. They were held to be *civiliter mortui* (civilly dead).

Religious worship. See PUBLIC WORSHIP REGULATION; WORSHIP, PLACE OF.

Relinquishment, forsaking, or giving up. When a priest or deacon of the Church of England has resigned his office, he may execute a deed of relinquishment, and after a certain period he becomes incapable of acting in any way as a priest or deacon and loses all privileges attached to the office and is freed from all liabilities and disabilities to which he would otherwise have been subject (Clerical Disabilities Act, 1870). A deed of relinquishment can be vacated under the Clerical Disabilities Act, 1870 (Amendment) Measure, 1934. See HOLY ORDERS; RESIGNATION.

Reliqua, the remainder or debt which a person finds himself debtor in upon the balancing or liquidation of an account; hence reliquary, the debtor of a *reliqua*; as also a person who only pays piecemeal.

Reliques, remains, such as the bones, etc., of saints, preserved with great veneration as sacred memorials; they were forbidden to be used or brought into England in 1606.

Rem, Action in. By proceedings *in rem* the property in relation to which the claim is made, or the proceeds of such property in court, can be made available to answer the claim, and be proceeded against. See ADMIRALTY ACTION; ARREST.

Rem, Information in. When any goods were supposed to become the property of the Crown, and no one appeared to claim them or to dispute the title, as in the case of treasure-trove, wrecks, waifs, and estrays seized by the Crown's officers, after such seizure an information was usually filed in the Exchequer, and thereupon a proclamation was made for the owner (if any) to come in and claim the effects, and at the same time there issued a commission of appraisement to value the goods, after the return of which and a second proclamation made, if no claimant appeared, the goods were supposed derelict, and condemned to the use of the Crown; and when in later times forfeitures of the goods themselves, as well as personal penalties on the parties, were inflicted by Act of Parliament for transgressions against the laws of the customs and excise, the same process was adopted in order to secure such forfeited goods for the public use, though the offender had escaped justice; see the Crown Suits Act, 1855, as to the Crown paying costs. See ACTION.

Rem, Judgment in, an adjudication pronounced upon the status of some particular subject-matter by a tribunal having competent jurisdiction and concluding all persons (not merely the parties to the proceedings) from saying that the status of the thing adjudicated upon was not such as declared by the adjudication (*R.* v. *Harrington* (1855) 4 E. & B. 780; *Castrique* v. *Imrie* (1870) L.R. 4 H.L. 414). Where a court *rei sitae* has control over the thing and jurisdiction to decide as to its disposition, the adjudication is conclusive against the world. The chief instances are in the Admiralty courts, foreign judgments declaring the status of a ship, matrimonial causes, grants of probate or administration, condemnation of goods by a competent tribunal, and as to highways (*Wakefield Corporation* v. *Cooke* [1904] A.C. 31).

Remainder [Lat. *remanentia*], that expectant portion, remnant, or residue of interest which, on the creation of a particular estate, is at the same time limited over to another, who is to enjoy it after the determination of such particular estate (Co.Litt. 93a).

After 1925 remainders can operate only as equitable interests, and in that manner they can be created in respect of personalty as well as realty; and see the Law of Property Act, 1925, s. 4, as to the construction of equitable interests.

A remainder may be limited in all freehold estates, but not strictly and technically in chattels real and personal, although these may be limited over after a previous limitation or a partial interest in them. It might formerly be limited by way of use (which was, in practice, the usual method), as well as by a conveyance deriving its effect from the common law.

In the same land there may at the same time be an interest in possession, and an interest or several interests in remainder, and an interest in reversion.

When the interest in possession is determined, the interest in remainder, if any, otherwise the interest in reversion, becomes an interest in possession, with priority as to the interests in remainder, when there are several, according to the order in which they are limited.

An interest in possession and an interest in remainder or reversion are several parts of the same interest. When there are a particular interest and a remainder, the several limitations give distinct interests to the persons to whom these limitations are made.

These interests (different as they are in their nature), and also a reversion, are with reference to the person by whom the limitations are made, and the connection and relative situation of the tenants, several parts of the same estate.

Interests are said to be in remainder or reversion according to the relative situation they bear to each other.

The interest which as to one man is an interest in remainder, may, as to another person, be an interest in reversion. Thus if A leases to B for life, with remainder to C in fee, and C leases to D for life, the interest of C is still a remainder in reference to the interest of B, but in reference to the interest of D it is a reversion.

So an interest which as to one person is an interest in possession, or a particular interest, may, as to another person, be an interest in reversion; and consequently there may be two reversions in the same land, as if A leases to B, B has the possession and A the reversion as between themselves; and if B leases to C, then as between B and C, C has the possession and B the reversion.

A remainder does not, like a reversion, arise by operation of law, but is always created by act of parties. It may be granted over, charged, devised, or barred by a prior tenant in tail.

The difference between a reversion and a remainder may be illustrated thus: if the gift were simply to A for life the reversion in fee simple would remain in the donor. But this consequence would be varied if the gift were to A for life, and after his death to B and his heirs; or to A for twenty-one years, and subject thereto, to B and his heirs; or to A and the heirs of his body (which would constitute an entailed interest) and upon A's death and failure of his issue, to B and his heirs. In any of these three cases B would take an interest in fee simple, giving him a right to the possession of the land upon the death of A, or the expiration of twenty-one years, or the extinction of A and his issue. But this interest is not called a reversion, as the land does not revert or return to the donor, but a remainder, being the residue or remnant of the whole interest conveyed, after subtracting A's interest, which in relation to the remainder, as in this, or to the reversion, as in the former, case is called a particular interest (Burton, Comp. 28).

Remainders are of three kinds: vested or executed; contingent or executory; and cross.

If A, a tenant in fee simple, granted land to B for life, and after B's death to C and his heirs, C's interest was termed a remainder in fee expectant on the death of B. A remainder chiefly differed from a reversion (*q.v.*) in that between the particular tenant (B) and the remainderman (C) no tenure existed from which it followed that no rent-service would be incident to a remainder. The remainder was said to be vested (that is, vested in interest), because it was ready to come into possession the moment B's estate happened to determine; in other words,

the existence of B's estate was the only thing which prevented C's estate from coming into possession; and, therefore, whenever B died, the land passed to C, if he was living, or, through his representatives, to his heir or devisee if he was dead. If, however, A had limited the land after B's estate to the heir of C, a living person, the remainder would not be ready to come into possession at once, because until C died there was no one to take the remainder; for *nemo est haeres viventis,* and during C's life there was no such person as his heir. So if land was limited to B for life, and after his death, if C should then be living, to D, D's remainder was not vested, because its coming into possession depended not merely on the determination of B's estate, but on its determination during C's life: hence such a remainder was termed a contingent remainder, being a remainder limited so as to depend on an event or condition which might never happen or be performed, or which might not happen or be performed till after the determination of the preceding estate. When the uncertainty was removed, the remainder became vested. The possibility that a remainder might never come into possession at all did not of itself make the remainder contingent: thus, if land was granted to A for life, remainder to B for life, B's remainder was vested, although he might die before A, and consequently never come into possession.

Every contingent remainder was formerly liable to destruction by the determination of the particular estate before the remainder vested: thus, suppose land was limited to A, a bachelor, for life, and after his death to his eldest son and the heirs of his body, and in default of such issue to B and his heirs, then if A, before the birth of a son, forfeited or surrendered his life estate, or merged it by purchasing B's remainder in fee, the contingent remainder to his son would have been destroyed. To prevent this, the following plan was adopted in settlements and similar instruments giving contingent remainders to the children of a tenant for life: following the limitation of the estate to the tenant for life, an estate, to commence on the determination of his estate by any means during his life, was given to certain persons and their heirs during his life as trustees to preserve the contingent remainders, for which purpose they were, if necessary to enter on the premises, but to permit the tenant for life to receive the rents and profits during the rest of his life. These were called trusts to preserve contingent remainders. But the Real Property Act, 1845, s. 8, enacted that contingent remainders should not be liable to be destroyed by the forfeiture, surrender or merger of any preceding estate of freehold; and by the Contingent Remainders Act, 1877, no contingent remainder could be destroyed by the determination of the particular estate before the remainder vested, if the remainder would have been valid as a springing or shifting use, or executory devise, or other limitation, had it not had a sufficient estate to support it as a contingent remainder. Thus, if land was limited to A for life, with remainder to his eldest son who should attain twenty-one, and A died before any of his sons attained twenty-one, the remainder nevertheless took effect as soon as a son attained twenty-one. If, however, land was limited to A for life, with remainder to his eldest son who should attain twenty-five, the remainder would only take effect if the son attained twenty-five before A's death, because such a limitation could not take effect as an executory limitation by way of use or trust, being contrary to the rule against perpetuities. The only difference between a contingent remainder and an executory devise therefore was that the former was not affected by the rule against perpetuities, if it vested before the particular estate determined, but an equitable contingent remainder was void for remoteness if it infringed the rule against perpetuities (*Abbiss* v. *Burney* (1881) 17 Ch.D. 211). Contingent remainders were subject to a rule resembling that against perpetuities, for an estate could not be given to an unborn person for life, followed by any estate to any child of such unborn person; in such a case the estate given to the child of the unborn person was void. See PERPETUITY.

A remainder might be vested in interest and contingent as to the property comprised in it. Thus if land was limited to

A for life, remainder to the children of B in common in fee, each child of B on his birth in A's lifetime took a vested remainder in an undivided share, the amount of which was contingent on the number of children of B who might be born in A's lifetime. If the remainder was to the children of B whether born in the lifetime of A or not, the time for ascertaining the persons to take was also the death of A, unless the remainder was limited by an instrument executed after the passing of the Contingent Remainders Act, 1877, in which case the time was the death of B.

Cross-remainders arose when land was given in undivided shares to two persons A and B, for particular estates, in such a manner that upon the determination of the particular estates in A's share, the whole of the land went to B, and vice versa, the remainderman or reversioner not being let in till the determination of all the particular estates in both shares (Co.Litt. 195b). Cross-remainders still occur in settlements of land where, after limiting an entailed interest to each of the sons of the tenant for life in succession, provision is made for the failure of male issue by limiting it to the daughters in equal shares as tenants in common in tail, with a clause that on the death of any daughter without issue, her share (both original and accrued) shall go to the other daughters in tail, so that if all the daughters but one die without issue, that one takes everything, and the remainderman or reversioner in fee takes nothing unless and until they all die without issue.

The old rules relating to remainders were as follows:

(1) There must be a present or particular estate created which, if the remainder was vested, must be, at least, for years, but an *interesse termini* was sufficient; or, if the remainder was contingent, it must be an estate of freehold, expressly limited, or arising by a resulting or implied use in order to give such a remainder existence. A chattel interest would not support a contingent remainder, since, while the contingency was in suspense, there must be an ulterior estate of freehold vested in some person, for otherwise there would be no vested

freehold at law, which the law would not allow. There was, however, no necessity for a preceding freehold to support a contingent remainder for years; for such a remainder not amounting to a freehold, no freehold estate was requisite to pass out of the grantor in order to give effect to a chattel remainder.

The statute 1844, 7 & 8 Vict. c. 76, converted future contingent remainders into executory interests which were not hampered in the same way, but the Real Property Act, 1845, repealed this Act, and restored the rules relating to contingent remainders to their pristine vigour although the Act had abolished real actions on which they were largely based. This Act, however, provided that the accidental determination by forfeiture, surrender or merger of a preceding estate of freehold should not affect the estate in contingent remainder, but it was not until the Contingent Remainders Act, 1877, that the liberal purpose of the Act of 1844 was restored by providing that a contingent remainder which would have been valid as a springing or shifting use or executory devise or other limitation had it not had a sufficient estate to support it as a contingent remainder should be capable of taking effect as a springing or shifting use or executory devise or limitation. The Act of 1877 was repealed by the Law of Property (Amendment) Act, 1924, Sch. 10.

(2) The particular estate and the remainders must be created by the same deed or instrument, but a will and codicil might be fairly denominated the same instrument, for they took effect at the same time; and a deed giving a power, and the appointment exercising such power, were esteemed the same deed.

(3) The remainder must vest in the grantee during the particular estate, or the very instant it determined. But an estate limited on a contingency might fail as to one part, and take effect as to another, wherever the preceding estate was in several persons in common or in severalty; for the particular tenant of one part might die before the contingency, and the particular tenant of another part might survive it. Posthumous children were capable of taking in remainder in the same manner as if they had been born in their father's lifetime, and the remainder vested in them while yet *in ventre matris*: see the statute 1698, 10 Wm. 3, c. 22.

(4) A contingent remainder must be limited, upon a legal event, to someone who might by common possibility be in being, at or before the determination of the particular estate.

(5) It was not necessary for the support of a contingent remainder that the preceding estate of freehold should continue in the actual seisin of the rightful tenant; it was sufficient that there subsisted a right to such preceding estate at the time the remainder vested, provided such right was a present subsisting right of entry preceding the contingency, and not a right of action. It was necessary to distinguish between a right of entry and a right of action. If A was disseised by B, then, while the possession continued in B, it was a mere possession unsupported by any presumption of right, and A might restore his possession by an entry on the land without any previous action. If A entered and B defended his possession, and the question was tried in a possessory action, the gist of it must be who had the better title to the possession, and A must necessarily recover. Thus far the party disseised, even during the disseisin, was considered in law to be the rightful tenant. But if B continued in possession of the estate till his decease, the law, at his decease, cast the possession upon his heir; thus, upon B's decease his heir acquired possession by act of law, and his title, though immediately derived from a person who himself acquired it by wrong, was so far respected in law that A could not restore his possession by entry, and could only recover it by action. This removed A's title one degree farther than when he was able to restore his possession by entry, and was therefore said to reduce him to a right of action, and it was called a right of action in contradistinction to a right of entry.

(6) Where a contingent remainder was limited to the use of several persons who did not all become capable at the same time, notwithstanding it vested in the person first becoming capable, yet it divested as to the proportions of the

persons afterwards becoming capable, before the determination of the particular estate.

(7) If a condition was annexed to a particular estate, making it void on a given event, and a remainder was limited to take effect not only on the determination of the particular estate but on the destruction of that estate, by the effect of the condition the remainder was void, the common law rule being that a stranger might not take advantage of a condition, but only the grantor or his heirs. But if the condition for defeating the prior estate was to operate on one event, and the remainder was to arise on another and totally different event, the remainder would not be void, but the particular estate would be discharged from the condition. If A made a feoffment to B, a widow, for life, provided that if she married again then her estate should cease, and immediately after her death or second marriage the estate should enure to B in fee, this was a bad remainder, because it was limited to take effect not only on the determination of the widow's estate but also on the event mentioned in the condition to cut that estate short, namely, her second marriage; but if the remainder had been introduced without the words " or second marriage," then it would have been a good contingent remainder, and the condition would be viewed as surplusage. So, if the limitation had been to the widow *durante viduitate,* the remainder would have been good, as then her death or second marriage would have been the natural period for the determination of her estate. But if the remainder had been introduced by the words " from and immediately after the determination of that estate," it would be liable to objection on the ground that the remainderman would be taking advantage of the condition unless the word " determination " could be construed to refer to the death only of the widow and not to her second marriage. But such a remainder was supported, as a conditional limitation, in wills and conveyances under the Statute of Uses, 1535. A remainder commenced when the particular estate determined; it was, as it were, a continuance of the same estate; it was a part of the same

whole. A conditional limitation was not a continuance of the estate first limited but a different and separate estate. It was not to commence on the determination of the first, but the first was to determine when the latter commenced. It was the commencement of the latter which rescinded and destroyed the former, and not the ceasing of the former which gave existence to the latter. The particular estate and remainders were, in fact, one and the same estate. The estate first appointed and the conditional limitations were separate and distinct estates. See CONTINGENT REMAINDER; CROSS-REMAINDERS; EXECUTORY DEVISE; VESTED REMAINDER.

Remainderman, a person entitled to an expectant estate.

Remand. To remand a defendant or prisoner in a proceeding before a magistrate or justices of the peace is to adjourn the hearing to a future date, and to order that the defendant, unless admitted to bail, be kept in custody in the meantime. Children and young persons may be remanded to the care of a local authority (Children and Young Persons Act, 1969, s. 23).

Remand centres; remand homes. The statutory provisions relating to remand centres and remand homes were repealed by the Children and Young Persons Act, 1969, Sch. 6. Children and young persons in trouble are sent to community homes. See ss. 35–59.

Remanent pro defectu emptorum (they are left on my hands for want of buyers), a return made in an appropriate case by a sheriff with regard to goods taken under a *fieri facias.* See VENDITIONI EXPONAS.

Remanentiam, Ad. An estate *ad remanentiam* meant, in the time of Glanville, an estate in fee simple.

Remanet, an action which has been set down for trial at one sittings, but has not come on, so that it stands over to the next sittings. See R.S.C., Ord. 35, r. 3, notes.

Costs incurred for witnesses, etc., are allowed to the party ultimately prevailing.

The word also means the unexpired part of a sentence in criminal law.

Remanet in custodia (Rem. custod.) (he remains in custody). In the time of imprisonment on mesne process, an action in the King's Bench was properly commenced, when the defendant was in custody, by an entry of *rem. custod.* in the marshal's book.

Remedial statutes, statutes which are made to supply such defects and abridge such superfluities in the common law as arise from the general imperfection of all human laws, from change of time and circumstances, from the mistakes and unadvised determinations of unlearned judges, or from any other cause. This, being effected either by enlarging the common law where it is too narrow and circumscribed, or by restraining it where it is too lax and luxuriant, has occasioned a division of remedial statutes into enlarging and restraining statutes (1 Bl. Comm. 86).

Remedy, the means by which the violation of a right is prevented, redressed, or compensated. Remedies are of four kinds: (1) by act of the party injured, the principal of which are self-defence, recaption, distress, entry, abatement and seizure; (2) by operation of law, as in the case of retainer and remitter; (3) by agreement between the parties, *e.g.*, by accord and satisfaction, and arbitration; and (4) by judicial remedy, *e.g.*, action or suit. The last are called judicial remedies, as opposed to the first three classes, which are extrajudicial. As to the distinction between a remedy and a right, see LIMITATION OF ACTIONS; and as to equitable injuries and equitable remedies, see INJURY.

The minute variation permitted from the standard of weight and fineness prescribed for coins is known as a remedy (Coinage Act, 1971, s. 1, Sch. 1 Pt. I. See TOLERANCE.

Remembrancers. There were, in the Exchequer, three officers known as Remembrancers: the Queen's Remembrancer, the Lord Treasurer's Remembrancer, and the Remembrancer of the First Fruits. The office of the last-mentioned was abolished by the Queen Anne's Bounty Act, 1838, s. 1. The office of the Lord Treasurer's Remembrancer (who was concerned with the collection of the hereditary revenues of the Crown) was abolished by the enactment which in 1833 abolished the office of the Clerk of the Pipe (*q.v.*), who had kept the accounts of those revenues.

The Queen's Remembrancer performed duties connected with recoveries of penalties and debts due to the Crown; he kept in his office the documents relating to the passing of lands to and from the Crown, and he had functions in connection with English Bills (see BILL OF COMPLAINT). The Queen's Remembrancer Act, 1859, s. 1, provided that he should cease to exist as a separate officer, and that he should be a Master of the Court of Exchequer. Under the Judicature Act, 1873, s. 77, he was attached to the Supreme Court, and under the Judicature (Officers) Act, 1879, ss. 6, 8, he was transferred to the Central Office, and made a Master of the Supreme Court. The Senior Master of the Queen's Bench Division holds the office of Queen's Remembrancer. His duties as Queen's Remembrancer now consist mainly of certain functions connected with the selection of sheriffs (*q.v.*) and swearing in of the Lord Mayor of London, the trial of the pyx (*q.v.*), and acknowledgments of homage for Crown lands (Queen's Remembrancer Act, 1859, s. 43) (Bonner, *Office of King's Remembrancer*). See QUEEN'S REMEMBRANCER.

The Remembrancer of the City of London is an official who represents the corporation before parliamentary committees, accompanies the sheriffs when they wait on the sovereign in connection with any address from the corporation and attends courts of aldermen and common council when required.

Remise, to surrender or return; to release. In old releases the operative words were " remise, surrender and quit claim," all of which were of practically the same meaning (Co.Litt. 264b).

Remission, a pardon under the Great Seal; a release.

Remit; Remission. As in the majority of cases, a court of appeal sits merely to decide questions of law, and has not the machinery to carry its decisions into effect, it is obliged, when it reverses or varies the decision of an inferior tribunal in such a way as to make further steps necessary, to remit or send back the case to the inferior tribunal, so that such steps may be taken there as are necessary to carry the decision into effect. Thus, supposing a court gives judgment for the defendant in an action in which, if the plaintiff were successful, inquiries would have to be taken, then, if the House of Lords or Privy Council reverses that decision and gives judgment for the plaintiff, it remits the case to the lower court in order that the inquiries may be taken, or it may remit the case with directions as to the relief to be granted to the plaintiff. This is sometimes called remitter.

In Privy Council practice, on a cause being remitted to the inferior court, a document called a remission is in some cases (*e.g.,* ecclesiastical appeals) required to be issued. It is a kind of writ commending the judge to resume and proceed with the cause.

Remitment, the act of sending back to custody: an annulment.

Remittance, money sent by one person to another, in specie, or by bill of exchange, cheque, or otherwise.

Remitted actions. By the County Courts Act, 1959, s. 45, the High Court may remit to the county court any action brought in the High Court where (1) the plaintiff's claim is founded either on contract or tort and the amount claimed or remaining in dispute does not exceed £750, whether the counterclaim (if any) exceeds or does not exceed £750; or (2) the only matter remaining in dispute is a counterclaim, founded on contract or tort, not exceeding £750; or (3) by s. 50, the plaintiff's claim is for recovery of land, with or without a claim for rent or mesne profits, by a landlord against a tenant (or some one claiming by, through, or under him), whose term has expired or been determined or has become liable to forfeiture for non-payment of rent, and the action could have been brought in the county court. Certain equity proceedings may be transferred to the county court (s. 54), and also certain Admiralty proceedings (s. 59), probate proceedings (s. 62), and applications to attach debts or bring execution against members of a firm (s. 146). Interpleader issues may also be remitted to the county court if the amount or value of the matter in dispute does not exceed £750 (s. 68). See COUNTY COURTS.

Remittee, the person to whom a remittance is sent.

Remitter. Where he who has the right of entry in lands, but is out of possession, obtains afterwards the possession of the lands by some subsequent, and, of course, defective title, he is remitted or sent back, by operation of law, to his ancient and more certain title (3 Bl.Comm. 19, 189).

The possession which he has gained by a bad title is *ipso facto* annexed to his own inherent good one; and his defeasible estate is utterly defeated and annulled by the instantaneous act of law, without his participation or consent. As if A disseises B, *i.e.,* turns him out of possession, and afterwards demises the land to B (without a deed) for a term of years, by which B enters, this entry is a remitter to B, who is in of his former and surer estate. But if A had demised to him for years by deed or by matter of record, there B would not have been remitted. For if a man by deed takes a lease of his own lands, it binds him, because a man never can be allowed to affirm that his own deed is ineffectual; the same law holds, if it had been by matter of record. See RECONTINUANCE; REMIT.

Remittitur damna (or damnum). When one of the parties to an action in the Court of King's Bench obtained judgment for damages which he was either not entitled to, or was willing to abandon, he made an entry on the record called a *remittitur damna,* by which he gave up or remitted those damages. Thus, if the jury gave greater damages than the plaintiff had claimed by his pleading, the mistake was rectified by entering a *remittitur damna* as to the excess. So when the defendant, in an action of replevin, obtained judgment by default, he was entitled not only to a return of the goods replevied, but also to damages for being deprived of them, which had to be assessed by a writ of inquiry; but the damages being usually trifling in amount, they were generally remitted, in order to save the expense of a writ of inquiry.

Remittitur of record, when a judgment of the Court of King's Bench was affirmed or reversed in the Court of

Exchequer Chamber on a writ of error, there was a *remittitur* of record (or transmission of the transcript of the record) to the King's Bench to be entered up at the foot of the judgment there. This was made unnecessary by a rule of court made in 1834.

Remonstrance, a petition to Parliament that something which is in contemplation shall not be done (Husband, *Collection of Remonstrances*).

Remote parties, parties to a bill of exchange who are not in direct relation to each other.

Remoteness, want of close connection between a wrong and the damage, as cause and effect, whereby the party injured cannot claim compensation from the wrongdoer. See CAUSA CAUSANS; MEASURE OF DAMAGES.

The term is also often used to signify an infraction of the rule against perpetuity, a limitation exceeding the prescribed limits being said to be void for remoteness: see the Law of Property Act, 1925, s. 163. See PERPETUITY.

Remoto impedimento emergit actio (Wing. 20). (An impediment being removed, an action emerges.) Quoted by Wingate in support of various propositions such as that a man shall not have execution against the king's debtor, because the king ought to be paid first; yet if the plaintiff will undertake to pay the king's debt, he may have execution for both the debts.

Removal. The casual poor of a parish (as opposed to its settled poor) were only entitled to relief in that parish until they could be removed to their parish of birth or settlement, under an order of removal made by two justices of the peace, unless they had acquired the status of irremovability. See IRREMOVABILITY; POOR LAW; SETTLEMENT OF PAUPERS.

An action commenced in the Central Office of the High Court may be removed to a district registry, and an action proceeding in a district registry may be removed into the Central Office by the defendant in certain cases (Ord. 4, r. 6). See JUDGMENT.

A cause may in certain cases be removed from a county court to the High Court (County Courts Act, 1959, ss. 43, 44, 49, 58), or from the High Court to the county court. See REMITTED ACTIONS.

As to the removal of judgments, see JUDGMENT.

A cause may be in general removed from an inferior court into the High Court by certiorari (*q.v.*).

Removal of goods to prevent distress. The Distress for Rent Act, 1737, if the removal of his goods by a tenant be fraudulent, or clandestine, allows the landlord to follow and distrain upon the goods for thirty days, wherever they are.

Removal of surface soil. Improper removal of surface soil from agricultural land for sale is an offence under the Agricultural Land (Removal of Surface Soil) Act, 1953.

Remover, the transfer of a suit or cause from one court to another (11 Co.Rep. 41).

Renant, or **Reniant** [Lat. *negans*], denying: see the statute 1540, 32 Hen. 8, c. 2.

Rencounter, a sudden meeting, as opposed to a duel, which is deliberate.

Render, to yield, give again, or return; to yield or pay, as to render a rent (Co. Litt. 214).

Some kinds of heriots were said to lie in render, that is, the tenant was bound to give the heriot to the lord. Hence, profits are divided into profits lying in render, or those which the tenant is bound to yield or pay, such as rent, and profits lying in prender, which the person entitled to must take for himself (Co.Litt. 142a). See PRENDER; PROFIT.

Where a mine, quarry or the like is leased, it is sometimes stipulated that a certain proportion of the minerals gotten shall be delivered to the lessor by way of rent or royalty. This is called a render. It is a royalty in kind. See ROYALTY.

Rendition, surrender of a suspected or convicted person under mutual arrangements between members of the British Commonwealth.

Renegade [Lat. *renegare*, to renounce], one who has changed his profession of faith or opinion: one who has deserted his church or party. See APOSTASY.

Renewal of lease, a re-grant of an expiring lease for a further term. Where a lease contains a covenant by the lessor for renewal, this covenant is commonly subject to the condition that the covenants in the lease shall have been performed by the lessee, and this condition is strongly enforced by the court (*Finch* v. *Underwood* (1876) 2 Ch.D. 310).

An option to renew a lease can be exercised by conduct if the relevant provision calls for no notice to be given (*Gardner* v. *Blaxhill* [1960] 1 W.L.R. 752).

Leases may be surrendered in order to be renewed, without a surrender of under-leases, by virtue of the Law of Property Act, 1925, s. 150, replacing the Landlord and Tenant Act, 1730, s. 6, before which Act a surrender of each under-lease was necessary.

As to covenants for perpetual renewal, see *Wynn* v. *Conway Corporation* [1914] 2 Ch. 705.

By the Law of Property Act, 1922, s. 145, Sch. 15, perpetually renewable leases are converted into terms of 2,000 years from the date of the commencement of the existing term. The conversion is without prejudice to the covenants and conditions of the lease or the trusts, powers, limitations, rights and equities or defects in title affecting the original term. The long term may be terminated by ten days' previous notice on any date on which the original lease would have expired, apart from renewal. Every assignment or devolution of the term must be registered with the lessor, his solicitor, or agent, within six months at a fee of a guinea (£1·05) in substitution for similar covenants (if any) in the lease, and a further covenant for production of the lease and proof of right of renewal to the lessor, etc., and endorsement by the lessor of notice of such production, is also implied. Disputes as to notices to quit or right to renewal and other matters are referred to the Minister of Agriculture, Fisheries and Food, and fines payable upon renewal are converted into annual rents. Liability for rent and breach of covenant attaches to the tenant only for so long as he holds the term, even though he may be the original lessee. As to leases falling within these provisions, see *Parkus* v. *Greenwood* [1950] Ch. 644.

Long leases or leases with perpetual right of renewal, taking effect as demises for 2,000 years, may be granted, but any contract to renew an existing lease for a term exceeding sixty years from the termination of the original lease is void, and apparently this contract cannot be entered into until less than twenty-one years of the existing term is unexpired (Law of Property Act, 1925, s. 149 (3)). Corresponding provisions are made in regard to subleases with perpetual right of renewal. Copyholds held with a perpetual right of renewal are converted into enfranchised freehold by the Law of Property Act, 1922, s. 135, Sch. 12. Subleases with perpetual right of renewal become leases for 2,000 years under the Law of Property Act, 1922, s. 145, Sch. 15.

By the Small Holdings and Allotments Act, 1908, s. 44, a local authority which has compulsorily hired land for the purposes of the Act can obtain a compulsory renewal of the lease.

The Landlord and Tenant Act, 1927, made provision for the renewal of leases by way of compensation for improvements and increase in value due to goodwill. The Leasehold Property (Temporary Provisions) Act, 1951, provided for the renewal of tenancies of shops. The Landlord and Tenant Act, 1954, replaces these provisions and provides that a tenancy of business premises shall not come to an end unless terminated in accordance with the Act. See further the Law of Property Act, 1969, ss. 1–15.

Renewal of writs. It is provided by R.S.C., Ord. 6, r. 8, that no writ of summons shall be in force for more than twelve months; but upon application before the expiration of the twelve months, it may be renewed for twelve months from the date of such renewal, and so from time to time during the currency of the renewed writ, so as to be available to prevent the operation of any statute whereby the time for the commencement of an action may be limited (*Hewett* v. *Barr* [1891] 1 Q.B. 98). See WRIT OF SUMMONS.

Renounce, to give up a right. An executor who declines to take probate of the will of his testator is said to renounce probate. Where any person renounces probate of a will of which he is appointed executor, his right ceases and goes and devolves as if he had not been appointed (Administration of Estates Act, 1925, s. 5; Non-Contentious Probate Rules, 1954, r. 35).

A renunciation is a document by which a person appointed by a testator as his executor, or a person who is entitled to take out letters of administration of the estate of an intestate in priority to other persons, renounces or gives up his right to take out probate or letters of administration; the document is filed in the Probate Registry. The word renunciation is also commonly used as synonymous with disclaimer (*q.v.*) where the latter word is used generally in connection with a right, interest, or office. See RETRACTATION.

The stamp duty on a letter of renunciation of shares, etc., was abolished by the Finance Act, 1949, s. 35, Sched. VIII.

Renovant, renewing.

Rent [Lat. *reditus*; Norm. Fr. *rente*; *render,* to yield], a periodical payment due by a tenant of land or other corporeal hereditament; it is usually payable in money, but it may also be reserved in fowls, wheat, spurs or the like (Co.Litt. 142a).

When land is let free of rent and the landlord wishes to be able to obtain an acknowledgment of the tenancy when necessary, a nominal rent is frequently reserved, consisting of one peppercorn a year to be paid when demanded.

Rent may be regarded as of a twofold nature—first, as something issuing out of the land, as a compensation for the possession during the term; and secondly, as an acknowledgment made by the tenant to the lord of his fealty or tenure. It must always be a profit, yet there is no necessity that it should be, as it usually is, a sum of money; for spurs, capons, horses, corn, and other matters may be, and occasionally are, rendered by way of rent; it may also consist in services or manual operations, as to plough so many acres of ground and the like; which services, in the eye of the law, are profits. The profit must be certain, or that which may be reduced to a certainty by either party; it must issue periodically, though it may be reserved every second, third, or fourth year; it must issue out of the thing granted, and

not be part of the land or the thing itself.

Rents are of several kinds.

Rent service is always incident to tenure; in other words, it is that which is due when one man holds land of another by fealty (or any other service) and rent; as where a man holds land of another in fee simple at a rent reserved before the statute *Quia Emptores*, 1289 (see FEE FARM), or where an owner of land leases it to another for 99 years at a yearly rent. In the latter case the rent is an incident to the reversion of the lessor or reversioner and passes with it if he grants it to another. Payment of a rent service may be enforced by distress (*q.v.*).

If the rent is severed from the reversion (as where either is assigned without the other) it becomes a rent in gross.

A rack rent is a rent of the full annual value of the land, or near it.

When land is leased to a person on condition that he erects certain buildings on it, the rent reserved (which is small in comparison with the rent of the land when built on) is called the ground rent. When the lessee has erected the building, he may sub-let at a rack rent (calculated at an amount sufficient to repay to him with a profit the amount expended in building the house and also to cover the ground rent), or he may take from the sub-lessee a fine amounting to not much less than what he has expended on the house, reserving a rent a little larger than the ground rent; this is generally called an improved ground rent.

When a mine, quarry, brick-works, or similar property is leased, the lessor usually reserves not only a fixed yearly rent but also a royalty or galeage rent, consisting of royalties (*q.v.*) varying with the quantity of minerals, bricks, etc., produced during each year. In this case the fixed rent is called a dead rent. A footage rent is a rent payable for every acre a foot thick of minerals, and so in proportion for a greater or less thickness. A spoil-bank rent is a sum payable according to the quantity of rubbish from a mine deposited on land belonging to the lessor.

As to double and penal rent, see HOLDING OVER.

A rentcharge is where a rent is payable in respect of land to a person who has no reversion in it, and a right to distress is given him by express agreement between the parties: as where a man (since the statute *Quia Emptores*, 1289) conveys land in fee to another, reserving to himself and his heirs a certain rent with the right of distress, or if a man seised of land grants to another a yearly rent issuing out of it with a clause of distress (Litt. 217).

The rule against perpetuities (*q.v.*) does not apply to any powers or remedies for recovering or compelling the payment of a rentcharge charged on land or the income of land under s. 121 of the Law of Property Act, 1925, or charged on another rentcharge under s. 122 of the same Act (Perpetuities and Accumulations Act, 1964, s. 11). But this does not apply to instruments taking effect before the commencement of the Act (s. 15 (5)).

Formerly where a rent (not being a rent service) was reserved or created without a clause of distress, the grantee had no remedy by distress, and hence the rent was called a rent seck (*redditus siccus*, a dry rent). So if the owner of a rent service granted the rent to another, reserving the fealty to himself, the grantee had only a rent seck. But this distinction between a rentcharge and rent seck was abolished by the Landlord and Tenant Act, 1730, s. 5, which gave the owner of every rent seck a right of distress for it: so that every rent created by grant is now in effect a rentcharge.

Before the statute *Quia Emptores,* 1289, a person could convey land in fee simple to be held of him and his heirs, reserving a rent service from the grantee. Some instances of rents thus created still exist either under the name of fee farm rents (see FEE FARM RENT) or of quit rents, so called because in consideration of their payment the tenants are quit or discharged of all other services. Such rents were frequently due both by the freeholders and the copyholders of manors; they were sometimes called customary rents, being due by custom; or rents of assise, from being fixed in amount; and those of the freeholders were frequently called chief rents (*q.v.*). The fee farm rents payable to the Crown for the lands of religious houses were known as rents resolute.

Every rent, except a rent service incident to a reversion, is an incorporeal hereditament. It may belong to a man in fee, or in tail, or for any other interest.

The Law of Property Act, 1925, s. 121, gives a right of entry and distress for the recovery of any annual sum charged on land or the income of land (not being rent incident to a reversion). The Law of Property Act, 1925, s. 191, provides that quit rents, chief rents, rentcharges and other perpetual charges on land may be redeemed at prices to be fixed by the Ministry of Agriculture, Fisheries and Food.

Small rentcharges were frequently granted for the mere purpose of qualifying the grantee for the parliamentary franchise, as a forty-shilling freeholder, under the statute 1429, 8 Hen. 6, c. 7, but this kind of qualification was abolished by the Representation of the People Act, 1884, s. 4.

As to the period of limitation after which the right of recovering a rentcharge is barred, see *Shaw* v. *Crompton* [1910] 2 K.B. 370.

Fore-hand-rent means rent payable in advance (2 Bl.Comm. 14 *et seq.*; Co.Litt. 144a, note 5).

The Law of Property Act, 1925, s. 205 (xxiii), declares that rent includes a rent service or a rentcharge or other rent, toll or duty, royalty or annual or periodical payment in money or money's worth, reserved or issuing out of or charged upon land, but does not include mortgage interest; rentcharge includes a fee farm rent.

Rentcharges held in fee simple in possession or for a term of years absolute (see LEASE) are legal estates. All other rentcharges and rents, such as for life or remainder, etc., are equitable interests (Law of Property Act, 1925, s. 1 (8)); but s. 149 converts leases for life or determinable with life into terms of years absolute.

The Law of Property Act, 1925, s. 122, enables a rentcharge to be created out of another rentcharge with power to appoint a receiver upon default for twenty-one days.

Rent is not due till midnight of the day upon which it is reserved, although sunset is the time appointed by law to make a proper demand of it, to take advantage of a condition of re-entry or to tender it, in order to save a forfeiture; but the demand should be made before sunset, so as to allow sufficient light to count the money; and the person making the demand or tender must remain on the land till the sun has set. It may lawfully be made payable on a Sunday (*Child* v. *Edwards* [1909] 2 K.B. 753). Where rent is reserved generally and no such mention is made, as is usual, of half-yearly or quarterly payments, nothing is due until the end of the year.

Rent is considered as of a higher nature than even a debt due on an instrument under seal, as between the parties themselves. This is the effect of *Davis* v. *Gyde* (1835) 2 A. & E. 624, where a distress for rent after a bill of exchange had been given for it was held good; but in *Bramley* v. *Palmer* [1895] 2 Q.B. 405, it was held that the giving of such a bill was some evidence of an agreement by the landlord to suspend his remedy by distress during its currency; but the ordinary words " yielding and paying " import a payment in cash (*Henderson* v. *Arthur* [1907] 1 K.B. 10). Rent in arrear due by the executors of a tenant was, before the Administration of Estates Act, 1869, of a higher degree than simple contract debts, and of equal degree with specialty debts; but that Act abolished the priority (*Shirreff* v. *Hastings* (1877) 6 Ch.D. 610); see now the Administration of Estates Act, 1925, s. 34.

As to the apportionment of rents, see the Law of Property Act, 1925, ss. 77, 190. See APPORTIONMENT.

Rent allowances. See the Housing (Finance) Act, 1972, Pt. II; Rent Act, 1974, s. 11, Sch. 4.

Rent book. The Landlord and Tenant Act, 1962, requires the landlord of residential premises to supply the tenant with a rent book when the rent is payable weekly. This does not apply where the rent includes board (s. 1). Where the landlord is a company the tenant may demand the names and addresses of the directors and the secretary (s. 3).

Rent rebates. See the Housing (Finance) Act, 1972, Pt. II (ss. 18–26); Furnished Lettings (Rent Allowances) Act, 1973; Rent Act, 1974, Sch. 4.

Rent restriction. The control of rents and mortgage interest had its origin in the Increase of Rent and Mortgage Interest (War Restrictions) Act, 1915, and has persisted in one form and another to the present day, when it is regulated by the Rent Act, 1968, which consolidated all the earlier Rent Acts.

The Increase of Rent and Mortgage Interest (Restrictions) Act, 1920, consolidated the legislation from 1915 to 1919 and provided a system of control of rents (repealed in 1957), security of tenure and control of mortgages over the majority of unfurnished dwelling-houses leased to tenants. The Act of 1920 was amended in 1923, 1933 and 1935 so as to decontrol many of the more valuable houses but these remained tenancies controlled under the Act of 1920 as amended called " old control." Much of the ambit of " old control " is similar to the " new control " imposed in 1939 (see below) and is now to be found in Pts. I and II of the Act of 1968, but the differences are preserved in the Act of 1968, Sch. 14. " New control " was imposed over most dwelling-houses which were let by the Rent and Mortgage Interest Restrictions Act, 1939. The Rent Act, 1957, decontrolled many dwelling-houses and provided that no new tenancies should be controlled. It substituted a new type of rent limit now to be found in the Act of 1968, Pt. V. The Rent Act, 1965, brought under control most of the tenancies which had been decontrolled by the Act of 1957, but subjected them to a new form of rent regulation. Such tenancies are termed " regulated tenancies " and are now dealt with in Pts. III and IV of the Act of 1968. The Leasehold Reform Act, 1967, s. 39, provides that as from November 27, 1967, tenancies for a term exceeding twenty-one years at a rack rent become regulated tenancies and are no longer protected under Pt. I of the Landlord and Tenant Act, 1954.

Part I of the Act of 1968 (ss. 1–9), defines the ambit of control over " protected tenancies," which are the tenancies controlled under the Acts of 1920 and 1939 and the tenancies regulated under the Act of 1965. A tenancy is a protected tenancy if the rateable value does not exceed the amounts specified by s. 1 of the Act of 1968, and the Counter-Inflation Act, 1973, s. 14, Schs. 5, 6. Important exclusions from the above are tenancies under which no rent is payable or a low rent is payable, tenancies of dwelling-houses bona-fide let at a rent which included payments in respect of board, attendance or the use of furniture (Act of 1968, ss. 2, 7 (3)), tenancies where the landlord is the Crown, or the Duchy of Cornwall or a government department (s. 4). or local authority (s. 5; Housing Finance Act, 1972, Sch. 9). A tenancy may be a controlled tenancy although part of the premises are used for business purposes (Act of 1968, s. 9; Housing Finance Act, 1972, Sch. 11). The statutory continuance of a protected tenancy is called a statutory tenancy and the tenant a statutory tenant so long as he occupies the dwelling-house as his residence (Act of 1968, s. 3, Sch. 1). Limitations on the recovery of possession in the case of protected tenancies or statutory tenancies are imposed by Pt. II of the Act of 1968 (ss. 10–19, Schs. 1, 3) as amended by the Housing Act, 1969, Sch. 10; the Agriculture Act, 1970, s. 100 and the Agriculture (Miscellaneous Provisions) Act, 1972, s. 24). The upper limits of rent of tenancies formerly subject to the Act of 1965 (regulated tenancies and statutory tenancies) are controlled by Pt. III of the Act of 1968 (ss. 20–38), as amended by the Housing Act, 1969, Sch. 3 paras. 6, 13, Sch. 10; the Rent (Control of Increases) Act, 1969, s. 5 (1), Sch. para. 7 and the Housing Finance Act, 1972, s. 42, Sch. 11. Rents of regulated tenancies are registered under Pt. IV of the Act of 1968 (ss. 39–51) as amended by the Housing Act, 1969, ss. 52, 56, 83, Sch. 3 para. 7, Sch. 10; the Rent (Control of Increases) Act, 1969, ss. 5 (2), 6 (3); the Housing Finance Act, 1972, s. 39, Sch. 11 and the Rent Act, 1974, Sch. 1 Pt. II. Limits on the rent of tenancies formerly controlled by the Acts of 1920–1939 (controlled tenancies) are imposed by

Pt. V of the Act of 1968 (ss. 52–67) as amended by the Housing Act, 1969, Sch. 8 para. 32.

Part III of the Housing Finance Act, 1972 (ss. 27–34) provides for the conversion into regulated tenancies of controlled tenancies of houses which possess the standard amenities, are in good repair and are fit for human habitation. Conversion depends on the issue by the local authority of a qualification certificate. Part IV of the Act of 1972 (ss. 35–48) as amended by the Housing Rents and Subsidies Act, 1975, ss. 9, 17, Sch. 6 Pt. III, provided for a gradual general conversion of controlled tenancies to regulated tenancies. An exception is made in respect of premises declared unfit for habitation. Parts V, VI of the Act of 1972 (ss. 49–70) impose on housing authorities a duty to charge fair rents.

Part VII of the Rent Act, 1968 (ss. 85–92) restricts the right to ask for or receive a premium on the grant and assignment of protected tenancies and certain furnished lettings. The provisions as to premiums are penal in nature.

Part IX of the Act of 1968 (as amended by the Rent Act 1974, Sch. 1 Pt. II) contains provisions as to shared accommodation (ss. 101, 102), protection of sub-tenants (ss. 103, 104), rents of subsidised private houses (s. 110 as amended by the Housing Finance Act, 1972, Sch. 11), county court jurisdiction (Act of 1968, ss. 105, 106, as amended by the Administration of Justice Act, 1970, s. 47), service of notices on landlord's agents (Act of 1968, s. 109, as amended by the Housing Finance Act, 1972, Schs. 9, 11), restrictions on levying distress for rent (Act of 1968, s. 111). It is an implied term in all protected tenancies that the tenant shall afford to the landlord access to the dwelling-house and all reasonable facilities for executing repairs (s. 112).

A notice to quit any dwelling-house is to be of not less than four weeks (Rent Act, 1957, s. 16).

As to the protection of a tenant from harassment, and eviction without due process of law. See the Rent Act, 1965, Pt. III; Criminal Justice Act, 1972, s. 30 HARASSMENT; LANDLORD AND TENANT.

Additional powers of controlling rents are contained in the Counter-Inflation Act, 1973, s. 11.

The Rent Act, 1968, Pt. VI (ss. 68–84), Sch. 10) provided a measure of protection to tenants of furnished lettings through rent tribunals. Part VI was amended by the Tribunals and Inquiries Act, 1971, Sch. 4; the Housing Finance Act, 1972, s. 89; the Local Government Act, 1972, s. 205, Sch. 30 and the Rent Act, 1974, s. 1 (4), Sch. 4.

By the Rent Act, 1974, the provisions of the Rent Act, 1968, relating to statutory tenancies, protected tenancies and protected tenancies extend to furnished tenancies but no protected furnished tenancy or statutory furnished tenancy is a controlled tenancy (ss. 1, 6–8, Sch. 1). Consequential amendments are made to the Act of 1968, Sch. 2 Pt. II in relation to the recovery of possession of premises let on furnished tenancies (Act of 1974, s. 3). Applications for registration of a new rent before the three years specified in ss. 44 and 48 have expired (Act of 1974, s. 4). For transitional provisions affecting furnished lettings which become furnished tenancies, see the 1974 Act, s. 5. As to furnished sub-tenancies, see s. 13. As to the power of a county court in an action for possession to reduce the period of a notice to quit, see s. 14. Certain tenancies are excluded from protection. These are (a) a tenancy granted to a student by his university or similar institution, (b) a holiday tenancy and (c) tenancies granted by resident landlords (s. 2, Sch. 2).

For the powers of the court as regards the matrimonial home when the marriage is terminated by divorce, etc. see the Matrimonial Homes Act, 1967, s. 7; Rent Act, 1968, Sch. 15.

See DISTRESS; HOUSING; LOCAL GOVERNMENT; OVERCROWDING; PUBLIC HEALTH; RECOVERY; RENT ALLOWANCES; RENT REBATES.

Rent tribunals. See RENT RESTRICTION.

Rentcharge. See RENT.

Rente [Fr.], an annuity. *Rentes* is the term applied to the French government funds, and *rentier* to a fundholder or other person having an income from personal property.

Rente viagère [Fr.], a life annuity.

Rents and profits. A devise of the "rents and profits," or "rents," of land is, in the absence of evidence to the contrary, a devise of the land itself (*Blann* v. *Bell* (1852) 2 De G. M. & G. 781).

Renunciation. See RENOUNCE.

Renvoi, a term employed in private international law to denote the sending, or determination, of a matter to or according to the law of a tribunal outside the jurisdiction where the question arose. Apparently, the courts of France, Italy and Germany will apply the law of nationality and where the law of nationality, as in England, applies the law of the domicile, the latter law appears to have been applicable under the local law in Germany (*Re Askew* [1930] 2 Ch. 259), and Italy (*Re Ross* [1930] 1 Ch. 377), and, in France, as to movables (*Re Annesley* [1926] 2 Ch. 692). As to Spain, see *Re Duke of Wellington* [1948] Ch. 118.

Repairs. See LANDLORD AND TENANT.

Reparatione facienda, De, a writ to enforce the duty of carrying out repairs. Thus it lay for a man who had a right of passage over a bridge against another man who was under a duty to keep the bridge in repair but had failed to do so (New N.B. 281; Fitz.N.B. 127).

Repatriation. This is said to take place when a person regains a nationality which he had abandoned or lost. (See STATUTORY ALIEN.) It is the reverse process to expatriation (*q.v.*)

Repeal, a revocation or abrogation. Repeal of one Act of Parliament by another is either express or implied, the rule being that a later Act repeals a former one if contradictory thereto: *leges posteriores priores contrarias abrogant.* By the Interpretation Act, 1889, s. 11, re-enacting Lord Brougham's Act, 1850, s. 5, where an Act passed after 1850 repeals a repealing enactment, it does not revive any enactment previously repealed; where it substitutes other provisions, the repealed enactment remains in force until the substituted provisions come into operation. By the Interpretation Act, 1889, s. 38, where any Act passed after January 1, 1890, repeals and re-enacts any provisions of a former Act, references in any other Act to the provisions so repealed are to be construed as references to the provisions so re-enacted, as had been already specially provided in the Public Health Act, 1875, s. 313, and the Factory and Workshop Act, 1878, s. 102: see *R.* v. *Minister of Health, ex p. Villiers* [1936] 2 K.B. 29.

The effect of an implied repeal is the same as that of an express repeal; but the leaning of the courts is against implied repeal (*West Ham* v. *Fourth City Mutual Building Society* [1892] 1 Q.B. 654).

Repellitur a sacramento infamis (Co. Litt. 158). (An infamous person is not to be permitted to take the oath.) Coke is speaking of the challenge (*q.v.*) of a juror *propter delictum*. The maxim could also have been used to illustrate the old law under which infamy resulted from conviction of perjury, forgery, gross cheats, etc., and disqualified a man from being a witness.

Repertory, a classified inventory.

Repetition, a recovery of money paid under mistake (Civil Law).

Repetitum namium, a second or reciprocal distress, in lieu of the first, which was eloigned. See ELONGATOR.

Repetundae, or **Pecuniae repetundae,** the terms used to designate such terms of money as the *socii* of the Roman State, or individuals, claimed to recover from magistrates, *judices,* or *publici curatores,* which they had improperly taken or received in the *provinciae,* or in the *urbs Roma,* in the discharge of the *jurisdicto,* or in their capacity of *judices,* or in respect of any other public function. Sometimes the word *repetundae* was used to express the illegal act for which compensation was sought, as in the phrase, *repetundarum insimulari damnari*; and *pecuniae* meant, not only money, but anything that had value. Original inquiry was made into this offence, *extra ordinem ex senatus consulto,* as appears from the case of P. Furius Philus and M. Matienus, who were accused of it by the Hispani (Smith's Dict. of Antiq.).

Repleader, to plead again. The motion for a repleader was made when, after issue joined and verdict thereon, the pleading was found (on examination) to have miscarried, and failed to effect its proper object of raising an apt and material question between the parties. A repleader might become necessary where the issue had been defectively joined.

Replegiare, to replevy; to redeem a thing detained or taken by another, by giving sureties. See REPLEVIN.

Replegiare de averiis, a writ brought by one whose cattle were distrained or put in pound, on any cause, by any person, on surety given to the sheriff to prosecute or answer an action (Fitz.N.B. 68).

Replegiari facias, an original writ which issued out of the Chancery commencing an action of replevin, superseded by the Statute of Marlbridge, 1267, c. 21.

Repletion, where the revenue of a benefice is sufficient to fill or occupy the whole right or title of the graduate who holds it (Canon Law).

Repleviable, that which may be taken back or replevied.

Replevin [Old Fr. *pleige, plege,* a pledge or bail; *plevine,* a giving security; *plevir la fey,* to pledge one's word; Law Lat. *plegius,* a pledge; *plegiare,* to pledge; *praebere fidem,* to pledge one's word], a redelivery to the owner of a pledge or thing taken in distress (Brit. 54b, 55a, 180a; Co.Litt. 145b; 2 Bl. Comm. 150).

Replevin is a personal action to recover possession in specie of goods unlawfully taken (generally, but not exclusively, applicable to the taking of goods distrained for rent), by contesting the validity of the seizure, whereas, if the owner prefers to have damages instead, the validity may be contested by an action of trespass of unlawful distress. The pledge or thing taken in distress is redelivered to him by the registrar of the county court of the district within which it was taken, upon his undertaking and giving security to try the validity of the distress or taking, in an action of replevin to be forthwith commenced by him against the distrainer, and prosecuted with effect and without delay either in the county court or in the High Court, and to restore it if the right be adjudged against him; after which the distrainer may keep it in distraint subject to the law of distress.

REPLEVIN

See the County Courts Act, 1959, ss. 104–106.

It is a general rule that whoever brings replevin ought to have the property of the goods either general or special in him at the time of the taking, and it lies against him who takes the goods and also against him who commands the taking, or against both. Whatever may be distrained may be replevied.

In cases of distress for rent the replevy should be made before the expiration of five days (or fifteen, if the Law of Distress Amendment Act, 1888, s. 6, applies) after the distress, otherwise the distrainer may sell the goods; though, indeed, they may be replevied at any time before they have been sold (*Jacob v. King* (1814) 5 Taunt. 451).

An action for replevin may be commenced in the High Court, and if the replevisor wishes to proceed in that court, he must at the time of the replevying give security sufficient to cover the alleged rent or damage for which the distress is made, and the probable costs of the cause, conditioned to commence and prosecute an action of replevin in that court, a week from date, and to prove that he had ground to believe that the title to some hereditament, or to some toll, etc., was in question, or that such rent or damage exceeded £20, and to make return of the goods, if return adjudged. In the county court the action must be commenced within a month (County Courts Act, 1959, s. 105).

In avowries and cognisances for rent were set forth, as in a statement of claim, the nature and merits of the defendant's case, to show that the distress taken by him was lawful, and to entitle him to a judgment *de retorno habendo*. The technical difference between an avowry and cognisance was this: where the action was against the principal or landlord, he made avowry, that is, he avowed taking the distress in his own right; where, on the other hand, it was against a bailiff or servant, he made cognisance, that is, he acknowledged the taking in right of the principal or landlord; and where it was against both, the one avowed and the other made cognisance. The action of replevin is now rarely brought, it being usually more convenient to sue for damages for illegal distress.

Originally, the only remedy in cases of wrongful distress was the writ of replevin (*replegiari facias*), under which the proceedings were in the sheriff's county court; but by the Statute of Marlbridge, 1267, c. 21, the sheriff was authorised to grant replevins without this writ. If the goods had been eloigned (*q.v.*), the replevisor might have a writ of *capias in withernam* (*q.v.*), under which the sheriff took the distrainor's own goods as a punishment. If the plaintiff in an action of replevin was non-suited he was allowed a writ of second deliverance, under which the goods were again delivered to him; but if he was non-suited in the second action, the defendant obtained a writ of return irreplevisable, which was an absolute bar to the plaintiff's claim (3 Bl.Comm. 147).

The two latter proceedings were impliedly abolished by the abolition of non-suits (*q.v.*), See GAGE; GAGER DE DELIVERANCE; PROPRIETATE PROBANDA.

Replevisable. Goods for which replevin proceedings can be taken are said to be replevisable. Where goods are delivered under a contract, they are irreplevisable, because a wrongful taking is essential to replevin proceedings.

Replevy, or **Replevish,** to let a person to mainprise on surety; also to redeliver goods which have been distrained to their owner, upon his giving pledges in an action of replevin.

Repliant, or **Replicant,** a litigant who replies, or files or delivers a replication.

Replication. In matrimonial suits the pleading delivered by the petitioner to the answer of the respondent was formerly termed the replication and is now known as the reply.

In criminal proceedings by indictment, the replication is the pleading following the plea.

Under the old practice of the Court of Chancery and the common law courts, the replication was the pleading filed or delivered by the plaintiff in answer to the defendant's plea or answer. In Chancery, however, the replication had for many years been merely a joinder of issue (*q.v.*), special replications (which were used where the defendant introduced new matter into his plea or answer) having been superseded by the practice of amending the bill (Mitford, Pl. 321). See AMENDMENT; PLEADING; REPLY.

Reply, what the plaintiff, petitioner or other person who has instituted a proceeding says in answer to the defendant's case.

In an action in the High Court a plaintiff on whom a defendant has served a defence must serve a reply if he needs to plead any matter specifically. If no reply is served there is an implied joinder of issue on that defence. If the defendant has counterclaimed there must be a defence to counterclaim. A reply and defence to counterclaim must be in the same document. A reply and defence to counterclaim must be served before the expiration of fourteen days after service of defence or counterclaim (R.S.C., Ord. 18, rr. 3, 8, 14). No pleading subsequent to a reply may be served without the leave of the court (Ord. 18, r. 4).

When a case is tried or argued in court, the speech or argument of the plaintiff in answer to that of the defendant is called his reply. See OPENING, ETC.; RIGHT TO BEGIN; TRIAL.

In criminal cases, where any witness, other than the accused, is called for the defence, counsel for the prosecution is entitled to reply (Criminal Procedure Act, 1865, s. 2; Criminal Evidence Act, 1898, s. 3; Criminal Justice Act, 1948, s. 42 (1)).

The time at which the prosecution is entitled to that right is after the close of the evidence for the defence and before the closing speech (if any) by or on behalf of the accused. Formerly either of the law officers had a right to reply in all cases but this right has been abolished (Criminal Procedure Act, 1865, s. 2; Criminal Evidence Act 1898, s. 3; Criminal Procedure (Right of Reply) Act, 1964).

As to affidavits in reply, see AFFIDAVIT.

Under the old practice of the Chancery and common law courts, to reply was to file or deliver a replication (q.v.).

Report. Under the old practice in Chancery, when an inquiry was referred to the Master, he gave the result in a report, which was filed in an office called for that reason the Report Office. In more modern practice, chief clerks' certificates, petitions, etc., were also filed there (see CERTIFICATE). After the abolition of the Masters in Chancery (q.v.), the Report Office was added to that of Records and Writs by the Court of Chancery Act, 1855, and is now amalgamated with the Central Office (q.v.).

The judgment of the Judicial Committee of the Privy Council on an appeal or reference is technically a report to the Crown in Council, giving the opinion of the court on the question involved in the case. See JUDICIAL COMMITTEE, ETC; REFER.

Report, Law, a published account of a legal proceeding, giving a statement of the facts, the arguments on both sides, and the reasons the court gave for its judgment (Co.Litt. 293a).

Reports by barristers published with the reporter's name or otherwise sanctioned by persons of standing in the profession are cited in argument as precedents, and are of more or less authority according to the reputation of the reporter and of the judges whose decisions are reported.

Regular law reporting appears to have commenced about the end of the thirteenth century with the Year Books (q.v.). It was carried on by a succession of reporters in the various courts until 1865. In that year the Council of Law Reporting commenced a series of reports covering all the superior courts which took over the regular reporters. But this series is not official, all reports made by barristers and published on their responsibility being equally regular.

For information regarding the authority of the various old reports, see Wallace, *The Reporters,* 1882; continued to 1865 by Fox, *Handbook of the English Law Reports,* 1913. See also Daniel, *History and Origin of the Law Reports,* 1884.

For a list of law reports and their abbreviations, see *Where to Look for your Law,* Sweet and Maxwell.

Report Office. See REPORT.

Reporter, a barrister who reports legal proceedings. See LAW REPORT.

Reports, The, Coke's reports from 1572

to 1616, which are usually quoted as Rep. or Co.Rep. They are divided into thirteen parts, and the modern editions are in six volumes.

Reposition of the forest. In the law of the forest, this meant the reafforesting of forest lands which had been made purlieu (*q.v.*) (Manwood).

Repositorium, a storehouse or place wherein things are kept; a warehouse (Cro.Car. 555).

Representation, standing in the place of another for certain purposes, as heirs, executors, or administrators. See ADMIN-ISTRATOR; EXECUTOR; PERSONAL REPRE-SENTATIVES; REAL REPRESENTATIVES.

One person is said to represent another when he takes his place. Thus, an agent represents his principal, an heir his ancestor, an executor his testator, and an administrator the intestate whose estate he administers. As to parliamentary representation, see HOUSE OF COMMONS; HOUSE OF LORDS.

In the law of intestacy, the rule of representation is that rule of law by which the children or other descendants of a deceased person, who, if he had lived, would have taken property by virtue of an intestacy, stand in his place, so as to take the property which he would have taken if he had lived. See DESCENT; DISTRIBUTION; NEXT-OF-KIN; PER CAPITA.

In the law of contracts, a representation is a statement or assertion made by one party to the other, before or at the time of the contract, of some matter or circumstance relating to it. If a seller of goods simply represents them as worth a high price, while in fact they are not, this gives the buyer no right either to rescind the contract or to bring an action for damages. See CAVEAT EMPTOR.

A representation of simple commendation or expectation at or before a contract of which the other party can or should form his own opinion is not as a rule actionable. An innocent misrepresentation of fact gives no ground for damages, but may give a right to rescind the contract. If made at the time of sale of personal chattels, it may be a warranty provided it appears to have been so intended (*Pasley* v. *Freeman* (1789) 3 T.R. 634), and in that case, being a collateral contract, it may be proved by parol or extrinsic evidence, if the principal or written contract is wholly silent on the subject (*De Lassalle* v. *Guildford* [1901] 2 K.B. 235; *Heilbut Symons & Co.* v. *Buckleton* [1913] A.C. 30). See RESCIND.

In equity, on principles which are now applicable in all courts (Judicature Act, 1925, ss. 36 *et seq.*), even though a representation may not amount to fraud, or a warranty, its untruth may be a ground for resisting specific performance (*Redgrave* v. *Hurd* (1882) 20 Ch.D. 1), or for rescinding the contract (*Newbigging* v. *Adam* (1887) 34 Ch.D. 582). See RESCIND.

The Statute of Frauds Amendment Act, 1828, s. 6, enacts that no action shall be brought whereby to charge any person upon or by reason of any representation or assurance made or given concerning or relating to the character, conduct, credit, ability, trade or dealings of any other person, to the intent or purpose that such other person may obtain credit, money, or goods, unless such representation or assurance is made in writing, signed by the party to be charged therewith. A signature by an agent is not sufficient, so that a bank is not liable on the signature of the manager of one of its branches (*Swift* v. *Jewsbury* (1874) L.R. 9 Q.B. 301; *Hirst* v. *West Riding Banking Co.* [1901] 2 K.B. 560). See CONDITION; CONTRACT FOR SALE OF LAND; DECEIT; WARRANTY.

Representation of the laity. See the Synodical Government Measure, 1969, Sch. 3 Pt. V.

Representation of the people. See ELECTOR.

Representative, a person who represents or takes the place of another. The executor or administrator of a deseased person is called his personal representative, because he represents him in respect of his estate. Formerly, where there was realty the executor or administrator and also the heir were called the real representative (*q.v.*) because they represented the deceased as regards the realty; see now the Settled Land Act, 1925, s. 117 (xviii), and the Administration of Estates Act, 1925, s. 55 (xi).

If the plaintiff sues, or any of the

defendants is sued, in a representative character, this must be stated on the writ, and must also appear in the title or heading of the statement of claim R.S.C., Ord. 6, r. 3 (*Re Tottenham* [1896] 1 Ch. 628). A representative action is one brought by a member of a class of persons on behalf of himself and the other members of the class (R.S.C., Ord. 15, r. 12). In the proceedings before judgment the plaintiff is, as a rule, *dominus litis* (*q.v.*), and may discontinue or compromise the action as he pleases; therefore a member of the class who is dissatisfied with an order obtained by the plaintiff cannot appeal against it; he may, however, apply to be made a defendant, and, in a proper case, may obtain the conduct of the proceedings (*Watson* v. *Cave* (1881) 17 Ch.D. 19). As soon as judgment is given for the plaintiff he ceases to be *dominus litis,* and all members of the class who are willing to contribute to the expenses of the suit may join in, and take the benefit of, the subsequent proceedings.

Representative body. See WELSH CHURCH.

Reprieve [Fr. *reprendre*, to take back], the withdrawal of a sentence for a time, whereby the execution of it is suspended (4 Bl.Comm. 394). It may be granted either by the court or by the Crown. It may take place *ex mandato regis,* at the mere pleasure of the Crown; or *ex arbitrio judicis,* either before or after judgment, as, where the judge is not satisfied with the verdict, or the indictment is insufficient, or any favourable circumstances appear in the criminal's character, in order to give time to apply to the Crown for either an absolute or a conditional pardon; or *ex necessitate legis,* as where a woman is capitally convicted and pleads her pregnancy; or if the criminal becomes *non compos.* In two cases the court is bound to grant a reprieve, namely, where a female prisoner under sentence of death is found to be pregnant (Sentence of Death (Expectant Mothers) Act, 1931; Criminal Appeal Act, 1968, Sch. 5), and where a prisoner becomes insane after judgment (3 Co.Inst. 4; 4 Bl.Comm. 395). See JURY.

The Crown can, of course, reprieve as well as pardon or commute.

Reprimand, a formal and public stigmatisation of an offence addressed by a judge to a convicted offender, or by an official superior to an inferior, generally in substitution for any other punishment. Discharge, with reprimand, on payment of costs, was the penalty for a first offence under the Wild Birds' Protection Act, 1880, s. 4, in the case of a sparrow or other non-scheduled bird. See BIRDS.

Members of the armed forces may be sentenced by court-martial to reprimand or severe reprimand (Army Act, 1955, ss. 71, 72; Air Force Act, 1955, ss. 71, 72; Naval Discipline Act, 1957, s. 43; Armed Forces Act, 1971, ss. 36, 38).

Reprisal, the taking of one thing in satisfaction for another; recaption (*q.v.*). See CAPIAS IN WITHERNAM.

Reprisals. In international law, reprisals include every species of means, short of war, employed by one State to procure redress for an injury committed by another State. The term therefore includes embargo and retorsion (*q.v.*). Reprisals are negative when a State refuses to fulfil an obligation, and positive when they consist in seizing the subjects or property of the offending State. The reprisals above described were sometimes called special, as opposed to general reprisals, which were only used in time of war, and consisted in authorising any individuals whatever, whether suffering from private grievances or not, to act against the subjects of the opposed State. See LETTERS OF MARQUE; PRIVATEERS.

The word is now more generally used as meaning acts of retaliation during the course of a war for breaches of the usages of war. Thus the execution of prisoners by one belligerent might result in like steps being taken by the other belligerent.

Reprise, a deduction, such as a rent-charge, from the gross annual rent or value of lands. The word is used chiefly in such expressions as "above all reprises"; thus the Augmentation of Benefices Act, 1831, s. 1, referred to "the clear yearly value, above all reprises, of the rectory."

Reprobata pecunia liberat solventem (9 Co.Rep. 79). (Money refused frees him who tenders it.) The money must however be paid into court to support a plea of tender before action. See TENDER.

Reprobation, in ecclesiastical law, the propounding of exceptions to facts, persons, or things.

Rep-silver, money paid by servile tenants to their lord, to be quit of the duty of reaping his corn.

Republication of a will or codicil is where it is re-executed by the testator. Re-execution may take place when the will or codicil has been revoked and the testator wishes to revive it. Such re-publication as is effected by re-execution is now the only republication known to the law. The Wills Act, 1837, s. 22, provides that no will or codicil, or any part thereof, which is in any manner revoked, shall be revived otherwise than by the re-execution thereof, or by a codicil executed in the same way as a will, and showing an intention to revive the same; and that when any will or codicil which is partly revoked and afterwards wholly revoked, is revived, such revival shall not extend to so much thereof as has been revoked before the revocation of the whole thereof, unless an intention to the contrary is shown. Every will re-executed, or republished, or revived by any codicil is deemed to have been made at the time at which it is so re-executed, republished, or revived (s. 34). See PUBLICATION; REVIVAL.

Repudiation, the refusal to accept a benefice; the repudiation of a liability; the renunciation of a contract, which renders the repudiator liable to be sued for breach of contract, and entitles the other party, on accepting the repudiation, to treat the contract as at an end (*Mersey Steel and Iron Co.* v. *Naylor* (1884) 9 App.Cas. 434).

Repugnant, contrary to or inconsistent with. Thus, if A grants land to B in fee simple, upon condition that he shall not alienate it, this condition is repugnant to the estate, that is, inconsistent with the nature of a fee simple, and therefore void (Co.Litt. 206b).

The rule of construction is that, if there is no other way of arriving at the meaning, in a will the later of two contradictory clauses prevails, but in other writings the earlier. Conditions which are repugnant to a previous gift or limitation are void (*Bradley* v. *Peixoto* (1797) 3 Ves. 325; *Britton* v. *Twining* (1817) 3 Mer. 184; *Stogdon* v. *Lee* [1891] 1 Q.B. 661). See RESTRAINT ON ALIENATION.

As to repugnant gifts by deed or will, see INCONSISTENCY.

Reputation, credit, honour, character, good name. Injuries to one's reputation, which is a personal right, are defamatory. See CHARACTER; LIBEL; SLANDER.

In the law of evidence, matters of public and general interest, such as the boundaries of counties or parishes, rights of common (*Warwick* v. *Queen's College, Oxford* (1871) 6 Ch. 716), claims of highway (*Austin's Case* (1672) 1 Vent. 18ґ), etc., are allowed to be proved by general reputation, *e.g.*, by the declarations of deceased persons made *ante litem motam*, by old documents, etc., notwithstanding the general rule against secondary evidence. So, evidence of the conduct of a family, as proved by a surviving member of it, is admissible in questions of pedigree.

As to a manor by reputation, see MANOR.

As to the connection of a mark or name with goods, see TRADE MARK.

Reputed ownership. The doctrine of reputed ownership was first introduced into the bankruptcy laws by the statute 1623, 21 Jac. 1, c. 19, s. 11, with the object of protecting the creditors of a trader from the consequences of the false credit which he might acquire by being suffered to have in his possession, as apparent owner, property which does not really belong to him. If the circumstances in which the property is in the trader's possession, order or disposition, are such as to lead to a fair and reasonable inference, on the part of persons likely to have dealings with him, that he is the owner, and if the real owner is a consenting party, then on the trader becoming bankrupt, that property is divisible among his creditors. The doctrine does not apply to property comprised in a registered bill of sale, nor does it apply in cases where (as in the case of furniture held by an hotel keeper upon the hire-purchase system) there is a custom or usage of trade rebutting the presumption of ownership. (See ORDER AND DISPOSITION.) The Bankruptcy Act, 1883, s. 44 (iii), made the doctrine applicable to all goods possessed, etc., by any bankrupt, whether a trader or a non-trader in his trade or business; and that enactment is reproduced in the Bankruptcy Act, 1914, s. 38 (2) (c). It is still inapplicable in the case of a bankrupt who carries on no trade or business. As to the conduct of the owner, see *Simeons* v. *Durand* [1928] 2 K.B. 66.

The Law of Distress Amendment Act, 1908, s. 4 (as amended by the Consumer Credit Act, 1974, Sch. 5 Pt. I), enables a landlord to distrain on goods comprised in any settlement made by a tenant or on goods in the possession, order and disposition of such tenant by the consent and permission of the true owner under such circumstances that such tenant is the reputed owner thereof. See DISTRESS; HIRE-PURCHASE; TRUE OWNER.

Request. A request may give rise to an implied or tacit promise. Thus, if I request a workman to do work for me, I tacitly agree to pay him for it. If I request a person to do something for me without an express promise to pay him but in circumstances from which a promise to pay him can be implied, and after he has done it I promise to pay him, I am liable for the payment.

In some cases a request will itself be implied by the law (*quasi*-request): thus, if A has been compelled to do that which B is legally compellable to do, the law may imply a request by B to A to do the act. See CONTRACT; PROMISE; QUASI-CONTRACT.

Request, Letters of. Suits are sometimes brought before the Dean of Arches, as original judge, the cognisance of which properly belongs to inferior jurisdiction within the province, but in respect of which the inferior judge has waived his jurisdiction under a form of proceeding known in the canon law as letters of request. See LETTERS OF REQUEST.

Request-notes, applications to obtain a permit for removing excisable articles.

Requests, Courts of, tribunals of a special jurisdiction for the recovery of small demands, which were abolished by the County Courts Act, 1846, with a few exceptions. See COURTS OF REQUESTS.

Requisition, a demand by the enemy from the inhabitants of occupied territory or by an enemy naval force from a coastal place of supplies in kind, as distinct from contribution (*q.v.*).

Requisitioned houses. See the Requisitioned Houses Act, 1960; Housing Finance Act, 1972, Sch. 11 Pt. III.

Requisitioning, demanding necessaries for a military force, as billets or vehicles (Army Act, 1955, ss. 154, 165). Land was requisitioned during the war of 1939–45 under the Defence (General) Regulations, 1939, reg. 51, made under the Emergency Powers (Defence) Act, 1939. Compensation for requisitioned property was assessed under the Compensation (Defence) Act, 1939. Provision was made with regard to requisitioned property by the Landlord and Tenant (Requisitioned Land) Acts, 1942 and 1944, the Requisitioned Land and War Works Acts, 1945 and 1948, and the Requisitioned Houses and Housing (Amendment) Act, 1955.

Requisitions on title, a series of inquiries and requests which arise upon a title, made on behalf of a proposed purchaser or mortgagee, and which the vendor or mortgagor is called upon to satisfy and comply with. In the case of sales, they are often curtailed by the conditions of sale. See ABSTRACT OF TITLE; CONDITIONS OF SALE.

When a contract for the sale of real property has been entered into, and the vendor has delivered the abstract of title to the purchaser, the latter goes through the abstract, and if there are any defects in or questions as to the vendor's title, he puts his objections into writing and delivers them to the vendor. These are called requisitions, because they require the vendor to remove the defects or doubts pointed out. A formal contract of sale always stipulates that the requisitions shall be made within a certain time after the delivery of the abstract. It also generally stipulates that the title shall commence with a certain document, and that no requisitions shall be made in respect of the earlier title; not infrequently it is provided that no requisitions shall be made in respect of some specified defect in the title which the vendor is unable to remove. See VENDOR AND PURCHASER.

Rere county: Rier county, a supplementary county court held by the sheriff on the day after the county court. It was for, amongst other things, the receipt of the various moneys which the sheriff collected for the king: see the statute 1308, 2 Edw. 2, c. 5, and the Statute of Westminster II, 1285, c. 38 (2 Fleta 67).

Reredos, an ornamental screen covering the wall at the altar (*Philpotts* v. *Boyd* (1875) L.R. 6 C.P. 435).

Rerum progressu offendunt multa, quae in initio praecaveri seu praevideri non possunt (6 Co.Rep. 40). (In the course of events many mischiefs arise which at the beginning could not be guarded against or foreseen.) Coke cites this as illustrating the danger of innovations in the common law.

Rerum suarum quilibet est moderator et arbiter (Co.Litt. 223). (Everyone is the manager and judge of his own affairs.) That is to say, a man may do as he likes with his own. But Coke had not anticipated the course of modern legislation.

Res [Lat., a thing], any physical or metaphysical existence, in which a person may claim a right. In an Admiralty action *in rem*, the *res* is the ship, cargo or other property proceeded against. See ACTION; ARREST; BAIL; IN PERSONAM.

Res accessoria sequitur rem principalem. (The accessory follows the principal.) See ACCESSORIUM NON, ETC.

Res adirate, an action to recover goods from another into whose hands they had come and who refused to deliver them up (3 Holds. H.E.L. 322).

Res communes, things incapable of appropriation, such as light or air.

Res furtivae, stolen goods.

Res generalem habet significationem quia tam corporea quam incorporea, cujuscunque sunt generis, naturae sive speciei, comprehendit (3 Just.Inst. 182). (The word "thing" has a general signification, because it comprehends corporeal and incorporeal objects, of whatever nature, sort, or species.)

Res gestae (the things done), the facts surrounding or accompanying a transaction which is the subject of legal proceedings; all facts so connected with a fact in issue as to introduce it, explain its nature, or form in connection with it one continuous transaction. The phrase is chiefly used in the law of evidence, the rule being that evidence of words used by a person may be admissible (notwithstanding the general rule against derivative evidence), on the ground that they form part of the *res gestae*, provided that evidence of the act which they accompanied is itself admissible, and that they reflect light upon or qualify that act. Therefore, where a woman went to be examined by a surgeon with a view to effecting a policy of insurance on her life, and a few days afterwards stated to a friend that she was ill when she went, and that she was afraid she would not live until the policy was made out, and then her husband could not get the money, evidence of these statements was held admissible in an action on the policy, on the ground that as the woman's previous statements to the surgeon were admissible in evidence, her statements to her friend were also admissible, being part of the *res gestae*, that is, as following and explaining her previous statements. Similarly on an indictment for treason in leading on a riotous mob, evidence of the cry of the mob is admissible, because it forms part of the *res gestae*. So too on an indictment for rape are the cries of the woman who is being ravished (*R.* v. *Lillyman* [1896] 2 Q.B. 167). In *Ratten* v. *R.* [1972] A.C. 378, a woman's voice was heard on the telephone " get me the police please." Shortly afterwards the caller was shot dead by her husband who asserted that his gun had gone off accidentally while he was cleaning it. The Privy Council held that the words were admissible as part of the *res gestae*. See EVIDENCE.

Res integra, a point governed neither by any decision nor by any rule of law, which must therefore be decided upon principle.

Res inter alios acta alteri nocere non debet (Wing. 327; Co.Litt. 132; Broom, 648). (A transaction between strangers ought not to injure another party.) This means that persons are not to be prejudiced by the acts or words of others, to which they were neither party nor privy, and which they consequently had no power to prevent or control. In other words, a person is not to be affected by what is done behind his back. Thus, the evidence of a witness in one cause cannot usually be made available in another cause between other parties (*Duchess of Kingston's Case* (1771) 20 How.St.Tr. 335; *Higham* v. *Ridgway* (1808) 10 East 109). See JUSJURANDUM INTER, ETC.

Res ipsa loquitur (Cro.Jac. 508). (The thing speaks for itself.) This maxim means only that in certain cases one fact raises a prima facie presumption of another fact unless and until the contrary is proved; thus where a ship under way collides with a ship at anchor, that is prima facie evidence of negligence on the part of the ship which is in motion.

The principle embodied in this maxim applies in an action for damages resulting from the negligence of the defendant where it is shown that the thing which caused the accident was under the management of him or his servants and that the accident was such as in the ordinary course of things would not have happened if proper care had been exercised by him or his servants. It is used in actions for negligence where no proof of negligence is required beyond the accident itself, which is such as to involve a prima facie inference of negligence on the part of the defendant, *e.g.*, a collision between two trains upon a railway (*Carpue* v. *London, Brighton, and South Coast Ry.* (1844) 5 Ex. 787). See also *Moore* v. *R. Fox & Sons* [1956] 1 Q.B. 596 (gas apparatus exploding); *Richley* (*Henderson*) v. *Faull* [1965] 1 W.L.R. 1454 (unexplained violent skid).

Res ipsa loquitur means that a plaintiff prima facie establishes negligence where (i) it is not possible for him to prove precisely what was the relevant act or omission which set in train the events leading to the accident; but (ii) on the evidence as it stands at the relevant time it is more likely than not that the effective cause of the accident was some act or omission of the defendant, or of someone for whom the defendant is responsible, which act or omission constitutes a failure to take proper care for the plaintiff's safety (*per* Megaw L.J. in *Lloyde* v. *West Midlands Gas Board* [1971] 1 W.L.R. 749 (gas explosion injuring householder).)

Where the maxim applies the onus is thrown on to the defendant of disproving negligence, but if he does so the action fails (*Swan* v. *Salisbury Construction Co.* [1966] 1 W.L.R. 204).

A rule similar to *res ipsa loquitur* may apply in criminal proceedings where the defendant offers no explanation for a road accident (*Wright* v. *Wenlock* [1971] R.T.R. 228).

Res judicata. A final judgment already decided between the same parties or their privies on the same question by a legally constituted court having jurisdiction is conclusive between the parties, and the issue cannot be raised again. The principle of estoppel *per rem judicatam* applies where the question before the court was substantially the issue decided in previous proceedings whether or not there was an express finding in terms (*Duedu* v. *Yiboe* [1961] 1 W.L.R. 1040). Estoppel *per rem judicatam* may arise from a default judgment (*Kok Hoong* v. *Leong Cheong Mines* [1964] A.C. 993). The judgment may have been given by a foreign court (*Tarleton* v. *Tarleton* (1816) 4 M. & S. 21). A matter which is *res judicata* cannot be further gone into; but if the decision was obtained by fraud it can be set aside (*Cole* v. *Langford* [1898] 2 Q.B. 36). The underlying principle supporting a plea of *res judicata* is that it is desirable that litigation should end, and that it is undesirable that a person should be vexatiously pursued in litigation in regard to a matter that has already been decided (*Society of Medical Officers of Health* v. *Hope* [1959] 1 Q.B. 462; affirmed [1960] A.C. 551). Criminal proceedings do not constitute *res judicata* as regards civil proceedings arising out of the same facts (*Caine* v. *Palace Shipping Co.* [1907] 1 K.B. 670; *Palace Shipping Co.* v. *Caine* [1907] A.C. 386; *Anderson* v. *Collinson* [1901] 2 K.B. 107).

The rules for civil cases of estoppel *per rem judicatam* do not apply in their strictness to criminal cases (*Hailsham R.D.C.* v. *Moran* (1966) 64 L.G.R. 367). See ESTOPPEL.

Res judicata pro veritate accipitur (D. 50, 17, 207; Co.Litt. 103a). (A judicial decision is conclusive until reversed, and its verity cannot be contradicted.) But a judgment *inter partes* only binds the parties and their privies; as regards other persons, it is *res inter alios judicata.* See

IN PERSONAM; JUDGMENT; RECORD; RES INTER ALIOS ACTA.

Res mancipi. The *res mancipi* of the civil law were land—in historical times, land on Italian soil—slaves, and beasts of burden, such as horses and oxen; and the mode of conveyance by which they were transferred was called a *manicipium* or mancipation. Distinguished from them was another class called *res nec mancipi,* things which did not require a mancipation, *i.e.*, things which could be transferred by a simpler mode of assurance, and were held to pass by mere delivery.

Res nullius, a thing which has no owner.

Res perit domino. (The loss falls on the owner.) For illustrations of this maxim, see *Taylor* v. *Caldwell* (1863) 32 L.J.Q.B. 164; *Krell* v. *Henry* [1903] 2 K.B. 740. See also the Sale of Goods Act, 1893, ss. 7, 20, 32, 33. See DAMNUM SENTIT, ETC.; MORA DEBITORIS, ETC.

Res petita, a thing claimed.

Res sua nemini servit (4 Macq.Sc.App. Cas. 151). (No one can have a servitude over his own property.) This maxim of the civil law applies also in our law. See EASEMENT.

Res universitatis, things belonging to a corporation, the use of which is common to the members.

Resale. Sometimes (and in sales by auction under conditions of sale invariably) a vendor reserves the right of re-selling if the purchaser makes default in payment of the purchase-money, and in some cases (*e.g.*, on a sale of perishable articles or after notice of intention to resell) the vendor may do so without having reserved the right under the Sale of Goods Act, 1893, ss. 39, 48.

The maintenance by contractual and other means of minimum resale prices in respect of goods supplied for resale in the United Kingdom is restricted by the Resale Prices Act, 1964, and the Restrictive Trade Practices Act, 1956, ss. 24–27. Resale price maintenance is abolished except where it can be shown to be in the public interest. Except in the case of exempted goods, any term in a contract relating to the goods which provides for minimum prices to be charged on the resale of the goods in the United King-

dom is void. The inclusion of such a term in a contract is unlawful, so too are the publication of minimum resale prices, discrimination by a supplier against a dealer who has cut prices, except where the goods have been used as loss leaders. Jurisdiction in matters arising out of the Act is given to the Restrictive Practices Court to which applications are made for exempting goods from the provisions of the Act. The burden of proving that resale price maintenance is to the benefit of the public lies on the applicant. See also RESTRICTIVE TRADE PRACTICES.

See LOSS LEADERS.

Resceit, or **Receit** [Lat. *receptio*], an admission or receiving of a third person to plead his right in a cause already commenced between two other persons: see the statute 1390, 13 Ric. 2, st. 1, c. 17.

Where a cause has been commenced between two persons, the admission of a third person to plead was known as *resceit* or reception. The admittance of a plea by one or the other of the parties to a cause was also known as *resceit* (Co.Litt. 192; Broke 205; 3 Nels.Abr. 146).

Resceit of homage, the lord's receiving homage of his tenant at his admission to the land (Kitch. 148).

Rescind; Rescission. Rescission, or the act of rescinding, is where a contract is put an end to by the parties, or one of them. Thus, a contract is said to be rescinded where the parties agree that it is to be at an end, or where one of the parties is entitled to avoid it by reason of the act or default of the other party, and elects to do so by giving notice of his election to the other party, by setting up the invalidity of the contract as a defence to proceedings taken by the other party, or by instituting proceedings to have the contract judicially set aside (judicial rescission). (See RESTITUTIO IN INTEGRUM.) The most frequent instances of rescission by one party occur where there is fraud or misrepresentation and in certain cases where there is a failure of performance by one of the parties in an essential part of the contract. If a party to a contract fails to comply with a condition precedent, or by his own act makes the performance of the contract impossible, the other party may rescind the contract. A unilateral mistake in a contract in no way attributable to the conduct of the non-mistaken party does not constitute a ground for rescission (*Riverlate Properties* v. *Paul* [1975] Ch. 133). A right of rescission will be lost if the person entitled to rescind has elected to waive rescission (*Butler* v. *Croft* (1973) 27 P. & C.R. 1). See AFFIRM.

A contract may be rescinded on the ground of misrepresentation even if innocent and the fact that the misrepresentation has become a term of the contract or that the contract has been performed does not act as a bar to the right to rescind (Misrepresentation Act, 1967, s. 1). It is not necessary to prove that the representation went to the root of the contract. It is sufficient if the representation is material and tended to induce the formation of the contract (*Root* v. *Badley* [1960] N.Z.L.R. 736). Damages may be recovered when a contract has been entered into on the strength of a misrepresentation whether fraudulent or innocent. Damages for innocent misrepresentation may be awarded as an alternative to rescission (s. 2). Provisions in an agreement excluding liability for misrepresentation are void (s. 3) but this section does not affect the right of a principal to restrict his agent's authority (*Overbrooke Estates* v. *Glencombe Properties* [1974] 1 W.L.R. 1335).

In certain cases there is a right of rescission.

A contract for the sale of land commonly contains a power for the vendor to rescind the contract if the purchaser makes or insists upon any objection or requisition which the vendor is unable or unwilling to comply with; the Law of Property Act, 1925, ss. 42, 45, precludes the vendor from rescinding in certain cases, and this facility will not assist the vendor in case of a serious defect in title or substantial misrepresentation (*Hardicke Co.* v. *Lipski* [1901] 2 Ch. 666; *Baines* v. *Tweddle* [1959] Ch. 679. Where a purchaser rescinds under a power in the contract he has a lien for his deposit (*Whitbread & Co.* v. *Watt* [1902] 1 Ch. 835), but before 1926 the purchaser in the absence of misrepresentation was precluded from recovering his deposit if he chose to rescind upon an objection which he was precluded by statute from taking

under an open contract, or by the conditions in the contract (*Scott* v. *Alvarez* [1895] 2 Ch. 603). Under the Law of Property Act, 1925, ss. 45 (11), 49 (2), the court can, if it thinks fit, order the return of any deposit where the court refuses to grant specific performance or in any action for the return of the deposit.

Rescous [Old Fr. *rescosse*; *rescorre*, to release; Late Lat. *reexcutere*, to shake off again; *recupperare*, to take from, to receive or recover], rescue (*q.v.*).

Rescript, the answer of the Roman emperor when consulted by a particular person on some difficult question; it was equivalent to an edict or decree; a counterpart.

Rescriptum principis contra jus non valet (Reg.Civ.Jur.). (The prince's rescript avails not against legal right.) And so in our law no grant of the Crown can prejudice the course of justice, and the Crown can make no grant in violation of the common law or of the rights of the subject. See PROCLAMATIONS, ROYAL.

Rescue, the act of forcibly and knowingly freeing a person from an arrest or imprisonment (4 Bl.Comm. 131).

In the case of a person arrested in a civil action, the rescuer was liable to an action by the plaintiff for the loss thereby caused to him, and to attachment for contempt of court (3 Bl.Comm. 146).

In the case of a prisoner arrested in criminal proceedings, the punishment for a rescue varies with the degree of the offence for which the person rescued was in custody. See ESCAPE; OBSTRUCTING JUSTICE.

Rescue of persons in the custody of the law has been dealt with by a number of statutes beginning with the statute 1295, 23 Edw. 1. Aiding a prisoner to escape is an indictable offence by the Prison Act, 1952, s. 39, replacing the Prison Act, 1865, s. 37.

Rescue lies where a person distrains for rent or services, or for damage feasant, and is desirous of impounding the distress, and another person rescues the distress from him. The party distraining must be in possession of the distress, otherwise there cannot be a rescue. If the distress was unlawful, the owner may lawfully rescue the goods; if the distress was lawful, the rescuer is liable to an action by the distrainor. The action of rescue has fallen into disuse; the usual remedy is by an action under the Distress for Rent Act, 1689, s. 3; Administration of Justice Act, 1965, Sch. 2, which gives treble damages to the person aggrieved. When a distress is taken without cause, or contrary to law, the tenant may lawfully make rescue before it is impounded and is in the custody of the law. The Pound Breach Act, 1843, s. 1 (amended by the Justices of the Peace Act, 1949, Sch. 7 Pt. III; Criminal Justice Act, 1967, Sch. 3 Pt. I), gave a summary remedy for pound breach and rescue in certain cases after a distress for damage feasant.

A rescue in law is where the cattle, etc., come again into the possession of the owner without his act, and he refuses to deliver them to the distrainor (Co.Litt. 161a).

See DAMAGE FEASANT; DOUBLE DAMAGES; POUND; POUND-BREACH.

Rescuer. The doctrine of voluntary assumption of risk, *volenti non fit injuria*, does not apply where the plaintiff has, under an exigency caused by the defendant's wrongful act or omission, faced a risk to rescue another person, or his goods, from imminent danger where the defendant ought reasonably to have foreseen that the plaintiff would be likely to act as he did (*Haynes* v. *Harwood* [1935] 1 K.B. 146; *Hyett* v. *Great Western Ry.* [1948] 1 K.B. 345).

A stranger is entitled to intervene with the sole object of rescuing a person being attacked and of restoring the peace and is entitled to do what is reasonable for the purpose (*R.* v. *Duffy* [1967] 1 Q.B. 63). It is possible for a person whose negligence causes an accident to owe a duty of care to a rescuer. His liability can extend to damages for nervous shock (*Chadwick* v. *British Railways Board* [1967] 1 W.L.R. 912).

Rescussor, a person committing rescous or rescue (*q.v.*).

Resealing. The Administration of Estates Act, 1971, ss. 1–7, ended the need to reseal grants of probate and letters of administration as between the courts of England and Wales, Scotland and Northern Ireland.

Reseiser, a retaking by the king of lands where an *ouster le main* (*q.v.*) or proceedings thereon had been misused (Staundf.Praerog. 26; Chitty, *Prerogatives of the Crown*, 350).

Reservatio non debet esse de proficuis ipsis, quia ea conceduntur, sed de reditu novo extra proficua (Co.Littl. 142a). (A reservation ought not to be of the profits themselves, because they are granted, but from the new rent apart from the profits.)

Reservation, a clause in a deed whereby the feoffor, donor, lessor, grantor, etc., reserves some new thing to himself out of that which he granted before by the same deed; it most commonly and properly follows the *tenendum* (Shep.Touch. 80). See DEED.

The commonest instance of a reservation is the rent in an ordinary lease (Litt. 215).

A reservation in a conveyance of land by A to B operates by reason of s. 65 (1) of the Law of Property Act, 1925, by means of mere reservation and not re-grant. Accordingly, it is to be construed against A and not against B (*Cordell* v. *Second Clanfield Properties* [1969] 1 Ch. 9).

A reservation, in the proper sense of the word, cannot, it seems, be validly made in favour of a stranger to the deed, but the same effect may be produced by a grant, covenant or condition in favour of the stranger, for since the Real Property Act, 1845, s. 5, he need not be a party to the deed. It is said that a reservation to a stranger creates an implied covenant in his favour (Bythewood, Conv. iv, 420).

As to the difference between a reservation and an exception, see EXCEPTION.

Reservation of the Sacrament, a keeping aside of part of the consecrated bread of the Eucharist for the communion of the sick. Reservation of the Sacrament is an offence punishable by deprivation (*Oxford (Bishop)* v. *Henly* [1909] P. 319). See SACRAMENT.

Reserve, an amount which is not derived from the necessity to provide for a known or anticipated liability. A capital reserve is one which is not free for distribution through the profit and loss account. The creation of secret reserves by a company is prevented by the requirement that when an amount written off or retained to provide for depreciation, renewals or diminution in the value of assets or any amount provided for a known liability or for the purpose of preventing undue fluctuations in taxation is in excess of what in the opinion of the directors is reasonably necessary for the purpose, the excess shall be treated as a reserve (Companies Act, 1948, Sch. 8 para. 27; Companies Act, 1967, s. 9, Schs. 1, 2).

Reserve forces. The Army Reserve Act, 1950, replacing prior Acts on the subject, establishes an army reserve consisting of two classes. The first class consists of men transferred to the army reserve, men serving in the army reserve for a term of part-time service within the meaning of the National Service Act, 1948, and men enlisted or re-engaged in pursuance of the Army Reserve Act, 1950, for service in army reserve. The second class consists of men who, being out-pensioners of Chelsea Hospital or having served in any of the regular forces for not less than the full time of their original enlistment, may be enlisted or re-engaged therein in pursuance of the Army Reserve Act, 1950 (s. 1; Revision of the Army and Air Force Acts (Transitional Provisions) Act, 1955, s. 3, Sch. 2 para. 13 (1); Army and Air Force Act, 1961, Sch. 2; Reserve Forces Act, 1966).

The Air Force Reserve Act, 1950, provides that the air force reserve shall consist of men transferred to the air force reserve in pursuance of the Air Force Act, 1955, men serving in the air force reserve for a term of part-time service within the meaning of the National Service Act, 1948, and men enlisted or re-engaged therein in pursuance of the Air Force Reserve Act, 1950 (s. 1; Revision of the Army and Air Force Acts (Transitional Provisions) Act, 1955, s. 3, Sch. 2 para. 14 (1); Army and Air Force Act, 1961, Sch. 2).

By the Army Reserve Act, 1950, s. 10, and the Air Force Reserve Act, 1950, s. 10, the whole or part of the army reserve and the air force reserve may be called out to aid the civil power in the preservation of the public peace.

The reserve forces of the navy are composed of the royal naval reserve, established by the Royal Naval Reserve (Volunteer) Act, 1859, which consists of officers and men from the merchant service who receive an annual retaining fee; the royal fleet reserve, formed of time-expired members of the navy and marines; and the royal naval volunteer reserve (Royal Naval Reserve Acts, 1859 to 1927).

Further provisions relating to the reserves are contained in the Auxiliary and Reserves Forces Act, 1949, the Reserve and Auxiliary Forces (Training) Act, 1951, the Reserve and Auxiliary Forces (Protection of Civil Interests) Act, 1951, the Auxiliary Forces Act, 1953, and the Revision of the Army and Air Force Acts (Transitional Provisions) Act, 1955, s. 3, Sch. 2; the Army and Air Force Act, 1961, Sch. 2 and the Reserve Forces Act, 1966, Sch. 1.

Reserve liability, that portion of the share capital of a company which it has resolved shall not be capable of being called up except in the event and for the purposes of the company being wound up (Companies Act, 1948, s. 60).

Reserved shares, unsubscribed shares, *i.e.,* shares which the company is authorised to issue but which have not been issued and are reserved for future issue.

Reservoirs. Reservoirs now come under the control of the regional water authorities. See WATER. Water authorities may afford recreational facilities on reservoirs and other waters (Countryside Act, 1968, s. 22). Reservoirs are among the improvements which may be made with capital trust money under the Settled Land Act, 1925, s. 83, Sch. 3 Pt. I.

Reset, the receiving or harbouring an outlawed person.

Resettlement. Where land has been settled on a marriage, and the eldest son has attained twenty-one during his father's lifetime, and thus acquired an entailed interest in remainder, it is usual for the father as protector (*q.v.*) to give his consent to the son's entailed interest being barred on condition of a resettlement being made. The terms of such a resettlement generally are that the interest of the son shall be cut down to a life interest, with remainder to his children (if he should marry) successively in tail, subject to the usual provisions for his widow and younger children (see JOINTURE; PORTION), while the father on his side charges his life interest with an annuity for the son and a jointure for the son's widow, as a provision for them before the son's interest comes into possession. Such a resettlement will not, however, be supported in equity if it appears from the unfairness of its terms or otherwise not to have been understood by the son. See DISENTAILING DEED; ENTAIL; OVERREACHING CLAUSE; SETTLEMENT.

Resiance, residence, abode, or continuance.

Resiant, a resident. The term was chiefly used in speaking of manors (Old Nat.Br. 85; Kitchin 33). See COURT LEET.

Resiant rolls, those containing resiants (residents) in a tithing, etc., which were called over by the steward on holding courts leet.

Residence. This word is used in law to denote the fact that a person dwells in a given place, or, in the case of a corporation, that its management is carried on there: thus, if a company is formed in England for the purpose of carrying on a trade (such as mining or manufacturing) in a foreign country, but its business is under the control of a board of directors in England, the company is said to have its residence in England. A company is resident for tax purposes in the country where its central management and control are exercised even though according to its memorandum and articles the central management and control ought to be exercised in a different country (*Unit Construction Co.* v. *Bullock* [1960] A.C. 351). In the case of a person, residence connotes the idea of home, or at least of habitation, and need not necessarily be permanent or exclusive. The word denotes the place where an individual eats, drinks, and sleeps, or where his family or his servants eat, drink, and sleep (*R.* v. *North Curry (Inhabitants)* (1825) 4 B. & C. at p. 959).

Residence is of importance in several ways: first, as an element in ascertaining a person's domicile (*q.v.*), secondly, as determining whether he is subject to the authorities having jurisdiction or powers within the district where he resides, thirdly as forming part of some of the qualifications for voting at parliamentary and municipal elections.

Sometimes a distinction is drawn between actual and constructive residence, the latter term being used to mean that a person has the liberty of returning, and also the intention of returning, whenever he pleases, to the place at which he usually resides, although he may be actually absent from it for some time.

Residence also means the continuance of a parson or vicar on his benefice. It is upon the supposition of residence that the law styles every parochial minister an incumbent.

See NON-RESIDENCE; PLACE OF ABODE; PLURALITY.

Residens, a tenant bound to live on the land of his lord. He was called also *homme levant et couchant,* and in Normandy, *resseant du fief* (Leg. Hen. 1, c. 43).

Resident, an agent, minister, or officer residing in any distant place with the dignity of an ambassador; the chief representative of the government at certain princely states. Residents are a class of public ministers inferior to ambassadors and envoys; but, like them, they are under the protection of the law of nations.

Residual, or **Residuary,** relating to the residue; relating to the part remaining.

Residuary devisee, the person named in a will who is to take all the real property remaining over and above the other devises.

It is provided by the Wills Act, 1837, s. 35, that unless a contrary intention appears by the will, real estate or an interest therein comprised in a devise which fails or is void by reason of the death of the devisee in the lifetime of the testator, or by reason of such devise being contrary to law or otherwise incapable of taking effect, shall be included in the residuary devise (if any) contained in the will.

Residuary legatee, the person to whom the surplus of the personal estate, after the discharge of all debts and particular legacies, is left by the testator's will.

Residue, the surplus of a testator's or intestate's estate after discharging all his liabilities. In administering the personal estate of a testator or intestate, the debts, funeral and testamentary expenses and the costs of the administration are first paid, and what remains is the residue in the sense of the net personal estate; then, in the case of a testator's estate, the legacies, annuities, etc., are paid, and what remains is the ultimate residue or residuary estate in the ordinary sense of the word. Sometimes there is a residue within a residue, or a particular residue as opposed to a general residue: as where a fund is given to A subject to the payment thereout of certain legacies, so that if any of those legacies fail, they fall into the particular residue given to A, while the general residue of the estate is given to B.

A residuary bequest, that is, a bequest of the testator's residuary personal estate, passes all the personalty belonging to the testator at his death and not otherwise disposed of, including lapsed legacies. As to the effect of a residuary devise, see DEVISE; RESIDUARY DEVISEE. Where a testator does not effectually dispose of the residue of his property he dies intestate as to it, and it goes to his statutory next-of-kin. Unless it appears in the will that the executor was intended to have the residue, he will be deemed to be trustee for the next-of-kin (Executors Act, 1830, replaced by the Administration of Estates Act, 1925, s. 49): see *Att.-Gen.* v. *Jeffereys* [1908] A.C. 411. The distribution of the surplusage of an intestate's estate was provided for by the Statutes of Distribution, 1670 and 1685. The distribution of the estates of persons dying after 1925 is regulated by the Administration of Estates Act, 1925, as amended. See DISTRIBUTION; INTESTATE; LAPSE; WIDOW.

Resignatio est juris proprii spontanea refutatio (Godb. 284). (Resignation is a spontaneous relinquishment of one's own right.)

Resignation, the giving up a claim, office, or possession; also, the yielding up of a benefice into the hands of the ordinary, called by the canonists " renunciation "; and though it is synonymous with surrender, yet it is by use restricted to yielding up a spiritual living to the bishop, as surrender is the giving up of temporal land into the hands of the lord. Resignation of a benefice is usually done by an instrument attested by a notary. See HOLY ORDERS.

The office of a judge of the High Court or of the Court of Appeal may be vacated by resignation in writing under his hand, addressed to the Lord Chancellor, without any deed of surrender.

A member of the House of Commons cannot resign his seat. All he can do is to accept an office of profit under the Crown, which has the effect of vacating his seat. See CHILTERN HUNDREDS, ETC.

Resolution, a solemn judgment or decision; an expression of opinion or intention by a meeting (*q.v.*); a revocation of a contract.

As to the cases in which resolutions of the House of Commons varying or renewing taxation have statutory effect for a limited period, see the Provisional Collection of Taxes Act, 1968.

Resolutions of the members of a company are ordinary, special, or extraordinary. An ordinary resolution is one passed by a simple majority in number at an ordinary meeting. An extraordinary resolution is one passed by a majority of not less than three-fourths of such members as, being entitled so to do, vote in person or, where proxies are allowed, by proxy, at a general meeting of which notice specifying the intention to propose the resolution as an extraordinary resolution has been given. A special resolution is one passed by the same majority as that required in the case of an extraordinary resolution and at a general meeting of which not less than twenty-one days, notice, specifying the intention to propose the resolution as a special resolution, has been given (Companies Act, 1948, s. 141). The length of notice specified in the case of a special resolution may be waived by a majority of the members if the provisions of the section are fulfilled. At any meeting for the passing of an extraordinary or special resolution the chairman's declaration that the resolution is carried is, unless a poll is demanded, conclusive evidence of the fact without proof of the number or proportion of votes recorded in favour of or against the resolution (Companies Act, 1948, s. 141).

In bankruptcy proceedings, an ordinary resolution is one decided by a majority in value of the creditors present (personally or by proxy) at the meeting, and voting on the resolution; a special resolution is one passed by a majority in number and three-fourths in value of the creditors present (personally or by proxy) at the meeting, and voting on the resolution (Bankruptcy Act, 1914, s. 167).

Resoluto jure concedentis resolvitur jus concessum (Mackeld., Civ. Law 179). (The grant of a right comes to an end on the termination of the right of the grantor.) But the Settled Land Act, 1925, permits a tenant for life to grant leases of lands for longer than his own life. See NEMO POTEST PLUS, ETC.

Resolutory condition, one the accomplishment of which revokes a prior obligation.

Resort. As to places of public resort, see PUBLIC PLACE.

Resort, Court of last, a court from which there is no appeal; for example, the House of Lords or the Judicial Committee of the Privy Council.

Respectu computi vicecomitis habendo, De, a writ directed to the Treasurer and the barons of the Exchequer; it commanded them to respite (*q.v.*) the account of a sheriff (Reg.Orig. 139).

Respectum, Challenge propter honoris. See CHALLENGE.

Respiciendum est judicanti, ne quid aut durius aut remissius constituatur quam causa deposcit; nec enim aut severitatis aut clementiae gloria affectanda est (3 Bract. 105; 3 Co.Inst. 220). (A judge should see to it that nothing either more lenient or more severe than the case itself warrants should be done; for no attempt should be made to achieve distinction either by severity or by leniency.)

Respite, to discharge or dispense with. Thus, a lord was said to respite homage when he did not exact it from his tenant (see FEALTY; HOMAGE). It also means to delay, or a delay. Thus, a court of quarter sessions which adjourns an appeal from one sessions to another was said to respite the appeal, and such an adjournment was termed a respite. To enter and respite an appeal is to enter the same, and postpone the hearing to a future day. Respite also means interval, reprieve, suspension of a capital sentence, forbearance, or continuation of time. There are respite of execution, of debt, and of a jury.

Respondeat ouster (let him answer over), the judgment which was given when a prisoner failed to substantiate a special plea in bar. Thus, if he pleaded *autrefois acquit* and failed to prove it, judgment was given that he answer over, or plead to the indictment again, in which case he might plead the general issue, not guilty (see PLEA). Now a prisoner always pleads not guilty in addition to a special plea in bar; and therefore, if he fails to substantiate it, judgment of *respondeat ouster* is not necessary, but the trial proceeds as if no special plea had been pleaded.

In ordinary common law actions, judgment of *respondeat ouster* was formerly given when the defendant pleaded a dilatory plea (*e.g.*, a plea in abatement) and failed, in which case he had to plead in bar. Now, however, pleas in abatement are abolished; the defence contains all the defendant's objections to the action, and they are all tried at the same time; judgment of *respondeat ouster* therefore no longer exists; power, however, is given by R.S.C., Ord. 33, r. 3, to decide questions of fact or law before the trial, and by Ord. 33, r. 4, to order some questions to be tried before the others. See also FACT.

Respondeat superior (4 Co.Inst. 114). (Let the principal answer.) Where there exists the relation of master and servant or of principal and agent, then the maxim *qui facit per alium facit per se* (*q.v.*) applies. If I agree with a builder to build me a house on land which in fact is not mine, I shall be liable for the trespass on the land; but I am not liable for any collateral negligence (such as the dropping of a brick on one lawfully using the highway) which may be done by him or his servants while the work is in progress and in the course thereof. See VICARIOUS RESPONSIBILITY.

Respondent, a person against whom a petition, *e.g.*, a divorce petition, is presented, a summons issued, or an appeal brought, just as a defendant is a person against whom an action is brought. See CO-RESPONDENT; DEFENDANT; PETITION.

Respondentia, the hypothecation of the cargo or goods on board a ship as security for the repayment of a loan, the term "bottomry" being confined to hypothecation of the ship itself; but now the term *respondentia* is seldom used, and the expression "bottomry" is generally employed whether the vessel or the cargo or both be the security. It is allowed in cases of extreme urgency, as a last resort and where communication with the owners is impossible. The shipowner must indemnify the owner of the cargo thus hypothecated. See BOTTOMRY; HYPOTHECATION; NECESSARIES.

Respondere non debet (he is not bound to answer), a plea by which the party claimed that he ought not to answer the pleading of his opponent as, for example, when he claimed to be entitled to some privilege (1 Chitty, *Pleadings*, 433).

Responsa prudentium (the answers of the learned in the law), the opinions and decisions of learned lawyers, forming part of the civil law.

Responsalis, he who was appointed by the tenant or defendant in an action in case of extremity and necessity to allege the cause of the party's absence, and to certify the court upon what trial he would put himself. By the common law a party could not appear by attorney without the king's special warrant; when this rule was relaxed *reponsales* became obsolete (Co. Litt. 128a). See ATTORNEY.

Responsalis ad lucrandum vel petendum, he who appears and answers for another in court at a day assigned; a proctor, attorney or deputy (1 Reeves 169).

Responsions, annual payments due by the military orders of knights, such as the Hospitallers (*q.v.*): see the statute 1540, 32 Hen. 8, c. 24.

Resseiser, the taking of lands into the hands of the Crown, where a general livery or *ouster le main* was misused (Staundf.Praerog.).

Ressortissant, a national.

Rest, a periodical balancing of accounts for the purpose of determining and allocating interest; a pause in the taking of accounts at which the net balance between receipts and expenses is ascertained, so that interest may be abated or charged according to the finding. There may be rests as between a trustee and his *cestuis que trust*, a mortgagee in possession and his mortgagor, an unpaid vendor and a purchaser who has been let into possession, or a tenant for life and the remainderman.

Rest also means the reserve fund of a bank, and more especially of the Bank of England.

Restaur, or **Restor,** the remedy or recourse which assurers have against each other, according to the date of their assurances; or against the master, if the loss arises through his default, as through ill loading, want of caulking, or want of having the vessel tight; also, the remedy or recourse a person has against his guarantee or other person, who is to indemnify him from any damage sustained (Encyc.Londin.).

Restaurant. See REFRESHMENT HOUSES.

Restitutio in integrum, a phrase borrowed from the civil law, where it was applied to cases where a person, who, according to strict law, had lost a right, was restored to his original position by the judgment of a court acting on equitable principles. In English law it is sometimes used to denote the equitable relief which is given in rescinding contracts on the ground of fraud, and in similar cases, where both parties can be restored to their original positions.

Restitutio in integrum meant the rescinding of a contract or transaction, so as to place the parties to it in the same position, with respect to one another, as they occupied before the contract was made, or the transaction took place. The *restitutio* here spoken of was founded on the edict. If the contract or transaction was such as not to be valid, according to the *jus civile* this *restitutio* was not needed, and it only applied to cases of contracts and transactions which were not in their nature or form invalid. In order to entitle a person to the *restitutio*, he must have sustained some injury capable of being estimated, in consequence of the contract or transaction, and not through any fault of his own, except in the case of one who was *minor xxv annorum*, who was protected by the *restitutio* against the consequences of his own carelessness.

The following are the chief cases in which a *restitutio* might be decreed:

In the case of *vis et metus*, when a man had acted under the influence of force or reasonable fear, caused by the acts of the other party, he had an *actio quod metus causa* for restitution against the party who was the wrongdoer; and also against an innocent person who was in possession of that which had thus illegally been got from him; and also against the *heredes* of the wrongdoer if they were enriched by being his *heredes.* If he were sued in respect of the transaction, he could defend himself by an *exceptio quod metus causa.* The *actio quo metus* was given by the *praetor,* L. Octavius, a contemporary of Cicero.

In the case of *dolus,* when a man was fraudulently induced to become a party to a transaction, which was legal in all respects saving the fraud, he had an *actio de dolo malo* against the guilty person and his *heredes,* so far as they were made richer by the fraud, for the restoration of the thing of which he had been defrauded; and if that were not possible, for compensation. Against a third party, who was in bona fide possession of the thing, he had no action. If he were sued in respect of the transaction, he could defend himself by the *exceptio doli mali.*

In the case of one who was *minor xxv annorum,* the minor could by himself do no legal act for which the assent of a *tutor* or *curator* was required; and, therefore, if he did such act by himself, no *restitutio* was necessary. If the *tutor* had given his *auctoritas* or the *curator* his assent, the transaction was legally binding; but yet the minor could claim *restitutio* if he had sustained injury by the transaction. There were, however, cases in which a minor could obtain no *restitutio;* for instance, when a minor with a fraudulent design gave himself out to be of age, when he confirmed the transaction after coming of age, and in other cases.

In the case of *absentia,* which comprehended not merely absence in the ordinary sense of the word, but absence owing to madness or imprisonment, and the like causes, *restitutio* was allowed.

In the case of *error,* or mistake, which comprehended such error as could not be imputed to blame, a man could always have *restitutio* when another was enriched by his loss.

In the case of *alienatio in fraudem creditorum facta,* when a man was insolvent (*non solvendo*), and alienated his property for the purpose of injuring his creditors, the edict of the *praetor* gave the creditors a remedy.

In the imperial times *restitutio* was also applied to the remission of a punishment, which could only be done by the imperial grace (Tac.Ann. xiv, 12; Plin. Ep. x, 64, 65; Dig. 48, 19, 27; Sand. Just.).

Restitution, the restoring of anything unjustly taken from another; also putting in possession of lands or tenements him who had been unlawfully disseised of them; a person being attained of treason, etc., he or his heirs might be restored to his lands, etc., by royal charter of pardon.

In civil actions, where a defendant appeals and the judgment is reversed, he is entitled to be restored to all he has lost by the execution of the judgment. Under the present practice he may obtain redress by application to the court, but a writ of restitution (formerly the only remedy) now lies only where no other remedy is available.

See RESTITUTION OF STOLEN GOODS.

Restitution of conjugal rights. See CONJUGAL RIGHTS.

Restitution of stolen goods. By the common law there was no restitution of goods upon an indictment, because it is at the suit of the Crown only; therefore the party was obliged to bring an appeal of robbery in order to have his goods again; but a writ of restitution was authorised to be granted by the statute 1529, 21 Hen. 8, c. 11, and it became the practice of the court, upon the conviction of a felon, to order, without any writ, immediate restitution of such goods as were brought into court to be made to the prosecutor. The trial court has power to order that stolen goods or the proceeds thereof be restored to the owner or that a sum not exceeding the value of the goods be paid to the owner from money taken from the person convicted on his apprehension. The last named power may also be exercised in favour of an innocent purchaser of the goods who has been ordered to restore the goods to the true owner (Theft Act, 1968, s. 28; Criminal Justice Act, 1972, s. 6, Sch. 5). If there is any doubt about the title to the property, the order is suspended for twenty-eight days from the date of conviction and, if there is an appeal, the order is suspended until the determination of the appeal. If the appeal is successful the order for restitution is annulled. In any case the Court of Appeal may annul or vary the order. (Criminal Appeal Act, 1968, ss. 30, 42; Theft Act, 1968, s. 28 (5), Sch. 3 Pt. III; Criminal Damage Act, 1971, s. 8 (2)).

It is desirable that the person or body to whom a restitution order is directed should be specified (*Barclays Bank* v. *Milne* [1963] 1 W.L.R. 1241).

As to the tracing, following, and recovery of proceeds of fraud, see *Banque Belge* v. *Hambrouk* [1921] 1 K.B. 321.

Restitution, writ of. This writ is a writ of execution in aid of a writ of possession. See R.S.C., Ord. 45, r. 3; Ord. 46, r. 3 note.

Restitutione extracti ab ecclesia, De, a writ which lay for a person who had been forcibly removed from a church in which he had taken sanctuary: it commanded the sheriff to see that he was put back into the church from which he had been taken (Reg.Orig. 69).

Restitutione temporalium, De, a writ which issued to the sheriff commanding him to restore to a bishop who had been elected and confirmed, the temporalities of his bishopric (Fitz.N.B. 169; Roll. Abr. 880).

Restraining Act, the statute 1571, 13 Eliz. 1, c. 10. See Disabling Statutes.

Restraining orders. In the general sense of the term, a restraining order is an order of the High Court (under the original jurisdiction of the Court of Chancery) restraining a person from doing an act, *e.g.*, obstructing ancient lights; such orders are now more commonly called injunctions (*q.v.*).

Restraining statute, a statute which remedies a defect in the common law by restricting rights, such as the statutes 1559, 1 Eliz. 1, c. 19; 1571, 1 Eliz. 1, cc. 10, 20; 1572, 14 Eliz. 1, c. 11; 1575, 18 Eliz. 1, cc. 6, 11; and 1601, 43 Eliz. 1, c. 9, restraining bishops and others from granting leases binding on their successors for more than a limited time (1 Bl. Comm. 87; 5 Reeves, c. xxiii, 26).

Restraint of marriage. Marriage being an institution encouraged by the State, the general rule is that every contract the object of which is to restrain a person from marrying at all is void, and so is an agreement not to marry anyone except a specific person. As to conditions in restraint of marriage, the general rule is that such a condition is valid if it is a condition precedent. As to conditions subsequent, there is some difference in the case of real and personal estate. With regard to real estate, it would seem, on principle, that a condition subsequent is void if in general restraint of marriage but is valid if in partial restraint. With regard to personal estate, a condition subsequent in general restraint of marriage is bad, whether there is a gift over or not, while a condition subsequent in partial restraint of marriage is good if there is a gift over, but not otherwise; thus the condition is good if there is a gift over if the legatee should marry a particular person, or without a particular person's consent. A condition restraining the second marriage of a man or a woman is valid (*Allen* v. *Jackson* (1875) 1 Ch. 399). A limitation of property until marriage is good, whether to a widow, a widower, or an unmarried person; but in the case of an unmarried person, it seems that to make the restriction valid there must be a limitation over in the event of the donee marrying, because such gifts are construed rather as provisions for the donee until marriage than as restraints on marriage. So that a condition in restraint of marriage may be void, while the same result might be attained by a limitation. See Condition.

Restraint of princes. See Restraints of Princes.

Restraint of trade. The general rule is that a man ought not to be allowed to restrain himself by contract from exercising any lawful trade or business at his own discretion and in his own way, the reason being that such a contract tends to deprive the public of the advantage of employing him, and would *pro tanto* create a monopoly. A contract in general restraint of trade is one which provides that one of the parties shall not carry on a particular trade at all, or shall carry it on under the control of another person who has a rival business, or the like; such contracts are, as a general rule, void (*Mitchel* v. *Reynolds* (1711) P.Wms. 181). A contract in restraint of trade may, however, be valid if it is reasonable in the interests of the parties and not unreasonable in the interest of the public (*Herbert Morris* v. *Saxelby* [1916] 1 A.C. 688). Thus an agreement by the vendor of a business for valuable consideration not to carry on business for a certain period within such an area as may be reasonable in the circumstances of the case may be upheld (*Nordenfelt* v. *Maxim Nordenfelt* [1894] A.C. 535). Such a stipulation is not infrequently inserted in an agreement of partnership, where the partner who is the owner of the goodwill wishes to be protected against a rival business being set up in his neighbourhood by the other partner when the partnership ccmes to an end. An employer cannot by covenant prevent mere competition by his employee after the termination of the employment, but he is entitled to protection for trade secrets and trade connection.

A lease containing a covenant in unreasonable restraint of trade is in the same position as a bare contract. If the unenforceable part is severable either party can rely on the remaining terms of the contract. There is no power to put the covenantor to his election between observing the covenant and surrendering the lease (*Amoco Australia Pty.* v. *Rocco Bros. Motor Engineering Co. Pty.* [1975] A.C. 561). See SOLUS AGREEMENT.

Restraint on alienation. Although conditions in restraint of alienation of an absolute interest in possession in either real or personal property are generally void on the ground of repugnancy (*q.v.*) (*Re Dugdale* (1888) 38 Ch.D. 176), gifts of a life interest or of income or apparently of a reversionary interest (*Churchill* v. *Marks* (1844) 1 Coll. 441) until alienation or charging are permissible if there is a gift over and the gift is properly expressed (*Re Mabbett* [1891] 1 Ch. 707); see the Trustee Act, 1925, s. 33. A settlement upon himself by a settlor determining his estate upon bankruptcy is void.

Restraint upon anticipation. See ANTICIPATION.

Restraints of princes. The expression occurs in marine insurance policies, bills of lading, etc., usually as part of the phrase "arrests or restraints of princes, rulers or peoples," being one of the group of contingencies against which provision is made. It covers any forcible interference with the voyage or adventure at the hands of the constituted government or ruling power of any country. See PRINCES, RULERS AND PEOPLES.

Restriction. Under the Land Registration Act, 1925, s. 58, a restriction is an entry on the register, usually requiring notice to or consent by a named person before any further dealing is registered. The restriction may be limited to a special class of dealings and may have a continuous effect unlike a caution (*q.v.*), which can only operate once. Restrictions are frequently entered for the protection of settled land. See INHIBITION.

Restrictive covenant. This is defined by the Land Charges Act, 1972, s. 2, Class D (ii), as a covenant or agreement (not being made between lessor and lessee) restrictive of the user of the land; and see s. 15 (2). Such a covenant is in the nature of an equitable easement restricting the use or enjoyment of certain land for the benefit of other land and binding on every owner (Law of Property Act, 1925, ss. 78, 79) of the servient land having notice of the covenant (*Tulk* v. *Moxhay* (1848) 2 Phil. 774). Upon sale of land under a building scheme, of which the restriction formed part, the purchasers of plots may enforce the covenant (*Elliston* v. *Reacher* [1908] 2 Ch. 665; *Drake* v. *Gray* [1936] 1 Ch. 465; *Re Union of London and Smith's Bank* [1933] Ch. 611). Under the Land Charges Act, 1972, s. 2, Class D (ii), a restrictive covenant made after 1925 must be registered as a land charge (*q.v.*), and under s. 4 (6), if not so registered before completion of the purchase, is void against a purchaser of the servient land for money or money's worth. See PRIORITY NOTICE; REGISTRATION OF TITLE TO LAND.

The Law of Property Act, 1925, s. 84 (set out in amended form in the Law of Property Act, 1969, Sch. 3), enables the Lands Tribunal to discharge or modify covenants.

A restrictive covenant may become obsolete. Whether it has done so or not is not entirely a question of fact (*Re Edwards' Application* (1960) 11 P. & C.R. 403).

Restrictive indorsement, an indorsement prohibiting the further negotiation of a bill of exchange or promissory note or cheque, by expressing that it is a mere authority to deal with the bill, etc., as thereby directed, and not a transfer of the ownership thereof, as, for example, if a bill is indorsed, "pay D only," or "pay D for the account of X," or "pay D or order for collection" (Bills of Exchange Act, 1882, s. 35).

Resrictive interpretation, strict interpretation.

Restrictive trade practices. The Restrictive Trade Practices Act, 1976, consolidates the relevant provisions of the Restrictive Trade Practices Acts, 1956 and 1968 and of the Fair Trading Act, 1973.

The Act of 1976, provides for the registration and judicial investigation of restrictive agreements as to goods, information agreements as to goods, restrictive agreements as to services and information agreements as to services. The enforcement of the Act is in the hands of the Director-General of Fair Trading (appointed under the Fair Trading Act, 1973), whose functions include the compiling and maintaining of a register of agreements subject to registration under the Restrictive Practices Act, 1976, and the taking of proceedings before the Restrictive Practices Court, constituted under the Restrictive Practices Court Act, 1976.

Restrictions or information provisions in any agreement may be found by the court to be contrary to the public interest. If so found, the agreement is void in respect of those restrictions or those information provisions. The Restrictive Trade Practices Act, 1976, applies to an agreement notwithstanding that it is or may be void under European Communities provisions. A restriction or information provision is presumed to be contrary to the public interest unless the court is satisfied that it is not under the circumstances specified in the Act.

The class of services which are subject to the Act are to be prescribed by the Secretary of State for Trade by statutory instrument.

Agreements important to the national economy may be exempted by the Secretary of State from the Act. Agreements holding down prices may be exempted from the Act by order of the Secretary of State or the Minister of Agriculture, Fisheries and Food.

Certain services are excluded from designation by the Secretary of State. These include legal, medical, dental, ophthalmic, veterinary and nursing services; the services of midwives, physiotherapists or chiropodists, architects, accountants, patent agents, parliamentary agents, surveyors, professional engineers or technologists, and ministers of religion; educational and university services (Sch. 1).

Certain exclusive dealings are exempted from the Act (Sch. 3 paras. 2, 7) and certain "know-how" agreements (Sch. 3 paras. 3, 8).

The Director-General of Fair Trading maintains and publishes lists in respect of which the Restrictive Practices Court has made, refused or discharged orders permitting exemptions from the provisions of the Act.

See RESALE.

As to agricultural marketing boards, see the Agriculture (Miscellaneous Provisions) Act, 1968, s. 45, Restrictive Trade Practices Act, 1976, Sch. 5.

Result. In law, a thing is said to result when, after having been ineffectually or only partially disposed of, it comes back to its former owner or his representatives. Thus, if A conveyed land to B and his heirs to the use of C for life, on C's death the use resulted to A, that is A or his heirs again became the owners of the land, because no disposition was made beyond C's life. This was a resulting use. A resulting trust is similar. See TRUST; USE.

When land is directed to be converted into money for a special purpose and the object fails, so that either the sale becomes unnecessary, or (if the sale has taken place) the proceeds are not required to be applied for the purpose directed, then the land or the proceeds of sale (as the case may be) result to the settlor or the person entitled to his land if he is dead. The same rule applies to the converse case of a conversion of money into land. Thus, if a testator directs his land to be sold, and the purposes for which he has directed the conversion, or some of them, fail to take effect (*e.g.*, by lapse), then the land, if it has not been sold, or the undisposed-of proceeds if it has, result to the person entitled to his land as if the conversion had not been directed; and this is none the less so where the testator has created a blended fund (*q.v.*). In the case of a total failure of the objects for which the conversion is directed, there is no difference whether the instrument is *inter vivos* or testamentary; that is, the property results to the settlor or his representatives in its original state. Thus, if a testator directs his land to be sold, and the proceeds to be divided between A and B, and they both predecease the testator, then the land goes to the person entitled to the testator's land as land. But in case of a partial failure of the purposes for which conversion is directed, the general rule is that where the instrument is one *inter vivos* (*e.g.*, a deed), the property results to the settlor in the condition into which he had directed it to be converted (whether realty or personalty), and therefore devolves as such on his death, unless he has otherwise disposed of it; while, where the instrument is a will, there is a distinction between conversion of land into money, and money into land; for if a testator directs a conversion of land into money, and some of the purposes fail, that part of the proceeds which is undisposed of results to the person entitled to the testator's land as money, so that on that person's death it devolves with the rest of his personalty, unless specially disposed of by him; but if a testator directs a conversion of money into land, and some of the purposes fail, the money which is undisposed of results to the person entitled to his personalty as personalty and not as land. See BLENDED FUND; CONVERSION; RECONVERSION.

Resulting trust, a trust created by operation of law. A resulting trust arises where an owner of property makes a disposition of the legal estate and there is nothing to show that he meant to deal with the equitable interest; but the Law of Property Act, 1925, s. 60, provides that in a voluntary conveyance executed after 1925, a resulting trust for the grantor will not be implied merely because the property is not expressed to be conveyed for the benefit of the grantee. It also arises where a purchaser of property takes the conveyance not in his own name but in that of some one else. In either of these cases the law creates a resulting trust, in the former case, in favour of the owner of the legal estate, and in the latter, in favour of the purchaser, *i.e.*, the man who paid the purchase money. A resulting trust terminates upon the creation or declaration of a trust of the property and accordingly there need not be any disposition in writing of the interest held under the resulting trust (*Re Vandervell's Trusts (No. 2), White* v. *Vandervell Trustees* [1974] Ch. 269).

The rule against perpetuities applies to a possibility of a resulting trust on the determination of a determinable interest in property (Perpetuities and Accumulations Act, 1964, s. 12). But this does not apply to an instrument taking effect before the commencement of the Act (s. 15 (5)).

Resulting use, an implied use. See RESULT.

A resulting use arose where the legal seisin was transferred, and no use was expressly declared, nor any consideration nor evidence of intent to direct the use; the use then remained in the original grantor, for it was not to be supposed that the estate was intended to be given away, and the Statute of Uses 1535, immediately transferred the legal estate to such resulting use. The Statute of Uses, 1535, was repealed by the Law of Property Act, 1925.

Resummons, a second summons, calling upon a person to answer an action where the first summons was defeated by any occasion. When, by death, etc., of the judges, they did not come on the day to which they were continued, for trial of causes, such causes might be revived or recontinued by resummons (Tomlin).

The demise of the Crown was an occasion which would formerly have defeated the first summons.

Resumption. This word is used in the statute 1452, 31 Hen. 6, c. 7, as meaning the taking again into the king's hands of lands which, upon false suggestion or other error, he had made livery of to anyone or granted by letters patent (Bro. Abr. 191).

Agricultural tenancy agreements frequently provide for resumption by the landlord, before the legal tenancy ends, of the land or part for building, etc., making an abatement of rent and giving compensation for damage to crops. Notice to quit part only being invalid at common law (*Doe* v. *Archer* (1811) 14 East 245), this resumption must be specially stipulated for; but in many cases recourse may be had to the Agricultural Holdings Act, 1948, s. 33, which provides that where a notice to quit is given by the landlord of an agricultural holding to a tenant from year to year for adjustment of boundaries or amalgamation of units or with a view to the use of land for the erection of farm labourers' cottages or other houses with or without gardens, the provision of gardens for farm labourers' cottages, or other houses, the provision of allotments, the provision of small holdings, the planting of trees, the opening or working of any coal, ironstone, limestone, brick-earth, or other mineral, or of a stone quarry, or a clay, sand, or gravel pit, or the construction of any works or buildings to be used in connection therewith, the making of a watercourse or reservoir, or the making of any road, railway, tramroad, siding, canal, or basin, or a wharf, pier, or other work connected therewith, it is no objection that the notice relates to part only of the holding.

As to counter-notice to quit the entire holding by the tenant upon notice by the landlord in regard to part of the land, see the Law of Property Act, 1925, s. 140 (2), as amended by the Law of Property (Amendment) Act, 1926, s. 2, and the Agricultural Holdings Act, 1948, Sch. 8.

The Small Holdings and Allotments Act, 1908, s. 46, as amended by the Land Settlement Facilities Act, 1919, s. 25, Sch. 2, and the Small Holdings and Allotments Act, 1926, s. 18 (2), Sch. 2, gives power of resumption of possession by a landlord of land compulsorily hired by a local authority when it is needed for industrial purposes.

Re-surrender. Where copyhold land had been mortgaged by surrender, and the mortgagee had been admitted, then on the mortgage debt being paid off, the mortgagor was entitled to have the land reconveyed to him, by the mortgagee surrendering it to the lord to his use. This was called a re-surrender. See COPYHOLD; RE-CONVEYANCE.

Retable, a shelf or ledge, at the back and above the level of the Communion Table, upon which ornaments can be placed. Its use has been declared legal by the Privy Council.

Retail, to sell goods in small parcels and not in gross. As to the sale by retail of intoxicating liquor see the Customs and Excise Act, 1952, s. 148 (4); Weights and Measures Act, 1963, s. 59.

Retainer, the engagement of counsel or solicitor to take or defend proceedings, or to advise or otherwise act for the client; the agreement between client and solicitor or between solicitor and counsel for professional services and that such services shall not be given to the opposite party; a document given by a solicitor to counsel, engaging counsel to appear for a party, either in some particular suit or action in prospect (which is called a special retainer), or in all matters of litigation in which such party may at any time be involved (which is called a general retainer). Subject to rr. 20 and 21 of the Retainer Rules (made by the Bar Council in 1938, see Boulton, *Conduct and Etiquette at the Bar*), a special retainer is binding if duly tendered, whether accepted or not, but there is no rule of the profession which makes a general retainer binding on counsel unless it is accepted by him.

By r. 20, when counsel has held a brief for any party in any proceeding he may not accept a general or special retainer or brief on an appeal from any decision in such proceeding for any other party without giving the original client the opportunity of retaining or delivering a brief to him for such appeal.

By r. 21, counsel cannot be required to accept a retainer or brief or to advise or draw pleadings in any case where he has previously advised another party on or in connection with the case, and he ought not to do so in any case in which he would be embarrassed in the discharge of his duty by reason of confidence reposed in him by the other party.

It is a rule of the profession that when a brief is offered or delivered to counsel, and he finds that another counsel has become entitled to a brief and has not been briefed, such first-named counsel ought first to ascertain personally (and not through his clerk) whether the other counsel waives his claim to a brief. If the claim is not waived, the first-named counsel ought, where practicable, to ascertain from the solicitor offering or delivering such brief whether there is any sufficient explanation why a brief has not been offered or delivered to such other counsel, and unless a satisfactory explanation is given ought to refuse or return the brief.

General retainers to counsel are divided into ordinary general retainers, applying to the Supreme Court and the House of Lords; limited general retainers, applying only to the courts specified therein; separate general retainers, applying only to the Privy Council, and separate general retainers, applying only to parliamentary committees. A general retainer gives counsel a right, and puts him under a duty, to accept a brief in every proceeding by or against his client, and it lasts for the joint lives of counsel and client unless there is a failure on either side to comply with this rule, except in the case of the appointment of counsel as a Law Officer, when all retainers are determined. A general retainer applies only to proceedings to which the client on whose behalf the retainer was given is a party, but not where the client appears jointly with another person.

A special retainer to counsel cannot be given until after the commencement of the proceeding to which it relates, with the exception of parliamentary business. With certain exceptions, a special retainer entitles counsel to receive, and binds him to accept, a brief in every stage of that proceeding. Circuit retainers, that is to say, retainers for a case at a particular assize, were included amongst special retainers, but have had no practical application since the coming into force of the Courts Act, 1971.

Retainers to barristers can be given only by a solicitor, with the exception of retainers from parliamentary agents or patent agents for any matter in which such persons can instruct counsel without the intervention of a solicitor.

Retainers to solicitors are either general or limited to some particular matter. The client can withdraw a retainer to solicitors for non-contentious business by notice at any time unless there is one entire contract (*J. H. Milner & Son* v. *Percy Bilton* [1966] 1 W.L.R. 1582).

Retainer of debts. An executor or administrator (not being a creditor-administrator, who is precluded from retaining by the form of the administration bond) had a legal right to retain his own debt out of the legal or equitable assets in priority to all other creditors of equal degree (*Att.-Gen.* v. *Jackson* [1932] A.C. 365), and before the costs of all parties, including the plaintiff (Administration of Estates Act, 1925, s. 34) (see EXECUTOR). The right was abolished by the Administration of Estates Act, 1971, s. 10.

Retaliation, the *lex talionis* (*q.v.*).

Retenementum, a withholding or deduction. In conveyances of land the words *sine ullo retenemento* (without any deduction) were frequently used in order to make it clear that the grantor conveyed his entire estate in the land (Cowel).

Retinentia, a retinue, or persons retained by a prince or nobleman.

Retire, as applied to a bill of exchange, usually means that an indorser has taken it up by paying his immediate or some subsequent indorsee, after which he is in a position to recover from the antecedent parties. But it is sometimes used in the case of an acceptor who has paid and extinguished the bill.

Certain lump sums paid on retirement are exempt from income tax (Finance Act, 1973, s. 14). As to transfer of businesses on retirement, see Finance Act, 1965, s. 34, and Finance Act, 1974, s. 34.

As to the retirement of a trustee, see TRUSTEE.

Retirement benefits. See the Social Security Act, 1975, ss. 12, 27–30, 39, 40; Social Security Pensions Act, 1975.

Retorna brevium, the returns of writs. See RETURNUS BREVIUM.

Retorno habendo. When the defendant had judgment in replevin for the return of the goods, there issued in his favour a writ *de retorno habendo*, whereby the goods were returned again into his custody, to be sold or otherwise disposed of, as if no replevin had been made. See ELONGATA; REPLEVIN.

Retorsion, retaliation. In international law, when a sovereign is not satisfied with the manner in which his subjects are treated by the laws and customs of another nation, he is at liberty to declare that he will treat the subjects of that nation in the same manner. This is called retorsion, but the term is little used. See EMBARGO; REPRISALS.

Retour sans protêt [Fr.] (return without protest), a request or direction by a drawer of a bill of exchange that should the bill be dishonoured by the drawee, it may be returned without protest or without expense (*sans frais*) (*q.v.*).

Retractation, in probate practice, is a withdrawl of a renunciation (*q.v.*). A retractation is only allowed in special cases. See the Non-Contentious Probate Rules, 1954, r. 35 (3).

Retractus aquae, the ebb or return of a tide.

Retraite. See RE-EXCHANGE.

Retraxit (he has withdrawn), a proceeding somewhat similar to a *nolle prosequi*, except that a *retraxit* was a bar to any future action for the same cause, whereas a *nolle prosequi* is not, unless made after judgment. In the old common law practice it was a mode of withdrawing from an action, and took place where a plaintiff or demandant abandoned his action at the trial, and thus lost his right of action altogether (Co.Litt. 138b). See DISCONTINUANCE; NON-SUIT.

Retreat. See DRUNKENNESS.

Retroactive effect, relation back of an act to a time prior to such act.

Retrocession, a reassignment of inheritable rights to the cedent or original assignor (Civil Law).

Retropannagium, after-pannage. See PANNAGE.

Rette, a charge or accusation (Co.Litt. 173b).

Return, a report by an officer of a court showing the manner in which he has performed a duty imposed on him. The present form of writ of *fi. fa.* directs the sheriff to "indorse on this writ immediately after execution thereof a statement of the manner in which you have executed it and send a copy of the statement to" the plaintiff (R.S.C., App. A, Form No. 53). If a return is required a notice may be served on the sheriff requiring him to comply with the direction on the writ. If the sheriff fails to comply he may be directed to do so by an order of the court obtainable on summons return-

able before a master (R.S.C., Ord. 46, r. 9).

Returns to writs were known by the first words of the old returns, which were given in Latin, *e.g., nulla bona, fieri feci, non est inventus, tarde,* etc. As to the return to a mandamus, see MANDAMUS.

As to the consequences of a false return, see FALSE RETURN.

Companies and other associations established under Acts of Parliament are in many cases required to send in periodical returns to a public officer with reference to their condition. Thus every company having a share capital is bound to send in a yearly return to the Registrar of Companies, giving a list of its shareholders, and showing the position of its capital, etc. (Companies Act, 1948, s. 124, Sch. 6; Companies Act, 1967, Sch. 7).

Returns of income for income tax purposes are required to be made each year under the Taxes Management Act, 1970, s. 8.

Return days. Under the old practice there were four days in each of the terms except Easter term, and five days in Easter term, on which writs were made returnable. These days were known as return days or days in bank.

Return irreplevisable. See REPLEVIN; RETURNUM IRREPLEGIABILE.

Return Office, a branch of the office of the Clerk of Enrolments (*q.v.*) to the Court of Common Pleas (*q.v.*).

Returnable. Writs of execution and many other kinds of writs are returnable, that is, the person to whom they are directed is bound or may be required to make a return to them. The term is, however, chiefly used with reference to the time when the writ is returnable. Some writs are returnable at a date named in them, while others, such as writs of execution, are returnable as soon as they are executed. By analogy to this use of the word, a summons is said to be returnable on the day appointed for hearing it.

Returning officers, the persons responsible for the conduct of parliamentary and local government elections.

The persons who are to be returning officers at parliamentary elections are set out in the Local Government Act, 1972, s. 40. In the case of a county constituency the returning officer is the sheriff; in the case of a borough constituency, the chairman of the district (*q.v.*) council; in the case of a London borough, the mayor of the borough; in the City of London and the Temples, the Lord Mayor. Most of the functions are discharged by the registration officer (*q.v.*) (Representation of the People Act, 1949, s. 18; Local Government Act, 1972, s. 40). The returning officers at local government elections are appointed by the county and district councils. In London the returning officers are the proper officers of the London boroughs (Local Government Act, 1972, s. 41).

Returno habendo. See RETORNO HABENDO.

Returnum averiorum, a judicial writ similar to the *retorno habendo* (Cowel).

Returnum irreplegiabile, the writ of return irreplevisable, a judicial writ addressed to the sheriff for the final restitution or return of cattle to the owner when unjustly taken or distrained, and so found by verdict, granted after a nonsuit in a second deliverance (Reg. Judic. 27). See REPLEVIN.

Returnus (or **Returna**) **brevium** (the return of writs), a manorial right, also acquired by some of the more important boroughs. The sheriff, on receipt of a writ from the king's court commanding him to summon a resident within the manor or borough, had to deliver the writ to the bailiff of the liberty for execution (1 P. & M. 583, 644).

Reus, a defendant, properly the debtor to whom the question was put. *Rei* meant the parties or litigants (Civil Law).

Reve, or **Greve,** the bailiff of a franchise or manor: an officer in parishes within forests who marks the commonable cattle.

Reveach, rebellion (Domesday).

Reveland, the land which in Domesday is said to have been thane-land, afterwards converted into reveland. It seems to have been land which, having reverted to the king after the death of the thane, who had it for life, was not granted out to any by the king, but rested in charge upon the account of the reve or bailiff of the manor (Spelman, *Feuds*, c. 24).

Revels, sports of dancing, masking, etc. formerly used in princes' courts, the inns of court, and noblemen's houses, commonly performed by night; there was an officer to order and supervise them who was entitled the Master of the Revels.

Revendication. Upon the sale of goods on credit, by the law of some commercial countries, a right is reserved to the seller to retake them, or he has a lien upon them for the price, if unpaid: and in other countries he possesses a right of stoppage *in transitu* (*q.v.*) only in cases of insolvency of the buyer. The civil law did not generally consider the transfer of property to be complete by sale and delivery alone without payment or security given for the price, unless the seller agreed to give a general credit to the buyer; but it allowed the seller to reclaim the goods out of the possession of the buyer, as being still his own property. *Quod vendidi, non aliter fit accipientis, quam si aut pretium nobis solutum sit, aut satis eo nomine datum, vel etiam fidem habuerimus emptori sine ulla satisfactione.*

French law gives a privilege or right of revendication against the buyer for the price of goods sold, so long as they remain in his possession. In respect of ships, a privilege is given by French law to a certain class of creditors, such as sellers, builders, repairers, mariners, etc., upon the ship which takes effect even against subsequent buyers, until the ship has made a voyage after the sale; and, by the general maritime law acknowledged in most countries, hypothecations and liens are recognised to exist for seaman's wages and for repairs of foreign ships, and for salvage.

Revenue, income, annual profit received from land or other funds; also money at the disposal of the Crown, *i.e.*, the executive. The chief sources are Crown property surrendered to the nation; taxation, *e.g.*, income tax, death duties, customs and excise, stamp duties; and miscellaneous holdings such as shares in certain undertakings and other profits or fiscal prerogatives of the Crown.

Revenue causes were peculiarly within the province of the Court of Exchequer, the practice of which in matters of revenue was regulated by the Queen's Remembrancer Act, 1859, ss. 9 *et seq.*, and the Crown Suits Act, 1865.

The jurisdiction of the Court of Exchequer was transferred to the High Court by the Judicature Act, 1873, s. 16, now the Judicature Act, 1925, s. 18 (2) (iv); but all causes which would have been within the exclusive cognisance of the Court of Exchequer were assigned to the Exchequer Division of the High Court by the Judicature Act, 1873, s. 34 (now the Judicature Act, 1925, s. 56 (2) (*a*)); but in 1881, by Order in Council, under the Judicature Act, 1873, s. 32, the Exchequer Division was merged in the Queen's Bench Division. The practice and proceedings on the revenue side of that division were, in general, not affected by the Rules of the Supreme Court. Revenue cases were transferred to the Chancery Division in 1950. See EXCHEQUER.

Revenue expenditure, expenditure from which benefits may be expected to be derived within a comparatively short period. See CAPITAL EXPENDITURE.

Revenue paper. See PAPER, REVENUE.

Reverend. This prefix to the name of a clergyman is not appropriated by the law to the clergy of the Church of England alone. It is not a title of honour or dignity, and a person prefixing it to his name does not thereby claim to be in holy orders. The use of the prefix is of comparatively modern origin. A parson in late medieval times was styled Sir Oliver Martext, or as the case might be. In the early part of the seventeenth century the prefix " Reverend " came to be used by the Puritan and Presbyterian ministers: somewhat later it was adopted by the parochial clergy, to whom it is applied in the preamble to the statute 1662, 14 Car. 2, c. 4; but it has been decided that the prefix may be used upon a tombstone, in a parish graveyard, of a Noncomformist minister (*Keet* v. *Smith* (1875) L.R. 4 A. & E. 398).

An archbishop is entitled " Most Reverend "; a bishop, " Right Reverend "; a dean, " Very Reverend "; and the inferior clergy, " Reverend " simply.

Reversal, the making of a judgment void for error (Lil.Abr. 481).

When, upon the return of a writ of error, it appeared that a judgment was erroneous, the senior judge pronounced the reversal of it. Down to, at any rate, the middle of the eighteenth century he did this in the ancient French form, the words of the reversal being: *Pur les errors avandit, et auter errors manifest in le record, soit le judgment reverse,* etc. (Trin., 22 Car. 2, B.R.).

A judgment might have been reversed without a writ of error, for matters foreign to or *dehors* the record, *i.e.,* not apparent upon the face of it, so that they could not be assigned for error in the superior courts, or by writ of error, which lay from all inferior jurisdictions to the King's Bench and thence to the Exchequer Chamber and the House of Lords. It was brought for mistakes as to matters of substance, appearing in the judgment or other parts of the record. See now R.S.C., Ord. 59.

Reverse, to undo, repeal or make void. A judgment is said to be reversed when it is set aside by a court of appeal.

Reverser, a reversioner.

Reversio terrae est tanquam terra revertens in possessione donatori, sive haeredibus suis post donum finitum (Co. Litt. 142b. (A reversion of land is, as it were, the return of the land to the possession of the donor or his heirs after the termination of the estate granted.)

Reversion [Lat. *revertor*], that portion left of an interest after a grant of a particular portion of it, short of the whole interest, has been made by the owner to another person. When a person has an interest in lands, and grants a portion of that interest, the possession of the lands, on the determination of the interest granted, returns or reverts to the grantor. This interest is what is called the grantor's reversion, or, more properly, his right of reverter. Thus a grant by the owner of the fee simple to A for life leaves in the grantor the reversion in fee simple, which is a present and vested interest which will commence in possession after the determination of A's life interest; and this is called the particular interest; particular, as being a part (*particula*) carved or sliced out of the larger interest or reversion.

Settled reversions of freehold or leasehold estates are reduced to equitable interests by the Law of Property Act, 1925, but the word is also used to mean the freehold or leasehold reversion to a lease or term of years absolute in which case there is an estate in possession of the rents and profits as well as in the freehold or leasehold reversion, which together may form a legal estate subject to the term.

The relationship of tenure exists between the owner of the reversion and the particular tenant, and therefore fealty (*q.v.*) is nominally due from the latter to the former. A rent service or other service may also be reserved by the owner of the reversion, and thus made incident to the reversion, so that if the reversion is alienated, the rent or service passes with it. The rent may be severed from the reversion, but the fealty cannot; therefore if the owner grants the reversion to another person, he may reserve the rent to himself, but not the fealty (Co.Litt. 142b). See ATTORNMENT; RENT.

A condition of re-entry may also be annexed to a reversion, and will pass with it on an assignment. As to the difference between a reversion and a remainder, see REMAINDER.

If A, being a tenant in fee simple, grants a lease to B, and B grants an underlease to C, reserving a rent, this rent is incident to B's reversion: consequently if A grants his reversion to B, this causes a merger or destruction of B's reversion, and, at common law, C's rent, being incident to it, would also be destroyed. B would be tenant in fee simple in reversion, but his right to the rent would be gone. To prevent this, the Law of Property Act, 1925, s. 139, replacing the Real Property Act, 1845, s. 9, provides that where the reversion expectant on a lease is surrendered or merges, the estate or interest next in reversion or remainder shall, for the purpose of preserving the incidents to the reversion so merged, be deemed to be the reversion expectant on the lease. In the case supposed, therefore, the rent payable by C would be converted into a rent incident to B's reversion in fee simple.

As to covenants running with the reversion, see COVENANT.

" Reversion " is also used to denote a reversionary interest (*q.v.*), *e.g.*, an interest in personal property subject to the life interest of some other person.

As to sales of reversions, see REVERSIONARY INTEREST.

Reversionary, that which is to be enjoyed in reversion.

Reversionary bonus, a distribution to policy-holders of an assurance company's profits after an actuarial valuation of the policies in force, by way of addition to the sum payable at maturity of the policy or death of the assured, as opposed to a cash bonus payable immediately.

Reversionary interest. Any right in property the enjoyment of which is deferred is a reversionary interest in the wide sense of the term; but reversionary interests, in the ordinary sense of the term, are interests in property which are not reversions or remainders in the strict sense, but are analogous to them. Thus, if personal property is limited to A for life, and after his death to B, this gives B a reversionary interest. Similarly, if A gives B a life interest in chattels, A retains a reversionary interest.

Reversionary interests were formerly recognised only by the Court of Chancery, being equitable interests. (See EQUITY.) They are usually created by means of trusts, the legal estate in the property being conveyed to trustees, as in the case of an ordinary marriage settlement of personal property. See SETTLEMENT.

Formerly there was a rule in equity that in the case of the sale of a reversionary interest in real or personal estate the purchaser was bound to show that he had given the fair market price for it, and if he was unable to do so the sale was set aside; this rule was abolished by the Sale of Reversions Act, 1867, replaced by the law of Property Act, 1925, s. 174, but, in cases of fraud or unfair dealing, equity still intervenes. See EXPECTANT HEIR; INADEQUACY.

Reversionary lease, one to take effect *in futuro*; a second lease to commence after the expiration of a former lease. Formerly it did not create any estate, but only an *interesse termini* (*q.v.*). The Law of Property Act, 1925, s. 149, abolished the doctrine of *interesse termini*; it also provides that a term at a rent or in consideration of a fine cannot be created to take effect more than twenty-one years from the date of the instrument purporting to create it. See OPTION; RENEWAL OF LEASE.

Reversioner, one who has a reversion.

Revert, to return: thus when the owner of an estate in land has granted a smaller estate to another person, on the determination of the latter estate the land is said to revert to the grantor. See REVER-SION; REVERTER.

Reverter, reversion. In feudal times, on every grant of land, a right remained in the grantor to the services of the grantee during the continuance of his estate, and to a return of the land on its expiration. Whether this right of the grantor depended on an estate for life or in fee, it was of the same nature and was called his reverter or escheat; but from the remoter probability of the return when the fee was granted, it became customary to call it, after a grant of the fee, his possibility of reverter; by degrees that expression was applied to those cases only where a limited fee had been granted, and the word escheat was applied to those where the grant had conferred an absolute estate in fee simple. A grant to a man and the heirs of his body was at common law a limited fee; and therefore, after such a grant a possibility of reverter was said to remain in the grantor. When the statute *De Donis*, 1285, converted such estates into estates tail, the return of the land was secured by it to the donor and was called his reverter. In all these cases, the words reverter and reversion are synonymous (Fearne on Cont.Rem. (10th ed.), p. 381).

A reverter after an estate in fee simple conditional is still called a possibility of reverter. See FORMEDON; POSSIBILITY.

The rule against perpetuities applies to possibilities of reverter expectant on the determination of a determinable interest in land and to analogous interests by way of resulting trust expectant on the determination of a determinable interest in personalty (Perpetuities and Accumulations Act, 1964, s. 12). But this does not apply to instruments taking effect before the commencement of the Act (s. 15 (5)).

The School Sites Act, 1841, provides for the reverter of land to the grantor if it ceases to be used for the purposes of the Act. A fee simple subject to such a right of reverter remains a fee simple absolute (Law of Property Act, 1925, s. 7). As to the effect of reverter on the trusts on which land is held, see *Re Ingleton Charity* [1956] Ch. 585.

Revesting. See RESTITUTION.

Review. Any party to taxation proceedings who is dissatisfied with the allowance or disallowance of any item or with the amount allowed in respect of any item may apply to the taxing officer to review his decision in respect of that item specifying his objections in writing (R.S.C., Ord. 62 r. 33).

See COMMISSION.

Review, Bill of, proceedings in the nature of proceedings in error; its object was to procure an examination and alteration or reversal of a final decree in Chancery duly signed and enrolled. The objects of this proceeding may now be attained by an appeal to the Court of Appeal. See APPEAL; BILL OF COMPLAINT.

A bill in the nature of a bill of review was filed where the decree had not been enrolled.

Review, Commission of, a commission which was sometimes granted in extraordinary cases to revise the sentence of the Court of Delegates when it was apprehended they had been led into a material error. See DELEGATES.

Revised Reports, a republication of such cases in the courts of law and equity from 1785 to 1865 as were considered to be of practical utility, edited by Sir F. Pollock.

Revised Statutes, a republication by government authority of such public general statutes as are still unrepealed, or parts of them. See ACT OF PARLIAMENT.

Revival; Revivor. The term "revival" is sometimes applied to wills. Thus, where a testator revokes a will, he is said to revive it if he subsequently re-executes it, or executes a will or codicil showing an intention to revive it.

Under the practice of the Court of Chancery when a suit became defective by the death, marriage or bankruptcy of one of the parties, or by an assignment of the subject-matter of the suit *pendente lite,* or by some other change in the interest of some of the parties, it was necessary to revive it, that is, take steps for carrying on the proceedings: this was generally done by an order of revivor obtained as of course; but in some cases a new bill, called a bill of revivor, had to be filed. The Common Law Procedure Act, 1852, s. 52, abolished bills of revivor and simplified the procedure on the subject in the courts of common law as well as in the Court of Chancery. R.S.C., Ord. 15, r. 7, provides for the continuance of all causes or matters in all divisions of the High Court notwithstanding the death or bankruptcy of any party.

In the common law courts, also, if six years had elapsed, or if one of the parties had died, after the recovery of a judgment, it was formerly necessary to revive it by writ of revivor, *scire facias* or suggestion (*q.v.*). Under the present practice in all the Divisions, when six years have lapsed from the recovery of a judgment, or any change has taken place in the parties to the judgment (*e.g.*, by death), execution can only be issued with leave: on the application for leave the court or judge may either order execution to issue, or may direct any question necessary to determine the rights of the parties to be tried (R.S.C., Ord. 46, r. 23). See ABATEMENT OF CIVIL PROCEEDINGS; JUDGMENT.

A statute-barred debt is revived by acknowledgment or part-payment (Limitation Act, 1939, s. 23).

As to the revivor of a criminal appeal after the death of the person convicted, see *R.* v. *Rowe* [1955] 1 Q.B. 573; *R.* v. *Jeffries* [1969] 1 Q.B. 120.

Revivor, Bill of, a bill filed to revive and continue the proceedings whenever there was an abatement of the suit before its final consummation either by death or marriage. Bills of revivor were abolished by the Common Law Procedure Act, 1852, s. 52.

Revocation [Lat. *revocare*, to recall], the undoing of a thing granted, or a destroying or making void of some deed which had existence until the act of revocation made it void. It may be either general, of all acts and things done before; or special, to revoke a particular thing (5 Co.Rep. 90).

To revoke an offer or authority is to withdraw it. Revocation is the operation of revoking. Revocation is of three kinds: by act of the party; by operation of law; and by order of a court of justice (judicial revocation).

Revocation by act of the party is an intentional or voluntary revocation. The principal instances occur in the case of authorities and powers of attorney and wills. The two former require no particular form of revocation. A will may be revoked by a subsequent inconsistent will or codicil, or by a writing declaring an intention to revoke, executed with the same formalities as a will, or by the burning, tearing, or otherwise destroying of the will by the testator, or by some person in his presence and by his direction, with the intention of revoking it (Wills Act, 1837, s. 20). As to alterations in wills, see ALTERATION.

A revocation in law, or constructive revocation, is produced by a rule of law, irrespectively of the intention of the parties. Thus, a power of attorney is in general revoked by the death of the principal. A will is revoked by the subsequent marriage of the testator, except, by the Law of Property Act, 1925, s. 177, when expressed to be made in contemplation of a particular marriage (*Sallis* v. *Jones* [1936] P. 43), and except when made in exercise of a power of appointment under which the property appointed would not, in default of appointment, pass to the personal representatives or next-of-kin of the testator (Wills Act, 1837, s. 18). As to powers of revocation, see POWER. As to the revocation of a guarantee, see GUARANTEE.

When a grant of probate or letters of administration has been improperly obtained, it may be revoked by the court at the instance of a person interested; a grant may also be revoked at the request of the grantee, for instance, where he had erroneously believed himself to be the next-of-kin of the deceased. After revocation the grant is produced at the registry, and cancelled.

An agency is determined in several ways. It may be determined by the principal, either expressly or impliedly, as by appointing another person to do the same act, where the authority of both would be incompatible.

The exceptions to the power of the principal to revoke his agent's authority at mere pleasure are: when the principal has stipulated that the authority shall be irrevocable, and the agent has also an interest in its execution; when an authority or power is coupled with an interest, or is given for a valuable consideration, or is a part of a security, unless there is a stipulation that it shall be revocable; and when an agent's act in pursuance of his authority has become obligatory, for *nemo potest mutare consilium suum in alterius injuriam.*

The agent may give notice to his principal that he renounces the agency; but if the principal sustains damage thereby, the agent is responsible therefor.

Agency is revoked by operation of law, as by the expiration of the period during which the agency was to exist or to have effect, or by a change of condition or of state producing an incapacity of either the principal or the agent, as mental disability, or where the party is made bankrupt, except as to such rights as do not pass to the trustee under the adjudication; death, unless the authority is coupled with an interest in the thing vested in the agent; extinction of the subject of the agency; ceasing of the principal's powers; or complete execution of the trust confided to the agent, who then is *functus officio*.

Where a person has been held out as an agent, the principal remains liable to persons who have no notice of revocation of the authority.

As to the position when the agent is constituted by power of attorney, see POWER OF ATTORNEY.

Revocation and new appointment. The appointor may reserve a power of revocation and new appointment in the deed of appointment, although not expressly authorised so to do by the assurance creating the power; and such a power may be reserved *toties quoties*. By a revocation the original power revives. When a deed of appointment contains no power of revocation it is absolute and cannot be revoked, although there may be a power of revocation in the assurance creating the power. When a power is executed by will, an express power of revocation need not be reserved, since a will is always revocable.

Revocatione parliamenti, a writ for recalling a parliament (4 Co.Inst. 44).

Reward. The Crown Court may order payment of a reasonable sum to a person who has been active in or towards the apprehension of any person charged with an arrestable offence and if a person is killed in attempting to take such offenders the court may order compensation to his wife or relatives (Criminal Law Act, 1826, ss. 28–30; Criminal Law Act, 1967, Sch. 2 para. 3, Sch. 3 Pt. III).

The offering of rewards by the government was discontinued on the ground that persons committed crimes for the purpose of obtaining rewards by false accusations, and the Home Office, though urgently requested to offer a reward for the discovery of a series of murders in Whitechapel in 1888, refused to do so. See Radzinowicz, *History of English Criminal Law*, vol. 2.

Where any public advertisement of a reward for the return of any goods which have been stolen or lost uses any words to the effect that no questions will be asked or that the person producing the goods will be safe from apprehension or inquiry or that any money paid for the purchase of the goods or advanced by way of loan on them will be repaid, the person advertising the reward and any person who prints or publishes the advertisement is liable on summary conviction to a fine not exceeding one hundred pounds (Theft Act, 1968, s. 23).

An offer for reward for information is a contract to pay the reward to the first person giving it and to him only, his motive being immaterial (*Williams v. Carwardine* (1833) 4 B. & Ad. 621).

See BRIBE.

Rex. See KING.

Rex est caput et salus reipublicae (4 Co.Inst. 124). (The king is the head and guardian of the commonwealth.)

Rex est legalis et politicus (Lane, 27). (The king is both legal and politic.) This dictum was issued in *Bates' Case* (1606) 2 St.Tr. 371, in support of the proposition that reasons politic are sufficient to guide judges. See BATES' CASE.

Rex n'est lie per ascun statute si il ne soit expressement nosme (Jenk., Cent. 307). (The king is not bound by any statute unless he is expressly named therein.)

Rex non debet esse sub homine sed sub Deo et lege quia lex facit regem (1 Bract. 5; 12 Co.Rep. 65; Broom 17). (The king ought not to be under any man, but under God and under the law, for the law makes the king.) This early conception of the king as a creation of the law is in marked contrast to the divine right theory which made the law a creature of the king, *a Deo rex, a rege lex.*

Rex non potest fallere nec falli (Grounds of Law, 438). (The king cannot deceive or be deceived.) The judges represent the king, but if they go wrong they do so in their personal capacities and not as the representatives of the king.

Rex non potest peccare (2 Rolle R. 304). (The king can do no wrong.) It is not to be presumed that the king will do or sanction anything contrary to law, to which he is subject. But if an evil act is done, it, though emanating from the king personally, will be imputed to his ministers, for whose acts the king is in no way responsible. Upon this principle, the Crown could not, before the Crown Proceedings Act, 1947, be prejudiced by the wrongful acts of its servants, nor by errors in letters patent, etc. See EADEM MENS, ETC.; REX NON DEBET ESSE, ETC.

Rex nunquam moritur (Branch, Max. 197). (The king never dies.) See IN ANGLIA, ETC.

Rex quod injustum est facere non potest (Jenk., Cent. 9). (The king cannot do what is unjust.) See REX NON POTEST PECCARE.

Rhandir, a part in the division of Wales before the Conquest; every township comprehended four gavels, and every gavel had four rhandirs, and four houses or tenements constituted a rhandir (Taylor's Hist. Gav. 69).

Rhetoric, the art of speaking not merely correctly, but with art and elegance.

Rhind-mart, Rynmart, a carcass from the herd; used in old north-country charters for any species of horned cattle.

Rhodes, Laws of, a code of sea laws reputed to have been compiled, probably between A.D. 600 and A.D. 800, in the island of Rhodes. They were declared by the Roman emperors to be binding on the world at large. The only one of them extant is the *lex Rhodia de jactu,* which declares that where goods are thrown overboard in order to lighten a ship so as to save the ship and the rest of her cargo, then all the owners of the ship and the cargo must share in the loss; and this is the general average of our own day. See Ashburner, *Rhodian Sea Laws.* See AVERAGE.

Rhodesia. As a result of a unilateral declaration by the Government of Rhodesia of the independence of Rhodesia, the Southern Rhodesian Act, 1965, was passed declaring that Southern Rhodesia is part of Her Majesty's dominions and empowering the United Kingdom Government to make whatever provision is necessary or expedient. This power is continued on a year to year basis.

Rial. See GOLD COINS.

Ribaud, a rogue, vagrant, whoremonger; a person given to all manner of wickedness.

Ribbon development. The Restriction of Ribbon Development Act, 1935, ss. 1–3, enabled a highway authority to control development along the frontages of certain roads. These powers were superseded by the general powers of control in relation to planning. See DEVELOPMENT.

Ribbonmen, associations or secret societies formed in Ireland, having for their object the dispossession of landlords by murder and fire-raising (Alison, Hist. of Europe, c. 20, s. 13).

Ricambio; Ricambrium. See RE-EXCHANGE.

Richmond. See HERALD.

Richmond Forest, a royal forest founded by Charles I. As to Richmond Park, see 2 Hall.Const.Hist. 14. See PARK.

Rider, an inserted leaf or clause: an additional clause tacked to a Bill passing through Parliament; an additional opinion put forward by a jury in a criminal case with their verdict, as, for example, a recommendation to mercy.

Rider-roll, a schedule or small piece of parchment added to some part of a roll, record or Act of Parliament (1 Bl. Com. 182).

Riding. From before the Norman, and possibly from the Danish, Conquest, Yorkshire and Lincolnshire were each divided into three parts known as ridings, or trithings, that is to say, thirds (1 Stubbs, Const.Hist. 127).

The ridings of Lincolnshire have for hundreds of years been known as Parts; they are Holland, Lindsey and Kesteven. In Yorkshire there were the North Riding, the West Riding, and the East Riding. For the present areas of local government, see the Local Government Act, 1972, Sch. 1.

Riding armed. The offence of riding or going armed with dangerous or unusual weapons is at common law a misdemeanour tending to disturb the public peace by terrifying the good people of the land. See OFFENSIVE WEAPONS.

Riding clerk. Each of the Six Clerks (*q.v.*) in turn kept for one year at a time the Controlment Book of all grants that passed the Great Seal, and during that year he was known as the Riding Clerk. Whether he did or did not ride is not clear, but during his year of office he was at one time allowed one horse-keep. The Six Clerks were superseded by the Clerks of Records and Writs.

Riding establishments. Riding establishments require to be licensed by the local authority who have powers of inspection and control (Riding Establishments Acts, 1964 and 1970); Local Government Act, 1974, s. 35, Sch. 6 para. 18, Sch. 8).

A riding school is not an agricultural activity and a tenancy of riding stables does not come within the Agricultural Holdings Act, 1948 (*Deith* v. *Brown* [1956] J.P.L. 736). A field let for grazing to a riding school is protected as an agricultural holding (*q.v.*) (*Rutherford* v. *Maurer* [1962] 1 Q.B. 16).

Riding furiously. Riding or driving furiously is an offence against the Highway Act, 1835, s. 78 (as amended by the Criminal Justice Act, 1967, Sch. 3 and the Statute Law (Repeals) Act, 1973, Sch. 1), and is punishable by fine up to £20 in addition to liability to a civil action. See also the Town Police Clauses Act, 1847, s. 28; the Metropolitan Police Act, 1839, s. 54; the Offences against the Person Act, 1861, s. 35 and the Road Traffic Act, 1972, s. 2.

Riding officers. See COAST BLOCKADE.

Rief. See REIF.

Riens in arrere or Riens arrear (nothing in arrear), a plea in bar used by the plaintiff in an action of replevin when he alleged that the rent had been paid or satisfied before the distress was taken; also a plea which was used in an action for debt for arrearages of account, whereby the defendant alleged that there was nothing in arrear. The reply which has taken the place of the plea in bar under the present practice was some-times called by the same name. See REPLEVIN.

Riens passe per fait (nothing passes by the deed), an exception used in an action on a deed (Broke).

Riens per descent (nothing by descent), the plea of an heir where he was sued for his ancestor's debts, and had no land from him by descent or assets in his hands (3 Cro. 151).

Riens per devise (nothing by devise), a plea that a defendant sued as devisee under a will was not devisee of any lands or hereditaments under the will.

Rier-county; Rere-county; Reer-county [Lat. *retro-comitatus*], close county, in opposition to open county; some public place which the sheriff appointed for the receipt of the king's money after the end of the county court. Fleta says it was *dies crastinus post comitatum.* See RERE-COUNTY.

Rifflare [Sax. *reife*], to take away anything by force.

Right [Teut. *recht*; Lat. *rectus*, right, straight], that which the law directs. That which is so directed for the protection and advantage of an individual is said to be his right. It has been described as a liberty of doing or possessing something consistently with law, or more strictly, the liberty of doing or possessing something for the infringement of which there is a legal sanction.

A right, in its most general sense, is either the liberty (protected by law) of acting or abstaining from acting in a certain manner, or the power (enforced by law) of compelling a specific person to do or abstain from doing a particular thing. A legal right is a capacity residing in one man of controlling, with the assent and assistance of the State, the actions of others. It follows that every right involves a person invested with the right, or entitled; a person or persons on whom that right imposes a correlative duty or obligation; an act or forbearance which is the subject-matter of the right; and in some cases an object, that is, a person or thing to which the right has reference, as in the case of ownership.

With reference to their ultimate object or purpose, rights and duties are either primary (substantive, original), or secondary (adjective, sanctioning).

Primary rights are those which can be

created without reference to rights already existing. Thus, if A contracts to pay me £50, my right to the payment of that sum is a primary right. Primary rights are of two classes: (1) those rights to which every member of the community is prima facie entitled; they consist of (a) personal (or absolute) rights, *e.g.,* the right to life, health and liberty of action, and (b) public rights, which are those rights by which every member of the community is prima facie entitled to use certain things which either belong to the State, or, if they belong to private persons, are subject to the right to public user; such are the rights of the public in respect of the sea, navigable rivers, highways, public parks, etc. (see PUBLICI JURIS); (2) those rights which arise from relation other than membership of a community, and include the ordinary rights arising from ownership, contract, marriage, and similar relations.

Secondary rights can arise only for the purpose of protecting or enforcing primary rights. They are either preventive (protective) or remedial (reparative).

Preventive or protective secondary rights exist in order to prevent the infringement or loss of primary rights. They are judicial when they require the assistance of a court of law for their enforcement, and extra-judicial when they are capable of being exercised by the party himself. The right to prevent a threatened injury by injunction, the right to take proceedings to obtain a judicial recognition of a right which might be lost by lapse of time or adverse user, the right to institute proceedings for the administration of the estate of a deceased person or the assets of an insolvent person or corporation, and the right to security against the commission of a crime; are instances of judicial preventive rights; and the right of self-defence is an instance of an extrajudicial preventive right. See ADMINISTRATION; DE BENE ESSE; LEGITIMACY; NE EXEAT REGNO; PERPETUATING TESTIMONY.

Remedial or reparative secondary rights are also either judicial or extra-judicial. They may further be divided into rights of restitution or restoration, which entitle the person injured to be replaced in his original position; rights of enforcement, which entitle the person injured to the performance of an act by the person bound; and rights of satisfaction or compensation. A right of entry or re-entry is an extrajudicial right of restitution, a lien is an extrajudicial right of enforcement, a right of distress or retainer is an extrajudicial right of satisfaction, the right of bringing an action of ejectment or detinue is a judicial restitutive right, the right of obtaining an injunction for specific performance and the right to compel the payment of a debt are judicial rights of enforcement, and the right of bringing an action of damages for breach or contract or tort is a judicial right of satisfaction. See REMEDY.

With reference to the nature of the obligation which they impose, rights are either *in rem* (real rights, general rights, rights against the whole world, *jura in rem*) or *in personam* (personal rights, relative rights, rights against determinate persons, *jura in personam*).

A right *in rem* is one which imposes an obligation on persons generally, that is, either on all the world or on all the world except certain determinate persons. Thus, if I am entitled to exclude all persons from a given piece of land, I have a right *in rem* in respect of that land; and if there are one or more persons, A, B and C, whom I am not entitled to exclude from it, my right is still a right *in rem*. So if I am entitled to the services of a servant, I have a right *in rem* which obliges all other persons not to interfere wrongfully with that relation. (See MASTER AND SERVANT; SERVICE.) A right *in rem* is always negative.

A right *in personam* is one which imposes an obligation on a definite person. Thus, if A agrees to pay me £50, my right to that sum against A is a right *in personam*, belonging to the class of primary rights. My right to liberty of action, so long as I do not interfere with other persons' rights, is a right *in rem*; if B infringes that right by imprisoning or assaulting me, I acquire a right to recover damages against him, which is a right *in personam* belonging to the class of secondary rights. Primary rights *in personam* are either affirmative (positive) or negative, according as they require for their performance an act or a forbearance. Thus, if A contracts with B not to carry on business in a certain place, B has a negative right against A. Primary rights *in personam* are also subject to the following divisions: absolute and conditional, legal and equitable, personal and transmissible, and of perfect and imperfect obligation. See CONTRACT; OBLIGATION.

"Right" is used by the old writers on real property law in the technical sense of a right which an owner of land had when he had been disseised, so that he had only the right of recovering possession either by entry or action. His estate was then said to be turned to a right. If A was disseised by B, and B died while in possession, so that the land descended to his heir, A could not recover possession by entry, but had to bring a possessory action (see DESCENT CAST); if A further suffered a certain time to elapse, or had judgment given against him in a possessory action, he could no longer recover by a possessory action, but only by an action on the right, meaning the right of ownership as opposed to the right to possession. Hence his estate was said to be turned to a mere, bare or naked right (Co.Litt. 266a, 345a). See ACTION.

"Right," like "title" (*q.v.*) sometimes connotes the idea of a mode of acquisition. Thus, a person is said to hold or own property in his own right, or in right of another (*in auter droit.*) If he purchases it, he obtains it in his own right; but if he acquires it as representing another person, he is said to take it *in auter droit*. The principal mode of taking personal property *in auter droit* is by executorship or administration, for the executor or administrator holds the goods of the deceased as his representative. The difference is of importance as regards the law of merger (*q.v.*).

In the phrase "of common right," the word "right" seems to be used in a somewhat similar sense. Thus, when it is said that the remedy of distress for arrears of a rent-service exists of common right, and that every freehold tenant of a manor has a right of common of pasture appendant of common right, it is meant that the right is created

by law, and not by agreement between the parties. See IN GROSS.

"Right" is used in law, as well as in ethics, as opposed to "wrong." Thus a person may acquire a title by wrong. See TITLE.

Right close, Writ of; Writ de recto clauso, a writ of right which lay for tenants in ancient demesne (*q.v.*) who had been ousted of their lands. It was addressed to the lord and commanded him to do right in his court. See RECTO, ETC.

Right in court. See RECTUS IN CURIA.

Right of action, the right to bring an action. Thus, a person who is wrongfully dispossessed of land has a right of action to recover it. See ACTIO PERSONALIS MORITUR CUM PERSONA; CAUSE OF ACTION; CHOSE; REMEDY.

In the old writers, "right of action" was commonly used to denote that a person had lost a right of entry (*q.v.*), and had nothing but a right of action left (Co.Litt. 363b). See RIGHT.

Right of entry, the right of taking or resuming possession of land by entering on it in a peaceable manner. See ENTRY.

Rights of entry are of two kinds. An original or mere right of entry is a right of entry and nothing more. Thus, where a person has been disseised of land, or where an estate has determined, so that he becomes entitled to the possession of the land, he has an original right of entry. This kind of right was formerly inalienable, but since the Real Property Act, 1845, s. 6, has been capable of being disposed of by deed (Law of Property Act, 1925, s. 4). It was sufficient to support a contingent remainder, if the estate of the disseisee was itself sufficient (1 Co.Rep. 66b).

A right of entry by the exercise of which an existing estate is defeated is a right attached to a reversion. It was formerly called a title of entry, to distinguish it from an original right of entry, because it could not be enforced by action, and was therefore not a right in the technical sense. It is also sometimes called a right of re-entry. The commonest instance of this kind of right occurs in an ordinary lease, in which it is usual to reserve to the lessor the right of determining the lease by re-entry if the lessee fails to pay the rent or perform the covenants. This kind of right is inalienable by itself, although since the statute 1540, 32 Hen. 8, c. 34, the benefit of the condition passes on an assignment of the reversion, so that the assignee can take advantage of any breach of the condition committed after the assignment (Law of Property Act, 1925, ss. 140, 141). The exercise of a right of re-entry for breach of a covenant or condition contained in a lease is restricted by the Law of Property Act, 1925, s. 146.

See CONTINUAL CLAIM; DESCENT CAST; FORCIBLE ENTRY; FORFEITURE; RIGHT OF ACTION; TITLE.

Right of representation and performance. See COPYRIGHT.

Right of way. See WAY.

Right patent, Writ of, a writ which lay for a tenant in fee simple, if, for instance, another had recovered the lands against him by default in a *praecipe quod reddat* (Fitz.N.B. 1).

It was abolished in 1833.

See PRAECIPE; RECTO, BREVE DE.

Right, Petition of. See PETITION OF RIGHT.

Right to begin. The right to begin on the hearing or trial of a cause, or the argument of a petition, etc., is the right of first addressing the court or jury. The right to begin is frequently of importance, as the counsel who begins has also the right of replying or having the last word after the counsel on the opposite side has addressed the court or jury. This rule is subject to the exception that where the second counsel at a trial before a jury does not call witnesses, the counsel who began has no right of reply.

The general rule is that the plaintiff has the right to begin if the affirmative of the issue is on him, or if the onus of proving any one material issue, or of proving the amount of damages, rests on him. Otherwise, if the affirmative of the issue lies on the defendant, he has the right to begin. If in replevin the defendant avows for rent in arrear, and the plaintiff replies *riens in arrere*, the plaintiff must begin. In any action where the plaintiff seeks to recover damages of an unascertained

amount, he is entitled to begin, though the affirmative be with the defendant.

In considering, however, which party ought to begin, it is not so much the form of the issue which is to be considered as the substance and effect of it, and the judge will consider what is the substantial fact to be made out, and on whom it lies to make it out. As a general rule, the party entitled to begin is he who would have a verdict against him if no evidence were given on either side. See R.S.C., Ord. 35, r. 7; Archbold, *Criminal Pleading,* paras. 442, 578.

In the Court of Appeal, and in all other civil appeals, the appellant's counsel begins.

On an appeal from the justices, the person who appears in support of the order of the justices begins.

Right, Writ of [Lat. *breve de recto*], a procedure for the recovery of real property after not more than sixty years' adverse possession; the highest writ in the law, sometimes called the writ or right proper. It was abolished by the Real Property Limitation Act, 1833, and was last used in *Davies* v. *Lowndes* (1835) 1 Bing. N.C. 597. See RIGHT CLOSE; RIGHT PATENT.

Rights, Bill of. See BILL OF RIGHTS.

Ring-dropping, a form of swindle worked by a rogue who deposits on the pavement a ring or other article apparently of value, but actually worthless, which he picks up afterwards in the view of some person to whom he then offers it at what seems to be a bargain price. It will amount to obtaining property by deception (Theft Act, 1968).

Ringing the changes. Where a seller is given a good coin in payment for goods, and by a sleight of hand substitutes for it a bad coin which he hands back to the purchaser and declares to be the coin which had been paid, and thereby obtains a second good coin from the purchaser, he is said to ring the changes. This, as regards the second good coin paid, is obtaining property by deception (Theft Act, 1968, s. 15) and, as regards the bad coin, is the offence of uttering counterfeit coin (Coinage Offences Act, 1936, s. 5 (1)).

Another swindle also known as ringing the changes consists in asking for change and then so confusing the person who gives the change that more than the proper amount is obtained. This is also obtaining property by deception (Theft Act, 1968, s. 15).

Rings. See SERJEANT-AT-LAW.

Riot, a tumultuous disturbance of the peace by three persons or more assembling of their own authority, with an intent mutually to assist one another against any who shall oppose them in the execution of some enterprise, and afterwards actually executing the same in a violent and turbulent manner to the terror of the people, whether the act intended were of itself lawful or unlawful.

A riot is an unlawful assembly which has actually begun to execute the purpose for which it assembled by a breach of the peace, and to the terror of the public (*R.* v. *Graham* (1854) 16 Cox C.C. 420). The moment when persons in a crowd, however peaceful their original intention, commence to act for some shared common purpose supporting each other and in such a way that reasonable citizens fear a breach of the peace, the assembly becomes unlawful (*R.* v. *Caird* (1970) 54 Cr.App.R. 499). But a riot cannot take place unless three persons at least are present. Every person convicted of riot is liable to be sentenced to fine and imprisonment.

By the Tumultuous Petitioning Act, 1661 s. 1 (amended by the Criminal Law Act, 1967, Sch. 3 Pt. I), more than ten persons coming to present a petition to the sovereign, and by the Seditious Meetings Act, 1817, s. 23 more than fifty persons assembling near Westminster when Parliament is sitting, constitute a riot.

In any case of riot, or even apprehended riot, all places where intoxicating liquors are sold may be ordered to be closed by justices of the peace, under the Licensing Act, 1964, s. 188.

The Riot Act, 1714, under which rioters could be called upon to disperse or become guilty of felony (commonly but inaccurately called " reading the Riot Act ") was repealed by the Statute Law (Repeals) Act, 1973, Sch. 1 Pt. IV. The Riot Act, 1714, did not affect the common law right and duty of justices to suppress a riot at any moment with whatever degree of force may be necessary;

nor did it affect the common law right of private persons, acting on their own initiative, to do the same.

Compensation is payable to persons whose property has been damaged by riot under the Riot Damages Act, 1886, as amended by the Police Act, 1964, Schs. 9, 10. For procedure see the Riot (Claims for Compensation) Regulations, 1921 (No. 1536). As to the elements which must have existed in the disturbance in order to constitute a riot within the meaning of this Act, see *Field* v. *Receiver for Metropolitan Police District* [1907] 2 K.B. 853; *J. W. Dwyer* v. *Metropolitan Police District Receiver* [1967] 2 Q.B. 970. Where rioters damage a ship in distress, the remedy is under the same Act as applied by the Merchant Shipping Act, 1894, s. 515.

See AFFRAY; ASSEMBLY, UNLAWFUL; DAMAGE; CRIMINAL; ROUT.

Riparia [Med. Lat.], water running between two banks; a bank (Magna Carta, 1215, c. 15) (2 Co.Inst. 478). See MAGNA CARTA.

Riparian, that which relates to or is connected with the bank of a river or other watercourse. A riparian proprietor or owner is a person who owns land through or past which a river runs; and riparian rights are those arising from such a property. A riparian owner whose land is nearer the source of the river is called an upper riparian owner as compared with one whose land is more remote from the source.

As to the rights of riparian owners, see WATER.

Riptowell, or **Reaptowel,** a gratuity or reward given to tenants after they had reaped their lord's corn or done other customary duties (Cowel).

Ripuarian Laws, a code of laws belonging to the Franks who occupied the country upon the Rhine.

Risk, in insurance, the danger, peril, or event insured against; the possibility of the loss happening under such circumstances as to make the underwriter liable; when this possibility has arisen (*e.g.,* by the departure of a vessel insured), the risk is said to commence or attach, and the assured's interest is said to be at risk. When the insurance is of such a nature that the peril which would make the underwriter liable for a total loss may happen as soon as the risk commences, the risk is said to be entire; if, on the other hand, some circumstance which would have contributed to the happening of the peril insured against has not taken place, the risk is divided or apportionable. For instance, if the vessel deviates, the underwriter is discharged, but inasmuch as if it had been lost before the deviation he would have been liable, he has run the whole risk, and the risk is therefore said to be entire; but if part of the risk insured against has not been run (as where part of the cargo insured has not been shipped), the risk is divided, and the assured is entitled to a return of that proportion of the premium which covered the risk not run.

When goods are declared in a charterparty to be carried at merchant's risk this does not exclude the charterer's right to general average (see AVERAGE) in respect of goods properly jettisoned; but it does exclude the right of the charterer to recover in respect of the improper or negligent acts of the master or crew.

See MORA DEBITORIS, ETC; RES PERIT, ETC.

Ritual, the prescribed mode of conducting religious services. The subjects with which it deals are decorations, whether temporary or permanent, of the church, ornaments of the church, vestments (technically known as the ornaments) of the minister, ceremonies, and rites.

The Privy Council is the tribunal which decides cases on these points; it reserves the right to reconsider its decisions, which, therefore, are not absolutely final. See Phill.Ecc.Law; Cripps, *Church and Clergy.*

Rivage, or **Rivagium,** a toll which was paid to the Crown for the passage of boats or vessels on certain rivers (Jacob).

Riveare, to have the liberty of a river for fishing and fowling (Jacob).

River authorities. These were established under the Water Resources Act, 1963, replacing river boards established under the River Boards Act, 1948. River authorities were abolished by the Water Act, 1973, s. 33 and their functions transferred to water authorities by s. 9. See WATER.

Rivers. A public navigable river is one which is navigable and in which the tide ebbs and flows; all other rivers on which navigation is carried on are private rivers over which the public have acquired a right or easement or navigation. The ownership of the bed of a public navigable river is prima facie in the Crown. As to the right of navigation, see NAVIGABLE; as to the right of fishing in a public river, see FISHERY.

All rivers and streams above the flow and reflow of the tide are prima facie private, although many have become by immemorial user or by Act of Parliament subject to public rights of navigation. The right of navigation gives no right of property, or of fishing. When a private river runs through land belonging to one person, he is prima facie owner of the bed; when a private river separates the lands of two owners, each is prima facie owner of the soil of the bed to the middle of the stream (*ad medium filum aquae (q.v.)*). See Coulson and Forbes on *Waters.*

See ALLUVION; CONSERVATORS OF RIVERS; DERELICTION; WATER.

Rivers, Pollution of. See POLLUTION.

Rixa, a dispute or quarrel (Civil Law).

Rixatrix communis, a common scold.

Road, a way or passage (see HIGHWAY; WAY); a secure place for the anchoring of vessels.

Road fund, a fund established pursuant to the Roads Act, 1920, s. 3, for the receipt and payment out (under the direction of the Minister of Transport and Civil Aviation) of moneys for road improvements under that Act and the Development and Road Improvement Funds Act, 1909. It was abolished by the Miscellaneous Financial Provisions Act, 1955, s. 4.

Road haulage. The Transport Act, 1968, Pt. V (ss. 59–94) regulates the carriage of goods by road. See further the Road Traffic Act, 1972, Sch. 7; Road Traffic (Foreign Vehicles) Act, 1972, s. 1, Schs. 1, 2; European Communities Act, 1972, Sch. 4 para. 9; Hydrocarbon Oil (Customs and Excise Act, 1971, s. 24, Sch. 6 para. 3; Transport (London) Act, 1969, Sch. 6; Road Traffic Act, 1974, Sch. 4; International Road Haulage Permits Act, 1975. As to drivers' hours, see the Transport Act, 1968, ss. 95–103; Road Traffic Act, 1972, Sch. 7; Road Traffic (Foreign Vehicles) Act, 1972, s. 1, Sch. 2; European Communities Act, 1972, Sch. 4 para. 9; Road Traffic Act, 1974, Sch. 4; Road Traffic (Drivers' Ages and Hours of Work) Act, 1976, ss. 2, 3. See also the Carriage of Goods by Road Act, 1965; *William Tatton & Co.* v. *Ferrymasters* [1974] 1 Lloyd's Rep. 203.

Road humps. The Road Traffic Act, 1974, s. 17, authorises experiments with artificial humps or depressions in a road designed to control the speed of vehicles.

Road, Rule of the. The common law rule of the road, as between all traffic other than pedestrian traffic, is that everyone keeps to the left except when overtaking, in which latter case the overtaking vehicle or horse keeps to the right. Infractions of the rule are punishable summarily under the Highway Act, 1835, s. 78 (as amended by the Highways Act, 1959, Sch. 25; London Government Act, 1963, Sch. 6 para. 70; Criminal Justice Act, 1967, Sch. 3 Pt. I; Statute Law (Repeals) Act, 1973, Sch. 1) for the purposes of which a motor-car or other mechanically propelled vehicle is, like a bicycle, a carriage.

The Highway Code, para. 29, expresses the rule as follows: " Keep to the left, except when you intend to overtake or turn right, or when you have to pass stationary vehicles or pedestrians in the road. Allow others to overtake you if they want to." Para. 138 provides " If you are riding a horse keep to the left. If you are leading a horse while riding another you should keep to the left and keep the led animal on your left." Para. 139 provides "If you are on foot and leading an animal on a road that has no footpath, walk on the right hand side of the road. Keep between the animal and the traffic and keep it close to the edge of the road."

Pedestrians can take whichever side they please.

Road service licence. A vehicle may not be used as a stage carriage (*q.v.*) as an express carriage (*q.v.*) without a road service licence (Road Traffic Act, 1960, ss. 134–140; Road Traffic Regulation Act, 1967, Sch. 6; Transport Act, 1968, ss. 21, 30; Local Government Act, 1972, Sch. 30). See also the London Government Act, 1963, ss. 14, 15, Sch. 5 Pt. I para. 25; Transport (London) Act, 1969, s. 24, Sch. 6).

Road traffic. See the Road Traffic Regulation Act, 1967, as amended; Road Traffic Act, 1972; Local Government Act, 1974, s. 35, Sch. 6 para. 20; Road Traffic Act, 1974, Sch. 5, Pt. II.

See ARREST; CARELESS DRIVING; DANGEROUS DRIVING; DRIVING LICENCES.

Road-ferry, is a ferry connecting the termination of a highway (*q.v.*) with the termination of another highway (Highways Act, 1959, s. 295 (1)). Power to construct and maintain road-ferries is contained in the Highways Act, 1959, ss. 26, 107, 220), and power to acquire land by agreement or compulsorily in s. 220.

Robbery. A person is guilty of robbery if he steals (see THEFT) and immediately before or at the time of doing so, and in order to do so, he uses force on any person or puts or seeks to put any person in fear of being then and there subject to force. A person convicted of robbery, or an assault with intent to rob is liable on conviction on indictment to imprisonment for life (Theft Act, 1968, s. 8). The offence of robbery at common law was abolished by s. 32.

Roberdsman, or **Robertsman,** a bold and stout robber or night thief, so called from Robin Hood, the famous robber, but, perhaps, a corruption of " robber's-man " (3 Co.Inst. 197).

Rod, a measure of sixteen feet and a half long, otherwise called a perch (*q.v.*). See BLACK ROD; PORTER; USHER.

Rodeo. See the Protection of Animals Act, 1934 and CRUELTY TO ANIMALS.

Rodknights, those who held by the tenure of riding with their lord from one manor to another (2 Brac. c. 35).

Roe, Richard, otherwise **Troublesome,** the casual ejector and fictitious defendant in ejectment, whose services are no longer invoked. See EJECTMENT; JOHN DOE.

Rogatio, testium. In making a nuncupative will, this is where the testator formally calls upon the persons present to bear witness that he has declared his will. See WILL.

Rogation [Lat. *rogatio*], the demand, by the consul or tribunes, of law to be passed by the people (Civil Law).

Rogation days, the Monday, Tuesday, and Wednesday before Ascension Day (*q.v.*). See FAST DAY; GRASS-WEEK; PARISH BOUNDARIES.

Rogation Sunday, the fifth Sunday after Easter. It is the Sunday preceding Ascension Day.

Rogation week [Lat. *rogando* (*Deum*), supplicating God], the second week before Whit Sunday; thus called from three fasts observed therein, the Monday, Tuesday, and Wednesday, called Rogation days, because of the extraordinary prayers then made for the fruits of the earth, or as a preparation for the devotion of Holy Thursday, or the Ascension of our Lord.

Rogatory letters, a commission from one judge to another requesting him to examine a witness. In the terminology of international law, this expression is used as a synonym for what in our law are known as letters of request (*q.v.*) addressed to foreign courts.

Rogue, a wandering beggar, vagrant, vagabond. As to incorrigible rogues and rogues and vagabonds, see VAGRANCY.

Rogus, a funeral pile; a great fire wherein dead bodies were burned; a pile of wood (Claus. 5 Hen. 3).

Rôle d'équipage [Fr.], the list of a ship's crew; a muster-roll.

Roll, a schedule of parchment which may be turned up with the hand in the form of a pipe (Staundf.P.C. 11). In ancient times all the principal records were written on pieces of parchment stitched together so as to form a long continuous piece, which was rolled up when not in use. Hence such records were called " rolls." This practice was followed up till the last century in the Court of Chancery when the practice of writing on rolls was abandoned for the more convenient method of inscribing in books. See ENROLMENT.

The Parliament Rolls are the records of the proceedings of Parliament, especially Acts of Parliament, and therefore when any misprint appears in a printed copy of a statute, the Parliament roll is consulted to correct the error. See ROLLS OF PARLIAMENT.

The Patent Rolls contain grants of liberties, privileges, lands, offices, etc., creations of peers, and other letters patent (*q.v.*), while the Close Rolls are the records of letters close (*q.v.*). There are also numerous other kinds of rolls of a similar nature, such as the charter rolls, fine rolls, liberate rolls, perambulation rolls, hundred rolls, exchequer rolls, etc.

The rolls above described form part of the public records of the kingdom and are kept at the Record Office in London. See DOMUS CONVERSORUM; MASTER OF THE ROLLS; RECORD OFFICE; ROLLS OFFICE OF THE CHANCERY.

The court rolls of manors were in ancient times long pieces of parchment, rolled up into convenient bundles; but in modern times the court roll was a large book in which the steward entered every transaction relating to the copyhold lands of the manor. See COPYHOLD; ROLL OF COURT.

The admission of every solicitor of the Supreme Court requires to be enrolled in a roll or book kept for that purpose by the Law Society (*q.v.*). A solicitor is said to be struck off the rolls when his name is taken out of this roll by the Law Society, either on his own application, where he wishes to cease to be a solicitor, or on the application of some one else, when he has been guilty of misconduct. See DISBAR; SOLICITORS.

In the old common law practice the steps in every action were entered on a roll, which was called the plea roll, the issue roll, or the judgment roll, according to the stage which the action had reached. This kind of roll no longer exists, the cause book (*q.v.*) and the books in which judgments are entered having taken its place (R.S.C., Ord. 42, r. 5).

Roll of court, the court roll in a manor, wherein the business of the court, the admissions, surrenders, names, rents, and services of the tenants were copied and enrolled.

Copyhold lands were lands held by copy of court roll; that is, the muniments of the title were copies of the roll or book in which an account was kept of the proceedings in the court of the manor to which the lands belonged. As to the custody and superintendence of the Master of the Rolls, see the Law of Property Act, 1922, s. 144A (added by the Law of Property (Amendment) Act, 1924, Sch. 2). See COPYHOLD; ROLL.

Rolled-up plea, a plea in actions for libel where the defence of fair comment is set up, by which the defendant alleges that so far as the words complained of consisted of allegations of fact, they were true in substance and in fact, and in so far as they consisted of expressions of opinion they were fair comment made in good faith and without malice upon the facts, which were matters of public interest. The defendant must give particulars stating which of the words complained of he alleges are statements of fact and of the facts and matters he relies on in support of the allegation that the words are true. (R.S.C., Ord. 82, r. 3 (2); *Lord* v. *Sunday Telegraph* [1971] 1 Q.B. 235). See FAIR COMMENT.

Rolling stock. By the Railway Rolling Stock Protection Act, 1872, railway rolling stock when out on sidings, etc., belonging to private occupiers, is exempted from distress for rent due from the occupiers. The rolling stock is protected from execution by the Railway Companies Act, 1867, s. 4.

Rolls Court, the room where the Master of the Rolls used to sit as a judge before the Judicature Acts, 1873–75.

Rolls, Master of the. See MASTER OF THE ROLLS.

Rolls of the Exchequer, rolls relating to the revenue of the country.

Rolls of Parliament, the manuscript registers of the proceedings of our old Parliaments. In these rolls are likewise a great many decisions of difficult points of law which were frequently, in former times, referred to the determination of this supreme court by the judges of both benches, etc.

Formerly all bills were drawn in the form of petitions which were entered upon the parliament rolls, with the king's answer thereunto subjoined; not in any settled form of words, but as the circumstances of the case required; and at the end of each parliament, the judges drew them into the form of a statute, which was entered on the statute rolls (1 Bl. Comm. 181). See ROLL.

Rolls of the Temple. In the two Temples there was a roll called the Calves-head Roll, wherein every bencher, barrister, and student, was taxed yearly at so much to the cook and other officers of the houses, in consideration of a dinner of calves-head, provided in Easter term (Orig.Jurid. 199).

Rolls Office of the Chancery, an office in Chancery Lane, London, which contained rolls and records of the Court of Chancery.

This house or office was anciently called *Domus Conversorum*, as being appointed by Henry III for the use of converted Jews, but their irregularities occasioned Edward II to expel them thence, upon which the place was deputed for the custody of the rolls.

Rolt's Act, the Chancery Regulation Act, 1862, which was passed at the instance of Mr. Rolt, M.P., who in 1867 became a Lord Justice of Appeal.

Roly-poly, a kind of roulette; also an old game called half-bowl, which was a combination of bowls and skittles (Brandt, *Gaming* 24).

Roman Catholics. Laws, commonly called the penal laws, were passed against Roman Catholics, generally under the name of Papists (*q.v.*) after the Reformation. The statute 1571, 13 Eliz. 1, c. 2, punished with the penalties of a praemunire (*q.v.*) any person bringing into this country any Agnus Dei, cross, picture, etc., from Rome; the statute 1605, 3 Jac. 1, c. 5, penalised the sale or purchase of Popish primers; the statute 1698, 11 & 12 Wm. 3, c. 4, punished any Papist assuming the education of youth with imprisonment for life. Exclusion from Parliament was effected by the requirement of a declaration against transubstantiation (*q.v.*) from members of either House by the statute 1678, 30 Car. 2, st. 2, and disfranchisement by the requirement of an oath of supremacy by the statute 1696, 7 & 8 Wm. 3, c. 27, s. 19; while the statute 1696, 7 & 8 Wm. 3, c. 24, effected (until 1791) exclusion from the profession of barrister, attorney, or solicitor by requiring a declaration against transubstantiation under the statute 1672, 25 Car. 2, c. 2.

Roman Catholic disabilities have now been almost completely removed, the Roman Catholic Relief Act, 1791, for freedom of worship with unlocked doors, and the Roman Catholic Relief Act, 1829, for enfranchisement and qualification for sitting in Parliament, being the main factors in the removal, and the Roman Catholic Charities Act, 1832, subjecting Roman Catholics to the same laws as Protestant dissenters with respect to schools and places for religious worship, education, and charitable purposes.

Diplomatic relations with the sovereign of the Roman States were allowed by the statute 1848, 11 & 12 Vict. c. 108, which, however, prohibited the sovereign of this country from receiving as ambassador accredited by him any priest, Jesuit (*q.v.*), or member of any other religious order bound in monastic or religious vows.

The Act of Settlement, 1700, however, requires the sovereign to be a Protestant; and the Roman Catholic Relief Act, 1829, contains a series of enactments directed to the gradual suppression and prohibition of Jesuits, and members of other religious orders, communities, or societies of the Church of Rome, bound by religious or monastic vows; the Act does not render void an absolute immediate bequest to individuals ascertained at the death of the testator (*Re Smith* [1914] 1 Ch. 937). The Roman Catholic Charities Act, 1832, provided for the banishment of the persons named therein.

Roman Catholics were debarred from holding in the universities of Oxford, Cambridge or Durham any professorship of divinity, or any office for which membership of the Church of England or holy orders of that Church was required (Universities Tests Act, 1871, ss. 1, 8), and also from holding any office in the colleges of Eton, Westminster or Winchester or, probably, in the other public schools properly so-called (Roman Catholic Relief Act, 1829, s. 16).

The Roman Catholic Relief Act, 1829, s. 12, provided that nothing in it shall extend to enable any person professing the Roman Catholic religion to hold the office of regent, nor to enable any person, " otherwise than he is now by law enabled," to hold the office of Lord Chancellor of Great Britain or Ireland, or of Lord Lieutenant of Ireland, or Commissioner to the General Assembly of the Church of Scotland. The Lord Chancellor (Tenure of Office and Discharge of Ecclesiastical Functions) Act, 1974, declared that " for the avoidance of doubt " the office of Lord Chancellor is and shall be tenable by an adherent of the Roman Catholic faith (s. 1). In that event, his visitational and functions and his gifts of patronage are to be exercised by the Prime Minister or some other Minister of the Crown (s. 2). The Office and Oath Act, 1867, permitted the Lord Chancellor of Ireland to be a Roman Catholic. The office was abolished by the Irish Free State (Consequential Provisions) Act, 1922.

The Roman Catholic Relief Act, 1926, repealed nearly all the remaining disabilities of Roman Catholics.

Roman law. See CIVIL LAW.

Roma-peditae, pilgrims who travelled to Rome on foot (Mat.Paris).

Rome Convention. See BERNE CONVENTION.

Romescot; Romefee; Romepenny, Peterpence (*q.v.*). The statute 1533, 25 Hen. 8, c. 21, ss. 1, 17, and the Act of Supremacy, 1558, s. 2, forbade the payment of Peterpence to the Pope of Rome.

Romilly's Act, the Charity Procedure Act, 1812.

Romney Marsh, a tract of land in Kent governed by certain ancient and equitable laws of sewers, from which, Coke said, commissioners of sewers might receive light and direction (4 Co.Inst. 276).

At a very early period it was placed under the government of a body incorporated as the bailiff, jurats and commonalty of Romney, but it does not now exist as a separate unit for any purpose of local government. The management of the sea walls and the drains which preserved it from inundation by the sea was anciently in the hands of twenty-three lords of manors known as the Lords of the Marsh or Lords of the Levels; they also have ceased to exercise functions; but the special drainage laws of the marsh have to a large extent been preserved in modern Acts of Parliament.

The town of Romney, from which the marsh is named, is one of the Cinque Ports.

See Derville, *Level of Romney Marsh.*

Roncaria; Runcaria, land grown with brambles or briar: scrub (1 Co.Inst. 5).

Rood. This measure of land contains forty square perches (*q.v.*) or 1,210 square yards, and is one-fourth of an acre (Weights and Measures Act, 1963, s. 10, Sch. 1 Pt. II).

Rood; Roodloft. The rood was the holy cross and was anciently known as the holy rood.

In ecclesiastical law, the rood is a representation of the Crucifixion, placed over the line dividing the choir or the chancel of a church from the nave, and the roodloft is the structure supporting the rood. The legality of either the one or the other depends upon whether they do or do not lead to what is regarded by the ecclesiastical courts as superstitious worship.

Rood day. This meant either September 14, which was the Feast of the Exaltation of the Cross, or May 3, which was the Feast of the Invention (or Finding) of the Cross.

Rooks. Rooks are animals *ferae naturae* and no action is maintainable for scaring them away from a rookery by discharging guns near it (*Hannam* v. *Mockett* (1824) 2 B. & C. 934). As to the qualified right of property, and therefore of action, *ratione impotentiae* in regard to young birds' nests, see ANIMALS FERAE NATURAE.

Root of descent, stock of descent. See DESCENT.

Root of title. To be a good root of title to land, a document must deal with the absolute ownership of the land and must be at least fifteen years old and must contain nothing to throw any doubts on the title of the party disposing of the land. See TITLE.

Rope-dancers. Unlicensed booths and stages for rope-dancers and mountebanks are public nuisances, and may, upon indictment, be suppressed, and the keepers of them fined (1 Hawk.P.C. 75, s. 6).

Ros, a kind of rushes, which some tenants were obliged by their tenure to furnish their lords withal.

Rose noble. See FARTHING OF GOLD.

Rosland, heathy ground, or ground full of ling; also, watery and moorish land (Co.Litt. 5a).

Roster, a list or table. by which duty etc. is regulated.

Rota, the system by which succession to the functions of a temporary office is regulated among the persons who are to discharge them; a list showing the order in which persons are to be selected to perform particular duties. As to the selection of judges for the rota for the trial of election petitions, see the Judicature Act, 1925, s. 67.

Rotelanda; Rotelandia, Rutland. The Statute of Rutland, 1284, is also known as the Statutum de Rotelanda (or Rothlan). See RUTLAND.

Rother-beasts, oxen, cows, steers, heifers, and suchlike horned animals (Jacob).

Rothlan, Rotelanda (*q.v.*).

Rotuli, the roll (*q.v.*). See ROLL.

Rotulus Wintoniae, the Roll of Winton. In the *Descriptio compilata per Dominum Ingulphum, Abbatem Monasterii Croyland,* it is alleged that King Alfred had caused a survey of England, somewhat on the lines of Domesday, to be made, and that this had been recorded in a roll, kept at Winton or Winchester, which had been lost before the time of Ingulf. Ingulf, who died in 1109, was the Abbot of Croyland; but the work alleged to have been compiled by him is now generally regarded as a forgery dating from the early part of the fifteenth century, and there is no reason for believing that the Roll of Winton ever existed.

Rouge Croix. See HERALD.

Rouge Dragon. See HERALD.

Roulette. See GAMING.

Roundabout. For the rule of the road at a roundabout, see the Highway Code, arts. 81–84. See also WHIRLIGIG.

Round-robin, a circle divided from the centre, like King Arthur's Round Table, whence its supposed origin. In each compartment is a signature, so that the entire circle, when filled, exhibits a list without priority being given to any name. A common form of round-robin is simply to write the names in a circular form. For an account of perhaps the most famous round-robin on record, in which Johnson's friends ventured to criticise his epitaph of Goldsmith, see Boswell's *Johnson,* ed. by Birkbeck Hill, vol. iii, p. 82.

Rout, a disturbance of the peace by persons assembling with an intention to do a thing which, if it be executed, will make them rioters, and actually making a motion towards its execution. A rout is an unlawful assembly which has made some motion towards the execution of the common purpose of the persons asembled. It is, therefore, intermediate between an unlawful assembly and a riot (*q.v.*).

Taking part in a rout seems to be a misdemeanour at common law, but prosecutions for it are unknown, the persons who might be charged with rout being always charged with unlawful assembly, if with anything. See ASSEMBLY, UNLAWFUL.

Roy. See KING.

Royal arms. The Trade Marks Act, 1938, s. 61, provides as follows: "If any person, without the authority of His Majesty, uses in connexion with any trade, business, calling, or profession, the Royal Arms (or arms so closely resembling the same as to be calculated to deceive) in such manner as to be calculated to lead to the belief that he is duly authorised so to use the Royal Arms, or if any person without the authority of His Majesty or of a member of the Royal Family, uses in connexion with any trade, business, calling, or profession any device, emblem, or title in such manner as to be calculated to lead to the belief that he is employed by or supplies goods to His Majesty or such member of the Royal Family, he may, at the suit of any person who is authorised to use such arms or such device, emblem, or title, or is authorised by the Lord Chamberlain to take proceedings in that behalf, be restrained by injunction from continuing so to use the same: Provided that nothing in this section shall be construed as affecting the right, if any, of the proprietor of a trade mark containing any such arms, device, emblem, or title to continue to use such trade mark." See TRADE MARKS.

The Patents Act, 1949, s. 92, provides as follows: "The grant of a patent under this Act shall not be deemed to authorise the patentee to use the Royal Arms or to place the Royal Arms on any patented article. If any person, without the authority of His Majesty, uses in connection with any business, trade, calling, or profession the Royal Arms (or Arms so nearly resembling them as to be calculated to deceive) in such manner as to be calculated to lead to the belief that he is duly authorised to use the Royal Arms, then, without prejudice to any proceedings which may be taken against him, under s. 61 of the Trade Marks Act, 1938, he shall be liable on summary conviction to a fine not exceeding £20: Provided that this section shall not affect the right, if any, of the proprietor of a trade mark containing such Arms to continue to use such trade mark." See PATENTS.

The word "royal" may be used in such a way as to negative any suggestion of the enjoyment of royal patronage (*Re Royal Worcester, etc., Application* [1909] 1 Ch. 459). As to the use of the Prince of Wales's feathers and motto, see *Re Imperial Tobacco Co.* [1915] 2 Ch. 57. See ARMORIAL BEARINGS.

Royal assent, the act by which the Crown agrees to a bill which has already passed both Houses of Parliament. The royal assent may be given by the sovereign in person in the House of Lords, the Commons standing at the bar. The forms observed are as follows: the Lords being assembled in their own House, the sovereign or the commissioners seated, and the Commons at the bar, the titles of the several bills which have passed both Houses are read, and the sovereign's answer is declared by the Clerk of the Parliaments in Norman-French. To a bill of supply, the assent is given in the following words: *Le roy* (or *la reyne*) *remercie ses loyaux sujets, accepte leur bénévolence et ainsi le veult.* To a private bill it is thus declared: *Soit fait comme il est désiré.* To general public bills it is given in these terms: *Le roy* (or *la reyne*) *le veult.* Should the sovereign refuse assent, it is in the phrase *Le roy* (or *la reyne*) *s'avisera*. As acts of grace and amnesty originate with the Crown, the Clerk, expressing the gratitude of the subject, addresses the throne as follows: *Les prelats, seigneurs, et communs, en ce présent parlement assemblés, au nom de tout vos autres sujets remercient tres humblement votre majesté et prient à Dieu vous donner en santé bonne vie et longue.* The moment the royal assent has been given, that which was a bill becomes an Act, and instantly has the force and effect of law as from the beginning of that day, unless some time for the commencement of its operation has been specially appointed (*Tomlinson* v. *Bullock* (1879) 4 Q.B.D. 230).

An Act of Parliament is duly enacted if Her Majesty's assent thereto, being signified by Letters Patent under the Great Seal signed with Her Majesty's own hand (a) is pronounced in the presence of both Houses in the House of Lords in the customary manner or (b) is notified to each House of Parliament sitting separately, by the Speaker of that House or in the case of his absence by the person acting as such Speaker (Royal Assent Act, 1967 (s. 1 (1)). The power of Her Majesty to declare Her Royal Assent in person in Parliament and the manner in which an Act of Parliament is required to be endorsed in Her Majesty's name remain unaffected (s. 1 (2)). The Royal Assent by Commission Act, 1541, is repealed (Act of 1967, s. 2 (2)). The Crown Office Rules Order, 1967 (No. 802) made under the Crown Office Act, 1877, s. 3 (1), prescribes the three forms to be used for Letters Patent signifying the Royal Assent to bills by Commission, by Commission with prorogation and by Notification.

Elizabeth I at the end of one session rejected forty-eight bills agreed to by both Houses. The power of rejection was exercised in the year 1692 by William III, who at first refused, but in two years afterwards yielded, assent to the bill for triennial parliaments; and for the last time in 1707, when Queen Anne refused her assent to a Scottish militia bill (Dodd's Parl.Com. 94). See Erskine May, *Parliamentary Practice*.

Royal bounty. See BOUNTY.

Royal College of Physicians. This body was incorporated by royal charter dated September 23, 1518. The charter empowers the college to make by-laws to regulate the affairs of the college and the conduct of its members.

The college consists of fellows (F.R.C.P.), members (M.R.C.P.) and licentiates (L.R.C.P.). A fellow cannot sue for his fees (see MEDICAL PRACTITIONER); and he, like a member, cannot engage in trade, or dispense medicines, or practise in partnership, or buy or sell a partnership (by-law clxxviii).

Under an agreement made in 1883 pursuant to the Medical Act, 1858, s. 19 (replaced by the Medical Act, 1956, s. 12), the college and the Royal College of Surgeons (*q.v.*) set up a joint examination board, and every person passed by that board is entitled to become L.R.C.P. or M.R.C.S. as the case may be. See PHYSICIAN.

Royal College of Surgeons of London. This body exists under a royal charter granted in 1843. It consists of fellows (F.R.C.S.) and members (M.R.C.S.)

Neither fellows nor members of the Royal College of Surgeons would appear to be, as such, under the same restrictions as to fees, partnerships etc., as apply to fellows and members of the Royal College of Physicians. See BARBERS CHIRURGEONS; MEDICAL PRACTITIONER; SURGEON.

Royal Courts of Justice, the statutory name, by the Judicature Act, 1925, s. 222, replacing the Judicature (Officers) Act, 1879, s. 28, of the Law Courts, on the north side of the Strand, between St. Clement Danes Church and Chancery Lane, in which the business of the Supreme Court is transacted. The erection of buildings for bringing together into one place all the superior courts of law and equity, the Probate and Divorce Courts and the Court of Admiralty, recommended by a Royal Commission in 1858, was authorised by the Courts of Justice Building Act, 1865, and the Courts of Justice Concentration (Site) Act, 1865. The Royal Courts were formally opened by Queen Victoria on December 4, 1882, and opened for business on January 11, 1883, the judges' chambers and other offices having been opened for business in January, 1880. Prior to the opening, the Chancery Division occupied courts at Lincoln's Inn, and the Queen's Bench and Probate, Divorce, and Admiralty Division occupied courts adjoining Westminster Hall.

Guildhall Sittings for the transaction of City of London *nisi prius* business were held in the Guildhall, but provision was made by the Courts of Justice Building Act, 1865, s. 20, for removing such business to the Royal Courts on request of the Common Council, which request having been made, the business was removed accordingly, an Order in Council directing in May, 1883, that London causes were to be tried for ever thereafter at the Royal Courts. But in 1891 the Judicature (London Causes) Act, 1891, directed that, notwithstanding the Act of 1865 and any Order in Council thereunder, sittings might be held in the City of London by judges of the High Court; and two judges commenced to hold such sittings in November, 1891; but such sittings have been discontinued. See COMMERCIAL COURT.

Royal draught, a right to take a limited kind of fishing throughout the whole of a river by the officer of the Crown as conservator, or the officer of the grantee of such conservancy, who in some rivers appears to have had a right to take a net down the river through all the private fisheries in it at stated periods (Moore, *Fisheries*, 81).

Royal fish. See FISH, ROYAL.

Royal forests, a hunting territory for the sovereign's princely delight and pleasure. See FOREST; FORESTRY.

Royal grants, conveyances of record. They are of two kinds, letters patent, and letters close, or writs close.

Royal household. As to the salaries, etc., of certain officers of the royal household, see the Ministerial and other Salaries Act, 1975, s. 3, Sch. 1 Pt. IV.

Royal mail. See POST OFFICE.

Royal marine volunteers. The Naval Forces Act, 1903, s. 2 (1), authorised the raising of this force, which, when on duty, was to be on the same footing as the marines; but the force was not in fact raised. Power is given to the Admiralty to raise and maintain the Royal Marine Forces Volunteer Reserve (Royal Marines Act, 1948, s. 1 (1)).

Royal marines, a force first raised in 1755 to replace the soldiers of the army who since 1664 had been detailed for duty on ships of war. They are under the control of the Admiralty. They are subject to the Army Act, 1955, and also to the Naval Discipline Act, 1957. As to the royal marines reserve, see the Reserve Forces Act, 1966.

Royal marriages. By the Royal Marriages Act, 1772, no descendant of George II may marry without the previous consent of the sovereign, signified under the Great Seal, unless above the age of twenty-five, in which case the marriage may take place after twelve months' notice, unless disapproved by Parliament. See MARRIAGE.

Royal Military Asylum. See DUKE OF YORK'S SCHOOL.

Royal mines, gold and silver mines. The Crown has a right of pre-emption of any gold or silver found in mines of copper, tin, iron, or lead, by virtue of the statutes 1688, 1 W. & M. c. 30, s. 4; and 1693, 5 & 6 W. & M. c. 6. See MINERALS.

Royal Mint. See MINT.

Royal parks. See PARK.

Royal Patriotic Fund. See PATRIOTIC FUND.

Royal prerogative. See PREROGATIVE.

Royal proclamations. See PROCLAMATIONS, ROYAL.

Royal title. By a proclamation dated May 28, 1953, issued under the Royal Titles Act, 1953, the royal title is Elizabeth II, by the Grace of God of the United Kingdom of Great Britain and Northern Ireland and of Her other Realms and Territories Queen, Head of the Commonwealth, Defender of the Faith. Previously, the words " British dominions beyond the seas " had been added in pursuance of the Royal Titles Act, 1901, and the title of Empress of India had been added in pursuance of the Royal Titles Act, 1876, to the royal titles given under the Union with Scotland Act 1706, and the Union with Ireland Act, 1800.

The forms adopted at the same time by other member States of the Commonwealth are:

Australia: Elizabeth II, by the Grace of God of the United Kingdom, Australia and Her other Realms and Territories Queen, Head of the Commonwealth, Defender of the Faith.

Canada: Elizabeth II, by the Grace of God of the United Kingdom, Canada and Her other Realms and Territories Queen, Head of the Commonwealth, Defender of the Faith.

Ceylon: Elizabeth II, Queen of Ceylon and of Her other Realms and Territories, Head of the Commonwealth. See SRI LANKA.

New Zealand: Elizabeth II, by the Grace of God of the United Kingdom, New Zealand and Her other Realms and Territories Queen, Head of the Commonwealth, Defender of the Faith.

The Republic of India, while not owing allegiance to the Crown, remains a member of the Commonwealth and acknowledges the Queen as Head of the Commonwealth.

Royal Victorian Order. This Order was founded in 1896. It includes Knights Grand Cross (G.C.V.O.), Knights Commanders (K.C.V.O.), Commanders (C.V.O.), and Members (M.V.O.).

Royal warrant, a writing, issued by some royal official, under which a tradesman is authorised to act in such and such a capacity (as chemist or tailor, for instance) for some member of the royal family. No such writing has any force in law, but the Trade Descriptions Act, 1968, s. 12, makes it an offence falsely to pretend that goods or services are supplied with royal approval. The royal warrant more particularly known to the law is one of the instruments by which the sovereign exercises executive authority under statute or the common law. Such a royal warrant is generally used as a mere working part of the machinery of government, but it can occasionally be used as a substitute for an Act of Parliament. Thus, the purchase of commissions in the Army was abolished by royal warrant of July 20, 1871, after the government of the day had failed to secure the same result by Act of Parliament.

Royalty, a payment reserved by the grantor of a patent, lease of a mine or similar right, and payable proportionately to the use made of the right by the grantee. It is usually a payment of money, but may be a payment in kind, that is, of part of the produce of the exercise of the right. See RENT.

Royalty also means a payment which is made to an author or composer by a publisher in respect of each copy of his work which is sold, or to an inventor in respect of each article sold under the patent.

Rubric, directions printed in books of law and in prayer-books, so termed because they were originally distinguished by red ink.

Rubric of a statute, its title, which was anciently inscribed in red letters. It serves to show the object of the legislature, and thence affords a means of interpreting the body of the Act. Hence the phrase, an argument *a rubro ad nigrum (q.v.).*

See MARGINAL NOTES; PREAMBLE.

Rubricas, constitutions of the church founded upon the statute 1551, 5 & 6 Edw. 6, c. 1; the Act of Uniformity, 1558; and the statute 1662, 14 Car. 2, c. 4.

Rudmas-day [Sax. *rode*, cross], the feast of the Holy Cross. There are two of these feasts: one on May 3, the Invention of the Cross; and the other on September 14, called the Holy Roodday, the Exaltation of the Cross. See ROOD DAY.

Rule, a regulation made by a court of justice or a public office with reference to the conduct of business therein. Most rules are made under the authority of an Act of Parliament, and then have the same effect as an enactment of the legislature; such are the rules of court made by the judges under the Judicature Act, 1925.

" Rule " also signifies an order or direction made by a court of justice in an action or other proceeding. The term " order " included " rule " (Judicature Act, 1873, s. 100). The term was confined to the Queen's Bench Division, being borrowed from the practice of the old common law courts. After the Judicature Acts, 1873–75, rules were used mainly in connection with certiorari, mandamus, habeas corpus, *quo warranto,* and similar matters.

RULE

A rule is either (1) absolute in the first instance, or (2) calling upon the opposite party to show cause why the rule applied for should not be granted; a rule of the latter kind is called a rule to show cause, or a rule nisi, because if no sufficient cause is shown, the rule is made absolute; otherwise it is discharged. Thus the court in the first instance may make an order absolute *ex parte* for the issue of a writ of habeas corpus or it may grant an order nisi. See MOTION; OF COURSE; SIDE-BAR.

"Rule" sometimes means a rule of law. Thus we speak of the rule against perpetuities, the rule in *Shelley's Case* (1580) 1 Co.Rep. 93b, etc. See LAW; PERPETUITY; SHELLEY'S CASE, ETC.

A rule of court generally means a rule of procedure. Sometimes, however, it means an order made by a court in a particular action or matter: thus a compromise of an action may, if approved by the court, be made an order of the court in which the action was brought. The making of a compromise a rule of court gives it the same effect as if the terms of the compromise were contained in an order of the court. See *Re Grimthorpe* [1908] 1 Ch. at p. 669; *McCullum* v. *Country Residences* [1965] 1 W.L.R. 657.

Rule of the War of 1756, the principle that colonial trade between the metropolitan territory of a State and its colonies, which is closed to third States in time of peace, is enemy trade in time of war even though such trade is carried on by neutrals.

Rules, Liberty of the. See LIBERTY OF THE RULES.

Rules of court, orders regulating the practice of the courts; orders made between parties to an action or suit.

General rules regulating the practice of the courts, both of common law and equity, have from time to time been made by the courts in pursuance of the powers of various Acts of Parliament. See as to the common law courts, which promulgated consecutive rules without any division into orders, Day's *Common Law Procedure Acts*; and as to the Court of Chancery, which promulgated orders subdivided into rules, Morgan's *Chancery Acts and Orders*.

The scheme of the Chancery Procedure Acts was that the orders made thereunder should come into force as soon as made, subject to the power of Parliament to annul them afterwards (Chancery Procedure Act, 1858, s. 12), while that of the Common Law Procedure Acts was that rules made thereunder should not come into force until they had lain before Parliament for three months: see the statute 1850, 13 & 14 Vict. c. 16, and the Common Law Procedure Act, 1852, s. 223. The practice under the Judicature Act, 1875, s. 25, followed that of the Chancery Procedure Acts, allowing rules to come into force as soon as made, but requiring them to be laid before each House of Parliament, an address from which within a limited time might invalidate them; and the Rules Publication Act, 1893, also provided for the consideration by any public body interested of draft rules, and for the consideration by the authority making the rules of suggestions by any such body.

A large body of orders subdivided into rules was appended to the Judicature Act, 1875, s. 17, which allowed a majority of the judges to alter, annul, or add to them from time to time. The Appellate Jurisdiction Act, 1876, s. 17, as amended by the Judicature Act, 1881, s. 19, delegated this power to a committee, commonly called the Rule Committee, of any five or more of eight judges, to whom were added two practising barristers and two practising solicitors by the Judicature (Rule Committee) Act, 1909. The rules made from time to time under the authority of these Acts are called "Rules of the Supreme Court." They were consolidated with amendments in 1883 by the Rules of the Supreme Court, 1883. They were frequently amended and an entire revision was carried out in two stages in 1963 and 1965. All the previous rules were revoked by S.I. 1965 No. 1776. They may be cited as the Rules of the Supreme Court, 1965 (R.S.C., Ord. 1, r. 1). The rules have the force of a statute (*S.S. Hontestroom* v. *S.S. Sagaporack* [1927] A.C. 37, *per* Lord Sumner at p. 47; *Donald Campbell & Co.* v. *Pollak* [1927] A.C. at p. 804).

By the Interpretation Act, 1889, s. 14, "Rules of Court" means, when used in relation to any court, rules made by the authority having for the time being power to make rules or orders regulating the practice and procedure of such court, and as regards Scotland, includes Acts of Adjournal and Acts of Sederunt.

See MOTION; NEW TRIAL.

Rules of good husbandry. These are laid down in the Agriculture Act, 1947, s. 11.

Rules of the Supreme Court. See RULES OF COURT.

Ruling cases, cases having much the same character and effect as leading cases (*q.v.*).

Rump Acts, the ordinances, or Acts, passed by Parliament, without the concurrence of the king, between August 26, 1642, and the Restoration in 1660 (Blount).

Run, to take effect in point of place, as of the king's writ in given localities; or in point of time, as of the Limitation Act, 1939.

Run with the land, Run with the reversion. A covenant is said to run with the land either leased or conveyed in fee when either the liability to perform it, or the right to take advantage of it, passes to the assignee of that land. A covenant is said to run with the reversion to land leased when either the liability to perform it, or the right to take advantage of it, passes to the assignee of that reversion (*Spencer's Case* (1583) 1 Sm.L.C. 1; *Dyson* v. *Forster* [1909] A.C. 98).

A covenant running with the land enures for the benefit of the covenantee, his successors in title and the persons deriving title under him or them; and in connection with restrictive covenants " successors in title " includes owners and occupiers for the time being of the land intended to be benefited (Law of Property Act, 1925, s. 78).

A corresponding provision is made in regard to the burden of such covenants, and these covenants may relate to some act relating to the land notwithstanding that the subject-matter is not in existence. In none of these cases of benefit or burden of covenants it is necessary that the successors in title or assigns or other persons should be expressly referred to. In regard to covenants running with the reversion upon conveyance, assignment, or severance, or on cesser of a lease as to part of the land, see the Law of Property Act, 1925, ss. 140–142, replacing the statute 1540, 32 Hen. 8, c. 34, the Law of Property Amendment Act, 1859, s. 3, the Conveyancing Act, 1881, ss. 10–12, and the Conveyancing Act, 1911, s. 2. Under the Law of Property Act, 1925, s. 140, as amended by the Law of Property (Amendment) Act, 1926, where the assignee of part of a reversion to an agricultural holding could give notice to quit in respect of that part, the lessee had the right within one month of the notice to give notice to determine the lease as to the whole of the land demised (*Bebington* v. *Wildman* [1921] 1 Ch. 559) but this provision was repealed by the Agricultural Holdings Act, 1948, Sch. 8.

See COVENANT.

Runcaria, land full of brambles and briars (Co.Litt. 5a).

Runcilus, Runcinus, a load-horse, a sumpter-horse, a cart-horse.

Rundlet, or Runlet, a measure of wine, oil, etc., containing eighteen gallons and a half: see the statute 1484, 1 Ric. 3, c. 13.

Running days. In a charterparty " days " or " running days " means, in the absence of custom, all days, whether working or non-working, and includes Sundays and holidays. But custom may, as in the City of London, make " days " or " running days " equivalent to working days, that is to say, may make " days " or " running days " exclude Sundays and holidays. See LAY DAYS.

Running down case, an action for damages for negligent driving of a vehicle.

Trial should be without a jury except in very special circumstances (*Hennell* v. *Ranaboldo* [1963] 1 W.L.R. 1391; *Ward* v. *James* [1966] 1 Q.B. 273).

For counsel's fees, see [1975] C.L.Y. 2628.

Ruptari or **Ruttarii,** soldiers (Mat. Paris).

Ruptum, broken. In the *Lex Aquilia,* *ruptum* meant *corruptum,* or spoliation in any way (Civil Law).

Ruptura, arable land, or ground broken up.

Rural chapters. See CAPITULA RURALIA.

Rural dean. Rural deans, or *decani rurales*, existed during the Anglo-Saxon period. It was then their duty to exercise many of the functions subsequently exercised by the archdeacon. About the thirteenth century, the archdeacon took over most of the work of the rural deans, and comparatively little was heard of them until within the last hundred years. Now they form part of the machinery of every diocese. They are required to execute all processes and writs directed to them by the bishop, and to report to him on the lives of the clergy of the various parishes within the respective rural deaneries; but these latter duties are largely theoretical.

Every archdeaconry is an aggregation of rural deaneries.

See KALENDAE.

Rural deanery, the circuit of an archdeacon's and rural dean's jurisdictions. Every rural deanery is divided into parishes.

Rural development boards. See the Agriculture Act, 1967, ss. 45–57 as amended.

Rural district council. See DISTRICT.

Russell Gurney's Acts, the Criminal Law Amendment Act, 1867, the Larcency Act, 1868, and the Medical Act, 1876. See RECORDER'S ACT.

Russell's (Lord John) Act, the Marriage Act, 1836.

Russia Company. See MUSCOVY COMPANY.

Rustici, churls, clowns, or inferior country tenants, who held cottages and lands by the services of ploughing and other labours of agriculture for the lord. The land of such ignoble tenure was called by the Saxons *gafalland*; it was afterwards socage tenure, and was sometimes distinguished by the name of *terra rusticorum* (Paroch.Antiq. 136).

Ruta, things extracted from land, as sand, chalk, coal and other such matters (Civil Law).

Rutland, Statute of, the Statute of Rothlan, 1284, touching the recovery of the king's debts. It was repealed by the Sheriffs Act, 1887, s. 39.

Rutter of the Sea [Fr. *routier, route*]. See OLERON, LAWS OF.

Rye. See GUARANTEED PRICES.

Rylands v. Fletcher. The rule in *Rylands* v. *Fletcher* (1868) L.R. 3 H.L. 330 imposes liability irrespective of proof of negligence for damage done to another's property by the escape of things which are brought or kept on land otherwise than in the course of a natural user of the land and which are likely to do damage if they escape.

S

S., section. See BRANDING.

S.C., same case.

In Scotland it is an abbreviation for the reports called Sessions Cases.

S.G., *salutis gratia,* for the sake of safety. These letters appear on a Lloyd's policy.

S.I., statutory instruments (*q.v.*).

S.L.R., Statute Law Revision Act. Every few years since 1861 a Statute Law Revision Act was passed to remove from the statute book Acts or parts of Acts which had become obsolete or which had been impliedly repealed by subsequent legislation or, as has been the case since 1890 as regards many

preambles to statutes, which Parliament thought superfluous.

The quasi-repeal effected by the Statute Law Revision Acts differs from other repeals. It is in the main clerical only. The Acts were passed chiefly in order to cut down the vast body of statute law to such dimensions as would permit of its publication in the comparatively small number of volumes known as the *Statutes Revised*; and a Statute Law Revision Act sometimes contains an express provision to ensure that the legal effect, if any, of anything repealed by the Act remains notwithstanding such repeal: see *e.g.,* the Statute Law Revision Act, 1953, s. 1.

The reform of the statute law is currently being carried out, in accordance with recommendations of the Law Commission (*q.v.*), by the Statute Law (Repeals) Acts, 1971, 1973, 1974, 1975, 1976.

S.P., *sine prole,* without issue; d.s.p. means *demisit sine prole, i.e.,* died without issue.

S.R. & O., statutory rules and orders (*q.v.*).

S.S., Collar of, a collar or necklace of gold, weighing about four pounds, worn over his official robes by the Lord Chief Justice on State occasions. It consists of twenty-eight "S" shaped links, with what is known as a "garter-knot" between each two links, and with the Beaufort badge of the portcullis and the rose, the badge of Henry VII, as a pendant. Formerly the Chief Justices of the Exchequer and the Common Pleas wore similar collars: that used by Sir Edward Coke descended to the successive Chief Justices of the Common Pleas until the Common Pleas ceased to exist. The collar worn by the Chief Justice of the Common Pleas consisted of twenty-seven "S" links and twenty-six knots, and weighed 20½ oz. avoirdupois. That used by Sir Alexander Cockburn has been in use by the Lord Chief Justices of England down to the present day. Sir Alexander Cockburn who died in 1880, left it to his successors as an "office-loom": but the law would not appear to recognise such an entity—the case of the Pusey Horn (see CORNAGE) is quite different—and there would appear to be nothing in law to prevent a Chief Justice, or his personal representative, from disposing of the collar. Lord Ellenborough, when he retired in 1818, retained for himself the collar which had been worn for a hundred and fifty years by the Chief Justices of the King's Bench. See Purey-Cust, *Collar of S.S.*

S.V. See SUB VOCE.

Sabbatum, the Sabbath; used in Domesday as meaning peace. See SUNDAY.

Sabbulonarium, gravel, a gravel-pit, or money paid for the privilege of digging gravel.

Sable, the heraldic term for black. It is called saturn by those who blazon by planets, and diamond by those who use the names of jewels. Engravers commonly represent it by numerous perpendicular and horizontal lines crossing each other.

Sac, jurisdiction, especially manorial jurisdiction; the privilege enjoyed by a lord of a manor of holding courts, trying causes, and imposing fines. It was usually joined with "soc," and sometimes also with "toll" and "team." All the four words had a meaning practically identical.

Saca, cause, sake.

Sacabere, Sacaburth, Sakabere, he who is robbed, or by theft deprived of his money or goods, and puts in surety to prosecute the felon (3 Bract. 32, 150).

Saccularii [Lat.], cut-purses.

Saccus, a sack. See BROCHIA.

Saccus cum brochia, a service or tenure of finding a sack and a broach (pitcher) to the sovereign for the use of the army (2 Bract. 16). See BROCHIA.

Sack. As regards wool, the statute 1340, 14 Edw. 3, st. 2, c. 4, enacted that the sack ought to contain twenty stones, and each stone fourteen pounds.

Sacquier, an officer whose business was to load and unload vessels laden with salt, corn, or fish, to prevent the ship's crew defrauding the merchant by false tale, cheating him of his merchandise.

Sacrament. In the Church of England there are two sacraments only, baptism and the supper of the Lord; confirmation, penance, orders, matrimony and extreme unction are not recognised as sacraments (Art. 25). The term sacrament is commonly used to mean the Holy Communion. Reviling the sacrament was punishable by fine and imprisonment (Sacrament Act, 1547, s. 1 (repealed)) and administration of the sacrament in both kinds is enjoined unless necessity otherwise requires, and the statute enacts that the minister shall not without lawful cause deny the same (s. 8). In the Roman Catholic Church the cup is not administered to the laity.

For a clergyman to refuse without lawful cause to administer the sacrament to a parishioner is an offence against the laws ecclesiastical (*Jenkins* v. *Cook* (1876) 1 P.D. 80). The Holy Communion cannot be refused to a person because he has married his deceased wife's sister (*Thompson* v. *Dibdin* [1912] A.C. 533); and see Canon 27 and the ante-Communion rubrics in the Prayer Book. The reservation of the sacrament was held to be unlawful in *Bishop of Oxford* v. *Henly* [1907] P. 88.

Sacramentum, an oath. The *sacramenti actio* was a form of action in the civil law.

Sacramentum si fatuum fuerit, licet falsum, tamen non committit perjurium (2 Co.Inst. 167). (A foolish oath, though false, makes not perjury.)

Sacrilege, larceny from a church. By the Larceny Act, 1916, s. 24 (repealed), breaking and entering any church, chapel, meeting-house, or other place of divine worship, and committing any felony therein, or being therein and committing any felony therein and breaking out of the same, was a felony punishable by imprisonment for life. The offence was for a long time capital, the last execution having taken place in 1819. Under the statute 1554, 1 Mar. sess. 2, c. 3 (repealed) (which was passed for the protection of Roman Catholic places of worship), any person who unlawfully pulled down, defaced or broke any altar, crucifix or cross in any church, chapel or churchyard was liable, on summary conviction, to imprisonment for three months, or until he repented (Spelman, Hist.Sacri.).

Sacrilege also meant the alienation to laymen of property given to pious uses (Par.Ant. 390).

Sacristan, a sexton, anciently called *sagerson* or *sagiston*; the keeper of things belonging to divine worship.

Sadberge, a denomination of part of the county palatine of Durham (Camd. Brit.).

Saemend, an umpire, arbitrator (Anc. Inst.Eng.).

Saevitia [Lat.], cruelty. See CRUELTY.

Safe means of access. A duty to provide a safe means of access to work and a safe place of employment is imposed by the Factories Act, 1961, s. 29. This duty is to be replaced by a duty defined by regulations made under the Health and Safety at Work, etc., Act, 1974, s. 1, Sch. 1.

Safe system of working. A master owes a duty at common law to his servant to exercise due care and skill in respect of the adequacy of plant, the competence

of fellow employees and the propriety of the system of work (*Wilsons & Clyde Coal Co.* v. *English* [1938] A.C. 57). The question whether a safe system of working has been provided is one of fact, not law, and previous decisions on other facts are of no authority in a later case (*Qualcast (Wolverhampton)* v. *Haynes* [1959] A.C. 743). See SAFE MEANS OF ACCESS.

Safe-conduct, convoy (*q.v.*); guard through an enemy's country; a document allowing such a journey. It is a prerogative of the Crown to grant safe-conducts.

In the ancient collections of original writs there are given forms of safe conducts issued by the king to aliens desirous of entering the kingdom. These safe conducts directed the royal officers to provide for the security of those holding them. They had to be enrolled in the Chancery and to be produced on demand: see the statutes 1297, 25 Edw. 1, c. 30; 1446, 25 Hen. 6, c. 5; 1536, 28 Hen. 8, c. 1.

At present a safe-conduct is a pass issued to an enemy subject by the authorities of a belligerent State.

Safe-guard, a protection of the Crown to one who is a stranger who fears violence from some of its subjects for seeking his right by course of law (Reg. Brev. 26).

In war it means protection granted for persons or property, sometimes by posting men, sometimes by putting up a notice (Holland, Lect. 375).

It also means a party of soldiers, or a single sentry posted from such party, detached for the protection of some person or persons, or village, house or other property.

Safeguarding of industries. See KEY INDUSTRIES.

Safe-pledge, a surety appointed for one's appearance at a day assigned (Bract.). See SALVUS PLEGIUS.

Safety at sea. See the Merchant Shipping (Safety Convention) Act, 1949 (as amended). See LIFEBOATS; LOAD LINE.

Sagaman, a tale-teller; secret accuser.

Sagibaro, Sachbaro, a judge (Leg.Inae, c. vi).

Sailing instructions, written or printed directions delivered by the commanding officer of a convoy to the several masters of the ships under his care, by which they are enabled to understand and answer his signals, and to know the place of rendezvous appointed by the fleet in case of dispersion by storm, by an enemy, or otherwise. Without sailing instructions no vessel can have the protection and benefit of convoy (*Anderson* v. *Pitcher* (1800) 2 Bos. & P. 164).

St. Briavel's. See GALE.

St. Christopher. See the West Indies Act, 1967.

Saint-German, Christopher, a legal writer, born about 1460, who published in 1523 a handbook of English law entitled *Dialogus de Fundamentes Legum et de Conscientia.* There were numerous editions, at first in Latin and afterwards in English; and for more than two hundred years the book was in general use by law students. The English edition of 1721 is, like others, entitled " *Doctor and Student or Dialogues between a Doctor of Divinity and a Student in the Laws of England,*" etc.; and the work is generally known as *Doctor and Student.*

St. John of Jerusalem, Knights of, Hospitallers (*q.v.*).

St. John of Jerusalem, Order of. The Order derives from the ancient Order of Knights Hospitaller. See HOSPITALLERS. The Order was revived and granted a royal charter in 1888, as a separate British Order of St. John. The Order maintains the St. John Ambulance and Brigade which provides a body of trained and uniformed volunteers for attendance wherever First Aid is needed.

St. Leonard's (Lord) Act, the Law of Property Amendment Act, 1859.

St. Lucia. See the West Indies Act, 1967.

Saint Martin-le-Grand, Court of. A writ of error formerly lay from the sheriff's courts in the City of London to the court of hustings, before the mayor, recorder and sheriffs; and thence to justices appointed by the royal commission, who used to sit in the church of St. Martin-le-Grand; and from the judgment of those justices a writ of error lay immediately to the House of Lords (Fitz.N.B. 32).

Saint Michael and Saint George, Order of. The Most Distinguished Order of Saint Michael and Saint George was founded in 1818 in order to provide titles of reward for public service in the Mediterranean. It is now used for all the overseas dominions. It includes Knights Grand Cross (G.C.M.G.), Knights Commanders (K.C.M.G.) and Companions (C.M.G.).

Saint Patrick, Order of. The Most Illustrious Order of Saint Patrick was founded in 1788. The Grand Master was formerly the Lord Lieutenant of Ireland.

St. Peter ad Vincula, Feast of, August 1. See GULE OF AUGUST.

St. Vincent. See the West Indies Act, 1967.

Saints' days. See FEASTS.

Saisie-arrêt [Fr.], an attachment of property in the possession of a third person.

Saladine tax (tenth, tithe), a tax imposed in England in 1188 by Henry II, at the request of Pope Innocent III, and in France, to defray the expenses of the Crusade undertaken by Richard I of England and Philip Augustus of France against Saladin, the Sultan of Egypt and Syria, then going to besiege Jerusalem. Persons who went on the Crusade were exempt, as also were religious communities. The tax was one-tenth of all goods and chattels; it did not extend to land or to wearing apparel, books or arms. Juries were emloyed to assist in the assessment. It was the first tax on personal property.

Gibbon remarks that when the necessity for this tax no longer existed, the Church still clung to it as too lucrative to be abandoned, and thus arose the tithing of ecclesiastical benefices for the Pope or other sovereigns. In the preamble to the statute 1531, 23 Hen. 8, c. 20, it is recited that the court of Rome exacted great sums of money under the title of annates or first-fruits, which were first suffered to be taken within the realm for the defence of Christian people against infidels (Encyc. Londin.).

Salary, a recompense or consideration generally periodically made to a person for his service in another person's business; also wages, stipend, or annual allowance. See RECEIPT.

The ancients derive the word from *sal*, salt, the most necessary thing to support human life being thus mentioned as a representative of all others (Plin.H.N. xxxi, 42).

Sale, a transfer of property or of a right from one man to another, in consideration of a sum of money, as opposed to barters, exchanges and gifts (*q.v.*) (2 Bl. Comm. 446).

Almost any right may be transferred for a price, but the term " sale " is only applied to cases where the whole right of the seller is transferred, not to cases where he creates a new or limited right in consideration of a money payment: thus a mortgage or lease is not a sale. Every sale includes the agreement or bargain, the payment of the price, and the delivery or conveyance of the property. Sometimes the three transactions take place simultaneously, as where I go into a shop, select an article, pay the price and take it away, and then the transaction is a simple sale. But either the payment of the price, or the delivery (or conveyance) of the property, or both, may be postponed to a future time, giving rise to a contract or agreement to do something *in futuro*. In the case of chattels, such a postponement does not prevent the property or ownership from passing from the seller to the buyer, provided that the thing sold is existent and ascertained, and that the contract of sale fulfils the legal requisites and therefore the " sale " is complete as soon as the contract has been entered into: such a transaction is called a bargain and sale (*q.v.*) or an executed contract of sale, although the contract has not been performed. The law is contained in the Sale of Goods Act, 1893 (as amended). But in the case of an agreement for the sale of land or of unascertained goods (*e.g.*, ten sheep to be selected from a given flock), the ownership does not pass, and therefore the sale is not complete until the land has been conveyed, or the goods ascertained: such a transaction is an executory contract of sale. See APPROPRIATION.

Ordinarily the person who sells is the owner of the property or his agent, but in some cases a person may sell property which does not belong to him, *e.g.*, a sheriff who has taken goods in execution. So a person may have a power of sale over property without having the ownership of it; as in the case of an ordinary mortgagee of land or a pledgee of chattels. (See MORTGAGE; POWER.) So when a person has a charge on property, he may take proceedings in the High Court to have it sold in satisfaction of the debt. This is sometimes called a judicial sale. See HYPOTHECATION.

Again, a sale is usually a voluntary act, but in some cases the owner of property may be compelled to sell it by the order of a court: thus in an action for partition the court may order a sale instead of a partition (*q.v.*) if the nature of the property makes that course preferable, and then even the non-assenting co-owners are ordered to join in the conveyance, or the conveyance is effected without their concurrence. See VESTING ORDER.

Public authorities are frequently empowered to purchase land, etc. See COMPULSORY PURCHASE.

All causes and matters for the specific performance of contracts between vendors and purchasers of land are assigned to the Chancery Division, as are also all causes and matters for the partition or sale of land (Judicature Act, 1925, s. 56 (1) (b)).

See CONTRACT; RESALE; VENDOR AND PURCHASER; WARRANTY.

Sale, Bill of. See BILL OF SALE.

Sale by the court. It sometimes happens that in the course of an action in the Chancery Division a sale of property becomes necessary, as, for instance, in administration suits, also, under the Administration of Estates Act, 1925, s. 38, or in actions to enforce mortgages. After an order has been made for sale, the further proceedings take place before the master in chambers. An estate, when sold by the court, is usually sold by public auction, but a private advantageous offer may be accepted at once, without going to an auction. For the procedure on sales by the court, see R.S.C., Ord. 31.

Sale notes. See BOUGHT AND SOLD NOTES.

Sale of Goods Act. The Sale of Goods Act, 1893, codified the law of the sale of goods. For amendments see the Law Reform (Enforcement of Contracts) Act, 1954, s. 2; Administration of Justice Act, 1965, s. 22; Misrepresentation Act, 1967, s. 4; Criminal Law Act, 1967, s. 10, Sch. 3 Pt. III; Theft Act, 1968, s. 33, Sch. 3 Pt. III; Supply of Goods (Implied Terms) Act, 1973; Consumer Credit Act, 1974, Sch. 4 para. 3.

An infant or person by mental incapacity or drunkenness incompetent to contract must pay a reasonable price for necessaries sold and delivered to him (Sale of Goods Act, 1893, s. 2).

Formerly, a contract for the sale of goods of the value of £10 or more was not enforceable by action unless the buyer accepted and received part, or gave something in earnest to bind the contract, or unless some note or memorandum in writing of the contract was made and signed by the party to be charged or his agent in that behalf (s. 4), but this section was repealed by the Law Reform (Enforcement of Contracts) Act, 1954, s. 2. The Sale of Goods Act, 1893, s. 7, provides that a contract for the sale of specific goods which have perished without the knowledge of the seller is void. The Act of 1893, as amended by the Supply of Goods (Implied Terms) Act, 1973 and the Consumer Credit Act, 1974, Sch. 4 paras. 3, 4 makes provision as to conditions and warranties, sale by sample, transfer of property as between seller and buyer (rules being laid down for ascertaining the time when the property passes), transfer of risk, transfer of title, effect of sale in market overt and of conviction for theft on the property in stolen goods, time and place of delivery, effect of delivery of short or excessive quantity, delivery by instalments and delivery to a carrier, right of the buyer to examine the goods, liability of the buyer for not taking delivery, right of lien or right to retain the goods, right to stop in transit if the buyer becomes insolvent notwithstanding any sale by the buyer, actions by the seller for the price and actions for non-acceptance, actions by the buyer for non-delivery, specific performance, or breach of warranty.

Goods are defined as including all chattels personal (and therefore all animals) other than things in action and money, and in Scotland all corporeal movables except money, also emblements, industrial growing crops, and things attached to or forming part of the land which are agreed to be severed before sale or under the contract of sale. A warranty is defined as meaning an agreement with reference to goods which are the subject of a contract for sale, but collateral to the main purpose of such contract, the breach of which gives rise to a claim for damages, but not to a right to reject the goods and treat the contract as repudiated; as regards Scotland, a breach of warranty is deemed to be a failure to perform a material part of the contract. See SALE OF RETURN.

As to international sales of goods, see the Uniform Laws on International Sales Act, 1967 and S.I. 1972 No. 973; Supply of Goods (Implied Terms) Act, 1973, ss. 5, 6. 7.

See AGENT; APPROPRIATION; ASSUMPSIT; AUCTION; BILL OF SALE; BOUGHT AND SOLD NOTES; BREAD; BROKER; C.I.F.; CAVEAT EMPTOR; COAL; CONDITIONS OF SALE; CONTRACT; CONVERSION; DAMAGES; DAMNUM SENTIT DOMINUS; DEL CREDERE; DELIVERY; DEPOSIT; EARNEST; EXCHANGE; F.O.B.; FACTOR; FACTORS ACT; GOODS BARGAINED AND SOLD; GOODS SOLD AND DELIVERED; HIRE-PURCHASE; HORSE; INFANT; INNKEEPER; LIEN; MARKET OVERT; MERCHANDISE MARKS; MISREPRESENTATION; MISTAKE; NECESSARIES; OPTION; PLEDGE; QUALITY OR FITNESS; RESALE; RESCIND; SALE OR RETURN; STATUTE OF FRAUDS; STOPPAGE IN TRANSITU; TEA; WARRANTY; WEIGHTS AND MEASURES.

Sale of land. See ABSTRACTS OF TITLE; ASSIGN; AUCTION; BENEFICIAL OWNER; CAVEAT EMPTOR; COMPENSATION; COMPLETION; CONCEALMENT; CONDITIONS OF SALE; CONTRACT OF SALE; CONVEYANCE; COVENANT; DEED; DEPOSIT; ESTATE CLAUSE; FEE; FINE; FURTHER ASSURANCE, ETC; GRANT; HABENDUM; LAND REGISTRIES; MEMORANDUM; MISDESCRIPTION; MORTGAGE; OPERATIVE WORDS; PARCELS; PARTICULARS; PURCHASER WITH-

OUT NOTICE; RECITALS; REQUISITIONS; RESALE; SEARCHES; SETTLED LAND; SPECIFIC PERFORMANCE; STATUTE OF FRAUDS; SURRENDER; TITLE; TRUST; WORDS OF LIMITATION.

Sale of offices. See PUBLIC OFFICES, SALE OF.

Sale of settled estates. See SETTLED LAND.

Sale or return. By the Sale of Goods Act, 1893, s. 18, when goods are delivered to the buyer on approval or on sale or return or other similar terms, *e.g.,* on trial (*Elphick* v. *Barnes* (1880) 5 C.P.D. at p. 326), the property therein passes to the buyer when he signifies his approval or acceptance to the seller or does any other act adopting the transaction (*London Jewellers* v. *Attenborough* [1934] 2 K.B. 206), and if he does not signify his approval or acceptance to the seller but retains the goods without giving notice of rejection, then, if a time has been fixed for the return of the goods, on the expiration of such time, and, if no time has been fixed, on the expiration of a reasonable time. What is a reasonable time is a question of fact.

As to unsolicited goods, see UNSOLICITED GOODS AND SERVICES.

Salford Hundred Court of Record, an inferior and local court of record having jurisdiction if the cause of action arose wholly or in part within the hundred of Salford. (See HUNDRED.) The court was abolished on January 1, 1972, by the Courts Act, 1971, s. 43. See also Sch. 5 para. 12.

Salic, or **Salique** [*lex salica*], an acient and fundamental law of the kingdom of France, usually supposed to have been made by Pharamond, or at least by Clovis, in virtue of which males only could reign. Henry I borrowed from it in compiling his laws.

It is an error to suppose that the Salic law was established purely on account of the succession of the Crown, since it extended to private persons as much as to the royal family.

The Salic law had not in view a preference of one sex to the other, much less had it a regard to the perpetuity of a family, a name, or the succession of land. It was purely a law of economy which gave the house, and the land dependent on the house, to the males who should dwell in it, and to whom it consequently was of more service.

In proof of this, the title of allodial lands of the Salic law may be thus stated: if a man died without issue, his father or mother succeeeded him; if he had neither father nor mother, his brother or sister; if he had neither brother nor sister, the sister of his mother; if his mother had no sister, the sister of his father; and if his father had no sister, the nearest relation by the male.

Salisbury Court. See PRIVILEGED PLACES.

Salmon. This includes all fish of salmon species (Salmon and Freshwater Fisheries Act, 1975, s. 41 (1)). See CLOSE SEASON; FISHERY; KIPPER TIME; SATURDAY'S SLOP; TROUT.

Salt. As to the standards of measurement, etc. on the sale of salt other than cut lump salt, see the Weights and Measures Act, 1963, s. 21, Sch. 4 Pt. VIII. As to agricultural salt, see Sch 7 Pt. III.

Salt duty in London, a custom in the City of London called granage, formerly payable to the Lord Mayor, etc., for salt brought to the port of London, being the twentieth part. See GRAINAGE.

Salt silver, one penny paid at the feast day of St. Martin, by the tenants of some manors, as a commutation for the service of carrying their lord's salt from market to his larder (Paroch.Antiq. 496).

Salt works. These are regulated under the Alkali, etc., Works Regulation Act, 1906. See also the Clean Air Act, 1956. See SMOKE.

Salus populi est suprema lex (11 Co. Rep. 139; Bac.Max. 12). (The safety of the people is the supreme law.) Thus a condition in a will divesting property in the event of a beneficiary entering the naval or military service of the country is void (*Re Beard* [1908] 1 Ch. 383). See NECESSITAS PUBLICA, ETC.

Salute. The salute or salus was a gold coin, of the value of twenty shillings, coined by Henry V and Henry VI, not as part of the English coinage, but for circulation in the parts of France held by them. On it the arms of England and

France were stamped and quartered. There was also half-salute. See BLANK.

Salvage, allowance or compensation made by maritime law to those by whose exertions ships or goods have been saved from the dangers of the seas, fire, pirates or enemies.

This was allowed by the laws of Rhodes, Oleron and Wisby, and is also allowed by all modern maritime States; the person who saves goods from loss or imminent peril has a lien upon them, and may retain them till payment of salvage. In this, however, the maritime law differs from the common law. No doctrine similar to salvage applies to things lost upon land, nor to anything except ships or goods in peril at sea (*Falcke* v. *Scottish Imperial Insurance Co.* (1886) 34 Ch.D. at p. 248).

Under the Administration of Justice Act, 1956, ss. 1, 3, and the Administration of Justice Act, 1970, s. 2, the Admiralty Court of the Queen's Bench Division has jurisdiction, and fixes the sum to be paid, adjusts the proportions, and takes care of the property pending the suit; or, if necessary, directs a sale and divides the proceeds between the salvors and the proprietors. In fixing the rate of salvage, the court has regard, not only to the labour and perils of the salvors, but also to the situation in which they stand to the property saved, to the promptitude and alacrity manifested by them, and the value of the ship and cargo, and the danger from which they were rescued. In some cases as much as half of the property saved has been allowed as salvage; in others only a tenth.

As to the jurisdiction in salvage of the county courts, see the County Courts Act, 1959, ss. 55–61.

The assistance must be voluntary, and not under any contract or duty, and must involve skill, enterprise and risk on the part of the salvors (*The Cleopatra* (1878) 3 P.D. 145). Salvors have a retaining lien for their remuneration on the property rescued. (See LIEN.) In the absence of an agreement between the salvors and the owners of the property salved, the court will assess the amount which ought to be paid to the salvors. In doing so the court will have regard to the skill, enterprise and risk involved, and

to the fact that if their efforts had been unsuccessful, they would not have been paid anything (*Aitchison* v. *Lohre* (1879) 4 App.Cas. 755). The court will refuse to enforce an exorbitant salvage agreement (*The Silesia* (1880) 5 P.D. 177). See TOWAGE.

The crew of a ship are not entitled to salvage or any unusual remuneration for extraordinary efforts they have made in saving her, it being their duty as well as interest to contribute their utmost upon such occasions, the whole of their possible service being pledged to the master and owners. Neither are passengers entitled to anything for the ordinary assistance they may have afforded a vessel in distress. But a passenger is not bound to remain on board a ship in danger, if he can leave her; and if he performs any extraordinary service, he is entitled to a proportionable recompense (Merchant Shipping Act, 1894, ss. 544–565). Salvage includes all expenses properly incurred by the salvor in the performance of the salvage services (s. 510 (2)). See SUE AND LABOUR CLAUSE.

The law of wreck and salvage is applied to aircraft by the Civil Aviation Act, 1949, s. 51.

By analogy, the term "salvage" is also used in cases which have nothing to do with maritime perils, but in which property has been preserved from loss by the last of several advances by different persons. In such a case, the person making the last advance is frequently entitled to priority over the others, on the ground that, without his advance, the property would have been lost altogether. This right, which is sometimes called that of equitable salvage, and is in the nature of a lien, is chiefly of importance with reference to payments made to prevent leases or policies of insurance from being forfeited, or to prevent mines and similar undertakings from being stopped or injured (*Saunders* v. *Dunman* (1878) 7 Ch.D. 825).

See CINQUE PORTS; PRIZE SALVAGE.

Salvage loss, the difference between the amount of salvage, after deducting the charges, and the original value of the property.

Salvage money, money paid as salvage. Officers and men of the navy get it for salvage services to vessels other than naval vessels.

Salvo [Lat., *salvo jure*], without prejudice to.

Salvor, a person who renders assistance to a ship or vessel in distress, whereby he becomes entitled to a reward. See SALVAGE.

Salvus plegius, safepledge, or bail, for appearance (4 Bract., c. 2).

Sample, a small quantity of a commodity exhibited at public or private sales as a specimen. Where goods are warehoused, certain small specified quantities may, by the regulations of the customs, be taken out as samples without payment of duty (Customs and Excise Act, 1952, s. 83).

On a sale of goods by sample, conditions are implied that the bulk shall correspond with the sample, that the buyer shall have a reasonable opportunity of comparing the bulk with the sample, and that the goods shall be free from any defect rendering them unmerchantable which would not be apparent on reasonable examination of the sample (Sale of Goods Act, 1893, s. 15). As to implied conditions in a hire-purchase contract, see the Supply of Goods (Implied Terms) Act, 1973, s. 11; Consumer Credit Act, 1974, Sch. 4 para. 35.

As to samples for the purpose of analysis, see the Food and Drugs Act, 1955. See ADULTERATION.

Sancta, relics of saints, upon which oaths were made.

Sanction, a penalty or punishment provided as a means of enforcing obedience to a law.

The evil which will probably be incurred if a command is disobeyed or a duty broken is frequently called a sanction, or an enforcement of obedience. The command or the duty is said to be sanctioned or enforced by the chance of incurring the evil (Austin).

For sanctions against Rhodesia, see, *e.g.,* the Southern Rhodesia (Prohibited Trade and Dealings) Order, 1966 (No. 1595).

Sanctuary, any place in which neither the civil nor the criminal process of the law could be executed. But, against a man in sanctuary, civil proceedings could be taken and effect given to them, except by the taking of the defendant's body in execution.

The privilege of sanctuary existed in England from a period commencing soon after the conversion of the Saxons to Christianity. Its effect was that a person accused of any crime except treason or sacrilege might by flying to any church or churchyard, or even to certain other places in Westminster, Wells, Norwich, or York, or in London to Whitefriars or the Savoy, within forty days, on confession and taking oath of abjuration (*q.v.*) of the realm, escape to a foreign country, under the disability of not being able to return without the royal licence. If arrested during the forty days, he might put in the plea of sanctuary. The privilege was attended by attainder of blood and forfeiture of goods.

Sanctuary and adjuration were abolished by the statute 1623, 21 Jac. 1, c. 8, after having been restricted by the statutes 1534, 26 Hen. 8, c. 13; 1535, 27 Hen. 8, c. 19; and 1541, 33 Hen. 8, c. 15. See PRIVILEGED PLACES.

Sanctus bell. At the Sanctus of the Mass (which is anterior to the consecration and, therefore, also to the elevation) a bell is rung at each of the three repetitions of the word *sanctus*. In the communion service in the Church of England, a bell is sometimes rung at the elevation of each of the elements during the consecration prayer; it has been decided that it is illegal to fit the church bell so that, from inside the church, it can be tolled for this purpose or be used as a *sanctus* bell (*Re St. John the Evangelist* [1909] P. 6; *Re St. Mary, Tyne Dock* (*No.* 2) [1958] P. 156).

Sand. There is at common law no right in the public to dig and carry away sand, stones, etc., from the foreshore. The fact of certain members of the public having been permitted to take seaweed and sand in small quantities will not affect the title of the claimant to foreshore unless such practices have been long continued, and not interrupted, and of large extent (Moore, *Foreshore*, 656, 660). As to rights in Devon and Cornwall, see the statute 1610, 7 Jac. 1, c. 18.

See also the Coast Protection Act, 1949, s. 18. There may be a common of digging akin to common of estovers or of turbary giving a commoner a right to take sand, gravel, stones and clay. See COMMON.

As to the standards of measurement etc. on the sale of sand and ballast see the Weights and Measures Act, 1963, s. 21, Sch. 5.

The opening and extension of sand and gravel pits is controlled as development. See DEVELOPMENT.

Sand gavel, a payment made by tenants to the lord of the manor of Rodley in Gloucestershire for liberty to dig gravel (Cowel).

Sand grouse, birds frequenting sandy tracts in various parts of Europe, Asia and Africa, with feet feathered like those of the British grouse. They are not, however, grouse for legal purposes, nor, indeed, are they generally found in these islands. A number of them, having migrated over to England about 1888, were promptly exterminated; and the Sand Grouse Act, 1888, was passed for the protection of any future visitants. The Act is replaced by the Protection of Birds Acts, 1954 to 1967.

Sane memory, perfect and sound mind and memory.

Sang, Sane [Old Fr.], blood.

Sanguine, or **Murrey,** blood-colour, called in the arms of princes dragon's tail, and in those of lords sardonyx. It is a tincture of very infrequent occurrence, and not recognised by some writers. In engraving it is denoted by numerous lines in saltire.

Sanguinem emere, a redemption by villeins, of their blood or tenure, in order to become freemen.

Sangius, the right or power which the chief lord of the fee had to judge and determine cases where blood was shed (Dugd.Mon., 1021).

Sanitary Acts, enactments protecting the public health by provisions for the inspection and removal of nuisances, etc.; especially those so called in, and repealed by, the Public Health Act, 1875, Sch. 5. See PUBLIC HEALTH.

Sanitary authority. The name, under the Public Health Acts prior to the Public Health Act, 1936, of the authorities for the purposes of those Acts. See LOCAL BOARDS OF HEALTH; METROPOLITAN BOARD OF WORKS; NUISANCE; PUBLIC HEALTH; QUARANTINE; RATE.

Sanitary control of ships. This is provided for by regulations made under the Public Health Act, 1936, s. 143.

Sanitary inspectors. These officials are now known as public health inspectors (Sanitary Inspectors (Change of Designation) Act, 1956.)

Sans ceo que [Nor. Fr.], without this. See ABSQUE HOC; WITHOUT THIS.

Sans frais, without expense. See RETOUR SANS PROTÊT.

Sans nombre. As applied to rights of common, this means not a common for innumerable beasts, but for a number not certain, the limit being fixed by some other standard than that of number (Y.B. 11 H. 6, 22b).

Common of pasture in gross *sans nombre* is a right to turn on the common so many cattle as the common will maintain beyond the cattle of the lord and those who have common appendant and appurtenant there. As applied to common of pasture appurtenant, the term *sans nombre* can mean no more than that the measure of the right is levancy and couchancy (*q.v.*) (*Benson* v. *Chester* (1799) 8 T.R. 401).

Sans recours [Fr.], without recourse to me. A bill of exchange may be so marked by the indorser or any other party (Bills of Exchange Act, 1882, s. 16), apparently absolving him from liability as such party under the bill.

Saoi [Sax., *sagol,* a staff], a tipstaff or serjeant-at-arms.

Sarcle, to hoe. The statute 1351, 25 Edw. 3, c. 1, speaks of the "time of sarcling."

Sarclin-time, the time or season when husbandmen weed the corn.

Sarculatura una, a tenant's service of one year's weeding for his lord (Paroch. Antiq. 403).

Sark, one of the Channel Islands (*q.v.*).

Sarkellus, a medieval unlawful engine for taking fish.

Sart, a piece of woodland turned into arable. See ASSART.

Sassons, a corruption of Saxons: a name of contempt formerly given to the

English, while they affected to be called Angles. Sassenach is the name given by the Gaelic inhabitants of Scotland and Ireland to their "Saxon" or English neighbours (O.E.D.).

Satisdare, to guarantee the obligation of a principal (Civil Law).

Satisdation, satisfaction; suretyship (Civil Law).

Satisfaction, legal compensation; the recompense for an injuury done, or the payment of money due and owing; the exhaustion of an obligation by performance (*q.v.*), or some act equivalent to performance. Thus, where a debt is due by one person to another, payment by the debtor or retainer by the creditor produces satisfaction of the debt.

In equity, the doctrine of satisfaction is chiefly made use of in cases where satisfaction is implied from the ambiguous acts or language of testators or settlors. Thus, if a parent bequeaths a legacy to a child by way of portion, and afterwards (*e.g.*, upon the marriage of the child) gives him a sum by way of portion, the latter sum operates as a satisfaction of the former, either completely or *pro tanto*; that is, the child cannot claim the legacy on the death of the parent. So if a testator gives a legacy to his creditor, it operates as a satisfaction of the debt, provided that the legacy is equal to or greater than the debt, and that no contrary intention appears.

The doctrine of satisfaction of legacies, portions, and debts means the gift of a thing with the intention, either express or implied, that it is to be taken either wholly or partly in extinguishment of some prior claim or demand. Of course, it is open to a donor expressly to provide that his subsequent gift shall be a satisfaction of a prior demand, so as to prevent such donee from claiming both. With regard to implied or presumed satisfactions, they are divided into the three following classes:

(1) The satisfaction of legacies by portions, otherwise called the ademption of legacies. It was laid down in *Ex p. Pye* (1811) 18 Ves. 140, that where a parent, or a person *in loco parentis,* gives a legacy to a child, not stating the purpose with reference to which he gives it, the court understands him as giving a portion; and as the court leans against double portions, if the father (or quasiparent) afterwards advances a portion on the marriage, or preferment in life, of that child, though of less amount, it is a satisfaction of the whole, or in part, *i.e.,* if the portion is equal to or greater than the legacy, it operates as a total ademption of such legacy; but if it is of a lesser amount than the legacy, such portion will then only adeem the legacy *pro tanto.*

(2) The satisfaction of a portion by a legacy. The rule is that wherever a legacy given by a parent, or a person *in loco parentis,* is as great as, or greater than, a portion or provision previously secured to the legatee upon marriage or otherwise, then, from the leaning against double portions, a presumption arises that the legacy was intended by the testator as a complete satisfaction. When the legacy is not so great as the portion or provision, it is then only a satisfaction *pro tanto* (*Hinchcliffe* v. *Hinchcliffe* (1797) 3 Ves. 516). A bequest of the whole or part of a residue will, according to its amount, be presumed a satisfaction of a portion either in full or *pro tanto.*

(3) The satisfaction of a debt by a legacy. Subject to any expression or indication in the will to the contrary, if a debtor bequeaths to his creditor a sum of money as great as, or greater than, the debt, without taking any notice at all of the debt, this is deemed a satisfaction of the debt, so that the creditor cannot have the debt and also the legacy —a doctrine founded upon the maxim *debitor non praesumitur donare.*

Sometimes satisfaction is distinguished from ademption (*q.v.*), the former being applied to cases where a person has entered into an agreement or covenant to settle property on another, and afterwards gives that person an equal or greater benefit by his will, in such a manner that he must be presumed to have intended the gift to operate as a satisfaction of his agreement or covenant, and not to be an additional benefit; while ademption is the converse case of a person giving property by will and afterwards giving a similar benefit by deed impliedly in satisfaction of the former gift. The distinction lies in the difference between revocable and irrevocable instruments, and is of importance in this respect, that in cases of satisfaction the persons intended to be benefited have the right to elect which gift they will take, whereas in cases of ademption there is no such right (*Chichester* v. *Coventry* (1867) L.R. 2 H.L. 71).

See ACCORD; CUMULATIVE; DEBITOR NON, ETC.; ELECTION; PERFORMANCE; QUIETUS.

Satisfaction of bill of sale. When a bill of sale is satisfied, a memorandum may be ordered to be written on the registered copy of the bill of sale (R.S.C., Ord. 95, r. 2).

Satisfied terms. See OUTSTANDING TERM; TERM.

Saturday's slop or **slap** [Scot. *slap, gap*], a space of time from evensong on Saturday till sun-rising on Monday, in which it was not lawful to take salmon in Scotland and the northern parts of England; where fishing was by cruive, the trap had to be open during that period. See CLOSE SEASON.

Saunkefin [Fr. *sang qui fin*], a failure of issue; the determination of the lineal race; a descent of kindred (Brit. c. 119).

Sausages. Where no standard is laid down for the meat content of sausages, it is a question of fact whether they amount to articles of the quality and substance demanded by the purchaser (*Williams* v. *Hurrells Stores* [1954] C.L.Y. 1361; *Marston* v. *Loney* [1955] C.L.Y. 1112).

As to the standards of measurement etc. on the sale of sausage meat, see the Weights and Measures Act, 1963, s. 21, Sch. 4 Pt. II.

Saver default, to excuse default, as where a man having made default in appearance came afterwards and showed a good cause, such as the fact that he had been in prison when he should have appeared.

Savigny. Friedrich Carl von Savigny, was born on February 21, 1779, at Frankfort-on-the-Main; became professor at Marburg, Landshut and Berlin, where he was made minister for the revision of the statutes; and died on October 25, 1861. He founded the historical school of jurisprudence. His principal works are: *The Right of Possession* (translated into English by Sir Erskine Perry); *The Capacity of our Age for Legislation and Jurisprudence* (translated into English by A. Hayward, under the title of *The Vocation of our Age, etc.*); *History of Roman Law in the Middle Ages*; *System of Modern Roman Law*; and *The Law of Obligations*.

Savings banks, institutions for the safe custody and increase of small savings.

Trustee savings banks are regulated by the Trustee Savings Bank Acts, 1969 and 1976.

The Post Office Savings Banks Acts, 1954 and 1966, were repealed by the National Savings Bank Act, 1971: see NATIONAL SAVINGS BANK.

As to the liability of a trustee savings bank for conversion, see *Knight and Searle* v. *Dove* [1964] 2 Q.B. 631.

For exemption from tax, see the Income and Corporation Taxes Act, 1870, ss. 339, 414; Finance Act, 1973, s. 13.

Savings, Director of. The functions of the Postmaster-General (*q.v.*) as to savings have been transferred to a Director of Savings (National Savings Bank Act, 1971, s. 1; National Debt Act, 1972, s. 1). See NATIONAL SAVINGS BANK.

Savour, to partake of the nature of; to bear affinity to. Money in any way connected with land, *e.g.,* money secured by mortgage of real or leasehold property, or a legacy charged on land, was said to " savour of the realty," and prior to the Mortmain and Charitable Uses Act, 1891, could not be bequeathed to a charity.

Savoy, one of the old privileged places (*q.v.*) or sanctuaries. See SANCTUARY.

Saxon-lage, the law of the West Saxons.

Scabini. In the charter of Henry VIII, the wardens of King's Lynn are termed *scabini*.

Scaccarium, a chequered cloth resembling a chess-board which covered the table in the Exchequer, and on which, when certain of the king's accounts were made up, the sums were marked and scored with counters. Hence the Court of Exchequer or *curia scaccarii* obtained its name (3 Bl.Comm. 44). See EXCHEQUER.

Scalam [Lat., *ad scalam*, at the scale], the old way of paying money into the Exchequer.

Payment was said to be by the scales

(*ad scalam*) when, upon a payment into the Exchequer, sixpence was added to each twenty shillings in order to compensate for deficiency in weight: and this was said though no scales were used.

Scales. See WEIGHTS AND MEASURES.

Scandal, a report or rumour, or an action whereby one is affronted in public.

Scandal in pleadings is injurious, by making the records of the court the means of perpetuating libellous and malignant slanders; and the court, in aid of the public morals, is bound to interfere to suppress such indecencies.

It is provided by R.S.C., Ord. 18, r. 19, that scandalous matter may be ordered to be struck out from any pleading, and by Ord. 41, r. 6, from affidavits.

Objection may be taken to an interrogatory on the ground that it is scandalous (Ord. 26, r. 1, note).

Scandalum magnatum. The making of defamatory statements regarding persons of high rank, such as peers, judges, or great officers of State, was known as *scandalum magnatum*, and the person guilty of it was liable, not only in damages, but also to punishment under the statutes 1275, 3 Edw. 1, c. 34; 1378, 2 Ric. 2, st. 1, c. 5; and 1388, 12 Ric. 2, c. 11. The action for damages lay, without proof of special damage, in respect of words which ordinarily were not actionable without such proof. Thus where a clergyman said from the pulpit, "The Lord of Leicester is a wicked and cruel man and an enemy to the Reformation," the Earl of Leicester recovered a verdict for £500. There had, however, been no proceedings for *Scandalum magnatum* for two hundred years; the statutes on the subject were repealed in 1887.

Scavage, Schevage, Schewage, or **Shewage,** a toll or custom, extracted by mayors, sheriffs, etc., of merchant strangers, for wares showed or offered for sale within their liberties. It was prohibited by the statute 1503, 19 Hen. 7, c. 7. See PACKAGE; SCHOLANDA.

Scavaidus, the officer who collected the scavage money.

Scavenger. In the City of London, and in other places, scavengers were formerly included amongst the minor municipal officers. Thus the statute 1694, 6 & 7 Will. & Mar., c. 4, exempted apothecaries from serving as constables, scavengers, and other parish and ward officers. The scavenger in this sense did not himself clean the streets, but he saw, or was supposed to see, that it was done. Thus in Aberystwyth in 1835, churchwardens and overseers of the poor were selected for the office, and they got paupers to do the actual scavenging. See DUSTBINS.

Sceat. In the Anglo-Saxon period this was a coin corresponding approximately to a penny.

Sceppa salis, an ancient measure of salt, the quantity of which is now not known.

Schaffa, a sheaf.

Schar-penny, Scharn-penny, or **Schorn-penny,** a small duty or compensation paid by some tenants for non-observance of the duty of penning their cattle at night in the lord's yard, as in some cases they were obliged to do for the benefit of the lord's manure pit.

Schedule, a small scroll; an inventory; a writing additional or appendant, as a list of fixtures in a lease or details of any matter contained in the body of a deed, or of enactments repealed and other supplementary matter in an Act of Parliament.

Scheduled territories, the countries, formerly part of the sterling area, designated in the Exchange Control Act, 1947, Sch. 1, as substituted by S.I. 1972 nos. 930, 2040, under which they are confined to the United Kingdom, the Channel Islands, the Isle of Man, the Republic of Ireland and Gibraltar.

Scheme, a document containing provisions for regulating the management or distribution of property, or for making an arrangement between persons having conflicting rights. Thus, in the practice of the Chancery Division, where the execution of a charitable trust in the manner directed by the founder is difficult or impracticable, or requires supervision, a scheme for the management of the charity will be settled by the court. The Charity Commissioners have concurrent jurisdiction with the High Court, subject to appeal against any order of the Commissioners brought to the High Court by the Attorney General or by the charity, or any of the charity trustees or by any person removed from any office or employment (Charities Act, 1960, s. 18). See CHARITY COMMISSIONERS; CY-PRES.

Under the Companies Act, 1948, ss. 208, 209, the court may approve a scheme for the reconstruction of a company. See INCLOSURE.

Scheme of arrangement. See ARRANGEMENTS BETWEEN DEBTORS AND CREDITORS.

Schetes, usury (Rot.Parl., 14 Ric. 2).

Schilla, a little bell used in monasteries.

Schireman, a sheriff; an earl.

Schirrens-geld [Sax. *shiregeld*], a tax paid to sheriffs for keeping the shire or county court.

Schism Bill, the Schism Act, 1713, which restrained Protestant dissenters from educating their own children, and forbade all tutors and schoolmasters to be present at any conventicle or dissenting place of worship. It was repealed in 1718.

Scholanda, a place comprising shops, seldas and penthouses where goods were permitted by the lord of the manor to be sold, and where schewage, or toll, might be extracted from merchant strangers. Shoe Lane, London, is a corruption of Scholanda (Williams, *Early Holborn*). See PACKAGE.

Scholarship. Scholarship income is exempt from income tax: Income and Corporation Taxes Act, 1970, s. 375.

Scholefield's Act, the statute 1860, 23 & 24 Vict. c. 84, which related to adulteration of food.

School. The Elementary Education Act, 1870, s. 3, defined an elementary school as one at which elementary education was the principal part of the education there given. Under the Education Act, 1921, s. 170 (1), it meant (except in the case of courses of advanced instruction given in pursuance of the Act) a school or department of a school at which elementary education was the principal part of the education there given, and did not include any school or department of a school at which the ordinary payment in respect of the instruction from each scholar exceeded ninepence a week, or any school carried on as an evening school under the regulations of the Board of Education, or a continuation school. A public elementary school was defined by the Elementary Education Act, 1870, s. 7, as an elementary school at which

a child, if the parent so desired, received no religious instruction, which was at all times open to inspection by the official inspectors, and which was conducted in accordance with the Education Code (*q.v.*): and the Education Act, 1921, s. 27, was to the same effect.

The Education Act, 1944, s. 8 (as amended by the Education (Miscellaneous Provisions) Act, 1948, s. 3) provides that it shall be the duty of local education authorities to provide schools for primary education and schools for secondary education. Primary and secondary schools maintained by a local education authority, not being nursery schools or special schools, are, if established by a local education authority, known as county schools and if established otherwise are known as voluntary schools (s. 9). County schools include what were formerly known as provided schools. Voluntary schools are the denominational schools formerly known as non-provided schools. An independent school is one which is not maintained by a local education authority and in respect of which the Secretary of State for Education does not make a grant to the proprietor. See COUNCIL SCHOOL; EDUCATION; PUBLIC SCHOOLS.

Schools of anatomy are regulated by the Anatomy Acts, 1832 and 1871.

As to the use of a school room for parish (*q.v.*) or (in Wales) community (see COMMUNITIES) purposes, see the Local Government Act, 1972, s. 134. As to the rating of county and voluntary school premises see the General Rate Act, 1967, s. 30.

The court will take judicial notice of the practice that a parent who withdraws his child from a fee-paying school without giving a term's notice must pay a term's fees (*Mount* v. *Oldham Corporation* [1973] 1 Q.B. 309).

As to sex discrimination, see the Sex Discrimination Act, 1975, ss. 22–36.

School attendance committee, a body formed for the purpose of enforcing attendance of children at school in every district which was not within the jurisdiction of a school board (Elementary Education Act, 1876, s. 7 (2)). Its powers and duties were transferred to the local education authority (*q.v.*), by the Education Act, 1902, s. 5. School attendance is now enforced under the Education Act, 1944, s. 40 (amended by the Criminal Justice Act, 1967, Sch. 3 Pt. I; the Children and Young Persons Act, 1969, Sch. 5 para. 13).

School boards, bodies corporate created by the Elementary Education Act, 1870, for the purpose of providing and conducting public elementary schools other than those provided by the various religious denominations and by private persons.

Their powers and duties were transferred to the local education authorities by the Education Act, 1902, s. 5.

School crossings. See the Road Traffic Regulation Act, 1967, ss. 24, 25; Local Government Act, 1972, Sch. 19 Pt. II para. 12; Road Traffic Act, 1974, Sch. 5 Pt. II, Sch. 6 para. 7; *Wall* v. *Walwyn* [1974] R.T.R. 24.

Schoolmaster. In *Fitzgerald* v. *Northcote* (1865) 4 F. & F. 656, the defendant to an action of trespass for an assault and battery pleaded that he was the headmaster of a school of which the plaintiff was a pupil, and that the plaintiff combined with other pupils for purposes subversive of the discipline of the school, and the plea was held good. As to the extent of the powers of a schoolmaster in this respect, see *Cleary* v. *Booth* [1893] 1 Q.B. 465. As to the power of an assistant teacher in a public elementary school to administer corporal punishment, see *Mansell* v. *Griffin* [1908] 1 K.B. 160, 947.

The duty of care of a schoolmaster towards his boys is that of a careful parent (*Williams* v. *Eady* (1893) 10 T.L.R. 41; *Rich* v. *London County Council* [1953] 1 W.L.R. 895; *Lyes* v. *Middlesex C.C.* (1962) 61 L.G.R. 443).

As to remuneration, see the Remuneration of Teachers Act, 1965.

Science and Art Department. This was, from its origin in 1837 down to 1856, a branch of the Board of Trade. In 1856, when the Education Department was formed, it became a branch of that department; but it received a charter of incorporation in 1864, and from that time it was practically a distinct department. Its place was, however, taken by the Board of Education under the Board

of Education Act, 1899, s. 2 (1), and it ceased to exist.

Science, Minister of. See Atomic Energy.

Science Research Council. See the Science and Technology Act, 1965. The Council took over the activities of the National Institute for Research in Nuclear Science (s. 3 (2)). The Council for Scientific and Industrial Research and the Department of Scientific and Industrial Research were dissolved (s. 3 (1)).

Scienter [Lat. *scienter*, knowingly], an allegation in a pleading that the defendant or accused person did a thing knowingly.

At common law it was necessary, in order to make a person who kept a domestic animal answerable for any harm it had done to prove that the defendant knew that it had a mischievous propensity to do that kind of harm; proof of this knowledge was called proving scienter. Liability in such cases is now under the Animals Act, 1971, s. 2. See Animals, Liability for.

Scientia utrinque par pares contrahentes facit (3 Burr. 1910). (Equal knowledge on both sides makes the contracting parties equal.) Thus, they are put on the footing essential to the conclusion of a valid contract of marine insurance, with regard to which the law is that the insurer has a right to know every material fact known to the insured unless disclosure is waived by the insurer (Marine Insurance Act, 1906, s. 18 (c)).

Scientology. A national of the E.E.C. may be excluded from entry into the United Kingdom because of association with the cult of scientology (*Van Duyn* v. *Home Office* [1975] Ch. 358). The Church of Scientology of Toronto cannot be defamed by an article published in Canada referring to a German Society of Scientology (*Church of Scientology of Toronto* v. *International News Distributing Co.* (1974) 48 D.L.R. (3d) 176).

Sciethman, a pirate or thief.

Scilicet [Lat. *scire licet*], that is to say, to wit; abbreviated *scil.* or *sc.*

This is not a direct and separate clause, nor a direct and entire clause, in a conveyance, but *intermedia*; neither is it a substantive clause of itself, but it is rather to usher in the sentence of another, and to particularise that which was too general before, or distribute that which was too gross, or explain that which was doubtful; and it must neither increase nor diminish the premises nor *habendum,* for it gives nothing of itself; but it may make a restriction where the precedent words are not so very express but that they may be restrained (Hob. 171).

Scintilla juris, a spark or fragment of right. If a conveyance of land was made to A and his heirs to the use of B and his heirs until the happening of a certain event and then to the use of C and his heirs, the use was executed in B and his heirs, so that A had no seisin left in him. If then the event happened, the question was, who was seised to the use of C? At one time it was supposed that on the happening of the event the original seisin reverted back to B, so that he was seised to the use of C, and that meanwhile a possibility of seisin, or *scintilla juris,* remained in him. This doctrine was always discountenanced by the best authorities, and was abolished by the Law of Property Amendment Act, 1860, s. 7.

Scintilla juris et tituli, a spark of right and title. See SCINTILLA JURIS.

Scire facias (that you cause to know), a writ founded upon some record, such as a judgment, letters patent, etc., directing the sheriff to make known to (*scire facias*) or warn the person against whom it is brought to show cause why the person bringing it should not have advantage of the record, or (as in the case of a *scire facias* to repeal letters patent, Crown grants, charters and franchises) why the record should not be annulled and vacated.

Writs of *scire facias* were abolished by the Crown Proceedings Act, 1947, Sch. 1.

Scire fieri inquiry, a writ issued against an executor against whom judgment had been obtained for a debt due by his testator when the property of the testator had been found insufficient (*i.e.,* when the sheriff had returned *nulla bona* to a *fieri facias de bonis testatoris* without returning a *devastavit*), and the executor was supposed to have committed a *devastavit.* It commanded the sheriff that

in case there should be no goods of the testator remaining in the hands of the executor, he should summon a jury to inquire if the defendant had wasted the goods of the testator; and if a *devastavit* were found, that he should warn the defendant to show cause why the plaintiff should not have a *fieri facias de bonis propriis* against him. The name was componded of the names of the three proceedings, *scire facias, fieri facias,* and inquiry, of which the process consisted. See DEVASTAVIT; FIERI FACIAS; JUDGMENT.

Scirewyte, the annual tax or prestation paid to the sheriff for holding the assizes or county courts (Paroch. Antiq. 573).

Scite, or **Site** [Lat. *situs*], the setting or standing on any place; the seat or situation of a capital messuage, or the ground whereon it stands.

Scitum, a decree of the Roman people, sometimes abbreviated SCTm.

Scold [*communis rixatrix*], a troublesome and angry woman who, by brawling and wrangling amongst her neighbours, breaks the public peace, increases discord, and becomes a public nuisance to the neighbourhood.

Such a woman was indictable at the sheriff's tourn (*q.v.*), where she was punishable with the cucking-stool (*q.v.*). See CASTIGATORY.

The offence of being a common scold was abolished by the Criminal Law Act, 1967, s. 13.

Sconce, a mulct or fine.

Scot, a fee payable under the Saxon kings for church services, in the name of church scot, light scot, soul scot (burials), and Rome scot.

Scot and lot [Sax. *sceat*, part], a customary contribution laid upon all subjects according to their ability. Whoever were assessed to any contribution, though not by equal portions, were said to pay scot and lot.

The inhabitants of a borough who were liable for the rates were described as paying scot and bearing lot therein.

The word " scot " was used alone as meaning a tax.

See CHURCH SCOT; SCOTALE; SCOTTARE.

Scot and lot voters, voters in certain boroughs entitled before the Representation of the People Act, 1832, to the franchise in virtue of their paying this contribution; the rights of those living in 1832 were preserved by that Act.

Scotale, Scotal, an alehouse kept by an officer of the forest, at which inhabitants of the forest had to drink in order to secure the favour of the officer. The keeping of such a house was prohibited by the *Carta de Foresta* (*q.v.*). The word is derived from scot, in the sense of a tax, and ale.

Scotare; Scottare, to pay scot or customary dues; said anciently of tenants.

Scotland and Ireland. As to service of a writ, by leave of a judge, upon a defendant resident in Scotland or Ireland, see R.S.C., Ord. 11 (*Williams* v. *Cartwright* [1895] 1 Q.B. 142). Process for compelling the attendance of witnesses from Scotland or Ireland before English courts and vice versa might be issued under the Judicature Act, 1925, s. 49. Appeals from courts in Scotland and Northern Ireland are heard by the House of Lords under the Appellate Jurisdiction Act, 1876, s. 3; see also the Irish Free State (Consequential Provisions) Act, 1922, Sch. 1 para. 6 (3).

Acts of Parliament passed since the Union bind Scotland unless they are expressly or impliedly limited to England (*Westminster Fire Office* v. *Glasgow Provident Investment Society* (1888) 13 App. Cas. at p. 716). As to the position of Northern Ireland and the Republic of Ireland, see IRELAND.

The Union with Scotland Act, 1706, confirmed twenty-five articles of union, gave Scotland sixteen representative peers in the House of Lords (see HOUSE OF LORDS), and forty-five representative members in the House of Commons.

A Secretary for Scotland, now a Secretary of State (*q.v.*), was established by the Secretary for Scotland Act, 1904.

Scots, assessments by commissioners of sewers. See SCOT AND LOT VOTERS.

Scots judgments. It is desirable that the decisions in the Scottish courts and in the courts of this country should, if possible, be uniform (*Chislett* v. *Macbeth & Co.* [1910] A.C. at p. 224).

Scots law is mainly derived from the civil law, and differs in many points from the English.

Scottare, to pay scot, tax, or customary dues.

Scrap metals. Scrap metal dealers must be registered in a local authority register (Scrap Metal Dealers Act, 1964, s. 1). Dealers must keep a record of dealings (ss. 2, 3). Additional requirements may be imposed on convicted dealers (s. 4). Acquisition of scrap metal from a person apparently under the age of sixteen years is an offence. Any person selling scrap metal to a dealer who gives a false name and address is guilty of an offence (s. 5). Constables have a right of entry and inspection (s. 6). As to partnerships, see s. 7. " Scrap metal dealer " and " scrap metal " are defined in s. 9. The Act replaces the Old Metal Dealers Act, 1861, and some other enactments relating to dealings in old metals. It also replaces ss. 538 to 542 of the Merchant Shipping Act, 1894, which regulated the business of marine store dealers.

Scraping the defendant's conscience, the amendment of the interrogatory part of the old bill in Chancery in order to make the defendant give plain answers instead of the evasive answers previously given by him.

Scribere est agere (2 Rol.Rep. 89). (To write is to act.) That is to say, to write anything is to do an overt act within the meaning of the law relating to treason, if the writing is published. In the case in which these words are cited the accused " inclosed *son liver* in a box sealed up and *sic secretment* conveyed it *al Roy* " —which was held to be publication of the manuscript.

Scrip. A scrip certificate (or shortly " scrip ") is an acknowledgment by a company or the issuers of a loan that the person named therein (or more commonly the holder for the time being of the certificate) is entitled to a specified number of shares, debentures, bonds, etc. It is usually given in exchange for the letter of allotment, and in its turn is given up for the shares, debentures or bonds which it represents. Scrip is chiefly used in the case of bonds and shares which are payable by instalments, so that they cannot be issued until all the instalments are paid; therefore as soon as bonds or shares have been allotted to a subscriber or applicant, a scrip certificate, certifying that, on due payment of the unpaid instalments, the bearer will be entitled to receive bonds or shares to the amount of the certificate, is given to the allottee (see ALLOT). Scrip certificates are negotiable instruments (*Goodwin* v. *Robarts* (1875) L.R. 10 Ex. 337; *Rumball* v. *Metropolitan Bank* (1877) 2 Q.B.D. 194).

There were formerly companies (called scrip companies) in which the scrip was not required to be exchanged for shares, the scripholders being the shareholders. These unincorporated companies with shares transferable by delivery were in contemplation of law nothing but great partnerships with some special features, and the members were liable in the same way as members of any other partnership. Partnerships of more than twenty persons must be registered as companies under the Companies Act, 1948, ss. 429, 434; Companies Act, 1967, ss. 119, 120.

" Scrip certificate " seems to be a contraction for " subscriptions certificate," that is, a certificate of the amount subscribed for by the applicant.

See COMPANIES.

Scrip dividend, a dividend otherwise than in cash. It may take the form of a dividend or bonus out of capitalised reserves satisfied by the issue of fully paid shares or by the discharge of cancelled liability or partly paid shares previously issued. Finance companies frequently issue as dividends shares or debentures in other companies.

Script, a writing; the original or principal document.

In probate practice, it means a will, codicil, draft of will or codicil, or written instructions for the same. If the will is destroyed, a copy or any paper embodying its contents becomes a script, even though not made under the direction of the testator. See AFFIDAVIT.

Scriptae obligationes scriptis tolluntur, et nudi consensus obligatio contrario consensu dissolvitur. (Written obligations are superseded by writings, and an obligation of naked assent is dissolved by naked assent to the contrary.) This was a rule of the civil law. See QUOMODO, ETC.

Scripture, the canonical books of the Old and New Testaments; see the Articles of Religion, art. VI. See CHRISTIANITY.

Scrivener [Ital. *scrivano*; Fr. *escrivain*]. A scrivener, also called a money scrivener, was a person who received the money of his clients for investment. Pending its investment, he could use it for his own purposes without having to account for any profits which he might make. He, like a banker, traded in money, and, like other traders, he could be made a bankrupt under the statute 1624, 21 Jac. 1, c. 19, s. 2; but it was decided in *Adams* v. *Malkin* (1814) 3 Camp. 539, that an attorney who occasionally acted as a scrivener could not, *qua* scrivener, be made a bankrupt.

Scriveners ceased to exist as a separate class about 1760. In Boswell's *Life of Johnson* it is related that one Jack Ellis, a contemporary of Johnson and mentioned by him with great respect, was the last of the scriveners. The Bankruptcy Act, 1869, Sch. 1, however included amongst traders persons using the trade or profession of a scrivener, receiving other men's moneys or estates into their trust or custody. But though there are now no scriveners *eo nomine*, the Scriveners' Company of the City of London still exists; and any notary who practices within its jurisdiction must take up the freedom of the company (Public Notaries Act, 1801, s. 13). See NOTARY.

Scroll, a mark which supplies the place of a seal.

Scrope's Act, the Parochial Assessments Act, 1836.

Scrope's or **Scroop's Inn,** an obsolete law society, also called Serjeants Place, opposite to St. Andrew's Church, Holborn, London. See SERJEANTS-AT-LAW.

Scruet roll, a record of the bail accepted in cases of habeas corpus (3 St.Tr. 134).

Scruple, one third of a drachm (Weights and Measures Act, 1963, s. 10, Sch. 1 Pt. V) but a scruple is no longer a unit of measurement (s. 10 (9)).

Scrutator, a bailiff appointed to look after the king's rights to flotsam, jetsam, etc. (1 Hargrave, *Tracts*, 23).

Scrutiny, an inquiry into the validity of the votes recorded for the successful candidate at an election. It may be claimed if the unsuccessful candidate alleges in his petition that he has in fact a majority of lawful votes. It involves a trial of the validity of each vote objected to.

Sculpture. The work of a sculptor is " artistic work," and is the subject of copyright (Copyright Act, 1956, s. 3).

Scutage, a tax or contribution raised by those who held lands by knight's service in commutation of such service towards furnishing the king's army, at the rate of one, two, or three marks for every knight's fee. The statute 1660, 12 Car. 2, c. 24, abolished military tenures. See ESCUAGE.

Scutagio habendo, a writ which lay against tenants by knight's service to serve in the wars, or send sufficient persons, or pay a certain sum (Fitz.N.B. 83).

Scute, a fifteenth-century French gold coin of the value of 3s. 4d. It was worth one-half of the English noble (*q.v.*) (Rot. Parl. 1 Hen. 6).

Scutella, a scuttle; anything of a flat or broad shape like a shield.

Scutella eleemosynaria, an alms-basket.

Scuttling, the intentional casting away of a ship, for the sake of the insurance money, etc. (*Samuel* v. *Dumas* [1924] A.C. 431).

For practice where scuttling is to be pleaded see *Probatina Shipping Co.* v. *Sun Insurance Office* [1974] Q.B. 635

Scutum armorum, a shield or coat of arms.

Scyldwit, a mulct for any fault (Leg. Hen. 1).

Scyra, a fine imposed upon such as neglected to attend the *scyre-gemot* courts, which all tenants were bound to do.

Scyre-gemot, or **Sciremot,** a court held by the Saxons twice every year, by the bishop of the diocese and the ealdorman in shires which had ealdormen: and by the bishop and the sheriff where the counties were committed to the sheriff, etc., wherein both the ecclesiastical and temporal laws were given in charge to the county (Seld., *Titles of Hon.*).

Se defendendo, in self-defence. Homicide *se defendendo* is excusable manslaying in defence of one's own life, when attacked and put in jeopardy. See HOMICIDE.

Sea. The main or high seas are part of the realm of England, for thereon the courts of Admiralty have jurisdiction, but they are not subject to the common law. The main sea begins at the low-water mark, but between the high-water mark and the low-water mark, where the sea ebbs and flows, the common law and Admiralty have *divisum imperium,* an alternate jurisdiction, the one upon the water when it is full sea, the other upon the land when it is an ebb. See FORE-SHORE; FOUR SEAS.

The jurisdiction of the Admiralty within three miles of the low-water mark was discussed in *R.* v. *Keyn* (1876) 2 Ex.D. 63, where it was held that the Central Criminal Court had no jurisdiction to try for manslaughter the foreign captain of a foreign ship which, in passing within three miles of the British shore, ran into a British ship and sank her; but this state of the law was altered by the Territorial Waters Jurisdiction Act, 1878, s. 2, which enacts that any offence committed by a person, whether a British subject or not, within one marine league of the coast, although it may have been committed on board or by means of a foreign ship, is an offence within the jurisdiction of the Admiralty. As to the jurisdiction of the Crown Court to try a case of theft alleged to have been committed in Scottish waters, see *R.* v. *Devon Justices* [1924] 1 K.B. 503.

See FRONTAGER; HIGH SEAS; NAVIGATION; QUEEN'S CHAMBERS; TERRITORIAL WATERS.

Sea fisheries. See FISHERY.

Sea laws, laws relating to the sea, as the laws of Oleron, etc.

Sea lawyer, a captious sailor; an idle litigious long-shorer, more given to question orders than to obey them; an amateur lawyer.

Sea letter; Sea brief, a document which must be carried by every neutral vessel in waters where she is liable to meet the warship of any nation which is at war with another. It is issued by the government of the State to which the neutral ship belongs, and specifies the name of the master, the name and description of the vessel, her cargo, the port of departure and the port of destination. It is used to protect her from capture.

Sea marks. See BEACON.

Sea rovers, pirates and robbers of the sea.

Seal, wax or wafer with an impression. By the Law of Property Act, 1925, s. 73, deeds executed after 1925 must be signed or, in case of illiterates or blind persons, marked) as well as sealed.

By R.S.C., Ord. 38, r. 10, the seal of any officer or department of the Supreme Court is sufficient to authorise as evidence any document or copy of a document. As to the seal of district registrars, see the Judicature Act, 1925, s. 9.

The formality of affixing a seal to a document is one of the oldest modes of expressing an intention to be bound by it, derived from the times when few persons could sign their own names. It is still a solemn mode of expressing assent to a written instrument, and when done with that intention makes the instrument a deed; the intention is generally expressed by the additional formality of delivery (*q.v.*). See DEED; EXECUTION; SIGNATURE.

Every corporation (*q.v.*) aggregate must have a common seal, for being an invisible body, it cannot manifest its intention by any personal act or discourse, but only acts and speaks by its common seal, except where it is represented by an officer, agent or attorney, and in a few cases where it would be inconvenient to require the seal, *e.g.,* in everyday matters of business (*Wright & Son* v. *Romford Borough Council* [1957] 1 Q.B. 431).

As to the seal of a company, see the Companies Act, 1948, ss. 32–36.

As to the seals of the Crown, see GREAT SEAL; PRIVY SEAL; SIGN MANUAL; SIGNET.

As to the forgery of seals, see the Forgery Act, 1913, ss. 5, 18.

Seal day, motion day in the Court of Chancery. On motion day the Great Seal (*q.v.*) was brought into court for the purpose of sealing motion papers. Accordingly the expression " the Seal is closed " meant that motions were over for that day.

Seal fisheries. Close times for fur seals were established under the Seal Fishery Act, 1875, the Behring Sea Award Act, 1894, and the Seal Fisheries (North Pacific) Acts, 1895 and 1912. See also GREY SEALS.

Seal Paper. Before the Judicature Acts, 1873–75, there was issued before the commencement of each of the sittings a list, known at the Seal Paper, specifying the business to be done each day in the Courts of the Lord Chancellor, the Master of the Rolls, the Lords Justices, and the Vice-Chancellors.

Sealer [Lat. *sigillator*], an officer of the Court of Chancery who sealed writs, etc. According to the Sealer of the year 1798, his attendance was perpetual, he did business at all hours and he had no holidays (*Commons Committee Reports*, 1803, Vol. 13, p. 252): but nevertheless he, along with the Deputy Sealer and the Chaff Wax (*q.v.*) and the Deputy Chaff Wax, was abolished by the Court of Chancery Act, 1852, s. 23. See SPIGURNEL.

Sealing up. Where a party to an action has been ordered to produce a document, part of which is either irrelevant to the matters in question or is privileged from production, he may, by leave of the court, seal up that part, if he makes an affidavit stating that it is irrelevant or privileged. The sealing up is generally done by fastening pieces of paper over the part with gum or wafers. But where books are in constant use the party producing them will, as a matter of convenience, be allowed merely to cover up the irrelevant or the privileged parts during the inspection, subject, if so required, to his making an affidavit that nothing relevant has been covered up.

Seamen, persons engaged in navigating ships, barges, etc., upon the high seas. Those employed for this purpose upon rivers, lakes, or canals are denominated watermen.

The term seamen includes everyone employed in any capacity on board ship except masters, pilots, and duly indentured and registered apprentices (Merchant Shipping Act, 1894, s. 742).

The Merchant Shipping Act, 1970, contains provisions with regard to the engagement and discharge of crews (ss. 1–6), wages, etc. (ss. 7–18), safety, health and welfare (ss. 19–26), offences by seamen (ss. 27–38), civil liability for absence without leave (s. 39), for smuggling (s. 40) and for fines imposed under immigration laws (s. 41), trade disputes involving seamen (s. 42), manning and certification (ss. 43–51), disqualification of seamen, inquiries and investigations (ss. 52–61), relief and return of seamen or masters left behind (ss. 62–64, 67), the property of deceased seamen or masters (ss. 65–67), documentation, reports and returns (ss. 68–75), stowaways, etc. (ss. 77–79), uniform (s. 87), deserters (s. 89).

As to seamen in the navy, see the Naval Discipline Act, 1957. See NAVY.

Seaplane. The regulations for preventing collisions at sea may be applied to seaplanes (Civil Aviation Act, 1949, s. 52). See AIR NAVIGATION.

Search. In international law, the right of search is the right on the part of ships of war to visit and search merchant vessels during war, in order to ascertain whether the ship or cargo is liable to seizure. Resistance to visitation and search by a neutral vessel makes the vessel and cargo liable to confiscation. Numerous treaties regulate the manner in which the right to search must be exercised. See CONTRABAND.

Powers of search by customs officers are contained in the Customs and Excise Act, 1952.

Search warrant, an order authorising a person therein named to enter a specified building and seize certain specified goods. If it is made to appear by information on oath before a justice of the peace that there is reasonable cause to believe that any person has in his custody or possession or on his premises any stolen goods, the justice may grant to a constable a warrant to search for and seize the same. An officer of police not below the rank of superintendent may give a constable written authority to search any premises for stolen goods (a) if the person in occupation of the premises has been convicted within the preceding five years of handling stolen goods (*q.v.*) or any offence involving dishonesty and punishable with imprisonment, or (b) if a person who has been convicted within the previous five years of handling stolen goods has within the preceding twelve months been in occupation of the premises. A person authorised to search premises for stolen goods may enter and search the premises accordingly and may seize any goods he believes to be stolen goods (Theft Act, 1968, s. 26).

Such a warrant must be in the possession of the person executing it. He can, if need be, enter by force, but he should first demand admission.

Under many Acts, search warrants may be issued to search for many things ranging from adulterated bread to explosives, or to search for girls detained in a brothel.

Searchers. Officials known by this name were appointed under the statute 1335, 9 Edw. 3, st. 2, c. 9, to see that no sterling or bullion was exported and no base money imported at the various ports.

The term was also applied generally to officers appointed to search ships, etc., for dutiable or contraband goods: see the statute 1495, 11 Hen. 7, c. 13. See AULNAGER; CUSTOMER; TRONOUR.

Searches. Registration under the Land Charges Act, 1972, in the Land Registry or in the local registries of any incumbrance which is required to be registered under that Act is notice (*q.v.*) to a purchaser and all persons connected with the land affected (Law of Property Act, 1925, s. 198). Searches are necessary, not only in the Land Registry, but at the office of the local authority for local land charges. Searches may be made personally in each of the registers under the Land Charges Act, 1972, but the usual practice is to apply for and obtain an official certificate of search. An official certificate of search at the Land Registry covers all the registers there, *viz.*: pending actions; writs and orders affecting land, such as writs of execution or orders appointing a receiver, bankruptcy petitions and receiving orders; deeds of arrangement; and land charges under the Land Charges Act, 1972, s. 2. The certificate is good against any charge registered between its date and completion of the purchase if the purchase is completed within fourteen days (Law of Property (Amendment) Act, 1926, s. 4). See PRIORITY NOTICE.

At the Land Registry the application for search must be made in the names of each beneficial or estate owner affected during the period required for registration. For local land charges, on the other hand, registration is made against the land affected and the danger of an accidental omission of the name of an interim owner or incumbrances is avoided. Searches against land registered under the Land Registration Act, 1925, are not necessary as a rule, the subject-matter being entered on the register except for the local land charges, which are not covered by this Act. Searches against companies for mortgages or charges for securing money may be made at Bush House, London, under the Companies Act, 1948, s. 95. See the Land Charges Act, 1972, s. 3 (7) (8). But the Bush House register does not effectively protect registered land. See REGISTRATION OF TITLE TO LAND.

In proper cases, searches should also be made at the Central Office for deeds enrolled there, see ENROLMENT, or the Record Office if not kept at the Central Office.

Searches in the registries do not absolve the party from making the usual prudent inquiries as to tenancies, over-riding interests (*q.v.*) in regard to registered land, etc., or inspections before purchase, or for tithe annuities.

See ANNUITY; JUDGMENT; LAND CHARGE; LAND REGISTRIES; LIS PENDENS.

Sea-reeve, one who in a seaport looked after the maritime jurisdiction of the lord, kept the foreshore clean, and collected wreck (Spelman).

Seas, Beyond the. At common law this means not being in Great Britain. By the Mercantile Law Amendment Act, 1856, s. 12, which related to absence beyond the seas as a ground for extension of the period for bringing actions, it meant not being in Great Britain, or Ireland, or the Channel Islands, or the Isle of Man. Absence beyond the seas has no effect under the Limitation Act, 1939. See LIMITATION OF ACTIONS.

Seashore, the space of land between high-water and low-water mark. It belongs to the Crown, or, by grant from the Crown, to the lord of the manor or other grantee of the Crown, and the public have no right over it for bathing (*Blundell* v. *Catterall* (1821) 5 Bl. & Ald. 268; *Brinckman* v. *Matley* [1904] 2 Ch.

313). See COAST PROTECTION; FORE-SHORE.

Seat belt. A driver is not guilty of contributory negligence by reason alone of his failure to wear a seat belt where such failure is due to an opinion honestly held and shared by many sensible people (*Froom* v. *Butcher* [1974] 1 W.L.R. 1297, following *Challoner* v. *Williams* [1974] R.T.R. 221, not following *Pasternak* v. *Poulton* [1973] 1 W.L.R. 476; *Parnell* v. *Shields* [1973] R.T.R. 414; *Toperoff* v. *Mor* (*Note*) [1973] R.T.R. 419; *McGee* v. *Francis Shaw & Co.* [1973] R.T.R. 409). See also *Wickstead* v. *J. Murphy & Sons* [1975] C.L.Y. 2455; *Smith* v. *Blackburn* [1974] R.T.R. 533; *Drage* v. *Smith* [1975] R.T.R. 1; *James* v. *Parson* [1975] R.T.R. 20; *Freeborn* v. *Thomas* [1975] R.T.R. 16; *Chapman* v. *Ward* [1975] R.T.R. 7; *Down* v. *Schacter* [1975] R.T.R. 238. Where injuries resulting from a road accident would have been prevented or lessened if a seat belt had been worn, the failure to wear it amounts to contributory negligence. Where the injuries would have been altogether prevented by the wearing of a seat belt, the damages should be reduced by 25 per cent.; where the injuries would have been a good deal less severe, the reduction should be 15 per cent. (*Froom* v. *Butcher* [1976] Q.B. 286).

Seaweed. The lord of the manor cannot acquire an exclusive right to cut seaweed below low-water mark, unless by grant from the Crown, or such long and undisturbed enjoyment as to give him a title by prescription (*Benest* v. *Pipon* (1830) 1 Knapp. 68). Nor is there at common law a general right in the public of entering on the seashore to take seaweed even between high-water and low-water mark (*Hamilton* v. *Att.-Gen.* (1880) 5 L.R.Ir. 555). See Moore, *Foreshore*.

Seaworthiness. The question whether a ship is or was at a given time seaworthy is chiefly of importance with reference to the liability of the owner and the underwriters or insurers in the event of her loss. In this use of the term, " seaworthiness " means that the vessel is in a fit state, at the time of sailing, as to repair, equipment, and crew, and in all other respects, to encounter the ordinary perils of the voyage insured. Where there is no agreement to the contrary, a shipowner who contracts for the conveyance of merchandise in his ship, or contracts for her insurance, impliedly warrants that she is seaworthy; that is to say, if she is lost, and it turns out that she was not seaworthy at the time of sailing, in the one case the owner is liable to the owner of the goods for their loss, and in the other case the insurers or underwriters are discharged from liability under the policy, notwithstanding the *bona fides* and honesty of the shipowner (*Cohn* v. *Davidson* (1877) 2 Q.B.D. 455).

It is provided in all charterparties that the vessel chartered shall be tight, staunch, and strong, well-apparelled, and furnished with an adequate number of mariners, sufficient tackle, provisions, etc. If the ship is insufficient in any of these particulars, the owners, though ignorant of the circumstances, will be liable for whatever damage may in consequence be done to the goods of the merchant, and if any insurance has been effected upon her it will be void. In a voyage policy a warranty of seaworthiness is implied, but not in a time policy (*Dudgeon* v. *Pembroke* (1877) 2 App. Cas. 284); but see the Carriage of Goods by Sea Act, 1971, ss. 1, 3, Sch. art. III 1, art. IV 1, and the Merchant Shipping Act, 1894, ss. 457, 459; *Maxine Footwear Co.* v. *Canadian Government Merchant Marine* [1959] A.C. 589.

If, in the course of proceedings for desertion, it is alleged by one-fourth or, if the crew is over twenty, by five, of the seamen belonging to a ship that by reason of unseaworthiness, overloading, defective equipment, or the like, she is not in a fit condition to go to sea, the court having cognisance of the case may have the ship surveyed (Merchant Shipping Act, 1894, s. 463). A naval court (*q.v.*) may order a survey of any ship which is the subject of investigation (s. 483 (1) (*j*)). See the Merchant Shipping Act, 1970, Sch. 5.

Provision is made by the Merchant Shipping Act, 1894, for the proper equipment and survey of ships in the interest of passengers.

Every person who sends or attempts to send, or is party to the sending of, or takes, a ship to sea in an unseaworthy state, so as to endanger the life of any person on board, is guilty of a misdemeanour, unless he proves that he used all reasonable means to make her seaworthy (Merchant Shipping Act, 1894, s. 457).

Seck [Lat. *siccus*, dry or barren]. Rent seck is a rent charge without a clause of distress. Rent seck *idem est quod redditus siccus*, for that no distress is incident to it (Co.Litt. 144a).

The Law of Property Act, 1925, s. 44, gives a power of distress. See RENT.

Seck was applied to certain services and obligations to signify that they created no tenure between the person from whom and the person to whom they were due, as opposed to those services of homage, fealty, and escuage, which could not become seck or dry, but made tenure whereunto distresses, escheats and other profits were incident (Co.Litt. 151a).

At the present day, the term is hardly ever used except in the phrase " rent seck."

See CAMBIUM; RENT.

Second deliverance, Writ of, a judicial writ which lay after a nonsuit of the plaintiff in replevin (*q.v.*), and a *retorno habendo* of the cattle replevied, adjudged to him that distrained them, commanding the sheriff to replevy the same cattle again, upon security given by the plaintiff in the replevin for the redelivery of them if the distress was justified. It was a second writ of replevin (Fitz.N.B. 68).

Second distress. A landlord has a power at common law to make a second distress for the same rent, but a second distress for the same rent is not to be made if there was enough which might have been taken on a first distress (*Hutchins* v. *Chambers* (1758) 1 Burr. 579).

Second mortgage, a mortgage or charge ranking after a prior mortgage or charge, *i.e.*, after a first mortgage.

Second surcharge, Writ of. If after admeasurement of common, upon a writ of admeasurement of pasture, the same defendant surcharged the common again, the plaintiff might have had this writ of second surcharge *de secunda superoneratione*, which was given by the Statute of Westminster II, 1285, c. 8.

Secondary, an officer who is next to the chief officer (2 Lil.Abr. 506).

The Secondary of the City of London was a permanent officer of the Corporation who held also the office of High Bailiff of Southwark. He occupied a position analogous to that of a sub-sheriff, and performed, in the name of the sheriffs, duties which would elsewhere devolve upon the sub-sheriff. Down to 1871 there were two Secondaries.

There were formerly a number of officers immediately subordinate to a principal officer who were described as Secondaries, there being the Secondary of the Fine Office, the Secondary of the Office of Privy Seal, Secondaries to the Clerks of the Crown and the Chief Clerk in the Court of King's Bench, etc. The Secondary to the Chief Clerk had a deputy. There are now deputy chairmen of the Board of Customs and Excise; such officers, if the ancient terminology were still used, would be the Secondaries of the Board of Customs and Excise.

Secondary conveyances, those which presuppose some other conveyance precedent, and only serve to confirm, alter, retain, restore, or transfer the interest granted by the original conveyance. They are otherwise called derivative, and are: releases, confirmations, surrenders, assignments and defeasances. See CONVEYANCE.

Secondary education. See EDUCATION.

Secondary evidence, that species of proof which is admitted on the loss of primary evidence. There are no degrees of this evidence; for example, if a letter is lost it may be as good to recite it from memory as to produce a copy. It is the province of the judge to decide whether a document produced is original or not, and until he decides it is not, no secondary evidence can be put in. See EVIDENCE; HEARSAY; NOTICE TO ADMIT; NOTICE TO PRODUCE.

Secondary use, a use limited to take effect in derogation of a preceding estate, otherwise called a shifting use, as a conveyance to the use of A and his heirs, with a proviso that when B returns to England, then to the use of C and his heirs.

Seconds, assistants at a duel. If either of the principals is killed, his adversary, and also the seconds, are all guilty of murder.

Secret. A solicitor, and also a barrister, is bound by law not to disclose his client's secrets; the same rule does not appear to apply as between medical men and their patients (*Kitson* v. *Playfair* (1896) *The Times*, March 28). As to privileged communications, however, the privilege is that of the client, not of the solicitor. The clerk of a professional or business man is under an implied contract not to disclose professional or trade secrets which he has learned in the course of his employment (*Merryweather* v. *Moore* [1892] 2 Ch. 518; *Amber Size & Chemical Co.* v. *Menzel* [1913] 2 Ch. 239).

As to official secrets, see OFFICIAL SECRETS. As to secrets of the confessional, see CONFESSION (TO PRIESTS).

As to secret commission, corruptly taken by an agent from the party with whom he is employed by his principal to transact business for such principal, see COMMISSION; CORRUPT PRACTICES.

Secret profits, profits made by an agent (*q.v.*), as such, for which he has not accounted to his principal.

Secret reserve, a reserve which is not disclosed in the accounts or balance sheet. The Companies Act, 1948, Sch. 8, contains provisions aimed at preventing the creation of secret reserves. See RESERVE.

Secret service. See the Civil List and Secret Service Money Act, 1782.

Secret trusts. Where a testator gives property to a person, on an express or implied promise by the legatee or devisee that he will hold it in trust for another person, this is called a secret trust (*Re Blackwell* [1929] A.C. 318). The rule is that if the secret trust would have been valid as an express trust it will be enforced against the legatee or devisee, while if it would have been invalid as an express trust, the gift fails altogether, so that neither the devisee or legatee, nor the object of the trust, takes any benefit by it.

Secretary, one entrusted with the management of business; one who writes for another; the head of a Government department; an officer of a company, or club, etc.

A modern company secretary is not a

mere clerk but an officer of the company with extensive duties and responsibilities, and he has ostensible authority to sign contracts connected with the administrative side of the company's affairs (*Panorama Developments (Guildford)* v. *Fidelis Furnishing Fabrics* [1971] 2 Q.B. 711). He is liable for misfeasance under the Companies Act, 1948, s. 333. He is entitled to preferential payment on account of salary in a winding up under the Companies Act, 1948, s. 319 (*Cairney* v. *Back* [1906] 2 K.B. 746). Every company must have a secretary and a sole director cannot also be secretary (s. 177).

Secretary at War, an official whose office dated from the reign of Charles II. He was always a member of one House of Parliament or the other, and had some control over army finances. He is to be distinguished from the Secretary of State (*q.v.*) for War, who took over his duties when the Colonial Office was formed in 1854. The office of Secretary at War was abolished by the Secretary at War Abolition Act, 1863.

Secretary of Bankrupts, an officer of the Lord Chancellor. His office was abolished by the statute 1852, 15 & 16 Vict. c. 77, s. 2.

Secretary of Decrees and Injunctions, one of the officials of the Court of Chancery whose office was abolished by the Court of Chancery Act, 1852, s. 23. The duties were performed in 1798 by a firm of law stationers, who acted as deputies for the holders of the office (*Commons Committees Reports*, 1803, Vol. 13, p. 260).

Secretary of Presentations. See PRESENTATION OFFICE.

Secretary of State. Acts of Parliament frequently speak of " the Secretary of State " as if there were only one. But the expression means " one of Her Majesty's Principal Secretaries of State for the time being," unless a contrary intention appears (Interpretation Act, 1889, s. 12 (3)). The principal Secretaries of State are the Secretary for Foreign and Commonwealth Affairs, for the Home Department, for the Environment, for Employment, for Energy, for Prices and Consumer Protection, for Social Services, for Industry, for Trade (who is also President of the Board of Trade), for Defence, for Education and Science, for Scotland, for Wales, and for Northern Ireland.

The salary of a Secretary of State is £13,000 a year provided that not more than twenty-one salaries are paid at the same time (Ministerial and other Salaries Act, 1975, s. 1,Sch. 1).

The first Secretary of State whom we know of was John Maunsell, in the reign of Henry III. The title Principal Secretary of State first occurs in 1476. Soon afterwards the Secretary of State ceased to be a mere writer of the royal orders and became a minister. The Secretary of State for the Home Department, or the Home Secretary, is the lineal official descendant of the original Secretary of State, and exercises all his functions which have not been specifically transferred to the Secretaries of State other than the Home Secretary. Until 1539 there was only one Principal Secretary of State; for the next two hundred years there were two, one for the Northern Department, who was concerned with the Northern European Powers, and the other, for the Southern Department, who was concerned with the other European Powers, domestic affairs, Ireland and the colonies.

From 1707 to 1746 there was a third Secretary of State, the Secretary of State for Scotland; and from 1768 to 1782 there was a fourth Secretary, the Secretary of State for the Colonies, the latter being, as regards the " plantations " (*q.v.*) the successor of the Board of Trade and Plantations (see BOARD OF TRADE), and being himself replaced in 1782 by the Home Secretary.

In 1782 the Northern Department became the Foreign Office, and the Southern Department became the Home Office with Ireland and the colonies under its charge. A Secretary of State for War was created in 1794, the colonies being put under his care. In 1854 two more Secretaries of State, one for India and the other for the colonies, were created, the Secretary for War being left with only the army to look after; the Secretary of State for Air was created by the Air Force (Constitution) Act, 1917, s. 8.

Down to 1921 the Home Office was,

in theory, the channel of commmunica-
tion between the Crown and the Lord
Lieutenant of Ireland, who, in theory,
was responsible for the government of
that country, but the Home Office had in
fact nothing to do with Ireland.

Each Secretary of State can do anything which any one of the others is
empowered to do; but for purposes of
administrative convenience each of them
confines himself to such matters as
properly appertain to his own department.

Secretary of the Briefs, an officer
(receiving about £80 a year in fees) of the
Court of Chancery whose duty it was to
make out briefs for applicants (*Commons
Committees Reports,* 1803, Vol. 13, p.
262). The brief was a process commanding the sheriff to summon or attach a
defendant (*Termes de la Ley*).

Secta [Lat. *sequendo*], a suit; the
witnesses or followers of a plaintiff; a
following. The word was chiefly used to
denote a service, due by custom or prescription, which obliged the inhabitants of
a particular place to make use of a mill,
oven, kiln or similar structure (*secta ad
molendinum, ad furnum, ad torrale,* etc.).
In such a case the owner of the mill, oven
or kiln had an action against any
inhabitant who " withdrew his suit," that
is, went to another mill, oven or kiln.
The theory was that the mill or other
structure had been erected by the ancestors of the owner for the convenience
of the inhabitants, on condition that
they should use it to the exclusion of
any other (3 Bl.Comm. 235).

In the old common law practice, *secta*
meant the followers or witnesses whom
the plaintiff brought into court with him
to prove his case. The actual production
of the *secta* had been disused since the
reign of Edward III; but the declaration
in every action contained a fictitious
statement on the subject, until comparatively modern times (Potter, Leg.Inst.
254).

Secta ad curiam, De, a writ which lay
against one who failed to perform suit
at the sheriff's county court or at the
court baron.

Secta ad furnum, suit to a public
oven, or bakehouse.

Secta ad justiciam faciendam, a service

which a man was bound to perform by
his fee (Bract.).

Secta ad molendinum, a writ which
lay where a man, by usage, had ground
his corn at the mill of a certain person,
and afterwards went to another mill with
his corn, thereby withdrawing his suit
to the former (Fitz.N.B. 123).

It was abolished by the Real Property
Limitation Act, 1833, s. 36.

Secta ad torrale, suit to a kiln or malt-
house.

Secta curiae, suit and service done by
tenants at the court of the lord (Cowel).

**Secta facienda per illam qui habet
enitiam partem, De,** a writ which lay to
compel the eldest of coparceners to perform suit and service for the others. The
eldest had the *enitia pars* (*q.v.*) (Reg.
Brev. 177).

Secta non faciendis, a writ for a woman
who, for her dower, did not have to
perform suit of court (Reg.Brev. 174).

**Secta quae scripto nititur a scripto
variari non debet** (Jenk., Cent. 65). (A
suit which is based upon a writing ought
not to vary from the writing.)

Secta regalis, the obligation to attend
twice a year at the sheriff's tourn, which
was in theory the king's leet.

**Secta unica tantum facienda pro pluri-
bus haereditatibus,** a writ under which a
man was exempted from doing more than
one suit and service in respect of lands
which he held of one lord, not as the heir
of one person, but as the heir of several.

Sectares, bidders at an auction (Civil
Law).

Sectatores, suitors of court, who
amongst the Saxons, gave their judgment
or verdict in civil suits upon the matter
of fact and law (1 Reeve 22).

Sectis non faciendis, De, a writ of
exemption from suit and service which
lay for a doweress (Reg.Orig. 174).

Secular, not spiritual; relating to
affairs of the present world (*in seculo*).

Secular clergy, parochial clergy who
performed their ministry *in seculo,* and
were contradistinguished from the regular
clergy, who lived in monasteries, by
rules (*regulae*).

Secunda superoneratione pasturae, De,
a writ which lay where one against whom
a writ of admeasurement had been sued
out again surcharged the common

1623

(Statute of Westminster II, 1285, c. 8). See SECOND SURCHARGE, WRIT OF; SURCHARGE.

Secundum naturam est, commoda cujusque rei eum sequi, quem sequuntur incommoda (D. 50, 17, 10). (It is natural that the advantages of anything should follow him who the disadvantages follow.) See QUI SENTIT, ETC.

Secundum statutum. See APPEARANCE, SEC. STAT.

Secundum subjectam materiam, with reference to the subject-matter. The meaning of a word or phrase is often governed by the context.

Secured creditor. See CREDITOR.

Secured debts. See DEBT.

Securitate pacis, De, a writ of security for the peace which issued out of the Chancery for anyone threatened with death or bodily harm by another (Reg. Orig. 98).

The modern procedure is to bind to the peace before a justice.

Securitatem inveniendi quod se non divertat ad partes exteras sine licentia regis, De. Anciently the king could issue against any man a writ requiring him to find security that he would not betake himself to foreign parts without licence from the king. It was superseded by the writ *ne exeat regno* (*q.v.*) (Fitz.N.B. 115).

Security, something which makes the enjoyment or enforcement of a right more secure or certain.

A security may be a personal security; or a security on property (called in jurisprudence a real security); or a judicial security.

A personal security consists in a promise or obligation by the debtor or another person, in addition to the original liability or obligation intended to be secured. Sometimes the security consists of an instrument which facilitates the enforcement of the original obligation or extends its duration, as in the case of a bond, bill of exchange, promissory note, etc., given by a debtor for an existing debt, the liability on such instruments being easy of proof. When the security consists of a promise or obligation entered into by a third person it generally takes the form of a guarantee (*q.v.*), bond, promissory note, or the like. See SURETY.

A security on property is where a right over property exists, by virtue of which the enforcement of a liability or promise is facilitated or made more certain. This is of two kinds, active and passive. An active security is where the creditor (or promisee) has the right of selling the property for the purpose of satisfying his claim, as in the case of a pledge or a mortgage with a power of sale. A mortgage of a freehold interest in land is sometimes called a real security, as opposed to a security on leaseholds or other personalty. A passive security is where the creditor has the right of keeping the property until his claim is satisfied, but not of selling it; such are possessory liens. Between these two classes stand certain rights which entitle the holder to take proceedings to have the property dealt with so as to satisfy his claim; such are charges in the restricted sense of that word. (See CHARGE; HYPOTHECATION.) The important characteristic of a security on property is that in the event of the debtor being bankrupt, absconding or dying the right can nevertheless be enforced by means of the property. See CREDITOR.

Securities on property are also either specific or shifting. Thus, an ordinary mortgage on land is a security on specific property; the mortgagor can deal only with the land subject to the mortgage, and the mortgagee does not by his mortgage acquire any right to other property belonging to the mortgagor. A shifting or floating security, on the other hand, is a security on all property which comes under a certain description at the time when the rights of the parties have to be ascertained. Thus, a mortgage or bill of sale on fixtures, machinery or the like, in a given building, may be so framed as to cover articles of a like description placed in the building after the date of the security, with or without a clause empowering the mortgagor to take away any articles and replace them by others of equal value (*Holroyd* v. *Marshall* (1862) 10 H.L.C. 191). So a debenture may form a charge on the property for the time being of a company, including stock in trade or book debts, etc.; so that it may sell its stock in trade and buy new stock in trade, or receive book debts and create new ones in such a way that, when the time comes for enforcing the security, the property then subject to it may be quite different from what it was when the security was given. As soon as proceedings are taken which necessitate an enforcement of the security (*e.g.*, if the company goes into liquidation), the security becomes fixed, and no further change is possible (*Re Panama Co.* (1870) L.R. 5 Ch. 318).

A judicial security exists where a right is enforceable by means of the powers vested in a court of law. Thus, a judgment is enforceable by execution against the property, and (in some cases) against the person of the defendant; and, therefore, a judgment creditor who has taken the proper steps to enforce his judgment is a secured creditor. (See CREDITOR; JUDGMENT.) To this class may also be referred cognovits, warrants of attorney, garnishee orders, stop orders, charging orders and notices in lieu of distringas.

With reference to its origin, a security is either created by agreement of the parties or by operation of law; a mortgage or bond is an instance of the former class, a retaining lien of the latter.

With reference to the purpose for which they are created, securities may be divided into ordinary securities, namely, those created to secure the payment of a debt or the performance of an obligation between private persons; and securities given in legal proceedings. Securities given in legal proceedings are of various kinds.

In ordinary actions, security is in some cases required to be given to secure a right in question in the litigation; to this class belong stop orders, proceedings in lieu of distringas, attachment of debts, payment of money and transfer of stock into court, and deposit of property in court. In criminal and summary proceedings the defendant or prisoner is sometimes allowed to go at large on giving bail or entering into his own recognisance, instead of being detained in custody. (See BAIL.) A person may also be required to give security to keep the peace. See ARTICLES OF THE PEACE; BREACH OF THE PEACE; RECOGNISANCE.

Security is sometimes required to be given in relation to the proceedings themselves. See SECURITY FOR COSTS.

As to security on removing causes from inferior course, see REMOVAL.

In a secondary sense, " security " denotes an instrument by which a security is created or evidenced, such as a bond, bill of exchange, debenture, scrip, etc. See NEGOTIABLE INSTRUMENTS; STOCK.

Security for costs. In certain cases a plaintiff, before proceeding with his action, may be required to give security for the costs of it (R.S.C., Ord. 23, rr. 1, 3). The principal cases in which security may be required are the following: where the plaintiff is resident abroad, but if he resides in Scotland or Northern Ireland security will not be required: *aliter*, if in the Republic of Ireland (*Wakely* v. *Triumph Cycle Co.* (1924) 40 T.L.R. 15); where he misdescribes his residence, or is keeping out of the way; where he is only a nominal plaintiff and is insolvent; where he is a privileged person, *e.g.*, an ambassador's servant (*Goodwin* v. *Archer* (1727) 2 P. & W. 452), but not an ambassador (*Duke de Montellano* v. *Christin* (1816) 5 M. & S. 503); where the plaintiff is a limited company (Companies Act, 1948, s. 447). But security cannot be required from a plaintiff on the mere ground of poverty or insolvency; or from a defendant, unless by reason of a counterclaim he is really in the position of a plaintiff; or from a person compelled to litigate. Security for costs may extend as well to past as future costs.

In any cause or matter in which security for costs is required the security is to be of such an amount, and be given at such times, and in such manner and form, as the court directs (R.S.C., Ord. 23, r. 2).

As to security for the costs of an appeal, see Ord. 59, r. 10 (5).

Security for good behaviour. See BREACH OF THE PEACE; SURETIES OF THE PEACE AND GOOD BEHAVIOUR.

Secus, otherwise.

Sede plena, when a bishop's see is not vacant.

Sederunt, Acts of, ordinances of the Court of Session in Scotland, made originally under authority of the Scots

Act of 1540, c. 93, and later enabling Acts, which may be said to be equivalent to the *regulae generales* of the English courts. Acts of Sederunt regulate procedure in Scots litigation, terms of membership of legal societies, etc.

Sedition, the offence of publishing orally or otherwise any words or document with the intention of exciting disaffection, hatred or contempt against the sovereign, or the government and constitution of the kingdom, or either House of Parliament, or the administration of justice, or of exciting persons to attempt, otherwise than by lawful means, the alteration of any matter in Church or State, or of exciting feelings of ill-will and hostility between different classes.

If the matter so published consists of words spoken the offence is called the speaking of seditious words. If it is contained in a document or the like, the offence is called a seditious libel.

A seditious conspiracy is where two or more person agree to do any act for the furtherance of any seditious intention.

Sedition is an offence against the Crown and government, not capital and not amounting to treason.

On a verdict or judgment by default against any person for composing, printing or publishing any seditious libel tending to bring into hatred or contempt the person of the sovereign or the government and constitution of the United Kingdom as by law established or either House of Parliament, or to excite the public to attempt the alteration of any matter in Church or State as by law established otherwise than by lawful means, the court may make an order for the seizure of all copies of the libel, etc. (Criminal Libel Act, 1819, s. 1).

Political meetings of more than fifty persons within one mile of Westminster Hall, except for parliamentary election purposes, are unlawful on any day on which Parliament is sitting (Seditious Meetings Act, 1817, s. 23).

Taking or administering oaths for a seditious purpose is unlawful (Unlawful Oaths Acts, 1797 and 1812).

Seducing to leave service, an injury for which a master may have an action for damages. See LABOURERS, STATUTE OF.

Seduction, inducing a girl or woman to part with her virtue (*R.* v. *Moon* [1910] 1 K.B. 818). An action of seduction could be brought by a parent or person standing *in loco parentis* for enticing away or debauching the girl *per quod servitium amisit* (*Evans* v. *Walton* (1867) L.R. 2 C.P. 615). The cause of action was abolished by the Law Reform (Miscellaneous Provisions) Act, 1970, s. 5.

See [Lat. *sedes*], the diocese of a bishop.

Seeds. The sale of seeds is controlled by regulations made by the Minister of Agriculture, Fisheries and Food. The Minister controls the importation of seeds (Plant Varieties and Seeds Act, 1964, ss. 16–41; Agriculture (Miscellaneous Provisions Act) 1968, ss. 43, 52, Schs. 7, 8; Trade Descriptions Act, 1968, s. 41, Sch. 2; European Communities Act, 1972, s. 4, Sch. 3 Pt. III, Sch. 4 para. 5 Sch. 7.

Seignior, or **Seigneur,** a lord of a fee or manor or seignory (*q.v.*). A seignior in gross was a lord without a manor, simply enjoying superiority and services.

Seigniorage, a royalty or prerogative of the Crown, whereby an allowance of gold and silver, brought in the mass to be exchanged for coin, is claimed; the profit made at the Mint on the coinage of money. The levying of a duty on all coined money was one of the royal prerogatives. Edward III is stated to have levied a duty of five shillings for coining a pound weight of gold. The statute 1421, 9 Hen. 5, st. 2, c. 2, gave the king seigniorages of five shillings for coining a pound weight of gold, and of fifteen pence for coining a pound weight of silver. The statute 1666, 18 Car. 2, c. 5, s. 1, put an end to seigniorages by providing that all gold and silver brought to the Mint should be coined without any charge for assaying and coining. Since then no seigniorage has been charged on gold: but the statute, 1816, 56 Geo. 3, c. 68, s. 9, provided that for the coining of every pound weight of silver the Mint should charge four shillings. The Acts of 1666 and 1816 were repealed by the Coinage Act, 1870 s. 20, which, while providing that all gold coin brought to the Mint should be assayed and coined free of charge (s. 8), provided that the Mint might issue silver coins of the weight and fineness set out in the First Schedule, the effect being that the Mint could purchase silver at such a price in the open market that there was always a profit on the silver coinage. In 1870 there was a profit of about 9 per cent.; and in 1906 the price of silver was so low that there was about 112 per cent. But the war of 1914–18 caused such an increase in the price of silver that silver coin was being coined at a very heavy loss to the Mint. The Coinage Act, 1920, put an end to that state of things by providing that silver coins instead of being, as they were under the Act of 1870, thirty-seven parts of silver to three parts of alloy, should be half silver and half alloy; and this had the effect of again giving the Mint a profit on the coinage of silver. The Coinage Act, 1946, substituted cupro-nickel, an alloy containing three parts of copper and one part of nickel, for the silver coinage. The cupro-nickel coins issued now are of the denominations of fifty, ten and five new pence.

Bronze coinage has always been merely token money, and until recent times there has always been a profit on it to the Mint. It was unknown before 1660. The question of the prerogative right to seigniorage never arose in connection with it.

See COIN; COPPER COINS.

Seignory, a manor or lordship; the relation of a feudal lord to his tenant, and to the land held by him. If before the statute *Quia Emptores,* 1289 (*q.v.*), A, a tenant in fee simple, conveyed his land to B to hold of A as his tenant, then A's rights against B in respect of services, fealty, etc., and his interest in the land in the event of an escheat or forfeiture by B or his successors in title, would constitute a seignory. Since the statute *Quia Emptores,* 1289, no seignory can be created. Owing to the feudal incidents of tenure (fealty, etc.) having now become obsolete, and to the rent services anciently reserved having become almost valueless, seignories in freehold land are seldom of any practical importance; in most cases indeed they cannot be traced. Consequently almost the only seignories now in existence are those of lords of manors, for a manor does not

exist unless there are at least two free tenants, that is, tenants of freehold land forming part of the manor who hold of the lord by a service of some kind. Hence a manor is sometimes said to consist of demesnes and seignories.

A seignory is sometimes distinguished by the services incident to it, *e.g.*, a seignory by fealty and rent service; or by the position of the lord *e.g.*, seignories paramount and mesne seignories. (See MESNE; PARAMOUNT). A seignory may also be either appendant, that is, attached to a manor; or in gross, when it has been severed from the manor to which it originally belonged. On the conveyance of a manor the seignories appendant to it pass with it; a seignory in gross must be conveyed by a deed of grant, a seignory being an incorporeal hereditament. Originally a seignory differed but little from a reversion.

Seignory sometimes means the land or district over which the rights of the lord extend. See FRANCHISE; LIBERTY.

Seised in demesne as of fee. See DEMESNE.

Seisin [Old Ger. *bisazjan*; Ang.Sax. *biseltan,* to take possession of, beset; Old Fr. *saisir*; Late Lat. *sacire, saisire,* to take possession of land; Fr. *seisine,* possession of land], feudal possession; the relation in which a person stands to land or other hereditaments when he has in them an estate of freehold in possession; such a person is said to be seised of the land (Co.Litt. 266b, 330b).

Seisin is opposed (1) to possession, which, in its technical sense, is only applied to leaseholds and other personal property; and (2) to occupation, which signifies actual possession (Williams, *Seisin.* See OCCUPATION; POSSESSION.

Seisin was possession of such an estate in land as was anciently thought worthy to be held by a free man (*Leach* v. *Jay* (1878) 9 Ch.D. 42; *Copestake* v. *Hoper* [1908] 2 Ch. 10; *Thackray* v. *Norman* [1914] W.N. 303).

With reference to its nature, seisin is either actual, or in law. Actual seisin, or seisin in deed, is where the freeholder is himself in possession or occupation of the land, or where it is occupied by a person claiming under him, and not having an estate of freehold in the land, *e.g.*, a lessee for years (Co.Litt. 15a).

Seisin in law is that seisin which an heir had when his ancestor died intestate seised of land and neither the heir nor any other person had taken actual possession of the land. Thus, if a man had two farms, Blackacre and Whiteacre, the former of which he let to a tenant for years, and the latter he occupied himself then, on his death intestate, his heir had actual seisin of Blackacre from the moment of the death, because the possession of the tenant was looked upon as the possession of the freeholder; but of Whiteacre the heir had merely a seisin in law until he entered and took possession, and then he had actual seisin of Whiteacre too. The term "seisin in law" was sometimes applied to the interest of a reversioner or remainderman expectant on an estate of freehold, but inaccurately, because the seisin was in the tenant of the estate of freehold. Actual seisin of incorporeal hereditaments is obtained by exercising the rights of which they consist, *e.g.*, receiving a rentcharge or presenting to an advowson (Litt. 235, 565).

With reference to the nature of the property, a tenant in fee simple is said to be seised in his demesne as of fee of such things whereof a man may have manual occupation, possession or receipt, as of lands, tenements, rents and such like. But of such things as do not lie in such manual occupation, etc., as of an advowson of a church and such like, there he was said to be seised as of fee and not in his demesne as of fee. The distinction was of importance only under the old system of pleading (Litt. 10). See DEMESNE.

Since the abolition of the rules as to descent cast and *seisina facit stipitem* (*q.v.*), and the introduction of modern forms of conveyance, which do not require livery of seisin (*q.v.*) the doctrine of seisin has lost almost all its importance. Under the old law, when an heir obtained seisin of land on the death of his ancestor, and then himself died intestate, the land went to his heirs and not to the heirs of his ancestor. This was called a mesne seisin, because it was intermediate between the two deaths, and

the heir was called a mesne heir or mesne person. See POSSESSIO FRATRIS.

Another kind of seisin was simple seisin, namely, that nominal or formal possession which a lord was entitled to take on the death of a tenant in fee simple in order to assert his right of seignory, as opposed to the full or beneficial seisin of the tenant's heir (Brit. 178b).

Quasi-seisin was the possession which a copyholder had of the land to which he had been admitted. The freehold in copyhold lands being in the lord, the copyholder could not have seisin of them in the proper sense of the word, but he had a customary or quasi-seisin, analogous to that of a freeholder.

Equitable seisin is analogous to legal seisin, that is, it is seisin of an equitable estate in land. Thus, a mortgagor is said to have equitable seisin of the land by receipt of the rents. See DISSEISIN; POSSESSION. Actual possession, clothed with the receipt of the rents and profits, is the highest instance of an equitable seisin.

Seisin, Covenant for. In a conveyance of an estate in fee simple this was a covenant to the effect that the vendor was, at the date of the conveyance, seised of a good and indefeasible estate of inheritance in fee simple. This came in course of time to be generally omitted, as it was always followed by a covenant for the right to convey in fee simple; and the latter covenant was in itself sufficient for all purposes. See COVENANT.

Seisin, Livery of, formal delivery of possession, called by the feudists investiture of a fee or feudal estate. It was applicable to corporeal hereditaments, while incorporeal hereditaments such as a remainder or easement were conveyed by writing under seal. After the Real Property Act, 1845, s. 2, all corporeal hereditaments might be conveyed by deed, and by the Law of Property Act, 1925, s. 25, conveyance by livery of seisin was abolished. See FEOFFMENT.

Seisina facit stipitem (6 Fleta 14). (Seisin makes the stock of descent.) Before the Inheritance Act, 1833, the rule of intestate succession to real estate was that descent must be traced from the person last seised, i.e., in possession. The

Inheritance Act 1833, enacted that descent should be traced from the last purchaser, *i.e.*, the last person entitled who did not inherit (see PURCHASE), and the rule is still applicable in ascertaining the heir under equitable limitations provided for by the Law of Property Act, 1925, ss. 130–132, and the Administration of Estates Act, 1925, s. 51. See DESCENT; NON JUS, ETC.

Seisina habenda, a writ for delivery of seisin to the lord of lands and tenements, after the sovereign, in right of his prerogative, had had the year, day and waste on a felony committed, etc. (Reg.Brev. 165).

The fuller title of the writ was *de seisina habenda quia rex habuit annum, diem, et vastum* (for having seisin because the king was entitled to a year, a day and waste).

Seizure. In the law of copyholds, seizure was where the lord of copyhold lands took possession of them in default of a tenant. It was either seizure *quousque*, or absolute seizure. When a copyhold tenant died intestate, his heir was bound to come to the lord for admittance within a certain time, and pay the fine on admittance; if he did not appear, the lord might seize the land *quousque* (*i.e.*, " until " he did appear), and enjoy the rents and profits in the meantime. Where the lord seized land for a forfeiture, escheat, etc., this was an absolute seizure. The lord might also take heriots by seizure, and the same remedy was given for things lying in franchise, as waifs, wrecks, estrays, etc.

In the law of procedure, seizure is sometimes a species of execution. Thus, a sheriff executes a writ of *fi. fa.* by taking possession of the chattels of the debtor. (See FIERI FACIAS.) Seizure also takes place when goods are confiscated as a punishment for smuggling or carrying contraband of war.

In international law, seizure means the provisional detention of ships or cargo by a belligerent, subject to confirmation by a prize court, as distinct from capture.

Sel, denotes the bigness of a thing to which it is added, as *Selwood*, a big wood.

Selborne's (Lord) Act, the Powers of Appointment Act, 1874.

Selda [Sax. *selde*, a seat], a shop, shed or stall in a market; a wood of sallows or willows; also a saw-pit (Co.Litt. 4).

Selden. John Selden was born in 1584, and died in 1654. He wrote *Mare clausum*, proving that the sovereignty over the narrow seas had been exercised from the earliest times by England, in reply to the *De mari libero* of Grotius, who disputed the English claims. Selden wrote also *Dissertatio historica ad Fletam*; *Notes on Fortescue*; and other works on tithes, titles of honour, etc.

Select committee. See COMMITTEE.

Select vestry, a vestry consisting of not less than twelve nor more than 120 householders, elected in parishes adopting the Vestries Act, 1831, known as Hobhouse's Act, which was repealed (except s. 39, as to charity estates), so far as it related to parish meetings in rural parishes, by the Local Government Act, 1894.

The Select Vestries Bill is the title of a Bill always formally read a first time in the House of Lords at the beginning of a new session before the House proceeds to debate the king's or queen's speech, as an assertion of its independence. The corresponding Bill in the House of Commons is the Outlawries Bill, for the more effectual preventing of clandestine outlawries. No further steps are taken on either Bill.

Selecti judices, Roman judges returned by the praetor, drawn by lot, and subject to be challenged, and sworn like our juries (3 Bl.Comm. 366).

Selective employment tax (S.E.T.). This was a tax imposed by the Finance Act, 1966, s. 44, read with the Selective Employment Payments Act, 1966. It was abolished by the Finance Act, 1972, s. 122.

Self-build society means a housing association (see HOUSING SOCIETIES) whose object is to provide for sale to, or occupation by, its members, dwellings built or improved principally with the use of its members' own labour (Housing Act, 1974, s. 12). For tax relief see s. 120.

Self-defence. Life and limb are of such high value in the estimation of the law that it pardons even homicide if committed *se defendendo*, or in order to preserve them. See DEFENCE; HOMICIDE.

Self-defence may be pleaded on a

charge of making an affray (*q.v.*) (*R.* v. *Sharp,* [1957] 1 Q.B. 552).

Self-help, action by an injured party to obtain redress without recourse to a court. See ABATEMENT OF NUISANCE.

Self-incrimination. See CRIMINAL EVIDENCE.

Self-murder. See FELO DE SE.

Selion of land [Fr. *sillon*], a ridge of ground rising between two furrows, containing no certain quantity (*Termes de la Ley*).

Seliones were strips into which the open fields (*q.v.*), before the general inclosure of the country, were divided (Seebohm, *Village Community*).

Semble, it appears. Used in judgments and textbooks to introduce a proposition of law which is not intended to be stated definitely.

Semestria, the collected decisions of the emperors in their half-yearly councils (Civil Law).

Seminaufragium, half shipwreck, as where goods are cast overboard in a storm; also, where a ship has been so much damaged that her repair would cost more than her worth. See CONSTRUCTIVE TOTAL LOSS.

Semi-plena probatio, a semi-proof; the testimony of one person, upon which the civilians would not allow any sentence to be founded. See UNUS NULLUS RULE.

Semper in dubiis benigniora praeferenda (11 Moo.P.C.C. 343). (In doubtful matters the more liberal construction should always be preferred.)

Semper in obscuris, quod minimum est sequimur (D. 50, 17, 9). (In obscure matters we should always follow that which is the least obscure.) But where the words of a document are obscure to such a degree that they have no meaning, the court will not invent a meaning. See AMBIGUITY.

Semper ita fiat relatio ut valeat dispositio (6 Co.Rep. 76). (A word is, if possible, always made to relate back to antecedent words in such a way as to give effect to a disposition in a will.) This maxim is part of a much longer maxim quoted in connection with the construction of a will.

Semper paratus, always ready. In an action of assumpsit (*q.v.*) the form in which tender was pleaded was known as a *semper paratus.* See UNCORE PRIST.

Semper praesumitur pro legitimatione puerorum; et filiatio non potest probari (Bract.; Co.Litt. 126a). (The presumption is always in favour of the legitimacy of children; and filiation cannot be proved.) See FILIATIO NON, ETC.

Semper praesumitur pro matrimonio. (The presumption is always in favour of the validity of a marriage.) See MARRIAGE.

Semper praesumitur pro negante (10 Cl. & F. 907). (The presumption is always in favour of the negative.) On an equal division of votes in the House of Lords the question passes in the negative (*R.* v. *Millis* (1884) 10 Cl. & F. 634; *Paquin* v. *Beauclerk* [1906] A.C. 148). If the court is equally divided (as in *R.* v. *Archbishop of Canterbury* (1848) 11 Q.B. 483, on the question whether the opposition to the confirmation of a bishop was merely formal or not) things remain as they were before the court was applied to; *e.g.*, a rule for a mandamus is discharged. See PARIBUS SENTENTIIS, ETC.

Semper specialia generalibus insunt (D. 50, 17, 147). (Specialities are always included in generalities.) See GENERALIA SPECIALIBUS, ETC.; MAJUS CONTINET, ETC.; SPECIALIA GENERALIBUS, ETC.

Sen, justice (Co.Litt. 61a).

Senage, money paid for synodals.

Senate of the Inns of Court and the Bar. This was constituted by resolution at an Extraordinary General Meeting of the Bar on June 3, 1974. It came into being at the end of July, 1974. The officers of the Senate are the President, the Chairman, the Vice-Chairman and the Treasurer. The members are the Attorney-General, the Solicitor-General and the Chairman of the Council of Legal Education for the time being *ex officio,* twenty-four Bench representatives appointed by the Benchers of the four Inns of Court (*q.v.*), twelve hall representatives elected by the subscribing hall members of the Inns of Court, thirty-nine Bar representatives elected by members of the Bar and not more than twelve additional members appointed by the Senate.

The Senate has the following standing committees: Executive Committee,

Finance Committee, Accommodation Committee, Planning Committee, Library Committee, Law Reform Committee, Consolidated Regulations and Transfer Committee, Trust Funds Committee, Chambers Loans Sub-Committee, and Benchers Sub-Committee. In addition there is a Steering Committee consisting of the officers and chairmen of the principal committees of the Senate and the Bar Council, which meets weekly during term time.

Other committees may be constituted by the Executive Committee. At least one meeting of the Senate must be held in or immediately before each Sittings (*q.v.*).

Within the framework of the Senate there is a new Bar Council which is an autonomous body for the purposes of its separate powers and functions in the performance of which it is not subject to any direction of the Senate. It is its duty to maintain the standards, honour and independence of the Bar, to promote, preserve and improve the services and functions of the Bar, and to represent and act for the Bar generally as well in its relations with others and also in all matters affecting the administration of justice. The officers of the Bar Council are the Chairman and Vice-Chairman of the Senate. The members are the Treasurer of the Senate, the Attorney-General, the Solicitor-General and the leader of each circuit (or his deputy) for the time being, *ex officio* and the Bar representatives to the Senate. Not more than twelve members may be co-opted. Committees of the Bar Council are: Bar Committee, Professional Conduct Committee, International Relations Committee, Young Barristers' Committee, Fees and Legal Aid Committee, Taxation and Retirement Benefits Committee.

The functions of the Professional Conduct Committee are to investigate and sift complaints, to prefer and prosecute disciplinary charges and to make recommendations on matters of professional conduct and etiquette to the Bar Committee of the Bar Council. Any charge of professional misconduct against a barrister is heard and determined by an *ad hoc* Committee of the Senate. Professional misconduct includes any conduct unbecoming a barrister.

The Council of Legal Education is reconstituted and continues as an educational charity on behalf of the Inns of Court. The Chairman is a person elected by the Senate. The Dean of the Council of Legal Education for the time being is an *ex officio* member. The other members are twelve members of the Senate. There is power to co-opt members.

The offices of the Senate are at 11 South Square Gray's Inn.

Senators of the College of Justice. The judges of the Court of Session in Scotland are Senators of the College of Justice; see the Scots Act of 1540, c. 93.

Senatus consulta (ordinances of the senate), public Acts among the Romans, which regarded the whole community; abbreviated S.C.

Senatus decreta (decisions of the senate), private Acts among the Romans, which concerned particular persons or personal matters.

Seneschal [Old Ger. *sein,* a house; *schale,* an office], a steward; also one who has the dispensing of justice (Co. Litt. 61a; Kitch. 13; Cooke's Jurisp. 102).

The High Seneschal was the Lord High Steward (*q.v.*), and the *Seneschal de la Hotel de Roy* was the Lord Steward of the King's Household.

Seneschallo et mareshallo quod non teneant placita de libero tenemento, a writ which lay to the Court of the Marshalsea (*q.v.*) prohibiting it from entertaining any action relating to freehold (Reg.Brev. 185).

Seneucia, widowhood.

Seney-days, play-days, or times of pleasure and diversion.

Senior. The expression " senior counsel " (or " senior ") means a barrister who is a Queen's Counsel. See JUNIOR.

Sense (of words). See SECUNDUM SUBJECTAM MATERIAM.

Sensu honesto, to interpret words *sensu honesto* is to take them so as not to impute impropriety to the persons concerned.

Sentence, a definite judgment pronounced in a criminal proceeding. The length of a sentence for a common law offence is at large and in the discretion of the court (*Verrier* v. *D.P.P.* [1967] 2 A.C. 195). In the case of indictable offences except murder, on conviction of which the court is bound to pronounce a sentence of imprisonment for life (see CAPITAL OFFENCES; CAPITAL PUNISHMENT), and treason, the extent of the sentence is within a given maximum left to the discretion of the court, such few maximum sentences as previously were enjoined having been abolished by the Penal Servitude Act, 1891.

A sentence imposed, or other order made by the Crown Court (*q.v.*) takes effect from the beginning of the day on which it is imposed unless the court otherwise directs. The Crown Court has power to vary a sentence or order within twenty-eight days of imposing or making it (Courts Act, 1971, s. 11). A magistrates' court has a similar power to vary within fourteen days (Criminal Justice Act, 1972, s. 41).

The Crown Court or a magistrates' court may defer (for a maximum of six months) passing sentence on an offender for the purpose of enabling the court to have regard to his conduct after conviction and where appropriate the making by him of reparation for his offence and to any change in his circumstances. Deferment requires the consent of the offender (see *R.* v. *Fairhead* [1975] 2 All E.R. 737). The power of the Crown Court to bind over an offender to come up for judgment (see BIND OVER) is unaffected (Powers of Criminal Courts Act, 1973, s. 1; *R.* v. *Crosby* (1975) 60 Cr.App.R. 234). But where a court defers passing sentence, it has no power at the same time to make a common law bind over order or make any order in respect of a suspended sentence (*R.* v. *Dwyer* (1974) 60 Cr.App.R. 39) or commit the offender for sentence to a Crown Court (*R.* v. *Birtles* [1975] 1 W.L.R. 1623).

Powers of absolute or conditional discharge are conferred by ss. 7, 12, 13. As to further offences, see s. 8. As to breach of a conditional discharge by a young offender, see s. 9. A conditional dis-charge may be substituted for probation (s. 11).

Where an offender is convicted on indictment of an offence against any enactment he may be sent to prison for not more than two years in the absence of specific provisions for imprisonment. An attempt is not to be punished more severely than the substantive offence (s. 18). As to imprisonment of persons under seventeen or under twenty-one years of age, see YOUNG OFFENDERS.

An offender is not to be sentenced to imprisonment, Borstal training or detention in a detention centre if he is not legally represented unless he has had the opportunity to obtain legal aid (Powers of Criminal Courts Act, 1973, s. 21).

Suspended sentences of imprisonment may be passed under the Powers of Criminal Courts Act, 1973, ss. 22–27.

See FINE; FIRST OFFENDERS; PERSISTENT OFFENDERS.

By the Infanticide Act, 1938 (as amended by the Criminal Law Act, 1967, Sch. 3 Pt. III), in certain cases a verdict of infanticide may be returned notwithstanding that the circumstances were such that, but for the Act, they would have amounted to murder.

Formerly, in sentencing any misdemeanant to imprisonment without hard labour, the court might order him to be treated as a misdemeanant of the first division of misdemeanants, and not as a criminal prisoner (Prison Act, 1865, s. 67), and the Prison Act, 1898, s. 6, provided for prisoners being divided into three divisions. Hard labour and prison divisions were abolished, together with penal servitude, by the Criminal Justice Act, 1948, s. 1, and imprisonment substituted.

The Children and Young Persons Act, 1933, s. 53 (1) (as substituted by the Murder (Abolition of Death Penalty) Act, 1965, s. 1 (5)), provides that sentence of imprisonment for life is not to be imposed on a person under the age of eighteen at the time the offence was committed nor shall sentence of death be pronounced or recorded against such person, but in lieu thereof the court shall sentence him to be detained during Her Majesty's pleasure.

The Sentence of Death (Expectant

Mothers) Act, 1931, s. 1, provides that where a woman convicted of an offence punishable with death is found to be pregnant, the sentence to be passed on her shall be a sentence of imprisonment for life instead of sentence of death.

Upon a conviction on indictment of several offences, whether on separate indictments or on separate counts in the one indictment, the court may, in general, order that the sentences be either consecutive or concurrent. Where a prisoner is convicted of several offences the judge has a discretion to award consecutive sentences which total more than the maximum permitted for any one of the offences taken by itself. In exercising that discretion no account should be taken of possible remission for good conduct (*R.* v. *Blake* [1962] 2 Q.B. 377).

Sentence in ecclesiastical procedure is analogous to judgment (*q.v.*) in an ordinary action. A definitive sentence is one which puts an end to the suit as regards the principal matter in question.

An interlocutory sentence determines only some incidental matter in the proceedings.

See DECREE.

Sententia contra matrimoniam nunquam transit in rem judicatam (7 Co. Rep. 43). (A sentence against marriage never becomes *res judicata*.) But this maxim is cited merely in argument, and it is, in fact, the reverse of the truth; for the judgment of a matrimonial court is conclusive.

Sententia interlocutoria revocari potest, definitiva non potest (Bac.Max. 20). (An interlocutory sentence may be recalled, but not a final.) This was a rule of the civil law. See ACTUS INCEPTUS, ETC.

Sententia non fertur de non liquidis (Jenk., Cent. 7). (A court does not decide except upon clearly defined points.) See OPORTET, ETC.

Separaliter [Lat.], separatively or distributively.

Separate estate. The common law did not allow a married woman to possess any property independently of her husband, but when property was settled to her separate use and benefit, equity treated her, in respect to that property, as a *feme sole*, or unmarried woman. A wife's separate property might be acquired by a pre-nuptial contract with her husband, or by gift, either from the husband or from any other person.

Where property was given to a married woman to her separate use absolutely (*i.e.*, without a limitation over after her death), and she died without having disposed of it, her husband took it *jure mariti*. See JUS MARITI.

The Married Women's Property Act, 1882, almost abolished the common law distinction between married and unmarried women in respect of property, and the Married Women's Property Act, 1893, s. 1, provided that every contract entered into by a married woman otherwise than as agent should be deemed to be a contract entered into by her with respect to and to bind her separate property whether she was or was not in fact possessed of or entitled to any separate property at the time when she entered into such contract; should bind all separate property which she might at that time or thereafter be possessed of or entitled to; and should also be enforceable against all property which she might thereafter while discovert be possessed of or entitled to; but this did not render available to satisfy any liability or obligation arising out of such contract any separate property which at that time or thereafter she was restrained from anticipating.

The Law Reform (Married Women and Tortfeasors) Act, 1935, provides that a married woman is capable of acquiring, holding and disposing of property, rendering herself liable in contract or tort, suing or being sued in contract or tort, and being subjected to bankruptcy law and the enforcement of judgments and orders in all respects as if she were a *feme sole* (s. 1, as amended by the Law Reform (Husband and Wife) Act, 1962, s. 3 (2), Sch.), and that her property shall belong to her in all respects as if she were a *feme sole* (s. 2, as amended by the Married Women (Restraint on Anticipation Act, 1949, s. 1, Sch. 2)).

See ANTICIPATION; COVERTURE; MARRIED WOMEN'S PROPERTY.

Separate opinion, an individual opinion of a member of an appellate court who agrees with the conclusions of the majority judgment but not with its reasoning.

Separation. If a husband and wife cannot agree so as to carry out the purpose of their union, they may resolve to live apart. A deed of separation, containing the terms and conditions upon which an actual and immediate separation is to be arranged, will be valid, so far as relates to the trusts and covenants of the husband; but if it contemplate a contingent or future separation it is void, as being opposed to the policy of marriage and the well-being of the community.

The concurrence of trustees is not essential, and a deed of separation will be binding on the wife as well as the husband, though entered into without the intervention of a trustee (*McGregor* v. *McGregor* (1888) 21 Q.B.D. 424; *Sweet* v. *Sweet* [1895] 1 Q.B. 12).

The court will decree specific performance of an agreement to execute a deed of immediate separation if based upon sufficient consideration (*Gibbs* v. *Harding* (1870) L.R. 5 Ch. 336).

If, after the separation, the husband and wife are reconciled, and live together again, that circumstance will put an end to the agreement, and determine the separate allowance.

See HUSBAND AND WIFE; JUDICIAL SEPARATION; SEPARATION ORDER.

Separation order. See MATRIMONIAL PROCEEDINGS IN MAGISTRATES' COURTS.

Separatists, seceders from the Church. They, like Quakers, solemnly affirm, instead of taking the usual oath, before they give evidence. See the statute 1833, 3 & 4 Wm. 4, c. 82, and the Oaths Act, 1888. See AFFIRMATION.

Separia, several or severed and divided from other ground (Paroch.Antiq. 336).

Septennial Act, 1715. By this Act (enlarging the time from three years) a parliament had continuance for seven years unless sooner dissolved. By the Parliament Act, 1911, s. 7, five years was substituted for the seven years fixed by the Septennial Act, 1715.

Septuagesima, the third Sunday before Quadragesima Sunday (*q.v.*) in Lent, being about the seventieth day before Easter.

Septum, an inclosure; any place paled in.

Sepultura, an offering to the priest for the burial of a dead body.

Sequatur sub suo periculo, a writ which lay where a summons *ad warrantizandum* was awarded, and the sheriff returned that the person had nothing whereby he might be summoned; then issued an *alias* and a *pluries,* and if he came not in on the *pluries,* this writ issued (Old N.B. 163). See WARRANTY.

Sequela causae, the process and depending issue of a cause for trial.

Sequela curiae, suit of court, *i.e.,* the court of the lord.

Sequela molendina. See SECTA AD MOLENDINUM.

Sequela villanorum, the family retinue and appurtenances to the goods and chattels of villeins (*q.v.*), which were at the absolute disposal of the lord (Paroch.Antiq. 216).

It meant everything that villeins had. Where a lord sold his villein he sold *nativum meum cum tota sequela sua* and the *sequela* included the children of the villein.

Sequendum et prosequendum, to follow and prosecute a cause. Thus a guardian was admitted *ad prosequendum* for his ward.

Sequester, to renounce; to set aside from the use of the owners.

Sequestrari facias, a writ issued for the purpose of enforcing a judgment against a beneficed clergyman, when a *fi. fa.* has been issued and returned *nulla bona* (R.S.C., Ord. 47, r. 5). It commands the bishop of the diocese to enter into the benefice and sequester the rents and profits until the debt is satisfied. The bishop executes the writ by issuing a sequestration (*q.v.*). See LEVARI FACIAS; SEQUESTRATION; WRIT.

The Sequestration Act, 1871, provides that on sequestration the bishop of the diocese shall appoint a curate and assign a stipend; see also the Benefices Sequestration Measure, 1933.

Sequestratio, the separating or setting aside of a thing in controversy, from the possession of both the parties contending for it; it was twofold—voluntary, when done by consent of all parties, and necessary, when a judge ordered it (Civil Law).

Sequestration, where, by some judicial or quasi-judicial process, property is temporarily placed in the hands of persons called sequestrators, who manage it and receive the rents and profits.

In the procedure of the High Court, a sequestration is a means of enforcing obedience to a judgment or order requiring a person to do an act, *e.g.,* pay money into court, deliver up a chattel, etc. (R.S.C., Ord. 45, r. 1; Ord. 46, r. 5). It can be issued against a debtor as if he had been arrested (Debtors Act, 1869, s. 8). It is a writ or commission directed to certain persons (usually four in number, one of them being usually a sheriff's officer) nominated by the person prosecuting the judgment, and empowering them to enter upon and take possession of all the real and personal estate of the disobedient person and to collect the rents and profits of his real estate and all his personal estate until he performs the act required. The sequestrators are officers of the court, and are bound to account for what they receive. (See ASSISTANCE, WRIT OF; PRO INTERESSE SUO). It is a prerogative process and was formerly confined to the Court of Chancery and the Courts of Probate and Divorce. It has no return, and is granted upon a return of *non est inventus* by the serjeant-at-arms, or by a sheriff on an attachment. It is an appropriate remedy for enforcing an order for alimony or maintenance (*Coles* v. *Coles* [1957] P. 68). It is a mode of enforcing an order against a corporation in the case of the order having been wilfully disobeyed (*Stancomb* v. *Trowbridge U.D.C.* [1910] 2 Ch. 190).

A bank has a duty without any specific order of the court to make full disclosure to and to pay out what may be demanded by sequestrators (*Eckman* v. *Midland Bank* [1973] I.C.R. 71 (N.I.R.C.)).

When a *fi. fa. de bonis ecclesiasticis* or a *sequestrari facias* is directed to a bishop, he issues a sequestration, which is in the nature of a warrant addressed to the churchwardens, requiring them to levy the debt out of the profits of the debtor's benefice.

In ecclesiastical law, where a benefice becomes vacant, a sequestration is usually granted by the bishop to the churchwardens, who manage all the profits and expenses of the benefice, plough and sow the glebe, and provide for the necessary cure of souls. They are bound to account for the profits to the new incumbent. Sequestration is also usually granted in a cause of spoliation (*q.v.*), or as a punishment (*e.g.,* for nonresidence), or as a mode of compelling payment of money for dilapidations, or the like.

See ASSISTANCE, WRIT OF; SEQUESTRARI FACIAS.

Sequestro habendo, a judicial writ for discharging a sequestration of the profits of a church benefice, granted by the bishop at the sovereign's command, thereby to compel the parson to appear at the suit of another; upon his appearance, the parson may have this writ for the release of the sequestration (Reg. Judic. 36).

Serf, the slave of feudalism. See SERVI.

Seriatim [Lat.], severally, and in order.

Serjeantia idem est quod servitium (Co. Litt. 105). (Serjeanty is the same as service.)

Serjeants [Lat. *servientes*], bailiffs of the hundred, etc. (see SERJEANTS OF THE PEACE), and officials of the nature of tipstaves (*q.v.*).

The Common Serjeant is a judicial officer in the City of London. See COMMON SERJEANT.

There are inferior serjeants such as serjeants of the mace in corporations, and serjeants of manors.

Serjeants-at-arms, officers of the Crown, whose duty is nominally to attend the person of the sovereign, to arrest traitors, to attend the Lord High Steward (*q.v.*) when sitting in judgment on traitors, and the like.

They are in old books called *virgatores,* because they carried silver rods gilded, as they now do maces, before the sovereign (2 Fleta, 38).

Two of them attend on the two Houses of Parliament, and each has a deputy; the office of him in the House of Commons is the keeping of the doors and the execution of such commands, especially touching the apprehension of any

1635

SERJEANTS

offender, as that House enjoins him. Another of them attended on the Lord Chancellor or Lord Keeper, in the Chancery, and one on the Lord Treasurer of England; also one upon the Lord Mayor of London on extraordinary solemnities. The Serjeant-at-Arms of the House of Lords attends the Lord Chancellor or other person acting as Speaker of that House; this is his only duty as an official of that House except, very occasionally, the attachment of offenders: but he also invariably holds the unpaid office of Lord Chancellor's Serjeant-at-Arms, and in the latter capacity he is the Serjeant-at-Arms of each of the judges of the Chancery Division, and may be ordered by any of them to enforce orders as to the custody of wards or to arrest persons in contempt.

Serjeants-at-law, or **of the coif** [*servientes ad legem*], otherwise called serjeants counter, the highest degree in the common law, as doctors in the civil law; but, a doctor of law was superior to a serjeant, for the very name of a doctor is magisterial, but that of a serjeant only ministerial (Spelman).

Serjeants-at-law were made by the sovereign's writ, addressed to such as were called, commanding them to take upon them that degree by a certain day (Fortescue, c. 50; 3 Cro. 1; Dyer, 72; 2 Co.Inst. 213).

Serjeants-at-law were barristers of superior degree, to which they were called by writ under the Great Seal. They formed an Inn called Serjeants' Inn. Formerly they were supposed to serve the Crown (hence their name, serjeants or *servientes ad legem*); but in more modern times the degree was conferred on eminent counsel as a distinction, without reference to their services to the Crown. Serjeants had precedence over junior barristers; but only serjeants with patents of precedence (*q.v.*) took precedence of Queen's Counsel. They formerly had a right of exclusive audience in the Court of Common Pleas, which was abolished by the statute 1846, 9 & 10 Vict. c. 54; an attempt to do this by royal warrant under the Sign Manual had been declared illegal in *Re Serjeants-at-law* (1840) 6 Bing.H.C. 235. When a serjeant was appointed, it was customary for him to appear in the Court of Common Pleas and to go through the form of opening a real action by reading the count (*q.v.*) therein: this was called "counting." It was also customary for him to present gold rings, bearing a motto, to the other serjeants, to all the high officials and nobility present at the instalment feast and to the judges and others; this was called "giving rings." See REGARD.

The degree of Queen's Counsel gradually supplanted that of serjeant, and the abolition by the Judicature Act, 1873, s. 8, of the rule requiring every judge of the superior courts of common law to be a serjeant made the extinction of the order of serjeants merely a question of time. Since 1868, no person except a judge designate had taken the degree, which, however, was never formally abolished.

For some period at some date before 1497, the serjeants held, as an Inn, certain premises opposite the Church of St. Andrew in Holborn (Williams, *Early Holborn*). These premises were subsequently known as Scrope's Inn. They were, in 1497, the property of Lord Scrope.

From 1443 to 1758 the serjeants held, as an Inn, the buildings in Fleet Street which are still known as Serjeants' Inn. When the last renewal of the Fleet Street lease expired in 1758, the serjeants who had lived in that Inn migrated to the other Serjeants' Inn in Chancery Lane. The Chancery Lane Inn (known as Old Serjeants' Inn) was held from 1416 upon a series of leases renewed from time to time, until in 1854 the freehold was acquired from the Bishop of Ely. Old Serjeants' Inn was sold in 1877, and the proceeds amounting to £57,000 were divided among the serjeants. The site is now occupied by Nos. 5, 6 and 7, Chancery Lane.

Lord Lindley, who became a serjeant in 1875 and died in 1921, was the last survivor of the Order of the Coif. That was the collective title of the serjeants.

See COIF; FARYNDON INN.

See Manning, *Serviens ad Legem*; Pulling, *Order of the Coif*.

Serjeants of the household, officers who executed functions within the royal household: see the statute 1541, 33 Hen. 8, c. 12.

Serjeants of the peace. In medieval times the peace officers included county serjeants, those of the hundreds, the forests, the baronies and the franchises. They were entrusted with the preservation of peace, the repression of crime and the execution of the orders of the courts of justice. Their duties included the making of arrests and distraints, the placing of persons under attachment by sureties to appear for trial, the service of summonses and the collection of some of the profits of jurisdiction (Stewart-Brown, *Serjeants of the Peace*). See PELF; PUTURE.

Serjeanty, or **Searjeanty,** or **Seargeanty,** or **Sergeanty** [Norm. Fr. *serjantie*; Lat. *serviens,* a servant], service. Serjeanty was a service due to the Crown for lands held of it and which could not be due to any other lord. It was divided into *grand* and *petit.* See GRAND SERJEANTY; PETTY SERJEANTY; TENURE.

The Law of Property Act, 1922, s. 136, provides that the services incident to grand and petit serjeanty are preserved (following the statute 1660, 12 Car. 2, c. 24, as to grand serjeanty) and are declared not to be manorial incidents, but the special tenure, if any, is free and common socage, or if copyhold, is enfranchised under the Act.

Sermo est animi index (3 Bulst. 260). (Speech discloses what is in the mind.) See OS DEMONSTRAT, ETC.

Sermo relatus ad personam intelligi debet de conditione personae (4 Co.Rep. 16). (Words referring to any man must be taken as referring to him in his occupation.) Thus to say of an attorney that he deals corruptly, means prima facie that he does so *qua* attorney.

Sermones semper accipiendi sunt secundum subjectum materiam et conditionem personarum (4 Co.Rep. 14). (Words are always to be taken in the sense which they would ordinarily have in relation to the subject-matter and to the occupation of the persons spoken of.) Thus the word " layman " ordinarily means one who is not a clergyman: but it means one who is not a barrister or a solicitor when, for instance, it is said that laymen are in general not acquainted with such and such a proposition of law (See SECUNDUM SUBJECTAM MATERIAM.

Servage. There was said to be servage when tenants, besides paying rent, had to provide labour for the lord. In the law of tenure it was in fact a particular kind of service (*q.v.*). King John was said to have brought the Crown of England in servage to the see of Rome: see the statute 1377, 1 Ric. 2, c. 6 (Co.Inst. 174).

Servants. See MASTER AND SERVANT.

Servi, bondmen, or servile tenants. They were of four sorts: such as sold themselves for a livelihood; debtors sold because they were unable to pay their debts; captives in war, retained and employed as perfect slaves; and *nativi,* servants born as such, solely belonging to the lord. There were also said to be *servi testamentales,* those who were afterwards called covenant-servants.

Servi redemptione, criminal slaves in the time of Henry I (1 Kemble, *Saxons,* 197).

Servi testamentales, covenant-servants.

Service [Lat. *servitium*], that duty which a tenant, by reason of his estate, owes to his lord. There are many divisions of this duty in our ancient law books, as into personal and real, urban and rustic, free and base, continual and annual, casual and accidental, intrinsic and extrinsic, certain and uncertain, etc. (2 Bl.Comm. 60). See TENURE.

Divine or spiritual services were services of a religious nature, either certain, as in the case of tenure by divine service (*q.v.*), or uncertain, as in the case of frankalmoign (*q.v.*). Temporal services were services which could be performed by a secular person, and were either free, namely such as were not unbecoming the character of a soldier or a freeman to perform, as to serve under his lord in the wars, to pay him rent, etc., and also those incident to tenure in grand serjeanty (*q.v.*); or base or villein services, namely such as were fit only for peasants or persons of a servile rank, as to plough the lord's land or make his hedges. Certain services were such as were fixed in quantity, as to pay a certain rent, or to plough a field for three days every year; examples of uncertain services were to do military service, or to plough the lord's land when called upon. Accidental or casual services were wardship, relief, heriots and other things, more commonly called incidents (*q.v.*). In the tenure of knight's service, some services due by the tenant were called foreign, *servitia forinseca,* because they were due to the king and not to the lord: such was the military service in the field due by a tenant by knight's service (Co.Litt. 75b). See FOREIGN.

Customary services arose by immemorial custom, as where the inhabitants of a place had from time immemorial been accustomed to grind their corn at a certain mill: such a custom gave rise to the obligation on the part of the mill-owner to maintain the mill and all provisions for grinding (servants, etc.), and on the part of the residents to take their corn to be ground there and not elsewhere (Hob. 189; Willes, 654). See SECTA; SUBTRACTION.

Service, Contract of. In the law of contract, service is the relation between master and servant. A contract by which one person binds himself to serve another is called a contract of service. As to the rights and duties arising from such a contract, see MASTER AND SERVANT.

In order to support claims for damages against seducers and abductors, the meaning of "service" was strained so that if a daughter lived with her father, this was a sufficient service to support an action by the father against the man who raped, seduced or enticed her. See ENTICEMENT; SEDUCTION.

Service franchise, a franchise given by the Representation of the People Act, 1884, s. 3, to male persons occupying, by virtue of their service of employment, a dwelling-house not occupied by their master. See ELECTORAL FRANCHISE.

Service, loss of. See PER QUOD SERVITIUM AMISIT; SEDUCTION.

Service occupation, a kind of licence whereby a servant is required to live in the house in order the better to do his work. If the servant is given an interest in the land separate and distinct from his contract of service then he is a tenant. The distinction depends on the truth of the relationship and not on the label that is put upon it (*Torbett* v. *Faulkner* [1952] 2 T.L.R. 659).

Service of process. In procedure, service is the operation of bringing the contents or effect of a document to the know-

ledge of the person concerned. It is of two kinds. Writs of summons, orders for disobedience to which process of contempt may be issued, and some other judicial documents, require either direct or substituted service. (R.S.C., Ord. 65, r. 1). Direct service is effected by actually bringing the document to the person or thing to be served. In the case of a person such service is called personal. Thus, in an ordinary action, personal service of the writ of summons is effected by handing a copy of the writ to the defendant, and showing him the original if he asks to see it (r. 2). An example of direct service on a thing (which might be called real service) occurs in an ordinary admiralty action *in rem* against a ship, where service of the writ of summons is effected by affixing the original writ for a short time to the mast of the vessel, and taking it off, leaving a copy affixed in its place (R.S.C., Ord. 75, r. 11). Analogous to this is the mode of serving a writ for the recovery of land in the case of vacant possession, where a copy of the writ is posted on some conspicuous part of the property; this mode of service also partakes of the nature of substituted service.

The object of substituted service is to provide the best means available under the circumstances for bringing the effect of the document to the knowledge of the party, when he is keeping out of the way, or his whereabouts are not known. The usual mode of effecting substituted service is by directly serving the document on some person likely to bring it to the knowledge of the party (*e.g.,* his wife, agent, etc.), or by advertising notice of it, or by sending a copy by post to the party's address (Ord. 65, r. 4). See NOTICE; NOTICE OF WRIT, ETC.

Analogous to substituted service is the practice called "accepting service," which is done by the solicitor for the party to be served indorsing on the writ a statement that he accepts service of the writ on behalf of the defendant (Ord. 10, r. 1 (2)).

A solicitor is required to give notice to the Law Society of any change in his business address within fourteen days from the date on which the change takes effect (Solicitors Act, 1974, s. 84).

Certain documents which are merely the foundation for other proceedings do not require direct or substituted service, but are left at the address of the person for whom the document is intended, or of his solicitor, if he is represented by a solicitor. (See ADDRESS FOR SERVICE.) Summonses, notices of motion, petitions, and certain other documents, are served in this manner; if served between 12 noon on a Saturday and midnight on the following day or after 4 p.m. on any other weekday, the service counts from the Monday following that Saturday or the day following that weekday, as the case may be (Ord. 65, r. 7). As to pleadings, see DELIVERY.

As to the expression " service by post," in a statute, by the Interpretation Act, 1889, s. 26, service by post is deemed to be effected on properly addressing, pre-paying, and posting a letter containing the document to be served, and unless the contrary is proved, to have been effected at the time at which the letter would have been delivered in the ordinary course of post. As to service by post, see Ord. 65, r. 5. See POST.

Any notice to or by lessees or mort-gagors, and any notice affecting property required by any instrument unless a con-trary intention appears, must be in writing and may be effected by registered letter through the post (Law of Property Act, 1925, s. 196).

Service out of the jurisdiction. This may be allowed by the court or a judge in certain specified cases. There are restrictions upon the allowance of such service upon a defendant resident in Scotland or Northern Ireland (R.S.C., Ord. 11). As to the exercise of discretion in giving leave, see *Watson & Sons* v. *Daily Record* [1907] 1 K.B. 853.

Service, Secular, worldly service, as contrasted with spiritual or ecclesiastical.

Service voters. Persons in the armed forces may vote by proxy. See PROXY.

Serviens ad legem, sergeant-at-law (*q.v.*).

Servient tenement, the land over which an easement is exercised, as the dominant tenement is that to which the easement is attached. See EASEMENT.

Servientibus, certain writs touching servants and their masters violating the statutes made against their abuses (Reg. Brev. 189).

Servitia personalia sequuntur personam (2 Co.Inst. 374). (Personal services follow the person.) Quoted by Coke as showing that where there was a lord paramount, a mesne lord and a tenant, and the mesne lord had made default in rendering the customs and services due to the lord paramount, then the customs and services to be rendered to the lord paramount by the tenant in order to obviate distraint did not include services, such as homage, fealty, etc., which were annexed to the person of the mesne lord (Statute of Westminster II, 1285, c. 9). See MESNE.

Servitiis acquietandis, De, a writ by means of which a tenant obtained redress when he had been distrained for services by a lord to whom he owed no service (Reg. Judic. 27).

Servitium, service.

Servitium feodale et praediale, a per-sonal service, but due only by reason of lands which were held in fee (2 Bract. c. 16).

Servitium forinsecum, a service which did not belong to the chief lord but to the king (2 Dugd.Mon. 48).

Servitium, in lege Angliae, regulariter accipitur pro servitio quod per tenentes dominis suis debetur ratione feodi sui (Co.Litt. 65). (Service, by the law of England, means the service which is due from the tenants to the lords by reason of their fee.)

Servitium intrinsecum, that service which was due to the chief lord alone from his tenants within his manor (3 Fleta).

Servitium liberum, a service to be done by feudatory tenants, who were called *liberi homines,* and distinguished from vassals, as was their service, for they were not bound to any of the base services of ploughing the lord's land, etc., but were to find a man and horse, or go with the lord into the army, or attend the court, etc. It was called also *servitium liberum armorum.*

Servitium regale, royal service, or the prerogatives which, within a royal manor, belonged to the lord of it; they were generally reckoned to be the following, *viz.,* power of judicature in matters of property, and of life and death in felonies and murders; right to waifs and estrays; minting of money; assize of bread and beer, and weights and measures (Paroch. Antiq. 60).

Servitor, a serving man; particularly applied to students of Christ Church, Oxford, upon the foundation, similarly to sizars at Cambridge.

Servitors of bills, messengers sent by the Marshal of the King's Bench to serve bills or writs: see the statute 1401, 2 Hen. 4, c. 23.

Servitude, such apprenticeship as gives a right of admission to the freedom of a borough or to the City Companies. See COMPANIES, CITY; FREEDOM OF A BOROUGH.

In the civil law, servitudes were certain portions or fragments of the right of ownership separated from the rest, and enjoyed by persons other than the owner of the thing itself.

Servitus, slavery.

Servus ordinarius, a slave holding some special post in an establishment, as cook, baker, etc. (Civil Law).

Servus poenae, a penal slave; a convict, e.g., one sent to the mines or condemned to fight with wild beasts. The status was abolished by Justinian (Civil Law).

Servus vicarius, an attendant or assistant of a *servus ordinarius,* often purchased by the latter out of his *peculium* (Civil Law).

Seskyn; Sesken. See SUSKIN.

Session, Court of, the supreme civil court of Scotland.

Session, Great, of Wales, a court which was abolished by the Law Terms Act, 1830.

The jurisdiction of the Great Session of Wales, which was first established by Henry VIII, was similar to that of judges of assize in England. Later it was exercised by two barristers, who sat for eighteen days only, into which period all the litigious business had to be compressed.

Session of Parliament, the sittings of the Houses of Lords and Commons, which are continued, day by day, by adjournment, until the parliament is prorogued or dissolved. See PARLIAMENT.

Sessions of the peace, sittings of justices of the peace for the execution of those powers which are confided to them by their commission, or by charter, and by statute.

Every meeting of two or more justices in the same place, for the execution of some power vested in them by law, whether had on their own mere motion or on the requisition of any party entitled to require their attendance in discharge of some duty, is a petty or petit session. See OPEN COURT; PETTY SESSIONS; QUARTER SESSIONS.

Set. See SETT.

Set-off. In an action to recover money, a set-off is a cross claim for money by the defendant, for which he might maintain an action again the plaintiff, and which has the effect of extinguishing the plaintiff's claim *pro tanto,* so that he can only recover against the defendant the balance of his claim, after deducting what is due by him to the defendant (R.S.C., Ord. 18, r. 17). Thus, if A sues B for £100, while he owes B £75, a set-off would have the effect of reducing A's claim to £25. The object of this is to prevent cross-actions. See CIRCUITY OF ACTION.

The subject of a set-off under the former practice was a cross debt or claim, on which a separate action might be sustained, due to the defendant from the plaintiff. It was a defence created by the statutes 1728, 2 Geo. 2, c. 22, and 1734, 8 Geo. 2, c. 24; it had no existence at common law, and could only be pleaded in respect of mutual debts of a definite character, and did not apply to a claim founded in damages, or in the nature of a penalty, and the debt must have been due in the same right and between the same parties, and must not have been a mere equitable demand. The defendant could not avail himself of a set-off unless it was specially pleaded and particulars thereof delivered with the plea.

Under the Judicature Acts, 1873–75, mutual claims of any kind, whether for debts or damages, can be set off against one another; but in practice the term " set-off " is generally applied to mutual debts or claims for liquidated amounts, so that one can be deducted from the other: while cross claims in respect of damages, which are unliquidated, are distinguished as " counterclaims " (*q.v.*).

As to the limitation of a set-off or counterclaim, see LIMITATION OF ACTIONS.

In the practice of the old common law courts, where there were cross judgments in the same or different actions, in the same or different courts, between parties substantially the same, whether for debt (or damages) and costs, or for costs alone, either party might set off the amount of his judgment against that of the other by obtaining a rule or order to enter satisfaction in both actions for the amount of the smaller debt. This practice was made obsolete by the full powers of set-off given by the Judicature Acts, 1873–75.

A person may not in any proceedings by the Crown make any counterclaim or plead a set-off if the proceedings are for the recovery of, or the counterclaim or set-off arises out of a right or claim to repayment in respect of, any taxes, duties or penalties (R.S.C., Ord. 77, r. 6 (1)).

As to set-off in bankruptcy, see MUTUAL CREDITS.

See COUNTERCLAIM.

Sets of bills. It has been common, from a very early period, for the drawer to draw and deliver to the payee several parts, commonly called a set of the same bill of exchange (*q.v.*), any one part of which being paid, the others are void. This is done to obviate inconveniences from the mislaying or miscarriage of the bill, and to enable the holder to transmit the bill by different conveyances to the drawee, so as to ensure the most speedy presentment for acceptance and payment. The general usage in England and America is for the drawer to deliver a set of three parts of a bill to the payee or holder (Byles on *Bills*).

By the Bills of Exchange Act, 1882, s. 71, where a bill is drawn in a set, each part of the set being numbered and containing a reference to the other part, the whole of the parts constitute one bill.

Sett and sale, Action of, an action by a part-owner of a ship claiming that the others should buy his share or sell their own or that the ship should be sold.

Settle. To settle property is to limit it, or the income of it, to several persons in succession, so that the person for the time being in the possession or enjoyment of it has no power to deprive the others of their right of future enjoyment. See SETTLEMENT.

The term " settle " was also applied to paupers. See SETTLEMENT OF PAUPERS.

To settle a document is to make it right in form and in substance. Documents of difficulty or complexity are frequently settled by counsel. (See CONVEYANCER.) In Chancery practice every order (except orders for time and a few others) is settled by the registrar in the presence of the parties, unless they agree as to its form, in which case the " settling " consists in their signing the draft as approved. See MINUTE; PASS; REGISTRAR.

Settled account. See ACCOUNT SETTLED.

Settled land. For the purposes of the Settled Land Acts, 1882 to 1890, settled land meant land, and any estate and interest therein, which was the subject of a settlement; and settlement meant any instrument, or any number of instruments, under which any land, or any estate or interest in land, stood for the time being limited to or in trust for any persons by way of succession (Settled Land Act, 1882, s. 2). The Settled Land Acts, 1882 to 1890, are repealed by the Settled Land Act, 1925.

Prior to 1856 settled estates could not be sold or leased except under the authority of some power in the settlement by which they were settled, or of a private Act of Parliament. The Leases and Sales of Settled Estates Act, 1856, as amended by the statutes 1858, 21 & 22 Vict. c. 77; 1864, 27 & 28 Vict. c. 45; and 1874, 37 & 38 Vict. c. 33, gave powers to the Court of Chancery, with the concurrence of the parties interested, to direct sales and leases of settled estates, and also enabled tenants for life, without application to any court, to make certain leases binding on the parties in remainder. The Settled Estates Act, 1877, consolidated these Acts.

The Settled Land Act, 1882, though not repealing the Act of 1877, rendered its provisions comparatively useless. The main objects of the Settled Land Acts, 1882 to 1890, were to liberate tenants for life from the control of their trustees, and to enable them to improve settled land out of the proceeds of the sale of part of it, or permanently to convert the whole or part of the settled land into money and receive the income derived from its investment instead of the rents of the estate. The Acts regarded the tenant for life as the person most interested in the welfare of the estate, and empowered him to do almost anything that a judicious owner would wish to do, subject to the exception that he could not receive the purchase money on the sale of the estate; that had to be paid at his option either into court or to the trustees of the settlement.

Under the Settled Land Act, 1925, the fee simple in possession or term of years absolute in settled land is vested in an owner who may transfer the property to a purchaser for value free from the limitations and trusts of the settlement. To effect this, the entire legal estate comprised in the settlement is vested in the tenant for life or in a person on whom the like powers have been conferred instead of being merely subject to the power of disposition freed from the settlement which had been given to the tenant for life by the Settled Land Acts, 1882 to 1890.

By the Settled Land Act, 1925, s. 4 (1), it is provided that settlements of a legal estate in land *inter vivos* shall be effected by two deeds, namely, a vesting deed and a trust instrument, and if effected in any other way shall not operate to transfer or create a legal estate. See TRUST INSTRUMENT; VESTING INSTRUMENT.

A settlement includes one or more instruments whereby land stands limited in trust for persons by way of succession, for any person in possession, in tail, for a legal estate subject to a limitation over, for a base or determinable fee or corresponding interest in leasehold land, being an infant, for a legal estate, or limited in trust for any person for a legal estate contingently on the happening of any event, or (formerly) limited to or in trust for a married woman of full age in possession for a legal estate or any other interest with a restraint upon anticipation, or charged voluntarily or in consideration of marriage or by way of family arrangement with any payment of any rentcharge for life or less period or any capital or annual or periodic sum for portions, advancement, maintenance or other bene-fits with or without terms of years for securing the same. Where a settlement consists of more instruments than one it is commonly called a compound settlement (*Re Du Cane & Nettlefold* [1898] 2 Ch. 96; *Re Munday & Roper* [1899] 1 Ch. 275; *Re Wimbourne & Browne* [1904] 1 Ch. 537). References in the Settled Land Act, 1925, to a settlement extend to any compound settlement to which the land may be subject (*Re Ogle's Settled Estates* [1927] 1 Ch. 229).

Settlement does not include land held on trust for sale (Law of Property (Amendment) Act, 1926): see *Re Ryder and Steadman's Contract* [1927] 2 Ch. 62.

By the Settled Land Act, 1925, s. 4 (2), the vesting deed must convey the land to the tenant for life or statutory owners for the legal estate the subject of the settlement, or if the legal estate is already vested in the tenant for life or statutory owner, must declare that the land is vested in him for that estate. The expression "tenant for life" includes persons having the powers of a tenant for life, such as tenants in tail, tenants in fee simple subject to executory limitations over, and an estate owner of land subject to family charges, and formerly a married woman subject to restraint upon anticipation (ss. 19 (1), 20, 26, 117 (1) (xxviii)).

A vesting instrument must be executed in favour of each successive tenant for life or statutory owner upon his becoming entitled, and if the legal estate is held by statutory owners, they must also at his request execute a vesting deed in favour of the tenant for life upon his becoming entitled. The vesting deed constitutes the tenant for life's title to deal with the legal estate, and a purchaser for value from him under that title is not concerned with anything outside the vesting instrument so far as relates to equitable interests affecting the estate except that it is incumbent on the purchaser to identify the land conveyed with the land comprised in the settlement, so as to see that the person conveying is the person in whom the land ought to be vested as tenant for life or statutory owner and that the trustees have been properly constituted (s. 110). An estate owner in fee simple in possession or entitled to a term of years absolute subject to family charges may declare that the legal estate is vested in him on trust to give effect to those charges, etc., and thereupon subject to the appointment of trustees, he may exercise the powers of a tenant for life (s. 21). A similar result can be attained by way of trust for sale (Law of Property Act, 1925, s. 2), but the owner may also convey the legal estate simply as owner in fee or of the term subject to the charge (Law of Property (Amendment) Act, 1926).

Where there is no tenant for life or person having the powers of a tenant for life, any person of full age on whom such powers are by the settlement conferred and in any other case the trustees of the settlement have the powers of a tenant for life. These persons having the powers of a tenant for life are called statutory owners and come into existence in the event of land being limited in trust contingently on a future event, or in case of a discretionary trust, or a trust for accumulation, or in other cases where there is no person being a tenant for life or having his powers in possession of the property (ss. 20, 26).

Wide powers of sale, mortgage, leasing, improvement and investing capital money are conferred on tenants for life. Improvements are classed under three heads, the cost of which the tenant for life (a) is not required, or (b) may be required by the trustees or the court, or (c) is unconditionally required, to replace by instalments of income into capital money Sch. 3.

Capital money must be paid to the trustees of the settlement, being at least two in number, or a trust corporation (s. 18).

The powers given by the Act are not assignable, and any contract not to exercise them is void (s. 104); and any prohibition against any exercise of the powers is forbidden (s. 106); the tenant for life is however to be regarded as a trustee in exercising the powers of the Act (s. 107): see Re Hunt [1906] 2 Ch. 11. The case of property settled not by a strict settlement, i.e., as land, but through the medium of a trust for sale, was provided for by the Settled Land Act, 1882, s. 63,

which gave the statutory powers to the person entitled to receive the income of the sale moneys. This was found to create a difficulty, the question arising whether a sale ought to be effected by the trustees for sale or the tenant for life; but the Settled Land Act, 1884, ss. 6, 7, restored the rights of the trustees under the trust for sale, unless and until an order had been made by the court authorising the tenant for life to sell (Re Harding's Estate [1891] 1 Ch. 60). By the Law of Property (Amendment) Act, 1926, settlements by way of trust for sale are excluded from settlements which are regulated by the Settled Land Act, 1925, and trustees for the purposes of the Settled Land Act, 1925, have no general power of sale against the tenant for life. On the other hand, trustees for sale under trusts for sale have all the powers of a tenant for life (Law of Property Act, 1925, ss. 28 et seq.).

The principal mansion house on any settled land, and the park and grounds occupied therewith, cannot be sold without the consent of the trustees of the settlement or an order of the court (Gilbey v. Rush [1906] 1 Ch. 11), unless the settlement if made before 1926 provides to the contrary, or the settlement if made after 1925 imposes a condition that it is not to be sold without such consent or order (Settled Land Act, 1925, s. 65); heirlooms cannot be sold without an order of the court (s. 67.)

Settlement, an instrument by which property, or the enjoyment of property, is limited to several persons in succession. Generally, the word " settlement " implies a deed or an instrument equivalent to a deed (such as articles or agreement for a settlement); but a settlement may be and often is made by will, and occasionally by private Act of Parliament. The settlement may consist of any number of documents under which land stands limited to, or in trust for, persons by way of succession, when the settlement is described as a compound settlement.

The most important kinds of settlements are marriage, or ante-nuptial, settlements, post-nuptial and voluntary settlements, and family settlements or resettlements (q.v.). Settlements are also sometimes directed by a court to be entered into by the parties to a proceeding, such as those ordered by the Chancery Division upon the marriage of wards of court. The Family Division has power to order the settlement of property and the variation of settlements when a marriage is dissolved. See MAINTENANCE.

A marriage or ante-nuptial settlement is an instrument executed before a marriage, and wholly or partly in consideration of it, for the purpose of regulating the enjoyment and devolution of real or personal property. Such settlements are sometimes distinguished as real and personal settlements, a real settlement being one in which the property is throughout treated as land, so that if a person entitled under it dies, his share goes to the person who takes his realty, while a personal settlement is one in which the property is either personalty or realty directed to be turned into money, and therefore treated as personalty. See CONVERSION, EQUITABLE.

An ordinary settlement of personalty or realty directed to be sold (the object of which is to make an equal provision for all the children) consists of a conveyance of (or agreement to convey) the property to trustees, to be held by them in trust for the settlor until the marriage takes place (which generally is a few hours after the execution of the settlement), followed by a declaration of the trusts on which it is to be held after the marriage, namely, to pay the income to the husband for life (assuming that the property is brought into trust by him), and after his death to the wife for life, and after the death of the survivor to hold the property in trust for the issue of the marriage in such shares as the husband and wife jointly, or the survivor of them, shall have appointed, or in default of and subject to any appointment upon trust for all the issue who attain twenty-one, or (being daughters) marry, in equal shares, with an ultimate trust by which, if there is no issue of the marriage, the property reverts to the husband or settlor. If the property is brought into settlement by the wife, the income is first given to the wife for her life, formerly for her separate use with a restraint on anticipation (*q.v.*). In addition there are provisions as to the securities in which the trustees are to be at liberty to invest the settled property, covenants to settle after-acquired property, hotchpot, advancement clauses, and provisions for the appointment of new trustees. See ACCUMULATION; MAINTENANCE.

A marriage settlement of real property, where the object is to retain the estate in the family (hence sometimes called a family settlement, or, more commonly, a strict settlement), has, in the most simple case, where the intended husband is seised in fee of the property, the following principal objects: (1) to make provision for the wife: this is effected by securing the payment to her of two annuities; the one, payable during her husband's lifetime, called pin-money; the other, payable after his death, called a jointure; (2) to provide for the payment of gross sums of money, called portions, to such of the younger children of the marriage as attain majority; and (3) to provide that the property charged with these provisions for the wife and younger children shall go as a whole to the eldest son. These objects are effected by limiting a long term to trustees to secure the pin-money, followed by another long term to other trustees to secure the jointure, followed by another long term to secure the portions; subject to these terms, the land is limited to the husband for life, with remainder to the sons of the marriage successively in tail; failing sons and their issue, it is limited to the daughters as tenants in common in tail; and failing daughters and their issue, it is limited to the settlor in fee.

These are the traditional limitations of personalty and realty settlements, but they are often modified nowadays with a view to minimising modern penal taxation and to securing greater flexibility, so that, for instance, capital can be made available should the income prove insufficient. As to the taxation of income derived from a settlement see the Income and Corporation Taxes Act, 1970, ss. 434–459 as amended by the Finance Act, 1971. See Potter and Monroe, *Tax Planning with Precedents*.

A marriage settlement often contains a covenant by the husband or wife to settle all property exceeding a certain amount in value which may be acquired by him or her after the marriage. Such a covenant generally binds the covenantor to settle not only property in which he or she had no interest at the time of the marriage, but also interests which were contingent, and, in some cases, even vested at the time of the marriage, such as reversions.

Voluntary settlements are settlements made otherwise than for valuable consideration. (See VOLUNTARY.) A post-nuptial settlement (*i.e.*, one made by a husband on his wife or family after the marriage without some new consideration) is a voluntary settlement. Formerly, under the statute 1584, 27 Eliz. 1, c. 4, a voluntary settlement of land was defeated by a subsequent conveyance by the settlor to a purchaser for value, but the Law of Property Act, 1925, s. 173, replacing the Voluntary Conveyances Act, 1893, provides that no voluntary conveyance of any date, which was made in good faith and without fraudulent intent, shall be liable to be defeated by any later conveyance. A voluntary settlement of any property is void if the settlor becomes bankrupt within two years from its date (Bankruptcy Act, 1914, s. 42), and it is also void if he becomes bankrupt within ten years from its date, unless it is proved that at the time of making it he was able to pay all his debts without the aid of the property comprised in it. A voluntary settlement is also void if it falls within the purview of the Law of Property Act, 1925, s. 172, replacing the statute 1571, 13 Eliz. 1, c. 5. See FRAUDULENT CONVEYANCES.

Stamp duty on settlements was abolished by the Finance Act, 1962, ss. 30 (1), 34 (7), Sch. 11 Pt. V.

Settlement, Act of. By the Act of Settlement, 1700, the Crown is limited to the heirs of the body of the Princess Sophia, Electress of Hanover (daughter of James I's daughter, the Queen of Bohemia, and mother of George I), being Protestants, and various provisions are made for securing religion, laws and liberties.

Settlement estate duty, the further estate duty levied under the Finance Act, 1894, ss. 5, 17; abolished by the Finance Act, 1914, s. 14.

Settlement of paupers, the fixture of persons on becoming poor persons in a particular parish, to which was attached a right, first regulated by the Poor Relief Act, 1662, to be maintained by that parish and a liability to be removed thereto. In the early part of the nineteenth century, the law of settlement, in consequence of the increased facilities for locomotion, led to frequent litigation between parishes, which was gradually diminished by the introduction of the status of irremovability, upon acquiring which a poor person was no longer liable to be removed. A person was deemed to be settled in the county or county borough in which he was born until shown to have derived or acquired a settlement elsewhere. A person might derive a settlement from a parent or husband, acquire a settlement by residence, apprenticeship, estate, renting a tenement, or paying rates or taxes, or be presumed to be settled by reason of an estoppel (Poor Law Act, 1930). The poor law was abolished by the National Assistance Act, 1948. See NATIONAL ASSISTANCE BOARD; POOR LAW.

Settling day, the day on which transactions for the account are made up on the Stock Exchange. In consols they are monthly; in other investments, twice in the month.

Settlor, a person who makes a settlement (*q.v.*). As to the effect of conveying as settlor, see COVENANT.

Seven Bishops, Case of the. See BISHOPS.

Sever; Severable; Severance. To sever is to divide, and severable is that which is divisible. The Law of Property Act, 1925, s. 36, provides that no severance of a joint tenancy of a legal estate is permissible, but this does not affect the right to sever a joint tenancy in an equitable interest; thus a joint tenancy in an equitable interest is severed when one of two joint tenants transfers his interest to a stranger, because the other tenant and the stranger are then tenants in common (Co.Litt. 191a, 164b). See JOINT TENANCY.

When a claim is composed of several parts, and some of them may be put forward or enforced without the others, the latter are said to be severable, and the act of severing them is called severance; thus where a person brings an action in an inferior court for causes which are partly within and partly without the jurisdiction of the court, he is allowed to sever them by abandoning the latter part of his case, so as to keep the action in the inferior court.

When two or more defendants to an action put in separate defences, instead of joining in one defence, they are said to sever.

Severance is also the act of removing fixtures, growing crops, or minerals from land. As to the effect of severance, see GROWING CROPS; MINERALS.

When part only of land is taken compulsorily, compensation may be claimed for severance. See INJURIOUS AFFECTION. See APPORTIONMENT OF CONTRACTS; ENTIRE; SEVERAL; SEVERALTY.

Several. This is opposed to " joint." Thus tenants in common of land were said to be seised by several titles, so that if they were disseised each had a separate right of action, while joint tenants were seised by a joint title, and therefore if they were disseised they had to bring one action to recover the land. A covenant by several persons may be several, the effect being as if each had covenanted by a separate instrument, or joint, the effect in the latter case being that any covenantor who is sued can require the others, or the survivors of the others, to be sued also. In deeds, covenants by more than one person for the doing of a certain thing are commonly expressed to be both joint and several, or other words to the like effect. See JOINT.

As to the several hereditaments, see HEREDITAMENT; as to a several pasture, see PASTURE.

Several covenant, a covenant by two or more separately.

Several fishery, where a person has an exclusive right to fish in water either on his own soil or on the soil of another. See FISHERY.

Several inheritance, an inheritance conveyed so that it descended to two persons severally, by moieties, etc. See INHERITANCE.

Several tail, where land is entailed on two separately.

Several tenancy [*tenura separalis*], a tenancy which is separate, and not held jointly with another person.

Severalty. Property is said to belong to persons in severalty when the share of each is ascertained (so that he can exclude the others from it) as opposed to joint ownership, ownership in common, and coparcenary, where the owners hold in undivided shares (Litt. 243; 2 Bl. Comm. 179). See ESTATE.

Usually when land is held in severalty, it is divided so that each of the owners has a part to himself, but they may agree that one shall have the land for one part of the year, another for another, and so on, and in this case also they are said to hold in severalty (Co.Litt. 4a, 167a, 180a). See INHERITANCE.

The term severalty is especially applied to the case of adjoining meadows undivided from each other but belonging, either permanently or in what are called shifting severalties, to separate owners, and held in severalty until the crops have been carried, when the whole is thrown open as pasture for the cattle of all the owners, and in some cases for the cattle of other persons as well: each owner is called a severalty owner, and his rights of pasture are called severalty rights, as opposed to the rights of persons not owners. See COMMON; COMMONABLE; DOLE; LAMMAS LANDS; LOT MEADS; OPEN FIELDS; SHACK.

When a number of persons are owners, and an exclusive share is allotted to each for a certain time, at the expiration of which the shares are again distributed, so that the occupation varies or shifts from time to time, they are said to hold by shifting severalties. The most usual instance of shifting severalties occurs in the case of open fields and other commonable lands, where the severalty holding of each owner varies sometimes by rotation, sometimes by lot, while in some places the choice was formerly awarded to the best runner or wrestler, or determined by other fantastic methods, but since the general inclosure of the country such instances have become rare (Elton, Comm. 31).

Severance, separating or severing. See SEVER.

Seward, or **Seaward,** one who guards the sea-coast; *custos maris.*

Sewer, a trench, channel, or pipe through which water or sewage flows.

" Sewer " originally meant an open trench or channel, made for carrying off surplus water from land near the sea or a river, or from marshy ground.

The Court of Commissioners of Sewers was a temporary tribunal, erected by commission under the Great Seal, which used to be granted *pro re nata* at the pleasure of the Crown and later at the discretion of the Lord Chancellor, Lord Treasurer, and Chief Justices, pursuant to the Statute of Sewers, 1531. Their jurisdiction was to overlook the repairs of the banks and walls of the sea-coast and navigable rivers and with the consent of a certain proportion of the owners and occupiers, to make new ones, and to cleanse such rivers, and the streams communicating therewith. They were a court of record, and might proceed by jury, or upon their own view, and might make orders for the removal of annoyances, or the conservation of the sewers within their commission according to the customs of Romney Marsh, or otherwise. They might also assess necessary rates upon the owners of land, and, on refusal of payment, might levy by distress of goods and chattels.

By the Land Drainage Act, 1861, the Crown might, upon the recommendation of the inclosure commissioners, direct commissions of sewers and give them jurisdiction for the construction of new, and maintenance and improvement of old, works. The Act included all commissions of sewers granted by the Crown for the time being in force, and provided for the constitution of elective drainage districts, and for the appointment of boards therein, with the same powers as commissioners of sewers.

The Land Drainage Act, 1930, repealed the Statute of Sewers, 1531, and the Land Drainage Acts, 1861 to 1929, and made provision for the creation of drainage districts, drainage boards, catchment areas and catchment boards. It was amended by the River Boards Act, 1948, and the Land Drainage Act, 1961. Land drainage is now regulated under the Water Act, 1973. See LAND DRAINAGE.

The Public Health Act, 1936, ss. 14–52, deals with sewers, drains, cesspools and water-closets, replacement of earth closets by water-closets, and kindred matters. See DRAIN; PUBLIC SEWER. See also the Public Health Act, 1961, ss. 12–23, 50; London Government Act, 1963, Sch. 9 Pts. I, II, Sch. 11 Pt. I para. 35; Local Government Act, 1972, Sch. 14 paras. 35, 36, Sch. 30; Water Act, 1973, ss. 14–16; G.L.C. (General Powers) Act, 1967, s. 24; the Control of Pollution Act, 1974, Sch. 2 paras. 6–10, Sch. 3 para. 27.

As to metropolitan sewers, see the London Government Act, 1963, s. 40, Sch. 11.

As to the discharge of trade effluents into public sewers, see the Public Health (Drainage of Trade Premises) Act, 1937; London Government Act, 1963, Sch. 10, Sch. 18 Pt. II; S.I. 1965 No. 654, s. 24 (2) (*c*); Water Act, 1973, ss. 14–16, Sch. 9; Control of Pollution Act, 1974, ss. 43–45, Sch. 2 paras. 13,14. See WASTE.

As to the collection of charges for sewerage disposal see the Water Act, 1973, ss. 30, 32a; Water Charges Act, 1976.

Sex change. A person born biologically male cannot contract a valid marriage as a woman despite a sex-change operation (*Corbett* v. *Corbett* (*orse. Ashley* [1971] P.110).

Sex discrimination. Discrimination against women on the grounds of sex is the subject of elaborate prohibitions under the Sex Discrimination Act, 1975. Sex discrimination against men, married persons, and by way of victimisation are also covered (ss. 1–5). See also the Equal Pay Act, 1970 (set out as amended in Sch. 1 Pt. II of the Act of 1975), the Employment Protection Act, 1975, Sch. 16 Pt IV para. 13, and the Sex Disqualification (Removal) Act, 1919. See WOMAN.

Sexagesima Sunday, the second Sunday before Lent, being about the sixtieth day before Easter.

It intervenes between Septuagesima (*q.v.*) and Quinquagesima (*q.v.*) Sundays.

Sexhindeni, or **Sexhindmen,** the middle thanes valued at six hundred shillings. See HINDENI HOMINES.

Sextery lands, lands given to a church or religious house for maintenance of a sexton or sacristan.

Sexton [Law Lat. *sacristanus,* a

sacristan], a person who in pre-Reformation times had charge of sacred vessels, vestments and other things belonging to divine worship. In some of the cathedrals, the office of sacristan or sexton, in its ancient sense, is still held by a minor canon. Now, the sexton is sometimes merely a person who has charge of the church and its contents, and who rings the church bell, in which case the appointment generally lies with the church-wardens; but the incumbent generally appoints if, as is sometimes the case, the sexton is clerk as well as sexton, or if, as happens in some parishes, the sexton merely looks after the churchyard and digs graves. In many places, however, the sexton, without regard to the particular nature of his duties, is elected by the parishioners in select vestry or by the churchwardens and the parishioners. His tenure of office, like everything else connected with him, also depends upon local custom; in some cases he holds merely during pleasure, while in others it is a freehold for life except in case of proved misconduct. In 1739 it was decided that a woman could hold the office.

There is no presumption that the office of sexton in an ancient parish church is a freehold for life (*R.* v. *Dymock* (*Vicar and Churchwardens*) [1915] 1 K.B. 147).

The power to appoint and dismiss the sexton is held jointly by the incumbent and the parochial church council (Parochial Church Councils (Powers) Measure 1956, s. 7). The duties of the sexton are to cleanse the church, to open the pews, to fill up the graves, to provide candles and other necessaries, and to prevent disturbance in the church.

Sexual offences. The Sexual Offences Act, 1956, consolidated with amendments, a large number of statutory provisions relating to sexual crimes and abduction, procuration and prostitution of women and kindred offences.

In proceedings before examining justices inquiring into a sexual offence a child under fourteen is not to be called as a witness for the prosecution but written statements taken from the child are prima facie admissible in evidence (Children and Young Persons Act, 1963, s. 27).

As to the length of imprisonment for certain offences against young girls, see the Indecency with Children Act, 1960, s. 2.

A matrimonial order may be made on conviction of any offence under the Sexual Offences Act, 1956, ss. 1–29. See MATRIMONIAL PROCEEDINGS IN MAGISTRATES' COURTS.

See ABDUCTION; ABOMINABLE CRIME; ABUSING CHILDREN; BESTIALITY; BUGGERY; CARNAL KNOWLEDGE; CORROBORATION; DEFECTIVES; DEFILEMENT OF GIRLS; DRUG; INCEST; INDECENCY; INDECENT ASSAULT; PROCURATION OF WOMEN; PROSTITUTE; RAPE; SODOMY; SOLICITATION.

Shack, to ramble or go at large; a liberty of winter pasturage in Norfolk. A common of shack is the right of persons occupying lands lying together in the same common field to turn out their cattle after harvest to feed promiscuously in such field (*Corbet's Case* (1585) 7 Co. Rep. 5).

It sometimes happens that a number of adjacent fields, though held in severalty, that is, by separate owners, and cultivated separately, are, after the crop on each parcel has been carried in, thrown open as pasture to the cattle of all the owners.

Arable lands cultivated on this plan are called shack fields, and the right of each owner of a part to feed cattle over the whole during the autumn and winter is known as common of shack, a right which resembles but is not identical with common because of vicinage. It is also known as shackage and common of shacker, and the shack lands are sometimes called " the known lands," to distinguish them from an ordinary common, in which there is no distinction of property, and more frequently " half-year lands," from the period during which they are open to pasture.

Common of pasture in open meadows (see OPEN FIELDS) is of very much the same nature as common of shack.

Shaftesbury's (Lord) Act, the Liberty of Religious Worship Act, 1855.

Sham plea, a vexatious or false defence, resorted to under the old system of pleading for purposes of delay and annoyance.

Shandy, a mixture of beer and lemonade or ginger beer. Sale to a person under eighteen is an offence against the licensing laws unless it is proved that the beer sold was of a strength which does not require an excise licence (*Hall* v. *Hyder* [1966] 1 W.L.R. 410).

Share, a portion of the capital of a company. The ownership of a share entitles the holder to receive a proportionate part of the profits of the company, and to take part in the management of its business, in accordance with the articles of association or other regulations of the company, which also regulate the mode in which shares may be transferred. See MEETING; RESOLUTION; SHAREHOLDER.

Where the property is vested by charter or Act of Parliament in a body corporate, the shares of the individual corporators in the concern itself are personal, not real, estate; for such shares are merely the rights which each individual possesses as a partner to a share in the surplus profit derived from the employment of the capital, which is a mixed fund, consisting in part of personal chattels, as well as lands and fixtures. Shares in all companies which are within the Companies Act, 1948, are personal property; and in many cases of companies incorporated by special Act the shares have been expressly declared to be personal property. Before 1926 the question whether shares in other undertakings were real or personal property turned upon the nature of the shares, *i.e.,* whether the holder could call for a specific part of the land itself or only a share of the profits. See UNDIVIDED SHARES IN LAND.

When the amount of a share has been paid to the company, it is said to be fully paid up; and if the company is a limited one, the liability of the holder of the share is then at an end. Shares may be issued by a company as fully paid up (*e.g.,* in consideration of services or works rendered to the company by the person to whom they are issued). A company may convert its fully paid shares into stock (*q.v.*) (Companies Act, 1948, s. 61). A share certificate is an instrument under the seal of the company, certifying that the person therein named is entitled to a certain number of shares: it is prima facie evidence of his title thereto (s. 81), but it is not a negotiable instrument. A share warrant to bearer is a warrant or certificate under the seal of the company, stating that the bearer of the warrant is entitled to a certain number or amount of fully paid-up shares or stock; coupons for payment of dividends may be annexed to it; delivery of the share warrant operates as a transfer of the shares or stock; it is a negotiable instrument (s. 83). See SCRIP.

As to simplified transfer, see STOCK.

The expression "shares" in a will passes stock (*Morrice* v. *Aylmer* (1875) L.R. 7 H.L. 717).

As to shares in ships, see SHIP.

Share options and share incentive schemes. See the Income and Corporation Taxes Act, 1970, s. 186; Finance Act, 1972, ss. 77–79; Finance Act, 1974, s. 57, Sch. 14 Pt. II.

Share premium account, the account to which must be transferred any premium (*q.v.*) derived from the issue of shares, whether for cash or otherwise (Companies Act, 1948, s. 56). The provisions of the Act as to reduction of capital apply as if this account were paid-up share capital.

Shareholder, a person who has agreed to become a member of a company, and with respect to whom all the required formalities have been gone through (*e.g.,* registration, signing of deed of settlement, or the like). A shareholder by estoppel is a person who has acted and been treated as a shareholder, and consequently has the same liabilities as if he were an ordinary shareholder. Thus, a person who has acted as a shareholder may be liable for the debts of the company, although he has never been registered as a shareholder, and is therefore not a shareholder in the full sense of the word. So also a person will be treated as a shareholder if he has entered into a valid contract to take shares.

Sharepushing, calling from house to house endeavouring to sell shares. The Prevention of Fraud (Investments) Act, 1958, prohibits dealing in securities without licence from the Department of Trade. See also the Protection of Depositors Act, 1963, ss. 1 (3), 21; Criminal Justice Act, 1972, Sch. 5; *R.* v. *Grunwald* [1963] 1 Q.B. 935 (meaning of "reckless"); *R.* v. *Linnell* [1969] 1 W.L.R. 1514.

Sharing. A sharing of accommodation so as to exclude the operation of the Rent Restriction Acts involves the simultaneous use of a living room in such a manner that the privacy of the landlord or tenant, as the case may be, is invaded (*Neale* v. *Del Soto* [1945] K.B. 144; *Goodrich* v. *Paisner* [1957] A.C. 65).

Sharping corn, a customary gift of corn which, at every Christmas, the farmers in some parts of England give to their smith for sharpening their plough-irons, harrow-tines, etc. (Blount).

Shaw, a grove or wood, an underwood.

Shawatores, soldiers.

She. See HE.

Sheading, a riding, tithing, or division in the Isle of Man, where the whole island is divided into six sheadings, in each of which there is a coroner or chief constable appointed by a delivery of a rod at the Tynwald Court or annual convention (King, *Isle of Man,* 7).

Sheep. As to injuries to and damage by sheep, see ANIMALS, LIABILITY FOR. As to cruelty to sheep by allowing them to be infested with maggots, see *Potter* v. *Challens* (1910) 102 L.T. 324 and CRUELTY TO ANIMALS.

Sheep of a tenant are exempt from distress for rent conditionally, *i.e.,* if there is other sufficient distress on the demised premises, by the Statute of Marlbridge, 1267, c. 4, and this exemption extends to the sheep of an under-tenant (*Keen* v. *Priest* (1859) 28 L.J. Ex. 157).

See HILL FARMING; LIVESTOCK; RAM.

Sheep-heaves, small plots of pasture often in the middle of a waste, the soil of which may or may not be in the lord, but the pasture is private property, and is leased and sold as such (Cooke, *Inclos. Acts,* 44).

Sheep-heaves principally occur in the northern counties, and seem to be corporeal hereditaments, although they are sometimes classed with rights of common, but erroneously, the right being an exclusive right of pasture (Elton, Comm. 35). See PASTURE.

Sheep-scab. The Ministry of Agriculture, Fisheries and Food may by the Diseases of Animals Act, 1950, ss. 42, 43, replacing the Diseases of Animals Act, 1903, make orders prescribing, regulating, and securing the periodical treatment of sheep by dipping, or by the use of some other remedy for sheep scab (*Maclean* v. *Laidlaw* (1909) S.C.(J.) 68). See ANIMALS, DISEASES OF.

Sheep-silver, a service turned into money, which was paid in respect that the tenants used to wash the lord's sheep.

Sheep-skin, a deed; so called from the parchment it was written on.

Sheepwalk. A right of sheepwalk is the same thing as a foldcourse (*q.v.*).

Sheffield Marks. See the Trade Marks Act, 1938, s. 38, Sch. 2. See TRADE MARKS.

As to assaying Sheffield plate, see PLATE.

Sheffield University. The Sheffield University Act, 1914, extends the privileges of graduates of the university.

Shell fish. In *Bagott* v. *Orr* (1801) 2 B. & P. 472, the court affirmed the general common law right of the subject to take or catch shell fish on the seashore, but doubted whether any such common law right existed for the subject to take shells. See Moore, *Foreshore.*

As to the regulation of shell fish fisheries, see FISHERY.

A local authority may provide tanks or other apparatus for cleansing shell fish (Food and Drugs Act, 1955, s. 25; London Government Act, 1963, Sch. 18 Pt. II).

Shelley's Case, Rule in, a rule connected with the quantity of estate which a tenant might hold in realty. The rule in *Shelley's Case* (1580) 1 Co.Rep. 93b, was examined in *Van Grutten* v. *Foxwell* [1897] A.C. 658, and *Re Williams* [1952] Ch. 828. The rule was abolished by the Law of Property Act, 1925, s. 131.

The rule was that where a life estate of freehold, either legal or equitable, in realty (whether of freehold or copyhold tenure), was limited by any assurance to a person, and by the same assurance the inheritance of the same quality, *i.e.,* either legal or equitable, was limited by way of remainder (with or without the interposition of any other estate) to his heirs or the heirs of his body, such remainder was immediately executed in possession in the person so taking the life estate, the word " heirs " being treated as a word of limitation and not of purchase, so that the life-tenant took the inheritance, which was neither contingent nor in abeyance; that is to say, where the inheritance was to his heirs or right heirs he took the fee simple, and where it was to the heirs of his body an estate tail general. In Coke's Reports in verse the rule was rhymed thus:

Where ancestors a freehold take,
The words "his heirs" a limitation make.

Where land was limited to A for life, remainder to his right heirs, the rule did not treat this remainder as contingent, but conferred it upon A at once, whereupon his life estate merged in the remainder and he took the entire interest, *i.e.*, the fee simple. Again, where land was limited to A for life, remainder to B for life, remainder to the heirs male of A's body, the second remainder vested in A as a remainder in tail male general, and was not in contingency or abeyance, nevertheless waiting for, and continuing expectant on, the determination of B's life estate, which was expectant on A's death; but after A's death, and the determination of the mesne remainder to B, A's heir in tail male general enjoyed the land as heir, and not as purchaser.

The rule was of positive institution at variance with rules of construction; by applying the rule, the courts did not seek for the intention of parties, and strive for its accomplishment, but combated the intention. According to the assurance, two estates were created, a particular estate in the ancestor, and a remainder in his heirs, and in the absence of the rule, the heir would have taken an original and independent estate by purchase, not derived from nor controllable by his ancestor; but the operation of the rule placed the whole power over the inheritance in the ancestor, who could partially or totally defeat the expectation of his relation.

The Law of Property Act, 1925, s. 131, enacts that where an interest in any property is expressed to be given to the heir or heirs or issue or any particular heir or any class of heirs or issue of any person in words which, but for the section, would, under the rule of law known as the Rule in *Shelley's Case,* have operated to give to that person an interest in fee-simple or an entailed interest, such words shall operate in equity as words of purchase and not of limitation, and shall be construed and have effect accordingly, and in the case of an interest in any property expressed to be given to an heir or heirs or any particular heir or class of heirs, the same person or persons shall take as would in the case of freehold land have answered that description under the general law in force before the commencement of the Act.

The rule is called the rule in *Shelley's Case* because it was much discussed in that case, but the rule itself is of much more ancient date.

Sheppard's Touchstone. See DODERIDGE.

Shepway, Court of, a court held before the Lord Warden of the Cinque Ports. A writ of error lay from the mayor and jurats of each port to the Lord Warden in this court, and thence to the King's Bench. The civil jurisdiction of the Cinque Ports was abolished by the Cinque Ports Act, 1855 (Knocker, *Grand Court of Shepway*). See CINQUE PORTS; COURT OF BROTHERHOOD.

Shereffe, the body of the lordship of Cardiff, excluding the members of it (Powel's Hist.Wal. 123).

Sheriff, Shire-reeve, or **Shiriff** [Sax. *scire,* shire; *scyran,* to divide; *gerefa,* a guardian; Lat. *vicecomes*], the chief officer of the Crown in every county.

A high sheriff is appointed for every county and for Greater London (excluding the City of London) (Local Government Act, 1972, s. 219). The two sheriffs of the City of London are elected by the Corporation of the City (Sheriffs Act, 1887, s. 33). The duties of sheriffs include the charge of parliamentary elections, the execution of process issuing from the High Court and the criminal courts and the levying of forfeited recognisances. Most of his ordinary duties are performed by the under-sheriff and deputy.

The lord lieutenant (*q.v.*) of the county (*q.v.*) or of Greater London nominates three persons as being fit to serve as high sheriff (Sheriffs Act, 1887, s. 6; Administration of Justice Act, 1964, s. 19; Local Government Act, 1972, s. 219, Sch. 30). The Crown appoints one of them to be

SHERIFF

high sheriff. See Pricking for Sheriffs. If a sheriff dies in office, the appointment of another is the act of the Crown alone.

The Sheriffs Act, 1887, replaces enactment as to sheriffs from the statute 1275, 3 Edw. 1, c. 9, to the Judicature Act, 1881, s. 16. A high sheriff is appointed annually, having sufficient land within the county to answer the sovereign and the people. The high sheriff must within one month after his appointment is gazetted nominate some fit person to be his under-sheriff. In Greater London an under-sheriff is to be appointed for each London commission area. The area for which each under-sheriff is to act is prescribed by the Lord Chancellor. An under-sheriff is treated as the high sheriff's deputy except as regards the functions of returning officer (Sheriffs Act, 1887, s. 23; Administration of Justice Act, 1964, s. 19; Local Government Act, 1972, s. 219, Sch. 30).

As to the protection of the sheriff selling goods under an execution without notice of claims by third parties, see the Bankruptcy and Deeds of Arrangement Act, 1913, s. 15.

The ancient sheriff's courts of the City of London (q.v.) have fallen into disuse. See Common Pleader, etc.

Formerly the sheriff had judicial duties to perform as judge of the sheriff's county court (see County Court; Outlawry). He also held a court of record called the sheriff's tourn twice every year, which had the same functions and jurisdiction as the court leet (q.v.). See Mather, *Sheriff Law*; Morris, *Medieval Sheriff*. See Anglo-Saxon Laws; Bailiff; Bailiwick; Elegit; Inquiry, Writ of; Pricking for Sheriffs; Shire-Reeve; Westmorland.

Sheriffalty, Sheriffdom, Sheriffship, Sheriffwick, or Shrievalty [Lat. *vice-comitatus*], the office or jurisdiction of a sheriff.

Sheriff-geld, the rent or payment which the king received from the sheriff at the time when the office of sheriff was a source of profit (Rot. Parl., 50 Edw. 3).

Sheriff's Court in London. See City of London Court; Common Pleader.

Sheriff's officers, bailiffs, who are either bailiffs of hundreds or bound-bailiffs.

Sheriff's tourn or **rotation,** a court of record held twice every year, within a month after Easter and Michaelmas, before the sheriff, in different parts of the county, being indeed only the turn of the sheriff to keep a court leet in each respective hundred; this, therefore, was the great court leet of the county, as the county court was the court baron. The tourn was abolished by the Sheriffs Act, 1887, s. 18 (4).

Sheriff-tooth, a rent paid at an early period by certain tenants who held by the tenure of providing entertainment for the sheriff when sitting in his county court; a common tax formerly levied for the sheriff's diet.

Sherman; Shearman, one who used to shear woollen cloth, that is to say, remove the nap from it: see the statute 1503, 19 Hen. 7, c. 17.

Sherrerie, a word used by the authorities of the Roman Church to specify contemptuously the technical parts of the law, as administered by non-clerical lawyers (Bacon).

Shew cause, to appear (in obedience to a rule of court calling upon the party to appear and shew cause) and argue that the rule should not be made absolute. When an order, rule, decree or the like has been made nisi, a person who appears before the court and contends that it should not be allowed to take effect, is said to shew cause against it. Rules to shew cause are in many cases abolished by the Judicature Act, 1925. See Absolute Rule; Decree; Nisi; Rule.

Shewer; Shower. In the practice of the High Court, when a view by a jury is ordered, persons are named by the court to shew the property to be viewed, and are hence called shewers. There is usually a shewer on behalf of each party. See View.

Shewing [Lat. *monstratio*], being quit of attachment in a court, in plaints shewed and not avowed.

Shift marriage. When a man died having debts which his widow was unable to pay, she was obliged, if she contracted a second marriage, to leave her clothes in the hands of her creditors, and to go through the ceremony in her shift (4 Lecky, Hist. 23).

Shifting clause, in a settlement, is a clause by which some other mode of devolution is substituted for that primarily prescribed. Examples of shifting clauses are the ordinary name and arms clause (*q.v.*) and a clause by which a settled estate is destined as the foundation of a second family, in the event of the elder branch becoming otherwise enriched. These shifting clauses formerly took effect under the Statute of Uses, 1535. See SHIFTING USE; USE.

Shifting use, a secondary or executory use, which, when executed, operated in derogation of a preceding estate; as where land was conveyed to the use of A and his heirs, with a proviso that when B paid a certain sum of money, the estate should go to the use of C and his heirs. The legal estates thereby created are converted into equitable interests by the Law of Property Act, 1925, ss. 1, 39, Sch. 1 Pt. I. The instrument declaring the use is a settlement within the meaning of the Settled Land Act, 1925, s. 1 (ii) (*b*). See SHIFTING CLAUSE; SPRINGING USE; USE.

Shilling [Lat. *solidus*; Sax. *scilling*]. The shilling among the English Saxons passed for 5d.; afterwards it represented 16d., and often 20d.; in the reign of the Conqueror it was 12d. (Domesday). The equivalent is now five new pence. See SILVER COINS.

Shilwit. See CHILDWYTE.

Ship. The Merchant Shipping Act, 1894, s. 742, provides that " ship " includes every description of vessel used in navigation not propelled by oars.

A foreign-going ship includes every ship employed in trading, or going between some place or places in the United Kingdom, and some place or places situate beyond the following limits, that is to say, the coasts of the United Kingdom, the Channel Islands and the Isle of Man, and the continent of Europe, between the river Elbe and Brest inclusive. A home-trade ship includes every ship employed in trading or going within those limits (*Smith* v. *Veen* [1955] 2 Q.B. 277). A home-trade passenger ship means every home-trade ship employed in carrying passengers.

The Carriage of Goods by Sea Act, 1924, Sch. art. 1 and the Carriage of Goods by Sea Act, 1971, Sch. art. 1, define a ship as any vessel used for the carriage of goods by sea; the Merchant Shipping (International Labour Conventions) Act, 1925, s. 5, as any sea-going ship or boat of any description which is registered in the United Kingdom as a British ship including any British fishing boat entered in the fishing-boat register; and the Petroleum (Consolidation) Act, 1928, s. 24, as every description of vessel used in navigation, whether propelled by oars or otherwise. As to the jurisdiction of the courts over ships, see the Administration of Justice Act, 1956, ss. 1–3.

A vessel cannot be registered as a British ship unless owned wholly by British subjects, or a corporation formed under and subject to the laws of, and having its principal place of business in, the British Commonwealth (Merchant Shipping Act, 1894, s. 1 (as amended by the British Nationality Act, 1948, Sch. 4 Pt. I).

A British ship is personal property, but while on the high seas is deemed to be part of the soil of England: thus, persons born on board a British ship, whether in foreign territorial waters or not, are natural-born British subjects, and the British courts have jurisdiction in respect of crimes committed on the high seas on board British vessels.

The ownership of every registered ship is divided into sixty-four shares, all of which may belong to one person or they may be divided among several persons; but not more than sixty-four persons can be registered as part-owners of any one ship. (See PART-OWNERS.) Not more than five persons may be registered as joint-owners of any ship or of any share or shares therein (Merchant Shipping Act, 1894, s. 5). Any part-owner can transfer or mortgage any or all of the shares held by him; but to do so he must comply with the statutory provisions, as ships are not within the ordinary rules governing the assignment and hypothecation of chattels. See BILL OF SALE; MORTGAGE.

As to the hypothecation of ships, see BOTTOMRY; HYPOTHECATION; NECESSARIES; RESPONDENTIA.

As to the employment of ships, see AFFREIGHTMENT; BILL OF LADING; CHARTERPARTY; DEMURRAGE; FREIGHT; INSUR-

ANCE; LAY DAYS; LOSS; MANAGING OWNER, ETC.; MERCHANT SHIPPING; PILOTAGE; POLICY OF INSURANCE; RUNNING DAYS; SEAMEN; SEAWORTHINESS; SHIP'S HUSBAND; TRANSIRE.

The liability of shipowners (who are liable at common law, if carriers, as insurers of goods) is limited where there has been no actual fault or privity, to amounts varying with the tonnage of the ship. The owner of a British ship is protected against liability in respect of goods lost or damaged by fire on board the ship, and in respect of certain valuables, the true nature and value of which have not been declared on shipment, if lost or damaged by reason of any robbery, embezzlement, etc. (Merchant Shipping Act, 1894, ss. 502, 503; Merchant Shipping (Liability of Shipowners and Others) Act, 1958). Although the Carriers Act, 1830, extends to carriage by land only, where there is a contract for the carriage of goods partly by land and partly by sea, the carrier has the benefit of the Act as to the carriage by land (*Le Conteur* v. *L. & S. W. Ry.* (1865) L.R. 1 Q.B. 54); see also the Carriage of Goods by Sea Act, 1924; Carriage of Goods by Sea Act, 1971.

Taking away or using a vessel without authority is an offence under the Theft Act, 1968, s. 12.

See ADMIRAL; ADMIRALTY; AVERAGE; COLLISION OF SHIPS; COURT OF SURVEY; DERELICT; DETAINING OFFICER; LIMITATION OF LIABILITY; NAVIGATION ACTS; SALVAGE; WRECK.

Shipbuilding. Illegal shipbuilding is an offence under the Foreign Enlistment Act, 1870.

Credits and grants are available for the construction of ships and offshore installations under the Industry Act, 1972, ss. 10–12.

Ship-money, an imposition formerly levied on port-towns and other places for fitting out ships for the defence of the realm.

It had become obsolete, but was revived by Charles I, who attempted to levy it in the county of Bucks. Three writs were issued in 1634, 1635 and 1636 to the sheriffs instructing them to levy money for the purpose of providing ships

for the navy. John Hampden, a gentleman of the county, was accordingly assessed at 20s., which he declined to pay, and proceedings were taken against him in the Exchequer and judgment was given for the Crown (*Case of Ship Money* (1637) 3 St.Tr. 825). In Parliament resolutions were at once passed condemning the judgment, and it was reversed and the tax was abolished by the statute 1640, 16 Car. 1, c. 14.

Shipped bill of lading, a bill of lading which states that the goods have been shipped on board and not merely that they have been received for shipment.

Shipper, the owner of goods who entrusts them on board a vessel for delivery abroad, by charterparty or otherwise.

As to the responsibilities and rights of a shipper under a bill of lading see the Carriage of Goods by Sea Act, 1924, Sch.; Carriage of Goods by Sea Act, 1971, Sch.

Shippers are required to give an account of the goods intended to be shipped under the Harbours, Docks and Piers Clauses Act, 1847, s. 39, amended by the Criminal Justice Act, 1967, Sch. 3 Pt. I.

Shipping casualties. See the Merchant Shipping Act, 1970, ss. 55–58, 73 (replacing the relevant provisions of Pt. VI of the Merchant Shipping Act, 1894).

Shipping documents, documents sometimes attached to a bill of exchange. They consist of the invoice, the policy of insurance and the bill of lading.

Ship's agent. Under the Naval Agency and Distribution Act, 1864, every naval vessel when in commission must have an agent, who may not be in Her Majesty's service nor be a solicitor or proctor, to look after the claims of the officers and crew to special payments (such as those in salvage or in prize, or for the capture or destruction of enemy ships, etc.), to which they may become entitled. He receives as his remuneration $2\frac{1}{2}$ per cent. on moneys recovered. He must have a place of business within five miles of the General Post Office, London. He is subject to the Admiralty Court as if he were an officer thereof.

Ship's husband, an agent appointed by the owner of a ship to look after the repairs, equipment, management, and other concerns of the ship. His duties are to see to the proper outfit of the vessel, the repairs, tackle and furniture necessary for a seaworthy ship; to have a proper master, mate, and crew for the ship, so that in this respect it shall be seaworthy; to see to the due furnishing of provisions and stores; to see to the regularity of clearance from the custom-house of the registry; to settle contracts, and provide for payment of the furnishings requisite; to enter into charter-parties, or engage the vessel for general freight, under usual conditions, and to settle for freights and adjust averages with the merchant; and to preserve the proper certificates, surveys, and documents, in case of disputes with insurers or freighters, and to keep regular books of the ship. He must be registered under the Merchant Shipping Act, 1894, s. 59 (2). He does not attend to insurance; and sometimes his authority is limited to specific things. See AGENT; MANAGING OWNER, ETC.

Ship's papers, a ship's registry certificate, bill of lading, bill of health, charter-party, log, and other documents which show the character of the ship and cargo.

They are the documents required for the manifestation of the property of the ship and cargo. They are of two sorts: those required by the law of a particular country, as the certificate of registry, licence, charterparty, bills of lading and of health, required by the law of England to be on board all British ships; and those required by the law of nations to be on board neutral ships, to vindicate their title to that character, as the passport, sea-brief or sea-letter, proofs of property, muster-roll or *rôle d'équipage*, charter-party, bills of lading and invoices, log-book or ship's journal, and bill of health.

Shire [Sax. *scyran*, to divide], a part or portion of the kingdom; called also a county, *comitatus*. King Alfred first divided the country into *satrapiae*, or shires; shires into *centuriae* or hundreds; and *centuriae* into *decennae* or tithings (Leg. Alfred.; Brompton, 956; Hackwood, *Story of the Shire*).

Shire clerk. It was in the capacity of shire clerk that the sheriff held the old county court. The office was never held except by the sheriff.

Shiregemont; Shiremote. See COUNTY COURT; FOLCMOTE.

Shire-ground; Shire-land, such parts of the kingdom as had been formed into shires; see the statute 1535, 27 Hen. 8, c. 26, s. 24.

Shire-man, or **Scyre-man,** a judge of the county, by whom trials for land, etc., were determined before the Conquest.

Shiremote, an assembly of the county or the shire at the assizes, etc. See COUNTY COURT; FOLCMOTE.

Shire-reeve, the sheriff (*q.v.*). See REEVE.

Shochet, a Jewish butcher; in effect a member of a religious order invested by the Chief Rabbi with authority to kill and prepare meat in accordance with the Jewish ceremonial.

Shock. Damages may be recovered in respect of injury by shock, where it is a reasonably foreseeable consequence of the defendant's wrongful act or omission (*Hambrook* v. *Stokes Bros.* [1925] 1 K.B. 141; *Bourhill* v. *Young* [1943] A.C. 92; *King* v. *Phillips* [1953] 1 Q.B. 429; *Chadwick* v. *British Railways Board* [1967] 1 W.L.R. 912).

Shoeblacks in London must be licensed by the Commissioner of Police (Metropolitan Streets Act, 1867, s. 19).

Shooting. The right of shooting over land is a variety of the right of sporting (*q.v.*).

Shooting at vessels, aircraft or vehicles belonging to the navy or in the service of the revenue while employed in the prevention of smuggling is punishable with imprisonment for five years (Customs and Excise Act, 1952, s. 72).

Shooting galleries may be regulated by by-laws (Public Health Act, 1961, s. 75; London Government Act, 1963, s. 40).

Shop, a place where things are kept for sale, usually in small quantities, to the actual consumers. By the Shops Act, 1950, s. 74, " shop " includes any premises where any retail trade or business is carried on.

The Act provides that no young person between the ages of sixteen and eighteen shall be employed for more than the normal maximum working hours, that is, forty-eight hours in any week (s. 24), restricts night employment (s. 31), has special provisions as to the catering trade (s. 25), the sale of accessories for aircraft, motor-vehicles and cycles (s. 26), provides for weekly half-holidays (s. 1), and intervals for meals (s. 19).

Every shop must, save as otherwise provided, be closed not later than 1 p.m. on one weekday in every week, to be fixed by the occupier of the shop (Shops Act, 1950, s. 1; Shops (Early Closing Days) Act, 1965). General early closing hours are prescribed by the Shops Act, 1950, s. 2 and S.I. 1952 No. 1862. Special provisions relating to trading elsewhere than in shops are contained in the Act of 1950, s. 12 as amended by the Act of 1965, s. 4 and also to shops where more than one business is carried on (Act of 1950, s. 13, *Fine Fare* v. *Brighton Corporation* [1959] 1 W.L.R. 223), holiday resorts (Act of 1950, s. 51), shops where Post Office business is carried on (Act of 1950, s. 44; Act of 1965, s. 5 (2); Post Office Act, 1969, Sch. 8 Pt. I) and Shops at Airports (Shops (Airports) Act, 1962). The enforcement of the law is entrusted to the local authority (Act of 1950, s. 71). Fairs, bazaars or sales of work from which no private profit is derived are exempt (Act of 1950, s. 45; Act of 1965, s. 5 (2); Offices, Shops and Railway Premises Act, 1963, Sch. 2). Certain trades and businesses are exempted from the provisions as to the early closing day and from the provision of closing orders (Act of 1950, Schs. 1, 2; S.I. 1965 No. 1536; Post Office Act, 1969, Sch. 4 para. 51). There are provisions dealing with the sale of confectionery (Act of 1950, s. 6; S.I. 1952 No. 1862) and tobacco (Act of 1950, s. 4) and exemptions for exhibitions, etc. (Act of 1950, s. 42). Customers in the shop before closing time may be served or when the article is required in the case of illness (Act of 1950, ss. 1, 2). The sale of meals and food is excepted in certain circumstances (Act of 1950, s. 49). Hairdressers' and barbers' shops must be closed on Sunday (*q.v.*) but Jewish hairdressers may close on Saturday instead (Act of 1950, s. 67; Act of 1965, s. 4 (1) (*c*); Criminal Justice Act, 1972, s. 31). Other shops must be closed on Sundays (Act of

1950, s. 47) with certain exceptions such as for the sale of intoxicating liquors, refreshments, sweets, ice-cream, fruit, flowers, milk and cream, medicines, tobacco, newspapers, books, etc. (Act of 1950, Sch. 5). There are special provisions for Jewish traders provided they close on Saturday (Act of 1950, s. 53; Act of 1965, s. 4 (1) (*c*)). Goods may not be despatched to a customer at a time when the customer could not lawfully be served in the shop (Act of 1950, s. 55).

An incorporated company is bound by the Act (*Evans* v. *L.C.C.* [1914] 3 K.B. 315). A costermonger's barrow is not a place in which retail trade or business is carried on within s. 12 of the Shops Act, 1950 (*Kahn* v. *Newberry* [1959] 2 Q.B. 1).

As to standards of health, welfare and safety, see OFFICES.

The definition of shop in the Town and Country Planning (Use Classes) Order, 1972 (No. 1385) excludes launderettes, cafés and restaurants and hot-food shops.

Shop club, a thrift club (Shop Clubs Act, 1902).

Shop-lifting. Shop-lifting is theft and punishable on conviction on indictment with imprisonment for not exceeding ten years (Theft Act, 1968, ss. 1, 7). It is triable summarily with the consent of the accused (s. 29 (2); Magistrates' Courts Act, 1952, s. 19, Sch. 1). A custodial sentence is appropriate in most cases of persistent shop-lifting though such a sentence should usually be a short one (*R.* v. *Anderson* (1972) 56 Cr.App.R. 863).

It was a capital offence under the statute 1698, 10 Will. 3, c. 12, repealed by the statute 1826, 7 & 8 Geo. 4, c. 27, s. 1. As to arrest for shop-lifting, see *John Lewis & Co.* v. *Tims* [1952] A.C. 676.

Shore. See FORESHORE.

Short cause. A Master may order an action to be set down in the Short Cause List under R.S.C., Ord. 14, r. 6. For the practice in the Chancery Division in an action directed to be heard as a short cause, see Ord. 8, rr. 1–5, notes. See further Ord. 25, r. 3, notes; Ord. 34, r. 4, notes. As to Admiralty short causes, see Ord. 75, r. 31.

Short entry. This takes place when a

bill or note, not due, has been sent to a bank for collection, and an entry of it is made in the customer's bank-book, stating the amount in an inner column, and carrying it into the accounts between the parties when it has been paid. See ENTERING SHORT.

Short title. The statute 1845, 8 & 9 Vict. c. 16, s. 4, enacted that in citing the statute in other statutes and in legal instruments, it should be sufficient to use the expression, the Companies Clauses Consolidation Act, 1845. This originated the modern practice of giving short titles to Acts of Parliament. The practice is now invariably followed; but for years after 1845 a short title might or might not be given to an Act. Thus the statute 1893, 56 & 57 Vict. c. 31, had no short title until the Short Titles Act, 1896, gave it the short title of the Rivers Pollution Prevention Act, 1893.

Now, under an order of the House of Lords, every Bill must contain a section giving it a short title.

The Short Titles Act, 1896, gave short titles to 2,076 Acts of which 840 had been given short titles by the Short Titles Act, 1892, which it re-enacted. The Statute Law Revision Act, 1948, gave short titles to a further 158 Acts.

There are still, however, many Acts without short titles, and in the event of its being necessary to refer to any such Act in another Act or a legal instrument it must be referred to as, for instance, " An Act of the session of the 5th and 6th years of the reign of Her late Majesty Queen Victoria, chapter 52, intituled, ' An Act to Indemnify Witnesses who may give Evidence before the Lords Spiritual and Temporal on a Bill to exclude the Borough of Sudbury from sending Burgesses to serve in Parliament.' " See ACT OF PARLIAMENT; COLLECTIVE TITLE.

Shortened Services Act, the Act of Uniformity Amendment Act, 1872.

Short-ford. The custom of the city of Exeter was when the lord of the fee could not be answered rent due to him out of his tenement, and no distress could be levied, that he was to come to the tenement, and there take a stone, or some other dead thing of the tenement, bring it before the mayor and bailiffs;

and this he had to do seven quarter-days successively; and if, on the seventh quarter-day, he was not satisfied his rent and arrears, then the tenement was adjudged to him to hold for a year and a day; and forthwith proclamation was made in the court, that if any man claimed any title to the tenement, he must appear within the year and a day next following, and satisfy the lord of the rent and arrears. If no appearance was made, and the rent was not paid, the lord came again to the court and prayed that according to the custom the tenement should be adjudged to him in his demesne as of fee, which was done, and the lord from thenceforth had it to him and his heirs. This custom was called short-ford, meaning to foreclose (Izack, Antiq.Exet. 48; Cowel).

A like custom in London by the Statute of Gavelet, 1317, was called *forschot* or *forschoke*.

Shorthand-writers. Shorthand writers' notes are notes taken by a shorthand-writer of the evidence or arguments on the trial or hearing of an action for future use on a motion for a new trial or an appeal.

Under R.S.C., Ord. 68, an official shorthand note is taken in all witness actions, summonses and motions in the Chancery and Queen's Bench Divisions of the High Court unless the judge otherwise directs. A note is taken of the oral evidence, the judge's summing up, if any, and of the judgment. Any transcript required for the Court of Appeal must in the first instance be paid for by the appellant unless the judge or Court of Appeal grants a certificate for a free transcript. The costs of transcripts may be paid out of public funds in the case of persons in poor financial circumstances but the costs of persons receiving legal aid are payable out of the legal aid fund (see LEGAL AID). Any reference in Ord. 68 to a shorthand note includes a record made by mechanical means. The costs of the transcript are, unless the Court of Appeal otherwise directs, costs in the appeal. See also R.S.C., Ord. 62, r. 28.

The Lord Chancellor has directed that an official shorthand note shall be made of all judgments in the Court of Appeal. One copy of the transcript is filed in the

SHORTHAND

Bar Library, where it is indexed, and one copy is sent to the court from which the appeal lay. Parties desiring copies may obtain them from the shorthand writers on payment of the usual charges. Notes of unreported judgments of the Court of Appeal (Civil Division) are published in Current Law. See, *e.g.* [1974] C.L.Y. p. 67.

Criminal proceedings in respect of which an appeal lies to the Court of Appeal are recorded by means of shorthand notes or by mechanical means (Criminal Appeal Rules 1968, rr. 18–20, 25 (1)), made under the Criminal Appeal Act, 1968, s. 32.

Shorthand writers in any court are ineligible for jury service. See JURY.

Show of hands. Since the Ballot Act, 1872, the mode of election known as a show of hands (that is to say, by counting the hands of the electors which may be held up to indicate the candidate for whom each elector votes has formed no part of the procedure at any election for which the use of the ballot (*q.v.*) is prescribed. See HUSTING; RESOLUTION.

Shrievalty, the office of sheriff; the period of that office.

Shrievo, a corruption of sheriff.

Shroud-stealing. If any one, in taking up a dead body, steals the shroud or other apparel, it is an indictable offence; for the property therein remains with the executor, or whoever was at the charge of the funeral (3 Co.Inst. 110; 1 Hale, P.C. 535).

Shrove Tuesday, the day before Ash Wednesday (*q.v.*), anciently called also Fasten Tuesday, that is to say, the Tuesday which was the eve of the fast.

Si actionem, etc. Before Latin (see FRENCH) ceased to be used in pleadings, these words were part of the conclusion of a plea in bar; and from 1733 until 1834, the use of the same conclusion in English was obligatory. In English the conclusion was " prays judgment if the said plaintiff ought to have or maintain his aforesaid action against him." See ACTIO. NON.

Si autem sacramentum fatuum fuerit, licet falsum, tamen non committit perjurium (4 Bract. 188; 3 Co.Inst. 167). (But if an oath be foolish, he who takes it does not commit perjury, even though it be false.) The law does not concern itself with the question of the truth or falsity of an oath taken without legal sanction.

Si fecerit te securum (if he shall have given you security), a species of original writ, so called from the words of the writ, which directed the sheriff to cause the defendant to appear in court, without any option given him, provided the plaintiff gave the sheriff security effectually to prosecute his claim.

Si non omnes, a writ of association of justices, by which, if all in commission of oyer and terminer could not meet on the day assigned, it was allowed that two or more of them might finish the business. After the writ of association, it was usual to make out a writ of *si non omnes,* addressed to the first justices, and also to those associated with them, which, reciting the purport of the two former commissions, commanded the justices that if all of them could not conveniently be present, such a number of them might proceed, etc. (Fitz.N.B. 111, 186; Reg.Brev. 202).

Si quid universitati debetur singulis non debetur nec quod debet universitas singuli debent (D. 3, 4, 7, 1). (If anything is owed to an entire body it is not owed to the individual members, nor do the individual members owe what is owed by the entire body.) But partners are individually liable for every debt due by their firm. The maxim is, however, true of corporations aggregate.

Si quidem in nomine, cognomine, praenomine, legatarii testator erraverit, cum de persona constat, nihilominus valet legatum (Just. Inst. 2, 20, 29). (Though a testator may have made a mistake as to the name or names of the legatee, when it is certain who is the person meant, the legacy is nevertheless valid.) See FALSA DEMONSTRATIONE, ETC.

Si quis [Lat. if anyone]. The *si quis* is a notice posted in the parish church of a candidate for holy orders, stating that if anyone knows of any just cause why the candidate should not be ordained, then the bishop is to be informed of such just cause.

Si quis unum percusserit, cum alium percutere vellet, in felonia tenetur (3 Co. Inst. 51). (If a man kill one, meaning to kill another, he is held guilty of felony.) The law holds him guilty of murder or manslaughter, provided, of course, that the killing was unlawful.

Si recognoscant, a writ which lay for a creditor against a debtor who had acknowledged before the sheriff in the county court that he owed such and such a sum for money lent.

Sib, related by blood.

Sic [Lat. so, thus], a word put in brackets in a quoted passage to confirm that the quotation is exact, though its incorrectness or absurdity would suggest that is is not.

Sic utere tuo ut alienum non laedas (9 Co.Rep. 59). (Use your own property so as not to injure your neighbour's.) Use your own rights so that you do not interfere with those of another.

Any man can build a reservoir on his land; but he is bound to see that it does not burst and flood his neighbour's land. See AEDIFICARE IN, ETC.; OWNERSHIP.

Sica, Sicha, a ditch (2 Dugd.Mon. 130).

Sich, a little current of water, which is dry in summer; a water furrow or gutter.

Sicius, a sort of money current among the ancient English, of the value of 2d.

Sickness benefit. See the Social Security Act, 1975, ss. 14–20; Social Security Pensions Act, 1975.

Sicut alias, as at another time, or heretofore. This was a second writ sent out when the first was not executed. See ALIAS WRIT.

Side-bar rules; Side-bar. There was in Westminster Hall a bar or partition, known as the side-bar, from within which attorneys each morning of term moved the judges, on their way to the respective courts, for common rules known as side-bar rules. Such motions were made *ex parte*, and were granted as of course. Before 1825 the practice of moving at the side-bar had been discontinued, and common rules were obtainable in the rule office; but each such rule was expressed to have been obtained upon a side-bar motion and continued to be known as a side-bar rule. The common rules were such as the rule to plead, the rule to reply, the rule to rejoin, etc. See RULE.

Sidelings [*sidlingi*], meers or balks betwixt or on the sides of arable ridges of land (Cowel).

Side-men, or **Sidesmen (Synods-men),** two or three or more discreet persons acting as assistants to the churchwardens in collecting alms and maintaining order. They are elected by the annual parochial church meeting (Synodical Government Measure, 1969, Sch. 3 para. 8 (4) (*c*)).

In ancient parishes, as distinguished from parishes created under the New Parishes Acts and Measures, it is lawful, under Canon 90, to appoint annually, along with the churchwardens, "sidesmen," that is to say, two or three discreet persons who are required to sign a declaration that they will faithfully assist the churchwardens. In many places no sidesmen are appointed. In others, the appointment is quasi-permanent, the same persons being re-elected each year; and this is more particularly the case where the sidesmen are paid salaries and are supplied with gowns.

Sidenotes. See MARGINAL NOTES.

Siens, scions or descendants.

Sierra Leone. See the Sierra Leone Independence Act, 1961; Sierra Leone Republic Act, 1972. See COMPANIES, CHARTERED.

Sight, Bills payable at. By the Bills of Exchange Act, 1882, s. 10, replacing the Bills of Exchange Act, 1871, prior to which three days' grace was allowed, bills payable at sight are made equivalent to bills payable on demand.

Sigil [Lat. *sigillum*], seal, signature.

Sigla [Sax. *segel*], a sail (Leg.Ethel. c. 24).

Sign Manual, the signature or "royal hand" of the sovereign. It is called the Sign Manual because it is the actual signature of the sovereign, as distinguished from the operation of signing documents by the Signet (*q.v.*). Warrants for the use of the Great Seal or Wafer Great Seal are signed with the Sign Manual. See GREAT SEAL.

The royal signature is sometimes required by statute as evidence of the authority of the sovereign. Towards the end of the reign of George IV, the royal signature was, in consequence of the king's illness, by the statute 1830, 11 Geo. 4 & 1 Wm. 4, c. 23, authorised to be affixed for him by commission.

The expression is also sometimes used as meaning the signature of anyone's name in his own handwriting.

Signatories, those who sign, *e.g.*, those who sign the memorandum and articles of a company.

Signature, a sign or mark impressed upon anything; a stamp, a mark; the name of a person written by himself either in full or by initials as regards his Christian name or names, and in full as regards his surname, or by initials only (*In the Goods of Blewitt* (1880) 5 P.D. 116); or by mark only, though he can write (*Baker* v. *Dening* (1838) 8 Ad. & E. 94); or by rubber stamp (*Goodman* v. *Eban* [1954] 1 Q.B. 550); or by proxy (*Tennant* v. *London County Council* (1957) 121 J.P. 428).

A person signs a document when he writes or marks something on it in token of his intention to be bound by its contents. In the case of an ordinary person, signature is commonly performed by his subscribing his name to the document, and hence " signature " is frequently used as equivalent to " subscription "; but any mark is sufficient if it shows an intention to be bound by the document: illiterate people commonly sign by making a cross. See MARKSMAN.

The Statute of Frauds, 1677, s. 17, which formerly required a memorandum of a contract for the sale of goods in certain cases to be signed by the party to be charged, was held to be satisfied where the party wrote the memorandum forming the contract on a piece of paper on which his name was printed.

The only signature which a corporation aggregate can make is by its seal. In practice ordinary contracts by a trading company are generally signed by an agent or officer of the company on its behalf. See SEAL.

Signature is required to authenticate a will (see WILL), a deed after 1925 (Law of Property Act, 1925, s. 73), and a memorandum of certain contracts (see FRAUDS, STATUTE OF). Pleadings must be signed by counsel if settled by him, and if not, by the solicitor or the party (R.S.C., Ord. 18, r. 6). No fee to counsel is allowed on taxation unless

vouched by his signature (Ord. 62, App. 2 Pt. X, 2).

Signet, a seal commonly used for the Sign Manual (*q.v.*) of the sovereign. See PRIVY SEAL.

The Signet is a seal with which certain documents are sealed by a principal Secretary of State on behalf of the sovereign. Formerly, every bill for letters patent, after being signed with the Sign Manual, was sealed with the Signet, as a warrant or authority to the proper officer to affix the Privy Seal or Great Seal (as the case might be) to the grant. But the necessity of affixing the Signet in such cases was abolished by the statute 1851, 14 & 15 Vict. c. 82, s. 2, and the use of the Signet seems practically to have ceased. (See CLERKS OF THE PRIVY SEAL.) A writ *ne exeat regno* may be issued under the Signet, for this is but a signification of the sovereign's commandment, and nothing passes from him (2 Co.Inst. 556).

The Signet (or Privy Signet) is the principal of the three seals, the smallest of which is called the Cachet, by the delivery of which a Secretary of State is appointed to his office, and which he surrenders on ceasing to hold the office.

Significavit, the bishop's certificate on which a writ *de excommunicato* or *contumace capiendo* was issued (Ecclesiastical Courts Act, 1813, s. 1, Sch. A). CONTUMACY; DE CONTUMACE CAPIENDO; EXCOMMUNICATION.

The writ, which was also called a *significavit,* issued out of the Chancery upon certificate given by the ordinary of a man's standing excommunicate by the space of forty days, for keeping him in prison till he submitted himself to the authority of the Church. In *Ex p. Dale* (1881) 6 Q.B.D. 381, a *significavit* was issued against a clergyman for disobedience to an inhibition.

The word also referred to another writ, addressed to the judges, commanding them to stay any suit depending between such and such parties by reason of an excommunication alleged against the plaintiff, etc. (Reg.Brev. 7).

It also denoted a letter addressed to the king by the chancellor of Oxford University invoking his aid in dealing with persons rebellious to the chancellor's jurisdiction.

Signing judgment. The proper term is " entering " judgment. See R.S.C., Ord. 42, rr. 4, 5; Masters' Practice Directions, 19, 20. See ENTER.

Signs. See SKY SIGN.

Signum, a cross prefixed as a sign of assent and approbation to a charter or deed, used by the Saxons.

Silentiarius, one of the Privy Council: also an usher, who sees good rule and silence kept in court.

Silentium in senatu est vitium (12 Co. Rep. 94). (Silence in the senate is a fault.) This was cited by the judges in extenuation of their conduct in venturing to advise the council with regard to points of law upon which many peers had already expressed opinions.

Silicosis, an industrial disease in respect of which benefit is payable.

Silk gown. Queen's Counsel (*q.v.*) wear silk gowns; hence the expression " to take silk " means to become a Queen's Counsel.

Silva caedua, wood under twenty years' growth.

Silver. See BRITANNIA; STERLING.

Silver coins. The period of the Roman occupation being left out of consideration, the earliest silver coin in general circulation was the silver penny coined by Offa in the eighth century. This, and the succeeding pennies coined up to the time of the Conquest, were of much the same weight as those coined from 1066 to 1377, which again were practically of the same weight as the threepenny piece coined in the reign of Victoria, which weighed a little more than twenty-one grains.

Down to 1272 the penny was the only silver coin. Between 1272 and 1307 Edward I issued halfpennies and farthings, the weights of which were proportionate to their denominations. The penny continued to be issued down to some years after 1660; but its weight had gradually diminished. From twenty-two grains in 1272, it had dropped to eighteen grains in 1322; in 1412 it weighed only fifteen grains. Its weight after 1485 never exceeded twelve grains. From twelve grains it gradually sank to ten grains in 1527, to eight grains in 1552, and there was no further material reduction until the issue ceased soon after 1660. The farthing which, like the halfpenny, varied in weight with the penny, was not issued after 1543; and the halfpenny disappeared after the Protectorate. The penny, the halfpenny, and the farthing were the only silver coins down to 1327, soon after which year Edward III issued the groat. On its first appearance, the groat was only slightly smaller than the florin of Victoria which weighed 174 grains. In 1380 the groat weighed seventy-two grains, from which it gradually sank to thirty-one grains in the reign of Charles II. The half-groat was contemporaneous with the groat down to this time. In 1831 the groat was reissued with a weight of twenty-nine grains; but it was not again coined after 1856. This latest issue was popularly known as the fourpenny piece.

The shilling, weighing 144 grains (or just twelve times the weight of the contemporaneous silver penny), was first issued in 1504; and by the reign of Elizabeth I it weighed only ninety-two grains, which does not much differ from its weight in the reign of Victoria of eighty-seven grains. In 1543, when at the intermediate weight of 120 grains, the shilling was also known as the testoon. See FORMELLA.

The crown, weighing 480 grains as against the ninety-six grains contained in the shilling of the period, the half-crown, the sixpence and the threepence, weighing twenty-four grains, first appeared in 1552. The crown and the half-crown, with slightly varying weights, were issued during nearly every subsequent reign as well as during the Commonwealth and the Protectorate. The threepence continued to be issued occasionally down to 1685; but it was not coined from then until the reign of Victoria. The sixpence was issued concurrently with every issue of the shilling.

The twopenny, the three-halfpence and the three-farthing pieces were silver coins issued only during the reign of Elizabeth I. The twopenny was of practically the same weight as the half-groat.

Cromwell issued a two shilling piece or double shilling, weighing 163 grains, in 1658. It was the nearest early equivalent of the modern florin, which did not appear until the reign of Victoria.

SILVER

The pound, the shilling and the mark were in use as measures of money before the Norman Conquest; and, in an order of the High Court, the mark was used to measure a penalty so late as 1770. There never was such a coin as the mark, and, except as regards a few pounds weighing 1,858 grains (exactly twenty times the weight of the contemporaneous shilling), which, along with half-pound pieces, were coined by Charles I during the Civil War, there has never been such a coin as the pound. Originally a pound meant about 5,760 grains (the pound troy) of pure silver, a mark meant so much silver as weighed a mark or two-thirds of a pound weight, and a shilling meant one-twentieth part of a pound weight of silver; while a shilling was the equivalent of twelve of the early silver pennies, each of which was therefore approximately one two-hundred and fortieth part of the pound. By the reign of Charles I the pound, the shilling and the penny, were, or represented, only about one-third of their original weight in silver; and the same applied to the mark, which all through was two-thirds of the pound for the time being. But from the earliest times, the pound, the mark and the shilling were used as measures of money in Acts of Parliament, charters, deeds, etc., in the reservation of rents of land and in the buying and selling of goods, the gold coinage never being mentioned in any such matter.

Cupro-nickel coins were substituted for silver coins by the Coinage Act, 1946, s. 2, Sch.

See BLANK; COIN; COPPER COINS; DOITKIN; GALLEY-HALFPENNY; GOLD COINS; SEIGNIORAGE; SUSKIN.

Silver Scullery, Serjeant of the. See MASTER OF THE HOUSE.

Similiter [Lat., in like manner], the word used by the plaintiff or defendant in an action by which he signified his acceptance of the issue tendered by his opponent. When simply added to the adversary's pleading containing the tender of issue, it was in the following form: " And the plaintiff (or defendant) doth the like." When instead of being simply added to the pleading it was delivered to the opposite party as a separate instrument, it ran in the following form: " And the plaintiff,

as to the plea of the defendant by him above pleaded, and whereof he hath put himself upon the country, doth the like"; in which latter case it was called a special *similiter*. The use of the *similiter* was applicable only to issues of fact which were triable by the country (*i.e.*, a jury). The resort to a jury in ancient times could in general be had only by the mutual consent of each party; and it appears to have been with the object of expressing such consent that the *similiter* was in those times added in drawing up the record; and from the record it afterwards found its way into the written pleadings. Accordingly, no *similiter* or other acceptance of issue was ever necessary when recourse was had to any of the other modes of trial. Under the Common Law Procedure Act, 1852, s. 79, the *similiter* ceased to be necessary. The want of a *similiter* by the prosecutor in criminal cases was cured by the Criminal Law Act, 1826, s. 20.

Simony, a corrupt presentation or agreement to present to an ecclesiastical benefice; a deliberate act, or a premeditated will and desire, of selling such things as are spiritual, or of anything annexed thereto, by giving something of a temporal nature for the purchase thereof (Ayliffe, *Parergon*).

Thus it was simony for anyone to sell the next presentation to a living when it was vacant; and it was simony for a clergyman to purchase a next presentation even when the living is full (Simony Act, 1713, repealed by the Statute Law (Repeals) Act, 1971).

The word is derived from Simon Magus, who offered money to the Apostles for the power to work miracles (Acts viii, 18–24). Simony is an offence by the statute 1588, 31 Eliz. 1, c. 6, s. 5, which directs that the corrupt presentation shall be void and the presentation shall go to the Crown, and the Clerical Subscription Act, 1865, required a declaration against simony to be subscribed by every person about to be instituted or collated to any benefice or to be licensed to any perpetual curacy, lectureship, or preachership. This declaration, which was only to the effect that the declarant had not to the best of his knowledge been party to any simoniacal contract, is now superseded by a far more effective and specific declaration scheduled to the Benefices Act, 1898 (as amended by the Benefices Act, 1898 (Amendment) Measure, 1923, s. 5).

Simple contract, a contract made either orally or in writing but not under seal.

Formerly, simple contract debts were, in the administration of the estate of a deceased person, postponed to debts secured by instrument under seal, called specialty debts, but all such priority was abolished by the Administration of Estates Act, 1869, s. 1, replaced by the Administration of Estates Act, 1925, s. 32.

See LIMITATION OF ACTIONS.

Simple deposit, a deposit made, according to the civil law, by one or more persons having a common interest.

Simple trust, where property is vested in one person upon trust for another, and the nature of the trust, not being qualified by the settlor, is left to the construction of law. In this case the *cestui que trust* has *jus habendi,* or the right to be put into actual possession of the property, and *jus disponendi,* or the right to call upon the trustee to execute conveyances of the legal estate as the *cestui que trust* directs. See BARE TRUSTEE.

The Law of Property Act, 1925, s. 3 (3), and the Settled Land Act, 1925, s. 7 (5), enable a person entitled to a legal estate to have it conveyed to him. The Law of Property Act, 1925, Sch. 1 Pt. II, para. (3), as amended by the Law of Property (Amendment) Act, 1926, vested an estate existing on January 1, 1926, in the beneficial owner.

Simplex beneficium, a minor dignity in a cathedral or collegiate church without a cure of souls. The holding of such a dignity along with a parochial cure of souls never amounted to a plurality.

Simplex commendatio non obligat (D. 4, 3, 37). (The mere recommendation of goods by the seller imposes no liability upon him.) See REPRESENTATION.

Simplex justiciarius, a judge who was not chief in any court, a puisne (*q.v.*) judge.

Simplex obligatio. See SINGLE BOND.

Simplicitas est legibus amica (4 Co.Rep. 5). (Simplicity is the friend of the laws.)

That is to say, a natural interpretation is to be preferred to a forced construction. See NIMIA, ETC.

Simpliciter [Lat.], without involving anything not actually named.

Simul cum [Lat.], together with. Used formerly in indictments, as where the doing of an act was by " *X simul cum* divers others unknown," or in declarations (*q.v.*) where the writ was against two persons and the plaintiff declared against one of them *simul cum* the other.

Simulatio latens, a species of feigned disease, in which disease is actually present, but where the symptoms are falsely aggravated, and greater sickness is pretended than really exists.

Sinderesis, a natural power of the soul, set in the highest part thereof, moving and stirring it to good, and abhorring evil. And therefore *sinderesis* never sins nor errs. And this *sinderesis* our Lord put in man, to the intent that the order of things should be observed. And therefore *sinderesis* is called by some men the law of reason, for it ministers the principles of the law of reason, which are in every man by nature, in that he is a reasonable creature (*Doctor and Student,* 39).

Sine assensu capitali, a writ which lay where a bishop, dean, prebendary, or master of a hospital aliened the lands held in right of his bishopric, deanery, house, etc., without the assent of the chapter or fraternity, in which case his successor might have this writ (Fitz.N.B. 195).

Sine die [Lat. without a day, indefinitely], without a day being fixed. The consideration of a matter is said to be adjourned *sine die* when it is adjourned without a day being fixed for its resumption. See ADJOURNMENT; EAT INDE SINE DIE.

Sine prole, without issue. See S.P.

Sinecure [Lat. *sine,* without; *cura,* care], an office which has revenue without any employment.

Sinecure rector, a rector without cure of souls. In former times the rector of an advowson had power, with the proper consent, to entitle (that is, appoint) a vicar to officiate under him, so that two persons were instituted to the same church. By degrees, the rectors who had entitled vicars got themselves excused from residence, and devolved the whole spiritual cure upon the vicars. In such a case the rectory became merely nominal, without cure of souls (*sine cura*), and was hence called a sinecure.

Provision for the suppression of sinecure rectories and for the endowment out of their revenues of the vicarages or the perpetual curacies previously dependent on them was made by the Ecclesiastical Commissioners Act, 1840, ss. 48, 54, 55, and the Ecclesiastical Commissioners Act, 1841, s. 17.

Singapore. See the Singapore Act, 1966.

Singing in streets. See STREET MUSICIANS.

Single bond [Lat. *simplex obligatio*], a bond merely for the payment of money, or for the performance of some particular act, without any condition in or annexed to it (*Re Dixon* [1900] 2 Ch. 561). Shylock called the bond which he took from Antonio a single bond: *Merchant of Venice*, Act I, Scene 3. He may have called it so because it was given by Antonio alone without sureties.

Single combat, Trial by. See BATTEL, ETC.

Single entry, an entry made to charge or to credit an individual or thing, as distinguished from double entry, which is an entry of both the debit and credit account of a transaction. See DOUBLE ENTRY.

Single escheat, when all a person's movables fell to the Crown, as a casualty, because of his being declared rebel. See ESCHEAT; FORFEITURE; HORNING, LETTERS OF.

Single woman. See AFFILIATION.

Singular. By the Interpretation Act, 1889, s. 1, re-enacting the statute 1850, 13 &14 Vict. c. 21, s. 4, it is enacted that words in Acts of Parliament passed after 1850 importing the singular shall include the plural, and the plural the singular, unless the contrary intention appears.

Singuli in solidum. Joint and several obligors are said to be liable *singuli in solidum*.

Sinking fund, a fund formed for the redemption of a debt by the periodical accumulation of fixed amounts by the borrower.

" Sinking fund " for the redemption of debentures does not, necessarily, connote accumulation at compound interest or any like mode of application (*Re Chicago & N.W. Granaries Co.* [1898] 1 Ch. 263).

Sipessocna, a franchise, a liberty or a hundred (Leg.Hen. 1, c. 6).

Sise, assize.

Sisters. Coke says, *omnes sorores sunt quasi unus haeres*—all sisters are, as it were, one heir. See COPARCENER.

Site value. Where a condemned house is compulsorily purchased the compensation is based on the value of the cleared site (Housing Act, 1957, s. 29). Compensation under Pt. III of the Housing Act, 1957, is also site value (s. 59 (2)). Additional payments may be made for well-maintained houses (ss. 30, 60), owner-occupiers, etc. (s. 31). See also the Housing Act, 1961, Sch. 3 para. 6; Housing Act, 1969, Sch. 8 para. 7, Sch. 10.

Sithcundman, the high constable of a hundred.

Sittings. The sittings of the Supreme Court are four in number: the Hilary Sittings, commencing on January 11, and ending on the Wednesday before Easter Sunday; the Easter Sittings, commencing on the second Tuesday after Easter Sunday and ending on the Friday before Whit Sunday; the Trinity Sittings commencing on the second Tuesday after Whit Sunday and ending on July 31, and the Michaelmas Sittings commencing on October 1, and ending on December 21 (R.S.C., Ord. 64, r. 1; Long Vacation Order, dated February 3, 1950).

Formerly the sittings of the Courts of Chancery and common law were regulated by the terms (*q.v.*), and hence were distinguished as sittings in and sittings after term. Terms were abolished and sittings substituted for them by the Judicature Act, 1873, s. 26.

The sittings of the officers of the Supreme Court extend over the whole year (R.S.C., Ord. 64, r. 7), with the exception of Saturdays and Sundays, Good Friday, the Tuesday after Easter Sunday, Christmas Day, bank holidays and such other days as the Lord Chancellor may direct (R.S.C., Ord. 64, r. 7).

As to the hours during which the offices of the Supreme Court are open, see the Supreme Court Offices (Hours of Business) Order, 1963.

Sittings of the High Court may be held, and any other business of the High Court may be conducted at any place in England or Wales. The places at which the High Court sits outside the Royal Courts of Justice and the days and times when the High Court sits outside the Royal Courts of Justice are determined by directions given by the Lord Chancellor (Courts Act, 1971, s. 2).

Sittings at the Royal Courts of Justice include sittings in chambers as well as in court (*Petty* v. *Daniel* (1886) 34 Ch.D. 172).

Sittings in banc, sittings of the judges on the benches of their respective courts at Westminster, at which they decided matters of law and transacted other judicial business, as distinguished from *nisi prius* sittings, at which matters of fact were tried. See DIVISIONAL COURTS.

Sittings in camera. See CAMERA.

Situs [Lat.], situation, location. As a rule a debt is locally situated where the debtor resides (*Re Helbert Wagg & Co.'s Claim* [1956] Ch. 323). See further as to the situs of choses in action, *F. & K. Jabbour* v. *Custodian of Israeli Absentee Property* [1954] 1 W.L.R. 139, and *Re Banque des Marchands de Moscou* (No. 2) [1954] 1 W.L.R. 1103.

Sive tota res evincatur, sive pars, habet regressum emptor in venitorem. (If a purchaser is evicted from the whole or part of the things sold, he has a right to be indemnified by the vendor.)

Six Acts, also called the Gagging Acts, the statutes 1819, 60 Geo, 3 & 1 Geo. 4, cc. 1, 2, 4, 6, 8, 9; portions of c. 1 (the Unlawful Drilling Act, 1819), and c. 8 (the Criminal Libel Act, 1819), are still unrepealed.

The six Acts prohibited the training of persons to arms; authorised general searches and seizure of arms; prohibited meetings of more than fifty persons for the discussion of public grievances; repressed with penalties and confiscation seditious and blasphemous libels; and checked pamphleteering by extending the newspaper stamp duty to political pamphlets.

Six Articles, Law of the, the statute 1539, 31 Hen. 8, c. 14, entitled "An Act abolishing Diversity in Opinions." Any person who expressed any opinion, either orally or in writing, contrary to the real presence was to be burned as a heretic and anyone who spoke or wrote against communion in one kind only for the laity, against the celibacy of the clergy, against the binding force of vows of chastity, or against private masses or against auricular confession was to suffer death as a felon without benefit of clergy. These were the Six Articles. Anyone bound by vows of celibacy who married, was also a felon without benefit of clergy. The statute was amended by the statute 1540, 32 Hen. 8, c. 10, which required conviction to be on the oath of twelve men, and was repealed by the statute 1547, 1 Edw. 6, c. 12, s. 2, and by the Act of Supremacy, 1558.

Six Clerks. Formerly there were in the Court of Chancery six officials, collectively known as the Six Clerks. Each of them was known as a Six Clerk. They seem to have descended from the six *clerici praenotarii* of the Chancery (2 Fleta, cc. 13, 15).

In the reign of Elizabeth I they were, in theory, the only attorneys of the court; but in practice they were the intermediaries between solicitors and the court. Later their duties corresponded to those subsequently performed by the Clerks of Records and Writs (*q.v.*). The statute 1833, 3 & 4 Will. 4, c. 94, provided that until the number of Six Clerks had been reduced to two, no vacancies should be filled, and there were in fact only five Six Clerks when the Court of Chancery Act, 1842, s. 1, abolished them. The Act of 1842 transferred some of their duties to the Clerk of Enrolments in Chancery (*q.v.*), and others to the Clerks of Records and Writs (*q.v.*). See CLERKS OF THE CHANCERY; CLERKS OF THE ROBE; SIXTY CLERKS.

See Braithwaite, *Six Clerks in Chancery.*

Six-day licence, a liquor licence containing a condition that the premises in respect of which it is granted shall be closed during the whole of Sunday, granted under the Licensing Act, 1964, s. 65.

Sixhindi, servants of the same nature as rodknights (*q.v.*) (Anc.Inst.Eng.).

Sixpenny Writ Office, an office of the old Court of Chancery. The head of the office was known as the deputy. He received in 1798 a salary of £100 a year, in return for which he had to attend every public day at the Cursitors, Six Clerks and Subpoena Offices, and to take an account of the writs sealed; to receive the duty on them and the duty on extra writs at the Crown Office, and to receive from the Purse Bearer the duty on all writs received at private seals; to pay the Sealer, the Deputy Sealer, the Chaff Wax, the Deputy Chaff Wax, the Gentlemen of the Chamber, and the Messenger of the Great Seal their salaries out of the duty each term, and to pay the surplus, after deducting the receiver's salary, to the Clerk of the Hanaper. He collected duties to an average annual amount of about £600 (*Reports from Committees of the House of Commons,* 1803, p. 250).

The office seems to have been abolished about 1852 at the time that the Sealer (*q.v.*) and the Chaff Wax (*q.v.*) and other such officials disappeared.

Sixty Clerks. From an early period, the Six Clerks (*q.v.*) employed assistants, who had, however, no legal status until in 1596 they were made officers of the court, eight of them being assigned to each of the Six Clerks. This number of eight was increased a little later to first nine and then ten, so that in fact they became the Sixty Clerks. They received a percentage of the fees payable to the Six Clerks. Some were later known as the Sworn Clerks and others as Clerks in Court. They were abolished by the Court of Chancery Act, 1842, s. 1.

Skating. Parks and recreation grounds may be enclosed in time of frost to protect ice for skating (Public Health Acts Amendment Act, 1907, s. 76; London Government Act, 1963, s. 40).

Skeleton bill, one drawn, indorsed or accepted in blank.

Sketch. The making of sketches in court is prohibited (Criminal Justice Act, 1925, s. 41).

Skilled witnesses. See EXPERT.

Sky sign. Advertisements by way of sky signs are controlled under the Town and Country Planning Act, 1971, s. 63. See ADVERTISEMENT.

Skyvinage, or **Skevinage,** the precincts of Calais.

Slander. A false and defamatory statement concerning a person made by word of mouth or in other transient form is a slander, giving rise to a right of action for damages: (i) if it imputes to the plaintiff the commission of a crime punishable with imprisonment for a first offence, or the having some contagious disorder which may exclude him from society, or is calculated to disparage him in his office, profession, calling, trade or business (Defamation Act, 1952, s. 2), or if it imputes unchastity or adultery to any plaintiff being a woman or girl (Slander of Women Act, 1891); or (ii) if it has caused the plaintiff special damage. The first kind is called slander actionable *per se,* and the latter kind is called slander actionable by reason of special damage. Thus, if one man falsely says of another that he is a thief or a swindler, or a leper, or that, being a lawyer, he is a rogue, this is slander actionable *per se.* In the case of words imputing unchastity to a woman, the costs are as the costs in other actions, if there has been special damage, but if the words are actionable only under the Slander of Women Act, 1891, the plaintiff can recover no more costs than damages unless the judge certifies that there was reasonable cause for bringing the action. Mere words of abuse are not actionable (*Fields* v. *Davis* (1955) *The Times,* May 25).

The publication of words in the course of the performance of a play is, with certain exceptions, treated as publication in a permanent form (Theatres Act, 1968, ss. 4, 7).

A statement in itself defamatory is not actionable if it is privileged (*q.v.*).

See APOLOGY; DEFAMATION; JUSTIFICATION; LIBEL; MALICE.

Slander of goods, a false and malicious statement, whether by word of mouth or in writing, with reference to goods manufactured and sold by the plaintiff (*White*

v. *Mellin* [1895] A.C. 154). Where a reasonable man would give serious credence to an unfavourable comparison of the plaintiff's goods with those of the defendant, a reasonable cause of action for slander of goods will lie and a statement of claim alleging slander of goods will not be struck out under R.S.C., Ord. 18, r. 19 (*De Beers Abrasive Products* v. *International Electric Co. of New York* [1975] 1 W.L.R. 972). See SLANDER OF TITLE.

Slander of title, a false and malicious statement, whether by word of mouth or in writing, with reference to a person's title to some right or property belonging to him, as where a person falsely alleges with some improper motive that the plaintiff has a defective title to land, or to a patent. Slander of title is not actionable unless special damage results from it (*Haddan* v. *Lott* (1854) 15 C.B. 411), or unless the words are calculated to cause damage to the plaintiff in respect of his office, profession, calling, trade or business (Defamation Act, 1952, s. 3).

A written slander of title is sometimes called a libel in the nature of slander of title (*Hart* v. *Hall* (1877) 2 C.P.D. 146).

Slate mines. See MINE; QUARRY.

Slaughterhouses. A slaughterhouse is any building, premises or place used in connection with the business of killing animals whose flesh is intended for human consumption (Slaughterhouses Act, 1974, s. 45). It includes any place for the confinement of animals awaiting slaughter or for the keeping, or subjecting to any treatment or process, products of the slaughtering of animals there (s. 34). A slaughterhall is that part of a slaughterhouse in which the actual slaughtering or dressing of carcasses takes place (s. 34). As to knackers' yards see KNACKER.

Provisions for the licensing and regulation of private slaughterhouses and knackers' yards are contained in ss. 1–14. Local authorities may provide public slaughterhouses, cold stores and refrigerators (ss. 15–18). Methods of slaughter are dealt with in ss. 36–38. Slaughtermen require to be licensed (s. 39). Local authorities are the council of a district (see DISTRICT COUNCIL), London borough (see LONDON) or the Common Council of the City of London (see LONDON) (s. 45).

See also the Local Government Act, 1974, s. 35, Sch. 6 para. 26, Sch. 8, amending ss. 18 and 40 (9) of the Slaughterhouses Act, 1974.

A person licensed under s. 39 of the Slaughterhouses Act, 1974, may, without a firearms (*q.v.*) certificate have in his possession a slaughtering instrument and ammunition therefor in any slaughterhouse or knacker's yard in which he is employed and they may be stored without a firearms certificate (Firearms Act, 1968, s. 10; Slaughterhouses Act, 1974, Sch. 3).

Slave. In *Smith* v. *Gould* (1705) Ld. Raym. 1274, where the defendant had taken a negro alleged to be the slave of the plaintiff, it was held that the action of trover did not lie, inasmuch as the negro was not the slave, that is to say, the chattel, of his alleged master, but that an action lay in trespass *quare captivum suum cepit,* inasmuch as the negro, if a captive, was therefore a villein; but it does not appear that any further action was taken. In *Sommersett's Case* (1772) Lofft. 1, it was held that once a negro slave had set foot on English soil he was a free man and was entitled to be discharged on habeas corpus.

Slave trading, an indictable offence punishable with imprisonment for fourteen years (Slave Trade Act, 1824, s. 10). Piratical slave trading is the offence of carrying away or assisting in carrying away any person from any part of the British dominions for the purpose of his being dealt with as a slave (s. 9). It is punishable with imprisonment for life.

The Slave Trade Act, 1873, consolidated the Acts for carrying into effect treaties for the more effectual suppression of the slave trade.

It is an offence to decoy any native of any Pacific island not subject to the jurisdiction of any civilised power for the purpose of removing him elsewhere (Pacific Islanders' Protection Act, 1875); see also the Slave Trade (East African Courts) Acts, 1873 and 1879.

Slavery, that civil relation in which one man has absolute power over the liberty of another. It cannot subsist in England (*Sommersett's Case* (1772) Lofft. 1).

The system of colonial slavery was abolished by the Slavery Abolition Act, 1832.

Sledge, a hurdle to draw traitors to execution (1 Hale P.C. 82).

Sleeping partner, a partner who puts his money into a partnership but takes no active part in the management of it. He is liable to the full extent of his assets, as is any other partner, to satisfy creditors of the partnership.

Sliding. See SNOW.

Slip. In negotiations for a policy of marine insurance, the agreement is in practice concluded between the parties by a memorandum called the slip, containing the terms of the proposed insurance, and initialled by the underwriters. Although, under the Marine Insurance Act, 1906, s. 22, which requires every contract of marine insurance to be expressed in a policy, the slip is not itself enforceable, it is for many other purposes of legal effect; thus, where a slip has been initialled, the assured need not communicate to the insurer facts which afterwards come to his knowledge material to the risk insured against, and the non-disclosure of those facts will not vitiate the policy afterwards executed, although it would do so if there were no slip. The slip is in fact a binding contract for the issue of the policy.

Slip order, R.S.C., Ord. 20, r. 11, under which clerical mistakes and accidental slips in judgments or orders, and consequential errors, may be corrected in a summary way on motion or summons.

Slippa, a stirrup. There is a tenure of land in Cambridgeshire by holding the sovereign's stirrup.

Slough-silver, a rent which was paid to the owner of the castle of Wigmore in commutation of the service of rendering certain days' work in harvest (Cowel).

Slum clearance. See the Housing Act, 1957, Pt. III. See also the Housing (Slum Clearance Compensation) Act, 1965, and the Housing Act, 1969, ss. 65–69.

Small bankruptcy, a bankruptcy administered as a summary case where the assets are not likely to exceed £300. The official receiver acts as trustee.

Small debts courts, courts of request and courts of conscience superseded by the County Courts Act, 1846.

Small dwellings. The Small Dwellings Acquisition Acts, 1899 to 1923 (see the Housing, etc. Act, 1923, s. 25 (6)), enable county councils and district councils to advance money to enable persons to become owners of houses. Power to make advances and to guarantee loans is given by the Housing (Financial Provisions) Act, 1958, ss. 43–45. See also the House Purchase and Housing Act, 1959, ss. 3, 31, Sch. 2; the Housing Act, 1964, s. 57 (8); the Fire Precautions Act, 1971, s. 36 (8); the Local Government Act, 1974, s. 37. See HOUSING.

Small holding colonies. Land could be acquired for this purpose under the Small Holding Colonies Acts, 1916 and 1918, as amended. The Acts were repealed by the Agriculture Act, 1970, Sch. 5 Pt. III.

Small holdings. Small holdings are regulated by the Agriculture Act, 1970, ss. 37–65, as amended by the Agriculture (Miscellaneous Provisions) Act, 1972, ss. 9, 26, Sch. 6, and the Local Government Act, 1972, ss. 131, 272, Sch. 30. The Small Holdings and Allotments Acts, 1908 and 1926, as amended were repealed as regards small holdings by the Agriculture Act, 1947, s. 67, Sch. 8.

Small lotteries. See LOTTERY.

Small tenements. The Small Tenements Recovery Act, 1838, was repealed by the Rent Act, 1965, Sch. 7 Pt. II.

Small tithes, or **Privy tithes,** all personal and mixed tithes, and also hops, flax, saffrons, potatoes, and sometimes, by custom, wood.

Smallpox. See VACCINATION.

Smell. See NUISANCE.

Smoke. The production of smoke in large quantities may be a ground for a civil action or for a prosecution for a nuisance at common law (*R.* v. *Dewsnap* (1812) 16 East 194). See CHIMNEYS.

Consumption of smoke is proscribed by the Public Health Act, 1936, ss. 101–106, the London Government Act, 1963, s. 40, the Clean Air Acts, 1956 and 1968, the Housing Act, 1964, s. 95, the Control of Pollution Act, 1974, ss. 75–81, Sch. 2 para. 26, Sch. 4; the Consumer Credit Act, 1974, Sch. 4 para. 16; S.I. 1974 No. 482, art. 14; S.I. 1974 No. 2170.

Compensation for smoke arising out of the use of public works may be claimed under the Land Compensation Act, 1973. See NUISANCE.

Smoke-farthing. See FUMAGE; PENTE-COSTALS.

Smokesilver, a modus of 6d. in lieu of tithe-wood.

Smoking. See TOBACCO.

Smugglers Act, the statute 1745, 19 Geo. 2, c. 34.

Smuggling, the offence of importing or exporting prohibited goods, or of importing or exporting goods without paying the duties imposed on them. Goods so imported are liable to confiscation, and offenders are liable to forfeit a penalty of three times the value of the goods or £100 whichever is the greater, and to imprisonment for two years (Customs and Excise Act, 1952, s. 45). See DRUGS, DANGEROUS; SHOOTING.

Snottering silver, a small duty which was paid by servile tenants in Wylegh to the abbot of Colchester.

Snow. Nuisances arising from snow may be prevented by by-laws of local authorities under the Public Health Act, 1936, s. 81; London Government Act, 1963, s. 40, Sch. 11 Pt. I para. 17. If an obstruction arises in a highway from accumulation of snow, the highway authority is required from time to time, and within twenty-four hours after notice thereof from a justice of the peace to cause the same to be removed (Highways Act, 1959, s. 129 (as substituted by the Highways (Amendment) Act, 1965, s. 1); London Government Act, 1963, s. 16, Sch. 6 para. 46; Courts Act, 1971, Sch. 9 Pt. I; Local Government Act, 1972, Sch. 21 para. 51). Sliding on snow in the street to the common danger is an offence under the Town Police Clauses Act, 1847, s. 28, and the Metropolitan Police Act, 1839, s. 54 (17). By the Town Police Clauses Act, 1847, s. 28, snow thrown down so as not to fall on a passer-by is excepted from the list of

things which may not be thrown down from a roof.

Snuff. Offences in relation to snuff are set out in the Customs and Excise Act, 1952, ss. 173, 176, 191.

Soap. The excise on soap was repealed by the statute 1853, 16 & 17 Vict. c. 39.

As to the standards of measurement, etc., on the sale of soap, see the Weights and Measures Act, 1963, s. 21, Sch. 7 Pt. VI.

Soc, Sok, Soka, jurisdiction; a power or privilege to administer justice and execute laws; also a shire, circuit, or territory (*Merttons* v. *Hill* [1901] 1 Ch. 842). See SOKE.

Soca, a seigniory or lordship, enfranchised by the king with liberty of holding a court of his soc-men or socagers, *i.e.,* his tenants.

Socage [Ang.Sax. *soc, socn,* jurisdiction; Fr. *soc,* a ploughshare], land held by free suitors of the lord's courts, often, in ancient times, by the service of ploughing the lord's land for so many days in the year (Co.Litt. 86).

Socage is a kind of tenure, distinguished from the tenure of frankalmoign (*q.v.*) by its services being certain and of a temporal nature, and from the tenure of knight's service (*q.v.*) by its services having been originally agricultural. See SERVICE; TENURE.

Socage was originally of two kinds, free socage and villein socage, according as the services were free or base. Thus, where a man held land by fealty and a fixed rent, the tenure was free socage (Litt. 117).

Free socage was of two kinds, socage *in capite* (*q.v.*) and common socage, but the former has been abolished. Common free socage is the modern ordinary freehold tenure. The exceptions were, until abolished by the Law of Property Act, 1922, borough-english, gavelkind, etc. (*q.v.*).

Socagium idem est quod servitium socae; et soca idem est quod caruca (Litt. 119). (Socage is the same thing as the service of the soc; and the soc is the same thing as the plough.) Littleton is probably wrong as regards the first of these statements: the word is probably derived from a word meaning jurisdiction. See SOCAGE.

Soccager, a tenant by socage.

Socer [Lat.], the father of one's wife; a father-in-law.

Social need. See the Local Government Grants (Social Need) Act, 1969.

Social security. See the Social Security Act, 1975; the Supplementary Benefits Acts, 1966 to 1975; Employment Protection Act, 1975, ss. 111–113; the Social Security (Consequential Provisions) Act, 1975, and the Social Security Pensions Act, 1975.

The courts will interfere with the decisions of social security appeals tribunals only in case of want of jurisdiction, non-observance of the rules of natural justice (*q.v.*) or if their decisions are wholly unreasonable (*R.* v. *Preston Supplementary Benefits Appeal Tribunal, ex p. Moore* [1975] 1 W.L.R. 624).

Social Security, Ministry of. The Ministry was dissolved and its functions transferred to the Secretary of State for Social Services by S.I. 1968 No. 1699.

Social Services, Secretary of State for. By the Ministry of Social Security Act, 1966, the functions of the Ministry of Pensions and National Insurance and of the National Assistance Board were transferred to the Minister of Social Security. These functions and the functions of the Ministry of Health were transferred to the Secretary of State for Social Services by S.I. 1968 No. 1699.

The Department of Health and Social Security is responsible for the administration of the National Health Service in England, for the welfare services run by local authorities in England (Local Authority Social Services Act, 1970), for the medical and surgical treatment of war pensioners, for the ambulance and first aid services in emergency (Civil Defence Act, 1948), and for social security services, including war pensions, national insurance, family allowances and supplementary benefits. It has functions relating to food hygiene and welfare foods. It represents the United Kingdom on the World Health Organisation of the United Nations. Responsibility for the health services in Wales has been transferred to the Secretary of State for Wales.

Socida, a contract of hiring upon condition that the bailee take upon himself the risk of the loss of the thing hired (Civil Law).

Societas Ieonina, that kind of society or partnership by which the entire profits belong to some of the partners in exclusion of the rest, so called in allusion to the fable of the lion, who, having entered into partnership with other animals for the purpose of hunting, appropriated all the prey to himself. It was void. Other *societates* were *negotionis alicujus* (partnership); *unius rei vel certarum rerum*; *universorum bonorum*; *universorum quae ex quaestu veniunt*; and *vectigalium* (collection of taxes) (Civil Law).

Société anonyme, an association where the liability of all the partners is limited (French Law). See LIMITED COMPANIES.

Société en commandite. See COMMANDITE.

Societies. Associations designated by the name of "society" include building societies (*q.v.*), friendly societies (*q.v.*), industrial and provident societies (*q.v.*), loan societies (*q.v.*), literary and scientific societies (*q.v.*), and other benevolent or useful societies: see, *e.g.*, the Companies Act, 1948, s. 19.

Societies, Unlawful, societies whose members are obliged to take any oath or enter into any engagement prohibited by the Unlawful Oaths Acts, 1797 and 1812 (as amended by the Criminal Law Act, 1967, Sch. 3 Pt. III).

Society of Gentlemen Practisers. See LAW SOCIETY.

Socii mei socius meus socius non est (D. 50, 17, 47). (The partner of my partner is not my partner.) See PARTNER.

Socman, one who held in socage (*q.v.*).

Socmanry, a free tenure by socage.

Socna, a privilege, liberty, or franchise.

Socome, a custom of grinding corn at the lord's mill. Where the grinding was obligatory the custom was known as bond socome, and where it was voluntary the custom was called love socome.

Sodomy, unnatural sexual intercourse by a man whether with a man or a woman, so called from Sodom (Gen. xiii, 13). In the criminal law it is known as buggery. See ABOMINABLE CRIME.

A homosexual act in private between two consenting persons over the age of twenty-one is not an offence (Sexual

Offences Act, 1967, s. 1 (1) (2)). A man is to be treated as doing a homosexual act if, and only if, he commits buggery (*q.v.*) with another man or commits an act of gross indecency with another man or is party to the commission by a man of such an act (s. 1 (7)). As to homosexual acts by soldiers, airmen or sailors, see s. 1 (5). As to homosexual acts on merchant ships, see s. 2. As to punishment for buggery with another man of or over the age of sixteen, see s. 3. Procuring others to commit homosexual acts is an offence under s. 4. Living on the earnings of male prostitution is punishable under s. 5. Premises resorted to for the purpose of homosexual acts are to be treated as a brothel (*q.v.*) (s. 6). Prosecutions require the consent of the Director of Public Prosecutions (s. 8). There is a time limit of twelve months on certain prosecutions (s. 7). Notwithstanding that homosexual behaviour between consenting adults is no longer an offence an allegation that a witness is a homosexual is an imputation on his character (*q.v.*) so as to justify the character of the person making the allegation being given in evidence (*R.* v. *Bishop* [1975] Q.B. 274).

Sodor and Man, a bishopric annexed to the province of York by the statute 1541, 33 Hen. 8, c. 31: see also the Sodor and Man Act, 1838. The bishop is not a lord spiritual, the lands with which the see was endowed being held, not of the king directly, but of a subject, who nominated the bishop, till 1829, when the lordship of the Isle of Man was purchased by the Crown (Selborne, *Defence of the Church of England*, 5th ed., p. 45).

As to the bishop's salary and expenses, see the Church Commissioners (Miscellaneous Provisions) Measure, 1975 (No. 1).

Soil. Removal of surface soil from agricultural land without planning permission is an offence (Agricultural Land (Removal of Surface Soil) Act, 1953).

Soit droit fait al partie [Nor.-Fr.], let right be done to the party.

Soke, a manor or lordship (*Beauchamp* v. *Winn* (1873) L.R. 6 H.L. at p. 243).

Soke-land. See BOND-LAND.

Sokemanry, the tenure of land by a sokeman or socman (*q.v.*); and also the socmen collectively.

Sokemanries were lands and tenements which were not held by knight's service, nor by grand serjeanty, nor by petit, but by simple services, being, as it were, lands enfranchised by the king or his predecessors from their ancient demesne.

Sokemans, tenants of socage-lands (3 Bl.Comm. 100).

Soke-reeve, the lord's rent-gatherer in the soca.

Sola bill, a single bill of exchange, as distinguished from one in a set, the latter being marked as " first (second or third) of exchange," and the former as " sola of exchange." See SETS OF BILLS.

Solarium, a sollar, upper room or garret (Jacob).

Solatium, solice; a sum paid to an injured party over and above the actual damage by way of solace to his wounded feelings.

Sold note. See BOUGHT AND SOLD NOTES.

Soldiers. See ARMY.

Soldiers' wills. See NUNCUPATIVE WILL.

Sole, not married, single, alone; also separate and apart.

Sole agent, an expression of which the meaning is to be ascertained by construction of the contract (*Snelgrove* v. *Ellringham* (1881) 45 J.P. 408; *Lamb* v. *Goring Brick Co.* [1932] 1 K.B. 710). The appointment does not preclude the principal from selling on his own behalf (*Bentall* v. *Vicary* [1931] 1 K.B. 253). See SOLUS AGREEMENT.

Sole, Corporation, one person and his successors who are incorporated by law in order to give them some legal capacities and advantages, particularly that of perpetuity, which in their natural persons they could not have had; as the sovereign, a bishop, parson, etc. The word " successors " was formerly essential in order to pass the fee simple in a grant to a corporation sole; without it, a life estate only passed (Co.Litt. 94b).

Words of limitation are not now necessary to convey land to a corporation sole (Law of Property Act, 1925, s. 60), and any property vested in a corporation sole, including the Crown, passes to his successors unless disposed of by him, and on his death does not pass to his personal representatives (Administration of Estates Act, 1925, s. 3 (5); Law of Property Act, 1925, ss. 180, 181). As to the property on a dissolution, see *Hastings Corporation* v. *Letton* [1908] 1 K.B. 378.

In a conveyance to a corporation aggregate, words of limitation are unnecessary, and indeed meaningless (*Re Woking U.D.C.* (*Basingstoke Canal*) *Act*, 1911 [1914] 1 Ch. at p. 307).

Sole tenant [*solus tenens*], he who holds lands by his own right only, without any other person being joined with him.

Solemn form. See PROBATE.

Solicitation. It is an indictable offence to solicit and incite another to commit a crime, although no felony be in fact committed (*R.* v. *Higgins* (1801) 2 East, 5).

Solicitation by a prostitute is an offence under the Street Offences Act, 1959, s. 1. See LOITERING. Placing an advertisement in a shop window does not come within the section (*Weisz* v. *Monahan* [1962] 1 W.L.R. 262; *Burge* v. *D.P.P.* [1962] 1 W.L.R. 265). It is an offence for a man persistently to solicit or importune in a public place for immoral purposes (Sexual Offences Act, 1956, s. 32). The time limit for prosecutions under s. 32 is twelve months (Sexual Offences Act, 1967, s. 7). The accussed may claim to be tried by a jury (s. 9).

"Kerb-crawling" after prostitutes is not soliciting within s. 32 of the Sexual Offences Act, 1956 (*Crook* v. *Edmondson* [1966] 2 Q.B. 81).

There is no distinction between persistently importuning and persistently soliciting (*Field* v. *Chapman* (1953) *The Times*, October 9).

Solicitor, a person employed to conduct the prosecution or defence of an action or other legal proceeding on behalf of another, or to advise him on legal questions, or to frame documents intended to have a legal operation, or generally to assist him in matters affecting his legal position.

"Solicitor of the Supreme Court" was the title given by the Judicature Act, 1843, s. 87, to all attorneys, solicitors and proctors, and it is continued by the

Solicitors Act, 1974, s. 87 (1). Prior to the Judicature Act, 1843, attorneys conducted business in the common law courts, solicitors conducted business in the Court of Chancery, and proctors conducted ecclesiastical and Admiralty business; but it was the general custom, although any person might be admitted to practise as an attorney or solicitor only, to be admitted to practise as an attorney and solicitor also.

To qualify to act as a solicitor a person must, in accordance with regulations, (a) be admitted as a solicitor, (b) have his name on the roll of solicitors and (c) have in force a practising certificate issued by the Law Society (Solicitors Act, 1974, ss. 1, 28). No person may be admitted as a solicitor unless he has obtained a certificate that the Law Society is satisfied (a) that he has complied with the Society's training regulations (see s. 2) and (b) as to his character and suitability to be a solicitor. A person on obtaining such certificate may be admitted by the Master of the Rolls or his deputy (s. 3). A person who has served as assistant to a clerk to the justices (*q.v.*) may be admitted under the Justices of the Peace Act, 1949, s. 20 (3). Overseas solicitors may be admitted under the Solicitors Act, 1974, ss. 4, 5. An admitted solicitor is entitled to have his name entered in the roll of solicitors kept by the Law Society on payment of a fee not exceeding £15 (ss. 6, 7). He may, on application, have his name removed from the roll (s. 8). Practising certificates are issued by the Law Society under ss. 9–13 on payment of the prescribed fee. Every practising certificate issued in November or December bears the date of November 1. Practising certificates issued later bear the date of issue. Practising certificates expire on October 31 (s. 14).

The making by the Solicitors Disciplinary Tribunal (*q.v.*) or by the court (ss. 50–55) of an order suspending a solicitor from practice and an adjudication in bankruptcy operate to suspend his practising certificate (ss. 15–17). The inclusion of a solicitor's name in an official list published by authority of the Law Society is prima facie evidence that he holds a practising certificate. The absence of his name is prima facie evidence that he is not qualified to practise (s. 18).

Solicitors have the right to practice as solicitors in the Supreme Court, in any county court, in all courts and before all persons having jurisdiction in ecclesiastical matters and in all matters relating to applications to obtain notarial faculties (see NOTARY) (s. 19). It is an offence for an unqualified person to act as a solicitor (s. 20) or to pretend to be a solicitor (s. 21) or to draw or prepare an instrument of transfer or charge of registered land or make any application or lodge any document at the Land Registry or draw or prepare any other instrument relating to real or personal estate or any legal proceeding unless the act was not done for or in expectation of any fee, gain or reward (s. 22 (1)). This does not apply to a barrister or duly certificated notary (see NOTARY) public or any public officer acting in the course of his duty or to a person employed merely to engross any instrument, application or proceeding (s. 22 (2)). " Instrument " does not include (a) a will or other testamentary instrument, (b) an agreement not under seal, (c) a letter or power of attorney or (d) a transfer of stock containing no trust or limitation thereof (s. 22 (3)). It is an offence for an unqualified person to prepare papers for probate or letters of administration unless the act was not done for or in expectation of any fee, gain or reward. This does not apply to a barrister or a duly certificated notary public (q.v.) (s. 23 (4)). These provisions are applied to a body corporate by s. 24. No costs are recoverable in respect of anything done by an unqualified person acting as a solicitor (s. 25). The time limit for prosecuting for an offence is two years from the commission of the offence or six months from its first discovery by the prosecutor, whichever period expires first (s. 26). An alien may become a practising solicitor (s. 29). As to Scottish solicitors see s. 30.

The professional practice, conduct and discipline of solicitors is regulated by rules made by the Council of the Law Society with the concurrence of the Master of the Rolls. If a solicitor fails to comply with the rules any person may complain to the Solicitors Disciplinary Tribunal (q.v.) (ss. 31, 46–49, 87).

The accounts to be kept by a solicitor are dealt with in ss. 32–34.

If a solicitor is suspected of misconduct or has been adjudged bankrupt, or made a composition or arrangement with his creditors or has been committed to prison or is suffering from mental ill-health or has been struck off the roll or suspended the Council of the Law Society may take steps to deal with the situation (s. 35, Sch. 1). Loss or hardship suffered in connection with a trust owing to the dishonesty of a solicitor or from failure by a solicitor to account for money which has come into his hands may be the subject of a grant by the Law Society out of the Compensation Fund to which every solicitor who applies for a practising certificate is required to contribute (s. 36, Sch. 2). A grant may also be made to a solicitor who suffers loss or hardship in consequence of some act or default of a partner or employee (s. 36 (2) (c)). This grant may be by way of loan (s. 36 (3)–(6)). Indemnity rules concerning indemnity against loss arising from claims in respect of civil liability incurred by a solicitor or an employee may authorise the establishment of a fund and may authorise the Law Society to take out insurance and may require solicitors to take out insurance (s. 37).

A solicitor who is a justice of the peace for any area may not act as solicitor before the justices of that area, nor may any partner of his. If the area is divided into petty sessional divisions this prohibition does not disqualify him or his partner from appearing before justices of a petty sessional division for which he does not ordinarily act (s. 38).

No solicitor may wilfully and knowingly act as agent for an unqualified person (s. 39) or commence or defend actions while in prison (s. 40). No solicitor, without the permission of the Law Society, may employ a person who, to his knowledge, has been struck off the roll or suspended (s. 41). Failure by a person to disclose the fact that he has been struck off or suspended is an offence. Proceedings may be commenced within six months of the first discovery of the offence by the prosecutor but no proceedings may be commenced except by or with the consent of the Attorney-General (s. 42). Dishonest clerks may be prohibited from employment by a solicitor (ss. 43, 44). The Lord Chancellor may appoint "lay observers" to examine complaints by the public of the Law Society's treatment of a complaint of a solicitor (s. 45).

A solicitor is an officer of the court and is subject to the jurisdiction of the court (ss. 50–55).

The remuneration of solicitors is regulated by orders made under s. 56. The remuneration of solicitors in conveyancing and non-contentious business is in general regulated by the Solicitors Remuneration Order, 1882, as amended. The Solicitors' Remuneration Order, 1972 (No. 1139), provides that in place of scale charges solicitors may charge for non-contentious business such sum as may be fair and reasonable in all the circumstances. In certain circumstances the client may apply to the Law Society for a certificate as to whether the charge is fair and reasonable. In determining the amount of a solicitor's remuneration for transactions such as compulsory purchase the proper approach is to take a broad look at all the circumstances of the case and in particular the general nature of the business followed by a consideration of the factors specified in art. 2 of the Order (*Property and Reversionary Investment Corporation* v. *Secretary of State for the Environment* [1975] 1 W.L.R. 1504). But a solicitor and his client may make an agreement as to his remuneration. The agreement must be in writing signed by the client or his agent in that behalf. A taxing master has power to inquire into the fairness of the agreement (s. 57). As to the remuneration of a solicitor-mortgagee, see s. 58.

The costs to be allowed to a solicitor in contentious business are regulated by R.S.C., Ord. 62. A solicitor may make an agreement for his remuneration but he may not purchase a share in litigation or agree to be paid only in the event of success (s. 59). As a general rule the costs of a solicitor where there is a contentious business agreement are not subject to taxation. A provision in the agreement relieving the solicitor for negligence, etc., is void (s. 60). No action can be brought on a contentious business agreement but the court may, on application, enforce the agreement or set it aside. A taxing officer on application may examine the agreement and allow it or reduce the amount payable under it, or set it aside and order costs covered by it to be taxed as if it had never been made (s. 61). See further ss. 62–64. A solicitor may take security for costs in respect of any contentious business to be done by him (s. 65 (1)). If a client refuses to make a reasonable advance on account of costs, the solicitor may cease to act for him (s. 65 (2)). In determining the remuneration of a solicitor in respect of contentious business the taxing master may have regard to the skill, labour and responsibility involved and may allow interest on the solicitor's disbursements. He may also allow interest on money of the client improperly retained by the solicitor (s. 66). A solicitor's bill of costs may include disbursements (including counsel's fees) before they are made but they must be described in the bill as not yet paid and may be disallowed on taxation if not paid (s. 67). As to the power of the court to order the solicitor to deliver a bill of costs, see s. 68; in general, no action may be brought to recover a solicitor's costs for one month after delivery of the bill of costs (s. 69), but he may exercise a right of set-off for them (*Brown* v. *Tibbetts* (1862) 11 C.B. (N.S.) 855). He has a general lien for his costs on the papers of his clients (*Re Rapid Road Transit Co.* [1909] 1 Ch. 96). He may obtain a charging order for his costs (s. 73; S.I. 1974 No. 1273). Taxation may be ordered on the application of the party chargeable with a bill of costs or by the solicitor (s. 70); and on the application of a third party (s. 71). See also s. 72. As to county court costs, see s. 74.

Every solicitor who holds a practising certificate has the powers of a commissioner for oaths (*q.v.*). A solicitor may not exercise these powers in a proceeding in which he is solicitor to any of the parties or in which he is interested (s. 81).

For the purpose of any statutory provision or custom whereby the qualification of a solicitor for holding office depends upon his having been admitted and enrolled for a prescribed period, the period of enrolment of a solicitor who before admission was a barrister is deemed to include any period after his call to the Bar during which he was in practice or employment as a barrister (s. 82).

Solicitors practise as advocates before magistrates at petty sessions, in county courts, at arbitrations, at judges' chambers, at coroners' inquests, in sheriffs' and secondaries' courts, in the Court of Bankruptcy and before the Land Tribunal. The Lord Chancellor may give directions that solicitors shall have rights of audience in Crown Courts. See Practice Directions dated December 7, 1971, and February 10, 1972 ([1972] C.L.Y. 2725).

A clerk to licensing justices may not himself or by his partner or clerk act as solicitor to or agent for any person at any licensing sessions or before justices of the peace or the Crown Court in any relevant proceedings (Licensing Act, 1964, s. 28; Courts Act, 1971, Sch. 8 para. 42 (1)).

The immunity of a barrister (*q.v.*) from claims in negligence may extend to a solicitor doing litigation work which could have been done by counsel (*Rondel* v. *Worsley* [1969] 1 A.C. 191).

The Crown Court has jurisdiction to order a solicitor to pay costs personally and the solicitor has no recourse to a higher court where the order is made in circumstances relating to trial on indictment (*R.* v. *Martin Smith* [1975] Q.B. 531).

Communications made to a solicitor in his professional character by a client are privileged; but the privilege is that of the client, not of the solicitor. Transactions between a solicitor and his client are subject to special scrutiny by the courts (*Demerara Bauxite Co.* v. *Hubbard* [1923] A.C. 673). A solicitor who takes a benefit under a will prepared by him must be prepared to remove the suspicion which attaches to such a gift (*Wintle* v. *Nye* [1959] 1 W.L.R. 284).

Solicitors, solicitors' articled clerks and legal executives in the employment of solicitors are ineligible for jury service. See JURY.

A solicitor engaging in contentious business is not to be treated as doing so in the course of any ancillary credit business (Consumer Credit Act, 1974, s. 146).

The professional services of a barrister can be obtained only through a solicitor except where a judge requests a barrister to defend gratuitously a prisoner about to be tried on indictment or where a barrister undertakes a dock-defence (*q.v.*).

A barrister is not forbidden by any express rule of professional etiquette from accepting instructions, and a fee, direct from a client for non-contentious business, such as drafting a marriage settlement; but the Bar Council has expressed the view that such a course is undesirable.

Value added tax (*q.v.*) is chargeable on reimbursement of out-of-pocket expenses as part of the consideration paid for a supply of services by a solicitor (*Rowe & Maw* v. *Customs and Excise Commissioners* [1975] 1 W.L.R. 1291).

See ATTORNEY; BANKER; CHARGING ORDER; LAW SOCIETY; OFFICIAL SOLICITOR; SERVICE OF PROCESS; SOLICITORS' DISCIPLINARY TRIBUNAL.

See Cordery on *Solicitors*.

Solicitor-General, the second of the Law Officers (*q.v.*). His functions are political as well as legal, for he is almost invariably a member of the House of Commons. He acts as the deputy or assistant of the Attorney-General (*q.v.*) (Law Officers Act, 1944, s. 1). The office is conferred by patent, and is held at the pleasure of the Crown. The Solicitor-General receives a salary of £11,000 a year (Ministerial and other Salaries Act, 1975, s. 1, Sch. 1) and cannot since 1895 take private business. Attached to the household of a queen consort, there is an officer called the Solicitor-General. See Norton-Kyshe, *Attorney-General and Solicitor-General*.

Solicitors at law, a society of solicitors in Edinburgh formerly enjoying an exclusive right to practise in the inferior courts.

Solicitors before the Supreme Courts, S.S.C., a body of solicitors practising in Edinburgh, incorporated in 1797.

SOLICITORS

Solicitors Disciplinary Tribunal. This consists of practising solicitors of not less than ten years' standing and persons who are neither solicitors nor barristers appointed by the Master of the Rolls. Applications and complaints under the Solicitors Act, 1974, are made to the Tribunal (s. 46). The Tribunal has power to strike the name of a solicitor off the roll or to require a solicitor to answer allegations contained in an affidavit. The Tribunal may deal with an application by a former solicitor whose name has been struck off the roll to have his name restored to the roll. The Tribunal may also suspend a solicitor from practice, impose a fine (not exceeding £750) on him or make an order as to payment of costs. The Tribunal may impose any punishment for which express provision is made by the Act (s. 47). Orders of the Tribunal are filed with the Law Society. The file is open to inspection. An order of the Tribunal may be enforced as an order of the High Court. Appeals from orders of the Tribunal in respect of convicted clerks (s. 43 (3)) or on the refusal of the Tribunal to restore a former solicitor's name to the roll are heard by the Master of the Rolls. Other appeals lie to the High Court. The decisions of the Master of the Rolls and of the High Court are final (s. 49). The Tribunal takes the place of the disciplinary committee constituted under the Solicitors Act, 1957, s. 46 (Solicitors Act, 1974, s. 89 (5)).

Solidatum, absolute right of property.

Solidum. To be bound *in solido* is to be bound for the whole debt jointly and severally with others; but where each is bound for his share, they are said to be bound *pro rata parte*.

Solidus legalis, a coin equal to 13s. 4d.

Solinus terrae, two plow-lands and somewhat less than a half; perhaps 160 acres (Domesday; Co.Litt. 5a; Jacob). See SULUNG.

Solitary confinement. The consolidating statutes relating to the criminal law passed in 1861 provided for sentences of imprisonment with or without solitary confinement in the discretion of the court, and also that no offender should be kept in solitary confinement for a longer period than one month at a time, nor three months in the space of a year;

the Prison Act, 1865, s. 17, enjoined the preventing of criminal prisoners from holding any communication with each other: this was repealed by the Prison Act, 1898. In every prison special cells are provided for the confinement of refractory or violent prisoners (Prison Act, 1952, s. 14 (6)).

Sollar. In a mine a sollar is a horizontal wooden platform, sometimes made in a level, to facilitate the ventilation.

Soller; Solar; Solarium, an upper room or garret (Tomlin). See SOLARIUM.

Solomon Islands. See S.I. 1960 No. 1367.

Solus agreement. An agreement (usually in respect of petrol) that supplies shall be obtained only from one supplier. Such an agreement may be attacked as being in restraint of trade (*Regent Oil Co.* v. *J. T. Leavesley* (*Lichfield*) [1966] 1 W.L.R. 1210; *Esso Petroleum Co.* v. *Harper's Garage* (*Stourport*) [1968] A.C. 269; *Petrofina* (*Great Britain*) v. *Martin* [1966] Ch. 146; *Amoco Australia Pty.* v. *Rocco Brothers Motor Engineering Co. Pty.* [1975] A.C. 561). See also CLOG ON EQUITY OF REDEMPTION.

Repudiation of a solus agreement and acceptance of the repudiation thereof does not bring to an end a lease which cannot be severed from the agreement (*Total Oil Great Britain* v. *Thompson Garages* (*Biggin Hill*) [1972] 1 Q.B. 318). Breach of a solus agreement may be remedied by injunction (*Sky Petroleum* v. *V.I.P. Petroleum* [1974] 1 W.L.R. 576). Solus agreements are not *per se* prohibited by Article 85 of the EEC Treaty. They are potentially capable of being so prohibited, depending on the circumstances in each case surrounding it (*Brasserie de Haecht S.A.* v. *Wilkin* (*No. 23/67*) [1968] C.M.L.R. 26; *Esso Petroleum Co.* v. *Kingswood Motors* (*Addlestone*) [1973] C.M.L.R. 665; *Re a Brewery Solus Agreement* [1975] 1 C.M.L.R. 611).

Solutio, a discharge; the performance of that to which a person is bound (Civil Law).

Solutio pretii emptionis loco habetur (Jenk., Cent. 56). (The payment of the price stands in the place of the purchase.) This maxim is cited in connection with a decision that where A had bailed goods to B in such a way as to pass the property in them, then A, where he took the goods *clam et noctanter*, was guilty of felony.

Solutione feodi militis (or burgensis) parliamenti, De, a writ which lay for a knight of the shire or for a borough member or burgess whose constituents did not pay him the wages to which a Member of Parliament was entitled: see the statute 1543, 35 Hen. 8, c. 11.

Solvendo esse, to be solvent.

Solvere poenas, to undergo the punishment prescribed for an offence.

Solvit ad diem, a plea by the defendant, in an action on a bond, bill, etc., that he had paid on the day that the money was due.

Solvit ante diem, a plea that the money was paid before the day appointed.

Solvit post diem, a plea that the money was paid after the day appointed.

Solvitur in modum solventis. (Money is to be applied according to the wish of the person paying it.) See QUICQUID SOLVITUR, ETC.

Somaliland. See S.I. 1960 Nos. 205, 848, 1060.

Somers' Act, the statute 1695, 7 & 8 Will. 3, c. 25, which related to parliamentary elections.

Somerset. See HERALD.

Son assault demesne (his own assault), a justification in an action of assault and battery, on the ground that the plaintiff made the first assault, and what the defendant did was in his own defence. It was a plea of confession and avoidance. See PLEADING; STATEMENT OF DEFENCE.

Sontage, a tax of 40s. laid upon every knight's fee (Stow).

Sorcery. Prosecution for witchcraft, sorcery, etc., or for charging another with any such offences, was abolished by the Witchcraft Act, 1735; but the Act provided that persons pretending to use witchcraft, sorcery, etc., should suffer one year's imprisonment on conviction. The Act was repealed by the Fraudulent Mediums Act, 1951. See CONJURATION.

Sorites, a form of argument which consists in consolidating several syllogisms (see SYLLOGISM), in which the subject of the minor premiss is the same, so as to suppress the conclusion in every syllogism but the last, and the minor premiss in every syllogism but the first.

Sors, principal; to distinguish it from interest.

Sothsaga, or **Sothsage** [Sax. *soth*, rue; *saga*, testimony], history.

Soul-scot, a mortuary fee.

Sound. An action which is brought to recover damages is said to " sound in damages," *i.e.*, to have the essential quality of damages, as opposed to an action brought for the recovery of a specific thing, as debt, etc.

Soup. At certain courts where prisoners are tried on indictment, it is the custom, in cases which are not privately prosecuted, to hand out the briefs to counsel who are members of the bar-mess connected with the court and who regularly attend. In some cases only counsel who have been members of the mess for two or three years are eligible for such briefs, which are known as " soup," the reference being to the soup which used to be supplied, either gratuitously or at a low cost, to the poor or the unemployed at institutions known as soup-kitchens.

Sources of the law. See LAW; CUSTOM; PRECEDENT.

South Africa. The colonies of Cape of Good Hope, Natal, Transvaal, and Orange Free State were incorporated into the Union of South Africa by the South Africa Act, 1909.

The Union of South Africa became a republic outside the Commonwealth (South Africa Act, 1962).

South Sea Bubble. See BUBBLE ACT.

South Sea Company, a company incorporated in 1711 under a royal charter giving it a monopoly of trade to the south seas. The exclusive privilege of the company was abolished by the statute 1814, 55 Geo. 3, c. 57. The company, which was largely engaged in the whale fishery, continued to exist until 1850.

South Sea Fund, the produce of the taxes appropriated to pay the interest of such part of the national debt as was advanced by the South Sea Company and its annuitants. The holders of South Sea annuities were paid off, or received other stock in lieu thereof.

Southern Ireland. See IRELAND.

Souvenir land. Plots of land of inconsiderable size (often a foot square) have been sold, often to Canadians and Americans. They are bought for the sake of pure ownership or for sentimental reasons or commemorative purposes. Where such plots lie in an area of compulsory land registration their registration is apt to interfere with the proper work of the Land Registry. The Land Registration and Land Charges Act, 1971, excludes souvenir land from registration.

Sovereign, a chief or supreme person; a gold coin of the value of twenty shillings. See GOLD COINS; KING; QUEEN.

Sovereign power, or **Sovereignty,** that power in a State to which none other is superior.

Sowlegrove, February, so called in South Wales.

Sowne [Fr. *souvenue,* remembered]. Estreats which sowne are those which the sheriff cannot levy (4 Co.Inst. 107).

Spadarius, a sword bearer (Blount).

Spado, a eunuch; an impotent man (Civil Law).

Sparsim [Lat.], dispersedly.

Spatae placitum [Lat. *placitum*, plea; *spatha*, the short sword of the Roman legionary], the plea of the sword; a species of military court mentioned in a document of the reign of Henry III as having been held in Normandy by Henry II and Richard I; a court for the speedy punishment of military delinquents (Cowel).

This plea of the sword seems to have been distinct from the pleas of the sword anciently known as *placita gladii.* See PLEAS OF THE SWORD.

Speaker, the spokesman of the Commons; in modern times he is more occupied in presiding over the deliberations of the House than in delivering speeches on their behalf. The principal duties of the Speaker are to preside, as chairman of the House, at its debates when it is not in committee; to give a casting vote when the votes are equal (he has no original vote); to read to the sovereign petitions or addresses from the Commons, and to deliver in the royal presence, whether at the palace or in the House of Lords, such speeches as are usually made on behalf of the Commons; to reprimand persons who have incurred the dis-

pleasure of the House; to issue warrants of committal or release for breaches of privilege; and to communicate in writing with any parties, when so instructed by the House. In the case of Bills introduced under the provisions of the Parliament Acts, 1911 and 1949, he must certify that a money Bill is such, and in the case of Bills other than money Bills he must certify that the provisions of the Acts have been complied with, and must also give a certificate as to amendments introduced by the House of Lords. Any certificate given by him under the Act is conclusive.

"The Speaker" always means the Speaker of the House of Commons. He is always a member of the House of Commons, and is elected, subject to the approval of the Crown, on the first day that a new Parliament assembles.

When the House is in Committee of the Whole House the Chairman of Ways and Means or the Deputy Chairman of Ways and Means presides. Both of them, like the Speaker, are members, and like him are elected by the House; but in their case the royal approval is not required. The Chairman, or in his unavoidable absence, the Deputy Chairman, can act as Deputy Speaker in the absence of the Speaker.

The salary of the Speaker is £13,000 a year or such amount as is fixed by Order in Council (Ministerial and other Salaries Act, 1975, s. 1). As to pension see the Parliamentary and other Pensions Act, 1972, ss. 26, 29, 31. The Speaker has the use of a house in the Palace of Westminster (*q.v.*). He neither takes part in debates nor votes; the Lord Chancellor does both the one thing and the other in the Lords, and down to 1835 the Speaker of the Commons used sometimes to take part in debates when the House was in committee. In point of precedence outside the House he ranks next after the Prime Minister (*q.v.*) and the Lord President of the Council (*q.v.*). He is officially described as Mr. Speaker.

The Speaker's tenure of office is only during the continuance of the Parliament which elects him. For certain purposes connected with officers of the House he is, however, deemed to be Speaker between the dissolution of one Parliament and the meeting of the next (House of Commons Offices Act, 1846, s. 5), and in practice since 1835 the same Speaker is re-elected until, at the end of ten or fifteen years, he intimates his desire to retire. Then the House prays the sovereign to grant him some signal mark of favour; the sovereign replies that he is only too willing, but that he cannot act without the concurrence of the House; the House votes the retiring Speaker an annuity for his life, and the sovereign makes him a viscount. See, for instance, Mr. Speaker King's Retirement Act, 1971.

The Lord Chancellor (see CHANCELLOR, LORD) is *ex officio* the Speaker of the House of Lords though he is never spoken of by that title. He has no such position of authority as is held by the Speaker of the House of Commons. He has, for instance, no control of a disorderly peer. He is usually, but not necessarily, a peer, and unlike the Speaker of the House of Commons is under no obligation to preserve an impartial attitude, since he is a member of the government for the time being. He has always had a Deputy Speaker, and formerly there were two or more, but since the year 1815 there has been only one; the Chairman of Committees generally fills the office. In the absence of the Lord Chancellor and of the Deputy Speaker, it is competent to the House to appoint any peer to take the woolsack. The Lord Chancellor is the organ or mouthpiece of the House, and it therefore is his duty to represent the peers in their collective capacity, when holding intercourse with other public bodies or with individuals. He has not a casting vote upon divisions, for should the numbers prove equal the non-contents prevail. The Deputy Speaker of the Lords is appointed by the Crown.

Speaking demurrer, one in which new facts, which did not appear upon the face of a bill in equity, were introduced to support a demurrer (*q.v.*).

Speaking order, an order containing a statement of what has led to the decision of the court. Certiorari is available to quash a decision for error of law appearing on the face of an award of a statutory tribunal (*R.* v. *Northumberland Com-*

pensation Appeal Tribunal [1952] 1 K.B. 338).

Speaking with the prosecutor, an imparlance (*q.v.*) by a defendant convicted of a misdemeanour personally affecting the prosecutor, as where he has been assaulted; if the prosecutor declares himself satisfied, the court may see fit to inflict only a slight punishment.

Special. See AUTHORITY; JUDGMENT; POWER; RESOLUTION.

Special Acts of Parliament, local, personal, or private Acts; Acts which apply only to a particular kind of persons or things, as a particular undertaking to be constructed, or otherwise dealing with a particular area or person only, and therefore not overruled by the general terms of a general Act (*Taylor* v. *Oldham Corporation* (1876) 4 Ch.D. 410). But the term has received various statutory definitions; see *e.g.,* the public Health Act, 1875, s. 316, and the Railways Clauses Consolidation Act, 1845, s. 2. Thus the various Clauses Acts (*q.v.*) frequently describe as " special Acts " the particular Acts which may subsequently be passed regarding particular undertakings of the kind contemplated by the Clauses Acts. See LOCAL AND PERSONAL ACTS; PRIVATE ACTS, etc.

Special administration, one limited to a particular extent of time, or to a specified subject-matter, as distinguished from a general grant, *e.g.,* administration with the will annexed and *administratio de bonis non.* See ADMINISTRATION.

Special agent, one authorised to transact only a particular business for his principal, as distinguished from a general agent. See AGENCY.

Special bail. See BAIL.

Special bailiff, one chosen by a party, himself to execute process in the sheriff's hands; the appointment of such a bailiff relieves the sheriff of all responsibility. See BAILIFF.

Special case, a mode of obtaining a judicial decision on a statement of facts. Under R.S.C., Ord. 33, r. 3, the court may direct that a question or issue shall be stated by or in the form of a special case (see *Duncan* v. *Lambeth Borough Council* [1968] 1 Q.B. 747) but the parties cannot under this rule state questions of law in the form of a special case. If a special case is directed by the court it must be signed by counsel if settled by him, otherwise it should be signed by the solicitors or by the parties if appearing in person.

A special case is set down for hearing, and argued in court, after which judgment is given according to the rights of the parties. The court has power to draw inferences of fact; that is, to deduce from facts stated the existence of facts not expressly stated. See ADVICE OF COURT; DEMURRER; QUESTIONS OF LAW.

See CASE STATED BY ARBITRATOR; CASE STATED BY JUSTICES; CASE STATED BY TRIBUNALS.

Special commissioners. See INCOME TAX COMMISSIONERS.

Special constables may be appointed by the chief officer of police (see CHIEF CONSTABLE) (Police Act, 1964, ss. 16, 19, 34).

Special damage, such a loss as the law will not presume to be the consequence of the defendant's act, but which must be claimed in the pleadings; at the trial, it must be proved by evidence both that the loss was incurred and that it was the direct result of the defendant's conduct. A mere expectation of loss is not sufficient, though it may be taken into account in assessing general damages (*q.v.*).

Special defence. Formerly, in the county court a defendant had to give notice to the plaintiff when he intended to rely on a defence of set-off or counterclaim, infancy, coverture, statute of limitations, bankruptcy, equitable defence or the Statute of Frauds, 1677, s. 4, and if he failed to do so in one action he might be estopped from doing so in a subsequent action (*Humphries* v. *Humphries* [1910] 2 K.B. 521). Since 1936, there have been no special defences: the defendant is supposed to give notice of his defence in all cases, but he may appear and defend without delivering a defence, although the court may order him to pay any costs occasioned by his failure to deliver a defence. See DEFENCE.

Special demurrer, a demurrer for some defect in the form of the opposite party's pleading. It was abolished by Common Law Procedure Act, 1852, s. 51. See DEMURRER.

Special examiner. See EXAMINER.

Special finding, of a jury. See VERDICT.

Special hospital. Under the Mental Health Act, 1959, the Minister of Health (now the Secretary of State for Social Services) was given power to provide such institutions as appear to him to be necessary for persons subject to detention under the Act, being persons who, in the opinion of the Secretary of State, require treatment under conditions of special security on account of their dangerous, violent or criminal propensities. The Broadmoor Institution (see BROADMOOR ACT) which dealt with Broadmoor patients (formerly called criminal lunatics) and Rampton and Moss Side Hospitals for violent or dangerous mental defectives are deemed to be special hospitals (Act of 1959, ss. 97–99).

Special hours. Special hours certificates may be granted to licensed premises where music, dancing and substantial refreshment are provided (Licensing Act, 1964, s. 77).

Special indorsement, an indorsement in full on a bill of exchange or promissory note, which, besides the signature of the indorser, expresses in whose favour the indorsement is made. Thus: " Pay C. D. or order, A. B.," the signature of the indorser being subscribed to the direction. Its effect is to make the instrument payable to C. D. or his order only. See INDORSEMENT.

Special indorsement on writ. See STATEMENT OF CLAIM.

Special jury, a jury consisting of persons who, in addition to the ordinary qualifications, were of a certain station in society, as esquires, bankers, merchants, etc.

The Juries Act, 1949, ss. 18, 19 abolished special juries except City of London special juries in commercial cases and this exception was abolished by the Courts Act, 1971, s. 40.

Special licence, a licence granted by the Archbishop of Canterbury to authorise a marriage at any time or place whatever. See LICENCE; MARRIAGE.

Special manager, a manager appointed by the court under the Companies Act, 1948, s. 263, on the application of the official receiver as liquidator of a company.

Special notice. The Companies Act, 1948, s. 142, requires twenty-eight days' notice to be given to the company of intention to move certain resolutions and the company must give notice thereof to the members with notice of the meeting; this applies to notice of resolutions to remove auditors (s. 160), or directors (ss. 184, 185).

Special occupancy. Where an estate was granted to a man and his heirs during the life of a *cestui que vie*, and the grantee died without alienation, and while the life for which he held continued, the heir would succeed, and he was called a special occupant (Wills Act, 1837, ss. 3, 6). In case of death of the tenant *pur autre vie* after 1925, the equitable interest devolves on the special personal representatives of the deceased, and if he dies intestate, upon trust for sale for the benefit of persons entitled, under the Administration of Estates Act, 1925, s. 45, the old rules of descent having been abolished. See DESCENT; HEIR; OCCUPANCY.

As to a limitation or trust for a man and his heirs during the life of another, see AUTRE VIE; SHELLEY'S CASE, RULE IN.

Special Paper, a list kept in the courts of common law, and afterwards in the Queen's Bench Division, in which list special cases, etc., to be argued, were set down. See PAPER BOOK.

Special Paper days. In the common law courts this meant days on which cases in the Special Paper were argued. SEE PAPER DAYS.

Special parliamentary procedure. Where it is proposed to acquire compulsorily certain classes of land, the compulsory purchase order is of no effect until it has been laid before Parliament and brought into operation under the Statutory Orders (Special Procedure) Act, 1945 (as amended by the Statutory Orders (Special Procedure) Act, 1965). The Act applies to the acquisition of the land of local authorities, statutory undertakers and the National Trust, commons and open spaces and ancient monuments.

Special personal representatives, the personal representatives of a tenant for life in connection with settled land which has been settled otherwise than by his will or by way of trust for sale. They are the trustees of the settlement and their duties are to convey the land to the tenant for life or statutory owner entitled upon the death of the testator subject to provision by them for death duties (Law of Property Act, 1925, s. 16). If there is no appointment to that effect the testator will be deemed to have appointed the trustees of the settlement as the special representatives. Upon an intestacy, probate may be granted to them for the purpose (Settled Land Act, 1925, s. 7 (1); Administration of Estates Act, 1925, ss. 22–24). If the settlement has come to an end with the testator's death, these provisions do not apply (*Re Bridgett and Hayes' Contract* [1928] Ch. 163).

Special pleaders, members of an inn of court who devoted themselves mainly to the drawing of pleadings, and to attending at judge's chambers. If not called to the Bar, as was frequently the case in former times, when many special pleaders practised as such prior to being called to the Bar, they took out annual certificates.

Special pleaders no longer exist: Bar Council Annual Statement 1948.

See COMMON PLEADER, ETC.; DRAFTSMAN; PLEADER.

Special pleading, the science of pleading. It was a forensic invention, due to the dialectic genius of the Middle Ages. See PLEADING.

Special pleas, pleas not in the form of general issues, but which allege affirmative matter, as infancy, coverture, statute of limitations, etc. See DEFENCE; PLEA.

Special pleas in bar in criminal matters go to the merits of the indictment, and give a reason why the prisoner ought to be discharged from the prosecution: they are of four kinds, *viz.*, a former acquittal, a former conviction, a former attainder, or a pardon.

Special property, qualified property (*q.v.*).

SPECIAL

Special reasons. Where a person is convicted of an offence involving obligatory disqualification from driving a motor vehicle the court must order him to be disqualified for not less than twelve months unless the court for special reasons thinks fit to order him to be disqualified for a shorter period or not to order him to be disqualified (Road Traffic Act, 1972, ss. 93 (1), 105). If the court does not order disqualification on conviction, the court need not order particulars of the conviction to be endorsed on the driving licence if for special reasons it thinks fit not to do so (s. 101 (2)). A special reason is one which is special to the facts of the particular case and not a circumstance which is peculiar to the offender (*Whittal* v. *Kirby* [1947] K.B. 194).

A special belief on reasonable grounds that no offence was being committed is a "special reason" for justices not to endorse an offence on the driving licence (*Carlton* v. *Garrity* (1963) 62 L.G.R. 147). As to the defence of "laced drinks" see *R.* v. *Newton* [1974] R.T.R. 451; *Adams* v. *Bradley* [1975] R.T.R. 233. As to drugs, see AUTOMATISM.

Special referee. See REFEREE; REFERENCE.

Special reserve. See MILITIA.

Special roads may be constructed and reserved for specified classes of traffic (Highways Act, 1959, ss. 11–20; Highways (Miscellaneous Provisions) Act, 1961, s. 3; Town and Country Planning Act, 1962, Sch. 12; London Government Act, 1963, Sch. 6 para. 6; Highways Act, 1971, ss. 6, 11, 12, 15 (4), Sch. 12; Town and Country Planning Act, 1971, Sch. 23 Pt. II; Gas Act, 1972, Sch. 4 para. 1 (6); Local Government Act, 1972, Sch. 30; S.I. 1970 No. 1681, Road Traffic Act, 1974, Sch. 4 Pt. II).

Special schools. See EDUCATION.

Special tail, where an entailed interest (*q.v.*) is limited to the children of two given parents, as to A and the heirs of his body by B, his wife.

Special traverse, a form of plea abolished by the Common Law Procedure Act, 1852, s. 65. It consisted of two parts. The first part (known as the inducement) consisted of affirmative matter; the second part (known as the *absque hoc*) consisted of a denial, that is to say, a traverse in the proper sense of the word, and was introduced by the words "Without this, that." See SANS CEO QUE.

Special trust, where the machinery of a trust is introduced for the execution of some purpose particularly pointed out, and the trustee is not a mere passive depositary of the estate, but is called upon to exert himself actively in the execution of the settlor's intention; as where a conveyance is made to trustees upon trust to sell for payment of debts. See USE.

Special verdict. The jury have the right in all criminal cases to find a special verdict. Special verdicts should be obtained in only the most exceptional cases (*R.* v. *Bourne* (1953) 36 Cr.App.R. 125). If the Court of Appeal consider that a wrong conclusion has been arrived at by the court of trial on the effect of a special verdict, they may, instead of allowing the appeal, order such conclusion to be recorded as appears to them to be in law required by the verdict and pass such sentence in substitution for the sentence passed at the trial as may be authorised by law (Criminal Appeal Act, 1968, s. 5).

Where in any indictment or information any act or omission is charged against any person as an offence, and it is given in evidence on the trial of such person for that offence that he was insane, so as not to be responsible, according to law, for his actions at the time when the act was done or omission made, then, if it appears to the jury before whom such person is tried that he did the act or made the omission charged, but was insane as aforesaid when he did or made the same the jury must return a special verdict that the accused is not guilty by reason of insanity (Trial of Lunatics Act, 1883, s. 2 (1); Criminal Procedure (Insanity) Act, 1964, s. 1). (The special verdict was formerly "guilty but insane".)

Where on a trial for murder the accused contends (a) that at the time of the alleged offence he was insane so as not to be responsible, according to law, for his actions, or (b) that at that time he was suffering from such abnormality of mind as is specified in s. 2 (1) of the

Homicide Act, 1957 (diminished responsibility (*q.v.*)) the court must allow the prosecution to adduce or elicit evidence tending to prove the other of those contentions, and may give directions as to the stage of the proceedings at which the prosecution may adduce such evidence (Criminal Procedure (Insanity) Act, 1964, s. 6). An appeal lies to the Court of Appeal against a special verdict (Criminal Appeal Act, 1968, ss. 12, 13). Where a special verdict is returned or a finding is recorded that the accused is under a disability or where either result is arrived at on appeal the court must order the accused to be admitted to such hospital as may be specified by the Secretary of State (Criminal Procedure (Insanity) Act, 1964, s. 5; Criminal Appeal Act, 1968, ss. 6, 52 (1), 54, Schs. 1, 5, 7).

Specialia generalibus derogant. (Special words derogate from general ones.) See GENERALIA SPECIALIBUS, ETC.

Specialty, a contract under seal.

Specialty debts, bonds, mortgages, debts secured by writing under seal and recoverable at any time within, formerly, twenty years (Civil Procedure Act, 1883, s. 3), and now twelve years (Limitation Act, 1939, s. 1). They formerly ranked in the administration of the estate of a deceased person in priority to simple contract debts; but this distinction was abolished by the Administration of Estates Act, 1869 (Hinde Palmer's Act), replaced by the Administration of Estates Act, 1925, ss. 32, 34. See ASSETS; DEBT.

Specie, metallic money. Anything *in specie* is anything in its own form, not any equivalent, substitute, or reparation.

Specific bequest, a gift by will of a particular item of personal estate. See LEGACY.

Specific devise, a gift by will of a particular item of real property. See DEVISE.

Specific goods, goods identified and agreed upon at the time a contract of sale is made (Sale of Goods Act, 1893, s. 62).

A buyer of specific goods is no longer compelled to treat a breach of condition as a breach of warranty merely because the property in the goods has passed to him (s. 11 (1) (*c*); Misrepresentation Act, 1967, s. 4 (1)).

Specific legacy. See LEGACY.

Specific performance. The doctrine of specific performance is that where damages would be an inadequate compensation for the breach of an agreement, the contractor will be compelled to perform specifically what he has agreed to do. The principal instances of the jurisdiction occur in contracts for the sale, purchase or lease of land, or for the recovery of unique chattels, of which the Pusey Horn (see CORNAGE) is a well-known example. In such cases the court (*e.g.*, the High Court, in an action instituted in the Chancery Division) will order the defendant to carry out the sale, purchase, or lease, or deliver up the chattel, and will imprison him until he does so.

Equity sometimes enforces the actual accomplishment of a thing stipulated for, on the ground that what is lawfully agreed to be done ought to be done, and that damages at law for breach of the contract are not a sufficient compensation. The common law only gave damages to a suffering party for the non-performance of an executory agreement. The Common Law Procedure Act, 1854, however, imparted to the common law writ of mandamus a little more efficacy by provisions superseded by the Judicature Act, 1873, s. 24 (now the Judicature Act, 1925, s. 36), and the Mercantile Law Amendment Act, 1856, introduced a procedure for enforcing the specific delivery of goods sold in certain cases, superseded by the Sale of Goods Act, 1893, s. 52.

An award of damages may be combined with a decree for specific performance (Judicature Act, 1925, s. 36, replacing the Judicature Act, 1873, s. 24).

By the Law of Property Act, 1925, s. 49, where the court refuses to grant specific performance of a contract, the court has power to order the repayment of any deposit.

Contracts relating to the sale or lease of land will be specifically enforced, but not contracts relating to personal property except under very special circumstances, as where damages do not afford an adequate remedy. The court will not decree specific performance of a contract of personal service (*Lumley* v. *Wagner* (1852) 5 De G. & S. 485), but it will enforce a negative covenant by injunction if damages are not an appropriate remedy (*Warner Bros.' Pictures* v. *Nelson* [1937] 1 K.B. 209).

In order that a decree for specific performance may be obtained, the contract must be entered into by competent parties, or their lawfully authorised agents. The general rule is that all parties who can bind themselves at law are competent to enter into agreements which equity will enforce. The parties must contract willingly, without undue bias, and not under any improper influence. The terms of the contract must be understood by the parties without mistake or misapprehension, and must be certain and defined, importing a concluded agreement (*Douglas* v. *Baynes* [1908] A.C. 477). The contract must be entered into for valuable consideration, such as marriage or money, and not for merely good consideration, however meritorious it may be. While valuable consideration exists on the one side, there must be a promise or sale on the other, together with a mutuality of remedy between the parties. The contract must be evidenced by writing if so required by the Law of Property Act, 1925, s. 40, replacing part of the Statute of Frauds, 1677, s. 4. Equity, however, will entertain actions for the specific performance of contracts which, though within the statute, are not evidenced by writing in the following cases:

(1) Where a sale is ordered by a decree of a court, for the judgment of the court in confirming such a purchase takes the transaction out of the statute. It is, however, usual for the purchaser to subscribe a written or printed contract.

(2) Where a parol agreement has been so substantially performed in part as to render it inequitable not to enforce the whole of it (*Maddison* v. *Alderson* (1883) 8 App.Cas., p. 473).

(3) Where the absence of writing is due to the fraud of one of the parties.

(4) Where the land is partnership property. Where a partnership, or an agreement in the nature of a partnership, exists between two persons, and land is acquired by the partnership and the land is in the nature of stock-in-trade of the partnership, the court, without regarding the statute, will inquire of what the partnership stock consisted, whether that stock be land or any other kind of property.

(5) Where a suit is brought for the execution of an oral agreement fully set forth in the plaintiff's claim, and the defendant puts in his answer or defence thereto, and confesses the agreement.

The courts of England have jurisdiction to decree specific performance of a contract for the sale of land outside the jurisdiction against a defendant within it (*Richard West and Partners* (*Inverness*) v. *Dick* [1969] 2 Ch. 424).

By the Judicature Act, 1873, s. 34 (now the Judicature Act, 1925, s. 56 (1)), all causes and matters for the specific performance of contracts between vendors and purchasers of land, including contracts for leases, are assigned to the Chancery Division. Specific performance may be obtained of contracts up to £5,000 in the county courts under the County Courts Act, 1959, s. 52 (1) (*d*). See CAIRNS' ACT.

Specificatio, in the civil law, was a mode by which one person could acquire property belonging to another by making it into something different; as where a man made wine out of another's grapes; but the *specificator* was liable to make compensation to the original owner. *Specificatio* or specification is treated by Blackstone and others as a variety of accession (*q.v.*).

Specification. When a person applies for a patent, he must leave with his application a statement in writing describing the nature of his invention called the specification; the specification may be either complete or provisional (Patents Act, 1949, s. 3). If it is provisional the specification as a whole will consist of the title (*q.v.*), the provisional specification, the complete specification, the claims (*q.v.*), and the drawings or, in the case of a chemical invention, the samples or specimens. Specifications must neither cover more than is the proper subject of the patent, nor omit anything necessary to make the description intelligible. See DISCLAIMER; MEMORANDUM OF ALTERATION; PATENTS.

Speech, Freedom of. The Bill of Rights, 1688, provides that the freedom of speech and debates or proceedings in Parliament ought not to be impeached or questioned in any court or place out of Parliament. See PRIVILEGE.

Speed limits. There is no general limit on the speed of private motor-cars. On restricted roads the speed limit is generally limited to 30 miles an hour. A road is a restricted road if the street lamps are not more than two hundred yards apart (Road Traffic Regulation Act, 1967, ss. 71–73; Transport Act, 1968, Sch. 14 Pt. VI para. 1, Sch. 18 Pt. II; S.I. 1970 No. 1681). Speed limits may be imposed on roads other than restricted roads (Act of 1967, s. 74; Transport Act, 1968, Sch. 14, Pt. VI para. 1, Sch. 18). Temporary speed limits may be imposed (Act of 1967, s. 77; Transport Act, 1968, ss. 126, 130, Sch. 18). Speed limits may be imposed on vehicles of different classes (Act of 1967, s. 78). Fire engines, ambulances and police vehicles are exempt from speed limits if the observance of those limits would be likely to hinder the use of the vehicle for the purpose for which it is being used on that occasion (Act of 1967, s. 79; *Aitken* v. *Yarwood* [1965] 1 Q.B. 327).

For penalties for speeding see s. 78 (A), the Road Traffic Act, 1972, s. 203 (2); Road Traffic Act, 1974, Sch. 5 Pt. II.

Driving a motor vehicle at a speed exceeding the speed limit is an offence punishable on summary conviction by a fine of £50 (Road Traffic Regulation Act, 1967, s. 78A, inserted by the Road Traffic Act, 1972, s. 203). The court must order the endorsement of any driving licence held by the defendant unless for special reasons (*q.v.*) it thinks fit not to do so (Road Traffic Act, 1972, s. 101, Sch. 4 Pt. III para. 8). Disqualification may be ordered (Road Traffic Act, 1972, s. 93 (2), Sch. 4 Pt. III para 8). After two endorsements disqualification must be ordered for a period of not less than six months unless there are grounds for mitigation (s. 93 (3)). Whether or not disqualification is ordered, the court may order the defendant to be disqualified until he has passed a driving test (s. 93 (7)). The defendant must deliver his driving licence to the clerk of the court prior to the hearing or have it with him at the hearing (s. 101 (4)).

A person prosecuted for speeding may not be convicted solely on the evidence of one witness to the effect that, in the opinion of the witness, the person prosecuted was speeding. (Road Traffic Regulation Act, 1967, s. 78A (2)). This does not mean that there must be two witnesses. The evidence of one police officer supported by his own evidence of the reading of a speedometer or other device, is evidence of fact and not of opinion merely (*Nicholas* v. *Penny* [1950] 2 K.B. 466). There is no need for evidence that the speedometer has been tested (*Swain* v. *Gillett* [1974] R.T.R. 446). As to time-tables which involve speeding see the Road Traffic Regulation Act, 1967, s. 78A (4).

As to motor racing and speed trials see MOTOR RACING.

Speedometer. See ODOMETER; SPEED LIMITS.

Speedy execution. A plaintiff having obtained a verdict in a cause was not entitled to issue execution until fourteen days, unless a judge ordered execution to issue at an earlier period, which was called speedy execution (Common Law Procedure Act, 1852, s. 120). Now, immediate execution is the rule. See EXECUTION.

Spei emptio, the purchase of a chance, *e.g.*, of a succession.

Spes recuperandi, the hope of recovery. If it is entertained by a person in danger of death, it makes a declaration by him inadmissible in evidence, even though he in fact dies.

Spes successionis, an expectation of succession, as distinct from a vested right.

As to a grant of representation on the ground of *spes successionis* see the Practice Note issued by the Probate Registry dated December 17, 1951.

Spigurnel [Sax. *spicurran*, to shut up or enclose], an officer of the Chancery corresponding to the sealer (*q.v.*) of a later date. The office was one of dignity; thus it was for a long time held hereditarily by the great family of Bohun.

Spinning House, a prison at Cambridge used by the university authorities for the detention of light women convicted under a royal charter of April 26, 1561, as confirmed by the statute 1571, 13 Eliz. 1, c. 29, of associating for immoral purposes with undergraduates. In *Kemp* v. *Neville* (1861) 10 C.B.(N.S.) 523, the Vice-Chancellor was unsuccessfully sued by a Cambridge milliner committed by him after apprehension by a proctor, and in *Ex p. Hopkins* (1891) 61 L.J.Q.B. 240, the conviction of a woman upon a charge of walking with a member of the university was held bad. This jurisdiction was taken away by the statute 1894, 57 & 58 Vict. c. lx, ss. 4–12. That enactment applied to Cambridge the Universities Act, 1825, s. 3, which up to then had applied only to Oxford. The Universities Act, 1825, provides that any woman guilty of conduct such as had been punishable with detention in the Spinning House should be deemed an idle and disorderly person within the meaning of the Vagrancy Act, 1824. The effect is that any such person is now punishable only under the Vagrancy Act, 1824, s. 3.

Spinster, an unmarried woman, so called because she was supposed to be occupied in spinning; the " addition," or description, in deeds of a woman who has never been married. She is described, *e.g.*, as " Jane Brown, Spinster."

Spirits. The Spirits Act, 1880, consolidated the excise regulations relating to the distilling, rectifying and dealing in spirits; this Act is replaced by the Customs and Excise Act, 1952, ss. 93–115 (as amended); as to methylated spirits, see ss. 116–124 (as amended).

As to licences for the sale of spirits by retail, see INTOXICATING LIQUORS. As to barring of actions for the price of spirits sold in small quantities, see TIPPLING ACT.

Spiritual; Spiritualities. See GUARDIAN OF THE SPIRITUALITIES; SERVICE; TEMPORALITIES.

Spiritual corporations, corporations the members of which are entirely spiritual persons, and incorporated as such, for the furtherance of religion and perpetuating the rights of the Church. They are either sole, as bishops, certain deans, parsons and vicars; or aggregate, as dean and chapter, prior and convent, abbot and monks. See CORPORATION.

Spiritual courts, ecclesiastical courts (*q.v.*).

Spiritual lords, the archbishops and bishops of the House of Lords.

Spiritualism, pretending to hold communication with spirits. Under the Fraudulent Mediums Act, 1951, any person is guilty of an offence who with intent to deceive purports to act as a spiritualistic medium or to exercise any powers of telepathy, clairvoyance or other similar powers, or who, in purporting to act as a spiritualistic medium or to exercise such powers as aforesaid, uses any fraudulent device (s. 1 (1)). A person is not to be convicted unless it is proved that he acted for reward (s. 1 (2)). Anything done solely for entertainment is exempt (s. 1 (5)). An offence is punishable on summary conviction with a fine not exceeding £50 or imprisonment for a term not exceeding four months or with both; and on conviction on indictment with a fine not exceeding £500 or imprisonment for a term not exceeding two years or with both. Proceedings require the consent of the Director of Public Prosecutions. The Act repeals the Witchcraft Act, 1735, and so much of the Vagrancy Act, 1824, s. 4, as extends to persons purporting to act as spiritualistic mediums or to exercise any powers of telepathy, clairvoyance or other similar powers, or to persons who, in purporting so to act or to exercise such powers use fraudulent devices (s. 2).

Large gifts by an aged widow to a spiritual medium were set aside on the ground of undue influence in *Lyon* v. *Home* (1868) L.R. 6 Eq. 655.

Spirituality, that which belongs to a person as an ecclesiastic.

Spirituality of benefices, the tithes of land, etc.

Spital, or **Spittle,** a charitable foundation; a hospital.

Splitting a cause of action, suing for only a part of a claim or demand, with a view to suing for the rest in another action. The County Courts Act, 1959, s. 69, prohibits this in the county courts (*Grimbly* v. *Ackroyd* (1847) 1 Ex. 479).

Splitting Act, the statute 1695, 7 & 8 Will. 3, c. 25, relating to parliamentary elections.

Spoliation, a suit in a spiritual court by which an incumbent of a benefice suggests that his adversary has wasted (*spoliavit*) the fruits of the benefice, or received them to his prejudice. Such a suit lies by one incumbent against another to try which of them is the rightful incumbent where they both claim by one patron, and where the right of patronage does not come in question: *e.g.,* where a patron, erroneously believing his clerk to be dead, presents another; there the first incumbent may have a spoliation against the other. If, however, each of the incumbents claims by a different patron, so that the question of the ownership of the advowson is involved, the matter is for the civil courts.

Spoliatus debet ante omnia restitui. (The despoiled ought to get his property back before anything else.) This is the maxim governing the law as to the disposal of stolen goods. See MARKET OVERT; RESTITUTION; REVESTING.

Sponsalia, or **Stipulatio sponsalitia,** espousals; mutual promises to marry (Civil Law).

Sponsio judicialis, the feigned issue of the civil law. See FEIGNED ISSUES.

Sponsions, agreements or engagements made by certain public officers, as generals or admirals in time of war, either without authority, or in excess of the authority under which they purport to be made. They are invalid without ratification by the governments concerned.

Sponsor, a surety; one who makes a promise or gives security for another, particularly a godfather in baptism.

Sponsus, betrothed. The person who intended to marry a woman stipulated with the person who was to give her in marriage that he would do so, and on his part promised to marry her. *Sponsa* was the woman thus promised, and *sponsus* the man who promised to marry her (Civil Law).

Sponte oblata, a free gift or present to the Crown.

Sporting. The right of sporting, that is, of killing and taking game (*q.v.*) on another man's land is a profit *à prendre,* and, therefore, an incorporeal hereditament; it can only be conveyed by deed of grant; but if exercised by virtue of a contract it may take effect as an equitable profit *à prendre* without any deed (*Mason* v. *Clarke* [1955] A.C. 778). It is generally an exclusive or several right, that is, excluding the owner of the land from its exercise; but it may be a right of common. See COMMON.

As to the rating of sporting rights when severed from the occupation of the land, see the General Rate Act, 1967, s. 29.

See CHASE; FOREST; PARK; WARREN.

Shooting rats is not shooting for sporting purposes (*Morton* v. *Chaney* [1960] 1 W.L.R. 1312).

Sports. The duty of care which a competitor or participator in a sport or game owes to a spectator depends on the standard of conduct which the sport or game permits or involves and a spectator takes the risk of damage done to him by participants in the course of and for the purposes of that sport or game, notwithstanding that such damage may be the result of an error of judgment by the competitor, provided it is not reckless or deliberate (*Wooldridge* v. *Sumner* [1963] 2 Q.B. 43; *Wilks* v. *Cheltenham Homeguard Motor Cycle Club* [1971] 1 W.L.R. 668). The organisers of sporting events may effectively exclude their liability to spectators for accidents by displaying notices warning the public of the danger and stating that it is a condition of admission that they be absolved from liability for accidents " howsoever caused " (*White* v. *Blackmore* [1972] 2 Q.B. 651). Provision is made for safety at sports stadia and other sports grounds (Safety of Sports Grounds Act, 1975). As to allowance of expenditure on safety see the Finance (No. 2) Act, 1975, s. 49.

The Minister for Sport is a Minister of State in the Department of the Environment.

Sportula. or **Sportella,** a dole or largess either of meat or money given in the time of the Roman empire by princes or great men to the poor. It was properly the pannier or basket in which the meat was brought, or with which the poor went to beg it; thence the word was transferred to the meat itself, and thence to money sometimes given in lieu of it.

Spousal, marriage nuptials.

Spouse, a husband or wife.

Spouse-breach, adultery, as opposed to simple fornication.

SPREADING

Spreading false news concerning any great man of the realm was punishable at common law, and by the statute 1378, 2 Ric. 2, st. 1, c. 5. See SCANDALUM MAGNATUM.

Spring guns. The setting of spring guns, etc., calculated to destroy life or inflict grievous bodily harm on a trespasser, is a misdemeanour (Offences against the Person Act, 1861, s. 31). Damages are recoverable by a person injured by a spring gun, set without notice, from the person setting it (*Bird* v. *Holbrook* (1828) 4 Bing. 628). See MAN-TRAP.

Spring traps. Restrictions on the use of spring traps for the killing or taking of animals are imposed by the Pests Act, 1954, s. 5. For approved traps, see S.I. 1957 No. 2216; 1958 No. 24; 1966 No. 849; 1968 No. 645; 1970 No. 50.

Springing use, a form of use in the nature of an executory interest directing property in land to vest at a future period which did not coincide with the termination of a legal estate at common law. Upon a grant by A to B to the use of C, an infant, in fee on attaining twenty-one years of age, the use resulted to the settlor until, if ever, the period arrived and a good legal estate was conferred upon attaining that age by virtue of the statute. The use might be contingent, as in that case, or vested, as a grant to A to the use of B in fee upon the death of C, a stranger. If the grant defeated a previous legal estate and was not capable of being construed as a vested or contingent remainder, it might operate as a shifting use. Springing and shifting uses were resorted to in order to facilitate freedom of grant or conveyance of the legal estate in land by virtue of the Statute of Uses, 1535. Grants which would have created springing or shifting uses if they had been made *inter vivos* were good, apart from the Statute of Uses, 1535, if made by will at common law as executory devises, but apart, from statute (see CONTINGENT REMAINDER), executory devises like springing or shifting uses were not so construed if they were capable of taking effect by vesting as a remainder before or *eo instanti* with the determination of a particular freehold estate. The Statute of Uses, 1535, was repealed by the Law of Property Act, 1925, which also converted executory as well as all other future interests in land into equitable interests, and even before 1926, where the executory devise, shifting or springing use, or contingent remainder did not operate to create a legal estate but only an equitable interest, the rule as to failure of a preceding particular estate before the remainder could vest did not invalidate the equitable estate in remainder (*Re Freme* [1891] 3 Ch. 167). See USE.

Spur rial. See GOLD COINS.

Spurii [Gk. σποράδην, a hazard; Lat. *sine patre*, without a father], children conceived in prostitution.

Spy, a person not in military uniform who, acting clandestinely or on false pretences, obtains or seeks to obtain information in the zone of operations of a belligerent with the intention of communicating it to the hostile party (Hague Convention, 1899). A spy, who after rejoining his own army is captured by the enemy, must be treated as a prisoner of war, and incurs no responsibility for previous acts of espionage (Hague Convention, 1907, art. 31). A spy taken in the act may not be punished without previous trial (art. 30). The punishment of a spy rests in the discretion of the captor (Holland, Lect.Int. Law).

Squatter. If a squatter wrongfully encloses a bit of waste land, and builds a hut on it, and lives there, he acquires an estate in fee simple by his own wrong in the land which he has enclosed. He may, of course, be turned out by legal process until his title is confirmed by the Limitation Act, 1939; but as long as he remains he has an estate in fee simple. He is bound by a restrictive covenant entered into by a former owner even after he has acquired a statutory title (*Re Nisbet and Pott's Contract* [1906] 1 Ch. 386).

The summary procedure under R.S.C., Ord. 113 or C.C.R., Ord. 26 for claiming land summarily is available where persons remain in occupation of land without licence or consent (*McPhail* v. *Persons, Names Unknown* [1973] Ch. 447; *Greater London Council* v. *Jenkins* [1975] 1 W.L.R. 155). See also *G.L.C.* v. *Tully* (1976) 120 S.J. 555.

An electricity board is under no obligation to supply electricity to squatters

(*Woodcock* v. *South West Electricity Board* [1975] 1 W.L.R. 983). As to service of originating application see *Westminster City Council* v. *Chapman and Persons Unknown* [1975] 1 W.L.R. 1112. All persons on the premises should be evicted under an order for possession regardless of whether they were parties to the possession proceedings (*R.* v. *Wandsworth County Court* [1975] 1 W.L.R. 1314).

Squatter's title, the title acquired by one who, having wrongfully entered upon land, has occupied it without paying rent or otherwise acknowledging any superior title for such time that he acquires an indefeasible title. (*Williams Bros. Direct Supply* v. *Raftery* [1958] 1 Q.B. 159). See LIMITATION OF ACTIONS.

Squibs. Casting squibs in any thoroughfare or public place is an offence punishable by fine. See FIREWORKS.

In *Scott* v. *Shepherd* (1773) 2 Wm. Bl. 892, it was held that an action of trespass and assault lay against the original thrower of a squib which, after having been thrown about in self-defence by two other persons successively, put out the plaintiff's eye.

Squire, a contraction of "esquire." See ESQUIRE.

Squirrels. These are "vermin" for the purposes of the Forestry Act, 1967, s. 7. See POISON; RABBITS; VERMIN.

Sri Lanka. Ceylon has become a republic within the Commonwealth under this name (Sri Lanka Republic Act, 1972).

Stabbing, Statute of, the statute 1604, 1 Jac. I, c. 8, by which anyone who stabbed another who had no drawn weapon or had not first attacked was guilty of murder if the person attacked died within six months. See MALICIOUS INJURIES TO THE PERSON; MAYHEM; WOUNDING.

Stabilia, a writ of the time of Henry I, founded on a custom in Normandy that where a man in power claimed lands in the possession of an inferior, he petitioned the prince that it might be put into his hands till the right was decided. It did not apply in England.

Stabilitio venationis, the driving of deer to a stand.

Stabit praesumptio donec probetur in contrarium (4 Co.Rep. 71b; Hob. 297).

(A presumption will stand good until the contrary is proved.) But some presumptions are irrebuttable. See PRESUMPTION.

Stable-stand, one of the four matters upon proof of which there was prima facie evidence of killing, or attempting to kill, or to steal, deer in the royal forest. It consisted in being found with bent bow or cross-bow, or with hounds in a leash. The other three matters were dog-draw (actually hunting with hounds), back-bear (being in possession of a dead deer), and bloody-hand (being with bloody hands, etc.).

Stade, Stadium, a furlong.

Staff-herding, the following of cattle within a forest.

Under the forest law this was a right not merely to turn cattle into a forest to graze, but also the right to send a herdsman with them. The first right could be held without the second.

Stag, a stock exchange term for an applicant for shares of a new issue who applies with the intention of selling at a premium whatever shares may be allotted to him. See, *e.g.*, *R.* v. *Greenstein*; *R.* v. *Green* [1975] 1 W.L.R. 1353.

See DEER.

Stage carriage. A stage carriage is defined in the Road Traffic Act, 1960, as a public service vehicle (*q.v.*), carrying passengers at separate fares, not being an express carriage (*q.v.*) (ss. 117 (2), 118). See CAB.

Stage play. See THEATRE.

Stagiarius, a resident.

Stagnum, a pool. By this name the land and water pass (Co.Litt. 5a).

Stake, a deposit made to answer an event.

Stakeholder, a person with whom money is deposited pending the decision of a bet or wager (*q.v.*); a person who holds money or property which is claimed by rival claimants, but in which he himself claims no interest. See INTERPLEADER.

As to when money deposited in the hands of a stakeholder, to abide the event of a wager, may be recovered, see the Gaming Act, 1845, s. 18. A stakeholder of a sealed packet containing a document can be called upon to produce it upon a *subpoena duces tecum* (*R.* v. *Daye* [1908] 2 K.B. 333). If, on a sale of land, a deposit is paid to an estate agent while the sale is still subject to contract he holds it, in the absence of agreement to the contrary, as the vendor's agent and not as stakeholder and the vendor is liable to return it if the contract goes off and the agent becomes insolvent. *Semble*, the vendor is likewise liable if the agent is expressed to be a stakeholder (*Goding* v. *Frazer* [1967] 1 W.L.R. 286).

Apart from a special stipulation, it is not clear that a stakeholder converting the deposit into the property of either party before determination of the event is not acting in contradiction of his mandate.

Stale [Ang. Sax.], larceny.

Stale cheque, one which appears on its face to have been in circulation for an unreasonable time. A person who takes such a cheque takes it subject to equities and at his own risk. A banker may refuse payment of a stale cheque if the drawer has not directed him to pay it. What is an unreasonable time depends on the circumstances. By the custom of bankers, confirmation from the drawer is usually required when the cheque has been in circulation for six months before presentation.

Stale demand, a claim which has not been made for so long that it must be taken to have been waived.

Stallage, the liberty or right of pitching or erecting stalls in a fair or market or the money paid for the same; a payment due to the owner of a market in respect of the exclusive occupation of a portion of the soil within the market.

The right of stallage is a right for a payment to be made, to the owner of the market, in respect of the exclusive occupation of a portion of the soil, for the purpose of selling goods in the market (*Great Yarmouth Corporation* v. *Groom* (1862) 1 H. & C. 102). A voluntary bargain cannot be reopened on the ground that the stallage charge is unreasonable (*Att.-Gen.* v. *Colchester Corporation* [1952] Ch. 586).

See MARKETS AND FAIRS.

Stallarius, a master of the horse; also the owner of a stall in the market (Spelman).

Stallions. See HORSE BREEDING.

Stamp Act, the statute 1765, 5 Geo. 3, c. 12, for imposing stamp duties on American colonies; repealed by the statute 1766, 6 Geo. 3, c. 11.

Stamp duties. Stamps are used as a mode of raising taxes on written instruments, such as conveyances, leases, etc., by virtue of the Stamp Act, 1891. (See COMMISSIONERS OF INLAND REVENUE.) Stamps are either fixed in amount, or *ad valorem*, that is, proportionate to the value of the property dealt with by the instrument.

Adhesive stamps are sold separately, and are affixed and cancelled by the person whose duty it is to have the instrument stamped. Others are impressed with a die on the parchment or paper on which the instrument is written. Adhesive stamps can be used only where their use is expressly provided for (Stamp Act, 1891, s. 2). Provision is made by the Stamp Duties Management Act, 1891, ss. 9, 10, for the allowance (or repayment of the amount) of a stamp which has been " spoiled," that is, where, by some accident or mistake, the stamp itself has been rendered unfit for use, or the instrument on which it has been affixed or impressed has become useless before it came into operation; and in certain other cases. Appropriated stamps are stamps which can only be used for instruments of a particular description (Stamp Act, 1891, s. 10). An adjudication stamp is used to signify that the instrument has been submitted to the Commissioners of Inland Revenue, and that they are of opinion (if it is unstamped) that it is not chargeable with duty, or (if it is stamped) that it is duly stamped; and no question as to the proper stamp can then arise (s. 12). Where the stamp duty on an instrument depends upon the stamp on another instrument, the fact that the latter stamp duty has been paid may be evidenced by a stamp impressed for that purpose on the first instrument: this is called a denoting stamp (s. 11). No instrument executed in the United Kingdom, or relating to any property situate, or to anything done or to be done, in the United Kingdom, can be given in evidence or made use of, except in criminal proceedings, unless duly stamped (s. 14 (4)).

Bonds, conveyances, leases, mortgages and unit trust instruments must be stamped within thirty days of execution (s. 15 (2); Finance Act, 1962, s. 30 (1)). In the case of all other documents, the stamp may be affixed at any time after execution on payment of the unpaid duty, a penalty of £10, and interest on the duty at 5 per cent. per annum (Stamp Act, 1891, s. 15 (1)). But any instrument executed out of the United Kingdom may be stamped within thirty days from its arrival in this country, without payment of any penalty (s. 15 (3) (a)). The Commissioners are also empowered to stamp any instrument without payment of a penalty (s. 15 (3) (b)). For adaptation to decimal currency, see the Finance Act, 1970, s. 32, Sch. 7 para. 19.

Where a document unstamped or insufficiently stamped is produced in a judicial proceeding, it may be received in evidence on payment to the officer of the court of the unpaid duty, the penalty, and a further sum of £1 (s. 14 (1)).

By the Stamp Act, 1870, s. 17 (re-enacted by the Stamp Act, 1891, s. 14), reversing *Buckworth* v. *Simpson* (1835) 1 C.M. & R. 384, the stamp to be affixed to an unstamped document to render it admissible in evidence is not the stamp in accordance with the law at the time of affixing it, but the stamp in accordance with the law in force at the time when the document was executed.

A condition of sale framed with a view to precluding objection or requisition upon the ground of absence or insufficiency of the stamp upon any instrument is void.

Forgery of stamps and dies is an indictable offence (Forgery Act, 1913).

The amounts payable as stamp duties are set out in Sch. 1 to the Stamp Act, 1891, as varied by subsequent legislation.

Standard, that which is of authority, and the test of other things of the same kind; a settled rate.

Standing by, sanctioning by silence and inaction. See LYING BY.

Standing mute. See MUTUS.

Standing orders, rules and forms regulating the procedure of the two Houses of Parliament, each having its own. They are of equal force in every Parliament

except so far as they are altered or suspended from time to time.

Stannaries [Lat. *stannum*, tin; *stannaria*, a tin mine; Cornish *steán,* tin]. The stannaries are a district which includes all parts of Devon and Cornwall where any tin works are situate in actual operation. A stannary is a tin mine. The tin-miners of the stannaries have certain peculiar customs and privileges. See TINBOUNDING.

From very ancient times there were Stannary Courts in Cornwall for the administration of justice among the tinners therein, such courts being mentioned in charters of the reign of King John. In 1855 their jurisdiction was extended to Devonshire mines. Civil actions in respect of matters arising as to mines within the stannaries might formerly be brought in the Stannary Court, which was a court of record held before a judge called the Vice-Warden of the Stannaries; it also had power to wind up cost-book mining companies. Formerly an appeal lay to the Lord Warden of the Stannaries, and from him to the Privy Council, but this jurisdiction was transferred to the Court of Appeal by the Judicature Act, 1873, s. 18. The Stannary Court was abolished by the Stannaries Court (Abolition) Act, 1896; and the jurisdiction of the court was transferred to the county court.

The Stannaries Acts, 1869 and 1887, contain provisions relating to the regulation of mining partnerships working mines in the stannaries.

See Pearce, *Laws and Customs of the Stannaries*; *Procedure in the Court of the Vice-Warden.*

Staple, a public mart appointed by law to be held in Westminster, Newcastle, Bristol, and other places. A court was held before the mayor of the staple, which court was governed by the law merchant. It appears from statute 1390, 14 Ric. 2, that the staple goods of England then were wool, woolfells, leather, lead, tin, cloth, butter, cheese, etc.

The seaports from which wool, leather, tin and lead (collectively termed the staple) were exported, were from an early period called the staple, or *estaple*, towns; and the merchants of those towns had, from the reign of Edward I, a monopoly in the staple and were called the merchants of the staple, or, more shortly, the staplers. The king decided what should from time to time be the staple towns. The chief staple from 1390 to 1558 was at Calais. In each staple town there was a mayor of the staple (appointed at first by the king, but subsequently for the most part by the mayor of the town), and two constables of the staple. These mayors of the staple held staple courts, for the decision of matters touching the staple.

The Statute of the Staple, 1353 (see CORRECTOR, ETC.), regulated the staple towns. It was quite distinct from the Statute Staple (q.v.).

The merchants of the staple were incorporated as a merchant guild by a charter of Edward III; Elizabeth I renewed their charter; and Charles II finally incorporated them as the Mayor, Constables and Company of the Staple of England. The company still exists; but its monopoly had been destroyed even before the grant of the final charter: it has long since ceased to exercise any functions; and it has been judicially described as merely a dining club. In 1888 there were about thirty members. See Rich, *Ordinance Book of the Merchants of the Staple*; Selden Soc. vols. 23, 46, 49.

Staple Inn. See INNS OF CHANCERY.

Star; Starr [Med. Lat. *starrum*; Heb. *shetar*, a deed or contract]. The records of betrothals, settlements, sales of land, transfers of debt and other deeds, obligations, etc., executed by the Jews before their expulsion from this country, were known as *starra* or stars; they were written in two languages, either in Hebrew and Norman French or in Hebrew and Latin. Star also meant a schedule or inventory. See *Jewish Historical Society*, vol. 15; Lincoln, *The Starra*. See BENT.

Star Chamber [Lat. *camera stellata*; Fr. *chambre des estoylles*]. The court called by this name is commonly regarded as being the *Aula Regis* (q.v.), sitting in the Star Chamber, a room at Westminster. The jurisdiction of the court would, therefore, be all or some part of that residuary jurisdiction which remained after the severance of the Courts of Exchequer, Common Pleas, Queen's Bench and Chancery.

By the statute 1487, 3 Hen. 7, c. 1, the court was remodelled, and its jurisdiction placed upon a lawful and permanent basis. The statute empowered the Chancellor, Treasurer, and Keeper of the Privy Seal, or any two of them, with one spiritual and one temporal peer, and the Chief Justices of the Courts of King's Bench and Common Pleas, or in their absence, two other justices, to call before them and punish the following offences: combinations of the nobility and gentry, supported by liveries (that is to say, by retinues of followers wearing distinctive liveries); partiality on the part of sheriffs in making up the panels of jurors, or in making untrue returns of members; bribery in jurors; and riots and unlawful assemblies.

By the statute 1529, 21 Hen. 8, c. 20, the President of the King's Council was added to the list of judges; and by the statute 1539, 31 Hen. 8, c. 8 (which gave to the king's proclamations in ecclesiastical matters the force of law), all persons offending against such proclamations were to be tried before the Star Chamber, and punished with fine and imprisonment.

The jurisdiction of the court was defined by Bacon as extending to forces, frauds, crimes various of stellionate, and the incohations or middle acts towards crimes capital or heinous not actually committed or perpetrated.

The Star Chamber was of utility during the reigns of Henry VII and subsequent monarchs in its repression of the turbulence of the nobility and gentry in the provinces, and in its supplying a court of jurisdiction for matters which, as being of novel origin, were unprovided for by the existing tribunals, e.g., in the case of offences against proclamations in ecclesiastical matters. See CUSTOS MORUM.

The court enhanced the royal authority by supplying the executive with a speedy and effective machinery. Cardinal Wolsey improved and extended its jurisdiction. The very nature of its jurisdiction rendered its process liable to abuse; and Wolsey's connection with it was one of the principal causes of his unpopularity.

The Court was abolished by the statute 1640, 16 Car. 1, c. 10 (Selden Soc., vols. 16, 25; Scofield, *Court of Star Chamber*).

Star of India, Order of. The Most Exalted Order of the Star of India was founded in 1861. It consists of Knights Grand Commanders (G.C.S.I.); Knights Commanders (K.C.S.I.); and Companions (C.S.I.). No conferments have been made since 1947.

Stare decisis (to stand by things decided), to abide by former precedents where the same points come again in litigation, as well to keep the scale of justice even and steady and not liable to waver with every judge's opinion, as also because, the law in that case being solemnly declared and determined, what before was uncertain and perhaps indifferent is now a permanent rule which it is not in the breast of any subsequent judge to alter or swerve from according to his private sentiments, he being sworn to determine, not according to his private judgment, but according to the known laws and customs of the land, not delegated to pronounce a new law, but to maintain and expound the old one, *jus dicere et non jus dare* (Broom, Max 103). See PRECEDENT.

Stare in judicio, to sue; to litigate in a court.

Starr. See BENT; STAR.

Starr-Bowkett Society. A building society (*q.v.*).

State, a collection of persons occupying a certain territory, and having a legislative and executive organisation free from the control of any other human power. The name is sometimes given to bodies which are really only parts of a State, such as the separate organisations which collectively make up the United States of America, or to governments, such as those of Monaco, San Marino and Andorra, which are under the protection or control of other States; hence a State, in the ordinary and proper sense of the word, is described as an independent or sovereign State.

Every State consists of two parts, the sovereign part (which in England is the Crown and Houses of Parliament) and the subject part. In its external relations or dealings with other States the sovereign part, or a branch of it (in England the Crown), represents the State. The relations between independent States are governed by international law (*q.v.*). In its internal relations, that part of the sovereign government of a State which is entrusted with the executive power enforces the law dealing with the relations between it and the subject members of the State. It is, therefore, considered as representing the whole State, and hence the term "State" is frequently used in the sense of the executive power in a State, as when we say that public law deals (among other things) with the relations between the State and the private members of the community. (See LAW.) As the State has the power of enforcing the law, it cannot be subject to legal duties, for otherwise it would have to enforce the law against itself. See ACT OF STATE; PETITION OF RIGHT.

As one State cannot enforce a claim against another by legal procedure, it follows that no member of any State can enforce a claim against another State by legal proceedings in any court of justice external to the latter State. Therefore, if a foreign State borrows money from an Englishman, or commits what in the case of a private individual would be a tort against him, no proceedings can be taken in the English courts to enforce the claim thus arising, even though the foreign State may have property within the jurisdiction of the English courts (*The Parlement Belge* (1880) 5 P.D. 197). This rule is subject to two apparent exceptions: (1) that if proceedings are taken by A against B in the English courts in respect of property in which a foreign State claims or is believed to have an interest, it may be made a party to those proceedings as defendant to enable it to come forward and sustain its claim; here, however, it is obvious that the foreign State, though in form a defendant, is really a plaintiff; (2) that if a foreign State takes proceedings in the English courts against a private individual, the defendant can institute a cross-action or set up a set-off or counterclaim against the plaintiff as if the foreign State were a private person (*U.S.A.* v. *Wagner* (1867) L.R. 3 Eq. 724).

"State" in the old books sometimes

stands for " estate " (Co.Litt. 206b). Conversely, Cecil, in the reign of Elizabeth I, was termed Secretary of Estate instead of Secretary of State.

State trials, trials relating to offences against the State, or illustrative of the law relating to State officers of high rank, or cases raising important points of constitutional and international law. The best collection is Howell's *State Trials*, in 34 volumes, from 1163 to 1820. This was continued by a new series under the editorship of J. E. P. Wallis, in 8 volumes, bringing them down to 1858. Selections were brought out by J. Willis-Bund in 1880.

Stateless person, a person who is not a national of any State. See the Conventions on Stateless Persons 1954, Cmd. 9509 (ratified, 1959, Cmnd. 1098); 1961, Cmnd. 1825, 1977; 1973 Cmnd. 5447.

A stateless person may acquire British nationality under the British Nationality (No. 2) Act, 1964.

Statement. See ANSWER; BILL OF COMPLAINT.

Statement in lieu of prospectus. A public company which does not issue a prospectus on or with reference to its formation (or which has issued such a prospectus but does not proceed to allot any of the shares offered to the public for subscription), is required to file a statement in lieu of a prospectus before allotting any shares or debentures (Companies Act, 1948, s. 48).

Statement of affairs. A debtor against whom a receiving order is made must furnish to the official receiver a statement of his affairs, verified by oath, giving a list of his creditors, secured and unsecured, with the value of the securities, a list of bills discounted, and a statement of his property (Bankruptcy Act, 1914, s. 14).

Statement of claim. A statement of claim is a written or printed statement by the plaintiff in an action in the High Court, showing the facts on which he relies to support his claim against the defendant and the relief or remedy sought. Before a writ of summons is issued it must be indorsed with a statement of claim or with a concise statement of claim made or the relief or

remedy sought (R.S.C., Ord. 6, r. 2). The expression "special indorsement" is no longer used in this Rule. If the statement of claim is not indorsed on the writ, it must be served on the defendant before the expiration of fourteen days after the defendant has entered an appearance (R.S.C., Ord. 18, r. 1). For the practice on default of appearance, see Ord. 13.

In actions in the commercial list pleadings must be in the form of points of claim etc. (Ord. 72, r. 7).

Statement of defence. In the practice of the High Court, the defendant delivers in reply to the statement of claim a pleading called a statement of defence. The statement of defence deals with the allegations contained in the statement of claim, admitting or denying them, and, if necessary, stating fresh facts in explanation or avoidance of those alleged by the plaintiff. If the defendant wishes to set up a counterclaim (*q.v.*), he adds it to his defence, and the pleading is then called a statement of defence and counterclaim. See PLEADING.

A defendant who enters an appearance and intends to defend must serve his defence on the plaintiff before the expiration of fourteen days after the time limited for appearing or after the statement of claim is served on him, whichever is the later (R.S.C., Ord. 18, r. 1).

In actions in the commercial list pleadings must be in the form of points of defence etc. (Ord. 72, r. 7).

Statesman, a freeholder and farmer in Cumberland.

Statham. The learning of the law was put into a more methodical form by this author, who was a baron of the Exchequer in the time of Edward IV, in his *Abridgment of the Laws*, being a kind of digest containing most titles of the law, arranged in alphabetical order, and comprising under each head adjudged cases abridged from the Year-books (4 Reeves, c. xxv, 117).

Stationers' Hall, the Hall of the Stationers' Company, in the City of London, founded in 1553. Under the Copyright Act, 1842, s. 24, registration at Stationers' Hall was necessary, not to secure copyright, but as a condition precedent to the right to sue for an infringement. The Copyright Act, 1911, repealed all enactments referring to Stationers' Hall. The Copyright Act, 1956, contains no reference to Stationers' Hall; and no registration there is now required for any purpose. See COPYRIGHT.

Stationery Office, a Government office, established in 1786, which supplies the stationery and the books and other publications required by Parliament and the various public departments. It also has control of the printing required by Parliament and the departments. By letters patent dated October 3, 1888, the Controller of the Stationery Office is printer of all Acts of Parliament. The Office has no statutory origin: it is dependent for its existence on the annual vote of Parliament. By the Documentary Evidence Act, 1882, documents printed under the superintendence of the Office are receivable in evidence.

As to the finance of the Stationery Office, see the Government Trading Funds Act, 1973.

Statu liber, a slave made free or enfranchised by testament conditionally (Civil Law).

Statues. See ANCIENT MONUMENTS; ART, WORKS OF; PUBLIC STATUES.

Status. The status of a person is his legal position or condition; thus, when we say that the status of a woman after a decree nisi for the dissolution of her marriage with her husband has been granted but before it has been made absolute, is that of a married woman, we mean that she has the same legal rights, liabilities, and disabilities as an ordinary married woman. The term is chiefly applied to persons under disability (*q.v.*), or persons who have some peculiar condition which prevents the general law from applying to them in the same way as it does to ordinary persons.

The question of status is of importance in jurisprudence, because it is generally treated as a basis for the classification of law according as it applies to ordinary persons (general law, normal law, law of things), or to persons having a status, that is, a disability or peculiar legal condition, such as infants, married women, lunatics, convicts, bankrupts, aliens, public officers, etc. (particular law, abnormal law, law of persons).

" Status " is sometimes applied by analogy to things, as where we speak of a house having acquired the status of an ancient building. See ANCIENT MESSUAGES.

In the civil law the term indicated the position of a *persona*. A full Roman citizen must have possessed the *status libertatis*, *familiae*, and *civitatis*, which were sometimes called *tria capita*. The law of status thus classified men as slaves and free, citizens and aliens—as equals and unequals, so that it may be called the law of inequality.

Status de manerio (the state of a manor), the assembly of the tenants in the court of the lord to do suit and claim their rights and privileges.

Status mixtus, a state between peace and war.

Status quo, the state in which things are, or were. The expression is also found in the combinations *in statu quo* (in the state in which) and *in statu quo ante bellum* (in the state in which it was before the war).

Statuta Armorum, the Statutes of Arms. An enactment regulating the number of esquires whom a knight might take with him to a tournament is printed under this title in the *Statutes of the Realm* amongst the *Statutes of Uncertain Date*, and in the *Statutes at Large*, it is printed as of uncertain date under the title of *Statutum Armorum ad Torniamenta*.

Statuta de Moneta, the Statutes concerning Money. An enactment, consisting of several " statutes " (corresponding, to what are now called sections), is printed under these titles in the *Statutes of the Realm* amongst the *Statutes of Uncertain Date*, and in the *Statutes at Large* as 1292, 20 Edw. 1, sts. 4, 6.

Statutable or **Statutory,** that which is introduced or governed by statute law, as opposed to the common law or equity. Thus, a court is said to have statutory jurisdiction when jurisdiction is given to it in certain matters by Act of Parliament. See CONVEYANCE; DECLARATION, STATUTORY; MORTGAGE; PETITION.

Statute, an edict of the legislature; an Act of Parliament (*q.v.*); the term is usually confined to public Acts.

A statute is said to be declaratory when it does not profess to make any alteration in the existing law, but merely to declare or explain what it is; remedial, when it alters the common law; amending, when it alters the statute law; consolidating, when it consolidates or throws together, into one statute, several previous statutes relating to the same subject-matter, with or without alterations of substance; disabling or restraining, when it restrains the alienation of property; enabling, when it removes a restriction or disability; penal, when it imposes a penalty or forfeiture, as in the case of the statutes relating to game, smuggling, etc. See INFORMER; PENAL STATUTE; SUNDAY.

Sessional publication of the statutes began in 1484, by Maclinia. About the same time Maclinia printed a volume entitled *Nova Statuta*, containing the statutes from 1326 to 1483. The next printed collection was entitled *Magna Charta cum aliis antiquis statutis* (known as *Antiqua Statuta* or *Vetera Statuta*); it first appeared in 1508 and there were numerous reprints. This was followed about 1540 by the *Great Book of the Statutes*, from 1326 to 1534. In 1543 there was issued a volume containing all the statutes from Magna Charta, 1215, to 1504. In 1587 the *Whole Volume of Statutes at Large* from Magna Charta, 1215, to 1587 was printed, and this was several times reprinted with additions to the date of publication. Later editions of the *Statutes at Large* were compiled by Keble, 1676 (several times reprinted and brought down to date); by Hawkins (to 1734); by Cay (to 1757); by Pickering to 1761 in 24 volumes; and to 1800 by Ruffhead in 18 volumes, by Runnington in 14 volumes, and by Tomlins and Raithby in 10 volumes quarto and 20 volumes 8vo. The *Statutes at Large* means all the public general statutes, as distinguished from a collection of selected statutes, such as the old *Abridgments* and Chitty's *Statutes of Practical Utility* of our own time. An edition of the statutes from Magna Charta, 1215, to 1713, was printed between 1810 and 1822 in 10 volumes by the Record Commissioners from the original records, under the title of the *Statutes of the Realm*; alphabetical and chronological indexes were issued in 1824 and 1828. An edition of the statutes, prepared by the Statute Law Committee,

with all repealed Acts and parts of Acts omitted, coming down to 1878, was published by the government under the title of the *Statutes Revised*; a second edition brought down to 1920 was issued in 24 volumes; and a third edition brought down to 1948 was issued in 1951. As to the merits and the defects of various editions of the statutes, see Cooper, *Account of the Public Records*, c. vi. See LAW; S.L.R.; STATUTES OF UNCERTAIN DATE.

The principal works on statutes and their interpretation are Coke's *Second Institute*, Barrington on *The Statutes*, and Dwarris on *Statutes*, and in modern times, Maxwell on *The Interpretation of Statutes*, and Craies on *Statute Law*.

" Statute " sometimes means a kind of bond or obligation of record, being an abbreviation for " statute merchant " or " statute staple " (*q.v.*).

See ACT OF PARLIAMENT; CONSOLIDATION ACTS; MARGINAL NOTES; PUNCTUATION; RUBRIC OF A STATUTE; TAUTOLOGY.

Statute barred. Causes of action in respect of which proceedings cannot be brought because the periods laid down by the Limitation Act, 1939, have elapsed are said to be statute barred.

Statute fair, the half-yearly assemblage of labourers of both sexes at which they stood and offered themselves for hire and at which the rates of hiring fixed pursuant to the Statute of Labourers, 1349 (*q.v.*), were proclaimed; also called a hiring fair, or mop fair, or mop. See MARKETS AND FAIRS.

Statute labour. Under various ancient statutes the inhabitants of each parish were required either to do certain work, known as statute labour, annually upon the highways repairable by the parish, or to pay a composition. The last was the statute 1773, 13 Geo. 3, c. 78; it was repealed by the Highway Act, 1835.

Statute law revision. See S.L.R.

Statute merchant, a bond acknowledged before the chief magistrate of some trading town pursuant to the statute *De Mercatoribus*, 1285. Like a statute staple (*q.v.*), which was a bond acknowledged pursuant to the statute 1353, 27 Edw. 3, st. 2, before the mayor of the staple, that is to say, the grand mart for the principal commodities or manufactures of the kingdom, formerly held by Act of Parliment in certain trading towns, it was originally intended to encourage trade by providing a speedy remedy for recovering debts. Every statute merchant had to be sealed with the seals of the debtor and of the king, and enrolled. It was therefore a bond of record (see RECORD; ROLL), and the addition of the king's seal made it of so high a nature that on failure of payment by the debtor at the day assigned execution might be awarded without any mesne process to summon the debtor, or bringing in proofs, and thus it was called a pocket judgment. Under the writ *De statuto stabulae*, not only the body of the debtor might be imprisoned and his goods seized in satisfaction of the debt, but also his lands might be delivered to the creditor till out of the rents and profits the debt was satisfied; during that time the creditor was called tenant by statute merchant or statute staple, and had a chattel interest in the lands. Statutes merchant and statutes staple formerly charged the land of the debtor; but this privilege was abolished by the Judgments Act, 1864. See JUDGMENT; RECOGNISANCE; STATUTO MERCATORIO, DE.

Statute of Agreement, the Statute of Kenilworth, 1266.

Statute of Enrolments, 1536. This provided that sales of estates should not be valid unless made under seal and enrolled in one of the king's courts. See BARGAIN AND SALE.

Statute of Frauds, 1677. This was passed for the prevention of frauds and perjuries. With this object it enacted that leases of lands, tenements or hereditaments (except leases not exceeding three years, reserving a rent of at least two-thirds the value of the land) should have the force of leases at will only unless put in writing and signed by the parties or their agents. Assignments and surrenders of leases and interests in land were required to be in writing (ss. 1–3); under the Law of Property Act, 1925, ss. 53–55, replacing the Real Property Act, 1845, the leases and other instruments specified must be under seal. No action might be brought upon a special promise by an executor or administrator to answer damages out of his own estate, or upon a guarantee, or upon an agreement made in consideration of marriage, or upon a contract for the sale or lease of lands, etc., or any interest in or concerning them, or upon an agreement not to be performed within a year, unless the agreement was evidenced by writing signed by the party to be charged or his agent; the Law of Property Act, 1925, s. 40, reproduced the provisions of this section as to contracts relating to land, but the remainder of the section, other than the provision as to guarantees, was repealed by the Law Reform (Enforcement of Contracts) Act, 1954, s. 1; the consideration for a guarantee need not appear in the writing (Mercantile Law Amendment Act, 1856, s. 3). The sections relating to wills (ss. 5, 6, 19–23), are replaced by the Wills Act, 1837. Declarations or creations of trusts of lands etc., and assignments of trusts, except trusts arising by implication of law, were required to be in writing (ss. 7–9); these sections are replaced by the Law of Property Act, 1925, s. 53. Lands of a *cestui que trust*, when in the hands of his real representative, were liable to his judgments and obligations (ss. 10, 11); these sections are replaced by the Administration of Estates Act, 1925, s. 32. Estates *pur autre vie* were made devisable and liable to the owner's debts, and descendible, unless otherwise disposed of, to his personal representative (s. 12); this section was supplemented by the statute 1740, 14 Geo. 2, c. 20, s. 9, and was superseded by the Wills Act, 1837, ss. 3, 6 (see OCCUPANCY). No writ of execution against goods should bind the property therein until the writ was delivered to the sheriff to be executed; this section is replaced by the Sale of Goods Act, 1893, s. 26 (1), which provides that a bona fide purchaser shall have a good title to goods purchased before actual execution of the writ. No contract for the sale of any goods, wares and merchandises of the value of £10 or upwards was enforceable by action unless the buyer accepted and received part of the goods so sold, or gave something in earnest or part payment, or unless some note or memorandum of the contract was made and signed by the parties to be charged, or their agents; this section was replaced by the Sale of Goods Act, 1893, s. 4, which was repealed by the Law

Reform (Enforcement of Contracts) Act, 1954, s. 2. See TENTERDEN'S ACT.

Statute of Gloucester, the statute 1278, 6 Edw. 1.

Statutes of Jointures, the statute 1495, 11 Hen. 7, c. 20.

Statute of Stabbing. See STABBING.

Statute of Treasons, the Treason Act, 1351. See TREASON.

Statute of Uses, 1535. See USE.

Statute of Westminster I, the statute 1275, 3 Edw. 1.

Statute of Westminster II, the statute 1285, 13 Edw. 1.

Statute of Westminster, 1931, the statute which defines the constitutional position of the Dominions. See BRITISH COMMONWEALTH.

Statute staple, a bond of record acknowledged, pursuant to the statute 1353, 27 Edw. 3, st. 2, before the mayor of the staple, in the presence of the constables of the staple, or one of them; the only seal required for its validity was the seal of the staple, and therefore if the statute were void for any cause, it could not, as in the case of a statute merchant (*q.v.*), be proceeded on as a common obligation; and, wanting the sanction of the seal of the king, the sheriff, after the extent, could not deliver the lands to the conusee, but had to seize them into the king's hands; and in order to obtain possession of them, the conusee had to sue out a writ of *liberate*, which was a writ out of Chancery, reciting the former writ, and commanding the sheriff to deliver to the conusee all the lands, tenements, and chattels by him taken into the king's hands, if the conusee would have them, until he should be satisfied his debt. See STAPLE.

Statutes at Large. See STATUTE.

Statutes of Distribution. See ADVANCEMENT; DISTRIBUTION; NEXT-OF-KIN.

Statutes of Labourers. See LABOURERS.

Statute of Limitation. See LIMITATION OF ACTIONS.

Statutes of the Realm. See STATUTE.

Statutes of Uncertain Date. These are a number of statutes made before the reign of Edward III, to some of which no date has been assigned by anyone, while others are by some authorities attributed to dates which cannot be regarded as certain.

Statutes Revised. See STATUTE; S.L.R.

Statuti, advocates, members of the college (Civil Law).

Statuto mercatorio, De. There were two forms of this writ, one directed against a layman and the other against an ecclesiastical person. Where default was made in payment of a statute merchant by a layman, the writ commanded the sheriff to imprison him until the debt was satisfied; in the case of like default by an ecclesiastical person, the writ commanded the sheriff to levy the amount of the debt of the goods of such person (Reg.Brev. 146).

Statuto stapulae, or **stabulae,** a writ which lay to imprison and seize the lands and goods of a person who had forfeited the bond called statute staple (*q.v.*) (Reg. Brev. 151). See STATUTE MERCHANT.

Statutory alien. A natural-born British subject who had become an alien pursuant to the Naturalization Act, 1870, was entitled a "statutory alien," and could re-obtain his British nationality upon the same terms as those governing the naturalization of other aliens (Naturalization Act, 1870, s. 8). The Act was repealed by the Status of Aliens Act, 1914, after which there was no difference between a denaturalised British subject and any other alien.

Statutory declarations. The Statutory Declarations Act, 1835, substitutes declarations for oaths in a large number of cases. The expression statutory declaration in a statute means a declaration under that Act (Interpretation Act, 1889, s. 21). See DECLARATION, STATUTORY.

As to the punishment if a person knowingly and wilfully makes a statement false in a material particular in a statutory declaration, see the Perjury Act, 1911, s. 5.

Statutory exposition. When the language of a statute is ambiguous, and any subsequent enactment involves a particular interpretation of the former Act, it is said to contain a statutory exposition of the former Act.

Statutory instruments. Statutory rules and orders (*q.v.*) have been so called since the Statutory Instruments Act, 1946.

Statutory joint industrial councils. See

the Employment Protection Act, 1975, s. 90, Sch. 8.

Statutory meeting, the obligatory first general meeting of a company, for the purpose of which there must be prepared a statutory report (Companies Act, 1948, s. 130).

Statutory order. See SPECIAL PARLIAMENTARY PROCEDURE; STATUTORY RULES AND ORDERS.

Statutory owner. The Settled Land Act, 1925, s. 117 (1) (xxvi), defines " statutory owner " as meaning the trustees of the settlement or other persons who, during the minority of the tenant for life, or at any time when there is no tenant for life, have the powers of a tenant for life under that Act, but not including the trustees of the settlement, where by virtue of an order of the court or otherwise, the trustees have power to convey the settled land in the name of the tenant for life. Where land has been devised to an infant, the personal representatives, and in other cases, the trustees of the settlement, may be statutory owners (ss. 23–26, 110).

Statutory release, a conveyance which superseded the old compound assurance by lease and release. It was created by the statute 1841, 4 & 5 Vict. c. 21, which abolished the necessity for a lease for a year in such assurance. See RELEASE.

Statutory rules and orders. Most modern Acts of Parliament contain provisions authorising the Crown in Council, a Minister, a local authority, a corporation, or some other body to make rules, orders and regulations on particular subjects. The Rules of the Supreme Court and the orders which have been made with regard to diseases of animals are instances of the result of this delegation of authority. Such rules, orders and regulations, if validly made, have the same effect as if they were expressly enacted by Parliament. Where the Act provides that any rule, order or regulation shall be laid before Parliament and shall become of no effect if either House resolves that it be annulled, then, in the absence of such a resolution, no court can question its validity, but if no such reference to Parliament is provided for, and if there is no section declaring that it cannot be questioned in any court, then

it may be held to be *ultra vires* (*Daymond v. South West Water Board* [1975] 3 W.L.R. 865).

This delegation of authority by Parliament had taken place in a few instances during the first hundred and fifty years after the Revolution of 1688, but it became common only after the accession of Queen Victoria.

Since the Statutory Instruments Act, 1946, statutory rules, orders and regulations have been known as statutory instruments.

The Statutory Instruments Act, 1946, replacing the Rules Publication Act, 1893, directs that all statutory instruments shall be printed by the Queen's Printer and sold by him.

Since 1890 it has been customary to publish under official sanction from time to time the public and general rules, orders and regulations in force. These are known as the Statutory Rules and Orders Revised. There are then annual volumes which keep the collection up to date until another collection of those in force is published, as was the case in 1904 in 13 volumes. A third edition of Statutory Rules and Orders and Statutory Instruments Revised in 28 volumes was published in 1952.

Statutory tenant. See RENT RESTRICTION.

Statutory trusts. For the purposes of the Law of Property Act, 1925, land held upon the statutory trusts is held upon trust to sell the same and to stand possessed of the net proceeds of sale, after payment of costs, and of the net rents and profits until sale after payment of rates, taxes, cost of insurance and repairs and other outgoings, upon such trusts, and subject to such powers and provisions, as may be requisite for giving effect to the rights of the persons (including an incumbrancer of a former undivided share, or whose incumbrance is not secured by a legal mortgage) interested in the land (Law of Property Act, 1925, s. 35). Where an undivided share was subject to a settlement and the settlement remains subsisting in respect of other property and the trustees of the settlement are not the same persons as the trustees for sale, the settled portion of the proceeds of sale is to be handed over to the settlement trustees as capital money under the Settled Land Act, 1925. By the Law of Property Act, 1925, s. 25, the trustees have power to postpone a sale unless a contrary direction appears in the trust instrument. By the Law of Property (Entailed Interests) Act, 1932, entailed interests in undivided shares of land are to be treated and held as entailed interests in the proceeds of sale. As to the meaning of statutory trusts upon distribution on intestacy, in favour of the issue and other classes of relatives of the intestate *per capita* and *per stirpes*, see the Administration of Estates Act, 1925, s. 47, as amended by the Intestates' Estates Act, 1952 and the Family Law Reform Act, 1969, s. 3 (2). See WIDOW.

Statutory undertakers, persons authorised by statute to construct or carry on gas, electricity, water, transport, and other public undertakings.

Statutum affirmativum non derogat communi legi (Jenk., Cent. 24). (An affirmative statute does not derogate from the common law.) If a statute is really only affirmative, that is to say, declaratory, it obviously makes no alteration in either the common law or the statute law. See QUAE COMMUNI, ETC.

Statutum de Admensuratione Terre, the Statute for the Measuring of Land. An enactment is printed under this title in the *Statutes of the Realm* amongst the *Statutes of Uncertain Date*, and in the *Statutes at Large* as 1305, 33 Edw. 1, st. 6.

Statutum de Conspiratoribus, the Statute concerning Conspirators. An enactment is printed under this title in the *Statutes of the Realm* amongst the *Statutes of Uncertain Date*, and in the *Statutes at Large* as 1305, 33 Edw. 1, st. 3.

Statutum de Finibus et Attornatis, the Statute concerning Fines and Attorneys. An enactment is printed under this title in the *Statutes of the Realm* amongst the *Statutes of Uncertain Date*, and in the *Statutes at Large* as 1322, 15 Edw. 2.

Statutum de Gaveleto in Londinio, the Statute of Gavelet in London. An enactment is printed under this title in the *Statutes of the Realm* amongst the *Statutes of Uncertain Date*, and in the *Statutes at Large* as 1317, 10 Edw. 2. See GAVELET.

Statutum de Judeismo. See LES ESTATUS DE LA JEUERIE.

Statutum de Justic assign quod vocatur Rageman. See RAGEMAN, STATUTE OF.

Statutum de laboriis, a writ which lay for the arrest of a labourer who refused to work as required by the Statute of Labourers, 1349. See LABOURERS, STATUTE OF.

Statutum de Magnis Assisis et Duellis, the Statute concerning the Great Assises and Battle. An enactment is printed under this title in the *Statutes of the Realm* and in the *Statutes at Large* amongst the *Statutes of Uncertain Date*. It is not really a statute, and is in fact merely an extract from the *Brevia Placitata* (*q.v.*).

Statutum de Mercatoribus. See ACTON BURNEL.

Statutum de Moneta. See STATUTA DE MONETA.

Statutum de Moneta Falsa, the statute 1299, 27 Edw. 1.

Statutum de Nova Custuma. See CARTA MERCATORIA.

Statutum de Officio Coronatoris, the statute 1276, 4 Edw. 1.

Statutum de Pistoribus, the Statute concerning Bakers. An enactment is printed under this title in the *Statutes of the Realm* and in the *Statutes at Large* amongst the *Statutes of Uncertain Date*.

Statutum de Prerogativa. See PREROGATIVA REGIS.

Statutum de Protectionibus non Alloccandis, the Statute against allowing Protections. An enactment is printed under this title in the *Statutes of the Realm* amongst the *Statutes of Uncertain Date*, and in the *Statutes at Large* as 1305, 33 Edw. 1, st. 1. See PROTECTION, WRIT OF.

Statutum de Respectu Militiae Habendo, the Statute for Respiting of Knighthood. An enactment is printed under this title in the *Statutes of the Realm* amongst the *Statutes of Uncertain Date*, and in the *Statutes at Large* as the *Statutum de Militibus*, 1307, 1 Edw. 2. It purported to give some relief from the hardship of compulsory knighthood.

Statutum de Rotelanda. See ROTELANDA.

Statutum de Sacramento Ministrorum Regis, the Statute of Oaths of the King's Officers in the Eyre. An enactment is printed under this title in the *Statutes of the Realm* and in the *Statutes at Large* amongst the *Statutes of Uncertain Date*.

Statutum de Tenentibus per Legem Angliae, the Statute concerning Tenants by the Curtesy of England. An enactment is printed under this title in the *Statutes of the Realm* and in the *Statutes at Large* amongst the *Statutes of Uncertain Date*. It is really no more than an extract from 7 Glanvil, c. 18.

Statutum de Viris Religiosi. See MORT-MAIN.

Statutum de Wardis et Releviis, the Statute concerning Wards and Liveries. An enactment is printed under this title in the *Statutes of the Realm* amongst the *Statutes of Uncertain Date* and in the *Statutes at Large* as 1300, 28 Edw. 1.

Statutum Domini Regis de Terris Vendendis et Emendis, the Statute of our Lord the King concerning the Selling and Buying of Land. This is the title under which the statute *Quia Emptores*, 1289 (*q.v.*), is printed in the *Statutes at Large*.

Statutum Hibernie de Coheredibus, the Statute of Ireland concerning Coparceners. An enactment is printed under this title in the *Statutes of the Realm* as 1235, 20 Hen. 3, and in the *Statutes at Large* as 1229, 14 Hen. 3. It applied to Ireland the law of England as to land descending to coparceners. It has been said not to be a statute. In form it appears to be an instruction given by the king to his justices in Ireland, directing them how to proceed in a certain point where they entertained a doubt. It seems the justices itinerant in that country had a doubt, when land descended to sisters, whether the younger sisters ought to hold of the eldest, and do homage to her for their several portions, or of the chief lord, and do homage to him; and certain knights had been sent over to know what the practice was in England in such a case (1 Reeves, 259).

Statutum sessionum (the statute-sessions), a meeting in every hundred of constables and householders, by custom, for the ordering of servants, and debating of differences between masters and servants, rating of wages, etc. It meant the General Session held next, or within six weeks, after Easter, sitting under the statute 1562, 5 Eliz. 1, c. 4, s. 11, to settle the rate of wages of artificers, husbandmen, labourers and workmen.

Staunforde, the author of the *Pleas of the Crown*, in the reign of Philip and Mary. This book is written in French. Whole pages are frequently transcribed from Bracton.

Staunforde treats of his subject under three heads: first, of crimes; next, of the method of bringing delinquents to justice; and lastly, of trials and punishment.

Stay. A stay of proceedings in an action is a suspension of them: thus, if the plaintiff is ordered to do something and fails to do it, the proceedings may, under the inherent jurisdiction of the court, be ordered to be stayed until he complies with the order. Except so far as the court below or the Court of Appeal may otherwise direct, an appeal does not operate as a stay of execution or of proceedings under the decision of the court below (R.S.C., Ord. 59, r. 13). So also at any time after the presentation of a bankruptcy petition the court may, under the Bankruptcy Act, 1914, s. 9, stay any action, execution or other legal process against the debtor, unless the claim is one from which the debtor would not be released by discharge or unless the plaintiff is a secured creditor. By the Judicature Act, 1925, s. 41, the court has power to stay proceedings in cases where an injunction or prohibition could formerly have been obtained. Every court has an inherent jurisdiction to stay proceedings on the ground that they are an abuse of the process of the court (*Re Norton's Settlement* [1908] 1 Ch. at p. 479; *Egbert* v. *Short* [1907] 2 Ch. 205). An action shown by the pleadings to be frivolous or vexatious may be stayed under R.S.C., Ord. 18, r. 19. A stay of proceedings is sometimes produced *ipso facto*, without an express order to that effect, as where a party obtains an order for a new trial.

" Stay of proceedings " also sometimes means a total discontinuance of the action: thus, if an action in the Queen's Bench is compromised, the compromise takes the form of an order made, on summons, by a master to stay all further proceedings on the terms agreed by the parties. In the Chancery Division the term is also so used, but in strictness it is only accurate when a decree or judgment has been given, for in such a case the suit or action cannot be dismissed, because the court has adjudicated on it, and therefore all that can be done is to stay proceedings under the decree or judgment. Before decree or judgment the proper way of disposing of an action is either by discontinuance (*q.v.*), or by an order dismissing the action. After discontinuance there will be a stay of subsequent action until costs are paid (R.S.C., Ord. 21, r. 5).

Stealing. See KIDNAPPING; ROBBERY; THEFT.

Steam engines. At common law, steam engines were nuisances if and in so far as anyone was inconvenienced by such noise and smoke as emanated from them. The various Acts under which their use is legal on railways have taken away the remedy of proceedings for nuisance in respect of their use on a railway. Proceedings for damages are still available in case of negligent user; the production of smoke (*q.v.*) is restrained by statute; and a remedy for fires caused by railway engines is provided by the Railway Fires Acts, 1905 and 1923.

The Acts authorising the use of locomotives (*q.v.*) on highways do not exempt owners from liability for nuisance.

As to steam boilers, see BOILERS.

See ENGINE.

Steelyard; Stilyard; Stylehouse [Old Germ. *stâl*, a sample]. The Steelyard was established about 1250 by certain Hanse merchants near what was later called Ironbridge Wharf in the City of London, as a mart for their goods. The Hanse was deprived of its privileges by Edward VI, but remained in occupation of the Steelyard until it was expelled from England in 1597. The Hanseatic towns of Lubeck, Bremen, and Hamburg continued to own the Steelyard down to 1852, when they sold it to the South Eastern Railway Company. Part of Cannon Street Station stands on the site. See GUILDHALDA, ETC.

Stellionate [*stellionatus*], a kind of crime which is committed by a deceitful selling of a thing; as if a man should sell as his own estate that which is another's.

In the civil law, it meant granting a second mortgage without giving notice of the first; but the crime was not committed if the land was equal in value to all the charges upon it.

Stent. See EXTENT.

Sterbrech; Strebrech, the breaking, obstructing, or making less of a highway (*Termes de la Ley*).

Sterling, genuine; money; standard-rate. For a possible derivation of this term see EASTERLING. The term "sterling" was first applied to the English penny, and then to standard current coin in general. There is a reference in the time of Edward I to *denarius Angliae, qui vocatur sterlingus* (Co.Litt. 207b, n. 1; Wedgw.; Ducange).

Sterling was an early synonym of the penny, or *denarius*, as it was in medieval Latin. Fleta writes of *denar Angliae qui sterling appellatur*, and Stow writes: "Paid in starlings which were pence so called."

"Sterling" was used subsequently as meaning coin of standard weight and fineness.

As to the effect of an obligation expressed in terms of sterling in gold of a given fineness or by reference to the relations between sterling and gold, see *Feist* v. *Société Intercommunale Belge d'Electricité* [1934] A.C. 161.

A description of an article or of the metal in an article as sterling is to be presumed to be an indication that the article or the metal is silver of a standard of fineness of 925 parts per thousand (Hallmarking Act, 1973, Sch. 1 Pt. III).

By art. 106, of the Treaty of Rome, an English court must give judgment for a creditor residing in another member state in his own currency when that is the currency of the contract and the sterling rule no longer applies (*Schorsch Meier G.m.b.H.* v. *Hennin* [1975] Q.B. 416; *Miliangos* v. *George Frank (Textiles)* [1976] A.C. 443).

The making of claims and enforcement of judgments expressed in foreign currency is regulated, in general, by Practice Direction dated December 18, 1975. See [1976] 1 W.L.R. 83.

Stet, let it stand.

Stet billa. If a plaintiff in a plaint in the Mayor's Court of London had attached property belonging to the defendant and obtained execution against the garnishee, the defendant, if he wished to contest the plaintiff's claim, and to obtain restoration of his property, had to issue a *scire facias ad disprobandum debitum* (see SCIRE FACIAS); if the only question to be tried was the plaintiff's debt, the plaintiff in appearing to the *scire facias* prayed *stet billa*, that his bill original, *i.e.*, his original plaint, might stand, and that the defendant might plead thereto; the action then proceeded in the usual way as if the proceedings in attachment (which were founded on a fictitious default of the defendant in appearing to the plaint) had not taken place. See FOREIGN ATTACHMENT.

Stet processus. In the practice before the Judicature Acts, 1873–75, of the old common law courts, this was an entry on the record in an action whereby it was ordered, with the consent of the parties, that all further proceedings in the action should be stayed. It could only be made with the consent of both parties, and apparently could only be entered as to the whole record. As there is under the modern practice no record in an action, it is difficult to see how a *stet processus* could be entered, though it is believed that orders to that effect were made subsequent to the Judicature Acts, 1873–75; they took effect as an ordinary stay of proceedings.

Stethe, or **Stede,** the bank of a river; a place (Co.Litt. 4b).

Stevedore [Sp. *estivar*, to stow], a person employed to stow a cargo on board a ship.

A stevedore is a person whose business is to undertake the stowage (*q.v.*) or discharge of cargoes with a gang of men whom he hires and pays and is responsible for. Such a person, named a *stibador*, is mentioned in the *Consolato del Mare*. See Maclachan on *Merchant Shipping*.

A stevedore is not a party to the contract of carriage between shipper and carrier (*Midland Silicones* v. *Scruttons* [1961] 1 Q.B. 106).

Stew, an artificial oyster-bed; a vivarium; a breeding place for tame pheasants.

In the plural, as in the expression " the stews," it meant brothels, the existence of which was tolerated down to the reign of Henry VIII. In the Rolls of Parliament for 1436 we find: " No person that had dwelled in the common Stywes ": but the word is not used in any statute. It is said to be derived from the old French, *estuves,* a stove or hot bath, because frequenters prepared themselves by bathing.

Steward [Lat. *seneschallus*], a ward or keeper; one appointed in the stead of another.

The word was formerly used to denote an officer of the Crown, or of a feudal lord, who acted as keeper of a court of justice (Co.Litt. 61a), as for example, the Lord High Steward (*q.v.*); and there is still the Lord Steward of the Royal Household (*q.v.*).

Steward of a manor, the lord's deputy, who transacted all the legal and other business connected with the estate, and took care of the court rolls. The office was usually held by the lord's solicitor. Every manor had a steward, appointed by the lord, who theoretically acted as judge of the customary court baron and the court leet, and as registrar of the freeholders' court baron. His duties were rather ministerial than judicial, for his chief function was to receive surrenders of and grant admittances to the copyhold lands of the manor, and keep the court roll. See COPYHOLD; COURT BARON; COURT LEET; DAPIFER; MANOR.

Compensation was payable to the steward on the abolition of copyhold (Law of Property Act, 1922, Sched. XIV; Law of Property (Amendment) Act, 1924). Upon a vacancy for three months in the office and on other occasions the Lord Chancellor might upon default of the lord of the manor transfer the duties of the office to the Land Registry (Law of Property Act, 1922, s. 129).

Should there be joint stewards, one might act without the other (1 Scriv. 130).

The chief steward was usually appointed by deed, though he might be appointed by parol; but corporations had always to appoint by deed under their corporate seal.

The appointment of a steward was generally during the lord's pleasure; it might, however, be for years or for life, forfeitable by abuser, misuser, nonuser, or refuser. The steward's remedy for a disturbance of his office was an action on the case for consequential damages. The Queen's Bench Division might grant a mandamus to restore a steward to his office. A steward might depute or authorise another to hold a court. An under-steward or deputy might authorise another as sub-deputy, *pro hac vice*, to hold a court for him, such limited authority not being inconsistent with the rule *delegatus non potest delegare*.

Stick of eels, twenty-five eels. Ten sticks made a " bind."

Stickler, an inferior officer who cut woods within the royal parks of Clarendon, a woodcutter or stikker; an arbitrator; an obstinate contender about anything; a person who adheres strictly to convention; a judge in a Cornish wrestling match.

Stifling a prosecution, agreeing, in consideration of receiving a pecuniary or other advantage, to abstain from prosecuting a person. If the offence is an indictable offence of public concern, such an agreement is void and invalidates any transaction of which it forms part. (See COMPOUND; MISPRISION.) Where, as in the case of perjury, the offence is of public concern, the stifling of the prosecution is probably a misdemeanour at common law.

Still. As to licences to keep or use a still, see the Customs and Excise Act, 1952, ss. 226–228; Finance Act, 1967, s. 4 (5), Sch. 16 Pt. III.

Stillicidum, eavesdrop, the water which falls from the roof of a house in scattered drops (Civil Law).

Stint. A stint is a limit, and therefore a stinted right of common of pasture is one where the number of beasts allowed to be put on the common by each commoner is limited, as opposed to common *sans nombre.* (See SANS NOMBRE.) A right of pasture may also be stinted in respect of time. See VIEW AND DELIVERY.

Stint is also used in a special sense to denote the right of pasture of one of several persons who are tenants in common of land which they use as a common pasture ground for their cattle. Stinted pastures are grazing lands on moors, downs and wastes, which produce no crop, and which are open to each person who has a share in the pasture for a stinted or limited number of cattle. They are usually closed at certain seasons of the year for the better growth of the pasture, but are never held in severalty. The right of each joint owner of the herbage is known as a stint or cattle gate (Elton, *Commons*).

A stint is not a common, but a corporeal hereditament. See COMMON; HEREDITAMENT.

Sometimes the lord of a manor has a stint or limited right of pasture on the waste during a certain part of the year. See SHEEPWALK.

Stipend, a salary; settled pay; a provision made for the support of the clergy.

Stipendiary estates, feuds, estates granted in return for services, generally of a military kind.

Stipendiary magistrates, salaried magistrates appointed to act instead of, or along with, justices of the peace under the Administration of Justice Act, 1973. They must be barristers or solicitors of not less than seven years' standing. A person so appointed is a justice of the peace for the area to which he is appointed (s. 2).

A stipendiary magistrate can do things for which two ordinary justices are required (Magistrates' Courts Act, 1952, s. 121).

As to London, see METROPOLITAN STIPENDIARY MAGISTRATE.

Stipendium [Lat. *stips*, a piece of money; *pendere*, to weigh], wages, pay. Before silver was coined at Rome, the copper money in use was paid by weight.

Stipulated damage, liquidated damages (*q.v.*).

Stipulatio, an oral contract formed by question and answer. One party proposed a question (*stipulatio*) and the other responded to it (*promissio*). In the time of Gaius it was necessary to use a certain solemn form of words, but by the time of Justinian the question and answer could be embodied in any form of words which would express the intention of the parties. The contract was unilateral, the *promissor* only being bound, and the parties had to be present when the contract was entered into.

The *stipulatio* was the highest and most authentic contract known to the civil law, entered into through the medium of interrogatories and answers calculated to explain the nature and extent of the undertaking, to put the parties entering into it on their guard, and to show it to be their mature and deliberate act. It could not be impeached except for fraud or deceit, and could not be released or discharged except by an equally solemn proceeding, conducted by question and answer, called *acceptilatio* (Civil Law).

Stipulation, bargain; a recognisance of certain fidejussors in the nature of bail, taken in the Admiralty courts.

Stiremannus, a pilot or steersman (Domesday).

Stirpes. See PER CAPITA; PER STIRPES.

Stoc and stovel, a forfeiture which was incurred by one taken in the act of unlawfully carrying stoc (sticks) and stovel (fodder) out of woods.

Stock, a race, lineage, or family; the public funds, considered merely as perpetual annuities redeemable at the pleasure of the Government; the capital of a public company. What is now generally called the capital of a company was formerly called its "joint-stock," meaning the common or joint fund contributed by the members. The capital of a company is generally divided into shares (*q.v.*), so that shares and stock are in one sense the same thing: but the Companies Act, 1948, s. 455, enacts that "share" means share in the share capital of a company and includes stock except where a distinction between stock and shares is expressed or implied.

Stock also signifies a fund or capital which is capable of being divided into and held in any irregular amount. Thus, the ordinary Government funds such as Consols are called stocks, because a person can buy them in any amount (such as £99 as well as £100). A share or debenture, on the other hand, is of a fixed amount (such as £10, £50, £100), and is incapable of subdivision or consolidation. Many companies, however, have, under the Companies Act, 1948, s. 61 (1), and the Companies Clauses Consolidation Act, 1845, s. 61, the power of converting paid-up shares into stock, and of converting debentures into debenture stock. See DEBENTURE STOCK; SHARE.

Simplified transfer of certain securities is provided for by the Stock Transfer Act, 1963. Securities here means shares, stock, debentures, debenture stock, loan stock, bonds, units of a unit trust scheme, or other shares of the investments subject to the trusts of such a scheme, and other securities of any description (s. 4); S.I. 1974 No. 1214. See also the Finance Act, 1964, s. 24, Sch. 8 para. 10, Sch. 9; Post Office Act, 1969, s. 108 (1) (*f*).

Stock certificates. By the National Debt Act, 1870, it is provided that a holder of British Government stock may obtain a stock certificate, that is to say, a certificate of title to his stock or any part thereof, with coupons annexed, entitling the bearer of the coupons to the dividends on the stock (s. 26); that a certificate shall not be issued in respect of any sum of stock not being £50, or a multiple of £50, or exceeding £1,000 (s. 28); that a trustee of stock shall not apply for or hold a stock certificate, unless authorised to do so by the terms of his trust (s. 29); that no notice of any trust in respect of any certificate or coupon shall be receivable (s. 30); that where a stock certificate is outstanding the stock represented thereby shall cease to be transferable in the Bank books (s. 31); and that a stock certificate, unless a name is inscribed thereon, shall entitle the bearer to the stock therein described, and shall be transferable by delivery (s. 32). These sections are prospectively repealed by the Finance Act, 1963, s. 71 (7) except as to stock certificates outstanding at the date of repeal.

Stock exchange, a society of stockbrokers and dealers (or stockjobbers) for the conduct of the sale or purchase, on behalf of non-members, of Government securities and stocks or shares in public companies. The members of the "House" (as it is called) are re-elected annually and pay a substantial annual subscription.

The London Stock Exchange is an unincorporated private company. It has many rules which, unless they are recognised by the law, are binding upon its members only to such extent as they can be enforced by disciplinary action, such as expulsion, on the part of the committee. Upon persons who are not members the rules are not binding, unless in the eye of the law they are reasonable, and the law will not regard as reasonable any custom which is in violation of law. (*Neilson* v. *James* (1882) 9 Q.B.D. 546). It is indeed a question whether any such contract is not void to all intents and for all purposes. See CUSTOM; WAGER.

The Stock Exchange does not recognise in its dealings any other parties than its own members; every bargain, therefore, whether for account of the member effecting it, or for account of a principal, must be fulfilled according to the rules, regulations and usages of the Stock Exchange. No member or authorised clerk may carry on business in the double capacity of broker and dealer. As to jobbers' transfers, see the Finance Act, 1976, s. 127.

Power to suspend financial dealings is conferred on the Treasury by the Banking and Financial Dealings Act, 1971, s. 2.

Stockbroker, one who buys and sells stock as the agent of others. The statute 1733, 7 Geo. 2, c. 8 (known as Sir John Barnard's Act), required a stockbroker to keep a book called the broker's book, to enter all contracts for stock made by him on the same day, with the names of the parties and the day, and to produce such book when lawfully required; but this Act was repealed by the statute 1860, 23 Vict. c. 28. See BROKER.

Stockjobber, a dealer in stock; one who buys and sells stock on his own account on speculation. See STOCK EXCHANGE.

Stock-jobbing Act, the statute 1733, 7 Geo. 2, c. 8, entitled " an Act to prevent the infamous practice of stock-jobbing." It was repealed by the statute 1860, 23 & 24 Vict. c. 28; and stock-jobbing, if and when it amounts to wagering, is now dealt with like other kinds of wagers (*q.v.*). See BACKWARDATION; BARNARD'S ACT; CONTANGO; PUTTS AND REFUSALS.

Stockland, soke-land. See BOND-LAND.

Stocks. These consisted of two boards; on one side of each there were two semicircular holes; and, when the boards were fastened together, there were two circular apertures just large enough to encircle the ankles of an offender sitting behind the boards.

Sitting in the stocks for a certain number of hours was from very early times a common punishment for minor offences. It was frequently ordered by the court leet (*q.v.*). Subsequently it was prescribed by various statutes. Under the statute 1606, 4 Jac. 1, c. 5, s. 1, repealed by the Licensing Act, 1872, a person fined for drunkenness was, in default of payment, to sit in the stocks for six hours; and under the Sunday Observance Act, 1677, s. 2 (repealed), a criminal who, for instance, sold tobacco on a Sunday must, in default of payment of a fine or in default of sufficient distress, be set publicly in the stocks for the space of two hours.

The punishment of the stocks began to be disused about the beginning of the nineteenth century, but has not been expressly abolished; and stocks have been preserved in some country villages and towns; *e.g.*, at Woodeaton in Oxfordshire, in the churchyard at South Hayling in Hampshire and in the town hall of Much Wenlock in Shropshire.

Stolen goods. See ADVERTISEMENTS; POSSESSION; RECEIVING STOLEN GOODS; RESTITUTION; REVESTING.

Stone. A stone consists of fourteen pounds (Weights and Measures Act, 1963, s. 10, Sch. 1 Pt. V). See POUND. Formerly, the stone varied greatly (see FORMELLA). The statute 1495, 11 Hen. 7, c. 4, s. 2, enacted that there should be fourteen pounds to the stone of wool, yet even in 1845 the customary stone for wool was twenty-four pounds in some places. The customary stone for which the prices of beef and of mutton are quoted is or was, in some places, only eight pounds. See WEIGHTS AND MEASURES.

Stop list, a list maintained by a trade association of persons who offer or sell goods at a price above or below a certain price. Members of the association are forbidden to trade with a person on the stop list. As to when this is lawful, see *Thorne* v. *Motor Trade Association* [1937] A.C. 797; see also the Restrictive Trade Practices Act, 1956, s. 24.

Stop order. A stop order prohibiting the transfer, sale, delivery out, payment or other dealing with funds in court or any part thereof or the income thereon, without notice to the person applying for the order may be obtained by summons under R.S.C., Ord. 50, r. 10. A stop notice may be obtained from the court on affidavit under Ord. 50, rr. 11–14. An order prohibiting the transfer etc. of securities may be obtained from the Chancery Division by motion or summons (r. 15). For forms see R.S.C., App. A, Forms Nos. 79–81.

Stoppage in transitu, the right which an unpaid seller has to resume the possession of goods sold upon credit and to retain them until tender of the price where the buyer has become insolvent before they come into his possession (Sale of Goods Act, 1893, s. 44). Thus if A orders goods of B, and B dispatches them by carrier to A's address, but before they have been actually delivered he hears that A has stopped payment (s. 62 (3)), then B is allowed to countermand delivery before or at the place of destination, and to resume possession of the goods (*Lick-barrow* v. *Mason* (1787) 6 East 21). But it is not an unlimited right; for the seller cannot exercise it if he has parted with documents sufficient to transfer the property and the buyer, upon the strength of them, has sold the goods to a bona fide purchaser without notice (s. 47). The seller's right ceases as soon as the *transitus* is determined, whether by the goods arriving at their destination, or being delivered to a person on behalf of the buyer, or by the carrier agreeing, between himself and the buyer, to hold the goods for him, not as carrier, but as his agent (s. 45).

There is also a so-called right of stoppage *in transitu* in cases where there is in fact no transit, as where goods are sold whilst in the possession of a warehouseman, and some act remains to be done for the completion of the sale (Factors Act, 1889, s. 10). See DELIVERY ORDER; DOCK WARRANT.

Stopping up of highways. See EXTINGUISHMENT OF HIGHWAY.

Story. Joseph Story was born in 1779 at Marblehead near Boston, in the United States, became member of Congress in 1809, judge of the Supreme Court in 1811, professor at Harvard in 1829 and died on September 10, 1845. His principal works are *Equity Jurisprudence; Law of Bailments; Agency; Bills of Exchange; Promissory Notes; Partnership;* and *Conflict of Laws.*

Stowage, money paid for a room where goods are laid; housage; the mode of lading a ship.

Stowage of a cargo is primarily the duty of the shipowner and the master, and nothing absolves them from this obligation short of express agreement on the part of the charterer or the unambiguous usage of the port (*Anglo-African Co.* v. *Lanzed* (1866) L.R.C.P. 266). See STEVEDORE.

Stowaway. For penalties on and discipline of stowaways on ships, see the Merchant Shipping Act, 1894, s. 237; see also s. 313. As to stowaways on aircraft, see the Air Navigation (Stowaways) Order, 1940, arts. 1, 2, and the Colonial Air Navigation Order, 1949, art. 47.

Stowe [Sax.], a bank of a river; a place; a village (Domesday; Co.Litt. 4b).

Stradling v. **Stiles,** a burlesque report of an argument *in banco,* published in Martinus Scriblerus's works. It is, in part, the work of Fortescue, an eminent lawyer who subsequently became a baron of the Exchequer.

Stramineus homo, a man of straw, one of no substance put forward as bail or surety. See STRAW, MAN OF.

Strand Inn, an Inn of Chancery (*q.v.*).

Stranding, the running of a ship on shore or on a beach. Under the memorandum (*q.v.*) in an ordinary policy of marine insurance, the underwriters are not liable for damage sustained by certain perishable articles, unless in consequence of a general average, or a stranding of the ship. " Stranding " does not occur when a vessel takes the ground in the ordinary and usual course of navigation, in a tideway or harbour, upon the ebbing of the tide or the like, so that the vessel will float again on the flow of the tide; but it occurs if the vessel takes the ground by reason of some unusual or accidental occurrence, *e.g.*, in consequence of an unknown and unusual obstruction in the harbour.

Stranger. A person is said to be a stranger to a transaction when he takes no part in it, or no part producing any legal effect. Thus a person who is not a party to a deed, contract, etc., is said to be a stranger to it. (See PART; PRIVY.) So when a promise is made to a person, but he has neither taken any trouble or charge upon himself, nor conferred any benefit on the promisor, but the trouble has been sustained or benefit conferred by another, the promisee is said to be a stranger to the consideration. See CONSIDERATION.

A "stranger in blood" means a person in no degree of relationship to another. The Stamp Act, 1815, Sch., speaks of "any stranger in blood to the deceased." A bastard (*q.v.*) is a "stranger in blood" for certain purposes unless legitimated *per subsequens matrimonium* (Legitimacy Act, 1976, s. 5).

Statocracy [στρατος, an army; χράτυς, power], a military government.

Strator. or **Stretward,** a surveyor of the highways (2 Dugd.Mon. 187).

Straw, Man of, a person without means (13 L.Q.R. 344).

The term is used in connection with the transfer of shares to a man without means in order to escape calls, and of leases in order to escape liability in respect of covenants. In respect of shares such a transfer, for a nominal or without consideration, will not relieve the transferor of liability if the shares are those of a mine within the Stannaries Act, 1869 (see s. 35); but in every other case the transfer, if it completely vests the shares in the transferee as absolute owner, will relieve the transferor of liability (*De Pass's Case* (1859) 4 De G. & J. 544), except such as may, in the event of a winding-up, attach to him as being on the "B" list (see A AND B LISTS). As regards leases, such an assignment, unless it is in breach of a covenant not to assign without the consent of the lessor, will relieve the lessee of liability in respect of covenants running with the land, amongst which are included a covenant to repair or to put or leave in repair.

Straw bond, a bond upon which is used the names of fictitious persons or of persons unable to pay the sum contracted for.

Stray. See ANIMALS, LIABILITY FOR; ESTRAYS.

Stream. See RIVERS.

Street, a road with continuous houses on each side of it. Statutory definitions have extended the meaning of the term for the purposes of various Acts. The Towns Improvement Clauses Act, 1847, s.

3, declares it to include any road, square, court, alley and thoroughfare within the limits to which that Act applies. Definitions to much the same effect are contained in the Waterworks Clauses Act, 1847, s. 3, the Towns Police Clauses Act, 1847, s. 3, and the Public Health Act, 1875, s. 4. The Public Health (London) Act, 1891, s. 141, was equally comprehensive, and went even further by declaring that a road is not outside the definition merely because there are no houses along it. By the Public Health Act, 1936, s. 343, it includes any highway, including a highway over any bridge, and any road, lane, footway, square, court, alley or passage, whether a thoroughfare or not (*Att.-Gen.* v. *Laird* [1925] Ch. 318). By the Housing Act, 1957, s. 189 (1), it includes any court, alley, passage, square or row of houses, whether a thoroughfare or not. By the Highways Act, 1959, s. 295, it includes any highway and any road, lane, footpath, square, court, alley or passage, whether a thoroughfare or not. By the Street Offences Act, 1959, it includes any bridge, road, lane, footway, subway, square, court, alley or passage, whether a thoroughfare or not, which is for the time being open to the public; and the doorways and entrances of premises abutting on a street and any ground adjoining and open to a street. By the Road Traffic Act, 1960, it includes any highway and any bridge carrying a highway and any lane, mews, footway, square, court, alley or passage whether a thoroughfare or not. By the Betting, Gaming and Lotteries Act, 1963, s. 8, it includes any common close or common stair.

For provisions as to new streets see the Highways Act, 1959, ss. 157–172; Local Government Act, 1972, s. 188 (4).

A local authority has power to erect barriers in streets in the interests of public order, public safety, or the prevention of congestion of traffic (Public Health Act, 1961, s. 44; London Government Act, 1963, s. 40, Sch. 11 Pt. I para. 37; Criminal Damage Act, 1971, Sch. Pt. I; Local Government Act, 1972, Sch. 14 para. 40).

For power to attach lamps to buildings, see the Public Health Act, 1961, s. 45; London Government Act, 1963, Sch. 11

Pt. I para. 38; Local Government Act, 1966, s. 28 (4). Consent must be obtained to carry out works for pavement lights and ventilators (Public Health Act, 1961, s. 48).

The operation of a loudspeaker in a street is restricted by the Control of Pollution Act, 1974, s. 62. " Street " here means a highway and any other road, footway, square or court which is for the time being open to the public. See NOISE.

A " street " for the purposes of private street works cannot be defined according to the popular meaning of the word (*Warwickshire C.C.* v. *Atherstone Common Right Proprietors* (1964) 65 L.G.R. 439).

Street betting. See BETTING.

Street collections. See the Police, Factories, etc., (Miscellaneous Provisions) Act, 1916, s. 5; the House to House Collections Act, 1939; Police Act, 1964, s. 25 (4); Local Government Act, 1972, Sch. 29 para. 22.

Street musician. Power to deal with a nuisance caused by street musicians was given by the Metropolitan Police Act, 1864. See MUSICIANS IN LONDON STREETS. The matter may be dealt with by by-laws made under the Local Government Act, 1933, ss. 249, 250, the London Government Act, 1963, s. 8, Sch. 4 para. 29, the Local Government Act, 1972, ss. 235–238 and local Acts.

Street offences. Numerous street offences are listed in the Metropolitan Police Act, 1839, s. 54 (as amended by the Street Offences Act, 1959, ss. 1, 5, Sch.; the Post Office Act, 1969, Sch. 8 Pt. I; the Criminal Damage Act, 1971, Sch. Pt. I and the Statute Law (Repeals) Act, 1973) and the Town Police Clauses Act, 1847, s. 28 (as amended by the Street Offences Act, 1959, ss. 1, 5, Sch.; and the Police Act, 1964, Sch. 9) and the Rabies Act, 1974, Sch. Offences common to both Acts include riding or driving furiously, sliding on ice or snow, disturbance by ringing doorbells, discharging firearms, making bonfires, setting off fireworks and allowing ferocious dogs to be at large. The Act of 1839 also includes bill posting on buildings without the consent of the owner, blowing of horns or noisy instruments for the purpose of calling persons together or of announcing any show, or for the purpose of hawking, selling, distributing or collecting any article whatsoever, or of obtaining money, or alms, wilfully disregarding police regulations, after having been made acquainted with them, for regulating routes or preventing obstructions during public processions. The Act of 1847 also includes keeping swine and obstructing footways. Persons offending against the Acts are liable to apprehension by a contstable without a warrant and the Act of 1847 authorises imprisonment without the option of a fine. The penalties under each Act are up to £20 (Criminal Justice Act, 1967, Sch. 3 Pt. I).

See LOITERING; PROSTITUTES.

Failure to comply with the directions of a constable directing traffic or with the indications given by a traffic sign is an offence (Road Traffic Act, 1972, ss. 22, 23). This extends to traffic directions given for the purpose of traffic surveys (s. 22A, inserted by the Road Traffic Act, 1974, s. 6, overruling *Hoffman* v. *Thomas* [1974] 1 W.L.R. 374).

Leaving a vehicle on a road in a dangerous position is an offence under s. 24.

It is an offence to be towed or attempt to be towed by a motor vehicle without lawful authority or reasonable cause (s. 30).

Street performances. See CRUELTY TO CHILDREN.

Street playgrounds. See the Road Traffic Regulation Act, 1967, ss. 26, 26A, 27; Transport Act, 1968, ss. 126 (10), 130 (6), Sch. 14 Pt. II, Pt. VI paras. 15, 16, 17, Sch. 18 Pt. II.

Street refuge. A place of refuge for the protection of pedestrians crossing the carriageway. Power to construct and maintain street refuges is conferred by the Highways Act, 1959, s. 68. See *Ching Garage* v. *Chingford Corporation* [1959] 1 W.L.R. 959.

Street trading. See CRUELTY TO CHILDREN; HAWKER; HIGHWAY; PHOTOGRAPH.

Street works. See the Highways Act, 1959, ss. 173–213, as amended by the Building Societies Act, 1960, s. 76, Sch. 6, the Private Street Works Act, 1961, the Highways (Miscellaneous Provisions) Act,

1961, ss. 11, 12, and the Public Health Act, 1961, s. 11, Sch. 1 Pt. III.

Strep. See ESTREPE.

Stress. See PORTEOUS.

Strict settlement, a settlement of land the object of which is to keep the estates as far as possible in the male line, the eldest son taking for life or in tail with successive limitations in tail to the exclusion of the younger children, who are provided for by means of portions charged on the land. The limitations vary according to the circumstances of each particular case, but the following may be taken as usual limitations in the case of an ordinary settlement on marriage: to the husband for life, remainder, subject to a jointure rentcharge to the wife and a term for raising portions for the younger children, to the first and other sons in tail male, remainder to the first and other sons in tail general, remainder to the daughters as tenants in common in tail with cross remainders between them, remainder to the husband in fee. See SETTLED LAND; SETTLEMENT.

Strictissimi juris, of the most strict law.

Strictum jus, mere law in contradiction to equity.

Strike. The Industrial Relations Act, 1971, s. 167 (1) defined a strike as meaning a concerted stoppage of work by a group of workers, in contemplation or furtherance of an industrial dispute, whether they are parties to the dispute or not, whether (in the case of all or any of those workers) the stoppage is or is not in breach of their terms and conditions of employment, and whether it is carried out during, or on the termination of their employment. This section was repealed by the Trade Union and Labour Relations Act, 1974, which contains no definition of " strike " although the word is used in, *e.g.,* Sch. 1 para. 8. For a definition of " trade dispute " see the Act of 1974, s. 29. See TRADE DISPUTE.

For an earlier definition of strike see the Trade Disputes and Trade Unions Act, 1927, s. 8.

Striking off the roll, removing the name of a solicitor from the rolls of the court, and thereby desentitling him to practise. See SOLICITOR.

Striking out. A pleading or indorsement of a writ may be struck out if it is an abuse of process (*q.v.*). A defence may be ordered to be struck out if the defendant fails to comply with an order for discovery (R.S.C., Ord. 24, r. 16).

Strip. See SELION OF LAND.

Strip-tease performances, may amount to keeping a disorderly house at common law. See DISORDERLY HOUSE.

Strokehaul or snatch. A device for catching fish by foul hooking. Its use is prohibited by the Salmon and Freshwater Fisheries Act, 1975, s. 1.

Stuff gown, the robe worn in court by barristers who are not Queen's Counsel. See QUEEN'S COUNSEL.

Stupration [Lat. *stupro*], rape, violation.

Stuprum, every union of the sexes forbidden by morality (Civil Law).

Sturgeon, a royal fish, which, when either thrown ashore or caught near the coast, is the property of the sovereign (1 Bl.Comm. 290). See FISH ROYAL.

Sturges-Bourne's Acts, the Vestries Act, 1818, and the Poor Relief Act, 1819.

Style, to call, name or entitle one; the title or appellation of a person. See CALENDAR.

Suable, that may be sued.

Sub colore juris, under colour of the law.

Sub judice, in course of trial.

Sub modo, under condition or restriction.

Sub nom., Sub nomine, under the name.

Sub pede sigilli, under the foot of the seal.

Sub silentio, in silence.

Sub voce (s.v.), under the title.

Sub-agent; Sub-contractor. When an agent employs a person as his agent, to assist him in transacting the affairs of his principal, the person so employed is called a sub-agent. In the absence of an agreement to the contrary, there is no privity between the principal and the sub-agent; therefore, the principal is not liable to the sub-agent for his remuneration, and he cannot sue the sub-agent for negligence or misconduct; only the agent can be sued. But if the agent has an express or implied authority to employ a sub-agent, privity of contract arises between the principal and the sub-agent, and the principal may sue or be sued by the sub-agent.

Similarly, when a contractor makes a contract with a sub-contractor to carry out his contract, or part of it, there is no privity between the principal and the sub-contractor.

Sub-bois, coppice-wood (2 Co.Inst. 642). See SYLVIA CAEDUA.

Subinfeudation, where the inferior lords, in imitation of their superiors, began to carve out and grant to others minuter estates than their own, to be held of themselves, and were so proceeding downward *in infinitum* till they were stopped by legislative provisions. See TENURE.

Subinfeudation, while it was allowed, was what took place when a tenant in fee simple of land granted the whole or part of it to another person in fee simple, to hold of him as his tenant, so that the relation of tenure, with its incidents of fealty, services, etc., was created between them. The practice of subinfeudation being found to decrease the power and wealth of the great landholders (the barons), it was abolished by the statute *Quia Emptores,* 1289 (*q.v.*), as a result of which, if A held land of B in fee simple, and wished to grant it to C, he could only do so on the terms that C should hold it of B, and not of himself (A). See FEUDAL SYSTEM; SEIGNORY; TENURE.

Subjacent. See SUPPORT.

Subject, in logic, is that concerning which the affirmation in a proposition is made. See PREDICATE.

"Subject" also means a member of a community under a sovereign.

Subject to contract. As to the meaning of these words in connection with sales of land, see *Hussey* v. *Horne Puyne* (1878) 4 App.Cas. 311; *Curtis Moffat* v. *Wheeler* [1929] 2 Ch. 244; *Eccles* v. *Bryant* [1948] Ch. 93; *Graham & Scott* v. *Oxlade* [1950] 2 K.B. 257; *Dennis Reed* v. *Goody* [1950] 2 K.B. 277; *Christie, Owen and Davies* v. *Stockton* [1953] 1 W.L.R. 1353; *Munton* v. *G.L.C.* [1976] 1 W.L.R. 649. See GAZUMPING.

Sublato fundamento cadit opus (Jenk., Cent. 106). (If the foundation be removed, the building comes down.)

Sublato principali tollitur adjunctum (Co. Litt. 389). (The principal being taken away, its adjunct is also taken away.) Thus, under the old law, when the estate to which a warranty was annexed was defeated, the warranty was also defeated.

Sub-lease. See LEASE.

Sub-let. See LEASE; UNDERLEASE.

Sub-mortgage. See MORTGAGE.

Submersible apparatus. This means apparatus used, or designed for use, in supporting human life on or under the bed of any waters or elsewhere under the surface of any waters. Regulations may be made to ensure the safety of such apparatus and supporting apparatus (Merchant Shipping Act, 1974, ss. 16, 17, Sch. 5).

Submission. A submission to arbitration is an instrument by which a dispute or question is referred to arbitration (*q.v.*). When the reference is made by the order of a court or judge, the order is called a reference; submission denotes an agreement between the parties. Such an agreement may be either general (that is, an agreement to refer to arbitration all future disputes arising out of a specified matter), or particular (that is, an agreement to refer to arbitration a dispute which has already arisen). A general submission is commonly contained in articles of partnership. See RULES OF COURT.

Submit, to propound, as an advocate, a proposition for the approval or otherwise of the court.

Subnervare, to ham-string by cutting the sinews of the legs and thighs. It is said to have been a custom of semi-civilised savages *meretrices et impudicas mulieres subnervare* (to ham-string prostitutes and shameless women) (Jacob).

Subnotation, a rescript (*q.v.*).

Subordinate clause. See CO-ORDINATE.

Subordinate integer, in patent law, any part of a whole patentable machine or thing which is itself independently patentable.

Suborn. See SUBORNATION.

Subornation, the crime of procuring another to do a bad action.

Subornation of perjury, the procuring of a person to commit perjury. At common law it was, and under the Perjury Act, 1911, s. 7, it still is, punishable in the same way as perjury. The attempt to suborn perjury is also a misdemeanour, just as it was at common law.

SUBPOENA

Subpoena [Lat. *sub*, under; *poena*, penalty], a writ or summons issued in an action or suit requiring the person to whom it is directed to be present at a specified place and time, and for a specified purpose, under a penalty (*sub poena*) for non-attendance. The varieties of subpoena now in common use are the subpoena *ad testificandum*, called a subpoena *ad test.*, used for the purpose of compelling a witness to attend and give evidence, either in court or before an examiner or referee, and the subpoena *duces tecum*, used to compel a witness to attend in court or before an examiner or referee, to give evidence and also bring with him certain documents in his possession specified in the subpoena.

The subpoena bears a close analogy to the citation, or *vocatio in jus* of the civil and canon laws.

A person attending under a subpoena *duces tecum* to produce a document need not be sworn, and in that case he cannot be cross-examined. See DUCES TECUM, ETC.

A subpoena must, as a rule, be served personally within twelve weeks after the issue of the writ (R.S.C., Ord. 38, r. 17; Ord. 65, r. 2). See also Ord. 38, rr. 14–19. For subpoenas enforcing the attendance of witnesses in chambers see Ord. 32, r. 7.

Subpoenas ad testificandum and *subpoenas duels tecum* (*q.v.*) are not issued in criminal proceedings for the purpose of which a witness summons may be issued (Criminal Procedure (Attendance of Witnesses) Act, 1965, s. 8). See CRIMINAL EVIDENCE.

The court can set aside the subpoena in criminal as well as civil proceedings if it is not required bona fide and is an abuse of process (*R* v. *Baines* [1909] 1 K.B. 258).

In the county court, a subpoena is called in the rules a witness summons (C.C.R., Ord. 20, r. 8).

There was also the subpoena to show cause, which was served upon an infant when he came of age if a judgment against him during infancy had given him a day to show cause against it. See R.S.C., Ord. 80, r. 2, note.

Under the old Chancery practice, every suit was commenced by a writ of subpoena requiring the defendant to appear; hence in the old books "subpoena" is equivalent to "suit in equity" or "bill of complaint." Under the more modern practice, the subpoena was endorsed on the bill of complaint. Now every action is commenced by writ of summons. The subpoena to hear judgment was another kind used in Chancery practice: it was issued by the party setting down a cause for hearing and was served on the opposite party. If the party served did not appear at the hearing, the court might make a decree against him.

Subpoena Office in Chancery. This office, like the Sealer (*q.v.*), etc., was abolished by the Court of Chancery Act, 1852, s. 28, which transferred to the Clerks of Records and Writs such work as there was to be done.

Subreption. In ecclesiastical law this means the obtaining of a faculty, dispensation, etc., by a suppression of any material fact. See OBREPTION.

Subrogation, the substitution of one person or thing for another, so that the same rights and duties as attached to the original person or thing attach to the substituted one. Thus, if a person insures a ship which is lost by a collision caused by the negligence of another ship, he may recover the value of the ship from the underwriters, and then they are subrogated to his rights so as to be able to bring an action against the person who caused the collision. A similar rule applies in fire insurances and employer's liability insurances (*Lister* v. *Romford Ice & Cold Storage Co.* [1957] A.C. 555).

As between insurer and insured, the insurer is entitled to the advantage of every right of the insured connected with the insurance which was effected between them (*Assicurazioni Generali de Trieste* v. *Empress Assurance Corporation* [1907] 2 K.B. 814). But see *Yorkshire Insurance Co.* v. *Nisbet Shipping Co.* [1962] 2 Q.B. 330. The doctrine is not confined to insurance, but extends in equity to many other cases, *e.g.*, where money has been borrowed without authority but applied in payment of existing debts; in such cases the quasi-lender is entitled to stand in the shoes of the creditors thus paid (*Re Wrexham, etc., Ry.* [1899] 1 Ch. 440). See GUARANTY; INDEMNITY; INSURANCE.

A surrogate (*q.v.*) is a person subrogated, *quoad* certain matters, for the bishop.

Subscribe; Subscription. To subscribe is literally to "write under," and is sometimes opposed to "sign," because a signature is not necessarily placed at the end or bottom of an instrument. (See SIGN; WILL.) A subscribing witness is the same thing as an attesting witness. See ATTESTATION.

Subsequens matrimonium tollit peccatum praecedens. (A subsequent marriage removes the previous sin.) See BASTARD; LEGITIMATION.

Subsequent condition. See CONDITION SUBSEQUENT.

Subsidence. The Coal-Mining (Subsidence) Act, 1957, makes provision for the execution of remedial works and the making of payments in respect of damage caused by subsidence resulting from the working and getting of coal and other minerals worked therewith. See BRINE PUMPING; SUPPORT.

Subsidiary company, a company controlled by another company (Companies Act, 1948, s. 154). See HOLDING COMPANY.

A parent company and a subsidiary company, even a hundred per cent. subsidiary company, are distinct legal entities and in the absence of a contract of agency between the two companies, one cannot be said to be the agent of the other (*Ebbw Vale U.D.C.* v. *South Wales Traffic Area Licensing Authority* [1951] 2 K.B. 366).

Exemption from stamp duty may be claimed on a transfer of property to a subsidiary company (Finance Act, 1930, s. 42; Finance Act, 1938, s. 50; Finance Act, 1967, s. 27); see *Escoigne Properties* v. *I.R.C.* [1958] A.C. 549.

For the meaning of subsidiary for the purposes of taxation, see the Income and Corporation Taxes Act, 1970, s. 532.

Subsidy [Lat. *subsidium*, troops stationed behind in reserve, aid], assistance; an aid, tax or tribute granted to the Crown for the urgent occasions of the kingdom, to be levied on every subject of ability according to the value of his lands or goods.

From about the year 1300 to the reign of Anne this word had several different meanings. During the fourteenth and fifteenth centuries it generally meant the import and export duties on cloth, wool, leather and skins, and the tonnage and poundage granted to the Crown for special occasions: see the statutes 1353, 27 Edw. 3, st. 1, c. 4, and 1382, 5 Ric. 2, st. 2, c. 3. This meaning was preserved even after the Restoration: see the statutes 1660, 12 Car. 2, c. 4, and 1706, 6 Anne, c. 48. In the sixteenth century it meant mainly the tax of 4s. in the pound on land and 2s. 8d. in the pound on movables from time to time voted; it also had the wider general meaning of any tax imposed by Parliament.

The term was extended by Coke and others to the taxes known as tenths (*q.v.*) and fifteenths (*q.v.*). They also classified the duties on cloth, wool and leather as perpetual subsidies (apparently because they were granted almost as of course) and other taxes as temporary subsidies (apparently because their grant was not so common), but both the one kind and the other were in fact payable only when Parliament voted them.

The word now generally means financial assistance granted by the Crown, *e.g.*, the food subsidies under the Prices Act, 1974.

Substantial damages, damages which represent actual loss, whether great or small, as opposed to nominal damages.

Substantive law. See ADJECTIVE LAW.

Substituted executor, one appointed to act in the place of another executor, upon the happening of a certain event, *e.g.*, if the latter should refuse the office.

Substituted service, service of a writ or other document on some person representing the party to be served, instead of on him personally (R.S.C., 65 r. 4). Leave is sometimes given to effect the substituted service by means of advertisement. See SERVICE OF PROCESS.

Substitution; Substitutional; Substitutionary. Where a will contains a gift of property to a class of persons with a clause providing that, on the death of a member of the class before the period of distribution, his share is to go to his issue (if any), so as to substitute them for him, the gift to the issue is said to be substitutional or substitutionary. A bequest to such of the children of A as shall be

SUBSTITUTION

living at the testator's death, with a direction that the issue of such as shall have died shall take the shares which their parents would have taken, if living at the testator's death, is an example. Under such a gift the issue of children dead at the date of the will cannot take anything (*Re Brooke* [1953] 1 W.L.R. 439).

In the civil law, substitution was a conditional appointment of a *haeres*.

Substratum, bottom or basis. It is a ground for winding up a company that its substratum has gone, *i.e.*, that it has become impossible to carry on the basic activity for which the company was formed.

Subtraction, neglecting or refusing to perform any suit, service, custom, or duty, or to pay rent, service, tolls, etc. (3 Bl. Comm. 230).

The term was chiefly used in connection with services and tithes. In the law of real property, subtraction was where a person who owed any suit, duty, custom or other service to another withdrew or neglected to perform it; the principal services which were the subject of subtraction were fealty, suit of court, rent, and customary services. In the case of fealty, suit of court, and rent, the remedy was by distress; an action also lay for rent and for subtraction of customary services. See SECTA; SERVICE.

In ecclesiastical law, subtraction was the injury of withholding tithes from the rector or vicar. For this injury, a suit lay in the ecclesiastical courts, unless the tithes only amounted to £50 or under, or unless there was a dispute whether they were payable. After the commutation of tithes into rentcharges, for recovering which a special mode of proceeding by distress was provided, suits of subtraction became obsolete. See TITHES.

Suburbani, husbandmen.

Succession, where property passes on the death of a corporation sole to his successor; for as the heir inherited to the ancestor, so the successor succeeds to the predecessor (C.Litt. 8b).

In a conveyance of land to a bishop, parsons, or any other corporation sole, the limitation had formerly to be to him " and his successors "; if it was " to him and his heirs " or " in fee simple," he

took in his personal capacity, and if there were no words of limitation, he took for his life only (Co.Litt. 94b). See FEE; HEIR; WORDS OF LIMITATION.

The Law of Property Act, 1925, s. 60, provides that a conveyance to a corporation sole without the word " successors " passes the fee simple or other the whole interest of the grantor unless a contrary intention appears in the conveyance.

In some cases a corporation sole can also take personal property by succession (2 Bl.Comm. 430). See CHURCHWARDENS.

There are also statutory modes of succession: thus, where land is conveyed to trustees for persons associated together for religious, educational, literary, scientific or artistic purposes, it passes to their succesors in office without conveyance.

The succession of the Crown (the sovereign being a corporation sole) resembles the old law of descent of land except that, in the case of a sovereign dying and leaving no son but several daughters, the Crown descends to the eldest alone, and that it can only descend to Protestants (1 Bl.Comm. 191). See DEMISE.

Succession duty, a duty first imposed by the Succession Duty Act, 1853, on gratuitous acquisition, on death, of property in respect of which no legacy duty was payable, unless the property was specially exempted from succession duty. Under the Succession Duty Act, 1853, s. 10 (as amended by the Finance (1909–10) Act, 1910, s. 58 (1)), the rate was, in the case of acquisition (1) by a husband, wife, lineal ancestor or lineal descendant of the deceased, or the husband or wife of any such person, 1 per cent.; (2) by a brother or sister of the deceased or a descendant of such brother or sister, or the husband or wife of any such person, 5 per cent.; and (3) by any other person, 10 per cent. Under the Customs and Inland Revenue Act, 1881, s. 41, the Customs and Inland Revenue Act, 1888, and the Finance Act, 1894, s. 1, Sch. 1, where neither probate duty nor estate duty was payable, class (1) paid an additional 10½ per cent., and each of the remaining classes paid an additional 1½ per cent.

No succession duty was payable where the principal value of all successions on the same death did not amount to £100 (Succession Duty Act, 1853, s. 18).

Succession duty on property of which the successor was competent to dispose was payable on the market value thereof less the amount of estate duty payable (Finance Act, 1894, s. 18 (1)), and succession duty on property of which the successor was not competent to dispose was payable on the value, calculated according to the tables annexed to the Succession Duty Act, 1853, of an annuity equal to the annual income of the property (Succession Duty Act, 1853, ss. 21, 31).

A succession took place, within the meaning of the Succession Duty Act, 1853, where a person became beneficially entitled to or interested in property upon the death of another. The person so becoming entitled was called the successor, and the person from whom he derived his title or interest was called the predecessor. Thus, if A by deed settled property on B for life, and after his death on C, then on B's death a succession took place, C being the successor and A the predecessor. So, if A died intestate and entitled to land, a succession to his heir-at-law took place. Where a person exercised a general power of appointment which he had become entitled to exercise on the death of another person, he was deemed to be entitled to the property so appointed as on a succession derived from the donor of the power (s. 4). If, therefore, he exercised it by will, two successions took place on his death, one from the donor to the donee (appointor), and another from the appointor to the appointee. But where a person exercised a limited power which he had become entitled to exercise on the death of another person, the appointee (and not the appointor) was deemed to take the property as on a succession derived from the donor of the power (s. 4). The object of the Act being to impose a duty on all dispositions and devolutions of property not chargeable with legacy duty, the terms " succession," " successor " and " predecessor " were in effect applicable only to successions arising from settlements *inter vivos* of real and personal property, and from descents or testamentary dispositions of real and leasehold estates. (See LEASEHOLDS.) Where a testator directed real estate to be sold, the proceeds were chargeable (under the Legacy Duty Act, 1805) with legacy, and not with succession, duty. Both duties were abolished by the Finance Act, 1949, ss. 27, 28. See LEGACY DUTY.

Successor, one who follows in the place of another; the correlative of predecessor in the succession (Succession Duty Act, 1883). See PREDECESSOR.

Succurritur minori: facilis est lapsus juventutis (Jenk., Cent. 47). (A minor is to be assisted: a mistake of youth is easy.) See EXPECTANT HEIR ; IN JUDICIIS, ETC. ; MELIOREM CONDITIONEM, ETC.

Sudbury Borough. This was disfranchised by the statute 1844, 7 & 8 Vict. c. 53.

Sue. To sue a person is to bring a civil action against him.

Sue and labour clause, a clause in a policy of marine insurance introduced to make it clear that the assured and his agents or servants, *e.g.,* the master and crew, can take every step to recover the insured property in peril without loss of the rights under the insurance and will be repaid any expenditure which may be incurred by the assured or his agents or servants to avert the loss. The clause does not cover general average losses and contributions and salvage charges (Marine Insurance Act, 1906, s. 78 (2)) ; and see *Aitchison* v. *Lohre* (1879) 4 App.Cas. 755. The clause is usually in the following form: " In case of any loss or misfortune, it shall be lawful to the assured, their factors, servants and assigns, to sue, labour, and travel for, in, or about the defence, safeguard and recovery of the said goods and merchandises and ship, etc., or any part thereof, without prejudice to this insurance: to the charges whereof, we, the assurers, will contribute, each one according to the rate and quality of his sum herein insured."

It is the duty of the assured so to act (Marine Insurance Act, 1906, s. 78 (4)).

Suez Canal. By an agreement ratified by the Suez Canal Shares Act, 1876, 176,602 shares in the Suez Canal Company were acquired by the Crown by purchase from the Khedive of Egypt for about £4 million. The canal undertaking was compulsorily acquired by the Egyptian government in 1956.

Sufferance, Tenancy at. This is the least and lowest interest which can subsist in realty. It is a mere possession only. It arises when a person after his right of occupation, under a lawful title, is at an end continues (having no title at all) in possession of the land, without the agreement or disagreement of the person in whom the right of possession resides. Thus if A is a tenant for years, and his term expires, or is a tenant at will, and his lessor dies, and he continues in possession without the disagreement of the person who is entitled to possession, he is said to have the possession by sufferance, that is, merely by permission or indulgence, without any right: his occupation is deemed to be continued by the permission of the person who has the right, till it is proved that he withholds possession wrongfully.

An under-tenant who is in possession at the determination of the original lease, and is permitted by the reversioner to hold over, is a quasi-tenant at sufferance.

Where a man comes to a particular estate by the act of the party, there, if he holds over, he is a tenant at sufferance; but where he comes to the particular estate by act of law, there, if he holds over, he is no tenant at sufferance, but an abator (1 Co.Inst. 134 ; 2 Co.Inst. 271).

Tenancy at sufferance is created only by construction of law, and cannot originate in the agreement of the parties. For the agreement of the parties would pass an interest at will, or for a term, or from year to year, according to their intention. There exists no privity between the tenant at sufferance (who has but a mere possession) and the person entitled to possession ; yet such occupancy is not adverse to the title of the person who possesses the right of entry, unless he choose to consider it so ; but an adverse possession will take place on an entry and perception of the profits of the land by a person, without the reversioner's consent, after the death of a tenant at sufferance. This interest cannot be the subject of conveyance or transfer.

Since *laches* or neglect can never be imputed to the sovereign, a lessee of Crown lands holding them over after the determination of his interest in them is never considered a tenant by sufferance, but is deemed a bailiff of his own wrong, and so accountable to the Crown ; after office found (*q.v.*) he became absolute intruder.

This interest is put an end to whenever the true owner actually enters upon the lands, by which he declares the continuance of the tenant tortious and wrongful, or demands possession, or brings an action of ejectment to recover possession, which he may do without any previous demand. See TENANT AT SUFFERANCE.

Sufferance wharves, wharves on which goods may be landed before any duty is paid. They are appointed for the purpose by the Commissioners of Customs and Excise (Customs and Excise Act, 1952, s. 14). See also the Finance Act, 1966, s. 10.

Sufferentia pacis, a grant or sufferance of peace or truce (Rot.Claus., 16 Edw. 3).

Suffering a recovery. A tenant in tail who procured a common recovery of his land to be effected so that he could bar the entail was said to suffer a recovery. See RECOVERY.

Suffocation of young children. See the Children and Young Persons Act, 1933, s. 1 (2) (*b*).

Suffragan. Bishops are styled suffragan, a word signifying deputy, in respect of their relation to the archbishop of their province. But formerly each archbishop and bishop had also his suffragan to assist him in conferring orders, and in other spiritual parts of his office within his diocese. These are called suffragan bishops, and resemble the *chorepiscopi*, or bishops of the country, in the early times of the Christian Church. How this inferior order of bishops may be appointed and consecrated for twenty-five towns therein specified (including Thetford, Grantham, and Gloucester) is regulated by the Suffragan Bishops Act, 1534, which enacts that every archbishop and bishop disposed to have a suffragan should name to the king two honest and discreet spiritual persons, being learned and of good conversation, and that each of them should request the king to appoint one of them. Notwithstanding this statute, it was not until recent years, when the suffragans were appointed for a few of the specified towns, usual to appoint them. The Suffragans Nomination Act, 1888, however, empowers the Crown by Order in Council to add towns to those specified in the Act of 1534, and to change the sees of suffragans appointed before the passing of the Act, and the Suffragan Bishops Act, 1898, allows existing bishops to be made suffragans. The Act of 1534 allows a suffragan, for the better maintenance of his dignity, to have two benefices with cure. See BISHOP.

Suffragans should not be confounded with the coadjutors of a bishop, the latter being appointed, in case of a bishop's infirmity, to superintend his jurisdiction and temporalities, neither of which was within the interference of the former (Co.Litt. 94a, n. 3).

Suffrage [*suffragium*], vote; elective franchise; voice given in a controverted point; aid; assistance. See ELECTORAL FRANCHISE.

Suffragette, a woman who agitated for woman-suffrage in the later years preceding the war of 1914–18.

Sugar. The British Sugar (Subsidy) Act, 1925, provided for a subsidy on sugar and molasses manufactured in Great Britain from beet grown in Great Britain, and for excise duties on the products manufactured in Great Britain and Northern Ireland from beet grown there. The industry is now regulated by the Sugar Act, 1956, as amended by the European Communities Act, 1972, Sch. 3 Pt. II.

As to the standards of measurement, etc., on the sale of sugar, see the Weights and Measures Act, 1963, s. 21, Sch. 4 Pts. VIII, IX, XI.

Suggestio falsi, suggestion of falsity, an active misrepresentation, as opposed to *suppressio veri,* suppression of the truth. See MISREPRESENTATION; OBREPTION; SUBREPTION.

Suggestion, a surmise or representing of a thing; an entry of a fact on the record.

Formerly, changes of the parties to an action in the Queen's Bench Division could be entered on the roll (or record of the proceedings in an action) by a " suggestion " (that is to say, an allegation) of them; and this made the action continue in the names of the new parties so as to prevent abatement (*q.v.*). Now the practice in such a case is as mentioned under REVIVOR.

As to suggestion of breaches, see BREACH.

Sui juris [Lat.], of his own right. A person who is not a minor, nor insane, nor subject to any other disability, is said to be *sui juris.*

In the civil law, persons were divided into two classes, according as they were *sui juris* or *alieni juris.* Persons subject to the *potestas* of a father, or the *manus* of a husband, or the *mancipium* of a master, were said to be *alieni juris*; the class, therefore, included all persons having a father or other ascendant living (unless they had been emancipated or otherwise freed from the *patria potestas*); all married women who had been married with certain formalities; and all slaves. All other persons were *sui juris,* so that a child of a few years old, if he had no father or other ascendant living, and had not been adopted by anyone, was *sui juris,* although he was under disability.

In English law, the term *sui juris* is used in quite a different sense. A person is said to be *sui juris* if he is not subject to any general disability. Therefore, infants and mental patients and a few other persons are not *sui juris,* because they cannot enter into contracts or dispose of their property with the same freedom as ordinary persons. See CURATOR; DISABILITY; GUARDIAN; INFANT; MARRIED WOMEN; NEXT FRIEND.

Suicide, self-slaughter; a self-slaughterer. Suicide is where a person kills himself. Deliberate suicide by a sane person was formerly a felony, punishable by forfeiture of the offender's goods and chattels to the Crown, and by an ignominious burial in the highway with a stake driven through the body, and without Christian rites of sepulture; but after 1824 the only consequences were burial in a churchyard or other burying ground between 9 and 12 at night without Christian rites; and since 1882 interment is as described under BURIAL. In practice, very slight evidence was sufficient to induce a coroner's jury to return a verdict that the deceased killed himself while the balance of his mind was disturbed, *i.e.*, during temporary insanity, which made the suicide no crime.

The Suicide Act, 1961, abrogated the rule of law whereby it was a crime for a person to commit suicide.

Attempted suicide was a common law misdemeanour but as the completed act is no longer a crime the attempt to commit suicide cannot be a crime. Causing the death of another in the course of attempted suicide was murder (*R.* v. *Spence* (1957) 41 Cr.App.R. 80) but this is not necessarily now so. See MURDER.

A person who aids, abets, counsels or procures the suicide of another or an attempt by another to commit suicide is liable on conviction on indictment to imprisonment for a term not exceeding fourteen years (Suicide Act, 1961, s. 2 (1)). In the case of suicide he may be charged with and found guilty of murder (*q.v.*) or manslaughter (*q.v.*) (s. 2 (2)). Proceedings for an offence under s. 2 require the consent of the Director of Public Prosecutions (s. 2 (4)).

For self-destruction to be suicide it must be intentional (*Re Davis* [1968] 1 Q.B. 72). It must be proved by evidence. It can never be presumed (*R.* v. *City of London Coroner, ex p. Barber* [1975] 1 W.L.R. 1310). Satisfactory evidence of suicidal intent is always necessary to establish suicide as the cause of death (*R.* v. *Cardiff City Coroner, ex p. Thomas* [1970] 1 W.L.R. 1475).

The fact that a man commits suicide does not debar his widow on grounds of public policy from claiming damages under the Fatal Accidents Acts (*Pigney* v. *Pointers Transport Services* [1957] 1 W.L.R. 1127).

Suicide pact. Formerly, where two persons agreed to commit suicide and only one did so, the survivor was guilty of murder as an accessory before the fact. Now, where a person kills himself in pursuance of a suicide pact the survivor is guilty of the offence of complicity and is liable on conviction on indictment to imprisonment for a term not exceeding fourteen years. If the deceased was killed in pursuance of the suicide pact by the survivor or by a third person the survivor may be found guilty of manslaughter

(*q.v.*) but not of murder (Homicide Act, 1957, s. 4; Suicide Act, 1961, ss. 2, 3, Sch. 2).

Suing and labouring clause. See SUE AND LABOUR CLAUSE.

Suit, a following; any legal proceeding of a civil kind brought by one person against another (Co.Litt. 291a).

Suit includes action (Judicature Act, 1925, s. 225. The term is however, used in opposition to " action." Formerly the most important kinds of suit in this sense were those brought by bill of complaint (*q.v.*) and information (*q.v.*) in the Court of Chancery. A proceeding for nullity or dissolution of marriage, etc., in the Family Division is called a suit.

As to suit in the sense of a service, see SECTA ; SUIT OF COURT.

Suit covenant, where one has covenanted to do suit and service in his lord's court.

Suit custom, where service is owed time out of mind.

Suit of court, a service theoretically due from every tenant of land forming part of, or held of, a manor, and consisting in the duty of attending the courts held by the lord. Free tenants or tenants of freehold land were bound to attend (either personally or by attorney) their lord's court baron (*q.v.*), while copyhold tenants were bound to attend personally at the customary court. See SECTA; SERVICE ; SUBTRACTION.

Suit of the peace, prosecution. Thus, in the statute 1404, 5 Hen. 4, c. 15, it was declared that the king had pardoned (or agreed to stop) the suit of his peace for all offences with certain specified exceptions.

Suit silver, or **Suter silver,** a small annual sum paid by the tenants of some manors as a commutation for appearance at the court of the lord.

Suithold, a tenure in consideration of certain services to the superior lord.

Suitor, one who sues; a petitioner; a suppliant; a wooer.

Suitors' Deposit Account. Formerly suitors in the Court of Chancery derived no income from their cash paid into court, unless it was invested at their request and risk; but the Chancery (Funds) Act, 1872, provided that all money paid into court, and not required by the suitor to be invested, should be placed on deposit and bear interest at 2 per cent. per annum for the benefit of the suitor entitled to it. The sum required for the payment of this interest is produced by placing all money in court not required for meeting current demands in the hands of the National Debt Commissioners who invest it in government securities. This arrangement was called the Suitors' Deposit Account. See now the Supreme Court Funds Rules, 1927, rr. 73–80.

Suitors' Fee Fund, a fund arising partly from the fees of the Court of Chancery, and partly from the surplus income of the Suitors' Fund (q.v.). Out of it the salaries and other expenses of the Court of Chancery were paid. By the Courts of Justice (Salaries and Funds) Act, 1869, the Suitors' Fee Fund was transferred to the National Debt Commissioners and the salaries and expenses formerly paid out of it were charged on the Consolidated Fund.

Suitors' Fund, a fund belonging to the Court of Chancery, which consisted of two parts. Fund " A " consisted of government stocks resulting from the investment of so much of the money in court belonging to the suitors as was not required for current purposes. Part of the income arising from these investments was employed in paying certain expenses of the court, and the balance was invested in government stocks, which formed Fund " B." Subsequently the surplus income of both funds was annually added to the Suitors' Fee Fund (q.v.) By the Courts of Justice (Salaries and Funds) Act, 1869, the Suitors' Fund was transferred to the National Debt Commissioners, and the Consolidated Fund was made liable for the due payment of the money which belonged to the suitors and had been invested. See PAYMASTER-GENERAL.

The Official Solicitor (q.v.) of the Court of Chancery was originally called the Solicitor to the Suitors' Fund by reason of his duties in connection with that fund.

Sulh aelmyssan, plough arms (Anc. Inst.Eng.).

Sullery, a plough-land (Co.Litt. 5a).

Sulung [solinus terrae], a measure of land in Kent at the time of Domesday, equivalent to the hide or carucate (q.v.).

It was divided into four yokes, and each yoke into four virgates (2 Holds. H.E.L. 67).

Sumage, a toll levied from persons on horseback (Cromp. Juris. 191).

Summa est ratio quae pro religione facit (Co.Litt. 341). (An argument which is in the interest of religion carries very great weight.)

Summary, an abridgment, a brief compendium; a summary application is one made to a court or judge without the formality of a full proceeding. See PLENARY.

In procedure, proceedings are said to be summary when they are short and simple in comparison with regular proceedings, that is, in comparison with the proceedings which alone would have been applicable, either in the same or analogous cases, if summary proceedings had not been available. Summary proceedings are sometimes concurrent with regular proceedings, that is, either may be adopted.

Petitions, special cases, motions, and summonses, not being interlocutory proceedings in an action or suit, are instances (chiefly occurring in the Chancery Division) of summary proceedings in civil cases, as opposed to suits or actions. (See PETITION; SUMMONS.) There are also summary modes of putting an end to an action, without carrying it on to trial, e.g., by obtaining judgment where the defendant has no defence (see JUDGMENT) or by interpleader proceedings.

Summary conviction, conviction before the magistrates, as opposed to conviction by a jury.

Summary judgment, judgment under R.S.C., Ord. 14. See JUDGMENT; LEAVE TO DEFEND.

Summary jurisdiction, the jurisdiction of a court to give a judgment or make an order itself forthwith, e.g., to commit to prison for contempt, to punish malpractice in a solicitor, or, in the case of justices of the peace, a jurisdiction to convict an offender themselves instead of committing him for trial by a jury. The mode of exercising this latter jurisdiction, which is given in particular instances by very numerous particular statutes, is regulated generally by the Magistrates' Courts Act, 1952; the Criminal Justice

SUMMARY

Administration Act, 1962, s. 12 (3), Sch. 3 Pt. I; the Criminal Justice Act, 1967, ss. 27–30; the Criminal Justice Act, 1972, s. 47. See HUSBAND AND WIFE; SESSIONS OF THE PEACE.

Certain indictable offences by adults may be dealt with summarily with the consent of the accused. These are: offences under the Offences against the Person Act, 1861, s. 20 (malicious wounding or inflicting grievous bodily harm), s. 27 (abandoning or exposing a child), s. 47 (assault), s. 60 (concealing birth); offences under the Telegraph Act, 1868, s. 20 (disclosing telegrams); offences under the Stamp Duties Management Act, 1891, s. 13; offences under the Perjury Act 1911, s. 5 (statutory declarations); offences under the Forgery Act, 1913, ss. 2 (2) (*a*), 4, 7 (*a*); offences under the Criminal Justice Act, 1925, s. 36 (passports); offences under the Agricultural Credits Act, 1928, s. 11; offences under the Coinage Offences Act, 1936, ss. 4, 5, 7, 8, 12 (2); offences in relation to national insurance stamps; offences under the Post Office Act, 1953, ss. 53, 55–58; committing an indecent assault upon a person whether male or female; offences under the Sexual Offences Act, 1967, ss. 4 (2), 9 (1) (procuring buggery), s. 13 (gross indecency between men); some offences under the Theft Act, 1968; offences under the Criminal Damage Act, 1971, ss. 1 (1), 2, 3 (damage to property); aiding, abetting, counselling or procuring the commission of any of the foregoing offences or attempting to commit them or inciting their commission (Magistrates' Courts Act, 1952, s. 19, Sch. 1, as amended and extended).

A court of summary jurisdiction means in an Act of Parliament any justice or justices of the peace, or other magistrate by whatever name called, to whom jurisdiction is given by, or who is authorised to act under, the Summary Jurisdiction Acts, now the Magistrates' Courts Act, 1952 (Interpretation Act, 1889, s. 13 (11)), but does not include justices at a licensing meeting (*Boulter* v. *Kent Justices* [1897] A.C. 556).

Summer time. The Summer Time Act, 1972 (consolidating legislation dating back to the Summer Time Act, 1916), provides that the time for general purposes shall, during summer time, be one hour in advance of Greenwich mean time. Summer time is the period beginning at two o'clock, Greenwich mean time, in the morning of the day after the third Saturday in March or, if that day is Easter Day, the day after the second Saturday in March and ending at two o'clock, Greenwich mean time, in the morning of the day after the fourth Saturday in October (s. 1). The period of summer time may be altered by Order in Council and may also be fixed at two hours instead of one hour in advance of Greenwich mean time (s. 2). The Act makes provision for summer time in Northern Ireland, the Channel Isles and the Isle of Man (ss. 4–6). See TIME.

Summer-hus silver, a payment to the lords of the wood on the Wealds of Kent, who used to visit those places in summer, when their under-tenants were bound to prepare little summer-houses for their reception, or else pay a composition in money (*Custumale de Newington juxta Sittingburn, M.S.*).

Summing up, the recapitulation of evidence or parts of it by a judge to a jury, with directions as to what form of verdict they are to give upon it.

Counsel for each party has the right of summing up his evidence, if he has adduced any, and the judge finally sums up the whole. See REPLY; RIGHT TO BEGIN; TRIAL.

Summoneas, the initial word of a number of writs such as the *summoneas ad warrantizandum* (the process whereby the vouchee in a common recovery was brought in), the *summoneas in auxilium* (the aid prayer (*q.v.*)), etc.

Summoner. From the fourteenth to the eighteenth century this meant an officer who summoned persons to appear in various courts. See APPARITOR.

Summonitiones aut citationes nullae liceant fieri intra palatium regis (3 Co.Inst. 141). (Let no summonses or citations be served within the king's palace.) See *Att.-Gen.* v. *Dakin* (1870) L.R. 4 H.L. 338; *Combe* v. *De la Bere* (1882) 22 Ch.D. 316.

Summonitores Scaccarii, officers who assisted in collecting the revenues by citing the defaulters therein into the

Court of Exchequer; the summoners of the Exchequer.

Summons [Law Lat. *summoneas*, that you summon], a call of authority, an admonition to appear in court, a citation.

A summons is a document issued from the office of a court of justice, calling upon the person to whom it is directed to attend before a judge or officer of the court for a certain purpose. See DIRECTIONS, SUMMONS FOR; MOTION; PETITION; WRIT OF SUMMONS.

In the High Court a summons may be a summons in a pending cause or matter. Every other summons is an originating summons (R.S.C., Ord. 1, r. 4). A summons other than an originating summons is a mode of making an application to a judge or master in chambers (*q.v.*). They are therefore only used on applications which are either of subsidiary importance or which can be conveniently disposed of in chambers, such as applications for enlarging the time to take certain steps, for discovery and production of documents, for appointing examiners and receivers, for leave to sign judgment under R.S.C., Ord. 14 (see JUDGMENT), etc. In simple cases, the solicitors of the parties attend on their behalf: in difficult or important cases counsel are instructed.

In the Queen's Bench Division some summonses must be heard in the first instance by a master, and others by a judge. An appeal lies from a master to a judge in chambers, and from the judge to the Divisional Court. See CHAMBERS.

In the Chancery Division every summons is heard in the first instance before a master, but either party, if dissatisfied with the decision, is entitled to have the summons heard by the judge in chambers. This is called adjourning the summons to the judge. The judge may also adjourn the summons to be argued in court; or if he refuses to do so, the dissatisfied party may either move before the judge in court to rescind the order made in chambers or may appeal to the Court of Appeal. See CHAMBERS.

Civil proceedings in the High Court may be begun by writ (see WRIT OF SUMMONS), originating summons, originating motion or petition (R.S.C., Ord. 5, r. 1). Proceedings by which an application is to be made to the High Court or a judge thereof under any Act must as a general rule be begun by originating summons (r. 3). Other proceedings may be begun by writ or originating summons at the plaintiff's choice (r. 4), and in the Queen's Bench or the Chancery Division. The summons must be in one of the prescribed forms. These are no. 8 (originating summons between parties, appearance required); no. 9 (the like issued out of a district registry); no. 10 (originating summons between parties (appearance not required)); no. 11 (*ex parte* originating summons); no. 11a (for possession under Ord. 113) (R.S.C., Ord. 7, r. 2, App. A). Every originating summons must include a statement of the questions to be determined or on which the direction of the court is required, or, as the case may be, a concise statement of the relief or remedy claimed with particulars thereof. The summons must be indorsed as to capacity and as to the solicitor's name and address (R.S.C., Ord. 7, r. 3). The procedure governing an originating summons is laid down by Ord. 28.

If the question raised by the summons is one requiring argument it is generally adjourned into court. If it is a simple matter it will be determined in chambers. The summons may be taken out by any person interested and must be served personally on each defendant. (R.S.C., Ord. 10, r. 1; Ord. 65).

Under (R.S.C., Ord. 11, r. 9), an originating summons, or notice thereof, can be served outside the jurisdiction; Ord. 10 provides for substituted service.

In a county court action as soon as the plaint (*q.v.*) has been entered, a summons requiring the defendant to appear and answer the plaintiff's claim on a certain day is issued and served on the defendant; attached to it are the particulars of claim, if any, and indorsed on it are various notices for the guidance of the defendant. Where it cannot be served in time, successive summonses may be issued. In certain cases the plaintiff may obtain a default summons, which informs the defendant that unless within eight days after service he gives notice of his intention to defend the action, the plaintiff may sign judgment. The attendance of witnesses in county court actions is enforced by summons with or without a clause requiring the production of documents in their possession. See SUBPOENA.

In magisterial practice, a summons is the ordinary way of compelling the appearance of a person against whom a complaint, information or other proceeding has been brought. See WARRANT.

Summum jus, summa injuria. Summa lex, summa crux (Hob. 125). (Extreme law is extreme injury. Strict law is strict punishment.) *Summum jus* often regarded the words and letter of the common law, for remedy whereof the parties grieved prayed aid of chancery to bridle the extremity and reduce such rigour to equity and conscience (*Grounds of Law*, 319). See APICES, ETC.

Sumner, or **Sumpnour,** one who cites or summons.

Sumptuary laws, those in restraint of luxury, excess in apparel, etc., as the Statute of Nottingham, 1336, *de cibariis utendis.* They were mostly repealed by the statute 1603, 1 Jac. 1, c. 25 (2 Hall. Mid. Ages 493).

Sunday [Sax. *sunnan daeg,* the day of the sun], the first day of the week, the Lord's Day, termed in the Sunday Observance Act, 1677, the Lord's Day, commonly called Sunday. It is a *dies non juridicus,* but an arrest for crime can be effected on this day; and bail can arrest their principal and a sergeant-at-arms can apprehend.

The profanation of the Lord's Day by trading, unlawful pastimes was repressed by the statute 1448, 27 Hen. 6, c. 5; the Sunday Observance Act, 1625; the statute 1627, 3 Car. 1, c. 2; the Sunday Observance Act, 1677, and the Sunday Observation Prosecution Act, 1871, all of which have been repealed.

The Sunday Observance Act, 1780, enacted that a house, room or other place opened and used for public entertainment or amusement or public debate on Sunday to which persons were admitted on payment should be deemed a disorderly house (*q.v.*). The word "place" extends to a park (*Culley* v. *Harrison* [1956] 2 Q.B. 71). An offender is liable to a fine of £100 on summary conviction (Common Informers Act, 1951, s. 1). Notwithstanding the Act of 1780, cinemas may be open on a Sunday (Sunday Entertainments Act, 1932, s. 1 ; Sunday Cinema

Act, 1972, s. 1), and so may theatres (Sunday Theatre Act, 1972, s. 1). As to licensed premises, see the Licensing Act, 1964, s. 68. Dancing at a wedding reception is not any kind of public entertainment such as is forbidden on Sundays by s. 1 of the Sunday Observance Act, 1780 (*Roe* v. *Harrogate JJ.* (1966) 64 L.G.R. 465).

With the exception of Jewish factories, women and young persons are not to be employed in a factory on Sundays (Factories Act, 1961, ss. 93, 109). The closing of shops on Sundays is dealt with by the Shops Act, 1950, ss. 47–65 and the Shops (Early Closing Days) Act, 1965, s. 4. See SHOP.

The provision of the Shops Act, 1950, ss. 47, 48, restricting retail sales on a Sunday are not inapplicable merely because the sales in question take place from stalls within an exhibition for which an entrance charge is payable (*Randall* v. *D. Turner (Garages)* [1973] 1 W.L.R. 1052). A shop which is open for viewing only may be held to be open for the serving of customers (*Betta Cars* v. *Ilford Corporation* (1959) 124 J.P. 19). The penalties for Sunday trading were increased by the Criminal Justice Act, 1972, s. 31.

A warrant of arrest or a search warrant may be executed on a Sunday (Magistrates' Courts Act, 1952, s. 102); see *Magee* v. *Morris* [1954] 1 W.L.R. 806.

Rent may be payable on a Sunday; in *Child* v. *Edwards* [1909] 2 K.B. 753, it was held that at common law Sunday is not a *dies non.*

By the Bills of Exchange Act, 1882, s. 13 (2), a bill of exchange, a cheque (s. 73), or a promissory note (s. 89), may be dated on Sunday; but Sunday is a non-business day (*q.v.*).

Betting by way of bookmaking or by means of a totalisator may not take place on Sunday (Betting, Gaming and Lotteries Act, 1963, s. 5).

As to a six-day licence, which requires entire Sunday closing, see the Licensing Act, 1964, s. 65. As to Sunday closing in Wales see s. 66; Local Government Act, 1972, s. 20, Sch. 4, Sch. 25 para. 3.

The common law rule that no judicial act may be done on a Sunday does not apply to administrative tribunals even when required to act judicially (*Att.-Gen. of Canada* v. *Hirsch* (1960) 24 D.L.R. (2) 93).

By R.S.C., Ord. 3, r. 2 (5), where any limited time less than seven days from or after any date or event is appointed or allowed for doing any act, or taking any proceeding, Sunday is not to be reckoned in the computation of such limited time (*Milch* v. *Frankau* [1909] 2 K.B. 100).

Sunrise. In *Tutton* v. *Darke* (1860) 5 H. & N. 647, the question was raised whether the time of sunrise is to be reckoned from the first appearance of the beams of the sun above the horizon, or from the time when the entire sun has emerged.

Super altum mare [Lat.], upon the high sea.

Super falso et certo fingitur. (Fiction is made regarding something known to be false.) See FICTION.

Super praerogativa regis, a writ which lay against the widow of a tenant who had held from the king if she remarried without licence of the king (Fitz.N.B. 174).

Super statuto, a writ which lay against the king's tenants in chief if they, in violation of the Statute of Westminster II, 1285, cc. 12, 13, aliened their land without licence of the king.

Super statuto de articulis cleri, a writ which lay, under the *Articuli Cleri*, c. 6, (*q.v.*), against a sheriff who distrained the goods of a clerk in the glebe or on the king's highway.

Super statuto facto pour seneschal et marshal de roy, a writ which lay to restrain the Court of the Marshalsea (*q.v.*) from intermeddling with matters outside its jurisdiction.

Super statuto que nul ject dung. The statute 1388, 12 Ric. 2, c. 13 (which was repealed by the Statute Law Revision Act, 1856), was a kind of primitive Public Health Act, which enacted, amongst other things, that none should, under a penalty of £20 payable to the king, cast filth, of many specified kinds, into the ditches, rivers, etc., in or near towns. Where the statute was infringed, this writ lay to the sheriff commanding him to see that the

offensive deposits were removed forthwith. Persons aggrieved by nuisance caused in violation of the statute could recover damages in an action at law; and the Lord Chancellor could attach offenders.

Super statuto que nul soit victuailer, etc., a writ which lay against any officer (such as a mayor, etc.) of a city or borough whose duty it was to assise wine and victuals (that is to say, to fix measures for wines and weights of bread) if he infringed the Statute of York, 1318, c. 6, which provided that during his term of office he should not merchandise for wines or victuals either in gross or by retail.

Super statuto versus servantes et laborentes, a writ which lay under the Statute of Labourers, 1357 (*q.v.*), against one who employed servants or labourers who had unlawfully left the employment of another.

Another writ under the statute lay against one who had refused to work at the prescribed wages, and two more are mentioned under LABORARIIS.

Super visum corporis [Lat.], upon view of the body. A coroner's inquest must generally be so held; but may be dispensed with in certain cases. See CORONER.

Superannuation. The Superannuation Act, 1972, enables the Minister for the Civil Service to make, maintain and administer superannuation schemes for civil servants and persons in the employments specified in Sch. 1 to the Act (ss. 1–6). The Secretary of State may make provision by regulations for the superannuation of persons employed in local government service and other persons or classes of persons, for whom it is appropriate to make superannuation provision (ss. 7, 8). The Secretary of State may also by regulations make superannuation provision for teachers and persons engaged in health services, etc. (ss. 9–12). The Act also deals with pensions and other benefits applicable to judicial offices (s. 13), metropolitan civil staffs (s. 14), members of police forces, special constables and police cadets (s. 15), members of fire brigades (s. 16), persons employed by light-house authorities (s. 17; Finance Act, 1972, Sch. 28), employees of law societies (Legal Aid Act, 1974, s. 19), members and staff of certain Commissions (Superannuation Act, 1972, s. 19), officers and servants of certain river authorities (s. 20), employees of the British Airways Board (s. 21, as amended by S.I. 1973 No. 2175) and the pension schemes of various statutory bodies (s. 22). Miscellaneous and supplemental provisions are contained in ss. 23–30 of the Act. See also PENSION.

Supercargo, an officer in a ship whose business is to manage the trade. He is a person employed by commercial owners to take charge of the cargoes exported, to sell them abroad to the best advantage, and to purchase commodities for importation. He goes out and returns home with the ship, thus differing from a factor, who has a fixed residence.

Superficiarius, a builder upon another's land under a contract (Civil Law).

Superficies, the alienation by the owner of the surface of the soil of all rights necessary for building on the surface, a yearly rent being generally reserved; also a building or erection (Civil Law).

Superflua non nocent (Jenk., Cent. 184). (Superfluities are harmless.) See NON SOLENT, ETC.; UTILE, ETC.

Superflous lands, lands acquired under the Lands Clauses Consolidation Act, 1845, but not required for the purposes of the undertaking of the company. Such lands must be sold within ten years after the time limited for the completion of the undertaking, the person entitled to the lands from which they were originally severed, or, if he refuses, the adjoining owners, having a right of pre-emption (q.v.); and if the lands are not so sold, they vest in the adjoining owners (ss. 127, 128). See *Great Western Ry.* v. *May* (1874) L.R. 7 H.L. 283; *Dunhill* v. *North Eastern Ry.* [1896] 1 Ch. 121; *Att.-Gen.* v. *Sunderland Corporation* [1930] 1 Ch. 168.

Super-institution, the institution of one to an office to which another had been previously instituted; as where A was admitted and instituted to a benefice upon one title, and B was admitted and instituted on the title or presentment of another (2 Cro. 463).

A church being full by institution, if a second institution was granted to the same church this was a super-institution. The super-institution was properly triable in the spiritual court, but it was not triable there if induction had been given upon the first institution. The advantage of a super-institution was that it enabled the party who obtained it to try his title by ejectment, without putting him to his *quare impedit*; but many inconveniences thence following (*e.g.*, the uncertainty to whom tithes should be paid), this method was discouraged (Mirehouse, *Advowsons*, 189).

Superintendent registrar, an officer who superintends the registers of births, deaths and marriages. He is a salaried officer in every registration district, with a registrar in every approved sub-district appointed by the local authority and holds office during the pleasure of the Registrar-General (Registration Service Act, 1953, s. 6; Local Government Act, 1972, Sch. 29 para. 41).

Superior courts. See HIGH COURT OF JUSTICE; SUPREME COURT OF JUDICATURE.

Superior orders, a doctrine according to which superior orders are a justification of, or excuse for, war crimes.

Super-jurare. When a criminal endeavoured to excuse himself by his own oath, or the oath of one or two witnesses, and the crime objected against him was so plain and notorious that he was convicted on the oaths of many more witnesses this was called *super-jurare* (Jacob).

Supermarket. Where a customer buys goods in a supermarket the property in such goods passes at the time of payment (*Lacis* v. *Cashmarts* [1969] 2 Q.B. 400).

Superoneratione pasturae, De. Where a man had been impleaded in the old county court for surcharge (q.v.) of common and the case had been removed into one of the courts at Westminster, then, if he were again impleaded in the county court for surcharge the writ de superoneratione pasturae lay against him.

Supersedeas, a writ which signified in general a command, on good cause shown, to stay some ordinary proceedings which ought otherwise to proceed (Fitz. N.B. 236).

Supersedeas was a writ which stayed or put an end to a proceeding. Thus, if a certiorari (*q.v.*) had been wrongly issued, and had been returned, the court would grant a *supersedeas*. So where upon a petition in lunacy a person had been irregularly found a lunatic, or had been found a lunatic and afterwards recovered, the inquisition might be superseded or set aside on petition by him to the Lord Chancellor for a *supersedeas* (Lunacy Act, 1890, ss. 101–107).

The writ of *supersedeas* was of importance in the law of bailable proceedings, it being the means by which a defendant who had been arrested on mesne process obtained his discharge. A prisoner entitled to the writ was said to be supersedable.

Under the old practice in bankruptcy, when the proceedings were commenced by commission, the bankruptcy was put an end to *ab initio* by superseding the commission, which was done by writ of *supersedeas*. The same effect is now produced by annulling the adjudication. See ANNUL.

Superstitious uses and trusts. Dispositions of real or personal estate for propagating religious rites not tolerated by the law are void. A bequest for masses for the soul of the testator was formerly held to be void as being for a superstitious use, but this was overruled in *Bourne* v. *Keane* [1919] A.C. 815. See CHARITY.

Super-tax. This term was first employed in the Income Tax Act, 1918, s. 4, to denote an additional duty of income tax which was levied upon incomes of over £2,500, altered to £2,000 by the Finance Act, 1920. The duty was at the rate prescribed by Parliament in any year. It was replaced by surtax (*q.v.*) (Finance Act, 1927, s. 38).

Supervision. See WINDING UP.

Supervision order. Every person released from a detention centre is subject to supervision (Criminal Justice Act, 1961, s. 13, Sch. 1). So also are young short term prisoners (Criminal Justice Act, 1967, s. 63). A suspended sentence supervision order may be made under the Criminal Justice Act, 1972, s. 12.

Where an order is made as to the custody of a minor the court has power to order that the minor shall be under the supervision of a local authority or of a probation officer (Guardianship Act, 1973, ss. 2–4).

Supervisor, an overseer, whom a testator sometimes used to name in his will. See EXECUTOR.

Supplement, Oath in. See SEMI-PLENA PROBATIO.

Supplemental answer, one which was filed in Chancery for the purpose of correcting, adding to, and explaining an answer already filed.

Supplemental bill, an addition to an original bill in equity, in order to supply some defect in it. See BILL IN CHANCERY ; BILL OF COMPLAINT ; STATEMENT OF CLAIM.

There was also a bill in the nature of a supplemental bill. This bill and the supplemental bill were sometimes confounded ; but a prominent distinction between them seems to have been that a supplemental bill was properly applicable to those cases only where the same parties and the same interest remained before the court ; whereas a bill in the nature of a supplemental bill was properly applicable when new parties with new interests arising from events which had happened since the institution of the suit were brought before the court.

Supplemental claim, a further claim which was filed when further relief was sought after the bringing of a claim.

Supplemental deed, a deed which is expressed to be supplemental to a previous deed. Such a deed has the same effect as one indorsed (*q.v.*) on the previous deed; it takes effect as if it contained a full recital of the previous deed (Law of Property Act, 1925, s. 58, replacing the Conveyancing Act, 1881, s. 53).

Supplementary benefits. See SOCIAL SECURITY.

Suppletory oath, the oath of a litigant party in the spiritual and civil law courts.

Suppliant, the actor in, or party preferring, a petition of right. See PETITION DE DROIT.

Supplicavit, a writ which issued out of Chancery for taking surety of the peace, upon articles filed on oath, when one was in danger of being hurt in his body by another ; it was addressed to the justices of the peace and sheriff of the county, and was grounded upon the statute 1327, 1 Edw. 3, st. 2, c. 16, which ordained that certain persons should be appointed by the chancellor to take care of the peace, etc. (Fitz.N.B. 80).

This writ was seldom used, for when application had been made to the superior courts, they had usually taken the recognisances there, under the statute 1623, 21 Jac. 1, c. 8. See ARTICLES OF THE PEACE ; BREACH OF THE PEACE.

Supplicium, any corporal punishment; it included death (Civil Law).

Supply, Committee of. All Bills which relate to the public income or expenditure must originate with the House of Commons, and all Bills authorising expenditure of the public money are based upon resolutions moved in a Committee of Supply, which is always a committee of the whole House.

The House of Commons sits in Committee of Supply when resolutions are passed in favour of making to the Crown such grants as are necessary for all services (known as supply services) other than those services (known as Consolidated Fund Services) the expenses of which are charged on the Consolidated Fund (*q.v.*).

Supply, Ministry of. See the Supply Powers Act, 1975.

Support. The right of support to land is either a natural right or an easement.

Every proprietor of land is entitled to so much lateral support from his neighbour's land as is necessary to keep his soil at its natural level ; that is, his neighbour must not excavate so close to the boundary as to cause his land to fall or subside. Similarly, if one person is entitled to the surface of land, and the land beneath the surface belongs to another proprietor, the owner of the surface is entitled to vertical support as against him (*Humphries* v. *Brogden* (1848) 12 Q.B. 739) ; that is, the owner of the subjacent land must not cause subsidence of the surface unless he has an easement entitling him to do so. Land has a right to support from underground salt beds which must

not be removed by brine pumping (*Louis* v. *British Soda Co.* [1972] Ch. 123).

The right of an owner to the support of the surface in its natural position is a presumption of the common law and is not part of a grant of mines or power to work the same, and a power to let down the surface must be expressly granted in a lease (*Warwickshire Coal Co.* v. *Coventry Corporation* [1934] Ch. 488).

This natural right to support, whether lateral or vertical, does not extend to the case of land the weight of which has been increased by buildings, unless it can be shown that the land would have sunk if there had been no buildings on it.

The right to extraordinary support, that is, to the support of land on which buildings have been erected, and which consequently requires more support than it did in its natural condition, is an easement. It was formerly considered that such an easement was not within the provisions of the Prescription Act, 1832, s. 2, on the ground that it was a negative easement and the section only applied to positive easements, but it is now established that the easement of support may not only exist by virtue of an express grant, or in the case of an ancient messuage, but may also be acquired by twenty years' uninterrupted enjoyment (*Dalton* v. *Angus* (1881) 6 App.Cas. 740).

The easement of support to a building by a building, or the right of the owner of a building to have it lean against and be supported by a building belonging to his neighbour, stands in the same position. It may also arise by implied grant under a disposition by the owner of two tenements. See ANCIENT MESSUAGES ; EASEMENT ; LOST GRANT ; PRESCRIPTION.

The easement may be acquired by twenty years' uninterrupted, peaceable, and open enjoyment of the building. In the case of the removal of support, the cause of action arises when the damage occurs, and the Limitation Act, 1939, is no bar however long since the cause of the damage may have occurred, but depreciation in selling value caused by apprehension of future mischief gives no cause of action and the risk of future subsidence must not be taken into account (*West Leigh Colliery* v. *Tunnicliffe &* *Hampson* [1908] A.C. 27).

The right to support does not extend to support by underground percolating waters; abstracting these so as to let down the surface is *damnum absque injuria* (*Acton* v. *Burnell* (1843) 12 M. & W. 324; *Langbrook Properties* v. *Surrey County Council* [1970] 1 W.L.R. 161). As to the right of a gas undertaking to support for its gas mains, see *Newcastle-under-Lyme Corporation* v. *Wolstanton* [1947] Ch. 427. See SUBSIDENCE.

Suppressio veri, suppression of the truth, one of the classes of fraud. See SUGGESTIO FALSI.

Supra, above. This word occurring by itself in a book refers the reader to a previous part of the book, like *ante*.

Supra protest, after protest. There may be either acceptance or payment of a bill of exchange by a person other than the drawee or acceptor or other person liable, after it has been protested for non-acceptance or non-payment. The full term is " acceptance (or payment) supra protest for honour," *i.e.*, for the honour or in relief of the person liable. The rights and liabilities of the parties are regulated by the Bills of Exchange Act, 1882, ss. 65–68. See PROTEST.

Suprema potestas seipsam dissolvere potest (Bacon). (Supreme power can dissolve itself.)

Supremacy, sovereign dominion, authority, and pre-eminence.

Supremacy, Act of. By the Act of Supremacy, 1558, supreme ecclesiastical jurisdiction was united to the imperial Crown. See CROWN.

Supremacy, Oath of, the oath prescribed for nearly 200 years, together with the oath of allegiance, which was to be taken by various high officers and persons by the statute 1688, 1 W. & M. c. 8, and also by the Bill of Rights, 1688. It was to this effect: " I, A. B., do swear that I do from my heart abhor, detest, and abjure as impious and heretical this damnable doctrine and position, that princes excommunicated or deprived by the Pope, or any authority of the see of Rome, may be deposed or murdered by their subjects or any other whatsoever. And I do declare that no foreign prince, person, prelate, state or potentate hath or ought to have any jurisdiction, power, superiority, pre-eminence or authority,

ecclesiastical or spiritual, within this realm. So help me God."

This oath had to be taken by all clergy on their ordination until the passing of the Clerical Subscription Act, 1865, when there was substituted for the oaths of allegiance and supremacy a single oath, as prescribed by the statute 1858, 21 & 22 Vict. c. 48, to maintain the Protestant succession to the Crown and declaring that no foreign prince, prelate, state or potentate has or ought to have any jurisdiction, power, superiority, pre-eminence or authority, ecclesiastical or spiritual, within the realm.

The oath of supremacy was abolished by the Promissory Oaths Act, 1868, s. 9, and the Promissory Oaths Act, 1871. See OATH.

Supreme Court of Judicature, the court formed by the Judicature Acts, 1873–75, in substitution for the various superior courts of law, equity, admiralty, probate and divorce then existing, including the Court of Appeal in Chancery and Bankruptcy, and the Exchequer Chamber. It consists of two principal divisions, *viz.*, a court of original jurisdiction, called the High Court of Justice, and a court of appellate jurisdiction, called the Court of Appeal (Judicature Act, 1925, s. 1). Its title "supreme" is a misnomer, as the superior appellate jurisdiction of the House of Lords and Privy Council, which was originally intended to be transferred to it, has been allowed to remain. See COURT.

The Court of Appeal consists of a Civil Division and a Criminal Division. See COURT OF APPEAL; CRIMINAL APPEAL.

The High Court of Justice is that branch of the Supreme Court of Judicature which exercises (i) the original jurisdiction formerly exercised by the Court of Chancery, the Courts of Queen's Bench, Common Pleas and Exchequer, the Courts of Probate, Divorce and Admiralty, the London Court of Bankruptcy, the Court of Common Pleas at Lancaster, the Court of Pleas at Durham, and the courts of the judges or commissioners of assize, and (ii) the appellate jurisdiction of such of those courts as heard appeals from inferior courts. It is a superior court of record (see COURT), and was originally composed of the Lord

Chancellor, the Lord Chief Justice of England, the Master of the Rolls, the Lord Chief Justice of the Common Pleas, the Lord Chief Baron of the Exchequer, the three Vice-Chancellors of the former Court of Chancery, such of the puisne judges of the old common law courts as had not been transferred to the Court of Appeal, the judge of the former Probate and Divorce Court and the judge of the former Admiralty Court; and subsequently it has consisted of the Lord Chancellor and the judges of the High Court who were appointed after the Judicature Acts, 1873–75, came into operation.

The High Court was also originally divided into five temporary divisions, corresponding to, and composed of the same judges as, the old courts which it replaced, viz., the Chancery Division, the Queen's Bench Division, the Common Pleas Division, the Exchequer Division, and the Probate, Divorce and Admiralty Division, and it was enacted that most of the business which before the Act was within the exclusive jurisdiction of any one of the old courts should be assigned to the corresponding Division of the High Court, that is, the action or matter was to be commenced in that Division: thus actions for the execution of trusts were to be assigned to the Chancery Division, and proceedings relating to the revenue to the Exchequer Division, provision being made for the transfer of business from one Division or judge to another when necessary.

On the death in 1880 of the Lord Chief Justice of England and the Lord Chief Baron of the Exchequer who were in office when the Judicature Act, 1873, came into operation, a council of judges was held, and on the resolution then passed an Order in Council (which came into effect on February 26, 1881) was made under the Judicature Act, 1873, s. 32, abolishing the offices of the Lord Chief Justice of the Common Pleas and the Lord Chief Baron, and consolidating the three common law divisions, that is, the Queen's Bench, Common Pleas and Exchequer Divisions, into one division called the Queen's Bench Division, under the presidency of a Lord Chief Justice. (See COUNCIL OF JUDGES; QUEEN'S BENCH DIVISION.) The High Court now consists of three divisions, namely, the Chancery Division (see CHANCERY), the Queen's Bench Division (q.v.), and the Family Division (q.v.).

The Lord Chancellor may constitute an advisory committee to advise him on matters relating to the Supreme Court (Courts Act, 1971, s. 30).

Under the practice of the old common law courts, almost every question of law arising in an action, such as demurrers, motions for new trials, for leave to enter verdicts, etc., had to be heard by the full court (or court sitting in banc) composed of at least three judges. To allow of the continuance of this practice, at all events for some time, the Judicature Act, 1873, ss. 40, 41, provided for the sittings of Divisional Courts (see DIVISIONAL COURTS) of the High Court (not to be confounded with the Divisions of the High Court), to be composed of two or three (but not more) judges of the High Court, including, if practicable, one or more judges of the Division to which the business to be heard was assigned. In the Chancery, Probate, Divorce and Admiralty Courts, on the other hand, all the business was transacted before a single judge, each cause or matter in chancery business being marked for a judge by name, who heard all applications and questions in it from its commencement to its end. With the view of extending this practice to the common law divisions of High Court, the Appellate Jurisdiction Act, 1876, s. 17, provided that every action and proceeding in the High Court and all business arising out of the same should, so far as practicable and convenient, be heard and disposed of before a single judge, and that all proceedings in an action subsequent to the trial or hearing should be taken before the judge before whom the trial or hearing took place.

Supreption. See OBTREPTION.

Sur, upon. In the titles of real actions " sur " was used to point out what the writ was founded upon. Thus a real action brought by the owner of a reversion or seignory, in certain cases where his tenant repudiated his tenure, was called a writ of right sur disclaimer. So a writ of entry sur disseisin was a real action to recover the possession of land from a disseisor. See CUI ANTE DIVORTIUM ; CUI IN VITA ; ENTRY.

Sur cui in vita. See CUI IN VITA.

Sur disclaimer, Writ of right, a real action brought by the owner of a seignory or reversion where the tenant repudiated his tenure ; it was abolished by the Real Property Limitation Act, 1833.

Surcharge, an overcharge of what is just and right ; exceeding one's powers or privileges; a second or further mortgage.

To surcharge a common is to put more cattle thereon than the pasture or herbage will sustain, or than the commoner has a right to do. As to the remedy for this injury, see ADMEASUREMENT.

In lieu of the power of an auditor to surcharge under the Local Government Act, 1933, s. 228, the Local Government Act, 1972, s. 161, provides that where an item of account appears to a district auditor to be contrary to law, he may apply to the court for a declaration to that effect, unless the expenditure has been sanctioned by the Secretary of State. The court may order repayment of the amount by the person responsible. Where a person has failed to bring into account a sum which ought to have been included the auditor may certify a sum recoverable by the authority concerned from the person responsible. Persons at fault are liable to disqualification. The court in this section is the High Court but, if the amount involved is within the jurisdiction of the county court in actions of contract, the county court has concurrent jurisdiction. See R.S.C., Ord. 98; C.C.R., Ord. 46, r. 26.

Surcharge and falsify, a mode of taking accounts in Chancery, where the court treats the account as a stated account, but gives liberty to challenge any particular items. If any of the parties can show an omission for which credit ought to be given, that is a surcharge ; or if anything is inserted that is a wrong charge, he is at liberty to show it, and that is falsification (*Pit* v. *Cholmondeley* (1754) 2 Ves.Sen. 565). See R.S.C., Ord. 43, r. 5.

Sureties of the peace and good behaviour. A person convicted of an indictable offence other than murder may in addition to, or in substitution for, any other punishment, be required to enter into a recognisance (*q.v.*), with or without sureties, to keep the peace and be of good behaviour for a reasonable time to be specified in the order (*R.* v. *Edgar* (1913) 23 Cox 558; *R.* v. *Sandbach, ex p. Williams* [1935] 2 K.B. 192 ; Criminal Law Act, 1967, s. 7 (4)).

Upon a substantive application before justices, a person may be required to find sureties of the peace if articles of the peace (*q.v.*) are exhibited against him ; and he may be required to find sureties for his good behaviour in cases where, even though no fear of violence is proved, it is shown that he has incited to breaches of the law or is a common breaker of the peace, or is otherwise not of good behaviour. See ARTICLES OF THE PEACE.

At common law a justice may require sureties of the peace from anyone committing a breach of the peace in his view. Any court of record having criminal jurisdiction has, as auxiliary to that jurisdiction, the power to bind over to be of good behaviour a person (including a witness (*Sheldon* v. *Bromfield JJ.* [1964] 2 Q.B. 573)) who or whose case is before the court, by requiring him to enter into his own recognisances or to find sureties or both, and committing him to prison if he does not comply (Justices of the Peace Act, 1968, s. 1 (7) ; *R.* v. *Sharp* [1957] 1 Q.B. 552).

Sureties for good behaviour may be taken under the Justices of the Peace Act, 1361 ; *R.* v. *Aubrey-Fletcher, ex p. Thompson* [1969] 1 W.L.R. 872. " Good behaviour " includes " the peace," but " the peace " does not include " good behaviour." Thus one bound to the peace will not commit a breach of his recognisance if he incites to violation of the law ; but one bound to good behaviour will commit a breach of his recognisance if he assaults another.

A person ordered by a magistrate to enter into a recognisance to keep the peace has a right of appeal to the Crown Court (Magistrates' Courts (Appeals from Binding Over Orders) Act, 1956).

Surety, hostage, bondsman; one who gives security for another; one who is bound for another. A surety is a person who binds himself to satisfy the obligation

1729

of another person if the latter fails to do so; thus, if A owes B money, and C, for valuable consideration, promises B that he will pay him the money if A does not, here C is a surety for A, the principal debtor, and his promise constitutes a contract of suretyship. A surety is the same as a guarantor (*q.v.*), but the term is usually restricted to the case of a person who binds himself by a bond: thus, it is sometimes necessary for a person who enters upon an office to obtain sureties who bind themselves by a bond to answer for his acts and defaults in the performance of the office, either generally, or for a limited amount or a limited time. A security given in a judicial proceeding also generally takes the form of a bond or recognisance with sureties. See BAIL; RECOGNISANCE; SECURITY.

If a surety satisfies the obligation for which he has made himself liable, he is entitled to recover the amount from the principal debtor (*Badely* v. *Consolidated Bank* (1887) 34 Ch.D. 536). If one of several sureties is compelled to pay the whole amount or more than his share, he is entitled to contribution (*q.v.*) from his co-sureties (*Steel* v. *Dixon* (1881) 17 Ch.D. 825); and if one of them has become insolvent, the solvent sureties may be compelled to contribute towards payment of the whole debt as if the insolvent surety had never been liable.

A surety is entitled to the benefit of all the securities which the creditor has against the principal; so that if a debt is secured by a bond with a surety, and also by a mortgage, and the surety pays the debt, he is entitled to stand in the place of the mortgagee and obtain repayment out of the mortgaged property. By the Mercantile Law Amendment Act, 1856, s. 5, every surety who pays the debt or performs the duty for which he is liable is entitled to have assigned, to himself or a trustee, every judgment, specialty or other security held by the creditor, and to use the name of the creditor in any action or other proceeding.

If the creditor releases the principal debtor, this will discharge the surety from liability, unless the creditor reserves his rights against the surety; such a release is then in effect merely a covenant not to sue the principal debtor. (See JOINT; RELEASE.) The surety may also be discharged by a variation of the contract by the creditor, or by the substitution of a new contract before breach of the old one.

In the case of fidelity guarantees the security is discharged if a material alteration takes place in the risk, *e.g.*, a change of duties (*Pybus* v. *Gibb* (1856) 6 E. & B. 902), or upon non-disclosure by the person to whom the guarantee is given of a matter affecting the contract, such as dishonesty of the employee (*Phillips* v. *Foxall* (1872) L.R. 7 Q.B. 666); see also the Partnership Act, 1890, s. 18.

See Hewitson, *Suretyship, its Origin and History*; Rowlatt, *Principal and Surety*.

Surface. See LAND; MINERALS; SOIL; SUBSIDENCE; SUPPORT.

Surgeon, Chirurgeon, one who cures diseases or injuries by manual operation. See MEDICAL PRACTITIONER; PHYSICIAN.

The Royal College of Surgeons in England was incorporated by charter of September 14, 1843. It had, however, been previously incorporated.

As to the power of the college to make by-laws, see the Medical Act (Royal College of Surgeons of England) Act, 1875.

Surmise, a suggestion or allegation.

In ecclesiastical practice, an allegation in a libel (*q.v.*) is called a surmise. A collateral surmise is a surmise of some fact not appearing in the libel.

Surname, or **Sirname** [Fr. *surnom*], the description of a person written in ancient rolls over the Christian name, this only being inserted in the line; the addition taken from the sire or father, the family name, the name over and above the Christian name (Encyc.Londin.).

The surname is the part of a name which is not given in baptism, the last name, the name common to all members of a family. Surnames were originally acquired by accident and retained by custom.

A person can adopt any surname he pleases, provided he does so for no dishonest purpose; and he can do so without taking any formal steps (*Davies* v. *Lowndes* (1835) 1 Bing.N.C. 618), though it is usual to execute a deed-poll declaring

SURRENDER

the fact; the deed-poll is sometimes enrolled at the Central Office and advertised in the *London Gazette*. A more expensive course is to change the name and then to get a royal licence to use the new name: fees are payable at the Heralds' College.

A parent who is given custody or care and control of a child may not change the child's surname without the leave of a judge of the Family Division or the written consent of the other parent (Matrimonial Causes (Amendment) Rules, 1974 (No. 2168).

See Linell, *Law of Names*; BASTARD; NAME ; TRADE NAME.

Surplice fees, customary payments made to clergymen officiating at marriages, baptisms and funerals.

Surplus assets, what is left of a company's property after payment of debts and repayment of the whole of the preference and ordinary capital. Whether the preference shareholders are entitled to share in the surplus assets is a question of construction of the articles, but the court will not readily hold that the preference shareholders have bartered away their rights (*Re Metcalfe & Sons* (1933) 49 T.L.R. 23).

Surplusage, where there is something over or in excess.

Where A held land of B in fee at a certain rent (*e.g.*, five shillings), and B held the same land of C at a less rent (*e.g.*, one shilling), and C purchased A's estate, so that B's seignory or mesnalty (*q.v.*) became extinct, C was bound to pay to B a rent equal to the difference between A's rent and B's rent (*i.e.*, four shillings), and this was called a rent by surplusage (Co.Litt. 150b, 309b (n)).

When, upon a sheriff lodging his account with the Clerk of the Pipe (*q.v.*), it appeared that there was a balance due to him he could, down to 1716, obtain payment only by means of a record of surplusage, which was dilatory and expensive. The Estates Act, 1716, s. 7, enacted that in such case any sheriff (other than the sheriffs of the Welsh counties and of the counties palatine of Chester, Durham and Lancaster, none of which passed their accounts before the Clerk of the Pipe) could obtain payment from the Treasury upon producing a certificate of

surplusage from the Clerk of the Pipe, unless the surplusage was occasioned by the payment, under various statutes then in force, of rewards for the arrest of clippers, coiners, highwaymen and housebreakers. See QUIETUS.

In construing a statute it is sometimes proper to reject words as surplusage (*R.* v. *Vasey* [1905] 2 K.B. 748) ; so also in construing a will (*Smith* v. *Crabtree* (1877) 6 Ch.D. 591).

Surplusagium non nocet (Branch.Max.). (Surplusage does no harm.) See UTILE, ETC.

Surprise. Where a person enters into a contract, conveyance, or the like, with excessive haste or want of deliberation, this fact may give rise to the inference that there was no true consent, or that the consent was not free, and that the transaction ought therefore to be set aside on the ground of surprise or improvidence. See CATCHING BARGAIN ; UNDUE INFLUENCE.

In procedure, a judgment or order may be set aside, or a new trial ordered, on the ground of surprise, if the court thinks that substantial injustice has been done. See R.S.C., Ord. 59, r. 11, note. See NONSUIT; TRIAL.

Surrebutter. Under the common law practice before the Judicature Acts, 1873–75, this was the pleading which followed the rebutter. It was the last pleading bearing a name. See PLEADING ; REJOINDER.

Surrejoinder. Under the practice, before the Judicature Acts, 1873–75, both at common law and in Chancery, this was the pleading which followed the rejoinder. See PLEADING ; REJOINDER.

Surrender [*sursum redditio*], an assurance restoring or yielding up an estate, the operative verbs being " surrender and yield up." The term is usually applied to the giving up of a lease before its expiration: it generally means the giving up of a lesser estate to a greater; a release is the giving up of a greater to a less interest, enlarging the latter. The effect of a surrender is to pass and merge the estate of the surrenderor to, and into, that of the surrenderee.

A surrender is a yielding up of a life interest or a term of years to him who has the immediate reversion or remainder, wherein the life interest or term of years may drown (*i.e.*, merge) by mutual agreement between them (Co.Litt. 337b).

Thus, if A, being tenant in fee of land, grants a lease for years to B, and B surrenders the term to A, it ceases to exist, being merged in A's reversion. Surrenders are of two kinds—in deed and in law. A surrender in deed is one made by express words. By the combined operation of the Statute of Frauds, 1677, s. 3, and the Real Property Act, 1845, s. 3, now replaced by the Law of Property Act, 1925, ss. 51–55, every express surrender must be in writing, and every express surrender of a term of more than three years must be by deed. As to surrenders of leases by mortgagors or mortgagees in possession, see the Law of Property Act, 1925, s. 100. But there may be an implied surrender or, as it is called in the Statute of Frauds, 1677, a surrender by act and operation of law (*Phene* v. *Popplewell* (1862) 12 C.B.(N.S.) 334), by anything which amounts to an agreement by the tenant to abandon and by the landlord to resume possession of the demised premises, *e.g.*, by the delivery and acceptance of keys, by the parties entering into a new contract of tenancy, or by the landlord accepting a new tenant.

Surrenders in law take effect by implication or operation of law, without express words. Thus, if a lessee accepts a new lease incompatible with his existing lease, this operates as a surrender in law of the latter (Co.Litt. 338a). See MERGER.

A corporation created by charter may give up or surrender its charter to the Crown, unless the charter was granted under an Act of Parliament (*e.g.*, the Municipal Corporations Act, 1835) imposing indefeasible duties on the bodies to which it applied.

Surrender of copyholds. Copyholds, which were abolished by the Law of Property Act, 1922, were not, as a general rule, alienable by any of the common law assurances. The principal mode of aliening copyholds was by surrender. Every tenancy in copyholds, though practically amounting to more or less absolute ownership, was in theory merely a tenancy at will, which was incapable of being transferred as such by the tenant; for if he attempted to convey his interest by a common law conveyance, he forfeited his estate. (See TENANT AT WILL.) Hence, when a copyholder wished to transfer his interest in the land, he surrendered it into the hands of the lord, in favour of (technically, to the use of) the intended transferee, or surrenderee, as he was called; and the lord thereupon admitted the surrenderee, that is, accepted him as tenant in lieu of the surrenderor. (See ADMITTANCE.) A surrender (which is *vocabulum artis*) was the yielding up of a legal tenancy in a copyhold estate, either by express words or by operation of law, by the tenant after admittance, or by his lawfully appointed attorney, either in or out of court, to the lord of the manor in person, his chief steward, or under-steward; or, by special custom, to the bailiff, beadle, or reeve, or to certain tenants of the manor, either as a relinquishment or resignation of such estate, or as the medium of conveying or transferring it to another.

The essential part of a surrender was the giving up of the customary seisin to the lord; and where this was effectually done, the form of relinquishment was not essential, unless the rights of a third person were injured. Formal surrenders were made by the surrenderor delivering to the lord, steward, or other person taking the surrender, a rod, straw, glove, or other symbol which represented the seisin of the land. A memorandum of the surrender was entered on the court rolls, and a copy of it signed by the surrenderor and steward, and formerly on parchment, was delivered to the surrenderee. A mortgage of copyholds was generally effected by a conditional surrender, or surrender made upon condition that, on payment of the mortgage debt on a certain day, the surrender should be void. If the debt was not paid on the day fixed, the mortgagor still had an equity of redemption in the same way as if the land were freehold.

When a copyholder surrendered for valuable consideration, the land was bound both at law and in equity, and he was prevented from surrendering to any other person; but the whole legal estate remained in him, and he had a right to retain the possession, subject to his accounting for the mesne profits should the surrenderee be afterwards admitted; and if the surrenderor died, the estate devolved upon his customary heir, but he was a trustee for the surrenderee. A surrender was not affected by the death of the parties, and the transfer might notwithstanding be completed.

Surrenders of copyholds were governed by the same rules as common law conveyances.

An equitable interest in copyholds was not the subject of surrender, except in the instance of a surrender for the purpose of barring an entail, but it was assignable. The assignee of an equitable estate, on taking a surrender from the person in whom the legal copyhold interest was vested, might compel an admission upon the payment of a single fine.

Copyholds in some manors were not devisable at all, or devisable subject to restrictions. In many manors they were devisable only by the testator making a surrender to the uses of his will, and then devising the land as he wished; but this necessity was abolished by the statute 1815, 55 Geo. 3, c. 192; and, by the Wills Act, 1837, provision was made for the devise of copyholds in all cases.

Surrenders were originally made in court, that is, at a customary court baron (*q.v.*); surrenders made out of court (that is, at any other place or time) were in some cases invalid unless they were afterwards presented in court by the homage. Later, however, the entry of the surrender on the rolls of the manor was sufficient (Copyhold Act, 1894, s. 85, replacing the Copyhold Act, 1841, s. 89).

In the manor of Taunton Deane in Somersetshire, there was a peculiar conveyance known as a Dayne surrender, which was used when a copyholder alienated his tenement, but desired to retain a part for his own life. The purchaser was admitted to the whole of the land (which was called the Dayne tenement), and paid a fine of one-third of the amount of an ordinary admittance fine, and further made himself responsible for the heriot to be paid on the death of the tenant for life. On the death of the surrenderor, the whole land belonged to the Dayne tenant. A somewhat similar custom existed in the manor of Yetminster, in Dorset (Elton, *Copyholds*).

Surrender of fugitives. Penal laws of foreign countries are strictly local, and affect nothing more than they can reach and than can be seized by virtue of their authority. A fugitive who passes hither comes with all his transitory rights. He may recover money held for his use, and stock, obligations, and the like; and cannot be affected in this country by proceedings against him in the country which he has left, beyond the limits of which such proceedings do not extend (*Warrender* v. *Warrender* (1834) 9 Bligh at p. 119). He may, however, in certain cases be extradited. See EXTRADITION.

Surrender value, the cash price which an insurance company will pay for the surrender by the policy holder to the company of the policy and all claims thereunder.

Surrenderee, Surrenderor, the persons to or by whom surrender is made.

Surreption, subreption (*q.v.*).

Surreptitious, fraudulent, stealthy. For the difference between surreptitious and obreptitious fraud, see Sanchez, *De Matrimonio*.

Surrise, to forbear or neglect (Bract. 1, 5).

Surrogate, one who is substituted or appointed in the room of another, as by a bishop, chancellor, judge, etc.; especially an officer appointed to dispense licences to marry without banns.

Sursum redditio [Lat.], a surrender.

Surtax. This was a deferred instalment of income tax payable (in addition to income tax at the standard rate) by individuals whose total income exceeded a stated amount (Income and Corporation Taxes Act, 1970, ss. 28–36). As a separate tax it has ceased to exist and in lieu thereof income tax is charged at different rates according to the individual's total income (Finance Act, 1971, ss. 32–35).

Survey. See COURTS OF SURVEY; ORDNANCE SURVEY.

Surveyor, one who has the overseeing or care of another person's land or works. See HIGHWAY.

A Court of Surveyors was erected by the statute 1542, 33 Hen. 8, c. 39, for the benefit of the Crown. The court had long

SURVEYOR

fallen into disuse when the sections of the Act relating to the court were repealed by the Statute Law Revision Act, 1863.

In an action for damages arising out of a negligent survey the proper measure of damages is the amount of money which will put the plaintiff into as good a position as if the contract to survey the property had been properly fulfilled (*Philips* v. *Ward* [1956] 1 W.L.R. 471).

See Auctioneers; Building Contract; Estate Agent; Quantity Surveyor.

Survivorship, the living of one of two or more persons after the death of the other or others. In questions of construction of wills the difficulty generally arises in regard to the persons or class of or from whom the survivor is to be ascertained and whether the word has a natural or stirpital meaning (*Gilmour* v. *MacPhillamy* [1930] A.C. 712). For rules of construction, see *Re James's Will Trusts* [1962] Ch. 226. See Per Capita; Per Stirpes.

The word "survivor" when used in relation to an event or point of time predicates primarily that the propositus (*q.v.*) is alive at and after the point of time or the event in question (*Elliott* v. *Joicey* [1935] A.C. 209; *Re Hodgson* [1952] 1 All E.R. 769).

A person is said to be entitled by survivorship where he becomes entitled to property by reason of his having survived another person who had an interest in it. The most familiar example is in the case of joint tenants, the rule being that on the death of one of two joint tenants the whole property passes to the survivor. See Commorientes; Joint; Jus Accrescendi.

Sus. per coll., an abbreviation for *suspendatur per collum* (let him be hanged by the neck), which, while Latin was used in the courts (see French), was written by the judge or clerk of arraigns opposite the name of each prisoner against whom sentence of death had been pronounced (4 Bl.Comm. 403).

Suskin, a Dutch coin which was in use about the year 1400. It seems to have been of the same value as the English silver farthing. See Galley-halfpenny.

Suspected person. In order to bring a person within the charge of being a suspected person loitering with intent to commit a felony (Vagrancy Act, 1824,

s. 4; Penal Servitude Act, 1891, s. 7), the act which brings a man into the category of a suspected person must have occurred before he commits the act which causes his arrest but the two acts need not be separated by any particular length of time (*Ledwith* v. *Roberts* [1937] 1 K.B. 232; *Pyburn* v. *Hudson* [1950] 1 All E.R. 1006; *Cosh* v. *Isherwood* [1968] 1 W.L.R. 48).

Suspend, to forbid an attorney or solicitor or ecclesiastical person from practising for an interval of time.

Suspended sentence. A court which passes a sentence of imprisonment of not more than two years may suspend the sentence. If the offender commits another offence within two years punishable with imprisonment he may be sentenced to serve the original sentence with or without variations (Criminal Justice Act, 1967, ss. 39–42; Criminal Appeal Act, 1968, s. 11 (4); Courts Act, 1971, Sch. 8 para. 48, Sch. 11 Pt. IV; Criminal Justice Act, 1972, s. 11, Sch. 6).

Suspension, a temporary stop or hanging up of a right for a time.

An estate was said to be suspended when it was extinguished for a time, but might afterwards revive: thus, if a copyholder in his own right became seised of the manor in right of his wife, the copyhold interest in his land was suspended during the coverture; so if a person holding land in fee by certain rents or services acquired the seignory during his life, the rents, services, etc., were suspended during his life. See Unity of Possession.

Suspension is an ecclesiastical censure. It consists of disqualification of a priest or deacon or bishop for a specified time from exercising or performing without leave of the bishop any right or duty of or incidental to his preferment or from residing in the house of residence of his preferment or within such distance thereof as shall be specified in the censure (Ecclesiastical Jurisdiction Measure, 1963, s. 49 (1)). Where a censure of suspension has been pronounced against any such person, he may not be readmitted to his benefice or permitted to exercise the functions of his order unless he satisfies the bishop (or, where he himself is a bishop, the Upper House of Convocation of the relevant province) of his good conduct during the term of his suspension or inhibition (s. 49 (2)).

Suspension, Pleas in, pleas which showed some matter of temporary incapacity to proceed with the action or suit. See ABATEMENT, PLEAS IN.

Suspensory Act, 1914, an Act which suspended the operation of the Government of Ireland Act, 1914, and the Welsh Church Act, 1914, in consequence of the war with Germany.

Suthdure, the south door of a church, where canonical purgation was performed, and plaints, etc., were heard and determined.

Suzerain, a lord paramount.

Swainmote. See ATTACHMENT OF THE FOREST; SWEINMOTE, COURTS OF.

Swans. The white swan on other than private waters is a royal bird and the property of the Crown unless it bears a " swan mark " indicating that it is the property of a subject (*Case of Swans* (1592) 7 Co.Rep. 16a). A " swan mark " is a distinguishing mark which some person has, either by royal grant or prescription, acquired the right to use. A subject has also such property in a swan which is tame and kept on private waters as to make the stealing of the swan theft. The taking of swans' eggs by any person on land where he has not the right to kill game is punishable summarily (penalty 25p for each egg) under the Game Act, 1831, s. 24; but swans are not game. The whooper swan and Bewick's swan and their eggs are protected by special penalties under the Protection of Birds Act 1954, Sch. 1; as to other swans, see ss. 1, 2 (3), 6 (1). See Herbert, *Prescription*. See BIRDS.

The abolition of the prerogative rights of the Crown to wild creatures does not affect the right of Her Majesty to swans (Wild Creatures and Forest Laws Act, 1971).

Swarf-money, warth-money or guard-money, paid in lieu of the service of castle-ward.

Swaziland. See the Swaziland Independence Act, 1968, as amended by the Finance Act, 1969, Sch. 21 Pt. IX.

Swear, to put on oath, to administer an oath to. See OATH.

Swearing, the act of declaring upon oath.

There is a penalty for using profane language in the streets by the Town Police Clauses Act, 1847, s. 28, and the Metropolitan Police Act, 1839, s. 54 (12). The penalty for offences is £20 (Criminal Justice Act, 1967, Sch. 3, Pt. I).

See CURSING; OATH.

Swearing the peace, showing to a court that one has just cause to be afraid of another in consequence of his menaces, in order to get him bound to keep the peace. See ARTICLES OF THE PEACE.

Sweep. See CHIMNEY SWEEPERS.

Sweepstakes. A sweepstake as usually run is a lottery (*Allport* v. *Nutt* (1845) 14 L.R.C.P. 272; *R.* v. *Hobbs* [1898] 2 Q.B. 647; *Hardwick* v. *Lanes* [1904] 1 K.B. 204) and is therefore illegal under the Lotteries and Amusements Act, 1976, s. 1, unless it falls within the exceptions in ss. 3–6. See LOTTERIES.

Sweets. The expression "sweets" means any liquor which is made from fruit and sugar or from fruit or sugar mixed with any other material, and which has undergone a process of fermentation in the manufacture thereof, and includes British wines, made wines, mead and metheglin (Customs and Excise Act, 1952, s. 307 (1)). As to duties on sweets see ss. 139–142; Finance Act, 1969, s. 1 (5), Sch. 7 para. 2.

Sweinmote, Court of, one of the forest-courts, held before the verderers as judges, by the steward, thrice in every year, the sweins or freeholders within the forest composing the jury, the jurisdiction being to inquire into oppressions and grievances committed by the officers of the forests, and to receive and try presentments, certified from the court of attachments, against offenders in vert and venison (4 Co.Inst. 289). See ATTACHMENT OF THE FOREST.

Swimming baths. These may be provided by local authorities under the Public Health Act, 1936, ss. 221–234; London Government Act, 1963, s. 40. See BATHS AND WASHHOUSES.

Swings. See WHIRLIGIG.

Swoling of land, so much land as one's plough can till in a year; a hide of land.

Sworn brothers [*frates jurati*], persons who, by mutual oaths, covenant to share in each other's fortunes (Leg. Edw. Conf. c. 35).

Sworn clerks in Chancery. These officers were abolished by the statute 1842, 5 & 6 Vict. c. 103. See SIXTY CLERKS.

Syb and som, peace and security (*Termes de la Ley*).

Syllogism, the full logical form of a single argument. To a legitimate syllogism it is essential that there should be three, and no more than three, propositions, *viz.*, the conclusion, or proposition to be proved, and two other propositions which together prove it, and which are called the premises. There must be three terms, *viz.*, the subject and predicate of the conclusion, and another called the middle term, which must be found in both premises, since it is by means of it that the other two terms are to be connected together, *e.g.*, all men are mortal; John is a man; therefore John is mortal.

Sylva caedua [Fr. *subbois*], wood under twelve years' growth; see the statute 1371, 45 Edw. 3, c. 23.

Symbolaeography, the art or cunning rightly to form and make written instruments. It is either judicial or extra-judicial, the latter being wholly occupied with such instruments as concern matters not yet judicially in controversy, such as instruments of agreements or contracts, testaments or last wills (West's Symbol.).

Symbolic delivery. See SEISIN, LIVERY OF.

Symbolum animae [Lat.], a mortuary.

Symond's Inn, formerly an Inn of Chancery.

Synallagmatical, that which involves mutual and reciprocal obligations and duties.

Sychronise, to concur in time.

Syncopare, to cut short, or pronounce things so as not to be understood (Cowell).

Syndic, an advocate or patron; a burgess or recorder; an agent or attorney who acts for a corporation or university; an actor or procurator, an assignee.

Where a testator appointed a corporation aggregate to be his executor, administration with the will annexed used to be granted to their " syndic," that is, a person specially appointed by the corporation for the purpose (*In b. Darke* (1860) 29 L.J.P.M. & A. 71).

This procedure was found to be inconvenient when it became an ordinary thing for a testator to appoint as his executor one of the insurance or other companies which are prepared to act as trustees and executors; and now any such trust corporation can itself take out a grant of probate in its corporate name (Administration of Estates Act, 1925, s. 14 (3), replacing the Administration of Justice Act, 1920, s. 17).

The term syndic means generally a person appointed by a corporation to act for it as regards a particular matter. The University of Cambridge appoints various syndics; these persons are members of the committees known as syndicates, and would elsewhere be described as members of the Library Committee and so forth.

Syndicate, a body of persons taking part jointly in some venture or undertaking; a body of persons associated temporarily for the purpose of buying a private business or other property and selling it at a profit, usually to a limited company. Private companies formed to carry out and complete some pending operation or transaction, or some contemplated operation or transaction, are commonly called syndicates.

If several persons unite to subscribe for, or guarantee the subscription of, an issue of shares or bonds, with a view to dividing the risk and the profit, they are said to form a syndicate. Sometimes a syndicate is formed by persons who are individually possessed of property of the same description (generally shares, or the like), and wish to subject it to a common management, with a view to its realisation, after which each member takes the profit or loss accruing in respect of his proportion. A syndicate is a mere partnership unless it is registered as a company.

The word is also used as meaning a council or body of syndics (*q.v.*).

Syngraph. This was the same thing as the chirograph (*q.v.*) except that the word *syngraphum* was written in the middle of the deed instead of *chirographum*.

In the civil law it was a deed, bond or writing under the hands and seals of all the parties.

Synod, a meeting or assembly of ecclesiastical persons concerning religion, being the same thing in Greek as " convocation " in Latin. It is a synonym of " council " as the latter word is used in ecclesiastical law. Apart from the General Councils held at Rome, there was in England down to 1555 the National Council of all the English bishops and archbishops. The Synodical Government Measure 1969, s. 1 provides for the vesting by canon of the functions, authority, rights and privileges of the convocations (*q.v.*) of Canterbury and York in the General Synod of the Church of England. The text of the canon is set out in Schedule 1 to the Measure.

See CONVOCATION.

S. 4 and Sch. 3 deal with the constitution and function of Diocesan Synods; s. 5 and Sch. 3, 4 with those of Deanery Synods.

See also the Synodical Government (Special Majorities) Measure, 1971, and the Synodical Government (Amendment) Measure, 1974.

As to the authority of synods in the Church of England, see Canons 139–141.

Synodal, the contributions which were paid by the clergy to the bishop or the archdeacon upon the occasion of the Easter visitation. Synodals were sometimes termed synodies. Synodals were abolished by the Ecclesiastical Jurisdiction Measure, 1963, s. 82 (3).

Synodales testes, those who gave evidence at the synod. Anciently the urban and rural deans were the *synodales testes*, one of their duties being to inform the diocesan synod of notorious cases of misconduct amongst both laity and clergy. Subsequently the *testes* were a priest and two or three laymen for every parish; and later the churchwardens or the sidesmen (*q.v.*) performed, or were supposed to perform, similar functions.

T

T. Every person who was convicted of felony, short of murder, and admitted to the benefit of clergy, was marked with this letter upon the brawn of the thumb. The practice was abolished by the statute 1827, 7 & 8 Geo. 4, c. 27. See BENEFIT OF CLERGY.

T.R.E., the initials of the phrase *tempore regis Edwardi*, in the time of Edward the Confessor (1042–1066), referring to pre-Conquest law.

Tabard [Low Lat. *tabardum*], a short gown; a herald's coat; a surcoat.

Tabarder, one who wears a tabard or short gown; the name is still used as the title of certain bachelors of arts on the old foundation of Queen's College, Oxford.

Tabellio, a Roman official who reduced contracts and wills into proper form, and attested their execution.

Table. The Companies Act, 1948, ss. 8, 11, Sch. 1 contains model forms of articles of association.

Table A is the model form of articles of association of a company limited by shares, not being a private company.

Table B is the model form of memorandum of association of a company limited by shares.

Table C is the model form of memorandum and articles of association of a company limited by guarantee and not having a share capital.

Table D is the model form of memorandum and articles of association of a company limited by guarantee and having a share capital.

Table E is the model form of memorandum and articles of association of an unlimited company having a share capital.

Table rents, such of the revenues of a bishopric as were appropriated to household expenses. See BORDLANDS.

Table waters. This expression was defined by the Finance (New Duties) Act, 1916, s. 4 (2), as meaning any aerated waters and any beverages sold or kept for sale in bottles other than (*a*) any liquor for the sale of which an excise licence was required, and (*b*) syrups or other liquors intended to be used only in a diluted form. The Act imposed an excise duty of fourpence per gallon on such waters when they were sweetened or fermented, and of eightpence a gallon when they were of any other kind. On imported table waters there were customs duties at the same rates (Finance Act, 1916, s. 7 (1)). These were the first taxes on soda water and other such waters. They were repealed by the Finance Act, 1924.

Tabula de Amalfa. See AMALFI, ETC.

Tabula in naufragio [Lat., a plank in a shipwreck], a term used to denote the power of a third mortgagee, who, having obtained his mortgage without any knowledge of a second mortgage, could acquire the first incumbrance, and squeeze out and have satisfaction before the second. See ATTENDANT TERM ; TACKING.

Tabulae nuptiales, a written record of a marriage ; also an agreement as to the *dos* (Civil Law).

Tabularius, a notary (Civil Law).

Tacfree, exempt from rent, payments, etc.

Tacit. A communication of intention is said to be tacit when it consists of mere silence.

Taciturnity, keeping silent about a debt when a claim would have been natural, leading to an inference of payment.

Tack, a lease or contract of location; also an addition, supplement ; also cattle taken in by a tenant on agistment.

Tack duty, rent reserved upon a lease.

Tacking. In the law of mortgages, where land is mortgaged by ordinary deeds of mortgage to several persons in succession, each ignorant of the security granted to the other, the general rule is that they rank in order of date (or registration, where registration is necessary). But formerly the first mortgagee, who alone obtained a legal estate, had this advantage over the others, that if he took a further charge on a subsequent advance to the mortgagor, without notice of any intermediate second mortgage, he would have priority in respect of his subsequent advance over the second mortgagee: in other words, he was in the same position as if he had made his subsequent advance at the same time as he made his original advance. And if a third mortgagee, who had made his advance without notice of a second mortgage, could procure a transfer to himself of the first mortgage, and thus acquire the legal estate, he might tack or annex his third mortgage to the first mortgage, and so postpone the

second mortgagee: in other words, he was in the same position as if he had advanced the amounts of both the first and third mortgages at the date when the first mortgage was made. The term " tacking," though especially applied to the case of a subsequent mortgagee getting in the legal estate, was also applied to the first case given above, namely, that of a first mortgagee adding a subsequent advance to his first mortgage. The essentials to the operation of tacking were possession of the legal estate (*Brace* v. *Marlborough* (1728) 2 P.Wms. 491), and absence of notice, at the time of making the advance to be tacked, of the existence of the incumbrance which would be postponed (*Marsh* v. *Lee* (1669) 2 Vent. 337).

Tacking was abolished by the Vendor and Purchaser Act, 1874, s. 7. It was restored by the Land Transfer Act, 1875, s. 129, but was again abolished, except in the case of further advances made by a prior mortgagee, by the Law of Property Act, 1925, s. 94.

Tacking is to be distinguished from consolidation.

See CONSOLIDATION OF MORTGAGES ; FURTHER ADVANCE ; MORTGAGE ; PRIORITY.

Tail [Fr. *tailler*, to prune]. An estate tail was formerly a freehold of inheritance and is now an equitable interest which may be created in respect of personalty as well as realty by way of trust and which (if not barred or disposed of by will) devolves in equity on the person who would have taken realty as heir of the body or as tenant by the curtesy if the Law of Property Act, 1925, had not been passed (s. 130 (4)).

An entailment of land constitutes a settlement (Settled Land Act, 1925, s. 1).

An equitable interest in tail, is an interest limited to a person and the heirs of his body general or special, male or female, and was the creature of the statute *De Donis*, 1285. The interest, if the entail is not barred, reverts to the donor or reversioner if the donee dies without leaving descendants answering to the conditions annexed to the interest upon its creation, unless there is a limitation over to a third person on default of such descendants, when it vests in such third person or remainderman.

In order to create an estate tail by deed the words " heirs of the body " had to be used (*White* v. *Collins* (1719) 1 Comyns' Rep. 289, 301), or the word " heirs " with words of procreation of some kind to describe the body from whom the heirs were to proceed, or the person by whom they were to be begotten. After the Conveyancing Act, 1881, s. 51, the words " in tail " without the words " heirs of the body " might be used.

In a will technical terms of limitation were before 1926 not necessary, if upon construction it appeared that the words were terms of limitation and not gifts to children or issue as purchasers or otherwise; thus a devise to A and his issue, or to A and his seed (or children, or sons), or to A and his heirs male, or to A and his heirs lawfully begotten, or to A and if he died before issue, or not having issue, or not having a son, then to another, would have given an estate tail.

By the Law of Property Act, 1925, s. 130, an interest in tail or in tail male or in tail female or in tail special (in the Act referred to as an " entailed interest ") may be created by way of trust in any property real or personal, but only by the like expressions as those by which before 1926 a similar estate tail could have been created by deed not being an executory instrument in freehold land.

It is necessary to limit either to the heirs of the body, etc., or in tail, to create the interest (Law of Property Act, 1925, s. 131). Informal limitations which would have created an entail in wills or executory instruments but would not have created an estate tail by deed before 1926 are construed for this purpose according to their effect if they had been limitations before 1926 of personal property (Law of Property Act, 1925, s. 130).

Unbarred entailed interests devolve according to the general law in force before 1926. An entailed interest is only capable of being created by a settlement of real or personal property or the proceeds of sale thereof (including the will of a person dying after 1925), or by an agreement for a settlement in which the trusts to affect the property are sufficiently declared.

Subject to his powers and duties as tenant for life under the Settled Land Act, 1925, if a tenant in tail grants the fee simple in the property to another person and his heirs without barring the entail, only a qualified or base fee will pass, commensurate with the entailed interest, capable, however, of being rendered absolute by the barring of the entail, but, until it so barred, defeasible by the entry not only of the reversioner, or remainderman, when he becomes entitled to enter into possession but also of the issue in tail upon the death of the tenant in tail. After 1925 a devise by a tenant in tail in possession (but not after possibility of issue extinct) of an entailed interest operates as a bar of the entail and passes the fee (Law of Property Act, 1925, s. 176).

An entailed interest possesses or possessed the following incidents and privileges:

It was, like a fee simple, formerly subject to curtesy and dower (if not barred): see now the Law of Property Act, 1925, s. 130 (4).

With the exception of a tenant in tail after possibility of issue extinct who may be liable for equitable waste, the owner may commit waste upon it without being impeacheable for it, and so it is said may his grantee (3 Leon. 121); see now the Law of Property Act 1925, s. 135, as to equitable waste.

It is liable to every kind of debt to the extent of the debtor's interest in the estate and a trustee in bankruptcy may bar the entail (Fines and Recoveries Act, 1833, ss. 69 *et seq.*), and now by the Law of Property Act, 1925, s. 176, a tenant in tail in possession may dispose of the whole estate by will either expressly or by general reference to his entailed estates, and in that case it passes to his personal representatives and is liable for his debts.

It might have been lost by escheat; by forfeiture for treason or felony (but such forfeiture was abolished by the Forfeiture Act, 1870); or by extinguishment.

As estate owner, having an inheritable freehold, the tenant in tail has a right to the title-deeds which equity will secure to him (Settled Land Act, 1925, s. 98 (3)).

Although a tenant in tail must generally keep own interest, he is not bound to pay off any charge or incumbrance affecting the estate; if, however, he does so, the presumption is that he meant to exonerate the estate (for he might, if he pleased, have acquired the fee simple), unless he evinces the contrary intention by taking an assignment of the incumbrance to a trustee in trust for himself, or by some other express act. As to his powers as tenant for life in regard to the employment of capital money or otherwise to discharge incumbrances, see the Settled Land Act, 1925, ss. 16 (2), 69, 73.

He may, if in possession, exercise the powers of a tenant for life (Settled Land Act, 1925, s. 20).

This estate could not be merged, surrendered, or extinguished by the acquisition of the fee simple by the tenant in tail except by a tenant in tail after possibility of issue extinct (Co.Litt. 27b).

The issue in tail is not bound to complete, either at law or in equity, any contract made by the ancestor as tenant in tail, since he claims from the original grantor, and not from his immediate ancestor. If, however, he does any act towards completing such a contract, equity will compel its performance; see now the Settled Land Act, 1925, ss. 63, 90, replacing the Settled Land Act, 1890, s. 6, in regard to his powers as estate owner.

Neither was such issue bound to pay off his ancestor's incumbrances, nor to keep down the interest thereon; but he was liable to Crown debts under the statute 1542, 33 Hen. 8, c. 39, s. 75.

A tenant in tail might cut timber and dispose of it, without barring the entail; but if he sold the growing trees, the buyer must sever them during his life, otherwise the issue in tail would have been entitled to them as part of the inheritance; and the buyer, though obliged to pay the purchase-money, would not then have been allowed to sever them. These rights have not been impaired by the Settled Land Act, 1925.

If a tenant in tail granted estovers, or the vesture of his woods, to another, the grant determined with his death; for being a charge upon the inheritance, it

necessarily ceased when his power was determined.

The entail may be barred by the tenant in tail in possession or by the remainderman in tail with the consent of the protector of the settlement, though not by the issue in tail, except as a base fee (*q.v.*), under the Fines and Recoveries Act, 1833; but the entail of offices or dignities cannot be barred.

Before the statute *De Donis*, 1285, the donee could, after issue born, have alienated the land, whereby the issue would have been disinherited and the donor deprived of his right of reversion. This being the case, the statute declared that the will of the donor should be observed; and that an estate granted to a man and the heirs of his body should descend to the issue (he not having power to alienate the estate), and that in default of issue, the land should revert to the donor or his heirs. Estates tail were thus made inalienable, and neither the issue nor the remainderman could be barred. And many other inconvenient consequences were produced, which quickened the ingenuity of the judicature, until it produced, at length (in its efforts to recover the liberty of alienation), the complicated machinery of fines and recoveries. See Donis Conditionalibus; Fine; Recovery.

The modes of barring an estate tail were two, *viz.*, a fine, according to the statute law (which was a compromise of a fictitious action), giving a base fee commensurate with the existence of the issue upon whom the estate tail would (if unbarred) have devolved, and a recovery at common law (which was a real action carried on to judgment), giving the fee simple absolute. These were abolished by the Fines and Recoveries Act, 1833.

The Fines and Recoveries Act, 1833, s. 15, enacts that a tenant in tail, whether in possession, remainder, contingency, or otherwise, shall have power to dispose, for an estate in fee simple absolute, or for any less estate, of the lands entailed, as against all persons claiming the lands entailed by force of the estate tail, and also as against all persons whose estates are to take effect after the determination, or in defeasance, of any such estate tail.

Enrolment of deeds was abolished by the Law of Property Act, 1925, s. 133.

In order to prevent a son tenant in tail defeating a strict family settlement, against the wish of his father, the tenant for life, the legislature introduced a protector of the settlement, who is, in many respects analogous to the tenant to the praecipe (*q.v.*). The office of the protector is to grant or withhold his consent, which is required to enable a tenant in tail in remainder to bar those in remainder as well as his own issue, to the same extent as might have been effected by a recovery. An expectant tenant in tail may bar his own issue only unless he has the consent of the protector.

The protector's consent may be given by the same assurance as that by which the disposition is effected, or by a deed distinct from the assurance. His consent once given cannot be revoked.

Under the Legitimacy Act, 1976, a legitimated person, and any other person, is entitled to take any interest as if the legitimated person had been born legitimate (s. 5 (3)).

As to undivided shares see the Law of Property (Amendment) Act, 1932. See PROTECTOR ; RECOVERY ; SETTLED LAND.

Tail after possibility of issue extinct, Tenancy in. This interest arises out of a special entail as to the parentage of the issue, when the express condition has become impossible by reason of death. Thus, if land is entailed upon a man and his issue from a particular wife, if she dies without issue, the interest of the husband becomes reduced to a tenancy in tail after possibility of issue extinct. Only a donee in tail special can become such a tenant, for if the entail is general, such a tenancy can never arise ; for whilst he lives he may have issue, the law not admitting the impossibility of having children at any age. As an entailed interest is originally carved out of a fee simple, so this estate is carved out of a special entail.

There may be tenant in tail after possibility, etc., of a remainder as well as of a possession. Thus, if a grant for life was made, remainder to the husband and wife in special tail, and the husband died with-

out issue, the wife was tenant in tail after possibility, etc., of this remainder ; and if the tenant for life surrendered to her, as he might (an estate for one's own life being greater than an estate for the life of another), she was tenant in tail after possibility, etc., in possession (*Bowles's Case* (1616) 11 Rep. 81a).

This interest must be created by death ; it cannot arise out of any arrangement of the parties, but *ex dispositione legis*, and not *ex provisione hominis* ; if, therefore, land is given to a husband and wife and the heirs of their bodies, should they afterwards be divorced *causa praecontractus vel consanguinitatis vel affinitatis*, their estate is converted into a joint tenancy for life, and not into a tenancy in tail after possibility of issue extinct, because their interest has been altered by their own act, and not by the act of God. Such a tenancy can endure only for the life of the surviving donee in tail, who has no power under the Fines and Recoveries Act, 1833, s. 18, to bar the remainders or reversion over, and if he conveys his interest to another, such other will be only a tenant *pur autre vie*, and will be punishable for waste. Impossibility will not be presumed on account of age (Co.Litt. 28a).

The attributes of this interest are : the tenant is dispunishable for waste ; he may, therefore, not only commit it, but also convert to his own use the property wasted ; equity, however, will restrain him from committing wilful waste. The interest is liable to forfeiture. It will merge in a fee simple or fee tail immediately expectant thereon. The reversioner or remainderman takes upon the tenant's default.

The tenant has the powers of a tenant for life under the Settled Land Act, 1925, s. 20.

See TENANT IN TAIL AFTER POSSIBILITY

Tail gote. See GOTE.

Tailage [Fr. *tailler*], a piece cut out of the whole ; a share of one's substance paid by way of tribute ; a toll or tax (Cowel).

Taille, the fee which is opposed to fee simple, because it is so minced or pared that it is not in the owner's free power to dispose of it, but it is, by the first giver, cut or divided from all other, and tied to the issue of the donee. See TAIL.

Take and carry away. After 1733 (see FRENCH), it was, until 1916 (see INDICTMENTS), necessary, in an indictment for the common law offence of larceny, to aver that the prisoner " did feloniously take and carry away." See ASPORTATION.

Tale. See NARRATIO.

Tale quale. This signifies that goods are as sample when shipped, the liability for loss or deterioration in transit being the responsibility of the buyer.

Tales [Lat.], such men. If, when a jury has been summoned, a sufficient number of jurors do not appear, or, if by reason of challenges or exemptions, a sufficient number do not remain to make up the proper number, either party may pray a *tales,* that is, ask the court to make up the deficiency. A *tales* (which is pronounced as a disyllable) is a supply of such men as were summoned upon the first panel. For this purpose a writ of *decem tales, octo tales,* used to be issued to the sheriff; but by the Juries Act, 1974, if it appears to the court that a jury to try an issue before the court will be, or probably will be, incomplete, the court may, if the court thinks fit, require any persons who are in or in the vicinity of the court to be summoned (without any written notice) for jury service up to the number needed (after allowing for any who may not be qualified (see JURY) and for refusals and challenges (*q.v.*) to make up a full jury. The names of the persons so summoned are added to the panel and the court proceeds as if those so summoned had been included in the panel in the first instance (s. 6). The power of so summoning jurors may be exercised after balloting has began, as well as earlier, and if exercised after balloting has begun the court may dispense with balloting in respect of persons so summoned (s. 11 (2)). It was held in *R.* v. *Solomon* [1958] 1 Q.B. 203 that there cannot be a jury composed entirely of talesmen but this appears to conflict with the terms of s. 6 of the Act of 1974.

Talesman, a person summoned to act as a juror from amongst the bystanders in the court.

Talfourd's Acts, the Custody of Infants Act, 1839 (replaced by the Custody of Infants Act, 1873), and the Copyright Act, 1842 (replaced by the Copyright Act, 1956).

Taliation, Sureties of. See LEX TALIONIS.

Talion, law of retaliation. See LEX TALIONIS.

Talis interpretatio in ambiguis semper fienda est, ut evitetur inconveniens et absurdum (4 Co.Inst. 328). (Ambiguous words should be interpreted in such a way that inconvenience and absurdity are avoided.) At 1 Co.Rep. 52 the same maxim is quoted with the omission of the words *in ambiguis* and the addition of the words *et ne judicium sit illusorium* (and that the decision is not illusory).

Talis non est eadem. (The like is not the same.) See NULLUM SIMILE, ETC.

Tallage; Tailage, taxes generally. See DE TALLAGIO, ETC.; HIDAGE.

Tallagers, tax or toll-gatherers (Chaucer).

Tallagium facere, to give up accounts in the Exchequer, where the method of accounting was by tallies.

Tallia, commons in meat and drink.

Talliage. See TAILAGE.

Tally, or **Talley,** a stick of rectangular section across one side of which were cut notches denoting payments. The stick being split lengthwise so that on each half there was one half of each notch, the debtor retained one half of the stick as evidence of the payment and the creditor kept the other half as a record.

Tallies were used in the Exchequer (*q.v.*) from the earliest times: the two deputy chamberlains of the exchequer and the talley-cutter attended the Talley Court to deal with them. The statute 1783, 23 Geo. 3, c. 82, s. 2, provided that, when the then two chamberlains of the Exchequer should have ceased to hold office, the use of tallies should cease also; but tallies still continued in use until 1826, when the last of the chamberlains died. The old tallies were ordered to be destroyed by the statute 1834, 4 & 5 Wm. 4, c. 15, and destroyed they were in a fire which led to the burning down of the Houses of Parliament.

Tally trade, a form of trade under which goods are sold upon credit and are paid for by weekly instalments. A tallyman is a man carrying on such a trade. A tally was a common security for money in the days of Edward I (2 Reeves, c. 11, p. 253, n. (*b*)).

Talon, a certificate attached to a bond, which enables the holder to get a fresh supply of coupons when those originally attached to the bond have been used.

Taltarum's Case. In *Taltarum's Case* (1473) Y.B. 12 Edw. 4, 19, it was decided than an estate tail might be barred by a common recovery. See RECOVERY.

Tam quam; Tanquam, the action generally called a *qui tam* action, or penal action (*q.v.*), the name *tam quam*, like *qui tam*, being formed of words found in the phrase *qui tam pro domino rege quam pro se ipso* ; also a writ of error from inferior courts, when the error was supposed to be as well in giving the judgment as in awarding execution upon it, *tam in redditione judicii, quam in adjudicatione executionis.*

Tanganyika. See the Tanganyika Independence Act, 1961 ; the Tanganyika Republic Act, 1962. See also TANZANIA.

Tangible property, corporeal property.

Tanistry, or **Tanistria** [Irish *tanaiste*, lord ; *tan*, country], an ancient law of tenure in Ireland, which allotted the inheritance of lands, castles, etc., to the oldest and most worthy and capable house of the deceased's name and blood, without any regard to proximity. This, in reality, was giving it to the strongest, and naturally occasioned bloody wars in families, for which reason it was abolished in the reign of James I (Encyc.Londin. ; 3 Hall. Const.Hist., c. xviii, p. 377 ; Dav.Rep. 28).

Tanzania. See the Tanzania Act, 1969.

Tape recording. A tape recording is admissible in evidence provided the accuracy of the recording can be proved, the voices recorded can be properly identified and the evidence is otherwise admissible. A transcript of a tape recording, properly proved, may be put before a jury (*R. v. Ali* ; *R. v. Hussain* [1966] 1 Q.B. 688). The recording must be shown to be original (*R. v. Stevenson* ; *R. v. Hulse* ; *R. v. Whitney* [1971] 1 W.L.R. 1). In criminal proceedings, if the authenticity of the recording is disputed but the judge is satisfied that it is genuine, the recording should be placed before the jury (*R. v. Robson* ; *R. v.*

Harris [1972] 1 W.L.R. 651). A witness may refresh his memory of a conversation overheard by him from notes made from a tape recording (*R. v. Mills* ; *R. v. Rose* [1962] 1 W.L.R. 1152). Radar recordings are similarly admissible (*Sapporo Maru (Owners)* v. *Statue of Liberty (Owners)* [1968] 1 W.L.R. 739). A tape recording of a conversation is a document which is liable to be produced for inspection (*Grant* v. *Southwestern and County Properties* [1975] Ch. 185).

See TELEPHONE TAPPING.

Tarde venit, a return made upon a writ by the sheriff when it came to him so late that he could not execute it in time (Fitz. N.B. 38 ; Dalton, *Office of Sheriffs*, 163).

Tare, an allowance for the weight of a container of goods.

Tare and tret. See ALLOWANCE.

Tariff [Span.], a cartel of commerce; a book of rates ; a table or catalogue, drawn up usually in alphabetical order, containing the names of several kinds of merchandise, with the duties or customs to be paid for the same, as settled by authority or agreed on between the several States that hold commerce together.

The Customs Tariff Act, 1876, consolidated the then customs duties.

By the Import Duties Act, 1932, a general *ad valorem* customs duty of 10 per cent. was imposed on all imports with additional duties on special classes or descriptions of goods. The Act set up an advisory committee to make recommendations to the Treasury as to additional customs duties. Commonwealth preference was given by the Ottawa Agreements Act, 1932. These Acts, and amending Acts, are replaced by the Import Duties Act, 1958. See the European Communities Act, 1972, s. 4, Sch. 3, Pt. I. See CUSTOMS.

Tasmania, formery called Van Diemen's Land ; the name of Tasmania was substituted by Order in Council of July 21, 1855: see the statute 1828, 9 Geo. 4, c. 83, and the Australian Constitutions Act, 1850. For union with the Australian colonies, see AUSTRALIA.

Tath. In Norfolk and Suffolk the lords of manors anciently claimed the privilege of having their tenants' sheep brought at night upon their own demesne lands, there to be folded for the improvement of the ground, which liberty was called by the name of the tath (Spelman).

Tattooing. It is an offence punishable by fine on summary conviction to tattoo a person under the age of eighteen years except for medical reasons. It is a defence to show that there was reasonable cause to believe that the person tattooed was of or over the age of eighteen (Tattooing of Minors Act, 1969).

Tau, a cross (Selden).

Tauri liberi libertas, the liberty of a free bull; a common bull, because he was free to all the tenants within such a manor, liberty, etc. See BULL.

Tautology, describing the same thing twice in one sentence in equivalent terms; a fault in rhetoric. It differs from repetition or iteration, which is repeating the same sentence in the same or equivalent terms: the latter is sometimes either excusable or necessary in an argument or address; the former (tautology) never.

While there is a presumption against tautology in an Act of Parliament, in a complicated Act the presumption is not strong (*Philipson-Stow* v. *I.R.C.* [1961] A.C. 727, *per* Lord Reid).

Tavole Amalfitane, the laws of Amalfi (*q.v.*).

Tax [Wel. *tâsq*; Fr., Dut. *taxe*], an impost; a tribute imposed on the subject; an excise; tallage.

In public law, taxation signifies the system of raising money for public purposes by compelling the payment by individuals of sums of money called taxes.

Some general principles of taxation have been said to be:

(1) The subjects of every State ought to contribute to the support of the Government as nearly as possible in proportion to their respective abilities; that is, in proportion to the revenue which they respectively enjoy under the protection of the State. In the observation or neglect of this maxim consists what is called the equality or inequality of taxation.

(2) The tax which each individual is bound to pay ought to be certain and not arbitrary. The time, manner and quality of the payment ought to be clear and plain to the contributor, and to every other person.

(3) Every tax ought to be levied at the time, or in the manner, in which it is most likely to be convenient for the contributor to pay it.

(4) Every tax ought to be so contrived as both to take out and keep out of the pockets of the people as little as possible over and above what it brings into the public treasury of the State.

Taxes are either direct or indirect. A direct tax is one which is demanded from the very persons who are intended or desired to pay it. Indirect taxes are those which are demanded from one person, in the expectation and intention that he shall indemnify himself at the expense of another, such as the excise or customs. Taxes may be laid on any one of the three sources of income (rent, profits, or wages); or a uniform tax on all of them (5 Smith, Wealth of Nat., c. 2; 5 Mill, Pol.Econ., cc. 2, 3).

As to collection of tax, see COMMISSIONERS OF INLAND REVENUE; COMMISSIONERS OF CUSTOMS AND EXCISE. As to the collection of taxes for a limited period under the authority of a mere resolution of the House of Commons, see HOUSE OF COMMONS.

Taxation is of two kinds. Some taxes are imposed on persons generally, without reference to locality, to raise money for the public expenses of the country; other taxes are imposed on persons residing, or owning or occupying property, within a certain district, to raise money for the public expenses of that district. Taxes of the first class are sometimes called imperial, being required for the *imperium* or supreme government and sometimes parliamentary, because their amount is fixed by Parliament. Taxes of the second class are called local, parochial, municipal, etc., to denote that they are assessed and levied by local authorities. More often still they are called rates, and the term "taxes" is confined to imperial taxes. See RATE.

Imperial or parliamentary taxes include customs and excise duties, stamp duties, land tax, and income tax.

See CAPITAL GAINS TAX; CAPITAL TRANSFER TAX; CUSTOMS; DEATH

DUTIES; ESTATE DUTY; EXCISE; INCOME TAX; VALUE ADDED TAX.

See Dowell, *History of Taxation*.

Taxatio ecclesiastica, the valuation of ecclesiastical benefices made through every diocese in England, on occasion of Pope Innocent IV granting to Henry III the tenth of all spirituals for three years. This taxation was first made by Walter, Bishop of Norwich, delegated by the Pope to this office in 1253, and hence called *taxatio Norwicencis*. It was also called Pope Innocent's *valor*.

Taxation of costs, the mode by which certain officers of the various courts allow or disallow the sums claimed by the one party in an action from the other or by solicitors from their clients. In the Supreme Court taxation is carried out by taxing masters, registrars of the principal registry of the Family Division and the Admiralty Registrar (R.S.C., Ord. 62, r. 12). A principal clerk of the Supreme Court (Taxing Office) may be authorised to tax costs the taxation of which is within the powers of a taxing master (r. 13). One taxing officer may act for another (r. 15). For practice see Practice Note, June 4, 1974 [1974] C.L.Y. 2982, and Practice Direction, July 26, 1976 [1976] 8 C.L. 36.

In the County Court taxation of costs is a function of the registrar (C.C.R., Ord. 47, r. 1).

Taxing masters were first appointed by the statute 1842, 5 & 6 Vict. c. 103, which abolished the Six Clerks (*q.v.*). They are now appointed by the Lord Chancellor with the concurrence of the Minister for the Civil Service as to numbers and salaries (Courts Act, 1971, s. 26).

Taxation in an action, matter or other judicial proceeding, takes place where costs are awarded to a party and made payable either—(i) by his opponent, or (ii) out of a trust fund or the estate of a deceased person, etc. (R.S.C., Ord. 62, r. 28). In the former case, the taxation is optional, that is, the person who is ordered to pay the costs is entitled to have them taxed, but he may pay them without taxation if he likes: in the latter case, the taxation is generally compulsory, that is, the costs must be taxed for the protection of the persons interested in the fund or estate, unless they are all *sui juris* and dispense with taxation. Taxation of the latter kind appears to occur only in Chancery and probate actions.

When a party has reason to complain of the manner in which the master (or other officer) has taxed the costs, he may carry in objections before the master (or other officer), showing the items objected to, and apply to the master to review his taxation (Ord. 62, r. 33). If the objecting party is dissatisfied with the decision of the master, he may apply to a judge at chambers for an order to review the taxation, and the judge then decides whether the objection is well founded (r. 35). There is no further appeal except by leave (*Re Jerome* [1907] 2 Ch. 145).

As to the stage of proceedings at which costs are dealt with see Ord. 62, r. 4.

Taxation as between solicitor and client, which may be had whether the business is transacted in court or not, is only obtained upon the application of the party chargeable; until the expiration of a month from the delivery of a signed bill of costs the solicitor is disabled from suing the client upon such bill. See SOLICITORS.

See COSTS; HIGHER AND LOWER SCALE.

Taxatores. See AFFEERORS.

Taxers. From the foundation of the University of Cambridge until well into the nineteenth century there were two university officers called taxers, who fixed the rents of students' lodgings and the prices of commodities, and kept the standards of weights and measures.

Taximeter. By the London Cab and Stage Carriage Act, 1907, s. 6, the expression " taximeter " means any appliance for measuring the time or distance for which a cab is used, or for measuring both time and distance, which is for the time being approved for the purpose by or on behalf of the Home Secretary.

The relationship between a taxi-cab driver and the company owning the taxi-cabs is not usually that of master and servant but bailor and bailee (*Doggett* v. *Waterloo Taxi-Cab Co.* [1910] 2 K.B. 336). See CAB; HACKNEY CARRIAGES.

Taxing masters. See TAXATION OF COSTS.

Taxing officer. Each House of Parliament has a taxing officer, whose duty it is to tax the costs incurred by the promoters or opponents of private bills.

Taylor's (Michael Angelo) Act. See MICHAEL ANGELO TAYLOR'S ACT.

Tea. As to the standards of measurement etc., on the sale of tea, see the Weights and Measures Act, 1963, s. 21, Sch. 4 Pt. VIII. Tea was first taxed by the statute 1660, 12 Car. 2, c. 23, as a beverage at 8d. a gallon, and afterwards in the leaf at 5s. per lb. by the statute 1688, 1 W. & M. sess. 2, c. 6. Tea was charged with protective duties under the Import Duties Act, 1958, instead of revenue duties (Finance Act, 1962, ss. 3, 34 (7), Sch. 11 Pt. II; European Communities Act, 1972, s. 4, Sch. 3 Pt. II.

Teacher. See SCHOOLMASTER.

Team, or **Theame** [Sax. *tyman*, to teem or bring forth], a privilege granted by royal charter to a lord of a manor, for the having, restraining, and judging of bondmen and villeins, with their children, goods, and chattels, etc. (5 Glan. c. 2).

Teamster, a waggoner who carries goods for hire.

Technology, Ministry of. This ministry was created in 1964; see the Ministers of the Crown Act, 1964, s. 1, Sch. 1. The functions of the Ministers were transferred to the Secretaries of State for Trade and Industry and the title of the minister was changed to the Minister of Aviation Supply (S.I. 1970 No. 1537). The Ministry of Aviation Supply was dissolved by S.I. 1971 No. 719 and its functions transferred to the Secretary of State for Energy (S.I. 1974 No. 692).

Teding-penny, Tething-penny, Tithing-penny, a small duty to the sheriff from each tithing, towards the charge of keeping courts, etc., from which some of the religious houses were exempted by royal charter. See TITHING PENNY.

Teinland, thaneland (*q.v.*).

Telegraphiae, written evidence of things past (Blount).

Telecommunications. The Post Office has a monopoly of telecommunication in the British Islands, that is the conveyance through the agency of electric, magnetic, electro-magnetic, electro-chemical or electro-mechanical energy of (a) speech, music and other sounds, (b) visual images (c) signals imparting any matter otherwise than in the form of sound or visual images, and signals serving for the actuation or control of machinery or other apparatus. (Post Office Act, 1969, s. 24). Excepted from the monopoly are certain general classes of acts (s. 25) or transmissions by a broadcasting authority (s. 26) or things done under a licence granted by the Post Office (s. 27). Sending, by means of a public telecommunication service, a message or other matter that is grossly offensive or of an indecent, obscene or menacing character is an offence punishable on summary conviction by fine of £50. So also is the sending for the purpose of causing annoyance, inconvenience or needless anxiety a false message, so also is the persistent use of public telecommunication services to cause annoyance, inconvenience or needless anxiety (Post Office Act, 1969, s. 78). Programme distribution systems are required to be licensed by the Secretary of State for Industry (ss. 89, 90; S.I. 1974 No. 691).

Telegraphs. A telegraph means a wire or wires used for the purposes of telegraphic communication, with any casing, coating, tube, or pipe enclosing the same, and any apparatus connected therewith for the purpose of telegraphic communication (Telegraph Act, 1863, s. 3). This definition includes the telephone.

The rights and liabilities under the Telegraph Acts are vested in the Post Office by the Post Office Act, 1969, s. 21 (1). The "Telegraph Acts" for this purpose are the Telegraph Act, 1863, 1868, 1870 and 1878, the Telegraph (Isle of Man) Act, 1889, the Telegraph Acts, 1892, 1899, the Telegraph (Construction) Act, 1908, the Telegraph (Arbitration) Act, 1909, and the Telegraph (Construction) Acts, 1911 and 1916.

The functions under the Wireless Telegraphy Acts, 1949 and 1967, and the Commonwealth Telegraphy Act, 1949, are vested in the Secretary of State for Industry (Post Office Act, 1969, ss. 3, 4; S.I. 1974 No. 691). The Telegraph Act, 1863, ss. 9, 21, 23, the Telegraph Act, 1892, s. 5 (2) (*b*) and the Telegraph (Construction) Act, 1908, s. 2 are amended by S.I. 1974 No. 595, art. 3.

See WIRELESS TELEGRAPHY.

Telephone. See TELECOMMUNICATIONS.

Telephone tappings. There is no rule of

public policy excluding evidence obtained by private telephone tappings. Official assurances given by the Crown relate only to action by the police or the security services (*R.* v. *Senat* (1968) 52 Cr.App.R. 282). See also *R.* v. *Keeton* (1970) 54 Cr.App.R. 267 (evidence of police officer).

Television. The definition of wireless telegraphy (*q.v.*) in the Wireless Telegraphy Act, 1949, s. 19 (1), includes television.

The functions of the Postmaster-General under the Wireless Telegraphy Acts, 1949 and 1967, were transferred by the Post Office Act, 1969, s. 3, to the Minister of Posts and Telecommunications (*q.v.*) and thence to the Secretary of State for Industry (S.I. 1974 No. 691).

Television and local sound broadcasting services, other than those of the British Broadcasting Corporation, are a function of the Independent Broadcasting Authority (formerly the Independent Television Authority). See the Independent Broadcasting Authority Acts, 1973 and 1974 (Nos. 1 and 2).

As to the rating of hereditaments occupied for carrying on the diffusion by wire of sound or television programmes, see the Local Government Act, 1974, s. 19, Sch. 3, para. 9.

The court will take judicial notice of the fact that the reception of television has become a very common feature of domestic life (*Bridlington Relay* v. *Yorkshire Electricity Board* [1965] Ch. 436). A television interview is published wherever the broadcast is seen (*Gorton* v. *Australian Broadcasting Commission* (1974) 22 F.L.R. 181).

For the effect of the E.E.C. Treaty see *Italy* v. *Sacchi* (No. 155/73) [1974] 2 C.M.L.R. 177.

Telex, a telegraphic service whereby written messages can be sent directly between sender and recipient (Telex Regulations, 1965 (No. 1192) amended by S.I. 1968 No. 1258). The place where a contract is made by means of a telex communication is the place where the offeror receives the notification of the acceptance by the offeree (*Entores* v. *Miles Far East Corporation* [1955] 2 Q.B. 327).

Teller, Tallier, one who keeps a tally (*q.v.*); one who numbers; a numberer; a cashier in a bank. In the Exchequer there were four officers known as tellers, who received all moneys due to the king. They, with the auditor (*q.v.*) and the Clerk of the Pells, were abolished by the statute 1834, 4 & 5 Will. 4, c. 15, s. 1.

In Parliament two tellers are appointed to count the votes on a division in either House of Parliament.

Telligraph, Telligraphum [Lat. *tellus*, land; Gk. γράφω, to write], an Anglo-Saxon charter of land; a terrier (*q.v.*) (1 Reeves Hist.Eng.Law, c. 1, p. 10).

Tellworc, that labour which a tenant was bound to do for his lord, for a certain number of days.

Tementale, or **Tenementale,** a tax of two shillings upon every ploughland; a decennary (*q.v.*).

Temple, two Inns of Court, thus called because anciently the dwelling-place of the Knights-Templars. On the suppression of that Order, they were purchased by some professors of the common law, and converted into *hospitia*, or inns of court. They are called the Inner and Middle Temple, in relation to Essex House, which was also a part of the House of the Templars, and called the Outer Temple, because situated without Temple-bar. The rating authority for the Inner Temple is the Sub-Treasurer, for the Middle Temple, the Under-Treasurer (General Rate Act, 1967, s. 1). As to the making of the general rate see ss. 2 (5), 3. (Encyc. Londin.; Addison, *History of the Knights Templars*; Bellot, *Inner and Middle Temple*). See INNS OF COURT; MASTER OF THE TEMPLE.

Temporal lords, the peers of the realm; the bishops are not in strictness held to be peers, but merely lords of Parliament.

Temporalities, or **Temporals,** secular possessions, as distinguished from ecclesiastical rights; such revenues, lands, and tenements as archbishops and bishops have had annexed to their sees by the kings and others, from time to time, as they are lords of Parliament.

The temporalities of a bishop are all such things as he has by livery from the Crown, as castles, manors, lands, tenements, tithes, etc. During a vacancy of a bishopric the Crown has the custody of the temporalities, and (nominally) the rents and profits thereof. See GUARDIAN OF THE SPIRITUALITIES.

Temporality, the laity; secular people.

Temporary employer. Where injury is caused by the negligence of a servant who is, with the consent of his general employer, doing work for a temporary employer, the general employer is prima facie responsible. To shift the responsibility on to the shoulders of the temporary employer, the general employer must prove that the temporary employer has authority to direct, or to delegate to the servant, the manner in which the work is to be done (*Mersey Dock and Harbour Board* v. *Coggins and Griffiths (Liverpool)* [1947] A.C. 1).

Temporary estate duty, a duty of 1 per cent. on any estate or succession exceeding £100, which was made payable, in addition to probate duty (*q.v.*) or succession duty (*q.v.*), by the Customs and Inland Revenue Act, 1889, ss. 5–7. The duty was not payable in respect of property on which estate duty (*q.v.*) was payable (Finance Act, 1894, s. 1, Sch. 1 para. 1).

Temporary housing accommodation. Provision for temporary housing accommodation was made by the Housing (Temporary Accommodation) Acts, 1944 and 1945, the Housing Repairs and Rents Act, 1954, ss. 2, 19, and the Housing Act, 1957, s. 48.

Temptatio, or **Tentatio,** a trial or proof.

Tempus est edax rerum (12 Co.Rep. 5). (Time is a devourer of things.) If all the witnesses to a conveyance are dead, then violent presumption, which stands for a proof, is continual and quiet possession (*Grounds of Law,* 320). See EX DIUTURNITATE, ETC.

Tempus pessonis, mast-time in the forest, which is about Michaelmas to St. Martin's Day, September 29 to November 11 (Cowel).

Tempus semestre, half a year, and not six lunar months (Statute of Westminster II, 1285, c. 5).

Ten Hours Act, the statute 1847, 10 & 11 Vict. c. 29, which first limited the time of work for women and children in mills and factories; it was repealed by the Factory and Workshop Act, 1878. See FACTORIES.

Tena, a coif worn by ecclesiastics.

Tenancy [Law Lat. *tenentia*], the condition of a tenant; the temporary possession of what belongs to another by his consent.

Tenancy is the relation of a tenant to the land which he holds. Hence it signifies the estate of a tenant, as in the expressions "joint tenancy," "tenancy in common," and also the term or interest of a tenant for years or at will, as when we say that a tenant must remove his fixtures (*q.v.*) during his tenancy. In old writers, "tenancy" sometimes denotes the land itself: "the tenant may plead that the tenancy is *extra feudum* of him" (Co.Litt. 1b). See TENANT; TENURE.

Tenancy in common. Legal estates in undivided shares in land were abolished by the Law of Property Act, 1925, s. 1, which reduced the interest of tenants in common to that of *cestuis que trust* under a trust for sale of land. This interest is created when several persons have several distinct interests, either of the same or of a different quantity, in any subject of property, in equal or unequal shares, and either by the same act or by several acts, and by several titles, and not a joint title. A tenancy in common will, as a rule, be construed to exist wherever the instrument creating it indicates that the property is to be held in shares, equally, or in moieties, or the nature of the transaction is such as to preclude the intention of survivorship such as an acquisition of land by partners for the purposes of their business.

A tenancy in common differs from a joint tenancy in that joint tenants have one interest in the whole, and no interest in any particular part. Tenants in common have several and distinct interests in their respective parts which may be in unequal shares and for interests of unequal duration.

Tenants in common hold by unity of possession, because neither of them knows his own severalty, and therefore they all occupy promiscuously. This is the only unity belonging to the interest; for since the tenants may hold different kinds of interest, so there exists no necessary unity of interest, and there is no unity of title, for they may claim from different sources; also the interest may vest in each tenant at different times. There being no entirety of interest among tenants in common, each is seised of a distinct though undivided share ; they hold neither *per my* nor *per tout* (see PER MY ET PER TOUT) and consequently the *jus accrescendi* does not apply to them. This interest was subject to curtesy and dower. A tenancy in common may be dissolved by a voluntary deed of partition, or by the union of all the titles and interests in one tenant, by grant, devise, surrender, or otherwise, which reduces the whole estate to a severalty, or by compulsory partition.

Tenants in common are jointly absolutely entitled as against the trustees within s. 22 (5) of the Finance Act, 1965 (*Kidson* v. *MacDonald* [1974] 1 All E.R. 849).

See COPARCENARY ; ESTATE ; JOINT TENANCY ; PARTITION ; PRESCRIPTION ; SEVERALTY ; UNDIVIDED SHARES and UNITY OF POSSESSION.

Tenancy, Joint. See JOINT TENANCY.

Tenant, a person holding under an agreement for a lease ; a lessee ; one who holds land of any one. Strictly speaking, a tenant is a person who holds land ; but the term is also applied by analogy to personalty : thus we speak of a person being tenant for life or tenant in common of stock.

In its proper use, " tenant " connotes either estate or tenure. Every person who has an estate in land is a tenant ; thus, a person who has an estate in fee simple is a tenant in fee simple, and a person who has an interest in joint tenancy is a joint tenant. Again, every tenant holds the land by tenure, because all the lands and tenements in England in the hands of subjects are held mediately or immediately of the king (Co.Litt. 1a).

See LANDLORD AND TENANT ; LEASE ; STATUTORY TENANT ; TENURE ; TERM.

Tenant at sufferance, a person who has originally come into possession of land by a lawful title, and holds such possession after his title has determined, as where a tenant *pur autre vie* continues in possession after the death of the *cestui que vie*, or where a tenant for years holds over at the end of the term (Co.Litt. 57b).

A tenancy at sufferance is a chattel interest. See CHATTELS ; ESTATE.

At common law, a tenant at sufferance is not a trespasser until the lessor or person entitled to the possession enters on the land, because his continuance in possession is imputed to the laches of the lessor in not entering at once ; but this doctrine has been modified by statute. See HOLDING OVER ; SUFFERANCE, TENANCY AT.

Tenant at will, where lands or tenements are let by one man to another, to have and to hold to him at the will of the lessor, by force of which lease the lessee is in possession. In this case the lessee is called tenant at will, because he has no certain or sure estate, for the lessor may put him out at what time it pleases him (Litt. 68). See WILL, TENANCY AT.

Similarly the tenant may leave when he likes. He has a right to emblements (*q.v.*), and to remove his goods, etc., if he is turned out by the landlord. He is liable for voluntary waste.

A tenancy at will may be created by parol (if followed by entry) or by deed. It may be determined not only by the will of either party, but also if the tenant should assign his estate to another, or if he should commit waste (Co.Litt. 57a).

A lease at an annual rent, made generally without expressly stating it to be at will, and without limiting any certain period, is not a lease at will, but a lease from year to year. See TENANT FROM YEAR TO YEAR.

A purchaser of land is sometimes let into possession pending completion of the purchase as tenant at will, on payment of interest on the unpaid balance of the purchase-money (*Pearlberg* v. *May* [1951] Ch. 699).

A tenancy at will is a chattel interest in land. See CHATTELS ; ESTATE.

A tenancy at will is not a tenancy within the protection of the Landlord and Tenant Act, 1954 (*Wheeler* v. *Mercer* [1957] A.C. 416).

The court will be reluctant to infer the grant of a tenancy where no rent is paid and a domestic relationship exists (*Heslop* v. *Burns* [1974] 1 W.L.R. 1241).

Copyholds were in theory tenancies at will. See COPYHOLD ; SURRENDER OF COPYHOLDS.

Tenant by copy of court roll, a tenant by copy, a copyholder. See COPYHOLD.

TENANT

Tenant by the curtesy. See CURTESY.

Tenant for life, a person who is entitled to land or tenements either for the term of his own life or for that of another person. In the latter case he is called tenant *pur autre vie,* and the person for whose life the land is held is called the *cestui que vie* (Co.Litt. 41b). See OCCUPANCY.

A life interest may be created by deed or by will. At the present day life interests are principally created by settlements and wills: as where property is given to a man for his life, and after his death to his children. See ASSIGNMENT; HEIR; SURRENDER.

An ordinary tenant for life is not allowed to commit waste, but if his interest is given to him without impeachment of waste he may cut timber and open mines, etc., so long as he does not commit equitable waste. See EMBLEMENTS; IMPROVEMENT OF LAND SETTLED LAND; WASTE.

Where a person has a life interest in chattels (*e.g.* in a sum of stock), he is sometimes called a tenant for life.

Tenant for years, a person to whom land is let for any period. A tenant for years is liable for waste (*q.v.*). See FIXTURES; INTERESSE TERMINI; LANDLORD AND TENANT; LEASES; TERM.

Tenant from year to year, a tenant of land whose tenancy can only be determined by a notice to quit expiring at that period of the year at which it commenced. In the case of ordinary tenancies from year to year a six months' notice to quit is required. Thus, if a house is held on a tenancy from year to year, beginning at midsummer, and either the landlord or the tenant wishes to determine it, he must, at or before Christmas, give notice to the other to quit at midsummer following.

A tenancy of an agricultural holding (*q.v.*) can only be determined by a year's notice to quit. See NOTICE TO QUIT.

Whenever one person holds land of another, and there is no express limitation or agreement as to the term for which it is to be held, then, if the rent is a yearly rent even though payable with reference to divisions of the year (*e.g.*, quarterly), the tenancy is deemed to be a tenancy from year to year. But if the rent is calculated on a quarterly, monthly or weekly basis, the tenancy will be a quarterly, monthly or weekly tenancy. See TENANT AT WILL.

Tenant in fee. See FEE.

Tenant in tail. See TAIL.

Tenant in tail after possibility of issue extinct. Where tenements are given to a man and his wife in special tail and one of them dies without issue, the survivor is tenant in tail after possibility of issue extinct, because there is no possibility of issue being born capable of inheriting the estate (Litt. 3b).

So if tenements are given to a man and the heirs of his body by his present wife, and the wife dies without issue, then the husband is tenant in tail after possibility of issue extinct, because no issue by another wife could inherit the estate tail. Such a tenant is, in effect, only a tenant for his own life, for he cannot bar the entail (Fines and Recoveries Act, 1833, s. 18); and on his death the land will pass to the person next entitled in remainder or reversion. The tenancy has, however, some of the privileges of an entailed interest, *e.g.*, the tenant is not punishable for waste (Co.Litt. 27b). See TAIL AFTER POSSIBILITY, etc.

Tenant in tail ex provisione viri. A woman was said to be tenant in tail *ex provisione viri* where she had an estate tail, either alone or jointly with her husband, in any lands or hereditaments inherited or purchased by her husband, or given to the husband and herself by any of the ancestors of the husband. Such a tenant in tail could not bar the entail after the death of the husband, except with the consent of the issue in tail: see the statutes 1495, 11 Hen. 7, c. 20, and 1540, 32 Hen. 8, c. 36. This kind of estate no longer exists (Fines and Recoveries Act, 1833, s. 16).

Tenant to the praecipe. Before the Fines and Recoveries Act, 1833, if land was conveyed to a person for life with remainder to another in tail, the tenant in tail in remainder was unable to bar the entail without the concurrence of the tenant for life, because a common recovery could be suffered only by the person seised of the land. In such a case, if the tenant for life wished to concur in barring the entail, he usually conveyed

1750

his life estate to some other person in order that the praecipe in the recovery might be issued against the latter, who was therefore called the tenant to the praecipe. See PRAECIPE; RECOVERY.

Tenant-right. In agricultural districts, tenant-right signifies the right of a tenant to claim a beneficial interest in the land, notwithstanding the expiration of his tenancy. Different usages prevailed in different counties and districts, conferring on an outgoing agricultural tenant a claim to remuneration for various operations of husbandry, from reaping the advantage of which he was prevented by the termination of his tenancy. Thus, by the Lincolnshire tenant-right custom, if a tenant spread chalk or bones upon the land, the money expended in this operation was divided by a certain number of years (three to seven); and if the tenant quitted before the expiration of that period, he received from the landlord a part of his outlay, proportionate to the number of years of the period remaining unexpired. There was an implied contract by the landlord to pay this (*Faviell* v. *Gaskoin* (1852) 7 Ex. 273), and a custom throwing liability on the incoming tenant was bad (*Bradburn* v. *Foley* (1878) 3 C.P.D. 129), though as a matter of fact and for convenience the incoming tenant generally paid the compensation by agreement with the landlord. The rules regarding tenant-right are now statutory: as to the effect of custom, see the Agricultural Holdings Act, 1948, ss. 63, 64, 101; Agriculture Act, 1958, Sch. 1 Pt. I para. 16; Agriculture (Miscellaneous Provisions) Act, 1968, s. 10 (5). See CUSTOM.

Tenant-right estates meant a peculiar kind of customary freeholds, found in the north of England. Although they had incidents not properly belonging to copyhold tenure, and had some which savoured more of military tenure by knight's service, and differed from copyhold tenure in not being held at the will of the lord and in not being alienable by surrender and admittance, these customary tenant-right estates were not freehold, but copyhold (Elton 6). See CUSTOMARY FREEHOLDS.

Tenants by the verge. Such tenants were of the same nature as copyholders. The reason they were called tenants by the verge was that when they surrendered their tenements into the hands of their lord to the use of another they had a little rod by custom in their hands which they delivered to the steward or bailiff, and the steward or bailiff according to the custom delivered to him that took the land the same rod, or another rod, in the name of seisin (Litt. 78). See SURRENDER.

Tenants in common with cross remainders in tail, tenants in common each of whom takes his or her equitable share in tail. On failure of his or her issue that share falls to the remaining grantees or devisees as tenants in common in tail. On failure of issue of any of the remaining grantees or devisees, that share goes to the then remaining tenants in common in tail in the same way and so on until only one line of the original grantees or devisees is left. In wills, cross remainders in tail are generally implied if there is a gift to a class as tenants in common in tail with a gift over, but not if the grant is by deed.

Tende, to tender or offer (Old Nat.Br. 123).

Tender, an offer by a debtor to his creditor of the amount of the debt. The offer must be in money, which must be actually produced to the creditor, unless by words or acts he waives production: therefore, a mere statement by the debtor that he has the money in his possession ready for payment is not sufficient, even if the creditor says he will not receive it. But if the debtor brings the money in purses or bags, it is not necessary to show or count it, because that is "the usual manner to carry money in, and then it is the part of the party that is to receive it to put it out and tell it" (Co.Litt. 208a).

The offer must also be unconditional. It need not be made by the debtor personally to the creditor personally; it may be made through an authorised agent, and a tender to one of several joint creditors is sufficient. A tender under protest is good so long as no condition is imposed (*Greenwood* v. *Sutcliffe* [1892] 1 Ch. 1). A cheque paid by a banker is evidence of receipt by the payee although undorsed (Cheques Act, 1957, s. 3). See RECEIPT.

If a debtor has made a tender, and continues ready to pay, he is exonerated from liability for the non-payment, but the debt is not discharged. Therefore if he is sued he should plead the tender, and also allege that he always was and still is ready to pay the debt, and he must pay the money into court (R.S.C., Ord. 18, r. 16; Ord. 22, r. 1). If he can maintain the defence of tender and readiness to pay, he will be entitled to an order for his costs (R.S.C., Ord. 62, r. 5). If part only of the sum due is tendered in satisfaction of an entire claim, the tender will be bad and therefore will be no defence (*Read's Trustee* v. *Smith* [1951] Ch. 439).

By the Coinage Act, 1971, s. 2, it is provided that a tender of payment of money, if made in coins issued by the Mint in accordance with the provisions of that Act, and not called in (and in the case of gold coins, not become materially diminished in weight), shall be legal tender, in the case of gold coins for the payment of any amount, in the case of coins of cupro-nickel or silver of denominations of more than 10 new pence for the payment of any amount not exceeding £10, in the case of coins of cupro-nickel or silver of denominations of not more than 10 new pence for the payment of any amount not exceeding £5 ; in the case of bronze coins, for payment of any amount not exceeding 20 new pence ; in the case of other coins if made current by proclamation, for the payment of any amount not exceeding that specified in the proclamation.

Bank of England notes are legal tender for payment of any amount. See CURRENCY.

The term " tender " is also applied to goods when they are offered to a person in performance of a contract for their delivery.

Tender of amends. See AMENDS, ETC.

Tender of issue, joinder of issue.

Tenel le roy, the abode for the time being of the king: see the statute 1390, 13 Ric. 2, c. 3.

Tenement [Lat. *tenere*, to hold], that which may be held ; that which is the subject of tenure (*q.v.*). The term includes not only all corporeal hereditaments, but also all incorporeal hereditaments issuing as rents, estovers, commons, or other profits whatsoever granted out of land,

or uses, offices or dignities concerning land (Co.Litt. 19b, 20a).

Liberum tenementum, frank tenement, or freehold, is applicable not only to lands and other solid objects, but also to offices, rents, commons, advowsons, franchises, peerages, etc. (2 Bl.Comm. 16).

A personal hereditament, such as an annuity granted to a man and his heirs, is not a tenement. See ENTAIL ; HEREDITAMENT ; LAND.

" Tenement " also means a house: see, *e.g.,* the Towns Improvement Clauses Act, 1847, s. 167. See MESSUAGE.

Local authorities sometimes refer to separately rated parts of houses or flats as tenements.

As to " dominant " and " servient " tenements, see EASEMENT.

Tenement factory, premises where mechanical power from any prime mover within the close or curtilage of the premises is distributed for use in manufacturing processes to different parts of the same premises occupied by different persons in such manner that those parts constitute in law separate factories (Factories Act, 1961, ss. 121, 176).

Tenementary lands, the outlying parts of manors granted by thanes in the Saxon period to tenants at arbitrary rents. They seem to have been farms let to tenants as distinguished from what would now be called the home-farm (Spelman).

Tenementis legatis, a writ which lay for the determination of disputes as to wills of lands and tenements in the City of London and other corporate towns (Reg. Brev. 244).

Tenendas. In ancient charters granting lands this was the clause (commencing with the words *tenendas praedictas*) which set out the tenure upon which the lands were to be held. It corresponded to the *tenendum* of a deed.

Tenendum [Lat. to be held], the clause in a conveyance which indicated the tenure by which the grantee was to hold the land of the grantor—*tenendum de me et haeredibus meis sibi et haeredibus suis, per servitium,* etc. When the statute *Quia Emptores,* 1289, abolished subinfeudation, the clause was altered to indicate that the grantee was to hold of the superior lords

—*tenendum de capitalibus dominis*; but now it simply says that the land is to be held by the grantee, without mentioning of whom (Shep.Touch. 79). See HABENDUM ; QUIA EMPTORES ; TENURE.

Tenentibus in assisa non onerandis. The full title of this writ was *tenentibus in assisa non onerandis de damnis quamdiu disseisitores habeant unde damna levari possunt*, which indicates that where one had disseised another and then put a tenant into possession, the writ lay for the tenant in order to prevent his being sued by the person disseised as long as the disseisor had chattels upon which the person disseised could levy (Reg.Brev. 214).

Tenheded, or **Tienheofed** [Sax.], a dean.

Tenmentale, or **Tenmantale,** the number of ten men, which number, in the time of the Saxons, was called a decennary, and ten decennaries made a hundred ; also a duty or tribute paid to the Crown, consisting of two shillings for each ploughland (Encyc.Londin.).

It was stated in a law of Edward the Confessor to have been used in Yorkshire as meaning frithborgh (*q.v.*), and also as meaning the tithing (*q.v.*). It was also used in northern England during the twelfth and thirteenth centuries as an equivalent for carucage (*q.v.*).

Tenne, tawny, orange, or brusk; orange colour.

In engravings it should be represented by lines in bend sinister crossed by others barways. Heralds who blazon by the names of the heavenly bodies call it dragon's head, and those who employ jewels, jacinth. It is one of the colours called stainand.

Tennis. This game, which was declared illegal by the statute 1541, 33 Hen. 8, c. 9, was legalised by the Gaming Act, 1845, s. 1.

A lawn tennis club is within the definition of " business " in the Landlord and Tenant Act, 1954, s. 23 (2), and entitled to security of tenure under that Act (*Addiscombe Garden Estates* v. *Crabbe* [1958] 1 Q.B. 513).

Tenor; Tenour. The tenor of a document means, in ordinary conversation, its purport and effect, as opposed to the exact words of it. In law, in its correct usage, the reverse is the case, and tenor means the exact words of the document.

When the appointment of an executor is not express but only constructive, upon the construction of the will, he is called an executor according to the tenor (*In b. Lush* (1887) 13 P.D. 20). See EXECUTOR.

As to bills of exchange, see the Bills of Exchange Act, 1882, s. 88.

Tenor est pactio contra communem feudi naturam ac rationem in contractu interposita (Wright, Ten., 2nd ed., 21). (Tenure is a compact contrary to the common nature of the fee, which is introduced into the contract.)

Tenor est qui legem dat feudo (Craig, Jus.Feud., 3rd ed., 66). (It is the tenor of the feudal grant which regulates it.) See CUJUS EST, ETC. ; MODUS LEGEM, ETC.

Tenore praesentium, by the tenor of these presents ; *i.e.*, the matter contained therein, or rather the intent and meaning thereof (Cowel).

Tenores indictamenti mittendo, a writ by which an indictment was removed into the Queen's Bench from another court (Reg.Brev. 69). See CERTIORARI.

Tenseriae, a sort of ancient tax or military contribution.

Tentates panis, the assay (*q.v.*) of bread (Blount).

Tenterden's Acts, the Statute of Frauds Amendment Act, 1828, and the Prescription Act, 1832. The former supplemented the Statute of Frauds, 1677, by requiring writing for the following promises and engagements: an acknowledgment of a statute-barred debt (see ACKNOWLEDGMENT), a promise to pay a debt incurred, or a ratification of a contract made, during infancy (see INFANT), an executory contract for the sale of goods (see SALE of GOODS ACT), and a representation as to a person's character made to enable him to obtain money or goods upon credit.

Tenths [Lat. *decimae*], tithes ; also the tenth part of the annual value of every spiritual preferment, paid in early times to the Pope, transferred from the Pope to the Crown by the statute 1534, 26 Hen. 8, c. 3, and from the Crown, for the augmentation of small livings, to the Church by the statute 1703, 2 & 3 Anne, c. 20. See BOUNTY OF QUEEN ANNE ; FIRST FRUITS.

TENTHS

Tenths are the tenth part of the annual profits of an ecclesiastical benefice according to the valuation contained in the *valor beneficiorum* or king's books, compiled in Henry VIII's reign. By Order in Council made pursuant to Queen Anne's Bounty Act, 1838, s. 19, tenths were commuted for an annual payment of 17s. 6d. on each £100 of the clear annual value of a living. Benefices of an annual value not exceeding £50 had been freed from tenths in Elizabeth I's reign.

Ecclesiastical tenths must not be confounded with the tax consisting of one-tenth of every man's whole personal property, formerly levied by the Crown under the name of tenths. As in the case of fifteenths (*q.v.*) the amount payable was fixed in the reign of Edward III: so that when this tax disappeared in the reign of James I it was not anything like a tenth of the national personalty.

Tents. See CAMPING.

Tenure. Tenure in its general sense is a mode of holding or occupying: thus we speak of the tenure of an office, meaning the manner in which it is held, especially with regard to time (tenure for life, tenure during good behaviour), and of tenure of land in the sense of occupation or tenancy, especially with reference to cultivation and questions of political economy, *e.g.*, tenure by peasant proprietors, cottiers, etc.

In its more technical sense, tenure signifies the mode in which all land in England is theoretically owned and occupied. The rule is that only the Crown can be the absolute owner of land in England, because all land in the hands of subjects is held of some superior, and mediately or immediately of the Crown; that is, every person who is possessed of land is theoretically merely a tenant and owes obligations in respect of it either to the Crown or to an intermediate lord. The manner of his possession is called tenure, and the extent of his interest is called an estate (*q.v.*). The rule is a relic of the feudal system. See COPYHOLD; ESCHEAT; FEALTY; FEUDAL SYSTEM; HOMAGE; LORD; MANOR; SERVICE; TENANT; TENEMENT.

With reference to the relation between the lord and the tenant, a tenure is either perfect or imperfect. A perfect tenure is

where one person holds land of another, or of the Crown, in fee simple, and this is accordingly subdivided into (a) tenure *in capite* or in chief, which is the tenure existing between the Crown and those who hold land of it directly; and (b) mesne tenure, which is where one subject holds land of another. (See MESNE.) When land is held of a private person merely by reason of his having the seignory of that particular land, the tenure is technically called a tenure in gross, as opposed to the case of land being held of a person in his capacity of owner of a manor, county palatine or the like. Imperfect tenure is that which exists between a tenant of land and a person to whom he has granted a smaller estate than his own, as where a tenant in fee simple creates an estate for years. An imperfect tenure may be created by anyone at the present day, while a perfect tenure can now be created only by the Crown (Co.Litt. 108a; Co.Copyho. 48). See SUBINFEUDATION.

Temporal or lay tenures are those by which land is or used to be held by secular persons. They were of two kinds according as their services were originally free or base. To the former class (frank or freehold tenure) belonged (a) knight's service with its varieties (grand serjeanty, escuage, castle ward and cornage, which are commonly called feudal tenures *par excellence*, and which have been converted into common socage), and (b) free socage with its varieties (petty serjeanty, burgage tenure, borough-English and gavelkind). Base or villein tenures were (a) pure villeinage, and later copyhold and customary freehold tenures; and (b) privileged villeinage or villein socage, from which was derived tenure in ancient demesne. Copyhold ancient demesne and customary freehold were sometimes called customary tenures, because they depended on local custom, and not on the general law.

Ecclesiastical or spiritual tenures were tenure in frankalmoign, and tenure by divine service (*q.v.*).

The only tenures in land now existing with a few unimportant exceptions are free and common socage in fee simple, including enfranchised copyhold which is subject to paramount incidents; and a term of years absolute. The idea of tenure or holding derives from feudalism, which separated the *dominium directum* (the dominion of the soil), which it placed mediately or immediately in the Crown, from the *dominium utile* (the possessory title), the right to use the profits in the soil, designated by the term " seisin," which is the highest interest a subject can acquire (2 Bl.Comm. 59).

As regards the mode in which it was held, land was originally of two kinds, *viz.* (1) allodial (from *los*, signifying lot), over which the owner had entire and irresponsible dominion, which he could dispose of at his own pleasure, or transmit as an inheritance to his children ; the land was also attachable to answer the owner's debts, and could also be made available for commercial enterprise ; such tenure was acquired by the distribution of lands by lot among the Franks ; and (2) feudal (from *od*, possession, or estate, and *feo*, wages, pay), over which the owner had but a conditional dominion, acknowledging a superior lord, upon whose pleasure the tenure precariously depended, and without whose consent nothing could be done. This is the groundwork of the feudal system, which displaced the laws obtaining in this country at the time of the Norman Conquest.

Out of feudalism arose the maxim that all lands in the kingdom were originally granted by the king, and held mediately or immediately of the king, as lord paramount, in consideration of certain services to be rendered by the holder. There was no allodial land in England. Those who held immediately from the king were called tenants *in capite* (in chief), which was the most honourable tenure. This was of two kinds, either *ut de honore*, where the land was held of the king as proprietor of some honour, castle, or manor, or *ut de corona*, where it was held of him in right of the Crown itself. When these tenants granted portions of their lands to inferior persons they were called mesne (middle) lords or barons with regard to such inferior holders, who were styled tenants paravail, the ultimate tenants in possession, because they were supposed to make avail or profit of the land. The lands were called feuds (*feoda*),

either proper, which were purely military, given *militiae gratia* to persons qualified for military service ; or improper, which did not, in point of acquisition, services, and the like, strictly conform to the nature of mere military feuds, such as those which were sold and bartered for any equivalent, or granted free from all circumstances, or in consideration of any certain services.

Knight's service proper, or tenure in chivalry, was the original and most honourable species of tenure created by a determinate quantity of land called a knight's fee. Its extent was twelve ploughlands, that is, as much land as could be reasonably ploughed in one year by twelve ploughs, or, according to other authorities, 800 acres of land (others say 680), and its value in those times was £20 per annum. This tenure was granted by words of pure donation, *dedi et concessi* (I have given and granted) ; transferred by investiture, *i.e.*, by a solemn and public delivery of the very land itself by the lord to a vassal, in the presence of his other vassals ; and perfected by homage and fealty, homage being the acknowledgment of tenure, and fealty the solemn oath made by the vassal of fidelity and attachment to the lord.

The owner of a knight's fee was bound to attend the lord to the wars on horseback, armed as a knight, for forty days in every year, if called upon, and his attendance was his rent or service for the land he held, but the service was usually commuted by payment in the form of escuage or scutage. Among the incidents of this tenure were reliefs or payments upon succession, aids, or contributions to the lord, wardships and marriage of heirs succeeding in infancy and escheat.

Grand serjeanty was another species of tenure which some writers think was superior to knight's service, whereby the tenant was bound, instead of serving the king generally in the wars, to do him some special, certain, and honorary service in person, as to be marshal of his host, or high steward of England, or to carry his banner or his sword, or to be his butler, champion, or other officer at his coronation. In most other respects it was similar to knight's service, only he was not bound to pay aid or escuage ;

and whereas a tenant by knight's service paid £5 for a relief, a tenant by grand serjeanty paid one year's value of his land.

The statute 1660, 12 Car. 2, c. 24, enacted that the Court of Wards and Liveries, and all wardships, liveries, primer seisins and ousterlemains, values, and forfeitures of marriage, by reason of any tenure of the king or others, should be taken away; and that all fines for alienations, tenures by homage, knight's service, and escuage, and also aids for marrying the daughter or knighting the son, and all tenures of the king *in capite*, should also be taken away; and that all sorts of tenures held of the king or others should be turned into free and common socage, save only tenures in frankalmoign, tenures by copy of court roll, and honorary services of grand serjeanty; and that all tenures which should be created in future should be free and common socage.

The other subdivision of frank tenement is free socage, which, most probably, means plough-service (see SOCAGE). It is distinguished from knight's service in that it is held by a certain determinate duty; whereas tenure in chivalry or knight's service was uncertain and indeterminate. These free socage tenures are said by some persons to be the relics of Saxon liberty, which were left untouched by the Normans.

Included among free socage tenures were petit serjeanty, tenure in burgage, and gavelkind.

Petit serjeanty (*parva serjeantia*) resembled grand serjeanty, for as the latter was a personal service, the former was a rent or render, both tending to some purpose concerning the king's person. The service in petit serjeanty was the rendering annually to the king of some small implement of war, as a sword, a buckler, a bow without a string, or the like. Both the tenures in serjeanty must be held from the Crown. The lands and property which were granted to the Dukes of Marlborough and Wellington for their military services are held in petit serjeanty, each rendering annually a small flag or ensign, which is deposited in Windsor Castle. Existing incidents of tenures in grand and petit serjeanty are

saved as incidents in free and common socage by the Law of Property Act, 1922, s. 136.

Tenure in burgage was where houses, or lands which were formerly the site of houses, in an ancient borough were held of some lord by a certain rent. There were a great many customs affecting these tenures, the most remarkable of which was the custom of borough-English, evidently of Saxon origin, and so named to distinguish it from the Norman customs. See BOROUGH-ENGLISH.

As to gavelkind (*gyfe-eal-kyn*, given to all the kindred), see GAVELKIND.

The other great class of tenements was villenage, which was subdivided into pure and privileged villenage.

Pure villenage was the origin of copyhold tenures, or tenure by copy of court roll, at the will of the lord. See COPYHOLD; HERIOT; MANOR.

Privileged villenage, sometimes called villein-socage, was where lands had been held of the Crown from the Conquest. This was an exalted species of copyhold, held according to custom, and not according to the mere will of the lord. It subsisted until 1926 under the name of tenure in ancient demesne, which consisted of those lands or manors which appeared in Domesday Book to have been actually in the possession of the Crown in the reign of Edward the Confessor or William the Conqueror. These tenants were esteemed highly privileged, for they could not be compelled to relinquish their lands at the will of their superior, *et ideo dicuntur liberi*. This tenure was not abolished by the statute 1660, 12 Car. 2, c. 24.

Tenures in ancient demesne were of three kinds:

(1) Tenure in ancient demesne properly so called, which was a free holding by grant from the Crown. The tenants were bound, in respect of their lands, to perform some of the better sort of certain villein services, which were commuted into money rents.

(2) Privileged copyholds, customary freeholds or free copyholds, held of a manor which was ancient demesne, according to the custom of the manor, but not at the lord's will. These lands were in fact copyholds, and therefore the term customary freeholds is not strictly

correct; for although the tenants had an interest nearly as good as freehold, yet they had not a freehold interest.

(3) Copyholds of base tenure were lands of a manor which was ancient demesne, but held merely at the lord's will.

The old Saxon ecclesiastical tenures, which were continued under the Normans, were frankalmoign (free alms), by which religious corporations and their successors held lands of the donor without any service other than praying for the souls of the donor and his heirs; and tenure by divine service, to which was annexed some special divine service, as to sing so many masses, to distribute a certain sum in alms, etc., which were contradistinguished from free alms; for if unperformed the lord could distrain without complaining to the visitor.

The statute 1660, 12 Car. 2, c. 24, excepted these spiritual tenures from abolition, so that many were subsisting in 1925, but only the Crown could create them in modern times.

The Law of Property Acts, 1922 and 1925, extinguished the customs of borough-English and gavelkind and all tenures which were not immediately before 1926, freehold or leasehold, grand or petty serjeanty, or frankalmoign and converted them into free and common socage, or leasehold, and in the case of copyholds, excepting and reserving to the lord his property and rights, if any, to mines and minerals, franchises and privileges, etc., set out in the Law of Property Act, 1925, Sch. 12 para. 5. See COPYHOLD; ESCHEAT.

See Hazlitt, *Ancient Tenures*; Elton, *Tenures of Kent*.

Tenure by divine service, where an ecclesiastical corporation, sole or aggregate, held land by a certain divine service, as to say prayers on a certain day in every year, or to distribute alms. It was originally called tenure in alms, as distinguished from tenure in free alms (frankalmoign). It differed from frankalmoign in the service being certain, in consequence of which the lord might distrain if the service was not performed. Fealty was also due by the tenant (Litt. 137; 2 Bl.Comm. 102). See FRANKALMOIGN; SERVICE; TENURE.

Term. In the law of property, a term of years is where a man lets lands or tenements to another for a certain number of years, as in the case of an ordinary lease for seven years; the word " term " not only signifies the limit of time, but also the estate and interest that pass for that time, so that if a lease is surrendered before the expiration of the time, the term is at an end. A tenant for term of years is called in the old books a termor (Litt. 58; Co.Litt. 45b).

A term is personal property. See CHATTELS; ESTATE; LEASEHOLDS; SURVIVORSHIP.

A term of years granted for the purpose of occupation by the termor is usually called a lease (*q.v.*), while " term " generally signifies a long term of years granted, not for the purpose of occupation by the grantee, but as security for the performance of an obligation, such as the payment of money. Thus, when land is settled on the marriage of the owner, it is usual to provide for the payment of a jointure to the wife, and of portions for the younger children, without interfering with the possession of the estate by the husband. This is done by vesting long terms of years (from 99 to 1,000) in trustees, upon trust, out of the rents and profits of the estate, or by sale or mortgage thereof for the whole or any part of the term, to raise the money required, and upon trust to permit the tenant for life to receive the residue of the rents and profits. In practice, however, the power thus created of receiving the rents directly from the tenants, or of selling or mortgaging the term, is rarely exercised, except for raising gross sums (*e.g.,* portions), as it is to the advantage of the tenant for life to keep down the annuities so that he may not be disturbed in the possession of the land. Terms created in this manner are called pinmoney-terms, jointure-terms, portions-terms, etc., according to the purposes for which they are created. See SETTLEMENT.

When the purpose for which a term has been created is accomplished, the term is said to be satisfied.

Formerly, when a term had become satisfied, it was usual in some cases to keep it on foot " in trust to attend the inheritance," as it was expressed. Thus, if property subject to a long term was sold, so that the powers of raising portions, etc., out of the land were no longer exercisable, the purchaser often preferred to keep the term on foot, because it protected him from any unknown incumbrances on the freehold created by the former owner since the commencement of the term, such incumbrances being postponed until the expiration of the term. The purchaser, therefore, would have the term assigned to a trustee in trust for him, and to attend the inheritance. Such a term was called an attendant term, while an ordinary term was called a term in gross. The Law of Property Act, 1925, s. 5, replacing the Satisfied Terms Act, 1845, provides that a satisfied term shall cease and determine.

By the Law of Property Act, 1925, s. 153, replacing the Conveyancing Act, 1881, s. 65, where a residue unexpired of not less than 200 years of a term which, as originally created, was for not less than 300 years, is subsisting in land, without any trust or right of redemption affecting the term in favour of the freeholder or reversioner, and without any rent having a money value, then any person beneficially entitled, in right of the term, to possession of any land comprised in the term, or any person who is in receipt of the income of the land in right of the term, or in whom the term is vested in trust for sale, or any person in whom the term is vested as personal representative of any deceased person, may by deed declare that the term shall be enlarged into a fee simple. Thereupon the term is enlarged accordingly, and the person in whom the term was vested acquires the fee simple, subject to the same trusts, powers, rights, obligations, etc., as the term would have been subject to. Numerous instances had occurred in practice in which estates really held merely for the residue of long terms were practically treated as freehold. This section enabled such terms, when the residue was not less than 200 years and the original term had been not less than 300 years, to be enlarged into a fee simple. It does not apply to any term liable to be determined by re-entry for condition broken, or to any term created by sub-demise out of a superior term

which is itself incapable of being enlarged.

" Term " also signifies a portion of the year during which alone, according to the former practice of the courts, judicial business could be transacted. The four legal terms were in existence as early as the beginning of the thirteenth century, but the dates of commencement and ending appear to have varied during different periods: see the statutes 1540, 32 Hen. 8, c. 21; 1640, 16 Car. 1, c. 6; 1751, 24 Geo. 2, c. 48; 1830, 11 Geo. 4 & 1 Will. 4, c. 70; and 1831, 1 Will. 4, c. 3 (3 Holds., H.E.L. 674).

By the Judicature Acts, 1873–75, the division of the year into terms was abolished, so far as relates to the administration of justice, the year being now divided into sittings (*q.v.*) and vacations (*q.v.*); but the terms still exist for some purposes, *e.g.*, in computing the period required for a call to the bar by the Inns of Court. The terms for judicial business were Hilary, from January 11 to 31; Easter, from April 15 to May 8; Trinity, from May 22 to June 12; and Michaelmas, from November 2 to 25. The law dining terms are Hilary, Easter, Trinity and Michaelmas. See LAST DAY OF TERM; RETURN DAYS; SITTINGS.

In ecclesiastical procedure, term signifies a period. Thus, a term probatory is the time assigned by the court for the examination of witnesses.

Term in gross, a term which would have been attendant on the inheritance if it had been assigned by a purchaser of settled land to a trustee for himself, and while outstanding and not merged it was kept in existence upon an implied trust for the parties entitled according to their estates and interests. See ATTENDANT TERM; OUTSTANDING TERM; TERM.

Term of years absolute. The Law of Property Act, 1925, s. 205 (1) (xxvii), provides that a term of years absolute means a term of years in possession or reversion, whether or not at a rent, with or without impeachment for waste, subject or not to another legal estate and either certain or liable to determination by notice, re-entry, operation of law, or by a provision for cesser of redemption or in any other event other than the dropping of a life or the determination of a determinable life interest, but does not include any term of years determinable with life or lives or with the cesser of a determinable life interest, nor a term of years which is not expressed to take effect in possession within twenty-one years where required by the Act to take effect within that period, *i.e.*, leases at a rent or in consideration of a fine and not being leases of a reversion on a term (s. 149). Term of years includes terms for less than years or from year to year. See LAW OF PROPERTY ACT; TERM.

Termes de la Ley, the title of a book, first published in 1624, which was founded upon a work published in 1563 as *An Exposition of Certaine Difficult and Obscure Wordes and Termes of the Law.* This Exposition was a translation by William Rastell (a justice of the Queen's Bench, 1558–63) of the *Expositiones Terminorum Legum Anglorum,* published in 1527 by his father, John Rastell, a member of Lincoln's Inn and also a printer. See RASTELL.

Terminal charges, charges at each end of a journey by rail, such as those for collecting, loading, unloading and delivery, over and above the maximum charge for the actual conveyance of goods.

Terminating building societies, a diminishing class of societies which by their rules terminate at a fixed date or when a result specified in the rules is attained (Building Societies Act, 1962, s. 1 (2)).

Terminum, a day given to a defendant.

Terminus a quo, the starting point.

Terminus ad quem, the finishing point.

Terminus annorum certus debet esse et determinatus (Co.Litt. 45). (A term of years ought to be certain and determinate.) And so a lease of glebe lands by the incumbent for as many years as he shall be parson is not a lease for a term of years; for no one can foretell the date on which his incumbency will be terminated by death or otherwise.

Terminus et feodum non possunt constare simul in una et eadem persona (Bract.; Plow. 29; *Grounds of Law,* 321). (The term and the fee cannot simultaneously exist in full force in one and the same person.) See MERGER.

Termor, he who holds lands or tenements for a given number of years. See TERM.

Terra, arable land (Kennett's Glos.).

Terra affirmata, land let to farm.

Terra boscalis, woody land.

Terra culta, cultivated land.

Terra debilis, weak or barren land.

Terra dominica, or **Indominicata,** the demesne land of a manor.

Terra excultabilis, land which may be ploughed (1 Dugd.Mon. 426).

Terra extendenda, a writ addressed to an escheator, etc., to inquire and find out the true yearly value of any land, etc., by the oath of twelve men, and to certify the extent into the Chancery (Reg.Brev. 293).

Terra frusca, or **frisca,** fresh land, not lately ploughed.

Terra hydata, land subject to the payment of hidage (*q.v.*) (Selden).

Terra lucrabilis, land gained from the sea or enclosed out of a waste.

Terra Normanorum, land held by a Norman (Paroch.Antiq. 197).

Terra nova, land newly converted from wood ground or arable.

Terra putura, land in forests held by the tenure of furnishing food to the keepers therein (4 Co.Inst. 307). See PUTURE.

Terra sabulosa, gravelly or sandy ground.

Terra testamentalis, allodial land, or such gavelkind land as was disposable by will (Spelman).

Terra vestita, land sown with corn (Cowel).

Terra wainabilis, tillable land.

Terra warrenata, land which had the liberty or free-warren.

Terrae dominicales regis, the demesne lands of the Crown.

Terrae dominium finitur, ubi finitur armorum vis. (The dominium of the land ends where the power of arms ends.) See CANNON-SHOT RULE.

Terrages, an exemption from all uncertain services.

Terrarius, a landowner (Leg.Will. 1).

Terre-tenant, Tertenant [Norm. Fr., landholder], he who is in actual possession and enjoyment of land (Co. Lit. 271b; 2 Bl.Comm. 91).

The word is used in the old books to signify a person who had the seisin of land, as opposed either to the lord of whom he held it, and who merely had a seignory (*q.v.*), or to a person to whose use he was seised of the land, before the Statute of Uses, 1535. Thus, if before the Statute of Uses, 1535, A conveyed land by feoffment to B and his heirs, to the use of C and his heirs, B was called the terre-tenant or feoffee to uses, and C was called the *cestui que use*. See USE.

In the law of execution a terre-tenant was an owner in fee of land which he had acquired from a defendant who had suffered judgment. Formerly every judgment charged the land of the defendant, and if he died after judgment, execution might be issued against his heirs and terre-tenants. See JUDGMENT; LAND TENANTS.

Terrier, or **Terrar,** a register or survey of lands setting out the tenures and boundaries. Terriers of the church lands in every parish have from time to time been made pursuant to Canon 87 of 1603. When coming from proper custody, such as the registry of the bishop or the archdeacon, or the chest in the parish church, they are evidence of the facts properly stated in them.

Telligraph (*q.v.*) is an early synonym.

Terris, bonis et catallis rehabendis post purgationem. When a clerk who had been charged before the king's justices with a felony had, at the request of his bishop, been handed over to an ecclesiastical court and had been acquitted by that court, this writ lay for him to get back his lands, goods and chattels after his acquittal.

Terris, catallis et tenementis ultra debitum levatum, a writ which lay for one whose lands, chattels and tenements had been distrained for more than the amount due by him.

Terris liberandis, a writ which lay for one against whom there had been successful proceedings by attaint (*q.v.*): it enabled him to have a fine substituted for the various punishments to which he had become liable. A different writ of the same name was for the delivery of lands to an heir after homage and relief

had been performed (Reg.Brev. 232, 293).

Territorial; Territoriality. These terms are used to signify connection with, or limitation with reference to, a particular country or territory. Thus, "territorial law" is the correct expression for the law of a particular country or State (*e.g.*, England), although "municipal law" is more common. See EXRATERRITORIALITY; HIGH SEAS; JURISDICTION; LAW; QUEEN'S CHAMBERS.

Territorial army, a body of men first created as the territorial force by the Territorial and Reserve Forces Act, 1907, to replace the yeomanry and volunteers.

It is now the Territorial and Army Reserve (Reserve Forces Act, 1966, s. 1). As part of the volunteer reserve there is established a home service force members of which are not required to serve outside the United Kingdom, the Channel Islands and the Isle of Man (s. 2). The volunteer reserve may be called out if national danger is imminent or a great emergency has arisen (s. 5).

See COUNTY ASSOCIATIONS; VOLUNTEERS; YEOMANRY.

Territorial bay, a bay under national jurisdiction.

Territorial waters, that portion of the sea, up to a limited distance, which is immediately adjacent to the shores of any country, and over which the sovereignty and exclusive jurisdiction of that country extend. Until recently the generally recognised limit was three miles which was the range of cannon in the seventeenth century. Following on extensions of territorial limits by other countries the British fishery limits were extended to a distance of twelve miles, the inner six miles being exclusive of foreign fishing vessels (Fishery Limits Act, 1964). See also the Sea Fisheries Act, 1968, s. 6, Sch. 2 Pt. II.

See the Territorial Waters Jurisdiction Act, 1878, passed in consequence of the decision in *R.* v. *Keyn* (1876) 2 Ex.D. 63. Orders may be made under the Colonial Boundaries Act, 1895, extending the boundaries of a colony to include the continental shelf beneath the high seas contiguous to the colony's territorial waters. See CONTINENTAL SHELF.

In the Wireless Telegraphy Act, 1949, the expression "territorial waters" means territorial waters from time to time, their determination being governed by declarations of sovereignty from time to time by the Crown or waters recognised by international usage from time to time in so far as such usage is recognised in this country (*R. v. Kent JJ., ex p. Lye* [1967] 2 Q.B. 153).

Territorium nullius, territory which is not under the jurisdiction of a subject of international law.

Tertius interveniens, one who voluntarily interposes in a suit depending between others, with a view to the protection of his own interests (Civil Law).

Test, to bring one to a trial and examination; to ascertain the truth; a criterion; a declaration preliminary to admission to an office or corporate body. See UNIVERSITY.

Test Act, the statute 1672, 25 Car. 2, c. 2, which provided that all persons having any offices, civil or military (with the exception of some few of an inferior kind), or receiving pay from the Crown, or holding a place of trust under it, should take the oaths of allegiance and supremacy, subscribe a declaration against transubstantiation, and receive the sacrament of the Lord's Supper according to the usage of the Church of England. It was extended by the statutes 1714, 1 Geo. 1, st. 2, c. 13; 1729, 2 Geo. 2, c. 31; and 1735, 9 Geo. 2, c. 26; and was repealed by the statute 1828, 9 Geo. 4, c. 17. See NON OBSTANTE; RECUSANTS.

Test case, an action on the result of which liability in other actions depends (*Healey* v. *A. Waddington & Sons* [1954] 1 W.L.R. 688).

Testa de Nevill (Liber foedorum), a register, consisting of two volumes, containing transcripts of inquisitions (as to knights' fees, serjeanties, fees held in frankalmoign, escheats, etc.) made between 1190 and 1250. It appears to derive its name either from Jollan de Nevill, one of the justices in eyre who died in 1246, or from Ralph de Nevill, who was Accountant of the Exchequer and Collector of Aids about the same time. The original Testa has disappeared; but a copy of a portion was made in the fourteenth century and, after being for long in the chapter-house of Westminister, is now in the Record Office. It was printed in 1807 by the Record Commissioners. A more accurate edition was issued in three parts, between 1921 and 1931.

These books contain accounts of fees held either immediately of the king, or of others who held of the king *in capite*, and if alienated whether the owners were infeoffed *ab antiquo* or *de novo*, as also fees held in frankalmoign, with the values thereof respectively; of serjeanties held of the king, distinguishing such as were rented or alienated, with the values thereof; of widows, and heiresses of tenants *in capite*, whose marriages were in the gift of the king, with the values of their lands; of churches in the gift of the king, and in whose hands they were; of escheats, as well of the lands of Normans as others, in whose hands the same were, and by what services held; of the amount of the sums paid for scutage and aid, etc., by each tenant.

Testable. Anyone is said to be testable when he has capacity to make a will. Anyone of twenty-one years and over who is of sound mind is testable. The capacity to make a will must be distinguished from a special power to dispose of property by will. Thus a power given to a married woman by a settlement to dispose of property by will did not make her testable; before the Married Women's Property Acts (*q.v.*) she was testable only as regards property settled on her for her separate use. Under the Wills Act, 1837, s. 11, as amended and extended by the Wills (Soldiers and Sailors) Act, 1918, and the Navy and Marines (Wills) Act, 1953, anyone authorised by those Acts to make a will otherwise than in accordance with requirements of the Act of 1837 as to wills generally, is testable even though not twenty-one years of age. He was in fact testable, under the law before 1837, at the age of fourteen.

Testament [Lat. *testatum*, a declaration], a will of personal property: a will of land is not called a testament. The word "testament" is now seldom used,

TESTAMENT

except in the heading of a formal will, which usually begins—" This is the last will and testament of me, A. B., etc." See INOFFICIOUS TESTAMENT.

Testamenta latissimam interpretationem habere debent (Jenk., Cent. 81). (Wills ought to have the broadest interpretation.) See ULTIMA VOLUNTAS, ETC.

Testamentary. " Testamentary power " is the power of making a valid will, either generally, or with reference to particular kinds or dispositions of property. " Testamentary capacity " usually refers to the absence of some disability which prevents a person from making a valid will: thus, infants and mental patients have not testamentary capacity.

A paper, instrument, document, gift, appointment, etc., is said to be testamentary when it is written or made so as not to take effect until after the death of the person making it, and to be revocable during his life, although he may have believed that it would operate as an instrument of a different character. Thus, deeds of gift, marriage settlements, letters, etc., when executed with the formalities of a will, have been admitted to probate as testamentary instruments. The term " testamentary documents " of course includes wills and codicils, which are in form as well as in effect testamentary. See NOMINATION; SCRIPT.

Testamentary causes, proceedings in the Family Division of the High Court relating to the proving and validity of wills and intestacies, over which it acquired jurisdiction to the exclusion of the ecclesiastical courts by the Court of Probate Act, 1857, amended by the Court of Probate Act, 1858. See PROBATE.

Testamentary expenses. These include the costs of an administration action (*Penny* v. *Penny* (1879) 11 Ch.D. 440). The expression includes both death duties and expenses of administration as well as funeral expenses (*Re Berrey's Will Trusts, Greening* v. *Waters* [1959] 1 W.L.R. 30).

Testamentary guardian, one appointed by a parent's will over a child, pursuant to the statute 1660, 12 Car. 2, c. 24: see the Guardianship of Infants Act, 1925, s. 5. See GUARDIAN.

Testamenti facio, the ceremony of making a testament, as a testator, heir, or witness (Civil Law).

Testamenti, Secundum tabulas, according to the tablets or terms of the will. *Contra tabulas testamenti* meant in oppositon to the provisions of the will (Civil Law).

Testamentum, a will. There were the following varieties in the civil law: (a) *calatis comitiis,* made in time of peace in the *comita curiata* twice a year; (b) *procinctum,* made in time of war in the field; (c) *per aes et libram,* by the copper and the scales; the testator alienated his estate in early times by *mancipatio* to the heir, and in the time of Gaius to another person (*familiae emptor*) who represented the heir; the testator then announced his wishes orally or by written tablets, called the *nuncupatio;* (d) *praetorianum;* the *praetors* protected by *bonorum possessio* the persons intended to be benefited if the will was sealed by seven witnesses, although there had been no *nuncupatio;* (e) *tripertitum,* of triple origin; from the civil law was derived the necessity for the witnesses' presence together at the same time; from the imperial institutions, the signatures (*subscriptiones*) of the testator and witnesses; from the praetorian edict, the seals and the number of seven witnesses; and (f) *militare,* made by a soldier on active service, in writing or orally, without any formality.

Testamentum destitutum, an abandoned will, *i.e.,* when no one entered on the inheritance; it was one of the forms of *testamentum irritum* (Civil Law).

Testamentum, i.e., testatio mentis, facta nullo prosentis metu periculi, sed sola cogitatione mortalitatis (Co.Litt. 322b). (A testament, that is, the witnessing of the mind, made not in fear of present danger, but only by the thought of death.)

Testamentum omne morte consummatum (Co.Litt. 322b). (Every will is perfected by death.)

Testate, having made a will.

Testation, witness, evidence.

Testator, a man who makes a will or testament. See WILLS.

Testatoris ultima voluntas est perimplenda secundum veram intentionem suam (Co.Litt. 332b). The last will of a testator is to be thoroughly fulfilled according to his real intention.)

Testatrix, a woman who makes a will or testament.

Testatum, the part of an indenture beginning with the words " Now this indenture witnesseth ": it is also known as the witnessing clause. See BREVARIA TESTATA; DEED.

Testatum writ. Formerly a writ of execution could not be issued into a county different from that in which the venue in the action was laid, without first issuing a writ called a ground writ (q.v.) into the latter county, and then another writ, which was called a *testatum* writ, into the former. This was abolished in ordinary cases by the Common Law Procedure Act, 1852, s. 121. Now a *testatum* writ means merely a writ which is issued into a county other than that in which the venue was laid.

A *testatum* writ in the old sense seems to be still necessary when a *fieri facias de bonis ecclesiasticis* has been issued into one diocese, but the entire debt is not levied on it, and the plaintiff wishes to have the residue levied from the defendant's ecclesiastical goods and chattels in another diocese.

Teste, the concluding part of a writ, giving the date and place of its issue. It is so called because it begins with the words " Witness myself " (*teste meipso*), or similar words. Writs are tested (that is, the *teste* runs) in the name of the Lord Chancellor (R.S.C., Ord. 6, r. 1), or, if the office is vacant, in that of the Lord Chief Justice (Ord. 1, r. 7).

Writs were before the Judicature Acts, 1873–75, tested in the name of the Lord Chancellor if issuing from the Court of Chancery, or of the Lord Chief Justice if issuing from the Queen's Bench, etc.

Testes ponderantur, non numerantur. (Witnesses are weighed, not numbered.) See UNUS NULLUS RULE.

Testes qui postulate debet dare eis sumptus competentes. (Whosoever demands witnesses must find them in competent provision.) See CONDUCT MONEY.

Testibus deponentibus in pari numero dignioribus est credendum (4 Co.Inst. 279). (Where the number of witnesses is equal on both sides, the more worthy are to be believed.)

Testimoignes [Law Fr.], witnesses.

Testimonial proof, parol evidence (Civil Law).

Testimony, the evidence of a witness given *viva voce* in a court of justice or other tribunal. In the old books, " testimony " means " witness " (Co.Litt. 32b). See EVIDENCE; PERPETUATING TESTIMONY.

Testmoignes ne poent testifie le negative mes l'affirmative (4 Co.Inst. 279). (Witnesses cannot prove a negative, but an affirmative.) If a man is charged with being drunk, the evidence of witnesses who can prove merely that they have never seen him drunk is admissible.

Testoon. See SILVER COINS.

Textbook, a legal treatise which lays down principles or collects decisions on any branch of the law, *e.g.*, Chitty on *Contracts*; Clerk and Lindsell on *Torts.* They are not binding on the court, but some of them are by general consent treated as guiding authorities (*Ecclesiastical Commissioners* v. *Parr* [1894] 2 Q.B. at p. 428). Textbooks written by living authors who are practising barristers are not cited in the courts as authorities, although passages therefrom may be adopted as part of an argument, and are sometimes referred to by judges in their judgments as corroboration or otherwise of their opinion.

Thalweg [Ger.], the *medium filum* of a river. See AD MEDIUM FILUM, ETC.

Thames. The Thames Conservancy Act, 1894, s. 3, defined the Thames as meaning so much of the rivers Thames and Isis respectively as are between the town of Cricklade and an imaginary straight line drawn from the entrance to Gantlet creek in the county of Kent to the City stone opposite to Canvey Island in the county of Essex and so much of the river Kennet as is between the common landing-place at Reading in the county of Berks and the river Thames and so much of the river Lee and Bow creek respectively as are below the south boundary stones in the Lee Conservancy Act, 1868, mentioned and all locks, cuts, and works within the said portions of rivers and creeks: but no dock, lock, canal, or cut, existing at the passing of the Act of 1894 and constructed under the authority of Parliament and belonging to any body corporate established under such authority, and no bridge over the river Thames or the river Kennet belonging to or vested in any county council or municipal authority or to or in any railway company was to be deemed to form part of the Thames.

The Thames Conservators created by the Act were abolished by the Water Act, 1973, s. 33. See WATER.

See LONDON, PORT OF; SANITARY AUTHORITY.

The Local Government Act, 1929, transferred functions relating to the Thames embankments to the London County Council.

By the statute 1827, 7 & 8 Geo. 4, c. lxxv, the watermen, wherrymen, and lightermen of the Thames were consolidated into one body corporate, in the freemen and apprentices whereof was vested, subject to certain exceptions, the exclusive right of navigating that river for hire; and see the Thames Conservancy Act, 1894. The powers of this body were transferred to the Port of London Authority by the Port of London Act, 1908, s. 11. See CONSERVATORS OF RIVERS; WATERMEN.

Thanage of the king, a certain part of the king's land or property, of which the ruler or governor was called "thane" (Cowel).

Thane [Sax. *thegn*, a servant], an Anglo-Saxon nobleman: an old title of honour, perhaps equivalent to baron. There were two orders of thanes, the king's thanes and the ordinary thanes. Soon after the Conquest this name was disused. See THEGN.

Thanelands, such lands as were granted by charter of the Saxon kings to their thanes with all immunities, except the *trinoda necessitas.*

Thanksgiving, public, Day of. Such a day may be fixed by royal proclamation. (See FASTS.) When the day of payment of a bill of exchange falls on any such day, or on a day of public fast, the bill is payable on the succeeding business day. See DAYS OF GRACE.

Thavies' Inn, an inn of Chancery. See INNS OF CHANCERY.

Theame. See TEAM.

Theatre. The censorship of plays exercised by the Lord Chamberlain under the Theatres Act, 1843, was abolished by the Theatres Act, 1968, s. 1. The presentation of obscene performances of plays is prohibited by the Act of 1968, s. 2. It is a defence that the performance was for the public good (s. 3). Performance of a play may constitute a libel, or an incitement to racial hatred or a provocation of a breach of the peace (ss. 4–10). Theatres are required to be licensed (ss. 12–20); Local Government Act, 1972, s. 204).

The Theatrical Employers Registration Acts, 1925 and 1928, prevent persons of no substance from engaging companies and then abandoning them; all theatrical employers must be registered. But the Acts do not apply to a person or his agent who has a licence under the Theatres Act, 1968.

The theatrical profession possesses its own customs and its established usages are enforceable. Thus, a producer can terminate a play by a fortnight's notice and the run of the play then comes to an end (*Gubertini* v. *Waller* [1947] 1 All E.R. 746). As to the revocation of a licence to use a theatre for the purpose of producing plays, see *Winter Garden Theatre (London)* v. *Millennium Productions* [1948] A.C. 173. See NATIONAL THEATRE.

See also the Theatres Trust Act, 1976.

As to cinematograph exhibitions and theatres, see CINEMATOGRAPH.

Theft. The law relating to larceny, robbery, burglary, obtaining by false pretences, receiving stolen goods and kindred offences has been restated in the Theft Act, 1968.

A person is guilty of theft if he dishonestly appropriates property belonging to another with the intention of permanently depriving the other of it, whether or not the appropriation is made for gain or for the thief's own benefit. The words " thief " and " steal " are to be construed accordingly (s. 1). The Act defines " dishonestly " (s. 2), " appropriates " (s. 3), " property " (s. 4), " belonging to another " (s. 5) and " with the intention of permanently depriving the other of it " (s. 6). A person guilty of theft is liable on conviction on indictment to imprisonment for a term not exceeding ten years (s. 7).

Removal without lawful authority of articles from places open to the public is an offence punishable on conviction on indictment with imprisonment for a term not exceeding five years (s. 11). In proceedings for the theft of anything in the course of transmission, by post or otherwise, a statutory declaration as to the despatch, receipt or non-receipt of the property may be admissible (s. 27 (4)).

Control of a site by excluding others from it is prima facie evidence of " control " within the meaning of the Theft Act, 1968, s. 5 (1), of the articles (e.g., scrap metal) on the site. The presumption would not apply where articles of serious crucial consequence such as explosives or drugs are introduced to the site without the knowledge of the owner of the site (R. v. *Woodman* [1974] Q.B. 754).

See also ACCOUNTS, FALSIFICATION OF; BLACKMAIL; BURGLARY; FALSE PRETENCE; FRAUD; HANDLING STOLEN GOODS; JOY-RIDING; LARCENY; RESTITUTION; REWARD; ROBBERY; SEARCH WARRANT.

Theftbote [Sax. *theof*, thief; *bote*, compensation], compounding a felony by taking some payment from a thief to secure him from legal prosecution; the receiving back by the owner of the stolen goods or of some compensation, or the taking of a bribe by a person who ought to have brought the thief to justice. It may be committed by a person not the owner of the goods, and is complete when the agreement not to prosecute is made whether it is performed or not

(R. v. *Burgess* (1886) 16 Q.B.D. 141). See COMPOUNDING; HUSH-MONEY; REWARD.

In the *Statutum Walliae*, 1284, theftbote is mentioned as being illegal.

Theftbote est emenda furti capta, sine consideratione curiae domini regis (3 Co. Inst. 134). (Theftbote is the paying of money to have goods stolen returned, without having any respect for the court of the king).

Thegn, an Anglo-Saxon who held his rank sometimes by virtue of his official position, sometimes because he owned five hides of land, sometimes by virtue of his position in the Church, and sometimes because he was a successful trader. In fact, the term " thegn " became the *nomen generale* for the higher classes of society (2 Holds.H.E.L. 39).

Thegn-land, grants of bocland (*q.v.*) made to private individuals for specific purposes.

Thellusson Act, the Accumulations Act, 1800. See ACCUMULATION.

Thelonium, toll (*q.v.*). The *breve essendi quieti de thelonio* (writ to establish freedom from toll) lay for burgesses of a town exempt by charter from toll, for lords in ancient demesne who were exempt from toll, for ecclesiastical persons as regards toll on ecclesiastical goods, for merchant strangers as regards toll from which they were exempted by charter, etc. (Fitz.N.B. 226).

There was also the writ *de thelonio rationabili habendo*, which lay for one holding of the king in fee to recover toll from those holding under him (Reg. Brev. 87).

Thelonmannus, the toll-man or officer who received toll.

Them, or **Theme,** the right of having all the generation of villeins, with their suits and cattle (*Termes de la Ley*). See TEAM.

Themmagium, a commutation paid by bondsmen to one possessing team (*q.v.*) (Cowel).

Theoden, an under-thane; a husbandman or inferior tenant (Spelman).

Theof [Lat. *praedones*], offenders who joined in a body of seven to commit depredations.

Theosophus. The Theosophical Society in England is not a charity (*Berry* v. *St. Marylebone Borough Council* [1958] Ch. 406).

Theows, Theowmen, or **Thews,** slaves, captives or bondsmen (Spelman).

Thereabouts. See MORE OR LESS.

Thereupon. Where a statute directs that a person " shall thereupon " do so and so, this means " shall immediately."

Therm, a hundred thousand British thermal units (Gas Act, 1972, s. 48 (1)). Gas is charged for according to the number of therms supplied, that number being calculated on the declared calorific value of the gas (s. 25).

Thermal insulation. See the Thermal Insulation (Industrial Buildings) Act, 1957.

Thesaurus, Thesaurium, the treasury.

Thesaurus competit domino regi, et non domino libertatis, nisi sit per verba specialia (Fitz.Coron. 281). (A treasure belongs to the king, and not to the lord of a liberty, unless it be through special words.)

Thesaurus inventus, treasure-trove (*q.v.*).

Thesaurus inventus est vetus dispositio pecuniae, etc., cujus non extat modo memoria, adeo ut jam dominum non habeat (3 Co.Inst. 132). (Treasure-trove is an ancient hiding of money, etc., of which no recollection exists, so that it has now no owner.) See TREASURE TROVE.

Thesaurus non competit regi, nisi quando nemo scit qui abscondit thesaurum (3 Co.Inst. 132). (Treasure does not belong to the king, unless no one knows who hid it.)

Thesmothete [θεσμοθέιης], a law-maker; a law-giver.

Thetinga, a tithing.

Thing in action. See CHOSE.

Things, the subjects of dominion or property, as distinguished from persons. They are of three kinds: things real or immovable, comprehending lands, tenements, and hereditaments; things personal or movable, comprehending goods and chattels; and things mixed, partaking of the characteristics of the two former, as a title-deed, a term for years. The civil law divided things into corporeal (*quae tangi possunt*) and incorporeal (*quae tangi non possunt*). See CHOSE.

Thingus, a thane or nobleman, knight or freeman.

Third party, a person who is a stranger to a transaction or proceeding; in other words, someone who is not a party.

The phrase is used to introduce any one into a scene already occupied by two in a definite relation to one another, as principal and agent, guardian and ward, solicitor and client. See As AGAINST; STRANGER.

As to the insurance of motor vehicles against third party risks, see INSURANCE; MOTOR INSURERS BUREAU.

Where in an action a defendant who has entered an appearance (a) claims against a person who is not already a party to the action any contribution or indemnity, or (b) claims any relief or remedy substantially the same as that claimed by the plaintiff, or (c) requires that some question or issue should be determined as against the third party, he may issue a third party notice stating the nature of the claim or the question or issue and requiring the third party to enter an appearance in the action (R.S.C., Ord. 16, r. 1). If the third party fails to appear he will be bound by the judgment in the action or may have judgment given against him (r. 5). If he appears the party citing him must apply to the court for directions (r. 4). See the Judicature Act, 1925, s. 39.

A person may sometimes be liable for a tort even though it would not have been committed but for the intervention of a third party (*Baker* v. *Snell* [1908] 2 K.B. 825).

Third penny. See DENARIUS TERTIUS COMITATUS.

Thirdborrow, Thirdborough, the head man in a frankpledge, a conservator of the peace in a borough or manor (Lambard, *Duties of Constables*).

Thirdings, the third part of the corn growing on the land, due to the lord for a heriot on the death of his tenant, within the manor of Turfat, in Hereford (Blount).

Third-night-awn-hinde [*trium noctium hospes*]. By the laws of Edward the

Confessor, if any man lay a third night at an inn, he was called a third-night-awn-hinde, and his host was answerable for him if he committed an offence. The first night, for-man-night, or uncuth (unknown), he was reckoned a stranger; the second night, twanight, a guest; and the third night, an agen-hinde, a domestic (3 Bract.). See TWANIGHT GESTE.

Thirty-nine Articles. See ARTICLES, THE THIRTY-NINE.

This day six months, a parliamentary expression for "never," the date appointed for further debate on second reading of a Bill which the House has decided to reject.

Thistle, Order of the. The Most Ancient and Most Noble Order of the Thistle was founded in 1687. The knights (K.T.) are the sovereign, certain royal princes, and persons having property in or being otherwise specially connected with Scotland.

Thistles. An occupier of land is not liable in negligence for damage by thistle seeds being blown on to his neighbour's land (*Giles* v. *Walker* (1890) 24 Q.B.D. 656); but he may be liable in nuisance (*Davey* v. *Harrow Corporation* [1958] 1 Q.B. 60). See WEEDS, INJURIOUS.

Thistle-take. It was the custom within the manor of Halton, in Cheshire, that if, in driving beasts over a common, the driver permitted them to graze or take but a thistle, he should pay a halfpenny a-piece, called a thistle-take, to the lord of the fee. And at Fiskerton, in Nottinghamshire, by ancient custom, if a native or a cottager killed a swine above a year old, he paid to the lord a penny, which purchase of leave to kill a hog was also called thistle-take.

Thorium. See PLUTONIUM.

Thornton, a Chief Justice and author of a *summa* or abridgment of Bracton, containing most of the titles of the law in a concise form (2 Reeves, c. 11, p. 281).

Thorp, Threp, or **Trop** [Lat. *villa, vicus*]. This word at the beginning or end of the names of places means a street or village.

Thrave, or **Threave** [Nor. Fr.], twenty-four sheaves or four shocks of corn; a certain quantity of straw; also a herd, a drove, a heap.

Threats, or menaces of bodily hurt, through fear of which a man's business is interrupted, are civil injuries affecting the right of personal security, for which there is a remedy in damages.

The common law offence of obtaining property by threats was abolished by the Theft Act, 1968, s. 32. See now BLACKMAIL.

It is an offence to threaten a prospective witness to prevent him giving evidence, even though he is never actually called as a witness (*R.* v. *Grimes* [1968] 3 All E.R. 179n; *R.* v. *Kellett* [1976] Q.B. 372).

The sending of letters threatening to murder is punishable by imprisonment for ten years (Offences against the Person Act, 1861, s. 16). Threats to destroy or damage property constitute an offence under the Criminal Damage Act, 1971, s. 2.

Threats of personal injury, etc., are a ground for exhibiting articles of the peace (*q.v.*).

The Patents Act, 1949, s. 65, provides that where any person (whether entitled to or interested in a patent or an application for a patent or not) by circulars, advertisements or otherwise threatens any other person with proceedings for infringement of a patent, any person aggrieved thereby may bring an action against him, and may obtain a declaration to the effect that such threats are unjustifiable, and an injunction against the continuance of such threats and may recover such damage, if any, as he has sustained thereby, unless the person making the threats proves that the acts in respect of which the proceedings are threatened constitute or, if done, would constitute an infringement of a patent in respect of a claim in the specification which is not shown by the plaintiff to be invalid or an infringement of rights arising from the acceptance of a complete specification in respect of a claim therein which is not shown by the plaintiff to be capable of being successfully opposed.

The Registered Designs Act, 1949, s. 26, gives a similar remedy in respect of groundless threats of proceedings for infringement of designs.

Three-mile zone, the minimum extent of territorial waters (*q.v.*).

Threnges, vassals, but not of the lowest degree, of those who held lands of the chief lord.

Threshing machines. Threshing machines must be fenced (Threshing Machines Act, 1878, repealed by the Agriculture (Safety, Health and Welfare Provisions) Act, 1956, s. 1 (7)). See the Health and Safety at Work, etc., Act, 1974, ss. 29–32, Sch. 4; S.I. 1975 No. 45. See *Jones* v. *Richards* [1955] 1 W.L.R. 444.

Thrithing, a division consisting of three or four hundreds. See RIDING.

Throw out, to reject a Bill in Parliament.

Thrymsa, a Saxon coin worth four-pence (Du Fresne).

Thude-weald, a woodward, or person who looks after a wood.

Thwertnick, the custom of giving entertainments to a sheriff, etc., for three nights.

Thwert-ut-nay, a plea uttered in defence of a charge, equivalent to a downright no (E.H.R. No. 157).

Tichborne Case. A celebrated case in which one Arthur Orton, for falsely swearing in 1867 and afterwards that he was Sir Roger Charles Doughty Tichborne, who had been drowned at sea in 1854, was sentenced in 1873 to fourteen years' penal servitude. An extract from Orton's confession, sworn before a commissioner for oaths, is given in Best on *Evidence,* 10th ed., p. 517B; see also D.N.B. Supp., tit. *Orton*; Atlay, *Famous Trials of the Century.*

Ticket. For a railway passenger not to produce a railway ticket on request by an officer or servant of a railway company, or to pay his fare from the place whence he started, or to give the officer or servant his name and address, is summarily punishable by fine up to £10 (Regulation of Railways Act, 1889, s. 5; Transport Act, 1962, s. 84 (2); *Browning* v. *Floyd* [1946] K.B. 597). See FARE.

Tickets often contain notice of a condition exempting the party issuing the ticket from liability and such an exemption, if in clear terms and brought to the notice of the other party, exempts the first party from liability; it does not exempt his servants unless they are clearly included in the exemption (*Adler* v. *Dickson* [1955] 1 Q.B. 158). See EXEMPTION CLAUSE.

Ticket of leave. See PAROLE BOARD.

Tidal rivers. See NAVIGATION; RIVERS.

Tidal water. The Merchant Shipping Act, 1894, s. 742, provides that tidal water means any part of the sea and any part of a river within the ebb and flow of the tide at ordinary spring tides, not being a harbour.

In s. 6 of the Salmon and Freshwater Fisheries Act, 1975, " tidal water " is not confined to the area between high water mark and low water mark, but includes any part of the sea within territorial waters (*q.v.*) where there is a real and perceptible ebb and flow of the tide, whether lateral or vertical (*Ingram* v. *Percival* [1969] 1 Q.B. 548).

Tidd Pratt's Act, the Scientific Societies Act, 1843.

Tide surveyor; Tide supervisor. The tide surveyors used formerly to supervise the tidewaiters, and the tide supervisors supervised the tide surveyors.

Tidesman; Tidewaiter, a custom's officer who, as ships came into port with the tide (as they generally did before the dredging of ports and the advent of steam) was placed on board to enforce the customs regulations. See LAND-WAITER.

Tied house, a public-house subject to a covenant, made with the freeholder or lessor of the premises, to obtain all supplies of alcoholic liquor from a particular brewer. Such a covenant in a mortgage is a clog on the equity of redemption (*Noakes* v. *Rice* [1902] A.C. 24). A deduction was formerly allowed in computing the brewer's profits for the purposes of income tax in respect of the amount by which the rent was less than the rent obtainable from a free tenant (*Usher's Wiltshire Brewery* v. *Bruce* [1915] A.C. 433; *Nash* v. *Tamplin & Sons* [1952] A.C. 231), but this concession was withdrawn by the Finance Act, 1952, s. 26. See the Income and Corporation Taxes Act, 1970, s. 140.

Tiel, or Tel [Nor. Fr.], such. See NUL TIEL RECORD, ETC.

Tierce, the third part of a pipe, or forty-two gallons.

Tigh [Sax. *teag*], a close or inclosure.

Tigni immittendi, a servitude consisting of the right of inserting a beam or timber from the wall of one house into that of a neighbouring house, in order that it might rest on the latter, and that the wall of the latter might bear this weight (Civil Law).

Tignum, any material for building.

Tihler [Sax.], an accusation.

Timber. Timber, strictly speaking, includes only oak, ash and elm; but in places where timber is scant, and beeches or the like are converted to building for the habitation of man or the like, they are all accounted timber (Co.Litt. 53a; 1 Rol.Abr. 649).

All trees used according to the custom of the particular part of the country in question for what is popularly known as " timber " are included (*Dashwood* v. *Magniac* [1891] 3 Ch. 306). See TREE.

Timber and other trees form part of the land, and on the death of the owner they pass with it to the person entitled to his land, therein differing from growing crops. Timber when severed is personal estate.

Cutting down timber is a form of waste (*q.v.*), except so far as it is required for estovers (*q.v.*). If a tenant unimpeachable for waste cuts timber in a husbandlike manner it vests in him; otherwise, if timber is cut or blown down, it belongs to the tenant in fee (see WINDFALLS). Where timber is ripe for cutting a tenant for life impeachable for waste may sell it with the consent of the trustees or of the court, and retain one-fourth of the proceeds for himself (Settled Land Act, 1925, s. 66, replacing the Settled Land Act, 1882, s. 35).

Succession duty was payable where a person took by succession land with timber or other trees, not being coppice or underwood, on all sums exceeding £10 in any one year from time to time received from any sales of such timber, unless he commuted the duty (Succession Duty Act, 1853, s. 23). For relief from capital transfer tax in respect of woodlands see the Finance Act, 1975, Sch. 9. See ESTATE DUTY; SUCCESSION; SUCCESSION DUTY.

Until extinguishment as provided by the Law of Property Act, 1922, the lord's right to timber on copyhold land remained as an incident of the enfranchised tenure. The right was the whole value if the lord could enter and remove the timber, otherwise half the value.

As to timber as deck cargo see the Merchant Shipping (Load Lines) Act, 1967, s. 24 (2). See DECK CARGO.

As to promoting the production and supply of timber, see FORESTRY.

Timberlands. See FABRIC LANDS.

Timberlode, a service due by tenants to a lord which consisted in carrying to the lord's house timber felled in his woods.

Time. Before 1751 the legal year in England began on March 25, therein differing from the common usage in the rest of the kingdom, and the legal method in Scotland. The Gregorian calendar (the present calendar) was substituted for the Julian calendar by the Calendar Act, 1751.

The courts take judicial notice of the calendar, as settled by the Calendar Act, 1751. See CALENDAR; NOTICE.

Time in Acts of Parliament and legal instruments means, in Great Britain, Greenwich mean time (Statutes (Definition of Time) Act, 1880) (*Gordon* v. *Cann* (1899) 68 L.J.Q.B. 434). See SUMMER TIME.

In *R.* v. *Logan* [1957] 2 Q.B. 589, it was held to be no defence to a charge under the Army Act, 1955, s. 70, which came into force on January 1, 1957, that the offence was committed in Hong Kong at a time when it was still only December 31, 1956, in England.

The computation of time for purposes of procedure in the Supreme Court is regulated by Ord. 3. See FRACTION OF A DAY; LIMITATION OF ACTIONS; MONTH; PRESCRIPTION; REASONABLE TIME.

Time bargains are contracts for the sale of a certain amount of stock at a certain price at a future day, sometimes called putts and calls or refusals. See WAGER.

An offer with a limited time for acceptance may be revoked at any moment before the limited time has been reached, on the ground that the stipulation for time to consider is void for

1769

want of consideration (*Cooke* v. *Oxley* (1790) 3 T.R. 653; *Bristol Bread Co.* v. *Maggs* (1890) 44 Ch.D. 616; *Dickinson* v. *Dodds* (1876) 2 Ch.D. 463).

Time immemorial means from time whereof the memory of man is not to the contrary. See MEMORY; PRESCRIPTION.

At common law, time was always of the essence of the contract, but the equitable doctrine now recognised in all courts since the Judicature Act, 1873, s. 25 (7), replaced by the Law of Property Act, 1925, s. 41, is that time is not of the essence of the contract unless made so either expressly or by implication (*Dibbins* v. *Dibbins* [1896] 2 Ch. at p. 350). As to making time of the essence of the contract by notice, see *Stickney* v. *Keeble* [1915] A.C. 386, and *Re Barr's Contract* [1956] Ch. 551; see also the Sale of Goods Act, 1893, s. 10. See ESSENCE OF THE CONTRACT.

See DAY; MONTH; NIGHT; YEAR.

Time bargains. See WAGER.

Time charter, a charterparty for a period, as contrasted with a charterparty for a particular voyage.

Time out of mind. See MEMORY.

Time policy. See CONTINUATION CLAUSE; POLICY OF INSURANCE.

Timocracy [Gk.], an aristocracy of property.

Tin coinage. See COPPER COINS.

Tinbounding, a custom regulating the manner in which tin is obtained from waste land, or land which has formerly been waste land, within certain districts in Cornwall and Devon. The custom is that any person may enter on the waste land of another, and may mark out by four corner boundaries a certain area; a written description of the plot of land so marked out with metes and bounds, and the name of the person, is recorded in the Stannaries Court, now the county court, and is proclaimed on three successive court-days. If no objection is sustained by any other person, the court awards a writ to the bailiff to deliver possession of the " bounds of tin-work " to the " bounder," who thereupon has the exclusive right to search for, dig, and take for his own use all tin and tin-ore within the enclosed limits, paying as a royalty to the owner of the waste a certain proportion of the produce under

the name of toll-tin (Bainbridge on *Mines*, 4th ed., p. 146). The right of tin-bounding is not a right of common (see COMMON), but is an interest in land, and, in Devonshire, a corporeal hereditament. In Cornwall tin bounds are personal estate. See DEAN, FOREST OF; STANNARIES.

Tinel le roy, the king's hall, wherein his servants used to dine and sup. See the statute 1390, 13 Ric. 2, st. 1, c. 3.

Tineman, or **Tienman,** a petty officer in the forest, who had the care of vert and venison at night, and other duties.

Tinet, brushwood and thorns for making up fences.

Tinewald or **Tynwald,** the ancient parliament or annual convention of the people in the Isle of Man.

Tinkermen or **Trinkermen,** fishermen who destroyed the young fry in the river Thames by nets and unlawful engines. See TRINK.

Tinpenny, a tribute paid for the liberty of digging in tin mines.

Tips. A cloakroom attendant who agrees to take no wages and keep tips received is nevertheless entitled to the minimum wage applicable to an employee in that grade (*Pauley* v. *Kenaldo* [1953] 1 W.L.R. 187). A waiter's tips are not part of his wages (*Wrottesley* v. *Regent Street Florida Restaurant* [1951] 2 K.B. 277). Tips received by a taxi-cab driver are assessable to income tax (*Calvert* v. *Wainwright* [1947] K.B. 526).

Tips, disused. See the Mines and Quarries (Tips) Act, 1969, Pt. II.

Tipstaff. Tipstaves are officers, in the nature of constables, attached to the Supreme Court. They were originally appointed for the Court of King's Bench by the Marshal of the King's Bench Prison and for the Courts of Chancery, Common Pleas and Exchequer by the Warden of the Fleet Prison (Queen's Prison Act, 1842, s. 5); but by that Act the functions, in this respect, of those officials were transferred to the Lord Chief Justice (of the Queen's Bench as he then was) and to the Lord Chancellor, the Lord Chief Justice of the Common Pleas, and the Lord Chief Baron of the Exchequer. The appointment now lies with the Lord Chancellor and the Lord

Chief Justice. Since the abolition of imprisonment on mesne process, the functions of the tipstaves have been confined to arresting persons guilty of contempt of court, except in the Queen's Bench Division, where the tipstaff also has in theory charge of any prisoner brought before the court, or committed by the court, in the exercise of its criminal jurisdiction. Writs of attachment are executed by the sheriff and the tipstaff does not usually act unless the offender is actually in court.

Tithe commissioners, a body created by the Tithe Act, 1836, s. 2. See COPYHOLD COMMISSIONERS; LAND COMMISSIONERS; TITHES.

Tithe rentcharge. See TITHES.

Tithe-hay. See MEAD-SILVER.

Tithes, payments due by the inhabitants of a parish for the support of the parish church, and generally payable to the parson of the parish. In extraparochial places the king was entitled to the tithes (1 Bl.Comm. 284).

Tithes payable to a rector were called rectorial tithes, those payable to a vicar were called vicarial tithes, and those payable to a lay person were called lay tithes; the last belonged to the class of incorporeal hereditaments. As to exemptions from tithes, see MODUS DECIMARDI; NON DECIMANDO, DE; REAL COMPOSITION.

Originally tithes were paid in kind, and consisted of the tenth part of all yearly or periodical profits of certain descriptions, tithes being divisible into praedial, mixed and personal. Praedial tithes (so called from *praedium*, a farm) were profits arising immediately from the soil, *e.g.,* corn, grass, etc.; mixed tithes were those arising from animals deriving their nutriment from the soil, *e.g.,* wool, milk, etc.; personal tithes were those arising entirely from the personal industry of man; these last existed only in a few instances, as in the case of fish caught in the sea, or, by special custom, in rivers. Tithes payable in respect of cornmills were personal tithes. Tithes of mineral might also be payable by custom.

Tithes were also divided into (a) great tithes, comprehending the tithes of corn, peas, beans, hay and wood, and (b) small (or privy) tithes, which included all other

kinds of tithes. The distinction was important, because vicars were frequently endowed with small tithes only (2 Bl.Comm. 24n.).

By a series of voluntary agreements and compulsory awards made under the Tithe Acts, 1836 to 1891, a rentcharge varying with the price of corn was substituted for almost all tithes, whether payable in kind or under a modus or composition.

Commutation was effected in one of two ways, either by a voluntary parochial agreement, confirmed by the commissioners, or by a compulsory award of the commissioners. The value, either voluntarily agreed upon or awarded by the commissioners, was the amount of the total rentcharge to be paid in respect of the tithes in the parish, apportioned among the lands of the parish, having regard to their average tithable produce and productive quality; and such lands were absolutely discharged from the payment of all tithes, and, instead thereof, became subject to their portion of the rentcharge thenceforth payable to the former tithe-owner, by two half-yearly payments, fluctuating according to the price of corn. An advertisement was inserted by authority in the *London Gazette,* in January in every year, stating the average price of wheat, barley and oats for seven years ending on the Thursday before Christmas then next preceding; every rentcharge then was deemed of the value of as many hundredweights of 112lb. of wheat, barley and oats in equal quantities as it would have been competent to purchase according to the prices contained in such advertisement; and after every January 1 it varied so as always to consist of the price of the same quantities, according to the advertisement then next preceding.

Tithe rentcharges did not merge in the lands out of which they were payable by mere unity of ownership; but the owner might by deed or declaration approved by the Ministry of Agriculture and Fisheries cause a merger to take place.

Neither tithe nor tithe rentcharge was recoverable unless distress was levied or proceedings taken within two years of the time when the tithe or tithe rentcharge became due (Tithe Act, 1836, s. 81; Tithe Act, 1891, s. 10 (2)).

By the Tithe Act, 1891, tithe rentcharge was payable by the landowner to the tithe-owner. Every contract between landowner and occupier for payment of it by the occupier was void, and the occupier ceased to be bound by any such contract made before that Act, being made by the Act expressly liable, however, to repay to the landowner such sum as the landowner had properly paid on account of tithe rentcharge to the tithe-owner (*Tuff* v. *Guild of Drapers of the City of London* [1913] 1 K.B. 40). When the rentcharge was in arrear for twenty-one days, the remedy was, until 1891, in every case by distress on the land; but by the Tithe Act, 1891, in the case of land being let by the owner to a tenant, the remedy of distress by the tithe-owner was extinguished, and recovery through a receiver appointed by the county court of the district was substituted for it, except where the land was occupied by the landowner, in which case an officer of the court might distrain for it. The landowner also, in case of a contract before the passing of the Act binding the occupier to pay tithe, might recover by distress on the occupier any sum he had paid the tithe-owner on account of tithe. A remission of tithe rentcharge for any one year exceeding two-thirds of the annual value of the land out of which it issued might be obtained from the county court.

As to the consideration money formerly payable on the redemption of a tithe rentcharge and the discharge thereof by an annuity, see the Tithe Act, 1918, the Tithe Annuities Apportionment Act, 1921, and the Tithe Act, 1925, which contained provisions for the stabilisation of tithe rentcharge and transferred to Queen Anne's Bounty all tithe rentcharges attached to benefices, and contained provisions for the extinguishment of Queen Anne's Bounty rentcharges at the expiration of 85 years.

As to compulsory redemption of annuities of £1 or less, and annuities on numerous plots of building land, see the Tithe Act, 1846, s. 5; the Tithe Act, 1878, ss. 3, 6; the Tithe Act, 1918, s. 4, Sch. 1; and the Tithe Act, 1936.

The Tithe Act, 1936 (which was amended by the Tithe Act, 1951, and the Finance Act, 1958, s. 38), by s. 1, extinguished tithe rentcharge and freed land charged therewith. The Act creates redemption stock secured on the Consolidated Fund to be issued as compensation to persons interested in tithe rentcharge (s. 2). The substituted charge is a 60 years' annuity at the like rates charged on the enfranchised land and payable to the Crown (s. 3). A Tithe Redemption Commission was established (s. 4). It has since been dissolved and its functions transferred to the Inland Revenue (S.I. 1959 No. 1971). Owners are required to give particulars to the Inland Revenue (s. 5; Act of 1951, s. 2). All collecting lists and similar documents are to be placed at the disposal of the Inland Revenue (Tithe Act, 1936, s. 6). Stock is issued subject to specified deductions in Sch. 3 to the Act of 1936 and deductions set aside to provide for liabilities to repair chancels, etc., and the Bank of England is to issue the specified stock upon certificate of the Commission (ss. 7, 29, Sch. 3). A register of annuities indicating by reference to a map of the district and the land charged was provided for (Act of 1936, s. 9) but this provision was repealed by the Act of 1951, which, by s. 1, gave the Tithe Redemption Commission power to maintain registers where expedient. The ownership of land in respect of which an annuity is charged is provided for by s. 5 of the Act of 1951. Provision is made as to apportionment of, or extinguishing, certain annuities, and compulsory redemption, corn rents and extraordinary tithe rentcharge and the legal incidents of annuities (Act of 1936, ss. 10–13, 15, 29, as amended by the Act of 1951 and the Finance Act, 1958, s. 38, the Finance Act, 1962, s. 32, and the Corn Rents Act, 1963. Annuities are payable annually on October 1 (Finance Act, 1958, s. 38). As to recovery of annuities, see the Act of 1936, s. 16, as amended by the Act of 1951. The owner of the land charged means the estate owner in respect of the fee simple unless it is subject to a long lease of more than 14 years at a rent less than a rack-rent, when it is the owner of the term, or if there are successive sub-leases of the land, the owner of the ultimate lease on which the others are reversionary (Act of 1936, s. 17). Tithe rentcharge and extraordinary tithe rentcharge are defined (s. 47).

Charges under a scheme for the apportionment or redemption of corn rents or other payments in lieu of tithes are registrable as land charges Class A (Corn Rents Act, 1963; Land Charges Act, 1972, s. 2 (2) (*b*), Sch. 2).

As to the custody of the tithe apportionment and map by a parish council, see *Lewis* v. *Poole* [1898] 1 Q.B. 164; see also the Tithe Act, 1936, s. 36.

See Millard, *Tithes (History and Development); Law relating to Tithes.*

See OCCUPIER'S LIABILITY NOTICE.

Tithing, a Saxon subdivision of the hundred, replacing the name of township as the unit of local administration in some parts of England, the name still existing in Somerset and Wiltshire; the number or company of ten men with their families, knit together in a society, all of them being bound to the king for their peaceable and good behaviour, the chief of whom was called the tithing-man. See FRANKPLEDGE; TOWNSHIP.

Tithing-man, a peace-officer, an under-constable. Anciently it meant the chief member of a tithing, or group of ten men associated in the frankpledge. Later it came to mean the same as headborough (*q.v.*): see the statute 1662, 14 Car. 2, c. 12, s. 15.

Tithing-penny, a customary payment by the tenants of a manor to the lord; also a customary payment by the lords of manors at the old hundred court. See TEDING-PENNY.

Title [Norm. Fr. *title*; Lat. *titulus*, a label; a name, pretext or motive; a cause or basis of acquiring a right], a general head, comprising particulars, as in a book; an appellation of honour or dignity; the means whereby the owner of lands has the just possession of his property, *titulus est justa causa possidendi id quod nostrum est* (Co.Litt. 345b).

In the primary sense of the word, a title is a right. Thus a title of presentation is the right to present to a benefice. (See NEXT PRESENTATION.) This use of the word, however, is comparatively rare, and generally " title " means a right to property considered with reference either to the manner in which it has been acquired, or to its capacity of being effectively transferred.

The lowest and most imperfect degree of title consists in the mere naked possession, or actual occupation of the estate, without any apparent right or any shadow of pretence of right to hold and continue such possession. The next step to a good and perfect title is the right of possession, which may reside in one man while the actual possession is not in himself but in another. The mere right of property, the *jus proprietatis,* without either possession or even the right of possession is frequently styled the mere right, *jus merum*; and the estate of the owner is in such cases said to be totally divested and put to a right. A complete legal title exists where the right of possession is joined with the right of property (2 Bl.Comm. 196).

With reference to the modes by which they are acquired, titles are of two kinds, namely, (1) original, where the person entitled does not take with reference to any predecessor; as in the case of title by occupancy, by capture, by invention (patent, copyright, trade mark, etc.), and by creation (as where the Crown grants a peerage): and (2) derivative, where the person entitled takes the place of a predecessor; this latter class is divisible into (a) title by the lawful and voluntary act of one or both of the parties; *e.g.,* title by conveyance, gift, devise, bequest, etc.; in the case of realty this is called title by purchase: (b) title by operation or act of the law, including title by survivorship, forfeiture, limitation, prescription, bankruptcy, etc.: and (c) title by wrong or tort, which occurs in the case of wrongful possession, abatement, disseisin, intrusion, deforcement, usurpation, and purpresture. This last kind of title differs from the others in being liable to be defeated by the person rightfully entitled, until the title of the wrongdoer has become absolute by lapse of time (see LIMITATION OF ACTIONS): subject to this, a title by wrong is always deemed to be the most extensive right which the subject-matter admits of; thus a disseisor of land is seised of an estate in fee simple by wrong.

TITLE

With reference to their capacity of being effectually transferred, titles to land are of various kinds. Thus, a marketable title is one which goes back at least fifteen years; that is, the vendor must show a chain or transmission of title, by conveyance or other lawful means, from his predecessor or predecessors, commencing at least fifteen years ago. A safe holding title is one resting on the undisturbed possession of the vendor for twelve years adversely to persons not under disability. Where a person agrees to sell land without making any stipulation as to the title, he must show a fifteen years' title (Law of Property Act, 1925, s. 44; Law of Property Act, 1969, s. 23). The contract of sale sometimes stipulates that the title shall commence at a more recent date than fifteen years. The conveyance or other document with which the title commences is called the root of title, and if the vendor shows that he has the title which he is bound to prove, he is said to show a good title. The period was formerly thirty and, before that, forty years.

The Law of Property Act, 1925, replacing the Vendor and Purchaser Act, 1874, and the Conveyancing Act, 1881, contains a number of provisions similar to those usually inserted in ordinary contracts for sale of real property and leaseholds, so that a person who enters into an open contract now runs less risk of failing to show a sufficiently good title than formerly. But these provisions do not meet special defects.

Under the Land Registration Act, 1925, ss. 4–7, a person entitled to land may prove and register (1) an absolute title, being a title good against all the world (except incumbrancers and *cestuis que trust,* if any); or (2) a qualified title, being a title subject to specified reservations; or (3) a possessory title, being a title subject to all estates, rights, and interests existing at the time of registration. See LAND REGISTRIES.

The investigation of title is one of the principal branches of conveyancing (*q.v.*); and in that practice the word " title " has acquired the sense of " history " rather than of " right." Thus, we speak of an abstract of title (see ABSTRACT OF TITLE), and of investigating a title, and describe a document as forming part of the title to property.

The principal circumstances to be attended to in drawing conclusions as to title are—

1. That there be a deduction of title to the legal estate for a period of fifteen years, unless an earlier title was required under the Vendor and Purchaser Act, 1874, or the Conveyancing Acts, 1881 and 1882, as in the case of leaseholds, advowsons, etc. (Law of Property Act, 1925, ss. 44, 45; Law of Property Act, 1969, s. 23).

2. That the legal estate can be obtained free from any equities affecting it. A stipulation by the vendor that the purchaser of a legal estate shall accept a title made with the concurrence of an equitable beneficiary if title can be made free from equities under a trust for sale or under the Law of Property Act, 1925, or any other statute is void (Law of Property Act, 1925, ss. 42, 43).

3. That all the particular estates either were determined before 1926, or if no vesting deed, trust for sale, probate or grant of administration, or vesting order has been executed or granted or made since 1925 enabling the vendor to deal with the whole legal estate, that the whole estate can be conveyed under the Law of Property Act, 1925, to the purchaser or his trustee free from equitable interests unless the purchaser agrees to accept it subject to a family charge (Law of Property (Amendment) Act, 1926).

4. That no reversion or remainder is outstanding in the Crown, or in any stranger.

5. That there are no registered incumbrances which the purchaser cannot procure either to be extinguished or assigned (Law of Property Act, 1925, s. 43); and if there has been no dealing with the legal estate since 1925, that the purchaser can obtain the estate free from all equities which would have been registrable if they had been created or conveyed after 1925, and of which he has notice. See LAND CHARGES.

There are at least three species of doubtful titles: (1) where the title is doubtful by reason of some uncertainty in the law itself; (2) where the doubt is as to the application of some settled principle or rule of law; and (3) where a matter of fact upon which a title depends is either not in its nature capable of satisfactory proof, or, being capable of such proof, is yet not satisfactorily proved.

A good title to a freehold or leasehold estate is made whenever it appears that the legal estate in the property contracted for will become vested in the purchaser free from any equity which would be capable of being over-reached by a disposition on trust for sale made in pursuance of the Law of Property Act, 1925, s. 2 (2), as amended by the Law of Property (Amendment) Act, 1926, and free from all incumbrances not specially provided for in the contract. See CONDITIONS OF SALE.

As to documents of title, see DOCUMENT.

The rule of law whereby, in any legal proceedings, a person other than a party to the proceedings could not be compelled to produce any deed or other document relating to his title to land was abrogated by the Civil Evidence Act, 1968, s. 16 (1) (*b*)).

" Title " formerly had the technical sense of a right to avoid an estate by entry, as opposed to the remedy by action. Thus if A conveyed land to B upon condition not to alienate it in mortmain, and B broke the condition, A was said to have a title of entry, or title of mortmain; but he could not bring an action, and therefore had no right in the technical sense (8 Co.Rep. 153b). See RIGHT OF ENTRY.

In ecclesiastical law " title " signifies a cause for which a person may be ordained. The most common title is either a presentation to a vacant benefice or the fact that the candidate for ordination is about to be appointed by the bishop to some vacant benefice or curacy. Hence, title signifies a presentation to a benefice; and the church or living to which the minister is presented. In the Roman Catholic Church, titles or *tituli* are the churches in and near Rome which are assigned to cardinals.

By the Ecclesiastical Titles Assumption Act, 1851, the assumption of the title of archbishop or bishop of a pretended province or diocese, or archbishop or bishop of a city, place, or territory in England or Ireland, not being the see, province, or diocese of an archbishop or bishop recognised by law, was prohibited under penalties; but this Act (which was passed after great public excitement, in consequence of the division of England into Roman Catholic dioceses by Pope Pius IX, under Cardinal Wiseman, as Archbishop of Westminster) was never enforced, and was repealed by the Ecclesiastical Titles Act, 1871.

" Title " also signifies an appellation or address indicative of honour or dignity. Such titles are to a certain extent dependent on courtesy. Thus, no person can compel another to address or describe him by his title; but, so far as their use by the person himself is concerned, titles are matters of right, and, as it were, of property. The law, however, recognises the right of anyone to call himself by any name he pleases; and so a peeress who has divorced her husband will not be restrained from using the title which was legally hers only during the continuance of the marriage. Some titles are hereditary and descend in fee simple or in tail, according to the nature of their creation. See DIGNITY.

Titles of honour are a species of incorporeal hereditament (Co.Litt. 20a, n. 3). Accordingly a baronetcy was held to be " land " within the meaning of the Settled Land Act, 1882, so that heirlooms annexed to the baronetcy could be sold with the leave of the court (*Re Rivett-Carnac* (1885) 30 Ch.D. 136).

" Title " also signifies a description. Thus, in procedure, every action, petition or other proceeding, has a title, which consists of the name of the court in which it is pending, the names of the parties, and the " reference to the record " (*q.v.*); administration actions are further distinguished by the name of the deceased person whose estate is being administered. Every pleading, summons, affidavit, etc., commences with the title. In many cases it is sufficient to give what is called the " short title " of an action, namely, the court, the reference to the record, and the surnames of the first plaintiff and the first defendant, *e.g.* " In the High Court of Justice, Queen's Bench

Division. 1975, S. No. 311. *Smith* v. *Jones.*"

The title of a patent is the short description of the subject-matter of an invention which must be prefixed to every specification (see PATENTS), whether provisional or complete, of an invention. This is referred by the Comptroller to an examiner, and if the examiner reports that it does not sufficiently indicate the subject-matter of the invention, the Comptroller may refuse to accept the application for a patent or require amendment, but there is an appeal against any such decision.

Title, Covenants for. In every conveyance of real or personal property, certain covenants for title are implied by virtue of the Law of Property Act, 1925, s. 76, Sch. 2. Such covenants may be either limited or absolute (*David* v. *Sabin* [1893] 1 Ch. 523).

In a conveyance for valuable consideration, other than a mortgage, by a person expressed to convey as beneficial owner there are implied covenants that, notwithstanding anything done, omitted, etc., by the person conveying, or anyone through whom he derives title otherwise than by purchase for value, the person conveying has the right to convey; that the person to whom the conveyance is made shall quietly enjoy the subject-matter of the conveyance without disturbance by the person conveying, or any person claiming by, through, under, or in trust for the person conveying; that the subject-matter of the conveyance is free from incumbrances by the person conveying or anyone deriving title from him or from whom he derives title otherwise than by purchase for value, except as expressly mentioned in the conveyance; and that the person conveying, and every person claiming through him otherwise than by purchase for value, and anyone through whom he derives title otherwise than by purchase for value, will execute all such further assurances for more perfectly assuring the subject-matter of the conveyance to the person to whom it is made, as from time to time may reasonably be required.

In a conveyance of leasehold property for valuable consideration, other than a mortgage, by a person expressed to convey as beneficial owner the further covenant is implied that, notwithstanding anything done or omitted by that person or anyone from whom he derives title otherwise than by purchase for value, the lease creating the term is valid, unforfeited, unsurrendered, and in nowise become void or voidable, and that the obligations under the lease have been performed.

In these provisions purchase for value does not include a conveyance in consideration of marriage.

In a conveyance by way of mortgage or charge by a person expressed to convey as beneficial owner there is implied an unqualified covenant for right to convey, with the addition that if default is made in payment of the money intended to be secured or interest thereon, the person to whom the conveyance is made may thenceforth enter upon and enjoy the subject-matter of the conveyance, and with the benefit of the same covenants for freedom from incumbrance and further assurance as in the case of a conveyance for valuable consideration, other than a mortgage, by a person expressed to convey as beneficial owner.

In a conveyance by way of mortgage (including a charge or lien) of freehold property subject to a rent or leasehold property by a person expressed to convey as beneficial owner there is implied an unqualified covenant that the grant or lease is valid and in full force and is in nowise void or voidable, and that the person conveying or the person deriving title under him has paid the rent and performed the covenants and will pay the rent and perform the covenants under the lease, and will keep the person to whom the conveyance is made indemnified against actions for non-payment of rent or breach of covenant.

There are also implied a limited covenant for further assurance in a conveyance by way of settlement by a person expressed to convey as settlor; and against incumbrances in a conveyance by a trustee, mortgagee, etc., expressed to convey as trustee, mortgagee, personal representative, committee or receiver of a person of unsound mind or under an order of the court, etc.

For covenants implied in a conveyance

for value (not being a mortgage and not being a lease for rent) of any land affected by a rentcharge and for similar covenants upon assignment for value (not being a mortgage) of a lease, see the Law of Property Act, 1925, s. 77, Sch. 2. As to cross powers of distress and entry, see the Law of Property Act, 1925, s. 190. For covenants implied in respect of registered land, see the Land Registration Act, 1925.

Title-deeds. As to dealing with title-deeds as mere personal chattels, see *Swanley Coal Co.* v. *Denton* [1906] 2 K.B. 873. Properly speaking, however, they are not chattels; they are so closely connected with the land that they will pass, on a conveyance of the land, without being expressly mentioned; the property in the deeds passes out of the vendor to the purchaser simply by the grant of the land itself (Co.Litt. 6a).

The Law of Property Act, 1925, s. 45 (9), provides that a vendor shall be entitled to retain documents of title where he retains any part of the land to which the documents relate, or where the document consists of a trust instrument or other instrument creating a trust which is still subsisting or an instrument relating to the appointment or discharge of a trustee of a subsisting trust. In such a case he gives the purchaser an acknowledgment for production (Law of Property Act, 1925, ss. 49 (7) (8), 64). As a rule the estate owner (*q.v.*) is entitled to possession of the documents relating to his title (*Clayton* v. *Clayton* [1930] 2 Ch. 12).

By the Forgery Act, 1913, s. 18 (1), a document of title to lands includes any deed, map, roll, register, or instrument in writing being or containing evidence of the title or any part of the title to any land or any interest in or arising out of any land, or any authenticated copy thereof. See FORGERY.

Title-hunters, persons who, about the commencement of the seventeenth century, made a practice of gathering information respecting titles in order to discover some flaw in them by which lands might be brought into the net of the Exchequer commissioners with a view to the impeachment of the title on behalf of the Crown, or the extortion of blackmail for a new grant to cure the supposed defect in the title (Moore, *Foreshore*, 170).

To have and to hold, the words in a conveyance which showed the estate intended to be conveyed. Thus, in a conveyance of land in fee simple, the grant in the days of long forms was " to A and his heirs to have and to hold the said land unto and to the use of the said A his heirs and assigns for ever." Now the grant is " to A to hold the same in fee simple." See HABENDUM.

Toalia, a towel. There is a tenure of lands by the service of waiting with a towel at the coronation of the sovereign.

Tobacco. The growing of tobacco was formerly prohibited in any part of the United Kingdom, and any person growing it was liable to a penalty of £10 for every rood grown, recoverable by penal action. The preamble to the statute 1660, as Car. 2, c. 34, shows the origin of the prohibition to have been the protection and maintenance of the colonies and plantations in America, and of the commerce of this country with them; see also the statute 1663, 15 Car. 2, c. 7, and the Tobacco Cultivation Act, 1831. The Irish Tobacco Act, 1907, largely removed the restrictions as to growing tobacco in Ireland, and similar provision was made for Scotland and England by the Finance (1909–10) Act, 1910, s. 83, which removed all prohibition or restraint on the growing, making, or curing of tobacco in England and Scotland, and imposed an excise duty of 5s. for a licence to grow, cultivate, or cure tobacco: see now the Customs and Excise Act, 1952, ss. 173–194, as amended by the Finance Acts, 1962, 1963, 1964, 1966, 1967, 1970, 1974, 1975 (No. 2), 1976.

Under the Customs and Excise Act, 1952, s. 180, the Commissioners of Customs and Excise may authorise persons who hold such licences to grow tobacco for the sole purpose of obtaining an extract therefrom to be used, without payment of duty, in the manufacture of insecticides or sheepwash or for other purely agricultural or horticultural purposes.

By the Children and Young Persons Act, 1933, s. 7, it is an offence to sell cigarettes to a person apparently under sixteen, or to sell other forms of tobacco to such a person unless the seller had no reason to believe that such tobacco was for the use of that person. There is also power for certain persons to seize any tobacco or cigarettes in the possession of a person apparently under sixteen who is found smoking. The penalties were increased by the Children and Young Persons Act, 1963, s. 32.

Tobago and Trinidad. See the statutes 1848, 11 & 12 Vict. c. 22; 1855, 18 & 19 Vict. c. 107; and the Trinidad and Tobago Act, 1887. The British Caribbean Federation Act, 1956, provided for federation of these colonies with the other West Indian colonies. See the Trinidad and Tobago Independence Act, 1962. See TRINIDAD, ETC.

Toft, a place where a messuage has stood (2 Br. & Had.Com. 17); see *City of London Brewery* v. *Allhallows Church-wardens* (1947) 97 L.J. 107.

When land is built upon, it is a messuage, and, if the building afterwards falls to decay, it is called a toft, which is a name superior to land, and inferior to messuage (Plow. 170).

The term " toft " is specially applied to ancient tenements within a parish or other district, the owners or occupiers of which are entitled to rights of common or commonable rights over land situate in the parish. (See ANCIENT MESSUAGES; LAMMAS LANDS). The word, in its Latinised form, is found in old fines (*q.v.*) in collocation with the Latinised form of croft (*q.v.*) *e.g., cum toftis et croftis, toftum et croftum,* and so forth.

Toftman, the owner or possessor of a toft.

Togati, Roman advocates.

Tokens, small metallic discs which were issued from time to time by traders during the seventeenth and eighteenth centuries and the early part of the nineteenth century. Each bore the name of the person issuing it; and he pledged himself to redeem it in silver, on demand, for the amount stated on its face. They came into circulation owing to the scarcity of coins of small values. The use of them is prohibited by the Coinage Act, 1971, s. 9, replacing previous enactments.

Tolbooth, a prison, a custom-house, an exchange; also the place where goods were weighed. The ancient Tolbooth, or city prison, of Edinburgh was commonly called the Heart of Midlothian. It was built by the citizens in 1561 and removed, with the buildings in which it was incorporated, in 1817. A stone in the pavement marks the spot where it stood, on which it is said to be the custom for prisoners going for trial in the courts nearby to spit for luck.

Tolerance. As regards the coinage " tolerance " is synonymous with " remedy " (*q.v.*).

In the law of town and country planning, tolerance denotes the classes of development which are deemed not to be development and for which no planning permission is required. It also includes certain changes of user specified in regulations made under the Act. See DEVELOPMENT; USE, EXISTING.

Toleration Act, the statute 1688, 1 Will. & Mar. c. 18, confirmed by the statute 1711, 10 Anne, c. 6, by which all persons dissenting from the Church of England (except Papists and persons denying the Trinity) were relieved from such of the Acts against Nonconformists as prevented their assembling for religious worship according to their own forms, or otherwise restrained their religious liberty, on condition of their taking the oaths of allegiance and supremacy, and subscribing a declaration against transubstantiation; and in the case of dissenting ministers, subscribing also to certain of the Thirty-nine Articles. So much of the Toleration Act as excepted persons denying the Trinity from its benefits, and so much of the Blasphemy Act, 1698, as related to persons denying any one of the Three Persons in the Holy Trinity to be God, were repealed by the statute 1813, 53 Geo. 3, c. 160 (*Re Hewley's Charities* (1842) 9 Cl. & Fin. 355), and the Act was repealed, save for some minor provisions, by the Promissory Oaths Act, 1871.

Toll [Sax., Dut. *tol*; Dan. *told*; Wel. *toll*; Fr. *taille*], a tribute or custom paid for passage; also a liberty to buy and sell within the precincts of a manor, which seems to import as much as a fair or market.

A toll is a payment for passing over or using a bridge, road, ferry, railway, market, port, anchorage, etc. Frequently the right to demand tolls forms part of a franchise (*q.v.*), as in the case of ferries, markets, ports, etc. Turnpike, harbour and railway tolls were generally created by Act of Parliament; see *e.g.*, the Railways Clauses Consolidation Act, 1845, ss. 3, 86, 92 (*Hunt* v. *Great Northern Ry.* (1851) 10 C.B. 900).

As to the exercise of the right to take tolls in former cities, boroughs and urban and rural districts, see S.I. 1974 No. 482, art. 17.

Toll traverse was a sum payable for passing over the private soil of another, or over a private road, bridge, ferry, or the like. Toll thorough was a sum payable for passing over the public highway: to support a claim for such a toll (which is a franchise) a consideration must be shown, *e.g.*, repairs to the highway by the owner of the franchise. Port toll was a charge on goods brought into a port. Turn toll was a charge made for every beast brought to a market but not sold. A right of distress is incident to every toll, but the distress cannot be sold. See PRESCRIPTION; STALLAGE.

County courts have no jurisdiction in actions where the title to any toll, fair, market or franchise is in question (County Courts Act, 1959, s. 39 (1) (*b*)).

In Anglo-Saxon times it meant the right to take tallage (*q.v.*) of one's villeins (1 Holds., H.E.L. 20).

The exemption of the Post Office from tolls was abolished by the Post Office Act, 1969, s. 68.

Franchise tolls payable for admission to a market are an incorporeal hereditament and are not rateable (*Oswestry Corporation* v. *Hudd* [1966] 1 W.L.R. 363).

Toll an entry [Lat. *tollere*, to take away], to bar, defeat, or deny and take away a right of entry (Real Property Limitation Act, 1833, s. 39). See DESCENT CAST.

Toll dish. At an early period, when tolls on grain were paid in kind, this was a measure which held just the amount to be taken from each sack as toll.

Toll-gatherer, the officer who takes or collects toll.

Toll-thorough, when a town prescribes (*q.v.*) to have toll for such a number of beasts, or for every beast that goes through the town, or over a bridge or ferry belonging to it (Com.Dig.). See TOLL.

Toll-tin. See TINBOUNDING.

Toll-traverse, or **Travers,** toll taken for every beast driven across a man's land. He may prescribe (*q.v.*) and distrain for it *via regia* (*q.v.*) (Cro.Eliz. 710). See TOLL.

Tollage, any custom or imposition.

Toller, one who gathered tolls.

Tolsester, an old excise; a duty paid by tenants of some manors to the lord for liberty to brew and sell ale.

Tolsey, a place at which tolls were collected; a tolbooth; a place where merchants meet.

The Tolzey Court of Bristol (*q.v.*) was a local tribunal for civil causes.

Tolt, a writ whereby a cause depending in a court baron was taken and removed into a county court (Old Nat. Br. 4). See PONE.

Tolta, wrong, rapine, extortion.

Tolzey Court of Bristol. This, originally, was the court of the bailiffs of the hundred of Bristol. Subsequently it became merged in the Court of the Lord Steward of the King's Household (*q.v.*); Richard II in 1395 revived its separate jurisdiction by charter. It sat under the authority of a charter of Anne, dated July 24, 1710. Its jurisdiction included mixed and personal actions to any amount provided that the cause of action arose within the city. The recorder was the *ex officio* judge.

The court was abolished on January 1, 1972, by the Courts Act, 1971, s. 43. See also Sch. 5 para. 12.

Tombstones. Tombstones in churchyards, it seems, can only be erected with the consent of the incumbent, and he may refuse to allow objectionable inscriptions on tombs. Strictly speaking, only the consistory court can give permission for the erection of a tombstone in a churchyard, though in most cases the chancellor is content to delegate the power to the incumbent (*Re Woldingham*

TOMBSTONES

Churchyard [1957] 1 W.L.R. 811). Tombstones in the body of the church can only be erected by leave of the ordinary, given by a faculty, though it seems that the consent of the incumbent is usually sufficient or that of the rector, if the stone is to be erected in the chancel (*Beckwith* v. *Harding* (1817) 1 B. & A. 508; *Keet* v. *Smith* (1876) 1 P.D. 73). A tombstone, when properly erected, does not vest in the incumbent, although annexed to the church or churchyard, the freehold of which is in him; therefore the person who set it up, or the personal representatives of the deceased, have an action of trespass against anyone who defaces or removes it (3 Co.Inst. 301).

Gifts by will for the erection or maintenance of tombstones in churchyards are void, if unlimited in point of time, being contrary to the rule against perpetuities: gifts for the maintenance of tombstones or monuments forming part of the fabric of a church are valid because they are for the public benefit, and are therefore charitable. The incumbent can control inscriptions proposed to be inscribed on a tombstone, but his decision may be reviewed by the ordinary (*Pearson* v. *Stead* [1903] P. 66).

As to fees for monumental inscriptions, see *Twyford* v. *Manchester Corporation* [1947] L.J.R. 12.

See BURIAL; CHARITY; CHURCHYARD.

Ton. This consists of 2,240 pounds (Weights and Measures Act, 1963, s. 10, Sch. 1 Pt. V). See POUND. As to a metric ton, see KILOGRAMME.

Tonga. See the Tonga Act, 1970.

Tonnage, the estimated number of tons burden that a ship will carry, measured in accordance with regulations made under the Merchant Shipping Act, 1965, s. 1.

Tonnage also meant a duty on imported wines, imposed by Parliament, in addition to prisage (*q.v.*). The duty was at the rate of so much for every tun or cask of wine; and tunnage would appear to be the more correct form of the word. It was first levied in the fourteenth century and was granted for life to several kings. It became practically a fixed tax in the reign of Anne and was made perpetual by the statutes 1714, 1 Geo. 1,

c. 12, and 1716, 31 Geo. 1, c. 7. It was abolished by the statute 1787, 27 Geo. 3, c. 13. See the Customs and Excise Act, 1952, ss. 143–145.

Tonnage-rent. When the rent reserved by a mining lease or the like consists of a royalty on every ton of minerals gotten in the mine, it is often called a tonnage-rent. There is generally a dead-rent in addition. See RENT.

Tonne. See KILOGRAMME.

Tontine, a financial arrangement under which subscribers to a loan each receive for life an annuity, which increases as other subscribers die, so that ultimately the last survivor receives for whatever is left of his life an annuity amounting in the aggregate to the total of the original annuities.

Lorenzo Tonti, an Italian, invented this kind of security in the seventeenth century, when the governments of Europe had some difficulty in raising money in consequence of the wars of Louis XIV, who first adopted the plan in France.

The system was used on several occasions during the eighteenth century by the British Government. The last Act passed for the purpose was the statute 1789, 29 Geo. 3, c. 41, entitled an Act for raising a certain sum of money, by way of annuities, to be attended with the benefit of survivorship, in classes.

Tool setting. As to the application of the safety provisions of the Factories Acts to the operation of tool setting, see *Nash* v. *High Duty Alloys* [1947] K.B. 377 and *Norris* v. *Syndic Manufacturing Co.* [1952] 2 Q.B. 135.

Tools. As to privilege of tools from distress, see DISTRESS; in bankruptcy, see the Bankruptcy Act, 1914, s. 38; and as to privilege from execution of tools of trade of small value, see the Small Debts Act, 1845, s. 8, and the County Courts Act, 1959. The limit of exemption is £50 or such larger amount as may be prescribed (s. 124).

Tor, Toira, or **Tyrra,** a mount or hill.

Torrens' Act, the Artisans' and Labourers' Dwellings Act, 1868, passed at the instance of William McCullagh Torrens, M.P. It and other Acts on the same subject were repealed and replaced by the Housing of the Working Classes Act, 1885. See now the Housing Act, 1957.

Torrens' system, a system of registration of title to land which was introduced into the legal system of South Australia in 1858 at the instance of Sir Robert Torrens, the first Premier of the colony. It was subsequently adopted in all the other Australian states as well as in Canada.

Tort [Lat. *tortus*, twisted, crooked]. In its original and most general sense, " tort " is any wrong, as in the phrase executor *de son tort*. See EXECUTOR, ETC.

More commonly, however, " tort " signifies an act which gives rise to a right of action, being a wrongful act or injury consisting in the infringement of a right created otherwise than by a contract. Torts are divisible into three classes, according as they consist in the infringement of a *jus in rem*, or in the breach of a duty imposed by law on a person towards another person, or in the breach of a duty imposed by law on a person towards the public.

The first class includes (a) torts to the body of a person, such as assault, or to his reputation, such as libel, or to his liberty, such as false imprisonment; (b) torts to real property, such as ouster, trespass, nuisance, waste, subtraction, disturbance; (c) torts to personal property, consisting (i) in the unlawful taking or detaining of or damage to corporeal personal property or chattels; or (ii) in the infringement of a patent, trade mark, copyright, etc.; (d) slander of title; (e) deprivation of service and *consortium*.

The second class includes deceit and negligence in the discharge of a private duty. Thus, if A contracts with B to carry his servant C, and, in performing his contract, is guilty of negligence which causes bodily hurt to C, and consequent damage, by loss of his services, to his master, then A may be sued by B for breach of contract, and by C for negligence, that is for a tort. So, if a physician is guilty of negligence in treating a patient, he may be sued either for breach of contract or for tort. This kind of tort is called a tort arising out of contract, in opposition to a pure tort (*e.g.*, an assault).

The third class includes those cases in which special damage is caused to an individual by the breach of a duty to the public. Thus, if A does something which is not only a public nuisance but also causes special damage to B which is peculiar to B, A is liable to B for a tort.

These divisions were formerly of importance with reference to the question where, on the death of the person injured, or of the tortfeasor, the personal representatives could sue or be sued for the tort; the general rule was that the right to sue, and the liability to be sued, for torts to property passed to the personal representatives of the injured person, or of the tortfeasor, but that in other cases it did not. See ACTIO PERSONALIS, ETC.

The distinction between tort and contract was formerly important with reference to the limitation of actions (*q.v.*), and is still important in the law of bankruptcy, claims for unliquidated damages for tort not being provable.

Actions are divided into actions in contract and actions in tort; as to county court jurisdiction in actions of tort when claim is under £750 (except in libel, slander and seduction), and as to costs of actions of tort commenced in the High Court which could have been commenced in the county court, see the County Courts Act, 1959, ss. 39, 47. An action founded on tort has been held to include detinue (*Bryant* v. *Herbert* (1877) 3 C.P.D. 389), an action against a carrier for loss of goods by refusal to stop *in transitu* (*Pontifex* v. *Midland Ry.* (1877) 3 Q.B.D. 23), and an action for injury to a railway passenger (*Kelly* v. *Metropolitan Ry.* [1895] 1 Q.B. 944). The distinction between tort and contract is not a logical one and it is sometimes difficult to say whether a particular wrong is a tort or a breach of contract. If the claim of the plaintiff had been set out at large, pointing to some particular stipulation in the contract, which stipulation had been broken, the action would be founded on contract, but where it is only necessary to refer to the contract to establish the relationship between the parties and the claim goes on to aver a breach of duty arising out of that relationship, the action is one of tort (*Sachs* v. *Henderson* [1902]

1 K.B. 612). If the plaintiff has suffered an injury for which, apart from the contract, he could have recovered damages, it is a tort, although it may also be a breach of contract and notwithstanding that the tort has been suffered in the execution or purported execution of the contract (*Turner* v. *Stallibrass* [1898] 1 Q.B. 56).

Husbands and wives may now sue each other in tort (Law Reform (Husband and Wife) Act, 1962, s. 1).

The Post Office is not liable in tort for failure in carrying out its functions (Post Office Act, 1969, s. 29).

See DAMAGE; DAMNUM ABSQUE INJURIA; INJURIA; NEGLIGENCE; QUASI-TORT.

Tortfeasor, a wrongdoer, or one who commits a tort. See CONTRIBUTION; OMNIA PRAESUMUNTUR, ETC.

Tortious, wrongful. Formerly certain modes of conveyance (*e.g.*, feoffments, fines, etc.) had the effect of passing not merely the estate of the person making the conveyance, but the whole fee simple, to the injury of the person really entitled to the fee, and they were thence called tortious conveyances (Litt. 611). See FEOFFMENT; FINE.

Torture. It has been constantly said that the law of England has never recognised torture as a permissible means of extracting evidence. It is indeed true that there has never been any statute or any decision expressly legalising it, and that in 1628 the judges declared it to be illegal when it was proposed to torture Felton, the assassin of Buckingham, to make him disclose his accomplices. But it was commonly and notoriously inflicted during the reigns of the Tudors and of the first two Stuarts; and the legislature and the courts practically acquiesced. The statute 1535, 27 Hen. 8, c. 4, recited in the preamble that pirates could not be convicted unless upon the evidence of witnesses—whom the pirates were careful not to leave alive—or unless they confessed "which they will never do without torture or pains"; and Coke, although he wrote (3 Co.Inst. 35) "there is no law to warrant tortures in this land," went out of his way to say in 1600, at the trial of Essex for treason (1 St.Tr. 1338), that the queen had shown "over much clemency" inasmuch as no man had been

"racked, tortured or pressed." The use of torture was, in fact, habitually carried on under the orders of the king, of the Star Chamber and of the Privy Council down to the outbreak of the Civil War.

It was frequently the practice to torture by virtue of the royal warrant, a warrant of 1640, for instance, directing the Lieutenant of the Tower "to cause John Archer to be carried to the rack, and that there yourself," with two named "sergeants-at-law, shall examine him upon such questions as our said serjeants shall think fit to propose to him." It was abolished in England by the Bill of Rights, 1688, and in Scotland by the Treason Act, 1708, s. 8.

Torquemada in the Inquisition frequently employed torture, and it was only in 1816 that it was abolished by Papal Bull.

In Athens torture was applied to slaves. Aristotle was in favour of it. In Rome, under the republic, only slaves could be tortured, but under the empire it was applied to freemen in cases of *laesa majestas.* Cicero (*pro Sulla,* c. 28) emphatically denounced it as leaving no place for truth, and Seneca as forcing even the innocent to lie.

Torture as a punishment was down to recent times a part of the legal system. The *peine forte et dure* (*q.v.*), branding (*q.v.*) with a red-hot iron, and the pillory (*q.v.*) were practically torture. See Parry, *Hist. of Torture*; Jardine on *Torture.*

Tory, originally a nickname for the wild Irish in Ulster. An Act of the Irish Parliament for better suppressing tories, robbers, and rapparees, 1695, 7 Wm. 3, c. 21, was repealed by the Statute Law Revision Act, 1878. The name was afterwards given to, and adopted by, one of the great parliamentary parties. See WHIG.

Tot; Totted; Totting. To "tot" an item in the sheriff's account was to write opposite it the word "tot" or the letter "T" in order to indicate that he had levied the money and must account for it. Such an item was said to be totted; and the marking of an item in this manner was called totting. The word "totted" (or rather its Norman-French equivalent *tottee*) is to be found in the statute 1368, 42 Edw. 3, c. 9. A good debt to the

Crown was by the officer in the Exchequer noted for such by writing the word " tot " to it (Jacob). See NIHIL.

Total loss. See LOSS.

Totalisator. A contrivance for betting also known as the *pari mutuel* or any other machine of like nature whether mechanically operated or not (Betting, Gaming and Lotteries Act, 1963, s. 55 (1)). Bets on a totalisator are subject to pool betting duty (Betting and Gaming Duties Act, 1972, ss. 6–10). Totalisators are lawful when conducted by or with the authority of the Totalisator Board (*q.v.*) or on licensed tracks (ss. 4, 5, 7, 16, 17). See TOTALISATOR BOARD.

Totalisator Board. The Racecourse Betting Act, 1928, established the Racecourse Betting Control Board. It was reconstituted as the Horserace Totalisator Board by the Betting Levy Act, 1961, s. 7. By the Betting, Gaming and Lotteries Act, 1963, s. 12, it was constituted a body corporate with perpetual succession and a common seal. It is referred to throughout that Act as the Totalisator Board and corporate powers were conferred upon it by ss. 14, 15 and the Horserace Totalisator and Betting Levy Boards Act, 1972, ss. 1–4. The functions of the Board with respect to the approval of horse racecourses were transferred to the Horserace Betting Levy Board by s. 5.

The Totalisator Board has the exclusive right to provide facilities for pool betting and dividend betting on any horse race and any other event approved by the Secretary of State and to authorise other persons to do so. Bets other than pool bets may be accepted for any sporting event or any other event approved by the Secretary of State (Betting, Gaming and Lotteries Act, 1963, s. 14; Horserace Totalisator and Betting Levy Boards Act, 1972, ss. 1, 4).

Totidem verbis, in so many words.

Toties quoties, as often as something happens; as often as occasion arises. See for instance the statute 1667, 19 & 20 Car. 2, c. 4, where it was enacted that " such assignee may in like manner assign again and so *toties quoties.*"

Toujours et encore presz (Norm. Fr.], always and still ready. See TOUT TEMPS, ETC.

Tourism. The Development of Tourism Act, 1969, established the British Tourist Authority, and separate Tourist Boards for England, Scotland and Wales. See S.I. 1970 Nos. 1537, 1682.

Tourn. See SHERIFF.

Tout temps presz et encore est [Norm. [Norm. Fr.], the averment that a defendant " always was and still is ready " to pay the debt (Co.Litt. 33a). See SEMPER PARATUS; TENDER; UNCORE PRIST.

Touting. A person may be touting for custom in the street although he is standing on his own forecourt (*McQuade* v. *Barnes* [1949] 1 All E.R. 154).

Barristers and solicitors are not permitted to tout for work.

Towage. In admiralty law, a towage service is where one vessel is employed to expedite the voyage of another, when nothing more is required than to accelerate her progress, as opposed to a salvage service, which implies danger or loss. (See SALVAGE.) A towage service gives a right to remuneration; but, although in many cases where salvage has been claimed the court has decreed only towage remuneration, there are comparatively few cases in which suits have been instituted for mere towage. Claims for towage remuneration are generally enforced in courts having admiralty jurisdiction. See Bucknill, *Tug and Tow*.

Anciently the word was also used as meaning money paid to the owner of land for the use of land as a tow-path.

Towing path. There is no common law right in the public to pass along banks for the purposes of towing. Such rights depend on usage or prescription (*Ball* v. *Herbert* (1789) 3 T.R. 262). The right of towing may exist by custom on navigable rivers: see the statute 1503, 19 Hen. 7, c. 18. A towing path may be a highway to be used only for towing (*Winch* v. *Thames Conservators* (1872) L.R. 7 C.P. 471). See Coulson and Forbes on *Waters*.

Town [Sax. *tun*, a tithing or coll], any collection of houses larger than a village. In the technical sense of the word, a town is a collection of houses which has, or in time past has had, a church and celebration of divine service, sacraments and burials but if a town is decayed so that no houses remain, yet it is a town in law; every borough was a town but every town was not a borough (Co.Litt. 115b). A parish may by resolution take on itself the status of a town (Local Government Act, 1972, s. 245). See PARISH. In the old books, "upland town" seems to mean a town which is neither a city nor a borough (Co.Litt. 110b). See VILL.

Where there is such a continuous occupancy of houses that persons living in them may be said to be living in the same town, there the place may be said to be a town (*London and South Western Ry.* v. *Blackmore* (1879) L.R. 4 H.L. 611). A town is a congregation of houses so near to one another that the inhabitants may fairly be said to dwell together. The word is so used in the Lands Clauses Consolidation Act, 1845, s. 128. (See PRE-EMPTION.) The name of such a town is a matter of reputation.

Town and country planning. The modern law of town and country planning has its roots in the Town and Country Planning Act, 1947, which not only repealed all previous legislation (re-enacting however some important provisions of the Town and Country Planning Act, 1944) but enacted principles entirely new to planning law. It came into force on July 1, 1948. It was amended by the Town and Country Planning (Amendment) Act, 1951, and the Town and Country Planning Acts, 1953, 1954, and 1959. These Acts were consolidated by the Town and Country Planning Act, 1962, which came into operation on April 1, 1963. It was amended by the Town and Country Planning Act, 1963, the Control of Office and Industrial Development Act, 1965, Pt. III of the Industrial Development Act, 1966, and the Town and Country Planning Act, 1968. The Acts of 1962 to 1968, were consolidated in the Town and Country Planning Act, 1971, which came into general operation on April 1, 1972.

The Town and Country Planning Act, 1971, is now the principal Act relating to town and country planning in England and Wales (the comparable law in Scotland is contained in the Town and Country Planning (Scotland) Act, 1972).

The principal Act was amended by the Town and Country Planning (Amendment) Act, 1972, and by the Local Government Act, 1972, s. 182, Sch. 16.

The central authority under earlier legislation was first the Minister of Town and Country Planning and then the Minister of Housing and Local Government. The central authority under the 1971 Act is the Secretary of State for the Environment (acting through the Minister for Planning and Local Government). He is charged with the duty of securing consistency and continuity in the framing and execution of a national policy with respect to the use and development of land throughout England and Wales.

Local planning authorities are the county and district councils, the Greater London Council, so far as Greater London as a whole is concerned, and the London borough councils within their areas (Town and Country Planning Act, 1971, ss. 1 (1), 5, Sch. 3 paras. 1, 2; Local Government Act, 1972, s. 182 (1).

Joint planning boards may be constituted comprising two or more counties or districts (Act of 1971, s. 1 (2), Sch. 1; Act of 1972, s. 182 (1), Sch. 16 paras. 49, 52). Planning powers conferred on local planning authorities outside Greater London are, in general, exercisable both by county planning authorities and by district planning authorities (Act of 1972, s. 182 (2)).

The 1947 Act required local planning authorities to survey their areas and prepare development plans and any county planning authority which has not submitted a development plan may be required by the Secretary of State to do so in a prescribed period (Act of 1971, Sch. 5 para. 1 (1); Act of 1972, s. 183, Sch. 16 para. 6). A development plan, generally speaking, consists of a basic map and a written statement together with such detailed maps as are appropriate. Before it comes into operation a development plan must be approved by the Secretary of State. It must be reviewed at least once in every five years and may be reviewed at any time. This procedure is known as the "old style procedure" and it continues to apply to all areas to which the "new style procedure" contained in Pt. II of the 1971

Act has not been made applicable (Act of 1971, Sch. 5).

Under the "new style procedure" in Pt. II of the Act of 1971, every county planning authority is required to institute a survey of their area if they have not already done so. They may institute a fresh survey at any time and may be directed to do so (Act of 1971, s. 6; Act of 1972, s. 183 (1)). A report of the survey must be sent to the Secretary of State together with a structure plan for his approval. This must formulate the county planning authority's policy and general proposals for the development and use of the land in their area and relate these to general proposals from neighbouring areas (Act of 1971, s. 6; Local Government Act, 1972, s. 183). See further the Act of 1971, ss. 8–10, 10A, 10B, 10C; Town and Country Planning (Amendment) Act, 1972, ss. 1–3; Local Government Act, 1972, s. 183. Sch. 16 paras. 8, 9, 52, Sch. 30). Subject to the policy and proposals of the structure plan, the county planning authority may or may not be required to prepare local plans consisting of a map and a written statement, together with diagrams, illustrations and descriptive matter formulating in detail the proposals for the development and other use of land in the area covered by the local plan including measures for the improvement of the physical environment and the management of traffic (Act of 1971, ss. 11–18; Town and Country Planning (Amendment) Act, 1972, ss. 1 (2), (3); Local Government Act, 1972, s. 182 (3), Sch. 16 paras. 1–5, 12–14, 52). If the structure plan indicates an area as an action area, a local action area plan must be prepared (Act of 1971, s. 11 (6)). While local plans are being prepared opportunity must be afforded for representation about it to be made (Act of 1971, s. 12; Local Government Act, 1972, s. 183 (2), Sch. 16 paras. 2, 10, 52). When a local plan has been prepared and before it is adopted, objections to it may be made to the county planning authority which must be considered by them at a public local inquiry or otherwise (Act of 1971, s. 13) after which the local plan is adopted (Act of 1971, s. 14; Town and Country Planning (Amendment) Act,

1972, s. 3 (2); Local Government Act, 1972, s. 182 (3), Sch. 16 paras. 3, 52). The development plan consists of the structure plan and the local plans (Act of 1971, s. 20); Town and Country Planning (Amendment) Act, 1972, s. 4 (2)).

The "new style procedure" applies to those areas in which it is brought into operation by orders of the Secretary of State. Until such time as the new style procedure is applied to an area the old style procedure continues to apply (Act of 1971, s. 21, Schs. 5–7, Sch. 24 Pt. III; Town and Country Planning (Amendment) Act, 1972, s. 5 (2); Local Government Act, 1972, s. 182 (3), Sch. 16 para. 6).

The foregoing provisions are applied to Greater London with modifications (Act of 1971, s. 19, Sch. 4; Town and Country Planning (Amendment) Act, 1972, s. 4).

Notices required to be served under the Act of 1971 may be served in accordance with s. 278.

As to the default powers of the Secretary of State, see the Act of 1971, s. 276; Local Government Act, 1972, s. 182 (3), Sch. 16 paras. 47, 52; Local Government Act, 1974, s. 35, Sch. 6 para. 25 (12).

See ADVERTISEMENTS; CAMPING; COMPENSATION FOR PLANNING RESTRICTIONS; COMPULSORY PURCHASE; CONSERVATION AREAS; DEVELOPMENT; ENFORCEMENT NOTICE; EXTINGUISHMENT OF HIGHWAYS; HISTORIC BUILDINGS; INDUSTRIAL DEVELOPMENT; OFFICE DEVELOPMENT; PLANNING BLIGHT; PLANNING INQUIRIES; PURCHASE NOTICES; TREE; USE, EXISTING; WASTE.

Town crier, an officer in a town whose business it is to make proclamations. The time-honoured summons is "Oyez" (hear ye), repeated three times, accompanied by ringing a bell or blowing a horn.

Town development. The Town Development Act, 1952 (as amended), enables local authorities to provide houses, industry and other incidental services for the benefit of congested and overpopulated areas. For the purposes of the Act "town development" is development in a country district, called the receiving district, which will relieve congestion or overpopulation in another area called the exporting district.

For a parallel code for the relief of over-population and congestion see NEW TOWNS.

Town Police Clauses Act, 1847, an adoptive Act relating to obstructions and nuisances in streets, fires, places of public resort, hackney carriages, and public bathing and other matters for the order and good government of towns and other districts. The Act is still in force as amended.

Towns Inprovement Clauses Act, 1847, an adoptive Act relating to naming streets and numbering houses, improving lines of streets, ruinous and dangerous buildings, precautions during construction and repair of sewers, streets, and houses, and such matters in urban districts. It has been largely superseded by more modern legislation.

Township, the district of a town, tithing, or vill; a district of land containing a town, and under the same administration as the town itself. When a hamlet or other small collection of houses is adjacent to a town, but governed by separate officers, it is, for some purposes in law, looked upon as a distinct township (1 Bl.Comm. 115).

The township is the unit of the early constitutional machinery in England and the boundaries of the parish, and the township or townships with which it coincides, are generally the same, "parish" being properly the ecclesiastical term, and "township" the civil one (1 Stubbs, Const. Hist. 82).

Tracing. As to the rights of beneficiaries to trace assets which have been wrongly distributed, see *Minister of Health* v. *Simpson* [1951] A.C. 251.

Traction engine. See MOTOR TRACTOR.

Trade [Ital. *trutta*], traffic; intercourse; commerce; exchange of goods for other goods, or for money. See CUSTOM; RESTRAINT OF TRADE; TRADE MARKS; TRADER.

Trade, Board of. The Board of Trade is in theory a committee of the Privy Council, and by the Interpretation Act, 1889, s. 12, the expression means the Lords of the Committee for the time being of the Privy Council appointed for the consideration of matters relating to

trade and foreign plantations. The constitution of the Board rests on an Order in Council of March 5, 1784, by which amongst the members composing it are the Archbishop of Canterbury, the Speaker of the House of Commons, the Paymaster-General and the Master of the Mint.

The Board as so constituted in fact never met, and in practice was an ordinary administrative government department presided over by a President. The Secretary of State for Trade is also President of the Board of Trade. It is now the Department of Trade.

Trade description. The Trade Descriptions Act, 1968, replaced the Merchandise Marks Acts, 1887 to 1953.

The principal offences under the Act of 1968 are applying a false trade description to any goods and supplying or offering to supply any goods to which a false trade description is applied (s. 1, *Fletcher* v. *Budgen* [1974] 1 W.L.R. 1056). A trade description is an indication, direct or indirect, and by whatever means given of any of the following matters with respect to any goods or parts of goods: (a) any quantity, size or gauge; (b) method of manufacture, production, processing or reconditioning; (c) composition; (d) fitness for purpose, strength, performance, behaviour or accuracy; (e) any physical characteristics not included in the preceding paragraphs; (f) testing by any person and results thereof; (g) approval by any person or conformity with a type approved by any person; (h) place or date of manufacture, production, processing or reconditioning; (i) person by whom manufactured, produced, processed or reconditioned; other history, including previous ownership or use. (s. 2 (1)). The foregoing are to be taken, in relation to any animal, to include sex, breed or cross, fertility and soundness, and in relation to any semen to include the identity and characteristics of the animal from which it was taken and measure of dilution (s. 2 (2)). "Quantity" includes length, width, height, area, volume, capacity, weight and number (s. 2 (3)). A false trade description is a trade description which is false to a material degree. This includes misleading descriptions and indications (s. 3). What is meant by

" applying " a trade description is dealt with in s. 4, and trade descriptions in advertisement are dealt with in s. 5. A person exposing goods for supply or having goods in his possession for supply is deemed to offer to supply them (s. 6). False or misleading indications as to the price of goods are covered by s. 11, false representations as to Royal warrant by s. 12, false representations as to the supply of goods or services by ss. 13–15, offences and prosecution by ss. 18–23; Medicines Act, 1968, Sch. 5 para. 17. It is a defence to prove that the commission of the offence was due to a mistake or to reliance on information supplied or to the act or default of another person or to accident or some other cause beyond control and that all reasonable precautions were taken and due diligence shown. If the person charged is relying on the defence of the Act or default of another person or reliance on information supplied by another person, notice in writing must be served on the prosecution seven clear days before the hearing identifying or assisting in the identification of that other person. It is a defence for a person charged with supplying or offering to supply goods under a false trade description to prove that he did not know and could not with reasonable diligence have ascertained the falsity (Trade Descriptions Act, 1968, s. 24). Innocent publication of an advertisement is a defence (s. 25). The enforcement authorities are the local weights and measures (*q.v.*) authorities and their powers are dealt with in ss. 26–31. Goods may be seized under s. 28 but compensation may be obtained under s. 33. As to the country of origin of imported goods, see ss. 36, 42; Trade Descriptions Act, 1972.

For minor amendments of the Act of 1968, see the Medicines Act, 1968, Sch. 5 paras. 16, 17; Agriculture Act, 1970, ss. 6 (4), 87 (3), 113 (3), Sch. 5 Pt. V; Road Traffic Act, 1972, s. 63, Sch. 9 Pt. I; European Communities Act, 1972, s. 4, Sch. 3 Pt. III, Sch. 4 paras. 3, 4; Fair Trading Act, 1973, Sch. 13; Consumer Credit Act, 1974, Sch. 4 para. 28.

As to the sale of cars, see ODOMETER.

See FALSE TRADE DESCRIPTION.

Trade dispute. In the Trade Union and Labour Relations Act, 1974, " trade dispute " means a dispute between employers and workers, or between workers and workers, which is connected with one or more of the following: (a) terms and conditions of employment, or the physical conditions in which any workers are required to work; (b) engagement or non-engagement, or termination or suspension of employment or the duties of employment of one or more workers; (c) allocation of work or the duties of employment as between workers or groups of workers; (d) matters of discipline; (e) the membership or non-membership of a trade union on the part of a worker; (f) facilities for officials of trade unions, and (g) machinery for negotiation or consultation, and other procedures, relating to any of the foregoing matters, including the recognition by employers or employers' associations of the right of a trade union to represent workers in any such negotiation or consultation or in the carrying out of such procedures (s. 29 (1)). An act, threat or demand done or made by one person or organisation against another which, if resisted, would have led to a trade dispute with that other is to be treated as being done or made in contemplation of a trade dispute notwithstanding that because that other submits to the act or threat or accedes to the demand no dispute arises (s. 29 (5)). " Worker," in relation to a dispute to which an employee is a party, includes any worker even if not employed by that employer. " Employment " includes any relationship whereby one person personally does work or performs services for another (s. 29 (6)). As to disputes between a Minister of the Crown and workers, see s. 29 (2). As to matters arising outside Great Britain, see s. 29 (3). A dispute to which a trade union or employers' association is a party is treated as a dispute to which workers or, as the case may be, employers are parties (s. 29 (5)).

A strike held in protest against the Government's proposed legislation is not in furtherance of a trade dispute (*Associated Newspapers Group* v. *Flynn* (1971) 10 K.I.R. 17).

Once a trade dispute has terminated, efforts by workers to penalise other workers involved in the trade dispute by putting an embargo on them are tortious and will be restrained by injunction (*Hutchinson* v. *Aitchinson* (1970) 10 K.I.R. 69).

As to trade disputes involving seamen, see the Merchant Shipping Act, 1970, s. 42. See CONSPIRACY; PICKETING; STRIKE; TRADE UNION.

Trade facilities. By the Trade Facilities Acts, 1921 to 1926, the Treasury was authorised to guarantee, up to a maximum of £75 million, loans raised for purposes calculated to promote employment. The Acts are replaced by the Export Guarantees Acts. See EXPORT GUARANTEES.

Trade fixtures. See FIXTURES.

Trade label, a small piece of paper, etc., affixed to goods with a design of some kind printed thereon. The use of a trade label too closely resembling one already in use will be restrained by injunction.

Trade libel. See LIBEL.

Trade marks. At common law " trade mark " denotes any means of showing that a certain trade or occupation is carried on by a particular person or firm, including, therefore, not only trade marks in the narrower sense of the word, but also trade names (*q.v.*) and marks which are not in themselves, or in their origin, distinctive, but which have become known by custom and reputation as showing that goods or implements of trade are made, sold, or employed by a particular person or firm.

In a narrower common-law sense of the word, a trade mark is a distinctive mark or device affixed to or accompanying an article intended for sale, for the purpose of indicating that it is manufactured, selected, or sold by a particular person or firm. Trade marks of this kind were made registrable under the Trade Marks Registration Act, 1875, replaced by the Trade Marks Acts, 1938.

The Trade Marks Act, 1938, s. 68, provides that a trade mark means, except in relation to a certification trade mark, a mark used or proposed to be used in relation to goods for the purpose of indicating, or so as to indicate, a connection in the course of trade between the goods and some person having the right either as proprietor or as registered

user to use the mark, whether with or without any identification of that person, and means, in relation to a certification mark, a mark registered or deemed to have been registered under the Trade Marks Act, 1938, s. 37.

The owner of a trade mark has a right to its use in connection with the goods associated with it, and if that right is infringed by a sale of other goods under his mark, or a colourable imitation, or otherwise so as to be calculated to deceive a purchaser into believing that those goods are goods of his manufacture, sale or mark, the owner is protected by the common law action of passing off.

The Trade Marks Act, 1938, provides a further protection. Trade marks may be registered in the register of trade marks, of which the Comptroller-General of Patents, Designs and Trade Marks is the registrar, under Part A or B of the register (s. 1). The effect of registration in Part A is that the registered trade mark in itself becomes an exclusive and assignable property of the owner in connection with the class of goods for which it is registered, for the infringement of which the statutory remedies are available (s. 4). No action lies for infringement of an unregistered trade mark, but there may be a remedy for passing off the goods (s. 3). The effect of registration in Part B of the register is that the registration affords prima facie evidence that the registered proprietor has the exclusive right to use the trade mark but it is open to the defendant in an action for infringement to prove that the user of which the plaintiff complains is not likely to deceive or cause confusion or to be taken as indicating a connection in the course of trade between the goods and the proprietor or registered user of the trade mark (s. 5).

After seven years, registration under Part A is conclusive (s. 13). A registered trade mark can be assigned either in connection with or independently of the good-will of a business (s. 22); formerly it could only be assigned in connection with the goodwill of a business.

A county court may not entertain an action for infringement (*Bow* v. *Hart* [1905] 1 K.B. 693).

To be registrable in Part A of the

register, a trade mark must consist of one or more of the following things: (1) the name of a company, individual or firm represented in a special or particular manner; (2) the signature of the applicant for registration or of some predecessor in his business; (3) an invented word or invented words; (4) a word or words having no direct reference to the character or quality of the goods and not being according to its ordinary signification a geographical name or a surname; (5) any other distinctive mark (s. 9).

Colour may form one of the particulars which is specified with regard to a trade mark (s. 16). The registration of trade marks which are obviously improper is prohibited (s. 11). Registration is for a period of seven, formerly fourteen, years, but may be renewed from time to time (s. 20).

The Company of Cutlers in Hallamshire (see CUTLERS) have at Sheffield a branch register, known as the Sheffield Register, for trade marks used on metal goods and registered by persons carrying on business in or within six miles of Hallamshire (*q.v.*) (s. 38, Sch. 2); and there exists at Manchester a branch, known as the Manchester Branch of the Trade Marks Registry of the Patent Office, for the registration of trade marks for textile goods (s. 39; Courts Act, 1971, Sch. 11 Pt. II).

A trade mark may amount to a false trade description (Trade Descriptions Act, 1968, s. 34).

For the effect of the E.E.C. Treaty see *Van Zuylen Freres* v. *Hag. A.G.* (No. 192/73) [1974] 2 C.M.L.R. 127.

See GOODWILL; MERCHANDISE MARKS; PUBLICI JURIS.

Trade name, a name which by use and reputation has acquired the property of indicating that a certain trade or occupation is carried on by a particular person. (See GOODWILL.) The name may be that of a person, place or thing, or it may be what is called a fancy name (that is, a name having no sense as applied to the particular trade), or a word invented for the occasion and having no sense at all. It may be applied to goods, to a magazine, or any other subject of trade.

A trade name gives the person entitled to use it the right of preventing any other person from using it so as to induce purchasers to believe that his goods are the goods sold or manufactured by the original maker, and thus to injure the latter. Thus, where a firm had obtained a reputation for a particular kind of goods distinguished by the word " Glenfield," which was the name of the place where the goods had originally been manufactured, a person who sold the same kind of goods under the name " Glenfield " was restrained by injunction from so doing, although he had a small manufactory at the place called Glenfield, because it was apparent on the evidence that he used the word to induce the public to believe that in buying his goods they were buying the goods of the plaintiff, the original manufacturer.

See PASSING OFF.

Trade protection society, an organisation formed for the purpose of supplying subscribers with information as to the financial standing of persons desiring credit.

Trade secret. The disclosure of trade secrets obtained by breach of confidence or obtained under a contract, whether implied (as in the case of employees) or express, not to divulge them, will be restrained by injunction (*Cranleigh Precision Engineering* v. *Bryant* [1965] 1 W.L.R. 1293). An action with regard to trade secrets may be heard *in camera* if a public hearing would defeat the ends for which the action is brought. See CAMERA.

Disclosures of information of a trade secret obtained under the Control of Pollution Act, 1974, is an offence (s. 94).

Trade, Secretary of State for. The Department of Trade is responsible for general overseas trade policy, commercial relations and tariffs, including those aspects of relations with the European Economic Community; for the work of the British Overseas Trade Board in export services and promotions, overseas finance and planning; for companies legislation, the insurance industry, the insolvency service and the Patent Office; for civil aviation, marine and shipping policy, tourism, the hotel and travel industries, the newspaper industry, and the film industry.

Certain miscellaneous functions were

transferred to the Department of Trade from the former Department of Trade and Industry by S.I. 1974 No. 692, Sch. 1 Pt. III.

Trade unions. These were originally mere friendly societies consisting of artisans engaged in a particular trade, such as carpenters, bricklayers, etc.; but in course of time they acquired the character of associations for the protection of the interests of workmen against their employers. The principal objects of such societies are to increase the rate of wages, reduce the hours of labour, and bring about an equal division of work among a large number of workmen by establishing uniform minimum rates of wages. They attain these objects principally by negotiation but also by the legal means of strikes, *i.e.*, stoppage of work by all the members until their demands are complied with, and the process known as picketing (*q.v.*) or rattening (*q.v.*). Many trade unions are also friendly societies.

Formerly trade unions were not recognised by law; and, as a general rule, their regulations, being in restraint of trade, were illegal, and incapable of being enforced; but, by the Trade Union Act, 1871, this doctrine was abolished, and provisions (analogous to those applying to friendly societies (*q.v.*)) were made for the registration of trade unions, for the regulations to be contained in their rules, and for the appointment of trustees in whom the property of the union is to vest, etc. But no agreements between the members as to the conditions on which they are to work, or as to the payment of subscriptions or application of the funds, were enforceable in any court of law (s. 4).

It was decided in 1911 that trade union funds could not be applied to the support of members of the House of Commons or of other elected bodies. The Trade Union Act, 1913, permits a union to resolve, by a majority of the members voting at a ballot, to raise a fund for such purposes, but a rule discriminating against non-contributors to the fund is invalid (*Birch* v. *National Union of Railwaymen* [1950] 2 Ch. 602). The Act was amended and extended to employers' associations by the Trade Union and Labour Relations Act, 1974, Sch. 3 para. 2.

The Trade Disputes and Trade Unions Act, 1927, declared certain strikes and lock-outs illegal, and restricted the membership of trade unions of civil servants; it was repealed by the Trade Disputes and Trade Unions Act, 1946.

In *Allen* v. *Flood* [1898] A.C. 1, it was held that no action lay against a trade union delegate for maliciously inducing a man's employer to give him notice of dismissal. In *Quinn* v. *Leathem* [1901] A.C. 495, it was held that a combination of two or more persons without justification or excuse to injure a man in his trade by inducing his customers or servants to break their contracts with him or not to deal with him or continue in his employment is, if it results in damage to him, actionable.

It was held in *Taff Vale Ry.* v. *Amalgamated Society of Railway Servants* [1901] A.C. 426, that a registered trade union might be sued in its registered name, so as to be liable for the consequences of a strike instigated and regulated by its secretaries, but the effect of this decision, which created an exception to the rule that actions can be brought only against individuals or corporations and not against unincorporated associations, was overridden by the Trade Disputes Act, 1906, s. 4.

The Industrial Relations Act, 1971, was an attempt to establish conditions in which improved industrial relations could develop. It sought to surround the principle of free and voluntary collective bargaining with a positive framework of law which would permit interests other than those of parties to collective bargaining to be taken into account. The Act was bitterly opposed by the Trade Union Congress who succeeded in making it unworkable as a whole. The Act was repealed by the Trade Union and Labour Relations Act, 1974, but certain provisions thereof were re-enacted (s. 1, Sch. 1).

" Trade union " is defined in the Act of 1974 as an organisation (whether permanent or temporary) which either (a) consists wholly or mainly of workers of one or more descriptions and is an organisation whose principal purposes include the regulation of relations between workers of that description or those descriptions and employers or employers' associations (*q.v.*), or (b) consists wholly or mainly of (i) constituent or affiliated organisations which fulfil the conditions specified in para. (a) above (or themselves consist wholly or mainly of constituent or affiliated organisations which fulfil those conditions), or (ii) representatives of such constituent or affiliated organisations, and in either case is an organisation whose principal purposes include the regulation of relations between workers and employers or between workers and employers' associations (*q.v.*) or include the regulation of relations between its constituent or affiliated organisations (s. 28 (1)).

A trade union which is not a special register body (see below) is not and is not to be treated as a body corporate but (a) it is capable of making contracts; (b) all property belonging to the union is vested in trustees in trust for the union; (c) subject to its immunity in tort it is capable of suing or being sued in its own name; (d) proceedings for any offence alleged to have been committed by it may be brought against it in its own name, and (e) any judgment, order or award may be enforced by execution, committal for contempt or otherwise against union property as if the union were a body corporate (Trade Union and Labour Relations Act, 1974, s. 2 (1)). A " special register body " is an organisation whose name was on September 15, 1974, entered in the special register maintained under s. 84 of the Industrial Relations Act, 1971, and which for the time being is a company registered under the Companies Act, 1948, or is incorporated by charter or letters patent (Trade Union and Labour Relations Act, 1974, s. 30 (1); S.I. 1974 No. 1385).

A trade union which is not a special register body is not to be registered as a company under the Companies Act, 1948, and accordingly any registration of any such union under that Act (whenever effected) is void (Act of 1974, s. 2 (2)). No trade union is to be registered as a friendly society or a provident society (s. 2 (3)). A trade union other than a special register body which on September 15, 1974, was a body corporate ceases to be a body corporate (ss. 2 (4), 4, 19; S.I.

1974 No. 1358). The purposes of any trade union which is not a special register body are not, by reason only that they are in restraint of trade, unlawful so as (a) to make any member of the trade union liable to criminal proceedings for conspiracy or otherwise; or (b) to make any agreement or trust void or voidable, nor is any rule of a trade union which is not a special register body or, in so far as it so relates, any rule of any other trade union, unlawful or unenforceable by reason only that it is in restraint of trade (s. 2 (5)).

The Trade Union and Labour Relations Act, 1974, s. 5, provided that every worker should have the right not to be excluded from membership or be expelled from membership of a trade union or a branch or section of a trade union by way of arbitrary or unreasonable discrimination. A worker aggrieved by his exclusion or expulsion from any trade union, branch or section could apply to an industrial tribunal for a declaration that he was entitled to be a member of that union, branch or section and could apply to the High Court if it became necessary to enforce implementation of a decision of the industrial tribunal in his favour. The rights so given were not to prejudice or in any way reduce the common law rights of a person who had applied to join but had not been given membership of, or who claimed to be and to remain a member of, or who had been expelled from a trade union. S. 5 of the Act of 1974, was repealed by the Trade Union and Labour Relations (Amendment) Act, 1976, s. 1 (*a*)).

A member of a trade union who has been wrongfully expelled may recover damages from the union (*Bonsor* v. *Musicians Union* [1956] A.C. 104; *Santer* v. *National Graphical Association* [1973] I.C.R. 60).

In every contract of membership of a trade union, there is implied a term conferring a right on the member, on giving reasonable notice and complying with any reasonable conditions, to terminate his membership of the union (Trade Union and Labour Relations Act, 1974, s. 7; Trade Union and Labour Relations (Amendment) Act, 1976, s. 3 (1)).

An act done by a person in contemplation or furtherance of a trade dispute (*q.v.*) is not actionable in tort on the ground only (a) that it induces another person to break a contract or interferes or induces another person to interfere with its performance; or (b) that it consists in his threatening that a contract (whether one to which he is a party or not) will be broken or its performance interfered with, or that he will induce another person to break a contract or to interfere with its performance (Act of 1974, s. 13 (1); Act of 1976, s. 3 (2)). An act done by a person in contemplation or furtherance of a trade dispute (*q.v.*) is not actionable in tort on the ground only that it is an interference with the trade, business or employment of another person, or with the right of another person to dispose of his capital or his labour as he wills (Act of 1974, s. 13 (2)). An act which by reason of the foregoing is itself not actionable and a breach of contract in contemplation or furtherance of a trade dispute (*q.v.*) is not to be regarded as the doing of an unlawful act or as the use of unlawful means for the purpose of establishing liability in tort (s. 13 (3)). An agreement or combination by two or more persons to do or procure the doing of an act in contemplation or furtherance of a trade dispute (*q.v.*) is not actionable in tort if the act is one which, if done without any such agreement or combination, would not be actionable in tort (s. 13 (4)).

In general, no action in tort lies in respect of any act (a) alleged to have been done by or on behalf of a trade union which is not a special register body or by or on behalf of an unincorporated employers' association or (b) alleged to have been done, in connection with the regulation of relations between employers or employers' associations and workers or trade unions, by or on behalf of a trade union which is a special register body or by or on behalf of an employers' association which is a body corporate; or (c) alleged to be threatened or to be intended to be done as mentioned in paras. (a) or (b) above, against the union or association in its own name, or against the trustees of the union or association, or against any members or officials of the union or association on behalf of themselves and all other members of the union or association (s. 14 (1)). Subs. (1) above does not affect the liability of a trade union or an employers' association to be sued in respect of the following, if not arising from an act done in contemplation or furtherance of a trade dispute (*q.v.*), that is to say (a) any negligence, nuisance, breach of duty resulting in personal injury to any person or (b) without prejudice to para. (a) above, breach of any duty so imposed in connection with the ownership, occupation, possession, control or use of property (s. 14 (2)). " Personal injury " includes any disease or any impairment of a person's physical or mental condition (s. 14 (3)). As to peaceful picketing, see PICKETING.

No court may whether by way of (a) an order for specific performance of a contract of employment, or (b) an injunction restraining a breach or threatened breach of such a contract, compel an employee to do any work or attend at any place for the doing of any work (s. 16). There is a restriction on the grant of *ex parte* injunctions in connection with trade disputes (s. 17).

In general, any collective agreement made before December 1, 1971 (the date on which the relevant sections (ss. 34–60) of the Industrial Relations Act, 1971, were brought into force by S.I. 1971 No. 1761), or on or after September 16, 1974 (see S.I. 1974 No. 1385), is conclusively presumed not to have been intended by the parties to be legally enforceable unless the agreement (a) is in writing and (b) contains a provision which (however expressed) states that the parties intended that the agreement should be a legally enforceable contract (s. 18 (1)). Any such agreement which satisfies both conditions is conclusively presumed to have been intended by the parties to be a legally enforceable contract (s. 18 (2)). A part of a collective agreement may be legally enforceable (s. 18 (3)). A collective agreement which restricts industrial action must comply with certain conditions (s. 18 (4) (5)).

The expression " worker " as defined in s. 30 (1) of the Act, excludes the relationship of professional man and client, and excludes members of the naval, military or air forces of the Crown or of any women's service administered by the Defence Council and the police service. See further s. 30 (2).

Lists of trade unions and employers' associations (*q.v.*) are to be maintained by the Certification Officer (*q.v.*).

Provision is made by the Act as to the keeping of accounts (ss. 10–12).

Certain provisions of the Industrial Relations Act, 1971, are re-enacted with or without amendments in the First Schedule to the Trade Union and Labour Relations Act, 1974. It is the duty of the Secretary of State for Employment to maintain a code of practice for the purpose of promoting good industrial relations (Sch. 1 Pt. I paras. 1–3). An employee has the right not to be unfairly dismissed (Sch. 1 Pt. II paras. 4–14; Act of 1976, ss. 3 (5) (6), 7). No account is to be taken of pressure on an employer to dismiss unfairly (Act of 1974, Sch. 1 Pt. I para. 15). The jurisdiction and procedure of industrial tribunals (*q.v.*) is dealt with in Sch. 1 Pt. III paras. 16–25; conciliation procedure is dealt with in Sch. 1 Pt. IV paras. 26, 27; race relations in para. 28; redundancy payments in para. 29. Para. 30 deals with periods of continuous employment; nominations are dealt with in para. 31.

In general any provision in an agreement purporting (a) to exclude or limit the operation of the Act or (b) to preclude any person from presenting a complaint to or bringing any proceedings before an industrial tribunal is void (Sch. 1 Pt. IV para. 32 (1)). The foregoing does not apply to the cases specified in para. 32 (2).

Employment under the Crown falls within the Act with the modifications made by para. 33.

The amalgamation of trade unions, the transfer of engagements and alteration of name are facilitated by the Trade Union (Amalgamations) etc. Act, 1964 amended by the Trade Union and Labour Relations Act, 1974, Sch. 3 para. 10.

As to exemption from tax see the Income and Corporation Taxes Act, 1970, s. 338; Finance Act, 1975, s. 16.

Trade unions are excepted from Pt. II of the Insurance Companies Act, 1974, in respect of insurance to provide provident benefits and strike benefits. See INSURANCE. For exemption from the Consumer Credit Act, 1974, see s. 16. See CONSUMER CREDIT.

A trade union is responsible for action taken by shop stewards in furtherance of the union's policy (*Heaton's Transport (St. Helens)* v. *Transport and General Workers' Union* [1973] A.C. 15; *General Aviation Services (U.K.)* v. *Transport and General Workers' Union* [1974] I.R.C. 35), but are not liable for action taken by members of the union which is contrary to union policy and without its authority (*General Aviation Services (U.K.)* v. *Transport and General Workers' Union* [1975] I.C.R. 276).

As to " political " strikes, see *Sherard* v. *Amalgamated Union of Engineering Workers* [1973] I.C.R. 421. As to sex discrimination, see the Sex Discrimination Act, 1975, ss. 12, 49.

Trade unions are given extensive rights of information with regard to industry by the Industry Act, 1975, ss. 31–33; Employment Protection Act, 1975, ss. 17–21.

The Employment Protection Act, 1975, contains provisions with regard to trade union membership and activities (ss. 53–58) and public activities (s. 59), time off to look for work or seek training after dismissal (ss. 61, 62). If, as is likely, the employer becomes insolvent, the Act provides for priority of payments (ss. 63–69).

Recognition of a trade union means the recognition of the union for purposes of collective bargaining (Act of 1975, s. 11 (2)). See ADVISORY, CONCILIATION AND ARBITRATION SERVICE.

See CONSPIRACY; EMPLOYERS' ASSOCIATIONS; MASTER AND SERVANT; PICKETING; STRIKE; TRADE DISPUTE.

Trade usage. See USAGE.

Trader. Traders were formerly subject to special provisions of the bankruptcy law: thus, for instance, until the Bankruptcy Act, 1861, s. 69, made all debtors subject to the provisions of that Act, only traders could be made bankrupt; under the Bankruptcy Act, 1869, s. 6, the time allowed for compliance with a debtor's summons (*q.v.*) was shorter in the case of a trader than in the case of other persons; and under the Bankruptcy Act,

TRADER

1869, s. 15 (5), the doctrine of reputed ownership (*q.v.*) was confined to traders. " Trader " within the bankruptcy law included not only persons carrying on trades in the ordinary sense, but also bankers, ship-owners, and many similar classes, enumerated in the Bankruptcy Act, 1869, Sch. I. All these distinctions between traders and non-traders have been abolished, although until the Law Reform (Married Women and Tort-feasors) Act, 1935, a married woman could be adjudicated bankrupt only when carrying on a trade or business (Bankruptcy Act, 1914, s. 125 (1)).

Trading stamps. See the Trading Stamps Act, 1964, as amended by the Companies Act, 1967, Sch. 8 Pt. VIII, the Decimal Currency Act, 1969, Sch. 2 para. 22; the Criminal Damage Act, 1971, ss. 11, 12, Sch. Pt. II, the Finance Act, 1972, s. 29, the Supply of Goods (Implied Terms) Act, 1973, s. 16; Consumer Credit Act, 1974, Sch. 4 para. 24, Sch. 5 Pt. I.

Trading with the enemy, dealings with enemy aliens or persons resident in enemy or enemy-occupied territory. The Trading with the Enemy Act, 1914, provided that any person who traded with the enemy during the war of 1914–18 should be guilty of a misdemeanour. The Trading with the Enemy Act, 1939, made similar provision as regards the war of 1939–45. Provision was made for vesting enemy property in the Custodian of Enemy Property.

Traditio loqui chartam facit (5 Co.Rep. 1). (Delivery makes a deed speak.) That is to say, without delivery it is of no effect. See ESCROW; IN TRADITIONIBUS, ETC.

Tradition, the act of handing over; delivery.

Trafalgar Square. As this square is within one mile of Westminster Hall, no public meeting (*q.v.*) can be held there during any session of Parliament. It is the property of the Crown, which consequently can at any time refuse to allow any meeting to be held there. In practice the regulation of meetings within the Square is left to the Commissioner of Police. The Square is (under the Trafalgar Square Act, 1844) part of the Metropolitan Police District.

Traffic census. See TRAFFIC SURVEY.

Traffic Commissioners. There are traffic commissioners for each traffic area whose main duty is the issue of licences in respect of public service vehicles (*q.v.*) (Road Traffic Act, 1960, s. 120, as amended by the London Government Act, 1963, Sch. 18 Pt. II and the Transport (London) Act, 1969, Sch. 6).

Traffic directions. Drivers are required to comply with the directions of a constable or a traffic warden or with traffic signs (Road Traffic Act, 1972, ss. 22, 22A; Road Traffic Act, 1974, s. 6; S.I. 1970 No. 1958).

Traffic signs. See the Road Traffic Regulation Act, 1967, ss. 54–68, 75, as amended. Failure to comply with indications given by a traffic sign is an offence (Road Traffic Act, 1972, ss. 22, 22A; Road Traffic Act, 1974, s. 6). As to traffic signs during the execution of road works, see the Public Utilities Street Works Act, 1950, s. 8; Road Traffic Act, 1956, Sch. 9.

Traffic lights may be presumed to have been working properly in the absence of evidence to the contrary (*Tingle Jacobs & Co.* v. *Kennedy* [1964] 1 W.L.R. 638 n.). A driver has no absolute right to enter a road junction merely because traffic lights are in his favour (*Radburn* v. *Kemp* [1971] 1 W.L.R. 1502) but a driver entering a simple junction at green is not bound to look out for traffic entering the junction from other roads (*Sudds* v. *Hanscombe* [1971] R.T.R. 212). A traffic sign which must be illuminated during the night need not be in a fit state for illumination during daylight (*Stubbs* v. *Morgan* [1972] R.T.R. 459).

As to fire engines and traffic lights, see *Buckoke* v. *Greater London Council* [1971] 1 W.L.R. 760; *Wardell-Yerburgh* v. *Surrey C.C.* [1973] R.T.C. 462.

Traffic surveys. Failure to comply with the direction of a constable given for the purpose of a traffic survey is an offence (Road Traffic Act, 1972, s. 22A; Road Traffic Act, 1974, s. 6, overruling *Hoffman* v. *Thomas* [1974] 1 W.L.R. 374).

Traffic wardens. Traffic wardens are appointed by the police authorities (Road Traffic Regulation Act, 1967, s. 81; Transport Act, 1968, s. 131; Road Traffic Act, 1972, Sch. 7.) See the Functions of Traffic Wardens Order, 1970 (No. 1958).

Trail-baston, a commission to make inquiry as to persons who ill-treated jurors, sheltered malefactors or otherwise disturbed the peace. The commissioners were known as justices of trail-baston. The commission was issued under the Statute of Rageman, 1276, and fell into disuse before the end of the fourteenth century. It was the connecting link between the commission in eyre (*q.v.*) and the commission of oyer and terminer (*q.v.*) (4 Co.Inst. 186; 2 Reeves 277). See RAGEMAN, STATUTE OF.

Trailers. For statutory provisions regulating the use of trailers see the Road Traffic Act, 1972, ss. 34, 65, 190; Road Traffic Act, 1974, Sch. 6 para. 16, Sch. 7.

Trainbands, the militia; the part of a community trained to martial exercises.

Training, Military. Unauthorised military training is illegal, by the Unlawful Drilling Act, 1819. See SEDITION.

As to compulsory military training, see NATIONAL SERVICE.

As to physical training, see the Physical Training and Recreation Acts, 1937 and 1958.

Training Services Agency. See the Employment and Training Act, 1973, s. 1; Social Security Act, 1973, Sch. 28; Health and Safety at Work Act, 1974, Sch. 10.

Traitor [Lat. *traditor*], one who, being trusted, betrays; one guilty of treason. See TREASON.

Traitor's gate, the river gate of the Tower of London by which traitors, and State prisoners generally, were committed to the Tower.

Tramps. See CASUAL PAUPER; VAGABONDS.

Tramways, rails for conveyance of traffic along a road not owned, as a railway is, by those who lay down the rails and convey the traffic, the rails being level with the surface of the ground, which is, or may be, laid along a public road so that the space occupied by the line is available for ordinary wheeled traffic as well as for tramway cars. A tramway is constructed under a provisional order made pursuant to the Tramways Act, 1870, or under a private Act of Parliament, unless it is such a tram-

way as comes within the meaning of the term " light railway " (*q.v.*)

A local authority may purchase a tramway within six months after the expiration of twenty-one years from the time of authorisation of construction, or within six months after the expiration of every subsequent period of seven years, under the Tramways Act, 1870, s. 43, as amended by the Local Government Act, 1933 (*London Street Tramways Co. v. London County Council* [1894] A.C. 489). As to the powers of the Minister of Transport, see the Ministry of Transport Act, 1919, ss. 2, 5.

The abandonment of tramways is regulated by the Tramways Act, 1870, ss. 41, 42.

As to liability to a passenger, see *Clarke* v. *West Ham Corporation* [1909] 2 K.B. 858.

Trani, Laws of, a code of maritime law which originated in 1063 at the Italian seaport of Trani, situate on the Adriatic about eighty miles north of Brindisi. They are printed, with a translation, in Sir Francis Twiss' edition of the *Black Book of the Admiralty*, vol. 4. The full title of the code is the *Ordinamenta et Consuetudo Maris, edita per Consules Civitatis Trani.*

Transcript, a copy; anything written from an original; an official copy of certain proceedings in a court. Thus, any person interested in an account in the books of the Paymaster-General can obtain a transcript of it.

In the Privy Council, when an appeal was brought to the Judicial Committee, the appellant had formerly to see that a transcript of the proceedings and evidence in the court below was prepared and transmitted to the Colonial Office by the proper officer. What was formerly called the transcript is now known as the record, which is transmitted to the Registrar of the Privy Council.

See SHORTHAND-WRITERS.

Transcripto pedis finis levati mittendo in cancellarium, De, a writ which was used for certifying to the Court of Chancery the foot (or chirograph) of a fine (*q.v.*) levied before the justices in eyre (Reg.Brev. 169).

Transcripto recognitionis factae coram justiciariis itinerantibus, De, a writ which was used for certifying a recognisance taken before the itinerant justices (or justices in eyre) (Reg.Brev. 151).

Transept, the part of a church between the nave and the choir. In churches of the Gothic style the ends of the transept project on each side of the edifice. Prima facie the transept belongs to the incumbent and the churchwardens.

Transfer, to convey; to make over to another; the document by which property, as shares in a public company, is made over by one person to another.

In the law of property, a transfer is where a right passes from one person to another, either (1) by virtue of an act done by the transferor with that intention, as in the case of a conveyance or assignment by way of sale or gift, etc.; or (2) by operation of law, as in the case of forfeiture, bankruptcy, descent, or intestacy. A transfer may be absolute or conditional, by way of security, etc. See ASSIGNMENT; BILL OF SALE; CONVEYANCE.

" Transfer " is used principally in the sense of voluntary transfer, and is applied especially to the operation of changing the ownership of stock, shares, etc., whether by registering an assignment or other instrument, or by making a simple entry in the register kept for that purpose. The person making the transfer is called the transferor, and the person to whom it is made the transferee.

By the Companies Act, 1948, ss. 73, 75, shares or other interests of a member in a company are personal estate transferable in manner provided by the articles of the company, and a transfer of shares or debentures is not to be registered except on production of a proper instrument of transfer (as provided for by the articles). See also the Companies Clauses Consolidation Act, 1845, s. 14. See SHARE; STOCK.

In Chancery practice, stocks and other securities standing in the names of trustees, patients, and other persons, are sometimes ordered to be transferred into the name of the Accountant-General pending the proceedings, in order that they may be kept in safety until the time comes for them to be transferred out of court to the parties entitled. See CERTIFICATE; PAYMENT INTO COURT.

The Real Property Act, 1845, replaced by the Law of Property Act, 1925, s. 52, provides that a transfer of land and an assignment of a lease must be by deed. See DEED.

Land registered under the Land Registration Act, 1925, is transferred or conveyed by the execution of an instrument of transfer in the statutory form, and by the entry of the transfer on the register. The transfer of registered charges is similar. See CHARGE; LAND REGISTRIES.

A transfer of a mortgage takes place when the mortgage and the right to receive the mortgage debt are conveyed by the mortgagee, either alone or with the concurrence of the mortgagor, to a third person. Formerly, it was an advantage to obtain the concurrence of the mortgagor, in order that he might covenant with the transferee for payment of the debt, for otherwise the transferee was obliged to sue for the debt as attorney of the mortgagee; but now, under the Law of Property Act, 1925, s. 136, replacing the Judicature Act, 1873, s. 25 (6), the assignee of a debt can sue in his own name. See CHOSE.

As to the transfer of judgments, see JUDGMENT.

In procedure, " transfer " is applied to an action or other proceeding when it is taken from the jurisdiction of one court or judge and placed under that of another. Any action in the High Court may be transferred from one division to another, or (in the case of an action in the Chancery Division) from one group of judges to another (R.S.C., Ord. 4, rr. 3, 4). Any judge of the Chancery Division before whom an estate is being administered or a company is being wound up may transfer into his group any action pending elsewhere against the estate or the company (r. 5). See REMITTED ACTIONS.

As to simplified transfer of securities, see STOCK.

Transferee, the person to whom something is transferred.

Transference, the process by which an action is transferred to the representatives of a party to it who has died.

Transferor, the person by whom something is transferred.

Transgressione, De, the general name

1796

of the various writs with which the various actions of trespass were commenced.

Transhipment. If a ship is in distress in a foreign port, and the master is unable to carry the cargo further, he is generally entitled to tranship it, that is, put it on board another vessel and forward it to its destination, and thus earn the freight (*Rosetto* v. *Gurney* (1852) 11 C.B. 176). But he is not justified in doing so if it would increase the freight payable by the shipper of the cargo, or cause a loss to the owners of the ship (Abbott, *Shipping* 528–530).

Transire. In the law of merchant shipping, when a coasting vessel is about to sail from her port of lading, an account giving particulars of the ship and her cargo must be delivered in duplicate to the customs collector of the port. He returns the original account, dated and signed by him, and this constitutes the " clearance " of the ship, and the " transire " or pass for the cargo; that is, it is an authority to the customs officers to let the vessel sail. The transire must be delivered up to the collector at the port of discharge before any of the cargo is unladen. A general transire may be granted to a coasting ship (Customs and Excise Act, 1952, s. 59).

Transit; Transitus. See STOPPAGE IN TRANSITU.

Transit in rem judicatam (it passes into or becomes *res judicata*), a short mode of saying that when a person has obtained a judgment in respect of a given right of action, he cannot bring another action for the same right, but must take proceedings to enforce his judgment. See MERGER; RES JUDICATA.

Transit terra cum onere (Co.Litt. 231a). (Land passes with its burthen.) See QUI SENTIT, ETC.

Transitory actions, actions in which the venue might be laid in any county. See ACTION; VENUE.

Translation. In ecclesiastical law, this means the transfer of a bishop from one diocese to another. There is, of course, no consecration; but all the other formalities required for the creation of a bishop are observed.

Transmission machinery must be fenced under the Factories Act, 1937, s.

13. The Act does not aim at protecting against breakage of the machinery (*Carroll* v. *Andrew Barclay & Sons* [1948] A.C. 477).

See also *Hodkinson* v. *Henry Wallwork & Co.* [1955] 1 W.L.R. 1195 and, *Richard H. Thomas & Baldwins* v. *Cummings* [1955] A.C. 321.

Transport Commission. See BRITISH TRANSPORT COMMISSION.

Transport consultative committees. See the Transport Act, 1962, s. 56; Transport Act, 1968, ss. 54, 55, Sch. 18 Pt. I; Transport (London) Act, 1969, s. 25 (1); Chronically Sick and Disabled Persons Act, 1970, s. 14 (1).

Transport Holding Company. A body corporate created by the Transport Act, 1962, s. 29; the Transport Holding Company Act, 1968. Power to dissolve this body is given by the Transport Act, 1968, s. 53, and the Transport Holding Company Act, 1972.

Transport, Minister of. This Ministry was dissolved and transferred to the Department of the Secretary of State for the Environment, under whom there is a Minister for Transport (S.I. 1970 No. 1681). For earlier orders see S.I. 1959 Nos. 1768, 1829. See ENVIRONMENT, SECRETARY OF STATE FOR THE.

Transport Tribunal. The Railway Rates Tribunal established under the Railways Act, 1921, was renamed the Transport Tribunal by the Transport Act, 1947, s. 72, which transferred to it the jurisdiction of the appeal tribunal under the Road and Rail Traffic Act, 1933, s. 15, and of the Railway and Canal Commissioners. See also the Transport Act, 1953, s. 31; Transport Act, 1962, s. 57; Transport Act, 1968, s. 94, Sch. 10, Sch. 18 Pt. IV; Transport (London) Act, 1969, s. 27 (5), Sch. 6, and the Tribunals and Inquiries Act, 1971, Sch. 1.

Transportation. This began in the reign of Elizabeth I with the sending of offenders to the North American plantations, where they were employed in a servile capacity under royal warrant or under indentures entered into by them in order to escape other punishment. The practice was recognised by the statute 1597, 39 Eliz. 1, c. 4. This transportion by consent was superseded in 1717 by a system, which continued until 1853, under which a number of felonies were expressly made punishable by transportation. After 1776 transportation was at first to Africa and subsequently to Australia. Under the Transportation Act, 1824, which consolidated the previous Acts on the subject, the Crown was enabled to appoint places beyond the seas to which offenders might be conveyed and kept to hard labour, and the same Act empowered the Crown to substitute transportation for capital punishment without its being necessary to obtain the consent of the convict. The punishment of transportation was abolished, and that of penal servitude (*q.v.*) substituted, by the Penal Servitude Act, 1853.

Transubstantiation, the change of the substance of the bread and wine in the Supper of our Lord (Thirty-nine Articles of Religion, art. 28); a conversion of the whole substance of the bread into the body and of the whole substance of the wine into the blood, which conversion the Roman Catholic Church calls transubstantiation (Creed of Pope Pius IV, founded on c. iv, sess. xiii, of the Council of Trent).

A declaration against transubstantiation was required of all members of either House of Parliament by the statute 1678, 30 Car. 2, st. 2, c. 1, which had the effect of disabling Roman Catholics from sitting in either House till the passing of the Roman Catholic Relief Act, 1829.

Both the Bill of Rights, 1688, and the Act of Settlement, 1700, by an incorporation by reference of the statute 1678, 30 Car. 2, st. 2, c. 1, which was repealed by the Parliamentary Oaths Act, 1866, required the sovereign, on the first day of the meeting of the first Parliament next after his accession, sitting on the throne in the House of Lords in the presence of the lords and commons there assembled, or at his coronation (whichever should first happen), to make, subscribe and repeat aloud the declaration against transubstantiation, as also did, in the case of many officials, etc., the Test Act, 1672, and the Toleration Act, 1688. The declaration was as follows: " I A. B. do solemnly and sincerely in the presence of God profess testify and declare that I

do believe that in the Sacrament of the Lord's Supper there is not any transubstantiation of the elements of bread and wine into the body and blood of Christ at òr after the consecration thereof by any person whatsoever; and that the invocation or adoration of the Virgin Mary or any other saint, and the sacrifice of the mass as they are now used in the Church of Rome are superstitious and idolatrous, and I do solemnly in the presence of God profess, testify and declare that I do make this declaration and every part thereof in the plain and ordinary sense of the words read unto me as they are commonly understood by English Protestants without any evasion, equivocation or mental reservation whatsoever, and without any dispensation already granted me for that purpose by the Pope or any other authority or person whatsover or without thinking that I am or can be acquitted before God or man or absolved of this declaration or any part thereof although the Pope or any other person or persons or power whatsoever should dispense with or annul the same or declare that it was null and void from the beginning."

See now the Accession Declaration Act, 1910. See BILL OF RIGHTS.

Transvestism. See CROSS-DRESSING.

Traps. See SPRING TRAPS.

Travaux préparatoires, historical work. The English courts will not use *travaux préparatoires*, such as parliamentary debates, reports of commissions and the like, as an aid to the interpretation of a statute.

Travel agents. See HOLIDAY.

Traveller. Under the Licensing (Consolidation) Act, 1910, s. 61, intoxicating liquors were not to be sold at certain hours except to bona fide travellers, and a person was not to be deemed a bona fide traveller unless the place where he lodged during the preceding night was at least three miles distant from the place where he demanded to be supplied with liquor. The expression bona fide, which owed its origin to the Licensing (Scotland) Act, 1853, the Forbes-Mackenzie Act, merely pointed the distinction between those who travelled to drink, and those who drank to travel. The section was repealed by the Licensing Act,

1921. As to the obligation of an inn-keeper to entertain travellers, see *Sealey* v. *Tandy* [1902] 1 K.B. 296, and *R.* v. *Higgins* [1948] 1 K.B. 165. See INNKEEPER.

Traverse [Old Fr. *traverser*, to deny; Lat. *transversus*]. In the practice of the High Court, to traverse is to deny an allegation of fact. The term is used both in pleadings and in affidavits: thus if a plaintiff replies by simply joining issue on the statement of defence he traverses, that is, denies, all the material allegations in the defence (R.S.C., Ord. 18, r. 14). See CONFESSION AND AVOIDANCE; QUAE EST EADEM.

So, in an answer (*q.v.*) to interrogatories, a denial of the allegation impliedly contained in an interrogatory is a traverse, and may be either simple or subject to an explanation or admission previously given.

In an affidavit of documents, the paragraph stating that the deponent has no documents in his possession except those specified in the affidavit used sometimes to be called the traverse, because the affidavit was in the same form as if it were made in answer to an interrogatory. See SPECIAL TRAVERSE.

Traverse of office or inquisition was a mode by which a subject could, in certain cases, dispute an office or inquisition finding the Crown entitled to property claimed by him. It was a convenient remedy, on account of the difficulty of obtaining redress against the Crown by petition of right. One of the most usual instances of its use was in resisting extents (see EXTENT), in which case the defendant or traverser (*i.e.* the person claiming the property) entered an appearance and claim, followed by a plea or traverse disputing the debt alleged by the Crown, to which the Crown replied or demurred, and so on, until issue joined, when the cause was tried by a jury at Westminster. Judgment for the Crown on a traverse was that the subject took nothing by his traverse; if for the subject, it was judgment of *amoveas manus*, that the king's hands be amoved, etc.

Formerly, where a person indicted of a misdemeanour, but not actually in custody, traversed the indictment by pleading not guilty, the trial was postponed until the next assizes or sessions, and hence " traverse " came to mean " postpone." The Criminal Procedure Act, 1851, s. 27, provided that no person should be entitled to traverse, that is, postpone, the trial of any indictment.

Traverse, Toll. See TOLL-TRAVERSE.

Traversing answer; Traversing note. In suits under the practice in Chancery, where the defendant refused or neglected to file an answer to the bill, the plaintiff might file either a traversing answer or a traversing note, which produced the same effect as if the defendant had filed an answer traversing the case made by the bill. (See CONFESSO, BILL TAKEN PRO.) Now, in the corresponding case, the plaintiff sets the action down on motion for judgment under R.S.C., Ord 19, r. 7.

Traversum, a ferry.

Trawling. See SEA FISHERIES.

Treacher, Trechetour, or **Treachour,** a traitor.

Treachery, the crime committed by a person who, during the war of 1939–45, with intent to help the enemy, did or attempted or conspired to do any act designed or likely to give assistance to the naval, military or air operations of the enemy or impede such operations of the armed forces of this country or to endanger life (Treachery Act, 1940). See TREASON.

Treadmill, an instrument of prison discipline. It was composed of a large revolving cylinder, having ledges or steps fixed round its circumference; the prisoners walked up these ledges, and their weight moved the cylinder round, the principle being the same as that of the water-wheel used in old flour-mills. It was introduced into English prisons in 1818, and was for long a recognised means of causing prisoners to perform hard labour. By 1910 it had fallen into complete disuse.

Treason [Lat. *tradere*, to deliver up, betray; Fr. *trahir*, to betray; Lat. *proditio*, betrayal; Norm. Fr. *tresoun, tresun*]. Treason or *lèse-majesté* is an offence against the duty of allegiance, and is the highest known crime, for it

TREASON

aims at the very destruction of the commonwealth itself.

Treason, in its most general sense, is a crime committed by one person against another to whom he is bound by some tie of allegiance or subjection. It was formerly of two kinds, high treason and petit treason. The former now alone exists.

Five species of treason are declared by the Treason Act, 1351, as follows: if a man compasses or imagines the death of the sovereign, of his queen, or of their eldest son and heir; if a man violates the sovereign's companion (*i.e.*, his wife), or the sovereign's eldest daughter unmarried, or the wife of the sovereign's eldest son and heir; if a man levies war against the sovereign in his realm (after a battle has taken place, it is termed *bellum percussum*; before it, *bellum levatum*); if a man is adherent to the sovereign's enemies in his realm, giving to them aid or comfort in the realm or elsewhere; or if a man slays the chancellor, treasurer, or the justices assigned to hear and determine, being in their places doing their offices.

Further species have been created by subsequent statutes. Thus it is treason if a person endeavours to deprive or hinder any person, being the next in succession to the Crown, according to the limitations of the Act of Settlement, 1700, from succeeding to the Crown, and maliciously and directly attempts the same by any overt act: see the statute 1702, 1 Anne, st. 2, c. 9, s. 3. It is also treason if a person maliciously, advisedly, and directly, by writing or printing, maintains and affirms that any other person has any right or title to the Crown otherwise than according to the Act of Settlement, 1700, or that the sovereigns of this realm, with the authority of Parliament, are not able to make laws and statutes, to bind the Crown and the descent thereof (Succession to the Crown Act, 1707).

By the Treason Act, 1795, made perpetual by the Treason Act, 1817, compassing the death or injury of the sovereign, and expressing the same in writing or by any overt act, is made treason.

Treason must be prosecuted within three years from its commission, if committed within the realm, except in the case of a designed assassination of the sovereign (Treason Act, 1695).

Treason committed out of the British dominions is, by the statute 1543, 35 Hen. 8, c. 2, triable in the Queen's Bench Division. Two witnesses are required for a conviction, unless the prisoner confesses his crime (Treason Act, 1695, s. 2); the prisoner is entitled to have a copy of the indictment and lists of the witnesses and jurors delivered to him ten days before the trial (Treason Act, 1695, ss. 1, 7; Treason Act, 1708, s. 11). The Treason Act, 1842, s. 1, provides that these enactments shall not apply to attempts upon the life of the sovereign (s. 2).

The punishment of a convicted traitor is death by hanging, the ignominious adjuncts of drawing on a hurdle and quartering, etc., having been abolished, along with forfeiture and attainder, by the Forfeiture Act, 1870. The Crown can, however, direct that the traitor be beheaded (Treason Act, 1814, ss. 1, 2). By the Treason Act, 1842, treason consisting in the imagining bodily harm to the sovereign is triable just as murder is. By the same Act firing at the sovereign or striking him is punishable as a misdemeanour.

Petty treason was where a servant killed his master, a wife her husband, or an ecclesiastical person his superior, such a crime being considered a violation of private allegiance. Petty treason was abolished by the statute 1828, 9 Geo. 4, c. 31, s. 2 (replaced by the Offences against the Person Act, 1861, s. 8), which converted it into the crime of murder, from which it had differed only in its punishment.

See ACCESSORY; BURNING TO DEATH; DE FACTO.

Treason felony. Treason felony is, like treason, a purely statutory offence. By the Treason Felony Act, 1848, s. 3, if any person, within the United Kingdom or without, compasses to depose the sovereign, or to levy war against him, within any part of the United Kingdom, in order to compel him to change his counsels, or in order to intimidate or overawe Parliament, or to stir any foreigner with force to invade the United Kingdom, or any other of his dominions, and expresses such compassings by writing, or by open or advised speaking, or by any overt act, he is punishable, on indictment, with imprisonment for life.

Treasure trove [*thesaurus inventus*], money or coin, gold, silver, plate, or bullion found hidden in the earth or other private place, the owner thereof being unknown or unfound, in which case it belongs to the Crown, unless the owner appears to claim it. Bracton defines it as *vetus depositio pecuniae*. The right is not an incident of the feudal system but is a right belonging to the sovereign by virtue of the royal prerogative (*Lord Advocate* v. *Aberdeen University*, 1963 S.L.T. 361).

The Crown may grant the right to treasure trove found within a certain district to a private person, *e.g.*, the lord of the manor. (See DERELICT; FRANCHISE; MANOR; PREROGATIVE; WRECK.) In the absence of such a grant anyone concealing treasure trove which he might find was guilty of a common law misdemeanour.

The coroner has jurisdiction to hold an inquest, under the Coroners Act, 1887, s. 36, as to treasure trove; but his function is confined to ascertaining whether any given thing is or is not within the definition, and he cannot inquire as to who is entitled to it (*Att.-Gen.* v. *Moore* [1893] 1 Ch. 676). The common law offence of concealment of treasure trove was abolished by the Theft Act, 1968, s. 32. See Hill, *Treasure Trove*; Jervis, *Coroners*.

See THESAURUS, ETC.

Treasurer, one who has the care of money or treasure. See TREASURY.

There was a Lord High Treasurer of England, but the duties are now executed by commissioners. The Prime Minister generally fills the office of First Lord of the Treasury. See TREASURY.

Every local authority is under an obligation to make arrangements for the proper administration of its financial affairs and to appoint one of its officers for that purpose (Local Government Act, 1972, ss. 112, 151). The appropriate official in a county is the County Treasurer.

See UNDER TREASURER, ETC.

Treasurer's Remembrancer, he whose charge was to put the Lord Treasurer and the rest of the barons of the Exchequer in remembrance of such things as were called on and dealt in for the sovereign's behoof. See TREASURY.

Treasury, the place where treasure is deposited. It is that fiscal department of the government which controls the payments of the public money in accordance with the votes of the House of Commons. For this purpose it issues directions to the Exchequer (*q.v.*). The Lord High Treasurer is properly the head of this department; but, in practice, the functions of this official are discharged by several commissioners. The chief of these is called the First Lord; and he is, by custom, the Prime Minister, the head of the Cabinet (see CABINET), and of the whole executive, for which he is responsible in every department. The Chancellor of the Exchequer is the second commissioner, and there are five others. The management of the Treasury devolves upon the Chancellor of the Exchequer and, under him, the Paymaster-General (*q.v.*), the Chief Secretary, the Parliamentary Secretary and the Financial Secretary. As to salaries see the Ministerial and other Salaries Act, 1975, s. 1, Sch. 1.

The Interpretation Act, 1889, s. 12 (2), defines the expression "the Treasury" as meaning the Lord High Treasurer for the time being, or the Commissioners for the time being of Her Majesty's Treasury.

The Lord High Treasurer represents the Treasurer, who together with the Chancellor and the barons of the Exchequer exercised, under the Norman kings, general control over the royal revenues. See LORD TREASURER.

Treasury bills. Under the Treasury Bills Act, 1877, the Treasury, when authorised by any Act to raise money, may do so by means of bills (known as Treasury bills) payable not more than twelve months after date. Such bills have superseded Exchequer bills (*q.v.*) See also the National Loans Act, 1968.

Treasury Board. See LORD TREASURER.

Treasury Chest Fund, a fund not exceeding £1 million which the Treasury could employ to make advances for any public service, to be repaid out of moneys appropriated by Parliament to such service (Treasury Chest Fund Act, 1877, ss. 2, 3). The fund was wound up under the Finance Act, 1958, s. 39.

Treasury, First Lord of the. See LORD TREASURER.

Treasury notes, currency notes (*q.v.*).

Treasury Solicitor. The functions of the Solicitor for the Affairs of H.M. Treasury are dealt with in the Treasury Solicitor Act, 1876. They are much more extensive than those of a solicitor in the ordinary sense of the word. He need not be a qualified solicitor (Solicitors Act, 1974, s. 88), but when acting within his powers he can perform all the functions and claim all the rights which, in ordinary cases, are peculiar to a qualified solicitor. The office is generally held by a barrister. He is no longer Director of Public Prosecutions. See DIRECTOR OF PUBLIC PROSECUTIONS.

The Treasury Solicitor is also H.M. Procurator-General. " Procurator " is the Latin form of " proctor." The Treasury Solicitor, *qua* Procurator-General, has now no functions to perform. The Queen's Proctor (*q.v.*), however, belongs to his department.

Treating. The Corrupt Practices Prevention Act, 1854, s. 4, as amended by the Corrupt Practices Act, 1883, ss. 1, 2, and the Corrupt Practices Act, 1884, replaced by the Representation of the People Act, 1949, s. 100, enacts that a person who corruptly by himself or by any person before, during or after an election directly or indirectly gives or provides, or pays wholly or in part the expense of giving or providing, any meat, drink, entertainment or provision to or for any person for the purpose of corruptly influencing that person or any other person to vote or refrain from voting, or on account of that person or any other person having voted or refrained from voting, or being about to vote or refrain from voting, is guilty of treating, which is punishable as a corrupt practice. Every elector or proxy for an elector who corruptly accepts any such meat, drink, entertainment or provision

is also guilty of treating (3 Hallam, Const. Hist., c. 21, p. 302n.). See CORRUPT PRACTICES.

Treaty, the discussion of terms which precedes the conclusion of a contract or other transaction; negotiation; the act of treating; a compact between nations. It is the sovereign's prerogative to make treaties, leagues, and alliances with foreign States and princes.

In public and international law, a treaty is an agreement between the governments of two States. (See STATE.) Such an agreement is, of course, not enforceable by legal proceedings. (See INTERNATIONAL LAW; LAW.) In England, the power of making treaties with foreign States is vested in the Crown as part of its prerogative; but after the war of 1914–18, the Crown adopted a course which had previously been quite unknown, in agreeing to a treaty with France which stipulated that it, before ratification by the Crown, should be submitted to Parliament for approval (Anglo-French Treaty (Defence of France) Act, 1919). In some cases, however, treaties made by the Crown are not valid in the courts of this country unless concluded under the powers of an Act of Parliament. See EXTRADITION.

Treble costs; Treble damages. See COSTS; DOUBLE DAMAGES.

Trebucket, a tumbrel, castigatory, or cucking-stool. See CASTIGATORY; CUCKING-STOOL.

Tree. Overhanging branches may be cut by an adjoining owner without notice to the owner of the tree, provided that the adjoining owner does not go upon the land of the owner of the tree (*Lemmon* v. *Webb* [1895] A.C. 1). No right can be acquired by prescription for trees to overhang; and an action lies for damage to crops by overhanging trees (*Smith* v. *Giddy* [1904] 1 K.B. 448). See ADJOINING OWNERS; WINDFALLS.

Highway authorities and local authorities have power to plant trees, shrubs and plants of any description (Highways Act, 1959, s. 82; Highways (Miscellaneous Provisions) Act, 1961, s. 5; Land Compensation Act, 1973, Sch. 3). Trees, shrubs and other vegetation may be planted on dual carriageways and roundabouts (Act of 1959, s. 65; London

Government Act, 1963, s. 16 (2), Sch. 6 para. 21; Local Government Act, 1972, Sch. 21 para. 21, Sch. 30). Subject as above, no tree or shrub may be planted in a made-up carriageway or within fifteen feet from the centre of a made-up carriageway (Act of 1959, s. 123; *Stilwell* v. *New Windsor Corporation* [1932] 2 Ch. 155) except under licence from the highway authority (Highways Act, 1971, s. 43).

Power to lop overhanging trees, etc., which endanger or obstruct traffic or obstruct the view of drivers or the light from a public lamp is given by the Act of 1959, s. 134, amended by the Local Government Act, 1972, Sch. 21 para. 41, Sch. 30, and dangerous trees, etc., near roads may be dealt with under the Highways (Miscellaneous Provisions) Act, 1961, s. 10.

Power to lop trees overhanging any street or public road in order to prevent interference with a telegraphic line is given by the Telegraph (Construction) Act, 1908, amended by the Post Office Act, 1969, Sch. 4 para. 7.

A local planning authority may make provision for the preservation of trees, groups of trees and woodlands by means of Tree Preservation Orders. These orders need confirmation by the Secretary of State for the Environment unless no objection has been lodged (Town and Country Planning Act, 1971, s. 60; Town and Country Amenities Act, 1974, s. 10; Town and Country Planning (Tree Preservation Order) Regulations, 1969). A purchase notice requiring the purchase of the applicant's land may be served in the event of any consent under a Tree Preservation Order being refused (Act of 1971, ss. 60 (2) (*b*), 191 (1)). A person aggrieved by the making of a Tree Preservation Order may challenge the validity of the order by application to the High Court (ss. 242, 245; R.S.C., Ord. 94, rr. 1–3). A person contravening a Tree Preservation Order or interfering with trees in a conservation area is liable to penalties on summary conviction or on conviction on indictment (Act of 1971, s. 102; Town and Country Amenities Act, 1974, s. 10). Nothing in a Tree Preservation Order applies to the cutting down, topping, lopping or uprooting of a tree

(1) which is dying or dead or has become dangerous, or (2) in accordance with statutory obligations, or (3) so far as necessary to prevent or abate a nuisance (s. 60 (6); Town and Country Amenities Act, 1974, s. 10 (2)).

When granting permission for development a local planning authority must impose conditions and make Tree Preservation Orders whenever appropriate, to secure the preservation or planting of trees (Act of 1971, ss. 59, 60 (3)). The owner of land on which a tree (the subject of a Tree Preservation Order) dies or is removed or destroyed in contravention of the Order, must replace the tree unless the local planning authority absolve him from this responsibility (Act of 1971, s. 62; Town and Country Amenities Act, 1974, s. 10 (2)).

In urgent cases the local planning authority may make a provisional tree preservation order (s. 61). Trees in conservation areas (*q.v.*) are subject to special protection (Act of 1971, s. 61A inserted by the Town and Country Amenities Act, 1974, s. 8). The local planning authority are empowered to enforce these provisions subject to appeal to the Secretary of State for the Environment and to a further appeal (on law only) to the courts (ss. 103, 246; R.S.C., Ords. 55, 94).

A Tree Preservation Order is registrable as a local land charge (Local Land Charges (Amendment) Rules, 1948, r. 3).

The Forestry Commissioners have power to control the felling of trees (Forestry Act, 1967, ss. 9–36, as amended).

An owner of land is liable for damage caused by the roots of trees penetrating into adjoining property (*Morgan* v. *Khyatt* [1964] 1 W.L.R. 475). The owner of a tree which falls across the highway is not liable to pay the cost of its removal if he took reasonable care to secure that it did not fall (*Williams* v. *Devon C.C.* (1966) 65 L.G.R. 119).

See FORESTRY; TELEGRAPHS; TIMBER.

Treet [Lat. *triticum*], fine wheat (51 Hen. 3).

Tremagium, Tremesium, Tremissium, the season or time of sowing summer-corn, being about March, the third month. See HYPERNAGIUM.

Tremellum, granary.

Tresayle, a great-great-grandfather; the grandfather of a grandfather. The writ of tresayle was identical with the writ of cosinage. It lay upon ouster by abatement on the death of the grandfather's grandfather. See AIEL; BESAIEL; COSINAGE.

Trespass [Lat. *transgressio*], any transgression of the law less than treason, or misprision of treason.

Trespass is a generic name for various torts, most of them being distinguished by the Latin words formerly used in the appropriate writs.

The action of trespass lies where a trespass has been committed either to the plaintiff's person or property. A trespass is an injury committed with violence, and this violence may be either actual or implied; and the law will imply violence, though none is actually used, where the injury is of a direct and immediate kind, and committed on the person or tangible and corporeal property of the plaintiff. Of actual violence an assault and battery is an instance; of implied, a peaceable but wrongful entry upon the plaintiff's lands.

Trespass *vi et armis* (with force and arms) includes injuries to the person accompanied with actual force or violence, as in the case of battery and imprisonment, and the act of entering on another man's land without lawful authority. This latter kind of trespass (in which the " force " is implied or fictitious) is also called trespass *quare clausum fregit*, " because he (the defendant) broke or entered into the close " or land of the plaintiff. Not only entering a man's land, but also the acts of allowing cattle to stray into his land, or driving nails into his wall, or digging the minerals under his land, constitute trespass *quare clausum fregit*. To enable a person to bring an action of trespass " *qu. cl. fr.*," he must have actual possession of the land. Therefore, an heir of land could not maintain an action for a trespass committed before he took possession by entry. See POSSESSION; QUARE CLAUSUM FREGIT; VI ET ARMIS.

Where a person has by law the right to enter on the lands of another for a certain purpose, and, after entry, he does some positive act of misfeasance, then he is considered a trespasser *ab initio*, as if his entry had been unlawful (*Six Carpenters' Case* (1610) 8 Co.Rep. 146a). See AB INITIO; ADJOINING OWNERS.

A continuing trespass is one which is permanent in its nature; as where a person builds on his own land so that part of the building overhangs his neighbour's land.

For trespass by entry or user of land without right or beyond the limits of a right, no damage need be proved. Trespass by occupation of land is a continuing damage which is actionable from day to day so long as the trespassing person or object remains on the land. See SUPPORT.

The plaintiff must show that he was in possession at the time of the alleged trespass, and not merely that he had a right of possession or a licence which had been infringed, but having entered, or commenced an action for possession, he is entitled to sue for trespass from the date of the accrual of the right by the doctrine of trespass by relation, which is the basis of the action for mesne profits.

Jus tertii or the extraneous right of another who is not in possession is no defence to an action of trespass unless the defendant acted under it.

Another variety of trespass *vi et armis* is trespass *de bonis asportatis*, for the wrongful taking of chattels. Injuries committed to chattels while in the owner's possession (*e.g.*, by poisoning his cattle) are also classed under the head of trespass *vi et armis*. See FORCE AND ARMS.

In an action of trespass to the person it must be alleged and proved that the defendant acted intentionally or negligently (*Fowler* v. *Lanning* [1959] 1 Q.B. 426).

As to trespass on the case, see ACTION ON THE CASE.

Trespasser, one who commits a trespass. In general a person owes no duty to a trespasser, the rule being that a man trespasses at his own risk (*Grand Trunk Railway of Canada* v. *Barnett* [1911] A.C. 370; *Latham* v. *R. Johnson & Nephew* [1913] 1 K.B. 398; *Commissioner for Railways* v. *Quinlan* [1964] A.C. 1054). An occupier must not, however, injure a trespasser intentionally nor act with reckless disregard for his safety if he is aware of his presence. An occupier owes to a trespasser a duty to take such steps as common sense or common humanity would dictate to exclude or warn or otherwise, within reasonable and practicable limits, to reduce or avert the danger (*British Railways Board* v. *Herrington* [1972] A.C. 877). For there to be liability to a trespassing child there must be knowledge of facts which would fairly lead a humane and sensible man to draw the inference that there was a likelihood that in the absence of precautions some serious accident could happen (*Penny* v. *Northampton Borough Council* (1972) 72 L.G.R. 733). A person who has no express permission to enter another's land is not a trespasser if a licence to enter it is to be implied. Thus, the occupier of a dwelling house gives an implied licence to anyone coming on lawful business to come through the front gate and knock on the front door (*Robson* v. *Hallett* [1967] 2 Q.B. 939). An occupier of a field across which to his knowledge the public habitually walked was held liable to a person for injuries done to him by a vicious horse which the occupier of the field kept there (*Lowery* v. *Walker* [1911] A.C. 10). A man may be a trespasser even on a highway if he is using it for an improper purpose (*Harrison* v. *Duke of Rutland* [1893] 1 Q.B. 143). See SPRING GUNS.

Trestonare, to turn or divert another way.

Tret. See ALLOWANCE.

Trethings [Wel. *trethu,* to tax], taxes, imposts.

Treyts, taken out or withdrawn, as withdrawing or discharging a juror.

Trial, the hearing of a cause, civil or criminal, before a judge who has jurisdiction over it, according to the laws of the land. A trial is the finding out by due examination the truth of the point in issue or question between the parties, whereupon judgment may be given (Co. Litt. 124b).

A trial is that step in an action, prosecution or other judicial proceeding, by which the questions of fact in issue are decided. See FACT; ISSUE; QUESTIONS OF LAW.

At a trial by jury, the cause is called on, or the prisoner arraigned, before the jury is sworn. The parties may then challenge the jury. (See CHALLENGE.) The pleadings are opened by counsel for the plaintiff and the case stated to the jury; after this the witnesses for the plaintiff are examined by his counsel, the cross-examination being generally conducted by the senior counsel for the defendant. If the defendant's counsel objects to any question or any document, all the defendant's counsel are entitled to be heard on the objection, and all the plaintiff's counsel on the other side, and the senior counsel for the defendant in reply; and so if the plaintiff's counsel objects *mutatis mutandis.* If the plaintiff has evidence to rebut the issues of which the burden of proof lies on the defendant, he may either produce it at the same time as his other evidence, or reserve it until after the defendant has given affirmative evidence on the issue. At the end of the plaintiff's evidence, the defendant's counsel declares whether he will call witnesses; and if he does not, the plaintiff's senior counsel sums up his evidence, and the defendant's senior counsel next addresses the jury, and the judge sums up. If the defendant's counsel calls evidence, he immediately opens his case to the jury, and the witnesses are called and examined as in the plaintiff's case. The plaintiff is, in general, entitled to call witnesses to rebut the evidence of the defendant, if he has not already given all his evidence, which is more generally the case. Then the defendant's senior counsel sums up, and the senior counsel for the plaintiff replies upon the whole case. The judge then sums up. The verdict may be taken by the associate in the absence of the judge (*Hawksley* v. *Fewtrell* [1954] 1 Q.B. 228); but in a criminal trial the judge must be present.

In a criminal trial the effect of the pleadings is stated to the jury. In other respects the order of proceeding is the same. After conviction counsel for the defendant may address the court in mitigation, and counsel for the prosecution in aggravation, of his sentence. Sentence may be deferred to a future day.

In criminal cases, where the accused is charged on indictment, the trial is always by a jury. In civil cases in the High Court, trial is without a jury, unless the court otherwise orders; but where fraud is alleged, or in cases of libel, slander, malicious prosecution or false imprisonment, an order is made for trial by a jury on the application of either party unless the court or judge is of opinion that the trial thereof requires any prolonged examination of documents or accounts or any scientific or local investigation which cannot conveniently be made with a jury (Administration of Justice (Miscellaneous Provisions) Act, 1933, s. 6; Law Reform (Miscellaneous Provisions) Act, 1970, ss. 5, 7, Sch.; R.S.C., Ord. 33, rr. 4, 5). See JURY.

In the Chancery Division, when the trial is by affidavit it is commonly called a hearing, and all the counsel on both sides are heard in order, the senior counsel for the party first heard (plaintiff or petitioner) being heard in reply. When an issue is tried by oral evidence before the court itself, the common law practice is followed. In the Chancery Division actions are almost invariably tried by a judge alone, actions where a jury is thought desirable being usually transferred to the Queen's Bench Division.

The trial in the ecclesiastical courts mostly resembles the former course of an ordinary trial in Chancery.

In actions in the High Court, there are five principal modes of trial, viz., trial before a judge and jury, before a judge alone, before a judge with assessors, before an official referee (q.v.) with or without assessors, before a master or before a special referee (R.S.C., Ord. 33, r. 2). For trial by a circuit judge discharging the functions of an official referee, see Ord. 36, rr. 1–7; by special referee see Ord. 36, r. 8; by a master see Ord. 36, r. 9 and Ord. 14, r. 6 (2).

An " expedited hearing list " to secure the early disposal of short and simple cases in the Queen's Bench Division, particularly those involving sentences of imprisonment, disqualification for driving or possession of property, was introduced experimentally by Practice Direction of October 2, 1974 [1974] 1 W.L.R. 1219.

Trial before a judge and jury (formerly called trial per pais) is a mode of trial which was formerly peculiar to the superior courts of common law (see COUNTRY). By the Chancery Amendment Act, 1858, power was given to the Court of Chancery to summon juries to try questions of fact; but the power was seldom exercised.

It sometimes happens that the trial comes to a premature end by the non-appearance of one of the parties, or by nonsuit (q.v.), or the withdrawal of a juror (q.v.). If the plaintiff does not appear at the trial, the action is dismissed; if the defendant does not appear, the plaintiff must prove his case, so far as the burden of proof lies upon him. A verdict or judgment so obtained may be set aside by the Court of Appeal on terms (Judicature Act, 1925, s. 30; R.S.C., Ord. 59, r. 2). Sometimes a trial is ordered to take place before several judges and a jury; this was formerly called a trial at bar (see BAR, TRIAL AT), as opposed to the ordinary trial.

Where the judge who tried the action has misdirected the jury in point of law, or admitted evidence which ought to have been refused, or rejected evidence which ought to have been admitted, and by so doing has caused a miscarriage of justice, or where the jury have found against the weight of the evidence, or given excessive damages, and generally wherever it is clear that a fair trial has not been had, the party aggrieved may obtain an order for a new trial on motion made for that purpose. The whole proceedings on the trial are then gone through afresh, and, if the case is again not properly tried, a third trial may be ordered, and so on. (R.S.C., Ord. 59, r. 11).

The Court of Appeal has power to order a retrial in criminal cases. See NEW TRIAL.

The other modes of trial are similar to trial before a judge and jury, except that the calling and swearing of the jury, and the summing up by the judge, are necessarily absent. Where the trial is before a judge alone, the evidence is sometimes taken by affidavit. See AFFIDAVIT; EVIDENCE.

Admiralty actions involving nautical questions, e.g., actions of collision, are generally tried before a judge with Trinity Masters (q.v.) sitting as assessors.

Trial by the record was where issue was

joined as to the existence of a particular record (*q.v.*): such an issue was tried by the court itself on production of the record. Trial by certificate was where a fact could only be proved by the certificate of a public official: thus, the custom of the City of London in respect of foreign attachment was proved by the oral certificate of the recorder.

In county court actions, the course of proceedings resembles that on a trial in the High Court.

In criminal cases, the trial of a person accused of a crime usually takes place before a judge and jury at the Crown Court or the Central Criminal Court. The steps on a criminal trial are substantially the same as those above described, substituting " prosecutor " for " plaintiff," and " prisoner " for " defendant." (See ACQUITTAL; CONVICTION.) Obsolete modes of trial are those by ordeal, by the corsned, and by battle.

In cases of treason and felony, a nobleman was formerly entitled to be tried by his peers, that is, by members of the House of Lords. See CERTIORARI; HOUSE OF LORDS; LORD HIGH STEWARD.

Trial by battle. See BATTLE, TRIAL BY.

Trial in camera. See CAMERA.

Trial, Writ of. The Civil Procedure Act, 1833, s. 17, empowered the superior courts to order that the issues joined in any action of debt for not more than £20 should be tried before the sheriff or any judge of any inferior court of the county in which the action had been brought, and provided that effect should be given to such order by the issue of a writ known as a writ of trial. This enactment was repealed by the County Courts Act, 1867, s. 6, as being unnecessary in view of the jurisdiction which the county court had by then acquired.

Tribunal, the seat of a judge; a court of justice.

The word is commonly used to refer to a person or body exercising judicial or quasi-judicial functions outside the regular judicial system. A decision of such a tribunal can be questioned if an error of law appears on the face of the decision (*R.* v. *Northumberland Compensation Appeal Tribunal* [1952] 1 K.B. 338).

A domestic tribunal is subject only to

the instrument giving it jurisdiction and to the rules of natural justice. Unless the instrument states to the contrary, a person who is subject to examination by the tribunal is not entitled to be legally represented (*Pelt* v. *Greyhound Racing Association* (No. 2) [1970] 1 Q.B. 46, 67; *Enderby Town Football Club* v. *Football Association* [1971] Ch. 591). The courts will not interfere with the standards of professional behaviour, however high, set by a properly constituted disciplinary tribunal. In considering the appropriate penalty for a breach of such standards regard should be had to the extent to which those standards are known and accepted within the profession (*Re a Solicitor* [1975] Q.B. 475).

The Tribunals and Inquiries Act, 1971 (consolidating the Tribunals and Inquiries Acts, 1958 and 1966), continues in being the Council on Tribunals whose functions are to keep under review the constitution and working of the tribunals listed in Sch. I to the Act. There is to be an appeal on a point of law from decisions of certain tribunals. Statutory provision that orders or determinations shall not be called into question in any court are not to prevent the removal of proceedings into the High Court by order of certiorari or to prejudice the powers of the High Court to make orders of mandamus.

An appeal lies to the High Court on a point of law from a decision of the Secretary of State on an appeal to him from a determination of the Director General of Fair Trading (Tribunals and Inquiries Act, 1971, s. 13 (5A)); Consumer Credit Act, 1974, s. 42).

As to appeals etc. from industrial tribunals see s. 13 and the Employment Protection Act, 1975, Sch. 16 Pt. IV para. 14.

Tribunal of inquiry. A tribunal of Inquiry may be established by resolution of both Houses of Parliament for inquiring into a definite matter described in the resolution as of urgent public importance. As to the evidence before such a tribunal, see the Tribunals of Inquiry (Evidence) Act, 1921, and the Civil Evidence Act, 1968, s. 17 (1).

Tribunal of the Hague. See HAGUE CONFERENCE.

Tricycles. See BICYCLES.

Triding; Trithing, a riding (*q.v.*).

Tribute, a payment made in acknowledgment; subjection.

Tricesima, an ancient custom in a borough in the county of Hereford, so called because thirty burgesses paid 1d. rent for their houses to the bishop, who was lord of the manor (Lib.Nik.Heref.).

Tridingmote, the court held for a triding or trithing.

Triennial Acts. The Triennial Act, 1641, provided that if in every third year parliament was not duly summoned and assembled before September 3 it should assemble on the second Monday in the ensuing November. It was repealed by the Triennial Act, 1664, which provided that parliament should not be interrupted or discontinued above three years at the most.

The Triennial Act, 1694, provided that a new parliament should be called within three years after the dissolution of a former one and the utmost extent of time that any parliament should be allowed to sit was limited to three years. This Act was repealed by the Septennial Act, 1715, which extended the period of parliamentary duration to seven years. The Septennial Act, 1715, remained in force until the Parliament Act, 1911, enacted that five years should be substituted for seven years as the time fixed for the maximum duration of parliament.

Triens, a third part; also dower.

Triers; Triors, persons appointed by the court (when necessary) to decide challenges to jurors, where no jurors had been already sworn on the jury. As soon as two jurors were sworn, they decided all subsequent challenges. Challenges to the array were tried by the court itself (Bro.Abr. 122).

The Criminal Justice Act, 1948, s. 35, provides that challenges for cause shall be tried by the court.

See CHALLENGE; ELISORS.

Trina admonitio, the threefold warning. See PEINE FORTE ET DURE.

Trinepos, a male descendant in the sixth degree in direct line (Civil Law).

Trinidad and Tobago, islands in the West Indies forming one colony under the Trinidad and Tobago Act, 1887. Under the West Indian Court of Appeal Act, 1919, a court of appeal was created for Trinidad and Tobago, British Guiana, Barbados and the Leeward and Windward Isles. The British Caribbean Federation Act, 1956, provided for the federation of the West Indian colonies. See the Trinidad and Tobago Independence Act, 1962. See TOBAGO, ETC.

Trinity House. By the Merchant Shipping Act, 1894, s. 742, the Trinity House means the Master, Wardens, and Assistants of the Guild, Fraternity, or Brotherhood of the Most Glorious and Undivided Trinity and of St. Clement, commonly called the Corporation of the Trinity House of Deptford Strond. The Trinity House consists of ten Acting Masters (one of whom is a retired naval officer, the other nine being retired officers of the mercantile marine) and of a number of other Masters, some of whom have been Acting Masters who have ceased to perform active duties, the rest being peers, prominent politicians and members of the Royal Family. All the Masters are known as Elder Brethren.

The Trinity House received its charter in 1514. Under that and subsequent charters and statutes, including the statute 1566, 8 Eliz. 1, c. 13, and the Harbours, Docks, and Piers Clauses Act, 1847, it is entrusted with duties relating to pilotage (*q.v.*), lighthouses, beacons and sea marks. The enactment under which it deals with lighthouses, etc., is the Merchant Shipping Act, 1894, s. 634 (1) (*a*). The actual work of the Trinity House is done by the Acting Masters.

There are also Trinity Houses at Hull and Newcastle respectively, which, under various charters and the Pilotage Act, 1913, act instead of the main Trinity House as regards pilotage in districts adjoining those towns.

Trinity House outport districts, districts under the authority of subcommissioners appointed by the Trinity House, and any pilotage district declared to be a Trinity House outport district under the Pilotage Act, 1913, s. 52 (1).

Trinity Masters, Acting Elder Brethren of the Trinity House. If the decision of a question arising in an Admiralty action requires technical knowledge and experience in navigation, the judge or court is usually assisted at the hearing by two

Trinity Masters who sit as assessors (*q.v.*) and advise the court on questions of a nautical character. Trinity Masters also act as assessors of prize courts.

Trinity Masters are ineligible for jury service. See JURY.

Trinity sittings. The Trinity sittings of the Court of Appeal and of the High Court commence on the second Tuesday after Whit Sunday and end on July 31 (R.S.C., Ord. 64, r. 1). See SITTINGS; TERM.

Trinity Sunday, the Sunday next after Whit Sunday (*q.v.*).

Trinity term, one of the four legal terms, which began on May 22 and ended on June 12. See TERM; TRINITY SITTINGS.

Trink; Trinker; Trinkerman. A trink was a kind of fixed net used in the tidal part of the Thames; trinker was another form of the same word; and trinker or trinkerman meant a man who worked such a net; see the statutes 1423, 2 Hen. 6, cc. 12, 19.

Trinobantes, Trinonantes, or **Trinovantes** [Brit. *trie now hant*, inhabitants of the new city, *i.e.*, London], inhabitants of Britain, situated next to the Cantii northward, who occupied, according to Camden and Baxter, that country which now comprises the counties of Essex and Middlesex, and some part of Surrey. But in the time of Ptolemy their territories were not so extensive, as London did not then belong to them (Encyc.Londin.).

Trinoda necessitas. Under this denomination are comprised three distinct imposts, to which all landed possessions, not excepting those of the Church, were subject, *viz.*, *bryge-bót*, for keeping the bridges and high roads in repair (*pontis constructio*), *burg-bot*, for keeping the burgs or fortresses in an efficient state of defence (*arcis constructio*), and *fyrd*, or contribution for maintaining the military and naval forces of the kingdom (*expeditio*) (Anc.Inst.Eng.).

Triors. See TRIERS.

Tripartite, divided into three parts, having three corresponding copies; a deed to which there are three distinct parties.

Tripertitum testamentum, the form of will under Justinian, so called from its threefold origin. It had to be made before seven witnesses (as required by the *jus civile*), sealed with their seven seals (as required by the *jus honorarium*), and signed with their seven *subscriptiones* (as required by the constitutions of Theodosius II) (Civil Law).

Triplicatio, a rebutter; an equitable allegation by a plaintiff in answer to a *duplicatio* (Civil Law).

Triptych, a set of three pictures or carvings, set side by side in separate compartments, the outside compartments being hinged so that they can fold in over the central one. A faculty is required for the use of a triptych in connection with the altar of a parish church.

Tristis. Under the forest laws, this meant immunity from attending and assisting one who had the right of chase (1 Manw. 86).

Tritavia, a great-grandmother's great-grandmother; a female ascendant in the sixth degree (Civil Law).

Tritavus, a great-grandfather's great-grandfather; a male ascendant in the sixth degree (Civil Law).

Trithing, the third part of a shire or province; a riding. The county of York is divided into three ridings—East, West and North. See RIDING; TRIDING.

Trithing-reeve, a governor of a trithing.

Triumvir, a trithing man or constable of three hundreds; a member of a government consisting of three men.

Triverbial days [*dies fasti*], judicial days, when the courts were open for business; so called from the three words *do, dico* and *addico* (Civil Law). See DIES FASTI.

Trolley vehicle, a mechanically-propelled vehicle adapted for use upon roads without rails and moved by power transmitted thereto from some external source (Road Traffic Act, 1930, s. 121; Road Traffic Regulation Act, 1967, s. 104; Road Traffic Act, 1972, s. 196). Test certificates are not required; nor is third party insurance (Act of 1972, s. 198). A trolley vehicle has a power of manoeuvre not possessed by a tram (*Lancaster* v. *London Passenger Transport Board* [1948] 2 All E.R. 796).

Tron; Trona, a beam; the public weighing machine of a city or burgh (Fleta).

Such a machine was later known in

Scotland as the trone, or the king's trone, but these words do not seem to have been used in England.

Tronage [*tronagium*], a customary duty, or toll for weighing wool at the *trona* (*q.v.*) (Moore, *Foreshore*).

Tronator, a weigher of wool; an officer of the City of London who weighed all the wool brought into the City (*Book of Oaths*, edition of 1689, p. 129).

Tronour, an official in charge of the tron (*q.v.*). In this sense the word is Scottish rather than English and does not seem to have been used south of Newcastle-on-Tyne.

In the statutes 1344, 18 Edw. 3, st. 2, c. 4, and 1390, 14 Ric. 2, c. 10, the tronour is mentioned along with the finder (*q.v.*) and other such officers: he was some kind of customs officer.

Trophy money, money formerly collected and raised in London, and the several counties of England, towards providing harness and maintenance for the militia, etc.

Trout. By the Salmon and Freshwater Fisheries Act, 1975, s. 41, " trout " means any fish of the salmon family commonly known as trout and includes migratory trout, *i.e.*, trout which migrate to and from the sea, and char. There is prohibited the use of any firearm, otter, lath or jack, wire or snare, crossline or setline, spear, gaff (but see below), stroke-haul, snatch or other like instrument or a light for the purpose of taking or killing salmon (*q.v.*), trout or freshwater fish. A person may not have in his possession any of these instruments intending to use it to take or kill salmon, trout or freshwater fish. The throwing or discharging of stones or other missiles for the purpose of taking or killing salmon, trout or freshwater fish is also prohibited. These prohibitions do not apply to a gaff consisting of a plain metal hook without a barb or of a tailer as auxiliary to angling with rod and line (Salmon and Freshwater Fisheries Act, 1975, s. 1). No explosive, poison or other noxious substance or any electrical device may be used to take or destroy fish. No person may, without lawful excuse, destroy or damage any dam, floodgate or sluice with intent thereby to take or destroy fish (Salmon and Freshwater Fisheries Act, 1975, s. 5).

The use of fish roe for fishing for salmon, trout or freshwater fish is prohibited. So also is the taking, buying, selling, exposing for sale or having possession of unclean or immature salmon, trout or freshwater fish (s. 2).

Fishing for salmon or trout, except with rod and line, is restricted above or below any dam or any obstruction, whether artificial or natural, which hinders or retards the passage of salmon or trout or in any waters under or adjacent to any mill or in the head race or tail race of any mill or in any waste race or pool communicating with a mill or in any artificial channel connected with such dam or obstruction. This does not apply to any legal fishing dam not having a crib, box or cruive or to any fishing box, coop, apparatus, net or mode of fishing in connection with and forming part of such dam or obstruction for purposes of fishing. Scaring or disturbing salmon or trout is similarly restricted (s. 17).

As to obstructions (*e.g.*, fixed engines, fishing weirs, fishing mill dams, fish passes and gratings) to the passage of salmon and migratory trout, see ss. 6–18.

As to close seasons, see CLOSE SEASON.

Trover [Fr. *trouver*, to find]. This was an action on the case, properly called the action of trover and conversion, which might be maintained by any person who had a right to possession of goods, for recovering the value of such goods against another, who, having or being supposed to have obtained possession of such goods by lawful means, had wrongfully converted them to his own use. It originally lay only where the goods had been lost by the plantiff and found by the defendant, but it was in course of time allowed to be brought upon a fictitious allegation of the finding not required to be proved, but not formally abolished until the Common Law Procedure Act, 1852, s. 49.

Under the old common law there were four different remedies for the wrongful deprivation of goods, *viz.*, the actions of trespass to goods, detinue, replevin, and trover, which was the old name for an action of conversion. Trespass and trover were actions to recover damages merely, but the actions of detinue and replevin were both brought for the return of the goods. The actions of trespass and replevin could be maintained against anyone who took the goods out of the possession of the plaintiff; the actions of detinue and trover lay against any person who came into possession of the goods by any means and wrongfully withheld them from the plaintiff. In trespass and replevin the plaintiff was always in actual possession of the goods at the time when the defendant commenced the wrongful act.

An action for conversion (*q.v.*) is still commonly called an action of trover.

See DELIVERY, WRIT OF; DETINUE; TORT.

Troy weight [*pondus Trojae*], a weight having its name from Troyes, a city in Aube, France. See PONDUS REGIS.

An ounce troy consists of 480 of the 7,000 grains (*q.v.*) which go to the imperial pound (*q.v.*) (Weights and Measures Act, 1963, s. 10, Sch. 1 Pt. V). The pound troy is not referred to in a statute. The ounce troy consisted of twenty pennyweights (*q.v.*). The ounce troy is not to be used for trade except for the purpose of transactions in, or in articles made from, gold, silver or other precious metals, including transactions in gold or silver thread, lace or fringe (s. 10 (2)).

Truchman, an interpreter.

Trucial States. Certain states in the Persian Gulf for the foreign relations of which Her Majesty was responsible. See Aithison's *Collection of Treaties, Engagements and Sanads* (1933), Vol. XI, Part 2.

Truck Acts. The Truck Act, 1831, was passed to abolish the truck system. Under that system employers were in the practice of paying the wages of their workpeople in goods, or of requiring them to purchase goods at certain shops, which led to labourers being compelled to take goods of inferior quality at a high price. The Act made payment in money compulsory; and it applied to all artificers, workmen and labourers, except those engaged in certain trades, especially iron and metal works, quarries, cloth, silk and glass manufactories. It did not apply to domestic or agricultural servants. The Truck Act Amendment Act, 1887, s. 2, provides that the Act of 1831 shall apply

to workmen as defined by that part of the section which was added by the Statute Law (Repeals) Act, 1973, Sch. 2, that is to say, to all persons (other than seamen or domestic or menial servants) under a contract to perform any work or labour. This brought in agricultural labourers, but the Act of 1887, s. 4, provides that a contract may be made with an agricultural labourer for giving him food, drink, not being intoxicating, a cottage or other allowances or privileges in addition to money wages.

The Truck Act, 1896, regulates the conditions under which deductions may be made from wages for fines, for bad or negligent work or injury to materials, and for materials, tools, machines, etc., supplied by the employer.

The Truck Acts, 1831 to 1896, are enforceable by officers appointed by the Secretary of State. See S.I. 1974 No. 1887, made under the Health and Safety at Work etc. Act, 1974, ss. 15, 82.

A deduction from wages in respect of damages awarded to an employer in an action is a violation of the Acts (*Williams* v. *North's Navigation Collieries* [1906] A.C. 136); so too is a deduction from wages for the purchase of shares in an employing company (*Kenyon* v. *Darwen Cotton Manufacturing Co.* [1936] 2 K.B. 193).

The Payment of Wages Act, 1960, provides that notwithstanding the provisions of the Truck Acts, 1831 to 1940, and other legislation requiring wages to be paid in cash, an employed person, if he so requests in writing and his employer agrees, may have his wages or part of them paid by crediting his bank account with the amount due or by postal order, money order or by cheque.

An agreement between employer, union and employee whereunder the employer deducts union contributions from the employee's wages and pays the same direct to the union is not illegal under s. 2 of the Truck Act, 1831 (*Williams* v. *Butlers* [1975] 1 W.L.R. 946).

True bill [*billa vera*], the indorsement which the grand jury (*q.v.*) made upon a bill of indictment when, having heard the evidence, they were satisfied of the probable truth of the accusation. See INDICTMENT.

True owner. The " true owner " of goods in the " reputed ownership " (*q.v.*) of a bankrupt is the person, whether or not he is the legal owner, who is entitled to determine the state of things under which the bankrupt is the apparent owner (Bankruptcy Act, 1914, s. 38).

As to the meaning of the term *quoad* bills of sale, see BILLS OF SALE.

True, public, and notorious. These three qualities used to be formerly predicated in the libel in the ecclesiastical courts, of the charges which it contained, at the end of each article severally.

Trunk roads. See the Highways Act, 1959, ss. 7–10; Highways (Miscellaneous Provisions) Act, 1961, s. 2; London Government Act, 1963, Sch. 6 paras. 4, 5, Sch. 18 Pt. II; Road Traffic Regulation Act, 1967, s. 14 (1); Highways Act, 1971, ss. 11, 12; Local Government Act, 1972, Sch. 21 paras. 5, 6, Sch. 30. The Minister for Transport is the highway authority for trunk roads, *i.e.*, the national system of routes for through traffic (Highways Act, 1959, ss. 1, 7, replacing the Trunk Roads Acts, 1936 and 1946).

As to special roads see SPECIAL ROADS.

Trust. A trust is a confidence reposed either expressly or impliedly in a person (called the trustee) for the benefit of another (called the *cestui que trust*, or beneficiary), not, however, issuing out of real or personal property, but as a collateral incident accompanying it, annexed in privity to (*i.e.,* commensurate with) the interest in such property, and also to the person touching such interest, for the accomplishment of which confidence the *cestui que trust* or beneficiary has his remedy in equity only, the trustee himself likewise being aided and protected in the proper performance of his trust when he seeks the court's direction as to its management.

A trust, in its simplest form, is a relation between two persons by virtue of which one of them (the trustee) holds property for the benefit of the other (the *cestui que trust*), while as regards the rest of the world he (the trustee) is, for most purposes, absolute owner of it. The right of the *cestui que trust* to that benefit is enforceable as a personal right against only the trustee and those who have acquired interests in the trust property with notice of the trust. As between the trustee and *cestui que trust*, and those claiming under them, the *cestui que trust* is in effect beneficial owner of the trust property, either absolutely or with restrictions according to the nature of the trust. As trusts were formerly enforced only in equity, he is sometimes called equitable owner. See EQUITY; ESTATE; OWNERSHIP.

Every kind of property in which a legal interest may be given, whatever may be its quantity or quality, may be impressed with a trust, which equity will carry out without regard to form, provided its purpose does not contravene the policy of the law, or the principles governing the rights of property: for *qui haeret in litera haeret in cortice* (*q.v.*).

Trusts arise either by the act of the party or by operation of law.

Trusts arising by act of the party are either express or implied.

An express trust is one created by clear words: as where A gives property to B in trust for C, or otherwise expresses a clear intention that C shall have the benefit of it. A is called the author of the trust, or the settlor, testator, etc., according to the instrument by which the trust is created. As to where writing is required for the creation of trusts, see DECLARATION; SECRET TRUSTS; STATUTE OF FRAUDS.

Express trusts may be divided into trusts executed, perfect, complete, or constituted, and trusts executory, imperfect, incomplete, or directory.

With reference to the completeness with which they are expressed by the author of the trust, trusts are of two classes, *viz.*, those in which the objects of the trust are completely indicated, and those in which they are not. Trusts of the former class are again divisible into trusts executed and trusts executory. An executed trust is one in which the limitations of the equitable interest are complete and final; as if A conveys property in trust for B for life, and after his death in trust for C absolutely. In an executory trust the limitations of the equitable interest are intended to serve merely as minutes or instructions for perfecting the settlement at some future period; thus, a trust in marriage articles to settle land on the intended husband for life, with remainder to the heirs of the body of the husband and wife, is executory, because it contemplates a future settlement in accordance with the intention expressed by the articles, which is that such a limitation may be made as will give the husband a life interest only, with remainder to the eldest and other sons successively in tail. The distinction was formerly of importance in that, if the limitations in the articles had been treated as final (in other words, as an executed trust) they would, under the rule in *Shelley's Case* (1580) 1 Co.Rep. 93b (*q.v.*), have given the husband an estate tail, which would have enabled him to defeat the interests of the issue.

With reference to their purposes, trusts are either public or private. Public trusts are such as are constituted for the benefit either of the public at large or of some considerable portion of it answering a particular description, *i.e.*, trusts for charitable purposes. In private trusts the beneficial interest is vested absolutely in one or more individuals who are, or within a certain time may be, definitely ascertained, and to whom therefore collectively, unless under some legal disability, it is, or within the allowed limit will be, competent to control, modify or determine the trust. Public trusts are necessarily administrative (*q.v.*); private trusts, on the other hand, may be simple (passive) or special (active).

A simple trust is where property is vested in one person upon trust for another, and the nature of the trust not being prescribed by the settlor, it is left to the construction of law. In this case the *cestui que trust* has *jus habendi*, or the right to be put in actual possession of the property, and *jus disponendi*, or the right to call upon the trustee to execute conveyances as the *cestui que trust* directs; he is, in short, absolute equitable owner of the property. See TRUSTEE.

A special trust is where the machinery of a trust is introduced for the execution of some purpose particularly pointed out,

and the trustee is not, as before, a mere passive depositary of the estate, but is called upon to exert himself actively in the execution of the settlor's intention; as where a conveyance is to trustees upon trust to sell for payment of debts, or to pay the income to a given person during his life. See SETTLEMENT.

With reference to the obligations of the trustee, special trusts are divisible into imperative and discretionary. An imperative trust is where the trustee is bound to act in the manner directed; thus, if the property is given upon trust to sell, the trustee is bound to sell (though he may have power to postpone the sale). A discretionary trust is where the performance or exercise of the trust and not merely the mode of its exercise is left to the discretion of the trustee: as if property is given to B upon trust to apply it for the benefit of C or his wife and children during his life in such manner and so long as B in his discretion shall think best; such trusts are not infrequently inserted in wills and settlements when it is desired to prevent an allowance given to a spendthrift and his family from being assigned by him or taken by his creditors on his bankruptcy, because, as the trust cannot be enforced against the trustee, C has no interest capable of being sold or otherwise dealt with for the benefit of his creditors.

With reference to the mode in which they are to be exercised, special trusts are divisible into ministerial (or instrumental) and discretionary. Ministerial trusts are such as demand no further exercise of reason or understanding than every intelligent agent must necessarily employ; such is a trust to convey an estate to a certain person. Discretionary trusts are such as cannot be duly administered without the application of a certain degree of prudence and judgment; as where a fund is vested in trustees upon trust to distribute it among such charitable objects as the trustees shall think fit.

Trusts may arise by operation of law; such are constructive trusts, which arise when property which has been acquired in right of another is being retained by the trustee for his own benefit, or when a person obtaining the property knows or should know that another person has a prior right to the property or some part of or interest in it in equity; implied trusts, which arise under similar conditions, out of some special relationship between the parties by contract or otherwise; and resulting trusts, when the whole or any part of the property or interest in it is granted without any indication that it or such part or interest was intended for the benefit of the grantee or any person other than the grantor himself. See CONSIDERATION.

Trusts arising by operation of law are such as are not declared by the party at all, either directly or indirectly, but result from the effect of a rule of equity.

Trusts are also divisible into permanent trusts, when there is a continuing duty to be performed for the benefit of several persons in succession, and temporary trusts, when there is one particular duty only to perform. Again, trusts may be passive or active.

A trust being, in contemplation of equity, the substantial ownership of or control over property, the person having the ownership or power can create a trust in favour of another person or in his own favour in relation thereto co-extensive with his ability to dispose of it at law; as to the conveyance, see the Law of Property Act, 1925, s. 72 (3).

The Statute of Frauds, 1677, s. 7, replaced by the Law of Property Act, 1925, s. 53 (1) (b), requires that all declarations or creations of trusts or confidences of any lands, tenements, or hereditaments shall be manifested and proved by some writing, signed by the party who is by law enabled to declare such trust, or by his will, or else they are void. This provision does not affect the creation or operation of resulting, implied or constructive trusts, and does not include declarations of trust affecting chattels personal, which may be created by parol, provided they are to take effect during the life of their creator.

Since it is not necessary that a trust should be declared in writing, but only so manifested and proved, no form is requisite either as regards the nature of the instrument or the language; the statute will be satisfied if the trust can be established by any subsequent acknowledgment of the trustee, however

informally or indirectly made, as by a letter under his hand, by his statement of defence in an action, or by a recital in a deed, provided it relates to the subject-matter and the precise nature and object of the trust can be ascertained. A trust cannot be engrafted upon a will unless by a testamentary or codicillary paper executed with the statutory formalities, but if a devise or bequest of the legal estate is accompanied with any *mala fides* in the devisee or legatee, such as breach of an express or implied undertaking to execute the intent of making a provision for third persons, the court will establish such a trust.

A trust may be declared either directly or indirectly.

To create a trust by a direct or formal declaration, a person need only make his meaning clear as to the interest he intends to give, having regard as a rule to the technical terms of the common law or statutes in the limitations of a legal estate. Before 1926 an equitable entail would, in the case of an executory document or a bequest or devise by will, pass without the words " heirs of the body " or " in tail "; in the case of an executed document, apt words of limitation were necessary (*Re Moncton's Settlement* [1913] 2 Ch. 636; *Re Arden* [1935] 1 Ch. 326). By the Law of Property Act, 1925, s. 60, the fee simple or other interest which the grantor had power to convey will pass without words of limitation unless a contrary intention appears in the conveyance. As regard the creation of equitable interest corresponding to an estate tail in either realty or personalty the Act assimilates informal limitations in tail in executory instruments or wills to limitations of personalty, and directs that limitations in tail (without any reservation or qualification for the case of executory instruments or wills) must follow the precise form of legal limitations formerly necessary for the creation of such estates by deed (not being an executory instrument) (s. 130).

A precatory trust is properly a trust declared by a person by inference and not imperatively, and construed by the court in favour of the intention. Thus when property is given absolutely to any person, and he is recommended, or entreated, or wished, by the donor having power to command, to dispose of such property in favour of another, the recommendation, entreaty, or wish creates a trust, provided the words are so used that upon the whole they ought to be construed as imperative; and also provided that the subject of the recommendation, entreaty or wish, as well as the objects or persons intended to have the benefit of such recommendation, entreaty or wish, are certain and definite. There is not any inclination to extend the rule of construction which gives an imperative effect to precatory or recommendatory words.

Where, from the different parts of the instrument, it appears that the words are expressive of a mere expectation or wish, no trust will arise; as where the words are that the donee is to be kind to, or remember, certain objects or classes, or the like; or where the donor uses such expressions as " trusting to the justice of his successors," and it is to be inferred that it is their own sense of justice on which he relies. When the testator recommends, but adds that he does not absolutely enjoin, it is clear that the expressions are to be taken as precatory only, and not imperative. If it appears from the context that the first taker was intended to have a discretionary power to withdraw the whole or any part of the property from the objects of the wish or request, or if there are any words by which it is expressed or from which it can be implied that the first taker may apply the property to his own use, it will not be held that a trust is created.

In recommendatory trusts, if the words for any reason do not amount to a trust, or the intended trust fails in whole or in part, the absolute interest remains in the donee; and if the trust established does not exhaust the property given, the donee retains, in virtue of the gift, so much of the property as is not affected with the trust; but if property is given to a person as trustee only, if no trust is declared, or the trust declared or purporting to be declared fails, then there is a resulting trust for the donor or those claiming under him, and the donee can claim nothing beneficially, nothing being given to him but as trustee.

Any person may be appointed a trustee except an infant (Law of Property Act, 1925, s. 19), a person of unsound mind or convicted of felony, or a bankrupt or a corporation which has been dissolved (Trustee Act, 1925, s. 36; Mental Health Act, 1959, Sch. 7 Pt. I). As to the discretion of the court, see the Trustee Act, 1925, s. 41; Mental Health Act, 1959, Sch. 7 Pt. I. Formerly an alien (*q.v.*) could not be a trustee of realty. A corporation may be constituted a trustee of personalty, and also of realty upon charitable trusts; but not, formerly, upon private trusts unless the trustee is a trust corporation (*q.v.*) or the Public Trustee (*q.v.*). Equity will, however, supply a trustee where realty is devised to a corporation which is not capable of holding land as a trustee. It was formerly never advisable to select a married woman to be a trustee, on account of her inability to join in the requisite assurances without her husband's concurrence; but this difficulty was removed by the Married Women's Property Act, 1907, s. 1, replaced by the Law of Property Act, 1925, s. 170. In the case of receipt of capital money by trustees for sale of land or upon sale by tenants for life or statutory owners of settled land, the receipt must be by two trustees or a trust corporation. A personal representative selling for the purpose of administration can give a valid receipt (Law of Property Act, 1925, s. 27 (2); Administration of Estates Act, 1925, s. 39), but during a minority or if there is a life interest upon an intestacy or administration *cum testaments annexo*, administration will only be granted to two individuals (Judicature Act, 1925, s. 160 (1)).

On the death of a sole trustee, or the last of several trustees, the legal estate vests in his personal representative as if it were a chattel real (Conveyancing Act, 1881, s. 30, replaced by the Administration of Estates Act, 1925, s. 1).

A trust will be enforced wherever there is valuable consideration; but, if it is merely voluntary, the equitable interest will not be enforced unless an actual trust is created and no act remains to be done to complete the title of the trustees, for then consideration is not essential. An agreement founded on a meritorious consideration (*e.g.*, love and affection for a wife or children) will not be executed as against the settlor himself, but as between parties claiming under the settlor, if the court can act in favour of the meritorious consideration without inflicting a hardship on persons peculiarly entitled to protection, the voluntary agreement will in such a case be specifically executed (Law of Property Act, 1925, s. 172 (3)).

The rule is to carry into effect the object proposed by the trust unless it is in contravention of the public policy of the law, as, for instance, seeking to create a perpetuity, or accumulating annual income beyond the statutory limits.

By the Limitation Act, 1939, s. 19, replacing the Trustee Act, 1888, s. 8, a trustee may under certain circumstances plead lapse of time in answer to a claim against him for a breach of trust (*Re Somerset* [1894] 1 Ch. 231; *Howe* v. *Earl Winterton* [1896] 2 Ch. 626). See LIMITATION OF ACTIONS.

The Judicial Trustees Act, 1896, provides for the appointment of remunerated judicial trustees by the court on the application of either trustee or beneficiary. He has all the powers of any other trustee (*Re Ridsdel* [1947] Ch. 597). See JUDICIAL TRUSTEE.

By the Judicature Act, 1925, s. 56, the execution of trusts, charitable or private, is assigned to the Chancery Division.

As to variation of trusts, see TRUST, VARIATION OF.

The statutory investment powers of trustees are contained in the Trustee Investments Act, 1961. Trustees may divide the trust fund into two halves, one half to be invested in gilt-edged securities and the other half to the invested in " equities." The former statutory powers were contained in the Trustee Act, 1925, s. 1. As to the relationship between the Act of 1961 and other powers of investment see s. 3. Trustees are liable to make good any loss on unauthorised investments in the absence of statutory relief (Trustee Act, 1925, ss. 4, 8, 61)), or unless the breach was instigated by the *cestui que trust* (s. 62).

An investment trust is an agreement between a small number of persons (the trustees) and a comparatively large and fluctuating body of persons (generally called subscribers, certificate holders, or the like), that the trustees shall acquire and hold certain shares in companies and receive the income for the benefit of the subscribers, with power to sell any shares and reinvest the proceeds in other shares. Such an arrangement does not constitute the subscribers an association within the meaning of the Companies Act, 1948, and therefore does not require registration, even though the subscribers exceed twenty in number unless, possibly, the trustees exceed that number.

Trust corporation. By the Settled Land Act, 1925, s. 117 (1) (xxx), this means the Public Trustee or a corporation appointed by the court or entitled to act under the Public Trustee (Custodian Trustee) Rules, 1926. Trust corporations may exercise solely or jointly all the powers for the exercise of which two trustees at least would otherwise be required. See ADMINISTRATOR; SETTLED LAND; TRUST; TRUST FOR SALE.

These corporations include any company incorporated by special Act or royal charter or a company under the Companies Act, 1948, with an issued capital of not less than £250,000, of which at least £100,000 has been paid up in cash, or a company undertaking trust business for the navy, army, air force or civil service having as director or member any person nominated by one of the government departments referred to in the rules, or any company authorised by the Lord Chancellor in relation to any charitable, ecclesiastical or public trusts.

By the Law of Property (Amendment) Act, 1926, s. 3, " trust corporation " includes the Treasury Solicitor, the Official Solicitor and any person holding an official position prescribed by the Lord Chancellor, also trustees in bankruptcy and under deeds of arrangement, and certain corporations administering charitable, ecclesiastical or public trusts.

Trust for sale. It has always been common to create trusts for sale of land in settlements and well-drawn wills, with the effect of converting realty into personalty so that the proceeds devolved upon the beneficiaries as personalty unless they elected to take the property as realty (see CONVERSION), except that upon a lapse of the devise of realty in the testator's lifetime the property resulted to the heir-at-law (*Ackroyd* v. *Smithson* (1780) 1 Bro.C.C. 503). Another and more practical consequence was that the whole estate was vested as a rule in the trustees so that with or without the consent of any other person as directed by the donor or testator they could vest the whole estate in a purchaser without his seeing to the application of the purchase-money (Trustee Act, 1893, s. 14), and without participation of beneficiaries whose consent was not required.

Beneficiaries under a trust for sale have no estate in the land but only an interest in the proceeds so long as the trust continues. A testamentary trust for sale of leasehold land is subject to the rule in *Howe* v. *Lord Dartmouth* (1802) 7 Ves. 137, which applies in the absence of directions, express or implied, to the contrary, and which provides that where residuary personalty is settled by will upon persons in succession, wasting property must be sold and the proceeds invested in trustee or authorised investments with consequential attribution of capital and income among the beneficiaries according to their rights. Trusts for sale are to be distinguished from powers of sale, *e.g.*, a mere power does not effect conversion (*Curling* v. *May* (1734) 3 Atk. 255; *Re Thursby* [1910] 2 Ch. 181).

One of two trustees for sale can insist on the execution of the trust for sale if that will not defeat the purpose of the trust (*Jones* v. *Challenger* [1961] 1 Q.B. 176).

The Law of Property Act, 1925, provides for the duration or prolongation of the powers of sale until sale in favour of purchasers (s. 23), confers power to postpone a sale in the absence of a contrary intention (s. 25), and provides that, if consent is requisite, the consent of any two beneficiaries is sufficient in favour of a purchaser, and provides that the wishes of beneficiaries are to be consulted (s. 26). Proceeds of sale or capital money must be paid to not less than two trustees, whatever may be declared by the instrument creating the trust, or to a trust corporation, or to a sole personal representative acting under his powers as such. Receipts by these discharge the purchaser of a legal estate from seeing to the application of the purchase-money, but one trustee may act alone in all matters except where capital money arises on the transaction (s. 27); the trustees have all the powers of a tenant for life under the Settled Land Act, 1925, and land conveyed to them in exercise of those powers must be conveyed to them on trust for sale (s. 28 (1)). The destination of rents and profits until sale is provided for (s. 28 (2)), but without affecting the rule in *Howe* v. *Lord Dartmouth* (1802) 7 Ves. 137, in cases of trusts for sale of pure personalty (*Re Trollope* [1927] 1 Ch. 596). The trustees may partition the land (s. 28 (3)). As to overreaching equitable interests upon sale by properly appointed trustees for sale, see the Law of Property Act, 1925, s. 2 (2), 28.

A settlement of land upon trust for sale, even if the proceeds are settled, is not a settlement within the meaning of the Settled Land Act, 1926, s. 1 (7): see the Law of Property (Amendment) Act, 1926, Sch., and the Settled Land Act, 1925, ss. 3, 36.

Trusts for sale are conveniently created by two instruments, the conveyance of the land upon trust for sale and the instrument declaring the trusts of the proceeds. The Trustee Act, 1925, s. 35, requires two instruments on an appointment of new trustees. A will is not a conveyance of the legal estate, which now devolves upon the personal representatives by operation of law; it is a trust instrument only.

The Law of Property Act, 1925, s. 205 (1) (xxix), defines "trust for sale," unless the context otherwise requires, in relation to land, as an immediate binding trust for sale whether or not exercisable at the request or with the consent of any person and with or without a power at discretion to postpone the sale; but in its general legal sense the term is not restricted to that meaning.

Trust funds. In addition to the securities mentioned in the instrument creating the trust, trustees may invest trust funds in securities specified in the Trustee Investments Act, 1961, unless expressly forbidden by the trust deed. As to funds in court, see R.S.C., Ord. 22, r. 13, and the County Courts Act, 1959, s. 168.

Trust instrument. Under the Settled Land Act, 1925, ss. 9, 117 (1) (xxxi), a trust instrument includes, in relation to settled land, any instrument whereby the trusts of the settled land are declared, other than a vesting instrument or vesting conveyance. The trust instrument constituting a settlement must declare the trusts affecting the settled land, appoint or constitute trustees of the settlement, contain the power (if any) to appoint new trustees, set out any intended addition to or enlargement of the statutory powers, and (formerly) bear the proper *ad valorem* stamp payable by virtue of the vesting deed or otherwise in respect of the settlement (s. 4).

Certain instruments are deemed to be trust instruments though not complying with these requirements (s. 9).

A purchaser for value in good faith is not affected by the contents of the trust instrument and is not entitled to information in regard to it, except, *e.g.*, a purchaser taking title under the first vesting instrument (ss. 5 (2), 110). A trust instrument presumably includes an instrument containing the settlement of proceeds under a trust for sale (ss. 36, 117), but there is no express statutory definition of a trust instrument declaring the trusts under a trust for sale.

Trust territories, territories consisting mainly of the colonial possessions of the unsuccessful belligerents in the wars of 1914–18 and 1939–45, formerly known as mandated territories, and now administered under the supervision of the Trusteeship Council or the Security Council of the United Nations.

Trust, Variation of. The Variation of Trusts Act, 1958 (passed to overcome the difficulties raised by *Chapman* v. *Chapman* [1954] A.C. 429), gives the court jurisdiction to vary trusts on the application of any person interested, notwithstanding that the effect of the variation is to avoid tax. The court may vary a discretionary trust (*q.v.*) without considering whether the variation is for the benefit of the owner of the discretionary interest, but see *Re Steed's Will Trusts* [1959] Ch. 354. " Any person " includes an unascertained or unborn person (*Re Turner's Will Trusts* [1960] Ch. 122). A variation may be made *in futuro* (*Re Joseph's Will Trusts* [1959] 1 W.L.R. 1019). Applications should be made in open court (*Re Chapman's Settlement* (*No* 2) [1959] 1 W.L.R. 372; *Re Byng's Will Trusts* [1959] 1 W.L.R. 375). The reason for the desired variation should be given by affidavit (*Re Oakes' Settlement Trusts* [1959] 1 W.L.R. 502). See also the Finance Act, 1958, s. 22 and Practice Direction, July 27, 1976 [1976] 8 C.L. 201.

Trustee, a person who holds property upon trust (*q.v.*).

The office of a trustee is a personal one, and does not necessarily devolve or pass with the trust property. If one of several trustees dies, the office devolves on the survivors; the property also passes to the survivors, trustees being always made joint tenant. See JOINT TENANCY.

When any sole trustee of real estate dies it devolves, notwithstanding any testamentary disposition, on his personal representatives as if it were a chattel real (Administration of Estates Act, 1925, s. 1, replacing the Conveyancing Act, 1881, s. 30). Formerly, when a new trustee was appointed in the place of the deceased, his real or personal representatives had to convey the property to the new trustee by the same mode of conveyance (deed of grant, assignment, etc.) as that used in a conveyance by an absolute owner, and until that was done they held the property upon trust so to convey it, but they were not clothed with the office of trustee under the instrument creating the trust unless it so provided, and therefore they could not exercise any of the powers conferred by the trust. Now, however, under the Trustee Act, 1925, s. 40 (replacing the Conveyancing Act, 1881, s. 34), the deed appointing a new trustee contains a declaration (which is implied if not expressed) which vests the trust property in the new trustee or trustees, as joint tenants, as effectually as a conveyance formerly did.

Trusteeship is different from executorship. Therefore if a testator appoints A to be executor and trustee of his will, and A renounces the executorship, he remains trustee unless he executes a disclaimer of the office. See DISCLAIM; RENOUNCE.

Most instruments creating trusts contain a power of appointing new trustees: the power is generally vested in the beneficiaries or some of them, or in the trustees themselves, including the last survivor, his executors or administrators. As regards instruments under which there is no person having a power of appointing new trustees, and able and willing to act, a power of appointing new trustees to supply any vacancy by death, retirement, etc., was, by Lord Cranworth's Act, 1860, s. 27 (*q.v.*), vested in the surviving or continuing trustees or trustee or the acting executors or administrators of the last surviving or continuing trustee, or the last retiring trustee. These provisions were extended by the Conveyancing Act, 1881, s. 31, and the Trustee Act, 1883, s. 10, now replaced by the Trustee Act, 1925, s. 36. Under the Judicial Trustees Act, 1896, s. 1, a judicial trustee (*q.v.*) and, under the Public Trustee Act, 1906, s. 2 (1), the Public Trustee and a trust corporation, may be new trustees of a settlement; the Public Trustee or a trust corporation may be so appointed by anyone having power to appoint a private person as new trustee, but a judicial trustee can be appointed only by order of the court. Trust corporations can hold property in joint tenancy with an individual (Bodies Corporate (Joint Tenancy) Act, 1889): so also can the Public Trustee (Public Trustee Act, 1906, s. 2 (2)).

If a trustee cannot safely administer a trust, he may take out an originating summons or institute an action to have it executed by the court; and, in a proper case, the trustees or a majority of them may place the trust fund in the hands of the court under the Trustee Act, 1925, s. 63, replacing the Trustee Act, 1893, s. 42. If a trustee refuses or neglects to administer the trust, or is guilty of a breach of trust, or the like, any beneficiary may institute an action for the execution of the trust by the court. (See ADMINISTRATION ACTION; DISCRETION; EXECUTOR). The powers of trustees are suspended by the institution of a suit for the execution of the trusts, and they can only act with the sanction of the court.

Except in cases of fraud or of trust property wrongfully retained or converted, a trustee may plead the Statutes of Limitation (Limitation Act, 1939, s. 19, replacing the Trustee Act, 1888, s. 8). See BREACH OF TRUST.

Trustees are of two kinds, active and passive.

An active trustee is one who has to perform administrative duties, such as managing the trust property, receiving income and paying it over to the *cestui que trust*, etc. The duties and liabilities of such trustees are of infinite variety; but it may be said generally that a trustee is bound to take the same care in acting for his *cestui que trust* as he would, as a prudent man, in acting for himself: and that he must not derive or attempt to derive any benefit from the trust, unless he is authorised to do so by the terms of the trust. See BREACH OF TRUST; DISCRETION; NEGLIGENCE.

A passive trustee is one in whom property is vested simply for the benefit of another person. In such a case the trustee is bound to convey the property to the *cestui que trust*, or to dispose of it as he may direct, when the time comes for the *cestui que trust* to deal with it, and in the meantime to hold it on his behalf.

When the duties of an active trustee have come to an end, or when the time for the *cestui que trust* to claim possession of the trust property has come, so that in either case the trustee is compellable to convey the property to the *cestui que trust*, or deal with according to his directions, then the trustee is called a bare or dry trustee.

When an issue of debentures is intended to be secured by a charge on property, trustees are frequently appointed on behalf of the holders of the bonds or stock to receive and administer the property or the income thereof for their benefit, subject to provisions contained in a document called a trust deed.

As to trustees of charities, see CHARITY; OFFICIAL CUSTODIAN FOR CHARITIES.

The word "trustee" also used in a wide and inaccurate sense to denote that a person has the duty of carrying out a transaction in which he and another person are interested, in such manner as will be most for the benefit of the latter, and not in such a way that he himself might be tempted, for the sake of his personal advantage, to neglect the interests of the other. In this sense directors of companies are sometimes said to be trustees for the shareholders. The essential difference is that a trustee owns the trust property and deals with it as principal, subject to his equitable obligation towards his *cestui que trust*, while a director is rather an agent with a limited authority; and, moreover, a director is not debarred from using for his own personal benefit knowledge which he has acquired as director. A director of a parent company is not debarred from contracting with a subsidiary which has an independent board of directors (*Lingren* v. *L. & P. Estates* [1960] Ch. 572).

Directors are trustees of money standing to the credit of their company's bank account which they have authority to operate (*Selangor United Rubber Estates* v. *Cradock* (*No.* 3) [1968] 1 W.L.R. 1555).

As to the effect of conveying as trustee, see TITLE, COVENANTS, FOR.

Trustee in bankruptcy, a person in whom the property of a bankrupt is vested in trust for the creditors; his duty is to discover, realise and distribute it among the creditors, and for that purpose to examine the bankrupt's property, accounts, etc., to investigate proofs made by creditors, and to admit, reject, expunge or reduce them according to circumstances. (See PROOF.) He also has to keep various accounts of his dealings with the property, and of the course of the bankruptcy, which are audited by the committee of inspection and the Department of Trade (Bankruptcy Act, 1914, s. 92). The appointment of the trustee is regulated by the Bankruptcy Act, 1914, s. 19.

Trustee savings banks. See SAVINGS BANKS.

Tub, 60 lb. of tea.

Tuberculosis. Orders may be made under the Diseases of Animals Act, 1950, ss. 5, 85; Agriculture Act, 1970, s. 106 (3), declaring specified areas to be attested areas.

Tubman, a junior barrister whose place in the old Court of Exchequer was by the tub anciently used as a measure of capacity in excise cases. Except in Crown business, he took precedence in motions of all juniors, except the postman (*q.v.*). Like the postman, he disappeared when the Court of Exchequer ceased to exist.

Tug and tow. See TOWAGE.

Tumbrel, Tumbril, a cucking-stool (*q.v.*) or a ducking-stool used for the punishment of scolds; a dung-cart.

Tumultuous petitioning. See PETITION; RIOT.

Tun, a cask containing four hogsheads: see the statute 1377, 1 Ric. 3, c. 12; a measure of timber containing forty cubic feet: see the statute 1660, 12 Car. 2, c. 14; twenty hundredweight of coals: see the statute 1697, 9 Will. 3, c. 13. None of these measures is now recognised by the law.

Tungreve, a town-reeve or bailiff.

Tunnage. See TONNAGE.

Turbary [Lat. *turbus, turva,* turf], the liberty of digging turf upon another man's ground. It may be either by grant or prescription, and either appurtenant or in gross. It can be appurtenant only to a house, and can only be a right to take turf for fuel for such house. There can be no approver against common of turbary. See APPROVEMENT; COMMON.

Turf and twig. See LIVERY OF SEISIN.

Turf cutting. Land used for turf cutting is not agricultural land for purposes of derating (*Butser Turf and Timber Co.* v. *Petersfield Rural District Council* [1950] 1 All E.R. 288; *Meriden and Solihull Assessment Committee* v. *Tyacke* [1950] 1 All E.R. 939). See SOIL.

Turkey Company, the Levant Company (*q.v.*).

Turn, or **Tourn,** the great court leet of the county, as the old county court was the court baron; of this the sheriff was judge, and the court was incident to his office, wherefore it was called the sheriff's tourn, and it had its name originally from the sheriff making a turn of circuit about his shire, and holding this court in each respective hundred (2 Hawk.P.C. c. 10).

The tourn, which had long been obsolete, was abolished by the Sheriffs Act, 1887, s. 18.

Turnkey, a gaoler.

Turnpike. Turnpike roads were roads the cost of maintaining which was defrayed out of tolls levied upon passengers; turnpikes were the gates across such roads, which were opened so as to allow the passage of those who had paid toll; and the Turnpike Acts was the title of a large number of enactments for legalising the turnpike system, which originated early in the eighteenth century and came to an end before the termination of the nineteenth century.

Turnpike roads were generally in the nature of by-roads. The highways (*q.v.*) were the great arterial roads.

Turnpike roads did not fall within the operation of the Highway Act, 1835, but were regulated primarily by the local Acts relative to each particular road, which, though temporary, were, until about the middle of the nineteenth century, almost invariably renewed by the legislature from time to time as they were about to expire; they were also regulated by public general Acts, of which the principal was the Turnpike Roads Act, 1822, which applied (with few exceptions) to all turnpike roads, that is, all roads maintained by tolls, and placed under the management of trustees or commissioners for a limited period. This Act was repealed by the Statute Law Revision Act, 1890, with the exception of such provisions as are applied to dis-turnpiked roads by the Annual Turnpike Acts Continuance Acts, 1865 and 1870. There were at one time many thousand turnpike trusts. In 1864 they numbered above a thousand, but in 1879 they had been reduced to little more than two hundred, by expiration in accordance with the Annual Turnpike Acts Continuance Acts, 1865 and 1870, and they had before the end of the nineteenth century practically ceased to exist (Oke, *Turnpike Laws*).

Turpis causa, a base or vile considera-tion on which no action can be founded, the maxim being *ex turpi causa non oritur actio* (*Collins* v. *Blantern* (1766) 2 Wils. 341). See Ex Turpi Causa.

Turpis est pars quae non convenit cum suo toto (Plow. 161). (A part which does not fit in with the rest is out of place.) A properly drawn deed should admit of such interpretation as will make the part consonant with the whole. See Ex Antecedentibus, etc.

Tutela, guardianship for the purpose of managing the affairs and removing the legal incapacities of a person *sui juris* under the age of puberty (Civil Law).

Tutelage, guardianship; the state of being under a guardian.

Tutius semper est errare acquietando quam in puniendo, ex parte misericordiae quam ex parte justitiae (2 H.P.C. 290). (It is always safer to err by acquitting rather than by punishing, at the instance of mercy rather than of justice.)

Tutor, a guardian; a protector; an instructor.

In the civil law a tutor was a person on whom the law imposed the duty of *tutela* (*q.v.*) Tutors were of the following kinds: *Atilianus* or *Juliatitianus,* a tutor given to a pupil without one; *dativus,* a tutor appointed by an authorised magistrate; *fiduciarius,* a tutor holding office as if on a trust committed to him by the father, as where a *pater-familias* emancipated a descendant and then died leaving male descendants alive, who became fiduciary tutors of those emancipated; *honorarius,* a tutor excluded from the actual administration of a pupil's property; *legitimus,* a statutory tutor who succeeded to the office under the provisions of some statute or the Twelve Tables; *onerarius,* a tutor who actually administered a pupil's property; and *testamentarius,* a tutor appointed by will.

Tutor alienus; Tutor proprius. If a stranger entered into the lands of an infant within the age of fourteen, and took the profits, the infant might charge him as guardian in socage and he was called *tutor alienus,* and the right guardian in socage *tutor proprius* (Co. Litt. 124).

Tutorship, the office and power of a tutor.

Tutrix, a female tutor.

Twaite, a wood grubbed up and turned to arable (Co.Litt. 4b).

Twanight geste. In Saxon times this meant a guest staying for a second night at the house of another. He, and not the host, was responsible for injuries inflicted by him on a third person. See THIRD NIGHT, ETC.

Twelfhinde. In Anglo-Saxon law this meant persons whose property was valued at twelve hundred shillings or upwards. They were the highest rank of men and if any injury was done to such persons, satisfaction had to be made according to their worth.

Twelfth day, the Epiphany (*q.v.*).

Twelve-day writ, a writ issued under the Summary Procedure on Bills of Exchange Act, 1855, known as Keating's Act, for summary procedure on bills of exchange and promissory notes, abolished in 1880. The plaintiff was entitled to judgment unless the defendant within twelve days from service obtained leave to defend.

Twelvemonth. A twelvemonth means a year; but twelve months (plural) were formerly computed according to twenty-eight days for each month (6 Co.Rep. 62).

By the Law of Property Act, 1925, s. 61, "month" means calendar month unless the context otherwise requires. See MONTH.

Twyhinde. In Anglo-Saxon law this meant those whose property was worth two hundred shillings but did not exceed twelve hundred shillings.

Tyburn, the place where executions took place in former times; it was situate on the Oxford Road, not far from where the Marble Arch now stands. The execution was preceded by a procession from Newgate to Tyburn, the criminal being drawn in a cart, but this practice was abolished in 1783, and the sentences thenceforward carried out in front of Newgate. See Gent.Mag. 1783, pp. 974, 1060; *Croker Papers*, vol. iii, pp. 15, 16; Boswell's *Johnson*, ed. by Birkbeck Hill, vol. iv, p. 188.

Tyburn ticket, a certificate which was given to the prosecutor of a felon to conviction. It exempted him from parish and ward offices.

Tyhtlan, an accusation, impeachment or charge.

Tylwith, a tribe, house or family.

Tymborella, the tumbril (*q.v.*).

Tynwald, Court of, the Governor, Council and House of Keys (the legislative assembly) of the Isle of Man. After receiving the royal assent Bills are proclaimed in Manx and English on Tynwald Hill.

Tyth, tithe or tenth part.

Tything, a company of ten; a district; a tenth part. See TITHING.

Tzar, Tzarina, the title of the former emperors and empresses of Russia.

U

U.K., the United Kingdom (*q.v.*) of Great Britain and Northern Ireland.

U.N., the United Nations.

U.N.E.S.C.O., the United Nations Educational, Scientific and Cultural Organisation.

U.N.O., the United Nations Organisation (*q.v.*).

U.R., abbreviation of *uti rogas*, be it as you desire; this was a ballot, thus inscribed, by which the Romans voted in favour of a bill or candidate.

U.S.A., the United States of America (*q.v.*).

U.S.S.R., the Union of Socialist Soviet Republics.

Uberrimae fidei, of the fullest confidence, of the utmost good faith. A contract is said to be *uberrimae fidei* when the promisee is bound to communicate to the promisor every fact and circumstance which may influence him in deciding whether to enter into the contract or not. Contracts which require *uberrima fides* are those entered into between persons in a particular relationship, as guardian and ward, solicitor and client, insurer and insured (*London Assurance Co.* v. *Mansel* (1879) 11 Ch.D. 363; *Joel* v. *Law Union, etc., Insurance Co.* [1908] 2 K.B. 863). Contracts of suretyship and partnership, though not strictly contracts *uberrimae fidei*, are, when once entered into, such as to require full disclosure and the utmost good faith (*Phillips* v. *Foxall* (1872) L.R. 7 Q.B. 666; *Blisset* v. *Daniel* (1853) 10 Ha. 522).

A contract for the sale of land (*q.v.*) is not *uberrimae fidei*, but see the Law of Property Act, 1925, s. 183, as to fraudulent concealment of deeds, etc.

A barrister moving the court *ex parte* is under a strict obligation of *uberrima fides*.

Ubi aliquid conceditur, conceditur et id sine quo res ipsa esse non potest. (Where anything is granted, that is also granted without which the thing itself is not able to exist.) See CUICUNQUE, ETC.

Ubi cessat remedium ordinarium ibi decurritur ad extraordinarium (4 Co. Rep. 93). (When the ordinary remedy fails, then recourse is had to the extraordinary remedy.) This maxim was quoted in support of the contention that where the action of debt, which was an ordinary remedy, and an action on the case, which was an extraordinary remedy, both lay, then the plaintiff could bring only the action of debt; but the court held that the plaintiff could avail himself of whichever of the remedies he chose.

Ubi damna dantur, victus victori in expensis condemnari debet (C. 3, 1, 13; 2 Co.Inst. 289). (Where damages are given, the losing party ought to pay the costs of the victor.) This maxim taken from the civil law is quoted by Coke in his commentary on the Statute of Gloucester, 1278, c. 1, which made costs payable to anyone recovering damages.

Ubi eadem ratio ibi idem jus (Co.Litt. 191, 232). (Like reasons make like law.) See DE SIMILIBUS, ETC.

Ubi jus ibi remedium (Co.Litt 197b). (Where there is a right, there is a remedy.) See DAMNUM SINE INJURIA, ETC.; LEX SEMPER DEBIT, ETC.

Ubi lex aliquem cogit ostendere causam necesse est quod causa sit justa et legitima (2 Co.Inst. 269). (Where the law compels a man to show cause, it is incumbent that the cause be just and lawful.)

Ubi lex non distinguit, nec nos distinguere debemus (7 Co.Rep. 5). (We ought not to distinguish where the law does not do so.) Cokes cites the maxim as a warning against dividing allegiance into kinds other than those recognised by the law. See NEMINEM OPORTET, ETC.

Ubi non est principalis non potest esse accessorius (4 Co.Rep. 43). (Where there is no principal, there cannot be an accessory.) Quoted in support of a decision that if a principal were pardoned or " had his clergy," then no person could be arraigned as his accessory. See ACCESSORY.

Ubi nullum matrimonium, ibi nulla dos est (Co.Litt. 32). (Where there is no marriage there is no dower.) The right to dower was lost when there was a divorce *a vinculo*.

Ubi quid generaliter conceditur inest haec exceptio si non aliquid sit contra jus fasque (11 Co.Rep. 78b). (Where a grant is in general terms there is always an implied provision that it shall not include anything which is unlawful or immoral.)

Ubi supra, at the place above mentioned.

Ubi verba conjuncta non sunt, sufficit alterutrum esse factum (D. 50, 17, 110). (Where alternative conditions are imposed it is sufficient if one or the other of them is complied with.) See IN CONJUNCTIVIS, ETC.

Ubication, or **Ubiety** [Lat. *ubi*, where], local position.

Udal, allodial (*q.v.*).

Uganda. Uganda Independence Act, 1962; Uganda Act, 1964.

Ukaas, or **Ukase,** an Imperial Russian law, decree or ordinance.

Ullage [Lat. *uligo*, ooziness], the quantity of fluid which a cask wants of being full, in consequence of the oozing or evaporation of the liquor.

Ulna ferrea, the standard ell of iron, which was kept in the Exchequer for the rule of measure (2 Dugd.Mon. 383).

Ulnage, alnage (*q.v.*).

Ulnager, alnager (*q.v.*).

Ulpian, a Roman jurist who flourished in the time of Alexander Severus, about A.D. 222. The Code of Justinian is in great part founded on his works.

Ulster. See NORTHERN IRELAND.

Ulster Defence Regiment. See the Ulster Defence Regiment Acts, 1969 and 1973.

Ultima voluntas testatoris est perimplenda secundum veram intentionem suam (Co.Litt. 322). (Effect is to be given to the last will of a testator according to his true intention.) See BENIGNAE, ETC.; MENS TESTATORIS, ETC.

Ultimate destination, the doctrine that the real and final destination of goods to enemy territory or territory under enemy control is one of the elements of contraband (*q.v.*).

Ultimatum, or **Ultimation,** the last offer, concession, or condition.

In diplomacy an ultimatum means a demand, refusal to comply with which will be immediately followed by war with the nation which refuses.

Ultimogeniture, borough-English (*q.v.*).

Ultimum supplicium, the last or extreme punishment: death.

Ultra, beyond. Damages *ultra* means damages beyond a sum paid into court.

Ultra vires, beyond the powers.

A contract or similar act is said to be *ultra vires* a corporation when it purports to be entered into or done in pursuance of the powers conferred on the corporation, but is really beyond them. The doctrine does not apply to those things which are fairly incidental to what the company is empowered to do, although they may not be expressly authorised.

The doctrine is restricted by the European Communities Act, 1972. In favour of a person dealing with a company in good faith, any transaction decided on by the directors is deemed to be one which is within the capacity of the company to enter into. The power of the directors to bind the company is deemed to be free of any limitation under the memorandum or articles of association. A party to a transaction so decided upon is not bound to inquire as to the capacity of the company to enter into it or as to any such limitation on the power of the directors. He is presumed to have acted in good faith unless the contrary is proved (s. 9 (1)). *Ashbury Railway Carriage and Iron Co.* v. *Riche* (1875) L.R. 7 H.L. 653, and *Royal British Bank* v. *Turquand* (1856) 6 E. & E. 327 must now be read subject to the above.

The term *ultra vires* is used in another sense to signify that a certain act is not void as being beyond the powers of the corporation, but that it is not binding on the members who dissent from it because it is contrary to some provision, express or implied, for the protection of the shareholders; on this principle, if a company, being possessed of funds appropriated for a certain purpose, applies them to another purpose within its general powers, that appropriation will be *ultra vires* and only binding on the shareholders who consent to it.

If the powers of a corporation are given or acquired at common law or by custom or by charter, the corporation is a person at common law and may do anything which an ordinary person can do (*Wenlock* (*Baroness*) v. *River Dee Co.* (1885) 10 App.Cas. 354; *British South Africa Co.* v. *De Beers Consolidated Mines* [1910] 1 Ch. 354), subject to the consequences if the act is prohibited by the charter or by law directly or indirectly (*Jenkins* v. *Pharmaceutical Society of Great Britain* [1921] 1 Ch. 392). On the other hand, a corporation or company which is created by or under statute cannot do anything at all unless authorised expressly or impliedly by the statute or instrument defining its powers.

Ultra vires is also sometimes applied to an act which, though within the powers of a corporation, is not binding on it because the consent or agreement of the corporation has not been given in the manner required by its constitution. Thus, where a company delegates certain powers to its directors, all acts done by the directors beyond the scope of those powers are *ultra vires,* and not binding on the company, unless it subsequently ratifies them. An act which is *ultra vires* in the primary sense of the word is incapable of ratification.

Where a corporation acts *ultra vires* the remedy for a member is injunction;

for a stranger who has suffered injury the like remedy is available; and the Attorney-General can take proceedings, even though no person has suffered injury.

Umpirage, the performance of the duties of an umpire; arbitration, friendly decision of a controversy.

Umpire [Lat. *imperator, impar*]. A submission to arbitration usually provides that in case of arbitrators not agreeing in an award, the matters in dispute shall be decided by a third person, who is called an umpire. Such a provision is implied unless a contrary intention is expressed (Arbitration Act, 1950, s. 8). The umpire's authority commences when the arbitrators are unable to agree, but if there is a time limited for the award, his authority commences from such time. The umpire, when called upon to act, is generally invested with the same powers as the arbitrators, and bound by the same rules, and has to perform the same duties. See ARBITRATION.

Una cum omnibus aliis, along with all the other things. This was a form used in the granting part of old conveyances to add something to what had been already described.

Unborn persons. See EN VENTRE SA MÈRE; PERPETUITY.

Uncalled capital, the portion of the nominal value of shares issued by a company which has not yet been required to be paid.

Uncertainty. In the law of wills, the general rule is that where a testator has so expressed himself that it is impossible to ascertain what his intention was, the gift or provision so made is void for uncertainty. Thus, a will consisting merely of these words, " I leave and bequeath to all my grandchildren, and share and share alike," is too uncertain to be operative, although it may be conjectured that the word " all " was meant to precede the word " to." A gift is void for uncertainty if a testator bequeaths " some of my property " to A, or all his property, " to one of my sons."

In pleading, the general rule is that whatever is alleged must be alleged with certainty. An allegation suffering from the defect of uncertainty is liable to be struck out as embarrassing under R.S.C., Ord. 18, r. 19.

Unchastity. An oral imputation of unchastity in a woman or girl is actionable without proof of actual damage (Slander of Women Act, 1891). See SLANDER.

Unclaimed property. This devolves on the Crown at common law.

The Miscellaneous Financial Provisions Act, 1955, s. 5 (as amended by the National Debt Act, 1972, s. 15 (2)), provides that government stock, dividends and redemption moneys unclaimed for five years must be transferred to the National Debt Commissioners, but may be re-transferred to persons showing title thereto.

Dormant funds in court are regulated by the Supreme Court Funds Rules, 1927, r. 97.

By the Companies Act, 1862, Sch. 1, Table A, art. 72, dividends unclaimed for three years after having been declared might be forfeited by the directors for the benefit of a company under that Act; but the Act was silent as to capital stock. There was no similar provision in Table A to the Companies Acts, 1908, 1929, and 1948. Dividends are barred by the Limitation Act, 1939, at the end of twelve (formerly twenty) years (*Re Artisans, etc., Corporation* [1904] 1 Ch. 796). No period of limitation necessarily applies to capital stock, and in *Crawford* v. *Royal Exchange Insurance Corporation* (1884) *The Times,* April 29, stock on which no dividend had been paid since 1749 was handed over to the representative of a holder, who had taken out administration *de bonis non,* the amount recovered on £100 stock being about £3,000, £6,600 having been previously recovered by another plaintiff against the same defendants in respect of £200 stock on which no dividend had been paid since 1720 (*The Times,* December 11, 1883).

As to unclaimed funds or dividends in bankruptcy, see the Bankruptcy Act, 1914, s. 153.

Money at a bank on an ordinary current or drawing account is money lent to the banker by the customer, repayable upon and not until demand without which there is no cause of action (*Pott* v. *Clegg* (1849) 16 M. & W. 321; *Foley* v. *Hill* (1851) 2 H.L.C. 28; *Joachimson* v. *Swiss Bank Corporation* [1921] 3 K.B. 110); it follows from this that the Limitation Act, 1939, will not run for such money until six years after demand.

In the case of deposits with bankers for safe custody it would seem that the liability of the banker, if he retains custody, is a perpetual liability limited only by six years after demand and refusal (*Burdick* v. *Garrick* (1870) L.R. 5 Ch. at pp. 239, 240).

A finder of property has a title against all the world except the owner of it, but within what time, if any, he may convert it to his own use is doubtful. The practice of the police authorities appears to be that after a reasonable time and efforts to find the owner, the property will be returned to the finder, subject to conditions in case of property of value, and such property, of course, remains the property of the owner until his claim is barred by lapse of time. See FINDER OF LOST PROPERTY; LIMITATION OF ACTIONS.

Under the Metropolitan Public Carriage Act, 1869, s. 9 (5), the Home Secretary may make regulations for securing the safe custody and re-delivery of any property accidentally left in hackney or stage carriages, and fixing the charges to be paid in respect thereof, with power to cause such property to be sold or to be given to the finder in the event of its not being claimed within a certain time.

As to property which has come into possession of the police in connection with a criminal matter, see the Police (Property) Act, 1897. See RESTITUTION OF STOLEN GOODS.

Uncle and nephew. A nephew, the son of a deceased elder brother, was by the law in force before 1926, preferred in the inheritance to his uncle, a younger brother of the deceased. See DISTRIBUTION; NEPHEW.

Unconscionable bargain. See CATCHING BARGAIN.

Uncore prist, still ready. Where the defence to an action was that the money had been tendered on the day that it became due, the defendant pleaded

uncore prist and brought the money into court (Co.Litt. 207a). See SEMPER PARATUS.

Uncuth [Sax.], unknown.

Unde nihil habet. See DOWER, WRIT OF.

Under-Chamberlains of the Exchequer, two officers who cleaved the tallies and read them (see TALLY). They also made searches for records in the treasury, and had the custody of Domesday Book (Jacob).

Underground rooms. A closing order may be made in respect of an underground room which is unfit for habitation (Housing Act, 1957, s. 18; Housing (Underground Rooms) Act, 1959).

Under-lease, a grant by a lessee to another, called the under-lessee, or under-tenant, or sub-lessee, or sub-tenant, of a part of his whole interest under the original lease, reserving to himself a reversion; it differs from an assignment, which conveys the lessee's whole interest, and passes to the assignee the right and liability to sue and be sued upon the covenants in the original lease.

An under-lease for the whole term of the original lease amounts to an assignment (*Beardman* v. *Wilson* (1868) L.R. 4 C.P. 57).

A covenant not to under-let premises is not broken by an under-letting of part only of the premises (*Cook* v. *Shoesmith* [1951] 1 K.B. 752).

Between the original lessor and an under-tenant there is neither privity of estate nor privity of contract, so that these parties cannot take advantage, the one against the other, of the covenants, either in law or in deed, which exist between the original lessor and lessee (*Holford* v. *Hatch* (1779) 1 Dougl. 183; *Johnson* v. *Wild* (1890) 44 Ch.D. 146); but the lessor can distrain on the sub-lessee or take advantage of a condition of forfeiture (*Great Western Ry.* v. *Smith* (1876) 2 Ch.D. 253). By the Law of Property Act, 1925, s. 146 (4), as amended by the Law of Property (Amendment) Act, 1929, a sub-lessee can obtain relief from forfeiture of the superior lease. But the terms upon which relief will be granted are in the discretion of the court, and in certain cases the rent may be raised (*Ewart* v. *Fryer* [1910] 1 Ch. 499). A surrender by the lessee cannot prejudice the estate of the under-lessee.

Mortgages of leaseholds, where the covenants are onerous, have always been made by sub-demise, so as to avoid bringing the mortgagee into direct relation with the lessor and so rendering him liable to be sued on the covenants; but the mortgagee may often be in fact compelled to perform them in order to save his security from forfeiture under the proviso for re-entry in the lease. As to realisation, foreclosure, and retention by mortgagees under the Limitation Act, 1939, see the Law of Property Act, 1925, s. 89, as amended by the Law of Property (Amendment) Act, 1926.

For the purposes of the Law of Property Act, 1925, the term "lease" includes an under-lease unless the context otherwise requires (s. 205). To describe an under-lease as a lease in contracts and conditions of sale is generally a misdescription (*Re Beyfus and Masters' Contract* (1888) 39 Ch.D. 110).

See ASSIGN; FORFEITURE; LEASE.

Under-sheriff [Lat. *sub vicecomes*], the sheriff's deputy. See SHERIFF.

Undertaking, a promise. In the old books "undertaker" means a promisor (1 Salk. 27).

"Undertaking" is frequently used in the special sense of a promise given in the course of legal proceedings by a party or his counsel, generally as a condition to obtaining some concession from the court or the opposite party. Thus, where an interim or *ex parte* injunction is granted, the court generally requires the plaintiff to give an undertaking as to damages; that is, he must undertake that if it should subsequently turn out that he was not entitled to the injunction, and that its operation has caused injury to the defendant, he will pay to the defendant damages for the injury so sustained.

So, if an application is made for an injunction, and the defendant asks that it may be adjourned, he is generally required to give an undertaking not to commit the acts complained of in the meantime; if it is a question of infringement of a patent or the like, he some-times undertakes to keep an account of all articles made or sold by him during the period of the adjournment.

An undertaking may be enforced by attachment, or otherwise, in the same manner as an injunction. See R.S.C., Ord. 45, r. 5, note. In *Kemp* v. *Kemp* (1957) *The Times*, November 26, however, it was held that a writ of attachment could not issue for breach of an undertaking by a husband not to molest his wife, the correct remedy being by committal.

Where a solicitor gives an undertaking he is bound as a matter of professional etiquette himself to implement it unless the undertaking makes it plain that he does not intend to accept personal liability. The court does not, in practice, commit a solicitor for breach of an undertaking given by him unless it has previously made a mandatory order on him to perform his undertaking and he has failed to obey (*Re a Solicitor* [1966] 1 W.L.R. 1604). An undertaking to the court confers no personal right or remedy on any other party. The only sanctions for breach are imprisonment for contempt, sequestration or a fine (*Re Hudson* [1966] Ch. 207). Failure to comply with an undertaking to abate a nuisance may be visited with a substantial fine (*Shoreham-by-Sea U.D.C.* v. *Dolphin Canadian Proteins* (1972) 71 L.G.R. 261).

An acknowledgment for production and for delivery of copies and an undertaking for safe custody of documents is given when a person retains documents relating to property disposed of, *e.g.*, when only part of the property is disposed of. Such an undertaking in writing imposes on every possessor of the documents, so long as he has possession or control of them, an obligation to keep them safe, whole, uncancelled and undefaced, unless prevented from doing so by fire or other inevitable accident (Law of Property Act, 1925, s. 64 (9)). Sometimes only an acknowledgment for production and for delivery of copies is given, *e.g.*, by trustees.

In the Lands Clauses Consolidation Act, 1845, the Companies Clauses Consolidation Act, 1845, and similar Acts, applying to companies incorporated for the construction of works of public utility, "undertaking" means the works or undertaking, of whatever nature, which are authorised by the special Act incorporating the particular company. The question what is included in the "undertaking" of a company principally arises in cases where a company has created a mortgage or charge on its undertaking to secure debentures, or the like. The wording of the instrument creating the charge will determine whether the charge operates only on such property as was in existence at the date of its execution or whether it operates on all the property and revenues of the company, as a going concern, at the time when the security requires to be enforced. See DEBENTURE; SECURITY.

Under-tenant. See UNDER-LEASE.

Under-Treasurer of England [*vice-thesaurarius Angliae*], he who transacted the business of the Lord High Treasurer. This officer, who is mentioned in the statute 1597, 39 Eliz. 1, c. 7, was the principal assistant of the Treasurer, and acted in that office when a vacancy occurred. See TREASURY.

Underwriter, a person who joins with others in entering into a policy of insurance as insurer. Except where an insurance is effected with a company, a policy of marine insurance is generally entered into by a number of persons, each of whom makes himself liable for a certain sum, so as to divide the risk; they subscribe or underwrite the policy in lines one under the other, and thence to subscribe a policy is sometimes called "taking a line." Policies are usually effected through brokers. See ADJUSTMENT OF A LOSS; INSURANCE; POLICY OF INSURANCE.

"Underwriters" also means subscribers who (generally before a public issue by the company) offer to take all or a stated amount of the shares offered to and not taken up by the public. The sole consideration allowed is a commission at a rate which must be disclosed in the prospectus and must not exceed the rate authorised by the articles of association. This commission must not be confused with brokerage which companies are allowed to pay for placing their shares. A bona fide invitation to enter into an underwriting agreement does not require a prospectus (Companies Act, 1948, ss. 38, 417, Sch. 4 para. 11). See PROSPECTUS.

As to the taxation of underwriters see the Income and Corporation Taxes Act, 1970, s. 330, Sch. 10; Finance Act, 1973, s. 39, Sch. 16.

Undeveloped land. A duty on the site value, if over £50, of undeveloped land was imposed by the Finance (1909–10) Act, 1910. It was discontinued together with the other land value duties by the Finance Act, 1920, s. 57. See LAND VALUES DUTIES.

Undischarged bankrupt. Transactions by an undischarged bankrupt with any person dealing with him bona fide and for value in respect of any property, real or personal, acquired by the bankrupt after adjudication, are valid against the trustee if completed before he intervenes (Bankruptcy Act, 1914, s. 47). If an undischarged bankrupt obtains credit to the extent of ten pounds or upwards without giving notice that he is an undischarged bankrupt, or engages in any trade or business under a name different from that under which he was adjudicated bankrupt without disclosing the latter name, he is guilty of a misdemeanour (s. 155). See BANKRUPT; DISCHARGE; PROTECTED TRANSACTIONS.

Undivided shares in land. Before 1926 a legal estate in undivided shares in land was held by joint tenants, tenants in common, coparceners, and by husband and wife as tenants by entireties, but by the Law of Property Act, 1925, s. 1 (6), a legal estate is not capable of subsisting or of being created in an undivided share in land; such shares take effect as equitable interests only in the net proceeds of sale and of the rents and profits of the entirety of the land until sale, while the legal estate must be held by trustees for sale of the entire undivided property (ss. 1 (3), 34 (4), 205, Sch. 1 Pt. IV). See TRUST FOR SALE.

The legal estate of the trustees for sale in the joint tenancy in the entirety persists *ex necessitate rei*; severance of the legal estate in joint tenancy is prohibited, but the equitable interest in any shares may be disposed of and the incidents of a release of the legal estate by a joint tenant to the other joint tenants, and (by implication) the *jus accrescendi* (*q.v.*) are preserved (s. 36). Undivided shares can only be created by way of trust for sale under a trust instrument, or by a conveyance of the land to persons of full age in undivided shares having the effect of making the grantees, or if there are more than four, the first four named in the conveyance joint tenants upon the statutory trusts (*q.v.*) (Law of Property Act, 1925, s. 34; Settled Land Act, 1925, ss. 36, 117 (1) (xxxi)).

A trust for sale does not arise in the case of joint tenants for life who are constituted together as tenant for life by the Settled Land Act, 1925, s. 19 (2).

For the transitional provisions relating to land held in undivided shares at the commencement of the Act, see the Law of Property Act, 1925, Sch. 1 Pt. IV. As to testamentary dispositions in undivided shares, see the Law of Property Act, 1925, s. 34 (3). By the Law of Property Act, 1925, s. 36, where a legal estate (not being settled land) is beneficially limited to or held in trust for any persons as joint tenants, it is held on trust for sale in like manner as if the persons beneficially entitled were tenants in common (s. 34), but not so as to sever their joint tenancy in equity. A husband and wife are for all purposes of acquisition of property treated as two persons (s. 37). See ENTIRETIES, TENANCY BY.

For the equitable rights of persons entitled to undivided shares in the proceeds of land and the duties of trustees for sale, and as to the effect of contracts to convey undivided shares see the Law of Property Act, 1925, ss. 3, 23–33, 42 (6).

Undres, minors or persons under age not capable of bearing arms (1 Fleta, c. 2).

Undue influence, any influence, pressure, or domination in such circumstances that the person acting under that influence may be held not to have exercised his free and independent volition in regard to the act.

In the case of benefits or advantages obtained in certain relationships, the existence of this influence is presumed, *e.g.*, guardian and ward, a parent over a child upon or soon after attaining age

and the possession of property, a guide or instructor, medical advisers, ministers or professors of religion, managers of business (*Coomber* v. *Coomber* [1911] 1 Ch. 174), attendants upon or advisers of aged and infirm people. In such cases, in regard to transactions *inter vivos*, the onus of proving absence of undue influence lies on the person claiming the benefit of the disposition or act, and in some cases, *e.g.*, gifts by clients to their solicitors, the onus can only be discharged by showing not only that the relationship has ceased, but that the donor was acting under independent advice. In the case of wills, the onus is shifted and the person alleging undue influence is called upon for proof of the allegation (*Huguenin* v. *Baseley* (1807) 14 Ves. 273; *Lyon* v. *Holme* (1868) L.R. 6 Eq. 655; *Parfitt* v. *Lawless* (1872) L.R. 2 P.M. 462; *Allcard* v. *Skinner* (1881) 36 Ch.D. 145; *Low* v. *Guthrie* [1909] A.C. 278; *Wintle* v. *Nye* [1959] 1 W.L.R. 284).

As to transactions between engaged couples, see *Zamet* v. *Hyman* [1961] 1 W.L.R. 1442.

In election matters, undue influence is any force, violence, or restraint, or the infliction of, or threat to inflict, any injury, or the practice of any intimidation, in order to induce any person to vote, or refrain from voting, or on account of his having done so. See COR-RUPT PRACTICES.

Undue preference. As to avoidance of preference of a creditor within three months of bankruptcy, see FRAUDULENT PREFERENCE.

An electricity area board is not to show undue preference to any person or class of persons and is forbidden to exercise undue discrimination against any person or class of persons (Electricity Act, 1947, s. 37 (8); *South of Scotland Electricity Board* v. *Bristol Oxygen Co.* [1959] 1 W.L.R. 587).

As to undue preference or undue discrimination by the Post Office, see the Post Office Act, 1969, s. 11 (4).

Unemployment benefit. See the Social Security Act, 1975, ss. 14–20; Social Security Pensions Act, 1975.

Unenforceable. A contract is said to be unenforceable when, atlhough it may be a valid contract, it cannot be sued upon, *e.g.*, for want of written evidence when required by the Statute of Frauds, 1677, s. 4, or the Law of Property Act, 1925, s. 40. Such a contract may be enforceable in other ways, *e.g.*, by forfeiture of a deposit (*Monnickendam* v. *Leanse* (1923) 39 T.L.R. 445).

Unfair dismissal. See WRONGFUL DISMISSAL.

Unfree tenure, base tenure. See TENURE.

Unfrid [Sax.], one who has neither peace nor quiet.

Ungeld, an outlaw.

Unica taxatio. In a special award of *venire* where, of several defendants, one pleaded and one let judgment go by default, the jury who were to try and assess damages on the issue had also to assess damages against the defendant suffering judgment by default.

Uniformity, Acts of, the Book of Common Prayer Act, 1548, the Uniformity of Common Prayer, etc., Act, 1551, the Act of Uniformity, 1558, and the Act of Uniformity, 1662.

The Act of 1662 provides that ministers in any cathedral, collegiate or parish church or chapel or other place of public worship shall be bound to say and use the morning prayer, evening prayer, celebration and administration of both the sacraments and all other the public and common prayer in such order and form as is mentioned in the book annexed to the Act, and that the morning and evening prayers therein contained shall upon every Lord's day and upon all other days and occasions and at the times therein appointed be openly and solemnly read in every church, chapel or other place of public worship, and that resident incumbents keeping curates shall personally and at least once monthly read the prayer book service in their church, on pain of a £5 penalty, and that no person except an ordained priest shall be beneficed or administer the sacrament on pain of £100 penalty. There are savings for Latin prayers in the college chapels of Oxford and Cambridge Universities and in the convocations of either province.

The Act of 1662 is the Act of Uniformity *par excellence,* but the three preceding Acts of Uniformity each prescribed its own prayer book and all were confirmed by the Act of 1662, and are also included in the definition of " Act of Uniformity " contained in the Act of Uniformity Amendment Act, 1872, s. 1. These earlier Acts allow offences to be tried at assizes by judge and jury with diocesan assessors, and impose punishments on convicted offenders, imprisonment for life being the punishment on a third conviction.

The Prayer Book (Table of Lessons) Act, 1871, established a new lectionary; and the Act of Uniformity Amendment Act, 1872, authorises shortened, special, and additional services, provided that there is not introduced into an additional service any portion of the communion service, or anything, except anthems or hymns, which does not form part of the holy scriptures, or book of common prayer, and provided that the form and mode of use is approved by the ordinary. An alternative lectionary is provided by the Revised Table of Lessons Measure, 1922.

Uniformity of Process Act, the statute 1832, 2 Wm. 4, c. 39, by which personal actions, theretofore commenced by different processes in the Courts of King's Bench, Exchequer, and Common Pleas were first commenced by one process applicable to all three courts alike. See BILL OF MIDDLESEX: LATITAT; QUO MINUS.

Unigeniture, the state of being the only begotten.

Unilateral, one-sided.

Unilateral contract. When the party to whom an engagement is made makes no express agreement on his part, the contract is called unilateral, even in cases where the civil law attached certain obligations to his acceptance. A loan of money and a loan for use were of this kind (Civil Law).

Union. In the poor law, this meant any parish or union of parishes in which there was a separate board of guardians (Interpretation Act, 1889, s. 16). Union of parishes for the purpose of administering the laws for the relief of the poor were first effected under the statute of 1781, 22 Geo. 3, c. 83, known as Gilbert's Act, and afterwards under the Poor Law Amendment Act, 1834. As workhouses were usually established by poor law unions, the workhouse was sometimes called "the union." Poor law unions were abolished by the Poor Law Acts, 1930 and 1934, and the powers of guardians transferred to the county and borough councils. The poor law was abolished by the National Assistance Act, 1948. See NATIONAL ASSISTANCE.

In ecclesiastical law, a union consists of two or more benefices which have been united into one benefice. See BENEFICE.

As to the union of parishes, see PARISH.

Unit trusts. The principle of a unit trust is the purchase by a management company of a widely-diversified block of stock-exchange securities and the re-sale to the public of interests known as units, or sub-units, in this larger block. A service charge is made and added to the price of the sub-units, and represents the remuneration of the managers of the trust. In fixed trusts, the investments are stated in advance and may not be changed. In flexible or managed trusts, the managers are free to select the investments from a wider field and to change them as they in their judgment deem advisable. The Law of Property Act, 1925, s. 164, which prohibits the accumulation (*q.v.*) of income for excessive periods does not apply to a trust deed constituting a unit trust (*Re A. E. G. Unit Trust* [1957] Ch. 415).

The Prevention of Fraud (Investments) Act, 1958, s. 12, enables the Board of Trade to investigate the administration of any unit trust scheme.

As to apportionment between capital and income, see *Re Whitehead's Will Trusts* [1959] Ch. 579. As to stamp duty on a trust instrument of a unit trust scheme see the Finance Act, 1962, s. 30. For definition of a unit trust scheme see the Finance Act, 1946, s. 57; Finance Act, 1962, s. 30 (5). As to taxation, see the Income and Corporation Taxes Act, 1970, ss. 354–359; Finance Act, 1972, s. 93. As to capital gains tax, see the Finance Act, 1972, ss. 112, 113; Finance (No. 2) Act,

1975, ss. 63, 64. As to simplified transfer of units etc. see STOCK.

Unitarians, Protestant dissenters who do not hold the doctrine of the Trinity. They were excepted from the benefit of the Toleration Act, 1688, until the statute 1813 53 Geo. 3, c. 160, repealed the incapacities and penalties imposed by earlier statutes. The holding of Unitarian opinions was no offence at common law (*Re Hewley's Charities* (1842) 9 Cl. & Fin. 355). Trusts for the benefit of Unitarians are accordingly enforceable (*Shrewsbury* v. *Hornby* (1846) 5 Ha. 406; *Re Barnett* (1860) 29 L.J. Ch. 871; *Re Wall* (1889) 42 Ch.D. 510). See DISSENTERS.

Unitary State, a State in which the supreme authority rests in one centre. See CONFEDERATION; FEDERATION; PERSONAL UNION; REAL UNION.

Unitas personarum, unity of persons, as that existing for some purposes between husband and wife, or ancestor and heir.

United Kingdom. This comprises England, Wales, Scotland and Northern Ireland, but does not include the Channel Islands or the Isle of Man.

United Nations Organisation, an international organisation established at San Francisco on June 26, 1945. By the United Nations Act, 1946, effect may be given by Order in Council to measures of the organisation not involving the use of armed force.

Loss suffered by British subjects as a result of the acts of British forces may be actionable against the Crown notwithstanding the fact that such forces were at the time of the acts part of a United Nations force (*Att.-Gen.* v. *Nissan* [1970] 1 A.C. 179).

United States of America. These declared their independence on July 4, 1776, and it was acknowledged by England on September 3, 1783.

Unity of interest. This is applied to joint tenants, to signify that no one of them can have a greater interest in the property than each of the others, whereas, in the case of tenants in common, one of them may have a larger share than any of the others. See UNITY OF POSSESSION.

Unity of possession, where a piece of land which is subject to an easement, profit *à prendre*, rent, or similar right, comes into the possession of the person entitled to the easement or other right. At the present day, "unity of possession" is applied only to cases where the possession is temporary: as where the owner of land subject to an easement takes a lease of the dominant tenement, so that the easement is suspended by unity of possession during the lease; or where the owner of a rent evicts the tenant of the land out of which it issues, so that the rent is suspended by unity of possession. In the old books, "unity of possession" has a wider sense, and includes what is now more commonly called unity of seisin (*q.v.*) (Co.Litt. 188a, 313a).

Where a person has a right to two estates, and holds them together in his own hands, as if a person takes a lease of lands from another at a certain rent, and afterwards buys the fee simple, this is a unity of possession by which the lease is extinguished, because he who had before the occupation only for his rent, is now become lord and owner of the land (*Termes de la Ley*). See JOINT TENANCY; TENANCY IN COMMON.

As applied to joint tenants, tenants in common, etc., "unity of possession" is sometimes used to signify that they have an undivided possession (2 Bl. Comm. 180).

See JOINT TENANCY; PRIVITY; TENANCY IN COMMON.

Unity of seisin, where a person seised of land which is subject to an easement, profit *à prendre*, or similar right, also becomes seised of the land to which the easement or other right is annexed. The term is usually applied to cases where the seisin is that of a tenant in fee simple, and is equally high or "perdurable" in both pieces of land, so that the easement or other right is extinguished by the unity of seisin: as where a tenant in fee simple of land subject to an easement acquires an estate in fee simple in the dominant tenement. But if one piece of land is held for a conditional or determinable interest, then there is no unity of seisin sufficient to work an extinguishment (Co.Litt. 313). See UNITY OF POSSESSION.

Unity of time. This is applied to joint tenants to signify that the interest of each of them must arise at the same time: that is, one cannot take his share first, and then another come in after him. This rule, however, did not apply to estates created under the Statute of Uses, 1535, or by will. See UNITY OF INTEREST; UNITY OF POSSESSION.

Unity of title. This is applied to joint tenants to signify that they hold their property by one and the same title, while tenants in common may take property by different titles. See UNITY OF INTEREST; UNITY OF POSSESSION.

Universal agent, one who is appointed to do all the acts which the principal can personally do. Such a universal agency must be of the rarest occurrence, inasmuch as it would make such an agent the complete master, not merely *dux facti* but *dominus rerum*, the complete disposer of all the rights and property of the principal. The law will not from general expressions infer the existence of any such universal agency, but will rather construe them as restrained by the principal business in respect to which the authority was directed.

Universal legacy, a testamentary disposition by which the testator gave to one or more persons the whole of the property which he left at his decease (Civil Law).

Universal partnership, a species of partnership by which all the partners agreed to put in common all their property, *universorum bonorum*, not only what they then had, but also what they should acquire (Civil Law).

Universitas, a corporate body (Civil Law).

Universitas juris, the totality of the rights and duties inhering in any individual and passing to another as a whole at once; an estate or inheritance (Civil Law).

Universitas vel corporatio non dicitur aliquid facere nisi id sit collegialiter deliberatum, etiam si major pars id faciat (Dav. 48). (A university or corporation is not said to do anything unless it be deliberated upon collegiately, even though the majority of them do it.)

Universities and College Estates Acts. The sale and letting of the estates of the Universities of Oxford and Cambridge and Durham, and of the colleges therein, were regulated by the Universities and College Estates Acts, 1858, 1860 and 1898. These Acts are replaced by the Universities and College Estates Act, 1925, the Law of Property (Amendment) Act, 1926, and the Universities and College Estates Act, 1964.

University, an association of learners, and of teachers and examiners of the learners, upon whose report the association grants titles called degrees (such as Master of Arts, Doctor of Divinity), showing that the holders have attained some definite proficiency.

The English universities include those of Oxford and Cambridge (incorporated by the statute 1571, 13 Eliz. 1, c. 29, by the names of the Chancellor, Masters and Scholars of the University of Oxford and Cambridge respectively), Durham, London, Manchester, Newcastle, Birmingham, Liverpool, Leeds, Sheffield, Bristol, Reading, Nottingham, Southampton, Hull, Exeter, Leicester, Sussex, Keele, East Anglia, York, Lancaster, Essex, Warwick, Kent, Loughborough, Aston in Birmingham, City, Brunel, Bath, Bradford, Surrey, Salford and the Open University. There is also the University of Wales. The Scottish universities are those of St. Andrews, Glasgow, Aberdeen, Edinburgh, Strathclyde, Heriot-Watt (Edinburgh), Dundee, Stirling. In Northern Ireland there are the Queen's University of Belfast and the New University of Ulster; in the republic of Ireland, the University of Dublin (and Trinity College), and the National University of Ireland.

The Universities Tests Act, 1871, made provision for the removal of religious tests (*R.* v. *Hertford College* (1878) 3 Q.B.D. 693). The University of Dublin Tests Act, 1873, made similar alterations in the law with regard to the University of Dublin and Trinity College. The College Charter Act, 1871, provides that a copy of any application for a charter for a new college or university shall be submitted to Parliament as well as to the sovereign in Council.

By the Oxford University Act, 1854, commissioners were appointed with powers to frame statutes for the better government, etc., of Oxford University, and the colleges therein; and by the Cambridge University Act, 1856, other commissioners were appointed with the like powers as to Cambridge. By the Universities of Oxford and Cambridge Act, 1877, commissioners were appointed with the like powers as to both Oxford and Cambridge. The Universities of Oxford and Cambridge Act, 1923, established two bodies of commissioners, one for Oxford and the other for Cambridge, with power to make statutes and regulations for the universities and their colleges and halls, emoluments, endowments, trusts, foundations, institutions, etc.

As to the jurisdiction over undergraduates, see CHANCELLORS OF THE UNIVERSITIES, ETC.

The Sex Disqualification (Removal) Act, 1919, empowered universities to admit women to membership and degrees. As to sex discrimination see the Sex Discrimination Act, 1975, ss. 22–36.

Oxford and Cambridge had the franchise for two members each from the earliest times; London acquired it by the Representation of the People Act, 1867, ss. 24, 41–45, for one member, and the Scottish universities by the Representation of the People (Scotland) Act, 1868, s. 39. The Representation of the People Act, 1918, provided for the following university constituencies: Oxford, with two members; Cambridge, with two members; London, with one member; other English universities, with two members; Wales, with one member; and Scotland with three members. Men and women of full age and capacity who had received a degree (other than an honorary degree) at any university forming, or forming part of, the constituency, were entitled to be registered as parliamentary electors for a university constituency. The university franchise was abolished by the Representation of the People Act, 1948.

University courts. The Universities of Oxford and Cambridge from a very early date exercised, through the courts of their chancellors, a jurisdiction both civil and criminal, the jurisdiction being derived partly from numerous royal charters, which were confirmed by the statute 1571, 13 Eliz. 1, c. 29, and partly, in the case of Cambridge, from the Bishops of Ely, and, in the case of Oxford, from the Bishops of Lincoln.

UNIVERSITY

The Chancellor's Court of the University of Cambridge has fallen into abeyance, except as regards disciplinary matters, since the Cambridge Award Act, 1856, s. 18, which excludes from its jurisdiction all actions to which any person not a member of the university is a party and all criminal proceedings against any such person.

The ecclesiastical jurisdiction of the Chancellor's Court of the University of Oxford is obsolete; its functions in connection with probate were abolished by the Oxford University Act, 1860, s. 2; there is doubt as to whether it can exercise now the criminal jurisdiction which it formerly had in all cases (except treason, felony or mayhem) arising within the area of its jurisdiction in which a resident member of the university was either prosecutor or defendant; but its civil jurisdiction is still exercised. That jurisdiction is exclusive; it extends to all forms of action (other than actions relating to freehold) no matter what amount may be involved, and it extends to all parts of England. Thus in *Ginnett* v. *Whittingham* (1886) 16 Q.B.D. 761, it was held that the court had exclusive jurisdiction in an action for libel, where the alleged libel was published in London by a member of the university, and the plaintiff had never been in any way connected with the university or the city of Oxford. The vice-chancellor or commissary of the university or his deputy presides over the court. The deputy must be a barrister of five years' standing. As to appeals, see the Judicature Act, 1925, s. 209. See Salter, *Registrum Cancellarii Oxoniensis*; Snell, *Customs of Old England*.

See CHANCELLORS OF THE UNIVERSITIES, ETC.; COGNISANCE; HIGH STEWARD; JURY; PROCTOR; SPINNING HOUSE.

University press. At Oxford, the public press of the University is called the Clarendon Press; at Cambridge, the Pitt Press; at London, the Athlone Press.

Unjust enrichment, where a person unjustly obtains a benefit at the expense of another. In certain cases, *e.g.*, where money is obtained by mistake or through fraud or for a consideration which has wholly failed, the law implies a promise to repay it. The doctrine of unjust enrich-

ment, or *enrichement sans cause*, forms part of the law of Scotland and of various continental countries, but it is not recognised in English law (*Reading* v. *Att.-Gen.* [1951] A.C. 507). The principles on which restitution will be ordered are laid down in the decisions of the courts in actions for money had and received (*q.v.*) (*Boissevain* v. *Weil* [1950] A.C. 327).

See Goff and Jones, *Law of Restitution*.

Unlage (Sax.), an unjust law.

Unlawful. " Unlawful " and " illegal " are generally used as synoymous terms, but a distinction is occasionally drawn between them; " unlawful," as applied to promises, agreements, considerations and the like, is sometimes used to denote that they are ineffectual in law because they involve acts which, although not illegal (that is to say, positively forbidden), are disapproved of by the law, and are therefore not recognised as a ground of legal rights, either because they are immoral (*q.v.*), or because they are against public policy. (See POLICY.) It is on this ground that contracts in restraint of marriage or of trade are generally void. As a general rule, an unlawful agreement cannot be enforced, nor can money paid or property delivered under it be recovered back: *potior est conditio defendentis* (*q.v.*). " Unlawful " in relation to sexual intercourse means " illicit " (*R.* v. *Chapman* [1959] 1 Q.B. 100).

Unlawful assembly, an assembly of three or more persons for a purpose forbidden by law, such as that of committing a crime by open force, or with intent to carry out any common purpose, lawful or unlawful, in such a manner as to endanger the public peace, or to give firm and courageous persons in the neighbourhood of such assembly reasonable grounds to apprehend a breach of the peace in consequence of it. Assembly outside a building may be unlawful although no one outside the building is put in fear (*Kamara* v. *D.P.P.* [1974] A.C. 104). See ASSEMBLY, UNLAWFUL; PUBLIC MEETING; PUBLIC ORDER; RIOT; ROUT.

Unlawful drilling. See SEDITION.

Unliquidated, that which is not ascertained. See DAMAGES; JUDGMENT; LIQUIDATED DAMAGES; WRIT OF SUMMONS.

Unliquidated damages. When the amount to be recovered depends on all the circumstances of the case, and on the conduct of the parties, or is fixed by opinion or by an estimate, the damages are said to be unliquidated. See DAMAGES; LIQUIDATED DAMAGES.

Unmarried. Prima facie this means never having been married, but the context may show that it means not having a husband or wife (*Re Sergeant* (1884) 26 Ch.D. 575; *Blundell* v. *De Falbe* (1888) 57 L.J.Ch. 576).

Unnatural offence. See SODOMY.

Unneutral services, services which expose a neutral ship to the same treatment as if she were carrying contraband.

Unoccupied property. As to the rating of unoccupied property see the General Rate Act, 1967 (ss. 17, 17A, 17B, Sch. 1, as amended by the Local Government Act, 1974, ss. 15, 16. See also the Town and Country Planning Act, 1968, Sch. 9 para. 68; Town and Country Planning Act, 1971, Sch. 23 Pt. II; Local Government Act, 1972, Sch. 30.

Power to acquire unoccupied office premises is contained in the Community Land Act, 1975, ss. 28–36.

Uno flatu, with the same breath and the same intent.

Unques [Norm. Fr.], yet, still.

Unques prist, still ready. See UNCORE PRIST.

Unregistered companies may be wound up under the Companies Act, 1948, s. 399. (*Re Banque des Marchands de Moscou* [1958] Ch. 182).

Unseaworthy ships. Sending an unseaworthy (*Hedley* v. *Pinkney Steamship Co.* [1892] 1 Q.B. 58) ship to sea in such a state that the life of any person is likely to be endangered is a misdemeanour by the Merchant Shipping Act, 1894, s. 457, unless the person charged proves either that he used all reasonable means to insure the ship being sent to sea in a seaworthy state, or that her going to sea in such an unseaworthy state was under the circumstances reasonable and justifiable.

As to the meaning of unseaworthiness in a bill of lading, see *The Schwan* [1909] A.C. 450. See SEAWORTHINESS.

Unsolicited goods and services. Under the Unsolicited Goods and Services Act, 1971, a person who is sent goods with a view to his acquiring them may treat them as an unconditional gift, if the sender does not take them back within six months and the recipient within that period posts a notice to the sender stating the recipient's name and address and that the goods are unsolicited (s. 1). A person who demands payment for unsolicited goods is guilty of an offence punishable on summary conviction with a fine of £200 (s. 2). A demand for payment for an unauthorised entry in a directory is also an offence punishable on summary conviction with a fine of £400 or on indictment with a fine (s. 3 as amended by the Unsolicited Goods and Services (Amendment) Act, 1975). Sending unsolicited publications describing or illustrating human sexual techniques is an offence punishable on summary conviction with a fine of £100 for a first and a fine of £400 for any subsequent offence. No prosecution may be instituted except by, or with the consent of, the Director of Public Prosecutions (Act of 1971, s. 4). As to offences by corporations, see s. 5.

Unsound food. Powers for the inspection and seizure of unsound food are given by the Food and Drugs Act, 1955, ss. 8–11. The food and drugs authorities are specified in the Local Government Act, 1972, s. 198. As to the position of a wholesale butcher when unsound meat is seized while in the possession of the retailer to whom he sold it, see *Grivell* v. *Malpas* [1906] 2 K.B. 32, and as to the power of a butcher to obtain compensation when a prosecution results in an acquittal, see *Hobbs* v. *Winchester Corporation* [1910] 2 K.B. 471. See ADULTERATION.

Unsound mind. See MENTAL HEALTH.

Unsworn testimony. As to its admission in certain cases in civil and criminal proceedings in colonial courts, see the (Colonies) Evidence Act, 1843; as to the evidence of children, see the Children and Young Persons Act, 1933, s. 43.

Unthrift, a person of outrageous prodigality.

Unum est tacere, aliud celare. (It is one thing to be silent, another to conceal.) A seller is not as a rule bound to disclose defects, but if he takes active steps to conceal defects he may be guilty of fraud.

Unumquodque eodem modo, quo colligatum est, dissolvitur (*Grounds of Law*, 507). (Everything is loosed in the same way as it was bound.) This is not necessarily true. Thus a deed may be discharged by a simple contract (*Berry* v. *Berry* [1929] 2 K.B. 316). See EODEM LIGAMINE, ETC.; EODEM MODO QUO QUID, ETC.

Unus nullus rule, the rule of evidence of the civil law, that the testimony of one witness is equivalent to the testimony of none.

In English law corroboration is required on a summons for an affiliation order, and two witnesses are required on an indictment for treason or perjury, and for attestation of a will. The unsupported evidence of an accomplice, though legally admissible, is usually rejected by a jury under the direction of the judge (*Re Meunier* [1894] 2 Q.B. 415); the same procedure will usually apply to the uncorroborated testimony of a party in divorce proceedings or the claimant of property of a deceased person. With these exceptions, the rule of English law is that witnesses are weighed, not counted, *ponderantur testes, non numerantur.* See CORROBORATION.

Upholstery. See RAGFLOCK.

Upper bench [*bancus superior*], the style of the King's Bench during the protectorate of Cromwell. See BANCUS SUPERIOR.

Upset price, in sales by auction, an amount for which property to be sold is put up, so that the first bidder at that price is declared the buyer, if there is no higher bid.

Uranium. See PLUTONIUM.

Urari, a drug producing immobility, but not insensibility. It is not an anaesthetic for the purposes of the Cruelty to Animals Act, 1876, s. 5.

Urban district councils. See DISTRICT.

Ure, operation or effect. To put in ure, therefore, is to put in operation. See ENURE.

It also meant custom or practice: see the statute 1571, 13 Eliz. 1, c. 2, s. 1.

Urine. See BLOOD.

Usage, practice long continued (6 Co. Rep. 65).

Usage means a uniformity of conduct in respect to matters of common interest. Hence Coke says, in speaking of custom and prescription, " as for usage, that is the efficient cause or rather the life of both; for custom and prescription lose their being, if usage fail " (Co.Cop. 33). See CUSTOM; PRESCRIPTION.

Usage also meant a right of way, as Crooked Usage in Chelsea.

Usance [Fr.], the time in which bills of exchange between this country and a foreign country were formerly payable. The time varied for different countries. Thus, a usance between this country and Venice being three calendar months, a bill drawn on Venice at two usances and dated January 1 would fall due on July 1, subject to the allowance of days of grace. The practice of drawing bills at usances is obsolete, the same result being attained by specifying the time for which the bill is to run, but the term " usance " is still employed to signify the period for which bills on a foreign country are by the practice of merchants almost invariably drawn. If a foreign bill is drawn payable at sight, or at a certain period after sight, the acceptor will be liable to pay according to the course of exchange at the time of acceptance, unless the drawer expresses that it is payable according to the course of exchange at the time it was drawn, *en espèces de ce jour.*

Use [Lat. *usus*, use, the act of employing a thing; Lat. *opus*, Norm. Fr. *oes*, benefit]. There are two words " use " in law, which though spelled alike are etymologically and historically distinct.

In law, as in ordinary language, " use " denotes the act of employing a thing: thus, to cultivate land, to read a book, to inhabit a house, is to use those things.

In the case of corporeal things, use is one of the modes of exercising ownership. (See OWNERSHIP; USE AND OCCUPATION.) In the case of incorporeal things, use is a mode of acquiring and retaining certain rights. (See ENJOYMENT.) Thus, if A publicly makes use of his name or some peculiar word or token (not being a trade mark in the strict sense) in connection with his trade or occupation, he acquires the right to prevent other persons from using that name, work or token in such a way as to induce the public to believe that their business is carried on by A, and loses that right so soon as he discontinues the use. In the case of trade marks, registration is substituted for public user as a mode of acquiring title. See PUBLICI JURIS; TRADE MARKS.

Use also means " benefit "; thus, in an ordinary assignment of chattels the assignor transfers the property to the assignee for his " absolute use and benefit." In the expressions " separate use," " superstitious use," and " charitable use," use has the same meaning. More often, however, " use " has a technical meaning which can only be explained historically.

The common law treated the actual possessor for all purposes as the owner of the property. It was not difficult to find him out, since the possession of his estate was conferred upon him by a formal and notorious ceremony, technically called livery of seisin, which was performed openly and in the presence of the people of the locality.

The rules of the common law were evaded by a device founded by the monastic jurists upon a model furnished by the civil law. Two methods of transferring realty began to co-exist in this country—the ancient common law system, and the later invention, denominated uses.

Before the Statute of Uses, 1535, a use was in its nature equitable; it was a right in equity to the beneficial ownership of property the possession of which had been confided to another. The Court of Chancery, although without jurisdiction over the property, worked on the conscience of the apparent or legal owner.

Before the Statute of Uses, 1535, if one man (A) conveyed land by feoffment (then almost the only mode of conveyance) to another (B), with the intention, express or implied, that B should not hold it for his own benefit, but for the benefit of a third person (C), or of A himself, then B was said to hold the land " to the use," that is, for the benefit, of C or A. In the courts of common law the feoffee to uses (B) was looked upon as the owner of the land for almost all purposes, the

seisin or legal estate being in him. In the Court of Chancery, on the other hand, he was looked upon as merely the nominal owner; he was bound to allow the *cestui que use* (C) to have the profits and benefit of the land and to deal with it as he pleased. C was therefore the equitable or beneficial owner of the land. The " use " or beneficial ownership was treated like an estate, and descended on the intestacy of the *cestui que use* to his heir in the same way as the land would have done. A use was also devisable by will, although the land was not.

The person enjoying the beneficial right was called the *cestui que use*, or he to whose use the land was conveyed, and the person in possession, the feoffee to uses. Thus where A conveyed an estate to B to his (A's) own use or to the use of C, B was the feoffee to uses, and A or C, as the case might be, the *cestui que use*.

The use consisted of three parts: that the feoffee to uses should suffer the *cestui que use* to take the profits; that upon the request of the *cestui que use*, or notice of his will, the feoffee to uses would convey the estate to the *cestui que use* or his heirs, or any other person by his direction; and that if the feoffee to uses had been dispossessed, and the *cestui que use* disturbed, the feoffee to uses could re-enter or bring an action to recontinue his possession.

The properties of uses before the Statute of Uses, 1535, were as follows:

(1) They were descendible according to the rules of the common law relating to the inheritable estates of intestates: and the special customs of gavelkind, borough-English, and copyholds, determined the particular descent of uses. This is an illustration of the maxim, *aequitas sequitur legem*, equity follows the law.

(2) They were devisable even before the Statute of Wills, 1540.

(3) They were transferable, although at law they were mere choses in action.

(4) A *cestui que use* in possession of the land was deemed a tenant at will only, for he had neither *jus in re*, *i.e.*, an estate, nor *jus ad rem*, *i.e.*, a demand, and therefore he could bring no action, having neither title nor legal estate in the property.

(5) A widow could not be endowed nor

could a husband have his curtesy of a use, because the *cestui que use* had no legal seisin of the land. See DOWER.

(6) The *cestui que use* could be impanelled on a jury.

(7) The feoffee to uses, being complete owner of the land at law, performed the feudal duties, had power to sell and brought actions, and his widow became entitled to dower, and his estate was subjected to wardship, relief, and forfeiture for treason or felony. In fact, he was treated at common law as the absolute tenant of the fee.

(8) A use, being but the creature of equity, could not be taken in execution for the debts of the *cestui que use*; for there was no process at common law but against legal estates.

(9) A use, not being an object of tenure, was exempt from the oppressive burdens of the feudal system. It was not forfeitable for treason or felony, because it was not held of any person. This was afterwards broken in upon by the statute 1388, 12 Ric. 2, c. 3.

(10) At one time a use was not assets for the payment of debts by the heir or executor.

There appears to have been a distinction between a use and a trust, even before the Statute of Uses, 1535. A special trust appears to have arisen where the feoffee to uses was not only invested with the possession, rents and profits, but was under an obligation to deal with them in a special manner indicated by the feoffor. The special trust might be lawful or it might be a special trust unlawful, *i.e.*, one created for fraudulent purposes, so as to defraud creditors, to defeat the Statutes of Mortmain, and the like.

The statute 1377, 50 Edw. 3, c. 6, subjected the special trust to an execution by a creditor of the *cestui que trust*; while the statute 1503, 19 Hen. 7, c. 15, extended, for the first time, the estate of the *cestui que use*. (See EXTENT.) In general, however, there was but little difference in the terms use and trust. See ACTIVE USE; OFFICIAL USE; PASSIVE TRUST.

Objections to uses before the Statute of Uses, 1535, were as follows: —

(1) Estates passed by way of use, from one to another, by bare words only, without any solemn ceremony or permanent record of the transaction, whereby a claimant knew not against whom to bring his action.

(2) Heirs were deprived of their common law rights since uses were devisable.

(3) Lords lost their wardships, reliefs, marriages, and escheats, the trustees letting the *cestui que use* continue the possession, whereby the real tenants who held the lands could not be discovered.

(4) The king lost the estates of aliens and criminals; for they made their friends trustees, who kept possession, and secretly gave them the profits, so that their use was undiscovered.

(5) Purchasers were insecure; for the alienation of the *cestui que use* in possession was at common law a disseisin, and the statute 1483, 1 Ric. 3, c. 1, gave him power to alienate what he had; yet the feoffee might still enter to revest a remainder or contingent use, which was never published by any record or delivery whereby the purchaser could know of them.

(6) Uses were not subject to the payment of debts.

(7) Many lost their rights by perjury in averment of secret uses.

(8) Uses might be allowed in mortmain (Gilbert, *Uses*, c. 1, s. 8).

The Statute of Uses, 1535, used to be described in pleading as *Statutum de usibus in possessionem transferendis*. It became a pivot of English conveyancing. Its effect was that where any person was seised to the use of another, then the person enjoying the use was to be deemed to have the actual and lawful seisin, estate or possession corresponding to the use, and the statute transferred the (legal) seisin, estate or possession accordingly to the *cestui que use*.

The Statute of Uses, 1535, in effect enacted that where any person was seised of any lands or other hereditaments to the use, confidence or trust of another, the latter should be in lawful seisin, estate and possession of the lands for the same estate as he had in the use, and that the estate of the feoffee to uses should be deemed to be in the *cestui que use*. The effect of this was to convert uses into possession, or to make the *cestui que use*

1838

legal instead of equitable owner. The result was that if A conveyed land to B and his heirs to the use of C and his heirs, so that B acquired the seisin of the land, then the statute was said to execute the use by turning it into a legal estate; the seisin passed out of B and vested in C, who thus became legal owner of the land in fee simple. See SCINTILLA JURIS.

It has been said that one object aimed at by the statute was the total destruction of the use, by effecting an amalgamation of the legal and equitable interests; but this object, if it existed, failed owing to the equitable jurisdiction of the Court of Chancery and the judicial interpretation of the statute by the common law judges.

The circumstances necessary to the execution of uses under the statute were: —

(1) A person seised to the use.

(2) A *cestui que use in esse*.

(3) A use *in esse* in possession, reversion, or remainder.

(4) Every species of realty, except copyholds, whether corporeal or incorporeal, in possession, reversion, or remainder, might be conveyed to uses, but it must be *in esse*.

(5) There must be a seisin in the grantee, or feoffee, to uses at the time of the execution of the use.

(6) The use might be raised by a conveyance operating either by transmutation or non-transmutation of possession.

The Statute of Uses, 1535, did not operate to vest the legal estate in the *cestui que use* in the following cases: —

(1) Uses limited of copyholds, since no person could be introduced into the estate without the lord's consent; for if uses were permitted, there would then be effected a transmutation of the possession by operation of law, which would be contrary to the peculiarity of this kind of tenure. Yet shifting or springing uses might be limited by copyhold surrenders, so as to have the effect of divesting prior vested estates.

(2) Upon a demise to the grantee to uses of leaseholds and chattel interests. It is said that the statute contemplated freeholds only, and therefore employed the word seised; a tenant is only possessed of a leasehold for years. But the use declared upon a feoffment, etc.,

might be of a term of years and there was nothing to prevent the *cestui que use* from having the legal estate in the term to which the legal reversion could be released. See LEASE AND RELEASE.

(3) Active and constructive uses. When the use involved a direction to sell the estate and then divide the proceeds of the sale or pay debts, or to pay over the profits, or to convey to a child on attaining majority, or to reconvey on the repayment of a mortgage loan, the statute was precluded from the very nature of the transaction from converting such a use into a legal right to the land, and equity, therefore, compelled the trustee, who retained the legal estate notwithstanding the statute, to perform the duty confided in him. The trustee had the legal estate (if properly invested in him) in the following cases: a trust to permit a *feme covert* to receive the profits for, or to pay the same to, her separate use; and so of a trust to permit and suffer a party to receive and take the net rents and profits after discharge of outgoings.

(4) A second use, or a use upon a use. The common law judges determined that the statute could only operate upon one use, and where another use was superadded it was a mere nullity, since it was an interest unknown to the common law before the statute. This doctrine and its consequences have been explained thus: —

There were three conveyances, *viz.*, appointment to uses, bargain and sale, and covenant to stand seised, where there was no transmutation or change of possession but only a use raised in favour of the appointee, purchaser or covenantee, and a transmutation of the legal estate by virtue of the statute, while there were other conveyances, such as a feoffment or grant, which transmuted the possession at law, and no use was raised at all unless declared or implied upon the change in possession. Consequently if a use was declared upon a conveyance of the first kind, that use would be a use upon a use; in conveyances of the latter class, the use (if any) declared was the first, and the only use, on which the statute could work.

The following examples point out the operation of these two classes of transfers, *i.e.* (*a*) non-transmutation of possession, or (*b*) transmutation of possession, as to the vesting of the legal and equitable estates: —

Where A conveyed land, by appointment, bargain and sale, or covenant to stand seized, to B and his heirs, to the use of C and his heirs, to the use of, or in trust for, D and his heirs, this vested the legal estate or use in B and the equitable estate in D, C not taking any legal estate. But where A conveyed land by feoffment or grant to B and his heirs, to the use of C and his heirs, to the use of, or in trust for, D and his heirs, this gave B but a seisin, and vested the use or legal estate in C, and the equitable estate in D.

A release did not transmute the possession but it transvested the legal ownership and had the same effect as a feoffment or grant.

It was to avoid the divesting of the legal estate in the feoffee to uses that the practice grew up of a feoffment or grant by A to B and his heirs to the use of B and his heirs, or, in the usual form, unto and to the use of B and his heirs. A feoffment or grant to B and his heirs would have been perfectly good to transmute the possession and transfer the legal estate, but if a use arose expressly or by implication on that estate, B would have lost the legal estate without any transmutation of possession from him, and the additional words, so far from being superfluous, meant no more than to express the grant to be for the benefit of the grantee as his legal estate, subject, of course, to any trust that might have been engrafted on the grant.

Upon this doctrine that there could be no use upon a use, equity interfered, and treated D, the person having the second use, as the beneficiary, and compelled B, having the statute use, to deal with the estate for D's benefit as a trustee, and then giving the technical term of "trust" to D's second use, deprived the use properly so called of its beneficial interest, and revived the twofold system of one person holding the legal estate in the land, while the equit-able estate or the usufructuary right therein was actually enjoyed by another, and thus the Court of Chancery reasserted its jurisdiction over uses under the name of trusts.

Although the first use executed by the statute was called a use, and the second use not executed by the statute a trust, yet this phraseology was altogether arbitrary; for either word might be applied to either estate, since the particular interests enjoyed by the parties depended upon their position with regard to one another, and not upon the term employed in their denomination. The usual and strictly technical form was unto and to the use of B, to the use of D, or unto and to the use of B in trust for D, but it was immaterial whether it was in this form, so that a trust in name might be a use in effect, and *e converso*.

(5) Future executory and contingent uses could not be executed into legal estates by the statute until they arose.

(6) It is said that devises were not within the Statute of Uses, 1535, because it was passed before the Statute of Wills, 1540. But this was of no practical importance, since the courts, in their decisions, are guided by a testator's intention, and it was always held that if A devised land to B and his heirs, to the use of or in trust for C and his heirs, or in trust to permit C and his heirs to take the profits, it showed that the testator intended that C should have the legal estate in fee. And if there was a devise to the use of C for life, with remainder over, although it could not take effect by way of a use executed by the statute, because there was no seisin to serve the use, yet C would have the legal estate. Indeed, uses were executed in a will as if they were limited by deed, if such was the testator's intent (*Baker* v. *White* (1875) L.R. 20 Eq. 166).

The practical advantages of the system, subsequently to the Statute of Uses, 1535, were: —

Conveyances to uses legalised many dispositions which were void at common law, for uses might be suspended, revived, postponed, and accelerated in a way opposed to the rules of the feudal law. Amongst the most important relaxations thus introduced were the following: —

(1) A person could convey to himself, which he could not at common law, as it would have been absurd to give possession by livery of seisin to one's self. This was found to be convenient, especially in the following example: —

It frequently happened that upon the death or removal of trustees, it became necessary to fill up their number pursuant to a power for that purpose usually introduced into settlements of real property. In order to effect this it was formerly the practice for the old trustees to make a conveyance, which operated by way of transmutation of possession (either by release or grant), to the new trustees and their heirs, to the use of the old and new trustees and their heirs. Without the assistance, therefore, of the statute, it would have been necessary that the old trustees should have first enfeoffed some third person, who would have re-enfeoffed the old and new trustees jointly, thereby making two conveyances necessary. Indeed, in the case of terms for years, and other personal property, two assignments were required for this purpose, until the Law of Property Amendment Act, 1859, s. 21; by the Conveyancing Act, 1881, s. 50, freehold land might be conveyed by a person to himself jointly with another, and by the Law of Property Act, 1925, s. 72, to himself alone; this section also reproduces the last-mentioned two enactments.

(2) A conveyance could not be made by a husband to his wife, but by limiting a seisin to the grantee or releasee, the husband might declare the use to his wife, which the statute would execute.

(3) A man could not make his own heir a purchaser, even of an estate tail, for *filius est pars patris, haeres est pars antecessoris*; but a man might limit the use so as to make his heirs special take, either by purchase or by descent.

(4) No person could take a present interest in the *habendum* of a deed who was not named in the premises. But in a case where A enfeoffed B, *habendum* to B and C, their heirs and assigns, to the use of B and C, their heirs and assigns, it was resolved that, as C was not named

in the premises, he could take no possession originally by the *habendum*; and that the livery, made according to the intent of the indenture, did not give anything to C, because as to him it was void; but though the feoffment did not give any seisin to C, yet it did to B and his heir, which seisin was sufficient to serve the use declared to C. Therefore the use limited to B and C was good, and the statute executed it, but this limitation of the use in a bargain and sale to a person not named in the premises, after a previous disposition of it to the bargainee, would have been ineffective to pass the legal estate.

(5) If an estate was conveyed to two, the one being capable and the other incapable at the time of the grant, he who was capable took the whole; joint tenants could not take at different periods. But since the introduction of uses, if a feoffment was made in fee, to the use of a man and his future wife, though the whole estate would vest in the man at first, yet upon his marriage the wife would take jointly with him. So if a disseisin was had to the use of two, and the one agreed to it at one time, and the other at another, they became joint tenants.

(6) An estate of freehold could not be granted, apart from statute, at common law, to commence *in futuro*, nor could a contingent remainder be supported, without an express particular estate of freehold (see CONTINGENT REMAINDER), but by a conveyance under the Statute of Uses, 1535, a freehold could be created to commence *in futuro*, and future limitations would have been supported when no particular estate had been created, either as remainders or as springing uses.

(7) An estate could not at common law be limited upon a fee simple, *i.e.*, a fee simple could not be made to cease as to one person, and take effect by way of limitation upon a contingent event in favour of another; but such a limitation could take effect by way of shifting or springing use. A shifting or springing use, after a previous limitation of the fee, could not be barred by the *cestui que use* by any kind of conveyance, but where

it was limited upon an estate tail the tenant in tail could bar it.

(8) Every remainder, at common law, had to be limited so as to await the determination of the particular estate, before it could take effect in possession: but an abridgment of the particular estate, upon a certain condition, could be effected by a conveyance to uses, so as to accelerate the expectant estate into possession.

All estates which before the statute would have been good in equity and to which the statutes applied were, after the statute, good estates in law.

The statute only applied to cases where one person was seised of land or other hereditaments to the use of another. If, therefore, B was possessed of a term of years or a chattel, or was in quasi-seisin of copyhold land (all of which were incapable of true seisin), to the use of C, the statute did not execute this use, and the legal estate remained in B. The statute also did not execute a second use, or a " use upon a use," nor did it execute active uses, or uses which imposed some active duty on the grantee. If, therefore, land was conveyed to by A to B to the use of C to the use of D (which was a use upon a use), only the first use was executed; C became seised of the land in accordance with the statute, but he held it to the use of D as if the statute had never been passed. Again, if land was conveyed to B to the use (or upon trust) to pay over the rents and profits to C, this use was not executed, and therefore the legal estate remained in B.

Hence uses were of two kinds, uses at common law, or those which remained unaffected by the statute, and uses which operated under the statute.

Uses at common law included (a) all uses of leasehold and copyhold land and chattels, and (b) uses of freehold land or other hereditaments which were not executed by the statute because they were either " uses on uses " or active uses. A use at common law was seldom created under that name, almost the only instance being where a copyhold tenant surrendered his land to the lord to the use of some other person; here the lord was merely a trustee or instrument for

carrying the intended alienation into effect. See TRUST.

Uses which operated under the statute were those declared of land held by a freehold tenure for an estate of freehold, or of rents, services and most other hereditaments, except those (such as easements and profits à prendre) of which the enjoyment was inseparable from the possession. They were expressed or implied. If A conveyed land to B and his heirs to the use of C for life, without more, then the land vested in C for an estate for life, and the reversion in fee after C's estate resulted or returned to A, because it was not otherwise disposed of. Here the use to B was an express use, and the use to A was an implied or resulting use.

Uses were executed or executory. An executed use was one which took effect immediately, as where land was conveyed to B and his heirs to the use of C and his heirs. An executory use was one which was to take effect at some future time. Executory uses were of four kinds. (a) A springing use was one which was limited so as to commence in futuro, independently of any preceding estate; as where land was conveyed to B and his heirs to the use of C and his heirs on the death of D. Such a use did not take effect in derogation of any estate except that which resulted to the grantor or remained in him in the meantime. (b) A shifting or secondary use was one which was limited so as to shift from one person to another on the happening of a given event; in other words, such a use took effect in derogation of a preceding use; as where land was conveyed to B and his heirs to the use of C and his heirs, with a proviso that when D returned from Rome the land should be to the use of D and his heirs. (See EXECUTORY INTERESTS; LIMITATION.) (c) Uses which were limited or declared under powers. (See POWER.) (d) Future or contingent uses, being those which were limited to take effect as remainders: thus, if land was conveyed to B and his heirs to the use of C (a bachelor) for life, and after his death to his eldest son, this was a contingent use.

A thing could not be granted by way of use if the enjoyment of it was inseparable from the possession, such as annuities, ways, commons and authorities. Hence, where land was sold subject to an express reservation or exception of such rights, privileges or easements, the object had to be attained either by a regrant, or by a declaration that the land should remain to such uses as should give effect to the reservation or exception, and (subject thereto) to the uses declared to vest the land in the purchaser. The Conveyancing Act, 1881, s. 62, provided however that a limitation of freehold land to the use that a person might have an easement, right, liberty, or privilege over the land should operate to vest in possession in that person the easement, etc., so limited to him.

As to deeds to lead and declare uses, and to conveyances operating under the statute, see CONVEYANCE.

The Statute of Uses, 1535, was repealed by the Law of Property Act, 1925, s. 207, Sch. 7, and land directed by any statute or other instrument to be conveyed to uses is to be conveyed to a person of full age upon the requisite trusts (ss. 130–132); see also s. 65 (reservations in lieu of grants of rentcharges, easements, etc.); s. 66 (confirmation of past transactions); and s. 4 (equivalence in equity of former legal estates). See LAW OF PROPERTY ACT; SETTLED LAND; VOLUNTARY CONVEYANCE.

Use and occupation. A claim for use and occupation arises where a person has used and occupied the land of another with his permission but without any actual lease or agreement for a lease at a fixed rent. It is a claim for damages for breach of an implied agreement to pay for the use of a landlord's property. The Distress for Rent Act, 1737, s. 14, enacts that it shall be lawful for the landlord, where the agreement is not by deed, to recover a reasonable satisfaction for the land held or occupied by the defendant; and if in evidence on the trial of the action any parol demise, or any agreement (not being by deed) whereon a certain rent was reserved, shall appear, the plaintiff in such action shall not therefore be non-suited, but may make use thereof as evidence of the quantum of the damages to be recovered. The action is not for damages

ex delicto, because the action is not maintainable against a trespasser or wrongdoer. The claim is based on an implied or tacit contract to pay for the use of the land. An action for debt on the demise, but not upon covenant for use and occupation, was available at common law (*Gibson* v. *Kirk* (1841) 1 Q.B. 850). Occupation by the defendant must be proved.

Use classes. See DEVELOPMENT.

Use, Existing. See DEVELOPMENT.

User, use, the act of employing a thing. An owner can use land by keeping it in its virgin state for his own purposes. An owner of a powder magazine or a rifle range uses the land nearby for the purpose of ensuring safety even though he never sets foot on it. The owner of an island uses it for the purpose of a bird sanctuary even though he does nothing on it, except prevent people building there or disturbing the birds. A hospital which owns land adjoining it and leaves it in its virgin state for the benefit of its patients gets fresh air, peace and quiet and therefore uses the land for the purposes of a hospital (*Newcastle City Council* v. *Royal Newcastle Hospital* [1959] A.C. 248).

User de action, the bringing of an action in the proper county or venue (*q.v.*) (Brooke 64).

Uses to bar dower. When a conveyance of land was made to a person who was married before the Dower Act, 1833, and he wished to prevent his wife's right of dower from attaching to the land, it was conveyed to the following uses: to such uses as the purchaser should appoint; in default of appointment to the use of him and his assigns during his life; in the event of the determination of that estate by forfeiture or otherwise in his lifetime, to the use of a trustee during the life of the purchaser in trust for him; with an ultimate limitation to his heirs and assigns for ever. By this means the purchaser had a full power of alienation without having a greater estate in possession than an estate for life, to which the wife's dower did not attach, and the intermediate estate of the trustee prevented the remainder in fee simple from vesting in the purchaser in possession (and so becoming liable to dower) by any accidental merger of the life estate. See DOWER.

Usher [Fr. *huis*, a door], a door-keeper, an officer who keeps silence and order in a court. The office of Usher of the Court of Chancery was abolished by the Court of Chancery Act, 1852, s. 17.

The full title of Black Rod (*q.v.*) is the Gentleman Usher of the Black Rod.

The Usher of the White Rod or Principal Usher for Scotland is connected with England to the extent only that he is entitled to be present at a coronation. Under the Walker Trust Act, 1877, the office (which is hereditary) is vested in trustees under that Act; and when occasion arises a deputy is appointed by the sovereign.

Usque ad medium filum aquae, or **viae,** as far as the middle of the stream or road. See AD MEDIUM FILUM VIAE.

Usual covenants, covenants usually inserted in deeds having a similar scope to those in respect of which a question arises. The phrase occurs most frequently in connection with agreements for leases stipulating that the lease when granted shall contain " all usual covenants." What these are is a question of fact, but it may perhaps be laid down that at the present day covenants by the lessee to pay rent, to pay taxes, and to repair, and a qualified covenant by the lessor for quiet enjoyment, are usual, but that no others are, and in particular that the covenant not to assign or underlet without the leave of the lessor is not (*Hampshire* v. *Wickens* (1878) 7 Ch.D. 555; *Re Lander* [1892] 3 Ch. 41).

A proviso for re-entry on breach of covenants generally is not " usual," but a proviso for re-entry on breach of the covenant to pay rent is (*Hodgkinson* v. *Crowe* (1875) L.R. 10 Ch. 622; *Re Anderton* (1890) 45 Ch.D. 476).

Usual terms, a phrase in the common law practice, which meant pleading issuably, rejoining gratis, and taking short notice of trial. When a defendant obtained further time to plead, these were the terms usually imposed.

The phrase is often used informally upon declaring an order of court, according to the practice of the court, *e.g.*, " Stay of proceedings upon the usual terms pending an appeal." As a rule,

this means payment of the sum in question by the appellant, if defendant, the plaintiff giving security for repayment and an undertaking by his solicitor to abide any order for refunding if the appeal is successful, the costs of the application to be paid by the appellant (R.S.C., Ord. 59, r. 13).

Usucapio, usucaption; the enjoying, by continuance of time, of long possession, or prescription; property acquired by use or possession (Civil Law). See LIMITATION.

Usucapio constituta est ut aliquis litium finis esset. (Usucaption was instituted in order that there might be some end put to legal proceedings.) Usucaption in the civil law was ownership resulting from prolonged possession.

Usufruct, the right of reaping the fruits (*fructus*) of things belonging to others, without destroying or wasting the subject over which such right extended (Civil Law).

Usufructuary, the person enjoying the usufruct.

Usura est commodum certum quod propter usum rei (vel aeris) mutuatae recipitur; sed, secundario sperare de aliqua retributione, ad voluntatem ejus qui mutuatus est, hoc non est vitiosum (5 Co.Rep. 70). (Usury is a certain benefit which is received for the use of a thing (or of money) lent; but, secondly, to hope for a certain return at the option of the party who borrowed, this is not vicious.) See USURY.

Usura maritima [*foenus nauticum*], interest taken on bottomry or respondentia bonds, which being proportioned to the risk, was not affected by the usury laws; see the statute 1778, 19 Geo. 3, c. 37. See FOENUS NAUTICUM.

Usurpation, a keeping or holding by using that which is another's; an interruption of *usucapio*, or disturbing a man in his right and possession, etc. It is called intrusion in the civil and canon laws.

In the law of real property, usurpation is where a subject uses a royal franchise without lawful warrant (Co.Litt. 277b).

In ecclesiastical law, when a stranger who has no right presents to a church, and his clerk is admitted and instituted, he is said to be a usurper, and the wrongful act which he has done is called a usurpation. To recover his presentment and possession of the advowson, the patron must bring his action within six months from the induction of the usurper's presentee (Statute of Westminster II, 1285, c. 5). See NE ADMITTAS; QUARE IMPEDIT.

Usury. Originally usury had the same meaning as interest has at the present day, *viz.*, a periodical payment in consideration of a loan. Contracts could be avoided for usury above ten in the hundred (Co.Litt. 3b).

Many attempts were made to evade the statutes against usury by making the interest payable in the form of rents, annuities, etc., and in such cases the question was whether the stipulated payment was bona fide a rent or annuity, etc., or whether it was usury and the contract a usurious one within the statute (5 Co.Rep. 69).

Hence " usury " acquired the sense of interest above the rate allowed by those statutes, and the statutes making all such usurious contracts void became known as the Usury Laws. Eleven statutes from the statute 1545, 37 Hen. 8, c. 9, to the statute 1850, 13 & 14 Vict. c. 56, were repealed by the Usury Laws Repeal Act, 1854. The Consumer Credit Act, 1974, ss. 137–140, give the county court power to reopen extortionate credit bargains. See CONSUMER CREDIT. Canon 109, which includes usury among other offences, was made part of the Clergy Discipline Act, 1892. See Kelly, *History and Law of Usury.*

Usus est dominium fiduciarium (Bacon, Read.Stat.Uses). (Use is a fiduciary dominion.)

Ut poena ad paucos, metus ad omnes perveniat (*Grounds of Law*, 515). (Though few are punished, the fear of punishment affects all.) See IMPUNITAS, ETC.

Ut res magis valeat quam pereat (Noy, Max. 50). (It is better for a thing to have effect than to be made void.) See BENIGNAE, ETC.; VERBA ITA, ETC.

Utas [Fr. *octave*], the eighth day following any term or feast; octave (*q.v.*): see *Les Estatuz del Eschekere* where *la*

chise Pasche is translated as " the Utas of Easter."

Uterine brother [*uterinus frater*], a brother born of the same mother; *frater consanguineus* is a brother by the same father.

Utero-gestation, pregnancy.

Utfangtheft, outfangtheft (*q.v.*).

Uti possidetis, as you possess. The rule known as *uti possidetis* is that under which all property, whether movable or immovable, not specially provided for in the treaty terminating a war is to remain in the hands of the belligerent who happened to have possession of it when hostilities ceased.

Utile per inutile non vitiatur (Co.Litt. 227). (That which is useful is not marred by that which is useless.) See SUPERFLUA, ETC.

Utilis actio, an action granted by the praetor in the exercise of his judicial authority by means of an extension of an existing action (*actio directa*) to persons or cases not coming within its original scope (Civil Law).

Utilis annus, a year of *dies utiles*, made up by reckoning in succession only the days on which the plaintiff could bring his action, *i.e.*, when the praetor sat, and on which neither party was unable to appear in person or by procurator (Civil Law).

Utility goods, certain goods of everyday use which were not subject to purchase tax (Finance Act, 1952, s. 9).

Utlagato capiendo quando utlagatur in uno comitatu et postea fugit in alium, De, a writ which lay to take an outlaw when he was outlawed in one county and afterwards fled into another county.

Utlagus, or **Utlagatus,** an outlaw. See OUTLAWRY.

Utland, tenemental land.

Utlary [Norm. Fr. *utagarie*; Ang. Sax. *utlaga*], outlawry. See OUTLAW.

Utlepe, Utlesse, the escape of a felon from prison (Fleta).

Utrum. See ASSISA DE UTRUM.

Utter. In criminal law, to utter a forged document, die or seal, etc., or counterfeit coin, is to pass or attempt to pass it off as genuine when it is known to be forged. Uttering a forged document, seal or die is in general the same offence as that of forging the same document (Forgery Act, 1913, s. 6; Criminal Law Act, 1967, Sch. 3 Pt. III). As to uttering counterfeit money, see COIN.

Utter barristers, barristers who plead " without " the Bar, *i.e.*, " outer " barristers; all such counsel as are not Queen's Counsel or, formerly, serjeants-at-law. See APPRENTICII AD LEGEM; BARRISTER.

Uxor non est sui juris sed sub potestate viri (*Grounds of Law*, 516). (A wife is not *sui juris* (*q.v.*), but is under the government of her husband.) See OMNIA QUAE SUNT, ETC.

V

V., *versus,* against; also the mark of a vagabond. See AD SECTAM; BRANDING.

V.A., See VICTORIA AND ALBERT, ETC.

V.C., vice-chancellor.

V.G., *verbi gratia,* for the sake of example.

Vacant possession. See POSSESSION; SERVICE.

Vacant succession, an inheritance the heir to which was unknown.

Vacantia bona. See BONA VACANTIA.

Vacarius, commonly called Magister Vacarius, was a Lombard by birth. He introduced the study of the civil law into England and gave lectures on that subject at Oxford from 1149 to 1170. He compiled for the use of his students a digest of Justinian which was known as the *Liber pauperum*: an almost complete copy of this manuscript is preserved at Worcester.

Vacate, to cancel, to render of no effect.

Vacation. The vacations are the periods of the year during which the courts and chambers of the Supreme Court of Judicature are closed for ordinary business. There are, however, certain kinds of business which may be transacted during vacation, *e.g.*, applications for injunctions, for extension of time, etc., and for this purpose two vacation judges and a staff of officials attend in court periodically during the vacations. Provision is made for the trial or hearing during the Long Vacation of urgent causes, actions or matters in the Queen's Bench Division (R.S.C., Ord. 64).

The vacations are four, namely, the Christmas Vacation commencing on December 22 and ending on January 10; the Easter Vacation commencing on the Thursday before and ending on the second Monday after Easter Sunday; the Whitsun Vacation commencing on the Saturday before and ending on the second Monday after Whit Sunday, and the Long Vacation commencing on August 1, and ending on September 30 (R.S.C., Ord. 64, r. 1 (2)).

Vacation also signifies, in ecclesiastical law, that a church or benefice is vacant, *e.g.*, on the death or resignation of the incumbent, until his successor is appointed. See PLENARTY; SEQUESTRATION.

Vacatura, an avoidance of an ecclesiastical benefice.

Vaccaria, a dairy (Co.Litt. 5b).

Vaccination, inoculation with the virus of cowpox as a preventive of smallpox. It was first made compulsory by the statute 1853, 16 & 17 Vict. c. 100, gratuitous vaccination having been previously provided for in various enactments dating from 1840, all of which were repealed by the Vaccination Act, 1867. This Act was amended by the Vaccination Acts, 1871, 1874, 1898 and 1907. They were repealed by the National Health Service Act, 1946, s. 26, under which every local health authority is to make arrangements for vaccination against smallpox and immunisation against diphtheria, and, if so directed, against any other disease.

Vadiare duellum (to wage combat), where two contending parties, on a challenge, give and take a pledge of fighting.

Vadium [Lat. *vas*], a pledge or security (Civil Law).

Vadium mortuum, a mortgage or dead-pledge by which the pledgor loses the security and its fruits or interest which were taken by the pledgee or mortgagee until repayment or redemption. See MORTGAGE; VIVUM VADIUM.

Vadium ponere, to take bail or pledges for a defendant's appearance.

Vadium vivum. See MORTGAGE; VIVUM VADIUM.

Vadlet, the king's eldest son; hence the valet or knave follows the king and queen in a pack of cards (Barr. on Stat. 344).

Vagabonds. The provisions of the law with respect to vagrancy are directed against idle and disorderly persons, *e.g.*, unlicensed pedlars, beggars, etc.; rogues and vagabonds, *e.g.*, fortune-tellers, persons lodging in deserted buildings or the open air without visible means of subsistence, sellers of obscene prints, etc.; and incorrigible rogues, *e.g.*, persons twice convicted of being rogues and vagabonds, persons who escape from imprisonment as rogues and vagabonds, etc. These offences are punishable with imprisonment (Vagrancy Act, 1824). See VAGRANCY.

Vagabonds, Statute of, the statute 1547, 1 Edw. 6, c. 3. See BRANDING.

Vagrancy. The Act now in force is the Vagrancy Act, 1824. It is amended by the Vagrancy Act, 1838, as to re-commitment on failure to prosecute, appeal, and exhibition of obscene prints; by the Sexual Offences Act, 1956, s. 30, as to men living on earnings of prostitution; and by the Fraudulent Mediums Act, 1951, as to spiritualism. It points out three classes of persons, idle and disorderly persons; rogues and vagabonds; and incorrigible rogues.

Under the Vagrancy Act, 1824, s. 3, idle and disorderly persons include pedlars wandering abroad, and trading without a licence, common prostitutes wandering in the public streets or public highways (but not sitting in a motor-car (*Carnill* v. *Edwards* [1953] 1 W.L.R. 290)), or in any place of public resort, and behaving in a riotous and indecent manner, and persons wandering abroad, or placing themselves in a public place, street, highway, court, or passage, to beg, or gather alms (*Mathers* v. *Penfold* [1915] 1 K.B. 514). They are liable to a month's imprisonment. A fine not exceeding £1 (if the conviction is by one justice) or £5 (if conviction is by two or more justices) may be imposed instead of imprisonment (Magistrates' Courts Act, 1952, s. 27 (3)).

Under the Vagrancy Act 1824, s. 4, as amended by the Criminal Justice Act, 1925, s. 42, the Vagrancy Act, 1935, the Fraudulent Mediums Act, 1951, the Criminal Law Act, 1967, Sch. 2 para. 2, the Firearms Act, 1968, Sch. 1 paras. 3, 8, Sch. 2 paras. 14, 19, and the Theft Act, 1968, Sch. 3 Pt. I, rogues and vagabonds are persons committing any of the offences hereinbefore mentioned, after having been convicted as an idle and disorderly person, persons pretending to tell fortunes, or using any craft or device, by palmistry, or otherwise (*Monck* v. *Hilton* (1877) 2 Ex.D. 268) in order to deceive (*R.* v. *Entwistle* [1899] 1 Q.B. 846), persons wandering abroad or lodging in any barn or outhouse, or in any deserted or unoccupied buildings, or in the open air, or under a tent, or in any cart or wagon (not being a tent, cart or wagon with or in which they travel), and not giving a good account of themselves but not unless it is proved that they were directed to an accessible place of shelter where they could get free accommodation for the night and failed to apply for or refused shelter there, or that they are persistent wanderers abroad notwithstanding accessible shelter, or caused damage or were or were likely to be infectious with vermin or otherwise, persons wilfully exposing to view in any street, or shop in any street, road, or public place, any obscene picture, or other indecent exhibition, persons wilfully, openly, lewdly and obscenely exposing their person (*i.e.*, penis, *Evans* v. *Ewels* [1972] 1 W.L.R. 671), with intent to insult any female, persons wandering abroad, and endeavouring, by the exposure of wounds or deformities, to obtain alms, persons endeavouring to procure charitable contributions of any kind, under any false pretence, persons being armed with any gun or other offensive weapon, or having upon them any instrument with intent to commit an arrestable offence, persons being found in any dwelling-house or enclosed yard (*Goodhew* v. *Morton* [1962] 1 W.L.R. 210), garden, or area, for any unlawful purpose, suspected persons or reputed thieves frequenting any river, canal, street, highway, or any place of public resort, with intent to commit an arrestable offence and persons apprehended as idle and disorderly persons and violently resisting arrest. They are liable to three months' imprisonment. A fine not exceeding £1 (if conviction is by one justice) or not exceeding £100 (if conviction is by two or more justices) may be imposed instead of imprisonment (Magistrates' Courts Act, 1952, s. 27 (3)).

Under the Vagrancy Act, 1824, s. 5, as amended by the Criminal Justice Act, 1967, Sch. 6, and the Courts Act, 1971, Sch. 8, incorrigible rogues include persons escaping out of any place of legal confinement before the expiration of the term for which they have been committed, persons committing any offence subjecting them to be dealt with as rogues and vagabonds having been at some former time adjudged so to be, and persons apprehended as rogues and vagabonds and violently resisting arrest. They may be committed to the Crown Court either in custody or on bail, and may be imprisoned for one year (Vagrancy Act, 1824, s. 10; Courts Act, 1971, Sch. 8).

Possession of firearms by a person committing certain offences under the Vagrancy Act, 1824, s. 4, entails an additional punishment under the Firearms Act, 1968, ss. 17, 51, Schs. 1, 6 Pt. I.

Where an incorrigible rogue is committed by justices to the Crown Court, the Crown Court is not the convicting court and has no power to make a probation order (*R.* v. *Jackson* [1974] Q.B. 517).

Vagrants preventing children from receiving education are punishable under the Children and Young Persons Act, 1933, s. 10, as amended by the Education Act, 1944, Sch. 8; Criminal Justice Act, 1967, Sch. 3 Pt. I; Children and Young Persons Act, 1969, Sch. 5 para. 2, Sch. 6.

Vagrants, sturdy beggars; vagabonds.

Valeat quantum, let it have its weight, small or great. See QUANTUM VALEBANT.

Valec, Valect, or **Vadelet,** a young gentleman; a gentleman of the chamber; a personal attendant or servant. See VADLET.

Valentia, the value or price of anything.

Valor beneficiorum, the value of every ecclesiastical benefice and preferment, according to which the first-fruits and tenths were collected and paid. It was commonly called the king's books, by which the clergy were rated. See TENTHS.

Valor ecclesiasticus, a record of the whole of the property held by the Church in England, made by a commission appointed under the statute 1534, 26 Hen. 8, c. 3. It has been printed in six volumes (1810–34) as part of the *Record Commission Series*. The *Valor* was prepared for the purpose of enabling the Crown to collect the annates (*q.v.*) effectively: and it was also useful when the property of the monasteries came to be confiscated. The MS. of the *Valor* is defective: for instance, those parts relating to the whole diocese of Ely and to the counties of Berks, Rutland and Northumberland, and to much of the diocese of London, are missing. But along with the *Valor* is preserved another contemporary MS., entitled the *Liber valorum*, which covers the whole of England, though with less full details; and the blanks in the *Valor* have been filled in from the *Liber*, as far as may be.

Valore maritagii, De. See VALUE OF MARRIAGE.

Valsheria, the proving by the kindred of the slain, one on the father's side and another on that of the mother, that a man was a Welshman.

Valuable consideration. See CONSIDERATION; VALUE.

Valuation, the equivalent in money of any kind of property. Thus for the payment of estate duty, a valuation of property of all kinds had to be made.

When land is taken under statutory powers the compensation is assessed under the Land Compensation Act, 1961. See COMPENSATION.

As to valuation for rates and taxes, see ASSESSMENT; RATE; VALUATION LIST.

As to valuation of securities in administrative proceedings, see CREDITOR.

See SITE VALUE; VALUE.

Valuation list, a list of all the rateable hereditaments in a rating area prepared by Inland Revenue officers under the General Rate Act, 1967, ss. 67, 115; Local Government Act, 1972, Schs. 13, 30. See generally the General Rate Act, 1967, ss. 67–95; General Rate Act, 1970, s. 1; Superannuation Act, 1972, Sch. 8; Local Government Act, 1972, Schs. 13, 30; General Rate Act, 1975.

In construing a valuation list evidence of the intention of the valuation officer is not admissible but evidence may be given of the circumstances known to him (*Sussex Caravan Parks* v. *Richardson* [1961] 1 W.L.R. 561). See RATE.

Value, the utility of some particular object; the power of purchasing other goods which the possession of that object conveys. The one may be called value in use, the other value in exchange. The things which have the greatest value in use have frequently little or no value in exchange; and, on the contrary, those which have the greatest value in exchange have frequently little or no value in use. Nothing is more useful than water, but it will purchase scarcely anything; scarcely anything can be had in exchange for it. A diamond, on the contrary, has scarcely any value in use, but a very great quantity of other goods may frequently be had in exchange for it (1 Sm. Wealth of Nat. 37).

Value is often used as an abbreviation for " valuable consideration," especially in the phrases " purchaser for value," " holder for value," etc. The question whether a person acting in good faith has given value for property is often of importance when the person from whom he acquired it had not a perfect title as against some other person. Thus, if a trustee fraudulently sells the trust property to a bona fide purchaser for value, that is, to a person who had no reason to believe that it was affected with a trust, and gave a fair price for it, the *cestui que trust* has no claim against the purchaser. See BONA FIDES; CONSIDERATION; NEGOTIABLE INSTRUMENTS.

Value added tax. This tax (V.A.T.) was introduced by the Finance Act, 1972

(amended by the Finance Act, 1973, ss. 4–9; the Finance Act, 1975, ss. 1–4; and the Finance (No. 2) Act, 1975, ss. 19–21; Finance Act, 1976, ss. 17–23). It is a sales tax payable in reality by the ultimate consumer. Every sale is taxed but those purchasers in business who are not ultimate consumers can reclaim the tax which they have paid. They deduct such tax (called input tax) from tax which they receive on sales which they make (called output tax) (s. 3). It follows that a fully taxable business does not pay any V.A.T. but merely acts as a collecting agency on behalf of the Customs and Excise.

V.A.T. is a tax on the supply (a word of wide meaning) of all goods and services in the United Kingdom (Act of 1972, s. 1). It has a comprehensive coverage in that a supply which is neither of goods nor of services, for example, a patent licence, is treated as a supply of services (s. 5 (8)), therefore everything is taxable unless it is specifically exempt (see Sch. 5). A business making only exempt supplies, for example an insurance company, will have paid input tax on supplies to it, but being exempt, it has to bear this tax just as the ultimate consumer bears it, subject to corporation tax relief. Whereas if the insurance company were taxable it would bear no input tax. Exemption of a supply therefore confers no advantages save that of not having to keep records.

Zero-rating is to be distinguished from exemption. It means that tax is chargeable at a nil rate. The effect of notionally bringing the transaction within V.A.T. is that relief from input tax is obtained, by repayment if necessary, in the same way as for a fully taxable business. Exports (s. 12) and certain privileged items such as books and food (Sch. 4) are zero-rated.

Imports are taxed (s. 1) and V.A.T. is collected as if it were a customs duty (s. 2 (3)). V.A.T. is payable on imports of goods whether or not the importer is a business.

To sum up: V.A.T. is a tax on the final consumption of goods or services which is collected by instalments. The tax is charged on the " value added " by a taxable person at each stage in the process of production. In practical terms the

" value added " is the profit (including wages) of the taxable person computed on an invoice basis. Thus, the instalment of tax due at each stage is the amount chargeable on the difference between the cost of acquisition and the proceeds of sale. Whenever a taxable person supplies goods or services to another taxable person he charges him the basic cost of the goods or services plus the V.A.T. thereon and must give him a tax invoice showing the amount of these items. On the final sale to a non-business consumer the V.A.T. is added to the basic price but a tax invoice is not given. A person whose turnover is less than £5,000 per annum is not a taxable person.

The Council of the E.E.C. has issued Directives which bind member countries to introduce legislation for a value added tax.

Tax is not charged on any supply or import before April 1, 1973 (s. 47).

A White Paper (Cmnd. 4929) was issued in March 1972.

Purchase tax is abolished as from March 31, 1973 (ss. 54, 55), but a new tax, known as car tax (*q.v.*) is charged after that date (s. 52).

See also the Counter-Inflation Act, 1973, s. 12; Finance Act, 1974, ss. 5, 6.

Value of marriage, a writ known as *valore maritagii* which until 1660 lay against one who, holding by knight's service and being under age and unmarried, refused a marriage without disparagement offered by his lord. See DISPARAGEMENT; FORFEITURE OF MARRIAGE; MARRIAGE, VALUE OF.

Value payment, a payment for war damage, being an amount equal to the amount of the depreciation in the value of the hereditament caused by the war damage (War Damage Act, 1943).

Value received. This phrase is generally inserted in bills of exchange, but it is not necessary, since value is implied in every bill, as much as if expressed *in totidem verbis* (*White* v. *Ledwick* (1785) 4 Doug. 247).

If the bill or note is given for an illegal or an immoral consideration or without consideration, these words do not make it any the better; and if it is given for lawful and valuable consideration

they are superfluous (Bills of Exchange Act, 1882, s. 3 (4)).

Valued policy, a policy of insurance in which the sum at which the subject of the policy is insured is expressed (having been fixed by agreement between the parties), and so the value in case of loss need not (as a general rule) be proved. See POLICY OF INSURANCE.

Valuer, a person whose business is to appraise, or set a value upon, property.

Valvasor, or **Vidame,** a feudal title of dignity next to a peer (2 Co.Inst. 667). See VAVASOR.

Van Diemen's Land. See TASMANIA.

Vancouver's Island. See the statutes 1849, 12 & 13 Vict. c. 48, and 1858, 21 & 22 Vict. c. 99, s. 6. The British Columbia Act, 1866, provided for union with British Columbia. The British North America Act, 1930, confirmed an agreement between British Columbia and Canada.

Vang [Sax.], to stand for one at the font (Blount).

Vantarius, a precursor.

Varectum. See WARECTUM.

Variance, a discrepancy between a material statement in a pleading and the evidence adduced in support of it at the trial. At common law a variance, whether in a civil or a criminal proceeding, was a fatal defect, incapable of amendment; but this is no longer so. See AMENDMENT.

Variation of trusts. See TRUST, VARIATION OF.

Vassal [Ital., *vassallo*; Low Lat., *vassus*; Gall., *gwas*, a servant], one who holds of a superior lord; a subject; a dependant; a tenant or feudatory.

Vassalage, the state of a vassal; tenure at will; slavery.

Vasseleria, the tenure or holding of a vassal.

Vasto, De, a writ which lay against a tenant for life or for years who committed waste (Fitz.N.B. 55).

Vastum, waste (*q.v.*); also common land which was open to the cattle of the commoners (3 Bl.Comm. 227).

Vastum forestae vel bosci, that part of a forest or wood wherein the trees and underwood were so destroyed that it lay, in a manner, waste (Paroch.Antiq. 351).

Vattell. Emerich von Vattell was born at Couret, in Switzerland, in 1714 and died in 1767. He wrote *Droit de Gens* and *Questions de Droit Naturel.*

Vauderie, sorcery; witchcraft; the profession of the Vaudois (3 Hallam, Mid. Ages, c. 9, pt. 2, p. 386n.).

Vault. See CELLAR.

Vavasor [Low Lat. *vassi vassorum,* vassals of vassals]. the first name of dignity, next beneath a peer, was anciently that of *vidames, vice domini,* or *vavasors,* who were said to be *viri magnae dignitatis* (1 Bl.Comm. 403; Camden, Brit.; Reeves, c. 5, p. 26).

In Norman times vavasors were feudal tenants ranking next below barons. They seem to have been vassals of the barons.

Vavasory [*vavasoria*], the lands which a vavasor held (2 Bract.).

Veal-money. The tenants of the manor of Bradford, in the county of Wilts, paid a yearly rent by this name to their lord, in lieu of veal paid formerly in kind (Bract.).

Vectigal judiciarium, fines paid to the Crown to defray the expenses of maintaining courts of justice (3 Salk. 33).

Vectigal origine ipsa, jus Caesarum et regum patrimoniale est (Dav. 12). (Tribute, in its origin, is the patrimonial right of emperors and kings.)

Vegetables. See the Weights and Measures Act, 1963, s. 21, Sch. 4 Pts. VII, VIII, X.

Vehicles excise duty. See EXCISE.

Vejours [Lat. *visores*], persons sent by a court to take a view of any place in question, for the better decision of the right thereto; also persons appointed to view the result of an offence (O.N.B. 112).

It was formerly used as meaning persons sent by the court to view the corpse of a murdered man or to view a place in dispute in order to inform the court regarding it.

Velindre [Wel.], vill (*q.v.*).

Veltaria, the office of dog-leader or courser.

Veltarius [Old Germ. *welter*], one who leads greyhounds (Blount).

Venaria, beasts caught in the woods by hunting.

Venary. In the forest law, beasts of venary meant such as were got by hunting.

Venatio, hunting.

Vendee, one to whom anything is sold.

Vendition, sale, the act of selling.

Venditioni exponas (that you expose for sale), a judicial writ addressed to the sheriff, commanding him to expose to sale goods which he has already taken into his hands, to satisfy a judgment creditor (Reg. Judic. 33).

After delivery of this writ the sheriff is bound to sell the goods, and have the money in court on the return day of the writ. When a writ of *fieri facias* has been issued and the sheriff returns that he has taken goods, but that they remain in his hands for want of buyers, a writ of *venditioni exponas* may be sued out to compel a sale of the goods for any price they will fetch (R. S.C., Ord. 46, r. 1). See DISTRINGAS.

When a writ of extent in chief or in aid had been returned and no one appeared to claim the goods, etc., mentioned in the inquisition, a *venditioni exponas* issued directing the sheriff to sell them.

Venditor regis, the king's salesman. He exposed to sale goods and chattels which had been seized to answer any debt due to the king. The office was abolished in the reign of Edward II.

Vendor, one who sells anything, especially land. In the case of goods he is usually called a seller.

Vendor and purchaser. The law relating to vendor and purchaser includes such subjects as the particulars and conditions of sale of land, the contract of sale, the abstract of title, requisitions, searches, etc., and the preparation and completion of the conveyance. See COVENANT; SALE; SPECIFIC PERFORMANCE; TITLE; TITLE-DEEDS.

Vendor and purchaser summons. The Vendor and Purchaser Act, 1874, s. 9, replaced by the Law of Property Act, 1925, s. 49, enables any vendor or purchaser of any interest in land to apply in a summary way for the decision of the court in respect of any requisitions or objections or claims for compensation or any other question arising out of or connected with the contract not affecting its existence or validity. Proceedings are by way of originating summons (R.S.C., Ord. 5, r. 3). See DEPOSIT; ORIGINATING SUMMONS; SPECIFIC PERFORMANCE.

Vendor's lien. Where a vendor conveys land and the purchase money or part of it has not been paid, a lien arises as between the vendor and the purchaser, and persons claiming as volunteers, for so much of the purchase money as remains unpaid. The mere giving of security will not prevent the lien arising, unless it appears that the security was to be substituted for the lien. Similarly a purchaser will have a lien for prematurely paid purchase money (*Mackreth* v. *Symmons* (1808) 15 Ves. 329).

It must be registered under the Land Charges Act, 1972, s. 2, or it will be void against a purchaser, even if he has actual notice. See LAND CHARGE.

Vendue master, an auctioneer.

Venella, a narrow or straight way (1 Dugd.Mon. 488).

Venereal diseases. The treatment of venereal diseases by anyone other than a duly qualified medical practitioner is illegal (Venereal Disease Act, 1917, s. 1). The advertisement of any remedy for any such disease is illegal except in publications circulating amongst medical practitioners and chemists (s. 2; Medicines Act, 1968, s. 95, Sch. 6). Contravention of any provision of the Act can be punished summarily or on indictment (Venereal Disease Act, 1917, s. 3). Venereal disease means syphilis, gonorrhea or soft chancre (s. 4). See INDECENT ADVERTISEMENTS; INFECTIOUS DISEASES.

The imputation of venereal disease is actionable *per se* though merely oral. See SLANDER.

The communication of venereal disease by one spouse to another is cruelty as regards matrimonial law. See CRUELTY. It may be a ground for making a matrimonial order. See MATRIMONIAL PROCEEDINGS IN MAGISTRATES' COURTS.

Venia, a kneeling or low prostration on the ground by penitents; pardon.

Venia aetatis, a privilege granted by a prince or sovereign, in virtue of which a person under age is entitled to act as if he were *sui juris*, as if he were of full age.

Veniae facilitas incentivum est delinquendi (3 Co.Inst. 236). (Facility of pardon is an incentive to crime.)

Venire contra factum proprium, a subsequent act which is incompatible with a previous act.

Venire, Court of, a civil court at Kingston-upon-Hull with jurisdiction in all actions to any amount, held under the authority of charters granted by Henry VII, Henry VIII and Charles II.

Venire de novo. In criminal practice, this was a writ issued by the Queen's Bench on a writ of error (*q.v.*) from a verdict given in an inferior court, vacating the verdict and directing the sheriff to summon jurors anew, whence the name of the writ.

The *venire de novo* was the old common law method of proceeding to a new trial; it differed materially from granting a new trial, inasmuch as it was awarded from some defect appearing upon the face of the record, while a new trial was granted for matter entirely extrinsic. Where a verdict could be amended, a *venire de novo* was never awarded. If awarded, the party succeeding at the second trial was not entitled to the costs of the first. It has been superseded by a trial *de novo* (*R.* v. *Crane* [1921] 2 A.C. 299; *R.* v. *Dennis* (1924) 40 T.L.R. 420). See NEW TRIAL.

The Courts Act, 1971, Sch. 4 para. 4, provides that a writ or order of *venire de novo* shall no longer be addressed to the sheriff and shall be in such form as the court considers appropriate.

Venire facias, a writ in the nature of a summons to appear. Where an indictment had been removed into the Queen's Bench Division at the instance of the prosecutor, the writ might be moved for by the prosecutor if the defendant failed to appear; and where application was made to the Queen's Bench Division to amend a coroner's inquisition under its common law jurisdiction, the writ was in strictness necessary in order to bring the coroner before the court.

Anciently there were many forms of the writ. Their purposes were described by the various words following the words *venire facias.*

Venire facias ad respondendum, a writ to summon a person against whom an indictment for a misdemeanour had been found, to appear and be arraigned for the offence. It could be issued by the Queen's Bench, by a judge of assize, or by a court of quarter sessions. A warrant is now used instead. See DISTRINGAS; OUTLAWRY; WARRANT.

Venire facias de novo, a second writ to summon another jury for a new trial. See VENIRE DE NOVO.

Venire facias juratores, a writ commanding the sheriff to summon a jury. It was abolished by the Common Law Procedure Act, 1852, s. 104.

Venire facias tot matronas, a writ which was issued to the sheriff commanding him to summon a jury of matrons to execute the writ *de ventre inspiciendo.* See VENTRE INSPICIENDO, DE.

Venter, womb. In the old books it was equivalent to mother; as when Littleton speaks of a man having issue two sons " by divers venters," that is, by different wives; or of two brothers " by divers venters," meaning two brothers having different mothers (Litt. 6).

As to the cases in which a child will be held to be born in a testator's lifetime because it was at that time *en ventre sa mère,* see *Villar* v. *Gilbey* [1907] A.C. 139; *Elliot* v. *Joicey* [1935] A.C. 209.

Ventre inspiciendo, De. Where the widow of an owner of land was suspected of feigning herself with child in order to produce a supposititious heir to the estate, the heir presumptive might have a writ *de ventre inspiciendo,* to examine whether she was with child or not; and if she was, to keep her under proper restraint until delivered (1 Bl. Comm. 456).

Venue [Norm.Fr. *visne;* Lat. *vicenetum, visnetum*], the place where a jury are to come for trial of causes (Co.Litt. 125a, n. 2).

In criminal procedure, the venue was a note in the margin of an indictment, giving the name of the county or district within which the court in which the indictment was preferred had jurisdiction. Now there is no such note; but the commencement of the indictment indicates the place at which the accused is to be tried (Indictments Act, 1915, Sch. 1 r. 2). The common law rule is that, subject to statutory exceptions, the venue must be laid (that is, the indictment must be preferred in a court having jurisdiction) in the county where the offence was committed If a man is wounded in one

county and dies in another, the venue may be laid in either.

In the former common law practice, the venue was that part of the declaration in an action which designated the county in which the action was to be tried. It was inserted in the margin of the declaration thus: " Middlesex to wit," " London to wit," etc. Venue was of two kinds, transitory or local. It was transitory when the cause of action was of a sort which might have happened anywhere, in which case the plaintiff might adopt any county he pleased as a venue. It was local when the cause of action could have happened in one county only, and then the venue must have been laid in that county. Thus if the action were trespass for breaking the plaintiff's close, the venue had to be laid in the county where the close was situated, for such a trespass could have happened nowhere else. If it were trespass for assaulting the plaintiff, the venue was transitory, for such a cause of action might happen anywhere, and so, in general, in all cases of contract. Venue is now abolished, and the place of trial is fixed on the summons for directions; the place for its trial may be altered by order (R.S.C., Ord. 33, r. 4). See ACTION.

Venville tenants [*fines villarum*], tenants who inherited the rights granted in early times in compensation for the rights under forest law lost by disafforestation (Snell, *Customs of Old England*). See *Re Combe Down, etc., N. Bovey, Devon (No.* 2) [1976] 8 C.L. 21.

Vera copula. See CONSUMMATION.

Veray, true.

Verba accipienda sunt secundum subjectum materiem (6 Co.Rep. 62). (Words are to be interpreted in accordance with the subject-matter.) See SECUNDUM SUBJECTAM MATERIAM.

Verba aequivoca ac in dubio sensu posita intelliguntur digniori et potentiori sensu (6 Co.Rep. 20; Co.Litt. 73). (Words which are equivocal, and which are used in a doubtful sense, are to be taken in their more weighty and effectual sense.) Thus tenure *in capite* might be either of the king or of a subject; but when it was mentioned without qualification it was held to mean tenure of the king. And where a statute made a penalty recoverable in any court of record it was held that this meant only one of the four courts at Westminster although many minor courts were also courts of record.

Verba aliquid operari debent—debent intelligi ut aliquid operentur (8 Co.Rep. 94; Bac.Max. 3). (Words ought to have some operation—they ought to be interpreted in such as way as to have some operation.) See VERBA CUM, ETC.

Verba cartarum fortius accipiuntur contra proferentem (Co.Litt. 36a; Bac. Max. 3). (The words of deeds are to be interpreted most strongly against him who uses them.) Bacon styles this "a rule drawn out of the depth of reason." The rule was criticised in *Taylor* v. *St. Helens Corporation* (1877) 6 Ch.D. at p. 280, but was recognised in *Birrell* v. *Dryer* (1884) 9 App.Cas. 345 and *Lee* v. *Railway Executive* [1949] W.N. 373. In the case of a reservation it does not operate against the vendor, but may operate against the purchaser (*Bulstrode* v. *Lambert* [1953] 1 W.L.R. 1064). See CONSTRUCTIO, ETC.

Verba cum effectu accipienda sunt (Bac.Max. 3). (Words are to be interpreted in such a way as to give them some effect.) See VERBA ALIQUID, ETC.; VERBA DEBENT, ETC.

Verba de praesenti; Verba de futuro. A declaration in the presence of witnesses by A and B was known in the ecclesiastical law as a contract of matrimony *per verba de praesenti* when it was to the effect that they were man and wife, and as a contract of matrimony *per verba de futuro* when it was to the effect that they were betrothed, or, in modern parlance, engaged. See BREACH OF PROMISE; PER VERBA, ETC.

Verba debent intelligi ut aliquid operentur (8 Co.Rep. 94). (Words ought to be interpreted in such a way as to give them some effect.)

Verba generalia restringuntur ad habilitatem rei vel aptitudinem personae (Bac. Max. 10). (General words are restricted to the nature of the subject-matter or the aptitude of the person.) So if A is granted an annuity *pro concilio impenso et impendendo* (for past and future advice), this means his advice as to

medicine if he is a physician and his advice as to law if he is a lawyer.

Verba illata inesse videntur (5 Taunt. 337). (Words referred to are deemed to be incorporated.) See VERBA RELATA, ETC.

Verba intentioni, non e contra, debent inservire (8 Co.Rep. 94). (Words ought to be made subservient to the intent, and not the other way about.) See MENS TESTATORIS, ETC.

Verba ita sunt intelligenda ut res magis valeat quam pereat (Bac.Max. 3). (Words should be read in such a way as rather to give effect to the deed, etc., in which they are used than to render it nugatory). See BENIGNAE, ETC.

Verba posteriora, propter certitudinem addita, ad priora, quae certitudine indigent, sunt referenda (Wing.). (Subsequent words, added for the purpose of certainty, are to be referred to preceding words which need certainty.) See EX ANTECEDENTIBUS, ETC.; OPTIMA STATUTI, ETC.

Verba relata hoc maxime operantur per referentiam ut in eis inesse videntur (Co.Litt. 359). (Words to which reference is made in an instrument have the same operation as if they were inserted in the instrument referring to them.) By referring, in a document signed by the party, to another document, the person so signing in effect signs a document containing the terms of the one referred to. Incorporation by reference (*q.v.*) has the same effect as literal incorporation; and this applies to Acts of Parliament as well as to deeds and contracts generally. In the case of wills, a document will only be incorporated if it is an existing document and is identified as such in the will.

Verbal note, a memorandum or note, in diplomacy, not signed, sent when an affair has continued a long time without any reply, in order to avoid the appearance of an urgency which, perhaps, is not required, and, on the other hand, to guard against the supposition that it is forgotten, or that there is an intention of not prosecuting it any further.

Verbatim et literatim, word for word and letter for letter.

Verborum obligatio, a verbal obligation, contracted by means of a question and answer; the *stipulatio* (*q.v.*) (Civil Law).

Verborum obligatio verbis dissolvitur (D. 50, 17, 35). (An obligation created by words is dissolved by words; and so a verbal release of a verbal contract is effectual.) See EODEM LIGAMINE, ETC.

Verderer, an officer in the royal forest, whose office is to look to the vert, and see it well maintained; and he is sworn to keep the assize of the forest, and view, receive and enrol the attachments, and presentments of trespasses of vert and venison, etc. (Manw. 332). See FORTY DAYS COURT.

The forest law was abrogated by the Wild Creatures and Forest Laws Act, 1971, except in so far as it relates to the appointment and functions of verderers. See also DEAN, FOREST OF.

Verdict [Lat. *vere dictum*], the opinion of a jury on a question of fact in a civil or criminal proceeding. The verdict of a jury must usually be unanimous. The High Court may, where there are not less than eleven jurors, accept the verdict of ten of them, or if there are ten jurors, the verdict of nine of them. The verdict of a complete jury of eight in the county court need not be unanimous if seven of them agree on the verdict. The court may in any case accept a majority verdict with the consent of the parties. The parties may agree to proceed in any case with an incomplete jury (Courts Act, 1971, s. 39). A general verdict (formerly called a verdict at large) is where the jury find the point in issue generally, as where in a civil case they find for the plaintiff or defendant, or where, in a criminal case, they return a verdict of guilty or not guilty. A special verdict is where they find the facts of the case specially, that is, they say that certain facts have been proved, leaving to the court the application of the law to the facts thus found. The jury is entitled to find a general verdict in any case whether civil or criminal; and in any criminal case they may, if they think fit, find a special verdict. But special verdicts, are very unusual in criminal cases. If there are several issues, the verdict may be distributed, some issues being found for the plaintiff and some for the defendant. A verdict must comprehend the whole of the issues submitted to the jury, otherwise the judgment may be set aside. See PERVERSE VERDICT; SPECIAL VERDICT.

Where on a person's trial on indictment for any offence except treason or murder (*q.v.*), the jury find him not guilty of the offence specifically charged in the indictment but the allegations in the indictment amount to or include (expressly or by implication) an allegation of another offence falling within the jurisdiction of the court of trial, the jury may find him guilty of that other offence or of an offence of which he could be found guilty on an indictment specifically charging that other offence (Criminal Law Act, 1967, s. 6 (3)). Allegations of an offence include an allegation of attempting to commit that offence (s. 6 (4)).

When a jury have found a prisoner guilty of one offence and the facts prove another offence, the Court of Appeal may alter the verdict and sentence him for such other offence (Criminal Appeal Act, 1968, s. 3); and where a prisoner is convicted and sentenced on a special verdict, the Court of Appeal may, if they decide that the court below has drawn a wrong conclusion from the verdict, record such conclusion as is warranted by law and pass the appropriate sentence (s. 5).

Majority verdicts may be accepted in criminal cases if, in a case where there are not less than eleven jurors, ten of them agree and, in a case where there are ten jurors, nine of them agree on the verdict (Criminal Justice Act, 1967, s. 13 (1)). The court is not to accept a majority verdict of guilty unless the foreman of the jury has stated in open court the number of jurors who respectively agreed to and dissented from the verdict (s. 13 (2)). This is mandatory. A failure to comply renders the verdict invalid (*R. v. Barry* [1975] 1 W.L.R. 1190).

Where the prosecution offers no evidence the judge may order that a verdict of not guilty be recorded (Criminal Justice Act, 1967, s. 17).

Before the court accepts a majority verdict the jury ought to be urged to go out once more and endeavour to reach a unanimous decision. Nevertheless such a course is not mandatory (*R. v. James Milliken* (1969) 53 Cr.App.R. 330; *R. v.*

Wright (1974) 58 Cr.App.R. 444). If there is no prospect of obtaining the necessary majority the jury may be discharged (*R.* v. *Elia* (1968) 52 Cr.App.R. 342). For procedure see Practice Direction (C.A.) (Crime: Majority Verdicts) [1967] 1 W.L.R. 1198.

If the verdict is ambiguous the judge may properly question the jury so as to obtain an unambiguous verdict (*R.* v. *White* (1960) 45 Cr.App.R. 34).

When a coroner's jury find the death of a person without saying how he came by it, this is called an open verdict. See INQUEST.

In an action in the High Court, when the jury have found their verdict, the judge could formerly direct that judgment should be entered for any party, or adjourn the case for further consideration, or leave any party to move for judgment, but now he must direct judgment to be entered as he thinks right. (See MOTION FOR JUDGMENT.) Any party may also move for a new trial (see TRIAL), or apply to the Court of Appeal to set aside the judgment (R.S.C., Ord. 59, r. 2).

See ACQUITTAL; CONVICTION; FINDING; INQUISITION.

Veredictum, quasi dictum veritatis, ut judicium quasi juris dictum (Co.Litt. 226). (The verdict is, as it were, the dictum of truth, as the judgment is the dictum of law.)

Verge or Virge [Lat. *virgata*], the compass of the royal court which bounds the jurisdiction of the Lord Steward of the Household (Britt. 68).

At common law the coroner of the county had no jurisdiction within the compass of the royal court, which bounds the jurisdiction of the Lord High Steward of the Household, and comprehends a circuit of twelve miles round the residence of the court wherever held. This jurisdiction was called the verge, within which the Coroner of the Queen's Household, or, the Coroner of the Verge, had jurisdiction over all matters within the duty of a coroner, exclusive of the coroner of the county. In some cases the coroner of the county had jurisdiction concurrent with that of the Coroner of the Verge. The Lord

Steward (*q.v.*) now exercises a mere domestic jurisdiction over the members of the royal household; and the Coroner of the Queen's Household holds inquests only on the bodies of those dying within the limits of any place where the sovereign is residing (Coroners Act, 1887, s. 29).

As to the royal household, see Pegge, *Curialia; Collection of Ordinances.*

A verge of land is the same as a virgate, a quantity of land from fifteen to thirty acres. See YARDLAND.

A verge also meant a stick, or rod, whereby one was admitted tenant to a copyhold estate. Hence, copyholders were sometimes called tenants by the verge (Old N.B. 17). See TENANTS BY THE VERGE.

See BOARD OF GREEN CLOTH.

As to parking vehicles on the verge of a road see PARKING.

Vergelt, the Saxon fine for a crime. See WERGILD.

Vergers [Lat. *portatores virgae; virga,* a rod; Fr. *bédeaux d'église*], those who carry white wands before the judges, or before church dignitaries (Fleta, c. 38).

Formerly there were vergers or porters of the verge, who carried white wands before the judges of the Queen's Bench and of the Common Pleas. The minor official who carries the mace before the dean in a cathedral and before the vice-chancellor in the two ancient English universities is called a verger.

Verification. This was a part of the system of pleading used before the Common Law Procedure Act, 1852, s. 67. Any pleading subsequent to the declaration (*q.v.*) and alleging new matter concluded with a verification, consisting of the words: " And this the defendant (or plaintiff) is ready to verify " or (if it was intended that the matter pleaded should be tried otherwise than by a jury) of the words: " And this the defendant (or plaintiff) is ready to verify by the said record or to verify when, where and in such manner as the court shall order, direct or appoint " (3 Bl.Comm. 309). See GO TO THE COUNTRY.

Veritas, a quocunque dicitur, a Deo est (4 Co.Inst. 153). (Truth, by whomsoever pronounced, is from God.) Quoted by Coke when citing the practice of heathens, Saracens and Turks as to the inviolability of the persons of ambassadors and others *ejusdem generis*. It might also be quoted as showing that once the truth of evidence is accepted, the character of the witness who gives it is immaterial; his character is a relevant matter only in so far as it tends to show whether he is or is not telling the truth.

Veritas nihil veretur nisi abscondi (9 Co.Rep. 20). (Truth fears nothing but concealment.)

Veritas nominis tollit errorem demonstrationis (Bac.Max. 24). (The truth of the name cures error of description.) See PRAESENTIA, ETC.

Vermin. Rabbits were not vermin within the meaning of the (repealed) Gun Licence Act, 1870, s. 7 (4), which exempted an occupier of land from taking out a gun licence if he used a gun only for the purpose of scaring birds or killing vermin on his land. Nor were birds, no matter how destructive. The expression appears to include rats, mice, stoats, weasels and cats which have gone wild.

Orders may be made for the destruction of rabbits under the Pests Act, 1954. See RABBITS; RATS AND MICE.

A local authority is required to take steps for the cleansing of verminous premises or articles, and of verminous persons (Public Health Act, 1936, ss. 83–86; Public Health Act, 1961, ss. 35, 36; London Government Act, 1963, s. 40; Criminal Justice Act, 1967, Sch. 3 Pt. I). See also the Education Act, 1944, s. 54. Local authorities may require verminous premises to be cleansed before demolition (Housing Act, 1957, ss. 25, 44 (7)).

As to vermin in mines, see the Mines and Quarries Act, 1954, s. 95.

Verna, a slave born in his master's house (Civil Law).

Versificator. The *versificator regis*, or verse-maker to the king, existed as early as the time of Richard I. His *versificator* was Gulielmus Peregrinus, that is to say, Wandering William. One Master Henry was the *versificator* in 1250. By the reign of James I the *versificator* had been

replaced by the poet laureate (*q.v.*); but the precise period at which the change took place is uncertain.

Versus [Lat.], abbrev. *v.*, against. See AD SECTAM.

Vert [Fr. *verd*; Lat. *viridis*], otherwise called greenhue, everything which bears a green leaf within a forest which may cover a deer; but especially great and thick coverts. Vert, venison and inclosure were three of the requisites of an ancient legal park (*Pease* v. *Courtney* [1904] 2 Ch. 509).

In the law of the forest, vert meant anything, from a small shrub to a tree, which bore leaves and was in a forest. The trees were known as over-vert and the shrubs as nether-vert (Manw. pt. 2, p. 33).

The over-vert was also termed hautboys, and the nether-vert sub-boys. Special vert means all trees growing within the forest that bore fruit to feed deer, because the destroying of them was more grievously punished than the destroying of any other vert (*De la Warr* v. *Miles* (1881) 17 Ch.D. at p. 570).

Vert also meant the right, under a royal grant, of cutting green wood in the forest.

Vert also means green colour, called Venus in the arms of princes, and emerald in those of peers, and expressed in engravings by lines in bend.

Very lord and very tenant [*verus dominus et verus tenens*], an immediate lord and tenant, as where A held land of B without any mesne lord (Bro.Abr.). See LORD.

Vest; Vested. When a person becomes entitled to a right, estate, etc., it is said to vest in him.

An estate or interest may vest in one of two ways namely, in possession or in interest. An estate or interest is said to be vested in possession when it gives a present right to the immediate possession of property; while one which gives a present right to the future possession of property is said to be vested in interest: thus, if land is given to A for life, and after his death to B in fee, then A's interest is vested in possession while B's is vested in interest. If B dies before his interest vests in possession, it passes to his personal representatives. As a general rule, " vested " means vested in interest, as opposed to contingent (*q.v.*). Thus, remainders are divided into vested and contingent. See REMAINDER.

An estate or interest is said to be " vested subject to being divested " when it is vested but is defeasible on the happening of a particular event. Thus, where property is given to A, an infant, absolutely, with remainder over to someone else if he dies under twenty-one, he takes a vested interest determinable on his death under age. See CONDITION.

" Vest " is used specially to denote a transfer by or under an Act of Parliament. Thus, by the Bankruptcy Act, 1914, s. 18 (1), as soon as a person is adjudicated bankrupt, his property vests in the trustee for the time being: that is, the property is transferred to the trustee in the same way as if the bankrupt had executed a conveyance of it. A statutory transfer of this kind may be either absolute (as in the previous example) or limited: thus, where an Act of Parliament enacts that a street shall vest in a local authority, this means that the surface of the land, and so much of the soil as is necessary for its use as a street, shall be transferred to the authority.

Vested is also applied to rights, interests and expectancies with which it is considered the legislature ought not to interfere without giving compensation. Such are the rights of landowners, which are interfered with when an Act of Parliament is passed authorising the compulsory purchase of their land for public purposes.

Vesta, the crop on the ground.

Vested in interest, a term applied to a present fixed right of future enjoyment, as reversions, vested remainders, executory devises, future uses, conditional limitations, and other future interests, the present right of which is not referred to, or made to depend on, a period or event which is uncertain, although the period of enjoyment may be uncertain or conditional. See CONTINGENT LEGACY; CONTINGENT REMAINDER.

Vested in possession, a term applied to a right of present enjoyment actually existing.

Vested legacy. See LEGACY.

Vested remainder, an expectant interest which is limited or transmitted to a person who is capable of receiving the possession should the particular interest happen to determine: as a limitation to A for life, remainder to B in fee simple; here, as B is in existence he is capable (or his personal representatives, if he dies) of taking possession whenever A's death may occur. A vested interest may take effect though the preceding interest be defeated. Thus where an infant granted a lease for life with remainder over, and on majority he disagreed to the estate for life, but not with the remainder, the remainder was good, having been duly vested by a good title (Fearne, C.R. 308).

The person who is entitled to a vested remainder having a present vested right of future enjoyment, *i.e.*, an interest *in praesenti*, to take effect in possession and pernancy of the profits *in futuro*, can transfer, alienate, and charge it much in the same manner as an interest in possession (2 Cru.Dig. 204).

Interests in remainder can now only take effect as equitable interests (Law of Property Act, 1925, s. 1; Settled Land Act, 1925, s. 1).

Vesting assent. This is defined by the Settled Land Act, 1925, s. 117 (1) (xxx), as the instrument whereby a personal representative after the death of a tenant for life or statutory owner of the survivor of two or more tenants for life or statutory owners vests settled land in a person entitled as tenant for life or statutory owner. For its contents, see the Settled Land Act, 1925, s. 8, Sch. 1. See VESTING INSTRUMENT.

The term " vesting assent " should be distinguished from the ordinary assent by personal representatives which vests the property in a person who is not tenant for life or statutory owner (*Re Bridgett and Hayes' Contract* [1928] Ch. 163). See ASSENT OF PERSONAL REPRESENTATIVE.

Vesting declaration, a declaration in a deed of appointment of new trustees by the appointor that any estate or interest in the trust property is to vest in the new trustees. After the Conveyancing Act, 1881, the declaration operated to vest the property without any conveyance, and now, by the Trustee Act, 1925, s. 40, the effect is the same even if there is no such declaration except in case of mortgages, shares in companies and leaseholds held subject to a covenant against assignment.

When a compulsory purchase order has come into operation, a public authority may acquire the land by means of a general vesting declaration (Town and Country Planning Act, 1968, s. 30, Sch. 3); Land Commission (Dissolution) Act, 1971, Sch. 2 para. 2, Appendix A).

Vesting deed. See VESTING INSTRUMENT.

Vesting instrument, a deed, order of court, or assent, constituting the evidence under the Settled Land Act, 1925, of the title of a tenant for life or statutory owner to the legal estate in settled property as estate owner thereof. This evidence is essential for the settlement of a legal estate in land otherwise than by way of trust for sale (Settled Land Act, 1925, s. 4). The trusts are declared by a separate instrument called the trust instrument. The Settled Land Act, 1925, s. 5, provides that the principal vesting deed must state: —

(*a*) a description of the settled land;

(*b*) that the settled land is vested in the person or persons to or in whom it is conveyed or declared to be vested upon the trusts from time to time affecting the settled land;

(*c*) the names of the trustees of the settlement;

(*d*) any powers which are additional or larger than the statutory powers and are exercisable as statutory powers under the Act;

(*e*) the name of the person entitled under the trust instrument to appoint new trustees of the settlement.

References are permitted to any existing vesting instrument, but not as a rule to a trust instrument, except, *e.g.*, to a person taking title from a tenant for life under the first vesting instrument, etc. (Settled Land Act, 1925, ss. 5 (2), 110). See VESTING ASSENT; TRUST INSTRUMENT.

Vesting order. The Court of Chancery had, and the Chancery Division has, the power of making orders passing the legal estate in property without a conveyance. Also commissioners appointed by several modern statutes and others have power, by vesting order, to transfer legal estates without the necessity of a deed of transfer, *e.g.*, the Charity Commissioners or the Secretary of State for Education.

Vesting orders may be made under the Law of Property Act, 1925, s. 9; the Trustee Act, 1925, ss. 44 *et seq.*; the Settled Land Act, 1925, ss. 12, 16; and the Administration of Estates Act, 1925, ss. 38, 43.

Vestments. The effect of the Ornaments Rubric (*q.v.*), construed along with Advertisements of Elizabeth I (*q.v.*) and the Act of Uniformity, 1662, is to make the use at the Communion Service of the vestments known as the alb, the chasuble and the cope (all of which came into modern use only during the middle of the last century, about the time of what is popularly known as the Ritualistic Movement) illegal, except in cathedral and collegiate churches. They are, however, extensively used elsewhere and now the Vestures of Ministers Measure, 1964, regulates the vestments to be worn at the times of their ministrations.

Vestry, or **Vestiary,** a place or room adjoining to a church, where the vestments of the minister are kept; also, a parochial assembly commonly convened in the vestry, to transact the parish business. By custom in some parishes, and by the Vestries Act, 1831, in others, a select number of parishioners were chosen yearly to manage the concerns of the parish for that year. They were called a select vestry (*q.v.*).

The non-ecclesiastical functions of vestries are now exercised by the parish council or parish meeting. See PARISH. As to ecclesiastical functions see CHURCHWARDENS; PAROCHIAL CHURCH COUNCIL.

In the metropolis, the vestries were elected under the Metropolis Management Act, 1855, until they were superseded by the councils of the metropolitan boroughs under the London Government Act, 1899.

Vestura, a crop of grass or corn (Cowel).

It also meant a garment; metaphorically applied to a possession or seisin.

Vesture. If a man, being seised in fee of land, grants the vesture of the land to another man in fee, the land itself will not pass to the grantee, but only a particular right in the land; for thereby he shall not have the houses, timbertrees, mines, and other real things parcel of the inheritance, but he shall have the vesture of the land, that is the corn, grass, underwood, swepage and the like, and he shall have an action of trespass *quare clausum fregit* for any infringement of his right (Co.Litt. 4b).

A man may prescribe or allege a custom to have and enjoy *solam vesturam terrae* from such a day till such a day, and thereby the owner of the soil is excluded from pasturing or feeding animals there (Co.Litt. 122a).

It seems that a person may also prescribe for a sole vesture, excluding the owner from year's end to year's end. A right of *prima vestura* gives the right of mowing the first crop (Palm. 174).

The right of vesture seems to be an incorporeal hereditament. See PASTURAGE.

Vetera statuta, the ancient statutes commencing with Magna Carta, 1215, and ending with those of Edward II, including also some which, because it is doubtful to which of the three reigns of Henry III, Edward I, or Edward II to assign them, are said to be *incerti temporis*, of uncertain date (2 Reeves, c. 8, p. 85). See ANTIQUA STATUTA.

Veterinary surgeon [Lat. *veterinarius*, concerned with *veterinum*, a beast of burden], one skilled in the medical and surgical treatment of horses, cattle, sheep, dogs and other domesticated animals.

Before the Veterinary Surgeons Act, 1881, any person could practise, and describe himself, as a veterinary surgeon. There had, indeed, been founded in 1791 an association which in the year 1845 was incorporated by royal charter as the Royal College of Veterinary Surgeons; and it received supplemental royal charters in 1876 and 1879; but it had no control over the profession until the Veterinary Surgeons Act, 1881. The Act of 1881, was amended and extended by the Veterinary Surgeons Amendment Act, 1900, the Veterinary Surgeons Act (1881) Amendment Act, 1920, the Veterinary Surgeons (Irish Free State Agreement) Act, 1932, and the Veterinary Surgeons Act, 1948.

The present statute law is contained in the Veterinary Surgeons Act, 1966 which made fresh provision for the management of the veterinary profession, for the registration of veterinary surgeons and veterinary practitioners, for regulating their professional education and professional conduct. The governing body is the Council of the Royal College of Veterinary Surgeons.

Veterinary surgeons and veterinary practitioners are excusable as of right from jury service. See JURY.

As to avoidance of a sale of a horse on a certificate of a veterinary surgeon given after offer or acceptance of a bribe from the seller, see BRIBE.

As to fees for notifying diseases of animals and other matters, see the Diseases of Animals Act, 1950. See ANIMALS, DISEASES OF.

Vetitum namium, Vetito namii, Repetitum namium, a second or reciprocal distress, in lieu of the first, which has been eloigned. See NAM.

Veto, a prohibition, or the right of forbidding; especially applied to the refusal of the royal assent to a Bill in Parliament passed by the two Houses, *le roy* or *la reyne s'avisera*.

As applied to the charter of the United Nations the term means the power of the permanent members of the Security Council to prevent certain decisions by a refusal to concur in the vote when such concurrence is necessary.

Vexata quaestio [Lat.], an undetermined point, which has been often discussed.

Vexatious actions. A proceeding is said to be vexatious when the party bringing it is not acting bona fide, and merely wishes to annoy or embarrass his opponent, or when it is not calculated to lead to any practical result. Such a proceeding is often described as "frivolous and vexatious," and the court may stay it on that ground, both under its inherent jurisdiction and under R.S.C., Ord. 18, r. 19. See ABUSE OF PROCESS.

The High Court has inherent power to stay any action brought merely for the sake of annoyance or oppression (*Lawrence* v. *Norreys* (1890) 15 App. Cas. 210; *Haggard* v. *Pelicier Frères* [1892] A.C. 61). The Judicature Act, 1925, s. 51, replacing the Vexatious Actions Act, 1896, gives power to the court if satisfied, on the application of the Attorney-General, that any person has habitually and persistently instituted vexatious proceedings in any court to order that no proceedings shall be instituted by that person in any court without the leave of the court or a judge thereof. No legal proceedings instituted by such a person before the making of the order may be continued by him without such leave (Judicature (Amendment) Act, 1959). An order dismissing an action as frivolous and vexatious is an interlocutory order (*Re Page* [1910] 1 Ch. 489).

Vexatious indictments. The Vexatious Indictments Act, 1859, as amended by the Criminal Law Amendment Act, 1867, ss. 1, 2, provided that no bill of indictment for perjury, conspiracy, indecent assault, or certain other misdemeanours, should be presented to a grand jury, unless the prosecutor had been bound over by recognisance to prosecute, or unless the person accused had been committed to or detained in custody, or unless the indictment was preferred with the written consent of the Attorney-General. The Administration of Justice (Miscellaneous Provisions) Act, 1933 (which abolished grand juries and amended the law as to presentment of indictments), repealed the Vexatious Indictments Act, 1859, and the Criminal Law Amendment Act, 1867, s. 1, but not so as to affect any enactment restricting the right to prosecute in particular classes of cases.

Vi et armis (with force and arms), words formerly inserted in pleadings to characterise a trespass, but directed to be omitted by the Common Law Procedure Act, 1852, s. 49. See TRESPASS.

Vi laica removenda (for the removal of lay force), a writ which lay where two persons contended for a church, and one of them entered into it with a great number of laymen, and held out the other *vi et armis*; and he who was held out might have this writ addressed to the sheriff, that he should remove the lay force; but the sheriff could not remove the incumbent out of the church, whether he was there by right or wrong, but only the force (Fitz. N.B. 54).

The writ seems to have been applicable where an incumbent was hindered or disturbed in his possession of the benefice (*Ex p. Jenkins* (1868) L.R. 2 P.C. 258).

Via, the right to use a way for any purpose; also, by way of, or through, a given point to a destination.

Via regia, the highway or common road, called the king's way, because under his protection; it was sometimes called *via militaris* (4 Bract.).

Via trita est tutissima (10 Co.Rep. 142). (The much used road is the safest.) See CURSUS, ETC.; NOVITAS NON TAM, ETC.; OMNIS INNOVATIO, ETC.

Via trita via tuta (B.N.C. 45). (The much used road is the safe road.)

Viability, a capability of living after birth; extra-uterine life.

Viae servitus (servitude of way), a right of way over another's land.

Viaticum. In the Roman Catholic Church, this is the communion administered to the dying.

Vibration. This may amount to a nuisance, but regard must be had to the character of the locality (*Polsue* v. *Rushmer* [1907] A.C. 121); the aggrieved person is usually entitled to an injunction as well as damages (*Shelfer* v. *City of London Electric Lighting Co.* [1895] 1 Ch. 287). It may amount to a public nuisance (*Att.-Gen.* v. *P.Y.A. Quarries* [1957] 2 Q.B. 169).

Compensation for vibration arising out of the use of public works may be claimed under the Land Compensation Act, 1973. See NUISANCE.

Vicar, one who performs the functions of another, a substitute; also, the incumbent of an appropriated or impropriated benefice, as distinguished from the incumbent of a non-impropriated benefice who is called a rector.

A vicar is an incumbent appointed to an appropriated church. A vicar is therefore, in effect, a perpetual curate with a standing salary. See APPRO-PRIATION; CURATE; IMPROPRIATION; RECTOR; TITHES.

Every incumbent of a parish church not being a rector, who is authorised to solemnise marriage, baptisms, etc., and to take for his sole benefit the fees payable thereon, is a vicar for the purpose of style and designation, but not for any other purpose, and his benefice is a vicarage for the same purpose (Incumbents Act, 1868).

Vicarage, the benefice of a vicar; also his house (Incumbents Act, 1868, s. 2).

Vicar-general, an ecclesiastical officer appointed by a bishop to act by his authority and under his direction in matters purely spiritual, as visitation, correction of manners, etc., with a general inspection of men and things, in order to the preserving of discipline and good government in the church (Gibson, Codex, Int. xxii).

The vicar-general of this type, who was a survival from the pre-Reformation period, is obsolete. The modern vicar-general is a purely ministerial or judicial officer, not necessarily in holy orders, who, except in the province and diocese of Canterbury, holds also the office of official principal or of chancellor, and is designated as chancellor or official principal. The vicar-general of the Archbishop of Canterbury grants special marriage licences for all England, and has an office for that purpose in London. See CHANCELLOR OF A DIOCESE; OFFICIAL PRINCIPAL.

Vicarial tithes, petty or small tithes which were payable to the vicar. See TITHES.

Vicario deliberando occasione cujus-dam recognitionis capto, etc., a writ which lay for a spiritual person imprisoned upon forfeiture of a recognisance (Reg. Brev. 147).

Vicarious responsibility. A principal is liable for acts of his agent within the scope of his authority. If A, an innocent principal, by B his agent to report, misleads C, his selling agent, and C, relying on the report, innocently misleads the buyer, the buyer may recover damages against the principal for deceit if B's report was reckless and untrue (*London* *County Freehold Properties* v. *Berkeley Property Co.* (1936) 155 L.T. 190). The knowledge of the principal and his agent is one (*Pearson* v. *Dublin Corporation* [1907] A.C. 351); although the functions may have been divided and one only of the constituents has been guilty, the mind, and with it the guilt, if any, and the act are collectively the principal's, and his the responsibility: *qui facit per alium facit per se.* But in the absence of fraud on the part of the principal, knowledge by him of facts which render false a statement innocently made by his agent does not render the principal liable at common law (*Armstrong* v. *Strain* [1952] 1 K.B. 232) but he may become liable by reason of the Misrepresentation Act, 1967. See RESCIND; RESCISSION.

Vicarius non habet vicarium (Branch, Max. 5th ed., 380). (A delegate has no delegate.) See DELEGATUS NON, ETC.; DEPUTY.

Vicars choral, minor dignitaries of the choir of a cathedral or collegiate church who act as assistants to the canons.

Vice-admiral, an under-admiral at sea, or admiral on the coasts: a naval officer of a rank which is next to admiral (*q.v.*).

Vice-admiralty courts, tribunals established in British possessions beyond the seas with jurisdiction over maritime causes, including those relating to prize.

From the early part of the seventeenth century they were gradually established as various possessions were acquired. They acted under commissions from the Crown authorising governors of colonies to exercise such powers as in England appertained to the Lord High Admiral. Subsequently they were regulated by various statutes, the last of which was the Vice-Admiralty Courts Act, 1863.

The Colonial Courts of Admiralty Act, 1890, provided for the establishment of colonial courts of admiralty with a right of appeal to the Privy Council in all British possessions other than the Channel Islands, to which it was applied by Order in Council, whereupon the local vice-admiralty court was abolished. The Crown has power to declare that the Act shall apply either not at all or only to a limited extent to possessions which are not self-governing. The Act is amended in regard to the self-governing Dominions by the Statute of Westminster, 1931, ss. 1, 6, 11 and by the Acts by which independence was granted to various parts of the Commonwealth.

Vice-chamberlain, an officer next under the Lord Chamberlain, who, in his absence, has the rule and control of all officers appertaining to that part of the royal household which is called the chamber above stairs. He is the deputy of the Lord Chamberlain. He goes in and out with the Ministry of the day and is usually a member of the House of Commons. See CHAMBERLAIN, LORD.

Vice-chancellor [Lat. *vice-cancellarius*], a sub-chancellor. The first vice-chancellor (Sir Thomas Plumer) was appointed by the statute 1813, 53 Geo. 3, c. 24. He was styled Vice-Chancellor of England and was appointed to relieve the Lord Chancellor of some of his duties as a judge of first instance of the Court of Chancery. By the Court of Chancery Act, 1841, s. 19, two more vice-chancellors were appointed, partly to take over the equity business of the Court of Exchequer, but the number of three was not made permanent until 1852. The last who bore the title of Vice-Chancellor of England was Sir Lancelot Shadwell. Each vice-chancellor sat separately from the Lord Chancellor and the lords justices, to whom an appeal lay from his decisions: see the statutes 1851, 14 & 15 Vict. c. 4, and 1852, 15 & 16 Vict. c. 80, ss. 52–58. They became judges of the High Court (Judicature Act, 1873, ss. 5, 31), retaining their titles, but it was enacted that on the death or retirement of any one of them his successor should be styled a judge of the High Court. Vice-Chancellor Bacon (1870 to 1886) was the last of them. For a complete list of the equity judges since 1660, see Seton on *Judgments*. The title has been revived in favour of the senior puisne judge of the Chancery Division. See the Administration of Justice Act, 1970, s. 5.

So far back as the reign of Henry II there had been deputies who kept the Great Seal during the absence of the Chancellor and were known as vice-chan-

cellors; but they were not vice-chancellors in the modern sense.

The vice-chancellors and the Master of the Rolls (*q.v.*) were the judges of first instance of the Court of Chancery.

One of the vice-chancellors (usually the senior vice-chancellor) constituted a court of appeal in equity business from the county courts and the Chancery Court of Lancaster.

There is also a Vice-Chancellor of the Duchy of Lancaster, and at each of the two ancient universities there is a vice-chancellor as deputy for the Chancellor. See LORD CHANCELLOR; UNIVERSITY COURTS.

Vice-comes [Lat.], the equivalent for sheriff. The word is literally the equivalent of viscount, but the sheriff was the *vicecomes* for hundreds of years before viscounts (*q.v.*) were first created.

Vice-comes dicitur quod vicem comitis suppleat (Co.Litt. 168a). (The *vicecomes* (sheriff) is so called because he supplies the place of the *comes* (earl).)

Vice-comes non misit breve (the sheriff has not sent the writ), a continuance abolished by rules of court of 1853.

Vice-Constable of England, an officer in the time of Edward IV.

Vice-consul, a consular officer, which expression by the Interpretation Act, 1889, s. 12 (20), includes consul-general, consul, vice-consul, and any person for the time authorised to discharge their duties, and also consular agents. See CONSUL.

Vice-dominus, a sheriff (Ingulphus).

Vice-dominus episcopi, the vicar-general or commissary of a bishop (Blount).

Vice-gerent, a deputy or lieutenant.

Vice-Marshal, an officer who was appointed to assist the Earl Marshal.

Vice-president. The Lord Chancellor may appoint one of the Lords Justices of Appeal to be vice-president of the Court of Appeal (Judicature Act, 1925, s. 6 (4), as amended by the Judicature (Amendment) Act, 1935, s. 2 (1)).

Viceroy, the sovereign's lord-lieutenant over a kingdom. See INDIA.

Vice-Treasurer. See UNDER-TREASURER, ETC.

Vice-Warden of the Stanneries, the

judge of the Stannary courts. See STAN-NARIES.

Vicinage [Lat. *vicinetum*; Fr. *voisinage*], neighbourhood, or near dwelling; places adjoining. As to common because of vicinage, see COMMON.

Vicini vicinora praesumuntur scire (4 Co.Inst. 173). (Persons living in the neighbourhood are presumed to know the neighbourhood.)

Vicis et venellis mundandis, a writ which lay against the mayor or bailiff of a town, etc., for the clean sweeping of the streets and lanes (Reg.Brev. 267).

Vicontiel; Vicountiel, appertaining to the sheriff or *vice-comes.* Vicontiel writs were such as were triable in the old county court of the sheriff. Vicontiel rents were those which the sheriffs collected and accounted for to the Crown; the Fines Act, 1833, s. 12, made them part of the revenue of the Crown and collectable by the Commissioners of Woods and Forests (*q.v.*).

Vicountiel jurisdiction, that jurisdiction which belonged to the officers of a county, as sheriffs, commoners, etc.

Victor Townley Act, the statute 1864, 27 & 28 Vict. c. 29. It was passed in order to amend the statute 1840, 3 & 4 Vict. c. 54, under which a murderer named Victor George Townley, who had been duly convicted, was reprieved upon the ground of alleged insanity, although it was generally believed that he was in fact perfectly sane.

Victoria and Albert, Order of, an order founded in 1862 for ladies, who bear the appendix V. A. No members have been appointed for many years.

Victoria, State of. The colony of Victoria was separated from New South Wales by the Australian Constitutions Act, 1850; see also the Victoria Constitution Act, 1855, and the Australian Waste Lands Act, 1855. It was included as a State in the union of States (New South Wales, Victoria, South Australia, Queensland, Tasmania and Western Australia) by the Commonwealth of Australia Constitution Act, 1900. See AUSTRALIA.

Victualler. " Victualler " or " licensed victualler " is commonly used as meaning a publican. Anciently the word had a wider meaning and included brewers and bakers: see the statute 1530, 22 Hen. 8, c. 13.

Victualling house, a house at which food for consumption on the premises, but not lodging, is supplied to the public generally. The term applies to such places as eating-houses, tea-shops, restaurants, etc. A public-house at which luncheons, etc., are supplied· is also a victualling-house; but a hotel is not. See PUBLIC-HOUSE.

Vidame. See VAVASOR.

Vide [Lat., see], a word of reference; *vide ante,* or *vide supra,* refers to a previous passage and *vide post,* or *vide infra,* to a subsequent passage in a book.

Videlicet, abbreviated *viz.,* to wit, namely, that is to say. The word was used in pleading to precede the specification of particulars which did not have to be proved. Under the old system, when a pleader did not wish to be put upon strict proof of an averment as to time, he introduced it with a *videlicet*—" *videlicit* on the first day of December, etc.," or as the case might be. This was called " laying the time under a *videlicet.*" See SCILICET.

Vidimus, an inspeximus (*q.v.*) (Barr. on Stat. 5).

Viduitatis professio, the making of a solemn profession to live a sole and chaste woman.

Viduity, widowhood.

Vietnam, formerly Indo-China.

View, an inspection of property in controversy, or of a place where a crime has been committed, by the jury before or during the trial. When an action or other proceeding concerns an immovable thing, such as land or houses, it is sometimes desirable to have it seen and examined by the judge, jury, referee, etc., before the trial. A judge or jury may view any such property under R.S.C., Ord. 35, r. 8, and a referee, either with or without his assessors, can also view under Ord. 36, r. 4.

In any criminal case the judge may order that the jury or some of them (called " viewers ") may view a place in question (Juries Act, 1974, s. 14). A view is part of the evidence (*Karamat* v. *R.* [1956] A.C. 256; *Buckingham* v. *Daily News* [1956] 2 Q.B. 534). If witnesses are to be present and give evidence there, the judge should himself be present (*Tameshwar* v. *R.* [1957] A.C. 476). See SHOWER.

The old writ of view, which had formerly to be issued as a preliminary to any place being viewed by a jury in a civil action, was abolished by the Common Law Procedure Act, 1852, s. 114, which provided that all things which used to be done upon the writ could be done upon a rule or order to view.

No action lies for the obstruction of a view or prospect even though the value of property may be diminished thereby, unless the act amounts to a nuisance (*Campbell* v. *Paddington Corporation* [1911] 1 K.B. 869). Compensation is not payable under the Land Compensation Act, 1973, for interference with a view.

View and delivery. When a right of common is exercisable, not over the whole waste, but only in convenient places indicated from time to time by the lord of the manor or his bailiff, it is said to be exercisable after " view and delivery." See ASSIGNMENT OF WASTE; COMMON; STINT.

View of frankpledge. See FRANK-PLEDGE; COURT LEET.

Vifgage, *vivum vadium* (*q.v.*).

Vigil, the eve or next day before any solemn feast.

Vigilantibus, non dormientibus, jura subveniunt (2 Co.Inst. 690; 4 Co.Rep. 10; Hob. 347; Wing. 692). (The laws give help to those who are watchful and not to those who go to sleep.) This is quoted by Coke in connection with conduct described as *crassa et supina negligentia,* which, as he says, the statute under consideration never intended to relieve. See ACQUIESCENCE; CAVEAT EMPTOR; LACHES; LIMITATION OF ACTIONS; PRESCRIPTION.

Viis et modis, by ways and means. In the ecclesiastical courts, service of a decree or citation *viis et modis,* that is, by all ways and means likely to affect the party with knowledge of its contents, is equivalent to substituted service in the temporal courts, and is opposed to personal service. See SERVICE OF PROCESS.

Vill. A vill is in law the same thing as a town (*q.v.*) in the technical sense of that word. " Vill " seems originally to have been used in the same sense as the

Latin *villa,* and to have signified a mere collection of houses in the country, such as buildings on a farm or a manor (*villa ruralis*), in opposition to a walled town (*villa muralis*) namely, a city or borough (see VILLEIN). *Villa ruralis* appears to be the same thing as an " upland town " (see TOWN). The word " vill " is not used now except in dealing with the records of manors and with copyhold customs. The parish, in the civil sense, has superseded the vill (1 P. & M., H.E.L. 545, 594).

Villa est ex pluribus mansionibus vicinata et collata ex pluribus vicinis. Et sub appellatione villarum continentur burgi et civitates (Co.Litt. 115b). (A vill is a neighbourhood of many mansions, a collection of many neighbours. And under the term vills, boroughs and cities are contained.)

Villa regia, a manor held by the Crown.

Village. A vill or village may mean a manor, a parish, the out-part of a parish, a town, or a township, the simplest form of social organisation (1 Bl.Comm. 115; 1 Stubbs, Const.Hist. 82; Williams, *Common,* 39).

The following is the difference between a mansion, a village and a manor, *viz.*: a mansion may be of one or more houses, but it must be of one dwelling-house, and none near to it, for if other houses are contiguous, it is a village; and a manor may consist of several villages, or one alone (6 Fleta, c. 51).

Village green. See RECREATION GROUNDS.

Villainous judgment [*villanum judicium*], a sentence which was passed in, for instance, cases of conspiracy. It made the offender unworthy of credit; it debarred him from access to the king's courts, that is to say, it made him *legem liberam amittere*; and it involved the forfeiture of his lands and goods as well as imprisonment (*Termes de la Ley*; 4 Bl. Comm. 136; 4 Br. & Had.Comm. 153).

Villanis regis subtractis reducendis, a writ which lay for the bringing back of the king's bondmen who had been carried away by others out of his manors whereto they belonged (Reg.Brev. 87).

Villein or **Villain** [Norm. Fr. *vileyn*; Lat. *villanus,* one appertaining to a *villa* or farm], a man of base or servile condition; a bondman or servant; one who held by a base service.

Formerly there existed a class of persons in a position which was superior to downright slavery, but inferior to every other condition, known as villeins. They belonged principally to lords of manors. A villein was either a villein regardant, that is, annexed to the manor or land, or else in gross, or at large, that is, annexed to the person of the lord; thus, where a lord granted a villein regardant by deed to another person, he became a villein in gross. Villeins could not leave their lord without his permission, nor acquire any property; but they could sue anyone except their lord, and were protected against atrocious injuries by him (Litt. 181; Co.Litt. 117a; 2 Bl.Comm. 92).

Villeinage was never formally abolished, but it had become rare in Edward VI's reign, and it disappeared altogether under the Stuarts.

See CONFESSION; COPYHOLD; MANU-MISSION; MARKET; NEIFE; PRESCRIPTION; SERVICE; TENURE; VILLEINAGE.

Villein services, base, but certain and determined, services.

Villein socage, a holding of the king; a privileged sort of villeinage. See SOCAGE; VILLEINAGE.

Villein tenure. See SERVICE; TENURE.

Villeinage or **Villenage,** the status of a villein (q.v.); also an obsolete tenure, which existed where land was held of a lord of a manor by a villein, or by a free person by villein or base service (Litt. 172).

It gradually became either extinct or converted into copyhold tenure. There was also a kind of tenure in villeinage known as privileged villeinage or villein socage, which existed in certain lands of the Crown. The tenants of these lands could not be removed from their lands so long as they did their services, which differed from ordinary villein services in being certain. This kind of tenure gradually became converted into tenure in ancient demesne (q.v.) (Vinogradoff, *Villeinage in England*; Page, *End of Villeinage*). See COPYHOLD.

Vim vi repellere licet, modo fiat moderamine inculpatae tutelae; non ad sumendam vindictam, sed ad propulsandam injuriam (Co.Litt. 162). (It is lawful to repel force by force, so as it be done with the moderation of blameless defence; not to take revenge, but to repel injury.)

Vinagium [*tributum a vino*], payment of a certain quantity of wine instead of rent for a vineyard (2 Dugd.Mon. 980).

Vinculo matrimonii. See A VINCULO MATRIMONII; DIVORCE.

Vindex, a defender (Civil Law).

Vindicatio, a real action claiming property for its owner (Civil Law).

Vindicatory parts of laws, the sanction of the laws, whereby it is signified what evil or penalty shall be incurred by such as commit wrongs, and transgress or neglect their duty.

Vindictive damages, damages given on the principle of punishing the defendant, over and above compensating the plaintiff (*Whitham* v. *Kershaw* (1886) 16 Q.B.D. 613). See EXEMPLARY DAMAGES.

Vinter or **Vintner,** one who sells wine for consumption whether on or off the premises.

Vintners Company, one of the city companies. Freemen of the company are, under an ancient custom, entitled to sell foreign wines without licence anywhere in England. This privilege is recognised by statute (Customs and Excise Act, 1952, s. 166; Licensing Act, 1964, s. 199). See COMPANIES, CITY.

Viol [Fr.], rape (Barr. on Stat. 139)

Violation of safe conducts, an offence against the law of nations.

Violation of women. See RAPE.

Violenta praesumptio is manietimes plena probatio (Co.Litt. 6). (Violent presumption is often proof.) See PRAESUMPTIO VIOLENTA, ETC.

Viperina est expositio quae corrodit viscera textus (11 Co.Rep. 34; 2 Bulst. 179). (An interpretation which eats out the bowels of the text is like a snake.) See MALEDICTA, ETC.

Vir et uxor censentur in lege una persona (Jenk.Cent. 27). (Husband and wife are considered one person in law.) This is not generally true nowadays. See MARRIED WOMEN'S PROPERTY; OMNIA QUAE SUNT, ETC.; UXOR NON, ETC.; VIR ET UXOR SUNT, ETC.

Vir et uxor sunt quasi unica persona (Co.Litt. 112). (Man and wife are, as it were, one person.) If lands were given to

A and B (husband and wife) and C, a third person, and their heirs, A and B being one person took a moiety only of the rents and profits, with power to dispose only of one-half of the inheritance; and C, the third person, took the other half as joint tenant with them. This rule was not altered by the Married Women's Property Act, 1882 (*Re March* (1884) 27 Ch.D. 166; *Re Jupp* (1888) 39 Ch.D. 148), but any indication of an intention that husband and wife were to take separately would defeat the application of the doctrine (*Dias* v. *De Livera* (1879) 5 App.Cas. 135; *Re Jeffery* [1914] 1 Ch. 375); and now, by the Law of Property Act, 1925, s. 37, a husband and wife are for all purposes of acquisition of property treated as two persons. See ENTIRETIES, TENANCY BY.

Vir militans Deo non implicetur secularibus negotiis (Co.Litt. 70b). (A man fighting for God must not be involved in secular business.)

Virga, Virge, a staff or wand, a rod or ensign of office (Cowel). See VERGERS.

Virgate, a yard-land (*q.v.*). See VERGE.

Virge, Tenant by the, a species of copyholder who held by the verge or rod.

Virginia Company. See COMPANIES, CHARTERED.

Virgo intacta, an unblemished virgin.

Viridario eligendo, a writ which lay to the sheriff for the choice of a verderer in the forest (Reg.Brev. 177).

Virilia, the privy members of a man, to cut off which was felony by the common law, though the party consented to it (3 Bract. 144).

Virtute cujus, a clause in a pleading justifying an entry upon land, by which the party alleged that it was in virtue of an order from one entitled that he entered.

Vis [Lat.], any kind of force, violence, or disturbance to person or property. It was either *vis armata*, *i.e.*, *vis cum armis*, or *vis simplex*, *i.e.*, *vis sine armis* (1 Reeves, c. 6, p. 322).

Vis legibus est inimica (3 Co.Inst. 176). (Violence is inimical to the laws.)

Vis major, such a force as it is practically impossible to resist, *e.g.*, a storm, an earthquake, the acts of a large body of men, etc. The doctrine of *vis major* is that a person is not liable for damage if it was directly caused by *vis major*. *Vis major* includes many things described as the act of God (*q.v.*).

Visa, a register; the authentication of a passport by a foreign authority.

Viscount, or Vicount [Lat. *vicecomes*], an arbitrary title of honour, without any office pertaining to it, created by Henry VI (2 Co.Inst. 5; Barr. on Stat. 409).

A viscount is the fourth in rank of the peers; he ranks above a baron and below an earl. The title dates from 1440, when Henry VI conferred a viscounty on John, Baron Beaumont.

The sons and daughters of a viscount are all known simply as " the Honourable," and this is the case even when the viscount holds a barony. See PEERAGE; VICE-COMES.

Visit and search, a right, claimed and exercised by belligerents, to stop, visit and search neutral merchant vessels on the high seas and territorial waters, and confiscate contraband (*The Pellworm* [1918] A.C. 292). See SEARCH.

Visitation, a judicial visit or perambulation; the periodical visit of a bishop or archdeacon to his clergy at the principal church of the diocese or archdeaconry, when he delivers a hortatory address called a charge.

Ecclesiastical and eleemosynary corporations are visitable, or subject to visitation, that is, the law has appointed proper persons called visitors to visit, inquire into and correct all irregularities that arise in them. With regard to ecclesiastical corporations, the Crown is the visitor of the archbishops, and the archbishops of the bishops within their diocese, and the bishops are the visitors of all subordinate corporations, sole and aggregate. Hence, when an archbishop or bishop makes a circuit through his district to inquire into matters of church discipline, this is called a visitation (1 Bl. Comm. 480).

As regards lay eleemosynary corporations and other charities, the visitor is the founder, and his heirs, or a person appointed by him, or, in default of all of them, the Crown. The visitors of a charity superintend its internal management, but not (as a rule) the management of its estates and revenue.

VISITATION

The Court of Chancery exercised the right of visitation on behalf of the Crown, in whom the right of visitation and inspection lies, in default of special visitors: see the statute 1533, 25 Hen. 8, c. 21, and the Act of Supremacy, 1558, s. 2.

Jurisdiction exercised by the Lord Chancellor in right or on behalf of the Crown as visitor of any college, or of any charitable or other foundation, is not transferred to the High Court (Judicature Act, 1873, s. 17, replaced by the Judicature Act, 1925, s. 19 (5)).

As to the Lord Chancellor's visitors, see MENTAL HEALTH.

As to visitation of prisons, see PRISONS.

The judges of the High Court as visitors of the Inns of Court hear appeals from decisions with regard to the professional conduct of members of the Bar. See SENATE OF THE INNS OF COURT AND THE BAR. (*Re Marrinan* (1957) *The Times,* October 3).

Visitation books of heralds, compilations, when progresses were solemnly and regularly made into every part of the kingdom, between 1528 and 1686, to inquire into the state of families, their arms and pedigrees, and to register marriages and descents, which were verified to the heralds upon oath; they are allowed to be good evidence of pedigree.

Visiting forces. The Visiting Forces Act, 1952 (as amended), makes provision with respect to naval, military and air forces of certain countries visiting the United Kingdom, and to deserters and absentees without leave from such forces.

Visitor, an inspector incidental to and necessary for all eleemosynary, and many ecclesiastical and other corporations, endowed and other colleges, schools, hospitals and institutions. See VISITATION.

Visitor of manners, the regarder's office in the forest (1 Manw. 195). See REGARDER.

Visne [Lat. *visnetum*], a neighbourhood. *Visne* was an old name for a jury, because formerly the jurors were taken *de vicineto*, that is, out of the neighbourhood where the matters in question had taken place (Co.Litt. 125a).

Visus, view or inspection.

Visus Franciplegii, the View of Frankpledge. An enactment is printed under this title in the *Statutes of the Realm* amongst the *Statutes of Uncertain Date,* and in the *Statutes at Large* as 1323, 17 Edw. 2, st. 2. See FRANKPLEDGE.

Vital statistics. See REGISTRATION OF BIRTHS, ETC.

Vitilitigate, to litigate cavillously.

Vitium clerici nocere non debet (Jenk. Cent. 23). (An error of a clerk ought not to hurt.) This maxim is quoted only in connection with a clerical error by a clerk of the court in entering a judgment. See AMBIGUITY; FALSA, ETC.

Viva pecunia [Lat.], cattle, so called from being received during the Saxon period as money upon most occasions, at certain regulated prices.

Viva voce. See EVIDENCE; EXAMINATION.

Vivary or **Vivarye** [Lat. *vivarium*], a place where animals are preserved; a park, warren, piscary, etc. (2 Co.Inst. 100).

Coke says that a vivary signifies a fishpond or waters wherein fish are kept or nourished. If a man bought fish, as carp, bream, tench, etc., and put them in his pond, and died, the heir took them, and not the executors; they went with the inheritance, because they were at liberty, and could not be got without industry, as by nets, and other engines. It was otherwise if they were in a trunk or tank or the like, for in that case they went as personalty (2 Co.Inst. 199).

A man has a qualified property in fish confined in a small pond, tank, or stew, so that they can be caught at pleasure, and they may therefore be the subject of theft. See ANIMALS FERAE NATURAE; FISHERY.

Viver, or **Vivier,** a fish-pond (2 Co. Inst. 199).

Vivisection, the dissecting of animals alive, for the purpose of scientific experiments, which may only be practised by persons holding a licence from the Home Secretary, and subject to the restrictions imposed by the Cruelty to Animals Act, 1876. The Cruelty to Animals Act, 1876, provides that it shall be an offence to perform any painful experiment on any animal except subject to the restrictions imposed by the Act (s. 1), or to exhibit to the general public or to advertise any such experiment (s. 6); such experiments can be performed only by a person holding a licence from the Home Secretary, only for various specified purposes and under conditions as to anaesthetics insuring a minimum of pain (s. 3); such experiments must be made only in registered places (s. 7); experiments on dogs, cats, horses, asses or mules are specially restricted (s. 5). By the Protection of Animals (Anaesthetics) Acts, 1954 and 1964, all surgical operations upon domestic animals involving pain (with minor exceptions) must be carried out under an anaesthetic. See URARI.

See also the Dogs Act, 1906, as to stray dogs taken up by the police.

Vivum vadium, Vifgage (living pledge), when a person borrowed money of another, and granted to him an estate to hold till the rents and profits repaid the sum borrowed with interest. The estate was conditioned to be void as soon as the sum was realised. See WELSH MORTGAGE.

Vix ulla lex fieri potest quae omnibus commoda sit, sed si majori parti prospiciat utilis est (Plow. 369). (Scarcely any law can be made which is applicable to all things; but it is useful if it regards the greater part.) See AD EA, ETC.

Viz., *videlicet,* to wit, namely, that is to say. See VIDELICET.

Vocabulum artis, a word of art.

Vocatio in jus, a citation to law (Civil Law).

Vocational training. See DISABLED PERSON.

Vociferatio, an outcry; hue and cry (*q.v.*).

Void. An agreement or other act is said to be void when it has no legal effect, or not the legal effect which it was intended to produce. But an agreement which is void may subject the parties to penal consequences. Thus, an agreement amounting to a conspiracy would be admissible as evidence in criminal proceedings.

An act may be void either *ab initio* or *ex post facto.* Thus, if a contract is made without the true consent of the parties or for an immoral consideration it is void *ab initio.* No person's rights can be affected by it, whether he is a party or a stranger. In the case of a contract which is void for illegality, immorality, or on a similar ground, if money has been paid as the consideration of its performance, the party who has paid it may repudiate the contract and recover it back at any time before performance (*Bone* v. *Eckless* (1860) 29 L.J.Ex. 438). But when an illegal contract has been executed, money paid under it cannot usually be recovered back (*Andree* v. *Fletcher* (1789) 3 T.R. 266). See IN PARI DELICTO MELIOR EST CONDITIO POSSIDENTIS.

If a deed is properly entered into, and is afterwards altered in a material point by the fraud or laches of either party, it becomes void *ex post facto* as against him, so that he cannot enforce or take advantage of it. See AVOID; VOIDABLE.

Voidable. An agreement or other act is said to be voidable when one of the parties is entitled to rescind it, while until that happens it has the legal effect which it was intended to have. (See AVOID; RESCIND.) It can, however, be disputed only by certain persons and under certain conditions, and the right of rescission may be abandoned by the party entitled to exercise it. (See ADOPT; RATIFICATION.) If third persons acquire rights under a voidable contract or other transaction without notice and for value, they cannot afterwards be put in a worse position by its being set aside. Herein a voidable contract differs from a void contract, for in the latter case no third person can acquire rights under the contract unless the party against whom it is void elects to affirm it.

The principal examples of voidable transactions occur in the case of misrepresentation.

Voidance, the act of avoiding; ejection from a benefice.

Voire dire [Norm. Fr. *voire,* true; *dire,* to speak; Fr. *vrai dire*; Lat. *veritatem dicere,* to tell the truth], a sort of preliminary examination of a witness by the judge, in which he is required to speak the truth with respect to the questions put to him; if his incompetency appears from this examination or from extrinsic evidence, *e.g.,* on the ground that he is not of sound mind, he is rejected. A juror who has been challenged for cause may be examined on the *voire dire.* The form of the oath is as follows: " I swear by Almighty God that I will true answer make to all such questions as the court shall demand of me." The term applies also in the criminal law to statements made to a judge (after a prisoner has been convicted or has pleaded guilty) as to character or previous convictions.

Volatilia regalia, birds royal. See SWANS.

Volenti non fit injuria (Wing. 482; Plow. 501). (To a willing person no injury is done.) That to which a man consents cannot be considered an injury. This maxim is illustrated by the rule that no man can maintain an action of tort in respect of any act to the doing whereof he has consented (*Yarmouth* v. *France* (1887) 19 Q.B.D. at p. 653; *Dublin, etc., Ry.* v. *Slattery* (1878) 3 App.Cas. 1155; *Herd* v. *Weardale Co.* [1915] A.C. 67).

Consent or leave and licence is a defence in actions of tort or prosecutions unless the act amounts to the infliction of a serious physical injury or where the rights of the public as well as the individual sustaining harm have intervened. The public are interested in preventing one of their number from grievous bodily harm and from exhibitions which alarm the public conscience, such as prize-fights without gloves, duels, etc.

The maxim has also been invoked in cases where the person injured is alleged to have contracted to absolve the defendant from a known risk or from obligations, such as not to be negligent in the course of a contract (*Thomas* v. *Quartermaine* (1887) 18 Q.B.D. 685; (*Smith* v. *Baker* [1891] A.C. 325). Knowledge of the risk is not conclusive (*Dann* v. *Hamilton* [1939] 1 K.B. 509); it is only evidence from which consent may be inferred (*Letang* v. *Ottawa Electric Ry.* [1926] A.C. 725).

The performance of a duty in the face of imminent risk is not consent disentitling a plaintiff from his remedy (*Haynes* v. *Harwood* [1935] 1 K.B. 146; *Hyett* v. *G. W. Ry.* [1948] 1 K.B. 345). It may be otherwise if the risk was undertaken voluntarily and not under a duty. Contrast *Cutler* v. *United Dairies* [1933] 2 K.B. 297, with *Baker* v. *T. E. Hopkins & Son* [1959] 1 W.L.R. 966; *Videan* v. *British Transport Commission* [1963] 2 Q.B. 650.

The maxim does not normally apply to cases of spectators suing participants in games or sports (*q.v.*) because the maxim cannot apply in the absence of negligence (*Wooldridge* v. *Sumner* [1963] 2 Q.B. 43).

Volt, a measure of electrical potential. See the Weights and Measures Act, 1963, s. 10, Sch. 1 Pt. VI.

Volumus, we will. A clause commencing with this word was formerly used in the writ of protection and was called the *volumus*: see the statute 1390, 13 Ric. 2, st. 1, c. 16. See PROTECTION, WRIT OF.

Voluntarius daemon, a drunkard (Co. Litt. 247a).

Voluntary, without compulsion; without a consideration in return. A conveyance, settlement, gift or similar transaction is said to be voluntary when there is no valuable consideration for it. See CONSIDERATION; VOLUNTEER.

As a general rule a voluntary gift, conveyance or other executed transaction is valid as between the parties, and so is a voluntary contract, if under seal (see CONSIDERATION; CONTRACT); but this rule is subject to exceptions, principally in favour of the creditors of the person bound by the transaction. Thus, in the administration of the estate of a deceased person, his voluntary bonds and covenants are postponed to his other debts and obligations. (See ASSETS.) The court will not enforce specific performance of a voluntary covenant. As to the avoiding of voluntary conveyances and settlements, see FRAUDULENT CONVEYANCES; SETTLEMENT.

In equity it is a rule that in every case where one person obtains, by voluntary donation (gift, settlement, contract, etc.), a large pecuniary benefit from another, he is bound to show that the donor understood what he was doing, and that, if he cannot, the donation may be set aside at the instance of the donor or his representatives. See RESCISSION.

It is also a rule of equity that although no consideration is required for the validity of a complete declaration of trust, or a complete transfer of any legal or equitable interest in property, yet an incomplete voluntary gift creates no right which can be enforced. Thus, where a person possessed of a leasehold house and stock in trade purported to make a voluntary gift in favour of his grandson

A by indorsing and signing the following memorandum on the lease, "This deed and all thereto belonging I give to A from this time forth, with all the stock in trade," and by delivering the lease to A's mother on his behalf, it was held that there was no valid declaration of trust in favour of A.

Voluntary answer, one filed by a defendant in equity, without being called upon to answer by the plaintiff.

Voluntary conveyance, a conveyance by way of gift or otherwise without valuable consideration. It is liable to be defeated if fraudulent by a subsequent sale for value, but no voluntary disposition whenever made is deemed to have been made with intent to defraud by reason only that a subsequent conveyance for valuable consideration was made (Law of Property Act, 1925, s. 173, reproducing the statute 1584, 27 Eliz. 1, c. 4, as amended by the Voluntary Conveyances Act, 1893). Any conveyance made with intent to defeat or delay creditors may be set aside (*Twyne's Case* (1601) 3 Co.Rep. 80), unless the conveyance was made for valuable consideration and in good faith or for good consideration and in good faith to any person not having at the time of the conveyance notice of the intent to defraud creditors (Law of Property Act, 1925, ss. 172, 173, replacing the statute 1571, 13 Eliz. 1, c. 5). "Good faith " appears to mean good faith as between grantor and grantee, since an intent to defraud creditors is the gist of the action and must be proved *in limine*. As to the meaning of good consideration, see CONSIDERATION.

By the Bankruptcy Act, 1914, s. 42, any settlement of property not being in consideration of marriage or upon a sale or mortgage for valuable consideration or of property coming to the settlor after marriage in right of his wife is void if the settlor becomes bankrupt within two years in any case, and within ten years if the settlor was not at the time of the settlement able to pay his debts without the aid of the settled property and had not transferred the property to the trustees of the settlement at that time. Any agreement in consideration of marriage to make a future payment to or to settle future property on persons within that consideration if, as regards the future property, the settlor had no interest in it at the time, or if the money or property was not money or property in right of the settlor's wife or husband, is void against the trustee in bankruptcy if the agreement has not been performed at the date of commencement of the bankruptcy. Even if any such agreed payment or transfer was made before bankruptcy it may be avoided unless it was made more than two years before the bankruptcy or the settlor was able to pay all his debts at the time without the aid of such money or property, or unless the money or property was an expectation from a person named in the agreement and was paid or transferred within three months after coming into possession or control of the settlor. The beneficiaries may claim for dividend after the creditors have been satisfied. See FRAUDULENT CONVEYANCES.

Voluntary deposit, such as arises from the mere consent and agreement of the parties.

Voluntary dispositions *inter vivos* are chargeable with the like stamp duty (*q.v.*) as conveyances or transfers on sale with the substitution of the value of the property conveyed or transferred for the amount or value of the consideration for the sale (Finance (1909–10) Act, 1910, s. 74; Finance Act, 1942, s. 44; Finance Act 1962, Sch. 11, Pt. V; Finance Act, 1963, s. 64).

Voluntary liquidation. When a company is being wound up by resolution of its shareholders it is said to be in voluntary liquidation.

Voluntary oath, an oath administered in a case for which the law has not provided (Statutory Declarations Act, 1835). See OATH.

Voluntary schools. Under the Education Act, 1921, there were public elementary day schools not provided by the local education authority to which grants were made when recognised under the Act. Under the Education Act, 1944, s. 9, they are primary and secondary schools maintained but not established by a local education authority, not being nursery schools or special schools. They are denominated schools. Under s. 15 (as amended by the Education Act, 1946) they are classified as controlled schools, aided schools or special agreement schools.

Voluntary waste, that which is the result of the voluntary act of the tenant of property, as where he pulls down a wall, or cuts timber; opposed to permissive waste. See WASTE.

Voluntas donatoris in charta doni sui manifeste expressa observetur (Co.Litt 2). (The will of the donor, clearly expressed in his deed of gift, is to be observed.)

Voluntas facit quod in testamento scriptum valeat (D. 30, 1, 12). (The intention of the testator is what gives effect to a will.) See AMBIGUITY; MENS TESTATORIS, ETC.; VITIUM CLERICI, ETC.

Voluntas in delictis non exitus spectatur (3 Co.Inst. 57). (In crimes, the intention, and not the result, is looked to.) This maxim is of limited application. Unsuccessful attempts to commit crime are generally punished less severely than successful attempts (see AFFECTUS, ETC.); and there may be an offence even without criminal intent (see ACTUS NON, ETC.); but where A, intending to murder B, kills C by mistake, then A is guilty of murder; and compassing the death of the sovereign is treason the moment it is evidenced by an overt act.

Voluntas reputabatur pro facto (3 Co. Inst. 69). (The will is to be taken for the deed.) This is only occasionally true. See VOLUNTAS IN, ETC.

Voluntas testatoris est ambulatoria usque ad extremum vitae exitum (4 Co. 61). (The will of a testator is ambulatory down to the very end of his life.) A man may always alter his will; but there are limitations to this rule. See AMBULATORIA, ETC.; MUTUAL WILLS; OMNE TESTAMENTUM, ETC.

Voluntas testatoris habuit interpretationem latam et benignam (Jenk. Cent. 260). (The intention of a testator has always had a broad and benignant interpretation.) See IN CONTRACTIS, ETC.; IN TESTAMENTIS, ETC.; TESTAMENTA LATISSIMAM, ETC.

Volunteer. A person who gives his services without any express or implied promise of remuneration in return is called a volunteer, and is entitled to no remuneration for his services, nor to any compensation for injuries sustained by him in performing what he has undertaken. His claim was often defeated by the doctrine of common employment (*q.v.*) while that doctrine was in full force (*Degg* v. *Midland Ry.* (1857) 1 H. & N. 773), though later decisions limited its application (*Lomas* v. *Jones & Son* [1944] K.B. 4). But a person who, though he is not obliged to do an act, yet has an interest in doing it, is not necessarily a volunteer.

In the law of settlements and wills, a volunteer is a person who is merely an object of bounty, as opposed to a person who takes an interest for valuable consideration. Thus, an ordinary devisee or legatee is a volunteer; and if an appointment is made under a general power without consideration the appointee is a volunteer. So, in the case of a voluntary settlement or conveyance, the person on whom the voluntary settlement is made is called a volunteer. A person is a volunteer who takes under a voluntary conveyance, or who, though the conveyance may have been for value, is not within the scope of the consideration, *e.g.*, persons not issue of the marriage claiming under limitations in a marriage settlement. See VOLUNTARY.

Volunteers. The militia (*q.v.*) ballot was not used after 1815, and compulsory military service was, in modern times, unknown in this country until the war of 1914–18. The members of such supplementary forces as were from time to time voluntarily raised for military purposes in times of emergency were known as volunteers. More than 400,000 volunteers were enrolled during the Napoleonic wars under various Acts of George III. In 1859 fears of a French invasion led to the formation of many volunteer units; and their position was regularised by the Volunteer Act, 1863, and the later Acts extending and amending it. They (with certain exceptions such as the volunteer corps at Oxford, Cambridge and Eton) were transferred to the territorial army (*q.v.*) by Orders in Council made pursuant to the Territorial and Reserve Forces Act, 1907.

As to the volunteer reserve see now the Reserve Forces Act, 1966.

Vote, suffrage, voice given. See BALLOT; ELECTORAL FRANCHISE.

Voter, one who has the right of giving his vote or suffrage.

Votum, a vow or promise; *dies votorum* meant wedding-day (4 Fleta).

Vouch; Voucher. To vouch is to call upon, rely on, or quote as an authority. Thus, in the old writers, to vouch a case or report is to quote it as an authority (Co.Litt. 70a).

Hence, a "voucher" is a document which evidences a transaction, especially a receipt for the payment of money. In the practice of the Chancery Division, when an account is being taken in chambers, the accounting party has to produce vouchers for all payments of £2 or over claimed to have been made by him; smaller payments may be proved by the oath of the accounting party. This is called "vouching the account." Under R.S.C., Ord. 33, r. 3, the court or a judge may give special directions as to vouching, etc., and under Ord. 33, r. 4, it may be ordered that vouching, except in the case of contested items, be done in the office of the solicitor for the accounting party.

In the old law of real property, voucher (or "voucher to warranty") was where a person who was being sued for the recovery of land held by him called into court the person who had warranted the land to him, and required him either to defend the title against the demandant or to yield him land of equal value; the person thus called into court was called the vouchee. Double voucher was where the vouchee vouched the person who had warranted the land to him; and so with treble voucher, etc. A foreign voucher was where the vouchee was a foreigner, that is, a person out of the jurisdiction of the court in which the action was brought (Co.Litt. 101b).

In the fictitious proceedings called common recoveries, the vouchee (or ultimate vouchee if there were more than one) was usually the crier of the court, who was hence called the common vouchee (2 Bl.Comm. 349). See PRAECIPE; RECOVERY.

Real actions were abolished by the Real Property Limitation Act, 1833, s. 36, and the proceeding by voucher no longer exists. See WARRANTIA CARTAE; WARRANTY.

Vouchers are subject to tax under the Finance (No. 2) Act, 1975, ss. 36, 37. Luncheon vouchers are covered by an Extra-Statutory Concession. See MEAL VOUCHERS.

Vouche [Lat. *vocare*, to call], to call one to warrant lands. See VOUCH.

Vouchee, the person vouched in a writ of right.

Voucher, a witness, testimony; acquittance, or receipt. See VOUCH.

Vouchers, Statute of, the statute 1290, 20 Edw. 1, st. 1.

Vox emissa volat, litera scripta manet. (The spoken word is lost, the written word remains.)

Voyage policy, a policy of marine insurance against losses incurred during a voyage specified in the policy.

Vraic, seaweed. It is used in great quantities by the inhabitants of Jersey and Guernsey for manure, and also for fuel by the poorer classes. In *Benest* v. *Pipon* (1829) 1 Kn. 60, it was held that the lord of a manor in Jersey could not establish a claim to the exclusive right of cutting seaweed on rocks situate below low-water mark, except by a grant from the Crown, or by such long and undisturbed enjoyment of it as to give him a title by prescription.

Vulgaris purgatio, the ordeal. See JUDICIUM DEI.

W

W.S., writer to the signet. See SIGNET.

Wafer, a small circular piece of adhesive red paper which is affixed to a deed as a seal instead of sealing wax.

Wafer seal. The documents to which the wafer great seal is to be attached are prescribed by orders dated January 4, 1917, and October 7, 1919, and the

Wafer Great Seal Rules Order, 1955, made under the Crown Office Act, 1877, s. 4. See GREAT SEAL; PRIVY SEAL.

Waftors, conductors of vessels at sea. Edward IV appointed certain officials styled waftors, *custodes* and *conductores*, to guard English fishing vessels off the east coast. To waft meant to convey or safeguard a vessel on her voyage.

Wage [Lat. *vador*; Fr. *gage*], the giving of a security for the performance of anything; gage. To wage one's law meant to proceed to compurgation (*q.v.*). It also meant to plead. See NON-SUMMONS.

Wager. A wager consists of mutual promises between two persons that one will pay the other a certain sum of money if a certain event happens or is ascertained to have happened (*Carlill* v. *Carbolic Smoke Ball Co.* [1892] 2 Q.B. at p. 490). At common law a wager constituted a good contract, unless it was contrary to public policy, morality or the like (*Johnson* v. *Lumley* (1852) 12 C.B. 468); but by the Gaming Act, 1845, s. 18, all contracts by way of gaming or wagering are null and void, except so far as concerns subscriptions or contributions for prizes or money to be awarded to the winner of any lawful game, sport, pastime or exercise. There is nothing illegal in a wager: it is merely void. See UNLAWFUL.

In *Read* v. *Anderson* (1884) 13 Q.B.D. 779, it was held that a turf commission-agent might recover the amount of lost bets paid by him, but the Gaming Act, 1892, makes void any promise to pay any person any sum paid by him in respect of any contract made void by the Gaming Act, 1845, or any commission in respect of any such contract; the effect of this Act is that money paid by A for B at the request of B in discharge of bets lost by B to other persons cannot be recovered by A from B (*Tatam* v. *Reeve* [1893] 1 Q.B. 44). A promise to pay the amount of a lost bet in consideration of not being reported as a defaulter cannot be enforced (*Hill* v. *Hill* [1949] A.C. 530). This case overruled *Hyams* v. *Stuart King* [1908] 2 K.B. 696, in reliance on which many actions for unpaid debts had been brought. In *R.* v. *Weisz* [1951] 2 K.B. 611, it was held that to bring an action for a betting debt by means of a feigned issue was a contempt of court.

A cheque given for a bet on a game or pastime is deemed to have been given for an illegal consideration (Gaming Act, 1835, s. 1); it makes no difference that the cheque was drawn in a country where wagers are valid (*Moulis* v. *Owen* [1907] 1 K.B. 746), but money lent by cheque abroad for the purpose can be recovered (*Saxby* v. *Fulton* [1909] 2 K.B. 208), but not if it is lent by cheque here (*Carlton Hall Club* v. *Laurence* [1929] 2 K.B. 153). The deposit given to a stakeholder on a wagering contract may be recovered before it has been paid over (*Burge* v. *Ashley* [1900] 1 Q.B. 744).

Where gaming is lawful (see GAMING) the holder of a gaming licence may lawfully give cash or tokens in exchange for a cheque and the Gaming Acts, 1845 and 1892, do not effect the remedies for a dishonoured cheque (Gaming Act, 1968, s. 16).

Questions have arisen as to lawfulness of speculative transactions on the Stock Exchange, especially as regards "time-bargains" and "differences." A time-bargain is in form a contract to buy or sell shares or other securities, with an agreement (contemporaneous or subsequent) that the sale shall not be really carried out by delivery of the securities, but that one party shall pay to the other the difference between the market price of the security on the day when the contract was made and the day fixed for its performance. It is, therefore, a wager on the price of the security. The term "difference" is generally applied to the case where a person employs a broker to buy or sell stock for him on the understanding that when the day for completing the transaction arrives, the broker shall resell or rebuy the stock, and that the employer shall take the profit or bear the loss. A time-bargain is void as between the parties to it, but if a broker is employed to speculate in stocks, he can recover from his employer brokerage and "differences" in respect of all genuine contracts for buying and selling stock which he enters into with other persons.

Wager of battel. See BATTLE, TRIAL BY.

Wager of law [Lat. *vadatio legis*], a proceeding which consisted in a defendant's discharging himself from the claim on his own oath, bringing with him at the same time into court eleven of his neighbours (*compurgatores*) to swear that they believed his denial to be true. It was abolished by the Civil Procedure Act, 1833, s. 13, after long disuse except for a revival in *King* v. *Williams* (1824) 2 B. & C. 538. See COMPURGATION.

Wagering Act, the statute 1746, 19 Geo. 2, c. 37.

Wagering policies, those effected for gambling purposes, which are void by the Life Assurance Act, 1774. As far as marine insurance is concerned the matter is dealt with by the Marine Insurance Act, 1906, s. 4, and the Marine Insurance (Gambling Policies) Act, 1909. See INSURANCE.

Wagering policy, a policy effected on a life, ship, house, etc., in which the insurer has no insurable interest. See INTEREST.

Wages, money payable by a master to his servant in respect of services. (See MASTER AND SERVANT; MINIMUM WAGE; SERVICE, CONTRACT OF; TRUCK ACTS.) Some wages are preferential debts in bankruptcy (see DEBT). Wih reference to seamen's wages, the general rule used to be " freight is the mother of wages," so that if no freight was received no wages were payable; but this rule was abolished by the Merchant Shipping Act, 1854, s. 183, which is now replaced by the Merchant Shipping Act, 1894, s. 157. Seamen have a lien on the ship and freight for their wages. The lien cannot be renounced by agreement (Merchant Shipping Act, 1970, s. 16). Generally as to seamen's wages, see ss. 7–17. Claims for wages may be enforced by action *in rem* or *in personam.* Any court with Admiralty jurisdiction may deal with such a proceeding (Administration of Justice Act, 1956, ss. 1 (1) (*o*), 3, 5); the wages of a master are on the same footing as those of ordinary seamen (Act of 1894, s. 167).

No wages of any servant, labourer or workman can be attached by order of any court (Wages Attachment Abolition Act, 1870), except for maintenance. See MAINTENANCE.

An infant can recover wages up to £750 in the county court, by the County Courts Act, 1959, s. 80, as if he were of full age.

Particulars of work and wages must be given to pieceworkers (Factories Act, 1961, s. 135). Deductions from wages are restricted (s. 136). See TRUCK ACTS.

See AGRICULTURAL WAGES BOARD; CATERING WAGES COMMISSION.

Wages councils, councils established under the Wages Councils Acts, 1945 and 1948, upon whose recommendations orders were made by the Minister of Labour and National Service concerning wages and industrial conditions

These Acts were consolidated by the Wages Councils Act, 1959, amended by the Payment of Wages Act, 1960, s. 6 (4), the Civil Evidence Act, 1968, s. 17 (3), Sch., the Transport Act, 1968, ss. 94 (8), 165 (*d*), Sch. 18 Pt. IV, the Equal Pay Act, 1970, s. 4, the Trade Union and Labour Relations Act, 1974, Sch. 3 para. 9, and the Employment Protection Act, 1975, ss. 89–96, Sch. 7. The Secretary of State may convert wages councils into statutory joint industrial councils (Act of 1975, s. 90), and may abolish the latter (s. 93).

Wagessum [Fr. *vase,* mud], sea ground, mussel ouze (*Re Alston's Estate* (1856) 5 W.R. 189).

Waggonage, money paid for carriage in a waggon.

Waif or Waift, Weif or Weft [Law Lat. *waviatum*], goods found but claimed by nobody; that of which everyone waives the claim. Goods stolen and waived or thrown away by the thief in his flight (*bona waviata*), for fear of being apprehended, are given to the sovereign by the law, as a punishment upon the owner for not himself pursuing the felon and taking the goods away from him (Cro. Eliz. 694; 1 Bl.Comm. 297). See ESTRAYS; FRANCHISE; FUGATIVE'S GOODS; PREROGATIVE.

In ancient times a woman who failed to answer an accusation was waived, that is to say, was declared a waif. This had the effect of making the Crown, or lord of the franchise, entitled to seize the woman as if she were *bona waviata.* A woman could never be outlawed. See OUTLAWRY; WAIVE.

Wainable, gainable (*q.v.*); land which may be ploughed, manured, or tilled.

Wainagium or **Wonogium,** the countenance or contenement (*q.v.*) of a villein; that which is necessary for the cultivation of land; implements of husbandry (Barr. on Stat. 12). See GAINAGE.

Wain-bote, timber for waggons or carts.

Waiting clerks, officials of the Court of Chancery who, having served under articles of apprenticeship for three years with one of the Sixty Clerks (*q.v.*), were admitted to perform duties analogous to those of their masters, and they were appointed as sworn clerks when vacancies arose. They, along with the Six Clerks (*q.v.*) and the Sixty Clerks, were abolished by the Court of Chancery Act, 1842, s. 1.

Waive; waiver. A person is said to waive a benefit when he renounces or disclaims it, and he is said to waive a tort or injury when he abandons the remedy which the law gives him for it. A waiver may be either express or implied. Thus, if a tenant commits a breach of covenant, and thereby makes the lease liable to forfeiture, the lessor may waive the breach either by promising not to take advantage of it, or by receiving rent after knowing of the breach (*Davenport* v. *R.* (1877) 3 App.Cas. 115; *Central Estates* (*Belgravia*) v. *Woolgar* (*No.* 2) [1972] 1 W.L.R. 1048; *Welch* v. *Birrane* (1974) 29 P. & C.R. 102); the former is an express, the latter an implied, waiver. Formerly, if a lessor waived a right of re-entry for a breach of covenant, or the like, this operated as a waiver in law of all future breaches, so that the right of re-entry was destroyed. This rule was abolished in 1859; see APPORTIONMENT.

A woman who was " outlawed " was called waived, *waviata,* and not *utlegata* or *exlex,* for women were not sworn in leets or tourns as males of the age of twelve years or more were: and therefore men were called *utlegati, i.e., extra legem positi,* but women were *waviatae, i.e., derelictae,* left out or not regarded, because they were not sworn to the law (Co.Litt. 122b; Litt. 186). See WAIF.

Waiver clause, a clause in the prospectus of a joint stock company, or in an application for its shares, which, as in *Greenwood* v. *Leather Shod Wheel Co.* [1900] 1 Ch. 421 (where it was held bad), waived claims of shareholders against directors for damages caused by the issue of a prospectus not disclosing contracts. An honest waiver clause protected the defendant in *Calthorpe* v. *Tait* [1906] A.C. 24. These waivers were rendered void by the Companies (Consolidation) Act, 1908, s. 81 (4), replaced by the Companies Act, 1948, s. 38 (2).

Wake, an assemblage of persons, especially at night, to watch round a corpse between the death and the burial. By the Public Health Act, 1936, s. 165, it is unlawful to hold a wake over the body of a person who has died while suffering from a notifiable disease, and the occupier of any premises who permits or suffers any such wake to take place thereon, and every person who takes part in the wake, is liable to a penalty of £5.

A wake is also a concourse for pleasure held usually on a feast day following after a vigil connected with the local patron saint or some religious purpose (*Wyld* v. *Silver* [1963] 1 Q.B. 169; [1963] Ch. 243).

Wakeman, a watchman. Before the Reformation it was the title of certain officers of the town of Ripon, in Yorkshire, who, amongst other things, looked after the shrine of St. Wilfrid: afterwards, until 1604, it was the title of the official in Ripon who corresponded to the mayor of later times.

Wales. After Edward I conquered the Welsh the line of their ancient princes was abolished, and the eldest son of the King of England was created their titular prince, and the territory of Wales was then entirely annexed to the British Crown.

The *Statutum Walliae,* 1284, created the counties of Anglesey, Carnarvon, Merioneth, Flint, Carmarthen and Cardigan out of the Land of Snowdon (that is to say, the territory held down to 1282 by Llewelyn), and enacted that the Justice of Snowdon should have jurisdiction within them. The rest of Wales was under the jurisdiction of the Lord Marchers (*q.v.*), who had been given the right of holding their own courts.

The statute 1536, 27 Hen. 8, c. 26, which incorporated Wales with England, established the English county of Monmouth and the Welsh counties of Brecon, Radnor, Montgomery and Denbigh, and the same statute regularised the position of the Welsh counties of Pembroke and Glamorgan.

The statute 1543, 34 & 35 Hen. 8, c. 26, established the King's Great Sessions in Wales, which performed in all the twelve Welsh counties functions corresponding to those of assizes in England. These two statutes of 1536 and 1543 made the English law, but not the authority of the English courts, prevail in Wales, and practically abolished the jurisdiction of the Lords Marchers. The Court of Great Sessions was abolished by the Law Terms Act, 1830. In 1798 Wales was divided into four circuits, and there were eight judges with salaries amounting in the aggregate to £6,580 a year (*Commons Committees Reports*, 1803, Vol. 13, p. 203, 209–219). See Bowen, *Statutes of Wales*; Williams, Hist. Gt. Sess.

By the statute 1844, 8 & 9 Vict. c. 11, the manner of assigning sheriffs in Wales is assimilated to that obtaining in England.

By s. 3 of the Wales and Berwick Act, 1746, it was enacted that references in Acts of Parliament to England were to include Wales and Berwick. By the Welsh Language Act, 1967, s. 4, this does not apply to Wales in any Act passed after July 27, 1967.

As to the use of Welsh in legal proceedings, see the Welsh Courts Act, 1942, and the Welsh Language Act, 1967, s. 1. Welsh versions of official forms may be prescribed (ss. 2, 3, and orders made thereunder).

As to election forms in Welsh, see the Elections (Welsh Forms) Act, 1964.

Welsh-speaking inspectors of factories, mines, and quarries are provided for in Wales and Monmouthshire by the Factories Act, 1961, s. 145, and the Mines and Quarries Act, 1954, s. 171.

The local government areas and authorities in Wales are specified in the Local Government Act, 1972, ss. 20–38, 53–59, Schs. 4, 5. Monmouthshire and Newport have become part of Wales, see s. 20 (7). See LOCAL GOVERNMENT.

By the Welsh Church Act, 1914, the Church of England in Wales and Monmouthshire was disestablished and dis-

endowed. The operation of the Act was postponed, but eventually took effect from March 31, 1920. S. 23 of the Act abolished the right of ecclesiastical persons in Wales to grant marriage licences, but the section was repealed by the Welsh Church (Temporalities) Act, 1919, s. 6, and the right thereby restored (*Powell* v. *Church in Wales Representative Body* [1957] 1 W.L.R. 439).

See CHESTER; COUNCIL OF WALES; MARCHERS, LORDS; MONMOUTHSHIRE; RATIONABILE PARTE BONORUM, DE; WELSH CHURCH.

Wales, Prince of. See PRINCE OF WALES.

Wales, Statute of, the statute 1284, 12 Edw. 1 (2 Reeves, c. ix, 95).

Walescheria, the Welsh kindred of a murdered man (*Statutum Walliae*, 1284, cc. 3, 5).

Waleschery, the being a Welshman (Spelman).

Waliscus [Lat. *servus*], a servant, or any other ministerial officer (Leg. Jud., c. 34).

Walkers, foresters who have the care of a certain space of ground.

Walking possession. See FIERI FACIAS.

Walkways. Local authorities are empowered, by agreement with the owner of land, to construct footpaths known as walkways over, through or under buildings (Highways Act, 1971, s. 18; Local Government Act, 1972, s. 188 (6)).

Wall. A demise in writing of the " rooms situate on the first and second floors " of business premises prima facie includes the external walls of the two floors (*Goldfoot* v. *Welch* [1914] 1 Ch. 213). See PARTY WALL.

Waltham Black Act, the statute 1722, 9 Geo. 1, c. 22, also called the Black Act (*q.v.*).

Waltham Blacks, the gang against which the Black Act (*q.v.*) was directed.

Waltham Forest. See the statute 1849, 12 & 13 Vict. c. 81.

Wanlass, an ancient tenure of lands, *i.e.*, to drive deer to a stand, that the lord may have a shot (Blount, *Tenures*, 140).

Wapentake, or **Wapentachium,** the hundred (*q.v.*) in Yorkshire, Lincolnshire, Nottinghamshire, Derbyshire, Rutland,

and Leicestershire; the term is said to be derived from recognition of the local magistrate by touching his arms, but this is very questionable, though it unquestionably has reference to armed gatherings of the freemen (1 Stubbs, Const. Hist. 96).

War. The sovereign has the sole prerogative of making war or peace.

Where war actually prevails, the ordinary courts have no jurisdiction over the action of the military authorities (*Ex p. Marais* [1902] A.C. at p. 115). See ARMY; DECLARATION OF WAR.

War charities. By the War Charities Act, 1940, s. 11, replacing the War Charities Act, 1916, s. 10, " war charity " means any fund, institution, association or undertaking having for its sole or principal object or among its objects the relief of suffering or distress caused, or the supply of needs or comforts to persons affected by the wars of 1914–18 or 1939–45 and any other charitable purpose connected with the wars. To make any appeal, except in a place of public worship, for any war charity, unless the charity is registered or exempted from registration pursuant to the Act, is an offence (s. 1) punishable summarily with six months' imprisonment or a fine of £100 or both (s. 9). The Act provides for registration and for the proper management of war charities. The Charity Commissioners are given powers of regulation (ss. 3–5; Charities Act, 1960, Sch. 6). See BLIND PERSONS.

War crime, a violation of the rules of warfare. See the " Law Reports of Trials of War Criminals " prepared by the United Nations War Crimes Commission.

War damage. The War Damage Act, 1943 made provision for compensation for damage to land and goods as a result of enemy action or action taken against the enemy during the war of 1939–45. War Damage (Public Utility Undertakings) Act, 1949, the War Damage (Clearance Payments) Act, 1960, the War Damage Acts, 1964 and 1965, and the Town and Country Planning Act, 1971, s. 279.

War Department, a department from which the sovereign issued orders to the forces. This department was formerly united with the Colonial Office under an official called the Secretary at War, who was not a Secretary of State; but an additional Secretary of State was appointed, for affairs of war solely, in 1854: see the War Office Act, 1870.

By the Army (Annual) Act, 1909, certain powers formerly exercisable by the Secretary of State, and all powers of the Commander-in-Chief and the Adjutant-General under the Army Act, were transferred to the Army Council. See ARMY COUNCIL.

The War Department and the Army Council have been absorbed into the Ministry of Defence. See DEFENCE, MINISTRY OF.

War injury. Compensation for personal injuries caused to civilians by enemy acts or suffered in the course of combating or repelling the enemy, or caused by aircraft of the enemy or of the British or allied governments during the war of 1939–45 was provided for by the Personal Injuries (Emergency Provisions) Act, 1939.

War Loan. See FUNDS, PUBLIC.

War memorial. The War Memorials (Local Authorities Powers) Act, 1923, enables local authorities under certain circumstances to maintain and repair memorials vested in them. See also the Local Government Act, 1948, s. 133; Parish Councils Act, 1957, ss. 8, 15, Sch. 2; Local Government Act, 1972, ss. 251, 272, Sch. 29 para. 45, Sch. 30.

War of 1914–18. For legal purposes this was declared by an order made under the Termination of the Present War (Definition) Act, 1918, to have terminated on August 31, 1921. See DEFENCE OF THE REALM ACTS.

War of 1939–45. No Act corresponding to the Termination of the Present War (Definition) Act, 1918, was passed after the war of 1939–45, which terminated on different dates for different purposes. Thus an order made under the Courts (Emergency Powers) Act, 1943, declared that the emergency which was the occasion of the passing of the Courts (Emergency Powers) Act, 1939, terminated on October 8, 1950. The formal state of war with Germany ended on July 9, 1951 (*London Gazette*, July 6, 1951, supp. July 9, 1951).

War Office, the Government Department of which the Secretary of State for War was the head. See WAR DEPARTMENT.

War risks insurance. See the War Risks Insurance Act, 1939, the Restriction of Advertisement (War Risks Insurance) Act, 1939, and the War Damage (Amendment) Act, 1942.

War savings certificates. See the National Debt Act, 1972, s. 9.

War-time leases. See the Validation of War-time Leases Act, 1944.

War works. See the Requisitioned Land and War Works Acts, 1945 and 1948. See also the Land Powers (Defence) Act, 1958.

Ward; Wardship. A ward is an infant who is under the care of a guardian (*q.v.*). Wardship is the condition or status of a ward.

Formerly, if an action, suit or other proceeding relative to an infant's estate or person, and for his benefit, was instituted in the Chancery Division, the infant, whether plaintiff or defendant, immediately became a ward of court, although his father or testamentary guardian might be living. Thus, the institution of an action for the administration of property in which an infant was interested (*Brown* v. *Collins* (1884) 25 Ch.D. 56), or the payment into court under the Trustee Act, 1925, s. 63, of a fund in which he was interested, made him a ward of court.

By the Law Reform (Miscellaneous Provisions) Act, 1949, s. 9, no infant may be made a ward of court without an order of the court.

A ward of court cannot be taken out of the jurisdiction of the court, nor can any change be made in his or her position in life (as by marriage, adoption of a profession, etc.), without leave of the court, and the details of his or her education and maintenance are regulated by the court, namely, a judge of the Chancery Division sitting in chambers. The control of the court ceases when the infant becomes of age (*Bolton* v. *Bolton* [1891] 3 Ch. 270).

Proceedings in relation to the wardship of minors are assigned to the Family Division (*q.v.*) of the High Court (Administration of Justice Act, 1970, s. 1, Sch. 1).

A ward of court may be admitted to hospital as a mental patient on application made by leave of the court (Mental Health Act, 1959, s. 58) but a ward of court may not be received into guardianship under that Act (s. 58 (3)).

As to maintenance orders in respect of wards of court, see the Family Law Reform Act, 1969, s. 6. Wards of court may be committed to the care of the social services committee of a local authority (s. 7; Local Authority Social Services Act, 1970, ss. 2, 14, Schs. 1, 3).

In the law of tenure, wardship was the right to the custody of the land, and in some cases also of the person, of an infant heir of land. The right was a chattel real (Co.Litt. 200a).

See COURT OF WARDS, ETC.; INFANT; RAVISHMENT DE GARD; WARDS.

Warda, the custody of a town or castle, which the inhabitants were bound to keep at their own charge (1 Dugd. Mon. 372).

Wardage, payments made for the maintenance of watch and ward (*q.v.*) (*Domesday*).

Warden, a keeper; generally the term is used to denote an officer of the Crown. See CINQUE PORTS; DIES MARCHIAE; MARCHES; STANNARIES.

The Head of an Oxford college is sometimes styled Warden, *e.g.,* All Souls. The master of a city company is sometimes termed a prime warden. In the Society of Apothecaries (*q.v.*) there are a master, two wardens, etc. (Apothecaries Act, 1815).

Warden of the forest, an officer who bailed and discharged offenders and summoned the forest officers and others to the justice seat. See ATTACHMENT OF THE FOREST.

Wardens of the peace, conservators of the peace (*q.v.*) (1 Lamb.Eiren., c. 3).

Wardmote, a court held in every ward in London. See LONDON.

The wardmote inquest has power to inquire into and present all defaults concerning the watch and police doing their duty, to see that engines, etc., are provided against fire, that persons selling ale and beer are honest and suffer no disorders, nor permit gaming, and that they sell in lawful measures, that searches are made for beggars, vagrants, and idle persons, etc., and that they are punished.

Wardpenny, wardage (*q.v.*); also an annual payment made to a feudal superior as a commutation of military service.

Wards. The City of London has from an early period been divided into wards. See LONDON.

For the purpose of the election of councillors every metropolitan district is divided into wards, each returning a number of councillors which is divisible by three. Every non-metropolitan district is divided into wards each returning such number of councillors as may be provided by order. There is to be a separate election for each ward (Local Government Act, 1972, s. 6). As to parish wards, see ss. 16, 17. As to London boroughs see Sch. 2 para. 7.

Wards and Liveries, Court of, a court erected by Henry III, and abolished by the statute 1660, 12 Car. 2, c. 24.

Wards, Statute of, the statute 1300, 28 Edw. 1, c. 18.

Wardship, pupillage, guardianship; an incident to tenure in socage. See TENURE; WARD.

Wardship in chivalry, an incident to the tenure of knight's service.

Wardship in copyholds. The lord was guardian of his infant tenant by special custom.

Wardship of Infants. See WARD.

Wardstaff, a watchman's staff.

Wardwit; Warwit, freedom from wardage; a fine for not maintaining watch and ward.

Wardwrit, the being quit of giving money for the keeping of wards (Spelman).

Warectare, to plough up land designed for wheat in the spring, in order to let it lie fallow for better improvement, which in Kent is called summer-land (Jacob).

Warectum, Wareccum, Varectum, fallow (Co.Litt. 5b).

Warehouse. As used in, for instance, the Customs and Excise Act, 1952, s. 80, this means a store in which dutiable goods may be deposited without pay-

ment of duty until they are re-exported —in which case no duty is payable—or until they are taken out for consumption in this country. See DRAWBACK.

Warehouse receipt, a document of title to goods lying in a warehouse, signed or certified by or on behalf of the warehouse-keeper.

Warehousing system, the allowing of goods imported to be deposited in public warehouses, at a reasonable rent, without payment of the duties on importation if they are re-exported; or if they are ultimately withdrawn for home consumption, without payment of such duties until they are so removed, or a purchaser found for them. It has been in operation since the statute 1803, 43 Geo. 3, c. 132. See WAREHOUSE.

Warettum, the seashore covered by the neap tides (Moore, *Foreshore*, 393).

Wargus, a banished rogue (Leg.Hen. 1, c. 83).

Waring, Ex p., Rule in, the principle established in *Ex p. Waring* (1815) 19 Ves. 345, that securities held by the acceptor of a bill against his acceptances are available to the bill-holders if both acceptor and drawer are insolvent, even though the bill-holders had no knowledge that the securities had been appropriated for the purpose.

The rule only applies where there is a double insolvency and where there has been a specific appropriation of securities.

Warncistura, garniture, furniture, provision, etc.

Warning of a caveat, a notice to a person who has entered a caveat in the Principal Probate Registry to appear and set forth his interest. See CAVEAT.

Warnoth, a custom that if a tenant holding of the castle at Dover failed in paying his rent at the day, he should forfeit double, and for his second failure treble; the lands so held were called *terrae cultae et terrae warnoth* (2 Dugd. Mon. 589).

Warping, a means of fertilising land adjoining a tidal river and lying below high-water mark and above low-water mark. The land is artificially flooded through a sluice in an embankment and the water is not discharged until any sediment suspended therein has been deposited on the land. Capital moneys arising under the Settled Land Act, 1925, may be expended on warping (Settled Land Act, 1925, Sch. 3 Pt. I). Warping by a tenant is an improvement in respect of which the tenant cannot claim unless the landlord had consented in writing to the warping (Agricultural Holdings Act, 1948, Sch. 3 Pt. I).

Warrant, an authority; a precept under hand and seal to some officer to arrest an offender, to be dealt with according to due course of law; also, a writ conferring some right or authority, a citation or summons.

Warrants are used in executing process both in civil and criminal cases.

In ordinary actions, when a sheriff does not execute a writ either personally or by his under-sheriff, he must authorise a bailiff to execute it; and this authority is given by a document called a warrant. See BAILIFF.

The Criminal Procedure Act, 1853, s. 9, enables a judge of the High Court to issue a warrant for bringing up any prisoner or person committed for trial, to be examined as a witness in any court. See HABEAS CORPUS.

Under the old practice of the Admiralty Court, a warrant in a cause *in rem* corresponded to and was almost in the same words as the writ of summons in an Admiralty action *in rem* under the present practice. As to the warrant of arrest in an Admiralty action, see ARREST.

A warrant may be issued by a justice to arrest a person who has or is suspected of having committed an offence (Magistrates' Courts Act, 1952, s. 1 (as amended by the Courts Act, 1971, Schs. 8, 11 and the Local Government Act, 1972, Sch. 30), or on the non-appearance of the accused (Magistrates' Courts Act, 1952, s. 15 (as amended by the Magistrates' Courts Act, 1957, s. 4, and the Criminal Justice Act, 1967, s. 24 (2), Sch. 7), or on the non-appearance of the defendant against whom complaint is made (Magistrates' Courts Act, 1952, s. 47). A warrant may be issued for the arrest of a person who will not attend as a witness (Magistrates' Courts Act, 1952, s. 77, as amended by the Local Government Act, 1972, Sch. 30).

See ARREST; BACKING A WARRANT; BENCH WARRANT; EXTRADITION; SEARCH WARRANT.

Warrant of attorney. Originally, this meant the same thing as a power or letter of attorney (Co.Litt. 52a), but at the present day the term is used only to denote a written authority from a person enabling the person to whom it is given (the attorney) to enter an appearance for him in an action, and to allow judgment to be entered for the plaintiff, or to suffer judgment to go by default. Such a warrant is usually given to secure the payment of a sum of money, and is therefore qualified by a condition that it shall only be put in force if the debt is not paid by a certain day; this condition is expressed in a document called the defeasance, which also usually contains various stipulations designed to facilitate the execution of the judgment when obtained. The defeasance must be written on the same paper or parchment as the warrant (Debtors Act, 1869, s. 26), and its execution requires to be attested by a solicitor, who must explain the nature of the document to the debtor before he signs it (s. 24). It must be filed at the Central Office (Bills of Sales Department) of the Supreme Court within twenty-one days of its execution, and if affecting land, registered under the Land Charges Act, 1972, s. 6, every five years. (See LAND CHARGE.) If a warrant of attorney is obtained by fraud, duress, or misrepresentation, or upon illegal consideration, the court will order it to be delivered up to be cancelled, and will set aside all proceedings upon it, and also if a material alteration is made in it. If the warrant is good in part, and bad in part, the court will sustain it *quoad* the good part. If the fact of the consideration is doubtful, the court may direct an issue to try it. Warrants of attorney are not now of such frequent occurrence as formerly.

A warrant of attorney is given in contemplation of proceedings being necessary. A *cognovit* (*q.v.*) is given after proceedings have been commenced.

Warrantee, a person to whom a warranty is made.

Warrantia cartae, a real action which lay to enforce a warranty of title to land where the tenant was unable to avail himself of the warranty by voucher (*q.v.*) (Fitz.N.B. 134).

It was abolished by the Real Property Limitation Act, 1833, s. 36. See WARRANTY.

Warrantia diei, a writ which lay for the protection of one who was bound to appear on a certain day in an action but who was employed on the king's service so that he could not come (Fitz. N.B. 17).

Warrantizare nihil aliud est, quam defendere et acquietare tenentem qui warrantum vocavit in seisina sua (Co.Litt. 365a). (To warrant is simply to defend and ensure in peace the tenant who calls for warranty in his seisin.) The Real Property Limitation Act, 1833, s. 39, provided that warranty of lands should not defeat a right of entry.

Warrantor, a person who warrants; the heir of one's husband.

Warrantor potest excipere quod quaerens non tenet terram de qua petit warrantiam, et quod donum fuit insufficiens (Hob. 21). (A warrantor may object that the complainant does not hold the land of which he seeks the warranty, and that the gift was insufficient.)

Warranty, a term of a contract collateral to the main purpose of the contract; any agreement either accompanying a transfer of property, or collateral to the contract for such transfer (*Lawrence* v. *Cassell* [1930] 2 K.B. 83; *Miller* v. *Cannon Hill Estates* [1931] 2 K.B. 113), or to any other agreement or transaction. A warranty may be express or implied by law or statute.

Implied warranties have been said to underlie or to be the gist of actions for negligence or breach of duty arising out of the special relations between parties (*Coggs* v. *Bernard* (1703) 2 Ld.Raym. 909). See NEGLIGENCE.

As a general rule an express warranty, or a known usage, excludes any implication of warranty in regard to the same subject-matter: *expressum facit cessare tacitum.*

In the law relating to the sale of goods, a warranty is an agreement with reference to goods which are the subject of a contract of sale, but collateral to the main purpose of such contract, the breach of which gives rise to a claim for damages, but not to a right to reject the goods and treat the contract as repudiated (Sale of Goods Act, 1893, s. 62 (1)). Whether a stipulation in a contract of sale is a condition, the breach of which may give rise to a right to treat the contract as repudiated, or a warranty, depends in each case on the construction of the contract; a stipulation may be a condition though called a warranty in the contract (s. 11 (1) (*b*)).

A warranty of goods may constitute a defence to a criminal charge: see, for instance, the Rag Flock and Other Filling Materials Act, 1951, s. 23.

In the law of marine insurance, what is called a warranty is in fact a condition. The Marine Insurance Act, 1906, s. 33, provides for the release of the insurer from liability, unless the policy contains a provision to the contrary, if the warranty is not exactly complied with. The most usual express warranties are that a vessel is safe on a given day, and that she will sail or depart on a given day. The most important implied warranty is that the vessel is seaworthy at the commencement of the risk (s. 39). Warranty of documentation is a warranty that she has those documents which are required by international law or treaty to establish her national character. A continuing warranty is one which applies to the whole period during which the contract is in force: thus, an undertaking in a charterparty that a vessel shall continue to be of the same class as she was at the time the charterparty was made is a continuing warranty.

When a man holds himself out as the agent of another he is deemed to warrant his authority to act as agent, and if, and in so far as, he is without such authority as he purports to have, an action for breach of warranty of authority will lie against him for one damnified by such absence of authority.

On a sale of goods there is an implied warranty of freedom from encumbrances or charges and of quiet possession. Modified warranties are implied when the intention is to transfer only such title as the seller or a third person may have (Sale of Goods Act, 1893, s.

12; Supply of Goods (Implied Terms) Act, 1973, s. 1).

In the old law of real property, warranty was an obligation by the feoffor or donor of land (or other hereditaments) to defend the feoffee or donee in the possession of the land, and to give him land of equal value if he was evicted from it. A warranty was a real covenant. Warranties were either in deed, that is, expressed; or in law, that is, implied. Warranties in deed were of three kinds. (1) Lineal warranty was where the heir of the warrantor was, or might by possibility have been, entitled to the land by descent from the warrantor; this happened if a man seised of lands in fee made a feoffment of them by deed and bound himself and his heirs to warranty, and died, so that the warranty descended to his heir, who would otherwise have inherited the land. (2) Collateral warranty was where the heir of the warrantor could not by any possibility have been entitled to the land by descent from the warrantor; thus, if a younger son released with warranty to his father's disseisor, this warranty was collateral to his elder brother, because by no possibility could the latter in such a case claim the land as heir to his younger brother. (3) Where the conveyance to which the warranty was annexed immediately followed a disseisin, or operated itself as such (as where a father, being tenant for years with remainder to his son in fee, aliened in fee simple with warranty), this was called a warranty commencing by disseisin, and did not bar the heir of the warrantor (Litt. 703; Co.Litt. 370a, 373; 2 Bl.Comm. 302).

The operation of a warranty as against the heir of a warrantor in case the warrantee was evicted from the land was to compel him to yield the warrantee other land in its stead, to the extent of any land which had descended to him from the ancestor; and if he had no land by descent, then he was barred of all claim to the land warranted. This operation, however, was from time to time restrained by various statutes; and voucher (*q.v.*) and the writ of *warrantia chartae* (*q.v.*) were both abolished by the Real Property Limitation Act, 1833, s. 36, so that a warranty of land is now entirely inoperative. A fictitious warranty was the foundation of the proceeding called a common recovery (*q.v.*). Warranty was implied in certain cases; thus, the word "give" in a feoffment created a warranty binding on the feoffor during his life; and an exchange (*q.v.*) at common law created an implied warranty; these and other implied warranties were abolished by the Real Property Limitation Act, 1833, s. 3; covenants for title (*q.v.*) are however implied by the use of certain words as provided by the Law of Property Act, 1925, s. 76, Sch. 2.

See ASSETS BY DESCENT; REBUTTER; VOUCHER.

Warren [Dut. *waerande*; Fr. *guerenne*; Norm. Fr. *garrenne*; Low Lat. *warenna*, warren; Old High Ger. *waron*, to take care of, preserve]. A warren is the privilege of keeping and killing certain kinds of animals (especially hares and rabbits) on a piece of ground. As to what are beasts of warren, see GAME. A free warren was a franchise to have and keep certain wild beasts and fowls, called game, within the precincts of a manor, or other known place; in which animals the owner of the warren had a property, and consequently a right to exclude all other persons from hunting and taking them. It had to be derived from a royal grant, or from prescription, which supposed such a grant (*Beauchamp* v. *Winn* (1873) L.R. 6 H.L. at p. 238; *Robinson* v. *Duleep Singh* (1879) 11 Ch.D. 798; *Fitzhardinge* v. *Purcell* [1908] 2 Ch. 139). Franchises of free warren were abolished by the Wild Creatures and Forest Laws Act, 1971.

Warscot, a contribution usually made towards armour in the time of the Saxons.

Warth, a customary payment for castle guard.

Wash, a shallow part of a river or arm of the sea.

Washhouses, Public. See BATHS, ETC.

Washing-horn [Fr. *corner l'eau*], the sounding of a horn for washing before dinner. The custom was formerly observed in the Temple.

Washington, Treaty of. A treaty signed on May 8, 1871, between Great Britain and the United States as to certain differences arising out of the war between the northern and southern States, the Canadian fisheries, and other matters (Treaty of Washington Act, 1872).

The Rules of Washington lay down standards to be observed by a neutral in sea warfare, first formulated in the treaty.

The Treaties of Washington Act, 1922, enabled effect to be given to two treaties on the limitation of naval armaments. It was supplemented by the London Naval Treaty Act, 1930.

Waste [Lat. *vastum*], any spoil or destruction in houses, gardens, trees, etc., by a tenant; also uncultivated land.

In the law of real property, waste is land which has never been cultivated, as opposed to pasture and arable land, etc. The most important kind of waste is manorial waste, or that part of a manor which is subject to the tenants' rights of common, and hence " waste " is sometimes used improperly to denote any land subject to rights of common or similar rights, although under cultivation. (See COMMON; COMMONABLE; LAMMAS LANDS; MANOR; OPEN FIELDS; SHACK.) The soil of a manorial waste is vested in the lord of the manor, and he therefore is entitled to pasture his cattle on it. He is also entitled to the minerals under the waste, and may work them so that he does not unduly interfere with the commonable rights of the tenants. As to the inclosure of waste lands, see APPROVEMENT; INCLOSURE.

A local planning authority (*q.v.*) has power to take action with regard to neglected waste land which has become unsightly or offensive (Town and Country Planning Act, 1971, ss. 65, 104–107; Local Government Act, 1974, s. 35, Sch. 6 para. 25 (4), Sch. 8). See *Stephens* v. *Cuckfield* [1960] 2 Q.B. 373.

In the law of torts, waste is whatever does lasting damage to the freehold or inheritance of land, or anything which alters the nature of the property so as to make the proof of ownership more difficult, or to destroy or weaken the proof of identity, or diminish the value of the estate, or increase the burden upon it. It is either voluntary or permissive; the former is an offence of com-

mission, such as pulling down a house, converting arable land into pasture, opening new mines or quarries, etc.; the latter is one of omission, such as allowing a house to fall for want of necessary repairs, allowing land to remain flooded with water, etc. (Co.Litt. 52b).

A tenant in fee simple or in tail may commit as much waste as he likes; but the general rule is, that a tenant for life of freehold land is impeachable for waste, *i.e.,* he may not commit waste unless his interest is without impeachment of waste (or sans waste), as where it is expressly so given to him. See TENANT IN TAIL AFTER POSSIBILITY OF ISSUE EXTINCT.

Both for voluntary and permissive waste an action lay against a tenant, whether for life or years, by virtue of the Statute of Gloucester, 1278, c. 5, repealed by the Civil Procedure Acts Repeal Act, 1879. A tenant from year to year is liable for voluntary waste only. A mortgagor in possession will be restrained from cutting down timber, for as the whole estate is the security for the money advanced, the mortgagor ought not to be suffered to diminish it; but he may cut underwood of a proper growth at seasonable times; as to an estate under forestry management, see *Dashwood* v. *Magniac* [1892] 2 Ch. 253.

There are certain kinds of waste which courts of equity would always prevent, even where the tenant for life was unimpeachable for waste, and which are hence known as equitable waste.

Equitable waste (which is voluntary only) is an unconscientious abuse of the privileges of non-impeachability for waste at common law, whereby a tenant for life unimpeachable for waste will be restrained from committing wilful, destructive, malicious, extravagant waste, such as pulling down houses, cutting timber of too young a growth, or trees planted for ornament, or for shelter of premises; for, though in some cases *fortior est dispositio legis quam hominis*, yet that does not extend to encumber or spoil estates (*Garth* v. *Cotton* (1750) 1 Ves.Sen. 524, 546; *Baker* v. *Sebright* (1879) 13 Ch.D. 179).

By the Law of Property Act, 1925, s.

135, replacing the Judicature Act, 1873, s. 25 (3), it is provided that a life interest without impeachment of waste shall not confer upon the tenant for life any legal right to commit waste of the kind known as equitable waste, unless an intention to confer such right expressly appears by the instrument creating the interest. The Settled Land Act, 1925, s. 89, enables a tenant for life to effect authorised improvements without impeachment of waste. Where a tenant for life pulls down a building and erects a new one in such a way as to effect an improvement, the court will not interfere, this being what is called meliorating or ameliorating waste (*Doherty* v. *Allman* (1878) 3 App.Cas. 709).

The remedy for waste is an action for damages or an injunction.

As to the writ of waste, see ESTREPE; VASTO, DE.

Waste disposal. The collection and disposal of waste is dealt with by the Control of Pollution Act, 1974, Pt. I (ss. 1–30).

The collection of household waste is a function of district councils (*q.v.*), London borough councils, the Common Council of the City of London, the Sub-Treasurer of the Inner Temple and the Under-Treasurer of the Middle Temple. These bodies constitute "collection authorities." If requested, they may collect commercial waste and industrial waste. No charge is to be made for the collection of household waste except as otherwise prescribed (Control of Pollution Act, 1974, ss. 12, 30 (1)). See also CESSPOOL; PRIVY. A collection authority may require the occupier of premises to place the waste for collection in dustbins. The dustbins may be provided by the authority free of charge or on payment. If the occupier is unwilling to pay he must supply the dustbins himself (s. 13). Household waste consists of waste from a private dwelling or residential home or from premises forming part of a university or school or other educational establishment or forming part of a hospital or nursing home. Industrial waste consists of waste from a factory and any premises of a nationalised industry. It does not include waste from a mine or quarry. Commercial waste consists of waste from premises used for the purposes of a trade or business or for the purposes of sport, recreation or entertainment (s. 30 (3); *Iron Trades Mutual Employers Insurance Association* v. *Sheffield Corporation* [1974] 1 W.L.R. 107 (office waste paper)). A private dwelling includes a caravan on a caravan site (s. 30 (2)).

Penalties for interference with dustbins and refuse tips are provided by s. 27.

Special provisions are contained in s. 3 (3) as regards the deposit of noxious, poisonous or polluting waste. S. 88 imposes a civil liability in such cases.

Waste, Statute of, the statute 1292, 20 Edw. 1, st. 2.

Wasting assets, property with only a limited existence, *e.g.*, leaseholds. When residuary personalty is given by will to trustees for persons in succession it is the duty of the trustees (unless the will shows a contrary intention) to realise such parts of the estate as are wasting, perishable, or unauthorised by the will or the general law, or reversionary, and invest the proceeds in authorised investments (*Howe* v. *Dartmouth* (1802) 7 Ves. 117).

Wastors, thieves.

Watch. The watch was a body of constables on duty on any particular night.

Watch and ward [Teut. *watcht, wacta*; Lat. *custodia*]. One of the principal duties of constables is to keep watch and ward. Ward, *custodia*, is chiefly applied to the daytime, in order to apprehend rioters and robbers on the highways. Watch is applicable to the night only, and begins at the time when ward ends (1 Bl.Comm. 356). See CONSTABLES.

Watch committee. This was defined in the Police Act, 1964, s. 62, Sch. 8 as the police authority of a county borough. All boroughs (including county boroughs) have ceased to exist (Local Government Act, 1972, ss. 1, 20, Schs. 1, 30). See BOROUGH; COUNTY; COUNTY BOROUGH.

Watching and besetting. See BESET; PICKETING.

Watching and lighting. See LIGHTING AND WATCHING ACT.

Water. In the language of the law the term "land" includes water (2 Bl. Comm. 18).

WATER

An action cannot be brought to recover possession of a pool or other piece of water by the name of water only: it must be brought for the land which lies at the bottom, *e.g.*, " twenty acres of land covered with water " (Brownl. 142). See POOL.

If a man grants to another a piece of water on his land, all that the grantee takes is the right of fishing in it. By granting a certain water, though the right of fishing passes, yet the soil does not. Water being a movable, wandering thing, there can be only a temporary, transient, usufructuary property therein. " Water " does not include the land on which it stands, unless perhaps in the case of salt pits or springs, where the interest of each owner is measured by *builleries*, ballaries or buckets of brine (Burt. Comp. 550; Co.Litt. 4b).

Water is either public or private. Public waters are the sea and its branches and navigable rivers, the beds of which belong prima facie to the Crown. As a rule the soil of estuaries and of rivers (whether navigable or not) in which the tide ebbs and flows is vested in the Crown. (See HIGH SEAS; QUEEN'S CHAMBERS; RIVERS.) Private waters are rivers, streams, lakes and ponds, etc., the beds of which belong to private persons. Prima facie the soil of non-tidal rivers and lakes belongs to the owners of the adjoining land. Public waters are, as a rule, subject only to the public right of navigation, and to the right of access possessed by the owners of the adjoining shores or banks. See ACCESS; FRONTAGER; NAVIGABLE; RIPARIAN.

Private waters may be subject to a right of navigation by the public, as in the case of the Severn and other rivers.

The distinction between public waters and private waters subject to a public right of navigation is that in the case of the latter the owners of the soil may (as against the public) do what they like with the water and its bed so long as they do not obstruct the navigation.

Private waters passing through or between the lands of different proprietors may be subject to two kinds of rights, natural and acquired. Natural or proprietary rights are those possessed by every riparian proprietor, and consist principally in the right to have the water flow in its accustomed manner, without sensible disturbance or diminution by the superior and inferior riparian proprietors, and the right to the reasonable use of the water while it is flowing past his land, including its use for domestic purposes, for turning mills, etc.

Every riparian owner has a right to the uninterrupted flow of water (*McCartney* v. *Londonderry Ry.* [1905] A.C. 301), and may be liable for damage caused by neglect which prevents the free flow of water (*Finch* v. *Bannister* [1908] 2 K.B. 441); he is also entitled to receive the water in its natural character and quality (*Young* v. *Bankier Distillery Co.* [1893] A.C. 691).

The law is the same with regard to subterranean water flowing through a defined channel (*Chasemore* v. *Richards* (1859) 7 H.L.C. 349): but with regard to water which merely percolates through gravel, etc., the law is different, and a landowner can appropriate such water to the exclusion of a neighbour under whose land it would otherwise percolate (*Bradford* v. *Pickles* [1895] A.C. 587), although he may not so deal with it that it flows under his neighbour's land in a polluted state (*Ballard* v. *Tomlinson* (1885) 29 Ch.D. 115).

Acquired rights are those easements which entitle a riparian proprietor to interfere with a natural stream of water to an extent not justified by his natural or proprietary rights, *e.g.*, by diminishing or obstructing the flow of water, or by polluting it, etc., or which entitle him to the use of an artificial watercourse (*q.v.*). Acquired rights in respect of water may exist in the inhabitants of a district by virtue of a custom.

Any one who interferes with the natural channel of a stream must see that the works which he substitutes are sufficient to carry off the water, even in the case of extraordinary rainfall (*Greenock* v. *Caledonian Ry.* [1917] A.C. 556). These rights apply to water flowing in known channels whether above or below ground.

A man has a natural right to the benefit of the flow of a river or stream, such right commonly referring to a stream passing through his own land, and the banks of which belong either to himself on both sides, or to himself on one side and to his neighbour on the other, in which latter case (unless the stream is navigable, for then the bed of it, so far at least as the tide of the sea flows, presumably belongs to the Crown) the proprietor of each bank is considered as prima facie the proprietor also of half the land covered by the stream, i.e., *usque ad medium filum aquae.* A prescriptive prima facie right affecting water-courses (q.v.) or waterways (q.v.) is gained by twenty years' uninterrupted enjoyment, and an indefeasible right after forty years; when the land over which such rights are claimed has been held for a term of life, or a term exceeding three years, such term is excluded from the computation of the forty years in the event of the person entitled in reversion resisting the claim within three years after the term determines (Prescription Act, 1832).

A right of the public to enter upon land belonging to another to take water is not a profit *à prendre* and is not, apparently, a subject of prescription, but it may be acquired by custom or usage (*Gateward's Case* (1607) 6 Co.Rep. 59).

A prescriptive right to a watercourse is not lost by unity of possession because the right begins *ex jure naturae* and cannot be averted.

The foregoing rights are subject to the control of the abstraction and impounding of water imposed by the Water Resources Act, 1963, as amended. The abstraction of water requires a licence from the water authority subject to certain exemptions (ss. 23–35, 78; Water Resources Act, 1968; Water Act, 1973, Schs. 8, 9). The grant of a licence protects the holder against claims at common law (Act of 1963, s. 31). In some cases there is an entitlement to a licence as of right (Act of 1963, ss. 33–35; Act of 1973, Sch. 9). The impounding of water also requires a licence (Act of 1963, ss. 36, 37, 48; Act of 1973, Sch. 9; S.I. 1965 No. 319, Art. 5, Sch. 3 para. 2). Spray irrigation is subject to further restrictions (Act of 1963, ss. 45, 63, 105; Act of 1973, Schs. 8, 9). An owner of fishing rights may apply for revocation or variation of a licence (Act of 1963, s. 47).

As to abstraction and impounding of water by water authorities, see the Act of 1963, ss. 52–56. As to charges for licences, see the Act of 1973, ss. 30, 31. See also the Act of 1963, ss. 63, 64; Act of 1973, Schs. 8, 9. Discharges into underground strata are controlled by the Act of 1963, ss. 72–76; S.I. 1965 No. 319, Art. 5, Sch. 3 para. 2. See also as to discharges of water the Water Resources Act, 1971.

See also the Water Authorities (Miscellaneous Provisions) Order, 1974 (No. 607).

It is the duty of the Secretary of State for the Environment, the Secretary of State for Wales and the Minister of Agriculture, Fisheries and Food to promote a national policy for water in England and Wales including water supplies and resources, land drainage, sewerage, pollution, recreation, amenity and inland navigation (Water Act, 1973, s. 1). The effectuation of the national policy is entrusted to nine Regional Water Authorities in England and the Welsh National Water Development Authority together with an advisory body known as the National Water Council (ss. 2–8). The functions of water authorities are dealt with in detail in ss. 9–28. River authorities will cease to exist and their functions are transferred to water authorities. The water authorities have control of statutory water undertakers. Local authorities lose their water supply functions. Land drainage functions will be discharged by regional land drainage committees under the control of water authorities. For the meaning of "water resources," see the Water Resources Act, 1963, s. 2. See also the Control of Pollution Act, 1974, Sch. 3 paras. 27–30; Drought Act, 1976.

The Water Acts, 1945 to 1958, as amended, authorise the construction of waterworks and the supply of water to the public and the levying of rates. Water authorities under the Act of 1973 discharge their duties with regard to the supply of water through the statutory water companies (Act of 1973, s. 12, Schs. 8, 9). See also the London Government Act, 1963, Sch. 11 paras. 26–29. The Metropolitan Water Board was established by the Metropolis Water Act, 1902. Water authorities have power to fix and to demand, take and recover such charges for services performed, facilities provided or rights made available by them as they think fit (Water Act, 1973, s. 30). By agreement the charges may be collected by local authorities with the general rate (s. 32A, added by the Local Government Act, 1974, s. 38). There is no power under s. 30 of the Water Act, 1973, to demand charges in respect of sewage disposal from a ratepayer who is not connected to the authority's sewers. See *Daymond* v. *South West Water Authority* [1975] 3 W.L.R. 865; Water Charges Act, 1976 (refund of charges).

For minor amendments of the Act of 1973, see the Local Government Act, 1974, s. 42, Sch. 7 paras. 13, 14, Sch. 8. As to the rating of water hereditaments, see the Act of 1974, s. 19, Sch. 3 para. 1.

The pollution of water is the subject of the Control of Pollution Act, 1974, Pt. II (ss. 31–56).

A person is in general guilty of an offence if he causes or knowingly permits (a) any poisonous, noxious or polluting matter to enter any stream or controlled waters or any specified underground water, or (b) any matter to enter a stream so as to tend to impede the proper flow of the stream in a manner leading or likely to lead to a substantial aggravation of pollution due to other causes or the consequences of such pollution, or (c) any solid waste matter to enter a stream or restricted waters (s. 31). " Controlled waters " means the sea within three nautical miles from the coast, such other parts of the territorial sea adjacent to Great Britain as may be prescribed and any other tidal waters in Great Britain (s. 56 (1)). The discharge of trade and sewage effluent into rivers and coastal waters, etc., is governed by ss. 32, 34–42, 46, 52, 54–56. As to discharge into sewers, see ss. 43–45. Boats on rivers and restricted waters (see s. 56 (1)) with sanitary appliances may be prohibited or restricted by by-laws made by a water authority (s. 33). A water authority is under an obligation to deal with waste resulting from the provisions of s. 33 and to arrange for the washing out of appliances from the vessels affected thereby. The authority may arrange for facilities by way of water closets, urinals and wash basins for the use of persons from such vessels (s. 47). Unregistered vessels may be excluded by a water authority from its area (s. 48). It is an offence to cause deposits in a stream to be carried downstream in suspension and to cause or allow cut or uprooted vegetation to fall into the stream (s. 49). The water authority may obtain an order restricting an agricultural practice which is causing pollution (s. 51).

These provisions take the place of the relevant provisions of the Rivers (Prevention of Pollution) Acts, 1951 to 1961.

Polluting water containing fish is an offence under the Salmon and Freshwater Fisheries Act, 1975, s. 4.

A person may be guilty of causing pollution without proof of intention or negligence (*Alphacell* v. *Woodward* [1972] A.C. 824).

The Rivers (Prevention of Pollution) Act, 1961, deals with samples of effluent (s. 10; Control of Pollution Act, 1974, Sch. 3 para. 17). So does the water Resources Act, 1963, s. 113 (1); Control of Pollution Act, 1974, Sch. 3 para. 2.

The Water Act, 1945, contains powers to prevent the waste or contamination of water (s. 17) and to make by-laws for that purpose (ss. 19, 20); Control of Pollution Act, 1974, Sch. 2 para. 15, Sch. 4. A penalty is imposed for polluting water used for human consumption (Act of 1945, s. 21; Act of 1974, Sch. 2 para. 16).

As to the supply of water to houses, see the Public Health Act, 1936, s. 138; Water Act, 1945, ss. 30, 31, Sch. 4; Public Health Act, 1961, s. 78; Water Act, 1973, Sch. 8 para. 42, Sch. 9.

Notice should be given to a water authority of gauges and records kept by other persons (Water Resources Act, 1963, s. 17).

As to the rating of statutory water undertakings, see the Local Government Act, 1974, s. 19, Sch. 3.

Safety provisions in connection with reservoirs are contained in the Reservoirs (Safety Provisions) Act, 1930, and the Reservoirs Act, 1975.

Water authorities are under a duty to maintain, improve and develop the salmon, trout, freshwater and eel fisheries in their areas and they have powers of regulation and enforcement (Salmon and Freshwater Fisheries Act, 1975, ss. 28–37).

As to the right of fishing in public or private waters, see FISHERY. As to territorial waters, see TERRITORIAL WATERS. As to nuisances, see the Public Health Act, 1936, ss. 259–267.

Water supplied through pipes in return for payment is, like gas, capable of being stolen.

See ACCRETION; ALLUVION; CONSERVATORS OF RIVERS; DERELICTION; FERRY; FORESHORE; FRONTAGER; SHIP.

Water-bailiff, an officer in a seaport town whose duty it was to search ships; in the City of London it was the title of an official who supervised fishing boats coming to the Thames, collected river tolls, acted as master of the ceremonies to the Lord Mayor, and arrested, for debt or in criminal matters, persons on the river.

Under the Salmon and Freshwater Fisheries Act, 1975, a water bailiff appointed by the water authority has powers of search, entry, and arrest without warrant. He may require the production of fishing licences and has all the powers of a constable for the purpose of the enforcement of the Act (ss. 28–37).

Water closet. See PRIVY.

Water Space Amenity Commission. See the Water Act, 1973, s. 23.

Watercourse, an artificial channel (whether above or below ground) by which water is led from or over the land of one person to or over that of another (Brit. 153b).

The right of watercourse, in this sense of the word, is therefore the right of receiving or discharging water through another person's land, and is an easement, the tenement for the benefit of which the watercourse exists being the dominant tenement. See EASEMENT.

In some cases, however, it seems that where a watercourse passes over land for the discharge of water from the dominant tenement, the owner of the servient tenement may be entitled to have the flow of water through the watercourse uninterrupted, so that the dominant owner cannot stop or divert it. In such a case there are correlative easements, each

tenement and owner being dominant or servient, according to the easement which is in question: and the watercourse is, in law, practically indistinguishable from a natural stream.

The term "watercourse" is also sometimes applied to natural streams. The rights of receiving and discharging the water of a natural stream over the land of adjoining proprietors are not easements, but natural rights. See WATER.

Water-gage, a sea-wall or bank to restrain the current and overflowing of water.

Water-gang, a trench or course to carry a stream of water.

Water-gauge, an instrument to measure water.

Water-gavel, a rent paid for water or for fishing rights. See GAVEL.

Water-guard. See COASTGUARD.

Water-measure, a measure formerly used for the sale of coals in the Pool of London: see the statute 1670, 22 Car. 2, c. 11. It was larger than Winchester measure (*q.v.*).

Watermen. The Thames watermen were persons who used to ply upon the Thames, from Gravesend to Windsor, with small rowing boats, for the conveyance of passengers from shore to shore and up and down the river. They had from ancient times a monopoly of this business, and were a company known as the Company of Watermen. They and the lightermen, or men who worked with lighters, were formed into one company, under the name of the Watermen's and Lightermen's Company, by the statute 1699, 11 & 12 Will. 3, c. 21, which, together with nine other statutes, is recited in the preamble to the statute 1827, 7 & 8 Geo. 4, c. 75. The statute of 1827 made the company a body corporate with powers of registering boats, licensing watermen and lightermen, and regulating water traffic. These powers were transferred to the Port of London Authority by the Port of London Act, 1908, s. 11, which, however, still left the company their Hall—known as Watermen's Hall—a couple of adjoining houses and certain funds to the value of about £10,000. The company is not, and never was, one of the livery companies. See COMPANIES, CITY; THAMES.

Water-ordeal. See ORDEAL.

Waterscape, an aqueduct or passage for water.

Water-troughs. See DRINKING-FOUNTAINS.

Water-way. See NAVIGABLE.

Watt, a measure of electrical power. See the Weights and Measures Act, 1963, s. 10, Sch. 1 Pt. VI; S.I. 1963, s. 10, Sch. 1 Pt. VI. A kilowatt is 1,000 watts and a megawatt is one million watts (*ibid.*).

Waveson, goods floating upon the waves after a shipwreck; floating wreckage; flotsam. See JETSAM.

Waviata, Bona, goods stolen and waived or thrown away by the thief in his flight, for fear of being apprehended. They are given by the law to the Crown (1 Bl.Comm. 297). See WAIF.

Wax scot [Lat. *cerarium*], duty anciently paid twice a year towards the charge of wax candles in churches. See CERAGE.

Way [Sax. *waeg*; Dut. *weigh*; M. Goth. *vig, wig*], a road made for passengers.

There are three kinds of ways: (1) a footway (*iter*); (2) a footway and horse-way (*actus*), also called packe or pack and prime way; and (3) *via* or *aditus*, which contains the other two, and also a cart-way, etc.; and this is twofold, *viz.*, *regia via*, the king's highway for all men, and *communis strata*, belonging to a city or town or between neighbours and neighbours, also called *chimin* (Co.Litt. 56a).

All ways are divided into highways and private ways. A right of way strictly means a private way, *i.e.*, a privilege which an individual or a particular description of persons may have of going over another's ground. Such a right is an incorporeal hereditament.

A highway is a public passage for the sovereign and all his subjects, and it is commonly called the king's public highway. See HIGHWAYS.

Bridges are public highways. See BRIDGE.

A private right of way may be claimed by prescription and immemorial usage; thus where the inhabitants of a particular hamlet, or the owners or occupiers of a particular close or farm, have immemorially been used to cross a particular piece of land, a right of way is created by immemorial usage, which supposes a grant. By the Prescription Act, 1832, s. 2, it is enacted that no claim by custom, prescription, or grant, to any way or other easement, or to any watercourse or the use of any water which has been enjoyed twenty years without interruption, shall be defeated by showing the commencement of the right within the time of legal memory; and where the right shall have existed forty years, it shall be absolute and indefeasible, unless it appears to have been enjoyed by express agreement made for that purpose by deed or writing. The right must be proved by user down to the time of the commencement of the action; and, therefore, if there is no proof of user for the last four or five years, it is insufficient. Unity of possession operates as an extinguishment of a right of way by prescription (*Shury* v. *Pigott* (1627) 3 Bulstr. 339). See EASEMENT.

An agreement to move the position of a right of way on the servient tenement made with the concurrence of all interested parties does not break the prescription period (*Davis* v. *Whitby* [1973] 1 W.L.R. 629). To establish a right of way by prescription, periods of user of an original and a substituted way may be added together (*Davis* v. *Whitby* [1974] Ch. 186).

Although a landowner's agents' knowledge may be imputed to the landowner, the burden of proving such knowledge is upon the party seeking to establish a prescriptive right of way (*Diment* v. *N. H. Foot* [1974] 1 W.L.R. 1427).

A landowner who induces another to believe that a right of access will be given over the landowner's land, may be estopped from denying the existence of such right where the other has acted to his detriment in reliance upon the assurance given (*Crabb* v. *Arun District Council* [1975] 3 W.L.R. 847).

By the Highways Act, 1959, s. 34 (replacing the Rights of Way Act, 1932), where a way over land has been actually enjoyed by the public as of right and without interruption for a full period of twenty years, the way is deemed to have been dedicated as a highway unless there is sufficient evidence that there was no intention during that period to dedicate it (*Lewis* v. *Thomas* [1950] 1 K.B. 438; *Owen* v. *Bucks C.C.* (1957) 55 L.G.R. 373; *De Rothschild* v. *Bucks C.C.* (1957) 55 L.G.R. 595). The dedication could be made by a tenant for life and remainderman (*Farquhar* v. *Newbury District Council* [1909] 1 Ch. 12); and see the Act of 1959, s. 36, as to the rights of remaindermen or reversioners next entitled in possession. A statutory body has power to dedicate so long as this is not incompatible with its statutory objects (*British Transport Commission* v. *Westmorland C.C.* [1958] A.C. 126).

A quasi-private right of way may also be grounded on a special permission; as when the owner of lands grants to another a liberty of passing over his grounds, to go to church, market, or the like, in which case the gift or grant is particular and confined to the grantee alone; it dies with the person; the grantee cannot assign it, or justify taking another person in his company—it is a mere personal licence.

A right of way reserved in favour of a vendor in a conveyance is to be construed against him as grantor thereof (*St. Edmondsbury and Ipswich Diocesan Board of Finance* v. *Clark (No. 2)* [1975] 1 W.L.R. 468).

A right of way may also arise by act and operation of law; for if a man grants a piece of ground in the middle of his field, he at the same time tacitly and impliedly gives a way to come to it, and the grantee may cross the grantor's land without being a trespasser. Such a way of necessity is limited by the necessity which created it; and when such necessity ceases, the right of way also ceases. See EASEMENT.

Private rights of way are of various kinds. They may be limited (1) as to the intervals at which they may be used, *e.g.*, a way to church or market; (2) as to the actual extent of the user authorised, *e.g.*, a foot-way, horse-way, cart-way, carriage-way, a way for driving cattle, or drift-way, a way for carrying coals, etc.; and (3) as to the nature of the tenement to which the way is claimed, *e.g.*, a way to a shed used for storing wood.

A private right of way is either an easement (*q.v.*) or a customary right.

The obstruction of a private way is a disturbance (*q.v.*); the obstruction of a public way is a nuisance (*q.v.*).

Disturbance of way happens when a person who has a right of way over another's land, by grant or prescription, is obstructed by inclosures or other obstacles, or by ploughing across it, by which means he cannot enjoy the right of way, or at least not in so commodious a manner as he might have done. The remedy is usually by an action for damages. A right of way is often contested in an action of trespass. A person having a right of way over land is not entitled to recover damages for physical injury to the way caused by excessive user of the way by another dominant owner unless this substantially interferes with the right to pass and repass (*Weston* v. *Lawrence Weaver* [1961] 1 Q.B. 402).

A navigable river is deemed to be a highway; and if the water, which is the highway, changes its course and flows upon the land of another, the highway extends over the place where the water newly flows in like manner as it existed over the ancient course, so that the owner may not disturb it. With respect to navigable rivers there is this difference, however, between them and highways, that the right to the soil of a navigable river is not, by presumption of law, in the owners of the adjoining lands. See WATER.

Ferries may be said to be common highways, as they are a common passage over rivers. They differ, however, in some measure, as they are the private property of individuals, who may maintain an action for the disturbance of their rights. See FERRY.

Way, Under. A ship is under way when she is not at anchor or made fast to the shore or aground (*The Palembang* [1929] P. 246).

Way-bill, a writing in which is set down the names of passengers who are carried in a public conveyance, or the description of goods sent with a common carrier by land.

Way-going crop. See AWAY-GOING.

Wayleave, a right of way over or through land, *e.g.*, for the carriage of minerals from a mine or quarry, or for the hanging of electric cables over land. It is an easement (*q.v.*), being a species of the class called rights of way (see WAY), and is generally created by express grant or by reservation. A wayleave rent may be a fixed annual sum, or a sum payable according to the quantity of minerals drawn over the way, or a combination of the two. See RENT.

Mineral wayleave means any wayleave, airleave, waterleave or right to use a shaft granted to or enjoyed by a working lessee, whether above or under ground, for the purpose of access to or for the conveyance of the minerals, or the ventilation or drainage of the mine, or otherwise in connection with the working of the minerals (Finance (1909–10) Act, 1910, s. 24, repealed).

Waynagium, implements of husbandry (1 Reeves, c. v, 268). See WAINAGIUM.

Ways and Means, Committee of, a committee of the whole House in the House of Commons which determines the manner of raising the funds of which the Committee of Supply (*q.v.*) determines the expenditure.

Waywardens. The Highway Acts, 1862 to 1878, provided that in every parish forming part of a highway district there should annually be elected one or more waywardens. The waywardens so elected, and the justices for the county residing within the district, formed the highway board for the district. Each waywarden also represented his parish in regard to the levying of the highway rates, and in questions arising concerning the liability of his parish for repairs, etc. Waywardens and highway boards disappeared when the local authority was made the highway authority by the Local Government Act, 1894, s. 25 (1). See HIGHWAY.

Weald, Wald, Walt [Sax.], a wood or grove. The Weald of Kent is a part of the county which formerly was densely wooded.

Wealreaf, the robbing of a dead man in his grave.

Wealth, the actual and potential possessions and resources of individuals or a community, either convertible into terms of money, or measured by any other standard of value; all useful or agreeable things which possess exchange-value, or,

in other words, all useful and agreeable things except those which can be obtained in the quantity desired without labour or sacrifice (1 Mill, Pol.Eco. 10). See VALUE.

Weapon. See OFFENSIVE WEAPON.

Wear, or **Weir,** a dam or fence made across a river, or against water, formerly made of stakes interlaced by twigs of osier, and accommodated for the taking of fish, or to convey a stream to a mill. They are prohibited by Magna Carta, 1215, and other early statutes in navigable rivers (*Leconfield* v. *Lonsdale* (1870) L.R. 5 C.P. 657). They were prohibited for the purpose of catching salmon by the Salmon Fishery Act, 1861, unless lawfully in use at the time of the passing of that Act by virtue of a grant or charter or immemorial usage. Weirs and mill dams for taking or obstructing salmon and trout not in use before 1861 are prohibited by the Salmon and Freshwater Fisheries Act, 1975, s. 7.

Wear and tear, the waste of substance by the ordinary use of it. This expression commonly occurs in connection with leases, in which the lessee agrees to return the subject-matter of the lease at the end of the lease in the same state as it was at the beginning of it, " fair year and tear excepted " (*Manchester Bonded Warehouse Co.* v. *Carr* (1880) 5 C.P.D. at p. 513; *Terrell* v. *Murray* (1901) 17 T.L.R. 570; *Miller* v. *Burt* (1918) 63 S.J. 117; *Citron* v. *Cohen* (1920) 36 T.L.R. 560). As to how far this exempts the lessee, see *Taylor* v. *Webb* [1937] 2 K.B. 283; *Brown* v. *Davies* [1958] 1 Q.B. 117. See LANDLORD AND TENANT.

As to the insertion of the exception in a lease made by a tenant for life, see *Davies* v. *Davies* (1888) 38 Ch.D. 499.

Wed [Sax.], a covenant or agreement.

Wedbedrip, the customary service which inferior tenants paid to the lords in cutting down their corn, or doing other harvest duties.

Wedding presents. In the absence of any evidence to the contrary it may be assumed that wedding presents originating from one side of the family were intended for the husband and those from the other side were intended for the wife (*Samson* v. *Samson* [1960] 1 W.L.R. 190).

Wedding rings were required to be of not less than nine carats fineness (Wedding Rings Act, 1855, s. 1; Gold Wares (Standard of Fineness) Order, 1932). They are now regulated, with other articles made of precious metals, under the Hallmarking Act, 1973. See PLATE.

Weeds, Injurious. Spear thistle, creeping or field thistle, curled dock, broadleafed dock and ragwort and such other weeds as are specified in regulations made under the Weeds Act, 1959 (as amended by the Local Government Act, 1972, Sch. 30) which consolidated earlier legislation dating from 1921. The Minister of Agriculture, Fisheries and Food or any county council authorised by him may order the occupier of land to prevent the spreading of weeds. If the occupier fails to do so he is liable to be fined and the Minister or council may do the work and recover the cost of so doing from the occupier or if necessary, from the owner of the land. The Act confers powers of entry and inspection.

Weighage, a toll or duty paid for weighing merchandise.

Weighbridges. For the power of a highway authority to provide weighbridges see the Road Traffic Act, 1972, s. 200.

Weight of evidence, such superiority in the evidence for one side over that for the other as calls for a verdict for the first. When a new trial is asked for on the ground that the verdict is against the weight of the evidence, the judge who tried the cause may be consulted; as to the grounds for ordering a new trial, see R.S.C., Ord. 59, r. 11.

Weights and measures, instruments for reducing the quantity and price of merchandise to a certainty, that there may be the less room for deceit and imposition. See AVOIRDUPOIS; METRIC SYSTEM; TROY WEIGHT.

The adjustment of weights and measures is a prerogative of the Crown, and has from an early date been regulated by statute.

The Weights and Measures Act, 1878, established standard weights and measures to be used throughout the United Kingdom. The law is now contained in the Weights and Measures Act, 1963, as amended. It enacts that the yard (*q.v.*)

or the metre (*q.v.*) shall be the unit of measurement of length and the pound (*q.v.*) or the kilogramme (*q.v.*) shall be the unit of measurement of mass and fixes the relationship between the yard and the metre and the pound and the kilogramme (s. 1, Sch. 1 Pts. I, V). Limits of measurement and weights and measures lawful for use in trade are prescribed by s. 10, Schs. 1 and 3, which may be and have been amended by order (s. 10 (10)). Weighing or measuring equipment for use in trade must be passed as fit for use by an inspector of weights and measures and be stamped to that effect (ss. 11–17). Detailed provision is made in respect of transactions in particular goods by ss. 21–33 and Schs. 4–8. It is an offence to give short weight, etc. (s. 24). A warranty may be pleaded as a defence on a charge relating to quantity or pre-packing of goods (s. 25). Additional defences and safeguards for traders are contained in ss. 26–28, 33. Test purchases are authorised by s. 32. Inspectors of weights and measures are appointed by the local weights and measures authorities (ss. 41–46). The inspectors have powers of entry (s. 48) and obstruction of an inspector is an offence (s. 49).

The enforcement of the Trade Descriptions Act, 1968, is a function of every local weights and measures authority (ss. 26–31, 33).

See also the Local Government Act, 1974, s. 35, Sch. 6 para. 15, Sch. 8 (amending ss. 4 (2), 5 (3), 44 (1) of the Act of 1963).

The local weights and measures authority are an enforcement authority under the Consumer Credit Act, 1974, s. 161. See CONSUMER CREDIT.

A weights and measures inspector has implied licence to ask the occupier of a dwelling-house for permission to exercise his fuctions therein, but is a trespasser if he fails to do so (*Brunner v. Williams* (1975) 73 L.G.R. 266).

Before 1824 there was no uniform system of weights and measures. Sale by customary and local weights and measures was usual and legal. The Weights and Measures Act, 1824, s. 15, enacted that all contracts for the sale of goods should, unless the contrary was specified, relate to the standards of weights and measures established by that Act. The Act of 1824 was repealed by the Act of 1878, which for the first time made it impossible to sell except by standard weights and measures.

See ASSISA DE PONDERIBUS, ETC.; METRIC SYSTEM.

Weights of auncel. See AUNCEL WEIGHT.

Weir. See WEAR.

Weiring, warping (*q.v.*).

Well. Power to make by-laws as to wells is contained in the Public Health Act, 1936, s. 61 (as amended by the Public Health Act, 1961, ss. 4, 11, Sch. 1 Pt. III, Sch. 5 Pt. I). Power to deal with insanitary wells is contained in the Act of 1936, s. 141. As to London, see the London Government Act, 1963, s. 40.

Welsh Church. The Church of England, in so far as it existed in Wales (including Monmouthshire), was, as from March 31, 1920, disestablished by the Welsh Church (Temporalities) Act, 1919, s. 2. As to the dioceses affected, see BISHOPRICS. This disestablishment was provided for by the Welsh Church Act, 1914, the operation of which had been postponed by the Suspensory Act, 1914. Every ecclesiastical corporation in Wales became dissolved and the ecclesiastical law and the ecclesiastical courts ceased to operate in Wales (Welsh Church Act, 1914, ss. 2, 3).

The Church in Wales was deprived of its emoluments, but provision was made for the transfer to a representative body of churches, parsonages, certain of the endowments and also a sum of £1 million in respect of the commutation of existing interests of individuals: and the royal charter granted on April 15, 1919, pursuant to the Welsh Church Act, 1914, s. 13 (2), to hold land in mortmain. See also the Welsh Church (Amendment) Act, 1938. As to the right to grant marriage licences, see *Powell* v. *Church in Wales Representative Body* [1957] 1 W.L.R. 439. See WALES.

Welsh Development Agency. See the Welsh Development Agency Act, 1975.

Welsh mortgage, a conveyance of an estate redeemable at any time by the mortgagor on payment of the loan, the rents and profits of the estate being received in the meantime by the mortgagee, in satisfaction of interest, subject, however, to an account in Chancery, there being no covenant for the repayment of the loan, and the mortgagee being unable to compel either redemption or foreclosure. A Welsh mortgage differed from a *vivum vadium* or vifgage, which was a conveyance of property to the creditor and his heirs until out of the rents and profits of the estate he had satisfied the debt with interest; it was so called because neither debt nor estate was lost. The distinction between these securities was that in the vifgage the profits were applied in the periodical reduction of the debt, while in the Welsh mortgage they were applied in satisfaction of the interest, the principal remaining undiminished. In neither, however, was the estate ever forfeited (2 Br. & Had. Com. 299).

The Law of Property Act, 1925, s. 85, provides that a mortgage of an estate in fee simple is only capable of being effected at law either by a demise with a proviso for redemption or by a legal charge.

See LAND CHARGE; MORTGAGE.

Welsher, a person who receives money which has been deposited to abide the event of a race, and who has a predetermined intention to keep the money, and not to part with it in any event. As to whether, in an action of slander, the word is actionable without proof of special damage, see *Blackman* v. *Bryant* (1872) 27 L.T. 491; *Williams* v. *Magyer* (1883) *The Times*, March 1.

Wend, a certain quantity or circuit of land.

Wer, Were [*capitis aesimatio*], a pecuniary compensation for any injury; the value set on a man's life, varying with his rank, under the Anglo-Saxon laws. See WITE.

Werelada, a purging from the crime by the oaths of several persons according to the degree and quality of the accused.

Wergild, Weregild, Weregildum [Ang. Sax. *wer*, man; *geld*, satisfaction], the price of homicide or other enormous offences, paid partly to the Crown for the loss of a subject, partly to the lord whose vassal he was, and partly to the party injured or the next-of-kin of the party slain. This was the earliest award of damages in our law (4 Bl.Comm. 188).

West Indies. See the West Indies Acts, 1962 and 1967, the Anguilla Act, 1971, and the Immigration Act, 1971.

Westbury's (Lord) Act, the Land Registry Act, 1862. See LAND REGISTRIES.

Westminster, a city by express creation of Henry VIII. It was dissolved as a see and restored to the bishopric of London by Edward VI, and turned into a collegiate church, subject to a dean, by Elizabeth I.

The superior courts sat until 1822 in Westminster Hall itself, and after 1822 in courts opening into it—the Court of Chancery only upon the first day of certain sittings, after which it sat at Lincoln's Inn. The same course was observed under the Judicature Acts, 1873–75, by the Divisions representing the respective courts until the opening of the Royal Courts of Justice in 1883. See ROYAL COURTS OF JUSTICE.

It is provided by many Acts of Parliament, *e.g.*, by the repealed County Courts Act, 1850, s. 14, which gave an appeal from a county court, that certain jurisdiction shall be exercised by the courts " at Westminster." All such Acts are, by the Courts of Justice Building Act, 1865, s. 18, to be construed as if the Royal Courts of Justice had been referred to therein instead of the courts at Westminster.

Westminster Confession, a document containing a statement of religious doctrine drawn up at a conference of British and Continental Protestant divines at Westminster in 1643, which subsequently became the basis of the Scottish Presbyterian Church.

Westminster, Statute of, 1931. This Act confirmed and ratified certain declarations made by the delegates to the Imperial Conferences of 1926 and 1930, affecting Canada, Australia, New Zealand, South Africa, Ireland and Newfoundland. It provides that the Colonial Laws Validity Act, 1865, shall not apply to any law made by the Parliament of a Dominion (s. 2), gives power to the Parliament of a Dominion to legislate extraterritorially (s. 3), provides that the

Parliament of the United Kingdom shall not legislate for a Dominion except by consent (s. 4), and gives powers to the Parliament of a Dominion in relation to shipping (s. 5) and Courts of Admiralty (s. 6).

As to the right of appeal to the Privy Council, see *British Coal Corporation* v. *R.* [1935] A.C. 500; *Moore* v. *Att.-Gen. of Irish Free State* [1935] A.C. 484; *Att.-Gen. of Ontario* v. *Att.-Gen. of Canada* [1947] A.C. 127.

Westminster the First, Statute of, 1275, the name of the fifty-one chapters (each corresponding to what is now called an Act of Parliament) passed in 1275.

This statute, without extending the exemption of churchmen from civil jurisdiction, protected the property of the Church from the violence and spoliation of the king and the nobles; provided for freedom of popular elections, because sheriffs, coroners and conservators of the peace were still chosen by the freeholders in the county court, and attempts had been made to influence the election of knights of the shire, from the time when they were instituted; contained a declaration to enforce the enactment of Magna Carta, 1215, against excessive fines, which might operate as perpetual imprisonment; enumerated and corrected abuses of tenures, particularly as to marriage of wards; regulated the levying of tolls, which were imposed arbitrarily by the barons, and by cities and boroughs; corrected and restrained the power of the king's escheator and other officers; amended the criminal law; and dealt with procedure, civil and criminal (1 Campbell, *Lives of the Chancellors*, 167; 2 Reeves, c. 9, p. 107).

Westminster the Second, Statute of, 1285, the fifty chapters passed in 1285. The first of them is the statute *De Donis,* or *De Donis Conditionalibus* (2 Reeves, c. 10, p. 163). See TAIL.

Westminster the Third, Statute of, 1289, otherwise called the statute *Quia Emptores,* or *Quia Emptores Terrarum.* See QUIA EMPTORES.

Westmorland. The office of sheriff of this county was granted by King John to Robert de Veleripont and his heirs. Under this grant and various conveyances the office descended to Henry, Earl of

Thanet, who died in 1849 without issue. He purported to devise the office by will, but doubts arose as to whether it passed under this devise, or whether it passed to his heir, or whether it escheated to the Crown. The matter was settled by the statute 1850, 13 & 14 Vict. c. 30, which abolished all hereditary claim to the office and vested the appointment in the Crown as in other counties. The Sheriffs Act, 1887, s. 31, put the sheriffs of Westmorland in the same position as other sheriffs.

When the shrievalty was hereditary it descended to females as well as males. Anne, Countess of Pembroke, exercised the office in person, and, at the assizes at Appleby, sat with the judges on the bench (Co.Litt. 326n.).

West-Saxon-lage, the laws of the West Saxons. See DANELAGE.

Whales, like sturgeon, are royal fish, which when taken belong of right to the Crown; but the right to them may be vested in the lord of a manor or other subject by grant from the Crown, or by prescription (Williams, *Commons*, 292). See FISH ROYAL.

The whaling industry is regulated by the Whaling Industry (Regulation) Act, 1934 (as amended by the Sea Fish Industry Act, 1938). The Act prohibits the catching and treatment of whales within waters of the United Kingdom and provides for the licensing of whaling ships and whale-oil factories. As to ships registered in the independent countries of the Commonwealth see s. 17, as amended.

Wharf, a broad plain place, near some creek or haven, to lay goods and wares on that are brought to or from the water.

There are two kinds: legal wharves, which are certain wharves in all seaports appointed by commission from the Court of Exchequer, or legalised by Act of Parliament; and sufferance wharves, which are places where certain goods may be landed and shipped, by special sufferance granted by the Crown for that purpose. See SUFFERANCE WHARVES.

As to the implied warranty of fitness of a wharf for the unloading of a ship, see *The Moorcock* (1889) 14 P.D. 64.

See also the Harbours, Docks and Piers Clauses Act, 1847, s. 68, the Merchant Shipping Act, 1894, s. 492, and the Port of London (Consolidation) Act, 1920. Wharves may be approved under the Customs and Excise Act, 1952, s. 14; Finance Act, 1966, s. 10 (4), Sch. 13 Pt. II.

Wharfage, money paid for landing goods at a wharf, or for shipping and taking goods into a boat or barge thence (*London County Council* v. *General Steam Navigation Co.* (1907) 97 L.T. 863).

Wharfinger, the occupier of a wharf (Merchant Shipping Act, 1894, s. 492). The Port of London (Consolidation) Act, 1920, s. 2, defines a wharfinger as the occupier of a wharf, quay, warehouse or granary adjoining the Port of London mainly used for warehousing the goods, imported into the Port of London, of persons other than the occupier of such premises.

Wharfingers who transport goods of their customers by lighter from importing ships do not come under liability as common carriers (*Consolidated Tea Co.* v. *Oliver's Wharf* [1910] 2 K.B. 395).

As a rule, wharfingers have a general lien for the balance of their account.

Wharncliffe meeting, a meeting of the proprietors or members of a company held for the purpose of approving a Bill promoted by or conferring powers on the company, so called after the peer who was mainly responsible for the passing of the Standing Orders of the Houses of Parliament.

Wheat. The Agriculture Act, 1957, ss. 1–3, as amended by the Agriculture Act, 1967, s. 3; Agriculture Act, 1970, s. 11; European Communities Act, 1972, Sch. 3 Pt. II, secure to growers of wheat grown in the United Kingdom guaranteed prices and assured markets. See GUARANTEED PRICES.

Wheelage, duty or toll for carts, etc., passing over certain ground.

Whereas, a word which implies a recital of a fact. The word " whereas," when it renders the deed senseless or repugnant, may be struck out as impertinent, and will not vitate a deed in other respects sensible.

Whichwood Forest. As to the disafforesting of this, see the Whichwood Disafforesting Acts, 1853 and 1856.

Whig. This is said to be a word meaning sour milk. The name was applied in Scotland, in 1648, to those violent Covenanters who opposed the Duke of Hamilton's invasion of England in order to restore Charles I. Sir Walter Scott, however, gives a different derivation. Speaking of the rising of the Covenanters on this occasion, he says: " This insurrection was called the Whiggamores' Raid, from the word *whig, whig,* that is, *get on, get on,* which is used by the western peasants in driving their horses—a name destined to become the distinction of a powerful party in British history " (*Tales of a Grandfather,* c. 45).

The appellation of Whig and Tory to political factions was first heard of in 1679 (2 Hallam, Const.Hist., c. 12).

Whig and Tory differed mainly in this, that to a Tory the Constitution, inasmuch as it was the Constitution, was an ultimate point beyond which he never looked, and from which he thought it altogether impossible to swerve: whereas a Whig deemed all forms of government subordinate to the public good, and, therefore, liable to change when they should cease to promote their object. See TORY.

Whip. The whip (or, more fully, the whipper-in) of a pack of hounds is a man whose function it is to keep hounds from skirting, hunting rabbits, and doing other things which lessen the efficiency of the pack. Presents of cash to him at Christmas from members of the hunt are liable to income tax (*Wright* v. *Boyce* [1958] 1 W.L.R. 832).

The term is also applied to the members of Parliament who are detailed by the leaders of the various political parties for the duty of keeping other members of their party up to their work. They are paid the salaries prescribed by the Ministerial and other Salaries Act, 1975, s. 1, Schs. 1, 2.

See LORD TREASURER.

Whipping. This was a recognised part of the common law punishment for misdemeanours, and until the Whipping Act, 1820, it could be inflicted on women as well as on men. It was publicly inflicted, the misdemeanant sometimes being fastened to the tail of a moving cart. Under the Criminal Justice Administration Act, 1914, s. 36, no person could be whipped except under a statutory enactment. Such enactments were formally very numerous, more especially as regards boys under sixteen; as to the power of the justices to order whipping of a male child between seven and fourteen, see the Children and Young Persons Act, 1933, s. 60, Sch. III. Adult males might be whipped, *e.g.,* under the Criminal Law Amendment Act, 1912, when convicted on indictment under the Vagrancy Act, 1898, for the second time, or when convicted of certain offences against women under the Criminal Law Amendment Act, 1885, s. 2; and also for robbery with violence.

No offender could be whipped more than once for the same offence (Criminal Justice Administration Act, 1914, s. 36).

Whipping was abolished by the Criminal Justice Act, 1948, s. 1.

See CAT; CORIUM.

Whisky. See SPIRITS.

Whist drives. Whist drives for raising money to be applied for purposes other than private gain are legalised by the Gaming Act, 1968, s. 41. See GAMING.

Whit Monday was, by the Bank Holidays Acts, 1870 and 1875, made a bank holiday. These Acts were repealed by the Banking and Financial Dealings Act, 1971, which substituted the last Monday in May as a bank holiday (s. 1, Schs. 1, 2).

Whit Sunday, the seventh Sunday after Easter (*q.v.*). See FAST DAY; FEASTS.

White Book of London. This is printed under the title of the *Liber Albus* in No. 12 of the Rolls Series. It sets out the medieval customs and laws, including the maritime laws, of the City of London.

White fish. See FISHERY.

White Lyon Prison. See COURT OF CHIVALRY.

White meats, milk, eggs, butter and cheese and anything of which any of those things is an ingredient (Cowel).

The use of white meats during Lent was prohibited before the Reformation and up to 1643, when Henry VIII sanctioned it by proclamation. See PROCLAMATIONS, ROYAL.

White paper, an official memorandum issued by the government in which a problem and various considerations bearing on it are set out, and the policy which the government advocates, or is disposed to advocate, is stated.

White rents [Lat. *reditus albi*], payments received in silver or white money (2 Br. & Had.Com. 54). See ALBA FIRMA.

White rod. See USHER.

White slave traffic, traffic in prostitution. The protocol dated May 4, 1949, amends the international agreement for the suppression of the white slave traffic of 1904, and the international convention for the suppression of the white slave traffic of 1910. The Sexual Offences Act, 1956 prohibits the procuration and attempted procuration of young girls and women for purposes of prostitution, and strengthens the criminal law in relation to brothels, procurers and immoral trafficking in females.

White spur, a kind of esquire.

Whitecross Street Prison, a debtors' prison belonging to the sheriffs of London and Middlesex, to which the debtors, etc., confined in the Queen's Prison (*q.v.*) were removed in 1862. It ceased to be used after Holloway Prison was substituted in pursuance of the Queen's Prison Discontinuance Act, 1862, s. 12.

Whitefriars, a place in London between the Temple and Blackfriars, which was formerly a sanctuary, and therefore privileged from arrests. See ALSATIA; PRIVILEGED PLACES.

Whitehart silver, a mulct on certain lands in or near to the forest of Whitehart paid into the Exchequer, imposed by Henry III upon Thomas de la Linda, for killing a beautiful white hart which that king before had spared in hunting (Camd. Brit. 150).

Whitley councils, joint industrial councils formed to further co-operation between employers and employees.

Whitsuntide, the Feast of Pentecost, being the fiftieth day after Easter, and the first of the four cross-quarter days of the year.

Whitsuntide offerings were held assessable to income tax in *Slaney* v. *Starkey* [1931] 2 K.B. 148.

Whitsuntide farthings, pentecostals (*q.v.*).

Whittlewood Forest, As to disafforesting this forest, see the Whittlewood Disafforesting Act, 1853, and the Crown Lands Act, 1855.

Whole blood. A kinsman of the whole blood is he who is derived not only from the same ancestor, but from the same couple of ancestors. See BLOOD.

Wic, a place on the seashore or the bank of a river.

Wica, a country house or farm.

Wichencrif, witchcraft.

Widow, a woman whose husband is dead.

A widow is entitled equally with next of kin to administration of her deceased husband's estate subject to the discretion of the court (*In the Estate of Paine* (1916) 115 L.T. 935).

By the Administration of Estates Act, 1925, s. 46, as amended by the Intestates' Estates Act, 1952, the Family Provision Act, 1966, s. 1, and S.I. 1972 No. 916, a widow takes the whole of her deceased husband's estate if he dies intestate leaving no issue and no parent or brother or sister or issue of a brother or sister. If he leaves issue, the widow takes the personal chattels, £15,000 or such larger sum as may be fixed by the Lord Chancellor, free of death duties and costs with interest at 4 per cent. from the date of death, and a life interest in half the remainder of the estate. If he leaves no issue, but leaves a parent or a brother or sister or issue of a brother or sister, the widow takes the personal chattels, £40,000 free of death duties and costs with interest at 4 per cent. from the date of death, and a life interest in half the remainder of the estate.

Widow of the king. See KING'S WIDOW.

Widow-bench, the share of her husband's estate which a widow was allowed besides her jointure.

Widower, one whose wife is dead. A condition in restraint of the second marriage, whether of a man or a woman, is valid (*Allen* v. *Jackson* (1875) 1 Ch.D. 399).

Widow's benefit. See the Social Security Act, 1975, ss. 12, 24–26; Social Security Pensions Act, 1975.

Widow's chamber. Until the statute 1856, 19 & 20 Vict. c. 94, abolished all special customs as to the distribution of the estates of intestates, the widow of an intestate freeman of the City of London was entitled to the " widow's chamber," that is to say, her wearing apparel and the furniture of her bed-chamber (2 Bl. Comm. 518). See CUSTOM OF LONDON; LEGATORY.

Widow's quarantine. See QUARANTINE.

Wife [Sax. *wif*; Dut. *wiff*; Icel. *wyf*; Lat. *uxor*], a woman who has a husband. See HUSBAND AND WIFE.

Wife, Coercion of. At common law, there was a presumption that a wife who committed a crime in the presence of her husband acted under the coercion of her husband and was therefore not criminally responsible. This presumption never applied to specially heinous crimes, such as treason, murder or manslaughter, or to such crimes as keeping a brothel. It extended to some misdemeanours, such as the uttering of base coin. The presumption might in every case be rebutted; it did not arise where the husband was proved to have been physically incapable of coercion; and it did not apply where the wife committed a crime by the order of her husband but not in his presence.

The presumption was abolished by the Criminal Justice Act, 1925, s. 47, which provides, however, that on a charge against a wife for any offence other than treason or murder it shall be a good defence to prove that the offence was committed in the presence and under the coercion of the husband.

Wife's equity to a settlement. See EQUITY TO A SETTLEMENT.

Wife-swapping. See CONNIVANCE.

Wigreve, the overseer of a wood.

Wike, a farm (Co.Litt. 5a).

Wild animals. See ANIMALS FERAE NATURAE.

Wild birds. The Protection of Birds Act, 1954 (as amended by the Protection of Birds Act, 1954 (Amendment) Act, 1964, the Protection of Birds Act, 1967, the Nature Conservancy Act, 1973, Sch 1 and the Protection of Birds (Amendment) Act, 1976), makes it an offence to kill or take wild birds or take their nests or eggs except as provided in the Act. The Act replaces the Wild Birds Protection Acts, 1880 to 1908. See HAWKS; SAND GROUSE; SWANS.

Wildes. In the statute 1662, 14 Car. 2, c. 6, s. 17, which relates to highways, " wildes " is a misprint for " wealds."

Wild's Case, Rule in. The rule in *Wild's Case* (1599) 6 Co.Rep. 17, was as follows: where there was a devise to a person and his children, then, if there were children actually born at the time when the will was made, the parent and the children took a fee simple concurrently as joint tenants, unless there were words in the context to show that the children were not intended to take immediately; if there were such words, then, according to such intention as was disclosed, the parent either took an estate tail or else the parent took for life and the children took in succession to him as purchasers: if there were no children born at the date of the will, then the parent took an estate tail unless the context showed that he was to take for life and that unborn children were to take in succession to him as purchasers.

The rule did not apply to personalty (*Audsley* v. *Horn* (1858) 26 Beav. 195).

The Law of Property Act, 1925, s. 130, requires strict words of limitation for the creation of an entailed interest. See ENTAIL; TAIL.

Wilful, intentional or deliberate. Thus if a person accidentally strikes another, this is a battery giving rise to a right of action for damages, while, if he does it intentionally it is a wilful battery, for which the party injured may have an action of damages or a criminal prosecution. See BATTERY.

Similarly a wilful default is an act of omission done with intention (*Re Wood and Lewis's Contract* [1898] 1 Ch. 433). Mortgagees and other persons holding securities are liable for losses caused by their wilful default; hence if a mortgagee of land in possession does not avail himself of an opportunity of letting the land beneficially, he is bound to give credit for what he has thus lost by his wilful default. See MORTGAGE; NEGLIGENCE.

Will, a disposition or declaration by which the person making it (who is called the testator) provides for the distribution or administration of property after his death. It does not take effect until the testator's death (Wills Act, 1837, s. 24), and is always revocable by him. See NOMINATION.

Formerly " will " signified a testamentary disposition of land, as opposed to a testament (*q.v.*) but this distinction is obsolete. The rule was that *ultima voluntas in scriptis* was used where lands or tenements were devised, and *testamentum* when it concerned the chattels (Co.Litt. 111a).

The word " will " extends to a testament, and to a codicil, and to an appointment by will or by writing in the nature of a will in exercise of a power, and to a disposition by will and testament or devise of the custody and tuition of any child, by virtue of the statute 1660, 12 Car. c. 24, and to any other testamentary disposition (Wills Act, 1837, s. 1).

In the strict sense of the word, a will includes all testamentary dispositions by the testator in force at the time of his death; but in practice " will " signifies a testamentary document which is in form complete in itself, while additional or supplementary dispositions are called codicils. See CODICIL; TESTAMENTARY.

The Judicature Act, 1925, s. 172, replacing the Court of Probate Act, 1857, s. 91, provides that there shall, under the control and direction of the High Court, be provided safe and convenient depositories for the custody of the wills of living persons, and any person may deposit his will therein. The Administration of Justice Act, 1928, s. 11, makes provision as to the deposit of wills under the control of the High Court.

The right of testamentary alienation of lands is a matter depending on Acts of Parliament. Before the Statute of Wills, 1540, a will could not be made of land, and before the Statute of Frauds, 1677, a will could be made by word of mouth. Moreover, the testamentary power conferred by the Statute of Wills, 1540, did not extend to infants or married women. The Statute of Frauds, 1677, required wills of land to be in writing signed by three witnesses, and required nuncupative wills, where the estate bequeathed exceeded £30, to be proved by three witnesses, and to have been made at the time of the last sickness of the deceased, and in his dwelling-house or where he had resided ten days before, and provided that after six months no nuncupative will should be proved, unless the words or their substance had been committed to writing within six days, and that no probate should be granted till after fourteen days from the death of the testator. These enactments were repealed by the Wills Act, 1837.

No will made by any person under the age of eighteen years is valid (Wills Act, 1837, s. 7; Family Law Reform Act, 1969, s. 3 (1)); by the old law, an infant of the age of fourteen years if a male, or of twelve years if a female, could make a valid will of personalty, although not of realty.

Infants (except members of the forces on active service (Wills (Soldiers and Sailors) Act, 1918; Navy and Marines (Wills) Act, 1953; Family Law Reform Act, 1969, s. 3 (1)) and mental patients are wholly incapable of making wills while their disability lasts but the Court of Protection may make a will for a mental patient (Mental Health Act, 1959, ss. 103 (1) (*dd*), 103A; Administration of Justice Act, 1969, ss. 17, 18). All other persons have complete testamentary capacity. A person may also have a power of appointment by will over property not belonging to him (see POWER; TESTABLE). The court will grant probate of any instrument of a testamentary character if duly executed, leaving the question whether it is a valid exercise of the power to be decided by the proper tribunal, so that a testamentary document purporting to be made in execution of a power may be proved as a will and yet be invalid because it has not complied with the power. By the Wills Act, 1837, s. 10, every will executed in accordance with its provisions is declared to be, so far as respects the execution and attestation thereof, a valid execution of a power of appointment by will, although the power may have expressly required that a will made in exercise of it should be executed with some additional or other form of execution or solemnity. See APPOINTMENT, POWER OF; EXECUTE; POWER OF APPOINTMENT.

A person having testamentary capacity may dispose by will of all real and personal estate which he may be entitled to, either at law or in equity, at the time of his death, and which, if not so disposed of, would devolve upon his executor or administrator, including interests *pur auter vie,* and all contingent, executory and future interests in property, and all rights of entry (Wills Act, 1837, s. 3; Law of Property Act, 1925, s. 178). See OCCUPANCY; RIGHT OF ENTRY.

A will may be joint, or joint and mutual, and the wills of two or more persons may be mutual but not joint. A will is joint when two persons by the one instrument dispose of the things over which they respectively have testamentary power; a will is joint and mutual when made jointly by two persons each of whom takes benefits under the will of the other; and wills are mutual but not joint when each makes a separate will under which the other takes benefits. A joint will is the will of each testator, and will be admitted to probate as soon as he dies. Each maker of a mere joint will can at any time before his death revoke it in so far as it relates to what he personally can dispose of; a joint and mutual will or mutual wills can be revoked by either party during the lifetime of the other, but a joint and mutual will, or a mutual will, cannot be revoked by a survivor who takes benefits under the will of the testator who first died, and the survivor is in equity a trustee for the personal representatives of the deceased testator as regards whatever the deceased was to have taken under the will as it stood when the first of the testators died.

No particular form of words is required to make a valid will so long as the testator's intention can be ascertained; otherwise its provisions will fail from uncertainty (*q.v.*).

A will must in ordinary cases be in writing, and signed at the foot or end by the testator, or by someone in his presence and by his direction, and the signature must be made or acknowledged by the testator in the presence of two or more witnesses, who must be present together at the same time, and must attest and subscribe the will in the presence of the testator (Wills Act, 1837, s. 9; Wills Act Amendment Act, 1852). See ATTESTATION CLAUSE.

A devise or bequest to an attesting witness, or to his or her wife or husband, does not affect the validity of the will, but the gift is void (Wills Act, 1837, s. 15) unless the will is one made under the Wills Act, 1837, s. 11, and requiring no attestation (*Re Limond* [1915] 2 Ch. 240), that is to say, a will made by a soldier in actual military service, or by a mariner or seaman at sea, or by a member of the naval or marine forces in such circumstances that if he were a soldier he would be in actual military service (Wills (Soldiers and Sailors) Act, 1918; Navy and Marines (Wills) Act, 1953; Family Law Reform Act, 1969, s. 3 (1)). Such a soldier's or sailor's will could dispose only of personalty under the Act of 1837, s. 11, but under the Act of 1918, s. 3 (1), it can dispose of realty as well as of personalty. Such a will may be in the form of a letter or of anything else, provided it shows the intention of the testator. A gift to an attesting witness or his or her spouse is saved if the will is also attested by two independent witnesses (Wills Act, 1968).

A nuncupative will (*q.v.*) is when the testator without any writing declares his will before a sufficient number of witnesses. Before the Statute of Frauds, 1677, such wills were as valid for disposing of personalty as written wills; but by that statute they were laid under several restrictions, except when made by soldiers in actual service, or seamen or mariners at sea. By the Wills Act, 1837, nuncupative wills are altogether rendered invalid, except those made by soldiers or seamen in accordance with the old law. The Wills (Soldiers and Sailors) Act, 1918, s. 1, applies to nuncupative wills as well as to other wills under the Wills Act, 1837, s. 11, and the Act of 1918, s. 3 (1), makes realty devisable by any nuncupative will valid as regards personalty. As to the right of the non-commissioned ranks of the navy and marines to make nuncupative or other informal wills. See the Navy and Marines (Wills) Act, 1953.

If property is charged with payment of debts, and a creditor, or the wife or husband of a creditor whose debt is so charged, attests the execution of the will, such creditor may be admitted a witness to prove the execution of the will (s. 16).

An executor is not an incompetent witness (s. 17).

By the Law of Property Act, 1925, s. 177, if the will was made in contemplation of a particular marriage it will not be revoked by that marriage (*Sallis v. Jones* [1936] P. 43); otherwise the will is revoked unless it is a will made in exercise of a power of appointment when the estate thereby appointed would not, in default of appointment, pass to the executor or administrator, or persons entitled on intestacy (Wills Act, 1837, s. 18). No will is revoked by presumption of an intention on the ground of alteration in circumstances (s. 19). No will or codicil is revoked otherwise than as aforesaid, or by another will or codicil, or by the burning, tearing, or otherwise destroying the same by the testator, or by some person in his presence and by his direction, with the intention of revoking it (s. 20). No conveyance or other act made or done subsequently to the execution of a will, except an act by which the will is revoked, prevents the operation of the will with respect to such estate or interest in property as the testator has power to dispose of by will at the time of his death (s. 23).

No obliteration, interlineation or other alteration made after execution is valid except so far as the words or effect of the will before such alteration are not apparent, unless the alteration is executed as is required for the execution of the will. But the alteration is deemed to be duly executed if the signatures to the alteration of the testator and the witnesses are made in some part of the will (s. 21).

As a rule if the testator and each of his witnesses respectively signs his initials in the margin against or near each alteration or interlineation, it will be accepted for probate (*In b. Blewitt* (1880) 5 P.D. 116).

By the Law of Property Act, 1925, s. 175, contingent, specific or residuary devises of real or personal property carry the income; see also the Trustee Act, 1925, s. 31.

The Law of Property Act, 1925, s. 179, enables testators to incorporate the statutory will forms in their wills (Statutory Will Forms, 1925).

The Wills Act, 1837, s. 22, makes provision as to the revival of a revoked will. See REPUBLICATION.

A will is to be treated as properly executed if its execution conformed to the internal law in force in the territory where it was executed or in the territory where, at the time of its execution or of the testator's death, he was domiciled or had his habitual residence, or in a state of which, at either of those times, he was a national (Wills Act, 1963, s. 1). Additional rules validate a will executed on board a vessel or aircraft, a will of immovable property, the revocation of a will or part of a will and the exercise of a power of appointment (s. 2). A requirement of a foreign law that testators of a particular description are to observe special formalities or that attesting witnesses are to have certain qualifications, is to be treated as a matter of form notwithstanding any rule of that law to the contrary (s. 3). The construction of a will is not to be altered by reason of any change in the testator's domicile after the execution of the will (s. 4). Where there is more than one system of law in a country the appropriate system is to be chosen (s. 6). The Act came into operation on January 1, 1964. It does not apply to the will of a testator who died before that date (as to which see the Wills Act, 1861) but it applies to the will of a testator who died on or after that date whenever the will was executed (Act of 1963, s. 7).

A will is construed, with reference to the property comprised in it, to speak and take effect as if it had been executed immediately before the death of the testator, unless a contrary intention appears (*Re Chapman* [1905] A.C. 106; *Re Hewitt* [1926] Ch. 740). The effect of this is that if a legatee dies before the testator, the representatives of the legatee take nothing, the legacy lapsing for the benefit of the residuary legatee or next-of-kin. The Wills Act, 1837, s. 33, makes an exception from this rule of lapse in the case of legacies to children or other issue of the testator who may have died leaving issue living at the testator's death: in such a case the legacy takes effect as if the death of the legatee had taken place immediately after the testator's death. *Re Basioli* [1953] Ch. 367. As to legitimated children, see the Family Law Reform Act, 1969, s. 16; Legitimacy Act, 1976, ss. 5, 11, Sch. 2.

By the Law of Property Act, 1925, s. 176, a tenant in tail in possession may bar the entail by disposing of the entailed property by will, by a devise or bequest referring specifically either to the property or the instrument under which it was created or acquired, or to entailed property generally. If not so disposed of, the property does not become subject to his debts and liabilities. This does not apply to a tenant in tail after possibility of issue extinct or to a tenant in tail who is restrained by statute from barring or defeating the entail.

The Wills Act, 1837, s. 25, includes lapsed and void devises in a residuary devise. A devise of lands includes leaseholds as well as freeholds (s. 26). Words importing failure of issue mean issue living at the testator's death (s. 29).

A devise or bequest in general terms of real or personal property includes property subject to a general power unless a contrary intention appears (s. 27). Under the old law it was necessary that such a devise or bequest should refer either to the power or to the specific property which was the subject of it, in order that it might have that effect, and this is still the rule where the testator has only a special, as distinguished from a general, power of appointment.

Where any real estate is devised to a person without any words of limitation, the devise passes the fee simple or other the whole estate or interest which the testator had power to dispose of by will unless a contrary intention appears (s. 29).

Wills are not required to be in any particular form, but a well-drawn will usually contains the following clauses (or as many of them as may be required) in the following order: commencement (" This is the last will of me, A B, etc."); revocation of former wills; appointment of executors and guardians; specific legacies; general legacies; annuities; specific devises; residuary gift; clauses relating to property settled or given in trust; devise and bequest of trust and mortgage estates; testimonium. See SETTLEMENT; TRUST.

As soon as possible after the testator's death it is the duty of the executor to prove his will, either in common or in solemn form. (See PROBATE.) If there is no executor, letters of administration with the will annexed are granted. (See LETTERS OF ADMINISTRATION.) Before the probate is obtained, an executor may act as effectually in almost everything as if probate had been granted, and when granted it has relation back to the death of the testator. In the case of an administrator, on the other hand, acts done before the grant of administration are, as a general rule, not binding. Both rules are subject to exceptions.

Forgery of a will is punishable with imprisonment for life (Forgery Act, 1913, s. 2 (1)).

See ALIENATION; DEVISE; ESTABLISHMENT, ETC.; EXECUTION OF WILLS; HOLOGRAPH; LAPSE; LEGACY; MARRIED WOMEN'S PROPERTY; PROBATE; RESIDUE; WILD'S CASE, ETC.

Will, Tenancy at. This interest entitles the grantee to possession of land during the pleasure of both the grantor and himself, yet it creates no sure or durable right, and is bounded by no definite limits as to duration. It must be at the reciprocal will of both parties expressly or by implication and the dissent of either determines it (Co.Litt. 55a).

The grantee cannot transfer the interest to another, although after he has entered into possession he may accept a release of the inheritance from the grantor, for there exists a privity between them. It must end at the death of either party, for death deprives a person of the power of having any will. If a lessee for years accepts a tenancy at will in the property leased, his term of years surrendered.

A tenancy at will is created either by agreement of the parties or by construction of law.

A tenancy at will does not fall within the provisions of Pt. II of the Landlord and Tenant Act, 1954, whether it be created by operation of law or express agreement (*Hagee (London)* v. *A. B. Erikson and Larson* [1976] Q.B. 209).

WILL

The Law of Property Act, 1925, s. 54, enacts that a lease by parol for a longer term than three years shall have the force and effect of a tenancy at will only.

The grantee is entitled to emblements where his interest is determined by the grantor or by his death, and his personal representatives are entitled to them where the interest is determined by his own death; but if the grantee forfeits or determines the interest himself he is not entitled to them. He is not bound to maintain or repair the premises, but is liable for wilful waste.

The lessor can determine the interest by an express declaration that the grantee shall hold no longer; this should be made on the land or notice of it should be served on the grantee. But if he exercises any right of ownership, unless it is with the grantee's consent, inconsistent with the enjoyment of the interest, as entering upon the land, cutting down trees, or making a transfer or lease for years to commence immediately, the interest will be determined. So also if the grantee commits an act of desertion or does anything inconsistent with his interest, as assigning it to another person to the grantor's knowledge, or committing waste, but a verbal declaration that he will hold the land no longer does not determine the interest unless he at the same time waives possession.

If the grantor determine the interest, the grantee is entitled to ingress and egress to take away his goods and chattels without being a trespasser (Co.Litt. 56a).

A mere demand for possession by the grantor determines the interest (*Doe* d. *Nicholl* v. *M'Kaeg* (1830) 10 B. & C. 721).

See TENANT AT WILL.

William I, Laws of. William the Conqueror made but few changes in the national laws. He renewed the laws of Edward the Confessor with certain additions made by himself. Normans and English were in theory equal before the law, but the distinction of personal law was, for some purposes, allowed. The Normans were accustomed to the wager of battle (*q.v.*), the English to the ordeal and compurgation (*q.v.*). William allowed the men of each race to be tried by the customs of their own country.

He abolished the punishment of death and substituted for it that of mutilation. The forest laws which he introduced were marked by extraordinary harshness. He separated the ecclesiastical from the civil jurisdiction of the courts of law.

Wilmot's (Sir Eardley) Act, the Grammar Schools Act, 1840.

Win. In a covenant in a mining lease, to "win" a mineral means to put the ore in such a state that working can go on in the ordinary way.

It is doubtful whether it is necessary, in order to constitute the offence under the Gaming Act, 1845, s. 17, of "winning" money by cheating at play, that the person who has been cheated should actually pay over what he has lost.

Winchester Domesday. See WINTON DOMESDAY.

Winchester measure, measure according to the standards kept at Winchester until the statute 1835, 5 & 6 Will. 4, c. 63.

Winchester, Statute of, the statute 1285, 13 Edw. 1, which dealt with the preservation of the peace. See ARTICULI INQUISITIONES SUPER STATUTUM WINTONIAE; WYNTON, STATUTE OF.

Windas, or Windlass. See WANLASS.

Windfalls. In the law, this term is understood as meaning only trees blown down by the wind, though ordinarily it includes fruit, etc. See ADJOINING OWNERS.

Windfalls of timber (*q.v.*) belong, as between landlord and tenant, to the landlord if they are sound and to the tenant if they are dead (*Herlakender's Case* (1589) 4 Co.Rep. 92), and, in the case of settled land, windfalls of dead timber go to the tenant for life, while the proceeds of the sale of sound windfalls are treated as capital moneys (*Re Harrison's Trusts* (1885) 28 Ch.D. 220).

Winding up. As applied to a partnership or company, this is the operation of stopping the business, realising the assets and discharging the liabilities of the concern, settling any questions of account or contribution between the members, and dividing the surplus assets (if any) among the members. The term "winding up" is sometimes applied to the estates of deceased persons, but "administration" (*q.v.*) is the usual expression.

The winding up of a partnership is either voluntary (*i.e.*, by agreement between the partners) or by order of the court made in an action for the dissolution of the partnership. See DISSOLUTION.

The winding up of companies before the Companies Act, 1862, was effected under the Winding Up Acts, 1848 and 1849, and the Joint Stock Companies Acts, 1856 and 1858, which provided a machinery partly in Chancery, and partly in bankruptcy; after the Companies Act, 1862, all companies, except railway companies incorporated by Act of Parliament, were wound up under the Companies Act, 1862, in one of the three modes in which companies are now wound up under the Companies Act, 1948, *i.e.*, compulsory winding up by the court; voluntary winding up without the intervention of the court; and voluntary winding up under the supervision of the court.

The property of a company is collected and distributed first in discharge of its liabilities, and secondly, among its members according to their respective rights with a view to its dissolution. If the assets are not sufficient to meet the liabilities, a company is usually wound up by the court. In other cases the winding up is usually voluntary and conducted by the company itself either with or without the supervision of the court. The provisions of the Companies Act, 1948, govern a winding up in any of these three modes (s. 211). In any winding up the members who may be called upon to contribute are ascertained and their liability determined under ss. 212–217. (See CONTRIBUTORY.) Debts and claims of all kinds require to be proved and if not of certain value to be estimated justly (s. 316).

If the company is insolvent, the rights of secured or unsecured creditors, the admissibility of debts and claims, and the valuation of annuities and future or contingent liabilities are regulated according to the law of bankruptcy (s. 317). The Act provides for preferential payments and (if the company is registered in England) postpones the claims of debenture holders under any floating charge created by the company, but only so far as the assets are insufficient to meet the claims of the general creditors (s. 319).

Transactions which would be avoided against an individual in his bankruptcy as a fraudulent preference under the Bankruptcy Act, 1914, s. 44 (see FRAUDULENT PREFERENCE), are avoided, the commencement of the winding up being deemed to correspond with the presentation of a bankruptcy petition (s. 310); as to the date of commencement of a winding up by the court, see s. 229, and of a voluntary winding up, see s. 280. Floating charges created within twelve months of the commencement of the winding up are avoided unless the company was solvent immediately after the creation of the charge (s. 322). Onerous property may be disclaimed and rights under process of execution or attachment of creditors are restricted (ss. 323–327). Any company in liquidation must state on every invoice or order or business letter in which the name of the company appears that the company is being wound up (s. 338).

Winding up by the court may take place in pursuance of a special resolution of the company requiring it; or if default is made in delivering the statutory report to the registrar or in holding the statutory meeting; or on non-commencement of business within one year from incorporation; or on suspension of business for a year; or on reduction of members to less in number than seven, or, in a private company, below two; or on the company being unable to pay its debts; or whenever the court is of opinion that it is just and equitable that the company should be wound up (s. 222).

As from the commencement of the winding up by the court (s. 229), any disposition by the company of its property and any transfer of shares or alteration of the status of its members is void unless the court otherwise orders (s. 227); and every attachment, sequestration, distress or execution if made after commencement is void (s. 228); no action or proceeding may be proceeded with or commenced against the company except by leave of the court (s. 231); the liquidator or provisional liquidator takes the company's property into his custody or under his control.

Voluntary winding up may take place when the time for the duration of the company under the articles has expired and there has been a resolution of the company in a general meeting for a voluntary winding up; or when a special resolution has been passed to the same effect; or when an extraordinary resolution has been passed to the effect that the company cannot by reason of its liabilities continue its business and that it is advisable to wind up. Thereupon the business of the company ceases except for the purposes of a beneficial winding up, but the corporate state and powers of the company continue until it is dissolved (s. 281).

A member's voluntary winding up takes place where the directors or a majority of them have made a statutory declaration that the company will be able to pay its debts in full within twelve months from the commencement of the winding up (ss. 283–291); in the absence of this declaration the winding up is referred to as a creditors' voluntary winding up (ss. 283, 292–300).

Winding up subject to the supervision of the court takes place upon petition at any time after a company has passed a resolution for voluntary winding up. The petition gives the court jurisdiction over actions (ss. 312, 313). An order for winding up subject to the supervision of the court is deemed to be an order for winding up by the court with certain exceptions (s. 315, Sch. 11).

See ADMINISTRATION; BANKRUPTCY; CLAIM; CONTRIBUTORY; DIRECTOR; DISSOLUTION; LIQUIDATOR.

Window. See LIGHT.

Window box. Insecure window boxes are dealt with by the Town Police Clauses Act, 1847, s. 28. See also the Metropolitan Paving Act, 1817, s. 65, and the London Building Acts (Amendment) Act, 1939, s. 149 (*p.*).

Window cleaning. In urban districts, by the Public Health Act, 1875, s. 171, incorporating the Town Police Clauses Act, 1847, s. 28, as amended by the Criminal Justice Act, 1967, s. 92 (1), Sch. 3, an occupier of a house or other building or other person who orders or permits any person in his service to stand on the sill of any window in order to clean, paint, or perform any other operation on the outside of such window, or upon any house or any other building, unless such window is in the sunk or basement storey is, if the offence takes place in a street and to the obstruction, annoyance, or danger of the residents, liable to a fine up to £20 or to imprisonment for fourteen days, and a constable in whose view the offence is committed may take the offender into custody without warrant. As to the liability of occupiers and employers to window-cleaners sustaining injury, see *General Cleaning Contractors* v. *Christmas* [1953] A.C. 180; *Bates* v. *Parker* [1953] 2 Q.B. 231; *Drummond* v. *British Building Cleaners* [1954] 1 W.L.R. 1434; *Wilson* v. *Tyneside Window Cleaning Co.* [1958] 2 Q.B. 110.

Window tax, a tax first imposed by the statute 1695, 7 & 8 Will. 3, c. 18. It was levied upon the occupants of houses with more than a certain number of windows and increased as the number of windows in the house rose. It was continued under a number of statutes, the last of which was the statute 1808, 48 Geo. 3, c. 55, which was repealed by the House Duty Act, 1851, which substituted inhabited house duty (*q.v.*) for the window tax.

Windsor. See HERALD.

Windsor Forest, a royal forest covering an area of about 60,000 acres in the vicinity of Windsor Castle. It was founded by Henry VIII. It was disafforested by the statute 1812, 52 Geo. 3, c. 71; see also the statute 1815, 55 Geo. 3, c. 122.

Windsor, Knights of, retired military officers who have apartments and pensions at Windsor Castle. Some of them are in fact knights, but not in their capacity of Knights of Windsor, who, as such, are not knighted. From 1797 to 1892 there were also Naval Knights of Windsor (Naval Knights of Windsor (Dissolution) Act, 1892).

Wine. Adulteration of wine is dealt with under the Food and Drugs Act, 1955. (See ADULTERATION.) Formerly it was punishable under special Acts such as the statute 1660, 12 Car. 2, c. 25. The prices of various wines were regulated by various statutes. Thus, for instance, the statutes 1536, Hen. 8, c. 14, s. 2, and 1660, 12 Car. 2, c. 25, s. 13, empowered the Lord Chancellor etc., to fix prices, and the statute 1660, 12 Car. 2, 25, s. 12, enacted that Spanish wines were not to be sold at more than eighteenpence a quart, nor French wine at more than eightpence per quart, unless a higher price had been fixed.

As to misdescription of port wine and Madeira, see the Anglo-Portuguese Commercial Treaty Acts, 1914 and 1916.

As to the importation of wine, see the Customs and Excise Act, 1952, ss. 143–145. See CHAMPAGNE; PORT WINE.

Wine licences. See INTOXICATING LIQUORS.

Winter circuit. Originally this was an occasional circuit appointed for the trial of prisoners, and in some cases of civil causes, between Michaelmas and Hilary sittings (Winter Assize Act, 1876), but later the circuit held in spring was termed the winter circuit. See CIRCUIT.

Winter heyning, a season extending from November 11 to May 23 during which, in some of the royal forests, the commoners were deprived of rights of pasture in order that there might be sufficient feeding for the deer.

Winton Domesday [*Liber Wintoniae*], an account or survey of the city of Winchester made by order of Henry I.

Wireless telegraphy. The Wireless Telegraphy Act, 1949, replacing the Wireless Telegraphy Acts, 1904 to 1926, prohibits the establishment or use of any station for wireless telegraphy or the installation or use of any apparatus for wireless telegraphy except under the authority of a licence in that behalf. To constitute the offence of using wireless telegraphy apparatus to obtain information as to the contents of a message without appropriate authority contrary to s. 5 (*b*) (i) of the Act of 1949, no intent need be shown other than the intent to do the prohibited act (*Paul* v. *Ministry of Posts and Telecommunications* [1973] R.T.R. 245). A licence may be granted free to a blind person (Wireless Telegraphy (Blind Persons) Act, 1955). See also the Wireless Telegraphy Act, 1967.

Radio installations are required on seagoing ships (Merchant Shipping (Safety Convention) Act, 1949, ss. 3, 5, 6;

Merchant Shipping Act, 1970, s. 85, Sch. 1). See S.I. 1974 No. 1908.

See BROADCASTING; TELECOMMUNICATIONS; TELEGRAPHS; TELEPHONES; TELEVISION.

Wisby (or Wisbuy, or Visby), Laws of. These are the Water-Recht, or sea-law, of the Hanse town of Wisby in the island of Gotland. They contain the maritime mercantile code which, as a Copenhagen copy (dating from the fifteenth century) puts it, the skippers and merchants had resolved unto themselves as sea-law. These Laws of Wisby appear to have been based partly upon a code drawn up at Lubeck, of which a copy dated 1240 still exists, partly upon the Laws of Oleron (*q.v.*), and partly upon the maritime ordinances of Amsterdam, the latter being the medieval sea-code of those trading out of Amsterdam; and they formed the mercantile sea law of the Baltic. They, like the Laws of Oleron, the *Consolato del Mare* (*q.v.*) and other similar compilations, were cited as authorities by the English courts so late as 1759. These compilations, like the rest of the law merchant (*q.v.*), consisted of working rules drawn up by practical men of business, and the courts accepted these rules as law.

The Laws of Wisby are known in England chiefly through an abbreviated and somewhat inaccurate French version contained in Cleirac's *Us et Coustumes de la Mer*, published in 1647. A translation of a portion of the Laws of Wisby and of a portion of the Laws of Oleron is given in Malynes' *Lex Mercatoria*, 1686, and Justice's *Sea Laws*, 1705. See 3 Hallam, *Middle Ages* 334.

See HANSEATIC LAWS, ETC.

Wista, half a hide of land, or sixty acres.

Wit; Wite; Wyte. In Anglo-Saxon times this meant a penalty for murder or other serious offence against the person. See BLODWYTE; WITE.

Wit, To [Lat. *scilicet, videlicet, viz.*], to know, that is to say, namely.

Witam, the purgation from an offence by the oath of the requisite number of witnesses.

Witchcraft, conjuration (*q.v.*); sorcery. The Witchcraft Act, 1735, provided that no prosecution might be carried on against any person for witchcraft, sorcery, enchantment, or conjuration, or for charging another with any such offence, but that any person pretending to use any kind of witchcraft, etc., should be liable upon conviction on indictment to one year's imprisonment, and might be required to give sureties for good behaviour (*R.* v. *Stephenson* (1904) 68 J.P. 524). Offenders were deemed rogues and vagabonds under the Vagrancy Act, 1824, s. 4.

Prior to the Witchcraft Act, 1735, witchcraft was a capital offence: see the statute 1603, 1 & 2 Jac. 1, c. 12. A woman and her daughter aged nine years were hanged at Huntingdon for selling their souls to Satan as recently as 1716, this being the last execution in England for witchcraft. Pope Alexander VI nominated a commission against witchcraft in 1494; five hundred persons were burnt as witches in Geneva in 1515; Sir Matthew Hale condemned the Suffolk witches to be burnt in 1664 (6 *State Trials* 647); and a woman was burnt in Scotland in 1722, nine having been burnt after their own confessions in 1678.

Spiritualists could be dealt with under the Witchcraft Act, 1735, and the Vagrancy Act, 1824, s. 4 (*R.* v. *Duncan* [1944] K.B. 713). The Witchcraft Act, 1735, was repealed and the Vagrancy Act, 1824, s. 4, was amended by the Fraudulent Mediums Act, 1951. See SPIRITUAL-ISM.

Wite [Sax.], a punishment, pain, penalty, mulct, or criminal fine.

The *wite* was a penalty paid to the Crown by a murderer. The *were* was the fine a murderer had to pay to the family or relatives of the deceased, and the *wite* was the fine paid to the magistrate who presided over the district where the murder was perpetrated. Thus, the *wite* was the satisfaction to be rendered to the community for the public wrong which had been committed, as the *were* was to the family for their private injury (Bosworth, Anglo-Saxon Dict.).

Witekden, a taxation of the West Saxons.

Witena-gemot, or **Wittena-gemote** [Sax. *witta,* a wise man; *gemot,* a synod or council], the great council by which an Anglo-Saxon king was guided in all the main acts of government. It was composed of prelates and abbots, of the aldermen of shires, and of the noble and wise men of the kingdom. Whether the lesser thanes were entitled to a place is not certain (2 Hallam, *Middle Ages,* c. 8, pt. 1). See GREAT COUNCIL.

Witens, the chiefs of the Saxon lords or thanes, the nobles and wise men.

With costs. Judgment for a party " with costs " means that the judgment includes the right to recover his taxed costs from his opponent.

With profits policy, a policy of insurance under which bonuses from the insurance company's profits are allocated to the policy and increase its value, the premium being higher for such a policy than the premium for a " without profits " policy.

Withdrawal. A party who has entered an appearance in an action in the High Court may withdraw the appearance at any time with leave of the Court (R.S.C., Ord. 21, r. 1). See DISCONTINUANCE.

Withdrawal of a juror. At the trial of an action, when neither party feels sufficient confidence to render him anxious to persevere till verdict, or when the judge recommends that the action should not proceed further, the parties may by consent, for it cannot be done otherwise, withdraw a juror; and as that leaves the jury incomplete, there can be no verdict, and the trial comes to an end. The withdrawal of a juror in this way puts an end to the cause unless the withdrawal is upon terms which are not carried out; and if the action is afterwards proceeded with, an application may be made to the court or a judge to stay the proceedings (*Thomas* v. *Exeter Co.* (1887) 18 Q.B.D. 822). See DISCHARGE.

The court may, in certain cases, order a juror to withdraw (Juries Act, 1974, s. 11 (6)).

Withernam [Sax. *wieder,* other; *naam,* a taking], a taking again, reprisal. See AVERIIS CAPTIS IN WITHERNAM; CAPIAS; CAPIAS IN WITHERNAM.

Withersake, an apostate, or perfidious renegade.

Without day. Formerly, when a defendant in an action succeeded on a plea, the judgment in certain cases was that he should " go without day," or " go quit without day," that is, go free from the action without a continuance to any certain day; in other words, be discharged of further attendance. In some cases (*e.g.*, in case of nonsuit) this disposed of the action altogether, while in other cases it only suspended the action until the plaintiff remedied some defect in his title. See SINE DIE.

Without impeachment of waste. See ABSQUE IMPETITIONE VASTI; WASTE.

Without prejudice, a phrase used in offers, in order to guard against any waiver of right; also for the purpose of negotiating a compromise. Communications made without prejudice for the purpose of negotiating a compromise are not admissible in evidence (*Rabin* v. *Mendoza & Co.* [1954] 1 W.L.R. 271). If, however, they result in a concluded agreement they are admissible (*Att.-Gen.* v. *Dyer* [1947] Ch. 67). See PREJUDICE.

Without recourse to me [Fr. *sans recours*], a phrase used by an indorser of a bill or note, which protects him from liability (Bills of Exchange Act, 1882, s. 6). See SANS RECOURS.

Without reserve. See AUCTION.

Without this that. The words " without this that," *absque hoc* or *sans ceo que*, were the words used at the commencement of special traverses (*q.v.*).

Witness, a person who has knowledge of an event. As the most direct mode of acquiring knowledge of an event is by seeing it, " witness " has acquired the sense of a person who is present at and observes a transaction.

Hence, when a deed or other instrument is executed in the presence of a person, and he records the fact by signing his name on it, he is said to witness it, or to be an attesting witness. Formerly, the rule was that if there was an attesting witness within the jurisdiction, the document could not be put in evidence unless he was called to prove it; but this rule was abolished by the Evidence Act, 1938, s. 3. As to gifts to attesting witnesses in the case of wills, see WILL.

In procedure, a witness is a person who makes a *viva voce* statement to a judicial tribunal on a question of fact. (See EVIDENCE; EXAMINATION; FACT.) Witnesses are required to be sworn before their evidence is given (see OATH), unless

they have conscientious objections to taking an oath, or have no religious belief, in which case they make a solemn affirmation. See AFFIRM.

The general rule is that all persons are competent to give evidence, provided they have sufficient mental understanding. See COMPETENCY; CREDIT; VOIRE DIRE.

Every witness has a right to refuse to answer certain questions, such as questions the answer to which would have a tendency to expose the witness to criminal proceedings, or to a forfeiture or penalty. Liability to civil proceedings is not a ground of privilege. See ACCUSARE NEMO, ETC.; CONFIDENTIAL COMMUNICATIONS; PRIVILEGE.

As a general rule, every witness ought, in the first instance at least, to be presumed to be favourably disposed towards the party by whom he is called, and his examination should be conducted on that theory (see HOSTILE WITNESS). A zealous witness is one who endeavours to shape his testimony so as to make it as favourable as possible for one of the parties.

A witness must attend in court according to the requirement of his subpoena. If he has not been paid his lawful expenses, he may refuse to be sworn; but if he is once sworn, he must give his evidence.

In civil cases, as a rule, husband and wife are competent and compellable witnesses against each other (Evidence (Amendment) Act, 1853, s. 1). In criminal proceedings, husbands and wives are not compellable to disclose communications between each other (s. 3, as amended by the Civil Evidence Act, 1968, s. 16 (3)). See CRIMINAL EVIDENCE.

Notwithstanding any rule of law (*Russell* v. *Russell* [1924] A.C. 627) the evidence of a husband or wife is admissible to prove that marital intercourse did or did not take place between them during any period. (Matrimonial Causes Act, 1973, s. 48 (1)). See ADULTERY.

On the application of either party, all the witnesses on both sides are ordered to leave the court until called; and each is only called when his evidence is actually required. If a witness who has been ordered out of court remains, it is a contempt, if wilful, and may be treated as such; but his evidence is not rejected. Each witness remains in court after he has given his evidence, and is expected not to communicate with those outside; but it is no ground for quashing a conviction that the witnesses have been allowed to mix (*R.* v. *Fegredo* [1957] Crim.L.R. 50). But every party to the cause is entitled to be present throughout, though he be about to give evidence. The application is made either before the opening of the case, or before the first witness is called.

A witness cannot leave the precincts of the court without leave after the evidence of the side is over, nor even when the judge has begun to sum up, for any witness may at the discretion of the judge be recalled at any time before the verdict is given.

As to the extent of the obligation of the prosecution to call witnesses named on the back of the indictment see *R.* v. *Oliva* [1965] 1 W.L.R. 1028.

See ATTESTATION; CHARACTER; COMPETENCY; CONDUCT MONEY; CRIMINAL EVIDENCE; EXPERT; PERJURY; SUBPOENA.

Witnessing part. In a deed or other formal instrument, this is the part which comes after the recitals, or where there are no recitals, after the parties. It usually commences with a reference to the agreement or intention to be effectuated, then states or refers to the consideration, and concludes with the operative words and parcels, if any. Where a deed effectuates two distinct objects there are two witnessing parts.

The witnessing part is so called because it commences with the words " This deed witnesseth," meaning that the instrument is intended as a record of the transaction.

Witsom, goods driven to the shore, where there had not been for some space any wreck visible, whence they were anciently styled goods of God's mercy, *wit* in old English importing as much as *misericordia* in Latin (Philipot, *Villare Cantianum*).

Wittena-gemote. See WITENA-GEMOT.

Wold [Sax.], a down or open country.

Wolfeshead, or Wolferhefod [Sax.], the condition of such as were outlawed in the time of the Saxons, who if they could not be taken alive to be brought to justice might be slain and their heads brought to the king; for they were no more accounted of than a wolf's head, or what was afterwards called *caput lupinum* (3 Bract.).

Woman. By the Interpretation Act, 1889, s. 1, reproducing the statute 1850, 13 & 14 Vict. c. 21, s. 3, words in any Act of Parliament passed after 1850 importing the masculine gender include females unless the contrary intention appears.

Women became qualified to be registered as apothecaries by the Apothecaries Act Amendment Act, 1874, s. 5; as surgeons by the Medical Act (Royal College of Surgeons) Act, 1875, s. 2; and as medical practitioners by the Medical Act, 1876, s. 1.

The Sex Disqualification (Removal) Act, 1919, s. 1, provides that a person shall not be disqualified by sex or marriage from the exercise of any public function, or from being appointed to or holding any civil or judicial office or post, or from entering or assuming or carrying on any civil profession or vocation (see *Nagle* v. *Feilden* [1966] 2 Q.B. 633), or for admission to any incorporated society (whether incorporated by royal charter or otherwise), and that a person shall not be exempted by sex or marriage from liability to serve as a juror. A peeress in her own right is now entitled to a writ of summons to the House of Lords (Peerage Act, 1963, s. 6, overruling *Rhondda's (Viscountess) Petition* [1922] 2 A.C. 339. See SEX DISCRIMINATION.

The franchise was extended to women by the Representation of the People Act, 1918, and the Representation of the People (Equal Franchise) Act, 1928. See ELECTORAL FRANCHISE.

The Parliament (Qualification of Women) Act, 1918, provides that a woman shall not be disqualified by sex or marriage for being elected to or sitting or voting as a member of the House of Commons.

Under the British North America Act, 1867, s. 24, " persons " includes women (*Edwards* v. *Att.-Gen. for Canada* [1930] A.C. 124).

As to employment of women in factories, see the Factories Act, 1961, ss.

86–119, 119A; Employment Medical Advisory Service Act, 1972. The Mines and Quarries Act, 1954, s. 124 as amended by the Sex Discrimination Act, 1975, s. 21 (1), prohibits employment below ground in mines. See LAUNDRY.

At common law words imputing unchastity to a woman required special damage to be actionable; but this was put an end to by the Slander of Women Act, 1891. See SLANDER.

See MARRIED WOMEN'S PROPERTY.

Women and children, Offences as to. As to sexual offences, see ABDUCTION; ABORTION; BROTHEL; CARNAL KNOWLEDGE; EXPOSURE, INDECENT; INDECENT ASSAULT; PROCURATION OF WOMEN; PROSTITUTE; RAPE. As to other offences, see ABDUCTION; ASSAULT; BEGGAR; CRUELTY TO CHILDREN.

Wong [Sax.], a field (Spelman).

Wontner, a mole-catcher (Williams, *Commons* 102).

Wood plea court, a court anciently held twice a year in the Forest of Clun, in Shropshire, to settle all questions as to wood and agistments.

Wood-coin, a payment formerly made by the tenants of certain manors for the right of gathering dead wood.

Wood-corn, a certain quantity of grain paid by the tenants of some manors to the lord for the liberty to pick up dried or broken wood.

Wood-geld, or **Pudzeld.** This meant to be free from either money paid for wood cut in a forest, or money paid in order to secure the right of cutting wood therein (Co.Litt. 233a).

Wood-mote. See FOREST COURTS; FORTY-DAYS' COURT.

Woods and Forests, a Government Department which managed the Crown lands and collected the land revenue of the Crown. The department was presided over by two Commissioners, to whom the Minister of Agriculture and Fisheries was added as a third Commissioner, *ex officio*, by the Crown Lands Act, 1906; by an Order in Council of 1924, the name of the Commissioners was altered to the Commissioners of Crown Lands. The Crown Estate Act, 1956, s. 1, renamed them the Crown Estate Commissioners. See AGRICULTURE, FISHERIES AND FOOD, MINISTRY OF; COMMISSIONERS OF WOODS, ETC.; CROWN LANDS.

Woodward, an officer of the forest, whose duty consists in looking after the wood and vert and venison and preventing offences relating to the same (Manw. 189).

He was permitted to carry the weapon known as a forest bill,·but not a bow and arrows (4 Co.Inst. 293).

Woollen, Burial in. Formerly persons dying were to be buried in woollen on pain of £5: see the statute 1678, 30 Car. 2, c. 3, repealed by the statute 1814, 54 Geo. 3, c. 108.

Woolmer Forest. As to disafforesting, see the statute 1855, 18 & 19 Vict. c. 46; as to leasing, see the Crown Lands Act, 1855; and as to timber, see the statute 1812, 52 Geo. 3, c. 71.

Woolsack, the seat on which the Lord Chancellor sits in his capacity of Speaker of the House of Lords. It is not technically part of the House: and persons (such as members of Parliament) who are not peers occasionally sit upon part of it. If, as is theoretically possible, the Lord Chancellor were not a peer, he could not go beyond the Woolsack and the small space surrounding it. When the Lord Chancellor votes as a peer, he votes from the Woolsack; but if he desires to speak as a peer, he leaves the Woolsack and goes to his place in the House.

When, in the reign of Elizabeth I an Act was passed to prevent the exportation of wool, to keep in mind this source of national wealth woolsacks were placed in the House of Lords, whereon the judges sat. See also the statute 1539, 31 Hen. 8, c. 10, s. 8.

Words. See DEFAMATION.

Words of limitation; Words of procreation; Words of purchase. In a conveyance or will, words which have the effect of marking the duration of an estate are termed words of limitation. (See LIMITATION.) Thus, in a grant to A and his heirs, the words " and his heirs " are words of limitation, because they show that A is to take an estate in fee simple, and do not give his heirs anything. After the Conveyancing Act, 1881, s. 51, it was sufficient, in the limitation of an estate in fee simple, to use the words " in fee simple," without the word " heirs ";

now a conveyance of freehold land without words of limitation passes the fee simple or other the whole interest which the grantor had power to convey unless a contrary intention appears (Law of Property Act, 1925, s. 60).

To create an entailed interest certain words, known as words of procreation, must be used in order to confine the estate to the descendants of the first grantee, as in the usual form of limitation—" to A and the heirs of his body." Hence, a limitation to A and his heirs male would not create an entail, for want of words of procreation. It is sufficient to use the words " in tail " without the words " heirs of the body." Only those words of procreation above mentioned are effectual (Law of Property Act, 1925, s. 130). Formerly, while a gift to A and his children, or his issue or his offspring, would not, if used in a deed, create more than a life estate, if used in a will they created an estate tail.

Words of purchase are words which denote the person who is to take the estate. Thus, if land is granted to A for twenty-one years, and after the determination of that term to A's heirs, the word " heirs " does not denote the duration of A's estate, but the person who is to take the remainder on the expiration of the term, and is therefore called a word of purchase; the person to take is ascertained according to the law in force before 1926 (Law of Property Act, 1925, s. 132). Hence, " words of purchase " and " words of limitation " are opposed to one another. (See PURCHASE; SHELLEY'S CASE.) But there are cases in which words operate partly as words of purchase, and partly as words of limitation; thus, if an interest is limited to the heirs of the body of A, A being dead, these words are words of purchase to the extent that they give the interest to the person who fills the character of heir of the body of A (e.g., his eldest son B) by purchase and not by descent; but as they also have the effect of giving B an entailed interest, they are to this extent words of limitation.

Workhouse, a building for the accommodation of paupers in a parish or union (Poor Law Act, 1930, ss. 21–34). The poor law was abolished by the National Assistance Act, 1948, which made pro-

vision for reception centres and re-establishment centres, and imposes on local authorities the duty of providing residential accommodation for the aged and infirm. See also the Social Security Act, 1975. See POOR LAW; UNION; VESTRY.

Working classes. The earlier Housing Acts provided for the building of houses for the working classes. This limitation was removed by the Housing Act, 1949, s. 1. The expression is now descriptive of the lower-income groups (*Guinness Trust v. Green* [1955] 1 W.L.R. 872).

Working days. See RUNNING DAYS.

Working facilities. See MINERALS.

Working men's clubs, societies for the purpose of social intercourse, mutual helpfulness, mental and moral improvement and rational recreation (Friendly Societies Act, 1974, s. 7 (1) (*d*)). A working men's club may not divide its funds between its members (s. 9). The power to nominate a person to receive sums payable on death does not apply to a working men's club (s. 66 (4)). See FRIENDLY SOCIETIES.

Workmen. See COMMON EMPLOYMENT; LABOURERS' DWELLINGS; MASTER AND SERVANT; TRADE UNIONS; TRUCK ACTS; UNEMPLOYMENT INSURANCE; WORKMEN'S COMPENSATION.

Workmen's compensation. The Workmen's Compensation Act, 1897, introduced the principle of compensation for injured workmen by employers in a restricted number of trades. The gist of a right to compensation was accident arising out of and in the course of the employment causing personal injury to the workman (Workmen's Compensation Act, 1925, s. 1 (1)). The compensation was not damages for negligence or any other tort at common law or by statute, and an employer was not liable both for damages and compensation; but the workman or his representatives might elect between the remedies, and in an unsuccessful action for damages the court might assess or refer the question of compensation to the proper tribunal (Workmen's Compensation Act, 1925, s. 25). Compensation was not payable for an injury which did not disable the workman for at least three days from earning full wages in his employment, and serious and wilful misconduct might disqualify unless the injury resulted in death or serious and permanent disablement; contracting out was not allowed except under a scheme made under the Act (s. 1). Notice, verbal or written, was necessary within six months from the accident, or in case of death, from the time of death (s. 14).

The procedure was not by way of action, but by reference to an arbitrator, generally the county court judge, from whom an appeal lay to the Court of Appeal.

Compensation was payable in respect of personal injury by accident to the workman or his dependants, and the amount was based upon his average weekly earnings (s. 9). The minimum compensation payable in case of death of a workman who left dependants was from £200 to £300, and the maximum £600 (s. 8). The system was extended and the compensation increased by a series of Acts, and the system was superseded by the National Insurance (Industrial Injuries) Act, 1946. See the Industrial Injuries and Diseases (Old Cases) Acts, 1967, 1975.

Workshop. For the purpose of the Factory and Workshop Act, 1901, this meant hat works, rope works, bakehouses, lace warehouses, shipbuilding works, quarries, pit banks, dry-cleaning, carpet-beating, and bottle-washing works, and any premises named in Sch. 6 Pt. II to the Act, not being a factory where manual labour was used for gain, or for making, repairing, or adapting for sale any article, in premises to which the employer had a right of access, including laundries, as provided by the Factory and Workshop Act, 1907, s. 1. These Acts were repealed by the Factories Act, 1937. See FACTORIES.

Works, Ministry of. See PUBLIC BUILDINGS AND WORKS, MINISTRY OF.

Worscott [Old Eng.], to be free from the burdens of arms, *liberum esse de oneribus armorum* (Co.Litt. 71a).

Worship, a title of respect applied to a magistrate.

Worship, Place of. The Places of Worship (Enfranchisement) Act, 1920 (as amended by the Leasehold Reform Act, 1967, s. 40, Sch. 7 Pt. II), enables trustees of a leasehold interest in a place of worship or a minister's house to enlarge the interest into the freehold in not more than two acres (*Stradling* v. *Higgins* [1932] 1 Ch. 143).

The Places of Worship Sites Acts, 1873 and 1882, enable sites not exceeding one acre to be conveyed for purposes of worship. See PUBLIC WORSHIP.

A Mormon temple is not a place of public religious worship (*Church of Jesus Christ of Latter-Day Saints* v. *Henning* [1964] A.C. 420).

Wort, new beer unfermented or in the act of fermentation; the sweet infusion of malt or grain.

Worth, Wort [Sax. *weorth*], a curtilage or country farm.

Worthing of land, a certain quantity of land so called in the manor of Kingsland in Hereford; the tenants were called worthies (Jacob).

Wound, any lesion of the body, whether a cut, bruise, contusion, fracture, dislocation or burn. In surgery it is confined to a solution of continuity in any part of the body suddenly caused by anything which cuts or tears, with a division of the skin.

Wounding. Unlawfully and maliciously wounding or causing grievous bodily harm with intent to do grievous bodily harm to any person by any means is, by the Offences against the Person Act, 1861, s. 18 (amended by the Criminal Law Act, 1967, Sch. 3 Pt. III) punishable by imprisonment for life. As to the burden of proof where a defence of self-defence is set up, see *R.* v. *Lobell* [1957] 1 Q.B. 547. See MALICIOUS INJURIES TO THE PERSON; MAYHEM.

Wreccum maris significat illa bona quae naufragio ad terram pelluntur. (A wreck of the sea signifies those goods which are driven to shore from a shipwreck.)

Wreck, such goods, including the ship or cargo or any part, as, after a shipwreck, are afloat or cast upon the land by the sea. Formerly they were not wreck so long as they remained at sea in the jurisdiction of the Admiralty (Jacob).

By the Merchant Shipping Act, 1894, s. 510, " wreck " includes jetsam, flotsam, and derelict found in or on the shores of the sea or any tidal water.

As to the property in wreck, see Co.

WRECK

Litt. 261a; 1 Bl.Comm. 291; Williams, *Commons* 289; Moore, *Foreshore*.

By the common law, if a ship was lost at sea, and the cargo or a portion of it came to land, the goods saved belonged to the Crown under the name of wreck. This privilege was frequently granted to lords of manors. See FRANCHISE; MANOR; PREROGATIVE.

The strictness of the prerogative right to wreck was relaxed by early charters and by the statutes 1275, 3 Edw. 1, c. 4, and 1353, 27 Edw. 3, st. 2, under which the owners of shipwrecked goods were allowed to reclaim them within a year and a day, if they could identify them.

The term " wreck " is used in several senses, *e.g.*, a ship which is so damaged as to be unable to continue her voyage is a wreck for the purposes of the Merchant Shipping Act, 1894, s. 158, and the Merchant Shipping (International Labour Conventions) Act, 1925 (*The Olympic* [1913] P. 92; *Barras* v. *Aberdeen Steam Trawlers* [1933] A.C. 402). The old distinction appears to be that if property could be identified by its owner it was not wreck, *i.e.*, property which the Crown could claim as part of its prerogative.

The Merchant Shipping Act, 1894, ss. 511–528, deal with the custody of wreck by district receivers of wreck (as by the sheriffs of the counties under the ancient law), and the suppression of plunder by them, the claims of the owners within one year (s. 521) (formerly a year and a day), and the title of the Crown to unclaimed wreck except in cases where any other person has a right to wreck by royal grant (s. 522).

It is a branch of the coroner's office to inquire concerning shipwrecks and certify whether there has been a wreck or not, and who is in possession of the goods.

As to impeding a person saving his own or another's life from a wreck, see the Offences against the Person Act, 1861, s. 17. As to assaulting a magistrate, officer, etc., engaged in preserving a wreck or goods cast on shore, see the Offences against the Person Act, 1861, s. 37.

The Removal of Wrecks Act, 1877, and 1889, gave power to harbour and conservancy authorities to remove wrecks obstructing navigation and protected from obstruction lifeboats engaged in lifeboat service; these enactments are replaced by the Merchant Shipping Act, 1894, ss. 530–534.

The Protection of Wrecks Act, 1973, enables a Secretary of State to designate a restricted area round the sites of historic wrecks and around dangerous wrecks in United Kingdom waters.

Wreck commissioners, persons appointed by the Lord Chancellor under the Merchant Shipping Act, 1894, s. 477, to hold investigations (s. 466 (2)) at the request of the Department of Trade into shipping casualties (s. 464). Reports of their decisions are issued by H.M. Stationery Office. Similar investigations are in some cases made by stipendiary magistrates (s. 476). Preliminary investigations are also held by various officers of the coastguard and customs services, etc. (s. 465). See COURTS OF SURVEY.

Wreck-free, exempt from the forfeiture of shipwrecked goods and vessels, a privilege which the Cinque Ports enjoy by a charter of Edward I (Jacob).

Wrestling. Public exhibitions of wrestling and boxing may be controlled in London under the London County Council (General Powers) Acts, 1930, ss. 17–22, 1935, s. 55, 1936, s. 38, 1939, s. 5.

Writ [Lat. *breve*], a document under the seal of the Crown, a court or an officer of the Crown, commanding the person to whom it is addressed to do or forbear from doing some act. As to the issue and service of writs, see ISSUE; SERVICE OF PROCESS.

Writs are of two principal kinds, prerogative and of right (Co.Litt. 73b).

Prerogative writs are so called because they are issued by virtue of the Crown's prerogative, and not as part of the public administration of justice; writs belonging to the latter class are called writs of right, because the Crown is bound by Magna Carta, 1215, to issue them, while prerogative writs are granted at the discretion of the court, and only on a prima facie case being shown. The prerogative writs are or were the writs of mandamus, procedendo, prohibition, quo warranto, habeas corpus and certiorari; the Administration of Justice (Miscellaneous Provisions) Act, 1938, s. 7, substitutes orders of mandamus, prohibition and certiorari for the prerogative writs of mandamus, prohibition and certiorari. There were also statutory writs of mandamus (*q.v.*), which were grantable as of right, but orders of mandamus are substituted for these also (s. 8).

Writs of right are of two kinds, original and judicial.

An original writ was formerly the mode of commencing every action at common law (see ACTION ON THE CASE). It issued out of the common law side of the Chancery (see OFFICINA JUSTITIAE) and was under the Great Seal. To avoid the expense of original writs, other modes of beginning actions were devised with the connivance of the courts; but they were all abolished and the modern writ of summons introduced by the statute 1832, 2 & 3 Will. 4, c. 39. Original writs, however, continued some time longer to be used as modes of appealing from one court to another, as in the case of writs of error, writs of false judgment, etc., and the writ of error used in criminal proceedings, which was abolished by the Criminal Appeal Act, 1907.

The Real Property Limitation Act, 1833, abolished all writs in real and mixed actions (except in dower *unde nihil habet*, *quare impedit* or ejectment), expressly naming sixty abolished writs, *e.g.*, the writ of right *de rationabili parte*, of *quo jure*, of assize of *novel disseisin*, of entry *sur disseisin* in the *quibus*, of waste, of partition, and of *per quae servitia*.

A judicial writ is any writ which is issued by a court under its own seal, as opposed to an original writ. Judicial writs may be divided into (1) writs originating actions and other proceedings, of which the ordinary writ of summons (*q.v.*) is the commonest instance; (2) interlocutory writs, issued during the course of an action before final judgment, such as writs of inquiry, and recaption, and writs for enforcing obedience to interlocutory orders by attachment, sequestration, etc.; and (3) writs of execution. Writs of execution are of two kinds: some are issued in the first instance (*e.g.*, writs of *fieri facias*, sequestration, delivery, possession, *levari facias*, etc.), while others are only issued in aid of other writs, that is, when a writ of execution has been issued without producing the desired effect;

such are writs of *venditioni exponas*, *distringas*, *fi. fa. de bonis ecclesiasticis*, *sequestrari facias*, and the writ of assistance.

In the old books, " writ " is used as equivalent to " action ": hence writs are sometimes divided into real, personal and mixed. See ACTION.

See ALIAS WRIT; ASSISTANCE; ATTACHMENT; CLOSE ROLLS, ETC.; CURSITORS; DELIVERY, WRIT OF; DETAINER; DOWER, WRIT OF; ENTRY; ERROR; EXECUTION; FALSE JUDGMENT; HABERE FACIAS POSSESSIONEM; PLURIES; RETURN; TESTATUM; TESTE; TRIAL.

Writ of right, one which is grantable as a right, as opposed to a prerogative writ, which is issued only as a matter of grace or discretion. See WRIT.

In the old real property law, a writ of right was a real action which lay to recover lands in fee simple unjustly withheld from the owner. It might be brought in any case of disseisin, but was in practice only used where the disseisee had lost his right of entry or right to possession, as in other cases a possessory action (such as a writ of entry) was more convenient. It was called a writ of right, because it was brought to assert the right of property remaining in the owner, which was usually a mere right (see RIGHT). There were also writs in the nature of writs of right, such as the writ of right of dower (3 Bl.Comm. 193).

See RECTO; RIGHT CLOSE; RIGHT PATENT.

Writ of summons. In actions in the High Court, the writ of summons is a process issued at the instance of the plaintiff for the purpose of giving the defendant notice of the claim made against him and of compelling him to appear and answer it if he does not admit it. It is the first step in the action (R.S.C., Ord. 5, r. 1. Except in probate actions in which a writ cannot be issued out of a district registry (R.S.C., Ord. 76, r. 2), the writ of summons may be issued out of the Central Office or out of any district registry (Ord. 6, r. 7 (2)). In Admiralty actions writs *in rem* or *in personam* may be issued from the Admiralty Registry or any district registry. See ACTIONS AND MATTERS.

The writ consists of the body, the

memoranda and the indorsements. The body contains the title (*q.v.*) (that is, the reference to the record, the name of the court, division (and judge if necessary) and the names of the parties), the mandatory part (by which the defendant is ordered to enter an appearance), and the *teste* (*q.v.*). The memoranda specify the time within which the writ must be served and the place where the defendant may enter an appearance.

By R.S.C., Ord. 6, r. 2, before a writ is issued it must be indorsed (a) with a statement of claim or a concise statement of the nature of the claim made or the relief or remedy sought; (b) if the claim is for a debt or liquidated demand only, a statement of the amount claimed in respect of the debt or demand and for costs and also a statement that further proceedings will be stayed if within the time limited for appearing the defendant pays the amount claimed; (c) where the claim is for possession of land, with a statement showing (i) whether the statement relates to a dwelling-house and (ii) if it does whether the rateable value of the premises exceeds, in Greater London £400, and elsewhere £200; (d) where the action is brought to recover possession of goods, with a statement showing the value of the goods.

The writ must be indorsed with the name and address of the plaintiff's solicitor or, where the plaintiff sues in person, with the plaintiff's name and address (Ord. 6, r. 5). It must also be indorsed as to service by the person who served the writ (Ord. 10, r. 1 (4)). See R.S.C., Appendix A, Forms 1–5.

If the plaintiff sues or the defendant is sued in a representative capacity, such as executor, the indorsement must state in what capacity the plaintiff sues or the defendant is sued (R.S.C., Ord. 6, r. 3). Where the writ is indorsed with a claim for an account, a summary order for account may be sought under R.S.C., Ord. 43, r. 1. In probate actions the writ must be indorsed with (a) a statement of the nature of the interest of the plaintiff and of the defendant and (b) a memorandum signed by a master of the Chancery Division showing that the writ has been produced to him for examina-

tion and that two copies have been lodged with him (Ord. 76, r. 2).

In Admiralty actions *in rem* the writ of summons is in a special form; it is addressed to the owners of the ship or other property, and commands them to enter an appearance (R.S.C., Ord. 75, r. 3; Appendix B, Forms 1 and 2); and at any time after it has been issued a warrant may be issued authorising the arrest of the ship, etc. (Ord. 75, r. 5). The service (*q.v.*) of the writ and the execution of the warrant are effected simultaneously.

A writ remains in force for twelve months from its issue, but if service has not been effected within that time it may (if a judge so orders) be renewed for six months, by being sealed by the proper officer (Ord. 6, r. 8).

If there are several defendants to be served, or the whereabouts of a defendant is doubtful, or some similar reason exists, one or more concurrent writs (that is, writs to the same effect as the original writ and remaining in force for the same time) may be issued so as to facilitate service (Ord. 6, r. 6).

Before the Judicature Acts, 1873–75, the Court of Probate had power to cause questions of fact arising in suits or proceedings to be tried by a jury by means of an issue directed to one of the superior courts of law: the issues were contained in a document called a writ of summons.

Writ of trial. See the Civil Procedure Act, 1842, s. 17, repealed by the County Courts Act, 1867, s. 6.

Writer, a solicitor in Scotland.

Writer of the tallies, an officer of the Exchequer, who acted as clerk to the auditor of the receipt, who wrote upon the tallies the teller's bills. See TALLY.

Writers to the signet, designated by the letters W.S., or, in the case of three of the older established firms in Edinburgh, the letters C.S. (which stand for the words " Clerks to the Signet "), are the senior society of solicitors or law agents in Scotland. See SIGNET.

Writing. In any Act of Parliament, unless the contrary intention appears, this is construed as including printing, lithography, photography, and other modes of representing or reproducing words in a visible form (Interpretation Act, 1889, s. 20).

In the most general sense of the word, "writing" denotes a document, whether manuscript or printed, as opposed to mere spoken words.

A contract of guarantee and a contract relating to land are unenforceable by action unless evidenced by writing. Writing is essential to the validity of certain contracts and other transactions, *e.g.*, a bill of exchange or a will; and some transactions, *e.g.*, a conveyance of land, require a deed. See BILL OF EXCHANGE; CONTRACT; DEED; EVIDENCE; STATUTE OF FRAUDS; TENTERDEN'S ACT; WILL.

As to written and spoken defamation, see LIBEL; SLANDER.

Documents for the use of the Supreme Court must comply with the regulations contained in R.S.C., Ord. 66, r. 2.

In the old books, "writing" sometimes signifies a "writing sealed," that is, a deed, as opposed to "parol" (*q.v.*).

Writings obligatory, bonds. See BOND.

Writs close. See CLOSE ROLLS, ETC.

Writs for the election of members of Parliament. The Speaker of the House of Commons signs warrants for the issue of writs for by-elections.

Wrong, the privation of right, an injury; that which takes place when a right is violated or infringed.

Wrongs are generally divided into private and public. A private wrong is one which confers a remedy or right of redress on an individual: such are breaches of contract, torts, etc. A public wrong is one which renders the wrongdoer responsible to the community: such are crimes (*q.v.*) and other offences (*q.v.*), and generally all infringements of the rules of public law. See LAW.

The maxim that "No man can take advantage of his own wrong" means that a man cannot enforce against another a right arising from his own breach of contract or breach of duty (*Re London Celluloid Co.* (1888) 39 Ch.D. 206).

An estate gained by wrong is always a fee simple. A squatter may, of course, be ejected before the Limitation Act, 1939, has run in his favour, but as long as he remains he has seisin of the free-

hold to him and his heirs, "because wrong is unlimited and ravens all that can be gotten and is not governed by terms of the estates, because it is not contained within rules" (Hob. 323; Co. Litt. 181a; Williams, *Seisin* 7).

A squatter is bound by restrictive covenants affecting the land (*Re Nisbet* [1906] 1 Ch. 386).

As to estates or titles by wrong, see TITLE.

Wrongdoer. See CONTRIBUTION.

Wrongful dismissal, an unjustifiable dismissal of a servant by the master from an engagement for services for a fixed time or, if upon notice, before expiration of the period of notice. The servant may elect to treat the contract as repudiated (*General Bill Posting Co.* v. *Atkinson* [1909] A.C. 118; *Measures* v. *Measures* [1910] 2 Ch. 248), in which case he can recover remuneration for what he has actually done on a *quantum meruit* (*Cutter* v. *Powell* (1795) 6 T.R. 320), or if he treats the contract as continuing, he may sue for damages for loss of the employment and such wages as he has lost the opportunity of earning, taking into account the probability of finding another employment of the same kind and degree (*Brace* v. *Calder* [1895] 2 Q.B. 253). By custom, a domestic servant may be dismissed at any time on a month's notice or on payment of a month's wages (*Mould* v. *Halliday* [1898] 1 Q.B. 125).

Punitive damages are not recoverable and the plaintiff must take diligent steps to find other suitable employment (*Beckham* v. *Drake* (1849) 2 H.L.C. 579). The damages are the amount which the plaintiff has lost on the footing that the remuneration he would have received but for the dismissal would have been liable to tax (*Phipps* v. *Orthodox Unit Trusts* [1958] 1 Q.B. 314).

An employee has, in general, a statutory right not to be unfairly dismissed by his employer. The remedy for breach of that right is by way of complaint to an industrial tribunal and not otherwise (Trade Union and Labour Relations Act, 1974, Sch. 1, para. 4). For meaning of "dismissal," see para. 5 (as amended by the Employment Protection Act, 1975, Sch. 16 para. 8).

The question whether a dismissal was fair or unfair is determined in accordance with para. 6 (as amended by the 1975 Act, Sch. 16 Pt. III paras. 11, 12; Trade Union and Labour Relations (Amendment) Act, 1976, s. 3 (5) (6)). As to dismissal in connection with a lock-out, see s. 7; in connection with a strike or other industrial action s. 8 (as amended by the 1975 Act, Sch. 16 Pt. III paras. 1–5). The classes of employment excluded from the statutory right are detailed in Sch. 1 paras. 9, 11 (as amended by the 1975 Act, Sch. 16 Pt. III paras. 14, 15). The qualifying period of employment and the upper age limit of the employee are stated in paras. 10, 11 (as amended by the 1975 Act, Sch. 16 Pt. III para. 15). Certain contracts for a fixed term are excluded by para. 12. If a dismissal procedures agreement is in force it takes the place of the statutory provisions (paras. 13, 14). The fact that a dismissal was the result of pressure brought upon the employer is irrelevant (para. 15). Complaints of unfair dismissal are made to an industrial tribunal (see INDUSTRIAL TRIBUNALS) under para. 17 (as amended by the 1975 Act, Sch. 16 Pt. III para. 16). If the dismissal was to safeguard national security the complaint is to be dismissed (para. 18). Compensation for unfair dismissal is assessed under paras. 19, 20 (as amended by the 1975 Act, Sch. 16 Pt. III paras. 16, 17) and is recovered under para. 25.

See further the Employment Protection Act, 1975, ss. 71–80, Sch. 16 Pt. III.

Wydraught, a water-passage, gutter, or watering-place; sometimes mentioned in old leases of houses, in the covenant to repair (Jacob).

X

Xenodoceum, or **Xenodocheum,** an inn, a hospital (Cowel).

Xenodochy [ξενσδοχία], reception of strangers; hospitality (Encyc.Londin.).

Y

Yachts, vessels used primarily for purposes of pleasure. The provisions of the Merchant Shipping Act, 1894, with regard to the engagement and qualification of the crew do not apply to sea-going yachts (s. 262). Yachts not exceeding fifteen tons do not require to be registered (Merchant Shipping Act, 1894, s. 3 (1)), unless they are used for sea-fishing and have not been exempted from registration by Order in Council (ss. 370, 373). Yachts are exempt from compulsory pilotage (Pilotage Act, 1913, s. 11 (3)). The limitation of liability provided by the Merchant Shipping Act, 1894, s. 503, does not apply to a yacht of which the owner is in command, or which is racing under rules which make the owner impliedly contract to pay full damages. Yachts are exempt from the load line and loading provisions of the Merchant Shipping (Load Lines) Act, 1967. See s. 1 (c). The Commissioners of Customs and Excise may take steps to prevent smuggling by small craft (Customs and Excise Act, 1952, s. 68).

See the Customs Convention on the temporary importation of yachts for private use (Cmnd. 650).

A yacht is within the definition of "personal chattels" in the Administration of Estates Act, 1925, s. 55 (1) (x) (Re Chaplin [1950] Ch. 507).

Taking away or using a vessel without authority is an offence under the Theft Act, 1968, s. 12.

Yard [Sax. geard], an enclosed space of ground, generally attached to a dwelling-house, etc. See CURTILAGE.

The yard or the metre is the unit of

measurement of length in the United Kingdom (Weights and Measures Act, 1963, s. 1). It is a measure of three feet or thirty-six inches or 0·9144 of a metre (ss. 1, 10, Sch. 1 Pt. I). A square yard is a superficial area equal to that of a square each side of which measures one yard (s. 10, Sch. 1 Pt. II). A cubic yard is a volume equal to that of a cube each edge of which measures one yard (s. 10, Sch. 1 Pt. III). See FOOT; INCH.

Yardland [*virgata terrae*], a quantity of land differing in extent in different parts of the country, generally about twenty acres (Co.Litt. 5a, 69a; 2 Holds., H.E.L. 66). See FARDEL; PLOUGHLAND.

Year [Sax. *gear*], 365 days, twelve calendar months, fifty-two weeks and one day, or in leap-year (*q.v.*) 366 days, *i.e.*, fifty-two weeks and two days. (See TIME.) By the statute 1255, 40 Hen. 3, the increasing day in the leap-year, as well as the preceding day, were accounted one day only.

The first day of the year was altered for England from March 25 to January 1 in and after 1752 by the Calendar (New Style) Act, 1750, but as appears from the preamble to that statute, January 1 had been the first day of the year in Scotland and in other nations, and by common usage throughout the whole kingdom (2 Bl.Comm. 140). See CALENDAR.

Generally, when a statute speaks of a year it must be considered as twelve calendar and not lunar months (*Bishop of Peterborough* v. *Catesby* (1608) Cro. Jac. 166).

The financial year ends on March 31 (Interpretation Act, 1889, s. 22). The income tax year ends on April 5 (Income and Corporation Taxes Act, 1970, s. 2 (2)).

A quarter of a year contains by legal computation 91 days, and half a year contains 182 days (Co.Litt. 135b).

A year in a tenancy agreement at a weekly rental can mean 52 weeks and not 365 days (*Lamb* v. *Boyden* [1961] C.L.Y. 4906 (a county court case)).

As to leases for years, see LEASE; TENANT FOR YEARS; TERM.

Year and a day [*annus et dies*], a time which determines a right or works a prescription, etc., in some cases (Co.Litt. 254b; Jacob).

The owners of estrays (*q.v.*) must claim them within a year and a day, otherwise they belong to the Crown or a grantee from the Crown.

In order to make killing murder, it is requisite that the party die within a year and a day after the stroke received, or cause of death administered, in the computation of which period the whole day upon which the hurt was done is reckoned the first (3 Co.Inst. 53; 6 Co. Rep. 107; 4 Bl.Comm. 197).

See CONTINUAL CLAIM; WRECK.

Year Books, or **Books of Years and Terms,** reports, in a regular series, from the time of Edward II to Henry VIII. They are a series of reports of cases written in the Anglo-Norman language, commencing in the thirteenth century and extant either in manuscript copies or in print from 1290 to 1535, with a few gaps. There has been considerable controversy as to their origin. It is sometimes said that they were taken by the prothonotaries or chief scribes of the courts, at the expense of the Crown, and published annually; hence their denomination. Plowden stated that there were four reporters who had an annual stipend paid by the king, but doubts were cast on this by Sir Frederick Pollock and others. It appears to be now generally agreed that they were notes of cases taken by apprentices to the law (*q.v.*) and, as suggested by Bolland, probably copied by scribes in *scriptoria*; for there are varying manuscripts of the same years. At first the years were issued as separate volumes, some of those of Henry VI being among the first books printed in England. Between the years 1587 and 1638 the separate years were reprinted as a collection in ten small folio volumes misnamed the "quarto" edition, covering the reigns of Edward III to Henry VIII. In 1678–80 an edition in large folio, known as Maynard's edition, was issued. This contained eleven parts, some cases in the reigns of Edward I and Edward II being printed for the first time. In recent times, years 20 to 35, Edward I, were printed with a translation by A. J. Horwood in five volumes, and 11 to 20,

Edward III, with a translation by L. O. Pike in fifteen volumes. The Selden Society are now filling other gaps by the issue of original texts with translations. Citations of the Year Books are by the regnal years, folios and *placita* (*q.v.*), *e.g.*, Y.B. 14 Hen. 6, 18, 3. See LIBER ASSISSARUM; LONG QUINTO.

For an account of the origin and contents of the Year Books, see Bolland, *The Year Books*; for a list of the various editions, see Beale, *Bibliography of Early English Law Books*.

Year, day and waste [*annus, dies et vastum*], a part of the royal prerogative, whereby the Crown had for a year and a day the profits of lands and tenements of those attainted of petit treason or felony whosoever was lord of the manor whereto the lands or tenements belonged; and the right to cause waste to be made on the tenements by destroying the houses, ploughing up the meadows and pastures, rooting up the woods, etc. (unless the lord of the fee agreed for the redemption of such waste), afterwards restoring them to the lord of the fee (Staund. Praerog. 44; 4 Bl.Comm. 385).

This prerogative right was restricted by the Corruption of Blood Act, 1814, and ceased to exist (except, theoretically on attainder for treason) when forfeiture (*q.v.*) was abolished.

Year to year, Tenancy from. This estate arises either expressly, as when land is let from year to year, or by a general parol demise, without any determinate interest, but reserving the payment of an annual rent; or impliedly, as when property is occupied under a yearly rent, whether payable yearly, half-yearly, or quarterly; or when such tenant holds over, after the expiration of his term, without having entered into any new contract, and pays rent (before which he is a tenant on sufferance), in which case the tenant holds over on such terms of the old tenancy as are applicable to a tenancy from year to year and to the particular tenancy.

The qualities which distinguish a tenancy from year to year from a term of years and from a tenancy at will are (1) that it exists by construction of law alone instead of a tenancy at will in every instance where possession is taken with the consent of the legal owner and where a yearly rent has been paid, but without there having been any agreement conferring a legal interest; and (2) that, whether it arises from express agreement or by implication of law, it may, unless surrendered or determined by a regular notice to quit, subsist for an indefinite period, if the estate of the landlord will allow of it, or for the whole term of his interest where it is of a limited duration, unaffected by the death either of the landlord or the tenant, or by a conveyance of their estate by either of them; so that the assignees or personal representatives of the landlord or the tenant still continue the tenancy upon the original terms, and subject to the same conditions which the law, or the express agreement of the parties, has attached to it.

But the tenancy is liable at any time to be determined by a notice to quit from either party, which, when there is no agreement, or where the agreement is silent on that point, must be at least half a year's (not merely six months'), or where the Agricultural Holdings Act, 1948, applies, one year's, notice to give up possession at the expiration of the year, computing from the time when the tenancy commenced. An oral notice is sufficient unless the agreement requires it to be in writing (*Doe* v. *Crick* (1805) 5 Esp. N.P.C. 197). See TENANT FROM YEAR TO YEAR.

Years, Estate for. See TERM OF YEARS ABSOLUTE.

Yelverton's Act, the statute 1782, 21 & 22 Geo. 3, c. 48, of the Irish Parliament, extending the principle of Poynings' Act, 1495 (*q.v.*), to private estate Acts and shipping Acts.

Yeme [Lat. *hiems*], winter.

Yeoman, or **Yoman,** a man of a small estate in land; a farmer, a gentleman farmer; also, a 40s. freeholder not advanced to the rank of gentleman; the highest order among the plebians (2 Co. Inst. 668).

A yeoman was he who had free land of forty shillings by the year: who was anciently thereby qualified to serve on juries, vote for knights of the shire, and do any other act where the law required one who was *probus et legalis homo* (1 Bl.Comm. 406).

Yeomen ranked next after gentlemen in order of precedence. Nowadays the word has no meaning in the law.

Yeoman Usher, the deputy of Black Rod (*q.v.*), who appoints him.

Yeomanry, the collected body of yeomen; a denomination given to those troops of horse which were levied among the gentlemen and yeomen of the country, upon the same principle as the volunteer companies (National Defence Act, 1888; Militia and Yeomanry Act, 1901, s. 14). As to the former powers of the lords lieutenant of counties in reference to this force, see LORD LIEUTENANT.

For many years preceding the South African War of 1899–1902, this term was applied to the cavalry units of the Volunteers (*q.v.*). These units, which in some cases retain their original designation, were, by Order in Council made pursuant to the Territorial and Reserve Forces Act, 1907, transferred to the territorial army (*q.v.*).

Yeomen of the Guard, a corps of 140 old soldiers or non-commissioned officers appointed by the Constable of the Tower. The Captain of the Yeomen of the Guard is appointed by the sovereign and goes in and out with the Ministry of the day. The other officers are appointed by the sovereign on the recommendation of the captain; they are the lieutenant (who must have held the rank of lieutenant-colonel), the ensign (who must have been a major), and the Clerk of the Cheque and Adjutant and four "exons" or corporals, who must have held the rank of captain. The corps is not subject to military law and is under the Lord Chamberlain. Forty of the yeomen are warders of the Tower of London, the remainder are, in theory, the bodyguard of the sovereign; in reality, they are mere picturesque figures at State functions. They are and always have been privileged from arrest on civil process (2 Hall, Const.Hist. c. 9).

Yeven, or **Yeoven,** given; dated.

Yew trees. If a yew projects over an adjoining property and an animal having eaten projecting leaves is poisoned thereby, the owner of the yew is liable in damages (*Crowhurst* v. *Amersham* (1879) 4 Ex.D. 5). But a person having yew on his land, and being under no obligation to fence, is not liable for damage thereby caused to his neighbour's cattle when trespassing (*Ponting* v. *Noakes* [1894] 2 Q.B. 281).

Yield. In the law of real property, this means to perform a service due by a tenant to his lord. Hence the usual form of reservation of a rent in a lease begins with the words "yielding and paying," though now the words "yielding and" are often omitted.

Yielding and paying, the first words of the *reddendum* clause in a lease. See YIELD; REDDENDUM.

Ymbringe days. See EMBRING DAYS.

Yoke. See SULUNG; YARDLAND.

Yokelet [Sax. *jocelet*], a little farm, requiring but a yoke of oxen to till it.

York. In the archbishopric of York there were special customs as to the distribution of the estates of intestates. These customs were preserved by the Statute of Distributions, 1672, but were abolished by the statute 1856, 19 & 20 Vict. c. 94. As to restrictions on testamentary powers, see RATIONABILE PARTE, ETC.

The York Court of Record (formerly known as the York Sheriff's Court of Pleas) was created by a charter of 1936, and was held under a charter of 1664. It had, within the City of York, a jurisdiction which originally was unlimited but which under an Order in Council of May 17, 1890, was limited to claims not exceeding £10. It was abolished by the Local Government Act, 1972, s. 221, Sch. 28.

The provincial court of the Archbishop of York is called the Chancery Court of York (*q.v.*).

York, Duke of. See MILITARY ASYLUM OF CHELSEA.

York Herald. See HERALD.

York, Statute of, the statute 1318, 12 Edw. 2, st. 1, repealed by the Statute Law Revision and Civil Procedure Act, 1881. See SUPER STATUTO QUE NUL SOIT, ETC.

York-Antwerp Rules, optional rules of practice on the subject of general average for the assistance of shipowners, merchants, underwriters and average-adjusters for insertion in bills of lading, charter-parties and policies of insurance. The rules were adopted as a result of a conference of the Association for Reform and Codification of the Law of Nations at Antwerp in 1877 and have been revised on four occasions since, the latest revision being in 1974. See ADJUSTMENT OF A LOSS; AVERAGE.

Yorkshire land registries. These were regulated by the Yorkshire Registry Act, 1884, which replaced the various Acts under which they had been established and carried on in each of the three ridings, exclusive of the City of York; as to the North Riding, see the statute 1734, 8 Geo. 2, c. 6; as to the East Riding, see the statute 1707, 6 Anne, c. 62; as to the West Riding, see the statutes 1703, 2 & 3 Anne, c. 4, and 1706, 6 Anne, c. 20.

The Yorkshire deeds registries were closed by the Law of Property Act, 1969, s. 16. A certificate of the registration of an instrument in a Yorkshire deeds register endorsed on the instrument is conclusive evidence of the facts certified (s. 22).

See EASEMENT; LAND REGISTRIES; MEMORIAL.

Young person. In the Children and Young Persons Act, 1933, this expression means a person who has attained the age of fourteen years and is under seventeen years (s. 107).

A young person within the Merchant Shipping (International Labour Conventions) Act, 1925, is a person who is under the age of eighteen years (s. 5).

A young person within the Factories Act, 1961, is a person who is over compulsory school age but has not attained the age of eighteen years (s. 117 (1)).

Hours of employment are regulated by the Young Persons (Employment) Act, 1938 and the Factories Act, 1961, ss. 86–119, 119A; Employment Medical Advisory Service Act, 1972; Employment and Training Act, 1973, Sch. 3.

Neither the Crown Court nor a magistrates' court may impose imprisonment on a person under seventeen years of age. No court may impose imprisonment on a person under twenty-one years of age unless the court is of opinion that no other method of dealing with him is appropriate (Powers of Criminal Courts Acts, 1973, s. 19).

See CHILDREN.

Yrfe land, folcland (*q.v.*).

Yule [Dan. *jule*; Sax. *gehul, geola, geol*], the times of Christmas and Lammas.

Z

Zambia. Zambia Independence Act, 1964.

Zanzibar. See Zanzibar Act, 1963. See also TANZANIA.

Zealous witness. See WITNESS.

" Zebra " crossings. See PEDESTRIAN CROSSINGS.

Zetetick [ζητέω], proceeding by inquiry.

Zigari, or **Zingari,** gypsies (*q.v.*), held to be rogues and vagabonds in the Middle Ages; from Zigi, now Circassia.

Zollverein, a union of German states for uniformity of customs. It began in 1819 by the union of Schwarzburg-Sondershausen, and lasted until the unification of the then German Empire which included Prussia, Saxony, Bavaria, Württemberg, Baden, Hesse-Cassel, Brunswick, and Mecklenburg-Strelitz, and all intermediate principalities. This union was superseded by the formation of a Federal Council which took the place of the Federal Council of the Zollverein.

Zoonoses, the risk to human health from animal diseases, see the Agriculture (Miscellaneous Provisions) Act, 1972, s. 1.

BIBLIOGRAPHY

Abbott (G. J., Lord Tenterden): Shipping: Law relative to Merchant Ships and Seamen. 14th ed. 1901.

Abstract of New Forest Claims: An Abstract of all the claims on the New Forest, in the County of Southampton, entered at the Lord Chief Justice in Eyre's Court, adjourned from the Swainmote Court, held at Lyndhurst, the 27th of June, in the 22nd year of King Charles II, and held at Winton, the 29th Sep. 1670. 1776.

Adams (J.), Eject: Principles and Practice of Action of Ejectment. 4th ed. 1846.

Addams (J.): Reports of Cases in the Ecclesiastical Court, 1822–26. 1823–26.

Addison (C. G.): History of the Knights Templars. 3rd ed. 1853.

Aithison (Sir C. U.): Collection of Treaties, Engagements and sunnuds relating to India and neighbouring countries. 7 vols. 1862–65. Revised ed. 11 vols. 1892.

Alison (Sir A.): Hist. of Europe. 7th ed. 20 vols. 1847–48.

Allen (J.): Inquiry into the Rise and Growth of The Royal Prerogative in England. 2nd ed. 1849.

Amos, Fort. de Laud.: Amos (A.), Fortescue's De Laudibus Legum Angliae. 1825: see Fortescue.

Anc.Inst.Eng.: Ancient Laws and Institutes of England. Edited by B. Thorpe, 2 vols. 1840.

Anc.Inst.Wales: Ancient Laws and Institutes of Wales. Edited by A. Owen. Issued by the Record Commissioners. 1841.

Anglo-American Legal History, Select Essays in. 3 vols. 1907–09.

Anson: Law and Custom of the Constitution. 2 vols. Vol. I, 5th ed., 1909. Vol. II, 4th ed., 1935.

Antiq.Hibern.: Ancient Laws and Institutes of Ireland. 6 vols. 1865–1901.

Antiq. of Exeter: Exeter Receiver General's Accounts. 1752.

Archbold (J. F.): Archbold's Law and Practice relating to Pleading, Evidence and Practice in Criminal Cases. 39th ed. 1976.

—— Practice of the Court of Quarter Sessions. 6th ed. 1908.

Arnold (T. J.): Law of Municipal Corporations. 7th ed. 1935.

Arnould (J.): Law of Marine Insurance. 15th ed. 1961.

Ash (J.): Dictionary: New and complete Dictionary of England. 2 vols. 1775.

Ashburner (W.): Rhodian Sea Laws. 1909.

Attenborough (F. L.): Laws of the Earliest English Kings. 1922.

Ault (W. O.): Private Jurisdiction in England. 1923.

Austin (J.): Jurisprudence. 5th ed. revised. 2 vols. 1911.

Ayliffe (J.): Parergon Juris Canonici Anglicani. 1734.

Bac.Abr.: Bacon (M.). New Abridgment of the Law, 1736–66. 7th ed. 1832.

Bac.Max.: Bacon (F.). Collection of some of the principall Rules and Maxims of the Common Lawes of England. 1737.

Bacon: Bacon (F.). Complete Works. Collected and edited by James Spedding, R. L. Ellis and D. D. Heath, 14 vols. 1868–92.

Bacon (Francis, Lord Verulam): Read.Stat. Uses. Law Tracts. 8. Reading on the Statute of Uses. 2nd ed. 1741.

Bacon (N.): Government of England, Historical Discourse on the Uniformity of the. 5th ed. 2 parts in 1 vol. 1760.

Bacon: Office of the Vice-Admiral of the Coast: see Baker.

Baker (Sir S.): Office of the Vice-Admiral of the Coast. 1884.

Baldwin (J. F.): The King's Council in England during the Middle Ages. 1913.

Beale (J. H.): Bibliography of Early English Law Books [to 1600] [Ames Foundation]. 1926. Supplement, 1943.

Bell (G. J.): Comm. on Laws of Scotland. 7th ed. 2 vols. 1870.

Bell (W.): Dictionary and Digest of the Law of Scotland. 4th ed. 1890.

Bellot (H. H. L.): Inner and Middle Temple. 1902.

Bentham (J.): Works. 11 vols. 1843.

Bewes (W. A.): Romance of the Law Merchant. 1923.

Biener (F. A.): Geschichte der Novellen. Justinian's. 1824.

Bisset (A.), Life-Estates: Law of Estates for Life. 1842.

Bl.Comm.: Blackstone (Sir W.). Commentaries on the Laws of England. 1765. (For editions see Sweet & Maxwell's Bibliography of the British Commonwealth, Vol. 1.)

Black Books of Lincoln's Inn, 1422–1845. 4 vols. 1897–1902.

Block (Maurice): Dict. de la Politique. L'Europe polit. et soc. 2nd ed. 1892.

BIBLIOGRAPHY

Blount (T.): Law Dictionary. 1717.

—— Tenures: Fragmenta Antiquitatis; Antient Tenures of Land and Jocular Customs of some Mannors. 1679. 4th ed. by W. C. Hazlitt. 1874.

Bolland (W. C.): The General Eyre. 1922.

Bonner (G. A.): Office of the King's Remembrancer in England. 1930.

Book of Oaths, edition of 1689: Book of Oaths and severall Forms Thereof, both ancient and modern. By Richard Garnet. 2nd ed., 1689. 3rd ed., 1715.

Boulton (W. W.): Conduct and Etiquette at the Bar of England and Wales. 6th ed. 1975.

Bouvier (John): Law Dictionary. 2 vols. 16th ed. 1897.

Bowen (Ivor): Statutes of Wales. 1908.

Br. & Had.Com.: Broome and Hadley. Commentaries on the Laws of England. 4 vols. 1869.

Bract.: Bracton (Henry de). De Legibus et Consuetudinibus Angliae. 1250–1260. Edited by Sir Travers Twiss, 1878–83. Edited by G. E. Woodbine, another edition, 4 vols., 1915–42.

Brady (R.): Historical Treatise of Cities, and Burghs or Boroughs, showing the original, and whence and from whom they received their liberties, privileges and immunities; what they were, and what made and constituted a free burgh and free burgesses, as also when they first sent their representatives to parliament. 4th ed. 1777.

Braithwaite (T. W.): Six Clerks in Chancery; their Successors in Office, and the " Houses " they lived in. 1879.

Brandon (W.). For.Attach.: Customary Law of Foreign Attachment, and the Practice of the Mayor's Court of the City of London therein. 1861.

Britt.: Britton (John). [Code of the Laws of England.] 1540. English translations and notes by F. M. Nichols. 1901.

Bro.Ab.: Brooke (Sir Robert). La Graunde Abridgement. 2 vols. 1573.

Brompton (Johannes): Chronicon. Twysden (R.). Historiae Anglicanae Scriptores X. fol. 1652.

Broom (H.), Legal Maxims: Selection of legal Maxims Classified and Illustrated. 10th ed. 1939.

Broughton-Rouse (E. B.): Law of Heriots, their origin, etc. 1892.

Bucknill (A.): Tug and Tow, Law relating to. 2nd ed. 1927.

Bullen (E.): Law of Distress for Rent. 2nd ed. 1899.

Bulstr.: Bulstrode (E.). Reports in King's Bench, 1609–26. 3 vols. 1688.

Burge (W.), Col.Law: Commentaries on Colonial and Foreign Laws generally, and in their Conflict with each other and with the Law of England. 4 vols. 2nd ed. 1907–28.

Burnet (G.): Vindication of The Authority, Constitution and Laws of the Church and State of Scotland, in four conferences; wherein the Answer to the Dialogues betwixt the Conformist and the Non-Conformist is examined. 1673.

Burrows (M.): Cinque Ports. 4th ed. 1895.

Byles (Sir J. B.): The Law of Bills of Exchange. 23rd ed. Edited by Maurice Megrah and K. F. Ryder. 1972.

Callis (R.): Reading on the Statute of Sewers. 1622. 4th ed. by W. J. Broderip. 1824.

Calvo (C.): Dictionnaire de Droit International. 2 vols. 1885.

Cam (H. M.): The Hundred and the Hundred Rolls. An Outline of Local Government in Mediaeval England. 1930.

Cam.Brit.: Camden (William), Britannia. Various editions.

Camus (A. G.), Prof. d'Av.: Lettres sur la Profession d'Advocat et Bibliothèque Choisie des Livres de Droit, qu'il est le plus utile d'acquérir et de connaître. 2 vols. 5th ed. 1832.

Caradoc, Saint of Llancarfan, Historie of Cambria, now called Wales: a part of the most famous Yland of Brytaine, written in the Brytish Language above two hundred years past, translated into English by H. Lloyd, corrected and augmented by D. Powell. 6th ed. 1832.

Carew (R.): Survey of Cornwall. 1602. Reissued 1811.

Carr (C. T.): General Principles of the Law of Corporations. 1905.

Carson (T. H.): Prescription and Custom. 1907.

Carver (T. G.): Law of Carriage of Goods by Sea. 12th ed. 1971.

Cawston (G.) and Keane (A. H.): Early Chartered Companies, 1296–1858. 1896.

Chadwick (H. M.): Studies on Anglo-Saxon Institutions. 1905.

Challis (H. W.): Real Property Law. 3rd ed. 1911.

Cham. on Est.: Chambers (Sir R.). Treatise on Estates and Tenures. 1824.

Chamberlayne (E.), Prest.St. of Eng.: Angliae Notitia: or the Present State of England.

Chart de Forest: Great Charter of the Forest, declaring the Liberties of it, made at Westminster, 1224, and confirmed 1299. With some short observations taken out of Coke's Fourth Institute of the Courts of the Forests. 1680.

Chew (H. M.): The English Ecclesiastical Tenants-in-Chief and Knight Service, especially in the 13th and 14th Centuries. 1932.

Chitty (J.), Contracts: 21st ed. Edited by K. Scott and B. Clauson. 1955.

Chitty (J.), Pleadings: Treatise on Pleading and Parties to Actions with precedents. 7th ed. 3 vols. 1844.

Chitty (J., jun.); Prerogatives of the Crown. 1820.

Chitty Pr.: Chitty (J.). Practice of the Law in All its Departments. 3rd ed. 1837–42. 3 vols.

Chronicles of Great Britain and Ireland: (Rolls Series) Vol. 25. Letters of Robert Grosseteske. Ed. H. R. Luard. 1861.

Cleirac (E.): Us et Coustumes de la Mer, contenant les Jugemens d'Oleron, Ordonnances de Wisburg, de la Hanse-Teutonique, et autres pieces. 1671.

Clifford (F.): History of Private Bill Legislation, 1885–87. 2 vols.

Co.Copyh.: Coke (Sir Edward) Compleate Copyholder. With Supplement. 1673.

Co.Inst.: Coke (Sir Edward). Institutes of the Laws of England.
    1st Inst. Commentarie upon Littleton, 1628.
    2nd Inst. Treatise on Statutes, 1642.
    3rd Inst. Pleas of the Crown and Criminal Causes, 1644.
    4th Inst. Jurisdiction of the Courts 1644.

Co.Litt.: Coke (Sir Edward). Coke on Littleton being the First Institute of Coke's Institutes (*q.v.*). 13th ed. by Francis Hargrave. 1775.

Cohen (H.): History of the English Bar and Attornatus to 1450. 1929.

Collins (A.), Peerage Claims: Proceedings, Precedents and Arguments on Claims and Controversies concerning Baronies by Writ and other Honours. 1734.

Colquhoun (Sir P. P.): Summary of the Roman Civil Law. 4 vols. 1849–60.

Com.Dig.: Comyns (Sir J.). Digest of the Laws of England. 1762–67. 5th ed. 8 vols. 1882.

Cooke, Incl.: Cooke (G. W.). Acts for Facilitating the Inclosure of Commons in England and Wales. 4th ed. 1864.

Copinger (W. A.) and Skone James (F. E.): Law of Copyright. 9th ed. by F. E. and E. P. Skone James. 1958.

Cordery (A.), Solicitors: Law relating to Solicitors. 4th ed. 1935.

Coulson (H. J. W.) and Forbes (V. A.): Law of Waters, Sea, Tidal and Inland. 6th ed. 1952.

Cowel: Survey of the Duchy of Cornwall: *see* Carew.

Cowell (J.): Law Dictionary. 1727.

Crabb (G.), R. P.: Law of Real Property 2 vols. 1846.

Craig (Sir Thomas): Jus.Feud. 3rd ed. by J. Baillie. 1732.

Cressy (H. P.): Church History of Brittany. 1668.

Cripps (H. W.), Ch. & Cl.: Law Relating to Church and Clergy. 8th ed. 1937.

Cro.Eliz.: Croke's Reports, *temp.* Elizabeth I. 1582–1603.

Cro.Jac.: Croke's Reports, *temp.* James I. 1603–25.

Crompt.Juris.: Crompton (R.). L'Authoritie et Jurisdiction des Courts de la Maiestie de la Roygne. 1637.

Cruise (W.): Digest of the Laws of England respecting Real Property. 7 vols. 4th ed. 1804–07.

———— Fines, Essay on Nature and Operation of. 2 vols. 3rd ed. 1794.

Cunningham (T.): New and Complete Law Dictionary. 2nd ed. Vol. 1. 1771.

Dalton (M.), Office of Sheriffs: Officium Vicecomitum; the Office and Authoritie of Sherifs. 4th ed. 1700.

Daniel (W. T. S.): History and Origin of the Law Reports. 1884.

Daniell, Ch.Pract.: Chancery Practice. 8th ed. 1914.

Dav.: Davies (J.). Antiquae linguae Britannicae, nunc vulgo dictae Cambro-Britannicae, et linguae latinae dictionarium duplex. 1632.

Day (J. C.): Common Law Procedure Acts. 4th ed. 1872.

Deane (H. B.): Law of Blockade. 1870.

Derville (M. T.): Level of Romney Marsh. The Level and the Liberty of Romney Marsh in the County of Kent. An inquiry into the Origin, History and Present State of the Lords, Bailiff and Jurats, with some account of their Ancient Courts and Early Forms of Land Drainage Administration. 1936.

Dicey (A. V.): Conflict of Laws. 9th ed. Edited by J. H. C. Morris and others. 1973.

Doctor and Student: Saint-German (C.). 1530.

BIBLIOGRAPHY

Domat (J.): Civil Law in its Natural Order With Additional remarks on differences between the Civil Law and Laws of England. Translated by W. Strahan. 2 vols. 3rd ed. 1772.

Dowell (S.): History of Taxation. 2nd ed. 4 vols. 1888.

Du Cange: Glossarium ad Scriptores Mediae et Infirmae Latinatis. 1638.

Dugd., Antiq. of Warw.: Dugdale (Sir William), Antiquities of Warwickshire. 1656.

Dugd.Mon. Dugdale (Sir W.). Monasticon Anglicanum. 1655–73.

Dunglisson (R.): History of Medicine. 1872.

Dwarris (F.): Statutes, General Treaties on. 2nd ed. 2 pts. 1848.

Dyer: Dyer's Reports, King's Bench, 1513–82. 1585.

E.H.R.: English Historical Review. 1866–19—.

Eadm.: Eadmerus Monachus Cantuariensis Historiae Novorum sive sui Saeculi Libri IV (ab anno 1066 ad annum 1122), in lucem ex Bibl. Cottoniae emisit Joannes Seldenus et notas porro adjecit et spicilegium. 1623.

Eddy (J. P.): Distress, Law of. 2nd ed. 1939.

Edwards (W. D.): Compromises of Litigations. 1925.

Ellis (Sir Henry): General Introduction to Domesday Book. 2 vols. 1833.

Elphinstone (Sir H. W.), Norton (R. F.) and Clark (J. W.): Rules for the Interpretation of Deeds. 1885.

Elton (C. I.), Commons: Treatise on Common and Waste Lands. 1868.

—— Copyh.: Laws of Copyholds and Customary Tenures of Land. 2nd ed. 1893.

—— Tenures of Kent. 1867.

Emerigon (B. W.), Maritime Loans: Translated from the French.

Ency.Eng.Law: Encyclopaedia of the Laws of England. 17 vols. 2nd ed. 1906–19.

Encyc.Londin.: John Wilkes. Encyclopaedia Londiniensis. 24 vols. 1810–29.

Encyclopaedia of Planning, Compulsory Purchase and Compensation. General Editor: E. J. Rimmer; Vol. 1, D. Heap and H. J. Brown; Vol. 2, R. D. Stewart-Brown. Managing Editor, J. Burke.

Enever (F. A.): Bona Vacantia under the Law of England. 1927.

—— History of the Law of Distress for Rent and Damage Feasant. 1931.

Erskine (Thomas Erskine, 1st Baron): Defence of Lord George Gordon. 1781.

Essays in Anglo-Saxon Law. 1876.

Ewen (C. L.): Witch Hunting and Witch Trials. Indictments for Witchcraft from the Records of the 1,373 Assizes held from 1559 to 1736. 1929.

Fearne (C.): Cont.Rem. Essay on the Learning of Contingent Remainders and Executory Devises. 10th ed. 2 vols. By J. W. Smith. 1844.

Finch (Sir H.): Law: or, Discourse Thereof. 1613. 7th ed. 1759.

Fitz.N.B.: Fitzherbert (Sir Anthony). La Nouvelle Natura Brevium. 1534–37.

Fleta: Commentary on the Laws of England. 1647.

Forsyth (W.) Hortensius: Historical Essay on the Duties of an Advocate. 3rd ed. 1879.

Fortesc.: Fortescue (Sir J.). De Laudibus Legum Angliae. Cir. 1468. With notes by J. Selden, 1616: with notes by A. Amos, 1825.

Foss (E.): Judges of England, with sketches of their lives and notices connected with the Courts at Westminster, 1066–1864. 9 vols. 1848–1864.

Fost.: Foster (Sir Michael). Report of commission for trial of rebels in 1746; to which are added Discourses upon a few branches of the Crown law, viz., high treason, homicide, accomplices, and observations on the writings of Lord Hale. 3rd ed. 1809.

Fox (Sir J. C.): Handbook of English Law Reports. Part 1, from the last quarter of the 18th century to the year 1865. 1913.

—— History of Contempt of Court. 1927.

Gabel (L. C.): Benefit of Clergy in England in the later Middle Ages. 1929.

Gale (C. J.): Easements. 14th ed. by S. G. Maurice and R. Wakefield. 1972.

Gibb (A. D.): Students' Glossary of Scottish Legal Terms. 1946.

Gibson (E.): Codex Juris Ecclesiastici Anglicani. 2 vols. 2nd ed. 1761.

Gilb.Ch.: Gilbert (Sir G.). History and Practice of the High Court of Chancery. 1758.

Gilbert (Sir G.): Hist. View of Court of Exchequer. Historical view of the Court of Exchequer and of the King's Revenues there answered. 1738.

Giuseppi (M. S.): Guide to Public Records. Vol. I, Legal Records. 1923.

Glanvil (R. de): Tractatus de Legibus et Consuetudinibus regni Angliae. 1187–89.

Glen (W. C.): Poor Law Orders. 11th ed. 1898.

Godolphin (J.): Rep.Can. Repertorium Canonicum: or, Abridgment of the Ecclesiastical Laws of this Realm consistent with the Temporal. 3rd ed. 1687.

Goff (R.) and Jones (G.): Law of Restitution. 1966.

Goiten (H.): Primitive Ordeal and Modern Law. 2nd ed. 1926.

Gomme (G. L.): Primitive Folkmoots: or Open Air Assemblies in Britain. 1880.

Goodeve (L. A.): Modern Law of Personal Property. 9th ed. 1949.

Gothofredus (J.): De imperio Maris et de jure naufragii colligendi legeque Rhodia, etc. Genevae. 1637.

Grant (J.): Law of Corporations, as well Aggregate as Sole. 1850.

Green: Encyclopaedia of the Laws of Scotland. 14 vols., 1896–1904; 12 vols., 1909–14; 16 vols., 1926–35; 5 supplementary vols. 1931–52.

Green (G. M.): Death Duties. 7th ed. 1971.

Griffiths (A.): Chronicles of Newgate. 2 vols. 1884.

Gross (C.): Gild Merchants. 2 vols. 1890.

Grounds of Law: The Grounds and rudiments of law and equity, alphabetically digested; containing a collection of rules and maxims, with the doctrine upon them, illustrated by various cases, extracted from the books and records, to evince that these principles have been the foundation upon which the judges and sages of the law have built their solemn resolutions and determinations. 2nd ed. 1751.

Hackwood (F. W.): Story of the Shire: being the Lore, History and Evolution of English County Institutions. n.d.

Hale (Sir M.): De jure maris. Narrative legall and historicall touchinge the customes. See Moore (S. A.), History of the Foreshore. 1888.

—— Com.Law: History of the Common Law of England. 2 vols. 6th ed. by Charles Runnington. 1820.

—— Sheriff's Accounts. 1683.

Halk.Max.: Halkerston (P.). Latin Maxims and Rules in Law and Equity. 1823.

Hall (R. G.), Sea Shore: Rights of the Crown and Privileges of the Subject in the Sea Shores of the Realm. 2nd ed. 1875. See also Moore's History of the Foreshore. 1888.

Hall (W. E.): Foreign Jurisdiction of the British Crown. 1894.

—— International Law. 8th ed. 1924.

Hall.Lit.Hist.: Hallam (H.). Introduction to the Literature of Europe. 5th ed. 4 vols. 1855.

Hall.Const.Hist.: Hallam (H.). Constitutional History of England from Henry VII to George II. 6th ed. 3 vols. 1876–92.

Hallam (H.): Middle Ages. 3 vols. 1901.

Hanbury (H. G.): Modern Equity. 10th ed. 1976.

Hardy (Sir T. D.): Description of the Close Rolls in the Tower of London with an account of the early Courts of Law and Equity and historical illustrations. 1833.

—— Description of the Patent Rolls in the Tower of London, [with] an itinerary of King John, [and] observations. 1835.

Hargrave (F.): Law Tracts. Collectanea Juridica: consisting of Tracts relative to the law of England. 2 vols. 1791–92.

Harper (J. C.): Profit Sharing in Practice and Law. 1955.

Harrison (D.): Conspiracy as a Crime and as a Tort in English Law. 1924.

Hatsell (J.): Precedents of Proceedings in the House of Commons. 4 vols. 4th ed. 1818.

Hawke (M.): The Grounds of the Lawes of England. 1657.

Hawk.P.C.: Hawkins (W.). Pleas of the Crown, 1716–21. 8th ed. by John Curwood. 1824.

Haydn (J.): Dictionary of Dates. 25th ed. 1910.

Hazlitt (W. C.): Ancient Tenures. See Blount (T.). Fragmenta Antiquitatis; Ancient Tenures of Land and Jocular Customs of some Mannors.

Heap (D.): Outline of Planning Law. 6th ed. 1973.

Hearnshaw (F. J. C.): Leet Jurisdiction in England; especially as illustrated by the Records of Court Leet of Southampton. 1908.

Heath (Sir R.): Maxims and Rules of Pleading in Actions Real, Personal, and Mixt, Popular and Penal; from his manuscript, with additions [by W. B.], 1694; with notes by T. Cunningham. 1771.

Hengham (Sir Ralph de): Summa Parva Summae: Magna Hengham et Parva vulgo nuncupatae, ex vett. codd. MSS. in lucem proderunt (Appended to Fortescue, De Laudibus Legum Angliae). With notes by J. Selden, 1616. Edited by W. H. Dunham. 1932.

Herbert (T. A.): History of Prescription. History of the Law of Prescription in England. 1891.

Hewitson (T.): Suretyship, its Origin and History in Outline. 1927.

BIBLIOGRAPHY

Heywood (N. A.) and Massey (A. S.): Court of Protection Practice. 9th ed. 1971.

H.H.E.L.: Holdsworth (Sir W. S.). History of English Law. 1922–56.

Hill (Sir G. F.): Treasure Trove. The Law and Practice of Antiquity. 1934.

Hob.: Hobart's Reports, King's Bench, 1603–25. 1641.

Holingshed (Raphael), Chron.: Chronicles of England, Scotland and Ireland. 2 vols. 1577.

Holland (Sir T. E.): Lect.Int.Law. Lectures on International Law. Edited by T. A. Walker and W. L. Walker. 1933.

Holland: Elements of Jurisprudence. 12th ed. 1924.

Hone (N. J.): The Manor and Manorial Records. 2nd ed. 1925.

Hooper (W.): Law of Illegitimacy. 1911.

Horne (A.): Mirrour of Justices [and Diversity of Courts]. 1768.

Hov. or Hov.Ann.: Hoveden (Roger de) Annals: the History of England and of other countries of Europe from 732–1201. From the Latin, with notes and illustrations, by H. S. Riley. 2 vols. 1853.

Hume (D.): History of England. 8 vols. 1789–1806.

Hunter (S. J.): Elementary View of a Suit in Equity. 6th ed. 1873.

Husband (E.): Collection of Remonstrances. Exact Collection of all Remonstrances, Declarations, Votes, Orders, Ordinances, Proclamations, Petitions, Messages, Answers and other passages between the King's Majesty and his High Court of Parliament, December 1641 until March 21, 1643. 1643.

Hutchins (B. L.) & (A.): History of Factory Legislation. 3rd ed. 1926.

Hutton (W.): Courts of Requests, with cases determined in that of Birmingham. 1787. With a Memoir of the Author. 1840.

Illingworth (W.): Forestalling: Inquiry into the Laws, Ancient and Modern, respecting Forestalling, Regrating and Ingrossing, with cases, copies of records, and proceedings in Parliament. 1800.

Jackson (J.): The Law relating to the Formation and Annulment of Marriage: 1951.

Jacob (G.): Law Dictionary, 1729. 2 vols. 1835.

Jardine (D.): Torture. Reading on the Use of Torture in the Criminal Law of England previously to the Commonwealth. 1837.

Jeake (S.): Charters of the Cinque Ports. 1728.

Jeayes (I. H.): Court Rolls of the Borough of Colchester. 3 vols. 1921–41.

Jenk.: Jenkins (D.). Rerum Judicatarum Centuriae Octo. 1661.

Jenk.Cent.: Jenkins (D.). Eight Centuries of Reports. 1734.

Jenks (E.): History of the Doctrine of Consideration. 1892.

Jenkyns (Sir H.): British Rule and Jurisdictions beyond the Seas. 1902.

Jones (Sir W.): Bailments. Essay on the Law of Bailments. 4th ed. by W. Theobald. 1833–34.

Jurid.Rev.: Juridical Review (Quarterly). 1889 to date.

Justice (A.): Sea Laws. General Treatise of the Dominion of the Sea: and a compleat body of the Sea Laws, containing what is most valuable on that subject in Antient and Modern Authors, and particularly the antient Laws of the Rhodians and Romans; those of Oleron, Wisbuy and other Countries, as also the Sea Laws lately published in France. 1724.

Kahn-Freund (O.): Law of Inland Transport. Law of Carriage by Inland Transport, founded on Disney's Law of Carriage by Railway. 4th ed. 1965.

Kelly (P.), Cambist: The Universal cambist and commercial instructor. 2 vols. 3rd ed. 1836.

Kelly (J. B.): Summary and History and Law of Usury. 1835.

Kelsall (R. K.): Wage Regulations under the Statute of Artificers. 1938.

Kemble (J. M.): The Saxons in England. 2nd ed. 3 vols. 1876.

Kemp & Kemp: The Quantum of Damages. 4th ed. 1975.

Kennet (W.): Glossary. See Ken.Paroch. Antiq.

Ken.Paroch.Antiq.: Kennett (W.). Parochial Antiquities in the Counties of Oxford and Bucks. With a glossary. 1695.

Kerly (D. M.), Hist.Eq.: Historical Sketch of the Equitable Jurisdiction of the Court of Chancery. 1890.

Kimball (E. G.): Serjeanty Tenure in Mediaeval England. 1936.

Kiralfy (A. K. R.): Source Book of English Law. 1957.

Kitch.: Kitchin (J.). Courts Leet. 1589. 10th ed., 1623.

Knocker (E.): Grand Court of Shepway. Account of the Grand Court of Shepway holden on the Bredenstone Hill at Dover, August 28, 1861. 1862.

Kramer (S.): English Craft Gilds and the Government. 1905. Studies in their Progress and Decline. 2nd ed. 1927.

Kyd (S.): Law of Corporations. 2 vols. 1793–94.

Lambard (W.): Duties of Constables, Borsholders, Tything-men and such other lowe and Lay Ministers of the Peace. 1582.

——— Eirenarcha: or of the Office of the Justices of the Peace. 1581.

Lambard (W.), Perambulations of Kent: containing the description, Hystorie and Customes of that Shyre. 1576.

Langmead (T. P. Taswell-): English Constitutional History. 10th ed. 1946.

Lapsley (G. T.): County Palatine of Durham; a Study in Constitutional History. 1900.

Lauterpacht (Sir H.): Development of International Law by the International Court. 1958.

Law Reform: A Century of Law Reform. Twelve lectures. 1901.

Le Geyt (P.): Les Manuscrits sur la Constitution, les Lois et les Usages de Jersey. 4 vols. 1846–47.

Lea (H. C.): Superstition and Force: Essays on the Wager of Law, the Wager of Battle, the Ordeal, Torture. 4th ed. 1892.

Lecky (W. E. H.): Hist. of England in the Eighteenth Century. New ed. 7 vols. 1892.

Leg.Athel.: see Ancient Laws and Institutes of England.

Leges Canutae: see Ancient Laws and Institutes of England.

Leg.Etheld.: see Ancient Laws and Institutes of England.

Leges Inae: see Ancient Laws and Institutes of England.

Lewis (P.): Historical Inquiries Concerning Forests and Forest Laws, with topographical remarks upon the ancient and modern state of the New Forest in the County of Southampton. 1811.

Liber Custumarum: The Book of the Ancient Usages and Customes of the Town of Northampton to 1448. (C. A. Markham.) 1895.

Liebermann (F.): Die Gesetze der Angelsachsen, Bd. 1, Text und Uebersetzung, 1903; Bd. 2, erste hälfte Wörterbuch, 1906; zweite hälfte, Rechts und Sachglossar, 1912; Bd. 3, Einleitung, 1916.

——— Quadripartitus ein englisches Rechtsbuch von 1114, nachweisen und soweit bisher ungedruckt. 1892.

Lightwood (J. M.): Possession of Land. 1894.

Lil.Abr.: Lilly (J.). Practical Register: or, General Abridgment of the Law. 2 vols. 2nd ed., with Supplement. 1745.

Lincoln (F. A.): The starra. Their Effect on Early English Law and Administration. 1939.

Linell (A.): Law of Names, Public, Private and Corporate. 1938.

Lingelbach (W. E.): Merchant Adventurers of England, their laws and ordinances. 1902.

Litt.: Littleton's Tenures. Cir. 1481.

Litt.Epil.: Littleton's Tenures (q.v.). Epilogue to edition of 1813.

Lofft: Lofft's Reports and a Collection of Maxims (in Latin). 1790.

Lofft (Capel): Principia cum Juris Universalis tum praecipue Anglicani. 2 vols. 1779.

Lowndes (W.): Essay on Coins. Report containing an Essay for the amendment of the Silver Coins. 1695.

Lowndes and Rudolf: General Average. 10th ed. 1975.

Lushington: Affiliation and Bastardy. 7th ed. 1951.

Lyte (Sir H. Maxwell): Historical Notes on the Great Seal. 1926.

Macaulay (Lord T. B.): History of England. 5 vols. 1849–61.

McCull., Comm.Dict.: McCullough (J. R.). Dictionary of Commerce and Commercial Navigation. New edn. revd. 1869.

Macintyre (D.): Auctioneers and Estate Agents. 1957.

McKechnie (W. S.): Magna Carta: a commentary on the Great Charter of King John, with historical introduction. 2nd ed. 1913.

Maclachlan (D.): Merchant Shipping. 7th ed. 1932.

McNair (A. D.): Law of the Air. 3rd ed. 1964.

MacSwinney (R. F.): Mines; The Law of Mines, Quarries and Minerals. 5th ed. 1922.

Madox (T.): Form.Aug. Formulare Anglicanum: or, Collection of Ancient Charters and Instruments of divers kinds, placed under several heads, from the Norman Conquest to the end of the reign of Henry VIII. Pl. and facsim. 1702.

Madox (T.), Hist. and Ant. of Exchequer: History and Antiquities of the Exchequer of the Kings of England, from the Norman Conquest to the end of the reign of Edward II. 2 vols. 2nd ed. 1769.

Maine, Ancient Law, 1861: Reprinted with notes by Sir Frederick Pollock. 1930.

BIBLIOGRAPHY

Maitland (F. W.): Domesday Book and Beyond. 1897.

―――― Roman Canon Law in the Church of England. 1898.

―――― Select Essays in Anglo-American Legal History: *see* Anglo-American Legal History.

―――― Township and Borough. 1898.

Makower (F.): Constitutional History and Constitution of the Church of England. Translated from the German. 1895.

Malynes (G.): Lex Mercatoria. Consuetudo vel Lex Mercatoria; or, Antient Law Merchant. 1622.

Manning (J.): Exchequer Practice. Practice of the Court of Exchequer, Revenue Branch. 2nd ed., with appendix. 1827.

―――― Serviens ad legem. 1840.

Manwood (J.): Forest Laws. 1598.

Marchant (J. R. V.), Barrister-at-Law: Legal Position of Counsel. 1905.

Markby (Sir W.): Elements of Law, considered with reference to Principles of General Jurisprudence. 6th ed. 1905.

Mat.Paris: Matthew Paris. Chronica Maiora, 1217–1253. Ed. H. R. Luard. 7 vols. Rolls Series. Vol. 57. 1872–73.

Mather (P. E.): Sheriff Law. Sheriff and Execution Law. 3rd ed. 1935.

Maude (F. P.) and Pollock (C. E.): Laws of Merchant Shipping. 4th ed. 2 vols. 1881.

Maxwell: Complete List of British and Colonial Law Reports. 3rd ed. 1937.

Maxwell Leg.Bib.: A Legal Bibliography of the British Commonwealth. 5 vols. 2nd ed. 1955–57.

Maxwell (Sir P. B.): Interpretation of Statutes. 12th ed. 1969.

Maxwell-Lyte (Sir H. C.): Historical Notes on the use of the Great Seal of England. 1926.

May (Sir P. E.): Parliamentary Practice; Law, Privileges, Proceedings and Usage of Parliament. 18th ed. 1971.

Merewether (H. A.) and Stephens (A. J.): History of the Boroughs and Municipal Corporations of the United Kingdom. 3 vols. 1835.

Mews (J.) Digest: Annual Digest of English Case Law. Annually.

Mill (J. S.) Pol.Econ.: Principles of Political Economy. 1848.

Millard (P. W.): Law relating to Tithes. Law Relating to Tithe Rent Charge and other payments in lieu of Tithe. 3rd ed. 1927.

―――― Tithes and Variable Rentcharges. Some Aspects of their History and Development. 1933.

Milles (T.) Cat.of Hon.: Catalogue of Honor. 1610.

Mirehouse (J.): Advowsons, Law of. 1824.

Mirror: Horne (A.). Mirror of Justices [and Diversity of Courts]. 1768.

Mitchell (W.): Early History of the Law Merchant. 1904.

Mitford Eq.Pl.: Mitford (J. F. 1st Baron Redesdale). Treatise on the Pleadings in Suits in the Court of Chancery 1780. 5th ed. by J. W. Smith. 1847.

Molloy (C.): De Jure Maritimo et Navali; or Treatise of Affaires Maritime and of Commerce. 10th ed. 1778.

Mon.Angl.: Dugdale (Sir W.). Monasticon Anglicanum. 1655–73.

Montesquieu (Baron de): The Spirit of the Laws. Translated from the French. 1750. 6th ed. 1793.

Moore (S. A.) Hist.Foreshore: History and Law of the Foreshore. 1888.

Moore (S. A. and H. S.) Fisheries: History and law of Fisheries. 1903.

Morgan (G. O.) and Chute (C. W.): Chancery Acts and Orders. 6th ed. 1885.

Morris (W. A.): Early English County Court. An Historical Treatise with Illustrative Documents. 1926.

―――― Frankpledge System: Harvard Historical Studies No. 14.

―――― Mediaeval Sheriff: The Mediaeval English Sheriff to 1300. 1927.

Morris (J. H. C.) and Leach (W. Barton): Rule against Perpetuities. 2nd ed. 1962, with Supplement. 1964.

Murray (K. M. E.): Constitutional History of the Cinque Ports. 1935.

Neill (E. D.): History of Virginia Company of London. 1869.

New N.B.: Fitzherbert (Sir Anthony). New Natura Brevium; with a table of the most material things contained therein, composed by William Rastall, the Authorities in Law. 1652. 9th ed. with commentary by Lord Chief Justice Hale. 1793.

Nicholls (H. G.): Forest of Dean. 1858.

Nicholls (Sir G): Engl. Hist. History of the English Poor Law. 2 vols. 1854.

Nicholas (Sir Nicholas Harris), Editor: Proceedings and Ordinances of the Privy Council, 1386–1547: Record Commission. 7 vols. 1834–37.

Nicolas (N. H.): Adulterine Bastardy. 1836.

Nicolson (William): Leges Marchiarum or Border Laws. 1747.

Nokes (G. D.) Hist.Crime Blasph.: History of the Crime of Blasphemy. 1928.

North (The Hon. R.): Life of Lord-Keeper Guilford [and others], edited by A. Jessopp. 3 vols. 1890.

Norton (G.), City of London: Commentaries on the History, Constitution and Chartered Franchises of London, A.D. 1579–1664. 1869.

Norton (R. F.): Treatise on Deeds. 2nd ed. 1928.

Norton-Kyshe (J. W.): Attorney-General and Solicitor General. 1897.

—— Law of Gloves. 1901.

Noy, Maxims: Treatise of the Principal Grounds and Maxims of the Laws of this Kingdome. 1641. 9th ed. by W. M. Bythewood. 1821.

O.E.D. Oxford English Dictionary.

Odgers (W. B.): Century of Law Reform: see Law Reform.

Ogle (A.): Canon Law in Mediaeval England. 1912.

Oke (G. C.): Turnpike Laws. 2nd ed. 1861.

Old Nat.Br.: Old Natura Brevium, 1525. So called the publication of Fitzherbert's Natura Brevium (q.v.).

Oliphant (G. H. H.), Horses: Law of Horses, including the Law of Innkeepers, Veterinary Surgeons, and of Hunting, Racing, Wagers and Gaming. 6th ed. 1908.

Omond (G. W. T.): Lord Advocates of Scotland, from the close of the 15th century to the passing of the Reform Bill. 2 vols. 1883.

Oppenheim (L.): International Law. Vol. 1, 8th ed., 1955. Vol. 2, 7th ed., 1952.

Oughton (T.), Ordo Jud.: Ordo Judiciorum; sive Methodus procedendi in negotiis et Litibus in Foro Ecclesiastico Civili Britanico et Hibernico. 1738.

P. & M. H.E.L.: Pollock (Sir F.) and Maitland (F. W.). History of English Law before the time of Edward I. 2nd ed. 2 vols. 1898.

Page (T. W.): End of Villeinage in England. 1900.

Palgrave (Sir Francis): Essay on the . . . King's Council. Record Commission. 1834.

Palmer (Sir F. B.): Peerage Law in England. 1907.

Parkes (J.): History of the Court of Chancery. 1828.

Parry (L. A.): Hist. of Torture in England. 1934.

Paton (G. W.): Bailment in the Common Law. 1952.

Pearce (T.): Laws and Customs of the Stannaries in the counties of Cornwall and Devon; containing the Charter of Edward I, the Laws made in Parliament, several cases and pleadings, etc. 1725.

Pearce (T.): Procedure in the Court of the Vice-Warden: see Pearce, Laws of the Stannaries. 1725.

Pease (Howard): Lord Wardens of the Marches of England and Scotland. 1913.

Peel (W.): Practice of Ct. of Pass. Jurisdiction and Practice of Court of Passage, City of Liverpool. 2nd ed. 1934.

Perkins (J.): Profitable Book treating of the Laws of England. Translated from the French. 1555.

Philipot (T.): Villare Cantianum, or Kent surveyed and illustrated. 1659.

Phill.Ecc.Law: Phillimore (Sir R.). Ecclesiastical Law of the Church of England. 2nd ed. 2 vols. 1895.

Phill.Evid.: Phillimore (J. G.). History and Principles of the law of Evidence as illustrating our Social Progress. 1850.

Phill.Int.Law: Phillimore (Sir R.). Commentaries on International Law. 3rd ed. 1879–89.

Phipson (S. L.): Evidence. 12th ed. 1976.

Pike (L. O.): Constitutional History of the House of Lords. 1894.

Pike (L. O.), Hist.Cr.: History of Crime in England. 2 vols. 1873–76.

Pl.Com.: Plowden (E.). Commentaries or Reports [1550–80]. 1613. Translated from the French. 1761.

Plowden (E.): Commentaries or Reports. 1779.

Pollock (Sir F.) and Wright (R. S.): Possession in the Common Law. 1888.

Polychron.: Polychronicon Ranulphi Higden. Ed. C. Babington. Rolls Series No. 41. 1865–86.

Poth.Oblig.: Pothier. Law of Obligations or Contracts. Translated from the French by F. X. Martin. 2 vols. 1802.

Potter (D. C.) and Monroe (H. H.): Tax Planning with Precedents. 7th ed. 1974.

Potter (H.), Hist.Int.: Historical Introduction to English Law and its Institutions. 4th ed. 1958.

Powel (D.), Hist.Wal.: see Caradoc.

Praefatio ad Wilk. L. Anglo-Sax.: Wilkins (D.). Leges Anglo-Saxonicae Ecclesiasticae et Civiles. 1721.

Preston (R.), Abstracts: Essay on Abstracts of Title. 3 vols. 2nd ed. 1823–24.

Preston (R.): On Estates. 3rd ed. 1829.

Pritchard (T. S.): Jurisdiction, Practice and Procedure of the Quarter Sessions. 2nd ed. 1904.

Prynne, His.Coll.: Seasonable, legal, historical vindication and chronological collection of good old fundamental liberties, franchises, rights and laws of all English freemen, etc., evinced by parliamentary records, etc. 3 pts., 1654–57. Under the title Historiarchos, 1659.

BIBLIOGRAPHY

Puff. De Jur. Nat. et G.: Pufendorf. De Jure Naturae et Gentium. 1688.

Pulling (A.): Order of the Coif. 2nd ed. 1897.

Purey-Cust (A. P.): Collar of S.S. A History and a Conjecture. 1910.

Putnam (B. H.): Enforcement of the Statutes of Labourers during the First Decade after the Black Death, 1349–59. 1908.

—— Kent Keepers of the Peace, 1316–17. 1933.

Radzinowicz (L.): History of English Criminal Law. 3 vols. 1948–56.

Ranulphus de Diceto, Dean of St. Paul's: Ymagines Historiarum. From Twysden (R.), Historiae Anglicanae Scriptores X. 2 vols. 1652.

Redgrave (A.): Factory Acts. 22nd ed. 1972.

Reeves (J.): History of English Law from the Saxons to the end of the reign of Henry VII. 2 parts. 1783–84.

Reg.Brev.: Registrum brevium. 1531.

Reg.Judic.: Registrum Omnium Brevium tam Originalium, quam Judicialium. 1531.

Reports on the Dignity of a Peer: Reports from the Lords' Committees appointed to search the Journals, Rolls and other Records for all matters touching the Dignity of a Peer. 5 vols. 1820–29.

Rich (E. E.): Ordinance Book of the Merchants of the Staple: The Staple Court Books of Bristol, 1509–1601. Edited by E. E. Rich. 1937.

Ritson (J.): Office of Bailiff of a Liberty. 1811.

Robertson (G. S.): Civil Proceedings by and Against the Crown. 1908.

Robertson (Wm.): Phraseologia Generalis. 1681.

Robinson (T.): Common Law of Kent: or, Customs of Gavelkind, with appendix concerning Borough English. 5th ed. by C. D. Elton and H. J. H. Mackay. 1897.

—— Gavelkind: see previous entry.

Roscoe: Admiralty Jurisdiction and Practice. 5th ed. 1931.

Rot.Parl.: Rotuli Parliamentorum: ut et Petitiones et Placita in Parliamento [ab anno 1278 ad annum 1503]. 6 vols. 1767–77.

Rowlatt (S. A. T.): Principal and Surety. 3rd ed. 1936.

Rushworth (J.), Hist.Coll.: Historical Collections of Private Passages of State, Weighty Matters in Law, Remarkable Proceedings in Five Parliaments, 1618–48. 8 vols. 1659–80.

Russell (W. O.), Crime: On Crimes and Misdemeanours. 11th ed. 2 vols. 1958.

Ruth.Nat.Law: Rutherforth (T.). Institutes of Natural Law. 2 vols. 2nd ed. 1779.

Rymer (T.) and Sanderson (R.): Foedera, Conventiones, Literae et cujuscunque Generis Acta Publica inter Reges Angliae et alios quosvis Imperatores, Reges, Pontifices, Principes, vel Communitates ab 1066 ad nostra usque tempora. 20 vols. 1704–35.

Salmond (Sir J.): Jurisprudence. 12th ed. 1966.

—— Torts, 16th ed. 1973.

Salter (H. E.): Registrum Cancellarii Oxoniensis, 1434–69. Oxford Historical Society. Vols. 93, 94.

Samuels (H.): Factory Law. 6th ed. 1957.

Sand.Just.: Sandars (T. C.). Institutes of Justinian. 1883.

Sandys (C.): Consuetudines Kanciae; a History of Gavelkind and other remarkable customs in the County of Kent. 1851.

Saund.: Saunders's Reports, King's Bench. 1666–72.

Savigny (F. C. v.), Syst.: System des heutigen Römischen Rechts. 1867.

Schmitthoff (C. M.): Export Trade. 6th ed. 1975.

Schwarzenberger, Int.Law: 3rd ed. 1957.

Scofield (Cora): Court of Star Chamber. 1900.

Scott (W. R.): Joint Stock Companies. Constitution and Finance of English, Scottish and Irish Joint Stock Companies to 1720. 3 vols. 1910–12.

Scriven (J.): Treatise on the Law of Copyholds. 7th ed. 1896.

Scrutton (Sir T. E.): Contract of Affreightment as expressed in Charterparties and Bills of Lading. 18th ed. 1974.

Seebohm (F.): Customary Acres. 1914.

—— English Village Communities. 1926.

Selborne (R. P.): Defence of the Church of England against Disestablishment. 1886.

Seld.Hon.: see Seld. Titles of Honour.

Seld. Titles of Hon.: Selden (J.). Titles of Honour. 1672.

Selden (J.), De Duellis: Duello, or single combat: from antiquity derived into England, with the forms and ceremonies thereof. 1610.

Selden, Hist.Tithes: Selden (J.). History of Tythes. 1618.

Selden (J.): Mare Clausum. 1635.

Selden (John): Notes on Fortescue: De Laudibus Legum Angliae. 1616.

—— Notes on Hengham's Summae. 1616.

Sellers (M.): Acts and Ordinances of the Eastland Company of York. 1906. Royal Hist.Soc., 3rd Series, 11.

Selosse (L.): L'Ila de Serk. 2nd ed. 1929.

Senior (W.): Doctor's Commons and the Old Court of Admiralty. 1922.

Seton (H. W.): Judgments. 7th ed. 1912.

Shepp.Touch: Sheppard (W.). Touch-Stone of Common Assurances: or, Treatise opening the Learning of Common Assurances or Conveyances of the Kingdome. 1641. 8th ed. 1826.

Short (F. H.) and Mellor (F. H.): Crown Office Practice. 2nd ed. 1908.

Sidney (A.): Government, Discourses concerning. 3rd ed. 1751.

Skeel (C. A. S.): Council in the Marches of Wales. 1904.

Skene (Sir J.): De verberum significatione. The Exposition of the Termes and Difficill Wordes, conteined in the Foure Buikes of Regiam Majestatem; and uthers, in the Acts of Parliament, Infestments, and used in practicque of this Realme, with diverse rules and common places, or principalls of the Lawes. 1597.

Smith (Adam): The Wealth of Nations. 1776.

Smith (J. Toulmin): English Guilds. 1870.
―――― The Parish. Its Powers and Obligations at Law. 2nd ed. 1857.

Smith (J. W.): Action at Law, Elementary View of Proceedings in an Action at Law. 12th ed. 1876.

Smith (Sir W.) and Cheetham, Dict. of Antiq.: Dictionary of Christian Antiquities. 2nd ed. 2 vols. 1875–80.

Smith's L.C.: Smith (John W.). Leading Cases. 13th ed. 2 vols. 1929.

Snell (E. H. T.): Equity. 27th ed. 1973.

Snell (F. J.): Customs of Old England 1911.

Somner (W.): Dictionarium Saxonico-Latino-Anglicum voces phrasesque praecipuas Anglo-Saxonicas cum Latino et Anglica vocum interpretatione complectens; accesserunt Aelfrici Abbatis Grammatica. Latino-Saxonica, cum glossario suo ejusdem generis. 1652.

Spelman (Sir Henry), Feuds: The original growth, propagation and condition of feuds and tenures by knight-service. Spelmanni reliquiae, the posthumous works of Sir Hen. Spelman, relating to the laws of and antiquity of England. 1698.

Spelman: Glossary. 1626. 3rd ed., 1687.

Spelman (Sir H.), Hist.Sacri.: History and Fate of Sacrilege, from the beginning of the World to this day. 4th ed. 1895.

Spence (G.), Equitable Jurisdiction of the Court of Chancery: 2 vols. 1846–49.

Stair (Viscount): Institutes of the Law of Scotland. New edition. 2 vols. 1832.

Stanford (D. R.): Overseas Trade Corporations. 1957.

Staunford, Pl.C.: Staunford (Sir W.). Les Plees del Coron. 1557.

Staunf.Prerog.: Staunford (Sir W.). Exposition of the Kinges Prerogative collected out of the great Abridgement of Fitzherbert and other olde writers of the lawes of England. 7th ed. 1607.

Steer (J.): Parish Law. Civil and Ecclesiastical Government of Parishes and Relief of the Poor. 6th ed. 1899.

Stephen, Dig. of Crim. Law: Stephen (Sir J. F.). Digest of the Criminal Law. 9th ed. 1950.

Stephen, Hist.Crim. Law: Stephen (Sir J. F.). History of the Criminal Law of England. 3 vols. 1883.

Stephen (H. J.): Pleading. 7th ed. 1866.

Stephens (John), Procurations and Pentecostals: An historical discourse, briefly setting forth the nature of Procurations . . . and somewhat also of Synodals and Pentecostals. 1661.

Stewart-Brown (R.): Serjeants of the Peace. 1936.

Story (Judge): Bailments. 1832 (U.S.A.). 1839 (London).
―――― Commentaries on Equity Jurisprudence. 3rd Eng. ed. 1920.
―――― Confl. of Laws: Commentaries on the conflict of laws, foreign and domestic, in regard to Contracts, Rights and Remedies, and especially in regard to Marriages, Divorces, Wills, Successions and Judgments. U.S.A., 8th ed., 1883. G.B., 2nd ed., 1841.

Stow (J.), Annals: or, General Chronicle of England.
―――― Survey of London. 1755.

Street (H. A.): Ultra Vires. 1930.

Street (T. A.): Foundations of Legal Liability. 3 vols. 1906.

Stroud (F.): Judicial Dictionary. 5 vols. 4th ed. Edited by J. James. 1971–74.

Stubbs, Const.Hist.: Stubbs (W.). Constitutional History of England. 1874–78. Revised by G. Edwards. 1951.

Stubbs (W.): Select Charters and other illustrations of English Constitutional History from the earliest times to the reign of Edward I. 9th ed. 1913.

Sugden (E.): Practical Treatise on Powers. 8th ed. 1861.

Swinburne (H.), Spousals: Treatise of Spousals or Matrimonial Contracts wherein all the questions relating to that subject are ingeniously debated and resolved. 1686.

Tait (J.): The Mediaeval English Borough Studies in its Origins and Constitutional History. 1936.

BIBLIOGRAPHY

Tapping (T.): Cost Book, Readwin Prize Essay on. 2nd ed. 1854.

Tayl.Hist.Gavelk.: Taylor (S.). History of Gavel-Kind, with the etymology thereof. 1663.

Termes de la Ley: Rastell (W.). La Termes de la Ley. 1624.

Thoms (W. J.): Book of the Court. 1838.

Thorpe (B.), Editor: Ancient Laws and Institutes of England, comprising laws enacted under the Anglo-Saxon Kings from Aethelbirht to Cnut, with an English translation of the Saxon; the Laws called Edward the Confessor's; the Laws of William the Conqueror and those ascribed to Henry I; also Monumenta Ecclesiastica Anglicana from the seventh to the tenth century; and the ancient Latin version of the Anglo-Saxon Laws, with a glossary. 1840.

Tidd (W.), Pr.: Practice of the Court of King's Bench in Personal Actions. 9th ed. 1828–33.

Tristram (T. H.) and Coote (H. C.): Probate Practice. 24th ed. 1973.

Turk (M. H.): Legal Code of Alfred the Great. 1893.

Turner (R. W.): Equity of Redemption, its Nature, History and Connection with Equitable Estates Generally. 1931.

Turner (S.): Anglo-Saxons, History of, 1805. 2nd ed. 3 vols. 1799–1835.

Twiss: Black Book of the Admiralty. Edited by Sir T. Twiss. 1871–76.

Usher (R. G.): Rise and Fall of the High Commission (1535–1641). 1913.

Viner (C.): General Abridgment of Law and Equity. 24 vols. 2nd ed. 1791–95.

Viner Abr.: Viner (C.). Abridgment of the Modern Determinations in the Courts of Law and Equity; a supplement to Viner's Abridgment. 6 vols. 1799–1806.

Vinogradoff (P.): Oxford Studies in Social and Legal History. Vols. 8–9. 1926–27.

—— Villeinage in England: essays in English Mediaeval History. 1892.

Wallace (J. W.): The Reporters arranged and characterised; with incidental remarks. 4th ed. by F. F. Heard. 1882.

Walsing.: Walsingham (T.). Historia Anglicana, 1272–1422. Rolls Series, No. 28. 1863–64.

Warburton (J.): Treatise on History, Laws and Customs of Guernsey, containing the Précepte d'Assize. 1822.

Warren (S.), Law Studies: Popular and Practical Introduction to Law Studies, and to every Department of the Legal Profession. 3rd ed. 2 vols. 1863.

Warren (W. R.): Choses in Action. 1899.

Watk.Desc.: Watkins (C.). Essay towards the further elucidation of the Law of Descents. 1793. 4th ed. 1837.

Webb (S. and B.): Manor and Borough. 2 vols. 1908.

Webster (R. G.): Law Relating to Canals. 1885.

Wedg.: Wedgwood (H.). Dictionary of English Etymology. 2nd ed. 1872.

Wells (S.): Bedford Level, History of the Drainage of the Great Level of the Fens, called. 2 vols. 1830.

West (E.): Extents, Law of, with an Appendix of Cases (1686–1817). 1817.

Wharton (Henry): Anglia Sacra sive Collectio Historarium de Archiepiscopis et Episcopis Angliae a prima fidei Christianae susceptione ad annum 1540. 2 vols. 1691.

Wheaton (H.): International Law. 2 vols. Vol. 1, 6th ed., 1929. Vol. 2, 7th ed., 1944.

Where to Look for your Law: 14th ed. by C. W. Ringrose. 1962.

Wigram, Extrin.Evid.: Wigram (Sir J.). Rules of Law respecting the Admission of Extrinsic Evidence in Aid of the Interpretation of Wills. 5th ed. 1914.

Williams (E.): Early Holborn and the Legal Quarter of London. 2 vols. 1927.

Williams (G. L.): Crown Proceedings Act. 1948.

Williams (J.): Rights of Common and other Prescriptive Rights. 1880.

Williams (Joshua): Seisin of the Freehold. 1878.

Williams (O. C.): Historical Development of Private Bill Procedure. 1949.

Williams (W. R.), Hist.Gt.Sess.: History of the Great Sessions in Wales, 1542–1830, with the Lives of the Welsh Judges, Lists of Chamberlains, Chancellors, Attorney-Generals, and Prothonotaries of the Four Circuits of Chester and Wales, the Lord Presidents of Wales, and the Attorney-Generals and Solicitor Generals of the Marches. 1899.

Williams and Mortimer: Executors, Administrators and Probate. Being the 15th ed. of Williams on Executors and the 3rd ed. of Mortimer on Probate.

Wms.Saund.: Williams' (J.) Notes to Saunders Reports. 1799.

Willway (A. C. C.): Quarter Sessions Practice. 1940. Supplement to 1952.

Winfield (P. H.): Chief Sources of English Legal History. 1925.

—— History of Conspiracy and Abuse of Legal Procedure. 1921.

Wing.: Wingate (E.). Maximes of Reason; or, Reason of the Common Law of England. 1658.

Wood (J. G.): Laws of the Dean Forest and the Hundred of St. Briavels. 1878. Supplement to 1952.

Wood's Inst.: Wood (T.). An Institute of the Laws of England. 2 vols. 1720.

Woodbine (G. E.): Four Thirteenth Century Law Tracts. 1910.

Woodfall (W.): Landlord and Tenant. 27th ed. by L. A. Blundell and V. G. Wellings. 1968; Cumulative Supplement, 5th ed., by L. A. Blundell and V. G. Wellings. 1976.

Wright (C.) and Fayle (C. E.): History of Lloyd's from the Founding of Lloyd's Coffee House to the Present Day. 1928.

Wright (Sir M.), Ten.: Introduction to the Law of Tenures. 2nd ed., 1736. 4th ed., 1792.

Yates (J. B.): Rights and Jurisdiction of the County Palatine of Chester, the Earls, the Chamberlain and other Offices. 1854. (Chetham Soc.)